EVALUATION STUDIES REVIEW ANNUAL
Volume 5

Evaluation Studies

Review Annual

Evaluation Studies

Review Annual

Volume 5

Edited by
Ernst W. Stromsdorfer
and
George Farkas

SAGE PUBLICATIONS / BEVERLY HILLS / LONDON

For information address:

SAGE PUBLICATIONS, INC.
275 South Beverly Drive
Beverly Hills, California 90212

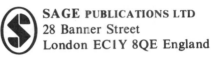

SAGE PUBLICATIONS LTD
28 Banner Street
London EC1Y 8QE England

Printed in the United States of America

International Standard Book Number 0-8039-1502-0

International Standard Series Number 0364-7390

Library of Congress Catalog Card No. 76-15865

FIRST PRINTING

Figure 1, p. 33, is adapted from T. Paul Schultz, "Estimating Labor Supply Functions for Married Women," in J. P. Smith (ed.) *Female Labor Supply: Theory and Estimation* (Princeton, NJ: Princeton University Press, 1980), by permission of the publisher.

Figure 2, p. 34, is adapted from Jerry A. Hausman and David A. Wise, "Social Experimentation, Truncated Distributions, and Efficient Estimations," *Econometrica,* 45(1977): 919-938, by permission of the Econometric Society.

CONTENTS

About the Editors

Ernst W. Stromsdorfer is Vice President and Director of Employment Research at Abt Associates Inc., Cambridge, Massachusetts. He is Project Director on several studies of subsidized employment and training programs for disadvantaged youth and low-income and welfare-prone individuals. Prior to joining Abt Associates he was Professor of Economics at Indiana University and Deputy Assistant Secretary for Evaluation and Research, U.S. Department of Labor. He has written and directed a variety of evaluation and labor market studies of employment and training programs and vocational and secondary education. He is a reviewer for a variety of journals including the *Journal of Human Resources,* and the *Industrial and Labor Relations Review.* His recent studies include *An Econometric Analysis of the Costs of Selected Manpower Programs,* with Kamran Moayed-Dadkhah and Bruno Oudet (a report for the U.S. Department of Labor); *Schooling and Work Among Youths from Low-Income Households,* with Suzanne Barclay, Christine Bottom, George Farkas, and Randall J. Olsen (a report for the Manpower Demonstration Research Corporation); "The Effectiveness of Youth Programs: An Analysis of the Historical Antecedents of Current Youth Initiatives" (in Anderson and Sawhill [eds.] *Youth Employment and Public Policy*); "Social Policies to Reduce Youth Unemployment: Lessons from Experience and the Potential of Recent Initiatives," with George Farkas (prepared for the Committee on Education and Labor, U.S. House of Representatives); "Youth Labor Supply During the Summer: Evidence for Youths from Low-Income Households" with George Farkas and Randall J. Olsen (forthcoming in *Research in Labor Economics,* R. Ehrenberg, ed.); and "The Youth Entitlement Demonstration: Program Impacts During the First 18 Months" with George Farkas, D. Alton Smith, Christine Bottom, and Randall J. Olsen (forthcoming from the Manpower Demonstration Research Corporation).

George Farkas is Senior Economist at Abt Associates Inc. and Principal Investigator on a study of subsidized employment for disadvantaged youth—The Youth Incentive Entitlement Pilot Project. He is also principal investigator on a study of net job creation for the proposed Employment Opportunities Pilot Projects—a subsidized employment and training program for low-income and welfare-prone families. Prior to joining Abt Associates he was Assistant Professor of Sociology and in the Institution for Social and Policy Studies, Yale University. He is a reviewer of sociological and economic submissions and projects for a variety of journals and organizations. His research specialties are econometrics, labor economics, and demography, and his recent publications include "Cohort, Age, and Period Effects Upon the Employment of White Females: Evidence for 1957-1968" *(Demography)* as well as the joint work with E. Stromsdorfer listed above.

Preface

This volume of the *Evaluation Studies Review Annual* presents important, rapidly evolving, but sometimes difficult, literature. We have attempted to select the best econometric analyses of social programs, experiments, and demonstrations completed in the last 18 months. Many of these make extensive use of recently developed statistical techniques, and as a group they represent the current state-of-the-art in quantitative program evaluation. Accordingly, the results they display are the most reliable answers to the social policy questions addressed. For this reason, policy analysts and program managers should find these results of great value.

But, technical sophistication has a cost. Some sections are difficult to read. To compensate for this, relatively extensive introductions have been written for each of the chapters, and each section of the book is prefaced by a descriptive and methodological discussion designed to highlight the most important findings while demonstrating the methodological relevance of the studies. The reader will find that these articles are indeed interrelated and present a coherent approach to the evaluation of policy regarding a wide range of social issues—with particular emphasis on income maintenance, subsidized job creation and training programs, vocational educational programs, housing programs, industrial safety regulation, and natural resource and public financial policy, among others.

We hope that the comprehensive and technical nature of these studies will make this volume a lasting reference for the student of research design and quantitative technique. The studies presented here show that even with an experimental or quasiexperimental design, properly specified behavioral models and complex quantitative techniques are required to measure program effects in an efficient and unbiased manner. The methods for doing so are only now beginning to be routinized.

We want finally to acknowledge the help we have received from many members of the Editorial Board as well as our colleagues in economics, sociology, and related professions. Our greatest thanks must be extended to the authors of these studies themselves. They have created literature well worth summarizing, and some have made special efforts to provide updates of ongoing work under very short deadlines.

Finally, we would like to acknowledge the secretarial and research assistance of Miss Annette Charest.

George Farkas
Ernst W. Stromsdorfer
Cambridge, Massachusetts

May 1980

Introduction

Ernst W. Stromsdorfer and George Farkas

In the 1970s, for the first time in history, large-scale social experiments were conducted in an attempt to understand the effects of social programs prior to their implementation. Accompanying this work has been the development of new analysis techniques that facilitate an unprecedented (in social science research) attention to potential biases and inefficiences in measuring experimental and quasiexperimental effects. And the results of these efforts are evoking more positive public comment than heretofore.

These experiments, and the methods used to evaluate them, are the major theme of this volume. As a result, the majority of the chapters are concerned with employment, education, or housing choices and outcomes for individuals. Policies and outcomes relating to marital stability, health and safety, energy and resource use, retirement from the labor force, and revenue sharing are also represented. In the final section, macroeconomic issues related to the circular flow within the economy, inflation, and public financial management are considered as an inevitable aspect of public spending to achieve social goals. The emphasis of the volume is economic, but the policy issues span a broad spectrum and the methods apply beyond the uses illustrated. Most of the authors are economists, but at least seven are sociologists. Some of the methods represent the latest in econometric innovation, yet can be applied to data far removed from economics. These methods, for the first time, address issues (such as self-selection and attrition bias) that arise, almost from first principles, in any empirical application of quasiexperimental methodology. The methods themselves appear complex, yet they are by-and-large related to each another and, taken as a group, represent the first fruits of an econometric revolution just gathering momentum. It seems inevitable that the decade of the 1980s will witness much further development along the lines presented here.

The volume, and this introduction, are each divided into eight sections. The first of these concerns methodology, and begins by discussing our organizing theme: the choice of a research design—particularly the choice of a control group—and the nature of statistical adjustments to be performed under differing experimental/control group strategies. The section summarizes the statistical issues and practical techniques involved in a variety of recently developed methods for coping with data collected (as data always *are* collected) under less than ideal statistical conditions. The chapters in this section present data from the Seattle and Denver and the Gary Income Maintenance Experiments. In addition, analytic themes and issues are raised which are then re-explored with other data in the following sections.

Each of the succeeding sections concerns a particular policy area, and with data arising from either designed or natural experiments. In each case the relevant section of our introduction summarizes policy developments and their relation to previous evaluation efforts and sets the selected chapters against this background of other efforts in the area. The strengths and weaknesses of the policy questions asked, the methods used, and the results obtained are compared, both within and between policy areas, and conclusions are drawn regarding the proper application and ultimate value of these methods. The theme is the comparison of program outcomes for an "experimental group" with some notion of the outcomes that "would have occurred for this group in the absence of the program." This is usually operationalized as a before/after comparison of experimental and control groups, a relatively straightforward operation if individuals are randomly assigned to one of the two groups, the experimental group alone undergoes an externally imposed treatment, and complete data are available on outcomes for all individuals. Since, in social science research generally, and in large-scale program evaluation particularly, none of these criteria are ever completely met, the experimental/control comparison becomes problematic. Methods recently developed to overcome these difficulties are introduced in Part I, and their use recurs in later sections. Our commentary strives to tie these together so that research strategy and the validity of research findings are clarified both for the practitioner and for the ultimate consumer of social policy research results.

I. METHODOLOGY

Selection and Attrition Bias

The first three chapters in this section are closely related, and, as a group, define the central methodological theme of the volume. This involves adjusting experimental and comparison group data for variables that have not been directly measured, but which both affect the outcome of interest and are not identically distributed between the two groups. If, in this situation, no adjustment is performed, the analyst is likely to be mislead regarding the true experimental effect. (That is, the effect due solely to the program.) This usually occurs when individuals are self-selected into experimental and control groups or when data on the study sample are nonrandomly missing. Perhaps the most important development for social science statistical methods during the 1970s was the realization that the difficulties associated with self-selection, censored samples (where some variables are unmeasured for certain individuals in the sample), truncated samples (where all variables are unmeasured for certain individuals who should be in the sample), and limited dependent variables (variables restricted to some subset of values: for example, weeks worked, which must be zero or above or the probability of being employed, which must lie between zero and one) all have a common foundation. This realization occurred simultaneously with the development of methods to deal with these situations, and it is within this econometric literature that our first three chapters belong.

Recognition of the potential importance of self-selection for social science theory and estimation goes back at least to the 1950s (see Lewis [1959] on estimating the effect of unions on wage rates), as does a social science concern for limited dependent variable models estimated by maximum likelihood. (Tobin's now well-known article on this, which appeared in 1958 and is the source of the model which has been named "tobit," deserves an award for "most ahead of its time.") Within the mathematical statistical literature, a concern with truncated distributions generally, and the truncated normal distribution particularly, recurs throughout this century. Indeed, methods for this situation go back at least to 1908,[1] and R. A. Fisher's *Mathematical Tables* (1931) include a tabulation of the truncated normal. Nevertheless, it was not until the close of the 1960s that the necessary models and methods of estimation began to be developed and adapted for social science use, and it is only now, at the close of the 1970s, that these methods are gaining widespread use within the profession.

Cragg (1971) works in the tobit framework, and Goldberger (1972) discusses self-selection bias, but the seminal papers are those of Gronau (1973, 1974) and Heckman (1974a, 1976). (See also Lewis, 1974, and Heckman, 1974b.) Here the concern is to estimate wives' labor force response to their own wage rate, and the technical difficulty is that of a censored sample—we do not observe the wage rates of wives not at work. Since, even among otherwise identical wives (e.g., wives with identical, measured background characteristics, such as age, race, and education), those with missing wage rates are likely to have rates that do not represent such rates as a whole, bias can result if our analysis is restricted only to those wives with complete data (those at work).

Gronau devised a method to cope with this problem, based on the existence of a variable (family income) that affects the wife's labor force participation but is presumed not to affect her wage offer. (Such an "identifying variable" will reappear in a later discussion.) The method involves classifying wives into categories based on family income and a number of other, predetermined variables. Then, with these other variables held constant, Gronau examined the trend in the mean wage rates of working wives as family income falls. Since income is presumed not to determine the wage offer, the mean observed wage rate for working wives should approach the true offered wage rate for all wives as we move to the groups of wives with higher labor force participation rates caused by their lower family income. By using the change in observed mean rates as family income falls, it is possible to infer the true mean of the wage offer distribution for all wives. Gronau found support for the notion that the wives who work are those with above average wage offers, so that analyses based on the subsample of working wives are likely to lead to biased results.

Heckman's solution to the problem is not unrelated to Gronau's but is much more far-reaching. He adapted the tobit model to a simultaneous equation framework, so that the wife's wage offer and labor supply equations (the latter being the decisions whether or not to work and the number of hours to work) are estimated jointly by maximum likelihood. With this approach, both the determinants of wage rates and the effect of wage rates on labor supply are estimated within one model, corrected for selectivity bias, and using all the data available. And, within Heckman's model, the individual's labor force participation decision is based on her comparison of the wage rate she is offered and her asking wage ("reservation wage"), so that the resulting parameter estimates are neatly tied to the economic theory of labor supply as labor and leisure choice. Indeed, it is claimed that with these methods we can now estimate the indifference curves that have so long adorned the theory textbooks. Certainly, these two papers (Heckman, 1974a, 1974b) are a remarkable tour de force.

Not content, Heckman (1976) went on to show the essential unity among models for self-selection, censored, and truncated samples, and for limited dependent variables. His work popularized the use of probit and tobit techniques in such a way as to rapidly revolutionize common econometric practice, pointed out the prevalence of these issues in a wide variety of economic and policy-related inquiries, and suggested a simple ordinary least squares (OLS) correction for some of the common occurrences of these problems. The chapter included in this volume dates from this period and can be regarded as a companion piece to the 1976 article. More recently, Heckman (1978a, 1978b) has extended the multivariate probit model to a variety of situations, including the analysis of panel data.

Meanwhile, others were working on these and related issues.[2] In an important series of papers, Amemiya (1973, 1974, 1978) provided the mathematics for estimating some of the models being developed. Goldfeld and Quandt (1972), Berndt et al., (1974) and Olsen (1977a) advanced the state of the art for maximum likelihood estimation. Hausman and Wise (1976, 1977a, 1977b, 1979 [included in this volume], 1980 [included in this volume]), Burtless and Hausman (1978 [included in this volume]) and Griliches et al. (1978) expanded these models and techniques and applied them within a variety of policy related contexts. Related advances and results are associated with the work of Cogan (1976), Schultz (1975), Maddala and Lee (1976), Maddala (1978), Lee (1979), Lee et al. (1980), and Olsen (1977b, 1978, 1979, 1980a, 1980b). A variety of recent articles, including many of those reprinted in this volume, have further contributed to this literature.

The papers mentioned above have the use of probit, tobit, and truncated normal distributions as a common basis. These lend themselves to being mixed and matched, so that every empirical situation involving missing data or other problems lead to a unique model with its own likelihood function, which is then maximized by numerical methods.[3] In general, similar models can be developed with the cumulative logistic (logit models) instead of the cumulative normal distribution function as a basis. These are generally easier to compute than those based on the probit but are less useful in a multiequation context. They form the basis of work by Nerlove and Press (1973, 1976), of important work on models of individual choice by McFadden (1974), Domencich and McFadden (1975) and Manski and Lerman (1977)[4], and of work by Tuma and others on continuous time Markov models of over-time change and sample attrition (see Tuma et al., Part I). We return below to a consideration of these latter models.

Sampling Frames for Longitudinal Surveys, Optimal Samples, Assignment to Treatment, and Balancing Covariates

One of the organizing themes of this volume is the distinction between designed and natural experiments. For practical purposes, the former refers to the situation in which the analyst is able to assign subjects to treatment status, while the latter refers to the situation in which this is not possible. The paper by Morris et al. raises a number of issues particularly relevant to designed social experiments. Their point of view provides an important complement to that of the authors of the first three chapters in this section, for while the latter strive to adjust experimental/control differences for deviations from ideal experimental conditions, Morris et al. are concerned with the best arrangement of these conditions. Thus, the first three chapters present methods appropriate to natural experiments and to the analysis of data from designed experiments after-the-fact of design or data availability flaws have been discovered, whereas the fourth chapter describes experimental arrangements that eliminate the need for such methods.

Morris et al. discuss issues arising from their work on the experimental portion of the Health Insurance Study, but their discussion applies far beyond this particular study. Specifically, the issues raised are directly relevant to evaluating the design and results from the Seattle and Denver Income Maintenance Experiments (chapters in this volume by Tuma et al., Keeley et al., Tuma and Robins, and Ohls), The Gary Income Maintenance Experiment (chapters by Hausman and Wise, Moffitt et al., Maynard and Murnane, and Kaluzny), Supported work (the chapter by Masters and Maynard), the Housing Allowance Demand Experiment (chapters by Friedman and Weinberg and Hausman and Wise), the Training in Community Living Program (the chapter by Weisbrod and Helming), and the Electricity Time-of-Day Pricing Experiments (chapters by Battalio et al. and by Aigner and Hausman).

Morris et al. place prominently the desire to find the most efficient, unbiased estimator of program effect that will be available in light of the practical difficulties involved in conducting a large-scale social experiment. Some of their points are: (a) Sampling frames for longitudinal surveys of experimentals and controls raise new practical survey issues associated with attrition and sample replenishment, among others; crossover designs with preenrollment in control group status followed by crossover to treatment status have their theoretical attractions but should probably be avoided because of the dangers associated with non-random attrition; (b) Most social experiments have over-sampled low-income individuals and households to choose an "optimal sample" that will be most cost-effective for the purpose at hand; the resulting stratification on an endogenous (changing) variable is to be distinguished from stratification on an exogenous (unchanging) variable, and is quite dangerous. (A similar point is made by Hausman and Wise, 1977b.); (c) Once again, in the interests of cost-effectiveness, many experiments have attempted to follow a plan designed to produce "optimal allocation of subjects to treatments." (See, for example, Conlisk and Watts, 1969; Conlisk, 1973); as with oversampling, however, this can build in bias—for example, applied to the Health Insurance Study, such a strategy might create a correlation between family health and the generosity of the experimental plan. The same rule applies to crossover designs—avoid them. Instead, keep the design simple and straightforward; (d) Simple random assignment is still a good design. If one wishes to increase efficiency, try proportional stratification. (See article for description.)

Models of Change in Continuous Time

The new method in the chapter by Tuma et al. (Part I) is a model of program impact, although as a byproduct it does provide a technique for dealing with sample attrition. From both methodological and substantive points of view, this is a remarkably innovative paper, whose statistical technique is likely to affect common practice for years to come. (See Tuma and Robins, this volume, for another application of the method.) As with many of the models described above, it is concerned to fit values for a limited, dependent variable and does so with maximum likelihood estimation. The specification of a logit model for a Markov transition process in continuous time, however, leads to a particularly felicitous result.

This chapter and its companions (Hannan et al., 1977, 1978) is the culmination of a long tradition of interest by sociologists in individual change over time, dating at least to Lazarsfeld's work in the 1940s (see Lazarsfeld et al., 1948). In the 1950s, sociological panel data were modeled within a Markov chain framework (Anderson, 1954; Anderson and Goodman, 1957; Blumen et al., 1955), a development that was continued and extended during the 1960s (Coleman, 1964; McGinnis, 1968) and consolidated during the first half of the 1970s (Spilerman, 1972a, 1972b; Singer and Spilerman, 1974, 1976).[5] Now, with their model of event histories in continuous time, Tuma et al. have provided what may be the most attractive analysis strategy yet devised for their situation.

The model is a finite-state, continuous-time Markov process. The Markov process assumes[6] that the probability of being in any particular state (for example, married or not) at a particular point depends only on the state of a previous point (and in the formulation here, background characteristics such as age, education, experimental/control status) and that, given the information concerning the state at this previous point, the state at any point previous to that is irrelevant.[7] With this assumption, the model becomes particularly simple, depending only on (unobserved) "instantaneous transition probabilities" between the states of interest. For example, if state 1 denotes being married and state 2 denotes being not married, r_{12} denotes the rate of marital dissolution and r_{21} denotes the rate of marital formation. Estimation is then nothing more than measuring the extent to which these rates depend on individual background characteristics. The finding that, in the Seattle and Denver Income Maintenance Experiment, the experimental group had a significantly higher marital dissolution rate than the control group is one of the major unanticipated findings of recent times. It has spawned a small industry of studies seeking to refute, confirm, or extend the results.

The Markov assumption is both the strength and potential weakness of the model. It gives the model simplicity and tractability, but it is a strong assumption, and, if false, could produce misleading results. To their credit, the authors are concerned with this possibility, and their demonstration that the model fits the data is convincing. That it does fit (where previous Markov models did not) is likely due to its allowance for population heterogeneity (dependence of the transition rates on individual background characteristics) and the provision to permit all effects to differ across successive periods (in this case, half-year intervals). With this many parameters to be estimated, a practical data reduction device has been created.

Omitted Variables, Process Analysis, and Other Styles of Evaluation Research

The exchange between Goodwin and Hannan et al. (included at the end of Part I) points up a number of issues which may be neglected by too much emphasis on the use of econometric models in policy research. This often comes down to a debate about the importance of variables that have been omitted from an econometric analysis (because they are difficult to measure, difficult to include in an econometric model, or simply because the analyst does not believe in their causal importance). Sometimes, however, it is claimed that noneconometric methods (for example, participant observation) can provide a more accurate estimate of a policy parameter. (See Nathan et al., 1978; Borus and Hamermesh, in Part VIII of this volume.) Indeed, the program operations people (as distinct from the research and evaluation groups) within federal agencies typically are most interested in "process analyses" which use observational techniques to summarize (and also to explore the more political and/or intangible) aspects of program operation and service delivery. The importance of the lessons to be learned from these should not be minimized. (For unexpected testimony on the importance of program administrative issues in social experiments, from the heart of the econometric camp, see Welch, 1978.)

The usual econometrician's response is that even if such variables are important, their omission from his analysis does not bias the results. In many cases, however, it should be possible to plan the econometric analysis to enhance the opportunity to include issues related to program administration and implementation. This is most feasible where there are more than a few program sites under study. (See Farkas et al. in Part III and Bishop et al. in Part VIII.)

II. LABOR FORCE PROGRAMS: DESIGNED EXPERIMENTS

Social experimentation on its current scale began with the support, during the 1960s, of Guy Orcutt, James Tobin, and Milton Friedman (among others) for a negative income tax program, and for income maintenance experiments to test for, and measure the magnitude of, the decreased labor supply expected as a result of such a program. Now, after the New Jersey, Gary, Seattle/Denver, and Rural Experiments, this work is just ending. Four of the chapters in this section are concerned with results from Gary and Seattle/Denver, while the fifth reports on the impact of a program (supported work) of direct job creation for those able to work. In the current political climate, this latter idea seems to be the most likely candidate for national implementation. (For descriptions of other programs based on the notion of subsidized job creation, see the chapters by Mallar et al. and Farkas et al. in Part III and by Borus and Hamermesh and Bishop et al. in Part VIII.)

Methodologically, the chapters in this section present an interesting variety. All compare outcomes for experimental and control groups—Masters and Maynard by the usual techniques of OLS regression, Keeley et al. and Moffitt with tobit models, such as described above, Tuma and Robins with the continuous-time, Markov model described above, and Burtless and Hausman with a new maximum likelihood technique which is perhaps the most innovative recent step down the "estimating indifference curves" path marked out by Heckman several years earlier.

The method of Burtless and Hausman (a very similar technique is applied to data from the Housing Allowance Demand Experiment in the Hausman and Wise paper reprinted in Part V of this volume) is an application of remarks by Sherwin Rosen (1974) on an earlier paper by Heckman (1974b). The goal is to go beyond simple experimental/control comparisons to a structural model of the effect of the program on labor supply and to do so while recognizing that because of the progressivity of tax rates (if not for other reasons), the individual's wage rate depends upon the number of hours he works. (This dependence has been assumed away in previous models.) By following Rosen's suggestion to work with the indirect utility function (which expresses utility as a function of prices and income—in labor supply studies the relevant price is the individual's wage rate, the "price" at which he gives up leisure) rather than the direct utility function (which expresses utility as a function of quantities of leisure and purchased goods—measuring the demand for leisure is equivalent to measuring the supply of labor), Burtless and Hausman are able to devise a procedure capable of coping with the nonconvex budget sets arising from the dependence of the wage rate on the number of hours worked. As illustrated in the chapter by Hausman and Wise analyzing Housing Allowance Demand Experiment data (Part V), such nonconvexity is likely to occur under a variety of proposed transfer programs.

The findings presented in Part II generally vindicate the Income Maintenance Experiments as viable research strategies. Despite earlier caveats, we now see that across the experiments the labor supply results are broadly consistent, showing small but significant diminutions in effort, most regularly for wives. The Supported Work evaluation results show a significant postprogram effect on employment and earnings for the AFDC group alone. (That there should be an effect, but for this group alone, is another example of the usefulness of experimentation for the discovery of unanticipated results.) The reader is referred to the *Times* editorial quoted at the beginning of this Introduction for a measure of the interest which has greeted these results.

III. LABOR FORCE PROGRAMS: NATURAL EXPERIMENTS

The selections in Part III report on evaluations of manpower and training programs related to Supported Work; but although each of these analyses involves experimental and control groups, none use random assignment to treatment status. Accordingly, they have been grouped as "natural experiments," whose data analysis is particularly vulnerable to selection bias.

In their present form, the large manpower and training programs mounted by the U.S. Department of Labor date at least to the 1960s (this ignores the Depression with the W.P.A. and other, related programs over the years), with one of the largest being that resulting from the Manpower Development and Training Act (MDTA). During the 1970s a group interested in more scientific evaluation of the effects of these programs formed in the Office of the Assistant Secretary for Policy, Evaluation and Research (ASPER) of the department, and initiated a number of econometric studies, often within an experimental/control group framework. The chapter by Ashenfelter dates from this period. (For another example, see Smith's paper on OSHA in Part VI.) The chapter by Kiefer provides an interesting complement to Ashenfelter's. It is also concerned with the evaluating the MDTA and uses similar methods, but is a later product of the same research program and thus also betrays some differences. Both Ashenfelter and Kiefer are working with less than an ideal control group—Ashenfelter's being selected from records in the Social Security Continuous Work History Sample, while Kiefer's was assembled from interviews with program-eligible nonparticipants in each of ten SMSAs where the program was conducted. Both authors attempt to control for the possible effects of selection by using individuals as their own control, modeling earnings growth both before and after the program period. Although their data and models differ, both studies find a small, positive program effect.

The Job Corps is a residential subsidized employment program for disadvantaged youths similar in spirit to Supported Work. But the evaluation of this program was not based on random assignment to treatment or control group, but rather a control group was "found" in much the same way as for the MDTA evaluation by Kiefer. Accordingly, the analysis by Mallar et al. uses both OLS regression and also the OLS correction for possible selection bias advocated by Heckman (Part I). The authors thus treat their analysis as involving simple experimental/control comparisons adjusted by regression, and comparisons adjusted by regression for unobserved differences (see their Table 4), a nice touch, since it permits us to see the extent to which these adjustments are important. The finding that the program has a positive effect for completers is significant as are their recent preliminary results that the magnitude of this effect increases with time out of the program (Personal Communication, C. Mallar to E. Stromsdorfer, March 21, 1980).

The Youth Entitlement Demonstration is another subsidized employment program, this time requiring school enrollment for program eligibility. In seven of the sites, sufficient funds are available to enroll all eligibles who apply, and the evaluation is proceeding with data from four of these, each of which has been assigned a matched control site. A sample of program eligibles was taken from each of the eight sites, so that as these are reinterviewed over time, and some of them join the program, a program participation function can be estimated. This permits at least two, distinct analysis strategies: (a) Outcomes for entire experimental and control sites, each taken as a whole can be compared. In this case the program is taken as an externally determined "treatment" to an entire site, and potential selection bias is avoided. (b) Program participants in the experimental sites can be compared with nonparticipants in these sites as well as with sample members in the control sites. In this case a selection correlation is required.

Since Wave II data are not yet available, the chapter by Farkas et al. concentrates on calibrating reduced-form and structural models with preprogram data. Of particular interest is their use of a probit and truncated normal to relax Heckman's (1974a) assumption that there are no fixed costs of working or demand-side distortions affecting apparent labor supply and also their relaxation of the usual normality (Gaussian distribution of the error term) assumption used in models to correct for selectivity bias (These developments are fully reported in Olsen, 1977b, 1978, 1979). Nonnormal residuals are easily confused with selection, and the way is cleared to estimate program labor supply and schooling effects even though wage rates are unobserved for youths not at work. The introduction of a "disemployment index" is particularly appropriate to the study of youth labor markets, and the econometric properties of the model are similar to Hausman's (1980) recent extension of the Burtless/Hausman (this volume) model to deal with fixed costs. (The disemployment index can be handled to impute a value to fixed costs. See Olsen, 1978.)

IV. EDUCATIONAL PROGRAMS: DESIGNED AND NATURAL EXPERIMENTS

There are only two chapters in this section, and, strictly speaking, neither concerns the evaluation of an educational program. They do, however, carry forward our themes of designed experiments and corrections for selectivity. And the Willis and Rosen paper raises issues of model specification, identification, and estimation that parallel those occurring in a number of other papers in this volume.

Maynard and Murnane use both OLS and tobit regression to estimate a model of school performance for the children of experimental and control households in the Gary Income Maintenance Tax Experiment. Theirs is a reduced-form model, so they can only speculate about the causes underlying the finding that the program had positive effects on the reading scores of younger children. Such effects, however, could plausibly be attributed to changes in family income and employment. The study stands out for having direct measures of school performance coupled with an experimental design.

The chapter by Willis and Rosen is something of a tour de force. They have combined the following elements in a way that is likely to influence the literature for some time to come: (a) The issue is the determinant of college attendance within a human capital framework. (b) The hypothesis is that individuals sort themselves according to ability with some abilities most likely to augment earnings when associated with a high school education, whereas the return to other abilities is best realized by going on to college. (c) The data set is the remarkable NBER-Thorndike-Hagen survey which contains early ability measures as well as earnings across a 20-year-span for more than 3,000 individuals. (d) The method is the two-stage estimator for selectivity as a switching regression proposed by Lee (1976, 1979). (e) The results are reasonably convincing.

Of particular interest in this paper is the centrality of the notion of a model of choice with explicit measures of the returns from each option for each individual and the clarity with which the identification assumptions for the selection model are revealed. The reduced-form probit permits calculation of the necessary term for the OLS selectivity correction needed to estimate the earnings function by the Heckman's method (this volume); the parameters of this earnings function are then entered into a re-estimated probit to yield a structural probit of the college attendance decision. This latter equation is identified only because the ability measures are hypothesized to affect college-going only through their effect on future potential earnings streams.

V. HOUSING PROGRAMS: DESIGNED EXPERIMENTS

This section provides, within the framework of designed experiments, an interesting contrast between constrained and unconstrained support (transfer) programs. It also contains two chapters, by Friedman and Weinberg and Hausman and Wise, that employ different methods with the same data. Since housing is a purchased good, these chapters are related to the health insurance and electricity demand papers in other parts of the volume. The concerns and methods are similar to those associated with the labor force program evaluations described above.

Friedman and Weinberg are evaluating the impact of the Housing Allowance Demand Experiment. Their paper examines the results for two treatment groups: unconstrained (resembling a general income support program such as that of the Income Maintenance Experiments) and housing gap. Under the latter plan, households receive allowance payments only if their dwelling units meet certain housing standards. For those who already meet these requirements, the constraint is nonbinding. For others, the income-induced increase in housing expenditures as a result of the program payment is sufficient to meet the standards, so they too are essentially unconstrained. However, there is a third group whom even the program payment leaves below the standard. If they wish to participate, they must allocate more of the payment to housing than is usual for them to allocate out of income. The existence of this group lends particular interest to the analysis.

The authors employ a relatively straightforward, "model-free" approach. The key assumption is that housing expenditures can be separated into "normal expenditures" plus an experimental effect with control households providing an important indication of the former. Serial correlation is used to improve prediction, and possible selection is accounted for by a procedure which uses control households to essentially "add back in" the mean of the error distribution for control households who did not meet the housing requirement. This procedure rests on the tautology that for the entire population, selectivity bias is zero and resembles the Entitlement Demonstration evaluation strategy (Farkas et al., this volume) of comparing entire experimental and control sites. Friedman and Weinberg find that selection is a factor and present both uncorrected and corrected estimates.

The paper by Hausman and Wise is more ambitious but different. For whereas Friedman and Weinberg examine the estimation of program effects, Hausman and Wise use the program data to estimate "normal behavior." They employ an approach similar to that of Burtless and Hausman (this volume), estimating demand elasticities within the context of an explicitly formulated model of utility maximization in the presence of a discontinuous budget constraint. (For Friedman and Weinberg's estimates of demand elasticities, see Friedman and Weinberg, 1980.) With this strategy, Hausman and Wise provide theoretically consistent estimates across the different subgroups of the sample, even though some of these may face linear, and others nonlinear, budget constraints. Their results appear to vindicate this strategy—estimates based on the different treatment plans are quite close.

Ohls and Kaluzny take a similar approach, analyzing the housing impact of the (unconstrained) income supplement from the Seattle/Denver and Gary Experiments. Their findings are consistent with Friedman and Weinberg's results for their unconstrained treatment group and suggest that a constrained transfer leads to greater expenditures on housing.

VI. HEALTH AND SAFETY PROGRAMS: DESIGNED AND NATURAL EXPERIMENTS

The chapters in this section are particularly interesting because of their audacity—how can we place monetary value on life and limb? And yet, this is done implicitly all the time; in public allocations to health care and research; in auto safety, airline safety, and, more generally, product safety regulation; and in industrial safety regulation. It is also done when we buy insurance and choose occupations and when we compensate accident victims or their survivors. The list could easily be multiplied. Each in its own way, the papers collected here provide innovative responses to the difficult issues arising in this area.

Viscusi approaches work-related hazards via hedonic prices; individuals reveal the costs they associate with hazardous working conditions by the compensating differentials they must receive to assume them. In this chapter, our theme of self-selection reappears—one's degree of risk-averseness and the existing structure of compensation determines the individual's choice. (This chapter is similar in spirit to that by Willis and Rosen in Part IV.) With these assumptions, Viscusi provides the first calculation of the implicit values placed on work-related injuries. These are admittedly shaky, yet the basic approach suggests a potentially fruitful line of inquiry.

The chapter by Smith takes an econometric approach to a politically controversial topic—the performance of OSHA and whether it should be expanded, contracted, or even eliminated. Smith faces the evaluation difficulty confronted in this volume—finding experimental and control groups to properly assess "what would have happened in the absence of the program."

The likely selectivity bias arising from OSHA targeting its inspections on the plant's injury rate caused Smith to abandon his planned comparison of inspected and uninspected plants and move instead to a comparison of "early" and "late" inspectees. He is clever and persistent in attempting to overcome the data difficulties confronting his analysis, and his results appear generally reliable, yet one wishes for at least a sample of plants that had been randomly assigned to inspection status.

Weisbrod and Helming do have random assignment, and in a program for treating the mentally ill, no less. In addition, they provide what is essentially a miniguide to benefit-cost analysis. If this stretches economics a bit far, the reader may be reassured by their conclusion: "the recipe for any useful benefit-cost analysis is to mix one measurement of economic science with several measures of creative art, and stir them with judgment."

VII. ENERGY AND RESOURCES PROGRAMS: DESIGNED AND NATURAL EXPERIMENTS

The short piece by Mead is an economist's overview of governmental performance in energy regulation. Not surprisingly, he thinks that the market would do a better job. The microbehavioral parameters which necessarily underly any discussion of macro-policy (e.g., how price-elastic is energy consumption?) are the subject of the following three chapters.

Battalio et al. report the results of a small field experiment designed to estimate the price elasticity of electricity use during the summer months in Texas. Their approach is a straightforward, involving random assignment to treatment group and control status and as the use of an error components model in the analysis. (Similar models are employed by Hausman and Wise in Part I, Ashenfelter and Kiefer in Part III, and Smith in Part VI.) The authors find that, at least under the conditions of this particular experiment, residential energy demand is not very responsive to price. But, the short duration, as well as other special conditions of this experiment, suggest the need for attempts to replicate the results.

Aigner and Hausman analyze data from the time-of-day electricity pricing experiment conducted in Arizona from May through October, 1976. Their concerns are methodological, and their model can be described as a joining of the usual methodology for estimating systems of demand equations with the correction for sample truncation. The reader of the chapters written by Jerry Hausman in Parts I, II, and V of this volume will recognize the approach.

The final chapter is unusually interesting as an example of the richness achieved by combining social psychological and economic approaches to studying the consumption of scarce resources. Using data on water consumption in four California water districts over a period of 96 consecutive months, Berk et al. use autoregressive moving average and error components models to measure the impact of both price and appeals for conservation on consumption. They find that both exert significant impacts, and are thus one of the first to demonstrate statistically the importance of nonprice variables. Similar studies of nonprice determinants of gasoline consumption, home heating oil use, and electricity consumption would be of great interest.

VIII. EVALUATION OF PUBLIC FINANCIAL POLICY

This section reflects a larger view of managing the federal budget and financing public programs. This seems particularly appropriate at the present time, with national attention on inflation, drastic developments in monetary and credit policy, the role of investment and "supply side economics" in productivity growth, and great pressure for a balanced federal budget. Because of these developments, many of the programs and policies reviewed in this volume may be scaled down or never implemented.

The chapter by Perry is an excellent review of the macroeconomics of inflation, written just prior to the recent inflationary acceleration and the major policy steps taken to combat it. In contrast to many recent writers, Perry feels that we have not lost the ability to explain inflation, and he sets out a scenario to account for trends over the last twenty years.

In this view, prices respond fully to wages (the major determinant of the costs of production), but the markup of prices over wages is variable, responding not only to demand conditions but also to "what has been happening to wages, prices, profit margins—or all three—or to what is expected to happen to them." Thus Perry believes that while there is a slow-growth, high-unemployment cure for inflation, it is extremely expensive in lost employment and output. It is interesting to note the link between Perry's concern with the economic impact of inflationary expectations and the finding of Berk et al. (Part VII) that the demand for scarce resources responds to exhortation. The current anti-inflationary policy contains both economic and exhortatory aspects—borrowed funds are being made more expensive, while the federal budget is balanced. (Any large impact of this latter action is more likely to occur as part of an exhortatory strategy than through the operation of economic forces.)

Ehrenberg provides an overview of a number of labor market policies, and thus complements the more narrow discussions in Parts II and III by showing the necessity to examine interrelations among programs and the place of each program and policy within the national economy. His discussion of the desire to increase employment without increasing the rate of inflation should be read in conjunction with the papers by Perry and by Bishop et al., and his discussion of public and private retirement policies (the topic of the chapter) complements that of Feldstein and Pellechio. Ehrenberg's conclusion that most of the retirement policies he examines have adverse effects on the level and distribution of employment and unemployment adds further emphasis to Feldstein's well-known dissatisfaction with the provisions of Social Security.

The paper by Feldstein and Pellechio is the most recent in a long series of studies in which Feldstein argues that Social Security has been a major force in depressing the United States savings rate, thus leading to the declines in investment and productivity which lie at the heart of our current economic malaise (see Fellner, 1980 for an extensive analysis from this point of view). Of particular interest is the use of microeconometric results to support an argument regarding macro-policy. In principle, all policy evaluation and discussion should proceed in this manner: individual-level behavior parameters are the correct guide to the performance of alternative policies.

The last three chapters form a set concerned with intergovernmental grants, public service employment, and the displacement which inevitably results. These follow up earlier work (Gramlich and Galper, 1973; Gramlich, 1978; Johnson and Tomola, 1977; Johnson, 1978; Wiseman, 1976) suggesting a down-side to the federal grants-in-aid, revenue sharing, and public service employment programs which grew so rapidly in the mid-1970s. This negative aspect is the displacement of local funds and unsubsidized workers by federal funds and federally subsidized workers so that the disemployment effects of these programs go a long way toward canceling their positive aspects. The extent to which this has occurred under CETA and other programs is controversial, but the problem has been considered serious enough to alter program regulations and to put the entire program in jeopardy.

Econometric estimates of the extent of displacement have generally been quite high, often approaching 100%, and Gramlich's results are consistent with these. Field monitoring estimates, however, have been much lower, typically closer to 20% (Nathan et al., 1978). The paper by Borus and Hamermesh cautions against too heavy a reliance on econometric results by showing the extent to which these may depend upon the modeling assumptions employed. This is not surprising in view of the small number of highly aggregated observations on which the study they review is based.

The displacement debate is partly responsible for the final chapter of the volume, for this is a research design for a labor market study to accompany the impact analysis of the Employment Opportunity Pilot Projects. These projects, the centerpiece of the Department of Labor's plan to reform the welfare program by replacing it with subsidized job creation for those able to work, are similar in basic design to the manpower and training programs discussed in Parts II and III. Now, however, the notion of program impact has been extended to include impacts on nonparticipants, an important widening of evaluation studies. The paper by Bishop et al. is the result of an unusual cooperative arrangement among three research contractors, and it provides a number of innovative aproaches to answering the questions that result from an expanded view of the potential scope of program effects. It seems likely that studies such as this one will regularly accompany impact analyses in the years to come. (Such a study is already underway for the Entitlement Demonstration.)

IX. CONCLUSION

As editors, looking back over the papers collected here, we are impressed. During the 1970s, econometric methods particularly appropriate to experimental/control comparisons under less-than-ideal circumstances have sprung up at the same time as large-scale social experimentation provided scope and substance to exercise the methodology. We believe that the resulting literature is extremely interesting.

It is customary at this point to cast a glance into the future and extoll the promise of the methods to come. We have no doubt that the line of econometric development begun with tobit will continue to proliferate, and that this is probably a good thing. We would, however, prefer that good experimental design, with random assignment, stratification only on exogenous variables, clearly defined treatments, and arrangements for minimum attrition, minimize the scope for complex methods. We are sure that by now Guy Orcutt is tired of asking "What is the treatment?"

NOTES

1. See Pearson and Lee (1908). We are grateful to Randy Olsen for this reference. For an updated version of this method see Olsen (1980a).
2. We ask the forgiveness of those omitted from mention in the suceeding paragraphs. At this point in the story the literature rapidly becomes too dense for adequate summary.
3. Maximum likelihood is a general estimation procedure that produces estimators with desirable properties under a variety of circumstances. In simple situations, such as those for which OLS regression is appropriate, the maximum likelihood estimator is identical to the estimator we are already accustomed to.
4. See Hausman and Wise (1978) for a probit analogue of these logit models.
5. For a relatively complete, user-oriented review of log-linear models for panel data, see chapter 7 of Bishop et al. (1975).
6. Markov was a mathematician who worked on stochastic processes (probabilistic events occurring through time). Markov models have long been a central theme within mathematical statistics.
7. Such a model is referred to as first-order Markov.

REFERENCES

AMEMIYA, T. (1978) "The estimation of a simultaneous equation generalized probit model." Econometrica 46: 1193-1206.
——— (1974) "Multivariate regression and simultaneous equation models when the dependent variables are truncated normal." Econometrica 42: 999-1012.
——— (1973) "Regression analysis when the dependent variable is truncated normal." Econometrica 41: 997-1016.
ANDERSON, T. W. (1954) "Probability models for analyzing time changes in attitudes," in P. Lazarsfeld (ed.) Mathematical Thinking in the Social Sciences. Glencoe, IL: Free Press.
——— and L. A. GOODMAN (1957) "Statistical inference about Markov chains." Annals of Mathematical Statistics 28: 89-110.

BERNDT, E. K., B. H. HALL, R. E. HALL, and J. A. HAUSMAN (1974) "Estimation and inference in nonlinear structural models." Annals of Econ. and Social Measurement 4: 653-665.

BISHOP, Y., S. FIENBERG, and P. HOLLAND (1975) Discrete Multivariate Analysis. Cambridge, MA: M.I.T.

BLUMEN, I., M. KOGAN, and P. J. McCARTHY (1955) "The industrial mobility of labor as a probability process." Cornell Studies in Industrial and Labor Relations, no. 6. Ithaca, NY: Cornell Univ. Press.

BURTLESS, G. and J. A. HAUSMAN (1978) "The effect of taxation on labor supply: evaluating the Gary Negative Income Tax Experiment." J. of Pol. Economy 86: 1102-1130. (Reprinted in this volume.)

CHAMBERLAIN, G. (1978) "On the use of panel data." Presented at the SSRC Conference on Life Cycle Aspects of Employment and the Labor Market, Mt. Kisco, NY.

COGAN, J. (1976) "Labor supply with time and money costs of participation." Santa Monica, CA: Rand. (mimeo)

COLEMAN, J. (1964) Introduction to Mathematical Sociology. Glencoe, IL: Free Press.

CONLISK, J. (1973) "Choice of response functional form in designing subsidy experiments." Econometrica 41: 643-656.

——— and H. WATTS (1969) "A model for optimizing experimental designs for estimating response surfaces." Proceedings of the Social Statistics Section, American Statistical Association.

CRAGG, J. (1971) "Some statistical models for limited dependent variables with application to the demand for durable goods." Econometrica 39: 829-844.

DOMENCICH, T. and D. McFADDEN (1975) Urban Travel Demand. Amsterdam (Netherlands): North-Holland.

FELLNER, W. (1979) Contemporary Economic Problems 1979. Washington, DC: American Enterprise Institute.

FISHER, R. A. (1931) Mathematical Tables, vol. I. Cambridge (England): Cambridge Univ. Press.

FRIEDMAN, J. and D. WEINBERG (forthcoming) "The demand for rental housing: evidence from the Housing Allowance Demand Experiment." J. of Urban Economics.

GOLDBERGER, A. (1972) "Selection bias in evaluating treatment effects: some formal illustrations." Discussion Paper, Institute for Research on Poverty. Madison: Univ. of Wisconsin.

GOLDFELD, S. and R. QUANDT (1972) Non-Linear Methods in Econometrics. Amsterdam (Netherlands): North-Holland.

GRAMLICH, E. (1978) "State and local budgets the day after it rained: why is the surplus so high?" Brookings Papers 1: 191-214.

——— and H. GALPER (1973) "State and local fiscal behavior and federal grant policy." Brookings Papers 1: 15-58.

GRILICHES, Z., B. H. HALL, and J. A. HAUSMAN (1978) "Missing data and self-selection in large panels." Annals de l'INSEE.

GRONAU, R. (1974) "Wage comparisons—a selectivity bias." J. of Pol. Economy (November/ December): 1119-1143.

——— (1973) "The intrafamily allocation of time: the value of the housewife's time." Amer. Economic Rev. 63: 634-651.

HANNAN, M. T., N. B. TUMA, and L. P. GROENEVELD (1978) "Income and independence effects on marital dissolution: results from the Seattle-Denver Income Maintenance Experiments." Amer. J. of Sociology 84: 611-633.

——— (1977) "Income and marital events: evidence from an income maintenance experiment." Amer. J. of Sociology 82: 1186-1211.

HAUSMAN, J. (1980) "The effect of wages, taxes, and fixed costs on women's labor force participation." J. of Public Economics.

——— and D. WISE (1980) "Discontinuous budget constraints and estimation: the demand for housing." The Review of Economic Studies. (Reprinted in this volume.)

——— (1979) "Attrition bias in experimental and panel data: the Gary Income Maintenance Experiment." Econometrica 47: 455-473. (Reprinted in this volume.)

—––— (1978) "A conditional probit model for qualitative choice: recognizing interdependence and heterogeneous preferences." Econometrica (March): 403-426.

—––— (1977a) "Social experimentation, truncated distributions, and efficient estimation." Econometrica (May): 919-938.

—––— (1977b) "Stratification on endogenous variables and estimation: the Gary Income Maintenance Experiment." (mimeo)

—––— (1976) "The evaluation of results from truncated samples: the New Jersey Income Maintenance Experiment." Annals of Economic and Social Measurement 5: 421-446.

HECKMAN, J. (1979) "Sample bias as a specification error." Econometrica (January): 153-162. (Reprinted in this volume.)

—––— (1978a) "Dummy endogenous variables in a simultaneous equation system." Econometrica (July): 931-960.

—––— (1978b) "Statistical models for discrete panel data developed and applied to test the hypothesis of true state dependence against the hypothesis of spurious state dependence." Annales de l'INSEE.

—––— (1976) "The common structure of statistical models of truncation, sample selection, and limited dependent variables and a simple estimator for such models." Annals of Econ. and Social Measurement. (December): 475-492.

—––— (1974a) "Shadow prices, market wages, and labor supply." Econometrica (July): 679-694.

—––— (1974b) "Effects of child care programs on women's work effort." J. of Pol. Economy 82, Pt. 2: S136-163.

JOHNSON, G. (1978) "Structural unemployment consequences of unemployment policies," in J. Palmer (ed.) Creating Jobs: Public Employment Programs and Wage Subsidies. Washington, DC: Brookings.

—––— and J. TOMOLA (1977) "The fiscal substitution effect of alternative approaches to public service employment policy." J. of Human Resources (Winter): 3-26.

LAZARSFELD, P., B. BERELSON, and H. GAUDET (1948) The People's Choice. New York: Columbia Univ. Press.

LEE, L. F. (1979) "Identification and estimation in binary choice models with limited (censored) dependent variables." Econometrica 4: 977-994.

—––— (1976) "Estimation of limited dependent variable models by two-stage methods. Ph.D. Dissertation, University of Rochester.

—––—, G. S. MADDALA, and R. P. TROST (1980) "Asymptotic covariance matrices of two-stage probit and two-stage tobit methods for simultaneous equations models with selectivity." Econometrica (March): 491-504.

LEWIS, H. G. (1974) "Comments on selectivity biases in wage comparisons." J. of Pol. Economy 82: 1145-1156.

—––— (1959) "Competitive and monopoly unionism," in P. D. Bradley (ed.) The Public Stake in Union Power. Charlottesville: Univ. of Virginia Press.

MADDALA, G. (1978) "Selectivity Problems in Longitudinal Data." Annales de l'INSEE.

—––— and L. F. LEE (1976) "Recursive models with qualitative endogenous variables." Annals of Econ. and Social Measurement 5: 525-545.

MANSKI, C. and S. LERMAN (1977) "The estimation of choice probabilities from choice based samples." Econometrica (November): 1977-1988.

McFADDEN, D. (1974) "Conditional logit analysis of qualitative choice behavior," in P. Zarembka (ed.) Frontiers of Econometrics. New York: Academic.

McGINNIS, R. (1968) "A stochastic process model of social mobility." Amer. Soc. Rev. 33: 712-722.

NATHAN, R. et al. (1978) "Monitoring the public service employment program." Report prepared for the National Commission for Employment Policy, Washington, DC (March).

OLSEN, R. J. (1980a) "Approximating a truncated normal regression with the method of moments." Econometrica. (forthcoming)

—––— (1980b) "A least squares correction for selectivity bias." Econometrica. (forthcoming)

————— (1979) "Tests for the presence of selectivity bias and their relation to specifications of functional form and error distribution." Working Paper 812. Yale University, Institution for Social and Policy Studies.

————— (1978a) "Note on the uniqueness of the maximum likelihood estimator for the tobit model." Econometrica (September): 1211-1216.

————— (1978b) "Two approaches to labor supply and selectivity bias—a reconciliation in terms of fixed costs." Working Paper 796, Yale University. Institution for Social and Policy Studies.

————— (1977) "An econometric model of family labor supply." Ph.D. Dissertation, University of Chicago.

PEARSON, K. and A. LEE (1908) "Generalized probable error in multiple normal correlation." Biometrika 6: 59-68.

ROSEN, S. (1974) "Comment." J. of Pol. Economy 82, Pt. 2: S164-S169.

SHULTZ, T. R. (1975) Estimating Labor Supply Functions for Married Women. Rand Report R-1265-NIH/EDA. Santa Monica, CA: Rand.

SINGER, B. and S. SPILERMAN (1976) "The representation of social processes by Markov models." Amer. J. of Sociology 82: 1-54.

————— (1974) "Social mobility models for heterogeneous populations," in H. Coster (ed.) Sociological Methodology 1973-74. San Francisco: Jossey-Bass.

SPILERMAN, S. (1972a) "The analysis of mobility processes by the introduction of independent variables into a Markov chain." Amer. Soc. Rev. 37: 277-294.

————— (1972b) "Extensions of the mover-stayer model." Amer. J. of Sociology 78: 599-626.

TOBIN, J. (1958) "Estimation of relationships for limited dependent variables." Econometrica 24-36.

TUMA, N., M. HANNAN, and L. GROENEVELD (1979) "Dynamic analyses of event histories." Amer. J. of Sociology (January): 820-854.

WELCH, F. (1978) "The labor supply response of farmers," in Palmer and J. Pechman (eds.) Welfare in Rural Areas. Washington, DC: The Brookings Institution.

WISEMAN, M. (1976) "Public employment as fiscal policy " Brookings Papers on Economic Activity 1: 67-104.

I

METHODOLOGY

As noted in the Introduction, the causes and cures for bias arising from limited dependent (truncated) variables, truncated samples (some observations entirely missing), censored samples (some observations missing certain variables—for example, through sample attrition from the postprogram survey in a two-wave, before/after evaluation design), and self-selection (for example, into experimental and control groups) are closely related. Since the resulting methodology is a central theme of this volume, we devote this space to summarizing its main features, with particular attention to practical model specification and computational issues. We therefore focus on the first three papers of this section. However, the other papers touch on these issues also: Morris et al. when they discuss the dangers of stratification on endogenous variables, and Tuma et al. when they show how their model can be used to account for sample attrition as an absorbing state. This introduction is divided into two parts. The first provides an overview of the statistical issues underlying the methodology, while the second is a short, practical guide to the methods appropriate to situations likely to confront the investigator.

1. STATISTICAL ISSUES ASSOCIATED WITH LIMITED DEPENDENT VARIABLES, SAMPLE SELECTION, AND ATTRITION

The technical issues associated with the use of truncated normal distributions in the central core of methods under discussion are clarified by considering three examples.

The first of these is simply that of a limited, dependent variable as considered by Tobin (1958). Figure 1 shows a dependent variable, such as hours or weeks at work, which is not permitted to be negative, and is positively associated with the X variable.[1] The figure resembles that usually employed to explain OLS regression in which at each X value, we imagine the distribution of the dependent variable to be normal (that is, Gaussian) and centered on the regression line. We see that this assumption is violated in the case of the limited dependent variable, since these normal distributions are truncated where they meet the X axis. As a result, OLS regression applied to this situation would erroneously attempt to fit a line through the trajectory of the dependent variable means conditional on X values, shown in the figure as $a^1b^1c^1$. Instead, the tobit model estimates the slope of the tobit index, abc, and recaptures the standard error of the truncated normal distribution. In general, a slope estimate based on $a^1b^1c^1$ will be a biased indicator of the slope of abc.

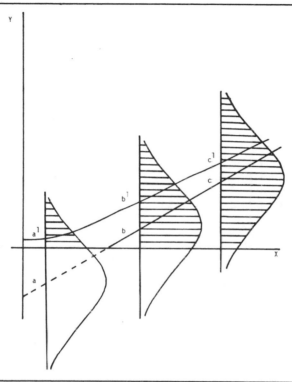

FIGURE 1: The Tobit Model for a Limited Dependent Variable (adapted from Schultz, 1975)

The second example shows the link between truncated samples and the limited dependent variable situation just considered. It is adapted from Hausman and Wise (1977a), who are concerned with the bias that can result from using OLS regression to estimate behavioral parameters from data collected for the evaluation of the New Jersey Negative Income Tax Experiment. The problem arises because the study sample does not fully represent the population but, rather, excludes families with incomes above one-and-one-half times the poverty level. We thus have a truncated sample (observations entirely missing in a nonrandom manner), a situation similar to, but different from, the tobit situation (Figure 1) where observations on the dependent variable alone are "piled up" at zero. (This latter case can be viewed as a censored sample, since some individuals—those with a score of zero—are lacking information on one variable.) This example of a truncated sample is shown in Figure 2.

Here is a situation reminiscent of Figure 1. As we move across values of X, the conditional mean of the dependent variable in the observed sample follows the path $a^1b^1c^1$, which is an erroneous guide to the true population path, abc. Once again we must recreate the truncated normal distribution to find the correct (population) slope of Y against X. And as before, the estimation involves maximizing a likelihood function tailored to the situation.

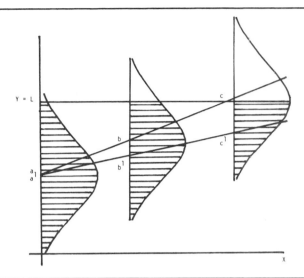

FIGURE 2:   A Sample Truncated at the Value L of the Dependent Variable
(adapted from Hausman and Wise, 1977a)

The final example shows that either self-selection into experimental and comparison groups or nonrandom sample attrition can lead to a situation quite similar to those already discussed. Figure 3 illustrates a situation in which the X variable is a program treatment—let us suppose it is weeks spent in a manpower training program. Here the comparison group comprises those with zero weeks, while the members of the experimental group receive a treatment whose intensity is measured by X. The dependent variable is some outcome measure of interest—for example post-program earnings.

If individuals are randomly assigned to treatment status, and there is no sample attrition, OLS regression will be adequate to estimate the true program effect given by the slope of the abc line. Suppose, however, that individuals are self-selected into treatment status, and that this occurs in such a way that the more ambitious individuals are disproportionately likely to volunteer for participation in the program. If such ambition is by itself a determinant of earnings, the distribution of earnings in the study sample will conform to that given by the shaded areas in Figure 3. (Darker shading corresponds to higher probabilities of observing the particular portion of the distribution.) That is, this distribution will shift upward with advancing X more rapidly than would be caused by the program effect alone. As a result, estimation via OLS produces the slope of $a^1 b^1 c^1$, an upwardly biased estimate of the true program effect.

The same figure can result from nonrandom sample attrition. Thus, in one scenario, even though individuals are randomly assigned to treatment status, successive waves of reinterviews designed to measure postprogram earnings are unable to locate all of the original sample members. If this occurs because ambitious members of the control group leave the locality in search of better job

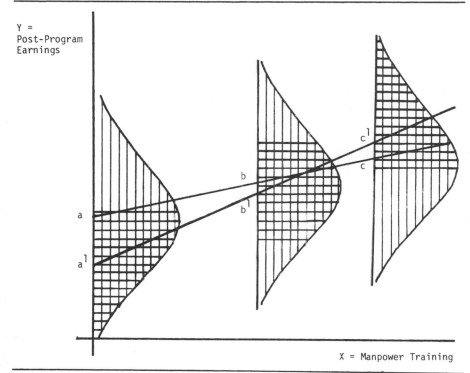

Y =
Post-Program
Earnings

X = Manpower Training

FIGURE 3: Self-Selection into Treatment Status

opportunities while ambitious members of the experimental group stay in the locality to be reinterviewed (possibly because their program experience has led to local job contacts) we are back in the situation of Figure 3. Of course, in either situation, if the variable "ambition" has been measured we can enter it into the OLS regression, thereby adjusting for its effect and still arrive at an unbiased estimate of program impact. But where there are unmeasured factors at work, methods such as those described by Barnow et al. (this volume), Heckman (this volume), and Hausman and Wise (this volume) are indicated.[2]

Practical application of these methods raises its own difficulties. Prominent here are the issues of (a) model specification; (b) identification; (c) assumptions regarding distributional shape; and (d) the choice of one among the several estimators that are often available. We leave further discussion of these more technical issues to our introductions to the various sections and to our head-notes for the chapters themselves.

2. A GUIDE TO PRACTICE

It is useful to distinguish two situations, either or both of which may confront the investigator. The first is nonrandom assignment to treatment status; that is, because of self-selection or other mechanisms, the variable that measures the program treatment must be considered endogenous rather than exogenous. The second is the situation in which program outcome observations are nonrandomly missing from the sample; observations are absent either through attrition from the "after" survey in a before/after design (censored sample), or because the basic sample is nonrepresentative of the population as a whole (truncated sample). Considered jointly, these situations define the four categories shown in Figure 4. We discuss the methodology for each of these in turn.

No Sample Attrition, Random Assignment to Treatment and Control

This is the ideal experimental situation. If Y is the outcome measure of interest, and T defines an individual's treatment status, we need only regress Y on T to measure the program's impact. More generally, one would include other predictors (X) in the equation to increase efficiency by decreasing the error variance in the regression. The result is the equation

$$Y = aX + bT + e. \qquad [1]$$

No Sample Attrition, Self-Selection to Treatment and Control

This is the case treated by Barnow et al. (and also, in passing, in the chapter by Heckman). It involves a two-equation system

$$Y_1 = a_1 X_1 + bT + e_1 \qquad [2]$$

$$Y_2 = a_2 X_2 + e_2, \qquad [3]$$

where Y_1 is the outcome measure and Y_2 is an index determining the individual's treatment status. That is

$$T = \begin{cases} 1 \text{ (experimental group) if } Y_2 > 0 \\ 0 \text{ (control group)} \qquad \text{if } Y_2 \leq 0. \end{cases} \qquad [4]$$

In addition, e_1 and e_2 are correlated, making [2] and [3] a simultaneous equation system. (If the error terms are uncorrelated once X_1 and X_2 are in the equations, the model reverts to the situation of [1].)

Several consistent estimators are available in this situation. The first one discussed by Barnow et al. (and originally made famous by Heckman) is the "inverse Mills ratio term" method. This involves first estimating [3] as a probit, then using the resulting coefficients to compute a new variable, which is the inverse of an expression known (for historical reasons) as the Mills ratio, and is usually denoted $\hat{\lambda}$. This term is then added as a regressor to [2], yielding

$$Y_1 = a_1 X_1 + bT + c\hat{\lambda} + e_1, \qquad [5]$$

	The Experimental/Control Dummy Variable is Endogenous (Self Selection Instead of Random Assignment)	
	No	Yes
Some Missing Observations for the Outcome Variable (Sample Attrition) No	1	2
Yes	3	4

FIGURE 4:   Four Program Evaluation Situations

which is estimated by ordinary least squares (OLS). The resulting value of b, the coefficient for the experimental/control dummy variable, is an unbiased estimate of the true program effect.

Several comments should be made regarding the properties of this procedure. First, its great advantage is that it is easy to perform and does not require exclusionary restrictions for identification. That is, because the probit specifies T as a nonlinear function of the X_2's, identification is assured and there is no need to find a variable among the X_2 set that can be assumed not to be among the X_1 set. Second, although the program effect estimate from this procedure is unbiased, the coefficient standard errors from the OLS regression are not. So significance tests require further calculations. In addition, it is possible in practice for the estimate of the correlation between e_1 and e_2 resulting from this procedure to fail to lie between −1 and +1. Finally, the method is based on the assumption that the joint distribution of e_1 and e_2 is bivariate normal. If this is false, the results can be misleading (Olsen, 1979). Under a different assumption, an even simpler procedure emerges (Olsen, forthcoming). This involves estimating the probability that an individual belong to the treatment group by OLS (linear probability model) rather than as a probit, using the resulting predicted values to form the expression $\hat{P} = 1$, and entering this term in equation 5 in place of $\hat{\lambda}$. This method however, does require identification via an exclusionary restriction.[3] In practice, the two methods appear to give quite similar results.

As pointed out by Barnow et al., there is a simple alternative to the inverse Mills ratio technique. After estimating the a_2 coefficient vector from the probit for equation 3, this can be used to form the probability $\hat{P}$ that an individual belongs to the treatment group, and $\hat{P}$ can be entered directly in equation 2 in place of the T dummy variable:

$$Y_1 = a_1 X_1 + b\hat{P} + e_1. \qquad [6]$$

If this model is estimated by OLS, the coefficient b for $\hat{P}$ will be an unbiased estimate of the treatment effect. Once again, identification is achieved by the nonlinearity of the probit, and standard errors are not correct. Equation 6 is the usual two-stage least squares estimator for simultaneous equations. Following

Olsen (forthcoming), it is possible to show that $\hat{P}$ can be estimated by OLS rather than as a probit; but in this case identification must be by exclusionary restrictions.

Greater efficiency results from estimating [2] and [3] jointly via maximum likelihood, and programs for doing so also usually provide correct standard errors. We briefly discuss these methods in the section below.

Sample Attrition, Random Assignment to Treatment and Control

Cell 3 of Figure 4 is the situation discussed by Heckman and Hausman and Wise. Heckman presents his OLS inverse Mills ratio method, while Hausman and Wise undertake maximum likelihood estimation of a three-equation model: one equation for the "before" outcome measure, one for the "after" outcome measure, and one to indicate sample attrition (missing information for the "after" measure). The issues are clarified by examining the following two-equation model designed to parallel that of equations 2 and 3:

$$Y_1 = a_1 X_1 + bT + e_1 \tag{2}$$

$$Y_2 = a_2 X_2 + cT + e_2. \tag{7}$$

Here we have the same outcome equation as before and are still interested in an unbiased estimate of the coefficient for the experimental/control dummy variable. But in this case Y_2 is an index determining the individual's attrition status. That is

$$A = \begin{cases} 1\,(\text{attritor}) \text{ if } Y_2 > 0 \\ 0\,(\text{non-attritor}) \text{ if } Y_2 \leqslant 0, \end{cases} \tag{8}$$

so that A is a dummy variable indicating whether an individual is an attritor, and the probability of this being the case is determined by the index of equation 7. As before, it is because of the correlation between e_1 and e_2 that bias potentially arises.

Heckman's solution to this situation is to estimate equation 7 by probit analysis, construct the $\hat{\lambda}$ term associated with sample attrition, and employ it as an additional regressor to yield

$$Y_1 = a_1 X_1 + bT + c\hat{\lambda} + e_1, \tag{5}$$

which is then estimated via OLS. The only difference between this and the methodology from the previous section is that here the Mills ratio term is associated with the probability of attrition, whereas before it was associated with the probability of membership in the experimental group.

Previous discussion of the properties of this method carries over to the attrition situation. In particular, it is possible to replace the $\hat{\lambda}$ term with $\hat{P} - 1$

estimated from a linear probability model for equations 7 and 8. Once again, this latter method requires identification by exclusion.

Maximum likelihood estimation has several attractions: It produces the most efficient estimator, eliminating the issue of deciding among several less than fully efficient OLS estimators; it produces correct standard errors; and it produces an estimate of the correlation between the error terms in the two-equation model that always lies between −1 and +1. The idea is simply to write out the likelihood function (the probability of having observed the sample data configuration expressed as a function of the model parameters), and then find the values of the parameters that maximize this function. The result is achieved by using the derivatives of the function in an iterative computing routine. One of the best, based on the Fletcher-Powell minimization routine, proceeds as follows:

> The parameter which determines the extent and direction of bias for OLS is ρ, the correlation between the error of the regression equation and the error term of the probit relation. For given values of ρ there is a unique maximum of the likelihood function with respect to the probit coefficients, the regression coefficients and the variance of the regression equation. When ρ is allowed to vary there may be multiple maxima of the log-likelihood function and in order to obtain the global maximum corresponding to consistent estimates a modified search procedure is used. First, the function is maximized conditional upon a number of values for ρ. The resulting plot of the 'concentrated' likelihood function will reveal the approximate neighborhood in which the function achieves its global maximum. In the second step the parameter values corresponding to the approximate maximum of the likelihood function are used as starting values and the likelihood function is maximized allowing all parameters (including ρ) to vary [Olsen, 1975].

This routine requires second derivatives, and, as always, extensive calculation. A method that uses only first derivatives has been developed by Berndt et al. (1974) and implemented in a computer program by the authors. Once again, extensive iteration is required. But the relative efficacy of the two methods is unclear.

The reader should know that estimating these models can produce results that differ a great deal from simple OLS estimates with the nonattrited sample, and the "corrected" estimates will occasionally appear to make no sense at all. This may be due to inappropriate assumptions regarding the variables and their appearance in each of the model equations, or it may be due to the incorrectness of the bivariate normal distributional assumption. A likelihood estimator that relaxes this assumption has been developed by Olsen (1979). As demonstrated in the chapter by Farkas et al., this model may outperform that based on bivariate normality.

Sample Attrition, Self-Selection to Treatment and Control

Cell 4 of Figure 4 leads to a three equation model:

$$Y_1 = a_1 X_1 + bT + e_1 \qquad\qquad [2]$$

$$Y_2 = a_2 X_2 + e_2 \qquad\qquad [3]$$

$$Y_3 = a_3 X_3 + cT + e_3, \qquad\qquad [7]$$

where Y_2 is an index determining the probability of assignment for T, the dummy variable for experimental/control status, and Y_3 is an index determining the probability of assignment for A, the dummy variable for attritor/nonattritor status. Here we must assume that correlations exist among all three error terms, so that three additional parameters enter the problem.

This situation is probably the most common one faced by evaluators, but it has rarely (if at all) been dealt with using the methods discussed here. In principle, a relatively large number of estimators can be constructed simply by mixing and matching the methods already proposed for self-selection and attrition. For example, two Mills ratio terms, one for each "problem," can be constructed and added to equation 2. Or $\hat{P}$ for program participation can be used in conjunction with a Mills ratio term to correct for attrition, and so forth. The practical difficulty is likely to come from the assumptions needed to assure identification, as well as from the form imposed on the joint distribution of the three error terms. Common sense suggests trying the correction under several different assumptions.

Maximum likelihood is appealing for estimating the system [2], [3], and [7], but the calculations themselves are likely to become quite cumbersome without further restrictions on the model. (The chapter by Hausman and Wise involves maximum likelihood estimation for a three-equation system—before, after, and attrition—and they simplify their problem by assuming that two of the error terms are correlated only through the correlation of each with the third.) Nevertheless, it seems likely that in the future there will be more exploration of techniques for dealing with this situation.

We have summarized a complex methodology, and the reader is urged to examine the papers in this section for points we have omitted. In general, the models and estimation techniques presented are in their infancy, but the literature can be expected to grow rapidly in the years ahead. In particular, we know very little about these and related econometric correction techniques when the dependent variable is categorical. If the dependent variable is limited, the Hausman and Wise model in this section can be extended to a before/after tobit with attrition (Smith, 1980). Work is currently proceeding on these and a number of related models, but the results must be handled with care. By comparison with the OLS world we are accustomed to, the new world of maximum likelihood estimation of tailor-made models can produce relatively opaque results that are particularly sensitive to assumptions regarding functional form and distributional shape. In addition, the novice may encounter difficulty with the computer software currently available. Caution is clearly advised.

NOTES

1. See Schultz (1975) for a similar figure and discussion.

2. Other situations where bias can arise include that in which the sample has been stratified on an endogenous variable. This has often been the case, for example, in the Seattle and Denver Income Maintenance Experiments (see Hausman and Wise, 1977b).

3. Without exclusionary restrictions, the probit method achieves identification by assuming that its particular nonlinear functional form just happens to be correct. This may be as good an arbitrary assumption as any other—but no better. A similar assumption for the linear probability model correction can be implemented by simply adding powers and products of the X_2 variables to the equation. In general, such identification by nonlinearity is a shaky proposition. With either method, identification by exclusion is preferred.

REFERENCES

BERNDT, E. K., B. H. HALL, R. E. HALL, and J. A. HAUSMAN (1974) "Estimation and inference in nonlinear structural models." Annals of Economic and Social Measurement 4: 653-665.

HAUSMAN, J. and D. WISE (1977a) "Social experimentation, truncated distributions, and efficient estimations." Econometrica (May): 919-938.

——— (1977b) "Stratification on endogenous variables and estimation: the Gary Income Maintenance Experiment." (mimeo)

OLSEN, R. J. (forthcoming) "A least squares correction for selectivity bias." Econometrica.

——— (1979) "Tests for the presence of selectivity bias and their relation to specifications of functional form and error distribution," Working Paper 812. New Haven, CT: Yale University, Institution for Social and Policy Studies.

——— (1975) "The linear regression model with informative sampling: a computer program." New Haven, CT: Yale University. (mimeo)

SMITH, D. A. (1980) "Memo on the three equation model: two tobits plus attrition." Cambridge, MA: Abt Assoc. (mimeo)

TOBIN, J. (1958) "Estimations of relationships for limited dependent variables." Econometrica 26: 24-36.

1

The importance of this chapter for the volume lies in the direct link it forges between the collection of simultaneous-equation methods for censoring and truncation and the central problem of many evaluations—nonrandom assignment to treatment and control. Whereas many econometric discussions make the link in passing (see the following chapter by Heckman, for example), few do so with such detail and readability as Barnow et al. The authors also place these methods within a literature on evaluation research that appears foreign to most econometricians. Accordingly, it is an ideal bridge between previous volumes of the *Evaluation Studies Review Annual* and the concerns of the present one.

The authors note that selectivity bias arises when treatment/control status is related to unmeasured characteristics that themselves are related to the program outcome under study. The focus is on unmeasured variables because we are in a multiple regression framework and believe ourselves able to adjust treatment/control mean differences for *observed* variables. The downside of this strategy is that we are unlikely to know the correct functional form, so that regression adjustments may never get us back to what would have been observed with random assignment. The positive implication is that even without the methods advocated, regression adjustments that control for many of the important variables may include sufficient variables correlated with those excluded such that further adjustments (such as those proposed by Barnow et al.) will make only a small difference. These are empirical questions, and it is best to employ the full range of methods available when faced with nonrandom assignment to treatment status.

The formal argument begins with a simple, additive linear model of program effect,

$$y = \alpha Z + w + e_0, \tag{1}$$

where z is treatment status and w is the (unobserved) preprogram "true ability" to achieve y—the outcome of interest. The issue is how an evaluator can convince his audience that the measured effect of z on y is free of any contamination (correlation between z and w), even though w is not available as an explanatory variable. (It is here that random assignment would be desirable.)

The authors now suppose that an observed variable t was used to determine assignment to treatment/control status. Although t is a score based on a composite of variables (some of them correlated with ability, w), "since t is the only systematic determinant of treatment status, t will capture any correlation between z and w." Thus, entering t alongside z in a regression equation will yield an unbiased estimate of program effect.

This argument can be elaborated. We are supposing that t has the property that holding it constant, assignment to treatment/control is random. That is, within categories of t (for a particular value of t), assignment to treatment status is uncorrelated with everything, in particular, with "ability" (w). This is the "perfect control variable," because with it in the equation, z is uncorrelated with every other variable, and so the coefficient for z must be unbiased.

Barnow et al. put this example in a real-world context by supposing that t is not precisely known, but that we have a vector of variables, x, some of which are correlated with (proxy for) ability (w), and some of which enter t. Entering these x variables alongside z in a regression equation will, in general, leave the z coefficient biased, with this bias depending on the covariance between z and w, conditional on x. The authors thus correct previous discussion in the evaluation literature by showing that everything depends on the *conditional* covariance of z and w.

After a digression, Barnow et al. finally derive the Mills ratio correction method. By assuming that both w and t depend upon x,

$$w = \theta'_1 \, x + e_1 \qquad\qquad [2]$$

$$t = \theta'_2 \, x + e_2, \qquad\qquad [3]$$

they isolate two sources of nonrandom selection—identical x variables affecting both w and t, and covariance (σ_{12}) between e_1 and e_2—and by substituting equation 2 into equation 1 they arrive at the following impact equation:

$$y = \theta'_1 \, x + \alpha Z + e_3. \qquad\qquad [4]$$

It is this equation, estimated jointly with [3] ($\sigma_{23} = \sigma_{12} \neq 0$) which is at the heart of the method.

Finally, the authors impose the assumption of bivariate normality for the error terms and derive the Mills ratio correction term to be added to equation 4. This derivation involves calculating the expected value of e_2 given x and either $z = 1$ or $z = 0$, and then using these to calculate the expected value of y given x and z. (A similar derivation appears in the following chapter by Heckman.) The chapter closes with a discussion of an alternate method and some of the practical difficulties in implementing the techniques (see the Introduction to this section for further discussion).

Issues in the
Analysis of Selectivity Bias

Burt S. Barnow, Glen G. Cain, and
Arthur S. Goldberger

1. INTRODUCTION

Selectivity bias arises in program evaluations when the treatment (or control) status of the subjects is related to unmeasured characteristics that themselves are related to the program outcome under study. The term "bias" refers to the potential misestimate of the effect of the treatment (or program) on the out-

Authors' Note: This is a revised version of the paper presented at the August 1978 meeting of the Econometric Society in Chicago. Burt S. Barnow is Acting Director of the Office of Research and Development, Employment and Training Administration, U.S. Department of Labor. Glen G. Cain and Arthur S. Goldberger are Professors of Economics at the University of Wisconsin—Madison. The research was supported in part by National Science Foundation Grant SOC 76-24428 and by the Institute for Research on Poverty with funds granted by the Department of Health, Education and Welfare. The ideas expressed herewith do not necessarily reflect those of the supporting agencies.

From Burt S. Barnow, Glen G. Cain, and Arthur S. Goldberger, "Issues in the Analysis of Selectivity Bias." Unpublished manuscript, 1980.

come. Selectivity bias is a concern whenever the assignment to treatment and control groups is not random, conditional on whatever observable explanatory variables, if any, are used in the analysis. So stated, it is clear that the issue of selection bias is pervasive in empirical research in economics because the assignment of observations to the different statuses defined by the predictor or explanatory variables of interest is seldom explicitly random. Thus, there should be a common ground in the methods used to analyze selectivity bias in program evaluation and econometrics, which are separate but increasingly overlapping fields.

In this essay we adapt techniques developed in the econometric analysis of labor markets—particularly by James J. Heckman (1974, 1976, 1978, 1979), G. S. Maddala (1976, 1978) and Maddala and Lung-fei Lee (1976)—to the bias problem in a conventional evaluation model. A resolution of the problem emerges under assumptions that are reasonably general.

The next section provides an institutional background by describing developments in program evaluation and in applied labor economics that deal with and illustrate the issue of selection bias. Section 3 introduces a simple model that illustrates formally the statistical issues, notes conditions when no bias exists and when the direction of bias is known, and points to several misunderstandings in the program evaluation literature. Section 4 surveys several econometric approaches in labor economics that have attempted to eliminate (or, equivalently, to quantify) the bias. Section 5, which is the core of the paper, applies the new econometric approach to the conventional evaluation model to indicate how the selection bias in this model may be resolved.

2. DEVELOPMENTS IN PROGRAM EVALUATION AND LABOR ECONOMICS INVOLVING SELECTION BIAS

Evaluation research began with the analysis of rather small-scale projects, mainly in medicine, experimental and social psychology, educational psychology, and economics. In economics, the benefit-cost approach was central; in the other disciplines, it was applied statistics. Since the mid-1960s evaluation research has been applied to large-scale governmental programs whose main purpose was to improve the well-being of a sizeable segment of society. Evaluation was not the main objective of the programs, which largely explains why random assignment to treatment and control groups was almost never employed. Nevertheless, ex post evaluations were publicly demanded because the successes or failures of the programs were major political issues.

The current practice of program evaluation research by economists is quite different from the ex ante evaluation of water resource projects and the like, which were the mainstay of traditional benefit-cost analysis.[1] In ex post evaluations, the first priority is to estimate the quantitative effect of the program, which logically precedes the determination of whether the benefits exceed the costs. This priority puts a greater emphasis on statistical models and has brought economic evaluation research closer to the approaches used in other disciplines.

Today, evaluation research is a huge enterprise in applied social science. The Evaluation Research Society was organized in 1976, and the journal *Evaluation* began in 1973 with a grant from the National Institute of Mental Health. Courses on the topic are offered in graduate schools of many universities, often in recently established departments or centers of public administration and policy research. A two-volume *Handbook of Evaluation Research,* intended as a text for graduate courses, includes a bibliography of some 1500 items, almost all post-1960 and by noneconomists.[2] Other books on evaluation would fill several shelves in one's bookcase, and these also tend to be recently published and written by noneconomists.[3]

The volume *Federal Program Evaluation* contains an inventory of approximately 1700 evaluation reports produced by and for 18 selected Federal agencies, covering the period 1973-1975. Many were written by researchers outside the government, but all were related to agency programs.[4] One may safely credit or blame the federal government, beginning with the Great Society programs of the Johnson administration, for making evaluation research the growth industry that it now is.

The topic of our article, selectivity bias, occupies a small part of the statistical methodology aspect of evaluation research, an aspect which is, itself, only a small part of the field. Nevertheless, selectivity bias can be given a broad interpretation, with implications and applications extending beyond evaluation research. For example, selectivity bias can be viewed broadly as a version of specification error in statistical models in which behavioral outcomes are functions of "predictor" or "explanatory" variables. In this version, the outcome of a program is examined in the same way as an outcome of a controlled experiment in a laboratory or, at the other end of the spectrum of research settings, as an outcome in a historical process measured with time-series data. There is a common framework used to measure the causal effect on the outcome of, respectively, the program, the laboratory treatment, or the historical event.

Selectivity concerns the presence of some characteristic of the treatment (or control) group that is both associated with receipt of the treatment and associated with the outcome so as to lead to a false attribution of causality regarding treatment and outcomes. So stated, selectivity bias is a version of omitted-variable bias, which is commonly analyzed under the rubric of specification error in econometric models. The unbiased measurement of causal effects is a broad and deep topic, and, as the eminent statistican W. Edwards Deming (1975) stated: "Evaluation is a study of causes."

In labor economics the issue of selection bias in evaluation models has been confronted directly in a number of recent studies. Training and educational programs deal with individuals who are either selected for the program or who are self-selected. If this selection is not fully known to the investigator, an unbiased measure of the treatment may be unobtainable (Ashenfelter, 1978; Garfinkel and Gramlich, 1973; Barnow and Cain, 1977). Regulatory programs usually deal with firms, and, again, there is selection by the agencies (or self-selection) for participation in the regulatory process. The apparent effects of the program may be biased because the outcomes may reflect unmeasured pre-existing characteristics of the selected firms. Evaluation of antidiscrimination and affirmative action programs are a case in point, and Heckman and Wolpin's (1976) study of the Office of Federal Contract Compliance of the U.S. Department of Labor deals explicitly with selection bias. Another example is the study by Smith (1975) of the impact on injuries of the "target industries program" of the Occupational Safety and Health Act (see also the critique by Triplett, 1975).

There are well-known examples of the selection bias issue in other areas of labor economics, which testify to the pervasiveness of the issue in empirical economic research. Attempts to measure the effect of unions on wages are especially interesting, because the selection is so varied in several dimensions. The units of observation may be industries, occupations, firms, or individuals. There is an element of self-selection among individual workers, dependent in part on the worker's preferences for unionism; there is selection by union organizers, dependent in part on the costs and benefits to the union of organizing the work place; and there is selection by employers through their hiring and personnel policies. Some twenty years ago Lewis (1959) discussed these potential selection biases in examining the union wage effect. Several recent econometric studies have attempted to model the selection of workers into union status in the course of estimating the union wage effect: Ashenfelter and Johnson (1972), Schmidt and Strauss (1976), Lee (1978), Leigh (1978), and Olsen (1978). The intricacies in this area are illustrated by noting that the bias may differ across demographic or social groups in the population. Ashenfelter (1972) estimated a larger union effect for blacks than whites, and Griliches (1976) estimated a relatively large union effect on the wages of young men age 17-27. Does selection operate differently among such groups of workers, and, if so, are differential biases a consequence?

Labor supply studies of women have probably provided the most explicit attention to the selectivity bias issue in economics. Here, the market wage of women is the analogue to the treatment in evaluation studies, and selectivity affects labor force participation and thus the observability of the market wage. A special feature here is that the sample for which a wage is measured is truncated—no wage is measured for nonworking women. In the typical program-evaluation design, the treatment variable is measured for both the treatment and control groups. Heckman provided an early analysis of this problem (1974) and a useful review article (1976). Ben-Porath (1973), Gronau (1973, 1974), and Lewis (1974) had earlier discussions of this application of selectivity bias, and Schultz (1980) and Hanoch (1980) have contributed more recent work.

Even those rare examples of economic research which use controlled experiments with random assignments to program status—namely, the negative income tax experiments—have been forced to confront selectivity bias. The issue arises with respect to attrition, particularly when the subjects leave the experiment for one of the existing welfare programs. Analyses of these experiments have included attempts at modeling attrition and of participation in welfare programs (Watts et al., 1977; Garfinkel, 1977).

Other studies in labor economics will be cited in Section 4 as illustrative of specific approaches to dealing with selectivity bias. Our message that the issue is important and pervasive in econometric research as well as in program evaluation research should be noncontroversial.

3. A SIMPLE FORMULATION OF THE EVALUATION MODEL

We examine that part of an evaluation that seeks to measure the effect of the program on a specific quantified outcome. Many aspects of a full evaluation are ignored in this narrow focus: the costs of the program, the dollar-equivalent value of the outcome, the administration of the program, the equity issues involved in the distribution of benefits and costs, the correspondence between measured outcomes and political objectives, the question of multiple objectives, and others.

For simplicity, assume that the outcome, y, is linearly related to the treatment status, z (defined by participation in the program), and to an unobserved variable, w, defined as the preprogram "true ability" to achieve the outcome. A pure random term, ϵ, completes the equation. In this hypothetical evaluation model, with y systematically related to z and w, there would be no need for any other "control" variables. The evaluator's interest is in the effect of z on y, given true ability, and, by assumption, w completely measures that true ability. In (1) below, α is the true treatment effect:

$$y = \alpha z - w + \epsilon. \qquad [1]$$

But this equation is nonoperational because w is unobserved (which, incidentally, is why assigning it a unit coefficient is innocent). How may the evaluator persuade an interested audience that the measured effect of z on y is free of any contamination from a correlation between z and w, given that w is not available as an explanatory variable? Random assignment to the z status is convincing in principle. But the integrity of randomization may be comprised in practice (by reliance on volunteers, by the absence of a double-blind design, by attrition), and, in any event, almost all programs deliberately use nonrandom assignments.

There should be widespread agreement among economists that random assignments are not essential to the estimation of unbiased treatment effects.[5] Unbiasedness is attainable when the variables that determined the assignment are known, quantified, and included in the equation (Goldberger, 1972; Barnow, 1975; Cain, 1975). Assume that an observed variable, t, was used to determine assignment into the treatment group (z = 1) and the control group (z = 0). In general, t, which we refer to as the selection variable, would be a score based on a composite of variables, some of which would be correlates of ability, w. Nevertheless, since t is the only systematic determinant of treatment status, t will capture any correlation between z and w. Thus the observed t could replace the unobserved w as the explanatory variable in [1]. In equation [2], β_1 would be unbiased, that is, equal to α:

$$y = \beta_1 z + \beta_2 t + \epsilon^* \tag{2}$$

The use of *either* w *or* t as an explanatory variable, then, will free z from the contamination which leads to selectivity bias.

"Modeling the selection process" is, of course, precisely what one claims to do when specifying a multiple regression that "holds constant" those traits of the unit of observation that affect the outcome *and* that are correlated with the input variable of interest. A purely random determinant of assignment would be harmless, where "random" refers to a selection variable—such as the flip of a coin—that does not affect the outcome. Theory is supposed to tell us which selection variables are associated with outcomes. As examples: How do persons get "selected into" different educational attainment categories or into union memberships, and how do the variables fully describing this process relate to an outcome variable such as earnings?

To illustrate the selection model briefly with an example that has spawned an extended controversy, assume z is participation in the Head Start compensatory educational program, y is the postprogram test score that is presumed to measure cognitive achievement, and let t represent the family income of the children. Assume, further, that those children for whom t is below the poverty line (t_p) are in the program ($z = 1$) and those with values of t above t_p are excluded ($z = 0$). Even though the correlation between w and t and the correlation between z and t are both negative, there is no bias in β_1 in model [2]. Figure 1 illustrates the magnitude of β_1 in the optimistic case that the program is beneficial.

A misunderstanding has arisen in the uses and interpretation of this model. In a seminal paper on evaluation methodology, the psychologist Donald T. Campbell (1969) suggested that this model, which he calls the "regression discontinuity" design, is severely restricted. But his reasons, in fact, do not apply. Campbell and Erlebacher (1970) say that the model requires a random assignment among "ties" on the boundary line of participation (t_p in our example), and that "We would learn about the effects of the program only for a narrow band. . . . We would wonder about its effectiveness for the most disadvantaged."[6] But model [2] uses the full range of t; "ties" are inconsequential and therefore no randomization is needed; and the entire range of values of t provides potential information for the effectiveness of the program, even for nonlinear or interactive effects. Figures 2A and 2B illustrate negative and positive interactions between the treatment and t. The nonlinear functional forms shown are chosen to avoid both deleterious and explosive treatment effects when t becomes large; such nonlinearities, of course, would have to be specified in the model.

Let us examine next the case where the selection process is not known precisely, in the sense that the available data do not permit quantification of t. Assume that there is available a vector x, composed of variables that are cor-

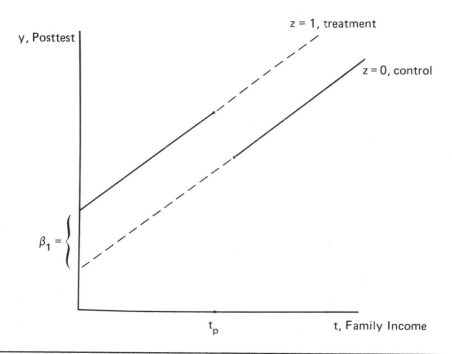

Figure 1 Nonrandom Assignment to Treatment and Control Groups Based on Family Income, t (Dashed lines represent nonobserved extrapolation of y, given t and the treatment/control status, z)

related with—that is, proxy for—ability, w. At the same time, x may include variables which enter t. The equation to be fitted is:

$$y = \gamma_1 z + \gamma_2 x + \epsilon^{**} \tag{3}$$

An estimate of γ_1 in this model will in general be biased for α. As discussed in our earlier papers, the bias depends on the covariance of z and w conditional on x and may be positive or negative. On this point, a misunderstanding arose in the well-known and often-cited paper by Campbell and Erlebacher (1970) dealing with an evaluation of Head Start. They argued that the direction of bias could be inferred on the basis of the x, z correlation:

> How can one tell which direction a matching bias will take? Only by having evidence of the nature of the population difference which matching attempted to overcome. . . . This undermatching [on true ability] showed up on the socioeconomic status ratings subsequently made [which showed a negative correlation between socioeconomic status and treatment status].[7]

It is the last sentence in the quotation that gave rise to the misunderstanding. In the example discussed, x was the socioeconomic status of the parents. Know-

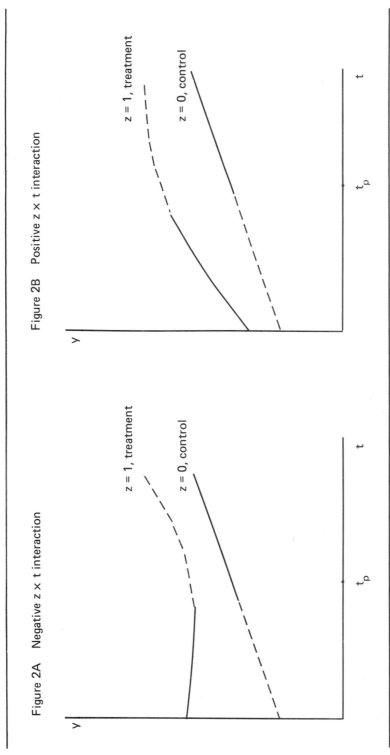

Figures 2A and 2B   Nonrandom Assignments to Treatment and Control Groups Based on Family Income, t, in Examples Where the Treatment Interacts with t*

*Dashed lines represent nonobserved extrapolations of y, given t and the treatment/control status. In Figure 2A the upper solid line, showing a negative interaction, is assumed to reach an asymptote rather than to decline indefinitely, thus avoiding a deleterious treatment effect at higher t values. Similarly in Figure 2B, a positive treatment $\times$ selection interaction increases at a decreasing rate and reaches an asymptote, thus preventing the treatment effect from exploding at higher t values.

ing that the x, w correlation is positive, one cannot infer that a negative x, z correlation biases down the Head Start (or z) effect. What determines the bias is the *conditional* covariance, $C(z,w|x)$ and not the unconditional covariance, $C(z,w)$.[8]

Consider the genreal empirical model represented by equation [3] above, in which the investigator has measures of x. As one polar case, x coincides with w, and there would be no bias in estimating the treatment effect regardless of the selection process. Here, $C(z,w) \neq 0$ but $C(z,w|x) = 0$ because x coincides with w. This polar case is presumably hypothetical, because w is unobserved. As another polar case, x coincides with t, and there is again no bias, as was discussed above in connection with equation [2]. Here again $C(z,w) \neq 0$, but $C(z, w|x) = 0$ because selection on t (= x) means that the only relation between w and z is that which is induced by the relation between w and t (= x), a source of correlation that is fully captured by x. A third polar case is that t, and therefore the z status, is random, like a coin flip. Here, again $C(z,w|x) = 0$, and indeed $C(z,w) = 0$.

This leaves the important case when w is unobserved and the selection is non-random and not fully measured. With no other outside information nothing can be said about the direction of bias. With information about the conditional covariances—in particular $C(z,w|x)$, but also $C(t,x|w)$ or its equivalent in sign, $C(z,x|w)$—direction of bias may be determined. With information about the distribution of the unobserved variables, t and w, along with information about the functional form relating t and w to x, it turns out—perhaps surprisingly—that the bias may be quantified, and, further, that this achievement does not require information about the signs of the relations, conditional or unconditional, among t, w, z, and x, beyond what may be directly measured on the basis of the observed values of z and x. The quantification (or equivalently the elimination) of bias in terms of the model of evaluation is demonstrated in Section 5. Let us first survey briefly the handling of selectivity bias in the recent econometric studies in labor economics.

4. APPROACHES TO SELECTION BIAS IN LABOR ECONOMETRICS

As we read the labor econometrics literature, it taps additional information about the selection process to obtain an unbiased estimate of the treatment effect when the observed x-variables exhaust neither t nor w. In essence, a selection equation with z as the dependent variable is specified, and restrictions are placed on it relative to the outcome equation (our [3]). The role of the restrictions is to purge the apparent treatment effect (γ_1 in our equation [3]) of any pre-existing differences between the treatment and control groups. In our reading, we detect two types of restrictions. The first specifies that one or more variables determining selection do not affect the outcome, and hence are excludable from the outcome equation. Thus, information on variables excluded from x is required. The second specifies a functional form for the relation between x and w, and a nonlinear relation between z and x. This leads to a nonlinear function of x in the outcome equation, which serves to control for any z, w relation that is net of x.

In distinguishing these two types of restrictions, we pass over what is no doubt the most common approach: simply assume away the selection bias after a diligent attempt to include a large number of variables in x that control for ability, w. The argument, or assumption, is that whatever the selection variables may be, beyond those include in x, they are unrelated to outcome. In the two-equation recursive formulation for z and for y, which we discussed above and present formally in section 5, this amounts to assuming that z is determined by x *and* a disturbance that is uncorrelated with the disturbance, ϵ^{**}, in equation [3] determining y. Most of the research estimating the effect of education (the treatment variable) on earnings (the outcome) adopts this approach. Also, the empirical estimates of the Head Start effect on test scores by Barnow and Cain (1977) fell in this category.

Two examples illustrate the first type of restriction—obtaining additional x's that have no effect on the outcome and using this information to identify the treatment effect. A trivial but universally accepted case is the coin flip. When the t variable is generated naturally by environmental or market forces, however, the assumption of "no effect on the outcome" will usually be controversial. For example, in a study of the effect of unionism on wage rates, Ashenfelter and Johnson (1972) variously assumed that the concentration ratio of the industry or the region of residence (South or non-South) determines the extent of union-ism, while concentration and region have no causal effect on wage rates. Thus those two variables are excluded from the structural equation for wages.[9]

The second type of restriction permits distinguishing between the way the x-variables affect selection from the way they affect outcomes (or, equivalently, the way they represent ability). Greenberg and Kosters (1973) analyzed the relation between labor supply (an outcome) and nonlabor income (the treat-ment). Their initial empirical work led them to specify a selection that involved differential tastes or preferences for asset accumulation (and, thus, for non-labor income). They used some of the x-variables from the labor supply equation to estimate asset preferences by a regression of observed assets on the selected x-variables. Predicted assets were included in the final labor supply equation, and identification of its effect was achieved by virtue of its nonlinear relation to x. The controversial feature of this procedure is that the specification of the nonlinear function between observed assets and the set of x-variables was some-what ad hoc.

More recent work, beginning with Heckman (1974), appears to be consider-ably more general. A nonlinear functional form in x that identifies the treatment effect is not imposed directly but rather emerges from two assumptions: one, that the distribution of the error terms in the equations for the omitted variables, w and t, is bivariate normal; and, two, that the functional forms relating w and t to x are known (in practice, known to be linear).

Heckman's model, dealing with the labor supply of women, is complicated by two features—simultaneity, which does not appear in the typical evaluation model, and the other, truncation, which does appear but is somewhat disguised. First, in the women's labor supply model, the analogue to the omitted ability variable is the "shadow price of time" in housework, and this is assumed to be affected by the outcome variable, hours of market work. Thus, a simultaneous-equation model is specified and, as with the Ashenfelter and Johnson model, additional identifying restrictions are required. Second, as mentioned earlier, the analogue to the treatment variable is the wage rate, and this is not observed for women who supply zero hours of market work. Thus, the distribution of wage rates is truncated and, unlike the treatment variable in program evaluation models, is not measured for all observations. This is only an apparent difference, however. In the evaluation model with differential ability between treatment and control groups, the two groups are effectively truncated (or censored) on ability, and the technique for correcting for the omitted variable bias is the same as the technique for correcting for the truncation bias.

5. UNBIASED ESTIMATION OF TREATMENT EFFECTS IN THE EVALUATION MODEL

We now sharpen the specification of the evaluation model in a way that will permit unbiased estimation of the treatment effect. The observable variables are y = outcome, z = treatment ($z = 1$ for treatment group, $z = 0$ for control group), and x = vector of covariates (including the constant). The unobserved variables are w = ability and t = selection, along with various disturbances to be introduced below. By definition of t, assignment to the two groups is determined by

$$z = \begin{cases} 1 & \text{if } t > 0 \\ 0 & \text{if } t \leqslant 0 \end{cases} \qquad [4]$$

By definition of w, outcome is determined by

$$y = w + \alpha z + \epsilon_0 \qquad [5]$$

where the disturbance ϵ_0 is normally distributed, independent of w and z, with expectation zero and variance σ_{00}.

Consider the joint probability distribution of w, t, and x in the initial population, that is, prior to selection and treatment. We suppose that

$$w = \theta_1' x + \epsilon_1 \qquad [6]$$

$$t = \theta_2' x + \epsilon_2 \qquad [7]$$

where θ_1 and θ_2 are coefficient vectors and where the disturbances ϵ_1 and ϵ_2 are bivariate-normal, independent of x (and of ϵ_o) with expectations zero, variances σ_{11} and σ_{22}, and covariance σ_{12}. Note that in [6]-[7] two sources of nonrandom selection are distinguished: w and t can be correlated via their common dependence on x, and via the correlation of their disturbances ϵ_1 and ϵ_2. Equations [6]-[7] are not intended to be causal: We need not say that x determines w or t. Rather the specification may be interpreted as purely descriptive of the joint probability distribution of w, t, and x.

Proceeding to the analysis, we substitute [6] into [5] to get the outcome equation:

$$y = \theta'_1 x + \alpha z + \epsilon_3 \qquad [8]$$

where $\epsilon_3 = \epsilon_1 + \epsilon_o$. Now ϵ_2 and ϵ_3 are bivariate-normal, independent of x, with expectations zero, variances σ_{22} and $\sigma_{33} = \sigma_{11} + \sigma_{oo}$, and covariance $\sigma_{23} = \sigma_{12}$. We seek $E(y \mid x, z)$, the expectation of outcome conditional on the covariates and the treatment dummy.

From [4] and [7] we see that the event z = 1 is equivalent to the event $\theta'_2 x + \epsilon_2 > 0$, and thus to $\epsilon_2 > - \theta'_2 x$, and thus to $(\epsilon_2/\sigma_2) > - \theta'x$, where $\sigma_2 = \sqrt{\sigma_{22}}$ and $\theta = (1/\sigma_2) \theta_2$. By the same argument, the event z = 0 is equivalent to $(\epsilon_2/\sigma_2) \leqslant - \theta'x$. Now ϵ_2/σ_2 is a standard normal variable independent of x. Since z is binary, it follows that

$$E(z \mid x) = \text{Prob} \{z = 1 \mid x\} = 1 - F(- \theta'x) = F(\theta'x), \qquad [9]$$

where $F(\cdot)$ denotes the standard normal cumulative distribution function. Further, it follows that

$$E((\epsilon_2/\sigma_2) \mid x, z = 1) = f(\theta'x)/F(\theta'x), \qquad [10]$$

$$E((\epsilon_2/\sigma_2) \mid x, z = 0) = -f(\theta'x)/(1 - F(\theta'x)), \qquad [11]$$

where $f(\cdot)$ denotes the standard normal density function (see Johnson and Kotz, 1970: 81). Using f and F as shorthand for $f(\theta'x)$ and $F(\theta'x)$ respectively, we can assemble [10]-[11] into

$$E((\epsilon_2/\sigma_2) \mid x, z) = z \, f/F - (1 - z)f/(1 - F)$$

$$= f(z - F)/((1 - F)F)$$

$$= h(x, z; \theta), \qquad [12]$$

say. Then $E(\epsilon_2 \mid x, z) = \sigma_2 h(x, z; \theta)$, and with the distributional information under [8] it follows that

$$E(\epsilon_3 \mid x, z) = (\sigma_{12}/\sigma_{22}) E(\epsilon_2 \mid x, z) = \mu h(x, z; \theta), \qquad [13]$$

where $\mu = \sigma_{12}/\sigma_2$ (see Johnson and Kotz, 1972: 112).

In view of [13], the expectation of [8] conditional on x and z is

$$E(y \mid x, z) = \theta_1' x + \alpha z + \mu h(x, z; \theta).$$ [14]

Since this is a conditional expectation function relating observable variables, its parameters, namely θ_1, α, μ, and θ can be estimated consistently by nonlinear least squares. We have thus established a method of obtaining an unbiased, or rather consistent, estimate of the treatment effect in our specification of the evaluation model. In doing so, we have simply restated the arguments in Heckman (1976) and Maddala and Lee (1976).

To estimate [14] in practice, a two-step procedure may be used. First, estimate θ by maximum-likelihood probit analysis of z on x, and insert those estimates $\hat{\theta}$ in place of θ in [12] to calculate $\hat{h} = h(x, z; \hat{\theta})$ at each observation. Second, estimate θ_1, α, and μ by *linear* least squares regression of y on x, z, and $\hat{h}$. This too provides consistent estimates.

A main theme in the evaluation research literature on selection bias is thus verified: linear regression of y on x and z produces biased estimates of α, the treatment effect. But in the present formulation, the precise source of the bias is apparent— namely, omission of the $h(x, z; \theta)$ variable in [14]. Once this term is included, least-squares regression gives a proper estimate of α. We observe from [14] that linear regression of x and z alone would give an unbiased estimate of α in the special case $\mu = 0$, that is $\sigma_{12} = 0$, that is $C(w, t \mid x) = 0$ or, equivalently, $C(w, z \mid x) = 0$. This verifies the results discussed informally in Section 3 concerning the absence of bias when assignment is purely random or purely on the basis of the observable covariates.[10]

A still simpler approach is also available. With the aid of [9] and [12] we recognize that conditional on x, $h(x, z; \theta)$ is a constant times $z - E(z \mid x)$, so that

$$E[h(x, z; \theta) \mid x] = 0.$$ [15]

Applying the iterated expectation rule to [14] then gives

$$E(y \mid x) = \underset{z \mid x}{E} \ (E(y \mid x, z)) = \theta_1' x + \alpha E(z \mid x) = \theta_1' x + \alpha F(\theta' x)$$ [16]

Indeed, [16] can be obtained directly from [8] (Maddala and Lee, 1976: 528), and thus holds without assuming normality for ϵ_0. Now [16] is also a conditional expectation function relating observable variables, so its parameters, θ_1, α, and θ are consistently estimated by nonlinear least squares. In practice, a two-step procedure may be used: First, estimate θ by maximum-likelihood probit analysis of z on x, and insert those estimates in place of θ to calculate $\hat{z} = F(\hat{\theta}' x)$ at each observation. Second, estimate θ_1 and α by *linear* least squares regression of y on x and $\hat{z}$. From this perspective, linear regression of y on x and z produces biased estimates of α because the variable z has not been purged of its endogeneity (for more formal discussion of these and alternate estimation procedures, see Amemiya [1978], Heckman [1978] and Lee [1979]).

We believe that this straightforward application of the Heckman-Maddala-Lee approach resolves in principle the problem of selectivity bias as it arose in evaluation research. Having reached that point, we must indicate that a number of serious problems require attention among which are the following:

(1) choice among alternative consistent estimation procedures
(2) high degree of collinearity in the second-step regressions
(3) robustness of estimators to non-normality of disturbances (Crawford, 1979)
(4) misspecification of original model, in which case the nonlinear terms h(x, z; θ) and F(θ'x) may be proxying for omitted variables or nonlinearities
(5) multiple selection rules (Waldman, 1979).

NOTES

1. Two early influential books in this tradition are McKean (1958) and Eckstein (1958).

2. *Handbook of Evaluation Research*, 2 vols. E. L. Struening and M. Guttentag (eds.) Beverly Hills, CA: Sage Publications, 1975. These volumes will be cited as HER, I and HER, II.

3. See Appendix.

4. *Federal Program Evaluation*, A Directory for the Congress, Compiled and Published by the U.S. General Accounting Office (Government Printing Office: Washington, DC, 1976). No information is given on the cost of these evaluations. Perhaps a conservative estimate of the average cost of an evaluation study is $50,000. This implies that $85 million was spent in the 1973-1975 period.

5. However, consider the following statement by the economist Alice Rivlin:

> A valid experiment requires that individuals be assigned to treatment or control groups by a random selection process. Chance must enter. A government official may find it far more difficult to explain to the public that he is allocating a scarce resource on the basis of chance than to defend some other selection criterion such as need or merit or 'first come, first serve.' But if such criteria are used, those not selected cannot validly be compared with the treatment group to establish the effectiveness of the treatment, because the two groups may differ in important ways [1971: 111-112].

6. Campbell (1969) is reprinted in HER, I, pp. 71-99. Campbell and Erlebacher (1970) is reprinted in HER, I: 597-617. The quotation in the text is on p. 615 of HER, I.

7. The quotation in the text is on p. 606 of HER, I.

8. Campbell and Erlebacher also referred to the fact that the analysts in the study they criticized had a more difficult time finding the "most disadvantaged" children among the control group (1970: 607). This proves nothing, however. The most disadvantaged children may be more difficult to recruit generally for either treatment or control groups. Or, the most disadvantaged control children who were found may have been lower on true ability than the treatment children of the same measured status.

9. Actually, their model was more elaborate than our two-equation, recursive representation, as they allowed for full simultaneity between union (selection), status, and wage rates (outcomes). Thus, they required additional identifying restrictions to estimate the effect of wage rates on union status, and used the restrictions that an industry's average educational level and percentage of females affect wage rates but have no effect on the extent of unionism. Clearly, these are also debatable assumptions.

10. There have been many recent attempts in the educational psychology literature to analyze selectivity bias in the evaluation model. Among these are Cronbach et al. (1977), Kenny (1975), Linn and Werts (1977), Overall and Woodward (1977), Porter and Chibucos (1975), Rubin (1974), and Weisberg (1978). These attempts all ran astray precisely because they focus on the linear regression

(or ANCOVA) of y on x, z, as indeed we did in our earlier papers (Goldberger, 1972; Barnow, 1973; Cain, 1975). Our use of the t-variable in the present formulation was stimulated by some ideas in Cronbach et al. (1977) and Weisberg (1978). The present approach requires no ex ante specification of the direction of selection—"creaming" vs. "scraping." The direction can be inferred ex post from the signs of the coefficients.

REFERENCES

AMEMIYA, T. (1978) "The estimation of a simultaneous-equation generalized probit model." Econometrica 46: 1193-1205.

ASHENFELTER, O. (1978) "Estimating the effect of training programs on earnings." Rev. of Economics and Statistics (February): 47-57.

———— "Racial discrimination and trade unionism." J. of Pol. Economy 80: 435-464.

———— and G. E. JOHNSON (1972) "Unionism, Relative Wages, and Labor Quality in U.S. Manufacturing Industries." International Economic Review 13: 488-508.

BARNOW, B. S. (1975) The effect of Head Start and socioeconomic status on cognitive development of disadvantaged children. Ph.D. Dissertation, University of Wisconsin.

———— and G. G. CAIN (1977) "A reanalysis of the effect of Head Start on cognitive development methodology and empirical findings." J. of Human Resources 12: 177-197.

BEN-PORATH, Y. (1973) "Labor force participation rates and the supply of labor." J. of Pol. Economy 81.

CAIN, G. G. (1975) "Regression and selection models to improve nonexperimental comparisons," in C. A. Bennett and A. A. Lumsdaine (eds.) Evaluation and Experiments: Some Critical Issues in Assessing Social Programs. New York: Academic.

CAMPBELL, D. T. (1969) "Reforms as experiments." Amer. Psychologist (April): 409-429. Reprinted in E. L. Struening and M. Guttentag (eds.) Handbook of Evaluation Research, 2 vols. Beverly Hills, CA: Sage, 1975. 1: 71-99.

———— and A. ERLEBACHER (1970) "How regression artifacts in quasi-experiemental evaluations can mistakenly make compensatory education look harmful," in Compensatory Education: A National Debate, Vol. 3, Disadvantaged Child. J. Hellmuth (ed.) New York: Bruner/Mazel.

CRAWFORD, D. L. (1979) "Estimating models of earnings from truncated samples." Ph.D. Dissertation, University of Wisconsin.

CRONBACH, L. J., D. R. ROGOSA, R. E. FLODEN, and G. G. PRICE (1977) "Analysis of Covariance in nonrandomized experiments: parameters affecting bias." Stanford Evaluation Consortium, Occasional Paper.

DEMING, W. E. (1975) "The logic of evaluation," in E. L. Struening and M. Guttentag (eds.) Handbook of Evaluation Research, 2 vols. Beverly Hills, CA: Sage, 1975. 1: 53-68.

GARFINKEL, I. (1977) "Effects of welfare programs on experimental response," pp. 279-302 in H. W. Watts and A. Rees (eds.) The New Jersey Income Maintenance Program, Vol. 3. New York: Academic.

———— and E. M. GRAMLICH (1973) "A statistical analysis of the OEO experiment in educational performance contracting." J. of Human Resources 8: 275-305.

GOLDBERGER, A. S. (1972) "Selection bias in evaluating treatment effects: some formal illustrations." Discussion Paper 123-172, University of Wisconsin, Institute for Research on Poverty.

GREENBERG, D. H. and KOSTERS, M. (1973) "Income guarantees and the working poor: the effect of income maintenance programs on the hours of work of male family heads," pp. 14-101 in G. G. Cain and H. W. Watts (eds.) Income Maintenance and Labor Supply. Chicago: Rand McNally.

GRILICHES, Z. (1976) "Wages of very young men." Journal of Political Economy 84, S69-S86.

GRONAU, R. (1974) "Wage comparisons—a selectivity bias." Journal of Political Economy 82: 1119-1144.

———— (1973) "The effect of children on the housewife's value of time." Journal of Political Economy 81.

HANOCH, G. (1980) "A multivariate model of labor supply: methodology and estimation," in J. P. Smith (ed.) Female Labor Supply: Theory and Estimation. Princeton, NJ: Princeton University Press.

HECKMAN, J. J. (1979) "Sample bias as a specification error." Econometrica 47: 153-162.

——— (1978) "Dummy endogenous variables in a simultaneous equation system." Econometrica 46: 931-960.

——— (1976) "The common structure of statistical models of truncation, sample selection, and limited dependent variables and a simple estimator for such models. Annals of Econ. and Social Measurement 5: 475-492.

——— (1974) "Shadow prices, market wages, and labor supply." Econometrica 42: 679-694.

——— and K. I. WOLPIN (1976) "Does the contract compliance program work? an analysis of Chicago data." Industrial and Labor Relations Rev. 29: 544-564.

JOHNSON, N. A. and S. KOTZ (1972) Distributions in Statistics: Continuous Multivariate Distributions. New York: John Wiley.

——— (1970) Distributions in Statistics: Continuous Univariate Distributions-1. Boston: Houghton-Mifflin.

KENNY, D. A. (1975) "A quasi-experimental approach to assessing treatment effects in the nonequivalent control group design." Psych. Bull. 82: 345-361.

LEE, L. (1979) "Identification and estimation in binary choice models with limited (censored) dependent variables." Econometrica 47: 977-996.

——— (1978) "Unionism and wage rates: a simultaneous equations model with qualitative and limited dependent variables." International Econ. Rev. 19: 415-433.

LEIGH, D. E. (1978) "An analysis of the interrelation between unions, race, and wage and nonwage compensation." Final Report for the U.S. Department of Labor, Department of Economics, Washington State University.

LEWIS, H. G. (1974) "Comments on selectivity biases in wage comparisons." J. of Pol. Economy 82: 1145-1156.

——— (1959) "Competitive and monopoly unionism," in P. D. Bradley (ed.) The Public Stake in Union Power. Charlottesville: Univ. of Virginia Press.

LINN, R. L. and C. E. WERTS (1977) "Analysis implications of the choice of a structural model in the nonequivalent control group design." Psych. Bull. 84: 229-234.

MADDALA, G. S. (1978) "Selectivity problems in longitudinal data." Annales de L'INSEE 30-31: 423-450.

——— (1976) "Self-selectivity problems in econometric models." Unpublished, Department of Economics, University of Florida.

——— and L. LEE (1976) "Recursive models with qualitative endogenous variables." Annals of Econ. and Social Measurement 5: 525-545.

OLSEN, R. J. (1978) "Comment on 'the effect of unions on earnings and earnings on unions: a mixed logit approach.'" International Economic Rev. 19: 259-261.

OVERALL, J. E. and J. A. WOODWARD (1977) "Nonrandom assignment and the analysis of covariance." Psychological Bull. 84: 588-594.

PORTER, A. C. and T. R. CHIBUCOS (1975) "Common problems of design and analysis in evaluative research." Sociological Methods and Research 3: 235-257.

RIVLIN, A. (1971) Systematic Thinking for Social Action. Washington, DC: Brookings.

RUBIN, D. B. (1974) "Estimating causal effects of treatments in randomized and nonrandomized studies." J. of Educ. Psych. 66: 688-701.

SCHMIDT, P. and R. P. STRAUSS (1976) "The effect of unions on earnings and earnings on unions: a mixed logit approach." International Econ. Review 17: 204-212.

SCHULTZ, T. P. (1980) "Estimating labor supply functions for married women," in J. P. Smith (ed.) Female Labor Supply: Theory and Estimation. Princeton, NJ: Princeton Univ. Press.

SMITH, R. S. (1975) "The estimated impact on injuries of OSHA's target industries program," presented at the ASPER-OSHA Conference on Evaluating the Effects of the Occupational Safety and Health Program, March, 1975.

TRIPLETT, J. E. (1975) "On the methodology of evaluating economic effects of government pro-grams: a comment on professor Smith's paper," BLS Working Paper 41, U.S. Department of Labor, May, 1975.

WALDMAN, D. M. (1979) Time Allocation of Young Men. Ph.D. Dissertation, University of Wisconsin.

WATTS, H. W., J. K. PECK, and M. TAUSSIG (1977) "Site selection representativeness of the sample, and possible attrition bias," pp. 441-446 in H. W. Watts and A. Rees (eds.) The New Jersey Income Maintenance Program, Vol. 3 New York: Academic.

WEISBERG, H. I. (1978) "Statistical adjustments and uncontrolled studies." Unpublished.

APPENDIX
SELECTED BOOKS ON EVALUATION RESEARCH

Evaluating the Labor Market Effects of Social Programs, eds. O. Ashenfelter and J. Blum. Industrial Relations Section, Princeton University, Princeton, N.J., 1976.

Readings in Evaluation Research, ed. F. G. Caro. New York: Russell Sage, 1971.

The Measurement of Policy Impact, ed. T. R. Dye. Tallahassee: Florida State University Press, 1971.

Policy Studies Review Annual, Vol. 2, ed. H. Freeman. Beverly Hills, CA: Sage Publications, 1978.

Evaluation Studies Review Annual, Vol. 1, ed. Gene V Glass. Beverly Hills, CA: Sage Publications, 1976.

Evaluation Studies Review Annual, Vol. 2, ed. M. Guttentag with S. Saar. Beverly Hills, CA: Sage Publications, 1977.

Handbook of Evaluation Research, Vol. II, eds. M. Guttentag and E. L. Streuning. Beverly Hills, CA: Sage Publications, 1977.

Public Expenditures and Policy Analysis, eds. R. Haveman and J. Margolis. Chicago: Markham, 1970.

S. Issac and W. D. Michael, Handbook of Research Evaluation, San Diego: Knopp, 1971.

Policy Studies Review Annual, Vol. 1, ed. S. S. Nagel. Beverly Hills, CA: Sage Publications, 1977.

Analyzing Poverty Policy, ed. D. B. James. Lexington, MA: D. C. Heath, 1975.

Evaluating Social Action Programs: Theory, Practice, and Politics, eds. P. H. Rossi and W. Williams. New York: Seminar Press, 1972.

F. P. Scioli, Jr. and T. J. Cook, Methodologies for Analyzing Public Policies, Lexington, MA: D. C. Heath, 1977.

Handbook of Evaluation Research, Vol. 1, eds. E. L. Streuning and M. Guttentag. Beverly Hills, CA: Sage Publications, 1975.

E. A. Suchman, Evaluative Research: Principles and Practices in Public Service and Social Action Programs, New York: Russell Sage, 1967.

Improving Experimental Design and Statistical Analysis, ed. J. C. Stanley. Chicago: Rand-McNally, 1967.

Evaluating Action Programs: Readings in Social Action and Education, ed. C. H. Weiss. Boston: Allyn & Bacon, 1972.

C. H. Weiss, Evaluation Research: Methods of Assessing Program Effectiveness. Englewood Cliffs, NJ: Prentice-Hall, 1972.

J. Wholey et al., Federal Evaluation Policy. Washington, DC: Urban Institute, 1970.

2

This chapter develops the ordinary least squares (OLS) "Mills ratio term" correction for selectivity bias. It complements the preceding chapter by Barnow et al. in that here the concern is with censored samples rather than nonrandom assignment to treatment status, and also in that this paper makes somewhat greater technical demands upon the reader.[1] The return to the increased difficulty is the attention to the standard errors as well as the mean values of the estimated coefficients.

After setting out the usual two-equation model (see the previous chapter or the Introduction to this section), Heckman provides an expression, $E(Y_1|X_1,$ sample selection rule) $= X_1\beta_1 + E(U_1|$ sample selection rule) that conveniently identifies the problem arising from non-random sample attrition (or a related situation). If the second term on the right side of this equation is nonzero, estimates of β_1 arrived at by the ordinary least squares method will be biased. The solution is to estimate this term and enter it into the impact equation for the observed sample. Doing so while assuming bivariate normality for the error terms leads to an estimate of λ, the inverse of Mill's ratio. (This term is calculated from the coefficients of a probit attrition equation estimated for the full sample.) The coefficient for the impact of this new regressor is an estimate of $\sigma_{12}/\delta_{22}^{1/2}$, where $\sigma_{12} = $ the covariance between the error terms in the impact and attrition equations and $\sigma_{22}^{1/2} = $ the standard error from the probit equation.

The presence of σ_{12} in this expression shows that if the error terms in the two-equation model are uncorrelated, there is no selectivity bias. A formal test of this proposition, however, requires the correct standard error for the $\hat{\lambda}$ coefficient. We also require the correct standard errors for the β_1 coefficients. These are available only after further computation. (See Heckman's chapter and Addendum.)

NOTE

1. See the Introduction to this Section for an overview of the various evaluation problems, their associated methods, and the inter-relations among these.

Sample Selection Bias as a Specification Error

James J. Heckman

THIS PAPER DISCUSSES the bias that results from using nonrandomly selected samples to estimate behavioral relationships as an ordinary specification bias that arises because of a missing data problem. In contrast to the usual analysis of "omitted variables" or specification error in econometrics, in the analysis of sample selection bias it is sometimes possible to estimate the variables which when omitted from a regression analysis give rise to the specification error. The estimated values of the omitted variables can be used as regressors so that it is possible to estimate the behavioral functions of interest by simple methods. This paper discusses sample selection bias as a specification error and presents a simple consistent estimation method that eliminates the specification error for the case of censored samples. The argument presented in this paper clarifies and extends the analysis in a previous paper [6] by explicitly developing the asymptotic distribution of the simple estimator for the general case rather than the special case of a null hypothesis of no selection bias implicitly discussed in that paper. Accordingly, for reasons of readability, this paper recapitulates some of the introductory material of the previous paper in, what is hoped, an improved and simplified form.

Sample selection bias may arise in practice for two reasons. First, there may be self selection by the individuals or data units being investigated. Second, sample selection decisions by analysts or data processors operate in much the same fashion as self selection.

There are many examples of self selection bias. One observes market wages for working women whose market wage exceeds their home wage at zero hours of work. Similarly, one observes wages for union members who found their nonunion alternative less desirable. The wages of migrants do not, in general, afford a reliable estimate of what nonmigrants would have earned had they migrated. The earnings of manpower trainees do not estimate the earnings that nontrainees would have earned had they opted to become trainees. In each of these examples, wage or earnings functions estimated on selected samples do not,

[1] This research was supported by a HEW grant to the Rand Corporation and a U.S. Department of Labor grant to the National Bureau of Economic Research. A previous version of this paper circulated under the title "Shadow Prices. Market Wages and Labor Supply Revisited: Some Computational Simplifications and Revised Estimates," June. 1975. An embarrassingly large number of colleagues have made valuable comments on this paper, and its various drafts. Particular thanks go to Takeshi Amemiya, Zvi Griliches, Reuben Gronau, Mark Killingsworth, Ed Leamer, Tom MaCurdy, Bill Rodgers, and Paul Schultz. I bear full responsibility for any remaining errors.

in general, estimate population (i.e., random sample) wage functions. Comparisons of the wages of migrants with the wages of nonmigrants (or trainee earnings with nontrainee earnings, etc.) result in a biased estimate of the effect of a *random* "treatment" of migration, manpower training, or unionism.

Data may also be nonrandomly selected because of decisions taken by data analysts. In studies of panel data, it is common to use "intact" observations. For example, stability of the family unit is often imposed as a requirement for entry into a sample for analysis. In studies of life cycle fertility and manpower training experiments, it is common practice to analyze observations followed for the full length of the sample, i.e., to drop attriters from the analysis. Such procedures have the same effect on structural estimates as self selection: fitted regression functions confound the behavioral parameters of interest with parameters of the function determining the probability of entrance into the sample.

1. A SIMPLE CHARACTERIZATION OF SELECTION BIAS

To simplify the exposition, consider a two equation model. Few new points arise in the multiple equation case, and the two equation case has considerable pedagogical merit.

Consider a random sample of I observations. Equations for individual i are

(1a) $\qquad Y_{1i} = X_{1i}\beta_1 + U_{1i},$

(1b) $\qquad Y_{2i} = X_{2i}\beta_2 + U_{2i} \qquad\qquad\qquad (i = 1, \ldots, I),$

where X_{ji} is a $1 \times K_j$ vector of exogenous regressors, β_j is a $K_j \times 1$ vector of parameters, and

$$E(U_{ji}) = 0, \qquad E(U_{ji}U_{j'i''}) = \sigma_{jj'}, \quad i = i'',$$
$$= 0, \quad i \neq i''.$$

The final assumption is a consequence of a random sampling scheme. The joint density of U_{1i}, U_{2i} is $h(U_{1i}, U_{2i})$. The regressor matrix is of full rank so that if all data were available, the parameters of each equation could be estimated by least squares.

Suppose that one seeks to estimate equation (1a) but that data are missing on Y_1 for certain observations. The critical question is "why are the data missing?"

The *population* regression function for equation (1a) may be written as

$$E(Y_{1i}|X_{1i}) = X_{1i}\beta_1 \qquad\qquad\qquad (i = 1, \ldots, I).$$

The regression function for the subsample of available data is

$$E(Y_{1i}|X_{1i}, \text{ sample selection rule}) = X_{1i}\beta_1 + E(U_{1i}|\text{sample selection rule}),$$

$i = 1, \ldots, I$, where the convention is adopted that the first $I_1 < I$ observations have data available on Y_{1i}.

If the conditional expectation of U'_{1i} is zero, the regression function for the selected subsample is the same as the population regression function. Least squares estimators may be used to estimate β_1 on the selected subsample. The only cost of having an incomplete sample is a loss in efficiency.

In the general case, the sample selection rule that determines the availability of data has more serious consequences. Suppose that data are available on Y_{1i} if $Y_{2i} \geqslant 0$ while if $Y_{2i} < 0$, there are no observations on Y_{1i}. The choice of zero as a threshold involves an inessential normalization.

In the general case

$$E(U_{1i} \mid X_{1i}, \text{sample selection rule}) = E(U_{1i} \mid X_{1i}, Y_{2i} \geqslant 0)$$

$$= E(U_{1i} \mid X_{1i}, U_{2i} \geqslant -X_{2i}\beta_2).$$

In the case of independence between U_{1i} and U_{2i}, so that the data on Y_{1i} are missing randomly, the conditional mean of U_{1i} is zero. In the general case, it is nonzero and the subsample regression function is

(2) $\qquad E(Y_{1i} \mid X_{1i}, Y_{2i} \geqslant 0) = X_{1i}\beta_1 + E(U_{1i} \mid U_{2i} \geqslant -X_{2i}\beta_2).$

The selected sample regression function depends on X_{1i} and X_{2i}. Regression estimators of the parameters of equation (1a) fit on the selected sample omit the final term of equation (2) as a regressor, so that the bias that results from using nonrandomly selected samples to estimate behavioral relationships is seen to arise from the ordinary problem of omitted variables.

Several points are worth noting. First, if the only variable in the regressor vector X_{2i} that determines sample selection is "1" so that the probability of sample inclusion is the same for all observations, the conditional mean of U_{1i} is a constant, and the only bias in β_1 that results from using selected samples to estimate the population structural equation arises in the estimate of the intercept. One can also show that the least squares estimator of the population variance σ_{11} is downward biased. Second, a symptom of selection bias is that variables that do not belong in the true structural equation (variables in X_{2i} not in X_{1i}) may appear to be statistically significant determinants of Y_{1i} when regressions are fit on selected samples. Third, the model just outlined contains a variety of previous models as special cases. For example, if $h(U_{1i}, U_{2i})$ is assumed to be a singular normal density $(U_{1i} \equiv U_{2i})$ and $X_{2i} = X_{1i}$, $\beta_1 \equiv \beta_2$, the "Tobit" model emerges. For a more complete development of the relationship between the model developed here and previous models for limited dependent variables, censored samples and truncated samples, see Heckman [6]. Fourth, multivariate extensions of the preceding analysis, while mathematically straightforward, are of considerable substantive interest. One example is offered. Consider migrants choosing among K possible regions of residence. If the self selection rule is to choose to migrate to that region with the highest income, both the self selection rule and the subsample regression functions can be simply characterized by a direct extension of the previous analysis.

2. A SIMPLE ESTIMATOR FOR NORMAL DISTURBANCES AND ITS PROPERTIES[2]

Assume that $h(U_{1i}, U_{2i})$ is a bivariate normal density. Using well known results (see [**10**, pp. 112–113]),

$$E(U_{1i} | U_{2i} \geq -X_{2i}\beta_2) = \frac{\sigma_{12}}{(\sigma_{22})^{\frac{1}{2}}} \lambda_i,$$

$$E(U_{2i} | U_{2i} \geq -X_{2i}\beta_2) = \frac{\sigma_{22}}{(\sigma_{22})^{\frac{1}{2}}} \lambda_i,$$

where

$$\lambda_i = \frac{\phi(Z_i)}{1 - \Phi(Z_i)} = \frac{\phi(Z_i)}{\Phi(-Z_i)},$$

where ϕ and Φ are, respectively, the density and distribution function for a standard normal variable, and

$$Z_i = -\frac{X_{2i}\beta_2}{(\sigma_{22})^{\frac{1}{2}}}.$$

"λ_i" is the inverse of Mill's ratio. It is a monotone decreasing function of the probability that an observation is selected into the sample, $\Phi(-Z_i)(=1-\Phi(Z_i))$. In particular, $\lim_{\Phi(-Z_i) \to 1} \lambda_i = 0$, $\lim_{\Phi(-Z_i) \to 0} \lambda_i = \infty$, and $\partial \lambda_i / \partial \Phi(-Z_i) < 0$.

The full statistical model for normal population disturbances can now be developed. The conditional regression function for selected samples may be written as

$$E(Y_{1i} | X_{1i}, Y_{2i} \geq 0) = X_{1i}\beta_1 + \frac{\sigma_{12}}{(\sigma_{22})^{\frac{1}{2}}} \lambda_i,$$

$$E(Y_{2i} | X_{2i}, Y_{2i} \geq 0) = X_{2i}\beta_2 + \frac{\sigma_{22}}{(\sigma_{22})^{\frac{1}{2}}} \lambda_i,$$

(4a) $Y_{1i} = E(Y_{1i} | X_{1i}, Y_{2i} \geq 0) + V_{1i},$

(4b) $Y_{2i} = E(Y_{2i} | X_{2i}, Y_{2i} \geq 0) + V_{2i},$

where

(4c) $E(V_{1i} | X_{1i}, \lambda_i, U_{2i} \geq -X_{2i}\beta_2) = 0,$

(4d) $E(V_{2i} | X_{2i}, \lambda_i, U_{2i} \geq -X_{2i}\beta_2) = 0,$

(4e) $E(V_{ji} V_{j'i} | X_{1i}, X_{2i}, \lambda_1, U_{2i} \geq -X_{2i}\beta_2) = 0,$

---

[2] A grouped data version of the estimation method discussed here was first proposed by Gronau [4] and Lewis [11]. However, they do not investigate the statistical properties of the method or develop the micro version of the estimator presented here.

for $i \neq i'$. Further,

(4f) $E(V_{1i}^2 | X_{1i}, \lambda_i, U_{2i} \geq -X_{2i}\beta_2) = \sigma_{11}((1 - \rho^2) + \rho^2(1 + Z_i\lambda_i - \lambda_i^2))$,

(4g) $E(V_{1i}V_{2i} | X_{1i}, X_{2i}, \lambda_i, U_{2i} \geq -X_{2i}\beta_2) = \sigma_{12}(1 + Z_i\lambda_i - \lambda_i^2)$,

(4h) $E(V_{2i}^2 | X_{2i}, \lambda_i, U_{2i} \geq -X_{2i}\beta_2) = \sigma_{22}(1 + Z_i\lambda_i - \lambda_i^2)$,

where

$$\rho^2 = \frac{\sigma_{12}^2}{\sigma_{11}\sigma_{22}}$$

and

(5) $0 \leq 1 + \lambda_i Z_i - \lambda_i^2 \leq 1$.

If one knew Z_i and hence λ_i, one could enter λ_i as a regressor in equation (4a) and estimate that equation by ordinary least squares. The least squares estimators of β_1 and $\sigma_{12}/(\sigma_{22})^{\frac{1}{2}}$ are unbiased but inefficient. The inefficiency is a consequence of the heteroscedasticity apparent from equation (4f) when X_{2i} (and hence Z_i) contains nontrivial regressors. As a consequence of inequality (5), the standard least squares estimator of the population variance σ_{11} is downward biased. As a consequence of equation (4g) and inequality (5), the usual estimator of the interequation covariance is downward biased. A standard GLS procedure can be used to develop appropriate standard errors for the estimated coefficients of the first equation (see Heckman [6]).

In practice, one does not know λ_i. But in the case of a censored sample, in which one does not have information on Y_{1i} if $Y_{2i} \leq 0$, but one does know X_{2i} for observations with $Y_{2i} \leq 0$, one can estimate λ_i by the following procedure:

(1) Estimate the parameters of the probability that $Y_{2i} \geq 0$ (i.e., $\beta_2/(\sigma_{22})^{\frac{1}{2}}$) using probit analysis for the full sample.[3]

(2) From this estimator of $\beta_2/(\sigma_{22})^{\frac{1}{2}}$ ($= \beta_2^*$) one can estimate Z_i and hence λ_i. All of these estimators are consistent.

(3) The estimated value of λ_i may be used as a regressor in equation (4a) fit on the selected subsample. Regression estimators of equation (4a) are *consistent* for β_1 and $\sigma_{12}/(\sigma_{22})^{\frac{1}{2}}$ (the coefficients of X_{1i} and λ_1, respectively).[4]

(4) One can consistently estimate σ_{11} by the following procedure. From step 3, one consistently estimates $C = \rho(\sigma_{11})^{\frac{1}{2}} = \sigma_{12}/(\sigma_{22})^{\frac{1}{2}}$. Denote the residual for the ith observation obtained from step 3 as $\hat{V}_{1i}$, and the estimator of C by $\hat{C}$. Then an estimator of σ_{11} is

$$\hat{\sigma}_{11} = \frac{\sum\limits_{i=1}^{I_1} \hat{V}_{1i}^2}{I_1} - \frac{\hat{C}}{I_1}\sum\limits_{i=1}^{I_1}(\hat{\lambda}_i\hat{Z}_i - \hat{\lambda}_i^2)$$

[3] In the case in which Y_{2i} is observed, one can estimate β_2, σ_{22}, and hence $\beta_2/(\sigma_{22})^{\frac{1}{2}}$ by ordinary least squares.

[4] It is assumed that vector X_{2i} contains nontrivial regressors or that β_1 contains no intercept or both.

where $\hat{\lambda}_i$ and $\hat{Z}_i$ are the estimated values of Z_i and λ_i obtained from step 2. This estimator of σ_{11} is consistent and positive since the term in the second summation must be negative (see inequality (5)).

The usual formulas for standard errors for least squares coefficients are *not* appropriate except in the important case of the null hypothesis of no selection bias $(C = \sigma_{12}/(\sigma_{22})^{\frac{1}{2}} = 0)$. In that case, the usual regression standard errors are appropriate and an exact test of the null hypothesis $C = 0$ can be performed using the t distribution. If $C \neq 0$, the usual procedure for computing standard errors *understates* the true standard errors and overstates estimated significance levels.

The derivation of the correct limiting distribution for this estimator in the general case requires some argument.[5] Note that equation (4a) with an estimated value of λ_i used in place of the true value of λ_i may be written as

(4a') $Y_{1i} = X_{1i}\beta_1 + C\hat{\lambda}_i + C(\lambda_i - \hat{\lambda}_i) + V_{1i}.$

The error term in the equation consists of the final two terms in the equation.

Since λ_i is estimated by $\beta_2/(\sigma_{22})^{\frac{1}{2}}$ $(= \beta_2^*)$ which is estimated from the entire sample of I observations by a maximum likelihood probit analysis,[6] and since λ_i is a twice continuously differentiable function of β_2^*, $\sqrt{I}(\hat{\lambda}_i - \lambda_i)$ has a well defined limiting normal distribution

$$\sqrt{I}(\hat{\lambda}_i - \lambda_i) \sim N(0, \Sigma_i)$$

where Σ_i is the asymptotic variance-covariance matrix obtained from that of β_2^* by the following equation:

$$\Sigma_i = \left(\frac{\partial \lambda_i}{\partial Z_i}\right)^2 X_{2i}\Sigma X'_{2i},$$

where $\partial \lambda_i/\partial Z_i$ is the derivative of λ_i with respect to Z_i, and Σ is the asymptotic variance-covariance matrix of $\sqrt{I}(\hat{\beta}_2^* - \beta_2^*)$.

We seek the limiting distribution of

$$\sqrt{I_1}\left(\begin{matrix}\hat{\beta}_1 - \beta_1 \\ \hat{C} - C\end{matrix}\right) = I_1\left(\begin{matrix}\Sigma X'_{1i}X_{1i} & \Sigma X'_{1i}\hat{\lambda}_i \\ \Sigma X_{1i}\hat{\lambda}_i & \Sigma \hat{\lambda}_i^2\end{matrix}\right)^{-1}\frac{1}{\sqrt{I_1}}\left(\begin{matrix}\Sigma X'_{1i}(C(\lambda_i - \hat{\lambda}_i) + V_{1i}) \\ \Sigma \hat{\lambda}_i(C(\lambda_i - \hat{\lambda}_i) + V_{1i})\end{matrix}\right).$$

In the ensuing analysis, it is important to recall that the probit function is estimated on the entire sample of I observations whereas the regression analysis is performed solely on the subsample of I_1 $(<I)$ observations where Y_{1i} is observed. Further, it is important to note that unlike the situation in the analysis of two stage least squares procedures, the portion of the residual that arises from the use of an estimated value of λ_i in place of the actual value of λ_i *is not* orthogonal to the X_1 data vector.

---

[5] This portion of the paper was stimulated by comments from T. Amemiya. Of course, he is not responsible for any errors in the argument.

[6] The ensuing analysis can be modified in a straightforward fashion if Y_{2i} is observed and β_2^* is estimated by least squares.

Under general conditions for the regressors discussed extensively in Amemiya [1] and Jennrich [9],

$$\operatorname*{plim}_{I_1\to\infty} I_1 \begin{pmatrix} \Sigma X'_{1i}X_{1i} & \Sigma X'_{1i}\hat{\lambda}_i \\ \Sigma X_{1i}\hat{\lambda}_i & \Sigma\hat{\lambda}_i^2 \end{pmatrix}^{-1} = \operatorname*{plim}_{I_1\to\infty} I_1 \begin{pmatrix} \Sigma X'_i X_{1i} & \Sigma X'_{1i}\lambda_i \\ \Sigma X_{1i}\lambda_i & \Sigma\lambda_i^2 \end{pmatrix}^{-1} = B,$$

where B is a finite positive definite matrix.[7] Under these assumptions,

$$\sqrt{I_1}\begin{pmatrix} \hat{\beta}_1 - \beta_1 \\ \hat{C} - C \end{pmatrix} \sim N(0, B\psi B')$$

where

$$\psi = \operatorname*{plim}_{\substack{I_1\to\infty \\ I\to\infty}} \left[\sigma_{11} \begin{pmatrix} \dfrac{\Sigma X'_{1i}X_{1i}\eta_i}{I_1} & \dfrac{\Sigma X'_{1i}\lambda_i\eta_i}{I_1} \\ \dfrac{\Sigma\lambda_i X_{1i}\eta_i}{I_1} & \dfrac{\Sigma\lambda_i^2\eta_i}{I_1} \end{pmatrix} + C^2\left(\dfrac{I_1}{I}\right) \begin{pmatrix} \displaystyle\sum_{i=1,i'=1}^{I_1}\sum \dfrac{X'_{1i}X_{1i'}\theta_{ii'}}{I_1^2} & \displaystyle\sum_{i=1,i'=1}^{I_1}\sum \dfrac{X'_{1i}\pi_{ii'}}{I_1^2} \\ \displaystyle\sum_{i'=1,i=1}^{I_1}\sum \dfrac{X_{1i}\pi_{ii'}}{I_1^2} & \displaystyle\sum_{i=1,i'=1}^{I_1}\sum \dfrac{\Omega_{ii'}}{I_1^2} \end{pmatrix} \right],$$

$$\operatorname*{plim}_{\substack{I\to\infty \\ I_1\to\infty}} \dfrac{I_1}{I} = k, \quad 0 < k < 1,$$

where

$$C = \sigma_{12}/(\sigma_{22})^{\frac{1}{2}},$$

$$\eta_i = (1 + C^2(Z_i\lambda_i - \lambda_i^2)/\sigma_{11}),$$

$$\pi_{ii'} = \left(\dfrac{\partial\lambda_i}{\partial Z_i}\right)\left(\dfrac{\partial\lambda_{i'}}{\partial Z_{i'}}\right)\lambda_i X_{2i}\Sigma X'_{2i'},$$

$$\theta_{ii'} = \left(\dfrac{\partial\lambda_i}{\partial Z_i}\right)\left(\dfrac{\partial\lambda_{i'}}{\partial Z_{i'}}\right) X_{2i}\Sigma X'_{2i},$$

$$\Omega_{ii'} = (\lambda_i\lambda_{i'})\left(\dfrac{\partial\lambda_i}{\partial Z_i}\right)\left(\dfrac{\partial\lambda_{i'}}{\partial Z_{i'}}\right) X_{2i}\Sigma X'_{2i},$$

where $\partial\lambda_i/\partial Z_i$ is the derivative of λ_i with respect to Z,

$$\dfrac{\partial\lambda_i}{\partial Z_i} = \lambda_i^2 - Z_i\lambda_i.$$

Note that if $C = 0$, $B\psi B'$ collapses to the standard variance-covariance matrix for the least squares estimator. Note further that because the second matrix in ψ is positive definite, if $C \neq 0$, the correct asymptotic variance-covariance matrix $(B\psi B')$ produces standard errors of the regression coefficients that are larger than those given by the incorrect "standard" variance-covariance matrix $\sigma_{11}B$. Thus

---

[7] Note that this requires that X_{2i} contain nontrivial regressors or that there be no intercept in the equation, or both.

the usual procedure for estimating standard errors, which would be correct if λ_i were known, leads to an understatement of true standard errors and an overstatement of significance levels when λ_i is estimated and $C \neq 0$.

Under the Amemiya-Jennrich conditions previously cited, ψ is a bounded positive definite matrix. ψ and B can be simply estimated. Estimated values of λ_i, C, and σ_{11} can be used in place of actual values to obtain a consistent estimator of $B\psi B'$. Estimation of the variance-covariance matrix requires inversion of a $K_1 + 1 \times K_1 + 1$ matrix and so is computationally simple. A copy of a program that estimates the probit function coefficients β_2^* and the regression coefficients $\hat{\beta}_1$ and $\hat{C}$, and produces the correct asymptotic standard errors for the general case is available on request from the author.[8]

It is possible to develop a GLS procedure (see Heckman [7]). This procedure is computationally more expensive and, since the GLS estimates are not asymptotically efficient, is not recommended.

The estimation method discussed in this paper has already been put to use. There is accumulating evidence [3 and 6] that the estimator provides good starting values for maximum likelihood estimation routines in the sense that it provides estimates quite close to the maximum likelihood estimates. Given its simplicity and flexibility, the procedure outlined in this paper is recommended for exploratory empirical work.

3. SUMMARY

In this paper the bias that results from using nonrandomly selected samples to estimate behavioral relationships is discussed within the specification error framework of Griliches [2] and Theil [12]. A computationally tractable technique is discussed that enables analysts to use simple regression techniques to estimate behavioral functions free of selection bias in the case of a censored sample. Asymptotic properties of the estimator are developed.

An alternative simple estimator that is also applicable to the case of truncated samples has been developed by Amemiya [1]. A comparison between his estimator and the one discussed here would be of great value, but is beyond the scope of this paper. A multivariate extension of the analysis of my 1976 paper has been performed in a valuable paper by Hanoch [5]. The simple estimator developed here can be used in a variety of statistical models for truncation, sample selection and limited dependent variables, as well as in simultaneous equation models with dummy endogenous variables (Heckman [6, 8]).

University of Chicago

Manuscript received March, 1977; final revision received July, 1978.

[8] This offer expires two years after the publication of this paper. The program will be provided at cost.

REFERENCES

[1] AMEMIYA, T.: "Regression Analysis when the Dependent Variable is Truncated Normal," *Econometrica*, 41 (1973), 997–1017.
[2] GRILICHES, ZVI: "Specification Bias in Estimates of Production Functions," *Journal of Farm Economics*, 39 (1957), 8–20.
[3] GRILICHES, Z, B. HALL, AND J. HAUSMAN: "Missing Data and Self Selection in Large Panels," Harvard University, July, 1977.
[4] GRONAU, R.: "Wage Comparisons—A Selectivity Bias," *Journal of Political Economy*, 82 (1974), 1119–1144.
[5] HANOCH, G.: "A Multivariate Model of Labor Supply: Methodology for Estimation," Rand Corporation Paper R-1980, September, 1976.
[6] HECKMAN, J.: "The Common Structure of Statistical Models of Truncation, Sample Selection and Limited Dependent Variables and a Simple Estimator for Such Models," *The Annals of Economic and Social Measurement*, 5 (1976), 475–492.
[7] ————: "Sample Selection Bias as a Specification Error with an Application to the Estimation of Labor Supply Functions," NBER Working Paper # 172, March, 1977 (revised).
[8] ————: "Dummy Endogenous Variables in a Simultaneous Equation System," April, 1977 (revised), *Econometrica*, 46 (1978), 931–961.
[9] JENNRICH, R.: "Asymptotic Properties of Nonlinear Least Squares Estimators," *Annals of Mathematical Statistics*, 40 (1969), 633–643.
[10] JOHNSON, N., AND S. KOTZ: *Distribution in Statistics: Continuous Multivariate Distributions.* New York: John Wiley & Sons, 1972.
[11] LEWIS, H.: "Comments on Selectivity Biases in Wage Comparisons," *Journal of Political Economy*, 82 (1974), 1145–1155.
[12] THEIL, H.: "Specification Errors and the Estimation of Economic Relationships," *Revue de l'Institut International de Statistique.* 25 (1957), 41–51.

Addendum to "Sample Selection Bias as a Specification Error"

James J. Heckman

This Addendum by the author corrects several errors in the original paper and sketches a method to be employed if the distribution of the residuals departs from normality. Similar work has been undertaken by Olsen (1979) and Goldberger (1980), among others; Olsen's method is illustrated in the paper by Farkas et al. in Part III. The potential importance of this issue is illustrated by the conclusion to Goldberger's paper:

> Our analysis suggests that the normal selection-bias-adjustment procedure is quite sensitive to modest departures from normality. This in turn suggests that a more general functional form for the truncated-mean function might be employed in practice. Or, one might be examining the data for departures from normality. . . . But one should not be too optimistic about the efficacy of those devices because in practice the linearity of the original true regression is itself questionable [1980: 13].

E.W.S.
G.F.

REFERENCES

GOLDBERGER, A. S. (1980) "Abnormal selection bias." University of Wisconsin, Department of Economics. (mimeo)
OLSEN, R. J. (1979) "Tests for the presence of selectivity bias and their relation to specifications of functional form and error distribution." Yale University: Institution for Social and Policy Studies Working Paper 812 (revised).

ADDENDUM

This addendum corrects several typographical errors in the original manuscript and one minor error in the text. A generalization of the test for the null hypothesis of no selection bias for a general non-normal model is also presented.

The typographical errors are as follows. In the paragraph beginning with "(3)" on page 157, "λ_i" and *not* "λ_1" should appear in the final sentence in the paragraph. In the following paragraph, the equation for $\hat\sigma_{11}$ should contain "$\hat{C}^2$" and not "$\hat{C}$", and "$\hat\lambda_i$" and not "$\hat\lambda_1$", so that the expression should be written

$$\hat\sigma_{11} = \frac{\sum\limits_{i=1}^{I_1} \hat{V}_{1i}^2}{I_1} - \frac{\hat{C}^2}{I_1} \sum\limits_{i=1}^{I_1} (\hat\lambda_i \hat{Z}_i - \hat\lambda_i^2).$$

On page 159, typographical errors appear in the expression for $\Theta_{ii'}$ and $\Omega_{ii'}$. The final term in each should read "X_{2_i}'" so that the correct expressions are

$$\Theta_{ii'} = \left(\frac{\partial\lambda_i}{\partial Z_{i'}}\right)\left(\frac{\partial\lambda_{i'}}{\partial Z_{i'}}\right) X_{2_i} \Sigma X_{2_{i'}}'$$

and

$$\Omega_{ii'} = \lambda_i\lambda_{i'} \left(\frac{\partial\lambda_i}{\partial Z_i}\right)\left(\frac{\partial\lambda_{i'}}{\partial Z_{i'}}\right) X_{2_i} \Sigma X_{2_{i'}}'.$$

The assertion on page 67 that "if $C \neq 0$, the correct asymptotic variance-covariance matrix (B ψ B$'$) produces standard errors of the regression coefficients that are larger than those given by the incorrect "standard" variance-covariance matrix σ_{11}B". is wrong. First, the "standard" variance-covariance matrix converges to $(\Sigma\eta_i/I_1)\sigma_{11}$B. Second, there is no necessary ordering of the two covariance matrices. The second matrix in ψ is positive semidefinite as asserted, but the first matrix in ψ is smaller than B^{-1} so long as some η_i are less than unity. Finally, the usual least squares estimate of σ_{11} general understates the true value of σ_{11} in large samples since

$$\text{plim } \Sigma \frac{\hat{V}_{1i}^2}{I_1} = \sigma_{11} \frac{\Sigma\eta_i}{I_1} \quad \text{and } 0 \leqslant \eta_i \leqslant 1.$$

Using the notation in the text, the "usual" least squares variance covariance matrix for the regression coefficients $\hat{\beta}_1$ converges to

$$\sigma_{11} \left(\frac{\Sigma \eta_i}{I_1} \right) B.$$

Recall that $0 \leqslant \eta_i \leqslant 1$. The correct variance-covariance matrix converges to

$$\sigma_{11} B \, \psi \, B'.$$

Denote the two matrices of ψ by ψ_1 and ψ_2 so $\psi = \psi_1 + \psi_2$. Thus the difference between the two covariance matrices is

$$\sigma_{11} B \left[\psi B' - \left(\frac{\Sigma \eta_i}{I} \right) I_{k_1+1, k_1+1} \right]$$

$$= \sigma_{11} B \, \psi_2 \, B'.$$

This matrix is clearly positive semidefinite, and the assertion made in the text is true.

In the general case, however, this result does not hold. By a judicious choice of X_{2_i} and X_{1_i} it is possible to construct examples in which the ordering of the co-variance matrices is reversed.

A test of the null hypothesis of no sample selection bias can be constructed without resort to the normality assumption used in the text. Assume that the joint density $h(U_{1_i}, U_{2_i})$ has finite moments and depends on a finite dimensional parameter set Θ. The second term on the right side of equation 2 in the text is

$$E(U_{1_i} | U_{2_i} \geqslant - X_{2_i} \beta_2) = \frac{\displaystyle\int_{-\infty}^{\infty} U_{1_i} \int_{-X_{2_i}\beta_2}^{\infty} h(U_{1_i}, U_{2_i}) dU_{2_i} \, dU_{1_i}}{\displaystyle\int_{-X_{2_i}\beta_2}^{\infty} h_2(U_{2_i}) dU_{2_i}},$$

where $h_2(\ )$ is the marginal density of U_{2_i}. This expression depends on $X_{2_i}\beta_2$ and Θ— the parameters generating the density of $h(\ )$. We record this dependence by writing

$$E(U_{1_i} | U_{2_i} \geqslant - X_{2_i}\beta_2) = K(X_{2_i}\beta_2; \Theta), \qquad [\text{A-1}]$$

where the functional form of K is specified once h is specified. Section 2 of the text gives an explicit expression for K when h is specified to be bivariate normal, but it is obvious that other joint densities generate other functional forms for K.

Suppose that the exact functional form for h is unknown. Is it possible to test the null hypothesis of no selection bias in this case? The answer is yes, provided certain additional conditions are met.

As in the text, a censored sample is assumed. The probability that observation i makes its way into the censored sample is, conditional on X_{2_i},

$$P_i(X_{2_i}) = \int_{-X_{2_i}\beta_2}^{\infty} h_2(U_{2_i}) \, dU_{2_i} = 1 - \int_{-\infty}^{-X_{2_i}\beta_2} h_2(U_{2_i}) \, dU_{2_i}.$$

P_i is a monotonic function of the term $X_{2_i}\beta_2$. Without knowledge of the density of h_2, the precise functional form of P_i is unknown. The probit function, however, plays a special role in approximating the unknown distribution function. It is the leading term of a Gram-Chalier type A or Edgeworth series (Kendall and Stuart 1971, I: 168-170; Cramer, 1946: 223) that, under conditions specified in these references, provides a convergent series approximation to any distribution function. Here we assume that the true underlying random variable is standardized so that it has zero mean and unit variance.

Thus

$$\int_{-\infty}^{Z_i} h_2(U) \, dU = \bar{\phi}(Z_i) + \frac{C_3}{3!} \bar{\phi}^{(3)}(Z_i) + \frac{C_4}{4!} \bar{\phi}^{(4)}(Z_i) + \ldots,$$

where $Z_i = -X_{2_i}\beta_2$ $\bar{\phi}$ is the unit normal distribution and $\bar{\phi}^{(j)}$ is the jth derivative of $\bar{\phi}$ and the C_j coefficients are functions of the moments of the underlying true distribution, which moments are assumed to exist. (See Cramer, 1946: 223 for an explicit derivation of these moments.) The $\bar{\phi}^{(j)}$ functions are known and in fact are Chebyshev-Hermite polynomials that are available on most computing machines.[1]

Define $D_i = 1$ if the observation makes its way into the censored sample and $D_i = 0$ otherwise. Then

$$P_i = E(D_i|X_{2_i}) = \bar{\phi}(-X_{2_i}\beta_2) + \frac{C_3}{3!} \bar{\phi}^{(3)}(-X_{2_i}\beta_2) + \frac{C_4}{4!} \bar{\phi}^{(4)}(-X_{2_i}\beta_2) + \ldots.$$

$$[A\text{-}2]$$

Running a nonlinear regression of D_i on the functions on the right side of the expression enables one under general conditions to estimate β_2, C_3, C_4, and so forth. In this fashion, one can approximate an arbitrary P_i function. A test of the probit assumption is a test that $C_3 = C_4 = \ldots = C_n = 0$.

Since $1 - P_i$ and $X_{2_i}\beta_2$ are monotonically related, one can insert $1 - P_i$ in place of $X_{2_i}\beta_2$ in expression A-1. Writing H_2 as the cumulative distribution function of h_2

$$P_i(X_{2_i}) = 1 - H_2(-X_{2_i}\beta_2)$$

so

$$-X_{2_i}\beta_2 = H^{-1}(1 - P_i(X_{2_i})),$$

and expression A-1 may be written as

$$E(U_{1_i}|U_{2_i} \geqslant X_{2_i}\beta_2) = K(-H^{-1}(1 - P_i(X_{2_i})); \Theta) = G(P_i; \Theta).$$

Assuming that the conditional mean of U_{1_i} is continuously differentiable to all orders, we may expand $G(P_i; \Theta)$ in terms of a power series in P_i. Thus, for point of expansion P_i, we may write

$$G(P_i; \Theta) = G(\bar{P}_i; \Theta) + \sum_{j=1}^{\infty} \frac{1}{j!} G^{(j)}(P_i; \Theta)(P_i - \bar{P}_i)^j. \qquad [A\text{-}3]$$

If there is no sample selection bias, $G^{(j)}(\bar{P}_i; \Theta)$ vanishes for all $j = 0, 1, \ldots$. In place of the unobserved P_i, we propose using $\hat{P}_i$ estimated from equation A-2.

The following procedure for testing the null hypothesis of no selection bias is proposed. Run a regression of Y_{1_i} on X_{1_i} and approximated G. Thus

$$Y_{1_i} = X_{1_i}\beta_1 + \sum_{j=1}^{k} \frac{G^{(j)}(\bar{P}_i; \Theta)}{j!} (\hat{P}_i - \bar{P}_i)^j + \epsilon_i, \qquad [A\text{-}4]$$

where ϵ_i is V_{1_i} (in the text) plus a term that arises from the approximations that arise from truncating the series at k terms and from using an estimated P_i in place of true P_i. Under the null hypothesis of no sample selection bias the estimated coefficients on $(\hat{P}_i - \bar{P}_i)^j$ for $j \geqslant 1$ will not be significantly different, statistically, from zero. This test is *exact* in the sense that under the null hypothesis there is no error of approximation in the disturbance term. Note that if X_{1_i} contains a constant term, it is not possible to estimate $G(\bar{P}_i; \Theta)$ so that the test must be performed on the coefficients of polynomials of order greater than zero. Failure to reject the null hypothesis implies that selection bias is present. Provided that sufficient terms are added in series expansions A-2 and A-3, the regression estimates of the parameters of equation A-4 provide an approximate method for estimating the model parameters (the β_1) in the presence of selection bias in the general non-normal case.[2] The quality of this approximation remains to be investigated.

A copy of the computer program that routinely performs the operations discussed in the text for the normal model is available. The program: (1) runs regressions with and without the correction term for sample selection bias and produces the correct standard errors; and (2) performs and reports the probit analysis needed to form the estimated λ_i and automatically forms the λ_i. The program is provided at cost on request from International Educational Services, 1525 East 53rd Street, Chicago, IL 60615.

For empirical applications of the methodology see, for example, the collection of papers on female labor supply edited by Smith (1980). Papers by the author, John Cogan and Giora Hanoch apply the methods developed in the text.

NOTES

1. It is clearly also possible to use a Taylor's series expansion for the distribution function. This would lead to a linear probability model for [A-2]. However, Kendall and Stuart, 1977 I, warn against this approach because of the high degree of inaccuracy involved.

2. It is not the case that the addition of one term of series [A-2] necessarily improves the approximation. The same is true of [A-3] in the general case.

REFERENCES

CRAMER, H. (1946) Mathematical Methods for Statistics. Princeton, NJ: Princeton Univ. Press.

KENDALL, M. G. and A. STUART (1977) Advanced Theory of Statistics, vol. 1. London: Griffin.

SMITH, J. [ed.] (1980) Female Labor Supply: Theory and Estimation. Princeton, NJ: Princeton Univ. Press.

3

This is the first of five papers in this volume reporting the results of the Gary Income Maintenance Experiment.[1] The authors have expanded the two-equation model employed in the papers by Barnow et al. and Heckman to a three-equation model incorporating before/after, experimental/control comparisons with a correction for nonrandom attrition. Estimation is by maximum likelihood, and the authors find that within a simple analysis of variance model, attrition bias is quite large. If sufficient regressors are included in the outcome equation, however, the remaining attrition bias is relatively insignificant. This finding reinforces the common observation that multivariate regression results are relatively robust under a variety of specification errors.[2]

Hausman and Wise specify a simple error components model of behavior at time periods 1 and 2:

$$y_{i1} = X_{i1} \beta + e_{i1}$$
$$y_{i2} = X_{i2} \beta + e_{i2}.$$

This model accounts for the persistence of individual behavior over time both in the X variables characterizing the individual and also with an unobserved individual-specific error term which contributes to the total error variance in the two equations.[3] The correlation between the error terms in the two equations, ρ_{12} (this is misprinted in the third line below expression [1.2]), measures the proportion of variance attributable to unobserved individual effects, and its generally large magnitude demonstrates the efficiency gains from using individuals as their own controls in a before/after design.

The authors then introduce a probit attrition equation 1.3 and derive the by now familiar outcome equation with inverse Mills ratio term added [1.4]. In addition, expression 1.5 shows that the conditional expectation of the time 1 outcome is also affected by attrition. Putting the two outcome equations together with the attrition equations yields the basic model [1.6]:

$$y_{i1} = X_{i1} \beta + e_{i1}$$
$$y_{i2} = X_{i2} \beta + e_{i2}$$
$$A_i = R_i \delta + e_{i3}.$$

The error terms in this specification are assumed to have a joint normal distribution with covariance matrix given by [1.7]:

$$\Sigma = \begin{matrix} \sigma^2 & \rho_{12}\sigma^2 & \rho_{12}\rho_{23}\sigma \\ & \sigma^2 & \rho_{23}\sigma \\ & & 1 \end{matrix}$$

An important (but untested) simplifying assumption is that the error terms from the time 1 outcome equation and the attrition equation are correlated only through the correlation of each with the error from the time 2 outcome equation.

Following this, Hausman and Wise write out the joint probabilities of observing the values of the outcome variables, with and without sample attrition. These expressions (1.8 and 1.9) are complex, and are probably the most difficult aspect of the paper. Their calculation enables the log likelihood function to be explicitly written out, and maximized via the algorithm of Berndt et al.[4]

The second section of the chapter is devoted to the application of this model to data from the Gary experiment. The focus is on black, male-headed households, only 65% of whom completed the experiment. Since this attrition may be related to endogenous variables, bias may result from uncorrected estimates based on complete data alone. The analysis proceeds in five stages, from simple to more complex models. In each case, the outcome variable is the logarithm of earnings, a specification that simplifies the problem since it does not involve a limited dependent variable.[5] (See the chapters by Moffitt and Burtless and Hausman in Part II for a different treatment of related issues.)

Hausman and Wise's first specification involves only three effect parameters, a pre-experimental mean, a time effect, and an experimental effect. This model, which is essentially an experimental/control, before/after comparison under the assumption that the groups have identical means in the preprogram period, leads to the conclusion that experimentals decreased their work effort by 6.4% as a result of the experiment. Since, however, the computed standard error is 8.3%, this is a relatively weak result.

The second model is similar, but this time an individual-specific error component is introduced. This leads to a very similar experimental effect estimate (work effort decreases by 6.2%), but with a smaller standard error. The third calculation uses this model, estimated jointly with the attrition equation. Now we find a stronger experimental effect—since its standard error is estimated at 4.5%.

Hausman and Wise's fourth model (section 2.D) estimates the experimental effect while controlling a variety of exogenous predictors, with and without a correction for attrition. Without this correction, the effect is estimated at minus 7.9% (standard error = 3.9%), whereas the corrected estimate is minus 8.2% (standard error = 4.0 percent). The authors conclude that the multivariate regression model is less sensitive to attrition bias than the simple analysis of variance model.

The final model estimates experimental effects separately by treatment group. The results suggest that the income guarantee, rather than the tax rate, is the significant aspect of the treatment. A similar result is achieved for husbands (the group under study by Hausman and Wise) via different methods in the papers by Moffitt and by Burtless and Hausman (Part II). Results for other groups (wives and female heads of households) are reported by Moffitt.

NOTES

1. See also Moffitt and Burtless and Hausman in Part II, Maynard and Murnane in Part IV, and Kaluzny in Part V.

2. See Hanushek and Jackson (1977: 84-86) for further discussion.

3. For related models see Ashenfelter and Kiefer in Part III. For a general exposition of these and related models see Kmenta (1971: 508-516).

4. Since the logarithm is a monotonic function that converts products into sums, it is standard practice to maximize the log likelihood function to find the values that maximize the likelihood function itself.

5. Smith (1980) extends the model to deal with this situation.

REFERENCES

HANUSHEK, E. A. and J. E. JACKSON (1977) Statistical Methods for Social Scientists. New York: Academic.

KMENTA, J. (1971) Elements of Econometrics. New York: Macmillan.

SMITH, D. A. (1980) "Memo on the three equation model: two tobits plus attrition." Cambridge, MA: Abt Assoc. (mimeo)

Attrition Bias in Experimental and Panel Data
The Gary Income Maintenance Experiment

Jerry A. Hausman and David A. Wise

CAREFUL ATTENTION TO SAMPLE DESIGN is an important consideration in both social experimentation and in panel surveys of individuals. Techniques of randomization and response surface design have been highly developed with the aim of obtaining the maximum amount of information from a given experiment or survey. In practice, however, social experimentation and panel data differ in one important respect from classical design assumptions as exemplified in the pioneering analysis of R. A. Fisher [4]. This difference arises from the fact that each individual in panel data is his own best control. In a classical experiment, seed might be planted in different plots at random and fertilized at different intensity levels chosen at random. Differences in yield would then be used to assess the effectiveness of the fertilizer. A characteristic of recent[2] social experiments is that individuals are surveyed before the experiment begins, and their pre-experimental behavior is then compared to their behavior after receipt of the ex-perimental "treatment." Information on controls, persons who receive no experimental treatment, is also obtained. However, it has been found that much more information is gained from the change in a given individual's behavior than by comparing differences in the average behavior of experimentals and controls. The reason for this finding is the presence of significant, unobserved individual effects. For instance, in a previous study of the earnings response of white males in the New Jersey negative income tax experiment (Hausman and Wise [10]) the authors found that about 85 per cent of the total variance in response was due to the variation in individual specific terms that persisted over time.

It is because of the importance of individual effects that the design of social experiments includes pre-experimental observations of individuals, and cor-responding data collection, and then the observation of the same individuals subject to experimental treatment over an extended period of time (ranging from two to fifteen years). But the inclusion of the time factor in the experiment raises a problem which does not exist in classical experiments—attrition. Some individu-als decide that keeping the detailed records that the experiments require is not worth the payment, some move, some are inducted into the military. In some experiments, persons with large earnings receive no experimental treatment benefit and thus drop out of the experiment altogether. This attrition may negate

[1] The research reported herein was performed pursuant to Contract Number HEW 100-76-0073 from the Department of Health, Education, and Welfare, Washington, D.C. The opinions and conclusions expressed herein are solely those of the authors and should not be construed as representing the opinions or policy of any agency of the United States government.

This study was part of continuing analysis of the Gary Experiment at MATHEMATICA POLICY RESEARCH. The authors also acknowledge research support of the National Science Foundation. Research assistance was provided by G. Burtless. We thank K. Kehrer, C. Mallar, and Zvi Griliches for their comments. An editor also provided helpful comments on an earlier draft of the paper.

[2] For example, the New Jersey, Gary, and Seattle–Denver income maintenance experiments and the health insurance experiment currently in progress, all sponsored by HEW.

From Jerry A. Hausman and David A. Wise, "Attrition Bias in Experimental and Panel Data: The Gary Income Maintenance Experiment," 47 (2) *Econometrica* 455-473 (March 1979). Copyright 1979 by the Econometric Society.

the randomization in the initial experimental design. If the probability of attrition is correlated with experimental response, then traditional statistical techniques will lead to biased and inconsistent estimates of the experimental effect.

Attrition is a problem in any panel survey, not only those conducted in conjunction with social experiments, where individuals are followed over time. Two important bodies of panel data, the Michigan Income Dynamics Survey and the National Longitudinal (Parnes) Surveys, for example, followed people for 5 and 10 years, respectively. While the attrition in these surveys has typically not been as severe as in social experiments, the same problems of potential bias arises, if attrition is not random.

In this paper we propose a method that uses a probability model of attrition, in conjunction with a traditional random effects model of individual response, to correct for attrition bias. The maximum likelihood procedure used provides consistent and asymptotically efficient estimates of the parameters of a structural model, including experimental response; and allows a test of whether or not non-random attrition has occurred. These procedures are closely related to previous models based on non-random samples by Hanoch [7], Hausman and Spence [9], Hausman and Wise [11], Heckman [14], Madalla and Nelson [17], and Nelson [20]. All of these models except Hausman and Wise considered the problem of non-random samples in the single period context. We consider the problem in a multi-period framework, due to its importance in both panel data and social experimentation. A modified scoring algorithm, first employed by Berndt, Hall, Hall, and Hausman [3], provides estimates at a reasonably small computation cost.

After formal discussion of the problem and statistical specification of our model, the method is used to estimate the earnings response of black males in the Gary Income Maintenance Experiment. Attrition bias is a potentially important problem in this experiment, but the extent of the bias seems to depend crucially on the specification of the model used to evaluate the experimental effect. Empirical results indicate a much greater bias with simple analysis of variance models than with behavioral specifications incorporating more exogenous variables. Attrition bias in a structural model estimating only a single experimental effect was found to be small although statistically significant. No attrition bias was found in a structural specification that allowed estimation of the effects of all four treatments. Simple analysis of variance estimates, however, were substantially affected by attrition.

1. STATISTICAL SPECIFICATION

Two statistical models are commonly used to analyze individual behavior over time. In this paper we will use the random effects specification, although the techniques can be applied in a straightforward manner to the fixed effects specification as well. Initially, we will concentrate on a two-period model. Later we will indicate the appropriate extension for more periods. The "linear regression" model used for individual behavior has the form

(1.1) $y_{it} = X_{it}\beta + \varepsilon_{it}$ $(i = 1, \ldots, N; t = 1, 2)$,

where i indexes individuals and t indexes time periods. In a social experiment X_{i1} may differ from X_{i2} because of experimental treatment, along with changes in individual characteristics which occur with the passage of time. Such changes, of course, may also occur in panel survey data. The residual in the specification is then decomposed into two orthogonal components, an individual effect μ_i, which is assumed to be drawn from an iid distribution and to be independent of the X_{it}'s, and a time effect, η_{it}, which is assumed to be a serially uncorrelated random variable drawn from an iid distribution. Thus, the assumptions on ε_{it} are:

(1.2) $\varepsilon_{it} = \mu_i + \eta_{it}$, $E(\varepsilon_{it}) = 0$, $V(\varepsilon_{it}) = \sigma_\mu^2 + \sigma_\eta^2 = \sigma^2$,
$\varepsilon_{it} \sim N(0, \sigma^2)$.

The contribution to the variance of the individual component σ_μ^2 is typically greater than σ_η^2 which highlights the importance of letting individuals serve as their own controls. The correlation between ε_{i1} and ε_{i2}, $\rho_{i2} = \sigma_\mu^2/(\sigma_\mu^2 + \sigma_\eta^2)$, often ranges from .4 to .9. The correlation coefficient indicates the proportion of total variance explained by the unobserved individual effect.

If attrition occurs in the sample, a common practice is to discard those observations for which y_{i2} is missing. But suppose that the probability of observing y_{i2} varies with its value, as well as the values of other variables. Then the probability of observing y_{i2} will depend on ε_{i2} and least squares will lead to biased estimates of the underlying structural parameters and the experimental response.

To develop a model of attrition, define the indicator variable a_i and let $a_i = 0$ if attrition occurs in period two, so that y_{i2} is not observed, and let $a_i = 1$ if attrition does not occur, so that y_{i2} is observed. Suppose that y_{i2} is observed if $A_i = \alpha y_{i2} + X_{i2}\theta + W_i\gamma + \omega_i \geq 0$, where W_i is a vector of variables which do not enter the conditional expectation of y but affect the probability of observing y_{i2}, θ and γ are vectors of parameters, and the ω_i are iid random variables. Substituting for y_{i2} leads to $A_i = X_{i2}(\alpha\beta + \theta) + W_i\gamma + \alpha\varepsilon_{i2} + \omega_i$. But since α and θ enter the specification in an equivalent manner, we combine them to form a "reduced form" specification which is $A_i = X_i\xi + W_i\gamma + \varepsilon_{i3}$. Define the vectors $R_i = [W_i, X_{i2}]$ and $\delta = [\xi, \gamma]'$. We assume that ε_{i2} and ω_i are normally distributed, and normalize by setting the variance σ_{33} of ε_{i3} equal to 1. Then the probabilities of retention and attrition are probit functions given, respectively, by

(1.3) $\mathrm{pr}\,(a_i = 1) = \Phi[R_i\delta]$ and
$\mathrm{pr}\,(a_i = 0) = 1 - \Phi[R_i\delta]$,

where $\Phi[\,\cdot\,]$ is the unit normal distribution function.[3] We could estimate the parameters of equation (1.3) as it is. However, our primary goal is to correct for the effects of attrition on estimates of the parameters in equation (1.1) by

---

[3] The specification of A_i and the normalization described in this paragraph were used by Hausman and Spence [9] in modeling non-random missing data. A comparable formulation, using an alternative normalization and specification for A_i, was suggested by Hausman and Wise [11, fn. 8, 9, and 10].

integrating it with the probability of attrition.

Suppose we estimate the model of equation (1.1) using only complete observations. The conditional expectation of y_{i2}, given that it is observed, is,

$$(1.4) \qquad E(y_{i2}|X_{i2}, a_i = 1) = X_{i2}\beta + \rho_{23}\sigma\frac{\phi(R_i\delta)}{\Phi[R_i\delta]},$$

where ρ_{23} is the correlation between ε_2 and ε_3. Thus, this procedure will lead to biased and inconsistent estimates of β unless $\rho_{23} = 0$.[4] Least squares estimates based on complete observations but using first period data only will also be inconsistent, even though attrition occurs only in the second period, if ε_{i1} and ε_{i2} have a common component. For then ε_{i1} and ε_{i3} will also be correlated. The expected value of y_{i1}, given that individual i is in the sample in the second period is given by

$$(1.5) \qquad E(y_{i1}|X_{i1}, a_i = 1) = X_{i1}\beta + \rho_{12}\rho_{23}\sigma\frac{\phi(R_i\delta)}{\Phi[R_i\delta]},$$

where $\rho_{13} = \rho_{12}\rho_{23}$.

The second term in equation (1.5) is smaller than the second term in the conditional expectation of y_{i2} in equation (1.4). But so long as individual effects exist across periods, attrition in one period will affect the estimates of all earlier periods, if only complete observations are used.

To recapitulate, we gather together the following definitions:

$$
\begin{aligned}
y_{i1} &= X_{i1}\beta + \varepsilon_{i1}, \\
(1.6) \quad y_{i2} &= X_{i2}\beta + \varepsilon_{i2}, \\
A_i &= R_i\delta + \varepsilon_{i3}.
\end{aligned}
$$

Attrition occurs if the index $A_i \leq 0$. From the conditional expectations of equations (1.4) and (1.5), we see that the critical parameter in the determination of attrition bias is the correlation ρ_{23} between ε_{i2} and ε_{i3}. We want a method of estimation that will yield asymptotically efficient and consistent estimates of the structural parameters of (1.6) and will allow a convenient test of the hypothesis that $\rho_{23} = 0$. We shall use a maximum likelihood procedure. The joint normal terms, ε_{i1}, ε_{i2}, and ε_{i3} have mean zero and covariance matrix

$$(1.7) \qquad \Sigma = \begin{bmatrix} \sigma^2 & \rho_{12}\sigma^2 & \rho_{12}\rho_{23}\sigma \\ & \sigma^2 & \rho_{23}\sigma \\ & & 1 \end{bmatrix},$$

where $\sigma_{11} = \sigma_{22} = \sigma^2$ and we have normalized by setting $\sigma_{33} = 1$. We need to consider two possibilities: $a_i = 1$ and $a_i = 0$. If $a_i = 1$, both y_{i1} and y_{i2} are observed

---

[4] A variance components estimator will also be inconsistent.

and the joint density of a_i, y_{i1}, and y_{i2} is given by

$$f(a_i = 1, y_{i1}, y_{i2}) = \text{pr}\,[a_i = 1 \mid y_{i1}, y_{i2}]f(y_{i2}\mid y_{i1})f(y_{i1})$$

(1.8)
$$= \Phi\left[\frac{R_i\delta + (\rho_{23}/\sigma)(y_{i2} - X_{i2}\beta)}{(1 - \rho_{23}^2)^{\frac{1}{2}}}\right]\frac{1}{(\sigma^2(1 - \rho_{12}^2))^{\frac{1}{2}}}$$

$$\phi\left(\frac{y_{i2} - \rho_{12}Y_{i1} - (X_{i2} - \rho_{12}X_{i1})\beta}{(\sigma^2(1 - \rho_{12}^2))^{\frac{1}{2}}}\right)\frac{1}{\sigma}\,\phi\left(\frac{y_{i1} - X_{i1}\beta}{\sigma}\right),$$

where the first term follows from the fact that the conditional density $f(\varepsilon_{i3}\mid\varepsilon_{i2})$ is $N((\rho_{23}/\sigma)\varepsilon_{i2}, 1 - \rho_{23}^2)$. If $a_i = 0$, y_{i2} is not observed and must be "integrated out." In this instance the fact that $f(\varepsilon_{i3}\mid\varepsilon_{i1})$ is $N(\rho_{12}\rho_{23}/\sigma)\varepsilon_{i1}, 1 - \rho_{12}^2\rho_{23}^2)$ leads to the expression,

$$f(a_1 = 0, y_{i1}) = \text{pr}[a_i = 0\mid y_{i1}]f(y_{i1})$$

(1.9)
$$= \left\{1 - \Phi\left[\frac{R_i\delta + (\rho_{12}\rho_{23}/\sigma)(y_{i1} - X_{i1}\beta)}{(1 - \rho_{12}^2\rho_{23}^2)^{\frac{1}{2}}}\right]\right\}\frac{1}{\sigma}\,\phi\left(\frac{y_{i1} - X_{i1}\beta}{\sigma}\right).\ {}^{5}$$

[5] An alternative formulation, suggested previously by Hausman and Wise [11], is to let

$$A_i = \alpha y_{i2} + R_i\tilde{\delta} + \omega_i,$$

where $R_i\tilde{\delta} = X_{i2}\theta + W_i\gamma$ and the ω_i are iid normal random variables assumed to be independent of ε_1 and ε_2. If we normalize by setting the variance of ω equal to 1, the covariance matrix of ε_1, ε_2, and ω is given by

$$\tilde{\Sigma} = \begin{bmatrix} \sigma^2 & \rho_{12}\sigma^2 & 0 \\ & \sigma^2 & 0 \\ & & 1 \end{bmatrix}.$$

If we now substitute for y_{i2} in the expression for A_i, we obtain

$$A_i = X_{i2}(\alpha\beta + \theta) + W\gamma + \alpha\varepsilon_{i2} + \omega_i = R_i\delta + \varepsilon_{i3},$$

with the covariance matrix for ε_1, ε_2, and ε_3 given by

$$\Sigma = \begin{bmatrix} \sigma^2 & \rho_{12}\sigma^2 & \rho_{12}\alpha\sigma^2 \\ & \sigma^2 & \alpha\sigma^2 \\ & & \alpha^2\sigma^2 + 1 \end{bmatrix}.$$

Expressions comparable to equations (1.8) and (1.9) are then given by

$$f(a_i = 1, y_{i1}, y_{i2}) = \Phi[R_i\delta + \alpha(y_{i2} - X_{i2}\beta)]\cdot f(y_{i2}\mid y_{i1})\cdot f(y_{i1})$$

and

$$f(a_i = 0, y_{i1}) = \left\{1 - \Phi\left[\frac{R_i\delta + \alpha\rho_{12}(y_{i1} - X_{i1}\beta)}{(1 + \alpha^2\sigma^2(1 - \rho_{12}^2))^{\frac{1}{2}}}\right]\right\}\cdot f(y_{i1}),$$

where explicit expressions for $f(y_{i2}\mid y_{i1})$ and $f(y_{i1})$ are the same as in (1.8) and (1.9).

In this formulation, attrition bias depends on the value of α and is zero only if α equals zero. A test for attrition bias is, of course, straightforward. To see the relationship between α and ρ_{23} in the specification used in the body of the paper, note that $\varepsilon_{i3} = \alpha\varepsilon_{i2} + \omega_i$, where ω and ε_2 are independent, can also be written as $\varepsilon_{i3} = \rho_{23}(\sigma_3/\sigma)\varepsilon_{i2} + \omega_i$, where $\alpha = \rho_{23}(\sigma_3/\sigma)$. Thus, $\alpha = 0$ if and only if $\rho_{23} = 0$. Normalizing by setting $\sigma_3^2 = 1$, instead of $\sigma_\omega^2 = 1$, would make the two specifications the same. In this specification, however, we have explicitly assumed that ω is independent from ε_1 and ε_2. But since we have not in the text specification attempted to identify the covariance between ω and ε_2, the two specifications are equivalent. We have not tried to distinguish correlation between ε_2 and ε_3 due only to the fact that ε_2 shows up in ε_3 from correlation between ω and ε_2.

The log likelihood function follows from equations (1.8) and (1.9). Order the observations so that the first s correspond to $a_i = 1$ and the remaining $T - s$ to $a_i = 0$. Then with k a constant the log likelihood function contains the unknown parameters β, δ, σ^2, ρ_{12}, ρ_{23}. It is given by

$$l = k + \sum_{i=1}^{s} \left\{ -\tfrac{1}{2} \log \sigma^2 - \frac{1}{2\sigma^2}(y_{i1} - X_{i1}\beta)^2 - \tfrac{1}{2} \log (\sigma^2(1 - \rho_{12}^2)) \right.$$

$$- \frac{1}{2\sigma^2(1 - \rho_{12}^2)}(y_{i2} - \rho_{12}y_{i1} - (X_{i2} - \rho_{12}X_{i1})\beta)^2$$

$$+ \log \Phi \left[\frac{R_i\delta + (\rho_{23}/\sigma)(y_{i2} - X_{i2}\beta)}{(1 - \rho_{23}^2)^{\frac{1}{2}}} \right]$$

$$+ \sum_{i=s+1}^{N} \left\{ -\tfrac{1}{2} \log \sigma^2 - \frac{1}{2\sigma^2}(y_{i1} - X_{i1}\beta)^2 \right.$$

$$\left. + \log \left[1 - \Phi\left(\frac{R_i\delta + (\rho_{12}\rho_{23}/\sigma)(y_{i1} - X_{i1}\beta)}{(1 - \rho_{12}^2\rho_{23}^2)^{\frac{1}{2}}} \right) \right] \right\}.$$

While it may appear complicated, the likelihood function has a simple structure defined in terms of normal density and distribution functions. It combines the variance components specification of the dependent variable y in equation (1.1) with the probit formulation of equation (1.3). The critical parameter for attrition bias is ρ_{23}; and inspection of the likelihood function demonstrates that if $\rho_{23} = 0$, the likelihood function separates into two parts corresponding to the variance components specification for y and the probit specification for attrition. Thus, if attrition bias is not present, generalized least squares techniques used to estimate equation (1.1) will lead to asymptotically efficient and consistent estimates of the structural parameters of the model, as expected.

We pause for a moment to consider identification of the parameters of A_i. Because of the specification of the equation determining A_i in equation (1.6), $A_i = \alpha y_{i2} + X_{i2}\theta + W_i\gamma + \omega_i$, all variables included in the conditional mean of y_{i2}, the vector X_{i2}, should also be included in R_i, the attrition specification vector. However, for (local) identification it can be shown that no variables "excluded" from X_{i2} need to be included in R_i. That is, the vector W_i need not appear in the specification of A_i. A heuristic argument for identification follows from noting that if the attrition bias parameter, ρ_{23}, is plus one or minus one and $\theta = 0$, then the second period attrition probability is identical to a Tobit specification where W_i does not appear in R_i. On the other hand, if $\rho_{23} = 0$, then the likelihood function factors into two distinct parts, a normal regression model and a probit equation. A consideration of the Hessian of the likelihood function for intermediate values of ρ_{23} establishes nonsingularity and thus local identification. When additional variables are included in W_i, the analysis remains the same.

The specified model of attrition extends in a straightforward manner to more than two periods. An attrition equation is specified for each period; it may include time effects. If once attrition occurs the individual does not return to the sample, then a series of conditional probabilities analogous to equations (1.8) and (1.9) result. The last period for which the individual appears in the sample gives information on which the random term in the attrition equations is conditioned. For periods in which the individual remains in the sample, an equation like (1.8) is used to specify the joint probability of no attrition and the observed values of the left hand side variables.[6]

Maximization of the likelihood function (1.10) yields estimates of β, δ, σ^2, ρ_{12} and ρ_{23}.[7] Numerical estimates based on the Gary experiment are presented in the next section.

2. ATTRITION IN THE GARY INCOME MAINTENANCE EXPERIMENT[8]

The primary goal of the income maintenance, or "negative income tax," experiments is to obtain estimates of potential labor supply and earnings responses to possible income maintenance plans.[9] Individuals in the experiments are surveyed to obtain retrospective data for a pre-experimental ("baseline") period, normally just prior to the beginning of the experimental period. Two groups are distinguished during the experimental period: controls and "experimentals." Controls are not on an experimental treatment plan, but receive nominal payments for completing periodic questionnaires. Experimentals are randomly assigned to one of several income maintenance plans. The Gary (Indiana) experiment had four basic plans defined by an income guarantee and a tax rate. The two guarantee levels were $4,300 and $3,300 for a family of four and were adjusted up for larger and down for smaller families. The two marginal tax rates were .6 and .4. The behavior of experimentals during the experiment can be compared to their own pre-experimental behavior and to that of the control group to obtain estimates of the effect of the treatment plans.

Persons received payments under the experimental plans according to a moving average scheme that took into account income in the previous six months in the determination of payments for a given month. This was to insure that payments did not vary widely with fluctuation in monthly income so long as average monthly income remained stable.[10]

[6] A similar model can be used for analysis of panel data in which missing an interview does not result in terminal attrition. A probability model similar to equation (1.3) is specified for each period. State dependence can be introduced in the probability model by conditioning on status in the previous period. Missing observations are then "integrated out" by the same procedure used to derive equation (1.9).

[7] We have used an algorithm proposed by Berndt, Hall, Hall, and Hausman [3]. It uses only first derivatives. It is similar to the method of scoring discussed by Anderson [1]. Nelson [20] reported difficulty in using second derivative methods (Newton-Raphson) in a similar problem. We began with least squares estimates of the parameters and our algorithm always converged to the global optimum. This procedure is computationally easier than using initial consistent estimates that could be obtained, for example, using methods discussed by Heckman [15].

[8] In addition to attrition, a potential problem is created because the sample is stratified according to our endogenous variable. We have found, however, that this problem does not lead to significant bias in parameter estimates. A paper on this topic, Hausman and Wise [13], or an appendix to this paper that considers the subject will be provided to the reader upon request to the authors.

[9] This summary of NIT experiments is only a brief outline. More detail is contained in Watts and Rees [23] and McDonald, Moffitt, and Kehrer [18]. For a discussion of the econometric theory of the response to a NIT, both Hall [6] and Hausman and Wise [10] are relevant.

[10] For a more detailed discussion of this procedure, see Kehrer, et al. [16].

Two broad groups of families were studied in the Gary experiment: black, female-headed households and black, male-headed households. There was little attrition among the first group, but the attrition rate among male-headed families was substantial. (See Moffitt [19].) Of our sample[11] of 585 black males for whom we had baseline data, 206, or 35.2 per cent, did not complete the experiment.[12] Among the 334 experimentals, the attrition rate was 31.1 per cent, while 40.6 per cent of the 251 controls failed to complete the experiment. This difference in attrition rates is not surprising since the experiment is much more beneficial to experimentals than to controls. Other characteristics of individuals may also affect attrition. The effect of these characteristics will be estimated using the model specified in Section 1.

We emphasize again that non-random attrition does not necessarily lead to biased estimates of a structural model of the type presented in equations (1.1) and (1.2). Attrition which is related only to the exogenous variables in a structural model does not lead to biased estimates, since these variables are controlled for in the statistical analysis. However, if attrition is related to endogenous variables, biased estimates result.

Attrition related to endogenous variables is easy to imagine. Beyond a "breakeven" point, "experimentals" receive no benefits from the experimental treatment. The breakeven point occurs when the guarantee minus taxes paid on earnings is zero. Thus, individuals with high earnings receive no treatment payment and may be much like controls vis á vis their incentive to remain in the experiment. But since high earnings are caused in part by the unobserved random term of the structural equation (1.1), attrition may well be related to it. In particular, attrition may be related to the random term in the earnings function for period 2, leading to correlation between ε_2 and ε_3 in equation (1.6).

We will present our empirical analysis in stages beginning with a simple analysis of variance model and proceeding to more elaborately parameterized structural models. To estimate the effect on earnings, say, of the treatment plans, it would appear that a straightforward and simple method is all that is necessary. We need only estimate experimental effects by comparing the mean responses of experimentals and controls; or, equivalently, by estimating the parameters in a simple analysis of variance model. There are, however, several reasons for using a more elaborate specification with more exogenous variables. If assignment to treatment groups is not in practice completely random, then we may want to control for other variables that affect earnings in order to obtain unbiased estimates of treatment effects. In addition, we may want to "parameterize" the experimental treatments in terms of income and wage effects in order to be able to predict the effect of plans not included among the treatment ones. (This, of course, may not make much sense with only two income guarantees and two tax rates.) Finally, we may want to

---

[11] The sample was put together for us by Mathematica Policy Research, who have primary reponsibility for analysis of the Gary experiment. Additional information on data availability can be obtained from Mathematica.

[12] While this attrition rate is high, attrition of black males in the New Jersey negative income tax experiment was so high that analysis of the experimental data for blacks was highly suspect. See Peck in Watts and Rees [23, Vol. 2, Part 6, Ch. 1].

use the experimental data just like any other survey data to estimate traditional earnings functions. We will see as we proceed that the possibility of attrition adds another dimension to consider in choosing a method of analysis.

We begin with a straightforward analysis of variance model because under usual assumptions underlying randomized controlled experiments it would be the most natural and appropriate method to obtain estimates of experimental effects. Controlled experiments are in fact designed to permit this method of analysis; they presumably obviate the necessity of controlling for individual characteristics other than experimental treatments.[13] We will see, however, that it may not be the most appropriate method of analysis when non-random attrition occurs.

A. A Simple Analysis of Variance Model

A simple analysis of variance specification is of the form:

(3.1) $\qquad E_{it} = \alpha + \delta_2 + \xi + \varepsilon_{it}$ $\qquad\qquad\qquad (i = 1, \ldots, N; t = 1, 2)$

where E is the logarithm of monthly earnings, α is the average of E over the pre-experimental period, δ_2 is a time (inflation) effect for period 2, ξ is the experimental effect, ε is a random term with zero mean for each i and each t, i indexes individuals, and t indexes time. The parameters of this model may be estimated by comparison of mean values of E for controls and experimentals for the two time periods.

The relevant information and parameter estimates are presented in Table I. Two important simplifications have been made for purposes of estimation. First, since only three observations are available during the experiment, each for a one month period, their average has been used to obtain a monthly earnings figure for the experimental period.[14] Second, the four experimental treatment groups have been treated as one. They will be distinguished in subsequent analysis. The average of the logarithms of earnings of controls increased by .1108 between the baseline and the experimental periods, while the increase for experimentals was only .0492. The time effect, δ_2, has been estimated by the difference between the average for controls in period 2 and the average over both controls and experimentals in period 1. The estimate is .1180 with a standard error of .1673. The

---

[13] A good treatment of analysis of variance estimation within the context of a social experiment is presented by Hall [6]. The analysis of variance models we have used closely parallel those suggested by Hall in analyzing the effect on white males of treatments in the New Jersey NIT experiment. Attrition among white males in that experiment was much less severe than among black males in this one (and in the New Jersey experiment, as well). We have argued verbally ourselves that simple analysis of variance models should be the preferred method of analyzing data from social experiments, at least to estimate initial experimental effects, because this method does take advantage of basic experimental design. Many of the efforts to obtain labor supply effects based on the New Jersey experiment, for example, seemed to fail largely because, in addition to ignoring truncation in sample selection, they also were overparameterized to control for many individual characteristics or as a concomitant of parameterization of experimental treatments. This more structural approach in many ways runs counter to the spirit and raison d'etre of elaborate social experiments.

[14] This averaging severely attenuates the unobserved individual effect in equation (3.2) below due to the high variance (transitory effect) in weekly observations. Average annual observations are much preferred, but were not available from the experiment.

TABLE I

AVERAGE EARNING FOR EXPERIMENTALS AND CONTROLS,
AND ESTIMATES OF PARAMETERS IN THE MODEL:
$$E_{it} = \alpha + \delta_2 + \xi + \varepsilon_{it}$$

	Average earnings	
	Period 1	Period 2
Experimentals	6.2584	6.3176
Controls	6.2710	6.3818

Parameter	Estimates	(standard errors)
Pre-experimental average, α	6.2638	(0.4517)
Time effect, δ_2	0.1180	(0.1673)
Experimental effect, ξ	−.0642	(0.0826)

experimental effect is estimated by the difference in the average for controls and experimentals in period 2. It is −.0642 with a standard error of .0826. Thus, the estimates do indicate a negative effect of the experimental treatments on labor earnings, but this method yields rather imprecise estimates. We also found, as in the New Jersey experiment, that hourly wages of experimentals and controls did not differ. Thus −.0642 per cent is a reasonable indicator of the effect of the experimental treatment on hours worked.

This method of estimation uses information for all persons in our sample of 585 by including data for those who dropped out to obtain the baseline means. (About one-third of the sample dropped out between periods 1 and 2.) But the experimental effect is calculated using only period 2 data; individual specific effects are not allowed.

B. An Analysis of Variance Model with Individual Specific Terms

An alternative analysis of variance specification is of the form:

$$(3.2) \qquad E_{it} = \alpha + \delta_2 + \xi + \mu_i + \eta_{it},$$

where the μ_i are random individual specific terms, and the η_{it} are independent and identically distributed with mean zero and a common variance. This formulation takes advantage of the correlation between the "random" component, $\mu_i + \eta_{it}$, of earnings in the two time periods. It essentially allows each individual to serve as his own control. But this advantage is gained at the expense of calculating the time effect δ_2 using only data for persons who did not drop out of the experiment—379 of the original 585 observations. It leads, however to a more precise estimate of the experimental effect ξ, the parameter of primary interest. Both methods yield unbiased estimates if the assumptions of equations (3.1) and (3.2) are correct.

An asymptotically efficient generalized least squares method has been used to estimate the parameters of equation (3.2).[15] The results are shown in Table II. The

---

[15] This estimator is the mixed estimator of combined variance components and fixed effects models. See Scheffé [**22**, Ch. 8].

standard error of the experimental effect is only about one-half as large as that obtained in the specification that ignores individual specific terms. The proportion of the total variance explained by the individual effects is .2212; it serves as an indicator of their importance. The estimate of the experimental effect remains about the same—a reduction in earnings of just over 6 per cent.[16] But it is still not significantly different from zero by conventional standards.

TABLE II

ESTIMATES OF PARAMETERS IN THE RANDOM INDIVIDUAL EFFECTS MODEL: $E_{it} = \alpha + \delta_2 + \xi + \mu_i + \eta_{it}$

Parameter	Estimates	(standard errors)
Pre-experimental average, α	6.2947	(0.0214)
Time effect, δ_2	0.0860	(0.0361)
Experimental effect, ξ	−.0621	(0.0419)

C. Analysis of Variance Model Corrected for Attrition

Although analysis of variance is the classical statistical method for analyzing the results of an experiment, the results may be biased by attrition. From the calculations in Section 1, we can see that attrition will lead to bias if either μ_i or η_i is correlated with the probability of attrition. We argued above that experimentals with higher than average income might be expected to have a higher attrition rate since they receive little or no benefit from the experiment. To check for possible attrition bias, the analysis of variance model of equation (3.2) was combined with the probability of attrition specification of model (1.3). Since analysis of variance has a straightforward regression interpretation, the likelihood function of equation (1.9) is maximized using the technique discussed in Section 2 with "dummy variables" associated with the analysis of variance effects. The attrition specification allows attrition to depend on variables that enter the structural model of earnings (discussed below) as well as other variables. They are:

Constant.

Experimental Effect: One for experimentals and zero for controls.

Education: Years of education.

Experience: Years of experience since starting work.

Income: Log of non-labor family income. It includes foodstamps, AFDC payments, public assistance, and earnings of other family members.

Union: A dummy variable that is one for union members and zero otherwise.

Poor Health: A dummy variable that is one if the individual said that his health was poor in relation to "others" and it limited the amount of work he did; otherwise the variable is zero.

The results are shown in Table III. The experimental effect is now estimated to be about 11 per cent and is significantly different from zero at conventional levels of significance. We found in Section 1 that attrition bias would be zero only if ρ_{23}

---

[16] The alternative fixed effects estimator, which takes μ_i to be a non-stochastic individual constant, yields an estimate of the experimental effect of −.0568 and a time effect of .0828.

TABLE III

PARAMETER ESTIMATES FOR THE ANALYSIS OF VARIANCE SPECIFICATION COMBINED WITH
THE ATTRITION MODEL

| Analysis of variance | | Attrition | |
Parameters	Estimates (standard errors)	Variables	Estimates (standard errors)
Pre-experimental average, α	6.2636 (0.0265)	Constant	$-.9210$ (.2608)
Time effect, δ_2	.1064 (.0408)	Experimental Effect	.2361 (.1131)
Experimental effect, ξ	$-.1098$ (.0453)	Education	.0172 (.0195)
		Experience	$-.0002$ (.0050)
		Income	.0934 (.0290)
		Union	1.2018 (0.1100)
		Poor Health	.2715 (.1013)
Attrition bias parameter ρ_{23}	$-.8213$ (.0449)	Earnings correlation ρ_{12}	.1697 (.0350)
Likelihood value	36.24	Earnings variance σ_{η}^2	.2147 (.0006)

were zero. Here we find a very precisely measured estimate of $-.8213$.[17] That is, persons with higher earnings, given other measured characteristics, are more likely to drop out of the experiment. Another method to test for attrition bias is to compare differences in estimates of α, δ_2, and ξ when a "correction" is made for attrition with estimates under the hypothesis that there is no attrition bias. Since under the null hypothesis that $\rho_{23} = 0$ the analysis of variance estimates for equation (3.1) are asymptotically efficient, the lemma of Hausman [8] can be applied to perform a specification test. The lemma states that the variance of the difference of the estimates is the difference of the respective variances. Concentrating on the experimental effect estimates, we see that the difference between the analysis of variance and maximum likelihood estimates is $-.0477$, with a standard error of .0171. The χ^2 statistic relative to the hypothesis of no difference has a value of 7.75. The hypothesis of no difference is rejected at any reasonable level of significance. Analysis of variance techniques which do not account for possible attrition bias lead to parameter estimates that differ substantially from the maximum likelihood estimates that take account of such bias. Furthermore, the maximum likelihood estimate of the experimental effect is significantly different from zero at usual levels of significance.

Finally, we note that experimentals appear to have a lower probability of attrition than controls. Higher non-labor income, poor health, and union membership are also associated with lower attrition rates, and the relevant

[17] The null hypothesis of $\rho_{23} = 0$ is rejected using a (Wald) χ^2 test. The χ^2 statistic with one degree of freedom is 334.6.

estimates are rather precisely measured. More education is estimated to be associated with less attrition and more work experience with more, but neither effect is measured with much precision.

We also estimated an analysis of variance model with a slightly more complex attrition specification. The estimates in Table III imply a probability of attrition for experimentals that is .047 less than for controls, if the probabilities are evaluated at the mean values of the other variables. To permit more general differences in the attrition behavior of experimentals and controls, we estimated a model with separate experimental and control coefficients on each of the attrition variables. That is, we allowed complete interaction between all variables and experimental status. However, none of the interactions was found to have a noticeable effect on attrition. None of the interaction terms was greater than one-fourth the size of the corresponding main effect. The attrition bias term ρ_{23} was estimated to be $-.8147$, nearly identical to the estimate of $-.8213$ found for the less complex specification, while the estimated experimental effect, $-.1098$, was identical to the one in the previous model. The maximum likelihood value of 36.62 barely exceeds the value of 36.24 found in Table III. The appropriate χ^2 likelihood ratio statistic (with five degrees of freedom) provides no evidence that the more complicated specification adds to our ability to predict attrition.

We have to this point been referring loosely to the difference between estimates that are corrected for attrition and those that are not as resulting from "attrition bias." This seems to be a correct interpretation since without attrition the analysis of variance model would presumably give an unbiased estimate of the experimental effect. We will see below, however, that the experimental effect estimated from a structural model is not altered much when a correction is made for attrition. Thus, it might be more appropriate to say that analysis of variance estimates of the experimental effect are less robust with respect to attrition than structural model estimates. Why this result might be expected is explained below.

D. *A Structural Model of Earnings Corrected for Attrition*

Structural models have been widely used in the analysis of income maintenance experiments. Such models permit estimation of the income and substitution effects which are needed to predict the response to plans which have not been included in the experimental design. However, to estimate a simple experimental response, it might be argued that only analysis of variance models are needed, given appropriate randomization in the original experimental design. If, in fact, allocation to treatment groups is completely random so that variables indicating treatment group are orthogonal to other exogenous variables that might influence earnings, addition of these variables will affect neither the experimental effect estimates nor their standard errors. If, however, treatment group assignment is not orthogonal to other exogenous variables, we cannot predict a priori whether estimates of the treatment effect from the structural model will be more or less precise than the simple analysis of variance estimates. On the one hand, the variance σ_η^2 is reduced by controlling for other determinants of earnings such as education and experience. On the other hand, additional variables use up degrees of freedom, thereby tending to increase the variance of parameter estimates.

We have, however, already found strong evidence of attrition bias within the context of the analysis of variance model, and are led to consider an alternative approach. Recall that the bias results from correlation between attrition and earnings in the second period. It may, in turn, be thought of as resulting from correlation between the error in the second period earnings equation and the probability of attrition. If exogenous variables that affect earnings, as well as attrition, are left out of the earnings equation, the correlation between attrition and the error in the earnings equation is magnified. Thus, if attrition is primarily related to exogenous variables in the structural model which are included in the stochastic term in the analysis of variance model, the structural model may be much less affected by attrition than the analysis of variance model.

We have estimated a variance components specification of the structural model $E_{it} = X_{it}\beta + \varepsilon_{it}$, with $\varepsilon_{it} = \mu_i + \eta_{it}$, as discussed in Section 1. Estimates are presented in Table IV. For comparison, generalized least squares estimates of the structural parameters (that are not corrected for attrition) have been included

TABLE IV[a]

PARAMETER ESTIMATES OF THE EARNINGS FUNCTION STRUCTURAL MODEL WITH AND
WITHOUT A CORRECTION FOR ATTRITION

Variables	With attrition correction: maximum likelihood estimates (standard errors)		Without attrition correction: generalized least squares estimates (standard errors)
	Earnings function parameters	Attrition parameters	Earnings function parameters
Constant	5.8539	−.6347	5.8911
	(0.0903)	(.3351)	(.0829)
Experimental effect	−.0822	.2414	−.0793
	(.0402)	(.1211)	(.0390)
Time effect	.0940	—	.0841
	(.0520)	—	(.0358)
Education	.0209	−.0204	.0136
	(.0052)	(.0244)	(.0050)
Experience	.0037	−.0038	.0020
	(.0013)	(.0061)	(.0013)
Income	−.0131	.1752	−.0115
	(.0050)	(.0470)	(.0044)
Union	.2159	1.4290	.2853
	(.0362)	(0.1252)	(.0330)
Poor health	−.0601	.2480	−.0578
	(.0330)	(.1237)	(.0326)
	$\hat{\sigma}_\eta^2 = .1832$	$l^* = 64.35$	$\hat{\sigma}_\eta^2 = .1236$
	(.0057)		
	$\hat{\rho}_{12} = .2596$	$\rho_{23} = -.1089$	$\hat{\rho}_{12} = .2003$
	(.0391)	(1.0429)	

[a] As an indication of computational costs for our sample of 585 observations, the GLS estimation which does not take account of attrition costs about $4.50 using TSP on the MIT 370-168 computer. The cost of maximum likelihood estimation of the attrition model ranged between $7 and $13 dollars, depending on the initial guesses of the parameters.

together with the maximum likelihood estimates that incorporate the effects of attrition. From the last column of the table, we see that the random effects model yields an estimated negative experimental effect of about 7.9 per cent.[18] The individual specific terms account for only 20 per cent of the total variance of the error term, as indicated by the estimated value of ρ_{12} in this model. As mentioned previously, this relatively low value probably results from using the average of only three monthly observations to calculate earnings. Annual figures would presumably include much less random noise. The coefficients on the right-hand side variables all have the expected sign and are measured rather precisely. In fact, the results agree closely with the estimates of Hausman-Wise [10, p. 429] based on data from the New Jersey experiment, where a primary consideration in estimation was correction for truncation bias introduced by the sample design.

Estimates of the parameters in the attrition model of equations (1.6) and (1.7) are presented in the first two columns of Table IV. The attrition bias parameter ρ_{23} is estimated to be $-.1089$. It indicates a small but statistically significant correlation between earnings and the probability of attrition. Although the estimate of the experimental effect is very close to the generalized least squares estimate, some of the other estimates differ substantially from the least squares values. The effect of income on earnings decreases by 23 per cent, while the effect of another year of education increases by 43 per cent. The experimental effect increases in magnitude from $-.079$ to $-.082$, an increase of 3.6 per cent.[19] Thus, within the context of a structural model, some attrition bias seems to be present, but not enough to substantially alter the estimate of the experimental effect. This is in marked contrast with the analysis of variance case, where attrition seems to affect the estimates significantly.[20]

Finally, we observe that non-labor income, poor health, and union membership are statistically significant and are estimated to reduce the probability of attrition. Experimentals are less likely to drop out than controls. The relevant estimates are not, however, precisely measured. Education and years of work experience are estimated to have small and statistically insignificant negative influences on retention in the sample. Recall that these are "reduced form" estimates in that the direct effect of these variables on attrition cannot be distinguished from their indirect effects through earnings.

Within the context of this structural model we also estimated a more complicated model of attrition, the same one used within the analysis of variance context.

---

[18] The experimental effect using a fixed effects model was estimated to be minus 6.4 per cent.

[19] Using the lemma of Hausman [8], the difference of .003 has an estimated standard error of .0097. Thus, the difference in the two experimental effect estimates is not statistically different from zero.

[20] Comparison with the analysis of variance model yields a likelihood ration of 56.22 with 5 degrees of freedom, which is significant at all reasonable test sizes. Note, however, that if it were not for attrition, unbiased estimates of the experimental effect would result from an analysis of variance if a correct experimental design were used. In fact, the experimental effect is just as precisely estimated in Table III as in Table IV, which indicates that while the coefficients of the additional variables are significant they do not help to obtain a more precise estimate of the experimental effect.

It allows for full interaction between the determinants of earnings and experimental status. Instead of allowing merely for an experimental effect as indicated by the estimates in Table IV, separate coefficients for experimentals and controls were distinguished for education, years of experience, non-labor family income, health, and union membership. As with the analysis of variance model, no significant differences in these coefficient estimates were found. None of the estimated interaction terms exceeded one-fourth the magnitude of the main effect terms.[21] The estimate of the attrition parameter ρ_{23}, however, decreased to only $-.040$. The experimental effect was estimated to be $-.0790$, almost identical to the generalized least squares estimate of Table IV.

E. A Structural Model of Earnings with Treatment Groups Distinguished

Because the more complicated model of attrition does not add much to the explanation of attrition, we returned to the non-interaction specification to estimate a final structural model. Instead of specifying a simple experimental effect, we allowed separate effects for each of the four experimental plans. The results are presented in Table V. The likelihood value increased to 71.59 as compared with a value of 64.35 in Table IV. The relevant likelihood ratio statistic, distributed as χ^2 with 6 degrees of freedom, has a value of 14.48. It is significant at the 2.5 per cent level. Although the individual experimental effects are not estimated precisely, their magnitudes are of interest. For convenience, the relevant estimates from the table have been reproduced in the tabulation below. Keep in mind that these estimates are rather imprecise.

		Tax Rate	
		High	Low
Guarantee	High	$-.115$	$-.093$
	Low	$-.001$	$-.083$

The effect of the guarantee seems to be large relative to the effect of the tax rate. For the high guarantee level, increasing the tax rate does not alter earnings substantially. For the low guarantee level, in fact, persons with a high tax rate are estimated to earn more than persons on the low tax rate plan.

Although it is normally assumed that the effect of an increase in the guarantee should be to reduce labor supply and thus earnings, the *average* effect to be expected from a decrease in the tax rate is not clear. While for an individual already receiving experimental payments (those "on" the experiment), the effect of a decrease in the tax rate may be to increase labor supply, it also brings onto the experiment some persons who were not receiving payments before—some of those above the initial breakeven point. These persons are likely to work less. The

---

[21] The maximizing value of the likelihood function increased to only 66.32 relative to the value of 64.35 without these interactions. The two values yield a likelihood ratio statistic of 3.94. This statistic under the null hypothesis of no interactions is distributed as χ^2 with 5 degrees of freedom, and has an expected value of 5.0. Thus, no significant interaction is found.

TABLE V

PARAMETER ESTIMATES FOR STRUCTURAL MODEL WITH FOUR TREATMENT
EFFECTS AND CORRECTION FOR ATTRITION

Variables	Earnings function parameters (standard errors)	Attrition parameters (standard errors)
Constant	5.8503	−.6692
	(0.0702)	(.3417)
High guarantee–High tax	−.1148	.5042
	(.0720)	(.2167)
High guarantee–Low tax	−.0930	.3990
	(.0610)	(.1774)
Low guarantee-High tax	.0009	.1255
	(.1027)	(.1601)
Low guarantee-Low tax	−.0831	.1843
	(.0746)	(.1483)
Time effect	.0831	—
	(.0533)	—
Education	.0209	−.0212
	(.0052)	(.0248)
Experience	.0083	−.0050
	(.0013)	(.0062)
Income	−.0129	.1785
	(.0056)	(.0488)
Union	.2186	1.4277
	(.0363)	(0.1273)
Poor Health	−.0606	.2843
	(.0335)	(.2483)
	$\hat{\rho}_{12} = .2614$	$\hat{\rho}_{23} = -.0562$
	(.0396)	(.0487)
	$\hat{\sigma}_{\eta}^2 = .1821$	$l^* = 71.59$
	(.0003)	

number brought onto the experiment by a decrease in the tax rate may be larger
when the guarantee is low than when it is high.

As might be expected, the experimental treatments have different effects on the
probability of attrition. Individuals with high guarantees are estimated to have a
substantially lower probability of attrition than persons with low guarantees.
Persons with high guarantees, of course, receive greater benefits from the
experiment.

To recapitulate a bit: We have used a model incorporating the probability of
attrition to estimate the treatment effect of the Gary income maintenance
experiment. First, we found a significant negative experimental effect on earnings
of about 8 per cent. This effect is due almost entirely to a decrease in hours
worked. We also found weak evidence that the guarantee level had a greater effect
on earnings than the tax level. (To estimate income and substitution effects, the
treatment plans would have to be parameterized in terms of implied net wage
rates and non-labor income and incorporated into a structural model of hours and
wages.) Second, while significant attrition bias is found in both the analysis of
variance and the structural models, it is much more serious in the analysis of

variance case. The analysis of variance estimate of experimental effect changes substantially when a correction is made for attrition. However, when a structural model is used, the experimental effect estimated by generalized least squares is found to be very close to the maximum likelihood estimates that incorporate the probability of attrition. Thus, the structural model seems more robust with respect to attrition bias.

3. CONCLUSION

We have specified a model of attrition and have proposed a maximum likelihood method of estimating its parameters. The model yields efficient estimates of structural parameters in the presence of attrition, as well as an estimate of a parameter that indicates the presence or absence of attrition bias. While the method was demonstrated using data from the Gary income maintenance experiment, it is applicable to any panel data. For instance, in the initial years of the National Longitudinal (Parnes) Survey, about 15 per cent of the young males "dropped out" of the survey. The majority of the dropouts entered the military either by the draft or through enlistment. It might well be the case, for example, that the random term in a model of earnings for these young men would be correlated with the dropout probability. Possibly persons with unusually low earnings are more likely to enlist in the armed forces than those with high earnings. This would lead to attrition bias if least squares estimators were used. Because attrition occurs from almost all samples of individuals who are followed through time, techniques which test for possible bias and correct for it when it is present should find many applications in the analysis of panel data, whether collected by traditional survey methods or in conjunction with social experiments.

Massachusetts Institute of Technology
and
Harvard University

Manuscript received June, 1977; final revision received January, 1978.

REFERENCES

[1] ANDERSON, T. W.: "Some Scaling Models and Estimation Procedures in the Latent Class Model," in *Probability and Statistics: The Harold Cramer Volume*, edited by O. Grenander. New York: 1959.
[2] AMEMIYA, T.: "Regression Analysis when the Dependent Variable is Truncated Normal," *Econometrica*, 41 (1973), 997–1016.
[3] BERNDT, E., B. HALL, R. HALL, AND J. HAUSMAN: "Estimation and Inference in Nonlinear Structural Models," *Annals of Economic and Social Measurement*, 3 (1974), 653–665.
[4] FISHER, R. A.: *The Design of Experiments*. Edinburgh: Oliver and Boyd, 1935.
[5] GOLDFELD, S. M., AND R. E. QUANDT: "The Estimation of Structural Shifts by Switching Regressions," *Annals of Economic and Social Measurement*, 2 (1973), 475–485.
[6] HALL, R. E.: "The Effects of the Experimental Negative Income Tax on Labor Supply," in *Work Incentives and Income Guarantees: The New Jersey Negative Income Tax Experiment*, edited by J. A. Pechman and P. M. Timpane. Washington: The Brookings Institution, 1975.

[7] HANOCH, G.: "A Multivariate Model of Labor Supply: Methodology for Estimation," September, 1976, mimeograph.

[8] HAUSMAN, J. A.: "Specification Tests in Econometrics," forthcoming in *Econometrica*, 46 (1978), 1251–1273.

[9] HAUSMAN, J. A., AND A. M. SPENCE: "Non-Random Missing Data," mimeograph, 1977.

[10] HAUSMAN, J. A., AND D. A. WISE: "The Evaluation of Results from Truncated Samples: The New Jersey Negative Income Tax Experiment," *Annals of Economic and Social Measurement*, 5 (1976), 421–445.

[11] ———: "Attrition and Sample Selection in the Gary Income Maintenance Experiment," mimeograph, 1976.

[12] ———: "Social Experimentation, Truncated Distributions, and Efficient Estimation," *Econometrica*, 45 (1977), 319–339.

[13] ———: "Stratification on Endogenous Variables and Estimation: The Gary Income Maintenance Experiment," mimeograph, 1977.

[14] HECKMAN, J.: "Shadow Prices, Market Wage, and Labor Supply," *Econometrica*, 42 (1974), 679–694.

[15] ———: "The Common Structure of Statistical Models of Truncation, Sample Selection, and Limited Dependent Variables and a Simple Estimator for Such Models," *Annals of Economic and Social Measurement*, 5 (1976), 475–492.

[16] KEHRER, K. C., E. K. BRUML, G. T. BURTLESS, AND D. N. RICHARDSON: "The Gary Income Maintenance Experiment: Design, Administration, and Data Files," mimeograph, 1975.

[17] MADDALA, G. S., AND F. D. NELSON: "Switching Regression Models with Exogenous and Endogenous Switching," *Proceedings of the Business and Economics Statistics Section, American Statistical Association*, 70 (1975), 423–426.

[18] McDONALD, J. F., R. A. MOFFITT, AND K. C. KEHRER: "The Negative Income Tax and Labor Supply: Methodological Issues and Analytic Strategy," mimeograph, 1976.

[19] MOFFITT, R. A.: "Selection Bias in the Analysis of Experimental Data: Empirical Results in the Gary Negative Income Maintenance Experiment," mimeograph, 1976.

[20] NELSON, F. D.: "Censored Regression Models with Unobserved, Stochastic Censoring Thresholds," mimeograph, 1976.

[21] QUANDT, R. E.: "The Estimation of the Parameters of a Linear Regression System Obeying Two Separate Regimes," *Journal of the American Statistical Association*, 53 (1958), 878–880.

[22] SCHEFFÉ, H.: *The Analysis of Variance*. New York: John Wiley and Sons, Inc., 1959.

[23] WATTS, H. W., AND A. REES (EDS.): *Final Report of the New Jersey Graduated Work Incentives Experiment*. Madison, Wis.: Institute for Research on Poverty, University of Wisconsin, Madison, 1974.

4

This chapter discusses design and evaluation issues arising as a result of work on the experimental portion of the Health Insurance Study. The focus is on methods for achieving the most efficient, unbiased estimator of program effects possible within real-world constraints. Unlike the other papers in this section, the emphasis here is on the provisions to be built into a classic experimental design to insure its proper functioning, rather than on statistical "fix-ups" to be taken when such provisions have not been made.

In four substantive sections the authors discuss issues associated with attrition and sample replenishment in longitudinal surveys, optimal samples and allocation to treatment (with particular attention to the dangers of stratification on an endogenous variable), and optimal balance of assignments to treatments, with particular attention to the method of "proportional stratification." In the belief that the reader can follow much of the argument without our assistance, we concentrate here on the two sections of the paper which involve explicit mathematical argument—that surrounding expressions 3.1-3.7, and 5.1-5.14.

The first of these employs a worked example to illustrate the dangers of strati-
fying on an endogenous variable. The example is simplified to reveal the essentials
of the problem, and yet may still be difficult to follow. Accordingly, we restate it
here in some detail.

Bias arises because of classification errors in using pre-experimental income as a
guide to income during the experiment. We suppose that both before and during
the experiment, 50% of the families fall into the low income group. (Income is
divided into two categories: low and high.) To oversample this group, we select our
sample so that f% of families have low pre-experimental income. Then $\bar{f} = (1 - f)$
have high pre-experimental income. (We choose f greater than .5.)

Since income changes over time, however, some of those classified as low or high
income during the pre-experimental period are no longer in this category during the
experiment. The authors make the simplifying assumption that the probability of
unchanging preduring classification is identical for those with either low or high
income during the pre-experimental period and define this probability as c. Then
$\bar{c} = (1 - c)$ represents both the percentage of those with low income who change
to high income, and also the percentage of those with high income who change to
low. As a result, the distribution of the sample according to pre- and during-experiment income categories is given by Figure 1. (This figure also shows the population
means for the outcome variable, u_{00}, u_{10}, u_{01}, and u_{11}, separately for the four
income categories.)

During the experiment, the true population means for the outcome variable are
weighted averages of those for each of the cells. Thus

$$u_0 = cu_{00} + \bar{c}u_{10} \tag{1}$$

$$u_1 = \bar{c}u_{01} + cu_{11} \tag{2}$$

are, respectively, the correct population values for the lower and upper rows of
Figure 1. (Unbiased estimates of these are shown in the paper as expression 3.5.)

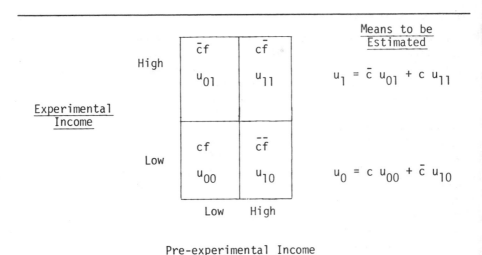

Figure 1 Sampling Proportions and Responses by Pre- and During-Experimental Income

Unfortunately, these are not the means of the statistics the analyst is likely to employ if he proceeds without reflection. Those statistics are, respectively,

$$\hat{u}_0 = \frac{n_{00}\bar{x}_{00} + n_{10}\bar{x}_{10}}{n_{00} + n_{10}} \qquad [3]$$

and

$$\hat{u}_1 = \frac{n_{01}\bar{x}_{01} + n_{11}\bar{x}_{11}}{n_{01} + n_{11}}, \qquad [4]$$

which are averages of the observed cell means, weighted by the observed cell proportions. (These expressions are reproduced in the chapter as 3.1 and 3.2.) The bias that results from using [3] and [4] as estimates of [1] or [2] can be calculated as follows.

Begin by observing that $u_{00} = cfN$, $n_{10} = \bar{c}fn$, and define the lower row sum, $n_{00} + n_{10} = f_c N$ where $f_c = cf + \bar{c}f$. (We define $\bar{f}_c = 1 - f_c$.) Then

$$E(\hat{u}_0) = \left(\frac{cf}{f_c}\right)u_{00} + \left(\frac{\bar{c}f}{f_c}\right)u_{01}, \qquad [5]$$

so that combining [5] and [1] we find

$$E(\hat{u}_0) - u_0 = \left(\frac{\bar{c}f}{f_c} - c\right)u_{00} + \left(\frac{\bar{c}f}{f_c}\right) - (1 - c)) u_{01}. \qquad [6]$$

Further manipulation of these expressions leads to

$$E(\hat{u}_0) - u_0 = \frac{cc(2f - 1)}{f_c} (u_{00} - u_{10}), \qquad [7]$$

which is reported in the chapter as expression 3.3.[1] (A similar expression results for the bias in $\hat{u}_1$.)

This derivation demonstrates that oversampling on an endogenous variable leads to bias unless weighted estimates are used. Morris et al. examine efficiency, concluding that even here there can be difficulty because "oversampling leads to uniformly higher variances if the oversampling rate exceeds the correct classification probability." The sum of these (and related results) is to caution strongly against stratification on an endogenous variable.

Finally, Morris et al. consider the issues surrounding optimal assignment of subjects to treatments. They suppose that subjects are classified into K strata (homogeneous groups defined on the basis of pre-experimental measurements) and are to be assigned to t treatments. The number of subjects enrolled in treatment i from stratum j is m_{ij}, with

$$n_i = \sum_j m_{ij}$$

being the total number assigned to treatment i. The proportion of subjects falling into stratum j is p_j.

If the true mean response of those in stratum j to treatment i is u_{ij}, and this is estimated by the sample mean x_{ij} of the m_{ij} observations in this cell, then

$$E(x_{ij}) = u_{ij} \qquad Var(x_{ij}) = \frac{\sigma^2}{m_{ij}}. \qquad [8]$$

(This is expression 5.1.) The average response to treatment i can be estimated as a weighted average across the strata, j,

$$\hat{u}_i = \sum_j p_j x_{ij}, \qquad [9]$$

which is unbiased and has variance

$$Var(\hat{u}_i) = \sigma^2 \sum_j \frac{p_j^2}{m_{ij}}. \qquad [10]$$

(This latter expression results from the fact that the variance of a sum of independent variables is the sum of the variances, applied to expressions 8 and 9.)

We now have an unbiased estimator with a known variance. The issue is how to assign subjects to treatments (specify the m_{ij}) so as to minimize this variance. That is, we wish to find the values of m_{ij} that give the minimum value of expression 10, while satisfying the adding-up constraint that

$$\sum_j m_{ij} = n_i.$$

This is a relatively easy problem once the (calculus) method of Lagrange multipliers is employed.[2] This involves constructing the function

$$L = \sigma^2 \sum_j \frac{p_j^2}{m_{ij}} - \lambda \left(\sum_j m_{ij} - n_i \right), \qquad [11]$$

taking its partial derivatives with respect to λ and the m_{ij}, setting these equal to zero, and solving the resulting equations for the m_{ij}. Doing this, one finds

$$m_{ij} = n_i p_j, \qquad [12]$$

or that subjects should be assigned to treatments proportionate to the share naturally arising in stratum j, so as to achieve the (already decided) n_i total observations for treatment i. This rule, called proportional stratification, is expression 5.5 in the chapter.[3]

Following this, the authors compare the efficiency of proportional stratification, simple random sampling, and proportional stratification with random nonacceptances. Once again they find that real-world conditions diminish the gains available from elaborate designs.

NOTES

1. Reasonably extensive use of relationships such as $\bar{c} = 1 - c$ and the definition of f_c is required, but the interested reader may enjoy the exercise.

2. For further discussion of this common solution to constrained minimization or maximization problems, see Fleming (1965: 129-131); Varian (1978: 264); or Hirshleifer (1976: 83).

3. The interested reader is invited to work through expressions 11 and 12 with two or three strata. The derivation is straightforward.

REFERENCES

FLEMING, W. (1965) Functions of Several Variables. Reading, MA: Addison-Wesley.
HIRSHLEIFER, J. (1976) Price Theory and Applications. Englewood Cliffs, NJ: Prentice-Hall.
VARIAN, H. R. (1978) Microeconomic Analysis. New York: Norton.

On the Theory and Practice of Obtaining Unbiased and Efficient Samples in Social Surveys

Carl N. Morris, Joseph P. Newhouse, and Rae W. Archibald

PREFACE

This report was written as part of the experimental design work for the Rand Health Insurance Study, supported by a grant (016B-7501-P2021) from the U.S. Department of Health, Education, and Welfare. It considers a number of problems that either have not been addressed in the literature on experimental design, or have been inadequately addressed. The report, which draws upon Rand experience in designing and operating the Health Insurance Study, should be of interest to analysts conducting longitudinal survey and social experiments, as well as to those interested in experimental design.

From Carl N. Morris, Joseph P. Newhouse, and Rae W. Archibald, "On the Theory and Practice of Obtaining Unbiased and Efficient Samples in Social Surveys," Rand Report R-2173-HEW, January 1978. Reprinted by permission of the Rand Corporation, Santa Monica, CA.

SUMMARY

This report takes up four problems in experimental design of social experiments that either have not been addressed or, in our view,
have been inadequately addressed in the literature. The first problem
concerns definition of the sampling frame when repeated sampling is
attempted and part of the population is transient. Sampling the transient population may not be feasible if a minimum length of participation is necessary. Even ignoring this problem, traditional sampling
rules may force inappropriate analyses, e.g., of partial families if a
new member cannot be included because that member would be given a
second chance to participate. Because such practices can lead to analytical bias, one should consider analytical aims when formulating
sampling rules. We illustrate how problems of defining a sampling
frame in a longitudinal study may arise, and give some practical suggestions for dealing with them. However, our major purpose is to call
attention to the sampling-frame problem, in the hope that new theory
and methods will be developed to deal with it.

The second problem we address concerns optimal choice of survey
samples. We consider two distinct, although related, issues--dispro-
portionate sampling of populations of greater interest (e.g., low income) and disproportionate sampling of neighborhoods with certain
characteristics (e.g., poor neighborhoods). We show that if the population of interest is described by a variable subject to measurement
error (e.g., current income as a measure of permanent income), disproportionate sampling can be inefficient relative to proportionate sampling, even for the favored group. Similarly, the oversampling of
neighborhoods that have many people with a desired characteristic can
also be less efficient relative to proportionate sampling. Before
using disproportionate sampling, the analyst should carefully review
the modeling assumptions that will be necessary and the likelihood of
misclassification.

The third problem we consider concerns the allocation of subjects
to treatments. The theory of optimal design pertains to this problem,

although we view its recommendations skeptically. If a functional form
is known, it is optimal to sample from certain portions of the distribution of a variable. For example, if a linear response to variation
in income is to be estimated, subjects with extreme incomes (both high
and low) provide minimum variance estimates. Because functional forms
are almost never known with certainty in social science research, a
design that assumes they are known may not be robust. It also is possible to exploit the dependence between a subject's characteristics and
the cost of improving precision (e.g., by using the Conlisk-Watts design model [2]). However, these gains are realized only if one is
willing to trust the assumptions made about the nature of responses
and the functional form (e.g., ruling out certain interactions). The
resulting design may provide little basis for testing these assumptions,
and if they are incorrect, the resulting analysis may produce biased
estimates. Finally, crossover designs have been suggested as a way to
reduce sample size. If practical, crossover designs are attractive;
however, we believe that crossover designs rarely can be used to advantage in social experiments.

In the final section, we discuss the problem of balancing covariates
when assigning subjects to treatments in the presence of field constraints. We prove that where nonacceptances of the enrollment offer
are random, the precision gains in estimating treatment contrasts by a
balanced sample will be degraded approximately in proportion to the
nonacceptance rate. We discuss practical reasons why avoidance of such
degradation was impossible in the Health Insurance Study.

I.   INTRODUCTION

Classical experimental design has been developed for studies that
use cross-sectional techniques, i.e., those that seek to make inferences
about a population from observations made at one point in time. Such
designs frequently attempt to satisfy the criteria of efficiency (minimum variance) and unbiasedness of estimates, and in doing so they often
assume that certain attributes of the population can be measured costlessly, instantly, and without error.

Field experiments (or social experiments) that involve economic
phenomena frequently will violate these assumptions. Time must pass
to gather data (e.g., data on labor supply in income maintenance experiments, data on medical care and on electricity consumption in health insurance and peak-load pricing experiments); thus, measurements are not
made on a population at one point in time. Furthermore, it is impossible in field experiments to measure individual or family attributes
costlessly or instantly, and the presence of error in such measurements
can substantially reduce the gains in efficiency that an optimal design
purports to achieve.

As a result of these constraints, and of the practical difficulties
of administering large-scale social experiments in real time, experimental design issues arise that have not been well addressed in the literature. Our purpose in raising them here is twofold: to give those who
will design field experiments the benefits of our experience in designing and implementing the experimental portion of the Health Insurance
Study (HIS); and to encourage the scientific community to rethink the
criteria and methods needed for design in these complicated situations.
Before we turn to the main issues of the report, however, a brief description of the HIS may be helpful for the reader.[1]

The HIS has several objectives, including: (1) to measure the insurance elasticity of demand for medical care services (i.e., the response to varying the portion of the expenditure that the participant
must pay out of pocket); (2) to determine if the insurance elasticity
of demand depends on permanent income; and (3) to determine what effects on health, if any, are observed from variation in the consumption
of medical care services because of differences in amount paid out of
pocket. To achieve these ends, some 2,800 families have been enrolled

in the experiment. The families are located in six geographic locations (Dayton, Ohio; Seattle, Washington; Fitchburg-Leominster, Massachusetts; Franklin County, Massachusetts; Charleston, South Carolina;
Georgetown County, South Carolina).

Each family in the HIS is enrolled in one of fourteen health insurance plans that vary the fraction of total expenditure to be paid
by the participant. The fraction is either 0, 25, 50, or 95 percent.
In addition, the family's financial exposure is limited to a certain
amount in any one year, an amount called the Maximum Dollar Expenditure
(MDE). Generally the MDE is set as a fraction of income, but in one
plan it is $150 per person. Some families are assigned to a Health
Maintenance Organization (HMO) (prepaid group practice), and their care
is free to them so long as it is received at the HMO. Families participate for either 3 years (70 percent) or 5 years (30 percent) to permit
measurement of transitory behavior at the beginning and end of the
experiment. Several years were needed to allow for transitory demand
to disappear (i.e., rates of consumption that do not reflect steady-
state behavior, such as restorative dentistry done on a one-time basis)
and for health status effects to appear.

During the period of participation in the experiment, families do
not use their own health insurance; rather, they assign the benefits
of that insurance to the experiment. They are paid lump sums (not based
on utilization) to ensure that they will not be worse off financially
by participating in the experiment. They do not have a choice of insurance plan within the experiment but are made an all-or-nothing offer
to participate in the plan to which they have been assigned.

Families were enrolled using the following procedure: (1) A
screening interview was administered to determine eligibility (the aged
and certain other populations are not eligible). (2) A baseline interview was administered to the eligible families to elicit certain information; in particular, information about health insurance policies. This
information, verified with the employer or insurance company, was used
as the basis for the guarantee to the families that they would not be
worse off by participating. (3) Following verification of the insurance
information, families were selected, assigned to insurance plans (experimental treatments), and offered a chance to enroll.

The experiment is well under way. All the required families are
enrolled, with about 75 percent of the ultimate number of person-years
having been completed as of December 1979.

II. LONGITUDINAL SURVEYS OF NONSTATIONARY POPULATIONS

Difficulties arise in the practice of repeated interviews of non-
stationary populations. These difficulties are not dealt with effectively by the existing theory and practice of survey sampling, which
usually assumes a stationary target population. A description of some
of these difficulties encountered in the HIS appears below. While our
purpose here is only to call attention to these problems, not to solve
them, we do discuss, later in this section, some practical methods for
reducing the difficulties. Real progress, however, will be achieved
only when new theory, methods, and standards are developed to deal directly with the complications of surveying nonstationary populations.

SAMPLING PROBLEMS

Contact with families in the HIS begins with a longitudinal (panel)
survey before the experimental phase and is followed by the longitudinal
experiment, lasting from 3 to 5 years. The preexperimental portion is
longitudinal, i.e., it involves a reinterview of subjects because families are administered screening interviews (preliminary, 10 minutes),
then baseline interviews (longer, in-depth), and finally enrollment interviews (when the insurance offer is made). Our concern here is focused
primarily on problems arising from these preexperimental surveys, which
in the HIS take a total of 6 to 9 months to complete, and might be expected to result in an unbiased sample for the experiment.[2]

Cross-Sectional vs. Longitudinal Sampling

The theory and practice of cross-sectional survey sampling (only
one interview) is now highly developed and widely used to obtain
nearly unbiased samples from specified target populations. When the
target population (e.g., a specified subset of individuals in a city)
can be enumerated and located, only the refusing respondents prevent

---

[2]We use the term "unbiased sample" loosely to mean that the probability of selection of each individual is completely known. Most
frequently, this means each individual has the same selection probability.

the sample from being unbiased. If refusal rate is low, the sampling
distribution can be assumed with confidence. When a human population
cannot be enumerated and located readily, standard practice requires that
dwelling units be listed and then sampled from that list as a basis for
locating individuals. The occupants of a dwelling at the time of the
"first knock" are considered to be in the sample; they are followed if
they move to another dwelling before the interview is actually conducted.
Hence, the sample switches from a dwelling sample to a sample of individuals at the first knock. This method works well so long as (a) almost all individuals are associated with exactly one dwelling unit at
any one time, (b) individuals who move can be found, and (c) the survey
period is short relative to changes in the population (due to vital
events, leaving the sampling area, etc.).

The successes of cross-sectional sampling foster expectations that
longitudinal sampling should produce equally good results. This is unrealistic, except in cases of relatively stationary populations. Longitudinal surveys cannot do as well. Even the concept of the "target
population" becomes ambiguous. The target population consists of those
individuals about whom the survey is to make inferences (in the HIS
these would be the populations in the six HIS experimental sites at the
end of the experiment who satisfy certain age and other eligibility
constraints). The "survey population" is the set of individuals who
make up the sampling frame during the preexperimental survey period.
These two populations often coincide for cross-sectional surveys (one
interview), since the period of analytical interest is the sampling
period, or nearly so. They cannot coincide for longitudinal surveys
of nonstationary populations.

Transient Population and a Long Period

Suppose the site has a transient population and the experimental
period is lengthy. Only by constantly replenishing the sample during
the experimental period is it possible to maintain the matching of
sample characteristics with those of the target population. This is
infeasible in the HIS because the survey population is the cross-section
of eligible people in each site at the time of the preexperimental

surveys and must remain fixed during the experiment. New entrants
(save for newborns and adopted children) are not allowed into the sample
during the experiment for two principal reasons. First, a minimum number of years of participation is required to allow long-term changes
in health status to occur. Individuals who have been used to replenish
the sample will not show these effects. Second, transitory behavior
may occur at the outset and at the end of the HIS if the participant's
own insurance differs from that provided by the experiment. For example,
the experimental insurance usually is more generous in that it covers
both dental and psychiatric expenses. To the extent that these are
durable goods, experimental families may purchase dental and psychiatric
care at the beginning and end of the experiment in greater quantity than
they would if their coverage were unchanging. Thus, their behavior differs from steady-state behavior. That individuals must be enrolled for
a substantial period of time also has implications for cross-over designs; these are taken up in Section IV.

Defining the Survey Population

A second difference with cross-section surveys arises because the
three surveys for the HIS during the preexperimental period (screening,
baseline, enrollment) make the survey population hard to define. The
screening survey can, and does in the HIS, provide a "first knock"
cross-sectional sample that is acceptably representative of the community by cross-sectional survey standards. The survey population at that
time is the "eligible" community during the screening period; thereafter
it must be modified. (In the HIS, the eligible community excludes certain families, on the basis of income exceeding $25,000 [1973 dollars],
the aged, the institutionalized, and certain students. Those whose
current insurance cannot be verified [e.g., held by an employer who will
not cooperate with the HIS] also are excluded. In a broader context,
eligibility also requires meeting certain space and time restrictions,
namely, that the individual reside within the sampling area during the
preexperimental surveys.)

The first new difficulties arise when the interviewer returns to
administer a second survey, the baseline survey, to an eligible family
that already has been screened. It may happen that

(a) The family has moved out of the sampling area.

(b) The entire family, or perhaps some of its members, has changed eligibility status since the screening period.

(c) The family has reconfigured; births, adoptions, deaths, marriages, divorces, or a member's coming of age and becoming a separate family, all act to produce family reconfigurations (which may include the formation of new families within the household).

The screening and baseline interviews are followed by the enrollment interview, which occurs several months after the baseline interview. The sampling problems occur again in this third interview. Sampling problems (a) through (c) occurred frequently in the HIS. As shown in Table 2, page 33, nonrefusal losses from the sample (moved, unable to locate, ineligible, unable to verify insurance) were about 22 percent, and the final enrollment sample in the HIS was slightly more than 105 percent of the original sample due to the discovery of new families.

Dating the Survey Population

In the presence of these events, the survey population cannot be dated to the screening period. If no effort is made to recoup moving and eligibility losses, the sample will be more stable than the eligible population at the time of each interview. Biased estimates can generally result from a standard analysis, because the sampling probabilities are modified in unknown ways. It is expensive and of negligible value to follow out-of-area movers in pursuit of an unbiased sample at the screening period. The HIS opted instead to administer both screening and baseline interviews to new families occupying those dwellings that housed out-of-area movers, and to follow only in-area movers. This partially atones for loss of the moving population, although not perfectly, because out-of-area movers are replaced by new families from both out of the area and within the area. It also moves the survey target population closer to the eligible population at the baseline period. Of course, the survey population cannot be updated entirely to the baseline period without returning to all households that, during the screening period, refused, were never at home, were vacant, or were not even contacted,

and attempting again to complete screening and baseline interviews.
Further, it would be necessary to return to households occupied by ineligible persons to determine if their eligibility status had since
changed. Therefore, individuals who were ineligible but became eligible
will not be represented in the sample; moreover, we will not know exactly how the community's population has changed over time, and so will
not have an appropriate denominator to compute sampling probabilities.

Oversampling

All these moving, eligibility, and reconfiguration difficulties
cause the baseline survey to oversample the population that is stable
during both the screening and baseline periods. The nonconstancy and
nonpredictability of eligibility characteristics causes this. By contrast, ineligibility due to age does not cause this problem, because
(ignoring deaths) future ages are totally predictable.

Family Reconfiguration in the HIS

The standard rule for treating the problem created by family reconfigurations is to ignore new persons joining the family between the
screening and the baseline interviews. The HIS, however, is especially
interested in families, because the family is the economic decision-
making unit, and because national health insurance may well apply to the
family unit. To take an example: Suppose a widower and his child are
insured by the HIS, but the stepmother is not because she married into
the family after the screening interview. This family's behavior will
match neither that of three-person, man-woman-and-child families with
all members insured (since the woman's expenditures in such families
affect whether the family meets the deductible), nor that of two-person,
father-and-child families (since the stepmother shares income and also
is likely to influence the child's demand for health care). Furthermore,
national health insurance is unlikely to exclude some family members,
such as the mother. A sampling procedure that excludes new family
members in order not to change their selection probability could therefore lead to biased estimates in the analysis of the HIS experimental
data. On the other hand, if some sampling bias is accepted in order

to enroll families as a unit, the utilization of health services as a function of family characteristics may actually be estimated with reduced bias. In the preceding example, inclusion of the new spouse clearly would aid the analysis. In fact, an estimate of the conditional distribution of utilization from a biased sample may be unbiased. The point is this: *A sampling design must consider the combined effects of two sources of bias, sampling biases and limitations (here, the incomplete family) imposed on the analysis.* An unbiased sample may not minimize bias of inferences concerning population parameters.[3]

PRACTICAL METHODS TO REDUCE LONGITUDINAL SAMPLING PROBLEMS

As noted earlier, our primary purpose is to call attention to the increased difficulties of sampling populations longitudinally, not to resolve them. A solution will be achieved only when the research community explicitly recognizes the longitudinal problem and provides generally acceptable standards and methods for dealing with it. We think the standards should be concerned with minimizing some function of both bias and variance of estimates in relation to cost. Acceptable sampling frames must include broader concepts than a specified population at a particular point in time.

While we will not attempt to make general recommendations, certain methods for reducing the magnitude of the problem have come to our attention in the course of designing the HIS. Related ideas in the context of assigning treatments are presented in Section V. Some of the following suggestions were used in the HIS and others were not. We are not claiming that we always made the proper choices for the HIS or that we would make the same choices now. When reasons for choice are given below, they are those that applied at the time of decision.

1. *Sample Replenishment.* As attrition takes place, new members with characteristics matching those lost can be brought into the study.

---

[3]The problem is analogous to the theory of the second best. Imposing the requirement of an unbiased sampling frame when there are resulting limitations on analysis is analogous to insisting that one marginal condition be satisfied when another cannot be.

This can reduce or eliminate sampling bias, but it also can be difficult, costly, and lead to incomplete data for subjects. A minor example
of sample replenishment in the HIS was replacing out-of-area movers
during the preexperimental survey period by the families who moved into
the vacated dwelling units.

2. *Sample Compensation*. If certain groups eventually will be
underrepresented, it may be advisable to overrepresent them initially.
In the HIS, those recently discharged from the military or leaving college could have been oversampled, because their cohorts will not be
picked up later.[4] While data were gathered at the baseline stage on
those soon to be discharged or graduated, this oversampling strategy
was not followed because these categories include only a minor segment
of the population, and because a proper oversampling rate was not known.

3. *Techniques for Shortening the Preenrollment Survey Period*. In
the first HIS site, the screening survey preceded the baseline by several months. In all other sites, a "doorstep screener" was used. The
interviewer attempted at first knock to complete the screening interview. After establishing family eligibility, a randomization table
(the randomization was based on income and family size for the purpose
of oversampling low-income families) was used to determine whether to
administer a baseline interview. If so, the family was asked to continue at that time or for an appointment to complete the baseline interview. By shortening the survey period, and generally reducing the
number of interview contacts, this strategy significantly reduced costs,
fielding time, and potential biases. It required more training of interviewers to make correct eligibility and randomization decisions,
because they cannot be made centrally.

Another similar tactic was used in the Los Angeles peak-load electricity pricing experiment (Manning et al., 1976) for the purpose of
shortening the time to enrollment. A random two-thirds of the households

---

[4] An HIS participant who enters the military is suspended; therefore, those with military experience will be underrepresented. College
dormitories were not sampled because of the mobility of students and
the likelihood that students would continue to use a student health
service even if national health insurance were enacted; as a result,
college students will also be underrepresented.

were asked to participate in the experiment on predesignated treatments at the end of the first interview. The remaining households were assigned to balance treatment variables later, after baseline data were available for the entire sample. This method appears to be very cost-effective, although it does somewhat restrict the ability to balance variables in assignment of subjects to treatments.

The method used by the peak-load pricing experiment was not applicable to the HIS because the HIS families had to have their insurance formally verified (which took at least 6 weeks) before an offer could be made. However, the HIS moved the enrollment period closer to the baseline period by selecting a portion of the enrollment sample before the baseline period was complete. Care must be taken when doing this; problems encountered are discussed in Section V.

4. *Crossover Designs with Preenrollment in Control Group Status.* In experimental situations, even though the treatments cannot be assigned immediately after completion of the baseline interview, it may be advantageous to preenroll interviewees in control group status at that time. Later they would cross over from control to treatment status. If this can be done, then transitory effects attributable solely to participating in an experiment may diminish before assignment of the treatments. While this does not alleviate many of the difficulties attributable to longitudinal sampling, it can lead to better comparisons among the treatments because some early attrition would be forced due to forms burden, and some refusals would occur before assignment of treatments. Other advantages are that participants will serve as their own control group while on the experimental measurement system, that the size of the entire control group is increased, and that analysis of those who refuse the offer of the experimental treatment is facilitated. The HIS did not use this method (except for a 2-year preenrollment group for part of the sample in South Carolina) primarily because of the additional risk of bias attributable to possible nonrandom attrition from the control group, unless quite large payments were made to the families. (By contrast, the magnitude of benefits received leads to low attrition during the experimental period.) Secondarily, it was costly to make preexperimental data available quickly for assignment of treatments.

5. *Rules for Following Movers and Reconfigured Families.* Standard survey practice is to follow individuals within the sampling area if this is possible. What if it is impossible? Under what circumstances should the person who moves into the vacated dwelling be interviewed instead? Which procedure is cost-effective? These issues become more complex if family units are to be sampled when divorce, separation, remarriage, and coming-of-age lead to reconfiguration and to creation of new family units.

Randomization, in conjunction with a change of viewpoint away from preserving a population of individuals and toward preserving the characteristics of the initial sample, offers one possibility. For example, if a husband and wife divorce and both remarry during the sampling period, then if the survey unit is the individual, both would be followed and their new spouses ignored. When the survey unit is the family, it may be preferable to follow the husband with probability one-half, and the wife with probability one-half, incorporating the new spouse, and ignoring the unselected family. Even though the new spouse has a second chance of being enrolled, certain characteristics are maintained: the wholeness of one husband-wife family is retained instead of changing the sample to include two partially enrolled families. This example is straightforward, but the matter becomes complex when one must consider the myriad combinations involving children and other members in the old and new family units, the inability to follow some members, and multiple family dwellings. We believe that much useful research could be carried out here.

6. *Connecting Cross-Sectional Surveys with the Panel Survey.* A cross-sectional survey of the site made after a panel has been selected will include two groups: those who might have been (or are) panel members because they were present and eligible during the preenrollment period; and those who could not have been because they were ineligible at the time (lived out of the area, etc.). Questions can be included on the cross-sectional survey that would provide information about which group included the interviewee. Analysis of such data would provide information about biases that might obtain because the panel was constrained to the more stable population. In particular, biases due to

selection of a nonrepresentative population along measurable dimensions (e.g., the stable population is older) can be relatively well estimated. However, any interaction between the experimental treatment and the transitory population cannot be measured by using a later cross-sectional sample.

In concluding this section, we wish to restate the main points.

Longitudinal surveys are different from cross-sectional surveys, and more difficult to carry out. A better understanding of the nature and problems of longitudinal surveys is needed by the scientific community so that proper standards can be agreed upon and suitable sampling methods developed.

Longitudinal surveys are not always more informative than cross-sectional ones; indeed, for many purposes they can be less informative. They gain because they permit estimation when experimental effects are time-dependent. Even when such models are not of interest, longitudinal experiments may be required if the number of experimental subjects is limited, if costs per year are constrained (but several years' support is available), if recall error requires frequent interview (e.g., asking a panel about consumption every month rather than asking once for annual consumption), if transitory behavior is expected, or if long-term effects are to be measured. In the absence of such conditions, a cross-sectional analysis will produce results earlier and may also be more accurate (in steady-state, a mean estimated from two positively correlated measurement periods on one subject has greater variability than a mean estimated from one measurement period on two subjects).

A goal of sampling should be to minimize a function of both variances and biases of the estimates finally generated by the analysis, subject to prescribed cost constraints. Because sampling errors are just one component of the total error, some sampling bias may be acceptable if this leads to decreased errors in the fitted analytical model, or reduced costs. Research on methods and standards for reinterview sampling should address these points.

III.   CONSTRAINTS ON CHOOSING OPTIMAL SAMPLES

Because the HIS sponsors had greater interest in the effects of
insurance on the low (permanent) income population than on other income
groups, it was agreed that the HIS would oversample low-income families.
This oversampling amounts to choosing a more efficient sample for analysis by not sampling proportionately. Since oversampling is required,
survey costs can also be reduced by overselection of low-income neighborhoods. Under certain circumstances, both kinds of oversampling can
be effective, but *our purpose here is to show that without strong modeling assumptions, the gains from each can be negligible or even negative.*

OPTIMIZATION WHEN CLASSIFICATION ERRORS EXIST

There is a fundamental difference between oversampling with respect
to a variable that varies randomly with time, as income does over the
several-year experimental period of the HIS, and one that is constant or
completely predictable, such as race, sex, or age. Oversampling a group
is desired for values of a variable that will occur during the experiment, but only the preexperimental values are available for this purpose. If the preexperimental variable is not perfectly correlated with
the experimental value, two difficulties arise. First, there will be
some regression to the mean so that the experimental value will not be
oversampled as strongly as the preexperimental value, causing the result
to be less efficient than desired. Second, unless researchers are in
a position to assert that no latent variables (omitted variables that
are partially correlated with the oversampling variable) exist, then an
analysis of experimental data must account simultaneously for the separate oversampling rates due to the preexperimental and to the experimental variables. This degrades precision, possibly to the extent that
proportional sampling would be more efficient than oversampling. Of
course, weighted analyses are also more cumbersome to conduct because
the weights must be carried throughout.

We shall illustrate these ideas with a simple example that will
permit numerical evaluation of the efficiency gains and losses. Suppose

each family falls into a "low income" or "high income" category on the basis of their income for the year immediately preceding the experiment, and that each of these two categories represents one-half of all families. Similarly, the average income of each family during the life of the experiment (permanent income would be another candidate for the variable of interest) falls into "low" and "high" categories, and again each is assumed to include one-half of all families. The assumption that each category corresponds to one-half the population is made for convenience only. Although more general situations may be treated, we keep matters simple here because our purpose is only to illustrate the problem caused by classification errors.[5]

The only data available for oversampling are preexperimental incomes, so the fraction f is designated as the proportion of the sample that is to have low preexperimental income, while $\bar{f} = 1 - f$ will have high income. Let c be the probability of correct classification. Because of the symmetry in this example, c is the probability that a preexperimental low (or high) income family is low (or high) during the experiment and $\bar{c} = 1 - c$ is the probability of changing income categories during the two periods. The case c = 1 corresponds to variables like race, age, and sex (assuming no errors in measurement of these variables). Ordinarily, c is greater than one-half, with c = .5 meaning that the preexperimental and experimental classifications are independent. Figure 1 contains the assumptions used for this presentation. Note in particular that the proportion of low-income families actually experienced, f_c, is less than f (for $f > \frac{1}{2}$), since $f_c = cf + \bar{c}\bar{f}$. For convenience, we also denote $\bar{f}_c = 1 - f_c = \bar{c}f + c\bar{f}$ to be the fraction of families with high incomes during the experiment.

The population means μ_{ij} are estimated unbiasedly by $\bar{x}_{ij}$, the mean response in cell i, j. Assume that var $(\bar{x}_{ij}) = \sigma^2/n_{ij}$ and that a total

---

[5] The problem discussed in this section arises whether the classification variable is continuous (e.g., income) or discrete (e.g., employment status), so long as the preexperimental values are not perfectly correlated with the experimental values.

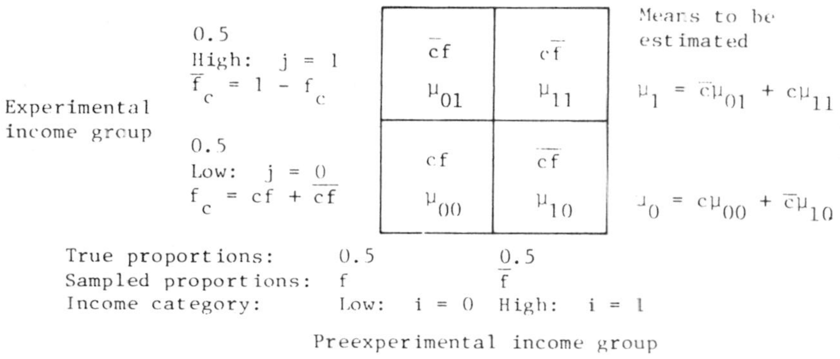

		Means to be estimated
0.5 High: $j = 1$ $\bar{f}_c = 1 - f_c$	$\bar{c}f$ $\bar{c}\bar{f}$ μ_{01} μ_{11}	$\mu_1 = \bar{c}\mu_{01} + c\mu_{11}$
0.5 Low: $j = 0$ $f_c = cf + \overline{cf}$	cf $c\bar{f}$ μ_{00} μ_{10}	$\mu_0 = c\mu_{00} + \bar{c}\mu_{10}$

Experimental income group

True proportions: 0.5   0.5
Sampled proportions: f $\bar{f}$
Income category: Low: $i = 0$ High: $i = 1$

Preexperimental income group

Fig. 1--Sampling proportions and responses μ_j and μ_{ij} for crossed income categories. $\bar{c} \equiv 1 - c$, $\bar{f} \equiv 1 - f$, μ_{ij} = mean of response of interest when the preexperimental income group is i and the experimental group is j; μ_j = mean response when the experimental group is j. The naturally occurring fraction is 0.5. Sampled fractions are f, 1 - f preexperimentally and f_c, 1 - f_c during the experiment.

of N families is used so that[6] $n_{00} = cfN$, $n_{10} = \overline{cf}N$, $n_{01} = \bar{c}fN$, and $n_{11} = \bar{c}\bar{f}N$. With these definitions, the mean responses during the experiment and the two quantities to be estimated are $\mu_0 \equiv c\mu_{00} + \bar{c}\mu_{10}$ for the low income group and $\mu_1 \equiv \bar{c}\mu_{01} + c\mu_{11}$ for the high income group.

If $\mu_{00} = \mu_{10}$ and $\mu_{01} = \mu_{11}$, so that the response for each income group during the experiment is independent of the preexperimental income categorization, then $\mu_0 = \mu_{00} = \mu_{10}$, $\mu_1 = \mu_{01} = \mu_{11}$, and *un-weighted*[7] estimates may be used:

---

[6] We ignore the unimportant complication that the n_{ij} actually are stochastic in order to streamline the presentation. In large samples, n_{ij} will be nearly equal to its expectation. Values in Table 1 (p. 18) under f = 1.0 are then interpreted as limiting values.

[7] We say "unweighted" because (3.1) and (3.2) are the simple averages ignoring the preexperimental income category, i.e., total response divided by total number of subjects in each experimental income category.

$$\hat{\mu}_0 = \frac{n_{00}\bar{x}_{00} + n_{10}\bar{x}_{10}}{n_{00} + n_{10}} , \qquad (3.1)$$

$$\hat{\mu}_1 = \frac{n_{01}\bar{x}_{01} + n_{11}\bar{x}_{11}}{n_{01} + n_{11}} . \qquad (3.2)$$

These estimates are unbiased if $\mu_{00} = \mu_{10}$ and $\mu_{01} = \mu_{11}$. If not, let $\delta_0 \equiv \mu_{00} - \mu_{10}$, $\delta_1 \equiv \mu_{01} - \mu_{11}$. Then (3.1) and (3.2) are biased by the amounts

$$E\hat{\mu}_0 - \mu_0 = \frac{c\bar{c}(2f - 1)}{f_c} \delta_0, \qquad E\hat{\mu}_1 - \mu_1 = \frac{c\bar{c}(2f - 1)}{\bar{f}_c} \delta_1, \qquad (3.3)$$

which are not zero unless $c = 1$ (or $c = 0$) or proportional sampling ($f = \frac{1}{2}$) has been used. Whether the estimates are biased or not, their variances are

$$\text{var } (\hat{\mu}_0) = \frac{\sigma^2/N}{f_c} , \qquad \text{var } (\hat{\mu}_1) = \frac{\sigma^2/N}{\bar{f}_c} . \qquad (3.4)$$

If δ_0 and δ_1 cannot be assumed to be zero, because the preexperimental income category is partially correlated (given experimental income) with the response, then although (3.1) and (3.2) are biased, the following *weighted* estimates are unbiased for μ_0 and μ_1:

$$\hat{\hat{\mu}}_0 = c\bar{x}_{00} + (1 - c)\bar{x}_{10} , \qquad \hat{\hat{\mu}}_1 = (1 - c)\bar{x}_{01} + c\bar{x}_{11} . \qquad (3.5)$$

Their variances are

$$\text{var } (\hat{\hat{\mu}}_0) = \frac{\sigma^2}{N} \frac{\bar{f}_c}{f\bar{f}} , \qquad \text{var } (\hat{\hat{\mu}}_1) = \frac{\sigma^2}{N} \frac{f_c}{f\bar{f}} . \qquad (3.6)$$

The values in (3.6) are always larger than the corresponding ones in (3.4) unless $c = 1$ or $f = \frac{1}{2}$. If $f = \frac{1}{2}$, weighted and unweighted estimates are the same; hence,

$$\text{var } (\hat{\mu}_0) = \text{var } (\hat{\hat{\mu}}_0) = \frac{2\sigma^2}{N}, \qquad \text{var } (\hat{\mu}_1) = \text{var } (\hat{\hat{\mu}}_1) = \frac{2\sigma^2}{N}. \quad (3.7)$$

When $f = \frac{1}{2}$, the variances (3.7) are therefore independent of the correct classification probability c, and, furthermore, unweighted estimates are unbiased [see (3.3)]. These are two strong advantages of choosing $f = \frac{1}{2}$ in this case, and in more general situations, of sampling proportionally.

We now are in a position to compute the variance of the weighted estimates with $f \geq \frac{1}{2}$ from (3.6), relative to the variance in (3.7) for $f = \frac{1}{2}$. These values appear in Table 1 for both income groups for the two cases $c = .5$ and $c = 1.0$. Since this ratio is linear in c, variance ratios for other values of c can be obtained by linear interpolation, as illustrated in Fig. 2.

Table 1 illustrates the major result of this section, that the variance for the unfavored group is always increased by oversampling,

Table 1

RATIO OF VARIANCES OF WEIGHTED ESTIMATES FOR VALUES OF $f \geq \frac{1}{2}$, FORMULA (3.6), RELATIVE TO THE VARIANCES WHEN $f = \frac{1}{2}$, FORMULA (3.7)

| | Low Income (Favored) Group $(f \geq \frac{1}{2})$ | | | High Income (Unfavored) Group $(\bar{f} \leq \frac{1}{2})$ | |
| | Variance Ratio | | | Variance Ratio | |
f	$c = 0.5$	$c = 1$	$\bar{f}$	$c = 0.5$	$c = 1$
0.5	1.00	1.00	0.5	1.00	1.00
0.6	1.04	0.83	0.4	1.04	1.25
0.7	1.19	0.71	0.3	1.19	1.67
0.8	1.56	0.63	0.2	1.56	2.50
0.9	2.78	0.56	0.1	2.78	5.00
1.0	∞	0.50	0	∞	∞

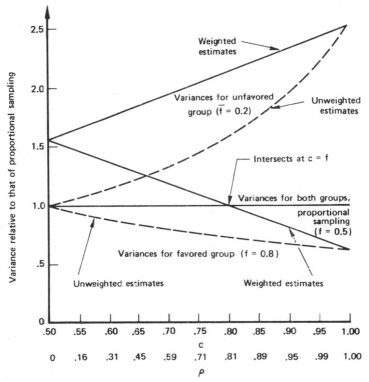

Fig. 2—Variances of weighted and unweighted estimates for the case $f = 0.8$, relative to variances resulting from proportional sampling. The horizontal axis is the classification probability c, or the corresponding correlation coefficient $\rho = \cos[\pi(1 - c)]$, between the preexperimental and the experimental values of the classification variable.

and for c near to 0.5, oversampling even harms estimation of the favored group. In fact, since the simple average of the two variance ratios for any value of c is $1/(4f\bar{f})$, independent of c, we may define this amount to be the overall increase in variance accepted in order to produce lower variances for the favored group. It is easy to see that even the favored group has larger variance than for proportional sampling if $c < f$. Hence: *oversampling leads to uniformly higher variances if the oversampling rate exceeds the correct classification probability.*

These ideas are illustrated for the case f = 0.8 in Fig. 2. The horizontal line going through 1.0 is the variance available if proportional sampling is used. The two solid sloped lines, which meet at 1.56 for c = 0.5 (see Table 1), are the variances from using the weighted estimates (3.5) when 80 percent of the sample is low income (preexperimentally) and 20 percent is high income (preexperimentally). If c ≤ 0.8, even the favored group does not improve on the variance for proportional sampling; hence the lines cross there. The variances of the unweighted estimates (3.1), (3.2) are the dashed curving lines, whose two values always average in excess of 1.0. The gains for the favored group are small for c near to 0.5 because substantial misclassification produces experimental samples that nearly match the population proportions. At c = 1, the unweighted and weighted estimates are the same, and so their variances also agree. At c = 0.5, the unweighted estimates have variance independent of the oversampling rate f (since $f_{.5}$ = 0.5 for all f) and therefore have relative variance equal to 1.

The horizontal axis is indexed not only by c but also by ρ, the value of the correlation coefficient that is consistent with c. It is computed from the formula $\rho = \cos[\pi(1 - c)]$, and is the correlation required between two normally distributed observations in order that the conditional probability of the second exceeding its median is c, given that the first exceeds its own median. (This formula is exact only for the case of two categories, each having probability one-half, as in the example.) Thus, in the case f = 0.8 of Fig. 2, correlations between preexperimental and experimental income less than 0.81 will lead to higher variances than for f = 0.5, *even for the favored group.*

The value ∞ for f = 1 and c = 0.5 in Table 1 raises an interesting point. If low incomes are the only ones of interest to the study, and if c < 1, then, to obtain unbiased estimates, it is necessary either to postulate that $\mu_{00} = \mu_{10}$ (that there are no latent variables partially correlated with preexperimental income) or to sample both preexperimental categories. That is, if $\delta_0 \neq 0$ in (3.3), any attempt to study low income preexperimental families by restricting the sample to low preexperimental incomes would be biased, because families with high preexperimental income, whose incomes drop later, would be excluded.

In summary, strong assumptions can eliminate the need to use weights
based on the preexperimental variables. In that case, oversampling can
be efficient if the probability of correct classification is high. If
a weighted analysis is needed, the oversampling may degrade precision
relative to proportional sampling, even for fairly high probabilities
of correct classification. We have illustrated this in the simple case
of estimating means, but this fact can hold for linear and other more
complicated models. An additional reason to avoid oversampling is that
a weighted analysis is more cumbersome to conduct than an unweighted
one. This is quite important if many different analyses and dependent
variables are being considered, because the weights must be used each
time, even for those dependent variables whose prediction is not improved by the oversampling.

PROBLEMS DERIVED FROM OVERSAMPLING NEIGHBORHOODS

If one decides to oversample certain categories, possibly because
classification errors are small, it may appear to be efficient to obtain
the sample by oversampling neighborhoods that are abundant with the
desired characteristics. This strategy reduces cost by decreasing the
number of screening interviews needed to produce the desired sample
proportions. If the analytical models legitimately can ignore the
neighborhood effects, the savings are real. Even when this simplifying
assumption cannot be made with confidence, such a sampling procedure
may be required and some bias accepted to keep costs within reasonable
bounds for studies that focus on individuals with uncommon characteristics.

But oversampling to reduce screening costs may not be cost effective. If the study must oversample low income families, the income
distributions in census tracts can be estimated from census data. This
information could be used to reduce the number of screening interviews
substantially if the between-census-tract variation in income is large
relative to the within-tract variation. However, a biased sample will
result if low income families in low income tracts differ systematically
in their responses from low income families in high income tracts. For
example, low income families in high income neighborhoods are often

young, single people living with their high income parents. These people probably differ in their responses from low income families in low income neighborhoods having different age, family size, and employment characteristics. Therefore, a weighted analysis would be required to avoid bias, and as stated earlier, this increases variances of estimates. We have constructed many models, similar to those presented above, where the fractional increases in variance resulting from this kind of strategy substantially exceeds the fractional decrease in costs. In such cases, these strategies are not cost effective for a given budget. Furthermore, oversampling of neighborhoods has other disadvantages: Derivation of a proper sampling scheme is costly and quite difficult. If done improperly, it can lead to biased estimates. In addition, weighted analyses are more difficult to conduct.

To summarize this section, two examples were considered where oversampling of a population in which the analyst has greater interest may be undesirable. Oversampling is common in these situations. More discussion of the problems of oversampling, involving treatment assignment, appears in Section V. Our view is that oversampling should be used only after reviewing both the additional modeling assumptions required to make the exercise advantageous and the likelihood of classification error.

IV. DIFFICULTIES WITH OPTIMAL ALLOCATION OF SUBJECTS TO TREATMENTS IN SOCIAL EXPERIMENTS

In the preceding two sections we discussed the difficulties of getting unbiased samples of transitory populations and of oversampling subpopulations in the presence of classification errors. In experimental situations there also are opportunities to control the manner in which subjects are allocated treatments, the purpose being to produce a more cost-effective experiment. In this section we briefly consider three of these options: (a) choosing the sample to be nonrepresentative of the survey population; (b) making unbalanced assignments of subjects to treatments; and (c) using a crossover design. In each of these cases extra modeling assumptions are required to avoid bias, assumptions we were unwilling to make in the context of the Health Insurance Study.

NONREPRESENTATIVE SAMPLES

Certain experimental subjects may be more valuable for the estimation of parameters or less costly than others, and may therefore be preferred for allocation to treatments. A simple example of this occurs if a linear regression function of one independent variable is to be estimated, in which case subjects with extremely low or high values on this variable (e.g., income) are much more informative than those with intermediate values. When more subjects are available for selection than are needed for assignment to treatments, the preferred subjects may be assigned to treatments and the others excluded from the sample. Unbiased estimates may be derived from such assignments if the assumed parametric distribution is correct, or, in the absence of such assumptions, if every member of the target population has positive probability of being assigned to the treatments and, in the analysis, subjects are weighted inversely to their selection probability. Of course, the weighted analysis may be inefficient.

More hazardous yet are samples with some subjects having no possibility of selection. This occurs in the simple linear response example. The exclusion of the intermediate subjects makes the estimation of a nonlinear model very difficult, and no weighted analysis can rectify the situation. The HIS did not follow this procedure by excluding middle income families, for example. While such a procedure would re-duce variances for estimating a linear effect of income on the response, we have no assurances that responses are linear in income, and there is a strong likelihood that middle income families differ importantly along other critical dimensions that are correlated with income.

Note that the problem here is one of determining a priori the ap-propriate parametric density function. Unfortunately, economic theory rarely gives much help with respect to functional form. Conlisk (1973) has proposed a decision-theoretic approach to this problem in which the analyst assigns probabilities to functional forms and then minimizes expected loss. While attractive conceptually, it is not clear how one proceeds in practice to assign zero probability to functional forms one will not consider, nor how one should think about appropriate probabil-ities (in some cases information from other studies can be helpful). In the absence of information concerning functional form, a self-weighting (representative) sample appears to us to be the best choice.

UNBALANCED ASSIGNMENTS OF SUBJECTS TO TREATMENTS

If the cost of including a subject in the experiment depends jointly on his characteristics and on the treatment to which he is assigned, then it may be possible to increase the sample size and precision of the ex-periment by exploiting this relationship. The allocation model of Con-lisk and Watts (1969) provides a means for computing the optimal sample allocation based on such a cost function, assuming a specified functional form.

For example, the cost of the Health Insurance Study could have been reduced by assigning those who had generous insurance before the experi-ment to the generous experimental insurance plans, and those with little or no insurance to the less generous plans. This would have eliminated the "worst-case" participation incentives paid to compensate those fam-ilies whose experimental insurance was inferior in any way to their pre-experimental insurance. It also would have been unwise. Families in poor health tend to purchase better insurance than they would were they

in good health (Phelps, 1976). Generous insurance plans therefore
would be overrepresented by unhealthy families and, as a result, comparisons between treatments would be biased unless the exact amount
of overrepresentation were known.

The New Jersey Negative Income Tax Experiment provides a second
example. The designers of this experiment found it less costly to put
higher income families on generous plans and lower income families on
less generous plans, and so generosity of the treatment and family
income are correlated. Of course the modeling assumption that income
does not interact with treatment generosity and that responses are
linear with income provides one way to unravel these effects. Presumably, such assumptions were made during the design of the New Jersey
experiment when it was decided that unbalanced assignment of incomes
would be cost effective. The alternative to making these modeling
assumptions is to use weighted estimates. But this will yield less
efficient estimates than would have resulted from balanced assignments
of subjects to treatments.

CROSSOVER DESIGNS

Thus far, we have considered designs in which subjects are exposed
to one treatment only. In a long experiment it may be possible to ex-
pose subjects to several treatments, one at a time—a crossover design.
If valid responses can be elicited in this fashion, then increased
precision for estimating treatment effects can be expected because each
subject acts as his own control. That is, comparisons between treatments can be made directly by observing the changed responses of each
subject as he changes treatments. This eliminates accounting for the
differences between subjects. Response variances are reduced by a
factor $1 - R^2$ if every subject is exposed to every treatment for an
equal length of time, where R^2 is the portion of the total variance
of the response of subjects attributable to differences between subjects.
Hall (1975) has argued that a crossover design could have reduced the
necessary sample size by a factor of six in the New Jersey Negative Income Tax Experiment. We doubt this. The responses from crossover experimentation will be invalid if there is transitory behavior at the

beginning or end of each treatment period that is not accounted for. Transitory behavior may exist for a variety of reasons. Learning effects produce transitory behavior if it takes time for the subject to become familiar with all the benefits of the treatment and to develop ways to take advantage of them (e.g., to find dentists or psychiatrists in the HIS). Put another way, the actual response to a treatment may be delayed. Or if the treatment benefits permit subjects to purchase durable goods, they may engage in transitory behavior in crossover situations by waiting to purchase these goods until they are on a generous treatment (e.g., elective surgery, dental work, and psychiatric care are likely to be purchased in greater quantity per unit time by a subject who is on a generous health insurance plan for only a short period than by one who has generous insurance for a long time). Changes in behavior resulting from the subject's heightened awareness of the experiment are more likely if the treatment is changed frequently.

In the face of time-varying experimental responses, the design must either (1) allow sufficient time within each treatment for transitory effects to disappear--this amount of time is likely not to be known a priori, and additional calendar time may be necessary to estimate it; or (2) estimate the rate of change in behavior and extrapolate to a steady-state value. The first solution in practice will defer the results in time, and therefore a larger sample with no crossover (but earlier results) may well be preferred; the second solution requires strong assumptions.

Unfortunately, time-varying experimental responses appear to be common. In peak-load pricing experiments for electricity, it takes time to adjust the household's stock of appliances; in income maintenance experiments, it takes time to search for a new job; in housing demand experiments, it takes time to locate new housing. Further, all involve aspects of durable goods. Thus, while crossover designs can be very useful, we doubt that they will prove to be desirable as a general design for the types of social experiments considered here.

V. OPTIMAL BALANCE OF ASSIGNMENTS TO TREATMENTS AND THE DIFFICULTIES OF ACHIEVING IT WITH FIELD CONSTRAINTS

For reasons just mentioned, imbalances among the treatment assignments and the target population, or imbalances among treatments, can lead to poor estimates of the treatment effects. Suppose then that it is desired to balance subjects across treatments as carefully as possible. The time-honored and simplest method for doing this is by simple random sampling (SRS): The available subjects are assigned at random to treatments in accord with the required sample size for each treatment, *without* regard to any preexperimental measurements made on the subjects. Of course some imbalance of the preexperimental measurements still occurs, but it is random; and if large samples are assigned to each treatment, only minor increases in variance are experienced relative to a perfectly balanced assignment. If sample sizes are not large, however, then the imbalances from SRS can be substantial, and more control over the sample is desired.

Classical ways to use preexperimental measurements to improve balance over SRS include proportional stratification and blocking. In the Health Insurance Study, the "Finite Selection Model" (FSM) was used as an alternative because it can handle more independent variables than the classical methods and does not require converting continuous variables, like income, to categorical variables (Morris, 1975). The method of proportional stratification involves dividing the sample into k strata on the basis of the preexperimental variables and then assigning subjects to treatments separately from each stratum, in proportion to the treatment size, using simple random sampling. Blocking, a special case of proportional stratification, can be used only if all the treatments are the same size, or if all treatment sizes are small integer multiples of the smallest treatment. The entire sample then would be broken into homogeneous groups of the proper size, and each group assigned to the treatments in proportion to their size by simple random sampling.

PROPORTIONAL STRATIFICATION TO IMPROVE BALANCE

Because the calculations can be carried out conveniently for proportional stratification, that case is treated in our examples here. Proportional stratification includes blocking as a special case, while it in turn is a special case of the FSM.

The notation needed is given in Fig. 3, below. Subjects are classified into k strata S_1, ..., S_k on the basis of their preexperimental measurements and are to be assigned to treatments T_1, ..., T_t, with N_i subjects assigned to treatment T_i. Hence $\Sigma N_i = N_+$ is the total number of subjects in the pool. The proportion of subjects available for selection in stratum j is p_j, so $\Sigma p_j = 1$. Because there may be refusals of the offer or other failures to enroll assigned subjects in treatments, n_i (with $n_i \leq N_i$) is the number actually enrolled in T_i.

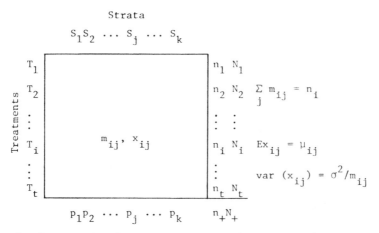

Fig. 3--Notation for assignment of subjects from k strata to t treatments.

The number of subjects actually enrolled in T_i from stratum j is m_{ij}, $\Sigma_j m_{ij} = n_i$. The true mean response to T_i in S_j is μ_{ij}, which is to be estimated by the sample mean x_{ij} of the m_{ij} observations in that cell. We assume

$$Ex_{ij} = \mu_{ij}, \qquad var\ (x_{ij}) = \frac{\sigma^2}{m_{ij}}\ . \tag{5.1}$$

The average response to T_i among these subjects is

$$\mu_i = \sum_j p_j \mu_{ij} , \qquad (5.2)$$

which is estimated unbiasedly by

$$\hat{\mu}_i = \sum_j p_j x_{ij} \qquad (5.3)$$

with variance

$$\text{var} (\hat{\mu}_i) = \sigma^2 \sum_j \frac{p_j^2}{m_{ij}} . \qquad (5.4)$$

The variances of contrasts between treatments are determined by formula (5.4). For example, the difference in effects of T_1 and T_2 is estimated by $\hat{\mu}_1 - \hat{\mu}_2$ with variance var $(\hat{\mu}_1)$ + var $(\hat{\mu}_2)$.

Suppose, first, that all assigned subjects actually enroll, so that $n_i = N_i$. Assuming that $(n_1, \ldots, n_t)$ is given, the uniformly best assignment scheme for all treatments--that which minimizes (5.4) for every i, subject to $\sum_j m_{ij} = n_i$--is proportional stratification:

$$m_{ij} = n_i p_j \qquad (5.5)$$

for all i, j, in which case

$$\text{var}_{\text{PROP}} (\hat{\mu}_i) = \frac{\sigma^2}{n_i} \qquad (5.6)$$

is the optimal variance. This is proved by minimizing (5.4) subject to $\sum_j m_{ij} = n_i$. Of course an exact identity for (5.5) may be impossible for any treatment because $n_i p_j$ may not be an integer. We ignore this complication.

Now suppose that some selected subjects fail to participate. If these subjects can be replaced by others from the same stratum, perfectly proportional samples still will be achieved. This sequential procedure was infeasible in the context of the HIS for reasons to be described later. Instead it was necessary to select N_i subjects, in excess of the n_i desired for each treatment ($N_i > n_i$), permitting the imperfect acceptance rate $\pi < 1$ to yield approximately the desired number n_i. Our purpose is to demonstrate how much the variance (5.6) increases when this happens. As a first step, the expected precision from simple random sampling will be determined.

We are supposing that the $\{p_j\}$ are defined by the sample, based only on the N_+ observations, and not on the entire universe. The variances realized from SRS will therefore be reduced because of finite sampling, as we shall see. Comparisons between SRS and the results of proportional stratification will also be made conditionally on the value of $\{n_i\}$, since the random mechanism that operates to produce these values is the same for either design method.

The sample is assumed to have been constructed as follows: The universe is assumed to be large (e.g., a city) and a simple random sample of N_+ subjects, eligible for treatment assignment, is obtained. The numbers $\{N_i\}$ are fixed in advance; $\Sigma_i N_i = N_+$ subjects are assigned to T_i either at random or by the method of proportional stratification. Let m_{ij}^* be the number of subjects assigned to T_i from S_j at this step, with $\Sigma_j m_{ij}^* = N_i$. If SRS is used, m_{ij}^* is random, whereas $m_{ij}^* = N_i p_j$ if proportional stratification is used. These subjects are enrolled with probability π, so, given m_{ij}^*, the number that actually accept on T_i from S_j are $m_{ij} \sim$ binomial (m_{ij}^*, π). [This notation means that the random variable m_{ij} has the binomial distribution with mean m_{ij}^*, π and variance m_{ij}^*, $\pi(1 - \pi)$.] Of course, it is m_{ij}, not m_{ij}^*, that affects variances in (5.4). We wish to compute the expected value of (5.4), i.e., $\sigma^2 E \Sigma p_j^2 / m_{ij}$, conditionally on this sampling scheme, on $\{n_i\}$, and on the sample of N_+ subjects, for both simple random sampling and proportional sampling. Formally, these expectations do not exist unless m_{ij} cannot be zero, but we shall interpret the expectations as conditional on the event that $m_{ij} \geq 1$. The approximate method used to obtain these expectations takes care of this problem. The results that follow are proved in the appendix.

Theorem 5.1. *The expected value of* (5.4) *under random sampling is approximately*

$$E_{SRS} \text{ var } (\hat{\mu}_i) \doteq \frac{\sigma^2}{n_i} \left[1 + \frac{k-1}{n_i} \left(\frac{N_+ - n_i}{N_+ - 1} \right) \right]. \tag{5.7}$$

Since σ^2/n_i is given by (5.6) as the variance for proportional stratification, the factor

$$1 + \frac{k-1}{n_i} \left(1 - \frac{n_i - 1}{N_+ - 1} \right) \tag{5.8}$$

is the expected fractional increase in variance from SRS relative to proportional stratification. When N_+ is large in relation to n_i, (5.8) simplifies approximately to

$$1 + \frac{(k-1)}{n_i}. \tag{5.9}$$

Note that (5.9) is the SRS variance for sampling from the universe, whereas (5.8) is smaller, because sampling without replacement from a universe of size N_+ is more efficient than from one of infinite size. Formulas (5.8) and (5.9) illustrate the well-known fact that SRS becomes less efficient as the number of subjects per treatment per stratum, n_i/k, decreases. SRS is asymptotically optimal as n_i/k becomes very large. But we believe that as n_+ increases in experiments as costly as the HIS, more treatments and more strata will be created, so that n_i/k ordinarily would not be large.

Turning to proportional stratification with $m_{ij}^* = N_i p_j$, formula (5.6) no longer will obtain because of random nonacceptances. Instead, conditional on n_i (the number of acceptances of T_i), the expected variance would be given by the following theorem.

Theorem 5.2. *The expected value of* (5.4), *assuming random acceptance of proportionally stratified offers* $(m_{ij}^* = N_i p_j$ *made to* T_i *from* $S_j)$, *is approximately*

$$E_{PROP} \text{ var } (\hat{\mu}_i) \doteq \frac{\sigma^2}{n_i} \left[1 + \frac{k-1}{n_i} \left(\frac{N_i - n_i}{N_i - 1} \right) \right]. \qquad (5.10)$$

To interpret Theorem 5.2, define

$$\psi_i \equiv \frac{n_i - 1}{N_i - 1} \cdot \frac{N_+ - N_i}{N_+ - n_i}, \qquad (5.11)$$

which depends on the acceptance rate n_i/N_i, and on N_i and N_+, but not on k or σ^2. If $n_i = N_i$, then $\psi_i = 1$; if $n_i = 1$, $\psi_i = 0$; and, in most instances, ψ_i is slightly less than, but fairly close to, the acceptance rate π. We may rewrite (5.10) in terms of ψ_i and (5.7) as

$$E_{PROP} \text{ var } (\hat{\mu}_i) \doteq (1 - \psi_i) E_{SRS} \text{ var } (\hat{\mu}_i) + \psi_i \text{ var}_{PROP} (\hat{\mu}), \qquad (5.12)$$

where $\text{var}_{PROP} (\hat{\mu}) \equiv \sigma^2/n_i$ is the variance achieved by proportional sampling (5.6). The quantity ψ_i therefore shows how much a random acceptance rate would be expected to cut into the gains due to proportional stratification. Roughly, the improvement over SRS would be reduced by a factor equal to the nonacceptance rate, $1 - \pi$.

To illustrate this improvement, the acceptance rate was about 0.58 in the HIS, with losses caused by refusal of the offer, refusal of the final interview, and other circumstances such as families having moved or become ineligible. A detailed breakdown of the HIS enrollment experience is shown in Table 2. Note that one-half of the 42-percent sample loss is due to nonrefusal attrition, and the other half is due to refusal of the enrollment interview or the actual offer of enrollment.

If $N_+ = 800$ families, a typical value, then for values of N_i at 10, 40 (where ψ_i is maximum), 75, 120, and 180, the corresponding values of ψ_i are 0.531, 0.557, 0.550, 0.537, and 0.515. Taking 0.54 as a typical value here, slightly less than the 58 percent acceptance rate, we would expect to have gained only about 54 percent of the improvement over SRS nominally available had proportional stratification been

Table 2

DISPOSITION OF THE HEALTH INSURANCE STUDY ENROLLMENT SAMPLE

HIS Enrollment	Dayton		Seattle[a]		Massachusetts[b]		South Carolina[c]		Total	
	No.	%	No.	%	No.	%	No.	%	No.	%
Families who completed baselines and were assigned to treatments	528	--	2054	--	1068	--	1232	--	4882	--
Families added to sample at enrollment interview[d]	(e)	--	101	5.2	46	4.5	89	7.8	236[f]	5.1[f]
Attrition due to nonrefusals[g]	106	20.1	414	20.2	264	24.7	245	19.9	1029	21.1
Enrollment refusals	32	6.1	404	19.7	238	22.3	356	28.9	1030	21.1
Enrolled	390	73.9	1236	60.2	566	60.0	631	51.2	2823	57.8
Families interviewed for enrollment	422	79.9	1640	79.8	804	75.3	987	80.1	3853	78.9
Refused interview	4	0.9	147	9.0	108	13.4	125	12.7	384	10.0
Refused offer to enroll	28	6.6	257	15.7	130	16.2	231	23.4	646	16.8
Enrolled	390	92.4	1236	75.4	566	70.7	631	63.9	2823	73.3

[a]Includes a fee-for-service sample, a health maintenance organization sample, and a control group.

[b]Fitchburg-Leominster and Franklin counties.

[c]Charleston and Georgetown counties (includes a preexperimental control group sample).

[d]Line 2 is a subset of line 1.

[e]Not available.

[f]Excluding Dayton. The percentage figure is calculated as 236/(4882-236).

[g]Families moved, could not be located, were ineligible, or were unable to verify insurance.

133

used in the HIS. In fact, proportional stratification was not used because it was infeasible with the large number of covariates considered in the HIS design, and the FSM was used instead. We believe that 54 percent of the nominal gain also provides a rough percentage for the actual improvement over SRS provided by the FSM after sample reduction in the field.

Two points need to be made in relation to (5.12). First, while the expected variance of $\hat{\mu}_i$ is given by (5.7), the actual amount varies randomly. When many treatments are involved, it is likely that some treatment effects will be estimated with much larger variance than (5.7) suggests. This is an additional argument against SRS. However, proportional stratification, even in the context of random nonacceptances, not only reduces the expected variance of the treatment effects, but it also reduces the variability of the actual precision from that expected. This is highly desirable, especially so in view of criticism that would likely occur if, after the sample was selected, it was observed that the actual assignments to treatments from strata were unbalanced (i.e., if m_{ij}/n_i were substantially different from p_j for some treatment stratum combinations). A second point is that the variances in (5.12) obtain with respect to the strata defined on the basis of the preexperimental observations. The gains from proportional stratification with respect to the experimental observations would be diminished if the correlation between the two sets of observations were imperfect. Of course, SRS does not suffer from this phenomenon.

If the variance of x_{ij} is not given by (5.1), but instead by v_{ij}/m_{ij} (i.e., depends on stratum and treatment), or if the objective function (5.4) is replaced by a more general one, such as

$$\text{var } (\hat{\mu}_i) = \sum_j W_{ij} \text{ var } (x_{ij}) , \tag{5.13}$$

with $W_{ij} \geq 0$ and fixed, then proportional stratification is not optimal. However, proportional stratification still is uniformly better than SRS, and formula (5.12) holds for the objective function (5.13). That is, even in this more general situation, the variance afforded by proportional sampling is a $(\psi_i, 1 - \psi_i)$ mixture of the proportional sampling variance resulting from no refusals, and of the expected SRS variance.

The discussion thus far has treated the n_i as given. Let n_i^* be the desired value for n_i, i.e., the desired number of subjects to be assigned to treatment T_i. If π is the acceptance rate, then $N_i = n_i^*/\pi$ selections would be made. Suppose the actual number of acceptances are random, so that n_i has a binomial distribution with parameters N_i and π. Then the mean of n_i is n_i^*; but since it may differ considerably from this value, some loss of overall precision would be expected. Suppose the n_i^* were derived by minimizing a weighted sum of the variances of $\hat{\mu}$, each given by (5.6), subject to a cost constraint which assumes that c_i is the cost of observing each subject on T_i. It is proved in the appendix, under the assumptions just made, that the weighted variance achieved for the optimal n_i^* is increased approximately by the factor

$$1 + \frac{1 - \pi}{E_c n^*} , \qquad E_c n^* \equiv \frac{\Sigma \, n_i^* c_i}{\Sigma \, c_i} . \qquad (5.14)$$

This ordinarily is fairly small. For example, with $\pi = 0.58$ and $E_c n^* = 35$ being the approximate average number of families enrolled on each HIS insurance plan, a 1.2-percent increase in variance results.

FIELD CONSTRAINTS IN THE HIS

We conclude this section by describing field constraints that acted in the Health Insurance Study to diminish the gains provided by the FSM. We have just showed that an imperfect acceptance rate reduces precision gains, unless the nonaccepting subjects are replaced by others from the same stratum. The sequential procedure needed to replace losses by subjects from the same stratum requires close contact with field operations. Although it is worth some effort to implement, this is more difficult than it may seem for the following five reasons.

First, the enrollment process is more efficient if enrollers have many cases to work at any one time rather than a few, with replacements arriving only as cases are closed. Thus, the majority of the cases to be assigned (N_+ in Fig. 3) should be assigned at the beginning of the enrollment period.

Second, at any particular time, families selected in the field are in one of four categories: (1) they have dropped out of the sample because of ineligibility, etc.; (2) they have accepted; (3) they have refused; (4) they are in an indeterminate state because the interviewers have not attempted to contact them, or they have been hard to contact, or their eligibility is being verified, or there has been a change in family composition since the baseline interview, or they are pondering the offer, and so on. The indeterminate category tends to be large through most of the enrollment period, and until it diminishes significantly, backup selections are not useful.

Third, a long interval, sometimes 6 weeks, elapsed between the time the field staff declared that a family could not be enrolled and the time a replacement selection could be fielded. Although quicker communications could have been designed, some of the clerical and data processing procedures necessary to maintain control in administering such a large survey would have had to be circumvented. Processing data about the refusal, making the new selection, preparing legal documents for the newly selected family, and integrating the new selections into the field schedule involved coordination among Rand and two subcontractors that required careful control procedures and, inevitably, time.

Fourth, the end of the field enrollment period in the HIS came not long after most families had achieved a final enrollment/nonenrollment status, and by that time it was too late for the field to enroll new families with enrollment complications. Replacing families near the end of the enrollment period could create a bias, because unless enrollers are given sufficient time to work on families with enrollment complications (e.g., replacing families who moved out, or are changing in composition, or are contemplating the offer), the experiment would be overloaded with problem-free families, and the acceptance rate would be lowered. Obviously, the responses of problem-free families to the treatments may well differ from those of the target population.

Fifth, the number of available backup families tends to be small in any stratum, unless large amounts are spent generating baseline interviews to purchase protection. Even if the true nonacceptance probability is the same for every stratum, random differences in the actual acceptance rate would deplete some strata of the necessary reserves, forcing some nonproportional stratification at the backup stage.

We will not consider the case in which the acceptance rate varies by stratum, or worse yet, varies on the basis of some unmeasured variable. The former problem can be corrected by using the true acceptance probabilities (although defining and estimating them may be difficult); the unmeasured variable problem is much harder.

The full benefits of proportional stratification in the HIS were reduced further by the need to make selections in "bursts." Burst is a term used in the HIS to refer to selections being made not one at one time, but in stages. The baseline period ended close to the beginning of the enrollment period so that we could reduce the number of transitory changes in the sample, reduce cost, and get the experimental data as early as possible. Because of the time lag between administration of the baseline and availability of machine-readable data for selection (often several months), we had to make selections before all baseline data were available. Thus, selections were made in stages, with each stage called a "burst." The number of bursts ranged from one to nine in the sites. Families that were harder to reach or whose insurance took longer to verify tended to appear in the later bursts. Because they are likely to differ systematically from other families (e.g., families living in multiple family units tended to be associated with later bursts), the burst itself was considered as a stratum. That is, each family was identified with a burst, and the assignment of families to treatments was made proportionally from each burst. Bursts degrade the efficiency gains of proportional sampling relative to random sampling because they reduce the number of options available for balancing the sample.

The final constraint we will mention here is that the overall acceptance rate π is not known until after enrollment is complete, and one must work with an estimate $\hat{\pi}$. In the HIS, π differed from site to site, so that we were operating under uncertainty in every case. Furthermore, in the early bursts, one cannot know for sure how many eligible families, which we shall call N_E, eventually will become available.

These two uncertainties make uncertain what portion of families should be assigned to treatments in early bursts, and what portion should be withheld. Substantial penalties are paid for significant errors in either direction. Two few assignments cause field schedules to slip and lead to low field morale because enrollers, ready to work, don't have enough to do. Eventually they become overworked near the end of the enrollment period, with the result that a full effort will not be made on the families selected with the final bursts. In this case some bias will result from undersampling those families. Of course, when it was realized later that more families should have been assigned from the early bursts, these selections would be made, but it is the release of these families that overburdens the field. On the other hand, too many selections from an early burst leads to overenrollment of that group, and if the enrollment targets (and budget) are not to be exceeded, the situation cannot be corrected later. If π and N_E are known, and if n_+ is the number of acceptances desired in the site, then the fraction of the burst that should be assigned is

$$\frac{(n_+/\pi)}{N_E} \, , \tag{5.15}$$

since n_+/π is the number of selections that eventually would have to be made to get n_+ acceptances, and N_E is the number of families eventually eligible for selection. Therefore the product

$$\pi N_E \tag{5.16}$$

must be estimated. The conservative approach would choose a high value for this product, making undersampling of the burst much more likely than oversampling, and compensating later. This means the field period must be extended enough to provide time to pursue the replacement families from the early bursts as the actual number needed becomes known later.

Our recommendation is to protect against this situation by earmarking a balanced fraction of the enrollments (we used 20 percent in the last sites) and instructing the field office to set them aside until the other enrollment selections have been fielded and followed up. This keeps options open until near the end of the fielding period and elimi- nates the lag time in the likely event that some of the remaining selec- tions must be used.

To summarize this section, blocking, proportional stratification, and the Finite Selection Model all can be used to improve the balance and precision of the estimates from an experiment. But the gains that they provide relative to simple random sampling are reduced by random nonacceptances, approximately in proportion to the nonacceptance rate. We discussed the principal reasons why, in the context of the HIS, a sequential procedure designed to replace nonaccepting families with others from the same stratum was infeasible, even though, if successful, such a procedure would reclaim the precision losses due to nonaccep- tances.

APPENDIX

Carl Morris

Definition: Given k, n_+, and $(N_1, \ldots, N_k)$, the random vector $(n_1, \ldots, n_k)$ of nonnegative integers with $\Sigma n_i = n_+$ is distributed as the *Multivariate Hypergeometric Distribution*, $\text{MHG}_k (n_+; N_1, \ldots, N_k)$, if

$$P(n_1 = n_1^*, \ldots, n_k = n_k^*) = \frac{\binom{N_1}{n_1^*} \cdots \binom{N_k}{n_k^*}}{\binom{\Sigma N_i}{n_+}} . \tag{A.1}$$

The first two moments of $\text{MHG}_k (n_+; N_1, \ldots, N_k)$ are

$$En_i = n_+ p_i , \qquad \text{var} (n_i) = n_+ p_i (1 - p_i) \frac{N_+ - n_+}{N_+ - 1} , \tag{A.2}$$

where $N_+ \equiv \Sigma N_i$, $p_i \equiv N_i/N_+$. The expected value of the reciprocal of the ith coordinate of MHG_k does not exist if $P(n_i = 0) > 0$, but

$$E\left(\frac{1}{n_i} \middle| n_i \geq 1\right) \doteq (1 + \gamma_i^2) \frac{1}{En_i} , \tag{A.3}$$

with γ_i^2 being the squared coefficient of variation of n_i given by

$$\gamma_i^2 = \frac{\text{var} (n_i)}{E^2 n_i} = \frac{1 - p_i}{n_+ p_i} \frac{N_+ - n_+}{N_+ - 1} . \tag{A.4}$$

Formula (A.3) is determined by noting that since

$$\frac{\mu}{X} = 1 - \left(\frac{X - \mu}{\mu}\right) + \left(\frac{X - \mu}{\mu}\right)^2 - \left(\frac{X - \mu}{\mu}\right)^3 \frac{\mu}{X} ,$$

for any random variable X with mean μ,

$$E \frac{\mu}{X} = 1 + \frac{\text{var } (X)}{\mu^2} - E\left(\frac{X - \mu}{X}\right)\left(\frac{X - \mu}{\mu}\right)^2 .$$

The remaining term $E[(X - \mu)/X][(X - \mu)/\mu)^2]$ is ignored, which is legitimate for the expectation in (A.3) involving the hypergeometric distribution, provided $P(n_i = 0)$ is small and γ_i is small. In the examples we have looked at, satisfying $n_+ p_i \geq 4$ and $\pi \geq 0.5$ [note that $1 - \pi \doteq (N_+ - n_+)/(N_+ - 1)$ in (A.4)], the right-hand side of (A.3) is smaller than the left-hand side, but by less than 4 percent, with diminishing error as $n_+ p_i$ increases. In Theorems (5.1) and (5.2), these errors are averaged over all strata, with smaller weights for small strata, thereby improving further the approximations in those theorems.

We turn to the proof of Theorems (5.1) and (5.2). Under the assumption of Theorem (5.1), N_i subjects are chosen at random for treatment T_i from the N_+ available. Then n_i accept at random from the N_i. Hence, the accepting subjects also are a random sample of size n_i from the N_+ available. Since the stratum sizes available are $(p_1 N_+, \ldots, p_k N_+)$, the conditional distribution of the numbers selected for T_i, i.e., of $(m_{i1}, \ldots, m_{ik})$, subject to $\Sigma_j m_{ij} = n_i$ with n_i given, is

$$(m_{i1}, m_{i2}, \ldots, m_{ik}) \sim \text{MHG}_k(n_i; p_1 N_+, \ldots, p_k N_+) . \qquad (A.5)$$

It follows from (A.2), (A.3), and (A.4) that

$$\sigma^2 E_{SRS} \Sigma p_j^2/m_{ij} \doteq \sigma^2 \Sigma p_j^2 \frac{1}{n_i p_j} \left(1 + \frac{1 - p_j}{n_i p_j} \cdot \frac{N_+ - n_i}{N_+ - 1}\right), \qquad (A.6)$$

and this reduces to (5.7).

Under the assumption of n_i random acceptances from N_i offers, where proportional stratification requires $m_{ij}^* = N_i p_j$ assignments to be made from S_j to T_i,

$$(m_{i1}, \ldots, m_{ik}) \sim MHG_k(n_i; p_1 N_i, \ldots, p_k N_i) \ . \qquad (A.7)$$

This is formally equivalent to (A.5), with N_i replacing N_+. Theorem (5.2) therefore follows from Theorem (5.1), with N_+ replaced by N_i.

Finally, (5.14) needs proof. If n_i^* minimizes $\sigma^2 \Sigma w_i/n_i$ subject to the budget constraint $\Sigma c_i n_i = C$, then

$$n_i^* \propto (w_i/c_i)^{\frac{1}{2}} \ . \qquad (A.8)$$

With $n_i \sim$ binomial $(n_i^*/\pi, \pi)$, then $En_i = n_i^*$, var $(n_i) = n_i^*(1 - \pi)$. The approximation (A.3) also holds for the binomial distribution; therefore,

$$E \ 1/n_i \doteq [1 + (1 - \pi)/n_i^*]/n_i^* \ .$$

It follows that

$$\sigma^2 E \ \Sigma \ w_i/n_i \doteq \sigma^2 \ \Sigma \ w_i/n_i^*[1 + (1 - \pi)/n_i^*]$$

$$= \sigma^2 \ \Sigma \ w_i/n_i^* \left[1 + (1 - \pi) \ \frac{\Sigma \ w_i/n_i^{*2}}{\Sigma \ w_i n_i^*/n_i^{*2}}\right]$$

$$= \sigma^2 \ \Sigma \ w_i/n_i^*[1 + (1 - \pi)/E_c n^*] \ , \qquad (A.9)$$

since $w_i/n_i^{*2} \propto c_i$. Formula (5.14) follows.

REFERENCES

1. Conlisk, John, "Choice of Response Functional Form in Designing Subsidy Experiments," *Econometrica*, Vol. 41, No. 4, July 1973, pp. 643-656.

2. Conlisk, John, and Harold Watts, "A Model for Optimizing Experimental Designs for Estimating Response Surfaces," *Proceedings of the Social Statistics Section*, American Statistical Association, 1969, pp. 150-156.

3. Hall, Robert E., "Effects of the Experimental Negative Income Tax on Labor Supply," in Joseph Peckman and P. Michael Timpane (eds.), *Work Incentives and Income Guarantees*, Washington: Brookings, 1975, pp. 115-147.

4. Manning, Willard G., Bridger M. Mitchell, and Jan P. Acton, "Design of the Los Angeles Peak-Load Pricing Experiment for Electricity," The Rand Corporation, R-1955-DWP, November 1976.

5. Morris, Carl, "A Finite Selection Model for Experimental Design of the Health Insurance Study," *Proceedings of the Social Statistics Section*, American Statistical Association, 1975, pp. 78-85; also published in the *Journal of Econometrics*, Vol. II, No. 1, September 1979, pp. 43-61.

6. Newhouse, Joseph P., "A Design for a Health Insurance Experiment," *Inquiry*, Vol. 11, No. 1, March 1974, pp. 5-27.

7. Phelps, Charles E., "Demand for Reimbursement Insurance," in Richard Rosett (ed.), *The Role of Health Insurance in the Health Sciences Sector*, New York: National Bureau of Economic Research, 1976.

5

The majority of chapters in this volume employ either single equation, cross-sectional models of program impact or expand this framework to two time periods to provide before/after comparisons. If equilibrium has been reached (change has ceased) during the postprogram period, such models will provide estimates of equilibrium level differences achieved by experimental and control groups. If, however, change has not ceased, only further data and model-fitting will capture the dynamic processes at work.

By contrast, the model of Tuma et al. is explicitly dynamic, using event history data to describe each individual's status at every moment. A strong simplifying assumption—the Markov property—is employed, and with this as a basis, the authors formulate a continuous time model of transitions between discrete states (in this case, married or not) that allows for the effects of population heterogeneity (individual characteristics, including treatment status, affect transition rates within a logit regression-like framework) and time dependence (time periods are introduced as with dummy predictor variables in a regression framework, so that the mean values and the determinants of transition rates vary by time period). Within this model it is also possible to correct for attrition bias (attrition is modeled as an absorbing state). Applying this model to data from the Seattle and Denver Income Maintenance Experiments led to the significant, and largely unanticipated, finding that an income guarantee increases marital dissolution. (In addition to the results reported below, see Hannan et al. 1977, 1978, and the debate between L. Goodwin and the authors reprinted at the end of this chapter.)

Tuma et al. specify an outcome variable, $Y(t)$, defining which of a finite set of values is observed for a given individual at time t. (In the empirical work later in the chapter, three possible values are used: married, unmarried, and attrited from the sample. The related paper by Tuma and Robins in Part II uses a similar model applied to the study of employment status.) The conditional probability of being in state k at time t, given that one was in state j at time u ($u < t$) is denoted $p_{jk}(u,t)$. The key parameters of the model are the unobserved "instantaneous rates of transition" from state j to state k at time t. Using the limit notion familiar from calculus, these are defined as

$$r_{jk}(t) = \lim_{\Delta t \to 0} \frac{p_{jk}(t, t + \Delta t)}{\Delta t}, \, j \neq k.$$

The authors then introduce the Markov assumption, which states that an individual's probability of occupying a particular state in the future is completely determined by his present state. This yields the familiar Markov property[1] of multiplicative transition probabilities (expression 4), which is then used to derive a number of properties of the model in continuous time (expressions 5-35).

Finally, the authors introduce their principle innovations. The first of these is the log-linear dependence of the instantaneous transition rates on exogenous characteristics of individuals (expression 36):

$$\ln r_{jk} = \theta_{jk} \, x.$$

The second is different parameters for this relation during each of several periods (expression 37):

$$\ln r_{jkp} = \theta_{jkp} \, Z_p,$$

where p denotes time periods and Z_p the exogenous variables for each time period. The goal is to estimate values for the θ, and this is accomplished by maximum likelihood. The necessary expressions (38-42) conclude this section of the paper.

The second section follows up previous work by the authors, applying the model to evaluating the impact of the Seattle and Denver Income Maintenance Experiments on marital dissolution. Treatment status is defined according to the level of the income guarantee, and whether it is for three or five years. (SIME/DIME labor supply results using the tax rate as well as the guarantee level to define treatment status are reported in the papers by Keeley et al. and Tuma and Robins in Part II.) Both time-independent and time-dependent models are estimated, the latter involving four periods of one-half year each, with only the experimental effects permitted to vary. (Other exogenous variables include normal income, a site dummy, a previous AFDC dummy, number of children, a dummy for children under six, the woman's age, her wage rate, and her years of schooling.)

The results of fitting the time-independent model (Table 1) show significant and large experimental effects increasing the rate of marital dissolution, accompanied by much smaller, and generally insignificant experimental/control differences for the rates of marital formation and sample attrition. The time-varying model estimates (Table 2) show these effects to be due to a very large effect during the first six months of the program, followed by smaller but persistent effects for the successive 18 months.

The chapter closes by examining the overall fit to the data and comparing the model's properties with those of competing approaches. A generally strong case is made for the appropriateness and usefulness of these methods.

NOTE

1. The reader wishing to better understand the fundamentals of these models might well begin with Markov chains—Markov process models in discrete rather than continuous time, often applied to panel data. For relatively nontechnical introductions to these, see Kemeny et al., (1958) or Coleman (1964). A more technical treatment is provided by Kemeny and Snell (1960) and Breiman (1969). The latter is a particularly readable and attractive treatment of a wide variety of probabilistic situations and models. See Bishop et al. (1975: Chapter 7) for estimation and inference with Markov chain models.

REFERENCES

BISHOP, Y., S. FIENBERG, and P. HOLLAND (1975) Discrete Multivariate Analysis. Cambridge, MA: M.I.T.
BRIEMAN, L. (1969) Probability and Stochastic Processes: With a View Toward Applications. Boston: Houghton Mifflin.
COLEMAN, J. (1964) Introduction to Mathematical Sociology. Glencoe, IL: Free Press.
HANNAN, M. T., N. B. TUMA, and L. P. GROENEVELD (1978) "Income and independence effects on marital dissolution: results from the Seattle-Denver Income Maintenance Experiments." Amer. J. of Sociology 84: 611-633.
——— (1977) "Income and marital events: evidence from an income maintenance experiment." Amer. J. of Sociology 82: 1186-1211.
KEMENY, J. G. and J. L. SNELL (1960) Finite Markov Chains. Princeton, NJ: D. Van Nostrand.
KEMENY, J. G., H. MIRKIL, J. L. SNELL, and G. L. THOMPSON (1958) Finite Mathematical Structures. Englewood Cliffs, NJ: Prentice-Hall.

Dynamic Analysis of Event Histories

Nancy Brandon Tuma, Michael T. Hannan, and Lyle P. Groeneveld

There is wide interest among sociologists in the study of change but little reflection of this interest in sociological research methods. In this paper we consider the advantages of and procedures for dynamic analysis of event-history data—data giving the number, timing, and sequence of changes in a categorical dependent variable. We argue for grounding this analysis in a continuous-time stochastic model. This permits the data to be fully utilized; it also allows a unified treatment of the various outcomes analyzed in the many approaches that use only part of the information contained in such data. We focus on the familiar continuous-time Markov model, summarize its properties, report its implications for various outcomes, describe extensions to deal with population heterogeneity and time dependence, and outline a maximum-likelihood procedure for estimating the extended model from event-history data. The discussion is illustrated with an empirical analysis of the effects of an income-maintenance experiment on change in marital status. We conclude by contrasting event-history analysis with cross-sectional analysis, event-count analysis, and panel analysis. We find that event-history analysis has substantial advantages over the other approaches.

Though most sociologists profess an interest in social processes—how social behavior and social systems change over time—this interest is seldom reflected in their research. They usually examine relationships among phenomena at only one point in time. Even when temporal data are used, as in

[1] We gratefully acknowledge the research assistance of Helen Garrison, Beverly Lauwagie, Marlos Viana, and Barbara Warsavage, and the helpful comments of anonymous referees. We appreciate the continuing support and encouragement of Robert G. Spiegelman, director of the Center for the Study of Welfare Policy, SRI International. Part of the analytic work reported herein was supported by the National Institute of Education Grant no. NIE-G-76-0082. The rest of the analytic work and all empirical research reported herein was performed pursuant to contracts with the states of Washington and Colorado, prime contractors for the Department of Health, Education, and Welfare under contract nos. SRS-70-53 and HEW-100-89-0004, respectively. During the period of this research, Hannan was a fellow at the Center for Advanced Study in the Behavioral Sciences and was supported by National Science Foundation grant BNS76-22943-A01. The opinions expressed in the paper are those of the authors and should not be construed as representing the opinions or policies of the states of Washington or Colorado or any agency of the United States government.

experiments and panel studies, sociologists seldom study dynamics—the time paths of change. Instead, the focus is on change from one equilibrium level to another, as measured, for example, by pre- and postexperiment differences or by levels at successive waves of a panel.

To some extent professed interests and actual research diverge because data suitable for dynamic analysis are scarce. But opportunities to collect such data are often bypassed because investigators are uncertain how to utilize detailed information on change over time. We are struck particularly by the failure of social scientists to gather and analyze dynamically data on changes in categorical variables. We hope to stimulate interest in the collection and analysis of what we call event histories. An event history records dates of events that occur for some unit of analysis. Examples of events include changes in categorical variables describing individuals—such as marital status, employment status, health status, and membership in voluntary associations—as well as those applying to social collectivities—such as changes in political regimes and outbreaks of strikes, riots, and wars.

This paper has two main goals. We wish to show the value of dynamic analysis of event-history data for the sociological study of change in categorical variables. We also wish to describe in some detail a practical procedure for making full use of event-history data to answer the kinds of questions that interest social scientists.

Section I begins by noting the wide range of empirical analyses permitted by event-history data—including, of course, application of existing techniques for analyzing cross-sectional and panel data. We argue that the use of continuous-time stochastic models allows a unified treatment of the outcomes analyzed in these other approaches, and the full use of the information in event-history data. Thus we take the position that event-history analysis should be linked to an explicit mathematical model of the social process being studied. We focus on a familiar model, the continuous-time Markov model introduced into sociology by Coleman (1964). We summarize properties of the model and its implications for various outcomes. We also describe extensions of it to deal with population heterogeneity and time dependence; these extensions make the model much more useful for sociological research. Section I concludes with an outline of a maximum-likelihood procedure for using event-history data to estimate and test the extended model.

Section II gives an empirical illustration. This involves an elaboration of the analysis presented in Hannan, Tuma, and Groeneveld (1977) of the effects of an income-maintenance experiment on change in marital status. To illustrate the extension dealing with population heterogeneity, we report estimates of the effects of experimental treatments on rates of marriage, marital dissolution, and experimental attrition. To illustrate the extension dealing with time dependence, we report estimates of how treatment effects vary over the experimental period. We conclude by showing that the estimated model not only provides much more information about the process than do other procedures more familiar to sociologists but also fits the data well—at least as well as the alternative procedures.

Finally, in Section III we contrast dynamic analysis of event-history data with other kinds of analysis. In particular, we compare it with cross-sectional analysis (assuming the process is in equilibrium), event-count analysis, and panel analysis. We find that when event-history data can be obtained, the strategy and procedures that we advocate have substantial advantages over these three alternatives.

A paper of this sort builds on a number of intellectual traditions and on contributions of previous authors. Our debt to classical mathematical sociology is obvious in our discussion of this model and its implications. Readers familiar with the causal-modeling (or structural equations) tradition should discern its influence on our approach to modeling causal structure and time dependence. In a companion paper (Tuma and Hannan 1978), we have sketched the genealogy of our statistical approach and have briefly reviewed some alternative estimation strategies.

I. CHOICE OF A MODEL

Any data set permits a variety of empirical analyses. When we analyze event histories, we have even more options than usual. This is seen clearly in the various dependent variables that can be selected from event histories. For example, consider how different investigators interested in marital stability might utilize marital histories to study changes in marital status. Some would study the probability of at least one marital dissolution within some fixed period. Others might study the average length of marriage. Others might choose to study the number of marital events during a fixed period. And some might analyze changes in the proportion of a population that is married.

What are we to make of the richness of the information contained in event histories? We certainly have no objection to different analysts focusing on different aspects of a problem. However, the various outcomes listed above are not independent. Moreover, none of them conveys all the information contained in an event history. We believe that much is gained from designing analyses that utilize all the information in an event history, that is, which use information on the number, sequence, and timing of events.

Our solution to this problem—not necessarily the only solution[2]—rests upon the recognition that we can infer each of the dependent variables listed earlier if we can describe each person's status at every moment in time.

---

[2] A simultaneous linear equations model might appear to be one alternative. However, the same exogenous variables appear in every equation, leading to underidentification of the structural parameters.

More generally, we can unify the analysis of various outcomes that can be extracted from event histories by building a model that describes the state of the categorical variable at every moment in time. This strategy has the advantage of parsimony—one model replaces several. It also has the advantage of dealing with the interdependence among the various outcomes. Of course, we expect to pay a price for such analytic power. In particular, we must make some restrictive assumptions about the process generating the events. Because of these assumptions, our model may fit sample data less well for any particular outcome at any arbitrary time than a model designed specifically to account for that outcome. After we have described our model and estimation procedure, we return to this issue as part of an extended empirical illustration of our methodology.

A Markov Model of Events

To use event histories fully, we must formulate an explicit model of the process generating the events. Because the model must account for states of categorical variables at every moment in time, and because the events can occur at any time, we choose continuous-time models. Exactly what type of model should be used depends on the substantive application; a variety of continuous-time models could be employed with the general methodology we propose. Here we concentrate on one type of model: a finite-state, continuous-time Markov model. We begin by stating briefly the formal assumptions of this model.[3]

Let $Y(t)$ be a random variable denoting the state of the categorical variable occupied by a member of a homogeneous population at time t. The set of all possible values of $Y(t)$ is called the state space of the process; this is assumed to be finite. Let $p_{jk}(u, t)$ represent the probability that someone in state j at time u is in state k at time t, $u < t$:

$$p_{jk}(u, t) = \Pr[Y(t) = k \mid Y(u) = j], \tag{1}$$

and let $P(u, t)$ denote the matrix of these transition probabilities, $P(u, t) = \|p_{jk}(u, t)\|$. For example, suppose that $j = k = 2 = $ married; then $p_{22}(u, t)$ stands for the probability that those married at time u are also married at time t.

Next we define $r_{jk}(t)$ as the instantaneous rate of transition from state j to state k at time t. The transition rate $r_{jk}(t)$ is the limit, as Δt approaches zero, of the probability of a change from j to k between t and $t + \Delta t$, per unit of time:

$$r_{jk}(t) = \lim_{\Delta t \to 0} \frac{p_{jk}(t, t + \Delta t)}{\Delta t}, \quad j \neq k. \tag{2}$$

---

[3] For a more thorough discussion, see Cox and Miller 1965, Feller 1968, Karlin and Taylor. 1975, or any other standard text on stochastic processes.

The rate of leaving state j at time t, $r_j(t)$, is as follows:

$$r_j(t) = \sum_{\substack{k \\ k \neq j}} r_{jk}(t) . \tag{3}$$

By the Markov assumption, the Chapman-Kolmogorov identity holds:

$$P(v, t) = P(v, u)P(u, t) \quad v \leq u \leq t . \tag{4}$$

Given this, and the usual additional assumptions (continuity, probabilities ranging between 0 and 1, etc.),[4] it can then be shown that

$$\frac{dP(u, t)}{dt} = P(u, t)R(t) , \tag{5}$$

where R is a matrix in which the j–kth off-diagonal element is the transition rate, $r_{jk}(t)$, and the jth diagonal element is the negative of the rate of leaving, $-r_j(t)$. In the time-independent case, $R(t) = R$, equation (5) has the solution:

$$P(u, t) = \sum_{m=0}^{\infty} \frac{R^m(t - u)^m}{m!} = e^{(t-u)R} , \tag{6}$$

where a matrix raised to the zero power is defined to equal the identity matrix I (so $R^0 = I$).

The first task in using such a model is specification of the state space, that is, the exhaustive and mutually exclusive set of discrete values of $Y(t)$. For example, in our analysis of the effects of income-maintenance treatments on marital stability (see Section II) the relevant states of $Y(t)$ are 1 (not married), 2 (married), and 3 (attrited). State 3 includes those who refuse to participate in the study, cannot be located, die, or emigrate outside the continental United States. Attrition is an absorbing state; it cannot be left. Thus R has the form:

$$R = \left\| \begin{array}{ccc} -r_1 & r_{12} & r_{13} \\ r_{21} & -r_2 & r_{23} \\ 0 & 0 & 0 \end{array} \right\| . \tag{7}$$

Although the elements of $P(u, t)$ cannot be written as explicit functions of the transition rates for a general matrix R, they can be so expressed when R has the form shown in (7). In particular, it can be shown that $P(u, t)$ has the elements:[5]

$$p_{jj}(u, t) = \frac{1}{(\lambda_1 - \lambda_2)} [(r_k + \lambda_1)e^{\lambda_1(t-u)} - (r_k + \lambda_2)e^{\lambda_2(t-u)}] , \tag{8}$$

---

[4] Mathematically these assumptions can be expressed as: $0 \leq p_{jk}(u, t) \leq 1$; $\Sigma_k p_{jk}(u, t) = 1$; $P(t, t) = I$.

[5] Eqq. (8) through (12) do not apply to a general three-state model, i.e., one in which r_{31} and r_{32} are greater than zero.

$$p_{jk}(u, t) = \frac{r_{jk}}{(\lambda_1 - \lambda_2)} [e^{\lambda_1(t-u)} - e^{\lambda_2(t-u)}],$$ (9)

$$p_{j3}(u, t) = 1 + \frac{1}{(\lambda_1 - \lambda_2)} [(r_{j3} + \lambda_2)e^{\lambda_1(t-u)} - (r_{j3} + \lambda_1)e^{\lambda_2(t-u)}],$$ (10)

$$p_{31}(u, t) = p_{32}(u, t) = 0,$$ (11)

$$p_{33}(u, t) = 1,$$ (12)

where $j = 1$ or 2, $k = 3 - j$, $\lambda_1 \neq \lambda_2$, and

$$\lambda_1 = -[r_1 + r_2 + \sqrt{(r_1 - r_2)^2 + 4r_{12}r_{21}}]/2,$$ (13)

$$\lambda_2 = -[r_1 + r_2 - \sqrt{(r_1 - r_2)^2 + 4r_{12}r_{21}}]/2.$$ (14)

The explicit inclusion of attrition as a state is an important feature of our application of a Markov model. All too frequently investigators with temporal data analyze only the fraction of the original sample that has not been lost through attrition by the time of some later measurement. This procedure implicitly assumes that attrition has no impact on the assessment of the effects of causal variables. By explicitly including attrition as a state, we avoid this highly dubious assumption. However, it is still necessary to assume that the same model applies both to those lost through attrition and to those who are not. This assumption could be incorrect but cannot be tested without a follow-up study of marital status changes among those who did not remain in the active sample.

The inclusion of attrition as a state complicates considerably both the derivation of equations and our discussion. For this reason, parts of our discussion are based on the two-state model in which there is no attrition:

$$R = \begin{Vmatrix} -r_1 & r_{12} \\ r_{21} & -r_2 \end{Vmatrix}.$$ (15)

Then we obtain

$$p_{jk}(u, t) = 1 - p_{jj}(u, t) = \frac{r_{jk}}{r_{12} + r_{21}} [1 - e^{-(r_{12}+r_{21})(t-u)}]$$ (16)

for $j, k = 1, 2$ and $j \neq k$.

Implications of the Model

We noted earlier that use of such a continuous-time stochastic model lets us derive implications about a variety of observable variables. In this section we show this by discussing a number of well-known results about Markov models.

Time between transitions.—It is widely known that for a Markov model the length of time between transitions has an exponential distribution whose parameter depends on the transition rates (see, e.g., Breiman 1969, chap. 7). In particular, let $F_j(t|u)$ represent the probability of a transition from state j before time t, given that state j is occupied at time u. $F_j(t|u)$ is usually called the cumulative probability distribution function or simply the probability distribution function. We can show that for models in which $R(t) = R$,

$$F_j(t|u) = 1 - e^{-(t-u)r_j} . \qquad (17)$$

Later we use the definition that

$$G_j(t|u) = 1 - F_j(t|u) . \qquad (18)$$

$G_j(t|u)$ is often called the survivor function because it gives the probability that a unit in state j at time u remains (or survives) in state j until time t. For models in which $R(t) = R$,

$$G_j(t|u) = e^{-(t-u)r_j} = e^{-(t-u)[\Sigma_k \ r_{jk}]} . \qquad (19)$$

This says, for example, that the probability that a marriage existing at time u survives until a later time t declines exponentially as the length of the interval $(t - u)$ increases. This monotonic decline occurs because it becomes increasingly likely as time t increases that either the marriage breaks up or the couple drops from the experiment.

We also use the probability density function:

$$f_j(t|u) = \frac{dF_j(t|u)}{dt} = \frac{-dG_j(t|u)}{dt} . \qquad (20)$$

It can be shown that in general

$$f_j(t|u) = r_j(t)G_j(t|u) . \qquad (21)$$

For the particular case in which $R(t) = R$, that is, in which the transition rates are constant over time,

$$f_j(t|u) = r_j e^{-(t-u)r_j} . \qquad (22)$$

The probability of a change from state j to some other state between t and $(t + dt)$ is approximately equal to $f_j(t|u)dt$. Equation (22) shows that this probability initially (i.e., at $[t - u] = 0$) equals r_j and declines exponentially as the length of the interval $(t - u)$ increases. In other words, the probability of leaving a state varies over time even when transition rates are constant. This is one of the main advantages of modeling social processes in terms of transition rates instead of probabilities of change.

The average duration of state occupancies (e.g., expected duration of marriages and of the intervals between marriages) when $R(t) = R$ is easily shown to be

$$E(t - u) = 1/r_j , \qquad (23)$$

where u and t denote the times of entry and exit, respectively, from state j.

Given that a change occurs at time t, r_{jk}/r_j is the conditional probability that k is the destination. Thus, with this model, we can account for both the probability of at least one change within any specified time interval and the conditional probability that a change involves movement into some specified state.

State probabilities.—We can also use the model to find the unconditional probability of being in any specified state at any point in time (e.g., the probability of being married at any specified time). Let $p_k(t)$ denote the unconditional probability of being in state k at time t, and $p(t)$ represent a row vector giving the probability distribution among the states at time t. It is easy to see that

$$p_k(t) = \sum_j p_j(u) p_{jk}(u, t) , \tag{24}$$

or

$$p(t) = p(u) P(u, t) . \tag{25}$$

Usually we are interested in $p(t)$ when $p(u) = p(0)$, the distribution at the start of the process.

For simplicity we begin by considering the two-state model, for example, for the study of marital stability when there is no attrition. Inserting equation (16) into (24), we obtain:

$$p_1(t) = p_1(0) e^{-(r_{12}+r_{21})t} + \frac{r_{21}}{r_{12} + r_{21}} [1 - e^{-(r_{12}+r_{21})t}] , \tag{26}$$

$$p_2(t) = p_2(0) e^{-(r_{12}+r_{21})t} + \frac{r_{12}}{r_{12} + r_{21}} [1 - e^{-(r_{12}+r_{21})t}] . \tag{27}$$

As time t becomes very large, $p_j(t)$ approaches a steady-state (or equilibrium) value: $p_1(\infty) = r_{21}/(r_{12} + r_{21})$, $p_2(\infty) = r_{12}/(r_{12} + r_{21})$. So $p_j(t)$ is a weighted average of the initial proportion in state j and the steady-state probability in state j. The weight given to $p_j(0)$ declines exponentially over time, while the weight given to the steady-state proportion in state j increases over time until it reaches one.

For the three-state model, for example, for the study of marital stability when there is attrition, we find (by substituting equations [8] through [12] into [24]) that:

$$p_1(t) = (e^{\lambda_2 t}\{(r_2 + \lambda_2)p_1(0) + r_{21}[1 - p_1(0)]\}$$
$$- e^{\lambda_1 t}\{(r_2 + \lambda_1)p_1(0) + r_{21}[1 - p_1(0)]\})/(\lambda_2 - \lambda_1) , \tag{28}$$

$$p_2(t) = (e^{\lambda_2 t}\{(r_1 + \lambda_2)[1 - p_1(0)] + r_{12}p_1(0)\}$$
$$- e^{\lambda_1 t}\{(r_1 + \lambda_1)[1 - p_1(0)] + r_{12}p_1(0)\})/(\lambda_2 - \lambda_1) , \tag{29}$$

$$p_3(t) = 1 + (e^{\lambda_2 t}\{\lambda_1 + r_{13}p_1(0) + r_{23}[1 - p_1(0)]\}$$

$$- e^{\lambda_1 t}\{\lambda_2 + r_{13}p_1(0) + r_{23}[1 - p_1(0)]\})/(\lambda_2 - \lambda_1) , \qquad (30)$$

where λ_1 and λ_2 are given by (13) and (14), respectively. It is important to emphasize that $r_1 = r_{12} + r_{13}$, $r_2 = r_{21} + r_{23}$ and that λ_1 and λ_2 depend on r_1 and r_2. Thus each of the above equations depends on the attrition rates, r_{13} and r_{23}.

Expected number of events.—Finally, we can derive relationships between the fundamental parameters of the model and the expected number of events that occur in any interval of time. This requires extension of the ordinary Poisson model of the number of events in a time interval, since the Poisson model assumes that only one kind of event can occur. Let $n_{jk}(0, t)$ denote the number of changes to state k between times 0 and t when state j is occupied at time 0, $0 \leq t$. For example, $n_{22}(0, t)$ stands for the number of marriages formed before t for a person who is married at time 0. It can be shown that for the two-state model (in which there is no attrition):

$$E[n_{jj}(0, t)] = \frac{r_{12}r_{21}t}{(r_{12} + r_{21})} + \frac{r_{12}r_{21}}{(r_{12} + r_{21})^2} [e^{-t(r_{12}+r_{21})} - 1] , \qquad (31)$$

$$E[n_{jk}(0, t)] = \frac{r_{12}r_{21}t}{(r_{12} + r_{21})} - \frac{r_{jk}^2}{(r_{12} + r_{21})^2} [e^{-t(r_{12}+r_{21})} - 1] , \qquad (32)$$

where $j, k = 1, 2$ and $j \neq k$. For the three-state model we find that:

$$E[n_{jj}(0, t)] = \frac{r_{12}r_{21}}{(\lambda_1 - \lambda_2)} \left[\frac{(1 - e^{\lambda_1 t})}{\lambda_1} - \frac{(1 - e^{\lambda_2 t})}{\lambda_2} \right] , \qquad (33)$$

$$E[n_{jk}(0, t)] = \frac{r_{jk}}{(\lambda_1 - \lambda_2)} \left[\frac{(r_k + \lambda_2)(1 - e^{\lambda_2 t})}{\lambda_2} - \frac{(r_k + \lambda_1)(1 - e^{\lambda_1 t})}{\lambda_1} \right] , \qquad (34)$$

$$E[n_{j3}(0, t)] = \frac{1}{(\lambda_1 - \lambda_2)} \left[\frac{(r_{jk}r_{k3} + r_{j3}r_k + r_{j3}\lambda_2)(1 - e^{\lambda_2 t})}{\lambda_2} \right.$$

$$\left. - \frac{(r_{jk}r_{k3} + r_{j3}r_k + r_{j3}\lambda_1)(1 - e^{\lambda_1 t})}{\lambda_1} \right] , \qquad (35)$$

where $j, k = 1, 2$ and $j \neq k$.

The point we wish to emphasize is that these diverse observable measures of event histories are all explicit functions of the rates that define the Markov model. It is not necessary that each of these relationships be estimated separately. Any one of them provides an approach to estimation. Once the rates have been estimated, the remaining quantities can be calculated using these functions. The empirical analysis in Section II uses them in evaluating the fit of our model.

Two Extensions of the Model

Markov models have been used quite often by sociologists in the past 20 years or so. In the simple form discussed above, these models have invariably failed to fit the data. Sociologists' efforts to increase realism and improve fit have concentrated on modification of two assumptions of the simple Markov model: time-dependence (see, e.g., Mayer 1972; Sørensen 1975; Tuma 1976) and population homogeneity (see, e.g., Blumen, Kogan, and McCarthy 1955; Coleman 1964, 1973; Land 1971; McFarland 1970; Spilerman 1972a, 1972b; Tuma 1976). These sorts of extensions are straightforward in the strategy we propose.

Population heterogeneity.—To this point we have assumed that the units studied are homogeneous, in other words, that their behavior is governed by the same, constant transition rates. Instead, following Coleman (1964, 1973) and Tuma (1976), we may assume that the same, constant rates only govern the behavior of units with identical values on a set of observable, exogenous variables. In other words, we may establish relationships between observable variables, denoted by x, and the rates of change in categorical variables. The main sociological interest in most analyses of event histories lies in testing hypotheses concerning the effects of exogenous variables on rates. For example, in analyses of marital histories produced by the income-maintenance experiments, we concentrate on testing hypotheses about effects of experimental treatments on rates of marital dissolution and remarriage.

To introduce such causal relationships, we must state an explicit dependence of the unobservable rates on the observable variables. In our empirical analysis, we assume a log-linear relationship between each transition rate and x:[6]

$$\ln r_{jk} = \theta_{jk} x , \quad \text{for all } j \text{ and } k, \; j \neq k , \tag{36}$$

where θ_{jk} represents a vector of parameters to be estimated. The log-linear relationship constrains r_{jk} to be positive for each individual, whatever the value of x, in accord with equation (2); we find that it usually fits data better than a linear relationship. We also assume that r_{jk} is finite for all j and k and for all individuals.

Time-dependence.—We have assumed to this point that the rates are con-

---

[6] As mentioned by an anonymous referee, we could have chosen to model r_j and m_{jk} ($= r_{jk}/r_j$) rather than r_{jk} as functions of exogenous variables. The choice involves a decision about the substantive nature of the process; it is not just a methodological issue. The approach suggested by the referee, which has also been advocated by Tuma (1976) and by Singer and Spilerman (1974), is appropriate when the decision to leave the current state and the choice of a destination are separate or sequential. In the example used in this paper, it seems reasonable to think that the decision to leave a state and the choice of a destination are not separate; therefore, we have not adopted this other approach. For other social processes it may, indeed, be preferable to model r_j and m_{jk} separately. The method of estimation and accompanying software described below can readily be used to estimate $r_j = e^{\alpha x}$ from data on the dates of entering and leaving state j.

stant over time. Sociologists are accustomed to thinking about population heterogeneity (i.e., causal relationships) but have not devoted much attention to issues involving time dependence of effects, that is, the manner in which causal relationships change over time. However, sometimes theory indicates that rates of change are some specific function of time. For example, Sørensen (1975) has argued that rates of leaving a job are exponentially declining functions of labor-force experience, while Tuma (1976) has specified a model in which rates of job leaving are second-order polynomials in duration in the job. Such parametric forms of time dependence may be accommodated without difficulty in the strategy we discuss.

Sometimes we do not have any a priori hypothesis concerning time dependence. In an experiment, we might expect transition rates during an initial adjustment period to differ from rates later on but be unsure whether initial rates should be larger or smaller than later rates. In these circumstances we can define a set of time periods and allow the effects of experimental variables to vary freely from period to period while remaining constant within each period. In this situation the time periods may be arbitrary, a disadvantage of this approach. However, in other situations, we may have some idea about points on the time axis when rates may change in some way. For example, rates of collective violence may change when there is a change in the political regime or during periods of warfare.

Mathematically stated, a model in which rates vary from one time period to another is:

$$\ln r_{jkp} = \theta_{jkp} z_p, \qquad \tau_{p-1} \leq t < \tau_p, \qquad (37)$$

where τ_p is the last moment in period p, $\tau_0 = 0$ is the starting time, z_p is a vector of exogenous variables affecting the rate in period p, and θ_{jkp} is a vector of parameters giving effects on r_{jkp} in period p. We illustrate the use of a model similar to this one below.

Estimation and Testing

The linear structural equations models with which sociologists have become quite familiar in recent years have made common the view that the estimation equation is identical to the model. But this is not necessarily the case. The equations relating observable outcomes (average duration, number of events, etc.) to the rates are all possible candidates for estimation equations, but they are not equally promising because they differ in complexity.

Building upon the work of Bartholomew (1957) and Albert (1962), we form maximum-likelihood estimators of rates (and of causal effects on rates) using data on the dates and kind of events. This approach offers a number of advantages in the present circumstances. First, maximum-likelihood estimators have good properties for large samples under fairly general conditions. Second, maximum-likelihood estimators retain their good properties under any monotonic transformation. Thus one can use maximum-likelihood estimators of rates to form maximum-likelihood estimators for expected durations and other monotonic functions of rates. Third, maximum-likelihood procedures permit a satisfactory solution of what is called the censoring problem. Data collected during an observation period too short to produce a change for every case are said to be censored, and errors of inference are likely if appropriate measures for dealing with censoring are not adopted (Tuma and Hannan 1978).

Assuming independent observations on the N different cases (units) being analyzed, we can write a likelihood function that uses all information in event histories—namely, the number, timing, and sequence of events. This information can be represented by the following kinds of variables: w_{mi} (a dummy variable that equals unity if case i's mth event occurs in the observation period), t_{mi} (the time of case i's mth event if $w_{mi} = 1$ and the time that case i is last observed if $w_{mi} = 0$), and v_{mji} (a dummy variable that equals unity if case i's mth event is observed and consists of a change to state j and otherwise equals zero). We define t_{0i} as the start of the observation period on case i and v_{0ji} as unity if state j is occupied by i at t_{0i} and otherwise as zero. Note that

$$\sum_{m=1}^{\infty} w_{mi}$$

equals the total *number* of events observed to occur to case i, while the t_{mi}'s are the *times* at which these events occur and the v_{mji}'s indicate the *sequence* of events.

For simplicity we begin with the likelihood equation that uses information on the first event only:

$$\mathcal{L} = \prod_{i=1}^{N} \prod_{j=1}^{n} \left\{ [G_j(t_1 | t_0, x)]^{(1-w_1)v_{0j}} \cdot [f_j(t_1 | t_0, x)]^{w_1 v_{0j}} \right.$$

$$\left. \cdot \prod_{k=1}^{n} [r_{jk}(x)/r_j(x)]^{-w_1 v_{0j} v_{1k}} \right\}, \tag{38}$$

where N is the number of cases, n is the number of states, and the subscript i on variables (namely, w_{mi}, t_{mi}, v_{mji}, and x_i) has been suppressed for clarity. The first term (in brackets), the survivor function, gives the probability that the first event has not occurred by time t_1 (see eq. [18]). Since any number raised to the zero power equals unity, the first term differs from unity only for those cases that have *not* experienced a first event ($w_1 = 0$) *and* are in state j at time t_0 ($v_{0j} = 1$). The second term is the probability density that the first event occurs at time t_1 (see eq. [20]). This term differs from unity only for those cases that have experienced at least one event ($w_1 = 1$) and are in state j at time t_0 ($v_{0j} = 1$). The third term is the probability that the first event consists of a move to state k, given that state j is left. This term differs from unity only for those cases that have experienced at least one event ($w_1 = 1$), that are in state j at time t_0 ($v_{0j} = 1$), and whose first event consists of a move to state k ($v_{1k} = 1$).

Equation (38) can be written more simply by substituting (21) into (38) and by then collecting terms:

$$\mathcal{L} = \prod_{i=1}^{N} \prod_{j=1}^{n} \left\{ [G_j(t_1 | t_0, x)]^{v_{0j}} \cdot \prod_{k=1}^{n} [r_{jk}(x)]^{w_1 v_{0j} v_{1k}} \right\}. \tag{39}$$

When $R(t) = R$, so that (19) holds, we can simplify this still more:

$$\mathcal{L} = \prod_{i=1}^{N} \prod_{j=1}^{n} \left\{ \prod_{k=1}^{n} [e^{-(t_1-t_0) r_{jk}(x)}]^{v_{0j}} \right\} \cdot \left\{ \prod_{k=1}^{n} [r_{jk}(x)]^{w_1 v_{0j} v_{1k}} \right\}, \tag{40}$$

$$\mathcal{L} = \prod_{j=1}^{n} \prod_{k=1}^{n} \left\{ \prod_{i=1}^{N} [e^{-(t_1-t_0) r_{jk}(x)}]^{v_{0j}} \cdot [r_{jk}(x)]^{w_1 v_{0j} v_{1k}} \right\}.$$

Note that the term in braces in (40) above does not depend on $r_{j'k'}$ where $j' \neq j$ and $k' \neq k$. Therefore, the maximum-likelihood estimates of a given r_{jk}—or of the effects of causal variables on r_{jk} as in (36)—can be obtained by maximizing the term in braces for that particular j and k. This fact is quite important in practice. It means that we can estimate selected transition rates without having data on *all* kinds of transitions. To estimate r_{jk}, we need data only on the times of all first events (t_1) for cases originally in state j ($v_{0j} = 1$) and on the outcome of first events (the value of v_{1k}). This means we can concentrate data collection and analysis on units originally in states of particular theoretical interest and can ignore events occurring to other units—unless we wish to model or predict the overall evolution of the entire process.

Equations (38) through (40) can be generalized in a straightforward way to the situation in which data on all observed events (and not just the first) are used in the estimation procedure. We give the equations corresponding to (38) and (40) only, leaving the intermediary equation to be supplied by the interested reader:

$$\mathcal{L} = \prod_{i=1}^{N} \prod_{m=1}^{\infty} \prod_{j=1}^{n} \left\{ [G_j(t_m | t_{m-1}, x)]^{(1-w_m) v_{m-1,j}} \right.$$

$$\cdot [f_j(t_m | t_{m-1}, x)]^{w_m v_{m-1,j}} \tag{41}$$

$$\left. \cdot \prod_{k=1}^{n} [r_{jk}(x)/r_j(x)]^{w_m v_{m-1,j} v_{mk}} \right\}.$$

When $R(t) = R$, this simplifies to:

$$\mathcal{L} = \prod_{j=1}^{n} \prod_{k=1}^{n} \prod_{m=1}^{\infty} \prod_{i=1}^{N} \left\{ [e^{-(t_m - t_{m-1})r_{jk}(x)}]^{v_{m-1,i}} \cdot [r_{jk}(x)]^{w_{mv} \, m-1, i^{v_{mk}}} \right\} . \quad (42)$$

Maximum-likelihood estimators of the parameters are found by maximizing $\mathcal{L}$ (or its logarithm).[7] The optimal asymptotic properties of maximum-likelihood estimators (consistency, asymptotic normality) are well known (e.g., see Dhrymes 1970). There is also evidence (Tuma and Hannan 1978) that the properties of the estimators obtained from (40) remain quite good even in small samples and with a high degree of censoring (i.e., when the mean of number of events is low).

A likelihood ratio test can be used to test nested models. Let $\mathcal{L}_\Omega$ be the likelihood for a model Ω with $q + s$ estimated parameters and $\mathcal{L}_\omega$ be the likelihood for the nested model ω that has s parameters constrained (usually to equal zero) and q parameters estimated. The likelihood ratio λ is defined to equal $[\max (\mathcal{L}_\omega)/\max (\mathcal{L}_\Omega)]$. Asymptotically $-2 \ln \lambda$ has a χ^2 distribution with q degrees of freedom, permitting us to test the fit of the model ω relative to the model Ω. Furthermore, it is possible to perform tests on the coefficients of individual variables using the estimated covariance matrix of the parameters (the inverse of the matrix of second derivatives of the natural logarithm of $\mathcal{L}$ with respect to the parameters). The square root of the variance of a parameter gives its estimated standard error, which can then be used in a standard fashion to calculate a t-statistic (or F-ratio) that tests whether the parameter differs from its value in the null hypothesis.

II. AN APPLICATION

To illustrate the models and methods discussed above we apply them to data on white women during the first two years of the Seattle and Denver Income-Maintenance Experiments (SIME/DIME). We combine data from Seattle and Denver.[8]

We have discussed the experimental design, nature of the sample, definitions of variables, and so forth earlier (Hannan, Tuma, and Groeneveld 1976, 1977). Here we use similar data that cover a period of 24 months instead of 18. We focus on estimating the effects of the three levels of income support (or guarantee) and the length of the treatment (three or five years). Because the design involved stratified random assignment to treatments, we include a number of preexperimental variables in the models: dummy variables representing six normal income categories, a site dummy

---

[7] A FORTRAN computer program called RATE has been developed to find the maximum-likelihood estimates of parameters in eqq. (36), (37), and (43), among others. Written documentation, test data, and test output are also available. For information, write the first author.

[8] For our definitions of marriage and marital dissolution, see Hannan et al. 1977.

(1 = Denver), a dummy variable for previous AFDC experience, number of children, a dummy variable for having any children under six, the woman's age, her wage rate, and her years of schooling.

Though other causal variables, as well as the experimental treatments, may have different effects on rates of events in different time periods, we are interested primarily in the time dependence of treatment effects. There are a variety of reasons for expecting the effects of experimental treatments to vary over the experimental period. Reasons for treatment effects to be smaller initially than later on include the possibilities that subjects do not fully understand the treatments at first and that they may need to search for an opportunity to change state (e.g., to find a marital partner). Reasons for treatment effects to be larger initially than later on include the possibility that the treatments become less salient as the end of the experiment approaches and the possibility that the treatments improve opportunities for a change for some fraction of subjects on the verge of changing marital status before the experiment. Indirect treatment effects (e.g., effects of treatments on work behavior, which in turn affect marital status) also can cause treatment effects to vary over time, but it cannot be predicted a priori whether indirect effects enhance or dampen the initial response. Our inability to predict the shape of the pattern of time variation is, of course, the reason for subdividing the observation period and letting rates vary from one period to another.

In the time-dependent models we began by using four time periods with end points of 0.5, 1.0, 1.5, and 2.0 years after the start of the experiment. These represented a compromise between two conflicting goals. First, we wanted the number of observed events per period to be large so that the standard errors of parameters would be comparatively small. Second, we wanted to have a large number of time periods so that we could detect the shape of the pattern of time variation (which according to our reasoning might decrease over time, rise over time, or rise and then decrease, etc.)

To improve the efficiency of estimation of effects still further, we estimated an equation that allowed treatment effects, but not the effects of other causal variables, to vary over time. This model can be represented as follows:

$$\ln r_{jkp} = \phi_{jk} x + \theta_{jkp} z_p, \qquad \tau_{p-1} \leq t < \tau_p, \qquad (43)$$

where x is the vector of other causal variables, z_p is a vector of experimental treatment variables, and p refers to one of P periods.

There is a constant term in ϕ_{jk} and each θ_{jkp}; however, for each transition j to k, only P of these $P + 1$ constants can be identified. Therefore, to achieve identification we arbitrarily constrain one of them to be zero.[9] The

[9] The same problem arises in regression analysis when dummy variables are used to represent categorical variables. One category must be omitted to achieve identification; the one chosen affects the interpretation of coefficients of the included dummy variables but does not affect predictions of the dependent variable.

P constants permit the rate of the control group to vary from one time period to another, even though the effects of other causal variables may not.[10]

The method of maximum likelihood can be used to estimate parameters in equation (43). The likelihood equation resembles (39) except that there is a different expression for the survivor function and each transition rate has an additional subscript p to indicate the time period to which it applies (for details, see the Appendix). In other respects procedures for estimating and testing the model and the effects of individual variables are the same as for a model with transition rates that are constant over time.

Results of the estimation could be reported in many different ways. Because the effect of a variable on the rate itself is of more interest than the effect on the log of the rate, we report the antilog of estimates $\hat{\theta}$. The antilog indicates the multiplier of the rate for a unit increase in a variable. For dummy variables, which we use to represent experimental treatments, the antilog of the coefficient of the variable is the ratio of the rate for those whose value on the dummy variable is unity to the rate for those in the omitted category. For example, if for some experimental treatment, $e^\theta = 2$, where θ is the coefficient of the dummy variable representing the experimental treatment, then the rate for those on the treatment is twice the rate for those in the control group. The percentage change in the rate for an experimental treatment relative to the rate for those in the control group is just $100\ (e^\theta - 1)$. Thus, if $e^\theta = 2$, the percentage change in the rate for this treatment relative to the rate for the control group is 100%.

Results for Time-independent Models

Table 1 gives the results for time-independent models of rates of marital status change and attrition. We have discussed similar results and their interpretation at length previously (Hannan et al. 1977; Tuma, Groeneveld, and Hannan 1976).[11] Here we comment briefly, concentrating on the effects of the support levels.

All four models improve significantly (at the .001 level) on a constant rate model. Inclusion of the set of experimental treatments improves significantly on a model that includes only the other causal variables in the case of the marital dissolution rate (.001 level), the attrition rate of married women (.10 level), and the attrition rate of unmarried women (.05 level), but not in the case of the remarriage rate.

Women in each support group have higher marital dissolution rates than women in the control group who are comparable in terms of values of other causal variables. Effects of the support levels are large (ranging from a

[10] The rate of the control group may vary over time because of aging, secular trends, etc.

[11] Although these papers do not explicitly mention attrition as a third state, the actual estimation procedures were the same as those reported here.

TABLE 1

EFFECTS OF VARIABLES ON RATES OF MARITAL STATUS CHANGE AND ATTRITION OF WHITE WOMEN: TIME-INDEPENDENT MODEL[a]

Variables	Marital Dissolution	Attrition of Married Women	Marital Formation	Attrition of Unmarried Women
Support level $3,800	2.29***	1.24	1.27	.86
Support level $4,800	2.06***	.96	1.08	.40**
Support level $5,600	1.57	.53	.80	.64
Three-year program	.86	.79	1.01	.91
Normal income levels ($):				
0–999	3.80***	2.52*	.31**	.82
1,000–2,999	2.71***	1.57	.48	.64
3,000–4,999	2.21***	.89	.53	.51
5,000–6,999	1.88**	1.09	.54	.60
7,000–8,999	1.21	1.06	.62	.65
Unclassified	4.13***	1.26	.64	1.12
One if on AFDC before enrollment	1.54**	.85	1.09	.81
One if any children under 6 yr.	.97	1.10	.83	.62*
Children (N)	.88**	.93	1.20**	1.01
Woman's age (yr.)	.97***	1.00	.91***	.95***
Woman's education (yr.)	.97	.95	1.02	.98
Woman's wage ($/hr.)	1.33**	1.41**	1.05	1.00
One if Denver	.90	1.85***	.92	1.79**
Constant	.10***	.04***	2.60	.73
N	1376	1376	914	914
Likelihood ratio test for model (17 df)	107.55***	26.52*	97.87***	32.16**
Likelihood ratio test for experimental effects (4 df)	18.78***	8.03*	2.91	9.54**

[a] Coefficients are the multipliers of the rate for a unit change in a variable, i.e., exp (θ). A coefficient of 1.0 means the variable has no effect.

* $.10 \geq P > .05$.

** $.05 \geq P > .01$.

*** $.01 \geq P$.

57% to 129% increase in the rate relative to comparable controls) and statistically significant at the .01 level, except for the highest support.

As expected, attrition rates among those with a financial treatment are lower than those among comparable controls, except in the case of married women on the low support. However, there is no clear pattern to the effects of the different support levels on attrition, and none of the individual coefficients is significant.

Results for the Time-dependent Models

We have estimated time-dependent (four-period) models of rates of dissolution, remarriage, and attrition (see Tuma, Hannan, and Groeneveld [1977] for a more detailed discussion). The results of these analyses indicated that experimental effects on attrition rates did not vary significantly over time or in any patterned way. Experimental effects on the remarriage rate were significant at the .10 level, but there was no particular pattern to these effects, suggesting that they resulted from chance alone. However, experimental effects on the dissolution rate had a striking pattern, so we focus on these.

Table 2 shows results of the experimental effects on the dissolution rate when the total observation period (24 months) is treated as a single period, four six-month periods, and two periods (the first six months and the remaining 18 months). In all three models inclusion of the set of experimental treatments improves significantly on a model that contains only the other causal variables.

Support level effects over the four periods are plotted in figure 1. The plot shows that all three support levels produce an exceptionally large increase in the rate during the first half-year of the experiment. Except for the $5,600 support level in the second half-year, effects of the support levels in periods two through four are positive and show no clear pattern of variation over time. This suggests that (1) the support levels have transitory effects on dissolution rates of white women that subside after six months, but (2) they also have nontransitory positive effects on the dissolution rate. Furthermore, the effect of each support level in the first six-month period relative to its effect in each subsequent period is about the same for all three support levels. Although there is a clear pattern of time-varying effects, the four-period model does not improve significantly on the one-period model.

With these findings in mind, we estimated a two-period model in which the first half-year is distinguished from the rest of the experimental period. Relative rates across support levels were constrained to be equal in the two periods (see table 2), but the rate relative to controls was allowed to vary from one period to the other. Treatment effects in this model vary significantly (.05 level) over time, according to both the likelihood ratio test and

TABLE 2

TIME-DEPENDENCE OF EFFECTS OF TREATMENTS ON MARITAL DISSOLUTION RATES OF WHITE WOMEN[a] ($N = 1,376$)

Periods (Years)	Support $3,800	Support $4,800	Support $5,600	Three-Year Treatment	Financial Treatment	Likelihood Ratio Test (χ^2) for Effects of Experimental Treatments	Degrees of Freedom	Likelihood Ratio Test (χ^2) for Time-dependent Effects of Experimental Treatments	Degrees of Freedom
One-period model:									
(0–2.0)	2.29***	2.06***	1.57	.86	...	18.78***	4	...	...
Four-period model:									
First period (0–0.5)	5.69***	3.37**	4.27**	.74	...	33.71***	16	14.80	12
Second period (0.5–1.0)	1.83	1.55	.71	.76	...				
Third period (1.0–1.5)	2.07*	1.75*	1.34	.68	...				
Fourth period (1.5–2.0)	1.53	2.23*	1.50	1.47	...				
Two-period model:									
First period (0–0.5)	1.96***	1.76**	1.35	.86	2.32**	23.33***	5	4.40**	1
Second period (0.5–2.0)	1.96***	1.76**	1.35	.86	...				

[a] All equations contain the other causal variables given in table 1. Coefficients are exp (θ) and indicate the multipliers of the rate. A coefficient of 1.0 means the variable has no effect.

* $.10 \geq P > 0.5$.
** $.05 \geq P > 0.01$.
*** $.01 \geq P$.

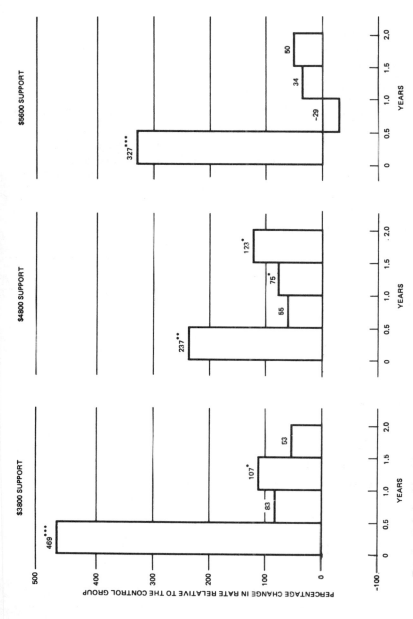

FIG. 1.—Relationship of income-maintenance support levels to marital dissolution rates of white women over time.
*.10 ≥ P >.05, **.05 ≥ P >.01, ***.01 ≥ P.

the *F*-test on a dummy variable for an effect of financial treatments in the first half-year.

The estimates for the two-period model (table 2) indicate that the effect of each support level is 2.32 times as large in the first half-year as it is thereafter. This is consistent with the possibility mentioned above that the treatments immediately changed the opportunities of some respondents on the verge of dissolving their marriages. But the treatments also seem to have changed the long-range opportunity structure. The effects of the support levels during the 0.5–2.0-year period are positive and significant (except for the $5,600 support), though 14%–15% lower than in the results for the time-independent model. Since the long-range impact of an income-maintenance program should not depend on transitory effects on rates during an initial adjustment period, the effects of the support levels in the 0.5–2.0-year period should provide more reliable estimates of the ultimate effects of income maintenance than estimates based on the one-period model.

How Well Does the Model Fit?

Markov models have a reputation for fitting data poorly. But our extensions of the Markov model should have helped to improve the ability of the model to fit the data. So far we have used likelihood ratio tests to assess the relative fit of a series of nested models. We have learned that some models do not improve upon others. Here we look at the absolute fit of the model and compare it with a common alternative.

Three main questions are involved in assessing our dynamic model: (1) To what extent do predictions based on our model differ systematically from observed values? (2) If there are systematic differences, are they related to the experimental treatments, causing us to make erroneous inferences about experimental effects on a particular outcome? (3) As compared with approaches that seek to minimize prediction errors for a single observable variable, how well does our model explain sample variation in outcomes related to marital stability?

In answering these questions we consider three kinds of outcomes: the probability of being in a given state (e.g., single) at any moment, the expected number of marriages and marital dissolutions in any given time interval, and the probability of leaving the original marital status in some time period. Our model implies that each of these is a function of marriage, dissolution, and attrition rates, as indicated in Section I. Thus for any woman we can use her support level and her values of other causal variables and the estimated effects of these variables to predict her rates of marriage, marital dissolution, and attrition. From the predicted rates we can then predict the kinds of outcome listed above. We chose to consider these outcomes at two arbitrary times: one and two years after the start of the experiment. For each woman used in our analysis of transition rates, we retrieved the observed outcomes listed in table 3. These variables were not used directly in estimating transition rates; nor, of course, are they independent of those data, which is the reason for having a single model. We also predicted each woman's outcomes using the estimated effects from the one-period models of remarriage and attrition and the two-period model of marital dissolution (see tables 1 and 2).

To detect systematic differences between predictions and observed values we report the mean residual for each outcome, that is, the mean difference between observed and predicted variables. We also report the observed mean of each outcome because the relative size of a systematic difference is of some interest too. With predictions from a linear regression model, the mean residual would be zero. This need not be the case with predictions from our model. The results in table 3 show that the mean residuals for our predictions are usually small in both absolute (the largest is .02) and relative terms. There is little indication of any overall pattern in these differences, except for the last four dummy variables, which have consistently positive mean residuals. It is well known that no change in status has tended to be under-predicted in sociological applications of Markov models (e.g., see Blumen et al. 1955). Our introduction of population heterogeneity has made this a comparatively small problem, but it has not erased it entirely.

Small mean residuals could hide systematic differences associated with different treatments, which is clearly undesirable if differences between outcomes for controls and for those on financial treatments are of interest. To answer the second question, we performed one-way ANOVA on the residuals for each outcome. Treatment differences in the residuals never even approached statistical significance. (The smallest probability was greater than .50.)

In addressing the third question, we focus on a single, common, inexpensive alternative—linear regression analysis. We regressed each observed outcome on the prediction from our model; we also regressed each of the 14 outcomes on initial marital status, treatments, and other causal variables used in our analysis of the transition rates. For both our model and the regression model we report R^2, the square of the correlation between the observed and predicted variables. Since we expected a poorer fit from our model than from one designed to minimize errors, we were surprised to find that for 10 of the 14 outcomes our model explains more of the sample variation than does linear regression analysis. Moreover, the advantage of our model in these 10 cases tends to be larger than the advantage of linear regression in the other four.

Though we have considered the predictions of our model for several outcomes at two arbitrary times, we have not yet seen how well it predicts the time path of these outcomes. Computational expense has forced us to examine the time path of only one outcome. We selected the proportion who

TABLE 3

OBSERVED AND PREDICTED VALUES OF ARBITRARY OUTCOMES

OUTCOME*	SAMPLE† SIZE	OBSERVED MEAN	OUR MODEL		LINEAR REGRESSION MODEL R^2	DIFFERENCE IN R^2
			Mean Residual	R^2		
Single at $t = 1$	1,917	.351	−.005	.675	.664	.011
Single at $t = 2$	1,917	.350	.002	.500	.481	.019
Married at $t = 1$	1,917	.598	.011	.631	.627	.003
Married at $t = 2$	1,917	.540	−.004	.439	.428	.011
Attrited at $t = 1$	1,917	.050	−.006	.008	.010	−.002
Attrited at $t = 2$	1,917	.111	.002	.025	.023	.002
No. of marital dissolutions, $t = 1$	1,917	.050	−.002	.050	.043	.007
No. of marital dissolutions, $t = 2$	1,917	.109	−.001	.083	.068	.015
No. of marriages, $t = 1$	1,917	.046	.002	.111	.087	.024
No. of marriages, $t = 2$	1,917	.086	−.006	.138	.109	.029
Continuously single to $t = 1$	705	.848	.004	.069	.072	−.003
Continuously single to $t = 2$	705	.740	.020	.092	.089	.003
Continuously married to $t = 1$	1,212	.885	.016	.022	.029	−.007
Continuously married to $t = 2$	1,212	.768	.017	.044	.045	−.001

* Except for the variables on number of marital events, the observed variables are dummy (0–1) variables.

† There were 705 initially single white women and 1,212 initially married white women, giving a total of 1,917 white women.

were unmarried at time t, conditional on not having been lost through attrition by time t. We chose this because it is similar to the most important policy outcome; because it should reveal whether experimental effects are confined to an initial, brief adjustment period; and because it depends about equally on our estimates of marriage, dissolution, and attrition rates. This choice provides a severe test of our method because it uses estimates of all four rates of change $(r_{12}, r_{13}, r_{21}, r_{23})$.

Figure 2 gives observed and predicted curves for this outcome by support level. Points on the observed curve are given by $N_{1j}(t)/[1 - N_{3j}(t)]$ where $N_{1j}(t)$ and $N_{3j}(t)$ are the number in treatment j at time t who are unmarried and lost through attrition, respectively. Points on the predicted curves are calculated as

$$\frac{1}{N_j} \sum_{i=1}^{N_j} \hat{p}_{1ji}(t)/[1 - \hat{p}_{3ji}(t)], \qquad (44)$$

where $N_j = N_{1j}(0) + N_{2j}(0)$ (the initial number in treatment j), and $\hat{p}_{1ji}(t)$ and $\hat{p}_{3ji}(t)$ are calculated for each woman i enrolled in treatment j using equations (28) and (30), respectively. Predictions are based on the one-period models of remarriage and attrition and on the two-period model of dissolution; they assume each woman has her assigned treatment.

We begin by considering the observed (squiggly) curves. First, note that the proportion of unmarried women at the start of the experiment differs

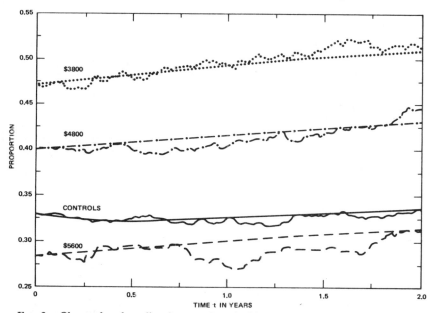

FIG. 2.—Observed and predicted proportion of white women who are single at time t, conditional on not having been lost through attrition by time t, by support level.

greatly from one treatment to another. These initial differences result from the use of a stratified random design in which marital status was a stratification variable. Unmarried women were more likely to be assigned to treatments with a lower support level. Because of this, a comparison of "posttest" levels is clearly inappropriate.

Next, notice that the observed curve for the control group is relatively flat, suggesting that there are no important "natural" time trends (due to aging, secular change, etc.). However, the observed curves for the three support levels show noticeable increases in the conditional proportion of unmarried women after two years ($+.039$ for the low support, $+.044$ for the medium support, and $+.031$ for the high support versus $+.009$ for the control group). Furthermore, the proportion of unmarried women among those on the financial treatments rises fairly steadily throughout the two-year period. This upward trend is quite apparent for the low and medium supports. It is less certain for the high support, which has the fewest subjects and the most extreme fluctuations about any overall time trend. There is little evidence that the proportion of unmarried women among those on financial treatments has reached a plateau within the first two years of the experiment, as we would expect if an equilibrium was attained during this period. This suggests that dynamic analysis is really needed to assess experimental effects accurately. We elaborate on this in Section III.

Now let us consider the fit between the (smooth) curves predicted by our model and the actual (squiggly) curves. We rely on visual inspection to compare the two sets of curves. On the whole, the fit is quite good except for the high-support group, for which the actual curve is noticeably below the predicted curve. Because only 240 women are in the high-support group, a change in status of a very few women makes a substantial difference in the observed curve. Hence the deviations for this group are less worrisome than they would be for a large group like the control ($N = 847$).

Our scrutiny of the implications of our model for various outcomes at arbitrary times has revealed no major disadvantages and even some small advantages. The model's primary advantage is, of course, its ability to predict the time path of a variety of interdependent outcomes reasonably well.

III. COMPARISON WITH OTHER APPROACHES

We return finally to an issue raised at the outset: the advantages of event-history analysis relative to other approaches. We continue to assume throughout this discussion that events are generated by a Markov process whose transition rates are log-linear functions of exogenous variables (36).

Obviously any comparison of alternative approaches depends on the assumptions about the process generating events. Following Coleman's (1964, 1968) work, nonetheless, we wish to challenge the still widespread view that substantive assumptions ought to be dictated by the form in which the data are collected. That is, we do not believe that sociologists ought to change their assumptions about the underlying process (their "model," in our terminology) when they shift from analyzing panel data, say, to analyzing cross-sections or event histories. In our view, a major advantage of formulating problems in terms of dynamic stochastic models is that we can use different data structures to estimate parameters of the same model. This provides a way of unifying a variety of data-analytic procedures.

We begin with an extended discussion of cross-sectional analysis because this has been—and will undoubtedly continue to be—the mainstay of sociological research. We then contrast event-history analysis with two other strategies that use temporal data: event-count analysis and panel analysis. Our discussion of each is brief. To the best of our knowledge, event-count analysis has not yet been developed (let alone applied) except for the most elementary kind of Markov model (a Poisson model). So our comments on it are intended to encourage the development of this approach. However, Singer and Spilerman (1974, 1976) have treated in detail the difficulties of panel analysis with categorical dependent variables. We review these mainly to emphasize that they are either absent or much less serious with event-history analysis.

Cross-sectional Analysis

Cross-sectional data give the state that each member of a sample occupies at a particular time t. Earlier we referred to the unconditional probability of being in a state j at time t as the state probability, $p_j(t)$. Given n possible states, there are only $(n - 1)$ unique state probabilities since the n probabilities must sum to unity. But, in general, there are $n(n - 1)$ unique transition rates. Because $n(n - 1) > (n - 1)$ for $n > 1$, it is immediately obvious that cross-sectional analysis does not allow all parameters of a model to be identified unless we can specify $(n - 1)^2$ of the transition rates, either on theoretical grounds or from a priori knowledge. With event-history analysis we can estimate all parameters. So event-history analysis is clearly preferable to cross-sectional analysis if we wish to understand a process fully or to predict other outcomes.

Under certain circumstances, however, cross-sectional analysis can supply useful information about the process generating events. It is worthwhile to identify these conditions. We begin by considering the situation in which the process has been operating a comparatively long time so that the distribution of the population across states is in equilibrium. For concreteness we again start with the two-state case.

Since the rates, r_{12} and r_{21}, cannot be negative, the two-state model implies that the probabilities of being in each state eventually reach stable, so-called steady-state, values:

$$p_1(\infty) = \frac{r_{21}}{r_{12} + r_{21}} = \frac{\exp[\theta_{21}x]}{\exp[\theta_{12}x] + \exp[\theta_{21}x]}$$

$$= 1/\{1 + \exp[(\theta_{12} - \theta_{21})x]\}\,, \tag{45}$$

$$p_2(\infty) = \frac{r_{12}}{r_{12} + r_{21}} = \frac{\exp[\theta_{12}x]}{\exp[\theta_{12}x] + \exp[\theta_{21}x]}$$

$$= 1/\{1 + \exp[(\theta_{21} - \theta_{12})x]\}\,. \tag{46}$$

Of course, individuals continue to change from one state to the other. That is, the model implies an equilibrium probability distribution on the aggregate level; it neither assumes nor implies equilibrium on the individual level.

Note that

$$\frac{p_1(\infty)}{p_2(\infty)} = \exp[(\theta_{21} - \theta_{12})x] \tag{47}$$

or

$$\ln\frac{p_1(\infty)}{p_2(\infty)} = \gamma_{12}x\,, \tag{48}$$

where $\gamma_{12} = \theta_{21} - \theta_{12}$. For example, this model implies that in the steady state, the log of the odds of being unmarried (rather than married) is linear in x. Equation (48) is the usual form of a binary logit model (Berkson 1944; Theil 1969, 1970), and if all members of x are dummy variables, then it is just a special case of Goodman's (1972) log-linear model of the odds ratio. Thus, when a population is in equilibrium, logit (or log-linear) analysis of cross-sectional data tells us the difference in the effects of variables on the two rates, r_{12} and r_{21}. Note that the finding of "no effect" for a variable in the cross-sectional logit analysis can be due to its equal effects on the two rates. That is, it should not be taken as evidence that a variable is irrelevant to the process, only that it has no net effect on the steady-state distribution.

Is there a similar connection between the general, n-state Markov model and multinomial logit analysis? Unfortunately, the answer is no. This can be proved by a single case. Consider $\ln[p_1(\infty)/p_2(\infty)]$ for the three-state model with attrition, which we have used in our empirical analysis. Though both $p_1(\infty)$ and $p_2(\infty)$ are zero (because eventually everyone "attrites"), they do have a finite ratio. We find that:

$$\lim_{t\to\infty}\ln\left\{\frac{p_1(t)}{p_2(t)}\right\} = \ln\left\{\frac{r_{21} + p_1(0)(r_{23} + \lambda_2)}{r_{12} + [1 - p_1(0)](r_{13} + \lambda_2)}\right\}. \tag{49}$$

The expression on the right-hand side is quite complicated and substitution of equations like (36) does not produce anything resembling a logit model in general. (If $r_{13} = r_{12}$, i.e., attrition rates for married and unmarried women are identical, then [49] does simplify to [48].)

However, an important class of Markov models—general birth and death models—does have a steady-state distribution that has the form of a multinomial logit model. In these models states can be ordered so that there can occur only transitions between neighboring states (e.g., in a three-state model transitions from one to three and from three to one are impossible). Then, for example, in a three-state model with ordered states, equations (47) and (48) continue to apply, and in addition:

$$\frac{p_2(\infty)}{p_3(\infty)} = \exp\left[(\theta_{32} - \theta_{23})\,x\right],\tag{50}$$

$$\ln\frac{p_2(\infty)}{p_3(\infty)} = \gamma_{23}\,x\ ,\tag{51}$$

where $\gamma_{23} = \theta_{32} - \theta_{23}$. Furthermore,

$$\frac{p_1(\infty)}{p_3(\infty)} = \frac{r_{32}r_{21}}{r_{12}r_{23}} = \exp\left[(\theta_{32} + \theta_{21} - \theta_{12} - \theta_{23})\,x\right].\tag{52}$$

The similarity in form of (52) to (47) and (50) means that there are no clues in cross-sectional data to tell us how to order the states. This must be done on theoretical grounds—or else we must have event-history data, which do permit us to observe what kinds of transitions can occur. But, if we know the order of states in a general birth and death model, cross-sectional multinomial logit analysis does let us make conclusions about the net effect of a variable on transition rates between states.

So far we have considered the situation in which the system is in equilibrium. We have indicated that in the steady state, the log of the odds of being in one state rather than another has a very simple form if states can be ordered. However, if the steady state has not been reached, the log of the odds of being in one state rather than another is a very complicated function of time, the transition rates, and the initial conditions—even for the very simple two-state case. This can be seen by forming the ratio of the right-hand sides of equations (26) and (27).

Suppose we perform cross-sectional analysis at two successive time points and determine that variables have very different effects. We cannot be certain what to conclude. Has the underlying process changed—that is, has the relationship between variables and transition rates altered? Or has the system just moved closer to its ultimate steady-state value? Without some form of temporal analysis we cannot answer these questions.

Social scientists have been so wedded to cross-sectional analysis that they seldom seem to reflect on the likelihood that equilibrium exists or on the length of time required for a system to reach a new equilibrium following some intervention or structural upheaval. We suspect that in most cases inertia greatly slows the speed with which social systems reach equilibrium. We note that the equilibrium assumption implicit in sociological theories prominent a few decades ago (e.g., functionalism) began to be attacked more than a decade ago. But these criticisms have barely begun to penetrate sociological methodology.

We will make our discussion of this issue more concrete by referring to our empirical illustration. Many analysts faced with data like ours might conduct some sort of logit analysis that assumes that equilibrium is reached within the experimental period. But can we expect the steady-state probability distribution of marital status to be approached during the three or five years of the experimental period? As social experiments go, SIME/DIME is long, so it might seem that this would happen. However, according to the models we have discussed, how long it takes to approach a new steady state (say, to within .01 of its ultimate value) depends on both preexperimental and experimental rates of marital status change. Our results imply that SIME/DIME is much too short for the steady state to be approached during the experimental period.

Marriage and dissolution rates are approximately equal to annual probabilities of forming and dissolving a marriage, respectively.[12] Among SIME/DIME's participants, who have incomes below the U.S. median, both rates are somewhat higher than in the overall U.S. population. In the environment facing the control group, $r_{12} = .10$ and $r_{21} = .05$ are fairly typical.[13] If an aggregate-level equilibrium exists at the beginning of the experiment, the initial probability of being unmarried is $.05/(.10 + .05) = .333$.

Our analyses reported in Section II indicate that for whites SIME/DIME has a negligible effect on marriage rates but roughly doubles the dissolution rate of those on most treatments. If the dissolution rate under income maintenance is twice that of the controls, that is, if $r_{21} = .10$, then according to the two-state model the equilibrium probability of being unmarried under income maintenance is $.10/(.10 + .10) = .50$. Thus the model predicts that under such conditions, the proportion of unmarried women in the population would eventually increase about 50% above its pre-income-maintenance value (from .333 to .500). However, the proportion of unmarried women would increase only by about .04, or about 13%, in the first two years (see fig. 2) and by about .09, or about 26%, in the first five years. It would take nearly 19 years to be within .01 of the steady-state proportion. If data on marital status of participants at any point during the three to five years of the experiment are analyzed cross-sectionally, the ultimate effect of income maintenance will be greatly underestimated. As we mentioned earlier, the

[12] If there is no attrition, the probability of a change in marital status before t is $1 - \exp(-r_{jk}t)$ (see eq. [17]). By a Taylor expansion this is approximately $1 - (1 - r_{jk}t) = r_{jk}t$. So when $t = 1$, the probability of a change is approximately r_{jk}.

[13] These numbers are obtained by rounding off the crude proportion of controls who marry (if initially unmarried) or end their marriages (if initially married) in the first year of the experiment.

observed curves for support levels in figure 2 do not suggest that a plateau or equilibrium has been reached within the first two years.

The only way to decide whether a system is in equilibrium is to collect data over time and to analyze it dynamically—that is, in a way that lets us study the time path of change in the phenomenon.

Event-Count Analysis

A number of sociological studies have analyzed the number of times a particular event occurs in some time period. For example, Spilerman (1970) analyzed the number of riots per city during the mid-sixties. We refer to this type of analysis as event-count analysis. We suspect that a number of surveys have asked such questions as "How many times have you been married?" and "How many times have you been divorced?" However, we are not aware of any event-count analyses in sociology where counts of more than one type of event are analyzed within a single model.

Given the assumptions of a Markov model we can derive expressions for the expected number of different types of events in some time interval. For example, for the two- and three-state models discussed in this paper, we derived the expressions given in equations (31) through (35). These equations, combined with observed data on the counts of different types of events, permit transition rates to be estimated by a nonlinear regression approach. That is, we can estimate rates—or the causal effects of variables on rates—by minimizing the sum over all units of the squared deviation between the observed count of events for each unit and that predicted by the model. This approach, which we have not yet used, has one inherent limitation: We know of no theorem (comparable to the Gauss-Markov theorem in linear regression analysis) that estimators obtained in this way will have optimal statistical properties—even in an infinite sample.

Maximum-likelihood estimators typically have optimal asymptotic properties. But to perform maximum-likelihood estimation we must know the probability-mass function for the count of events. To the best of our knowledge, the expression for this function has not yet been derived for a general n-state Markov model. In fact, it is not even clear that such an expression can be written in closed form for a general n-state model. The probability-mass function for the number of events can, of course, be written explicitly for certain special cases (e.g., a Poisson model), but it is mathematically intractable even for the two- and three-state models used in the illustrations in this paper.

Given these difficulties, it seems obvious that event-history analysis is preferable to event-count analysis. Nonetheless, event-count analysis deserves further study. Under some circumstances, event counts either already exist or are feasible to collect, while event histories or panel data cannot be obtained.

Panel Analysis

Panel data, which record the states occupied by members of a sample at a series of discrete points in time, are the temporal data most commonly available to sociologists. Singer and Spilerman (1974, 1976) have identified the following problems regarding estimation of transition rates in a general n-state Markov model from panel data.[14]

First, sometimes panel data on categorical variables cannot be embedded in—that is, described by—a Markov process. Moreover, sampling variability and measurement error can cause panel data to be unembeddable even though they are truly generated by a Markov process.

Second, even though the panel data may be describable by a Markov process, there may not be a *unique* matrix of transition rates that describe the data. Furthermore, the different matrices obtained in the nonunique cases may suggest substantially different qualitative conclusions (see, for example, Singer and Spilerman 1976, p. 31). Neither embeddability nor uniqueness is a problem in event-history analysis because maximum-likelihood estimators based on such data give unique estimates of rates—or of causal effects on rates.

Third, Singer and Spilerman (1976, pp. 44–48) note that small changes in an observed matrix of transition probabilities (due to sampling variability or measurement error) can sometimes lead to very marked changes in estimates of transition rates. This is clearly undesirable. However, in our experience in analyzing event histories, given a moderately large sample, fairly substantial errors in records on the occurrence or timing of events do not qualitatively alter estimated patterns of causal effects of variables on transition rates.[15] Insensitivity to sampling and measurement error is, we believe, an important advantage of event-history analysis. Because such errors are unavoidable, the sensitivity issue clearly deserves further study— in both panel and event-history analysis.

Fourth, estimation of transition rates from panel data is also sensitive to the length of the time interval between waves of the panel. When the time interval is large, each row of the matrix of transition probabilities approaches the steady-state probability distribution (see, for example, equations [8] through [12]). In this situation there are only $(n - 1)$ unique transition probabilities, rather than $n(n - 1)$. This means that the data contain no more information than cross-sectional data. However, if the time interval

[14] Some of these problems do not arise in certain special cases. For example, the first, second, and fifth problems mentioned below do not occur for the two-state model.

[15] We used this feature in Hannan et al. (1976) to eliminate the possibility that effects of income-maintenance treatment on the rate of marital dissolution were due to attrition bias. Our unpublished Monte Carlo studies show that random error in the timing of events has surprisingly small effects on the quality of maximum-likelihood estimators of rates obtained from event-history analysis.

between waves of the panel is very short, almost all members of the sample will be in their original state. This is not very informative either. With event-history analysis the length of the observation period cannot be too long. It can be too short—if no event has occurred. However, Tuma and Hannan (1978) have shown that with samples that are moderate in size, rates can be estimated well if as few as 10% of the sample have experienced an event. We have not seen comparable results based on panel analysis, but we suspect that it does not perform as well.

Fifth, we know of no way of estimating parameters in a general n-state Markov model from panel data when transition rates are functions of exogenous variables, as is almost always the case in problems of interest to sociologists. Singer and Spilerman (1974) have reported some work on estimating parameters from panel data generated by a mixture of Markov processes, when the mixture is described by some specified probability distribution. This work is helpful, but it still does not permit causal inferences to be made. As we have shown, causal relationships are easily studied with event-history analysis.

A sixth problem with panel analysis concerns the ability to study and detect time dependence in the process generating events. This appears to present a very difficult problem for panel analysis. As we have indicated, various kinds of time dependence can be investigated readily through event-history analysis.

Conclusions

Our conclusions are very simple. Event histories provide rich opportunities for answering fundamental sociological questions. We have shown how to analyze event histories when data are generated by a well-behaved stochastic process. The procedures we have outlined permit analysis of causal effects on the rates at which events occur and of time dependence in such rates. These procedures are simple to implement, and in our empirical application they yield good predictions about a variety of observable variables.

Event-history analysis offers substantial advantages over other common approaches to the study of causal effects on changes in qualitative variables. Since in many situations it is no more difficult to obtain information on the timing of events than the count of events, we urge that sociologists begin to collect and analyze such data.

APPENDIX

To write a likelihood equation like (39) for the model with transition rates that vary from one period p to another (43), we need the survivor function for state j, $G_j(t \mid u, x, z_p)$, where $u = t_{m-1}$ [the time of the $(m - 1)$th event] and t is some later time, $u \leq t$. The survivor function is obtained by solving the analogue of (21):

$$f_j(t|u, x, z_p) = r_{jp}G_j(t|u, x, z_p) , \tag{A1}$$

where $r_{jp} = \Sigma_k r_{jkp}$. Since $f_j(t|u, x, z_p) = -dG_j(t|u, x, z_p)/dt$, this implies that

$$\frac{dG_j(t|u, x, z_p)}{G_j(t|u, x, z_p)} = -r_{jp}dt . \tag{A2}$$

Integrating both sides from u to t, we obtain

$$\ln G_j(t|u, x, z_p) = - \int_u^t r_{jp}dt \tag{A3}$$

$$G_j(t|u, x, z_p) = \exp\left[- \int_u^t r_{jp}dt\right] . \tag{A4}$$

To eliminate the integral on the right-hand side of the expression above, define u'_p and t'_p as follows:

$u'_p = 0$ if $\tau_p < u$ or $t < \tau_{p-1}$ (state j is entered after period p ends
  or t occurs before period p begins);

$\quad = u$ if $\tau_{p-1} \leq u < \tau_p$ (state j is entered in period p) ;

$\quad = \tau_{p-1}$ if $u < \tau_{p-1} < t$ (state j is entered before period p begins
  and t occurs after period p begins);

$t'_p = 0$ if $\tau_p < u$ or $t \leq \tau_{p-1}$ (state j is entered after period p ends
  or t occurs before period p begins);

$\quad = \tau_p$ if $u < \tau_p < t$ (state j is entered before period p ends
  and t occurs after period p ends);

$\quad = t$ if $\tau_{p-1} < t \leq \tau_p$ (t occurs in period p);

where τ_p is the end of period p, as defined in the text. Using these definitions,

$$G_j(t|u, x, z_p) = \exp\left[-\sum_{p=1}^{P} (t'_p - u'_p)r_{jp}(x, z_p)\right]. \tag{A5}$$

So, analogous to (39), we can write the likelihood equation for the model given by (43) as:

$$\mathcal{L} = \prod_{j=1}^{n} \prod_{i=1}^{N} \prod_{m=1}^{\infty} \left\{[G_j(t_m|t_{m-1}, x, z_p)]^{v_{m-1,j}} \cdot \prod_{k=1}^{n}[r_{jkp}(x, z_p)]^{w_m v_{m-1,j} v_{mk}}\right\}. \tag{A6}$$

REFERENCES

Albert, A. 1962. "Estimating the Infinitesimal Generator of a Continuous Time, Finite State Markov Process." *Annals of Mathematical Statistics* 33 (June): 727–53.

Bartholomew, David J. 1957. "A Problem in Life Testing." *Journal of the American Statistical Association* 52 (September): 350–55.

———. 1973. *Stochastic Models for Social Processes.* 2d ed. New York: Wiley.

Berkson, J. 1944. "Application of the Logistic Function to Bioassay." *Journal of the American Statistical Association* 39 (September): 357–65.

Blumen, Isadore, Marvin Kogan, and Philip J. McCarthy. 1955. "The Industrial Mobility of Labor As a Probability Process." Cornell Studies in Industrial and Labor Relations, no. 6. Ithaca, N.Y.: Cornell University Press.

Breiman, L. 1969. *Probability and Stochastic Processes.* Boston: Houghton Mifflin.

Coleman, James S. 1964. *Introduction to Mathematical Sociology.* Glencoe, Ill.: Free Press.

———. 1968. "The Mathematical Study of Change." Pp. 428–78 in *Methodology in Social Research*, edited by H. Blalock and A. Blalock. New York: McGraw-Hill.

———. 1973. *The Mathematics of Collective Action.* Chicago: Aldine.

Cox, D. R., and H. D. Miller. 1965. *The Theory of Stochastic Processes.* London: Methuen.

Dhrymes, Phoebus. 1970. *Econometrics: Statistical Foundations and Application.* New York: Harper & Row.

Feller, William. 1968. *An Introduction to Probability Theory and Its Applications.* Vol. 1. 3d ed. New York: Wiley.

Goodman, Leo A. 1972. "A Modified Multiple Regression Approach to the Analysis of Dichotomous Variables." *American Sociological Review* 37 (February): 28–45.

Hannan, Michael T., Nancy Brandon Tuma, and Lyle P. Groeneveld. 1976. "The Impact of Income Maintenance on the Making and Breaking of Marital Unions: Interim Report." Research Memorandum 28. Menlo Park, Calif.: Stanford Research Institute, Center for the Study of Welfare Policy.

———. 1977. "Income and Marital Events: Evidence from an Income-Maintenance Experiment." *American Journal of Sociology* 82 (May): 1186–1211.

Karlin, Samuel, and Howard Taylor. 1975. *A First Course in Stochastic Processes.* New York: Academic Press.

Land, Kenneth C. 1971. "Some Exhaustible Poisson Process Models of Divorce by Marriage Cohort." *Journal of Mathematical Sociology* 1 (2): 213–32.

McFarland, David D. 1970. "Intragenerational Social Mobility as a Markov Process: Including a Time-Stationary Markovian Model That Explains Observed Declines in Mobility Rates." *American Sociological Review* 35 (June): 463–76.

Mayer, Thomas F. 1972. "Models of Intragenerational Mobility." Pp. 308–57 in *Sociological Theories in Progress*, edited by J. Berger, M. Zelditch, and B. Anderson. Vol. 2. Boston: Houghton Mifflin.

Singer, Burton, and Seymour Spilerman. 1974. "Social Mobility Models for Heterogeneous Populations." Pp. 256–401 in *Sociological Methodology 1973–1974*, edited by Herbert L. Costner. San Francisco: Jossey-Bass.

———. 1976. "The Representation of Social Processes by Markov Models." *American Journal of Sociology* 82 (July): 1–54.

Sørensen, Aage B. 1975. "The Structure of Intragenerational Mobility." *American Sociological Review* 40 (August): 456–71.

Spilerman, Seymour. 1970. "The Causes of Racial Disturbances: A Comparison of Alternative Explanations." *American Sociological Review* 35 (August): 627–49.

———. 1972a. "The Analysis of Mobility Processes by the Introduction of Independent Variables into a Markov Chain." *American Sociological Review* 37 (June): 277–94.

———. 1972b. "Extensions of the Mover-Stayer Model." *American Journal of Sociology* 78 (November): 599–626.

Theil, H. 1969. "A Multinomial Extension of the Linear Logit Model." *International Economic Review* 10 (October): 251–59.

———. 1970. "On the Estimation of Relationships Involving Qualitative Variables." *American Journal of Sociology* 76 (July): 103–54.

Tuma, Nancy Brandon. 1976. "Rewards, Resources, and the Rate of Mobility: A Non-Stationary Multivariate Stochastic Model." *American Sociological Review* 41 (April): 338–60.

Tuma, Nancy Brandon, Lyle P. Groeneveld, and Michael T. Hannan. 1976. "First Dissolutions and Marriages: Impacts in 24 Months of SIME/DIME." Research Memorandum 35. Menlo Park, Calif.: Stanford Research Institute, Center for the Study of Welfare Policy.

Tuma, Nancy Brandon, and Michael T. Hannan. 1978, in press. "Approaches to the Censoring Problem in Analysis of Event Histories." In *Sociological Methodology 1979*, edited by Karl Schuessler. San Francisco: Jossey-Bass.

Tuma, Nancy Brandon, Michael T. Hannan, and Lyle P. Groeneveld. 1977. "Variation over Time in the Impact of the Seattle and Denver Income Maintenance Experiments on the Making and Breaking of Marriages." Research Memorandum 43. Menlo Park, Calif.: Stanford Research Institute, Center for the Study of Welfare Policy.

6

The exchange between Goodwin and Hannan et al. raises a number of issues relating to what is omitted from econometric models and the uses of econometric results in policy formation. Goodwin argues that the SIME/DIME analysis[1] is seriously incomplete because it omits social psychological predictor variables and outcome variables such as child abuse, wife abuse, and measures of personal satisfaction. He believes, that, as a result of such omission, the results have been widely misinterpreted as evidence of negative program effects on participants.

The authors reply that their goal was simply to estimate experimental effects, and that the omission of the variables Goodwin favors has not biased their results. In this they are probably correct. But, it does appear that these results have been used to argue against national implementation of a negative income tax program. This outcome may have been less likely if some of Goodwin's substantive concerns had been more prominently featured in the analysis.

NOTE

1. The thrust of Goodwin's remarks is primarily toward the analysis in the two previous chapters by the authors, rather than the paper reprinted in this volume. The interested reader should consult all three chapters in the series to properly evaluate this controversy.

Limitations of the Seattle and Denver Income-Maintenance Analysis

Leonard Goodwin

In "Income and Independence Effects on Marital Dissolution" (*AJS* 84 [November 1978]: 611–33), Hannan, Tuma, and Groeneveld have reported on one of the most expensive and extensive experiments ever undertaken: the Seattle and Denver Income-Maintenance Experiment. Their consideration of the impact on families of providing a guaranteed income is of substantial professional and social importance.

The findings of the experiment received wide public attention during the hearings held in Washington, D.C., by Senator Daniel Moynihan (D-N.Y.) during November 1978.[1] Newspapers carried stories indicating the dangers of a guaranteed income because it caused family breakup. Hannan, Tuma, and Groeneveld should provide, I believe, a fuller view of that experiment for both the professional and lay publics. Several questions come to mind which may help facilitate fuller discussion.

[1] The Seattle and Denver results were presented by Dr. Robert C. Spiegelman at the hearings. He together with Lyle P. Groeneveld and Philip Robins also submitted a paper which warns of the marital dissolution effect that might accompany such national

Reprinted from "Limitations of the Seattle and Denver Income-Maintenance Analysis," 85(3) *American Journal of Sociology* 653-657 (November 1979), by Leonard Goodwin, by permission of the University of Chicago Press. © 1979 by the University of Chicago.

Was a formal model regarding family stability built into the design of the experiment? More specifically, were only the economic effects of the experiment considered as affecting family stability, or were social and psychological variables considered as well? The idea that a guaranteed income has an "independence effect" and an "income effect" is interesting, and the mathematical models presented add some validity to the concepts. But the approach is limited and incomplete.

To begin with, while the concept of an "independence effect" is interesting, it also seems misleading. Substantial difficulties are faced by any single parent head of household, monetary matters aside. It is hard to imagine many women welcoming this kind of "independence." Bearing on this issue are findings from a survey of several thousand persons in Chicago and New York designed by Goodwin and Wilson.[2] Respondents included the following: (1) mothers who head households and are applying for the work-training program for welfare recipients, the Work Incentive (WIN) Program; (2) mothers who head households and are applying for Unemployment Insurance (UI); (3) spouses of men who are applying for the WIN program; (4) spouses of men who are applying for UI.

Table 1 indicates how the women who already head households rate that status in comparison with women who are members of families with a male head. The table also presents orientations toward the goal of having a traditional family. (Differences in ratings of 0.20 points are significant at the .05 level of probability.) It is clear that all groups of women greatly prefer living in a family with a husband to heading a family themselves. While those women who already are heads of households are more accepting of that role than women in traditional families, their low ratings indicate that it is far from a good way of life.

TABLE 1

MOTHERS' ORIENTATIONS TOWARD TRADITIONAL
AND SINGLE-PARENT FAMILIES

	MEAN VALUES			
ITEMS RATED ON A 4-POINT SCALE RANGING FROM "NOT VERY GOOD WAY OF LIFE" TO "VERY GOOD WAY OF LIFE"	WIN Mothers $(N=663)$	UI Mothers $(N=187)$	WIN Spouses $(N=270)$	UI Spouses $(N=91)$
9. Being a single parent head of family...	1.84	1.70	1.45	1.53
13. Having a family where the husband, wife, and children live together......	3.64	3.67	3.84	3.79

programs as wage subsidies and guaranteed jobs (Spiegelman, Groeneveld, and Robins 1978, pp. 16–17). Nowhere in the paper are there data on family environments or relationships among spouses, nor is there any hint that marital dissolution might lead to an improved family environment for children under certain conditions.

[2] For further information on this study, see Goodwin and Wilson (1978).

If women choose to become single parent heads of families when given a minimal guaranteed income, it is not because of the money as such. Rather, the money creates the option for escape from a marital situation which is punishing to them and probably their children. The underlying causal variables are the negative situation. The authors do not deal with this possibility.

In order to make the critique more specific, I refer again to our survey. Respondents who were living with a mate were asked to rate the statement, "I have seriously thought of leaving my mate in the last few months," on a four-point scale ranging from Strongly Disagree to Strongly Agree. Responses of WIN spouses are of particular interest because these women are in a situation similar to that of the Seattle-Denver experiment spouses; namely, if the man leaves they will continue to receive governmental support. With those responses regarded as the dependent variable, a regression analysis was undertaken. The independent variables included the orientations toward family previously mentioned, orientations toward their mates, and various demographic characteristics such as earnings on their previous job (few were currently employed), liking of previous job, number of children, and household income.

The regression results indicate that six independent variables are significant in accounting for 36% of the variance of scores of WIN spouses on the question of leaving their mates. Five of the variables deal with interpersonal relations—for example, "Family life would be better if my mate worked harder at it." The other variable is the satisfaction found with previous job. The more the woman liked that job, the *less* likely she was to think of leaving her mate (pay on the last job was not significant).

While thinking about leaving one's mate is not the same as actually doing so, there is likely to be a connection. (Our followup interviews will test the connection between orientations and actions.) In any case, these findings suggest the potential significance of interpersonal relations in explaining marital dissolution.

If this suggestion is correct, concern should focus not only on the impact of income on marital dissolution but on how to improve the quality of marital situations. The provision of supplementary income to needy families should not be discarded merely because of the experimental findings; instead, provision for helping improve marital situations should be considered as an additional aid.

The authors' limited concern with substantive family issues occurs again in their discussion of results from one-child families. Such families did not conform to the "income" and "independence" models (p. 619). Instead of trying to interpret such findings (or bring other data to bear on them), the authors dismiss them with the observation that the overall predictability of the model is not markedly affected by whether the one-child families behave as predicted. It may be that the presence of only one child faces parents with a distinctly different social situation from the presence of more than one.

The limitations I have noted can be seen as indicating an apparent unwillingness to ask respondents directly about their feelings and expectations regarding life's contingencies and about their relationships with other persons. The limitations of such an approach are revealed further in the way the authors handle the comparison between welfare income and income from the experiment.

On pages 614, 619, and 620, the authors make a series of assumptions about welfare payments versus guaranteed income payments in order to develop a "welfare discount rate" to include in their estimate of the independence effect. It is assumed that welfare carries a stigma, that recipients have difficulty in obtaining payments, and that they lack knowledge about welfare rules. These assumptions may or may not be accurate. Why not have asked the Seattle and Denver participants about these matters? One might then have obtained measures which would have led to a more reasonable way of setting the so-called welfare discount rate.

In our own study, we found that a feeling of welfare stigma (family and friends looking down on one for receiving welfare) was a significant "predictor" in a regression equation of the expectation of men on welfare to be economically independent next year. The point is that measures of persons' perceptions of situations can be useful in estimating their actions. Without such measures, Hannan, Tuma, and Groeneveld are reduced to the inadequate procedure of adopting that discount rate which best predicts the desired results. In a similar vein, the authors try to estimate what wives think they can earn in the labor market (p. 619) without bothering to ask them what they think they can earn.

It is equally noteworthy that the authors do not mention important process and outcome variables. Was there more child abuse and wife abuse in families that eventually split than in those that did not or those in the control group? Were the environments of the families after the split better than what they were before even though the families were afterward headed by only one parent? How were men and women interpreting the impact of the experiment on their own lives and family situations?

Newspaper reports on the Moynihan hearings implied that family separations were bad and that the government should not support programs which encouraged separations. If in fact these splits provided a better family environment for children, that should be stated. Neither that statement nor its converse can be made if no data were gathered on the issue, which brings me to my last point.

It is my impression that the fundamental designs of all the income maintenance experiments were created by economists who had little concern for the kinds of noneconomic measures mentioned above. The narrowness of the research design has led to incomplete findings. The evidence of increased marital dissolution with a guaranteed income is not accompanied by evidence of what are probably more basic social and psychological reasons behind the event—pointing the way toward possibly helping certain families remain together—or by evidence of the conditions under which marital dissolution is beneficial.

Hannan, Tuma, and Groeneveld are in a position to comment on whether other data were gathered in the Seattle-Denver experiment that elucidate family functioning in relation to the family stability findings, or what kinds of data should have been or now should be collected from the families in the experiment. Their insights as noneconomists could lead to better research efforts in the future—research that would better illuminate what is happening "out there" and hence serve as a better guide to national problem solving.

LEONARD GOODWIN

Worcester Polytechnic Institute

REFERENCES

Goodwin, Leonard, and Julie Wilson. 1978. "Preliminary Report on the Impact of Federal Income Security Programs on Work Incentives and Family Stability." Mimeographed. Worcester, Mass.: Worcester Polytechnic Institute.

Spiegelman, Robert G., Lyle P. Groeneveld, and Philip Robins. 1978. "Additional Evidence on the Work Effort and Marital Stability Effects of the Seattle and Denver Income Maintenance Experiments." Testimony before the Subcommittee on Public Assistance of the Senate Finance Committee, November 15. Mimeographed. Menlo Park, Calif.: Stanford Research Institute International.

7

Reply to Goodwin

Michael T. Hannan, Nancy Brandon Tuma, and
Lyle P. Groeneveld

We have published three reports using data from the Seattle-Denver In-come-Maintenance Experiment (SIME/DIME) in this *Journal* (May 1977, November 1978, January 1979). Each focuses on analytic issues that we think should be considered prior to any attempt to draw implications for policy. Since Goodwin's comment gives heavy emphasis to policy matters, we begin by sketching the policy concerns that generated the research.

SIME/DIME, like the three other income-maintenance experiments, was designed to provide information about behavioral changes under a negative income tax (NIT) program and the effects of such changes on program costs. In our experiment, two possible behavioral changes were singled out for study: changes in labor supply and in marital status. The costs of an NIT program depend directly on both levels of work and the

Reprinted from "Reply to Goodwin," 85(3) *American Journal of Sociology* 657-661 (November 1979), by Michael T. Hannan, Nancy Brandon Tuma, and Lyle P. Groeneveld, by permission of the University of Chicago Press. © 1979 by the University of Chicago.

marital composition of the population. For example, increases in the number of families headed by one adult raise the costs to the public of an NIT program.

The attempts to address these questions with nonexperimental data face serious problems of determining the tax rates that low-income populations actually face. Various public transfer programs (AFDC, Food Stamps, Medicare, public housing subsidies. legal aid. unemployment insurance compensation, etc.) have complex rules of eligibility and tax the benefits of other programs in a bewildering manner. The main motivation for the experiments was the desire to control support levels and tax rates so that we could obtain meaningful estimates of structural relationships.

When the experiments were planned, policymakers and economists agreed that an NIT program would decrease labor supply. Moreover, economists tended to agree on the mechanisms involved. This consensus is reflected in the strong focus on labor supply and in the nature of the design of the experiments. In particular, families were assigned randomly to treatments within a stratification scheme designed to provide maximum information about labor supply responses.

No one pretended at that time to understand the likely impact of an NIT program on marriage. Many sociologists expressed private doubts that we would detect any impact. They claimed that a family's current financial situation influences marital stability only slightly and that enduring properties of individuals and marital relations are more important. Even those who thought that current financial circumstances affect marital stability predicted that experimental effects would be very slight. They told us that the typical changes in income in the experiment were too small and the length of the experiment was too short for such effects to be detectable. Also, some sociologists argued that an NIT program would stabilize marriage; others held that it would increase rates of dissolution. Given this dissensus, it made little sense to build a particular model of marital response into the assignment scheme.

Thus we have an experiment in which families with low to moderate incomes are assigned to a variety of NIT treatments or to a control group. Assignment is random within categories defined by combinations of race-ethnicity, marital status, and level of family income. The last restriction reflects the underlying emphasis on labor supply. However, we see only two major problems with using this population for assessing the impacts of an NIT program on rates of making and breaking marriages. First, because never-married adults were excluded from the study, we cannot estimate effects of an NIT program on the rate of first marriages. Second, because we did not study high-income families. we cannot estimate NIT effects for the whole population.

Our initial work, summarized in Hannan, Tuma, and Groeneveld (1977), revealed very substantial differences between experimental and control groups in the rate of marital dissolution. Moreover, couples with income guarantees similar to those in the existing welfare system showed large increases in the dissolution rate. Those on programs with the most generous guarantees showed a much weaker response. Our second report in this *Journal* (Hannan, Tuma, and Groeneveld 1978) sought to explain this pattern with a model incorporating three factors: an income effect, an independence effect, and a welfare discount that summarizes nonpecuniary differences between an NIT program and existing welfare programs. Our third report (Tuma, Hannan, and Groeneveld 1979) explored time variations in response.

Goodwin apparently accepts our basic findings, but finds our focus too narrow. He argues that our model is "limited and incomplete." We never intended any encyclopedic treatment of the causes of marital disruption. Instead we took as our problem understanding how the experimental treatments worked. We have tried to model the process by which changes in income guarantees and tax rates might affect rates of dissolution.

We relied heavily on the logic of experimentation. While never doubting that interpersonal relations affect marital stability, we recognized that randomization produced identical (within probability limits) distributions of such causal factors in treatment and control groups. Thus it is not reasonable to attribute the differences between control and experimental groups to initial differences on such factors.

We have shown that the treatments do affect behavior. We have not yet shown that changes in feelings and attitudes precede or accompany these behavioral changes. But we flatly dispute that either the importance of the findings or the appropriateness of our model depends on such analysis.

Goodwin concentrates on what our model ignores but does not take the trouble to understand the model. This is especially evident in his discussion of the independence effect. We argued that, ceteris paribus, improvements in the quality of the best alternative to marriage increase the rate of marital dissolution. Goodwin mentions the difficulties facing single parents and presents yet another illustration that most Americans prefer marriage to singleness. In this light, he finds it "hard to imagine many women welcoming this kind of 'independence.'" He goes on to argue that the income guarantees do not cause dissolutions and that, instead, an unpleasant situation in the marriage drives people out.

Careful readers will have noticed that our model holds that independence *modifies* the base rate of dissolution. Any marriage can be thought of as having some base rate given by demographic characteristics (e.g., duration of marriage, numbers and ages of children) and by the quality of interpersonal relations in the marriage. A woman's financial independence, according to our model, weakens or intensifies other effects. Thus an instance of brutality might cause an independent woman to leave her husband but a similar incident might not drive away a more dependent woman. The various factors we identify *combine* to produce a rate of dissolution; no effects are "more basic" than others.

Nor does Goodwin understand our discussion of family size interactions. We found, not surprisingly, that income and independence effects depend on family size. In the interest of using our large but not enormous sample efficiently, we wished to pool all observations and parameterize the family size interactions. The set of interactions we used fits reasonably well over-all, but the effect has the wrong sign for families with one child. Before exploring more complicated ways in which these effects depend on family size, we performed a likelihood ratio test of the model against a more constrained alternative in which the effect has the same sign for all family sizes. This test indicated that we could not reject the more constrained model. If this test had produced different results, we would certainly have gone in directions advocated by Goodwin.

We turn next to the question of what other data might be used to study the impact of the experiment on marriage and the family. The experiment did not ignore subjective data. We have records at several points in time of marital satisfaction, conflict, role differentiation, patterns of leisure activities, etc. We intend to report the effects of the experiment on such measures and to use them in explicating our main findings. We have not used them in our early studies of marital dissolution for one reason: most such data were collected during the experiment and thus may already reflect experimental responses.

Some measures of subjective variables were gathered at the beginning of the experiment in Denver. Thus if we wish to restrict ourselves to the Denver sample, we can use preexperimental measures of marital satisfaction, for example. We find that satisfaction does indeed have a significant effect on the rate of marital dissolution. Moreover, income effects are weaker and independence effects are stronger for couples who report dissatisfaction with their marriage. These results make good sense and accord with the spirit of our model. Nothing in these findings leads us to qualify the interpretations and conclusions in our published report. Then why not focus on the Denver sample? The problem is sample size. In any study of rare events, like marital dissolution, it is crucial to use large samples. If we restrict attention to Denver, standard errors of estimates increase. For example, we find that the interactions of marital satisfaction with experimental treatments (either support levels or income and independence effects) are not statistically significant even at the .10 level. Thus we judge that we will learn most by beginning with analysis of the entire sample and postponing the use of data on the quality of marital relations.

We are sympathetic to Goodwin's urging that we employ data on respondents' understandings. We wish we had attempted to measure welfare discounts at the beginning of the experiment. Unfortunately, we did not realize the importance of this issue to marital stability at that time (nor did anyone else as far as we can determine). Thus we must use indirect methods to estimate welfare discounts.

Finally, Goodwin expresses his dismay at the conclusions drawn by the press from the presentation of some of our findings to Senator Moynihan's subcommittee. We infer that Goodwin thinks that we have presented an unbalanced view of the problem in reporting an increase in the rate of dissolution of marriages without providing evidence on the costs or benefits of such dissolutions to family members.

Surely the calculation of such costs and benefits depends on value judgments. Some view as undesirable almost any dissolution in a family with young children. Others believe that at least the adults involved know their best interests and act accordingly. If so, one may argue that the quality of life improves for all involved. (See the interviews reported in the *New York Times* [February 5, 1979] for some such testimony.) We doubt that empirical findings will alter value judgments concerning these issues. For one thing, the issues have many dimensions. Individuals may argue in different directions on different dimensions. For example, Goodwin at one point stresses the hardships faced by divorced women and at another point suggests that some women may be better off to end their current marriages. Is dissolution a good thing? Such a question does not merit any simplistic answers. Our continuing research may shed some light on the various factual questions involved in judging the costs and benefits of dissolution. In no sense, however, will such findings settle the larger moral and political questions.

MICHAEL T. HANNAN and NANCY BRANDON TUMA
Stanford University

LYLE P. GROENEVELD
SRI International

REFERENCES

Hannan, Michael T., Nancy Brandon Tuma, and Lyle P. Groeneveld. 1977. "Income and Marital Events: Evidence from an Income-Maintenance Experiment." *American Journal of Sociology* 82 (May): 1186–1211.
———. 1978. "Income and Independence Effects on Marital Dissolution: Results from the Seattle-Denver Income-Maintenance Experiments." *American Journal of Sociology* 84 (November): 611–33.
Tuma, Nancy Brandon, Michael T. Hannan, and Lyle P. Groeneveld. 1979. "Dynamic Analysis of Event Histories." *American Journal of Sociology* 84 (January): 820–54.

II

LABOR FORCE PROGRAMS: DESIGNED EXPERIMENTS

This section contains two articles each from the Seattle/Denver and Gary Income Maintenance Experiments and one from the National Supported Work Demonstration. All are concerned with labor force outcomes—employment, hours worked, and earnings—yet the Income Maintenance and Supported Work evaluations have very different focuses. For the SIME/DIME and the Gary Experiment, the issue is "how large are the negative program effects?" That is, to what extent do program participants reduce their labor supply as a result of the program treatment—a guaranteed income support payment, reduced according to a "tax rate" applied to earnings? In this case, theory predicts a reduction in labor supply, and the only sense in which such a result can be seen as positive is that labor supply reductions may be small.[1]

By contrast, the Supported Work program treatment involves subsidized employment, so that participants are producing output of some real value during their time in the program. This work experience is also expected to lead to increased employment and earnings after the individual leaves the program, so that unambiguously positive program effects are (at least theoretically) possible. Manpower training programs of this sort have a long history,[2] but recent results, such as those in the chapter by Masters and Maynard, combined with a national political climate increasingly supportive of "work in return for benefits," have led to renewed emphasis on such programs, at least partly at the expense of pure income maintenance programs.[3]

EVALUATION DESIGN

The chapters in this section result from designed experiments with random assignment to treatment and control, yet none use simple experimental/control comparisons to measure program effects. Rather, all use regression-like strategy to increase efficiency, with the added argument for the SIME/DIME and Gary analyses that such calculations help to diminish bias arising from stratification on an endogenous variable. (See the paper by Morris et al. in Part I.) But despite the prevalence of a multivariate regression-like framework, the calculations undertaken in these chapters are quite different.

Masters and Maynard's goals and techniques are the simplest. They attempt only to measure before/after differences in the behavior of experimentals and controls, and they do this via ordinary least squares (OLS) regression with the treatment group distinguished by a dummy variable. Keeley et al. and Moffitt have a more elaborate goal—the use of program treatment variation to estimate behavioral labor supply parameters. Both authors use the tobit model (see the volume and Part I introductions), and Keeley et al. use over-time change to separate income and substitution effects with particular care. Burtless and Hausman are also interested in estimating labor supply parameters, but their model involves an innovative maximum likelihood approach to situations involving nonlinear budget constraints. Finally, Tuma and Robins use the model advanced by Tuma et al. (Part I) to examine experimental/control differences in employment during SIME/DIME. As in the Supported Work evaluation (Masters and Maynard), this is essentially a reduced-form rather than a structural model: Experimental/control differences, rather than fundamental behavioral parameters, are being estimated. Because of the SIME/DIME research design, however, the treatment is clearly defined by the variation in an income guarantee and wage rate (as altered by the tax rate), so that the causal mechanisms underlying Tuma and Robins' results are clear. This is less true for Supported Work where the question remains, "what is the treatment?"

THE ROLE OF THEORY

The design of the income maintenance experiments is closely related to theory and observation in the study of labor supply. Individuals were placed on experimental plans defined by the combination of an income guarantee and a tax rate that the guarantee reduces as earnings increase. One might take an agnostic view to the analysis of labor supply under such treatment plans, using dummy variables to measure, in a "model-free" way, the differences in response to different treatments. Labor supply theory suggests a more parsimonious approach.

According to this view, those provided with an income supplement should respond by purchasing more goods, one of these being leisure. That is, they should reduce their labor supply. Thus, the program income supplement by itself should decrease labor supply. Each treatment plan also involves a particular tax rate. This tax decreases the effective wage rate an individual receives for market work, and the tax rate defines the speed with which the program income supplement is reduced in response to earned income. A wage rate reduction has two consequences. The first of these is an income effect—at a given level of labor supply, a decreased wage rate means that fewer dollars are earned, so that fewer goods, including leisure, can be purchased. But this income reduction is always less than the basic income supplement, so that each treatment group experiences a net increase in unearned income and thus should respond with a decrease in labor supply.

The second consequence is a "substitution effect." With a lower wage rate, the relative price[4] of the good (leisure) has fallen, so that individuals should purchase more of it (substitute toward it). Once again, the program effect is expected to be a decrease in labor supply. The decomposition of changes in labor supply into (presumed) negative program income and substitution effects[5] is the sole empirical content of economic theory for the income maintenance experiments. The principle goal of the analysis was to estimate accurately the relevant magnitudes of effect.

WHAT HAVE WE LEARNED?

With clearly defined treatments, closely tied to a behavioral theory, the income maintenance analysis always has a "structural" content. That is, one feels some confidence that the causal mechanisms underlying the observed effects are correctly understood, and that the results can be extrapolated beyond the particulars of a given time and place. As a result, there is reason to believe that the program model could, if desired, be successfully replicated.

Keeley et al. find that, as expected, both program income and substitution effects decrease labor supply, with the strongest effect being the income effects for wives and female heads of households. The observed income effects are 2.5% for husbands, 16.6% for wives, and 7.4% for female heads, while the substitution effects are 2.9% for husbands, 5.3% for wives, and 3.7% for female heads.[6]

Finding a relatively weak labor supply response for husbands is corroborated by Moffitt and by Burtless and Hausman with the Gary data; these studies also find that the husbands response is due entirely to the income effect. Moffitt, however, found a stronger response for female heads than did Keeley et al., and essentially no response for wives. The latter phenomenon is attributed to demand side conditions in Gary—part-time jobs are almost nonexistent. This result points out the importance of estimating effects across several sites and measuring demand-side variables where possible. Different attempts in this direction are illustrated in the chapters by Farkas et al. (Part III) and by Bishop et al. (Part VIII).

As a result of the income maintenance experiments, we now have an agreed-upon theory and reasonably reliable estimates of empirical magnitudes to understand the likely effects of a national program. On this score, it is instructive to examine the results from Seattle/Denver and Gary, as well as from the rural experiment (Palmer and Pechman, 1978), to notice how much they have added to the original New Jersey experiment (Pechman and Timpane, 1975) in the scope of, and our confidence in the reliability of, the results.

Even as these results have become available, however, policy interest has shifted from income maintenance to subsidized job creation. Here the relevant theory and empirical magnitudes are less well understood, but much work is underway (Palmer, 1978). Nevertheless, the only analysis we have of Supported Work is based on simple experimental/control comparisons. Although the program seems to exert positive effects for some subgroups on some outcome variables, we do not know which aspects of the treatment are responsible for these effects. It is noteworthy that an attempt to answer this question was unsuccessful. That is, the analysts failed to discover (a) "What local conditions, administrative auspices, and implementation strategies seem to be conducive to success?" and (b) "What characteristics of the program model have the greatest impact on participant performance and behavior?"[7] Under the designs currently in use with employment and training programs, we understand the nature of the treatment only generally and the mechanisms of program effect only imprecisely. Thus, an important research agenda for the next decade is: "Why do employment and training programs work?"

NOTES

1. True positive results, however, may flow from the goods and increased time at home that can be purchased with the program income supplement. (See the chapter by Maynard and Murnane in Part IV and the chapters in Part V. For results suggesting that the Gary Experiment had a positive effect on infant birth weight, see Kehrer and Wolin [1979].)

2. For evaluations of an earlier version of a similar program idea, see the chapter by Ashenfelter and Kiefer in Part III.

3. For a discussion of some of the resulting initiatives, see the chapters by Mallar et al. on the Job Corps and by Farkas et al. on the Entitlement Demonstration (Part III) and the chapter by Bishop et al. on the Employment Opportunity Pilot Projects (Part VIII).

4. That is, the rate at which it can be traded for dollars to purchase goods in the market.

5. In economic theory, this is known as the Slutsky decomposition. See Addison and Siebert (1979: 69-85).

6. These are calculated from Table 4 in the chapter by Keeley et al.

7. See Board of Directors, MDRC, 1980: 40-41.

REFERENCES

ADDISON, J. T. and W. S. SIEBERT (1979) The Market for Labor: An Analytical Treatment. Santa Monica, CA: Goodyear.

Board of Directors, Manpower Demonstration Research Corporation (1980) Summary and Findings of the National Supported Work Demonstration. Cambridge, MA: Ballinger.

KEHRER, B. H. and C. M. WOLIN (1979) "Impact of income maintenance on low birth weight: evidence from the Gary Experiment." J. of Human Resources 14: 434-462.

PALMER, J. [ed.] (1978) Creating Jobs: Public Employment Programs and Wage Subsidies. Washington, DC: Brookings.

——— and J. PECHMAN [eds.] (1978) Welfare in Rural Areas: The North Carolina-Iowa Income Maintenance Experiment. Washington, DC: Brookings.

PECHMAN, J. and P. M. TIMPANE [eds.] (1975) Work Incentives and Income Guarantees: The New Jersey Negative Income Tax Experiment. Washington, DC: Brookings.

8

This chapter is important both for its methods and its findings. Methodologically, it is significant that experimental data are analyzed within a structural model of behavior so that parameter estimates of some generalizability results. In addition, the empirical model proposed here nicely mirrors the usual theoretical (comparative statics) discussion of behavior at two points in time. By contrast, most previous efforts have used cross-sectional data (different individuals at the same point in time) to estimate relations that are inherently dynamic (the same individuals at different points in time).[1]

Substantively, the findings presented here may be the most reliable of all the labor supply results generated by the various income maintenance experiments, and these findings—labor supply disincentives of 5.3% for husbands, 22% for wives, and 11.2% for female heads—appear both reasonable and in line with prior expectation. The Seattle and Denver Experiments can be counted successful both in producing labor supply results that "make sense" (this chapter and the succeeding one by Tuma and Robins) and also in producing other important, but unanticipated, findings (see Tuma et al., Part I).

Keeley et al. begin by summarizing the SIME/DIME experimental treatment: a payment scheme involving an income guarantee that declines according to a "tax rate" as earned income increases (expression 1). The result is experimental manipulation of an individual's unearned income and wage rate. According to labor supply theory, the latter has both an "income-compensated substitution" effect that are described in expressions 2 and 3, as well as in n. 9. (See also the Introduction to this section and the references cited there.) The authors exploit the preduring nature of their data to express these effects in finite difference form, with an individual's preprogram labor supply serving as his point of compensation (expression 4 and sections II.B and II.C). This is the basic model to be estimated.

The empirical strategy contains a number of interesting features. First, control families are assumed to experience no change in their wage rate or their disposable income (evaluated at preprogram labor supply) but are included in the regression to increase efficiency. Second, control variables in the regression include those that defined assignments to treatment status within the experiment. This attempts to reduce the bias associated with stratification on an endogenous variable (see Morris et al., Part I). Third, calculation of the program-induced change in disposable income is quite complex, since, in addition to being based on earnings and nonwage income in the preprogram period, items either taxed at 100% or reimbursed at 50- or 100% must be accounted for (see n. 26). Fourth, the authors ultimately estimate an equation in which the outcome variable is during-experiment labor supply, with pre-experimental labor supply among the predictors, rather than an equation in which the outcome variable is the difference of these, as their theoretical section has led us to expect (see Section III.B and expression 7). The consequences of this procedure are unclear (particularly because the authors do not report the b_1 coefficient in expression 7, nor the results of the alternate calculation to predict the labor supply difference).[2] Fifth, Keeley et al. use a wage equation estimated for those at work to impute wages to their sample. As they note, this does risk selectivity bias. (See the chapters by Barnow et al. and Heckman in Part I and Farkas et al. in Part III.) Finally, the tobit model is used for examination.[3] (For a quick description of this model see the introduction to Part I.)

Sections IV and V report the results of estimation and then use them to extrapolate to a potential national program. Disincentive effects come through clearly and are reported separately as income and substitution effects (Table 4). Table 5 provides one summary of the entire income maintenance research program: estimates of the differential labor supply disincentive of different program plans applied to population subgroups.

NOTES

1. Unfortunately, after proposing this model, the authors then actually estimate one in which the dependent variable is not a first-difference. More on this below.

2. The usual procedure to deal with errors in variables—the difficulty confronting the authors— is instrumental variables. The properties of the procedure they do use are not obvious.

3. For a less restrictive model, see Chapter 16.

The Estimation of Labor Supply Models Using Experimental Data

Michael C. Keeley, Philip K. Robins, Robert G. Spiegelman, and Richard W. West

For many years there has been interest in replacing the existing complex transfer system in the United States with a nationwide negative income tax (*NIT*) program.[1] The feasibility and desirability of an *NIT*, however, depend on its effects on aggregate labor supply (and its cost). Interest in predicting these aggregate effects has motivated considerable empirical research on labor supply. The first studies used existing data, usually cross-sectional, to estimate the parameters of labor supply functions.[2] Unfortunately, the range of estimates in these studies is disturbingly large and of limited usefulness to policymakers.[3] Consequently, a new approach to labor supply research has been followed social experimentation.[4]

Several experiments have been funded by the federal government to test the effects of alternative *NIT* programs on labor supply. The first experiment, the New Jersey Experiment, was conducted in New Jersey and Pennsylvania from 1968 to 1972.[5] Other experiments have taken place in Gary, Indiana from 1970 to 1974, and in rural areas of Iowa and North Carolina from 1969 to 1973. The largest and most comprehensive of these experiments began in 1971 in Seattle, Washington and Denver, Colorado and is still taking place.

In principle, a controlled experiment affords the opportunity to overcome most of the problems inherent in nonexperimental research, because in an experiment, the budget constraints of individuals are exogenously shifted in a measurable way. In practice, however, the experiments have been beset with their own unique set of econometric problems. These problems include the nonrandom assignment of experimental treatment, small samples, truncation of response, limited duration, participation in other welfare programs both before and during the experiment by sample members, and the selection of nonrepresentative samples.[6]

In this paper, a methodology is presented that attempts to deal with these problems. Experimental data from the Seattle and

*Economists, SRI International. The research reported in this paper was performed under contracts with the states of Washington and Colorado, prime contractors for the Department of Health, Education, and Welfare, under contract numbers SRS-70-53 and SRS-71-18, respectively. The opinions expressed in the paper are our own and should not be construed as representing the opinions or policies of the states of Washington or Colorado, or any agency of the *U.S.* government. An earlier version of this paper was presented at the Summer 1976 meetings of the Econometric Society and in seminars at the National Bureau of Economic Research and Mathematica Policy Research. Jodie Allen, Yoram Barzel, David Betson, Michael Boskin, Glen. Cain, Joseph Corbett, Irwin Garfinkel, David Greenberg, Terry Johnson, Richard Kaluzny, Richard Kasten, Robert Lerman, Stanley Masters, Myles Maxfield, Robert Moffit, Larry Orr, Harold Watts, and Robert Willis provided valuable comments on various drafts of this paper. We are, of course, solely responsible for the views presented and for any remaining errors. Helen Cohn, Diane Hollenbeck, Paul McElherne, Gary Stieger, and Steven Spickard provided expert programming assistance.

[1] Milton Friedman is usually credited with developing the concept of a negative income tax. Robert Lampman and James Tobin (1965) among others also made early contributions to the concept.

[2] An excellent collection of such studies is presented in Glen Cain and Harold Watts.

[3] See Keeley for a survey of these studies and a discussion of some of the econometric difficulties that lead to such a wide range of estimates.

[4] Heather Ross (1966) is credited with first conceiving the idea of an *NIT* experiment. Guy Orcutt and Alice Orcutt (1968) first published a paper outlining an experimental design.

[5] The New Jersey Experiment is described in David Kershaw and Jerilyn Fair. Watts and Albert Rees (1977a, b) and Joseph Pechman and P. Michael Timpane present the results from this experiment.

[6] See Henry Aaron, Keeley, and Keeley and Robins for a critical discussion of many of these problems.

Denver Income Maintenance Experiments (*SIME/DIME*) are used to estimate the parameters of a labor supply function.[7] These parameters are then used to predict the nationwide labor supply effects of alternative *NIT* programs.

The empirical response function estimated measures the change in labor supply over a two-year period. The Tobit method is used to estimate equations for single female heads of families, husbands, and wives. Nationwide aggregate labor supply responses to six alternative *NIT* programs are predicted by applying the response function to data from the March 1975 *Current Population Survey*.

The plan of the paper is as follows: Section I describes an experimental *NIT* program; Section II presents a theoretical model of the labor supply response to an *NIT*; Section III specifies the empirical model; Section IV presents the empirical results; Section V discusses policy implications; and Section VI presents the summary and conclusions.

I. Description of an Experimental NIT Program

An *NIT* program is characterized by a support (or guarantee) level S, and a tax rate t_e. The support level is the grant provided when other income is zero, and the tax rate is the rate at which the grant declines as other income increases. In a controlled *NIT* experiment, an effort is made to ensure that the influence of other tax and transfer programs is eliminated. Public transfers, therefore, are fully taxed, and positive taxes are reimbursed. Consequently, the payment a person receives depends on gross income and both experimental and nonexperimental tax rates.

For this discussion, it is assumed that nonexperimental net nonwage income (including public transfers) is zero and that both the nonexperimental and experimental tax rates are constant. These assumptions are relaxed in the empirical analysis. The

[7] For a description of *SIME/DIME*, see Mordecai Kurz and Spiegelman (1971, 1972).

payment P associated with a particular *NIT* program is determined as follows:

$$(1) \quad P = \begin{cases} S - t_e Y + t_n Y & \text{if } S + t_n Y \geq t_e Y \\ 0 & \text{if } S + t_n Y < t_e Y \end{cases}$$

where t_n is the nonexperimental tax rate and Y is gross income. The payment, if positive, is equal to the grant $S - t_e Y$, plus the positive tax reimbursement $t_n Y$.

Figure 1 shows a graph of the nonexperimental budget line (line ABT) and the experimental budget line (line ABE) of an individual enrolled in an *NIT* program. Point B, where the two budget lines intersect, is the point at which the payment becomes zero and is known as the tax break-even level. The tax break-even level of income, given by $S/(t_e - t_n)$, may be contrasted with the grant break-even level of income, given by S/t_e. The grant break-even level is the level of income at which the *NIT* grant $(S - t_e Y)$ becomes zero.

The program support level S is designated by the line ET. Under the assumption that the nonexperimental tax rate, t_n, is less than the tax rate of the *NIT* program under consideration, t_e, the absolute value of the slope of the new budget line (ABE) to the right of B is reduced.

The Seattle and Denver Income Maintenance Experiments are testing eleven different *NIT* programs. The programs are described in Table 1. A feature of *SIME/DIME* that distinguishes it from the other *NIT* experiments is the testing of programs in which the marginal tax rate declines as income increases. Families in *SIME/DIME* are enrolled for either three or five years.[8] Different durations are being tested, because of difficulties in inferring permanent effects from experiments of finite length. According to Charles Metcalf, substitution and income effects should vary according to the length of the experiment. In our empirical analysis, we formally test for such differences. The results of these tests are presented in Section IV.

[8] A small number of families are enrolled for twenty years but are not considered in this study.

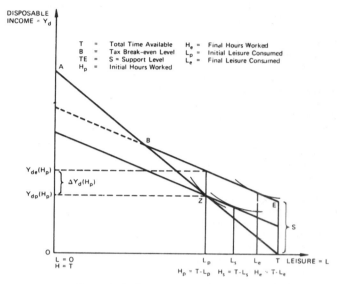

FIGURE 1. AN EXPERIMENTAL *NIT* PROGRAM

TABLE 1—PROGRAMS BEING TESTED IN THE SEATTLE AND DENVER
INCOME MAINTENANCE EXPERIMENTS
(1971 Dollars)

Support Level	Initial Tax Rate	Rate of Decline of Average Tax Rate per $1,000 of Income	Grant Break-Even Level	Tax Break-Even Level
$3,800	.5	0	$ 7,600	$10,250
3,800	.7	0	5,429	6,350
3,800	.7	.025	7,367	10,850
3,800	.8	.025	5,802	7,800
4,800	.5	0	9,600	13,150
4,800	.7	0	6,867	8,520
4,800	.7	.025	12,000	19,700
4,800	.8	.025	8,000	11,510
5,600	.5	0	11,200	15,700
5,600	.7	0	8,000	9,780
5,600	.8	.025	10,360	16,230

Note: The figures for the support level, the grant break-even level, and the tax break-even level are in 1971 dollars and are for a family of four with only one earner and no income outside of earnings. Adjustments are made to these figures for family size and for changes in the cost of living over time. Positive tax reimbursements include the federal income tax and social security taxes. The federal income tax assumes the family takes the standard deduction. State income taxes, which are relevant only for the Denver Experiment (there is no state income tax in Washington), are ignored in calculating the tax break-even level. Thus, the tax break-even level is slightly higher for the Denver Experiment.

II. Theoretical Analysis of the Labor Supply Response to an *NIT* Program

A. *The Model*

It is assumed that each individual maximizes a well-behaved utility function, $U(L, Y_d)$, where L is leisure and Y_d is consumption of market goods (or disposable income) subject to the budget constraint

$$(2) \qquad F \equiv wT + Y_n = wL + Y_d$$

where F is full income, w is the net wage rate, T is total time available, and Y_n is net nonwage income. Utility maximization implies that the individual has a labor supply function $H = H(w, Y_n)$, where $H = T - L$ is hours of work. Totally differentiating the labor supply function and substituting in the Slutsky equation[9] gives

$$(3) \quad dH = \left.\frac{\partial H}{\partial w}\right|_U \cdot dw + \frac{\partial H}{\partial Y_n}(Hdw + dY_n)$$
$$= \alpha dw + \beta(Hdw + dY_n)$$

where U is utility, α is the substitution effect, and β is the income effect.[10] The term $Hdw + dY_n$ is the total differential of disposable income, holding constant the initial supply of labor H.

The model given by equation (3) is specified in terms of unobservable differential changes. The differential change model implies that each individual's point of compensation should be his or her initial equilibrium labor supply. If differences in initial

[9] The Slutsky equation decomposes the total effect of a wage change on labor supply into a substitution effect and an income effect:

$$\frac{\partial H}{\partial w} = \left.\frac{\partial H}{\partial w}\right|_U + H\frac{\partial H}{\partial Y_n}$$

[10] For a family with more than one potential earner, the equation can be generalized to include cross-substitution effects. In our empirical formulation of this model, it is assumed that cross-substitution effects are zero, partly because the net wage changes of both spouses are highly correlated and their effects are difficult to distinguish empirically. An attempt to apply this model to nonexperimental cross-sectional data is presented in Orley Ashenfelter and James Heckman (1973, 1974). See, however, the critique of Jonathan Dickinson (1977).

labor supply across individuals are the result of differences in equilibrium or permanent labor supply, each person should be compensated at his or her initial position. In our application of the model, we follow this compensation procedure.[11] To measure substitution and income effects empirically, finite differences are used to approximate the unobservable differential changes. In discrete form, the model described in equation (3) becomes:

$$(4) \quad \Delta H \approx \alpha\Delta w + \beta(H_p\Delta w + \Delta Y_n) =$$
$$\alpha\Delta w + \beta\Delta Y_d(H_p)$$

where $\Delta Y_d(H_p)$ is the change in disposable income of an individual, holding constant his or her initial labor supply H_p.

B. *Analyzing the Response to an NIT Program*

Equation (4) states that the effects of shifts in the budget constraint on labor supply can be decomposed into a substitution effect, which depends on the change in the net wage rate Δw, and an income effect, which depends on the change in disposable income evaluated at initial hours of work, $\Delta Y_d(H_p)$. For a person placed on an experimental *NIT* program, Δw is equal to the gross wage rate times the difference between the pre-experimental and experimental tax rates,[12] and $\Delta Y_d(H_p)$ is equal to the payment the person would receive if initial labor supply were maintained. Referring again to Figure 1, consider a person below the break-even level who is in equilibrium at point Z before the imposition of an *NIT* program. The change in the quantity of leisure demanded is comprised of a substitution effect $(L_s - L_p)$ holding disposable income constant at initial labor supply, and an income effect $(L_e - L_s)$ holding relative prices (i.e., the

[11] If differences in initial labor supply are purely transitory, then such a procedure is not appropriate, because initial labor supply is not at an equilibrium position. Compensation at the initial position, however, ensures that the point of compensation is not endogenous.

[12] This assumes that the gross wage rate is unaffected by the program.

wage raᴇᴄ ᵣᴇlative to the price of goods) constant.[13] Disposable income is held constant by rotating the budget line through the initial equilibrium point Z, where, at the new net wage rate and new monetary full income, the consumer could still purchase the initial consumption bundle.

The analysis thus far focuses on the response of a given individual to a particular program. Because of differences in tastes or other unmeasured variables, however, there is considerable heterogeneity of the initial equilibrium positions of individuals.[14] In fact, the best empirical labor supply equations explain only about 20–30 percent of the variance in labor supply.[15] This suggests that on a given budget line there is a distribution of initial equilibrium positions. For simplicity, it is assumed that this distribution is the result of differences in tastes.

Because separate responses resulting from compensated wage changes and income changes are not observed for each person (only total response that results from both changes is observed),[16] some a priori restriction is needed to identify the model so that income and substitution effects can be measured empirically. The restriction we impose is to assume that different individuals have equal substitution effects and equal income effects at their initial equilibrium positions.[17] If, in fact, income and substitution effects differ among individuals, the empirical method used measures average income and substitution effects in the sample.

The assumptions underlying this model are different from those implicit in most cross-sectional studies.[18] Instead of assuming that each person has the same preference structure, it is assumed that differences in taste are reflected in differences in initial equilibrium labor supply, after controlling for differences in budget constraints. Therefore, there is no single utility function that is consistent with the model, although each person is assumed to maximize a well-behaved utility function.

C. *Implications of the Model*

The assumption that different individuals have equal substitution and income effects implies that response to a given *NIT* program depends on the initial equilibrium position. For example, a person with low income experiences a considerable change in disposable income and net wage rate, and a large response is expected. On the other hand, a person initially at the break-even level experiences a change only in the net wage rate. Response for this person consists only of a (Slutsky) substitution effect and is therefore smaller. Next, consider a person above the break-even level. This person experiences changes in disposable income and the net wage rate only if the elasticity of substitution in consumption is sufficiently large that the indifference curve through the initial point intersects the *NIT* segment of the new budget line. Thus, for a person initially above the break-even level, we would expect a very small probability of response. Finally, consider an individual who is not working: this person experiences a considerable change in disposable income and net wage rate, but has zero response.[19]

[13]This is the Slutsky, as opposed to the Hicks, decomposition.

[14]See Robert Hall (1975), and Heckman and Robert Willis for a discussion of heterogeneity.

[15]See Cain and Watts for a sampling of typical cross-section labor supply equations. These studies, however, analyze a measure of labor supply that does not correspond strictly to our concept of equilibrium labor supply. Instead, the studies use current labor supply, which is the sum of permanent or equilibrium labor supply, a transitory component, and a life cycle component.

[16]For persons at the tax break-even level initially, total response is a result of the (Slutsky) substitution effect.

[17]Although it may appear that we are assuming constant substitution and income effects for each person, this is not the case; indeed, it is impossible to have a labor supply function with constant income and substitution effects (see, for example, Dickinson, 1975, p. 31).

[18]It might be noted that the model described in this paper cannot be estimated using cross-sectional data. In a cross section, only one equilibrium position is observed, and the model is not identified.

[19]Response is subject to truncation because, at most, a person can reduce hours to zero. The estimation technique we employ accounts for this problem.

Thus, response depends on the initial equilibrium position.[20]

Differences in response to an *NIT* program arise, not because persons with different tastes for work have inherently different responses to changes in disposable income or net wage rates, but because individuals with different propensities to work (different initial equilibria on a given budget constraint) are offered different inducements to change their behavior. Those with the smallest propensities to work experience the largest changes in income.

A final implication of this model is that theory-free response models that compare the average response of persons on different programs are not meaningful. The reason for this is that persons with higher incomes (and therefore higher labor supplies) are assigned to the more generous programs in order to reduce the average cost of an observation.[21] Thus, because both response and assignment to program depend on the initial position, biased measures of program differences are obtained.[22] The response model used, however, controls for the nonrandom assignment by allowing response to be a function of preexperimental labor supply and by directly measuring the change in budget constraints caused by the *NIT*.

III. Empirical Specification

To estimate equation (4), data on heads of families in *SIME/DIME* are used. The change in labor supply ΔH, is equal to hours of work in the second year of the experiment H_e, minus hours of work in the year prior to the experiment H_p. The response variables, Δw and $\Delta Y_d(H_p)$, depend on the particular budget constraint, and on the preprogram equilibrium position. For reasons described below, several modifications are made to this equation regarding functional form, additional variables, missing data on wage rates for nonworkers, and nonlinearity of the budget constraints.

A. The Role of Control Families

Approximately 45 percent of the families in *SIME/DIME* serve as controls and are not eligible for payments. For these families, it is assumed that Δw and $\Delta Y_d(H_p)$ are zero.[23] Control families are included in the sample, however, to increase the efficiency of the estimated treatment effects.[24] Efficiency is increased because factors other than the experiment (such as changing economic conditions) cause labor supply to change over time. The inclusion of control families in the sample enables us to make a more precise distinction between experimental and nonexperimental effects. Variables used in this study to measure nonexperimental effects are called control variables. The control variables include all variables that affect assignment to experimental treatments.[25]

B. Calculating the Change in Disposable Income

The change in disposable income evaluated at the initial equilibrium hours of work

---

[20]Note that in a typical cross-sectional model, where it is assumed that gross wage effects and income effects are constant, response would not depend on the initial position (below break even and ignoring truncation), because the changes in nonwage income and the net wage rate do not depend on the initial position.

[21]Simple random assignment is not used in any of the *NIT* experiments. See John Conlisk and Kurz, and Keeley and Robins for a description of the *SIME/DIME* assignment model.

[22]If program dummy variables were interacted with all assignment variables, unbiased estimates of response could be obtained. Such a model would have far too many parameters, however, to be estimated with precision using our sample. See Spiegelman and West.

[23]Changes in the control budget constraints that have zero mean and are uncorrelated with the variables in the equation would not affect the consistency of the estimates.

[24]A comparison of least squares estimates for husbands, including and excluding control families, indicates that the coefficients of $\Delta Y_d(H_p)$ and Δw differ by less than 10 percent, while the standard errors are 16 percent larger when controls are excluded.

[25]The control variables include eight dummy variables for normal income categories, dummy variables for race (black/white) and site (Seattle/Denver), age, number of family members, number of children under 5 years of age, and Aid to Families with Dependent Children (*AFDC*) benefits in the year prior to enrollment.

is given by

$$(5) \quad \Delta Y_d(H_p) = Y_{de}(H_p) - Y_{dp}(H_p)$$

where $Y_{de}(H_p)$ is disposable income evaluated at H_p under the *NIT*, and $Y_{dp}(H_p)$ is disposable income evaluated at H_p before the *NIT*. For this study, $\Delta Y_d(H_p)$ is calculated on the basis of earnings and nonwage income in the year before enrollment in the experiment.[26] Thus, $\Delta Y_d(H_p)$ depends on both transitory and permanent components of labor supply. In theory, the change in disposable income should be measured at normal or permanent labor supply. Because there is likely to be a transitory component in our measure of labor supply, our estimate of the income effect will be biased because of the presence of errors in variables.[27] In a lengthier version of this paper available from the authors upon request, the bias is discussed and it is shown that the bias is not likely to be large if preexperimental labor supply is included on the right-hand side of the equation. For this reason, H_p is

---

[26] $\Delta Y_d(H_p) = S - SR100 - .5(SR50 - SA50) - [t - r(Y - E)](Y - E) + Q$, where S is the support level, t is the initial tax rate, and r is the rate of decline of the average tax rate. The term $SR100$ represents items taxed at 100 percent: bonus value of food stamps, welfare benefits other than *AFDC*, unemployment and workmen's compensation, veteran's survivors and disability benefits, training stipends net of tuition, fees and books, and social security benefits. The term $SR50$ represents items taxes at 50 percent: alimony and child support received and other support received. The term $SA50$ represents items reimbursed at 50 percent: alimony and child support paid and other support paid. The term Y represents items taxed as income: earnings, insurance benefits, pensions and annuities, payments from private disability plans, and a fraction of net worth. The term E represents items subtracted from income: child care expenses, care for the aged, and medical expenses. The term Q represents items reimbursed at 100 percent: federal and state income taxes and social security taxes. If $\Delta Y_d(H_p) > 0$, a family is defined as being below the tax break-even level; it is set equal to zero for families above the tax break-even level. Families receiving *AFDC* benefits prior to the experiment are required to give up their *AFDC* status in order to receive *NIT* payments. We subtract preexperimental *AFDC* benefits from $\Delta Y_d(H_p)$ for families below the tax break-even level.

[27] The substitution effect would also be biased to the extent that the preexperimental tax rate depends on preexperimental labor supply.

included among the explanatory variables, and H_e is used as the dependent variable.

C. *Calculating the Change in the Net Wage Rate*

The change in the net wage rate is given by

$$(6) \quad \Delta w = -W(t_e - t_p)$$

where W is the gross wage rate, t_e is the experimental tax rate, and t_p is the preexperimental tax rate. In calculating this variable from *SIME/DIME* data, two problems arise. First, the preexperimental tax function and many of the experimental tax functions are non-linear. Second, wage rates are not observed for nonworkers.

As mentioned earlier, a feature of *SIME/DIME* is the testing of declining tax rate programs. The effect of the declining tax rate programs is to make the experimental tax rate t_e an endogenous variable that depends on labor supply. To purge the tax rate of this endogeneity, we linearize the budget constraint around the preexperimental point and treat the individual as if he or she were on the tangent linear budget constraint. This procedure is deficient in that all final equilibrium points are not on the linearized budget constraint, although the rate of decline of the tax rate is small. Furthermore, because the experimental budget set is nonconvex for families on the declining tax rate programs, and because small changes in nonconvex budget sets may lead to large changes in behavior, the linearization may not be a reasonable approximation to the true budget set. To account for the linearization procedure during estimation, we include a dummy variable for persons on the declining tax rate programs.

The preexperimental budget constraint is also non-linear, because of the progressivity of the positive income tax system and the interrelations among tax rates in income-conditioned public transfer programs. Endogeneity is not a problem, however, because preexperimental labor supply is predetermined. The preexperimental tax rates are derived on the basis of preexperimental income and participation in certain income-conditioned tax and transfer programs. The income-conditioned programs we consider include federal and state income taxes, social security taxes, *AFDC*, Aid to Families with Dependent Children-Unemployed Parent (*AFDC-UP*), and Food Stamps. The tax rates are derived in accordance with the tax laws and the administrative regulations of the public transfer programs.[28]

Because wage rates are not observed for nonworkers, a wage equation is estimated for workers based on personal characteristics, and the equation is used to predict wage rates for the entire sample.[29] A variety of different wage equations can be specified; the wage equation we estimate is a simple linear formulation based on the human capital model of Jacob Mincer.[30] The change in the net wage Δw is calculated as the product of the predicted wage rate and the difference between the linearized preexperimental and experimental tax rates. Like $\Delta Y_d(H_p)$, Δw is set equal to zero for persons above the tax break-even level.

D. *Additional Experimental Variables*

Certain families on *SIME/DIME* are enrolled in manpower programs that provide counseling and subsidize training and educational activities.[31] To capture the effects of the three manpower programs of the experiment, dummy variables for each program are included in the empirical specification.

Many of the enrolled families are initially above the tax break-even level.[32] Even though the calculated values of Δw and $\Delta Y_d(H_p)$ are zero for families with preexperimental equilibria above the tax break-even level, some of these families will respond to the experiment.[33] Response above the break-even level is measured by defining three explanatory variables that capture the location of the family relative to the break-even level: a dummy variable signifying whether or not the family is above the break-even level, the break-even level of the

$$W = .800B + .110E + .036X - .00073X^2$$
$$(.049) \quad (.014) \quad (.008) \quad (.00020)$$
$$+ .590 \text{ for wives}$$
$$(.192)$$

$$W = .010B + .102E + .045X - .00098X^2$$
$$(.045) \quad (.013) \quad (.009) \quad (.00021)$$
$$+ .816 \text{ for female heads of households}$$
$$(.183)$$

where B is a dummy variable for race (black = 1), E is years of schooling, and X is experience (defined as age minus years of schooling minus 5). Standard errors are in parentheses. The R^2s are .112, .048, and .116, respectively. Because the variance of Δw would be dominated by the change in the tax rate no matter how complicated the wage equation, the results using a more complicated wage equation are likely to be similar to the results reported in this paper.

[28] See Kurz et al. for a discussion of how the positive tax rates are derived, and Maxfield for a discussion of how the transfer program tax rates are derived. There is some evidence that legal tax rates are an overestimate of the effective tax rates of public transfer programs. Legal tax rates are used in this paper because they are used in the computer program that extrapolates the experimental results to the national population.

[29] This approach follows Hall (1973) and Edward Kalachek and Frederick Raines. Reuben Gronau and Heckman (1974) demonstrate that the wage equation approach yields biased estimates for nonworkers, and they develop alternative estimation procedures. However, in this paper, the substitution effect is estimated as the coefficient of the change in the net wage rather than the coefficient of the gross wage rate. It is unlikely that small biases in estimating gross wages significantly affect the change variable, which depends primarily on the difference between the experimental and preexperimental tax rates. In a recent paper, Heckman (1976) finds that in a national sample of white married women (the National Longitudinal Survey) the selectivity bias in wage rates is quantitatively small.

[30] The estimated wage equations are

$$W = -.071B + .033E + .061X - .00106X^2$$
$$(.051) \quad (.012) \quad (.008) \quad (.00018)$$
$$+ 2.340 \text{ for husbands}$$
$$(.172)$$

[31] See Kurz and Spiegelman (1971, 1972) for a description of the manpower component of *SIME/DIME*.

[32] Based on preexperimental income, 10 percent of the single-parent headed families and 20 percent of the double-parent headed families in *SIME/DIME* are above the tax break-even level.

[33] Under the assumption that substitution effects are constant, it can be shown that families above the tax break-even level will respond only if income in excess of the break-even level is less than half of the absolute value of the change in income they would experience if they did respond [see Robins and West].

family earnings, and the amount of family earnings above the break-even level.[34]

E. *Estimation Procedure*

Because H_e cannot take on negative values and because there are numerous observations where $H_e = 0$, estimation of the model by ordinary least squares would yield inconsistent coefficient estimates. Furthermore, the estimates would be inefficient because the error term is heteroscedastic. To account for these statistical problems, we use a tobit model, which is designed to handle cases where the dependent variable is truncated normal.[35] The Tobit model may be written as

$$(7) \quad H_e = \max [b_0 + b_1 H_p + b_2 C$$
$$+ b_3 M + b_4 \Delta Y_d(H_p) + b_5 \Delta w$$
$$+ b_6 FABOVE + b_7 BREAK$$
$$+ b_8 EARNABV$$
$$+ b_9 DECLINE + e, 0]$$

where
$\quad H_e$ = experimental hours of work
$\quad H_p$ = preexperimental hours of work
$\quad C$ = vector of control variables
$\quad M$ = vector of manpower treatment variables
$\quad \Delta Y_d(H_p)$ = change in disposable income evaluated at preexperimental labor supply (thousands of dollars per year)

$\quad \Delta w$ = change in the net wage rate (dollars per hour)
$\quad FABOVE$ = dummy variable for persons above the tax break-even level
$\quad BREAK$ = break-even level of earnings (thousands of dollars per year)
$\quad EARNABV$ = family earnings above the break-even level (thousands of dollars per year)
$\quad DECLINE$ = dummy variable for persons on the declining tax rate programs.
$\quad e$ = random error term, assumed to be distributed normally with variance σ^2

The b_i and σ^2 are estimated by maximum likelihood using an iterative-maximization technique.

The parameters in a Tobit model cannot be interpreted in the same way as the parameters in a linear model. In a linear model, the treatment parameters are interpreted as the average response of the population to the imposition of a negative income tax. In a Tobit model, the treatment parameters give the average response only of persons who have nonzero labor supplies (interior solutions) before and after the imposition of a negative income tax. The response of all other persons is somewhat smaller in magnitude than that of persons with interior solutions because of the lower bound on the dependent variable. The coefficients of $\Delta Y_d(H_p)$ and Δw, however, can be interpreted as income and substitution effects for persons with interior solutions before and after the *NIT* program is implemented.

This empirical specification eliminates many of the problems associated with measuring the response to an *NIT* program. Nonrandom assignment by family income is taken into account because the response is allowed to vary with preexperimental income, which is the major assignment variable. Heterogeneity is partially controlled because individuals with identical budget

---

[34] Our specification of these above break-even variables is likely to suffer from errors of measurement of the same type as those present in $\Delta Y_d(H_p)$. To some extent, however, the procedure used to account for errors of measurement in $\Delta Y_d(H_p)$ should also account for this type of measurement error. The primary cause of bias in the above break-even variables is probably misclassification of persons who are near the break-even level preexperimentally; the specification would thus lead to overestimation of effects above the break-even level and underestimation of effects below the break-even level. In another paper, Robins and West present a model that unifies the response above and below the break-even level and find that the results are similar to those presented in this paper.

[35] See Takeshi Amemiya or Tobin (1958) for a discussion of the Tobit model.

TABLE 2—ESTIMATED EXPERIMENTAL EFFECTS ON LABOR SUPPLY
(Tobit Estimates)

Independent Variable	Coefficient		
	Husbands	Wives	Female Heads
Below break-even			
$\Delta Y_d(H_p)$	−34.4	−142.9[c]	−101.1[b]
	(27.3)	(44.4)	(39.4)
Δw	83.2[b]	168.0[a]	125.8[a]
	(37.1)	(91.2)	(65.9)
Above break-even			
FABOVE	−12.7	−430.8[a]	−344.8
	(174.6)	(255.6)	(291.3)
BREAK	−5.5	8.3	73.2
	(21.1)	(29.5)	(64.7)
EARNABV	11.5	47.5	35.1
	(27.3)	(42.0)	(55.6)
DECLINE	−86.3[b]	119.5	21.8
	(48.4)	(78.1)	(73.2)
x^2	21.55[c]	26.84[c]	20.24[c]
S	720	1,086	990
	(14)	(28)	(25)
$\bar{H}_e$	1,736	659	975
	(825)	(825)	(935)
N	1,592	1,698	1,358

Notes: Standard errors in parentheses; x^2 is the *chi*-square test for treatment effects (6 degrees of freedom); S is the standard error of estimate; $\bar{H}_e$ is the mean of the dependent variable, hours of work per year in the second year of the experiment; N is the sample size.
   [a]Indicates significance at 10 percent level.
   [b]Indicates significance at 5 percent level.
   [c]Indicates significance at 1 percent level.

constraints are allowed to respond differently. Preexperimental participation in other welfare programs is taken into account by including welfare income and tax rates in the definitions of the changes in disposable income and net wage rates. Finally, the estimation of substitution and income effects enables the prediction of labor supply response to *NIT* programs other than the ones being tested in *SIME/DIME*.

IV. Results

The sample consists of a subset of originally enrolled black and white family heads who remained in *SIME/DIME* for at least two years and for whom data were available at the time this study was undertaken.[36]

[36]About 800 Mexican-Americans are enrolled in the Denver Experiment but are excluded from the analysis in this paper because data were not available for them

The empirical model is estimated separately for female heads of households and for husbands and wives in two-parent headed households. The subgroups for analysis are defined as of the date of enrollment regardless of changes in marital status. This approach is used so that the estimates are not conditional on unchanged marital status.

when this study was undertaken. It has turned out to be a rather difficult task to build computer software that converts data from interview form into analytical files with reasonable flexibility and generality at low cost. SRI International is now in the process of building such computer software and processing interview data into a data management system. This system will enable users to construct their own analytical files from the basic data. When this data base system is complete, the Department of Health, Education, and Welfare, which is funding *SIME/DIME*, will release a public use file. In the interim, a copy of the data tape used for the analysis presented in this paper is available on request (at a nominal cost to cover copying and documentation).

TABLE 3—TESTS OF SITE, RACE, AND
EXPERIMENTAL DURATION DIFFERENCES IN RESPONSE

	Husbands	Wives	Female Heads
Site test	.53	.41	1.12
Race test	1.70	.52	1.34
Experimental duration test	.93	1.53	.41

Notes: Tests are based on ordinary least squares estimates. The race and site tests are performed by interacting each experimental variable with race and site dummies. The experimental duration test is performed by interacting Δw and $\Delta Y_d(H_p)$ with dummy variables for the three- and five-year programs. The coefficients of control variables are constrained to be the same in the tests. Numbers given are F-ratios with 6 and N degrees of freedom for the race and site tests, and 2 and N degrees of freedom for the experimental duration tests, where N is the sample size.

Table 2 displays the Tobit estimates for the experimental variables.[37] In Table 3, the results of tests of differences in response by race, experimental site, and experimental duration are presented. The various tests are performed using ordinary least squares to reduce computational expense.

For each group, there are statistically significant experimental effects on labor supply. The income effects are negative and statistically significant for wives and female heads, and the substitution effects are positive and statistically significant for all three groups. The F-statistics for site and race differences are not significant, implying that the hypotheses of equal experimental effects

[37] The results for the control and manpower variables are in an appendix available upon request from the authors.

in Seattle and Denver and for blacks and whites cannot be rejected. The tests of different substitution and income effects for persons on the three- and five-year experimental programs are not statistically significant; however, for all three groups, the substitution effect is larger and the income effect is smaller for persons on the three-year programs, a result consistent with the predictions of the model developed by Metcalf.[38] For families above the tax break-even level, only wives appear to be responding to the experiment. All three groups exhibit a response above the break-even level that declines in absolute value with distance from the break-even level.[39]

Table 4 presents estimated substitution and income effects evaluated at the sample means for persons below the break-even level who are working in both the pre-experimental and experimental periods (for example, persons for whom $H_e > 0$ and $H_p > 0$).

The estimated effects at the sample means

[38] *SIME/DIME* is uniquely structured to test the effects of experimental duration on behavioral response. Studies devoted to this issue are currently being undertaken.

[39] Because the functional form used for the experimental response could be considered fairly restrictive, we have estimated several less restricted versions of the model. These versions include the following sets of additional variables; 1) a dummy variable for having a financial treatment, 2) the change in the support level, 3) interactions of $\Delta Y_d(H_p)$ with preexperimental nonwelfare income, and 4) interactions of Δw and $\Delta Y_d(H_p)$ with *DECLINE*. Out of twelve tests of the null hypotheses that these additional variables have zero coefficients, only one, the test of 1) for wives, is significant at the 5 percent level; all the others are not significant at the 10 percent level.

TABLE 4—SUBSTITUTION AND INCOME EFFECTS AT THE MEAN
(Estimated Asymptotic Standard Errors in Parentheses)

	Husbands	Wives	Female Heads
Substitution effect at the mean $(\hat{b}_5 \Delta \bar{w})$	−55.7	−63.8	−59.1
	(24.9)	(34.7)	(31.0)
Income effect at the mean $[\hat{b}_4 \Delta Y_d(H_p)]$	−47.1	−198.6	−117.3
	(37.4)	(61.7)	(45.7)
Total effect at the mean	−102.8	−262.4	−176.4
	(33.0)	(55.1)	(43.6)
Mean hours of work in preexperimental period $(\bar{H}_p)$	1,922	1,194	1,577

indicate a substantial disincentive effect, particularly for women. In percentage terms, the effects are -5.3 percent for husbands, -22.0 percent for wives, and -11.2 percent for female heads of families. It is important to note that these effects are based on mean changes in disposable income and net wage rates that result from the set of programs being tested in *SIME/DIME*, rather than from any single *NIT* program.

V. Implications of the Results for a Nationwide *NIT* Program

One of the primary reasons for undertaking the *NIT* experiments is to provide policymakers with estimates of the labor supply effects of a nationwide *NIT* program. The model developed in this paper can be used to predict the labor supply effects of a variety of nationwide *NIT* programs, including programs that are different from those being tested in the experiments. We use the March 1975 *Current Population Survey* (*CPS*) to generate nationwide predictions.[40] The *CPS* is a weighted random sample of the *U.S.* population and contains information on about 50,000 households.[41] The predictions are derived by applying the estimated response function to each individual and then summing the estimated responses over all individuals. Only the responses of heads of families between the ages of 18 and 58 are considered; nonheads of households, households with only one member, and the elderly are omitted from the analysis.

Predictions are generated for six different *NIT* programs. The six programs have constant tax rates of 50 and 70 percent and support (guarantee) levels of 50, 75, and 100 percent of the poverty level ($5,000 for a family of four in 1974). Because the poverty level increases with family size, the support level also increases with family size. The nominal support level is constant across re-

[40] For a detailed description of the methodology used to generate the predictions, see Keeley et al. and Maxfield.

[41] The income data from the March 1975 *CPS* are annual data for the year 1974.

gions, and the *NIT* program is assumed to replace the existing *AFDC*, *AFDC-UP*, and Food Stamp programs. All other nonlabor income is taxed by the program at a rate of 100 percent.

The predicted labor supply responses are presented in Table 5 and are reported in two ways: first, the average responses for all participating families; and second, the average responses for the *U.S.* population. The average responses for the *U.S.* population include the responses of certain nonparticipants, as well as the responses of participants. The nonparticipants who respond are families that previously received welfare benefits and are above the break-even level of the *NIT* program. These families increase their labor supply when the welfare programs are replaced by the *NIT* program.

In interpreting the results, it is important to keep in mind that the responses vary not only because of changing guarantee levels and tax rates, but also because of a changing pool of participants. For example, as the tax rate increases (for a given guarantee), the pool of participants decreases. On the other hand, as the guarantee increases (for a given tax rate), the pool of participants increases. The manner in which the pools change depends on the distribution of income within the relevant population subgroup.

For participating husband-wife families, the magnitudes of the average responses are positively associated with both the guarantee and the tax rate. For participating female-headed families, the responses are positively associated with the guarantee, but do not vary with the tax rate. For both groups, the results indicate fairly sizable reductions in labor supply, ranging from between 10 and 21 percent for husband-wife families and between 0 and 15 percent for female-headed families.

The average responses of the *U.S.* population are quite small relative to the average responses of participating families because most families in the United States do not choose to participate in the program. While the magnitudes of the average responses again increase with the guarantee (as they

TABLE 5—AVERAGE LABOR SUPPLY RESPONSES TO A NATIONWIDE *NIT* PROGRAM FOR
ALL PARTICIPATING FAMILIES AND FOR ALL FAMILIES IN THE UNITED STATES

	Participating Families			All Families	
NIT Support Level	Change in Hours[b]	Percent Change	Number of Families[c]	Change in Hours[b]	Percent Change
NIT **Tax Rate 50 Percent**					
50 Percent of Poverty Level[a]					
Husbands	− 104	− 7.0		− 4	− 0.2
Wives	− 92	− 23.3		− 2	− 0.3
Total H/W	− 196	− 10.3	2.4	− 6	− 0.2
Female Heads	0	0.0	2.3	+ 16	+ 1.6
75 Percent of Poverty Level[a]					
Husbands	− 106	− 5.9		− 19	− 1.0
Wives	− 110	− 22.8		− 19	− 2.4
Total H/W	− 216	− 9.5	7.6	− 38	− 1.4
Female Heads	− 47	− 6.7	3.0	− 23	− 2.4
100 Percent of Poverty Level[a]					
Husbands	− 119	− 6.2		− 47	− 2.4
Wives	− 130	− 22.7		− 50	− 6.3
Total H/W	− 249	− 10.0	15.7	− 97	− 3.5
Female Heads	− 99	− 12.0	3.6	− 69	− 7.1
NIT **Tax Rate 70 Percent**					
50 Percent of Poverty Level[a]					
Husbands	− 136	− 10.8		− 2	− 0.1
Wives	− 111	− 29.9		0	0.0
Total H/W	− 247	− 15.1	1.3	− 2	− 0.1
Female Heads	− 10	− 2.7	2.0	+ 20	+ 2.1
75 Percent of Poverty Level[a]					
Husbands	− 157	− 11.2		− 9	− 0.5
Wives	− 126	− 32.5		− 5	− 0.6
Total H/W	− 283	− 15.8	2.8	− 14	− 0.5
Female Heads	− 47	− 9.3	2.5	− 12	− 1.2
100 Percent of Poverty Level[a]					
Husbands	− 164	− 10.1		− 23	− 1.2
Wives	− 144	− 32.0		− 18	− 2.3
Total H/W	− 308	− 20.6	5.8	− 41	− 1.5
Female Heads	− 95	− 14.9	3.0	− 52	− 5.3

Notes: Average hours of work per year for all husbands in the United States before response = 1,999. Average hours of work per year for all wives in the United States before response = 793. Average hours of work per year for all female heads in the United States before response = 974. Total number of husband-wife families in the United States = 39.8 million. Total number of female-headed families in the United States = 4.9 million.
[a] Poverty level was $5,000 per year for a family of four in 1974.
[b] Average change in hours of work per year due to *NIT*.
[c] Shown in millions.

do for participants), they decrease with the tax rate for both groups. This inverse relationship between the average *U.S.* response and the tax rate is an interesting and perhaps unexpected result that is a consequence of the fact that the number of participants decreases by an amount large enough to offset the effect of a larger response among participants. Thus, we find that the total disincentive effect of a nation-wide *NIT* program is smaller under higher tax rate programs.

VI. Summary and Conclusions

Social experimentation is a relatively new research tool that is being used to assess the behavioral effects and costs of alternative public transfer programs. Its success as a research tool depends on developing an empirical framework that exploits the advantages of experimental data (primarily, exogeneity of treatment) and at the same time accounts for the unique aspects of experimental design that create problems in the analysis (namely, nonrandom assignment, nonrepresentative samples, limited duration, the presence of other welfare programs, etc.).

In this paper, we present a framework for using experimental data to estimate the parameters of a labor supply response function. The nationwide aggregate labor supply effects of alternative *NIT* programs are obtained by applying these parameter estimates to a national data base. The results indicate that the labor supply responses to alternative nationwide *NIT* programs vary widely with the parameters of the program, and that for some programs, the aggregate labor supply responses are of considerable magnitude.

REFERENCES

H. J. Aaron, "Cautionary Notes on the Experiment," in Joseph Pechman and P. Michael Timpane, eds., *Work Incentives and Income Guarantees: The New Jersey Negative Income Tax Experiment*, Washington 1975, 88–114.

T. Amemiya, "Regression Analysis When the Dependent Variable is Truncated Normal," *Econometrica*, Nov. 1973, *41*, 997–1016.

O. Ashenfelter and J. Heckman, "Estimating Labor Supply Functions," in Glen G. Cain and Harold W. Watts, eds., *Income Maintenance and Labor Supply*, Chicago 1973, 265–78.

_____ and _____, "The Estimation of Income and Substitution Effects in a Model of Family Labor Supply," *Econometrica*, Jan. 1974, *42*, 73–85.

Glen G. Cain and Harold W. Watts, *Income Maintenance and Labor Supply*, Chicago 1973.

J. Conlisk and M. Kurz, "The Assignment Model of the Seattle and Denver Income Maintenance Experiments," res. memo. no. 15, Center Study Welfare Policy,

SRI International, July 1972.

J. Dickinson, "Implicit and Explicit Preference Structures in Models of Labor Supply," disc. paper no. 331-75, Instit. Res. Poverty, Univ. Wisconsin, Dec. 1975.

_____, "The Ashenfelter-Heckman Model and Parallel Preference Structures," disc. paper no. 411-77, Instit. Res. Poverty, Univ. Wisconsin, Dec. 1977.

Milton Friedman, *Capitalism and Freedom*, Chicago 1962.

R. Gronau, "Wage Comparisons—A Selectivity Bias," *J. Polit. Econ.*, Nov./Dec. 1974, *82*, 1119–143.

R. E. Hall, "Wages, Income, and Hours of Work in the U.S. Labor Force," in Glen G. Cain and Harold W. Watts, eds., *Income Maintenance and Labor Supply*, Chicago 1973, 102–62.

_____, "Effects of the Experimental Negative Income Tax on Labor Supply," in Joseph A. Pechman and P. Michael Timpane, eds., *Work Incentives and Income Guarantees: The New Jersey Negative Income Tax Experiment*, Washington 1975, 115–47.

J. Heckman, "Shadow Prices, Market Wages, and Labor Supply," *Econometrica*, July 1974, *42*, 679–94.

_____, "Sample Selection Bias as a Specification Error (with an Application to the Estimation of Labor Supply Functions)," mimeo., Univ. Chicago, Apr. 1976.

_____ and Robert Willis, "A Beta Logistic Model for the Analysis of Sequential Labor Force Participation by Married Women," *J. Polit. Econ.*, Feb. 1977, *85*, 27–58.

E. D. Kalachek and F. Q Raines, "Labor Supply of Lower Income Workers and the Negative Income Tax," in *Technical Studies*, The President's Commission on Income Maintenance Programs, Washington 1970, 159–86.

Michael C. Keeley, *The Economics of Labor Supply: A Critical Review*, forthcoming.

_____ and Philip K. Robins, "The Design of Social Experiments: A Critique of the Conlisk-Watts Assignment Model," mimeo., Center Study Welfare Policy,

SRI International, Mar. 1978.

———— et al., "The Labor Supply Effects and Costs of Alternative Negative Income Tax Programs," *J. Hum. Resources*, Winter 1978, *13*, 3–36.

David Kershaw and Jerilyn Fair, *The New Jersey Income Maintenance Experiment*, Vol. 1: *Operations, Surveys, and Administration*, New York 1976.

M. Kurz et al., "A Cross Sectional Estimation of Labor Supply for Families in Denver 1970," res. memo. no 24, Center Study Welfare Policy, SRI International, Nov. 1974.

———— and R. G. Spiegelman, "The Seattle Experiment: The Combined Effect of Income Maintenance and Manpower Investments," *Amer. Econ. Rev. Proc.*, May 1971, *61*, 22–29.

———— and ————, "The Design of the Seattle and Denver Income Maintenance Experiments," res. memo. no. 18, Center Study Welfare Policy, SRI International, May 1972.

Robert J. Lampman, *Ends and Means of Reducing Income Poverty*, Chicago 1971.

M. Maxfield, "Estimating the Impact of Labor Supply Adjustments on Transfer Program Costs: A Microsimulation Methodology," mimeo., Mathematica Policy Res., Feb. 1977.

C. E. Metcalf, "Making Inferences from Controlled Income Maintenance Experiments," *Amer. Econ. Rev.*, June 1973, *63*, 478–83.

Jacob Mincer, *Schooling, Experience, and Earnings*, New York 1974.

G. H. Orcutt and A. G. Orcutt, "Incentive and Disincentive Experimentation for Income Maintenance Policy Purposes," *Amer. Econ. Rev.*, Sept. 1968, *58*, 754–72.

Joseph A. Pechman and P. Michael Timpane, *Work Incentives and Income Guarantees: The New Jersey Negative Income Tax Experiment*, Washington 1975.

P. K. Robins and R. W. West, "Participation in the Seattle and Denver Income Maintenance Experiments, and Its Effect on Labor Supply," res. memo. no. 53, Center Study Welfare Policy, SRI International, Mar. 1978.

H. Ross, "A Proposal for a Demonstration of New Techniques in Income Maintenance," memo., Data Center Archives, Instit. Res. Poverty, Univ. Wisconsin, Dec. 1966.

R. G. Spiegelman and R. W. West, "Feasibility of a Social Experiment and Issues in Its Design," 1976 *Proc. Amer. Statist. Assn., Bus. and Econ. Statist. Sec.*, Washington 1976, 168–76.

J. Tobin, "Estimation of Relationships for Limited Dependent Variables," *Econometrica*, Jan. 1958, *26*, 24–36.

————, "Improving the Economic Status of the Negro," *J. Daedalus*, Fall 1965, *94*, 878–98.

Harold W. Watts and Albert Rees, (1977a) *The New Jersey Income Maintenance Experiment*, Vol. II: *Labor Supply Responses*, New York 1977.

———— and ————, (1977b) *The New Jersey Income Maintenance Experiment*, Vol. III: *Expenditures, Health, and Social Behavior, and the Quality of the Evidence*, New York 1977.

U.S. Bureau of the Census, *Current Population Survey*, Mar. 1975 (data tape).

9

This chapter complements the chapter by Tuma et al. in Part I and that by Keeley et al., above. The statistical model is essentially indentical to that of the former chapter, while the results can be viewed as an expansion of those reported by Keeley et al. This is because, as Tuma and Robins note (expressions 2 and 3), labor supply (total hours worked) is the product of the marginal probability of being employed and the conditional mean hours employed given that one is employed. Keeley et al. report program effects on total hours worked. Tumá and Robins help to explain these results by measuring program effects on the probability of employment. In so doing they also cast light on the dynamics of employment state transitions.[1]

For a guide to the model, the reader is referred to the volume introduction and the introductory notes to the paper by Tuma et al. in Part I. Perhaps the most important finding concerns the mechanisms by which the probability of employment decreases under a negative income tax (NIT). This results from longer spells of nonemployment, rather than from quits. A useful follow-up would ascertain those aspects of program operation (e.g., job search provisions) that might be manipulated to increase the labor supply of participants. (For further discussion see the comment by Goodwin in Part I and the paper on EOPP by Bishop et al. in Part VIII.)

NOTE

1. An explicit reconciliation of the Keeley et al. and Tuma and Robins results would be desirable. Of particular note is the fact that the Keeley et al. tobit estimation for total hours worked contains employment probability predictions. The match between these and Tuma and Robins' more detailed examination of employment rates would be instructive.

A Dynamic Model of Employment Behavior
An Application to the Seattle and Denver Income Maintenance Experiments

Nancy Brandon Tuma and Philip K. Robins[1]

In this paper we present a continuous-time model of changes in employment status. The model implies that the binary logit model describes the probability of employment in equilibrium: it also has implications for the probability of employment out of equilibrium and for the length of spells of employment and nonemployment. Parameters of the model can be readily estimated from employment history data using the method of maximum likelihood. In an application to data from the Seattle and Denver income maintenance experiments, we find that both the proposed model and the logit model reveal significant decreases in the probability of employment of family heads under NIT programs that decrease the net wage rate and increase nonwage income. Based on the proposed model, the decrease in the employment probability results primarily from a significant increase in the average length of spells of nonemployment.

From Nancy Brandon Tuma and Philip K. Robins, "A Dynamic Model of Employment Behavior: An Application to the Seattle and Denver Maintenance Experiments," *Econometrica*, 1980, forthcoming. Copyright 1980 by the Econometric Society.

1. INTRODUCTION

According to standard economic theory of household behavior (see e.g., Cain and Watts [3], Keeley et al. [7]), a negative income tax (NIT) program that decreases net wage rates and increases net nonwage income has a work disincentive. Possible behavioral manifestations of the work disincentive include (1) a reduction in the probability of employment and (2) a reduction in weekly hours worked by those employed. Analyses of labor supply that aggregate hours worked over a fairly long period (a year or even a quarter) do not allow these two effects to be separated.

Disentangling the two possible effects is important for both theoretical and practical reasons. The argument that the utility of workweek leisure differs from that of nonworkweek leisure (e.g., Hanoch [5]) suggests that individuals are not indifferent to working fewer hours per week while employed and having longer periods between episodes of employment, even if the total hours worked per year is the same. Separating the two possible effects is important for policy decisions because a number of current and proposed public transfer programs have eligibility requirements that are based, at least in part, on employment status.

Effects of program characteristics and other exogenous variables on the probability of employment are usually estimated from cross-sectional data giving the employment status of respondents at an interview. The methods most commonly applied to such data are logit and probit analysis.

We take another approach that has some advantages over the above methods. We develop a continuous-time model of changes in employment status. This model predicts that the usual logit model describes the probability of employment in equilibrium, assuming employment status is a dichotomous variable. In addition, the proposed model allows us to estimate to what extent an NIT program increases the rate at which individuals change from the employed to nonemployed state (i.e., shortens episodes of employment) and to what extent it decreases the rate at which persons change from the nonemployed to employed state (i.e., lengthens episodes of nonemployment). It also predicts the time path of change in the probability of employment following introduction of a new program. Finally, the proposed model enables us to deal explicitly with sample attrition, unlike the usual applications of cross-sectional and panel methods to the nonattrited sample in longitudinal studies.

Section 2 contains a description of the assumptions of the proposed model. Section 3 discusses its implications for various observable outcomes relevant to employment status. Section 4 describes the data from the Seattle and Denver income maintenance experiments (SIME/DIME), which we use in estimating the model. Methods of estimation and testing are given in Section 5. Section 6 reports results for both the proposed model and the usual logit model. Both models indicate that the NIT programs in SIME/DIME decrease the probability of employment, especially for wives and unmarried female heads. According to the proposed model, this decrease is almost solely due to lengthened eposides of nonemployment. Section 7 discusses some implications of the results.

2. MODEL

Consider the illustration in Figure 1 of the typical work history of an individual during a period from some arbitrary time 0 to a later time T. During the unshaded time interval (t_1, t_2), the person is not employed and works zero hours; during the shaded intervals (O, t_1) and (t_2, T), the person is employed and averages a positive number of hours worked. In this illustration the person, who is initially employed, leaves employment at t_1 and does not reenter employment until t_2. If we define a spell as a continuous period of time in a state (employed or not employed), then this example shows two employment spells and one spell in which the person is not employed.

Let $Z(t, X)$ denote the state occupied at time t by the person with a given vector of exogenous characteristics X such that

(1) $Z(t, X) = 1$ if employed at t,

         $Z(t, X) = 0$ if not employed at t.

In addition, let $p_z(t, X) = \text{prob } [Z(t, X) = z]$ and let $H_z(t, X)$ be the value of $H(t, X)$ when $Z(t, X) = z$. Thus, $H_0(t, X) = 0$ for all t and X. It is conventionally assumed (at least implicitly) that $H_1(t, X) = H_1(X)$ and that $p_1(t, X) = p_1(X)$—that is, that hours worked during employment and the probability of employment vary with X but do not vary over time. Then total hours worked in a period $(0, T)$ for a person with some X is given by:

(2) $L(0, T, X) = H_1(X)p_1(X)T.$

In this paper we retain the usual assumption that $H_1(t, X) = H_1(X)$ but formulate a model in which $p_1(t, X)$ may vary over time as well as over X. So

(3) $L(0, T, X) = H_1(X) \int_0^T p_1(t, X) \, dt.$

Due to limitations in the data currently available to us (see below), we actually make an even stronger assumption—that $H_1(X)$ is not affected by the NIT programs we study. We do not claim that this assumption is realistic, and intend to elaborate the model described below when data on hours worked during employment become available. However, it lets us partially assess the extent to which effects of an NIT program on total hours worked in a period (see Keeley et al. [7]) may result from effects of the probability of employment.

Thus, in this paper we concentrate on modelling the probability of employment and how this depends on exogenous variables X, including those describing an NIT program. Our approach consists of extending the standard first-order, finite-state, continuous-time Markov process to allow for effects of X.

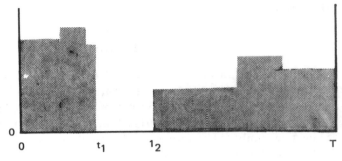

HOURS WORKED AT
TIME t, H(t)

TIME 1

Figure 1: A typical work history

The formal assumptions of this model are as follows. Let

(4) $p_{jk}(u, t, X) = \text{prob} [Z(t, X) = k \mid Z(u, X) = j]$, $u \leqslant t$,

and let $P(u, t, X)$ denote the matrix of these transition probabilities, $P(u, t, X) = p_{jk}(u, t, X)$, where j and k are any possible values of $Z(t, X)$. We define $r_{jk}(t, X)$ as the instantaneous rate of a transition (or change) from state j to state k at time t for given X:

(5) $r_{jk}(t, X) = \lim_{\Delta t \to 0} \dfrac{p_{jk}(t, t + \Delta t, X)}{\Delta t}$, $j \neq k$.

The rate of leaving j at time t, $r_j(t, X)$ is defined as:

(6) $r_j(t, X) = \sum_{\substack{k \\ j \neq k}} r_{jk}(t, X)$.

Under the Markov assumption, past history affects the future only through its influence on the state currently occupied. Then the Chapman-Kolmogorov equation holds:

(7) $P(v, t, X) = P(v, u, X)P(u, t, X)$, $v \leqslant u \leqslant t$.

Given additional innocuous assumptions (continuity, probabilities ranging from 0 to 1, etc.), it can then be shown that

(8) $\dfrac{dP(u, t, X)}{dt} = P(u, t, X)R(t, X)$,

where $R(t, X)$ is a matrix in which the jth diagonal element is $-r_j(t, X)$ and the jkth off-diagonal element is $r_{jk}(t, X)$. When $R(t, X) = R(X)$, (8) has the solution:

$$(9) \qquad P(u, t, X) = \sum_{m=0}^{\infty} \frac{R(X)^m (t - u)^m}{m!} \triangleq e^{(t-u)R(X)}$$

where by definition $R(X)^0 = I$, the identity matrix.

Markov models in which $R(t, X) = R$ (i.e., parameters are constants over time and within a population) have been applied to various problems in economics, sociology, and psychology, but rarely fit data well. Allowing parameters to vary within a population improves fit. The best known modification is the Mover-Stayer model (Blumen et al. [1]; McCall [8]), which assumes a certain fraction of the population cannot move, and the remainder can; both the fraction of stayers and the transition rates of movers are estimated from data. Others (e.g. Spilerman [11]; Frank [4]) have used a similar strategy, assuming some particular probability distribution of transition rates in the population. Though this strategy yields estimates that fit the data better than the assumption that there is a single R in the population, it does not relate rates of movement to characteristics X of the population or of the environment.

Our approach is to assume the following parametric relationship between transition rates and exogenous variables X:

$$(10) \qquad r_{jk}(X) = e^{\theta_{jk} X}$$

where θ_{jk} represents a vector of parameters to be estimated. The log-linear specification is preferable to a linear specification because it ensures that transition rates are positive.

Before discussing some implications and estimation of this model, we consider a frequent and troublesome problem in empirical studies that follow people over time—sample attrition. As time passes, collection of data on some persons initially in the study may become impossible due to death, emigration, loss of address, refusal to be interviewed, etc. It is a common practice to analyze only data on those who can be followed for a substantial portion (or all) of a study. This is a form of selecting a sample on the basis of an outcome. As shown in Section 3 below, it can lead to erroneous inferences.

To deal with this problem, we allow status at time t, $Z(t, X)$ to take on another value, in addition to those defined in (1):

$$(11) \qquad Z(t) = 2 \qquad \text{If the person is not observed after time } t \text{ (i.e. has attrited).}$$

We assume attrition is an absorbing state, i.e., that it cannot be left. Thus, $r_{21} = 0$ and $r_{20} = 0$ by assumption. We refer to the two-state model of employment in which attrition cannot occur as Model 1; for this model

$$(12) \quad R(X) = \begin{bmatrix} -r_0(X) & r_{01}(X) \\ r_{10}(X) & -r_1(X) \end{bmatrix} = \begin{bmatrix} -e^{\theta_{01}(X)} & e^{\theta_{01}X} \\ e^{\theta_{10}X} & -e^{\theta_{10}X} \end{bmatrix}$$

We refer to the three-state model of employment in which attrition can occur as Model II; for this model

$$(13) \quad R(X) = \begin{bmatrix} -r_0(X) & r_{01}(X) & r_{02}(X) \\ r_{10}(X) & -r_1(X) & r_{12}(X) \\ 0 & 0 & 0 \end{bmatrix}$$

$$= \begin{bmatrix} -(e^{\theta_{01}X} + e^{\theta_{02}X}) & e^{\theta_{01}X} & e^{\theta_{02}X} \\ e^{\theta_{10}X} & -(e^{\theta_{10}X} + e^{\theta_{12}X}) & e^{\theta_{12}X} \\ 0 & 0 & 0 \end{bmatrix}$$

3. IMPLICATIONS

In this section we consider implications of Models I and II for the conditional probability of employment, the unconditional probability of employment, and the expected duration of employment and nonemployment spells.[2] The differences in the implications of Models I and II show some possible consequences of ignoring attrition in analysis. We also relate implications of these models to the usual cross-sectional logit model.

Conditional (Transition) Probabilities

To find the unconditional probability of being in a state k (in particular, the probability of being employed) at time t, $p_k(t, X)$, we must first find the probability of being in state k, conditional on being in some state j at an earlier time u, i.e., $p_{jk}(u, t, X)$. The latter is given by (9), since transition rates are assumed to be time-invariant for any member of the population.

The elements of $P(u, t, X)$ cannot be written as explicit functions of transition rates for a general $n \times n$ matrix R, but they can be for Models I and II. For Model I:

$$(14) \quad p_{jk}(u, t, X) = 1 - p_{jj}(u, t, X)$$

$$= \frac{r_{jk}(X)}{r_{01}(X) + r_{10}(X)} (1 - e^{-[r_{01}(X)+r_{10}(X)](t-u)})$$

for $j = 0, 1$; $k = 1 - j$; and $u \leq t$. For Model II:

$$(15a) \quad p_{jk}(u, t, X) = \frac{r_{jk}(X)}{(\lambda_1 - \lambda_2)} \{e^{\lambda_1(t-u)} - e^{\lambda_2(t-u)}\},$$

$$(15b) \quad p_{j2}(u, t, X) = 1 + \frac{1}{(\lambda_1 - \lambda_2)} \{[r_{j2}(X) + \lambda_2] e^{\lambda_1(t-u)}$$
$$- [r_{j2}(X) + \lambda_1] e^{\lambda_2(t-u)}\},$$

$$(15c) \quad p_{20}(u, t, X) = p_{21}(u, t, X) = 0,$$

$$(15d) \quad p_{jj}(u, t, X) = 1 - \sum_{\substack{k \\ k \neq j}} p_{jk}(u, t, X),$$

where $j = 0, 1$; $k = 1 - j$; $\lambda_1 \neq \lambda_2$; and

$$(16a) \quad \lambda_1 = -\tfrac{1}{2}\{[r_0(X) + r_1(X)] - \sqrt{[r_0(X) - r_1(X)]^2 + 4r_{01}(X)r_{10}(X)}\},$$

$$(16b) \quad \lambda_2 = -\tfrac{1}{2}\{[r_0(X) + r_1(X)] - \sqrt{[r_0(X) - r_1(X)]^2 + 4r_{01}(X)r_{10}(X)}\}.$$

In both cases we continue to assume a log-linear relationship between a transition rate and exogenous variables as given by (10).

Though only of indirect interest in this paper, the above equations are potentially of direct use in other research contexts. First, these equations provide a basis for finding maximum likelihood estimates of $\{\theta_{jk}\}$ from panel data, i.e., data on states occupied by the sample at a series of discrete points in time. Second, if estimates of $\{\theta_{jk}\}$ are available, patterns of "runs" over time can be computed and compared with those observed to evaluate the fit of the model (for an example of this strategy, see Heckman [6]).

Unconditional Probabilities

The unconditional probability distribution at time t for a given X, $p(t, X) = (p_0(t, X), p_1(t, X), \ldots)$, depends on the distribution at an earlier time u, $p(u, X)$, and the matrix of transition probabilities, $P(u, t, X)$:

$$(17) \quad p(t, X) = p(u, X)P(u, t, X)$$

where in general $P(u, t, X)$ is the solution to (8). For Model I,

$$(18) \quad p_1(t, X) = 1 - p_0(t, X) = p_1(u, X) e^{-(t-u)[r_{01}(X)+r_{10}(X)]}$$
$$+ \frac{r_{01}(X)}{r_{01}(X) + r_{10}(X)} \{1 - e^{-(t-u)[r_{01}(X)+r_{10}(X)]}\}.$$

For Model II,

$$(19) \quad p_j(t, X) = \frac{1}{(\lambda_2 - \lambda_1)} \ [e^{(t-u)\lambda_2} \{r_{kj}(X) + p_j(u, X)[r_{k2}(X) + \lambda_2]\}$$

$$- e^{(t-u)\lambda_1} \{r_{kj}(X) + p_j(u, X)[r_{k2}(X) + \lambda_1]\}],$$

$$(20) \quad p_2(t, X) = 1 + \frac{1}{(\lambda_2 - \lambda_1)} \ [e^{(t-u)\lambda_2} \{r_{02}(X)p_0(u, X) + r_{12}(X)p_1(u, X) + \lambda_1\}$$

$$- e^{(t-u)\lambda_1} \{r_{02}(X)p_0(u, X) + r_{12}(X)p_1(u, X) + \lambda_2\}],$$

where $j = 0, 1$; $k = 1 - j$; λ_1 and λ_2 are given by (16a) and (16b), respectively; $p_0(u, X) + p_1(u, X) = 1$; and $u \leqslant t$.

These equations show that the probability distribution at time t depends in general on both the initial distribution at time u *and* all transition rates governing the process. Simplifications arise in certain situations, however.

First, consider the situation when Model 1 holds and time $t = t^*$ such that $(t^* - u)$ is very large. Then

$$(21) \quad p_1(t^*, X) = 1 - p_0(t^*, X) = \frac{r_{01}(X)}{r_{01}(X) + r_{10}(X)} = \frac{e^{\theta_{01}X}}{e^{\theta_{01}X} + e^{\theta_{10}X}}.$$

Furthermore,

$$(22) \quad \frac{p_1(t^*, X)}{p_0(t^*, X)} = \frac{e^{\theta_{01}X}}{e^{\theta_{10}X}} = e^{(\theta_{01} - \theta_{10})X}$$

or,

$$(23) \quad \ln\left[\frac{p_1(t^*, X)}{p_0(t^*, X)}\right] = (\theta_{01} - \theta_{10})X = \gamma_{10}X$$

where $\gamma_{10} = (\theta_{01} - \theta_{10})$. Thus, Model I implies that when t^* is such that $(t^* - u)$ is very large, there exists a steady-state probability distribution such that the logarithm of the odds of being employed are linear in the exogenous variables X. Equation (23) is just the conventional cross-sectional binary logit model. Note that a variable with "no effect" in cross-sectional logit analysis of the probability of employment *may* result from a variable having equal and opposite effects of the rates of entering and leaving employment (r_{01} and r_{10}, respectively). This means that "no effect" of a variable in cross-sectional logit analysis should not be taken as evidence that a variable is irrelevant to change in employment. To conclude this, we must find that the effect of X on both the rates of entering and leaving employment is zero.

Next consider the situation in which Model II holds and time $t = t^*$ such that $(t^* - u)$ is very large. Then

$$(24) \quad p_2(t^*, X) = 1.$$

That is, eventually everyone attrites, and the probability of being observed (either employed or not) is zero:

$$(25) \quad p_0(t^*, X) = p_1(t^*, X) = 0.$$

In spite of (25), the logarithm of the odds of being employed at t^*, conditional on being observed at t^*, does have a finite, nonzero limit:

$$(26) \quad \lim_{t^* \to \infty} \ln \left[\frac{p_1(t^*, X)}{p_0(t^*, X)} \right] = \ln \left\{ \frac{r_{01}(X) + p_1(u, X)[r_{02}(X) + \lambda_2]}{r_{10}(X) + p_0(u, X)[r_{12}(X) + \lambda_2]} \right\}.$$

Thus, the right-hand side of (26) depends on the initial distribution at time u and all transition in rates even when t^* is large enough that it does not vary over time. Furthermore, the right-hand side of (26) does not simplify to the cross-sectional logit model in general. However, if the attrition rates from states 0 and 1 are identical for all values of X, i.e., $r_a(X) = r_{02}(X) = r_{12}(X)$, then $\lambda_2 = -r_a(X)$ and (26) simplifies to (23), the cross-sectional logit model.

In sum, the equations above mean that a cross-sectional logit model and a Markov model with transition rates that are log-linear in exogenous variables imply the same probability of employment at a time t^* far from the origin u, as long as attrition is independent of employment status.

Duration of Spells

Knowing the effect of exogenous variables X on the duration of spells of employment and nonemployment is of considerable interest, especially because eligibility requirements for some current and proposed transfer programs depend on the length of time since a person left employment. For a Markov model with time-independent transition rates, the duration of spells is easily shown to be exponentially distributed (see, for example, Breiman, [2]). Let $G_j(t|u, X)$ represent the probabilty of remaining in state j until time t given X and occupancy of state j at time u; $G_j(t|u, X)$ is often called the survivor function for state j. When transition rates from j are independent of time but depend on X, $r_{jk}(X)$, we find that

$$(27) \quad G_j(t|u, X) = e^{-(t-u)\sum_k r_{jk}(X)}$$

where $k \neq j$. The probability density of leaving at time t is just

$$(28a) \quad f_j(t \mid u, X) = \frac{dG_j(t \mid u, X)}{dt},$$

$$(28b) \quad f_j(t \mid u, X) = \left[\sum_k r_{jk}(X) \right] e^{-(t-u) \sum_k r_{jk}(X)},$$

where $k \neq j$. Equation (28b) also gives the probability density of spells in state j that have duration $(t - u)$. From (28b) the expected duration of a spell in state j is just

$$(29) \quad E_j(t - u \mid X) = 1 \bigg/ \left[\sum_k r_{jk}(X) \right]$$

where $k \neq j$. For Model I

$$(30) \quad E_j(t - u \mid X) = e^{-\theta_{jk} X}$$

while for Model II

$$(31) \quad E_j(t - u \mid X) = [e^{\theta_{jk} X} + e^{\theta_{j2} X}]^{-1}.$$

4. DATA

The data used in the empirical analysis come from the heads of black and white families enrolled in the Seattle and Denver income maintenance experiments (SIME/DIME). About 4,800 families (2,000 in Seattle and 2,800 in Denver) were enrolled in the experiments.[3] Roughly 60 per cent of the families were assigned to one of 11 different financial treatments for a 3 or 5 year period; the remaining families received no financial treatment but were otherwise treated similarly.[4] The financial treatments consisted of selected combinations of three support (or guarantee) levels (S = $3,800, $4,800, or $5,600 per year for a family of four with an adjustment based on family size), three initial tax rates (τ_e = 0.50, 0.70, or 0.80), and two rates of decline in the average tax rate (d = .0.0, or 0.025 per $1000 of income per year). At enrollment a family with a financial treatment experiences a change in disposal income given by

$$(32) \quad \Delta Y = S - Y_0(\tau_e - Y_0 d - \tau_0), \quad \text{if right-hand side} \geq 0,$$
$$= 0, \quad \text{if right-hand side} \leq 0,$$

where Y_0 is the family's gross annual income at enrollment and τ_0 is its non-experimental tax rate.

The data have several features worth noting. First, enrollees had to meet several requirements: the family had to contain either two heads (i.e., a married couple) or one head with at least one dependent; family heads had to be between 18 to 58 years of age and be physically capable of working; pretransfer income (in 1971 dollars and adjusted for family size) had to be less than $9,000 per year in a family of four with one working head and under $11,000 per year in a four-member family with two working heads. The last criterion is the most important from a statistical viewpoint because it leads to a truncated sample. In particular, members of the sample are likely to have higher rates of leaving employment and lower rates of entering employment than the population at large. Correcting for this problem would greatly complicate the analysis, so we have ignored it in the analysis reported below.

Another important features of the SIME/DIME design is a stratified allocation of families to experimental treatments on the basis of four assignment variables: site, family type (one or two heads), race-ethnicity (black, white and Mexican-American), and normal income (seven levels of "typical" pretransfer family income adjusted for family size). Within any particular combination of the four stratification variables, assignment of a family to an experimental treatment was random. However, the probability of being assigned to a particular treatment varied across combinations of the stratification variables. For example, the probability of being assigned to a treatment with a high breakeven level increased with normal income.

The stratified random assignment to treatments causes problems in analyzing the effects of an NIT program on changes in employment status. If the effects vary with the assignment variables, then simple experimental-control differences may be misleading except for families with a particular combination of the stratification variables. Unfortunately the number of families within a combination is too small for this type of analysis. We are left with the not fully satisfactory alternative of using dummy variables to represent the stratification variables. This corrects for assignment to the extent that there are no important interactive effects of the stratification variables on rates of entering and leaving employment.

In addition to assignment variables, the explanatory variables X used in the analysis include a variety of other control variables likely to affect employment decisions as well as variables representing the experimental treatments. We have used two different representations of the financial treatments. One, which we call the dummy-variable representation, consists of a dummy variable that is unity for those enrolled on a financial treatment and zero otherwise. The second, which we call the parameterized representation, consists of the predicted changes in disposable income and in the net wage due to the financial treatment for those below the breakeven level at enrollment, and a dummy variable that is unity for those above the breakeven level at enrollment.[5] In both representations, an additional experimental treatment, program length, is indicated by a dummy variable that is unity for those with a three-year financial treatment,

Table I   Means of Variables by Employment Status of Spells

Variable	Husbands		Wives		Unmarried Female Heads	
	Employed	Not Employed	Employed	Not Employed	Employed	Not Employed
Number of family members	4.3	4.1	4.2	4.3	3.3	3.4
Number of children under 16	2.2	2.1	2.1	2.2	2.2	2.3
Age in years	32.9	31.9	30.1	30.3	34.3	32.7
Years of schooling	11.7	11.5	11.7	11.4	11.7	11.3
1 = Black	.38	.36	.46	.38	.54	.54
1 = Denver	.53	.49	.57	.52	.58	.50
Normal income level:						
Not determined	.02	.03	.02	.02	.04	.06
0-$1,000	.01	.03	.01	.02	.08	.20
$1,000- 3,000	.05	.09	.04	.07	.20	.27
$3,000- 5,000	.16	.22	.13	.17	.29	.26
$5,000- 7,000	.29	.29	.26	.28	.21	.12
$7,000- 9,000	.29	.23	.28	.28	.15	.09
$9,000-11,000	.17	.13	.24	.16	.02	.01
$11,000-13,000	.01	–	.02	.01	–	–
Weeks worked in year prior to enrollment	41.2	32.9	24.8	11.6	35.2	19.2
Net wage at enrollment predicted in $/hr.	3.29	3.26	2.19	2.15	2.41	2.36
Disposable income in year prior to enrollment ($)	6,612	5,615	7,116	6,283	3,945	2,514
1 = Financial treatment	.53	.56	.46	.51	.58	.61
Manpower:						
1 = Counseling only	.19	.20	.18	.17	.19	.19
1 = Counseling & 50% training subsidy	.24	.25	.25	.15	.23	.23
1 = Counseling & 100% training subsidy	.15	.15	.14	.14	.15	.16
1 = 3-year program[a]	.66	.66	.67	.69	.71	.80
Number of spells	2,991	1,837	1,692	2,189	1,523	1,418
Number of individuals	1,835	1,035	1,162	1,671	1,070	1,054

a. Calculated over financial families.

and is zero for all others. Table 1 lists means of the explanatory variables used in the analysis.

The dependent variables come from employment histories. Each interview collected extensive data on each family member's employment history since the previous interview (roughly 4 months earlier). The information gathered includes data (month, day, and year) at which employment started and ended.[6] In the analyses reported below "attrition" results from interviews refusals, residential mobility, expulsion for fraud, and changes in marital status.[7] Dates of attrition from the analytical sample are recorded as occurring at the date of the nearest completed interview, except in the case of deaths and marital status changes, which family members reported to the nearest day. The analyses in this paper use the employment-history data from the first six interviews after enrollment on the experiment, or roughly the first twenty-four months of the experiment.

5. ESTIMATION AND TESTING

We can estimate transition rates from any equation relating transition rates to an observable outcome (e.g., panel observations on employment status at a series of discrete points in time; duration in an employment status). However, some outcomes provide more useful information than others. For example, as discussed earlier, under certain conditions cross-sectional logit analysis gives an estimate of the difference between a variable's effects on the rates of entering and leaving employment. This information is certainly useful, but it cannot tell us the variable's separate effects on the two rates.

The SIME/DIME data are unusual in providing information on the number, timing and sequence of all changes in employment status, including attrition from the experiment. With such data the method of maximum likelihood can be used to estimate transition rates (or effects of variables on transition rates) in a simple and reliable way. The outcomes used as the "dependent variables" are the following: w_{mi}—a dummy variable that equals unity if case i's mth event occurs during the observation period; t_{mi}—the time of case i's mth event when $w_{mi} = 1$, or the time the case i is last observed when $w_{mi} = 0$; v_{mji}—a dummy variable that is unity if case i's mth event is observed and consists of a change to state j, and otherwise equals zero. By definition, t_{0i} is the start of the observation period on case i, and v_{0ji} equals unity if state j is occupied by i at t_{0i} and otherwise equals zero. Note that $W_i = \sum_{m=1}^{\infty} w_{mi}$ equals the total *number* of events observed to occur to case i, that the t_{mi}'s are the *times* that these events occur, and that the v_{mji}'s allow us to describe the *sequence* of events that occur to case i.

Assuming that observations on the N different cases in the sample are independent and that transition rates are time-independent functions of exogenous variables, we can write the likelihood function as:

$$(33) \quad e^{L} = \prod_{t=1}^{N} \prod_{m=1}^{\infty} \prod_{j=1}^{n} [G_j(t_m \mid t_{m-1}, X)]^{(1-w_m)v_{m-1,j}}$$

$$\cdot [f_j(t_m \mid t_{m-1}, X)]^{w_m v_{m-1,j}}$$

$$\cdot \prod_{\substack{k=1 \\ k \neq j}}^{n} \left[r_{jk}(X) \bigg/ \sum_{\substack{h=1 \\ h \neq j}}^{n} r_{jh}(X) \right]^{w_m v_{m-1,j} v_{mk}}$$

where n is the total number of states and subscript i (on w_{mi}, t_{mi}, v_{mji}, and X_i) has been suppressed for clarity. The first term (in square brackets), the survivor function, gives the probability that the mth event has not occurred by time t_m, given that the $(m-1)$th event is observable at t_{m-1} and consists of a move to j. The second term is the probability density that the mth event occurs at time t_m, given that the $(m-1)$th event is observed at time t_{m-1} and consists of a move to state j. The third term is the probability that the mth event is observed and consists of a move from j to k.

Equation (33) is a general expression that does not specify the form of the dependence of transition rates on exogenous variables. Assuming a log-linear relationship between r_{jk} and X, as in (10), (33) implies:

$$(34) \qquad L = \sum_{j=1}^{n} \sum_{k=1}^{n} L_{jk}$$

where

$$(35) \qquad L_{jk} = \sum_{i=1}^{N} \sum_{m=1}^{W_i} -v_{m-1,j}(t_m - t_{m-1}) e^{\theta_{jk}X} + w_m v_{m-1,j} v_{mk} \theta_{jk} X.$$

A few comments on (35) are useful. First, (35) applies not only to Models I and II, but also to any other model with a different state space or with different permissible transitions, as long as every transition rate is a time-independent, log-linear function of exogenous variables. For example, the state space could be redefined to distinguish unemployment from being out of the labor force. Then (35) could be used to estimate effects of X on rates of changing from employed to unemployed, etc.—as long as the data distinguish unemployment from being out of the labor force. (Unfortunately, the data available to us do not make this distinction.) Second, the summation over m has been changed from (1 to ∞) in (35) to (1, W_i) in (35) because v_{mji} and w_{mi} are zero for $m > W_i$. Thus this change converts a computationally infeasible summation into an easy one. Third, to estimate the effects θ_{jk} of X on the transition rate from j to k, we need only maximize L_{jk} because $L_{j'k'}$ does not depend on θ_{jk} for all $j' \neq j$ and all $k' \neq k$. Furthermore, maximization of L_{jk} requires knowledge of t_m, t_{m-1}, and v_{mk} only for events consisting of a move from $j(v_{m-1,j} = 1)$. So, for example, we need not estimate the effects of X on the attrition rate if we are only interested in effects of X on rates of entering and leaving employment. However, we *do* need to include information on the time of leaving j for all cases, and not just those who move to k. Excluding data on cases that move to other states (e.g., on those who drop out of the study) leads to estimates of θ_{jk} biased away from zero (Tuma and Hannan [13]). In fact, as long as we retain information on all cases who occupy j initially, the bias and variance of the maximum likelihood estimates of θ_{jk} are fairly small even when the sample is medium in size ($N = 100$) and the proportion of cases for which $W = 0$ is as high as 0.9 (Tuma and Hannan [13]).

Testing of nested models or of the effect of a single variance is straightforward. Furthermore, testing a model of the rate of a transition from j to k also requires maximization only of L_{jk} and not of L.

Let Ω represent a model of the rate of changing from j to k, and let ω denote another model in which a parameters in Ω are constrained to take certain values (usually zero). The likelihood ratio λ, defined as $(\max e^{L\omega})/(\max e^{L\Omega})$ has the property that $-2 \ln \lambda = -2(L_{\omega} - L_{\Omega}) = -2(L_{jk\omega} - L_{jk\Omega})$ is asymptotically distributed as chi-square with s degrees of freedom. We reject ω if the observed value of $-2 \ln \lambda$ exceeds the critical vlaue of chi-square with s degrees of freedom for the selected level of significance.

We can also test the effect of a single variable. The asymptotic variance-covariance matrix of parameters can be estimated by $[\partial^2 L_j / \partial \theta^2]^{-1}$ or since this matrix is block diagonal, by $[\partial^2 L_{jk} / \partial \theta_{jk}^2]^{-1}$. Because of the asymptotic normality of maximum likelihood estimators, we can use the estimated variances to perform standard t tests on individual members of θ_{jk}.

6. RESULTS

The empirical results for both the dummy variable and the parameterized representations of financial treatments are roughly consistent for those instances in which financial treatments had significant effects. However, the chi-square for the likelihood ratio test is larger for the dummy variable representation than for the parameterized representation, except in the case of the rate at which husbands entered employment. This suggests that on the whole the dummy variable representation fits the data at least as well as the parameterized representation. So we report only results for the dummy variable representation. (Results for the parameterized representation are available from the authors upon request.)

Table II gives the estimated effects of the NIT programs on the rates of entering and leaving employment for the husbands, wives, and unmarried female heads enrolled in SIME/DIME; the Appendix gives the estimated effects of other variables. Table II also provides estimates of the effects of the NIT programs on the probability of employment of those still observed (i.e., not attrited) by the end of the sixth experimental quarter. The latter estimates are obtained by cross-sectional logit analysis using the method of maximum likelihood (see Nerlove and Press [9]). Below we comment on the effects of the NIT programs on the rates of entering and leaving employment, and then compare these results to the cross-sectional logit results.

Rate of Leaving Employment

The estimated effect of the NIT treatments on the rate of leaving employment (r_{10}) is statistically significant only for husbands, although its effect is positive for all three groups. The estimate for husbands implies that men on the 5-year NIT program left employment at a rate roughly 25 per cent faster than comparable men not on the NIT. This finding is consistent with the usual view that an NIT program provides a work disincentive.[8] Note, however, that the 3-year program has a significant negative effect about the same magnitude as the positive effect of a 5-year NIT program. Consequently, husbands on one of the 3-year NIT programs do not leave employment faster than comparable men not on an NIT program.

Table II   Maximum Likelihood Estimates of Experimental Effects on Employment[a]

	Effect of 5-Year NIT Program	Additional Effect of 3-Year NIT Program	Likelihood Ratio Test for Treatment Effects (X^2) (d.f. = 2)	Number of Spells	Number of Individuals[c]
Husbands (N = 1964)[b]					
(1) Rate of leaving employment	.222[f] (.074)	−.221[f] (.077)	9.93[f]	2,991	1,835
(2) Rate of entering employment	−.251[f] (.077)	.256[f] (.080)	12.84[f]	1,837	1,035
(3) = (2) − (1)	−.473[f] (.107)	.477[f] (.151)			
(4) Probability of employment at 6th experimental quarter (logit)	−.275 (.231)	.378 (.242)	2.48	−	1,267
Wives (N = 1972)					
(1) Rates of leaving employment	.045 (.102)	−.160 (.112)	2.87	1,692	1,162
(2) Rate of entering employment	−.505[f] (.097)	.096 (.104)	45.77[f]	2,189	1,671
(3) = (2) − (1)	−.550[f] (.141)	.256[d] (.153)			
(4) Probability of employment at 6th experimental quarter (logit)	−.716[f] (.202)	.402[d] (.214)	14.06[f]	−	1,459
Female heads (N = 1511)					
(1) Rate of leaving employment	.031 (.117)	.005 (.115)	.16	1,523	1,070
(2) Rate of entering employment	−.437[f] (.117)	.057 (.118)	23.76[f]	1,418	1,054
(3) = (2) − (1)	−.468[f] (.165)	.062 (.165)			
(4) Probability of employment at 6th experimental quarter (logit)	−.550[e] (.226)	.286 (.221)	6.24[e]	−	1,130

a. Estimated asymptotic standard errors are in parentheses.
b. Number of husbands and wives differ due to missing data.
c. Some individuals in the analysis of the rate of entering employment are also in the analysis of the rate of leaving employment.
d. Significant at 10% level.
e. Significant at 5% level.
f. Significant at 1% level.

Rate of Entering Employment

The estimated effect of an NIT program on the rate of entering employment (r_{01}) is statistically significant at the .01 level for husbands, wives, and unmarried female heads. Those on an NIT program enter employment at a much slower rate than otherwise comparable persons who are not on an NIT program, which again supports the notion that an NIT acts as a work disincentive. The estimates imply that an NIT program decreases the rate of entering employment by 22.2 per cent for husbands, by 39.6 per cent for wives, and by 35.4 per cent for unmarried female heads. The effect of program length is positive for all three groups, but statistically significant only for husbands. The rate of entering employment for husbands on the 3-year program does not significantly differ from that of comparable men not on the NIT.

Probability of Employment

The cross-sectional logit analysis of the probability of employment (see row 4 of Table II) also indicates that an NIT program acts as a work disincentive. According to the logit estimates, an NIT program decreases the probability of employment at the end of the sixth experimental quarter. However, the decrease is statistically significant only for wives (.01 level) and unmarried female heads (.05 level). Once again we see that the effect of an NIT program is much smaller for those on the 3-year program. In fact, the probability of employment for husbands on a 3-year NIT program is somewhat higher for those who are not on an NIT program.

Recall from our earlier discussion (see Section 3) that the difference in a variable's effects on the rates of entering and leaving employment equals its effect in cross-sectional logit analysis on the probability of employment in a non-attrited sample *if* transition rates are time-independent, log-linear functions of exogenous variables, *if* attrition rates are independent of employment status, and *if* the time of the cross-section is far from the origin (the start of the experiment). These differences are given in row 3 of Table II.

Comparison of the third and fourth rows for each group shows that the two methods of estimating the effect of the NIT program on the probability of employment give qualitatively similar results. The actual numerical differences between the two sets of estimates are sufficiently small that they could result from sampling error.[9] Note, however, that the effect of the 5-year NIT program on the husband's probability of employment is significantly negative on the basis of the logit estimates (row 4). This difference in the implications of the two methods is partly because the estimated effect of the NIT program is larger in the transition-rate analysis and partly because the estimated standard errors for the effects of the NIT program on the probability of employment are uniformly smaller in the transition-rate analysis. Given the additional information used in the transition-rate analysis, the smaller standard errors seem reasonable, indicating an additional advantage of this procedure over cross-sectional logit analysis.

7. IMPLICATIONS OF RESULTS

In this section we report selected predictions for the SIME/DIME sample based on the estimated effects of variables on rates of entering and leaving employment. These predictions indicate the kinds of information that can be inferred from an analysis of transition rates but cannot be learned from cross-sectional analysis.

Probability of Employment

Table III gives the probability of employment 3, 6, 12, and 18 months after the start of SIME/DIME. The entries for enrollment are the actual observed proportion in each group who are employed at the start of the experiment. The

Table III Employment Predictions for the SIME/DIME Sample

	Husbands				Wives				Female Heads			
Prediction	Controls (1)	Financials, No NIT (2)	Financials, NIT (3)	Difference Due to NIT (4)	Controls (1)	Financials, No NIT (2)	Financials, NIT (3)	Difference Due to NIT (4)	Controls (1)	Financials, No NIT (2)	Financials, NIT (3)	Difference Due to NIT (4)
Probability of Employment at:												
Enrollment	.812	.784	.784	0	.369	.313	.313	0	.546	.519	.519	0
End of 1st quarter	.816	.784	.773	.011	.392	.345	.321	.024	.558	.526	.504	.023
End of 2nd quarter	.820	.785	.771	.014	.406	.364	.325	.039	.568	.532	.494	.038
End of 4th quarter	.823	.787	.770	.017	.421	.383	.330	.054	.579	.539	.484	.055
End of 6th quarter	.824	.788	.770	.018[b]	.428	.392	.332	.060	.584	.542	.480	.062
Steady state[a]	.824	.789	.770	.018[b]	.436	.400	.334	.067[c]	.589	.545	.474	.071[c]
	(.006)	(.008)	(.007)	(.010)	(.012)	(.012)	(.012)	(.017)	(.013)	(.015)	(.012)	(.019)
End of 6th quarter (logit)	.811	.778	.775	.003	.424	.388	.318	.070	.568	.527	.470	.052
Mean duration of employment (weeks)[a]	120.9	107.4	100.3	7.1	73.4	65.7	70.0	4.3	116.7	99.4	96.1	-3.4
	(5.8)	(5.0)	(4.5)	(5.7)	(4.0)	(3.6)	(4.0)	(4.8)	(8.1)	(6.8)	(5.6)	(7.9)
Mean duration of non-employment (weeks)[a]	25.4	28.9	31.0	2.1	108.6	111.2	172.4	61.2[c]	94.3	100.9	149.0	48.1[c]
	(1.7)	(2.0)	(2.1)	(1.7)	(6.0)	(6.2)	(10.0)	(9.9)	(7.3)	(8.3)	(11.2)	(10.4)

a. Estimated asymptotic standard errors are in parentheses. These standard errors are calculated using the theorem that var $(g) = (\partial g'/\partial \theta) \, var \, (\hat{\theta}) \cdot (\partial g/\partial \theta)$ where $g(\hat{\theta}, X)$ is the prediction equation, $\hat{\theta}$ is the vector of maximum likelihood estimates of parameters and var $(\hat{\theta}) = (\partial^2 \ln L/\partial \hat{\theta}^2)^{-1}$. Significance levels are reported only for the "difference due to NIT."

b. Significant at 10% level.

c. Significant at 1% level.

other entries are calculated from (18) using the estimates of effects of variables given in Tables II and the Appendix, and each person's values of the explanatory variables.

First, note that in each of the three groups, the proportion employed at enrollment is higher for controls (those not assigned an NIT program) than for financials (those assigned an NIT program). If everyone had the same probability of being assigned treatments, this difference would be unexpected. But assignment of treatments was random within combinations of stratification variables—pretransfer income, race, and site—each of which we would expect to be related to the probability of employment. So it is not surprising that controls and financials differ in the nonexperimental probability of employment.

Second, notice that even for controls the predicted probability of employment rises over time, especially for wives and unmarried female heads. This rise may result from secular trends or from the use of an income ceiling in selecting the sample. The income ceiling may have led to enrollment of families whose heads were less likely to be working preexperimentally than normally. If so, we would expect the probability of employment to drift upward as time passes, even for controls.[10]

Third, compare the predicted probability of employment after 18 months with the steady-state (equilibrium) probability. The differences are negligible for husbands and very small (under .01, about the size of the standard error) for wives and female heads. So differences between findings based on cross-sectional logit analysis at the end of 18 months and analysis of transition rates (see footnote 9) probably do not result from 18 months being too near the start of the experiment.

Fourth, compare the predicted probability of employment after 18 months based on the analysis of transition rates and that based on the cross-sectional logit analysis. For wives and unmarried female heads the predictions from logit analysis are usually within one standard error of the 18-month predictions based on the analysis of transition rates. The differences between the two predictions are slightly larger for husbands, but still fairly small. The similarity of these predictions suggest that the differences between the third and fourth rows of Table II result mainly from sampling error and from differences in the samples analyzed.

Finally, consider the difference in the steady-state (or long-run) probability of employment that is attributable to the NIT program. The results predict that, if the NIT programs continued indefinitely, there would be a significant decrease of roughly seven percentage points in the probability of employment of women in the SIME/DIME sample. There is also a decrease of about two percentage points for husbands; this decrease is significant at the .01 level.

Duration of Spells

Table III also reports the predicted mean length of spells of employment and nonemployment for husbands, wives, and unmarried female heads in the

SIME/DIME sample. We see that under an NIT program, the mean duration of employment decreases slightly for husbands and female heads and rises slightly for wives. Because these differences do not significantly differ from zero, we cannot be confident that an NIT program would have *any* long-run effect on the duration of employment. On the other hand, we see large and statistically significant increases in the mean duration of nonemployment spells of wives and female heads under an NIT program. The mean duration of nonemployment spells of husbands also rises slightly under an NIT, but is not significant.

These predictions suggest something about the mechanism by which the probability of employment decreases under an NIT program. This decrease could result from shorter spells of employment, longer spells of nonemployment, or both. The results obtained for the first two years in SIME/DIME indicate that the decreased probability of employment under an NIT is almost solely due to longer spells of nonemployment. This suggests that the introduction of an NIT program has not induced those who are employed to quit their jobs. However, the program has encouraged those who are either not employed initially or who leave employment during the experiment to take longer to regain employment.[11] What our analysis cannot reveal is whether longer spells of nonemployment under an NIT program result from people searching longer to find better jobs (either those with a higher wage rate or more pleasant working conditions) or from longer periods spent on leisure and work in the home. If the former, lengthened nonemployment might have long-term financial benefits that would at least partially outweigh the increased program costs resulting from the NIT's work disincentive.

Stanford University
    and
SRI International, Menlo Park, California.

Manuscript received October, 1977; revision received May, 1979.

APPENDIX

Table A-I   Maximum Likelihood Estimates of Effects of Nonexperimental and Manpower Treatment Variables on the Logarithm of the Rate of Leaving Employment

	Husbands	Wives	Female Heads
Constant	-1.863^c	-1.920^c	-2.217^c
	(.668)	(.491)	(.637)
Normal income level:			
not determined	$.437^b$	$-.134$	$-.399$
	(.187)	(.237)	(.385)
$0- 1,000	$-.326$	1.075^c	.432
	(.288)	(.324)	(.369)
$1,000- 3,000	$.444^c$	$-.059$	.359
	(.144)	(.193)	(.355)
$3,000- 5,000	$.489^c$	.039	.345
	(.104)	(.129)	(.350)
$5,000- 7,000	$.255^c$	$-.131$	$-.192$
	(.092)	(.106)	(.353)
$7,000- 9,000	.127	$-.157$	$-.064$
	(.094)	(.101)	(.353)
$9,000-11,000	—	—	—
$11,000-13,000	—	—	—
1 if Denver	$.267^c$	$.284^c$	$.277^c$
	(.056)	(.073)	(.079)
1 if Black	$-.153^b$	$-.240^c$	$-.281^c$
	(.060)	(.082)	(.079)
Age in years	$-.029^c$	$-.025^c$	$-.022^c$
	(.005)	(.006)	(.005)
Years of schooling	$-.051^c$	$-.019$	.021
	(.001)	(.057)	(.049)
Number of family members	$-.289^c$	$.274^c$	$-.172$
	(.110)	(.079)	(.113)
Number of children under 16	$.251^b$	$-.260^c$	.174
	(.110)	(.082)	(.116)
Weeks worked in year prior to enrollment	$-.023^c$	$-.018^c$	$-.013^c$
	(.002)	(.002)	(.003)
Manpower			
M1 (Counseling only)	$.125^a$	.000	$-.129$
	(.074)	(.100)	(.108)
M2 (Counseling + 50% subsidy)	.098	$.207^b$	$-.041$
	(.068)	(.087)	(.100)
M3 (Counseling + 100% subsidy)	$.139^a$	$.298^c$	.108
	(.084)	(.103)	(.114)
Preexperimental disposable income ($1,000's)	$-.017$	$-.016$	$-.040$
	(.014)	(.017)	(.023)
Preexperimental net wage (S/hr)	.004	$-.647$	$-.505$
	(.232)	(.526)	(.526)
Number of spells	2,991	1,692	1,523

a. Indicates significant at 10% level.
b. Indicates significant at 5% level.
c. Indicates significant at 1% level.

Table A-II   Maximum Likelihood Estimates of Effects of Nonexperimental
and Manpower Treatment Variables on the Logarithm of the
Rate of Entering Employment

	Husbands	Wives	Female Heads
Constant	−4.725[c]	−4.740[c]	−5.238[c]
	(.720)	(.453)	(.633)
Normal income level:			
not determined	−.070	.531[b]	−.576
	(.195)	(.219)	(.401)
$0- 1,000	−1.031[c]	−.534[a]	−.966[b]
	(.249)	(.306)	(.381)
$1,000- 3,000	−.592[c]	−.215	−.611
	(.143)	(.174)	(.371)
$3,000- 5,000	−.377[c]	−.138	−.453
	(.101)	(.124)	(.365)
$5,000- 7,000	.042	−.042	−.333
	(.092)	(.102)	(.365)
$7,000- 9,000	.132	.014	.023
	(.092)	(.096)	(.361)
$9,000-11,000	−	−	−
$11,000-13,000	−	−	−
1 if Denver	.757[c]	.551[c]	1.023[c]
	(.056)	(.068)	(.080)
1 if Black	−.405[c]	.276[c]	−.285[c]
	(.062)	(.077)	(.080)
Age in years	−.046[c]	−.021[c]	−.007
	(.005)	(.005)	(.005)
Years of schooling	.017	.156[c]	.013
	(.013)	(.052)	(.048)
Number of family members	−.174	.103	−.326[b]
	(.124)	(.097)	(.137)
Number of children under 16	.232[b]	−.120	.271[b]
	(.124)	(.098)	(.138)
Weeks worked in year prior to enrollment	.020[c]	.027[c]	.022[c]
	(.002)	(.002)	(.002)
Manpower:			
M1 (Counseling only)	−.132[a]	−.079	.072
	(.075)	(.092)	(.106)
M2 (Counseling + 50% subsidy)	−.240[c]	−.008	−.157
	(.069)	(.079)	(.101)
M3 (Counseling + 100% subsidy)	−.169[b]	−.210[b]	−.238[a]
	(.083)	(.100)	(.123)
Preexperimental disposable income ($1,000's)	.053[c]	−.021	.054[b]
	(.014)	(.015)	(.026)
Preexperimental net wage ($/hr)	.738[c]	−.726	.520
	(.250)	(.469)	(.425)
Number of spells	1,837	2,189	1,418

a. Indicates significant at 10% level.
b. Indicates significant at 5% level.
c. Indicates significant at 1% level.

NOTES

1. The research reported in this paper was performed pursuant to contracts with the states of Washington and Colorado, prime contractors for the Department of Health, Education and Welfare under contract numbers SRS-70-53 and SRS-71-18, respectively. The opinions expressed in the paper are those of the authors and should not be construed as representing the opinions or policies of the states of Washington and Colorado or any agency of the United States Government.

The authors wish to acknowledge the programming assistance of John McClure, Paul McElherne, Gary Stieger, and Craig Williams, and the helpful comments on an earlier version made by Lyle Groeneveld, Michael Keeley, Richard West, and anonymous referees.

2. Models I and II also have implications for the expected number of transitions (e.g., changes from employed to not employed) in a period. The equations are given in Tuma et al. [12].

3. About 800 Mexican-American families were enrolled in the Denver experiment. They are excluded in the analysis reported below because data on them were unavailable at the time of our study.

4. There were also three manpower treatments. These are controlled in the empirical analysis, but are not a major focus of our attention.

5. The procedure for constructing these variables is described in Keeley et al. [7].

6. The data do not include information on dates of movement between the traditional categories "unemployed" (i.e., "not employed but searching for work") and "out of the labor force" (i.e., "not employed and not searching for work"). The labor force status of each person can be determined for the dates of interviews but changes between interviews cannot be determined.

7. We plan to investigate models allowing changes in both employment status and marital status in future work, but data files for such analyses have not yet been constructed.

8. Throughout the discussion below, we are assuming that an NIT program, like the programs in SIME/DIME, decreases net wage rates and increases disposable income for those in families whose earned income is below the breakeven level. (In SIME/DIME the average decrease in the net wage is roughly $1 per hour while the average increase in disposable income is about $1250 per year.)

9. The observed differences could arise for several reasons. First, the attrition rate of those who are employed might differ from the attrition rate of those who are not employed. Second, the two methods of analysis are based on somewhat different samples, since those who attrite are excluded in the logit analysis. Third, the end of the sixth quarter may not be far enough from the start of the experiment for the probability of employment among those still observed to be near a steady-state value. An examination of these possibilities suggests that the third reason is not an important source of differences (see below), but that the first two reasons could be.

10. Robins and West [10] make a similar point in discussing hours worked per period.

11. Since this paper was written, data over a longer period of time (four years) have become available. Analyses of these data indicate that the date of leaving employment is significantly increased under an NIT program for husbands and unmarried female heads of families. Most of the effect on the probability of employment, however, is still due to longer spells of nonemployment.

REFERENCES

[1] BLUMEN, ISADORE, MARVIN KOGAN, and PHILIP J. McCARTHY: *The Industrial Mobility of Labor As a Probability Process*, Cornell Studies in Industrial and Labor Relations 6. Ithaca: Cornell University Press, 1955.

[2] BREIMAN, L.: *Probability and Stochastic Processes*. Boston: Houghton-Mifflin, 1969.

[3] CAIN, GLEN G., and HAROLD W. WATTS, Eds.: *Income Maintenance and Labor Supply*. Chicago: Rand McNally, 1973.

[4] FRANK, ROBERT H.: "How Long is a Spell of Unemployment?" *Econometrica*, 46 (1978), 285-302.

[5] HANOCH, G.: *Hours and Weeks in the Theory of Labor Supply*, R-1787-HEW. Santa Monica: The Rand Corporation, 1976.

[6] HECKMAN, JAMES J.: "Heterogeneity and State Dependence in Dynamic Models of Labor Supply," in *Conference on Labor Markets*, edited by J. Rosen. Chicago: University of Chicago Press, 1979.

[7] KEELEY, MICHAEL C., PHILIP K. ROBINS, ROBERT G. SPIEGELMAN, and RICHARD W. WEST: "The Estimation of Labor Supply Models Using Experimental Data." *American Economic Review*, 68 (1978), 873-887.

[8] McCALL, J. J.: "A Markovian Model of Income Dynamics," *Journal of the American Statistical Association*, 65 (1970), 1195-1203.

[9] NERLOVE, MARC, and S. JAMES PRESS: *Univariate and Multivariate Log Linear and Logistic Models*, R-1306-EDA/NIH. Santa Monica: The Rand Corporation, 1973.

[10] ROBINS, PHILIP K., and RICHARD W. WEST: "Participation in the Seattle and Denver Income Maintenance Experiments and Its Effect on Labor Supply." Research Memorandum 53, Center for the Study of Welfare Policy, SRI International, Menlo Park, California, March, 1978.

[11] SPILERMAN, SEYMOUR: "Extensions of the Mover-Stayer Model." *American Journal of Sociology*, 78 (1972), 599-626.

[12] TUMA, NANCY BRANDON, MICHAEL T. HANNAN, and L. P. GROENEVELD: "Dynamic Analysis of Event Histories." *American Journal of Sociology*, 84 (1979), 820-854.

[13] TUMA, NANCY BRANDON, and MICHAEL T. HANNAN: "Approaches to the Censoring Problem in Analysis of Event Histories," in *Sociological Methodology 1979*, edited by K. Schuessler. San Francisco: Jossey-Bass, 1978.

10

The question of whether to estimate reduced-form models to calculate simple experimental/control comparisons, or to estimate more elaborate structural models is a recurring issue in evaluation research.[1] Moffitt addresses the problem explicitly, and his solution is reasonable—both estimates are provided.

Reduced-form results are presented in Table 1. Specifications with either (a) before and during data stacked, and a dummy variable for the experimental group during the experiment, or (b) labor supply during the experiment regressed against an experimental/control group dummy variable (as well as preprogram labor supply and other control variables) give essentially the same result: significant negative effects for husbands and female heads but no effect for wives. Moffitt explains the surprising results for wives[2] by the fact that the Gary labor market provides few part-time jobs—those few wives holding such jobs may have been reluctant to give them up for a limited-duration experiment.

The structural model is a variant of the usual labor supply specification: Total hours worked are regressed against the wage rate and nonwage income. During- and pre-experimental observations are stacked together, so that the first-differences model proposed by Keeley et al. (Ch. 8) is not used. Nor is the estimated wage effect explicitly decomposed into income and substitution effects. (But such a calculation is provided in Moffitt, 1979.[3]) An averaging procedure approximates a nonlinear budget constraint (see Ch. 11) and the tobit model is used for estimation.[4]

The structural model results (Table 2) show relatively weak (negative) responses to the NIT income guarantee for husbands and female heads, and no significant response to the NIT tax rate. In combination with the results for the non-NIT variables, these findings suggest that social experiments ought to be run simultaneously in several sites with due attention given to intersite demand side differences.

NOTES

1. For further discussion of this issue see the introduction to Part III, the chapter by Farkas et al., and discussions in many of the other articles in this Volume.

2. Recall that the chapter by Keeley et al. found the strongest response to be among wives.

3. An unusual aspect of this calculation is that Moffitt uses the fact that almost all employed individuals work full-time to estimate total labor supply as a probit for whether or not the individual works 40 hours per week.

4. Near the end of the chapter, the author notes that a variety of sensitivity tests failed to disturb the basic results. Nevertheless, more explicit discussion of wage imputations corrected for selectivity and the calculation of the coefficient standard errors from a stacked tobit would have been desirable.

REFERENCE

MOFFITT, R. (1979) "A note on the effects of taxes and transfers on labor supply." Southern Econ. J. 45: 1266-1273.

The Labor Supply Response in the Gary Experiment

Robert A. Moffitt

ABSTRACT

The results of the Gary Negative Income Tax Experiment show significant work disincentives of 3 to 6 percent for husbands, 26 to 30 percent for female heads, but none for wives. The response of husbands is similar to those in other experiments. The response of female heads is somewhat larger than that in Seattle-Denver, the only other experiment reporting female-head results, because of a larger guarantee effect in Gary. The response of wives is very dissimilar to that in the other experiments, possibly because the Gary labor market offers few part-time possibilities for married women. In general, tax effects are much weaker than guarantee effects, which may also be a result of the steel-dominated, highly structured local labor market.

This paper is a brief summary of the central labor supply findings of the Gary Income Maintenance Experiment. A fuller and more detailed presentation will appear in the future in the Final Report of the Gary experiment. The experiment in Gary ran for three years, 1971–74, in Gary, Indiana, and

The author in the Department of Economics, Rutgers University, and is affiliated with Mathematica Policy Research.

* This research was performed at Mathematica Policy Research, Princeton, N.J., under contracts HEW-100-76-0073 and HEW-100-78-0059 from the U.S. Department of Health, Education, and Welfare. The author would like to extend special thanks to John Friedmann, David Horner, Kenneth Kehrer, and John McDonald for general moral support, persistent constructive criticism of the model, aid in the development of the data base, and correction of several important programming errors. Also, John Friedmann estimated the adjusted-mean responses, David Horner estimated the sample-selection equations, and John McDonald estimated the food-stamp-test equations. The author would also like to thank the following individuals for advice and comments at various points along the way: David Betson, Gary Burtless, Joseph Corbett, David Greenberg, Martin Holmer, Stuart Kerachsky, Charles Mallar, Charles Metcalf, Donna Vandenbrink, and Doug Wolf. In addition, Debra Tessier provided invaluable progamming assistance, and Caroline Roth supervised the data-file creation. In addition, the editor of this *Journal* and two anonymous referees provided valuable comments. [Manuscript received January 1979; accepted June 1979.]

From Robert A. Moffitt, "The Labor Supply Response in the Gary Experiment," 14(4) *Journal of Human Resources* 477–487 (Fall 1979). Copyright 1979 by the University of Wisconsin.

included approximately 1800 black families, 1000 of whom were female-headed and 800 of whom were families with husband and wife present. Like all the experiments, it operated on the principle of stratified random assignment to an experimental group that was eligible for payments or to a control group that was not. The families in the experimental group were assigned to one of four negative income tax plans, each with a different tax rate–guarantee combination. Tax rates of 40 and 60 percent were paired with guarantees of 75 and 100 percent of the poverty line for a family of a given size.

Results are presented below for the husbands, wives, and female heads in the experiment, and the findings are compared to those of other experiments, especially those of the Seattle-Denver experiment (Keeley and others [5]). The husbands' results are also compared to the Gary estimates of Burtless and Hausman [2]; however, they had no estimates for wives and female heads. The methodology is discussed in Section I, and the results are reported in Section II.

I. MODELS ESTIMATED

The logical first step in estimating the effect of an NIT experiment is to estimate the mean experimental-control group difference:

$$(1) \qquad L = \alpha T + \beta X + \epsilon$$

where L is some measure of labor supply, T is an experimental dummy variable equal to one if in the experimental group and zero if in the control group, X is a vector of exogenous socioeconomic characteristics, ϵ is a randomly distributed error term, and α and β are parameters. In such a model the coefficient α measures the experimental effect and represents the mean experimental-control labor supply differential adjusted for differences in X. Estimates of α are presented below. However, estimates of α are only a first step, for the mean experimental-control difference in a particular experiment cannot be generalized to a different population (e.g., with a different income distribution and a different percent of families below breakeven) or generalized to NIT programs with different tax rates and guarantees. A more structural model is needed for this purpose.

The labor supply model used here is an adaptation of the traditional model in which an individual's hours of work are a function of the net hourly wage rate and nonwage income:

$$(2) \qquad H = \gamma + \delta W(1 - r - t) + \eta(N + B_0)$$

where H = hours of work per month; W = gross hourly wage rate; r =

average non-NIT tax rate on earnings; t = average NIT tax rate on earnings; B_0 = NIT benefit per month at zero hours; and N = non-NIT nonwage income.

In this model, earnings are shown to be taxed by the NIT and by non-NIT programs (federal and state income taxes, other welfare programs, etc.). Nonwage income is shown to be composed of a basic NIT benefit (equal to $G - tN$, where G is the guarantee) and of non-NIT nonwage income (dividends, interest, etc., plus other welfare program guarantees minus taxes paid at zero hours). The tax rates r and t are average tax rates, meaning that they are averages of the marginal tax rates over the entire length of each individual's budget constraint. The reason for this procedure lies in the piecewise-linear nature of most budget constraints. For example, many experimentals with high wage rates go off the NIT if they work sufficiently long hours; they face a zero NIT tax rate over that portion of their budget constraint above the breakeven point. The averaging procedure assigns a value of t to such individuals, which is a weighted average of the positive, below-breakeven NIT tax rate and the zero, above-breakeven NIT tax rate. For experimentals who are below breakeven over the entire hours range, the average NIT tax rate is the same as the below-breakeven tax rate. The average non-NIT tax rate, r, is similarly constructed by averaging the marginal tax rates of AFDC (female head only) and those of the positive tax programs over the entire budget constraint.[1]

The averaging procedure only approximates the budget constraint and therefore only approximates the labor supply function. It is used here to provide flexibility and to avoid some of the difficulties in modeling the response to the entire budget constraint. Burtless and Hausman [2] have shown how this can be done with maximum-likelihood techniques. Their method appears to be superior to those used in previous experimental studies (see Moffitt and Kehrer [11] for a review). However, as shown below, the averaging procedure gives results very similar to those of Burtless and Hausman, at least on the subset of the sample which they analyzed (husbands), suggesting that the averaging procedure is not a bad approximation for the Gary sample. This is probably because very few individuals in the sample work part time, as a result of the Gary labor market's domination by the steel industry and its full-time, fixed-hours jobs. As a result, marginal changes in hours worked are infrequent.

---

1   The averages are calculated by taking the two endpoints on the budget constraint and deriving the slope of the line between them. Thus, $t = -(B_f - B_O)/WH_f$ and $r = \{1 - [(Y_f - N)/WH_f]\}$, where H_f is full-time hours, B_f is the NIT benefit at H_f, and Y_f in non-NIT disposable income at H_f. Full-time hours (173/month) was used because there are few workers in the sample who moonlight or work overtime. See Moffitt [9]. The NIT benefit is calculated taking tax reimbursement into account..

Equation (2) is modified slightly, but in an important way, to allow NIT and non-NIT variables to have different coefficients:

(3) $$H = \gamma + \delta'W(1 - r) + \delta''(-Wt) + \eta'N + \eta''B_0$$

This separation is important because it avoids "contaminating" the effect of the experimental stimulus with the effect of nonexperimental stimuli. If equation (2) were estimated, one could easily obtain estimates of δ and η which are primarily a result of behavioral responses to nonexperimental variables. This would defeat one of the main purposes of running an experiment, which is to obtain estimates *different* from those in nonexperimental data. In any case, the significance of the coefficient differences is an empirical question. However, despite the potential importance of separating the coefficients, this is the first experimental study to do so in a formal way.[2]

Equation (3) is estimated separately for husbands, wives, and female heads on a sample of about 600 husband-wife families and 750 female-headed families. Three major decisions are made regarding the selection of the analysis sample. First, several subgroups that are expected to have structurally atypical labor supply functions are deleted. These are the aged, the young, the self-employed, and the disabled. Second, families who left the experiment ("attriters") are included in the sample for the periods before their departure. Third, families who changed marital status during the experiment (i.e., went from husband-wife to single-headed or vice versa) are included in the sample and are classified according to their contemporaneous marital status. This decision is based upon previous research by Wolf [13], which showed that the Gary experiment had no effect on marital dissolution, implying that marital status can be treated as exogenous to the experiment.

One pre-enrollment observation and up to seven during-experiment observations are available from interview data. These are pooled into one regression,[3] and the pre-enrollment observation is "dummied out."[4] Independent variables for the number of other adults, the number and age

---

2 Whether nonexperimental coefficients are biased or not is another question, for they may differ from experimental coefficients for a number of other reasons. For example, the limited duration of the experiment may make NIT substitution effects larger and NIT income effects smaller than their respective non-NIT counterparts [8].

3 See below for mention of generalized least-squares estimation.

4 That is, the equation estimated is:
$$H = a + b(-Wt)D + cB_OD + dW(1 - r) + eN + fD + g(-Wt) + hB_O$$
where D is a dummy variable equal to 1 if the observation is during the experiment and 0 if pre-enrollment. Coefficients g and h measure pre-enrollment treatment differences (if any), and coefficients b and c measure the experimental effect, i.e., the effect *net* of any pre-enrollment difference that may exist.

distribution of children, the season at the time of the interview, the Gary unemployment rate at the time of the interview, and the presence of a multiple-family household are included. The estimation technique used is Tobit analysis, to account for the presence of zeros in the dependent variable. Sensitivity tests indicate that the estimates are not sensitive to these choices of sample, estimating technique, and method of controlling for pre-enrollment differences.[5]

II. RESULTS

Estimates of α in equation (1) are shown in Table 1. A range of estimates is provided by the use of two different statistical techniques to control for possible pre-enrollment experimental-control differences (see footnotes to the table). The table shows experimental effects on employment status and unconditional hours worked, indicating significant labor supply reductions for husbands and female heads, but not for wives. For husbands, employment-status reduction of 2.7 to 4.9 percent and unconditional-hours reductions of 2.9 to 6.5 percent occurred. For female heads, the employment-status and unconditional-hours reductions were from 26 to 30 percent.

The results for husbands are very similar to those from other experiments, where reductions ranged from 1 to 8 percent [11]; consequently, our confidence in the general order of magnitude of the male NIT response in Gary should increase. On the other hand, the results for wives are very different from those in the other experiments, where ranges were from 15 to 55 percent [11]. One possible explanation is the very low employment rate of wives—15 percent; less than 90 of the 545 wives in the combined experimental and control samples were working at pre-enrollment, which could have made differential experimental-control behavior difficult to detect statistically. However, the wives' employment rate was about the same at the beginning of the New Jersey experiment, where a substantial wives' response was found. The low employment rate in the New Jersey experiment was primarily a result of the income truncation in the experimental design [12, p. 26], so that transitory factors undoubtedly contributed to the low labor supply for wives for the year prior to that experiment. On the other hand, in Gary, where such truncation was negligible, the low employment rate was more a result of the structure of the labor market and the lack of

---

5   Also, attrition is ignored on the basis of the work of Hausman and Wise [3], who have shown that attrition in the Gary experiment does not have any substantial effect on the coefficients of a structural labor supply model. Although pre-enrollment differences are controlled for, no direct controls are used for the sample allocation model, whose effects were very weak in the Gary experiment.

TABLE 1
ESTIMATED MEAN EXPERIMENTAL-CONTROL LABOR SUPPLY DIFFERENCES[a]

Dependent Variable	Husbands		Wives		Female Heads	
	Net	Lagged	Net	Lagged	Net	Lagged
Employment status (1 if employed, 0 if not)	−.042**	−.023	.004	.003	−.055**	−.053***
Percent of control mean	−4.9	−2.7	2.8	2.1	−26.8	−25.8
Unconditional hours per month[b]	−9.53	−4.24	1.18	.32	−9.35	−8.23
Percent of control mean	−6.5	−2.9	5.0	1.0	−30.0	−25.9

a Taken from Robert Moffitt and John Friedmann, "Adjusted Mean Responses" in [7]. Net model includes both during-experiment and pre-enrollment observations: $L = \alpha TD + \beta X + \gamma T$, where D is a dummy equal to 1 if a during-experiment observation, and the X vector is as defined for equation (1). The lagged model includes only during-experiment observations: $L = \alpha T + \beta X + \delta L_P$, where L_P is the pre-enrollment value of labor supply. All equations are estimated with generalized least-squares assuming an error term with a completely random component and a constant individual component.

b No significance tests. See Moffitt and Friedmann.

** Coefficient significant at 95 percent level.   *** Coefficient significant at 99 percent level.

241

jobs for women. The Gary labor market is dominated by the steel industry and provides very few part-time jobs. This is illustrated by the index variable created by Bowen and Finegan [1, p. 774] to describe the degree to which the industry mix of the top 100 SMSAs is conducive to "female employment." The Gary SMSA ranks at the bottom of their list.

The results for female heads are considerably larger than the 12 percent response found in the Seattle-Denver experiment, the only other one that enrolled large numbers of female heads. The absolute magnitudes of the hours reductions in the two experiments are close to one another, but, given the much lower employment rate and hours worked in the Gary sample, a smaller response should be expected. The difference does not appear to be a result of different racial populations in each experiment because no statistically significant differences among the races were found in Seattle-Denver. Alternatively, the much lower AFDC standard in Indiana ($205 per month for a family of four in 1972) compared to Seattle ($294) and Colorado ($242) could have resulted in a stronger stimulus in Gary. However, the greater generosity of the Seattle-Denver NIT plans compensate for this difference. The net stimulus (i.e., the change in income net of AFDC) is about $100 per month or female heads in both experiments.[6] Another possibility is simply that the tax and guarantee elasticities are stronger in Gary. To explore this hypothesis, it is necessary to move to the estimates of equation (3).

Table 2 shows the estimated budget-line coefficients of equation (3).[7] For husbands, the results show a weak income effect (significant at the 20 percent level) with a mean elasticity of 5 percent, but an insignificant net-wage effect. These fairly inelastic responses are not exceptional for prime-age males. They are also identical to the estimates of Burtless and Hausman [2], who only examined males and also found an insignificant net-wage elasticity and a significant income elasticity of 5 percent. Although there are other important model differences between this study and theirs,[8] the most important is the different treatment of the nonlinearity of the budget constraint. The conformity of results indicates that, at least on this sample, the average-tax-rate procedure is not a bad approximation. The conformity may be a result of the highly structured Gary labor market, as has been

---

6   The change in the net wage is also not too different: $-.67$ per hour and $-.80$ per hour for Seattle-Denver and Gary, respectively.

7   Mean Tobit coefficients are presented because they are the relevant explanators of the *total* hours responses in Table 1. See McDonald and Moffitt [6]. The original beta coefficients can be obtained using the probabilities in the table footnotes. Estimates of the other coefficients in the equation are available in Moffitt [10].

8   In particular, Burtless and Hausman [2] (a) use log H as the dependent variable, thus not allowing zero hours, (b) constrain NIT and non-NIT coefficients to equality, and (c) constrain the income effect to be negative a priori.

TABLE 2
MEAN COEFFICIENTS IN TOBIT HOURS/MONTH REGRESSION[a]

	Husbands		Wives		Female Heads	
	Coefficient	Elasticity	Coefficient	Elasticity	Coefficient	Elasticity
NIT						
Income effect[b]	−5.85	−.05	4.07	.07	−6.35*	−.23
	(1.42)		(.58)		(1.91)	
Net wage effect	−3.60	−.01	12.67	.16	−4.61	−.12
	(.36)		(.65)		(.49)	
Non-NIT						
Income effect[b]	−24.53**	−.13	1.61**	.45	−4.94**	−.20
Net wage effect	−.621	−.01	5.55***	.46	−4.38**	−.27
	(.33)		(3.15)		(2.46)	

Note: Unsigned *t*-statistics are in parentheses.   * Significant at the 10 percent level.   ** Significant at the 5 percent level.   *** Significant at the 1 percent level.

a All coefficients evaluated at the mean value of the Tobit index. That is, if β is the vector of coefficients, X is the vector of independent variables, and F is the cumulative normal distribution function, the coefficients in the table are $\beta F(\beta X/\sigma)$. $F(\beta X/\sigma)$ equals .99, .15, and .21 for husbands, wives, and female heads, respectively.

b Divided by 100.

previously mentioned. About 65 percent of the husbands worked in a steel mill and only 7 percent worked part time (1 to 34 hours per week); the others worked about 38 hours per week or not at all. This lack of flexibility could make marginal hours adjustments difficult and, therefore, could make the averaging procedure, which throws away information on many intramarginal tax rates, a satisfactory approximation. It should also be noted that this aspect of the Gary labor market may also explain why no net wage (i.e., tax) effects were found here, as they have been in other experiments. Decreases in the tax rate may not increase work effort if marginal hours increases cannot be made.[9]

The results for wives show insignificant effects for both net wage and income, confirming the total lack of response discussed above. Again, the low employment rate (15 percent) of the sample may be part of the explanation, together with the occupational structure of the local labor market. Another indication of this constraint is that part-time work was very infrequent—9 percent of the sample—compared to the amount of part-time work among wives in other samples.

For female heads, the response shows a significantly negative income effect with an elasticity of .23, but an insignificant net-wage effect. The lack of a response to the tax rate again may be a result of inflexibility in the Gary labor market. But, like husbands, female heads did respond to the guarantee. Indeed, the magnitudes of the husbands' and female heads' coefficients are rather close to one another, perhaps because female heads also often must provide earnings for an entire family and may, therefore, be equally sensitive to changes in work incentives.

The size of the female-head guarantee effect goes a long way toward explaining why the response here is larger than that in Seattle-Denver. The comparable income effect in Seattle-Denver is less than one-third of the Gary effect (-2.02 vs. -6.35).[10] The effect of this difference on the response can be illustrated by applying the Seattle-Denver coefficients to the Gary guarantee and tax-rate stimuli. When this is done, the predicted Gary response of 26–30 percent falls by one-half (i.e., to 13–15 percent), and most of the difference between the Gary results and the Seattle-Denver percent response is thereby explained.

Why the Gary female heads have a stronger response to identical stimuli is unclear. The most likely explanation lies in the fact that the Seattle-Denver sample was composed of fairly high-income female heads, at least

9 Working overtime and moonlighting are ways to supplement hours, but virtually no individuals in the Gary sample did so.

10 The Seattle-Denver income effect is obtained by converting the income coefficient in Keeley and others [5, Table 3] to a monthly basis and multiplying by .21 to make it comparable to the results presented above in Table 2 (see footnotes to that table).

compared to that in Gary. For this reason, Seattle-Denver female heads may simply have had a higher level of commitment to work effort. For example, Seattle-Denver female heads worked an average of 80 hours per month, whereas Gary female heads worked only 31 hours. If there is a nonlinearity in the response to an NIT, with greater responses at lower income and hours levels, this could explain the difference.

Table 2 shows the coefficients on the non-NIT income variables. The most striking difference is in the magnitude and/or significance of the NIT and non-NIT coefficients: husbands have more significant and larger income effects, wives have significant net-wage effects, and female heads have more significant income effects.[11] (However, wives have a significant but positive non-NIT income effect.) Moreover, the coefficient differences are significant at the 5 percent level. These results show the importance of estimating NIT tax and guarantee coefficients separately from those of non-NIT income and could also further explain some of the above-mentioned differences between the NIT estimates in this study and those in other experimental studies such as Keeley and others [5], where the coefficients were constrained.

Numerous sensitivity tests were performed on equation (3). The equation was estimated with OLS and generalized least-squares rather than Tobit; pre-enrollment differences were controlled for by lagging the dependent variable instead of "netting out" pre-enrollment treatment differences; the data were averaged rather than pooled; only the middle year of the experiment was examined; a variety of wage instruments were used; and so on.[12] The results show that the estimates of the basic equation are quite robust, especially given the insignificance of many of the coefficients. Perhaps most notable is that none of these tests revealed any hidden response of wives.

III. SUMMARY

This paper has briefly reported the labor supply results of the Gary Income Maintenance Experiment. A 3 to 6 percent response of husbands and a 25 to 30 percent response of female heads were found. The male response is close to those in other experiments, but the female-head response is larger than that in Seattle-Denver. However, unlike other experiments, no wives' response was found. This may have been a result of the Gary labor market that offers very few part-time jobs. Also, the Gary labor market may have contributed to insignificant tax effects for both husbands and female heads.

---

11   Compensated substitution effects for all three groups are positive.
12   See Moffitt [10] or the upcoming Final Report for details

REFERENCES

1. William G. Bowen and T. Aldrich Finegan. *The Economics of Labor Force Participation.* Princeton, N.J.: Princeton University Press, 1969.
2. Gary Burtless and Jerry A. Hausman. "The Effect of Taxation on Labor Supply: Evaluating the Gary Negative Income Tax Experiment." *Journal of Political Economy* 86 (December 1978): 1102–30.
3. Jerry A. Hausman and David A. Wise. "Attrition Bias in Experimental and Panel Data: The Gary Income Maintenance Experiment." *Econometrica* 47 (May 1979): 455–74.
4. ———. "Stratification on Endogenous Variables and Estimation: The Gary Income Maintenance Experiment." Kennedy School Discussion Paper, 1978.
5. Michael C. Keeley, Philip K. Robins, Robert G. Spiegelman, and Richard W. West. "The Labor Supply Effects and Costs of Alternative Negative Income Tax Programs." *Journal of Human Resources* 13 (Winter 1978): 3–36.
6. John McDonald and Robert Moffitt. "The Uses of Tobit Analysis." *Review of Economics and Statistics* (forthcoming).
7. Mathematica Policy Research, Inc. "Central Findings Report of the Gary Income Maintenance Experiment." Forthcoming.
8. Charles E. Metcalf. "Making Inferences from Controlled Income Maintenance Experiments." *American Economic Review* 63 (June 1973): 478–83.
9. Robert Moffitt. "A Note on the Effects of Taxes and Transfer on Labor Supply." *Southern Economic Journal* 45 (April 1979): 1266–73.
10. ———. "The Labor Supply Response in the Gary Income Maintenance Experiment." Staff Paper 79A-02. Princeton, N.J.: Mathematica Policy Research, 1978.
11. Robert Moffitt and Kenneth Kehrer. "The Effect of Tax and Transfer Programs on Labor Supply: The Evidence from the Income Maintenance Experiments." In *Research in Labor Economics,* ed. Ronald G. Ehrenberg. Greenwich, Conn.: JAI Press, forthcoming.
12. Albert Rees. "The Labor-Supply Results of the Experiment: A Summary." In *The New Jersey Income Maintenance Experiment, Vol. II: Labor-Supply Responses,* eds. Harold W. Watts and Albert Rees. New York: Academic Press, 1977.
13. Douglas Wolf. "Income Maintenance, Labor Supply and Family Stability: An Empirical Analysis of Marital Dissolution." Ph.D. dissertation, University of Pennsylvania, 1977.

11

Burtless and Hausman analyze a subset of the Gary data considered by Moffitt (Ch. 10). Their results—no tax effect and a small income effect for male household heads—are similar. The methodology, however, is potentially important—the notion of duality from economic theory is combined with maximum likelihood estimation techniques to provide a framework for dealing with demand theory in the presence of nonlinear budget constraints. This chapter is concerned with the supply of labor (demand for leisure) under progressive taxation or a negative income tax treatment. (See also Hausman, forthcoming.) But the methods presented here could be applied well beyond this substantive area. (See the chapter by Hausman and Wise in Part V for an application to estimating the demand for housing under a variety of experimental subsidy schemes.) Thus, these methods are an important extension of the techniques for "estimating indifference curves" introduced by Heckman (1974a, 1974b).

A brief excursion into economic theory may aid in digesting this piece. It is usual to assume that individuals choose bundles of goods to maximize a "direct" utility function, $U(x_1, \ldots x_N, \text{leisure})$, where the x's represent goods purchased in the market and leisure is also thought of as a good. [1] Since more leisure means fewer hours at work, studying the demand for leisure is equivalent to studying the supply of labor. (It is for this reason that the figures in this article read from right to left.)

The solution to this optimization problem (choosing the quantities of goods so that the bundle maximizes utility) depends on prices, $p_1, \ldots p_N$, w (w = the wage rate is the price of leisure) and on the individual's nonlabor income, y. For each set of given values of these, there is a set of quantities $(x_1^*, \ldots x_N^*, \text{leisure}^*)$ that is optimal. If we indicate the level of utility associated with this bundle of goods as $v(p_1, \ldots p_N, w, y)$, we have defined the "indirect" utility function. As we shall see, an explicit representation of this function can be useful.

The issue is: how to proceed from theory to estimation? The usual answer is to assume that observed consumption represents individual optima, and use regression analysis to estimate a labor supply (leisure demand) function such as

$$\text{Hours} = k + \alpha w + \beta y, \qquad [1]$$

or,

$$\text{Hours} = k \, w^\alpha y^\beta. \qquad [2]$$

But this strategy is not available in the situation confronting Burtless and Hausman, since their subjects face a nonlinear budget constraint. As a result, no single wage rate can be found for use in equation 1 or 2. Instead, we must estimate the parameters k, α, β, by a maximum likelihood technique the involves calculating and comparing an individual's utility under alternate situations.

The indirect utility function is the key to this strategy. Using labor supply form (2) above, and combining it with Roy's identity (expression 6 in Burtless and Hausman) [2], the authors arrive at an explicit form for the indirect utility function:

$$v(w, y) = k \, \frac{w^{1+\alpha}}{1+\alpha} + \frac{y^{1-\beta}}{1-\beta} . \qquad [3]$$

(This is their expression 9.) It is remarkable to have this function explicitly, since it permits direct comparison of the individual utility associated with location on different budget line segments.

After specifying their model in stochastic form, Burtless and Hausman use the indirect utility function in just this way—as the key element of their procedure for arriving at the likelihood function necessary for parameter estimation. Thus, in the discussion occupying pp. 262-265 (accompanying Figure 6), the indirect utility function is used to solve for β^*, the individual's switch-over point between the two budget segments. [3] (See expression 14. Note also that there is a misprint in the text: expression 14 arises from the application of expression 9, not expression 10.) This leads directly to expressions 16 and 20, the terms in the likelihood function to be maximized across the sample. (See expression 21.)

NOTES

1. Which in one interpretation is used in "home production" of other goods.

2. For the duality theory underlying this procedure see Varian (1978: Chs. 1 and 2, particularly pp. 92-95) and Rosen (1974).

3. The income elasticity, β, determines the shape of the individual's indifference curve (the extent to which it is backward bending), and this in turn determines the location of the switching point.

REFERENCES

HAUSMAN, J. (forthcoming) "The effect of wages, taxes, and fixed costs on women's labor force participation." J. of Public Economics.

HECKMAN, J. (1974a) "Shadow prices, market wages, and labor supply." Econometrica (July): 679-694.

——— (1974b) "Effects of child care programs on women's work effort." J. of Pol. Economy 82, No. 2, Part II: S136-S163.

ROSEN, S. (1974) "Comment." J. of Pol. Economy 82 No. 2, Part II: S164-S169.

VARIAN, H. (1978) Microeconomic Analysis. New York: Norton.

The Effect of Taxation on Labor Supply
Evaluating the Gary Negative Income Tax Experiment

Gary Burtless and Jerry A. Hausman

A model of labor supply is formulated which takes explicit account of nonlinearities in the budget set which arise because the net, after-tax wage depends on hours worked. These nonlinearities may lead to a convex budget set due to the effect of progressive marginal tax rates, or they may lead to a nonconvex budget set due to the effect of government transfer programs such as AFDC or a negative income tax. The nonlinearities affect both the marginal wage and the "virtual" nonlabor income which the individual faces. The model is estimated on a sample of prime-age males from the Gary negative income tax experiment.

The economic theory of consumer choice derives consumer demands under the assumption of a constant price which is independent of quantity demanded by the consumer. Empirical estimation of consumer-demand functions then depends on a functional relationship between the price of a commodity and the amount of the quantity which is consumed. Many actual situations do not conform to these classical assumptions. Totally within the private sector, nonlinear prices may arise in industries with substantial fixed costs. Here average price and marginal price are not equal so the choice of the "correct" price to put in the demand function is not straightforward. Electricity prices are the most important example of this situation. The existence of government income tax and income

We would like to thank D. Carlton, A. Dixit, K. Kehrer, E. Lazear, R. Solow, and especially R. Hall for helpful conversations. This research was partly funded by HEW through Mathematica and by the NSF. The views expressed in this paper are the authors' sole responsibility and do not reflect those of the Department of Economics, the Massachusetts Institute of Technology, HEW, or the National Science Foundation.

transfer programs, however, is the primary source of nonlinear consumer prices. Net, after-tax wage rates almost always depend on the number of hours of work supplied. For instance, workers facing a progressive income tax have net wage rates that decline as gross earnings rise. Other important examples are AFDC programs and social security payments for individuals between 65 and 72 years of age. Here income transfers are accompanied by high marginal tax rates. These programs not only cause prices to be nonlinear but also cause budget sets to be nonconvex, which further complicates the theory and estimation of labor supply.

Most econometric studies of labor supply assume that the most preferred level of work effort for an individual depends on a single wage rate that is independent of the chosen level of hours of work. Thus the endogeneity of the net wage rate is ignored. When it has been considered, only reduced-form estimates have been computed. These estimates have the disadvantage that they depend on the particular sample information used and cannot be used to evaluate the expected effect of policy changes. In this paper we propose an alternative method of estimating labor-supply functions in the presence of nonlinear net wages. The technique follows from a structural model of individual labor-supply choice when the net wage depends on hours of work supplied. Thus individual choice depends on all net wages which comprise the budget set so that policy changes can be evaluated using the parameter estimates. The model we estimate has one other important difference from usual models of labor supply. We allow for a distribution of preferences in the population for the labor-leisure choice. This broadening of the traditional model seems called for by the observed data in which otherwise-identical individuals have widely differing labor-supply choices. Our findings confirm this observation since a very skewed distribution of preferences is observed.

The model developed here is used to evaluate the effects of a negative income tax (NIT) experiment in Gary, Indiana. In this experiment, income transfer payments were made to families on the basis of an income support level which depended on family size and a tax rate of either 40 percent or 60 percent. Beyond a given number of hours worked, an individual's earnings were taxed at the usual federal and state tax rates. A complicated budget constraint resulted which consisted of linear segments connected by kink points. We estimate the unknown parameters of the uncompensated labor-supply function together with the associated indirect utility function to evaluate the income and substitution effects of the NIT. An important question considered is, How large are the appropriate income and wage elasticities? We further consider the likely pattern of response to a NIT in the population. The estimates found here can be compared with labor-supply response estimates from other NIT experiments in New Jersey, Seattle, and Denver. Our findings imply that a NIT has only a very small effect on a substantial proportion of the population but that a significant number of individuals' labor-supply decisions may be affected quite substantially.

The first section of the paper discusses the problem of nonlinear net wages. It shows how a progressive income tax leads to a convex budget set, while government transfer programs like a NIT lead to nonconvex budget sets in which certain choices of hours worked can never be optimum. Thus the importance of knowing the form of both the labor-supply function and the associated indifference-curve map is emphasized. In Section II we use the modern theory of duality to derive the indifference-curve map through the indirect utility function. This utility function is derived from an ordinary specification of labor supply. Restrictions from the theory of consumer demand are derived so that the parameter estimates will not lead to violation of the theory of individual choice. Next we consider utility maximization and consumer choice in the presence of nonlinear net wages. We calculate the preferred point along a budget line at which individual choice jointly determines both hours worked and net marginal wage. To complete the specification of the model, we propose a stochastic specification which allows for both individual variation in preferences and the more traditional deviation between preferred hours of work and actual observed hours of work. Section IV discusses the operation of the Gary NIT experiment and the actual calculation of individual budget sets. Since some individuals acted as controls, we also consider budget sets of individuals facing only a progressive income tax. Potential data problems are also discussed. In Section V we present the results of maximum-likelihood estimation of our structural model. While an important income-elasticity response is found, no associated uncompensated wage-elasticity response seems to be present. Finally, we discuss the policy implications of the results and indicate possible future research.

I. Labor Supply with Nonlinear Net Wages

The economic theory of labor supply is a straightforward application of utility maximization. Individuals face a given market-determined wage along with prices of other consumption goods. Workers are assumed to choose the desired amount of hours of work which corresponds to the most preferred point on their budget sets.[1] In the familiar two-good diagram of hours supplied and expenditure on other goods, the slope of the budget set is the normalized wage $w = \tilde{w}/p$ and the intercept $y = \tilde{y}/p$ is normalized nonlabor income, where $\tilde{w}$ and $\tilde{y}$ are the market wage and nonlabor

---

[1] The theory of labor supply is sometimes stated as a theory of leisure demand given full income (see Becker 1965). However, we will treat hours supplied as the variable of interest, using a minus sign for hours worked in the utility function to maintain the usual monotonicity conventions. Also, in the econometric estimation, we will account for the fact that individuals may not be able to work their desired amount.

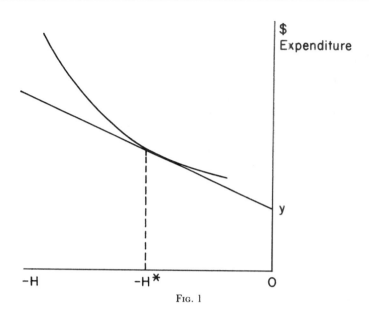

FIG. 1

income, respectively, and we use the price of the consumption good as the numeraire. In figure 1, $-H^*$ is the point which corresponds to the most preferred point created by the tangency of the indifference curve to the budget set. However, an important shortcoming of this analysis is the failure to incorporate the fact that the individual faces a nonconstant net wage, $w(1 - t)$, where t is the marginal tax rate. If t were a constant independent of labor supplied, and y were also independent of $-H$, then the budget line would simply be rotated counterclockwise. The previous analysis would be correct using the correctly measured net wage.

However, proportional tax systems are used only at the state and local tax level so that the analysis must account for nonlinear budget sets created by progressivity in tax formulas. Thus the budget set is piecewise linear, with kinks at points where income rises sufficiently to put the individual into the next higher tax bracket. The effect of a progressive tax system is to create a quasi-convex budget set like the one shown in figure 2.

In this highly simplified version of a progressive tax system, $-H_1$ and $-H_2$ correspond to the kink points induced by the tax system and $-H^*$ is the preferred amount of labor supply. This convex nonlinearity creates problems for the theory and estimation of labor supply. Theoretically, the usual comparative statics results must take account of the kink points and how their location depends on the gross wage. For estimation the problems are especially severe. Typical labor-supply specifications have the form

$$H = g(w, y, z, \varepsilon), \tag{1}$$

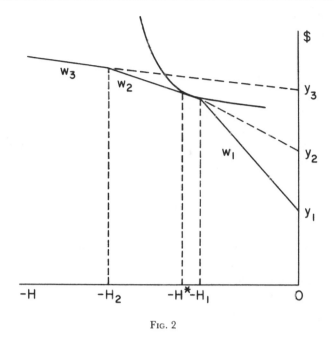

Fig. 2

where z is a vector of individual characteristics and ε is a stochastic term. Within the context of this type of labor-supply function, it is not obvious which net wage should be included as the variable explaining labor supply. Nor is it straightforward to decide which level of nonlabor income to specify. For instance, if the net wage corresponding to the second segment of the budget set of figure 2, w_2, were chosen, we might want to use "virtual income," y_2, corresponding to the intercept which equals nonlabor income of the budget set that the individual faces at the margin.[2]

Hall (1973) noted that a worker can be considered to be facing a linear budget constraint that is tangent to his actual budget set at the observed level of hours of work. For example, the individual facing the budget set drawn in figure 2 and observed to be working H^* hours can be considered to be facing a single wage rate, w_2, and a single level of virtual income, y_2. While this procedure is an important advance over using the gross wage, it cannot yield unbiased single-equation estimates because of the presence of the stochastic term ε in equation (1). Since both the net wage and virtual income are functions of hours worked, H, they will be correlated with ε, inducing a simultaneous-equations or errors-in-variables problem into the estimation procedure. Hausman and Wise (1976), Hurd

---

[2] Certainly the gross wage should not be used if substantial divergence exists between the gross wage and the net wage, since an upward-biased errors-in-variables problem will result.

(1976), and Rosen (1976) have each proposed different forms of instrumental variable procedures to account for the simultaneity problem. However, all these approaches are essentially "reduced-form" approaches to
the extent that predictions for alternative budget sets cannot be made on
the basis of the sample estimates.[3]

This problem of a nonlinear budget set would be solved if we had
sufficient knowledge about the form of the utility function. Suppose we
choose a particular form of the utility function and then adopt an additive
stochastic specification of the labor-supply function. The labor-supply
function can be written

$$H = h(w_1, w_2, w_3, y_1, y_2, y_3, z) + \varepsilon, \qquad (2)$$

where $h(\cdot)$ is the consumer's supply function for labor, derived from
maximizing the individual utility function.[4] Discrepancies from utility
maximization would be represented by ε, but since all the right-hand-side
variables can be treated as exogenous, the unknown parameters of the
utility function could be estimated. No problems of "which" net wage or
"which" level of nonlabor income to use would arise since they are fully
taken into account in the utility maximization.

When government programs beyond the progressive income tax are
considered, the situation becomes even more complex since the resulting
budget set may be nonconvex. Consider the operation of the NIT program
that we study empirically in this paper. An income transfer, T, is calculated on the basis of a family's income guarantee, the NIT marginal tax
rate, and family income. At the break-even point, $\tilde{H}$, in figure 3, the income
transfer is completely taxed away due to high family earnings, and the
earner returns to the federal and state income tax schedules. At this point
the net wage rate rises, creating a nonlinearity in the budget set. Not only
are four wage rates encountered, but an additional problem arises. Since
the break-even point represents a nonconvex kink point, there exists an
interval along the budget line in the vicinity of break even that may never
contain a global maximum if, as is generally assumed, indifference curves
are convex.[5] Furthermore, the exact size and location of this interval

[3] Another possible approach is to use an ordered probit model to estimate the probability
that an individual's preferred point is on a particular linear segment and then to estimate
hours worked as a random variable, which is censored at the kink points. Again, this approach
is reduced form since the probit model would change with different budget sets.

[4] Note that for nearly all utility functions $hp(\cdot)$ will be a complicated function of net wages
and nonlabor income. In fact, it will probably not exist in closed form for nonlinear budget
constraints. However, it can be calculated easily by numerical techniques on a computer. The
actual procedure used will be discussed in Sec. III. Heckman (1974a) proposed an alternative procedure in which net wages are estimated as a function of hours worked. If the form
of the budget set is known, this relationship would be exact so that a random variable, hours
worked, and an exact nonlinear transformation of it appear on both sides of the equation.
Also, nonconvex budget sets cannot be treated with this approach.

[5] None of the instrumental variable procedures takes account of this feature of the budget
set introduced by the nonconvexity.

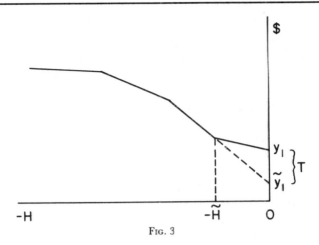

Fig. 3

depends on the specification and unknown parameters of the underlying utility function. Observed hours of work may sometimes fall in this interval if there are errors in optimization or institutional rigidities, but the implied restrictions on globally optimal hours should be taken into account in the estimation of labor supply.

The case of a nonconvex budget set emphasizes the importance of knowledge about the underlying utility function. This type of nonconvexity is encountered not only in the negative income tax but also in other earnings-related taxes or subsidies—for example, child-care payments, social security payments for individuals from 62 to 72 years old, AFDC, and food-stamp subsidies. Knowledge about the form of the utility function would permit estimation within the context of equation (2), although determination of the utility-maximizing point would be more complicated than in the previous case due to the nonconvexity of the budget set.

In this section we have specified the complications in the theory of labor supply which arise when individuals face nonlinear budget sets due to government tax and subsidy programs where the marginal tax rate is determined by earnings. The main problem for econometric purposes is the multiplicity of net wage rates which the individual faces in deciding on his labor supply. We have emphasized how knowledge of the utility function, up to its unknown parameters, would help to solve the problem. Yet all our empirical knowledge arises from observing the uncompensated labor-supply function of equation (1), since utility is never observed. In the next section we show how knowledge of the uncompensated labor-supply function can be used to derive knowledge of the utility function for purposes of econometric estimation.

II. Derivation of the Indirect Utility Function

Nonconvexity of the budget set requires specification of a parametric form for the indifference curves to determine the set of points which cannot correspond to utility-maximizing behavior. In the case of both convex and nonconvex budget sets, a complete model of consumer behavior requires knowledge of the indifference curve to determine the appropriate prices that the consumer faces. Two possible approaches to the problem are apparent. The direct approach is to specify a form of the direct or indirect utility function and then to derive the consumer-demand equations. For example, a Cobb-Douglas utility function could be specified leading to a leisure-demand (labor-supply) equation which can be estimated. This approach, taken by Burtless (1976), places strong restrictions on the labor-supply elasticities.[6] Less restrictive utility specifications such as the second-order flexible-form utility functions outlined by Diewert (1974) might also be used. However, the flexible-form specifications lead to complicated labor-supply equations which would be extremely difficult to estimate given a nonlinear budget set.

A second approach, which we will use here, arises from the theory of duality. In the context of consumer-demand theory, Roy (1947) did pioneering research, including the derivation of the identity relating consumer demand to the indirect utility function.[7] Define the consumers utility-maximization problem as maximizing a utility function $u(x)$ where $x = (x_1, \ldots, x_N)$, an N-dimensional utility function, subject to the budget constraint $p \cdot x \leq y$, where $p = (p_1, \ldots, p_N)$ is the vector of prices and y is the individual's income. Then the indirect utility function relates the maximum utility the consumer can attain, as a function of the exogenous variables p and y.[8] The function is determined by the solution to the utility-maximization problem

$$v(p, y) \equiv \max_{x} [u(x) : p \cdot x \leq y]. \tag{3}$$

Because utility is an unobserved variable, estimation can take place only by observing consumer demand. Here Roy's Identity simplifies matters since it relates consumer demand to the indirect utility function by the formula

$$x_i \equiv - \frac{\partial v(p, y)}{\partial p_i} \bigg/ \frac{\partial v(p, y)}{\partial y}, \qquad i = 1, \ldots, N. \tag{4}$$

[6] Since the first draft of this paper was completed, we have found Wales and Woodland (1977) using a CES utility function. However, they do not permit variation in preferences in the population as Burtless does.

[7] Hotelling, Wold, Samuelson, and Houthakker all made important contributions to the use of duality in consumer-demand theory. Other contributions and a review of the theory are found in Diewert (1974).

[8] For the present section we are assuming linear prices and a straight-line budget set.

We propose to use Roy's Identity "in reverse." That is, considerable empirical knowledge has been built up about labor supply together with the functional forms useful in estimating it. In fact, all our knowledge about the specific form of utility functions, both direct and indirect, must arise from observations of consumer demand. Thus our approach is to integrate Roy's Identity to derive the form of the indirect utility function rather than to specify the utility function a priori. The resulting indirect utility function will be consistent with consumer theory since it is derived using only the assumptions of utility maximization and consistent with the data to the extent that the specified labor-supply function is supported by observed behavior.[9]

Integration of equation (4) over all N goods raises the integrability problem that the function obtained must satisfy restrictions on the Slutsky matrix: rank $N - 1$, symmetry, and negative semidefiniteness. This integration would be difficult and also fruitless since we do not have observations over consumer demand for all goods. Instead, we simplify to a two-good case where the goods are labor supply and expenditure on all other goods. This two-good approach has been (implicitly) taken in almost all studies of labor supply. In order to aggregate $N - 1$ goods, justifications may be offered. A possible justification arises from assuming homogeneous weak separability of preferences between labor supply and the other $N - 1$ goods. This approach, due to Leontief, seems a reasonable assumption since labor supply differs so much from other consumption goods. It also permits the two-good approach to be applied to cross-section data where individuals do not face approximately the same prices.

Given a two-good model, the integrability problem dissolves. One diagonal element of the 2×2 Slutsky matrix determines the other three elements, since all expenditures not made on labor supply (leisure demand) must go to the remaining good. Thus the only requirements imposed by the theory of consumer demand are that the compensated labor-supply derivative with respect to the wage be greater than or equal to zero and that the indirect utility function be monotone nondecreasing in the wage and in nonlabor income.[10] Once we have estimated the unknown parameters in the indirect utility function we have obtained all the observable information possible about the consumer's indifference map. This information will, however, be sufficient to estimate the labor-supply effects of other government tax and subsidy programs.

To obtain the indirect utility function we need to specify a model of labor supply. We use the constant elasticity specification because it has

---

[9] Rosen (1974) emphasizes the importance of using the observed consumer behavior to achieve a proper specification of the utility function.

[10] The compensated derivative is positive, not negative, since work is supplied while leisure is demanded. These requirements correspond to the quasi-convexity and monotonicity properties of indirect utility functions. For further details see Diewert (1974, pp. 120–33).

been successfully used in other labor-supply investigations (Hausman and Wise 1976, Lillard 1977) and leads to a convenient indirect utility function. The labor-supply function is

$$h = kw^{\alpha}y^{\beta}, \tag{5}$$

where h is hours worked over the appropriate period, k is a constant determined by individual characteristics, w is the net wage, and y is nonlabor income.[11] Using Roy's Identity of equation (5) with the insertion of a negative sign since labor supply is a "bad,"

$$-kw^{\alpha}y^{\beta} = -\frac{\partial v(w, y)}{\partial w} \Big/ \frac{\partial v(w, y)}{\partial y}. \tag{6}$$

To derive the indirect utility function we use the implicit function theorem

$$kw^{\alpha} \, dw = -y^{-\beta} \, dy. \tag{7}$$

Then integrating both sides using the separability of the differential equation where c is the constant of integration,[12]

$$k\frac{w^{1+\alpha}}{1 + \alpha} = -\frac{y^{1-\beta}}{1 - \beta} + c. \tag{8}$$

We choose the constant of integration c as our cardinal measure of utility, and rearranging terms leads to the indirect utility function[13]

$$c = v(w, y) = k\frac{w^{1+\alpha}}{1 + \alpha} + \frac{y^{1-\beta}}{1 - \beta}. \tag{9}$$

Equation (10) is thus the indirect utility function that corresponds to the constant elasticity labor-supply function. The monotonicity properties are satisfied if utility is nondecreasing in w and y.[14] To derive the Slutsky matrix restriction on the indirect utility function, we use the Slutsky equation

$$\frac{\partial h}{\partial w} = s_{ww} + h\frac{\partial h}{\partial y}, \tag{10}$$

[11] Wage and income are both divided by the consumer-goods price deflator so we take the composite price of other goods as numeraire.

[12] Separability of the labor-supply function in the wage and nonlabor income is the crucial simplification which permits this approach. A more general specification is $h = kr(w)s(y)$. Note that the integration is only done locally over the range of the observed data so that boundary conditions can be ignored.

[13] In principle the direct utility function may be derived from the indirect utility function by a constrained minimization problem. For the constant elasticity specification a closed form does not exist. However, nowhere is the direct utility function needed, since labor supply and the effects of alternative tax and subsidy programs can be calculated solely from the indirect utility function and the expenditure function.

[14] These properties are satisfied globally with the limiting case of $\alpha = -1.0$ and $\beta = +1.0$, corresponding to the Cobb-Douglas specification.

where s_{ww} is the compensated wage derivative. Upon taking derivatives and simplifying,

$$s_{ww} = \frac{1}{h}\left(\frac{\alpha}{w} - \frac{\beta h}{y}\right).$$

(11)

Then the Slutsky restriction $s_{ww} > 0$ implies $\alpha > \beta hw/y$. Taking the expected case of $\beta < 0$,

$$\frac{kw^{1-\alpha}}{y^{1-\beta}} > \frac{\alpha}{\beta}.$$

(12)

This quasi-convexity condition is automatically satisfied if $\alpha \geq 0$, as we would expect for a sample of low-income males since $k > 0$. If $\alpha < 0$, then we would need to check the observations in the sample to make certain that inequality (12) holds.

In this section we have derived the indirect utility function corresponding to an ordinary model of labor supply using Roy's Identity. The sign restrictions to insure monotonicity and quasi convexity of the indirect utility function have also been derived. However, these derivations were based on the classical assumptions of linear prices and a straight-line budget constraint. Yet almost all government income tax and income transfer programs create nonlinear prices, leading to convex or nonconvex budget sets. In the next section we demonstrate how to calculate labor supply in the more complicated case using the derived indirect utility function.

III. Nonlinear Budget Sets and Stochastic Specification

A consumer is assumed to select his most preferred level of hours, H^*, on the basis of a set of preference parameters $\theta = (k, \alpha, \beta)$. Given values of these parameters, a worker facing a convex budget set of the type pictured in figure 2 or a nonconvex budget set of the type in figure 3 will choose a certain level of labor supply, and this choice may be calculated by using the indirect utility function. Note that direct use of the uncompensated labor-supply function is impossible due to the multiplicity of net wages faced by the consumer. In the case of a nonconvex budget set we must also ascertain the range of the interval around the break-even point that can never contain a utility-maximizing choice. Once the utility-maximizing problem is solved for a single individual, we proceed to a statistical specification that permits differences among individuals to be reflected in differences in the parameters of their indirect utility functions. Given the significant variation observed in hours worked for observationally equivalent individuals, it seems inappropriate to simply add an additive stochastic

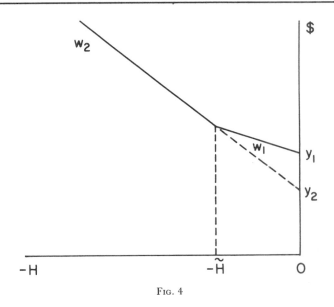

Fig. 4

disturbance to the estimated labor-supply function. Allowing for a distribution of preferences for work in the population is therefore an important component of our model of labor supply.

To demonstrate how preferred hours of work, H^*, are derived given an indirect utility function with parameters θ when an individual is faced with a nonlinear budget set, consider figure 4. The first budget segment is described by the slope, representing net wage w_1, and the intercept y_1, representing nonlabor income at zero hours of work. Similarly, the second budget segment is described by net wage w_2 and by virtual nonwage income y_2. For a given set of preference parameters the maximum indirect utility corresponding to the net wage w_1 and nonlabor income y_1 is calculated as $v_1(w_1, y_1)$. The preferred hours of work, $h_1(w_1, y_1)$, may be greater than the break-even point $\tilde{H}$, and thus the apparent utility maximum point may lie below the second budget segment in the interior of the budget set. Likewise, we calculate the maximum indirect utility, $v_2(w_2, y_2)$, and preferred hours of work, $h_2(w_2, y_2)$, corresponding to the net wage w_2 and virtual income y_2. Then the maximum maximorum, $v^*(w_1, w_2, y_1, y_2)$, which equals the greater of v_1 or v_2, determines the global maximum of hours of work, $H^*(w_1, w_2, y_1, y_2)$. Since the individual is better off on the boundary than he is in the interior for any number of hours worked, H^* will always lie along the boundary of the budget set. Figure 2 is treated in a similar manner. We restrict attention to the first two budget segments. Preferred hours, h_1 and h_2, are calculated in the manner described above. Note that h_1 and h_2 cannot both be feasible. If either h_1 or h_2 is feasible, the feasible choice is optimal, since it has greater utility than the most preferred attainable point along the other budget segment, which is the kink point, H_1. Alternatively, if neither h_1 nor h_2 is feasible, the preferred amount of labor supply corresponds to the kink point H_1. Extension to an indefinite number of budget segments follows by making similar comparisons of maximized utility corresponding to the net wage and virtual income of the different segments of the budget set.

Since the goal of empirical work is to estimate the unknown parameters of the uncompensated labor-supply function, we now specify a stochastic theory of labor-supply variation in a cross-section of individuals. Indexing individuals by i, we expect random differences to occur between observed hours supplied, H_i, and preferred hours of work, H_i^*. This random variation may be the result of measurement error, but a more important source of randomness arises because of unexpected variations in hours worked. Unexpected temporary layoffs, involuntary overtime, or short time due to cyclical downturns all provide potential reasons actual hours may diverge from "normal" hours associated with a given job. These variations in hours are unanticipated by the individual and cause his actual hours H_i to differ from his preferred hours H_i^*. As an empirical matter these sources of randomness turn out to explain only a very small fraction of the total variation of hours worked compared with variation in preferences among the population which we now specify.

Another form of randomness in the data occurs because of individual variation in tastes. Two individuals with the same personal characteristics who face the same budget sets may prefer to work substantially different amounts. From a policy standpoint these individual differences are very important in determining the response to alterations in the budget set induced by government programs. In estimating the unknown parameters k, α, and β, all may be specified to be functions of measurable and unmeasurable individual differences. However, this very general specification leads to an intractable estimation problem. In our empirical work a number of specifications were attempted using an instrumental variable estimator for the uncompensated labor-supply function. This experimentation suggested that k_i may best be treated as a function of measurable individual differences, while α_i and β_i are apparently independent of differences in measured personal characteristics. The actual specification used in this paper is presented, however, with the caveat that significant additional research is needed.

The constant term in the labor-supply function of equation (6) is therefore specified to be a function of measured individual differences. Since we have assumed that there will be random variation in uncompensated labor supply due to random divergences between actual hours H_i and preferred hours H_i^*, it will be convenient to subsume this random disturbance in our specification of the constant term. Thus,

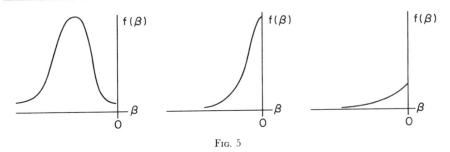

Fig. 5

$$k_i = \exp\left(Z_i\delta + \varepsilon_{2i}\right), \tag{13}$$

where Z_i is a vector of individual characteristics and ε_{2i} is assumed to be distributed $N(0, \sigma_2^2)$. The two other individual parameters α_i and β_i may both be expected to vary in the population. Technically both distributions are identified so that, given ideal data, the parameters of both distributions can be estimated. As a practical matter, estimation currently seems limited to allowing one of the two parameters to vary. Thus we decided to permit either α_i or β_i, but not both, to vary in the population. Empirical results led us to specify $\alpha_i = \bar{\alpha}$ a constant and to specify β_i as a random variable in the population.

The integrability conditions discussed in Section II impose restrictions on the possible distribution of the β_i. The wage elasticity $\bar{\alpha}$ is expected to be nonnegative in a sample of low-income workers. In addition, there is a strong expectation that the income elasticity is nonpositive, which implies that the integrability inequality of equation (12) is satisfied globally. A convenient distribution which imposes the negativity restriction on β_i is the truncated normal with the truncation point at zero. As figure 5 shows, a wide variety of shapes of probability densities can be accommodated with this specification. The individual parameter β_i can then be written as $\beta_i = \mu_\beta + \varepsilon_{1i}$ where $\dot{\varepsilon}_{1i} \sim TN(0, \sigma_1^2)$ with a truncation point from above of $-\mu_\beta$. We assume that ε_{1i} and ε_{2i} are independent sources of random variation. Given this stochastic specification, the unknown parameters of the model are $\theta = (\delta, \bar{\alpha}, \bar{\beta}, \sigma_1^2, \sigma_2^2)$, where $\bar{\beta}$ is the mean of the truncated distribution. We now use this stochastic specification to derive the likelihood function for a sample of observations.

The analysis is confined to budget constraints with only two linear segments, although generalization to more segments is straightforward. A control observation faces a convex budget set while an experimental one faces a nonconvex budget set of the type drawn in figure 4. The probability of the point actually observed, H_i, depends on the unknown parameters δ and α and the densities for β_i and ε_{2i}. Neglecting ε_{2i} momentarily, let us calculate the probability that a particular point, H, is the global maximum. For large negative values of β_i the individual will have a global maximum

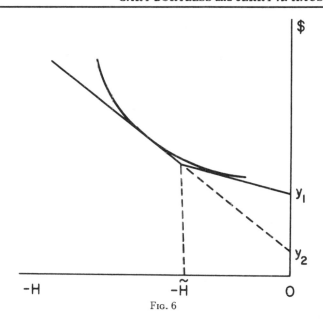

Fig. 6

on the first segment; H^*, the global maximum, will be less than the break-even point, $\tilde{H}$, and the net wage on the margin will be w_1 with associated virtual income y_1. As β_i increases toward zero the global maximum point moves along the first segment toward $\tilde{H}$, until a critical β_i is reached at which the individual is indifferent between a solution on the first segment and a solution on the second. This critical β_i, say β_i^*, depends on the underlying utility function and on the unknown parameters in that function. Using equation (10), β_i^* is calculated quite easily by solving the following equation:

$$\frac{e^{z_i\delta}w_{1i}^{1+\bar{\alpha}}}{1+\bar{\alpha}} + \frac{y_{1i}^{1-\beta_i^*}}{1-\beta_i^*} = \frac{e^{z_i\delta}w_{2i}}{1+\bar{\alpha}} + \frac{y_{2i}^{1-\beta_i^*}}{1-\beta_i^*}. \tag{14}$$

For every experimental observation, this equation must be solved for β_i^* each time the parameters change; however, the solution may be cheaply obtained on a computer. The indifference curve corresponding to β_i^* is drawn in figure 6, which illustrates that the break-even point $\tilde{H}$ cannot correspond to a utility maximizing point. As β_i rises from β_i^* to its limiting value, the global maximum moves upward along the second segment. Each value of β_i between $-\infty$ and zero, therefore, has an associated global maximum level of hours; the probability that a particular level of hours is a global maximum is the same as the probability of the associated income elasticity, β_i. We may now extend the analysis to observed hours of work by noting the relationship between observed hours, H_i, and desired hours of work effort, H_i^*,

$$\log H_i = \log H_i^* + \varepsilon_{2i}. \tag{15}$$

For any particular H_i, there are an infinite number of combinations of H_i^* and ε_{2i} that satisfy (15). By successively determining, for every possible H_i^*, the probability that the global maximum is H_i^* and the stochastic term ε_{2i} equals the difference between the logs of H_i^* and H_i, we can ascertain the probability that actual hours, H_i, will be observed. Letting $f(\beta)$ be the truncated normal density with associated distribution $F(\beta)$ and $\phi(\cdot)$ and $\Phi(\cdot)$ the standard normal density and distribution, respectively, the probability of observing H_i is

$$
PNC_i = \int_{-\infty}^{\beta_i^*} \frac{1}{\sigma_2} \phi \left(\frac{\log H_i - \log H_{1i}^*}{\sigma_2} \right) f(\beta) \, d\beta
$$
$$
+ \int_{\beta_i^*}^{0} \frac{1}{\sigma_2} \phi \left(\frac{\log H_i - \log H_{2i}^*}{\sigma_2} \right) f(\beta) \, d\beta, \tag{16}
$$

where $\log H_{ij}^* = Z_i \delta + \bar{\alpha} \log w_{ij} + \beta \log y_{ij}$ and j is an index of the budget segment. Evaluation of these integrals is equivalent to evaluation of a normal distribution $\Phi(z)$ and is thus inexpensive to perform on a computer.[15] The truncated density for β poses no problem since it is a normal density divided by a standard normal distribution which remains constant across all observations.

The case of a convex budget set is slightly different because there exists a range for β, say BL_i to BU_i, for which the utility maximizing point is at the kink point $\tilde{H}$ in figure 7. If the individual's β_i is considerably less than zero, the global maximum H_i^* will be on the first segment with associated net wage w_1 and nonlabor income y_1. If his income elasticity is quite near zero, the utility maximum will lie along the second segment corresponding to net wage w_2 and virtual and nonlabor income y_2. The range of β_i that places the utility maximum at the kink point is easily computed from the uncompensated labor-supply function. The lower point of the range, BL_i, is the greatest β_i on the first budget segment that leads to a utility maximum at the kink point,

$$
BL_i = \frac{\log \tilde{H}_i - Z_i \delta - \bar{\alpha} \log w_{1i}}{\log y_{1i}}. \tag{17}
$$

Correspondingly, the upper point of the range, BU_i, is the smallest β_i consistent with a global maximum on the second segment, and therefore

$$
BU_i = \frac{\log \tilde{H}_i - Z_i \delta - \bar{\alpha} \log w_{2i}}{\log y_{2i}}. \tag{18}
$$

All β_i's that lie between BL_i and BU_i thus lead to a utility maximum at the kink point, $\tilde{H}_i$. The probability that the observed level of hours H_i corresponds to a utility maximum at the kink point is

[15] See the Appendix for derivation of the evaluation procedure for the integrals.

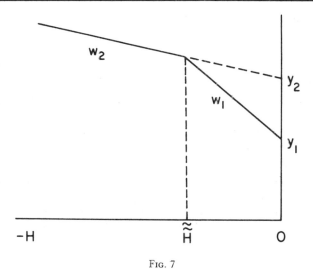

FIG. 7

$$pr\ (\log H_i^* + \log \varepsilon_{2i} = \log H_i \mid \log H_i^* = \log \tilde{\tilde{H}}_i) \cdot pr\ (\log H_i^* = \log \tilde{\tilde{H}}_i)$$

$$= \frac{1}{\sigma_2}\ \phi\ \left(\frac{\log H_i - \log \tilde{\tilde{H}}_i}{\sigma_2}\right) \int_{BL_i}^{BU_i} f\ (\beta)\ d\beta. \tag{19}$$

For observed hours of work H_i corresponding to β_i's outside the range BL_i to BU_i, the probabilities are similar to those calculated in equation (16). Thus for the case of a convex budget set the probability of observing actual hours worked H_i is

$$PC_i = \int_{-\infty}^{BL_i} \frac{1}{\sigma_2}\ \phi\ \left(\frac{\log H_i - \log H_{1i}^*}{\sigma_2}\right) f\ (\beta)\ d\beta$$

$$+ \frac{1}{\sigma_2}\ \phi\ \left(\frac{\log H_i - \log \tilde{\tilde{H}}_i}{\sigma_2}\right) [F\ (BU_i) - F\ (BL_i)] \tag{20}$$

$$+ \int_{BU_i}^{0} \frac{1}{\sigma_2}\ \phi\ \left(\frac{\log H_i - \log H_{2i}^*}{\sigma_2}\right) f\ (\beta)\ d\beta.$$

Given our stochastic specification of the model, we are able to specify the probability of observing actual hours worked as a function of the unknown parameter values. The natural method of estimation is then maximum-likelihood estimation, in which the unknown parameter values are chosen so as to maximize the probability of observing the sample. Our method can be extended, in principle, to cover the case of an arbitrarily large number of budget segments per individual, although this extension will not be undertaken here. In the next section we apply our methodology to evaluate the results of the Gary income maintenance experiment.

IV. Calculation of Budget Sets, Data, and Sample Considerations

We use the labor-supply model to estimate a structural model of labor supply for adult married males who participated in the Gary income maintenance experiment. The experiment, which took place from 1971 to 1974, had as participants residents of low-income neighborhoods in Gary, Indiana. All participants were black. The families were not chosen at random for the experiment, a problem which we will discuss later in this section. Participants in the Gary experiment were randomly assigned to one of four NIT plans or to control status. (Control families received no benefits except a small payment for their continued participation.) Each of the NIT plans can be described in terms of two parameters: the constant marginal tax rate and the basic support level. In two of the plans, wage and nonwage income was subject to a 40 percent tax rate; in the remaining two, income was taxed at a 60 percent rate. Two of the Gary NIT plans offered basic income supports, scaled according to family size, that were equal to slightly more than the poverty level. The other two plans offered basic supports, also scaled to family size, that were one-quarter less. All federal, state, and FICA income tax liabilities were fully reimbursed for income up to the break-even point $\tilde{H}$. Earned income above the break-even point was taxed according to the federal, state, and FICA tax tables.

Thus for individuals eligible for NIT payments, the intercept y_1 in figure 4 equals the NIT income guarantee plus net (after tax) nonwage income. The slope of the first budget segment, w_1, is determined by the worker's gross wage rate times one minus the experimental NIT tax rate. For the second segment of the NIT budget line, the virtual income intercept, y_2, and net wage, w_2, are calculated in the same manner as the second segment of a control individual's budget set, the calculation of which we now describe.

Control families are assumed to face a budget line with only two linear segments. This assumption results in a substantial simplification in budget lines, since the federal income tax schedule has a large number of kinks at lower levels of taxable income. However, low-income families face only one important kink in this schedule, one which occurs at the point where family exemptions and deductions are equal to countable family income. At that point the federal tax rate rises from 0 to 14 percent. Thereafter, the tax rate changes in relatively small steps. In calculating the budget lines for control individuals, we assume that the marginal tax rate along the first segment equals 5.85 percent for FICA plus the 2 percent Indiana state income tax rate. The second budget segment is calculated on the assumption that workers face an additional 18 percent marginal tax rate because of the federal income tax. The kink point $\tilde{H}$ is calculated by assuming that workers took standard income exemptions and used the low-income tax deduction available in 1973. Nonwage income is assumed to be nontaxable. The break-even point for individuals eligible for NIT payments $\tilde{H}$ always exceeds the income tax kink point $\hat{H}$ so that two segments are sufficient to characterize their budget sets.

Data on workers' hours, wages, nonwage income, and personal characteristics were taken from the first, fourth, and seventh of the periodic interviews administered to participants in the experiment during the period of NIT payments. To be included in the sample, workers must have responded to at least two of the three interviews.[16] Since we are interested in long-run labor-supply response, the measure of labor supply is an average of working hours in the three representative weeks during the experiment.[17] Individuals not observed to be working are omitted from the current sample. This feature of the labor-supply model may be modified by specifying and estimating a separate behavioral equation for an individual's participation in the labor force as Heckman (1974b) and Hanoch (1976) have done for women. This extension is not undertaken here since the sample consists of prime-age males who are heads of households. The proportion of the sample that does not participate in the labor force in this sample is quite small and, presumably, for a sample of average yearly hours worked the number of nonparticipants would decline even further. Nevertheless, we intend to add the behavioral equation for labor-force participation in future work on average yearly labor supply when such data become available.

A problem referred to in passing is that initial sample selection was not random but was based on current earnings. Thus the possibility of substantial bias exists since hours worked is one component of earnings.[18] Sample truncation did not occur in Gary, but families whose earnings are above 2.4 times the poverty limit were undersampled by a factor of three. Note that the cutoff line was substantially higher in Gary than in New Jersey, so that even if total truncation had occurred the effect on the conditional mean would be less.[19] In estimating the effects of the Gary NIT we used the consistent weighted estimator proposed by Hausman and

[16] Since approximately 35 percent of the individuals dropped out of the experiment with attrition of controls 10 percent higher than attrition for experimentals, a problem of attrition bias might occur. However, Hausman and Wise (1979), in a study of possible attrition bias on this sample, concluded that while it is serious for analysis of variance models, it does not pose a problem for structural models which control for individual characteristics and experimental-design parameters.

[17] A more long-run measure of labor supply is desirable, but such data are not available at the present time.

[18] In fact, in the New Jersey Negative Income Tax Experiment where sample truncation occurred at 1.5 times the poverty limit, Hausman and Wise (1976, 1977b) found that the ratio of estimated coefficients rose by a factor as high as 200 percent when sample truncation was accounted for.

[19] Hausman and Wise (1977c) propose and estimate a maximum-likelihood estimator which accounts for the nonrandom sample selection. However, they find little indication of bias in an earnings equation.

Wise (1979). Since the results differed only slightly from the nonweighted estimates, in discussing our results we will present only the nonweighted estimates. Apparently the combination of the high cutoff line of 2.4 times the poverty limit and the presence of an undersampled group above the cutoff led to little or no truncation bias.

In this section we have discussed computation of the nonlinear budget set for each individual, pointing out how marginal tax rates are computed. We then discussed the sample used from the Gary income maintenance experiment as well as possible biases resulting from attrition bias, non-labor-force participation, and truncation bias. In the next section we present the specification of the individual intercept k_i in the uncompensated labor-supply function as a function of individual characteristics. We then present and discuss our results, concluding with policy implications and ideas for future research.

V. Results

Both the uncompensated labor-supply function, equation (6), and the associated indirect utility function, equation (10), include the unknown parameters k, α, and β. It will be recalled that α and β are assumed to be independent of individual characteristics, while k is specified to depend on these characteristics through $k_i = \exp(Z_i \delta + \varepsilon_{2i})$. A wide variety of personal characteristics may affect tastes for work; the following were chosen by reference to earlier research on the NIT experiments: (1) constant—equal to one; (2) education—a dummy variable is used for individuals whose educational attainment is less than 9 years; (3) number of adults—number of persons aged 16 or more residing in the household; (4) poor health—a dummy variable is used if the individual reported his health to be "poor in relation to others" and zero otherwise; and (5) age—a variable equal to the age of the respondent minus 45 years was used if this age exceeded 45 years, otherwise the age variable was set to zero. The other unknown structural parameters of the model are the wage elasticity $\bar{\alpha}$ and parameters in the distribution of the income elasticity $f(\beta)$.

The sample consists of 380 individuals assumed to be independent observations. Once the budget lines have been determined for each individual, the unknown parameters can be estimated by the method of maximum likelihood. The log likelihood equals the sum of the logs of the probabilities of actual hours worked by the NIT-eligible individuals, log PNC_i, from equation (18), and the logs of the probabilities of actual hours worked by the control individuals, log PC_i, from equation (20). Thus the log-likelihood function has the form

$$L = \sum_{i=1}^{N_1} \log PNC_i + \sum_{i=1}^{N_2} \log PC_i, \qquad (21)$$

TABLE 1

Estimates of Labor Supply and Indirect Utility Function

Variable	Parameter Estimates
Constant	3.75043
	(.02555)
Primary education	.01078
	(.00558)
Adults (N)	.03300
	(.01272)
Poor health	−.02224
	(.00438)
Age	−.00869
	(.01347)
Wage elasticity, $\tilde{\alpha}$	.00003
	(.01632)
Mean income elasticity, $\bar{\beta}$	−.04768
	(.00465)
Variance of β distribution, σ_1^2	.06751
	(.00399)
Variance of ε_{2i}, σ_2^2	.00135
	(.00022)

Note.—Observations (N) = 380; log of the likelihood function = − 196.27. Asymptotic standard errors in parentheses.

where the number of experimentals N_1 and controls N_2 equals 247 and 133, respectively. Approximately 65 percent of the sample was eligible for the NIT. Because of technical reasons discussed in the Appendix, the likelihood function was maximized using the gradient method of Berndt et al. (1974) as well as the no-derivative conjugant gradient method of Powell (1964). Both techniques converged to the same maximum of the likelihood function. A variety of starting points converged to the same optimum, leading us to conclude that we have found the global maximum.

Results are presented in table 1. All the elements of k_i believed to affect tastes for work have the expected effects. Poor health reduced expected labor supply by 2.25 percent while a 60-year-old is expected to work 12 percent less due to his age, other things being equal. Increased family size, however, is related to higher levels of expected work effort, which leads to the conclusion that endogeneity of nonwage income is probably not a serious problem. Moreover, the effect of relatively low levels of educational attainment is in the expected direction, under the assumption that more educated workers have a wider variety of activities to pursue in their non-work time. The estimates of these parameters are relatively precise except for the effect of increased age; all except the coefficient of age are significantly different from zero at the 5 percent level.

The parameter estimates most important to the design of a negative income tax are the ones that measure work response to the level of the income guarantee and to the marginal tax rate. Our first finding is the lack of a perceptible effect on labor supply of variations in the NIT tax rate. The estimated wage elasticity is .00003 and, even at a range of two standard errors, is less than .04 in magnitude.[20] This estimate is well below the Hausman and Wise (1976) estimate for white males in the New Jersey NIT. This finding is consistent, however, with the Hausman and Wise (1977c) findings for the same Gary sample. Using a reduced-form earnings specification, they found the labor response to the level of the income guarantee to be much more important than the response to the marginal tax rate. While no direct effect of different marginal tax rates is found here, an indirect effect is present through the effect of taxes on a family's nonwage income. Consider two individuals with identical gross wage rates and nonwage income who are offered identical NIT income guarantees but have different NIT tax rates. They will have substantially different budget sets because the tax rate affects the locus of the break-even point $\tilde{H}$ in figure 4. The individual with the lower tax rate is more likely to work less than the break-even level of hours and is therefore likely to respond to a higher level of nonwage income than the individual with the higher NIT tax rate. Nonetheless, the finding of essentially zero wage elasticity leads to the conclusion that the wide variation in after-tax wage rates had little effect on labor supply among the black males in the Gary NIT experiment.

However, the estimate of the income elasticity was found to be quite significantly different from zero. The average income elasticity in the sample is estimated at $-.04768$. The wage elasticity and income elasticity estimates are not too dissimilar from a model estimated using instrumental variables. There, with no truncation of β, the estimate of $\bar{\beta}$ is $-.036$ with an asymptotic standard error of .022, while the wage elasticity $\bar{\alpha}$ is estimated to be .018 with an asymptotic standard error of .042. Neither coefficient estimate differs significantly from the maximum-likelihood estimates. To assess the effect of the income guarantee under the NIT, consider a family of four with one other adult present, with the worker in good health, under 45 years of age, and with a ninth-grade education (all near the mean of the sample). Using our estimates, the worker's expected preferred hours of work at a pretax wage of $3.50 per hour with the (convex) income tax budget set are 39.943 hours per week.[21] For comparison with a NIT plan, we assign an income guarantee of $3,500 and a marginal tax rate of 60 percent. Preferred hours of work fall to 36.985, a change of 2.958 hours per week or 7.69 percent.[22] Weekly income under the NIT rises to $119.07 from after-tax income of $115.54 without the NIT. Thus a significant

[20] Note that the integrability condition of eq. (12) is satisfied in the sample. When the distribution $f(\beta)$ was not truncated at zero, the estimate of $\bar{\alpha}$ was .0305, although the estimate was not very precise.

[21] It is important to take the expectation with respect to $f(\beta)$ rather than at the mean $\bar{\beta}$ due to the skewness of the $f(\beta)$ distribution. Thus we calculate $EH^* = \int H^*(\beta) f(\beta) d\beta$.

[22] This estimate is approximately equal to earlier estimates for the total response in the Gary sample by Kehrer et al. (1976) and by Hausman and Wise (1977b) who found an average response of 7.97 percent among NIT individuals.

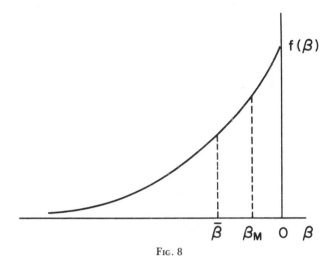

Fig. 8

work response to introduction of a NIT is found to exist, although its magnitude is not especially large. The effects of other NIT plans may be estimated in a similar manner, averaging over different family characteristics to find the average population response. In table 2 we present the expected response in the population for the average characteristics in Z to the different plans in the Gary experiment. Also included is the probability for each budget set that the individual will be "on the NIT"; that is, he is below the break-even point $\tilde{H}$ and is receiving benefits.

Since a distribution of income elasticities was estimated for the population, it is interesting to consider the estimated density $f(\beta)$. As figure 8 shows, the truncated normal distribution consists of the extreme left tail of a regular normal distribution. Thus while the mean $\bar{\beta} = -0.04768$, the median $\beta_M = -0.03331$, which means a substantial proportion of the population had a very low income elasticity. In fact, about 20 percent of the population is estimated to have an income elasticity of between 0 and 1 percent. Since the variance of ε_{2i} is very small compared with the variance of the β distribution, we can conclude that most of the observed variation in response to the NIT experiment results from differences in individual preferences rather than from random difference between the utility maximum and observed hours of work. Given this conclusion, we can interpret the estimate of the β distribution as suggesting that a small proportion of the Gary sample is substantially more responsive to the presence of an income guarantee in making their labor-supply decision than is the rest of the population. This pattern of response indicates that most individuals will vary their labor supply very little in response to the introduction of NIT plans similar to those used in the Gary experiment. A few individuals, however, will react with large reductions in labor supply. From estimates in the

TABLE 2

LOCATION OF 15 BUDGET LINES IN GARY EXPERIMENT

Financial Plan and Gross Wage/Hr ($)	w_1 ($)	w_2 ($)	y_1 ($)	y_2 ($)	Hours at Kink Point	Expected Hours	Change from Control (%)	95% Confidence Range of Expected Hours	Probability of below Break-even Point
Control:									
2.25	2.07	1.67	2.72	27.82	43.16	43.55	...	36.8, 45.38	...
4.25	3.92	3.15	2.72	27.82	22.85	40.37	...	36.8, 45.38	...
6.25	5.76	4.63	2.72	27.82	27.82	40.34	...	36.8, 45.38	...
40% tax/low guarantee:									
2.25	1.35	1.67	78.63	27.82	159.59	38.68	−11.8	34.15, 44.95	1.0
4.25	2.53	3.15	78.63	27.82	81.77	38.68	−4.3	34.15, 44.95	1.0
6.25	3.75	4.63	78.63	27.82	57.45	38.68	−4.2	34.15, 44.95	1.0
60% tax/low guarantee:									
2.25	0.90	1.67	78.09	27.82	65.42	38.69	−11.8	34.17, 44.96	1.0
4.25	1.70	3.15	78.09	27.82	34.63	39.62	−1.9	34.16, 43.48	.21
6.25	2.50	4.63	78.09	27.82	23.55	40.23	−.3	34.16, 45.38	.02
40% tax/high guarantee:									
2.25	1.35	1.67	102.63	27.82	234.97	38.27	−12.9	33.50, 44.85	1.0
4.25	2.53	3.15	102.63	27.82	120.39	38.27	−5.3	33.50, 44.85	1.0
6.25	3.75	4.63	102.63	27.82	84.59	38.27	−5.3	33.50, 44.85	1.0
60% tax/high guarantee:									
2.25	.90	1.67	102.09	27.82	96.66	38.29	−12.9	33.50, 44.84	1.0
4.25	1.70	3.15	102.09	27.82	51.17	38.29	−5.3	33.50, 44.84	1.0
6.25	2.50	4.63	102.09	27.82	34.86	39.38	−2.4	33.50, 45.38	.23

Gary sample, this responsiveness seems to be the result of increases in non-wage income rather than increases in the marginal tax rate on earned income. A possible explanation of this result is that some individuals take an increased amount of time in between jobs if they have an income guarantee. They do not search and find jobs with higher wages since the wage distribution remains virtually identical for control individuals and NIT individuals. Thus the income effect is much more important than the uncompensated wage effect in determining the response to introduction of a NIT.

VI. Conclusion

Given estimates of the unknown parameters in the uncompensated labor-supply function of equation (6) and the associated indirect utility function of equation (10), we could, in principle, do an applied welfare-economics analysis in designing a negative income tax to maximize various welfare measures subject to a budget constraint. However, since our estimate of α is zero, the derivative of the indirect utility function with respect to changes in the marginal tax rate is simply a constant proportional to the tax change since no direct labor-supply response is expected. Nor is the estimated-income response very high for most individuals. Thus we might more simply conclude that within the range of guarantees and marginal tax rates considered in the Gary NIT experiment the combination of a high guarantee and a high tax rate would lead to the fulfillment of one goal of a negative income tax, which is to provide a basic level of income support at the poverty line without at the same time causing payments to be made to families with relatively high levels of earnings or causing a substantial reduction in population labor supply.

Considerable future research is desirable for estimating the effect on labor supply of government programs which create nonconvexities in the budget set. These programs may induce large distortions on individual economic activity, and the size of this effect is an important consideration in evaluating such programs. The type of model developed here can be extended to cover a wide variety of such situations.

Appendix

Evaluation of the log-likelihood function requires evaluation of the integrals in equation (16) for nonconvex budget sets and equation (20) for convex budget sets. Two types of integrals are present. The more complicated integral has the form

$$\int_{-\infty}^{\beta_i^*} \frac{1}{\sigma_2} \phi \left(\frac{\log H_i - Z_i \delta - \alpha \log w_{1i} - \beta \log y_{1i}}{\sigma_2} \right) f(\beta) \, d\beta. \tag{A1}$$

The truncated normal density has the form

$$f(\beta) = \frac{\phi\left(\dfrac{\beta - \mu_\beta}{\sigma_\beta}\right)}{\sigma_\beta\left[1 - \Phi\left(\dfrac{\mu_\beta}{\sigma_\beta}\right)\right]}, \tag{A2}$$

where μ_β and σ_β are the parameters of the corresponding untruncated distribution. The standard normal density in the numerator can be combined with the other normal density in the integral. To combine the two densities, note that without truncation $\log H_i$ is distributed normally with mean $Z_i\delta + \alpha \log w_{1i} + \mu_\beta \log y_{1i}$ and variance $\sigma_\beta^2(\log y_{1i})^2 + \sigma_2^2$. Now considering the joint distribution of β and $\log H_i$, we write it as

$$f(\beta, \log H_i) = f(\beta \mid \log H_i) f(\log H_i) \tag{A3}$$

where $f(\cdot)$ stands for the appropriate density. The conditional density $f(\beta \mid \log H_i)$ (without truncation) is distributed normally with conditional mean $\mu_\beta + (\sigma_\beta^2 \log y_{1i})/[\sigma_\beta^2(\log y_{1i})^2 + \sigma_2^2](\log H_i - Z_i\delta - \alpha \log w_{1i} - \mu_\beta \log y_{1i})$ and conditional variance $\sigma_\beta^2\sigma_2^2/[\sigma_\beta^2(\log y_{1i})^2 + \sigma_2^2]$. Using equations (A3) and (A2) to simplify the integral of equation (A1) and evaluating it yields

$$\frac{1}{[1 - \Phi(\mu_\beta/\sigma_\beta)]} \int_{-\infty}^{\beta_i^*} f(\varepsilon_2 \mid \beta) f(\beta)\, d\beta$$

$$= \frac{1}{[1 - \Phi(\mu_\beta/\sigma_\beta)\sqrt{\sigma_\beta^2 \tilde{y}^2 + \sigma_2^2}}\, \phi\left[\frac{\log H_i - Z_i\delta - \bar{\alpha}\tilde{w} - \mu_\beta\tilde{y}}{\sqrt{\sigma_\beta^2 \tilde{y}^2 + \sigma_2^2}}\right] \tag{A4}$$

$$\times\, \Phi\left[\frac{(\beta_i^* - \mu_\beta)\sqrt{\sigma_\beta^2 \tilde{y}^2 + \sigma_2^2}}{\sigma_\beta\sigma_2} - \frac{\sigma_\beta\tilde{y}(\log H_i - Z_i\delta - \alpha\tilde{w} - \mu_\beta\tilde{y})}{\sigma_2\sqrt{\sigma_\beta^2 \tilde{y}^2 + \sigma_2^2}}\right],$$

where $\tilde{w} = \log w_{1i}$ and $\tilde{y} = \log y_{1i}$. The somewhat formidable expression on the right-hand side of equation (A4) is quite simple to evaluate, requiring evaluation of one normal density and two normal distributions where the distribution in the denominator remains constant across observations. The only other type of integral appears as the middle term in the convex budget set probability of equation (20). It is easily evaluated as

$$\frac{1}{\sigma_2}\, \phi\left(\frac{\log H_i - \log \tilde{\tilde{H}}_i}{\sigma_2}\right) [F(BU_i) - F(BL_i)]$$

$$= \frac{1}{\sigma_2[1 - \Phi(\mu_\beta/\sigma_\beta)]}\, \phi\left(\frac{\log H_i - \log \tilde{\tilde{H}}_i}{\sigma_2}\right)\left[\Phi\left(\frac{BU_i - \mu_\beta}{\sigma_\beta}\right) - \Phi\left(\frac{BL_i - \mu_\beta}{\sigma_\beta}\right)\right]. \tag{A5}$$

Two techniques were used to maximize the likelihood function. Convergence was obtained using the modified scoring method proposed by Berndt et al. (1974). Only first derivatives are required for this algorithm. However, as a check to make certain that the global maximum was achieved, the no-derivative conjugate gradient routine of Powell (1964) was also used to verify the parameter estimates. The reason for this caution is that, while the log-likelihood function of equation (21) is everywhere differentiable in the parameters, the derivatives are not everywhere continuous because of the kink point. While proofs of the usual large sample properties of maximum likelihood were not attempted in this nonregular case, consistency of the estimates would follow from the usual type of proof. However, proof of asymptotic normality of the estimates is complicated by the lack of continuous derivatives, and the reported asymptotic standard errors should be interpreted with this problem in mind. Starting values for the maximum-likelihood programs were estimated using an instrumental variable technique to predict the net wage and nonlabor income at the sample mean of 35 hours of work.

One last econometric note concerns the question of whether the gross wage should be treated as endogenous. Many studies in the past have treated it as endogenous, but the reasons advanced for the usual specification of a triangular system of a wage equation excluding hours in addition to the hours equation are not present here since we use the appropriate net wages. Previous studies used only one net wage, and since the level of utility-maximizing labor supply is observed with error the single net wage rate is also observed with an error that is correlated with the error between actual and preferred hours. Thus a simultaneous-equations problem existed. Here since all appropriate net wages are observed and used in the labor-supply specification the main cause of the simultaneous-equations problem will not occur. Nevertheless, in our preliminary investigations with the Gary data we did specify and estimate such a system making the gross (market) wage a function of personal characteristics. The results of the joint estimation were similar to those obtained when the gross wage was taken to be exogenous, and a specification error test of Hausman (1978) failed to reject the null hypothesis that the market wage could be treated as exogenous and measured without significant error. Thus simultaneous-equations estimation results are not presented in the paper.

References

Becker, Gary S. "A Theory of the Allocation of Time." *Econ. J.* 75 (September 1965) : 493–517.

Berndt, E. K.; Hall, B. H.; Hall, R. E.; and Hausman, J. A. "Estimation and Inference in Nonlinear Structural Models." *Ann. Econ. and Soc. Measurement* 3, no. 4 (October 1974) : 653–65.

Burtless, G. "Taxes, Transfers and Preferences for Work among Black Married Men." Mimeographed. Cambridge, Mass.: Massachusetts Inst. Tech., 1976.

Diewert, W. E. "Applications of Duality Theory." In *Frontiers of Quantitative Economics*, vol. 2, edited by Michael D. Intriligator and D. A. Kendrick. Amsterdam: North-Holland, 1974.

Hall, R. E. "Wages, Income and Hours of Work in the U.S. Labor Force." In *Income Maintenance and Labor Supply: Econometric Studies*, edited by Glen G. Cain and Harold W. Watts. Chicago: Rand McNally, 1973.

Hanoch, G. "A Multivariate Model of Labor Supply: Methodology for Estimation." Mimeographed. Santa Monica, Calif.: RAND Corp., 1976.

Hausman, J. A. "Specification Tests in Econometrics." *Econometrica* (1978), in press.

Hausman, J. A., and Wise, D. A. "Evaluation of Results from Truncated Samples: The New Jersey Income Maintenance Experiment." *Ann. Econ. and Soc. Measurement* 6 (1976) : 421–45.

———. "Econometrics of Nonlinear Budget Constraints: Estimating the Demand for Housing." Mimeographed. Cambridge, Mass.: Harvard Univ., 1977. (*a*)

———. "Social Experimentation, Truncated Distributions, and Efficient Estimation." *Econometrica* 45 (May 1977) : 919–38. (*b*)

———. "Stratification on Endogenous Variables and Estimation." Mimeographed. Cambridge, Mass.: Harvard Univ., 1977. (*c*)

———. "Attrition Bias in Experimental and Panel Data: The Gary Income Maintenance Experiment." *Econometrica* (1979), in press.

Heckman, James J. "Effects of Child-Care Programs on Women's Work Effort." *J.P.E.* 82, no. 2, pt. 2 (March/April 1974): S136–S163. *(a)*

———. "Shadow Prices, Market Wages, and Labor Supply." *Econometrica* 42 (July 1974): 679–94. *(b)*

Hurd, M. D. "The Estimation of Nonlinear Labor Supply Functions with Taxes from a Truncated Sample." Mimeographed. Stanford, Calif.: Stanford Univ., 1976.

Kehrer, C. C.; Kalvzny, R. L.; McDonald, J. F.; Moffitt, R. A.; Shaw, L. B.; and Stephenson, S. P. "The Initial Labor-Supply Findings from the Gary Income Maintenance Experiment." Mimeographed. Princeton, N.J.: Mathematica, 1976.

Lillard, L. "Estimation of Permanent and Transitory Response in Panel Data: A Dynamic Labor Supply Model." Mimeographed. Santa Monica, Calif.: RAND Corp., 1977.

Powell, M. J. D. "An Efficient Method for Finding the Minimum of a Function of Several Variables without Calculating Derivatives." *Computer J.* 7, no. 2 (July 1964): 155–62.

Rosen, Harvey S. "Taxes in a Labor Supply Model with Joint Wage-Hours Determination." *Econometrica* 44 (May 1976): 485–507.

Rosen, Sherwin. "Comment." *J.P.E.* 82, no. 2, pt. 2 (March/April 1974): S164–S169.

Roy, R. "La Distribution du revenue entre les divers biens." *Econometrica* 15, no. 3 (July 1947): 205–25.

Wales, T. J., and Woodland, A. D. "Labour Supply and Progressive Taxes." Mimeographed. Vancouver: Univ. British Columbia, 1977.

12

This chapter reports preliminary findings on the effect of Supported Work on a variety of outcomes, including employment and earnings, welfare dependence, criminal activities, and drug use. Because sample members had been randomly assigned to either an experimental or a control group, a simple comparison of mean values of the outcome measures for the two groups would have resulted in unbiased estimates of program effects. Both to increase the statistical precision of the estimates and to permit efficient estimation of program impacts for a large number of sample subgroups, however, regression techniques were used for most of the analysis.[1] All regression results are based on ordinary least squares techniques. But re-estimation of effects on selected outcome measures that are dichotomous or truncated, using probit or tobit analysis, respectively, yielded very similar results.

The findings are based on 19 months of follow-up data for 2830 of the 6500 sample members enrolled in the national Supported Work demonstration's research sample. [2] In many respects, the most relevant results are those for the 16-to-18-month period following enrollment in the demonstration sample, since they are findings for the early postprogram period. The authors found positive earnings effects over this period for the AFDC target group members, but no effects for members of the ex-addicts, ex-offenders or youth target groups. They also found evidence of reduced involvement in crime by experimentals in the ex-addict target group.

These results cover a very brief postprogram period and, as shown in the papers in Part III by Ashenfelter and by Mallar et al., employment and training effects are likely to vary significantly over time. Thus, it is of interest to examine more recent results from the Supported Work evaluation showing behavior over a more extended period. These results for the experimental/control employment rate differences for the four target groups during the postprogram period may be summarized as follows:[3]

Months After Enrollment		Target Group		
	AFDC	Ex-Addict	Ex-Offender	Youth
16-18	5.3**	−0.6	1.4	−2.1
19-21	8.1**	−0.4	0.8	2.8
22-24	7.4*	−0.4	1.5	−2.1
25-27	7.1*	2.4	−0.9	0.3
28-30		4.2	4.2	2.5
31-33		8.5	4.0	4.8
34-36		17.2**	5.7	7.5

* = statistically significant at the 10% level.
** = statistically significant at the 5% level.

These estimates are positive and show a marked tendency to increase over time. Only those for the AFDC group and for the ex-addict group during one 3-month period are statistically significant, yet the persistence of positive values for the other two groups during the 28- to 36-month period suggests a positive effect also may have occurred. For a discussion of the mechanisms possibly underlying these patterns, as well as for complete results for other outcome variables, see the reference in n. 3.

NOTES

1. To avoid problems of selection bias, the experimental group used for the analysis included all assigned to that treatment group whether they actually held a Supported Work job or not.

2. About 30% of the full demonstration sample had enrolled too recently to have completed their 18-month follow-up interview in time for inclusion on the analysis file used for this study. The sample used represents 64% of the sample enrollees who should have completed the requisite interviews to be included in the analysis, thus, as the authors note, raising the potential for selection-bias in the estimates of program impacts. However, selected re-estimations of results using Heckman's Mills ratio correction technique indicated that, in general, results were not biased due to interview nonresponse. (See Maynard et al., 1979, Appendix A.)

3. For the results reproduced here, see Board of Directors, MDRC (1980): Table 4-1, 5-1, 6-1, 7-1. See also Masters and Maynard, Dickson and Maynard, Maynard, and Piliavin and Gartner, forthcoming. Results for months 16 to 18, shown above, do not agree with those in the paper by Masters and Maynard (Ch. 12) due to differences in the samples available for the analyses: Masters and Maynard used a sample that included only 60% of the 4700 sample members who ultimately completed the 18-month follow-up interview.

REFERENCES

Board of Directors, MDRC (1980) Summary and Findings of the National Supported Work Demonstration. Cambridge, MA: Ballinger.

DICKINSON, K. and R. MAYNARD (forthcoming) Supported Work: Impacts for Ex-Addicts. New York: MDRC.

MASTERS, S. and R. MAYNARD (forthcoming) Supported Work: Impacts for the AFDC Target Group. New York: MDRC.

MAYNARD, R. (forthcoming) The Impacts of Supported Work for Young School Dropouts. New York: MDRC.

——— R. BROWN, and J. SCHORE (1979) The National Supported Work Demonstration: Effects During the First 18 Months After Enrollment. New York: MDRC.

PILIAVIN, I. and R. GARTNER (forthcoming) Supported Work: Impacts for Ex-Offenders. New York: MDRC.

Supported Work
A Demonstration of Subsidized Employment

Stanley L. Masters and Rebecca A. Maynard

Subsidized public employment programs have received considerable attention in recent years. The goals of such programs include reducing unemployment, increasing the earnings of the disadvantaged, and providing needed public services. This paper presents preliminary results from a large scale evaluation of one public employment program--the national Supported Work demonstration--and compares these findings with those of evaluations of other manpower programs designed to serve similar populations. Since a central feature of Supported Work is its emphasis on those with severe labor market handicaps, results for Supported Work should be relevant in considering the administration's current effort to focus CETA more heavily on the disadvantaged, especially those who are "structurally" unemployed. The first section describes the Supported Work program. The various components of its evaluation are described in the second section. Some preliminary results of

Masters is with the Institute for Research on Poverty. Maynard is with Mathematica Policy Research. This paper is based, in part, on research funded by and conducted on behalf of the Manpower Demonstration Research Corporation under its contract with Mathematica Policy Research to carry out, with the University of Wisconsin's Institute for Research on Poverty, major aspects of the evaluation of the national demonstration of Supported Work. Funding for this national demonstration comes from a number of federal agencies, but is channeled through the Employment and Training Administration, U.S. Department of Labor, as the lead federal agency, under Grant No. 33-36-76-01 and Contract Nos. 30-36-75-01 and 30-34-75-02. Researchers undertaking such projects under government sponsorship are encouraged to express their professional judgments freely. Therefore, points of view or opinions stated in this paper do not necessarily represent the official position or policy of the federal government or the sponsors of the demonstration.

From Stanley L. Masters and Rebecca A. Maynard, "Supported Work: A Demonstration of Subsidized Employment." Unpublished manuscript, 1980.

the program are presented in the third section, and, in the fourth section, results for other programs aimed at similar target groups are compared with the findings for Supported Work. We conclude with a discussion of several important qualifications and a consideration of alternative strategies for increasing employment opportunities for the disadvantaged.

THE PROGRAM

Supported Work is a transitional work experience program, designed for persons with serious employment difficulties. The four major target groups for the program are women who are long-term recipients of Aid to Families with Dependent Children (AFDC), ex-addicts, ex-offenders, and young school drop-outs. To ensure focusing on those in greatest need, the program enforces strict eligibility criteria and pays wage rates near the legal minimum wage. Through the imposition of formal eligibility criteria and the payment of wages near the legal minimum, the Supported Work programs sought to enroll those thought to benefit most from this special work experience. As can be seen from the data in Table 1, over 85 percent of the sample were black or Hispanic and few had completed high school.[1] On average, these individuals were employed only four to ten weeks during the year prior to their enrollment in the demonstration. These factors, together with the long-term welfare dependence of the AFDC group, the drug use and extensive criminal histories of the ex-addict group, and the recent incarceration and extensive criminal histories of the ex-offender group, mean that some special transitional employment experience, such as supported work, might be necessary for these groups to succeed in the regular labor market. It is also noteworthy that, on average, the Supported Work participants are considerably more disadvantaged than CETA enrollees with regard to both employment experience and schooling (Table 2).

A primary goal of Supported Work is to enable those who have had little, if any, successful experience in the labor market a chance to hold a job, to succeed in that job, and to move eventually into unsubsidized employment. As a result of a successful employment experience, both during and after participation in Supported Work, it is hoped that participants will become less dependent on welfare, and will be less likely to use drugs and to participate in criminal activities.

The program is based on the premise that participants can be successfully employed (and will engage in less deviant behavior) if they work in the company of their peers and under close supervision by technically qualified people who understand the work histories and personal backgrounds of their crew members. The goal is for these supervisors to enforce gradually increased standards of attendance, productivity, and performance until they resemble those for unsubsidized jobs. After 12 or 18 months, depending on the

TABLE 1

CHARACTERISTICS OF THE SAMPLE AT ENROLLMENT, BY TARGET GROUP

Characteristic	AFDC	Target Group Ex-Addict	Ex-Offender	Youth
Male (%)	0.0	80.9	94.7	88.6
Average Age	34.4	27.8	25.4	18.3
Race/Ethnicity				
Black, Non-Hispanic (%)	83.3	78.4	84.1	76.5
Hispanic (%)	10.2	7.1	8.7	13.9
White, Non-Hispanic (%)	6.5	14.5	7.2	7.4
12 or More Years of Education (%)	30.3	27.0	25.2	0.8
Currently Married (%)	3.1	23.5	12.9	4.5
Average Number of Dependents in Household	2.2	0.9	0.4	0.1
Ever Held a Job (%)	83.6	95.3	87.8	76.8
Average Number of Weeks Worked during Previous 12 Months	3.5	10.4	5.6	9.7
Average Earnings during Previous 12 Months ($)	220	1228	564	799
Average Number of Years Received Welfare	8.6	n.a.	n.a.	n.a.
Received Welfare during Previous Month (%)	99.9	41.3	20.0	10.9
Living in Public Housing (%)	38.5	16.1	21.6	26.7
Ever Used Drugs Regularly (other than marijuana) (%)	n.a.	90.3	38.6	5.9
Ever Used Heroin Regularly (%)	n.a.	87.0	33.1	3.8
In Drug Treatment during Previous 6 Months (%)	n.a.	90.9	11.2	1.9
Average Number of Arrests	n.a.	8.1	8.9	2.5
Average Number of Convictions	n.a.	2.8	3.0	0.7
Incarcerated during Previous 12 Months (%)	n.a.	27.4	91.5	20.7
Number in Sample	707	742	891	490

Note: These data were obtained through interviews administered to experimental and control group members at about the time the experimentals were enrolled in the demonstration. They refer to only those individuals included in the analysis discussed in this paper.

n.a. = data not available or not analyzed.

TABLE 2

PERCENTAGE DISTRIBUTION OF ENROLLEES IN SUPPORTED WORK AND CETA

BY CHARACTERISTIC

Characteristics at Enrollment	Supported Work	CETA--Fiscal Year 76	
		Adult Employability Development Component Titles I, II, VI	Public Service Employment Titles I, II, VI
Unemployed	97	50	48
Number of Continuous Weeks not Employed			
≤4	6	20	23
5-13	5	28	33
14-26	7	22	19
27-40	6	10	8
Over 40	76	20	17
Years of Schooling			
<12	60	38	22
12	30	43	42
>12	10	19	36

Source: Manpower Demonstration Research Corporation (1978).

Note: The data on Supported Work enrollees are based on data in the Supported Work Management Information System and those on CETA enrollees were obtained from Westat, Inc. (1977).

site, participants are required to leave Supported Work whether or not they have found other employment. This transitional aspect of the program is similar to limitations imposed on participation in many subsidized employment programs, but it is a major difference between Supported Work and sheltered workshops. Although participants are expected to learn some occupation-specific skills during the program, the emphasis of the program is on development of work habits, skills, and motivation that enhance employability. By succeeding at Supported Work jobs, participants also can develop an employment record that will distinguish them from an overall group that employers generally regard as poor risks.

The type of work is primarily construction and services, with ex-addicts and ex-offenders working mainly in construction and AFDC women working mainly in services. Although the jobs tend to be in relatively low-skill, labor-intensive activities where private sector wage rates are low, the work has ranged across many industries: most project days in the second contract year were spent in construction (34 percent) and service (46 percent) jobs, but 7 percent were in manufacturing, 4 percent were in agriculture and in transportation and communications, and 3 percent were in retail trade (MDRC, 1978).

The Supported Work demonstration is run nationally by the Manpower Demonstration Research Corporation (MDRC). Under MDRC's supervision, the program is operated at 21 sites by local organizations, which typically are independent agencies whose major or sole function is running the program. These agencies must supplement their national funding by marketing their output and/or by raising other local funding (e.g., grants from CETA prime sponsors). Supported Work is a new program in most of the cities and thus, in many cases, these organizations have established entire production operations in order to provide job experience of the desired type. At least in part because of their demonstration status, the Supported Work programs are small relative to the local labor markets. They typically range in size from about 75 to 200 slots, but a few programs have enrolled over 300 participants at one time.

The national funding of the program, while covering less than total expenses, provides a financial base that allows considerable flexibility in the choice of projects. Most of the work is done for the public and nonprofit sectors, and for a nominal charge, if any. The average net subsidy cost per person year (expenditures minus sales revenue) was over $13,000 in the first year, but declined to under $11,000 in the second year.[2/] However, the program wage of participants accounts for almost half of expenditures and the opportunity cost of this labor is low, resulting in the program's social cost being considerably lower than its expenditures.

The experience of the Supported Work programs to date demonstrates the feasibility of creating a small number of jobs for the members of its target groups. Greater difficulties, however, would undoubtedly be encountered in a large-scale national program, both because of increased administrative problems and the likelihood of greater opposition from both unions and private employers. Moreover, since administering agencies were chosen on the basis of grant applications, they are likely to be among the better qualified to run such programs. Finally, because the program is a demonstration, a considerable amount of technical and other support has been available.[3/]

THE EVALUATION DESIGN

The outcome measures of primary interest in the program evaluation relate to employment and earnings, welfare dependence, participation in criminal activities, and drug use. Largely as a consequence of these effects, it is also hypothesized that the program may lead to such outcomes as more stable lifestyles and improved living conditions.

For all target groups, it is expected that experimentals will have higher levels of employment and earnings than will controls. During the initial months after enrollment, these effects are expected to occur as a result of experimentals having the opportunity to hold a program job. While expectations with regard to post-program effects are less firmly held, it is expected that the Supported Work experience would have positive effects due to some combination of improved work habits, improved occupation-specific skills, a better work record to present to prospective employers, and the placement efforts of program operators. On the other hand, negative results are possible, especially to the extent that program participants become eligible for unemployment compensation as a consequence of their program employment and/or to the extent that experimentals take a substantial amount of time to secure their first job in the post-program period. Hypotheses concerning program effects on welfare dependence and other sources of income follow directly from the employment-related hypotheses: increased earnings lead to reductions in income-conditioned transfers, such as welfare, food stamps and Medicaid benefits.

There are several reasons to expect that an employment program such as Supported Work might reduce the criminal activities of members of the ex-addict, ex-offender, and youth target groups. First, by providing a legitimate means to obtain income, Supported Work might reduce the rate of recidivism among former offenders, especially for property crimes, and might deter first-time offenders. Second, the program may reduce crime by increasing the opportunity cost of deviant behavior, for example through the loss of program earnings as a result of arrest and incarceration. Third, the program may lead individuals to alter their self-perceptions and their attitudes concerning legitimate work.

Expectations as to the effects of Supported Work on the use of drugs
are more ambiguous. While it is hoped that employment in the supportive
environment of the program will reduce the likelihood and/or extent of drug
use, it is possible that either because of their higher incomes or their
association with ex-addicts on a daily basis, program participants might, in
fact, increase their drug use.

In order to test the above hypotheses, a large-scale evaluation of
Supported Work was built into the demonstration design--a feature which distinguishes this program from most previous subsidized employment programs.
This evaluation includes four main components: (1) an outcome analysis to
test various behavioral hypotheses noted above; (2) a benefit-cost analysis;
(3) a process analysis; and (4) a documentation study. In 10 sites, eligible
applicants for Supported Work were randomly assigned to an experimental or a
control group. This paper focuses on the outcome analysis, based on comparisons between these two groups, and uses data from a set of in-person interviews
administered at enrollment and at subsequent 9-month intervals for 18 to 36
months. The total sample for the demonstration evaluation includes about 6,500
persons evenly divided between experimentals and controls, about 4,700 of whom
completed the enrollment, the 9- and the 18-month interview. Ultimately,
about 3,000 sample members were interviewed 27 months and 800 were interviewed
36 months following enrollment. In this report, however, we present preliminary results for the outcome analysis based on 18 months of data for a sample
of 2,830 individuals who were enrolled in the Supported Work demonstration
between April 1975 and February 1977.[4/] The allocation of the analysis sample
by site and target group is presented in Table 3.

RESULTS

On average, experimentals stayed in their Supported Work jobs for
between 6 months (for the ex-offenders) and 9 months (for the AFDC sample).
In this section, we discuss the impact of this program experience on employment and earnings, welfare dependence and other sources of income, drug use
and criminal activities, both during the time when experimentals held their
Supported Work jobs and during the early months following their program
participation.[5/] These results are based on multiple regression estimates of
experimental effects. In addition to a dummy variable for experimental status,
control variables in the equations, measured from baseline interviews, included
site, age, sex, race, schooling, marital status, household size and composition, eligibility status, length of site operations, length of longest previous
job, weeks worked in previous year, job training in previous years, and income
from various sources during the previous month.

TABLE 3

SAMPLE ALLOCATION, BY SITE AND TARGET GROUP

| | | Target Group | | | Total | |
	AFDC	Ex-Addict	Ex-Offender	Youth	Number	(Percentage)
Site						
Atlanta	80	n.a.	n.a.	17	97	(3.4)
Chicago	138	163	128	n.a.	429	(15.2)
Hartford	50	n.a.	117	220	387	(13.7)
Jersey City	n.a.	286	119	156	561	(19.8)
Newark	171	n.a.	147	n.a.	318	(11.2)
New York	205	n.a.	n.a.	35	240	(8.5)
Oakland	37	43	147	n.a.	227	(8.0)
Philadelphia	n.a.	250	112	62	424	(15.0)
San Francisco	n.a.	n.a.	121	n.a.	121	(4.3)
Wisconsin	26	n.a.	n.a.	n.a.	26	(0.9)
Total Number	707	742	851	490	2830	(100.0)
(Percentage of Total)	(25.0)	(26.2)	(31.5)	(17.3)	(100.0)	

n.a. = not applicable.

EMPLOYMENT AND EARNINGS

As can be seen from Table 4, Supported Work led to greater employment and higher earnings among experimentals than controls (E–C), particularly during the period when experimentals were eligible for Supported Work jobs. These program effects were largest during the first 9-month period, when the percentage employed was between 39 and 63 points higher for experimentals than for controls. The effects on employment and earnings were largest for the AFDC target group, in part because AFDC experimentals tended to stay in Supported Work the longest. The relatively larger earnings differential for the AFDC group resulted from the greater hours differential and from the somewhat higher wage rate differentials between experimentals and controls as compared with the differentials between experimentals and controls in the other target groups.[6]

During the second 9-month period after enrollment, when between 34 and 68 percent of the experimental group members did not participate in the program at all, significant experimental-control differences persisted, although the magnitude of the differences declined substantially.[7] As in the first nine months, these differences were considerably larger for the AFDC than for the other target groups.

In many respects, the most interesting results are those for the 16- to 18-month period. By the start of this period about 92 percent of the experimentals had left their Supported Work jobs, and, thus, results for this period can be viewed as preliminary indications of post-program effects. As can be seen in Table 4, the only significant differences in employment-related outcomes during this period were for the AFDC target group. A significantly higher percentage of experimentals than controls in this group were employed during this period (41 versus 30 percent) and, on average, the experimentals worked 18 hours and earned $78 more per month than their control group counterparts. Contributing to these large differences for the AFDC group relative to those for the ex-addict, ex-offender, and youth groups was the AFDC controls having worked and earned substantially less than controls in the other target groups.

WELFARE AND OTHER INCOME

As shown in Table 5, the increase in earnings and, during the second 9 months, the increase in unemployment compensation benefits of experimentals relative to controls was accompanied by a substantial decrease in welfare dependence. Over the full 18-month period, a reduction in the percentage of experimentals receiving any benefits, together with a decrease in payments among many who continued to receive welfare after enrolling in the program, led to an average reduction in monthly welfare payments among experimentals of almost $100 for the AFDC group and of $30 for ex-addicts. In addition to this reduction in cash transfers, experimentals (in all but the youth group)

TABLE 4

EMPLOYMENT RATES, HOURS WORKED, AND EARNINGS

	Months 1-9		Months 10-18		Months 16-18	
	E – C	Control Mean	E – C	Control Mean	E – C	Control Mean
Employed (%)						
AFDC	62.9**	32.2	39.1**	36.4	10.4**	30.3
Ex-addict	47.9**	46.6	14.4**	50.0	-2.6	39.5
Ex-offender	38.9**	56.3	9.1**	55.9	3.6	42.8
Youth	48.4**	50.1	5.8	59.4	-5.3	47.4
Monthly Hours Worked		Program Hours		Program Hours		Program Hours
AFDC	115**	(131)	44**	(43)	18**	(7)
Ex-addict	79**	(102)	18**	(30)	-2	(6)
Ex-offender	74**	(99)	11**	(21)	1	(5)
Youth	88**	(104)	12**	(27)	-3	(7)
Monthly Earnings ($)		Program Earnings		Program Earnings		Program Earnings
AFDC	351**	(388)	152**	(130)	78**	(22)
Ex-addict	205**	(293)	55**	(92)	-1	(18)
Ex-offender	206**	(288)	45**	(67)	29	(19)
Youth	240**	(283)	40**	(77)	-2	(22)

**Statistically significant at the 5 percent level.

TABLE 5

INCOME FROM WELFARE AND OTHER SOURCES

	Months 1-9		Months 10-18		Months 16-18	
	E - C	Control Mean	E - C	Control Mean	E - C	Control Mean
Receiving Welfare (%)[a]						
AFDC	-5.9**	99.4	-11.4**	91.1	-15.0**	85.4
Ex-addict	-20.7**	50.9	-6.2**	48.5	-5.2	44.1
Ex-offender	-13.2**	30.7	-6.4**	29.7	-6.0**	25.3
Youth	-5.4	15.8	-1.3	21.8	-1.4	18.3
Monthly Welfare ($)						
AFDC	-110**	272	-82**	242	-72**	233
Ex-addict	-47**	94	-13*	89	-9	88
Ex-offender	-19**	36	-13**	45	-15**	47
Youth	-8*	21	-13**	33	-9	33
Monthly Food Stamp Bonus Value ($)						
AFDC	-20**	65	-18**	61	-15**	60
Ex-addict	-4**	20	-3	23	-2	23
Ex-offender	-3*	15	-3	15	-2	14
Youth	0	17	-6	16	-5	15
Monthly Unemployment Compensation ($)[b]						
AFDC	-2**	2	29**	4	47**	5
Ex-addict	-8**	11	21**	8	35**	9
Ex-offender	-4**	6	11**	9	14**	10
Youth	-5*	7	16**	6	24**	7
Monthly Earnings ($)						
AFDC	351**	59	152**	110	78	122
Ex-addict	201**	151	55**	194	-1	208
Ex-offender	206**	160	45**	224	29	233
Youth	240**	104	40**	175	-2	195
Total Monthly Income ($)						
AFDC	225**	409	88**	426	44**	430
Ex-addict	144**	288	51**	330	25	345
Ex-offender	167**	230	15	318	7	327
Youth	228**	161	9	265	-19	280

[a] Welfare income includes AFDC, GA, SSI, and other unspecified welfare income. Nearly all of the AFDC group's welfare income was from the AFDC program, while most of that received by the other target groups was from General Assistance programs.

[b] Except in New York, Supported Work did not participate in the Unemployment Compensation program. Thus, the experimental group's benefits would have been funded primarily by the federal Special Unemployment Assistance (SUA) program.

*Statistically significant at the 10 percent level.

**Statistically significant at the 5 percent level.

tended to receive lower food stamp bonuses than controls. Especially among the AFDC group, experimentals also tended to lose their Medicaid benefits as a result of their increased earnings: 75 percent of the AFDC experimentals, compared with 88 percent of controls, had a Medicaid card at the time of their 18-month interview.

The earnings gains more than compensated for the decrease in transfer payments. Consequently, experimentals increased their total income substantially relative to controls, especially during the early months of the program. On the other hand, the net return from working was less than the actual money earned due to the resulting decrease in welfare benefits. This was particularly true for the AFDC experimentals, whose total income increased by less than 75 cents for each dollar of earnings. Despite this substantial implicit welfare tax, we did not find that post-enrollment employment experiences were sensitive to expected welfare benefit reductions.[8]

DRUG USE

Supported Work had very little impact on drug use, even among the ex-addict group, virtually all of whom had been in drug treatment prior to enrolling in the program.[9] The only significant finding was that among the youth group, which reported relatively little drug use prior to enrollment in Supported Work, experimentals tended to be more likely than controls to use marijuana. However, this increase in marijuana use was not primarily in those sites that also enrolled ex-addicts.

CRIMINAL ACTIVITIES

Table 6 summarizes some of the key findings related to ex-addicts', ex-offenders', and youths' involvement in crime. In addition to the findings for the two 9-month periods, we have included results for the full 18-month period, since these provide a better indication of the cumulative effect of Supported Work on involvement in criminal activities. For the ex-addict target group, significantly fewer experimentals than controls (25 percent versus 36 percent) reported having been arrested during the 18-month period. A large portion of this differential in arrests was attributable to a reduction in robbery and drug-related arrests.[10] Experimentals in the ex-addict group also reported lower conviction and incarceration rates than did ex-addict controls.

Favorable results in terms of reduced involvement in crime were not observed for the ex-offender and youth target groups. Since similar employment results were observed for all three target groups, employment effects of the program cannot explain the difference in crime-related results among them. It may be, however, that the effect of Supported Work on legitimate income relieved one of the ex-addicts' main motivations for committing robberies or making illegal drug sales.

COMPARISON WITH OUTCOME RESULTS FOR OTHER PROGRAMS

This section compares the preliminary results for Supported Work with
those for other programs aimed at somewhat similar clients. These comparisons
should be treated cautiously because both the target groups and the evaluation
methods differ across programs. Although the direction of bias in the comparisons is not always clear-cut, the lack of a random control group in most
other studies is likely to result in an overestimation of the effect of the
programs being evaluated since, holding measurable variables constant, those
who are most eager to work are most likely to gain entrance to employment and
training programs. This section begins with a comparison of the AFDC target
group results with WIN evaluation results. The effects of Supported Work for
ex-offenders and ex-addicts are then compared with those of alternative programs for these groups. The section concludes with a comparison of Supported
Work results for youth with those for two other employment programs for youth:
Job Corps and the Neighborhood Youth Corps.[11]

COMPARISON WITH WIN EVALUATIONS

The Supported Work AFDC population is a subset of the WIN registrants.
The eligibility criteria for Supported Work include having received AFDC
continuously for at least the past three years and having had no job of more
than 20 hours per week during the past six months.[12] As a result of these
criteria, the work experience of Supported Work participants is considerably
less than that of WIN participants.[13] On the other hand, participation in
WIN is compulsory while participation in Supported Work is voluntary. Thus,
it may be that the Supported Work participants and corresponding control group
members are more eager to work than the average WIN enrollee.

The WIN program includes job search, education and training, and
subsidized employment components, but has as its ultimate objective employment in unsubsidized jobs. Recently, this program has been the subject of
extensive evaluation efforts, some of which are currently ongoing. Of the
two largest efforts, the results of one are presented in Schiller (1978),
while the other study by Ketron, Inc. (1979) is ongoing. Schiller (1978)
reports average earnings effects of WIN participation ranging from $25 per
month for women receiving job placement to $118 per month for those partici-
pating in on-the-job training (OJT) or public service employment (PSE).[14]
In comparison, Supported Work led to an average earnings gain of between $56
and $78 per month during the period immediately after leaving the program.[15]
The somewhat larger results for participation in PSE and OJT components of
WIN compared with Supported Work are due, in part, to the fact that both WIN
evaluations included some in-program earnings gains in their estimates while
the lower bound estimate of the Supported Work effect contains no program
earnings.

TABLE 6

ARREST RATES

	Months 1-9		Months 10-18		Months 1-18	
	E - C	Control Mean	E - C	Control Mean	E - C	Control Mean
Arrests (%)						
Ex-addict	-5.2*	21.7	-6.9*	19.6	-11.2**	35.9
Ex-offender	-4.1	32.4	3.1	21.8	-2.2	44.8
Youth	-2.8	19.1	1.0	15.0	-2.8	28.5
Arrested for Robbery (%)						
Ex-addict	-4.4**	5.5	-2.7**	3.5	-6.7**	8.8
Ex-offender	1.7	4.9	-1.0	4.5	0.2	8.9
Youth	-1.1	5.2	0.4	2.4	-0.8	7.7

*Statistically significant at the 10 percent level.

**Statistically significant at the 5 percent level.

Both the Supported Work results and those of the WIN evaluation show smaller earnings gains among those with more recent employment experience. This suggests that it may make sense to focus employment programs on those among the AFDC population who do not have recent labor market experience, which is consistent with the philosophy of the Supported Work program. The combined experience of WIN and Supported Work suggests that a sizable number of women receiving AFDC do, in fact, want to work and will take advantage of opportunities made available through subsidized employment.

COMPARISON WITH PROGRAMS FOR EX-OFFENDERS AND EX-ADDICTS

There has been a wide variety of programs to improve the employ-ability of ex-offenders. As described by Cook (1975) and by Taggart (1972), however, the evaluations of these programs have not resulted in optimistic conclusions. Taggart, for example, summarizes the evidence in the following passage (pp. 96-97):

> There is no proof that any single manpower service or strategy has had more than a marginal impact on its recipients, and no proof that any combination of services can make a substantial contribution. Some glimmerings of success have shown through and these should obviously be exploited; but overall, the results have been disappointing. On the basis of the existing evidence, it does not seem likely that the employment problems of offenders can be significantly alleviated by manpower programs, or that these programs will have a noticeable impact on the rate of crime.

The results of Supported Work for ex-offenders are consistent with these earlier results.

Among the more recent programs for ex-offenders, the Living Insurance for Ex-Prisoners (LIFE) program in Baltimore (Mallar and Thornton, 1978) pro-vides interesting results to compare with those of Supported Work. The sample of 432 participants was randomly assigned, in equal numbers, to one of four treatments: (1) $60 per week for three months after their release from prison, (2) job search assistance, (3) both, or (4) neither (control group). Job search assistance had very little effect, but, by the third quarter after the payments ended, those obtaining the cash transfer to help them get started were earning $29 per month more than the control group and were less likely to have been arrested or incarcerated since enrolling in the program. In con-trast, Supported Work appears to be having little impact on either criminal activity or post-program earnings of ex-offenders.

LIFE differs from Supported Work in three important respects: it provides income rather than employment; participants enroll immediately upon release from prison; and it is aimed at offenders with no history of drug or alcohol abuse but with a high chance of recidivism for theft.[16] This targeting may be especially important as evidenced by both the Supported Work findings and the fact that no positive results have been found for the TARP

program which is a larger-scale program of experimental treatments similar
to those in LIFE, undertaken in Georgia and Texas, but which enrolled a
random sample of released prisoners (see Stephens and Sanders, 1978, and
Smith and Martinez, 1978). The Supported Work program is similar to the
TARP program in that no effort is made to target the program on ex-prisoners
with a high probability of recidivism. In contrast to both LIFE and TARP,
however, Supported Work is not focused on those who have just been released
from prison. To be eligible, ex-offenders need have been incarcerated only
within the past six months.

The results from LIFE and TARP suggest that Supported Work might be
more effective for ex-offenders if it were targeted more carefully.[17/]
They also suggest that, since the LIFE program is less expensive than Supported Work, cash assistance may be more cost-effective than subsidized
employment for this target group.

In contrast to the number of employment-related programs for
ex-offenders, there have been very few programs aimed specifically at
ex-addicts. Two programs for which evaluation results are available are
the Wildcat program, which was a pilot program for the national Supported
Work demonstration, and the TREAT program, which provided job training and
part-time employment. There is some evidence that the Wildcat program
increased post-program earnings for experimentals but it did not have any
long-term effect on arrest rates (see Friedman, 1977, and Friedman, 1978).
However, since the sample is small (about 400) and random assignment was
not rigorously adhered to (e.g., no-shows, ineligibles, and a moderate percentage subjectively judged to be unqualified by program managers were
excluded from the experimental group), these findings should not be regarded
as definitive. The evaluation of the TREAT program, on the other hand,
shows no evidence of the program's having improved the participants' long-
term employment outcome (Bass and Woodward, 1978). However, there is some
indication that experimentals as compared with controls responded better to
drug treatment and weak evidence that they were arrested less often. The
arrest results observed for both TREAT and Supported Work suggest that
holding a job reduces the need for illegal income--at least for those with
only a moderate drug habit. It is still too early to know whether the crime
results for Supported Work will continue if the earnings results do not.
Nevertheless, the crime results are important even if they should only apply
to the in-program period.[18/]

COMPARISON WITH JOB CORPS AND OTHER PROGRAMS FOR YOUTH

Since the start of the War on Poverty in the mid-1960s, there have
been numerous employment and training programs aimed at disadvantaged youth.
These include the Job Corps and Neighborhood Youth Corps (NYC) of the
poverty program, various older CETA programs (including the Job Corps) and

the new CETA programs established by the Youth Employment and Demonstration
Projects Act of 1977.

Most CETA programs have been subject to relatively little evaluation,
due in part to their decentralization and diversity. More study has been
done of the programs of the 1960s, however, and a recent careful evaluation
has been done of the current Job Corps program. The early studies of NYC
and Job Corps found a small earnings effect (less than $200 per year) and
little evidence of any other positive post-program impact.[19] A more recent
Job Corps study by Mallar et al. (1978) found only small average gains in
post-program earnings for male Job Corps enrollees, but did find significant
reductions in criminal activity.[20] As a result, long-term program benefits
are predicted to exceed program costs, from societal, participant, and non-
participant perspectives.

The target populations for Supported Work and Job Corps are quite
similar. However, in contrast to Supported Work's emphasis on work experience, the Job Corps emphasizes education and training, as well. Its unique
feature relative to other employment and training programs is its residential
character. Quite possibly, the program is relatively successful, especially
in reducing crime, because of its emphasis on changing the youth's environment
by moving particpants to Job Corps centers. On the other hand, the results
may also represent the effect of greater self-selection biases than for other
youth programs (especially with regard to the crime results), since those who
are most eager to "go straight" may be most interested in attending a residential program.

CONCLUSION

In this section, we summarize the results for Supported Work, discuss
important qualifications, and consider alternative strategies for increasing
employment opportunities for the disadvantaged.

SUMMARY AND QUALIFICATIONS

The preliminary results for Supported Work, together with the review
of other evaluation studies, suggest that a sizable number of AFDC recipients
are eager, capable workers but are not able to overcome barriers to employment without the initial aid of a subsidized program. For ex-addicts,
ex-offenders, and youth, there do not appear to be any post-program earnings
effects of Supported Work, but there is evidence that the program led to
reduced crime among ex-addicts.[21]

These conclusions, however, are subject to some important qualifications. First, the results compare Supported Work with whatever programs
are available for controls rather than with the effect of no program.

Second, the length of follow-up is not yet sufficient to warrant any conclusions about the long-term effects of Supported Work. Third, the experimental-
control differences may be misleading to the extent that the program has
effects on nonparticipants. The implications of each of these problems will
be discussed briefly below. Then we discuss two alternative approaches for
dealing with the employment problems of the Supported Work target groups.

With regard to the effect of alternative programs on these results,
no important experimental effects were found for participation in either
education or training programs. Substantial participation in public employment programs was reported, with about 20 percent of the non-Supported Work
jobs likely to have been subsidized through programs such as CETA or WIN.[22/]
Although there is little difference in this percentage between experimentals
and controls, it is generally a little larger for controls. More important,
the overall nonprogram earnings were considerably greater for controls than
experimentals during the period under study. Thus, the earnings results for
Supported Work would probably be somewhat more positive in the absence of
these other subsidized employment programs.

The second qualification with regard to the results concerns the
limited post-program follow-up data currently available. Although the results
for months 16 to 18 presented here provide some useful information on post-
program labor market experiences, it is important to remember that from 5 to
10 percent of experimentals were still in the program at the start of this
period and that about 2 percent remained in the program at the end of the
eighteenth month. Furthermore, evidence from other studies concerning changes
in program impacts over time provides no clear indication as to whether these
early post-program results are likely to understate or overstate long-run
impacts.[23/] One factor, peculiar to the Supported Work demonstration, which
may have tended to depress temporarily post-program results is the receipt by
many experimentals of unemployment compensation (UC) upon their termination
from Supported Work.[24/] The longer-run impacts of having received UC payments are uncertain, however, since, although this alternative income source
may permit recipients to search longer and thus find better jobs, the longer
search time may partly negate the effect of Supported Work on job skills and
credentials. However, given the extent of UC receipt by experimentals as
compared with controls during the 16 to 18 month period, we might expect
effects on earnings at the end of 27 months to be larger than those observed
for this earlier period.[25/]

The third important qualification with regard to these results concerns the possibility of program effects on nonparticipants. The methodology
employed in this study implicitly assumes that there are no such effects.
In fact, however, the program may reduce employment among those with whom
experimentals are competing for post-program jobs and open up employment
opportunities for others who may be less likely to compete with experimentals

as a result of the program. Such changes in competition may result either during the program or in the post-program period. If wage rates are flexible, then the effects on nonparticipants should be mainly on wage rates. However, given minimum wages and various other "rigidities," both the employment and earnings of nonparticipants might be affected. For workers in the experimental group who are actively in the labor force before, during, and after the program it is unclear whether the net impact on nonparticipants would increase or decrease the benefits of the program, as measured by simple experimental-control group comparisons.[26] If workers in the experimental group would not have entered the labor force except for the program, however, this analysis suggests that the approach used here would tend to overestimate program benefits.[27] Since those in the AFDC target group are least likely to have entered the labor force in the absence of the Supported Work program, the results in Table 4 which suggest that the post-program employment and earnings effects are greatest for the AFDC group must be qualified accordingly. The only way to estimate the effects of an employment program on non-participants is to establish large programs in selected labor markets and then compare the experience in these labor markets with that in otherwise comparable labor markets where the program is not established.[28]

ALTERNATIVE POLICIES

In conclusion, we will briefly consider two alternative approaches to increasing the employment of the types of disadvantaged persons in the four Supported Work target groups. One is a program of tax credits or other subsidies to private employers for hiring disadvantaged workers. The other is to implement policies to stimulate aggregate demand in the economy, which will affect the availability of jobs for all kinds of workers.

One alternative to Supported Work is a program of tax credits or other subsidies to private employers who hire disadvantaged workers. An example of this approach is the federal Targeted Jobs Tax Credit Program, which went into effect in January 1979. Previous experience with such targeted tax credits in this country has not been very encouraging, however. For example, in discussing the experience with targeted wage subsidies such as the NAB-JOBS program of the late 1960s and the tax credit available to firms who have WIN enrollees, Hamermesh (1978, p. 97) concludes:

> The common thread in these few, limited wage subsidies is the failure of employers to respond to programs whose magnitude and expected effect on labor demand would seem to make them attractive. Experience suggests that there is a serious problem, either of resistance to paper work or reaction to the implication of a worker's eligibility (a stigma effect) that must be overcome if such subsidies are to have a strong impact.

In addition, if employers do use the subsidies on a large scale basis, they may do so mostly for workers they would have hired anyway or by substituting eligible workers for other needy but ineligible workers (e.g., displaced homemakers). Although it may be possible to overcome the difficulties experienced in previous private sector subsidy programs, the TJTC should not be assumed to have a high probability of dramatic success, either absolutely or relative to subsidized employment programs in the public sector that are targeted on the same disadvantaged groups.

The second alternative is to expand employment opportunities for the disadvantaged by increasing aggregate demand and, thus, increasing job opportunities for everyone. The well-known difficulty with this approach is its likely effect on inflation. The factors determining the extent to which a given increase in demand will lead to increases in output and employment as opposed to prices and wage rates is a most important topic. Some conclusions are fairly obvious. For example, demand increases that are targeted primarily on surplus rather than bottleneck sectors should be less inflationary than those having their primary impact on sectors already experiencing shortages. Similarly, increases in aggregate demand should have less effect on inflation when there is considerable slack in the economy than at times when the economy is producing near capacity. There does not appear to be much agreement on most other predictions, and even these may not be consistent with an extreme version of the monetarist position.

To analyze these policies we need to know more about the behavior of firms. During the past two decades, detailed work on the labor market behavior of firms and unions has been the subject of a diminishing proportion of the research of labor economists. Instead interest has shifted heavily toward human capital issues and the behavior of households. It may now be time for labor economists to put more emphasis on the demand side of the labor market, including the behavior of employers and unions.

NOTES

[1] The eligibility criteria for the youth group (ages 17 to 20 at enrollment) include being out of school and not having a high school diploma.

[2] These figures are taken from Manpower Demonstration Research Corporation (1978). Receipts represent approximately 20 percent of expenditures.

[3] The presence of a research evaluation does have some disadvantages, however, especially the need to recruit larger numbers of participants to accommodate the need for random assignment of half the entrants to a control group.
     It is the case, however, that a larger-scale program likely would have lower overhead costs per participant than were experienced for the demonstration.

[4] This sample includes only 64 percent of those who should, in principle, have completed all three interviews by the time the file was

created: 98 percent responded to the baseline interview, 80 percent to the
9-month interview, and 69 percent to the 18-month interview.

$\underline{5/}$A more detailed discussion of the results summarized here, including a discussion of the variance in results across sites and calendar years,
is presented in Maynard, Brown and Schore (1979).

$\underline{6/}$Wage rates during the program were set slightly below estimates of
market wage rates. The AFDC program wage is higher, relative to the estimated market wage, than is that for ex-offenders or ex-addicts both because
no sex differentials were established at sites that had ex-addict or
ex-offender target groups and because of minimum wage constraints at all
sites.

$\underline{7/}$It is noteworthy that during the second 9-month period, between
10 and 37 percent of the total earnings of experimental and control group
members was from public sector jobs. Such jobs were most prevalent among
the AFDC group, for which 20 percent of the experimental group's total
earnings (40 percent of its nonprogram earnings) and 37 percent of the
control group's earnings were from such jobs.

$\underline{8/}$This finding may seem to contradict the results of the numerous
studies that suggest that there are work disincentive effects associated
with welfare programs. However, welfare recipients who enrolled in
Supported Work may not be representative of the whole population of
recipients: individuals voluntarily applied to Supported Work, presumably
with some knowledge of the impact that both in-program and post-program
earnings would have on their welfare benefits.

$\underline{9/}$Reported drug use among the AFDC target group was very low, as
one would expect given that less than 2 percent of the AFDC population is
reported to have drug abuse problems (primarily analysis of the 1975 AFDC
Survey data). Thus, drug use data were not analyzed for this sample.

$\underline{10/}$For a portion of this sample, we compared interview data on
reported arrests with information obtained through state crime records and
found that both experimentals and controls under-report the occurrence of
an arrest (Schore et al., 1979). However, there was not a significant
differential between the two groups in the extent of under-reporting.

$\underline{11/}$Supported Work has not been compared with CETA programs, except
the Job Corps, mainly because these CETA programs have been subjected to
little careful evaluation. For a criticism of evaluations of CETA programs
that were based on very simple short-run performance indicators such as
initial placement rates, see Gay and Borus (forthcoming).

$\underline{12/}$According to interview data, about 90 percent of the sample met
these eligibility criteria.

$\underline{13/}$Over two-thirds of the Supported Work AFDC sample had not held
a job in the two years preceding their enrollment in the national demonstration, while just over one-third of the WIN participants fell into this
category. See Maynard et al. (1977).

$\underline{14/}$The more recent Ketron report presents estimates of median
effects of WIN on earnings that range from $18 per month for those partici-
pating in vocational training to $89 per month for those in the on-the-job
training component of the program. Both studies indicate that the orienta-
tion and education components of WIN have virtually no effect on subsequent
earnings. One of the main differences between these two studies is their
definition of the base period and their definition of post-program. The
PSE and OJT results in both studies include some in-program experience.
Furthermore, the Ketron results are based on very small sample sizes.

[15/] The $56 figure is obtained by subtracting the program earnings of experimentals. The difference between the two estimates represents the effects of assuming that, if they were not in the program, those with Supported Work earnings in months 16-18 would compensate by increasing their earnings from other jobs either completely (the $78 estimate) or not at all (the $56 estimate).

[16/] Those judged to have a relatively low probability of committing a theft crime and excluded from the LIFE experiment include those who were first-time offenders, had never committed a property crime, were over 45 years old and had been on work release for more than three months.

[17/] On a priori grounds, it might be argued that the program should be aimed at those just released from prison and, thus, needing help with financial and other adjustments. However, preliminary analysis of the data suggests that the results are not sensitive to the length of time since the individual's release from jail or prison.

[18/] As a result of the crime effects for ex-addicts, the benefit-cost results for Supported Work are more favorable (from both societal and non-participant perspectives) than those for the ex-offender and youth target groups. These benefit-cost results focus entirely on efficiency effects. Because of distributional considerations, the program may be regarded very positively, even though, for each target group, measured benefits are less than costs. See Kemper, Long and Thornton (1979).

[19/] See the literature review in Perry et al. (1975). See also the recent more negative results for these programs in Gay and Borus (forthcoming).

[20/] The Job Corps results apply mainly to the program as of about 1977, a period that is encompassed by our Supported Work analysis. The study is based on a comparison group design which focuses on differences in the changes over time in the dependent variables between enrollees and comparison group members. This approach appears as good as can be done in the absence of random assignment but cannot account for possible self-selectivity effects.

[21/] From conversations with program operators, it appears that, on average, the AFDC women are the most enthusiastic and cooperative workers. As noted previously, their average period of enrollment is also the longest, and that for ex-offenders is the shortest, although program operators appear to have the most difficulty with the youths.

[22/] Jobs explicitly identified as CETA/WIN account for about 20 percent of non-Supported Work jobs for AFDC and about 10 percent for the other three target groups. If other jobs with state and local government are included (on the assumption that some of those jobs are subsidized without the respondents being aware of this subsidization), then the percentage of CETA/WIN jobs may be as high as 40 percent for AFDC, 25 percent for youth, and 20 percent for ex-offenders and ex-addicts.

[23/] For example, Ashenfelter (1978) finds evidence that impacts of employment programs decay over time for male participants, but not for female participants. The recent evaluation of the Job Corps program (Mallar et al., 1978), however, shows some increase in effects over time, but this may be due to the time lag resulting from returning home from the centers, which is a unique feature of the Job Corps program.

[24/] Except for participants in the New York Supported Work program, such benefits were obtained through the Special Unemployment Assistance Program, which pays benefits to individuals who do not work in jobs covered by state UI systems, but otherwise have sufficient earnings to be eligible. The duration of benefits varies, but seldom exceeds 39 weeks. The program, which

began in 1975, was terminated for new claims at the end of 1977 and all payments ended July 1, 1978. Thus, the program should have a much more limited
impact on 27- and 36-month results.

[25/] In addition to the UC argument developed in the text, longer-run
effects might be larger than those observed for the 16- to 18-month period
if Supported Work enabled experimentals to obtain and hold jobs with better
prospects for promotion. Preliminary analysis of longer-term follow-up data
for these Supported Work samples indicate that, in general, the favorable
employment effects for the AFDC target group persist. However, conclusions
concerning longer-run impacts for the other target groups are less clear-cut.
At best, the results appear to be substantially less favorable than those for
the AFDC target group, and we may find, in fact, that there are no long-run
employment effects.

[26/] The experimental-control differentials are still appropriate for
estimating the benefits and costs of the program from the perspective of
participants. If the program affects the earnings of nonparticipants (whether
those in the control group or others), then experimental-control differentials
need not give unbiased estimates of benefits and costs from the social perspective. Due to the small size of the Supported Work program, the average
effects on nonparticipants are likely to be very small. Since many nonparticipants could be affected, however, the aggregate costs (or benefits)
to nonparticipants may be significant relative to the total cost of the
program.

[27/] For further discussion, see Johnson (1979). See also Bishop
(1979).

[28/] The Youth Incentive Entitlement Pilot Projects being run by the
Manpower Demonstration Research Corporation for the Department of Labor
represents an attempt to address labor market impacts in this manner. So
do the Employment Opportunity Pilot Projects currently being designed by
the Department of Labor.

REFERENCES

Ashenfelter, O. 1978. Estimating the effect of training programs on
   earnings. The Review of Economics and Statistics, 60:47-57.

Bass, U. and Woodward, S. 1978. Skills training and employment for
   ex-addicts in Washington: A report on TREAT. Washington, D.C.:
   U.S. Department of Health, Education and Welfare.

Bishop, J. 1979. The general equilibrium impact of alternative anti-
   poverty strategies. Industrial and Labor Relations Review, 32(2):
   205-223.

Cook, P.J. 1975. The correctional carrot: Better jobs for parolees.
   Policy Analysis, 1:11-54.

Friedman, Lee. 1977. An interim evaluation of the Supported Work experiment. Policy Analysis, 3(2):147-170.

Friedman, Lucy. 1978. The Wildcat experiment: An early test of Supported
   Work. New York: The Vera Institute of Justice.

Gay, R. and Borus, M. Forthcoming. Validating performance indicators for
   employment and training programs. Journal of Human Resources.

Hamermesh, D. 1978. Subsidies for jobs in the private sector. In J. Palmer (ed.), Creating jobs: Public employment programs and wage subsidies. Washington, D.C.: The Brookings Institution.

Johnson, G. 1979. The labor market displacement effect in the analysis of the net impact of manpower training programs. In F. Block (ed.), Evaluating manpower training programs. Supplement to Research in Labor Economics, vol. 1, Greenwich, Conn.: Johnson Associates, Inc.

Kemper, P., Long, D., and Thornton, C. 1979. The Supported Work evaluation: Final benefit-cost analysis, Princeton, N.J.: Mathematica Policy Research, Inc.

Ketron, Inc. 1979. Differential impact analysis of the WIN II program. Wayne, Pa.: Ketron, Inc. (draft, not to be quoted).

Mallar, C. et al. 1978. Evaluation of the economic impact of the Job Corps: First follow-up report. Princeton, N.J.: Mathematica Policy Research, Inc.

Mallar, C. and Thornton, C. 1978. Transitional aid for released prisoners: Evidence from the LIFE experiment. Journal of Human Resources, 13(2): 208-236.

Manpower Demonstration Research Corporation. 1978. Second Annual Report of the National Supported Work Demonstration. New York: Manpower Demonstration Research Corporation.

Maynard, R. et al. 1977. Analysis of nine-month interviews for Supported Work: Results of an early AFDC sample. New York: Manpower Demonstration Research Corporation.

Maynard R., Brown, R. and Schore, J. 1979. The National Supported Work Demonstration: Effects during the first 18 months after enrollment. New York: Manpower Demonstration Research Corporation.

Perry, C. et al. 1975. The impact of government manpower programs. Philadelphia, Pa.: Industrial Relations Unit, University of Pennsylvania.

Schiller, B. 1978. Lessons for WIN: A manpower evaluation. Journal of Human Resources, 13(4):502-523.

Schore, J., Maynard, R., and Piliavin, I. 1979. The accuracy of self-reported arrest data. Princeton, N.J.: Mathematica Policy Research, Inc.

Smith, C., Martinez, P. and Harrison, O. 1978. An assessment: The impact of providing financial job placement assistance to ex-prisoners. Huntsville, Texas: Texas Department of Corrections.

Stephens, J. and Sanders, L. 1978. Transitional aid for ex-offenders: An experimental study in Georgia. Atlanta: Georgia Department of Offender Rehabilitation.

Taggart, R. 1972. The prison of unemployment. Baltimore, Md.: Johns Hopkins University Press.

Westat, Inc. 1977. Characteristics of new enrollees who entered CETA programs during fiscal year 1976. Continuous Longitudinal Manpower Survey Report no. 6. Rockville, Md.: Westat, Inc.

III

LABOR FORCE PROGRAMS: NATURAL EXPERIMENTS

This section is concerned with measuring the impact of employment or training programs: the chapters by Ashenfelter and Kiefer on classroom training under the Manpower Development and Training Act, Mallar et al. on subsidized employment and training under the Job Corps, and Farkas et al. on subsidized employment and mandated schooling within the Youth Entitlement Demonstration. These programs are similar in design to the National Supported Work Demonstration reported by Masters and Maynard in Part II, but their evaluations are collected here because they are natural rather than designed experiments: Instead of random assignment to treatment status, they involve self-selected program participants and a "matched" control group of nonparticipants. As a result, the methodological themes of this volume assume particular prominence for these evaluations.

THE CHOICE OF A COMPARISON GROUP

Ashenfelter's chapter is one of the most reliable attempts to apply a quasi-experimental methdology to manpower program evaluation: He confronted a situation in which program planners and managers had made no provision for a control group. His solution—to use a sample drawn from social security earnings records—is both clever and adventuresome. It is also of interest to note that he tried two other means of assembling a comparison group—in one case using program dropouts, and in the other using the preprogram behavior of later program participants. His autoregressive model of earnings leads him to reject these groups as not evolving according to the same general earnings pattern as the program participants.

The chapter by Kiefer provides an interesting contrast, because it is a later evaluation of the same program. In this case, a control group was found as follows: "Trainees from 10 SMSA's were sampled and a subsample of the trainee group was matched on age, race, and sex to a sample of individuals from the same SMSA's who were eligible for training but did not participate in a program. Each member of the group of nonparticipants was matched to a member of the trainee group and interviewed as close as possible to the same time the trainee was interviewed." Kiefer's chapter is also of interest because the model he uses is related to, but significantly different from, Ashenfelter's.

The Job Corps evaluation by Mallar et al. employs a control group developed in a similar manner to Kiefer's. It also includes regression-adjusted experimental/control comparisons using Heckman's inverse Mills ratio term to correct for possible self-selection bias. (See Part I.) Finally, the Entitlement Demonstration evaluation study by Farkas et al. describes a design extending the strategy of a "found" comparison group. In this case, the program is administered within a SMSA, rural county, or major portion thereof, and a control site of generally similar location and demographic composition is selected. Random samples of program eligibles are then chosen in both experimental and control sites, and these are reinterviewed periodically throughout the life of the program. Some sample members in the experimental sites eventually join the program, permitting the estimation of a program participation function for these sites alone. This can be used to correct for self-selection bias, or, in an entirely different strategy, outcomes can be compared for experimental and control sites as entireties. With this strategy the treatment is exogenous, and self-selection bias is not an issue.

The Entitlement design permitting comparison of entire experimental and control sites, as opposed to the comparison of program participants and a found group of nonparticipants, raises an important, but often neglected, issue: The inability of a social experiment dealing with human subjects to really impose the treatment on them. Thus, many participants drop out of the program after only a few months. As a result, even with random assignment (as in the evaluation of the Supported Work Demonstration reported in Part II) many members of the experimental group have experienced very little exposure to the treatment. Thus, the "treatment" might more correctly be viewed as the *opportunity* to join a program of a particular type, so that self-selection is seen as necessarily an integral part of program outcome. From this perspective the treatment can be considered exogenous, and a research design comparing entire sites where the program was made available to those where it was not offered becomes particularly attractive.[1] (The Employment Opportunity Pilot Projects are a recent program embodying this research design. See the chapter by Bishop et al. in Part VIII.)

STATISTICAL MODELS

Ashenfelter considers a variety of statistical specifications designed to exploit fully the more than ten years of earnings information available for MDTA participants and the comparison group. His principle model (equation 7) employs a dynamic "earnings generation process" in which earnings from each post-program year are regressed on preprogram earnings, age, and a program-participation dummy variable.[2] Ashenfelter introduces one of the themes of our volume—bias possibly arising from self-selection into treatment status—by noting that this calculation fails to account for the possibility that an unmeasured individual-level component of earnings is correlated with trainee status even after including age and preprogram earnings in the equation. He then observes that the magnitude of the resulting bias is likely decreased if the dependent variable is taken to be a first difference in earnings, a calculation he then undertakes (equation 12 and Table 5). Ashenfelter also observes (n. 14) that if both sides of the equation are estimated in first-differences, bias should be eliminated altogether. He does not, however, provide this calculation.

Kiefer begins at essentially this point. His data are different than Ashenfelter's, his focus is on wage rates rather than earnings, and he has no interest in a dynamic model. Yet the kernel of this paper is contained in Ashenfelter's note 14. The point is that by taking deviations of all variables from their overtime means, unchanging but unmeasured individual-level effects are eliminated, as is their associated potential selection bias. The result is a quite simple specification, in which wages are regressed on an intercept, age, and a program-participation dummy variable. (See Kiefer's Table 3. Note, however, that this is estimated via generalized, rather than ordinary, least squares.) Kiefer also presents an instrumental variable estimate of the program effect, and notes the existence of a discrepancy between the two results. Taken together, however, they suggest that the effect of training is small and positive.

Mallar et al. focus on labor force outcomes of subsidized employment and training (although results for a variety of other outcome variables are also reported). The approach is similar to Ashenfelter's and Kiefer's, with before/after, experimental/control comparisons reported under a variety of model specifications. Of particular interest is the distinction the authors make among experimental group members according to whether they were program completers, partial completers, or early dropouts. For each of these groups (and separately by sex) eleven different specifications are used to examine program effects on weekly earnings. (See Table 4.) These begin with simple before/after mean differences, progress through regressions of postprogram earnings on an experimental/control dummy and other variables (including preprogram earnings), and end with a series of such regressions in which Heckman's inverse Mills ratio term is an added predictor. (Also of interest are the variables the authors report as successfully identifying this relation.)[3] The stability of the findings across the various specifications is an encouraging aspect of the results.

The Entitlement Demonstration is in an earlier state than the Job Corps, with outcome measures not yet available, so the chapter by Farkas et al. examines a number of modeling issues that can be addressed with preprogram data. One theme is that whereas reduced-form models leading to simple experimental/control comparisons (such as those discussed above) are important evaluation tools, it is also desirable to formulate and estimate structural models wherever possible. The gains from such a strategy are illustrated with models fit to the baseline evaluation data. Here the structural model is concerned with youth labor supply during the summer and contains a number of interesting features. A wage equation corrected for possible selectivity bias is estimated by maximum likelihood, both with and without the assumption of normal (Gaussian) residuals, and this assumption is shown to lead to potentially misleading results. A labor supply equation is then estimated via a truncated normal regression for hours worked, and in combination with the probit for employed at all (wage rate observed), this permits estimating both reservation wage rates and a "disemployment index" that measures fixed costs of working and demand side distortions. The highly significant constant term in the disemployment index demonstrates, in two stages, the superiority of modeling the probability of being employed and the hours worked by those employed in two stages—a probit combined with a truncated normal—rather than with a single tobit. (See Heckman, 1974, and the Introduction to Part I.) Indeed, the results presented here point up what should always have been obvious: The tobit is a rather restrictive specification, which does not always contain sufficient parameters to provide a good fit to both the probability of experiencing a particular outcome and also to the distribution of that outcome among those experiencing it.

The work for the evaluation of the Entitlement Demonstration is in an exploratory stage. As further data become available, the authors will fit reduced-form models to estimate basic program effects in a way similar to the other papers in this section. A variety of structural models will be fit to the (by then) several waves of data. The goal of this research program is reliable program effect estimates, the exploration of their underlying mechanisms, and a guide to the generalizability of the results.

RESULTS

The work by Ashenfelter and Kiefer on training programs and the study by Mallar et al. on the Job Corps are the most reliable to date. Their results, however, reflect continuing uncertainty regarding the magnitude of program effects. Ashenfelter finds statistically significant effects for a national sample of men and women who began training in the first three months of 1964. The results decay for men over the five-year follow-up period but hold steady for women. There is some concern that the results for women reflect selection bias that is uncorrected for in the model. (Nonresponse bias is also not adjusted for.) But the results of the Supported Work Experiment, where selection bias is not an issue, also show positive and significant effects for women (see Masters and Maynard, Part II). Thus, because of the nature of the sample, the methods used, and the corroborative evidence, one is disposed to place considerable policy weight on Ashenfelter's findings. But using related techniques with different data, Kiefer finds positive but insignificant effects in the third quarter after training. It is clear that some ambiguity remains.

Mallar et al. provide the most definitive estimates of Job Corps impact since the work of Cain (1967), who found cost-benefit ratios hovering around 1.0. But while the Mallar study is based on a much more appropriate data set, approximately half of the program benefits are due to decreases in criminal activity rather than to employment-related measures. And the gains from reduced criminality, being synthesized from several data sources, are likely less reliable than the estimates Mallar finds for improved labor market performance.

Thus, the picture is still mixed. Training programs have a positive effect, but this effect is not large; where positive results are observed, we still do not always understand the mechanisms underlying the outcomes. It may be tiresome by now, but the correct conclusion still seems to be: more analysis is needed.

NOTES

1. But consider the problem of whether two different sites can ever really be comparable. A better design might be a split-plot: Offer the program in only one half of each site.
2. This is the model generating the results reported in Tables 4 and 6 of Ashenfelter's chapter.
3. For a more complete guide to these methods and results, see Mallar et al. (1978, forthcoming).

REFERENCES

CAIN, G. G. (1967) Benefit/Cost Estimates for Job Corps. Madison, WI: University of Wisconsin, Institute for Research on Poverty.
HECKMAN, J. (1974) "Shadow prices, market wages, and labor supply." Econometrica 42: 679-694.
MALLAR, C. et al. (forthcoming) Evaluation of the Economic Impact of the Job Corps Program: Second Follow-Up Report. Prepared for Office of Program Evaluation, Employment and Training Administration, U.S. Department of Labor.
——— (1978) Evaluation of the Economic Impact of the Job Corps Program: First Follow-Up Report (December). Prepared for Office of Program Evaluation, Employment and Training Administration, U.S. Department of Labor.

13

Ashenfelter fits an "earnings determination function" (expression 1, rewritten as expressions 7 and 12 to include the effects of training) that includes previous earnings as a right-hand-side variable. The coefficient for this variable has no structural interpretation, but its presence in the equation may increase the efficiency with which the coefficient for the experimental/control group dummy variable is measured. In this model, the effects of training cumulate over time through the autoregressive earnings function, so that if we regress postprogram earnings for any particular year on preprogram earnings and the experimental/comparison group dummy variable, the cumulative program effect can be read off from the coefficient on the latter. This is the model given in the third line of expression 7 and used to estimate the effects reported in Tables 4 and 6. An important aspect of this specification is that since all lagged earnings are preprogram, estimating the program effect is not complicated by endogeneity.[1]

The other model estimated by Ashenfelter (expression 12 and Table 5) uses a first difference as the dependent variable to decrease the bias potentially associated with selection into experimental or control group on the basis of unmeasured personal characteristics. (A similar model, but without explicit lagged earnings measures, is estimated by Kiefer [Ch. 14].) Ashenfelter observes (n. 14) that using in addition a first difference on the right-hand-side should eliminate this bias altogether, but he does not try this since with so many years of data, such a model would yield program effect measures only after complex calculations, and then the standard errors would likely be large.

NOTE

1. With so many years available, it might be attractive to stack the data into one regression to estimate fewer parameters for the variables of no real substantive interest. (For one example of such

stacking, but with data at only two time points, see the article by Hausman and Wise in Part I.) However, in Ashenfelter's situation this would create a number of specification and estimation difficulties.

Estimating the Effect of Training Programs on Earnings

Orley Ashenfelter

GOVERNMENTAL post-schooling training programs have become a permanent fixture of the U.S. economy in the last decade. These programs are typically advocated for diverse reasons: (1) to reduce inflation by the provision of more skilled workers to alleviate shortages, (2) to reduce unemployment of certain groups, and (3) to reduce poverty by increasing the skills of certain groups. All of these objectives require that training programs increase the earnings of trainees above what they otherwise would be. For example, alleviating shortages by training more highly skilled workers should increase the earnings of these workers. Likewise, the concern for unemployed workers is derived from a concern for the decreased earnings of these workers; and if trainees subsequently suffer less unemployment, their earnings should be higher. Finally, training programs are intended to reduce poverty by increasing the earnings of low income workers.

Evaluating the success of training programs is thus inherently a quantitative assessment of the effect of training on trainee earnings.[1] It is an important process both because it helps to inform discussions of public policy by shedding light on the past value of these programs as investments and because it can provide a means of testing our ability to augment the human capital of certain workers. Although there have been many studies of the effect of post-school classroom training on earnings it is by now rather widely agreed that very little is

reliably known about the actual effects of these programs.[2] Three main problems account for this state of affairs: (1) the large sample sizes required to detect relatively small anticipated program effects in a variable with such high variance as earnings, (2) the considerable expense required to keep track of trainees over a long enough period of time to measure the full inter-temporal impact of training, and (3) the extreme difficulty of implementing an adequate experimental design so as to obtain a group against which to reliably compare trainees.[3] The purpose of this paper is to report on efforts to cope with this third problem using a data collection system that comes some way towards resolving the first two.

The basic idea of this data system is to match the program record on each trainee with the trainee's Social Security earnings history. The Social Security Administration maintains a summary year-by-year earnings history for each Social Security account over the period since 1950 that may be used, under the appropriate confidentiality restrictions, for this purpose.[4] In this paper I have concentrated on an analysis of all classroom trainees who started training under the Manpower Development and Training Act (MDTA) in the first 3 months of 1964 so as to ensure their having completed training in that year. In choosing to analyze trainees from so early a cohort something is clearly lost. On the one hand, the nature of the participants in these early years was considerably different than in the later years. In particular, programs geared

Received for publication February 9, 1977. Revision accepted for publication August 1, 1977.

* Princeton University.

This research was supported by ASPER, U.S. Department of Labor, but does not represent an official position of the Department of Labor, its agencies, or staff. I would like to thank Gregory Chow, George E. Ehrenberg, Roger Gordon, Zvi Griliches, George E. Johnson, Nicholas Kiefer, Richard Quandt, and Sherwin Rosen for helpful comments. I also owe a heavy debt to D. Alton Smith for computational and other assistance.

[1] See Reid (1976), for example, for a clear analysis of how knowledge of these effects is required in order to establish the impact of government training on the black/white wage differential.

[2] Surveys of many of these studies may be found in Stromsdorfer (1972) and O'Neill (1973).

[3] For further discussion of these points see Ashenfelter (1975).

[4] The idea for using these data to analyze the effectiveness of government training programs is apparently quite an old one, having been suggested by the National Manpower Advisory Committee (U.S. Department of Labor, 1972) to the Secretary of Labor at its first meeting in a letter dated October 10, 1962, the year of passage of the Manpower Development and Training Act. Actual efforts along these lines were ultimately reported by Borus (1967), Commins (1970), Farber (1970), and Prescott and Cooley (1972).

From Orley Ashenfelter, "Estimating the Effects of Training Programs on Earnings," 60(1) *Review of Economics and Statistics* 47-57 (February 1978). Copyright 1977 by North-Holland Publishing Company.

to the most easily trained during the high unemployment years of the early 1960s gave way to programs geared to the so-called disadvantaged worker in the late 1960s. This change shows up in program administrative statistics as sharp increases in early terminations (dropouts) from the training programs and a decline in the average age and education level of trainees. In more recent years the MDTA has given way to the Comprehensive Employment and Training Act and a considerable decentralization of administrative control to state and local governments. For both of these reasons it is unclear how relevant any results for this early cohort of trainees are for current discussions of public policy. At the same time, the study of this 1964 cohort offers several advantages. First, it is technically feasible to follow this cohort's progress in the labor market for many years after training, something which cannot be done with recent cohorts. Second, if convincing estimates of trainee effects can be generated for the early years of the program these may serve as benchmarks against which to assess the desirability of the subsequent changes in the focus of government efforts in this area.

The plan of the paper is as follows: Section I contains a discussion of the conceptual framework for the analysis, including its connection with the emerging literature on investments in human capital. Section II contains a further discussion of the data to be used and the empirical results, while section III is a discussion of the limitations of the results and the considerable additional research required in this area.

I. Earnings Generating Functions and Training

An adequate longitudinal data base on trainee earnings is not sufficient information for the analysis of the effect of training on earnings in a changing economy. It is also necessary to have an adequate comparison group of individuals against whom to benchmark the earnings of trainees so that general changes in earnings are not taken to be the effect of training. In the classical sample design some fraction of a training program's applicants would be randomly assigned to

training while the remainder would be reserved as a comparison group. For a variety of reasons, actual training programs have not been operated in this way and it therefore becomes necessary to look elsewhere for a comparison group. Although there are several possibilities, in this paper I have drawn on the 0.1% Continuous Work History Sample (CWHS) to serve this purpose.[5] The CWHS is a random sample of longitudinal earnings records on American workers that is maintained for general research purposes by the Social Security Administration. Since the trainee and comparison groups are obviously not being drawn from the same population it is thus necessary to control statistically for differences between the two groups. In order to do this it is necessary to have a specification of the earnings function that would prevail for both groups in the absence of the training program.

A. The Earnings Function

A useful specification of earnings determination in longitudinal data is

$$y_{it} = \alpha + \sum_{j=1}^{k} \beta_j y_{i(t-j)} + \sum_{j=1}^{k'} \beta_j' (A_i + t)^j + \epsilon_i + \epsilon_t + \epsilon_{it}, \tag{1}$$

where y_{it} is the earnings of the ith individual in period t, A_i is the age of the ith individual in period $t=0$, the α and β's are parameters, and the disturbance term $\epsilon_{it}' = \epsilon_i + \epsilon_t + \epsilon_{it}$ is taken to have an effect ϵ_i specific to an individual, an effect ϵ_t specific to the time period, and a remainder ϵ_{it} with zero expectation. In this framework current earnings are taken to be the sum of a polynomial in age and/or an

[5] I have also experimented with two other comparison groups. In one case dropouts from the program were used as a comparison group for completers of the program. In another case, trainees entering training in 1967 were used as a comparison group for the 1964 cohort of trainees. Both schemes led to large estimates of the effect of training on earnings, but in both cases the internal checks for similarity of the trainee and comparison group earnings structures that I report below for the CWHS comparison group led me to conclude that while the CWHS was far from ideal in this regard, it was more satisfactory for the 1964 cohort than were the alternatives. I am not so convinced that this would be the case with later cohorts where the selection criteria for program entrance had changed from enrollment of those most likely to be successful to enrollment of the disadvantaged worker.

autoregression in earnings plus the error components comprising fixed and random effects. The fixed effect ϵ_i presumably captures such factors as ability, motivation, or other previous investments in human capital by a specific worker, while the effect ϵ_t captures economy-wide movements in earnings. To the extent that these error components are removed in the estimation process it is worth observing that fitting equation (1) does not require explicit measurement of schooling level or any of the other unchanging variables usually taken to determine earnings. The effects of these variables on earnings are already captured in equation (1).

There are at least three alternative ways to rationalize the use of equation (1) as the basis for a predictor of earnings. At the most rudimentary level, surely any theory of the determination of earnings will imply that current earnings are the result of a variety of historical factors, such as education, experience, social class, and others, that influence earnings capacity. Moreover, good summary measures of this cumulative experience for a worker are surely his age and previous earnings. In effect, equation (1) exploits these rudimentary notions.

Alternatively, one may inquire as to whether equation (1) can characterize the known facts about the structure of earnings. One of these facts, for example, is the finding that over a wide range of the age distribution earnings increase with age, but at a decreasing rate.[6] It is obvious that the polynomial in (1) can accommodate these facts, but it is easy to see that the autoregression can do so also. Consider, for example, the first-order autoregression $y_t = \alpha + \beta y_{t-1}$. This difference equation has the solution $y_t = [y_0 - (\alpha/(1-\beta))]\beta^t + (\alpha/(1-\beta))$. For $0 < \beta < 1$ and $y_0 < \alpha/(1-\beta)$, earnings approaches the asymptote $\alpha/(1-\beta)$ gradually from below in just the manner of the empirical age-earnings profiles so often observed.[7]

Finally, equation (1) may also be rationalized as the end result of an optimal investment

program in human capital by individual workers. Rosen (1976) has called equations like (1) earnings generating functions, and one might reasonably characterize the emerging literature on the theory of optimum post-schooling investment as an attempt to define the restrictions on equations like (1) that arise if individuals are behaving so as to maximize $\sum_t y_t (1 + r)^{-t}$, the discounted value of lifetime earnings at the discount rate r. To see that equation (1) is consistent with such theories consider the income accounting equation so widely used in the analysis of human capital investments,

$$y_t = y_0 + \sum_{i=0}^{t-1} r_i c_i - c_t, \qquad (2)$$

where r_i is the average rate of return on the dollar investments c_i in the ith period.[8] The sum $y_0 + \sum r_i c_i$ is potential earnings in the tth period and is greater than actual earnings by the dollar costs of current investments, c_t. An optimal path for the accumulation of human capital implies optimizing paths for the r_i and c_i. Suppose first that these may each be approximated by polynomial functions in i. It is then an easy matter to show that (2) will take the form of a polynomial in age.[9] Alternatively, suppose that the sequences r_i and c_i may each be approximated by a weighted sum of power functions. It is then an easy matter to show that (2) takes the form of the solution of a difference equation that is the equivalent of the autoregressive component of (1).[10] Of course,

---

[6] See the extensive discussion by Mincer (1974).

[7] As an experiment, the fitted results of a regression of earnings in 1964 on earnings in 1963 in the CWHS comparison group for white males gives $\alpha = \$700$ (9.7), $\beta = 0.83$ (.003) (with estimated standard errors in parentheses), and a coefficient of determination (R^2) of 0.716. This implies a static age-earnings profile of $Y_t = \$4,118. + (Y_0 - 4,118.) (.83)^t$ which has the "typical" age-earnings shape.

[8] This accounting equation plays a large role in Becker's (1964) seminal work.

[9] Put $r_i = \sum a_m (i)^m$ and $c_i = \sum b_n (i)^n$ so that $r_i c_i = \sum d_j (i)^j$ where $d_j = a_m b_n$. Substituting into (2) then gives

$$y_t = y_0 + \sum_{i=0}^{t-1} \sum d_j (i)^j - \sum b_n (t)^n$$

$$= y_0 + \sum d_j \sum_{i=0}^{t-1} (i)^j - \sum b_n (t)^n$$

$$= y_0 + \sum d_j \sum_{k=1}^{j+1} \delta_k (t)^k - \sum b_n (t)^n,$$

where the δ_k coefficients are given implicitly by the formulas for the sum of the powers of the first $t-1$ integers, which is simply a polynomial in age.

[10] Put $r_i = \sum d_m (\lambda_m)^i$ and $c_i = \sum b_n (\mu_n)^i$ so that $r_i c_i$

the fact that the data are consistent with equation (1) is not a test of models of optimum post-schooling investment unless there are further restrictions deduced from the theory that may be imposed onto equation (1). After all, polynomial and/or power function approximations to the sequences r_t and c_t exist even if the latter do not result from an optimizing model. Nevertheless, it is important to observe here that equation (1) is not a priori inconsistent with such models.

B. The Effect of Training

To examine the effect of training on earnings it is convenient to re-write the Kth-order difference equation as a first order difference equation using the matrix notation $z_t = [y_t, y_{t-1} \cdots y_{t-k+1}]'$; $z_{t-1} = [y_{t-1}, y_t, \cdots y_{t-k}]'$; $d_{it} = [\alpha + \sum_j \beta_j'(A_t + t)' + \epsilon_t]\gamma$; where γ is a k-component vector with a unity in the first row and zeros in the remaining $k-1$ rows; $b_t = \epsilon_t \gamma$; and $u_{it} = \epsilon_{it} \gamma$. Letting B represent a matrix of order $(k \times k)$ with the elements of β_j as its first row and units below the diagonal, we may write equation (1) for the comparison group as

$$z_{it}^c = B z_{i(t-1)}^c + d_{it} + b_t + u_{it}. \tag{3}$$

and for the trainee participant group as

$$z_{it}^p = B z_{i(t-1)}^p + d_{it} + b_t + R_t + u_{it}. \tag{4}$$

where R_t is the incremental effect of training on trainee earnings in the tth period. Of course, $R_t = 0$ in the periods prior to training and it is likely that $R_t < 0$ during the training period. Equation (1) may now be read off of the top row of (3) or (4).

In this framework the amount by which the earnings of a trainee in the tth period are greater than they would have been in the absence of training cannot be obtained from equation (4) without further manipulation

---

$= d_j(\delta_j)^t$ where $d_j = a_m b_n$ and $\delta_j = \lambda_m \mu_n$. Substituting into (2) then gives

$$y_t = y_0 + \sum_{i=0}^{t-1} \sum d_j(\delta_j)^i - \sum b_n(\mu_n)^t$$

$$= y_0 + \sum d_j(1 - \delta_j)^t/(1 - \delta_j) - \sum b_n(\mu_n)^t$$

$$= B' + \sum d_j'(\delta_j)^t - \sum b_n(\mu_n)^t.$$

where $B' = y_0 + \sum d_j/(1 - \delta_j)$ and $d_j' = -d_j/(1 - \delta_j)$, which is the solution of a difference equation like (1) and is thus an alternative expression for it.

because the effects R_t will cumulate through the earnings generation process. To determine the effect of training on earnings in the tth period suppose that it is known that the period prior to the advent of training is the $(t-s)$th. Writing equation (4) repeatedly in lagged form and continuously substituting then gives

$$z_{it}^p = B^{s-1} z_{i(t-s)}^p + \sum_{\tau=0}^{s-1} B^\tau [d_{i(t-\tau)} + u_{i(t-\tau)} + R_{t-\tau}]$$

$$+ \sum_{\tau=0}^{s-1} B^\tau b_t$$

$$= B^s z_{i(t-s)}^p + d_{is}^* + R_s^* + b_{is}^* + u_{is}^* \tag{5}$$

where the second line reflects some obvious notational simplification. The same process applied to equation (3) then gives

$$z_{it}^c = B^s z_{i(t-s)}^c + d_{is}^* + b_{is}^* + u_{is}^* \tag{6}$$

for the comparison group individual. Comparing (5) and (6) it is clear that the term $R_s^* = \sum_{\tau=0}^{s-1} B^\tau R_{t-\tau}$ is the amount by which earnings are higher for trainees in the tth period than would have been the case in the absence of training. In more conventional terms, the discounted present value of the net private benefits of training (to the trainee) is simply $\sum_{s=1}^{\infty} R_s^*(1 + r)^{-s}$ at period $(t-s)$ when the discount rate is r.

For estimation purposes we may define the variable $p_i = 1$ for those who become trainees in the $(t-s+1)$st period and zero otherwise. Then observed earnings for the ith individual are

$$z_{it} = p_i z_{it}^p + (1 - p_i) z_{it}^c$$

$$= B z_{i(t-1)} + d_{it} + b_t + R_t p_i + u_{it}$$

$$= B^s z_{i(t-s)} + d_{is}^* + b_{is}^* + R_s^* p_i + u_{is}^*. \tag{7}$$

Since u_{is}^* is uncorrelated with $z_{i(t-s)}$ by construction and has expectation of zero as well, whether we fit the second line or the third line of equation (7) to the data is a matter of convenience. In the first case we merely regress earnings in each period on earnings in the k previous periods and include a dummy variable for trainee participation. In the latter case we regress earnings in each period on the earnings in the k periods prior to training and include a dummy variable for trainee participation. The latter scheme has the advantage that it provides direct estimates of the training effects because the R_s^* are treated directly as parameters for estimation. The former scheme requires considerable additional manipulation to obtain the training effects since they must be derived from the parameters of explicit interest and will consequently suffer from additional imprecision in estimation. On the other hand, as we shall see, the former scheme provides a much more convenient framework for handling the fixed individual effects b_i.

Finally, it should be observed that throughout the preceding discussion the hypothesis is maintained that the earnings generating functions are of the same form for the trainees and the comparison group members. This is a very strong assumption, and it is subjected to some limited tests below. In effect, one advantage of longitudinal data is that we may test the veracity of this hypothesis on the data for periods prior to the advent of training. If we find the earnings generating functions are different for the two groups prior to training this may serve as a signal of serious problems with the maintained hypothesis.

II. Data and Empirical Results

Table 1 contains sample statistics on the longitudinal earnings records of individuals aged 16 to 64 in four trainee and comparison groups broken down by race and sex. As can be seen from the table, all of the trainee groups suffer considerable declines in earnings in 1964, the year of training, and experience considerable increases in earnings after training. The table also reveals that the earnings of trainees tend to fall, both absolutely and relative to the comparison group, in the year prior to training. In retrospect this is not very surprising since the Department of Labor was instructed to enroll unemployed workers in the MDTA programs in this period and it is just such workers who would be most likely to want to enter a training program. Nevertheless, this result introduces considerable ambiguity into the empirical analysis for it suggests that some part of the observed earnings increase following training may merely be a return to a permanent path of earnings that was temporarily interrupted by one form of transitory labor market phenomenon or another. To the extent that this is the case the earnings generating functions of the trainee and comparison groups may differ considerably in the period just prior to training and cause considerable ambiguity in untangling the effect of training from the effect of this transitory phenomenon. To make the discussion concrete it is useful to continue in the context of a special case of equation (7).

A. Initial Estimates

In particular, suppose that $B = 0$ in equation (7) so that $B' = 0$ also and that $\beta_j' = 0$ for $j > 1$ so that $d_{it} = [\alpha + \beta_1'(A_i + t) + \epsilon_t]\gamma$. In this case there is no autoregressive component in earnings and merely a linear effect of age plus the fixed effects for the individual and time period. Although this might be a satisfactory approximation for short periods of time it is unlikely to be satisfactory over longer periods. Still, it is a convenient point of departure,

TABLE 1.—MEAN EARNINGS PRIOR, DURING, AND SUBSEQUENT TO TRAINING FOR 1964 MDTA CLASSROOM TRAINEES AND A COMPARISON GROUP

	White Males		Black Males		White Females		Black Females	
	Trainees	Comparison Group	Trainees	Comparison Group	Trainees	Comparison Group	Trainees	Comparison Group
1959	$1,443	$2,588	$ 904	$1,438	$ 635	$ 987	$ 384	$ 616
1960	1,533	2,699	976	1,521	687	1,076	440	693
1961	1,572	2,782	1,017	1,573	719	1,163	471	737
1962	1,843	2,963	1,211	1,742	813	1,308	566	843
1963	1,810	3,108	1,182	1,896	748	1,433	531	937
1964	1,551	3,275	1,273	2,121	838	1,580	688	1,060
1965	2,923	3,458	2,327	2,338	1,747	1,693	1,441	1,198
1966	3,750	4,351	2,983	2,919	2,024	1,990	1,794	1,461
1967	3,964	4,430	3,048	3,097	2,244	2,144	1,977	1,678
1968	4,401	4,955	3,409	3,487	2,398	2,339	2,160	1,920
1969	$4,717	$5,033	$3,714	$3,681	$2,646	$2,444	$2,457	$2,133
Number of Observations	7,326	40,921	2,133	6,472	2,730	28,142	1,356	5,192

because it allows a comparison of more sophisticated schemes against one that has been widely used in previous studies.

Now if $B = 0$, $R_s^* = R_t$ in equation (5) and this suggests a very simple estimator for R_t^*. In particular, equation (7) becomes

$$z_{it} = d_{it} + b_i + R_t p_i + u_{it}. \qquad (8)$$

Writing this relationship for period $t - s$ gives

$$z_{i(t-s)} = d_{i(t-s)} + b_i + u_{i(t-s)}. \qquad (9)$$

so that the difference between (8) and (9) is

$$z_{it} - z_{i(t-s)} = (d_{it} - d_{i(t-s)}) + R_t p_i$$
$$+ (u_{it} - u_{i(t-s)}), \qquad (10)$$

where $d_{it} - d_{i(t-s)} = [\beta_1' s + \epsilon_t - \epsilon_{t-s}] \gamma$ and is constant across individuals. According to (10), estimates of the training effects may be obtained by regressing the change in earnings from the period immediately preceding training to the tth period on a dummy variable indicating trainee participation. In using this procedure the individual b_i effects have been fully removed so that the effects on earnings of any variables that are unchanging have also been removed.[11]

Now the period $t - s$ is supposed to be the period immediately preceding training. However, there is no reason why this period must be used since with $R_t = 0$ in the periods prior to training any base period will do equally well. Suppose, however, that there is a decline of T dollars in the earnings of trainees relative to the comparison group in the period prior to training. If this decline is permanent, using a base period prior to the period $t - s$ will understate the training effect by T dollars. If the decline is transitory, and just offset by an increase of T dollars in earnings in the sequel, using a base period prior to the period $t - s$ will give an unbiased estimator of the true training effects. Just the reverse will be the case in these two situations if the base period is taken to be the $(t - s)^{th}$. There does not seem to be any way to remove this ambiguity in the results within

this framework, and so I have chosen to present results using both assumptions to see empirically how important this difficulty may be.

Estimates of the coefficients R_t obtained from fitting equation (10) to the data for white males are contained in table 2. As can be seen from the table, the estimates are sensitive to the base period used, varying by nearly $200 per year from highest to lowest. As expected, using 1963 as the base period produces the largest estimated training effects, although the second and third columns of table 2 indicate some discrepancy between the results using 1962 and 1961 as the base periods as well. Broadly speaking, these results indicate that training may have increased the earnings of white male trainees permanently by between $500 and $800 per year, and that foregone earnings were between $400 and $600 during the year of training.

TABLE 2.—CRUDE ESTIMATES (AND ESTIMATED STANDARD ERRORS), ASSUMING $B = 0$ AND $\beta_j' = 0$ FOR $j > 1$, OF THE EFFECT OF TRAINING ON EARNINGS DURING AND AFTER TRAINING. WHITE MALE MDTA 1964 CLASSROOM TRAINEES

Effect in (value of t)	Value of Effects for		
	$t - s = 1963$	$t - s = 1962$	$t - s = 1961$
1962	—	—	91 (13)
1963	—	−179 (14)	−88 (17)
1964	−426 (16)	−605 (18)	−514 (20)
1965	763 (20)	584 (22)	675 (23)
1966	697 (25)	518 (27)	609 (28)
1967	833 (28)	655 (30)	746 (31)
1968	745 (34)	566 (35)	657 (36)
1969	984 (37)	805 (39)	896 (40)

In this framework age enters equations (8) and (9) linearly only, and hence is eliminated from (10). It is a straightforward matter to relax this assumption. Taking the degree of the polynomial in age in (8) and (9) to be k' implies

---

[11] As a referee has pointed out, the b_i terms could be allowed coefficients different from unity and each other in equations (9) and (10) and equation (11) would be modified only to the extent that $z_{i(t-s)}$ would appear with a non-zero coefficient on the right-hand side. The disadvantage of this procedure is that the composite disturbance of (11) would then be correlated with $z_{i(t-s)}$, so that least-squares would no longer be a consistent estimator for (11).

that a polynomial in age of degree $k' - 1$ should enter equation (10). By the usual sum of squared errors criterion $k' = 3$ seemed satisfactory and this led to a regression of the change in earnings from the period immediately preceding training to the tth on a dummy variable indicating trainee participation and a quadratic in age. This procedure is very similar to many of the conventional earnings functions that have been estimated in the literature, but is perhaps an improvement because the individual b_i effects have been fully removed also. This, of course, is not possible with cross-sectional data alone.

Estimates of the coefficients R_t obtained from fitting this modified version of equation (10) to the data for white males for the sequence of values of t between 1962 and 1969 are reported in table 3. Again, there is no reason why the base period, $t - s$, cannot be taken to be any of the periods prior to training. As can be seen by comparing tables 2 and 3, the modification in equation (10) changes the estimates of the training effects R_t in two ways. First, all of the estimates of the training effects are considerably reduced, although they remain significantly greater than zero by the usual statistical criterion. Broadly speaking, the results in table 3 indicate that training may have increased the earnings of white male trainees permanently by between $200 and $500 per year, and that foregone earnings were between $500 and $700 during the year of training. Second, the results in table 3 differ only within sampling error as between those using 1962 and 1961 as the base years. Clearly the results in table 3 are based on a better specification of earnings determination than those in table 2 and are consequently to be preferred.

B. Additional Estimates

The specific assumption about the value of the matrix B used to generate simple estimators is convenient, but nevertheless unsatisfactory. Table 4 contains estimates of equation (7) for white males with $t - s = 1961$ and values of t ranging from 1962 through 1969. By the usual statistical criterion a linear term in age seemed adequate with this specification. The estimates in the first row of the table are essentially

TABLE 3.—ESTIMATES, ASSUMING $B = 0$, OF THE EFFECT OF TRAINING ON EARNINGS DURING AND AFTER TRAINING, WHITE MALE 1964 MDTA CLASSROOM TRAINEES

Effect in (value of t)	Value of Effects for		
	$t - s = 1963$	$t - s = 1962$	$t - s = 1961$
1962			52 (14)
1963		−238 (14)	−186 (17)
1964	−489 (15)	−728 (18)	−676 (20)
1965	605 (19)	368 (21)	419 (22)
1966	496 (25)	258 (26)	310 (27)
1967	532 (28)	294 (28)	345 (29)
1968	341 (33)	103 (33)	155 (34)
1969	472 (35)	234 (36)	286 (36)

estimates of the first row of the second line of equation (7) and they clearly imply that the assumption $B = 0$ is a poor empirical description of the data. These results also imply that the trainee and comparison group earnings functions differ with respect to intercept prior to training and that trainee earnings declined by some $300 to $400 in this period.[12]

The broad outline of the results in table 4 is consistent with the structure anticipated for them, although there are some anomalies. For one thing, moving down the columns of the table the coefficients of the lagged earnings variables begin to decay as would be expected from the fact that each successive row of the table is the uppermost row of the matrix B^s. This process seems to taper off more rapidly than it should, however. The age variable is measured in months and its coefficient should be read accordingly. The fact that these age coefficients are negative is not inconsistent with

[12] I have also tested these equations for structural differences in the other coefficients as between trainees and the comparison group. When the dependent variables are earnings in 1962, or 1966 through 1969, these differences are small, apart from intercepts. However, these results are only slightly reassuring regarding the assumption of equivalent earnings structures for the two groups, and this issue clearly deserves further attention.

TABLE 4.—ESTIMATED REGRESSION COEFFICIENTS (AND ESTIMATED STANDARD ERRORS) OF EQUATION (7) FOR WHITE MALE MDTA TRAINEES

The Dependent Variable is Earnings in	Constant	Training Variable	Coefficient of Earnings in					Age	R^2
			1961	1960	1959	1958	1957		
1962	536. (13.9)	−42.2 (13.0)	.679 (.005)	.115 (.006)	.071 (.006)	.021 (.007)	.031 (.006)	−1.98 (.434)	.78
1963	1072. (17.0)	−347. (16.0)	.558 (.006)	.136 (.007)	.086 (.008)	.031 (.008)	.030 (.007)	−6.70 (.534)	.65
1964	1665. (19.3)	−907. (18.2)	.465 (.007)	.133 (.008)	.073 (.009)	.043 (.009)	.049 (.008)	−12.2 (.604)	.55
1965	2405. (21.6)	139. (20.3)	.422 (.008)	.133 (.009)	.077 (.010)	.021 (.011)	.054 (.009)	−23.4 (.676)	.40
1966	3505. (28.1)	150. (26.5)	.481 (.010)	.173 (.012)	.117 (.013)	.019 (.014)	.090 (.011)	−41.6 (.881)	.35
1967	4190. (30.0)	138. (28.3)	.424 (.010)	.183 (.013)	.108 (.013)	.009 (.015)	.108 (.013)	−54.5 (.942)	.28
1968	5268. (35.7)	−7.3 (33.6)	.447 (.012)	.173 (.016)	.148 (.016)	.018 (.017)	.113 (.015)	−74.6 (1.12)	.24
1969	6009. (38.0)	62.8 (35.8)	.401 (.013)	.161 (.017)	.143 (.017)	.000 (.019)	.126 (.016)	−87.9 (1.19)	.20

the notion that earnings increase with age; the implied difference equations must be explicitly solved to examine the age-earnings profile.

One important deficiency of the results reported in table 4 is that no explicit attention is paid to the presence of the individual effects b_i in the estimation process. It should be made clear that ignoring these effects does not necessarily imply any bias for the estimated training effects, although it does imply inefficiency for the estimation method. There will be bias only if these specific effects are correlated with trainee participation after holding constant age and pre-training earnings levels.[13] Nevertheless, it is possible to examine this issue in somewhat more detail by writing equation (7) for the period $t - s + 1$ as

$$z_{i(t-s+1)} = Bz_{i(t-s)} + d_{i(t-s+1)} + b_i + R_{(t-s+1)}p_i + u_{i(t-s+1)} \qquad (11)$$

[13] Thus, suppose that schooling level is a component of the individual effect b_i. The least squares estimate of the training effect ignoring schooling will be $\hat{R}_s^* = \tilde{R}_s^* + n(b_i, p_i; z_{i(t-s)}, A_i + t)$, where $\tilde{R}_s^*$ is the least squares estimate of the training effect when accounting for variation in the b_i and $n(b_i, p_i; z_{i(t-s)}, A_i + t)$ is the regression coefficient of the omitted specific effect on the trainee participation variable in a multiple regression that controls for z_{t-s} and $A_i + t$. The point is that this last coefficient is likely to be considerably reduced because z_{t-s} is controlled, which would not be the case when we assumed $B = 0$ above.

and subtracting from (7) to get

$$z_{it} - z_{i(t-s+1)} = (B^s - B)z_{i(t-s)} + (d_{is}^* - d_{i(t-s+1)}) + (b_i^* - b_i) + (R_s^* - R_{t-s+1})p_i + u_{is}^* - u_{i(t-s+1)}. \qquad (12)$$

In (12) the individual effects $(b_i^* - b_i)$ are not zero, but they should be reduced. The results of fitting equation (12) to the data for white males for $t - s = 1960$ for various values of t are contained in table 5. As can be seen from the table the estimated training effects are increased slightly by this procedure, which is what one would expect if the individual effects b_i were negatively correlated with trainee status, as seems likely. Moreover, the coefficients of the lagged earnings variables in the successive rows of this table are estimates of the uppermost row of $B^s - B$ and should approach $-B$ if the underlying difference equation (1) is not explosive. If these conditions are satisfied, the implication of table 5 is that the coefficients of the lagged dependent variables are badly biased by the omission of the individual effects b_i, although the training effects do not seem to be severely affected.[14]

[14] Of course, simply fitting the second line of equation (7) in first-differences would eliminate the b_i effects completely. However, the resulting equation would then

TABLE 5.—ESTIMATED REGRESSION COEFFICIENTS (AND ESTIMATED STANDARD ERRORS) OF EQUATION (12) FOR WHITE MALE MDTA TRAINEES

The Dependent Variable is Earnings in	Constant	Training Variable	1960	1959	1958	1957	1956	Age	R^2
1962	420. (14.6)	6.9 (13.6)	−.110 (.005)	.037 (.006)	−.010 (.007)	.015 (.007)	.011 (.005)	−0.199 (.464)	.023
1963	908. (18.1)	−280. (16.9)	−.174 (.007)	.040 (.008)	−.011 (.009)	.015 (.009)	.006 (.007)	−6.55 (.577)	.060
1964	1468. (20.7)	−826. (19.3)	−.242 (.007)	.018 (.009)	−.003 (.010)	.028 (.010)	.011 (.008)	−12.0 (.658)	.123
1965	2187. (23.1)	227. (21.5)	−.272 (.008)	.018 (.010)	−.034 (.011)	.040 (.01)	−.001 (.008)	−23.1 (.733)	.180
1966	3335. (29.2)	230. (27.2)	−.192 (.010)	.060 (.013)	−.032 (.014)	.04 (.014)	.052 (.011)	−42.2 (.928)	.102
1967	3998. (31.3)	227. (29.0)	−.222 (.011)	.045 (.014)	−.048 (.015)	.057 (.015)	.053 (.011)	−55.1 (.993)	.149
1968	5096. (36.7)	79.3 (34.2)	−.217 (.013)	.086 (.016)	−.037 (.018)	.048 (.018)	074 (.013)	−75.7 (1.17)	.147
1969	5819. (39.2)	156.2 (36.5)	−.260 (.014)	.076 (.017)	−.059 (.019)	.062 (.019)	072 (.014)	−88.9 (1.25)	.192

C. Summary Empirical Results

Table 6 draws together the training effects estimated from fitting equation (7) to the data for each of the other three race-sex groups for $t - s = 1961$, 1962, and 1963 and for values of t from 1962 to 1969. Each of these training effect estimates is from a separate regression, as in table 4, but I have deleted the details of these results to conserve space. Taken together, the results in these tables constitute a summary of the substantive results of the application of the methods described above to the basic data on the 1964 MDTA classroom trainees. The results in the columns headed 1961 take 1961 as the base period year and confirm for all four groups that trainee earnings differed little from comparison group earnings in 1962, given the previous five years of earnings. At the present juncture the training effect estimates in these columns might reasonably be taken as lower limit estimates on the assumption that the earnings declines of trainees in 1963 were transitory and that the trainee groups would

provide estimates only of the terms R_t, while the estimates of R_t^* would depend in a complicated way on both the estimated terms R_t and the estimated matrix B, as the discussion surrounding equation (6) indicates. Since the terms R_t^* are the only coefficients of interest here I have not pursued this method.

have recovered from them in any event. Not surprisingly, the results in the column headed 1962 and using 1962 as a base earnings year differ only slightly from those in the first column. Likewise, at the present juncture the training effect estimates in the columns headed 1963 that use 1963 as the base year might reasonably be taken as upper limit estimates on the assumption that the earnings declines of trainees in 1963 would not have disappeared in the absence of training.

The conjunction of these results suggests several conclusions. First, all of the trainee groups suffered unpredicted earnings declines in the year prior to training. The estimates of these declines range from $150 to $350, being in the lower range for black trainees and the upper range for white trainees. This suggests that simple before and after comparisons of trainee earnings may be seriously misleading evidence on the effect of training on earnings even when a non-random comparison group is available to account for economy-wide earnings changes.

Second, for all groups there do appear to be significant foregone earnings as a result of the training process itself and these must be reckoned with in the calculation of the full social costs of training programs. These foregone earnings estimates fall between $900

TABLE 6.—ESTIMATED TRAINING EFFECTS (AND ESTIMATED STANDARD ERRORS) USING DIFFERENT BASE
PERIODS FOR VARIOUS GROUPS OF MDTA TRAINEES

Training Effect in	Black Males Base Period is			White Females Base Period is			Black Females Base Period is		
	1961	1962	1963	1961	1962	1963	1961	1962	1963
1962	− 18 (21)			− 88 (15)			− 22 (18)		
1963	− 248 (26)	− 231 (21)		− 317 (20)	− 238 (15)		− 165 (24)	− 146 (19)	
1964	− 454 (32)	− 439 (29)	− 273 (25)	− 412 (24)	− 349 (22)	− 142 (17)	− 154 (29)	− 139 (26)	− 25 (22)
1965	318 (38)	331 (36)	470 (34)	354 (28)	408 (26)	572 (24)	441 (36)	456 (34)	552 (32)
1966	372 (48)	393 (46)	530 (45)	364 (34)	414 (33)	559 (31)	517 (44)	532 (43)	627 (41)
1967	198 (52)	218 (51)	337 (50)	409 (38)	452 (37)	576 (36)	460 (51)	475 (50)	563 (48)
1968	93 (62)	115 (61)	235 (60)	365 (43)	405 (42)	514 (42)	364 (58)	379 (57)	465 (56)
1969	126 (67)	146 (66)	259 (66)	496 (47)	535 (46)	636 (46)	419 (65)	433 (64)	527 (63)

and $50, being in the upper end of this interval for males and the lower end of this interval for females.

Third, although there remains considerable ambiguity of interpretation, training does appear to have increased the earnings of all trainee groups. For males this effect is between $150 and $500 in the period immediately following training, but declining to perhaps half this figure after five years. For females this effect is between $300 and $600 in the period immediately following training and does not seem to decline in the succeeding years.

Finally, one may wonder how these crude estimates of the benefits from the MDTA programs in 1964 square up with the costs of these programs. In 1964 federal obligations for MDTA classroom training were around $1,800 per trainee, but this figure includes a considerable sum for trainee stipends. Assuming that stipend transfer costs differed only slightly from foregone earnings costs suggests that a permanent increase in earnings of perhaps $180 per year would be necessary for discounted benefits to equal costs at a discount rate of 10%. With the data available it is not possible to verify the satisfaction of this condition with any accuracy, but tables 4 and 6 suggest that it

may be roughly satisfied for the male cohorts and considerably exceeded for the female cohorts.

III. Concluding Remarks

This paper contains only the barest fragments of the results that might ultimately be obtained from a more complete use of the Social Security earnings records linked with the administrative records from various training programs. What is required for more complete results is a better treatment of evaluation issues in the design of programs and the development of better data and statistical methods. There is a large agenda for further research.

One of the most serious limitations in the use of Social Security earnings records is the truncation of the earnings record at the Social Security taxable maximum. Although this problem is likely to be unimportant for groups of workers with low earnings it is no doubt a serious problem for many groups. One solution to this problem would be to obtain the more detailed quarterly earnings data on trainees that are contained in the original Social Security employer records. Alternatively, statistical methods already exist for handling this problem in the conventional regression context and surely will be available soon for models with stochastic regressors as in equation (7).[15]

A second difficulty that must be coped with is the obvious problem of the selection bias in program participation that shows up clearly in these results. This problem may be extreme with respect to female trainees whose employment status may be the cause rather than the result of entrance to training. One solution to this problem would rely on more careful sample design with an explicit control on the selection procedure for program participation, but this approach has met enormous resistance by program managers.[16] An alternative approach may be to study the selection procedure more explicitly in the hope of identifying its structure.

Finally, the analysis of the attempt to augment the human capital of workers by post-schooling training programs contains only the smallest contact with the developing literature on human capital accumulation and earnings determination. Structural models where subsidies to training may be traced through for their effects on workers' choices and their implications for the life-cycle of earnings would be useful both for the development of a better framework for empirical work and for their normative implications for public policy.[17]

REFERENCES

Amemiya, Takeshi, "Regression Analysis When the Dependent Variable is Truncated Normal," *Econometrica* 41 (Nov. 1973), 997–1016.

Ashenfelter, Orley, "The Effect of Manpower Training on Earnings: Preliminary Results," in *Proceedings of*

[15] One discussion is Amemiya's (1973). Kiefer (1976) reports the results of using this method to examine the effect of training on earnings with a different data set and a model with fixed regressors. An excellent discussion of other problems encountered in using Social Security data in this context is contained in Assembly of Behavioral and Social Sciences of the National Research Council (1974).

[16] Some of the important issues involved are taken up by Cain (1975).

[17] Likewise, the role that these training subsidies play in the more general context of the equilibrium of labor markets deserves attention. See especially the discussion by Johnson (1978).

the *Twenty-Seventh Annual Winter Meeting of the Industrial Relations Research Association* (Madison: Industrial Relations Research Association, 1975).

Assembly of Behavioral and Social Sciences of the National Research Council, *Final Report of the Panel on Manpower Training Evaluation: The Use of Social Security Earnings Data for Assessing the Impact of Manpower Training Programs* (Washington, D.C.: Assembly of Behavioral and Social Sciences, National Research Council, National Academy of Sciences, 1974).

Becker, Gary, *Human Capital* (New York: Columbia University Press, 1964).

Borus, Michael, "Time Trends in the Benefits from Retraining in Connecticut," in *Proceedings of the Twentieth Annual Winter Meeting of the Industrial Relations Research Association* (Madison: Industrial Relations Research Association, 1967).

Cain, Glen, "Regression and Selection Models to Improve Nonexperimental Comparisons," in C. A. Bennett and A. A. Lumsdaine (eds.), *Evaluation and Experiment: Some Critical Issues in Assessing Social Programs* (New York: Academic Press, 1975).

Commins, William, *Social Security Data: An Aid to Manpower Program Evaluation* (McLean, Virginia: Planning Research Corporation, 1970).

Farber, David, "Using Social Security Records to Measure Change in Trainee Earnings Capacity," U.S. Department of Labor, Manpower Administration, unpublished paper, Nov. 1970.

Johnson, George, "The Labor Market Displacement Effect in the Analysis of the Net Impact of Manpower Training Programs," in Farrell Bloch (ed.), *Evaluating Manpower Training Programs* (Greenwich Conn.: Johnson Associates, Inc., 1978).

Keifer, Nicholas, "Econometric Essays in Labor Economics," unpublished Ph.D. dissertation, Princeton University, 1976.

Mincer, Jacob, *Schooling, Experience, and Earnings* (New York: National Bureau of Economic Research, 1974).

O'Neill, Dave, *The Federal Government and Manpower* (Washington, D.C.: American Enterprise Institute for Public Policy Research. 1973).

Prescott, Edward, and Thomas Cooley, "Evaluating the Impact of MDTA Programs on Earnings Under Varying Labor Market Conditions," University of Pennsylvania, unpublished paper, Dec. 1972.

Reid, Clifford, "Some Evidence on the Effect of Manpower Training Programs on the Black/White Wage Differential," *The Journal of Human Resources* 9 (Summer 1976), 402–410.

Rosen, Sherwin, "Human Capital: A Survey of Empirical Research," Department of Economics, University of Rochester, unpublished paper, Jan. 1976.

Stromsdorfer, Ernst, *Cost-Effectiveness Studies of Vocational and Technical Education* (Columbus, Ohio: The Center for Vocational and Technical Education, 1972).

U.S. Department of Labor, *Manpower Advice for Government* (Washington, D.C.: Manpower Administration, 1972).

14

Kiefer's work is similar to one portion of Ashenfelter's (Ch. 13) in that first differences are used to eliminate potential selectivity bias associated with unmeasured but unchanging individual characteristics. The omission of explicit measures of lagged earnings from the right-hand-side of the equation leads to a particularly simple model (expression 2) that in principle should eliminate such bias. In this model, the only predictors are the experimental/control dummy variable and age (to allow for nonlinearity). The results (Table 3) suggest a small positive effect of training. But, since this finding is for only a short postprogram period, and other results (Masters and Maynard in Part II and Ashenfelter and Mallar et al. in Part III) suggest that employment and training program effects vary over time, we must regard this finding as less than definitive. (See Kiefer [1978] for other results in a similar mode.)

The second set of estimates presented by Kiefer uses instrumental variables to eliminate remaining selectivity bias associated with unmeasured and changing individual characteristics.[1] The estimated training effect is larger, but its standard error has increased to such an extent that the result is not statistically significant. This difficulty often arises with instrumental variables and often limits the usefulness of such methods.

REFERENCE

KIEFER, N. (1978) "Federally subsidized occupational training and the employment and earnings of male trainees." J. of Econometrics 8: 111-125.

Population Heterogeneity and Inference from Panel Data on the Effects of Vocational Education

Nicholas M. Kiefer

This paper considers a model of earnings over time which incorporates individual effects and time effects without assuming that these effects are orthogonal to the variable of primary interest. The central coefficient is the effect of participation in a Manpower Development and Training Act training program on the earnings of trainees. Since the training status of (some) individuals in the sample changes during the period of the sample, both pre- and posttraining contrasts and trainee-nontrainee contrasts in earnings can be made. An estimate of the cross-section bias in a training coefficient can be made directly. The extent of the analogous bias in the education coefficient in regression studies is a point of current debate. The cross-section bias in the sample analyzed is large, and the estimated effect of training is small and positive.

Postschooling vocational education in the United States usually takes the form of on-the-job training, and the returns to this education are often attributed to the value of accumulated experience. However, a number of programs exist which attempt to teach particular market skills in a postschooling classroom setting. Participants in these programs typically have at least some prior experience in the labor

This paper was prepared for the U.K./U.S. Conference on Human Capital and Income Distribution held at King's College, Cambridge, March 1978. Financial support from the U.S. Department of Labor under contract J-9-M-7-0035 is gratefully acknowledged. The views expressed are not necessarily those of the U.S. Department of Labor, its agencies or staff. Useful comments on the early draft were made at the conference by several people, including O. Ashenfelter, R. Freeman, Z. Griliches, J. Heckman, R. Layard, S. Nickell, B. Weisbrod, and the discussant M. Blaug.

market. Given data on participants and nonparticipants, as well as pre- and posttraining data for both groups, models of the effects of training can be estimated using fixed-effects techniques. These techniques allow the freeing up of some extremely restrictive assumptions normally associated with estimating the returns to schooling. Several alternative models for relaxing the strongest assumptions and eliminating the potential cross-section bias in the schooling coefficient in a wage regression have been investigated (Griliches 1977). The problem is complex in the absence of pre- and postschooling labor market data. It is probably fair to say that no agreement on the magnitude of the cross-section bias has been reached. In the data analyzed here the bias in the cross-section estimate of the effect of training is substantial.

The focus of the present paper is on the exploitation of panel data on the pre- and posttraining wages of participants in classroom vocational educational programs authorized under the Manpower Development and Training Act (MDTA) of 1962 and similar data on nonparticipants. The possibility that selection into a training program may be associated with an unmeasured "fixed effect" which also affects the wage, that is, ability or unobserved background variables (this association could go either way—low-ability people might select themselves into the program or a program manager might select those potential trainees with the highest ability) is investigated. The "effects" are found to be important and to be correlated with the training variable.

This paper will abstract from the employment-earnings distinction in the effects of training in order to concentrate on exploiting the panel aspects of the data. It will have to be kept in mind, therefore, that coefficients reported below reflect not only effects of corresponding variables on wage rates but also their effect on employment probabilities. Heckman (1976) considers this point formally, and in a later paper (1977) offers discrete models for analyzing employment dynamics. An empirically tractable structural model of employment is provided in Kiefer and Neumann (1979). An obvious, but difficult, extension of the work reported here is to combine the wage-rate equations which are the topic of this paper with a model of employment. In a previous paper (Kiefer 1978) I considered employment and earnings separately but did not take full advantage of the panel data available.

Panel data on the earnings of employed individuals have been analyzed previously using variance-component techniques and, recently, a variance-component technique mixed with a simple autoregression (Lillard and Willis 1978). These models have maintained the assumption that all components of the error term are uncorrelated with all of the regressors, including choice variables such as education. This assumption is unnecessary if primary interest is in a coefficient of a variable which changes over the sample period or if primary interest is in earnings dynamics rather than levels. The results given below illustrate the sensitivity of the estimates to the assumed structure of the unobservables.

In Section I the model is described and its relation to models used for measuring the returns to education is examined. In Section II the data are described and estimates are presented. The possibility of endogenous training is considered briefly in Section III, and Section IV provides a conclusion.

I.   A Model with Individual and Time Effects

A basic specification of a model of wage-rate determination over time is $Y_{it} = X_i\beta_t + d_{it}\alpha_t + \epsilon_{it}$ where Y_{it} is the (log) wage of the ith individual in the sample at time period t, X_i is a vector of background variables which remain fixed over time for the ith individual, d_{it} is a vector of variables which change over time for each individual, β_t and α_t are parameter vectors, and ϵ_{it} is the error term. The error captures the influence of left-out variables and noise. In this paper X will contain the usual background variables included in earnings regressions and d will include only training status. Thus d_{it}, a scalar, is 0 for all individuals in the pretraining periods and 1 for trainees in the posttraining periods.[1]

One possible specification to start with is that the parameters are the same across periods and that $\epsilon_{it} = \gamma_t + u_{it}$ with $E(u_{it}) = E(X_i u_{it}) = E(d_{it} u_{it}) = 0$ and $E(u_{it} u_{i't'}) = w_{tt'}$, for $i = i'$; $= 0$ for $i \neq i'$. That is, after including time dummy variables in the regression equation the errors are orthogonal to the regressors and uncorrelated across individuals. In this specification the time variables are interpreted as capturing general growth or changes in the economy, common across individuals. The model of Lillard and Willis is a special case of this model with u_{it} being composed of an individual effect and an error following a simple autoregression.

The theory of human capital and the facts of life-cycle earnings (see Mincer 1974 and Becker 1975) suggest a second role for time variables in earnings regressions. Even without growth in the economy earnings would be expected to increase over time as individuals moved along their age-earnings paths. A "typical" age-earnings profile slopes steeply upward at young ages and slopes less steeply as age increases. The concave shape has been repeatedly verified and

---

[1] Note that the specification considered in this paper is not explicitly dynamic. An explicitly dynamic specification is considered by Ashenfelter (1978).

provides ample evidence for supposing that time effects will not necessarily be adequately captured by dummy variables which assume the same expected time path of earnings for each individual. Clearly, the expected growth in earnings will depend on the starting age.

One method of taking account of the dependency of time effects on age is to allow interaction between the time dummies and the age variable. This method is developed in more detail below when it it used in conjunction with a fixed individual effect. Allowing for appropriate movement of earnings over time affects the estimated training coefficient substantially, as might be expected considering the differences in mean ages (23.5 years for the trainees, 27.4 years for the controls).

Individual effects are represented by the decomposition $u_{it} = f_i + \mu_{it}$. If we are willing to assume that the f_i are orthogonal to the regressors then this model is a special case of that described above. It is appealing, however, to drop the assumption that the individual f_i are orthogonal to the regressors. As Mundlak (1978) points out, it is the assumption of orthogonality that is the critical difference between the fixed-effect and the random-effect model. In the fixed-effect specification it is assumed that $E(\mu_{it}) = E(X_i\mu_{it}) = E(d_{it}\mu_{it}) = 0$, but the f_i need not be uncorrelated with X_i and d_{it}. Therefore the problem of "ability bias," where ability is interpreted as a fixed effect, can be circumvented.

Writing the model out explicitly yields

$$Y_{it} = X_i\beta + d_{it}\alpha + \gamma_t + a_i\delta_t + f_i + \mu_{it} \tag{1}$$

where β and α have been assumed to be the same across periods, γ_t is the "time effect" in the tth period, a_i is the age (at the beginning of the sample period) of the individual, δ_t captures the nonlinearity in age of the age-earnings profile, and f_i is the individual effect. If the first period is the base period then the time effect in period t on the earnings of an individual of age a is $\gamma_t + a\delta_t$. Taking means over t and writing both sides of (1) in terms of deviations from means gives $Y_{it} - Y_i = (d_{it} - d_{i.})\alpha + (\gamma_t - \gamma.) + a_i(\delta_t - \delta.) + \mu_{it} - u_i$ where $x. = 1/T\Sigma_{t=1}^T x_t$ for any variable X. This can be written

$$\tilde{Y}_{it} = \tilde{d}_{it}\alpha + \tilde{\gamma}_t + \tilde{\gamma}a_t\tilde{\delta}_t + \tilde{\mu}_{it}, \tag{2}$$

defining the tilde operator. This equation no longer involves the fixed effect and can be easily estimated by generalized least squares, constrained so that the coefficient α is the same in each equation[2] and the

---

[2] There are $T - 1$ independent equations for each individual, where T is the number of periods. One equation is dropped because of the differencing out of the individual effects.

coefficients on the constants and on age are unconstrained. Intuitively, data on each individual are used to fix the level of his wage profile, data on all individuals are used to fix the average movement along the profiles, and the trainee-control contrast is used to estimate the effect of training.

This approach can be usefully compared with alternative methods of estimating the effects of training and with methods of estimating the returns to schooling. One approach is simply to regress post-training wage rates on background variables and a dummy variable indicating whether each observation was a trainee. This is analogous to the method of assessing the effect of schooling by regressing wage rates on years of schooling and interpreting the coefficient as a rate of return. If the training variable is correlated with the individual effects then the estimated coefficients will be biased. If no further information is available then the impact of training cannot be distinguished from correlation between training and the effects; interindividual contrasts in wage rates by training status simply do not provide enough information. In the case of the training programs studied here, additional information in the form of pretraining wage rates can be used to separate the impact of training from correlation between training and the individual effects.

In the case of estimating the returns to schooling, preschooling wage rates are typically not available. Consequently, alternative methods for dealing with potential ability bias have been developed. A starting point is to include measures of ability in the cross-section wage regressions. The difference between the estimated coefficient of schooling when ability is and is not included is sometimes interpreted as a measure of ability bias. This approach has led to a wide range of estimates of ability bias; Griliches (1977) gives an example in which the estimated percentage ability bias differs by a factor of 4 between two reasonable specifications estimated with the same sample.

Difficulty in measuring ability and in interpreting simple regressions including measures of ability as regressors has led to use of models of errors in measurement (Chamberlain 1977; Griliches 1977). Identification in these models is tricky, and a substantial amount of structure has to be put on the unobservables. Intuitively an unobservable variable is held constant by contrasting equations in which the unobservable is assumed to take the same value. In the model for estimating the effects of training considered above the unobservables of interest are the f_i, and they can simply be differenced away. In schooling models the structure is necessarily much more complicated; the cross-equation contrast has to be made across equations for earnings and test scores, and the unobservable will enter these equations with different coefficients.[3] This leads quickly to a factor-analytic formulation. This complication is avoided in the present model.

II. Data and Estimates

The data are from a 2½-year longitudinal survey taken under contract to the Office of Economic Opportunity and the Department of Labor. This paper is concerned with the data assembled on male participants in classroom vocational training programs under the MDTA and data collected on a group of nonparticipants for comparison purposes. Trainees from 10 Standard Metropolitan Statistical Areas (SMSAs) were sampled and a subsample of the trainee group was matched on age, race, and sex to a sample of individuals from the same SMSAs who were eligible for training but did not participate in a program. Each member of the group of nonparticipants was matched to a member of the trainee group and interviewed as close as possible to the same time the trainee was interviewed. Interviews took place when the trainee entered the program, upon leaving the program, 4 months after leaving the program, and 8 months later. Retrospective data on employment, earnings, and hours of work were collected. These data are described in detail in U.S. Department of Labor (1979).

In the present study data by quarter on 6 quarters are used—3 quarters before the trainees entered the programs and 3 quarters after leaving training. The sample analyzed here is restricted to those who reported wage rates in each of these 6 quarters. About one-third of the total sample available meets this restriction; this is about the fraction of observations available when other data sets (e.g., Michigan Income Dynamics) are restricted to household heads with earnings in each period. As mentioned in the opening paragraphs, this selection procedure results in some ambiguity in the interpretation of the coefficients. However, the subsample can be analyzed using simple techniques designed to exploit the panel aspects of the data. These techniques can then be compared with those used in other studies of earnings dynamics. About 600 observations survive the filter. Table 1 reports summary statistics.

The participants in the vocational training classes are somewhat younger than the nonparticipants in this sample and had on average slightly more schooling. There is considerable difference in the proportion married; 41 percent of the trainees versus 65 percent of the

---

[3] The part of the individual effect which is due to family background or familywise ability can sometimes be held constant by comparing siblings (Chamberlain and Griliches 1975; Taubman 1975). In this volume Griliches surveys this approach.

TABLE 1

SUMMARY STATISTICS BY TRAINING STATUS

	TRAINEES		NONTRAINEES	
VARIABLE	M	SD	M	SD
Age	23.5	6.0	27.4	7.7
Years of schooling	10.4	1.9	9.9	2.8
Proportion black	.53	.50	.62	.49
Proportion married	.41	.49	.65	.48
Proportion living in the:				
South	.17	.38	.22	.42
Midwest	.25	.43	.32	.47
West	.19	.40	.13	.33
Weeks in program	18.55	12.05	0	0
Wage rate:				
3 quarters before training	2.25	1.23	2.61	.98
2 quarters before training	2.33	1.24	2.64	.98
1 quarter before training	2.27	1.12	2.68	1.0
1 quarter after training	2.45	.85	2.87	1.1
2 quarters after training	2.61	.96	2.92	1.1
3 quarters after training	2.61	.96	3.01	1.2

NOTE.—The timing of the measurement of the posttraining wage rate for the nontrainees is explained in the text.

nontrainees in this sample were married. The nontrainee group had on average higher wages in each period, perhaps because they are older.

Table 2 reports the results of a period-by-period regression of wage rates on age and age squared, education, a race variable, a marital status variable, and the training dummy variable. The training variable takes the value one for trainees in each of these regressions. The coefficients on the background variables have the expected signs and reasonable values, and their similarity across periods suggests that some pooling might be advantageous. The schooling coefficient is somewhat lower than that found in random samples from the population, reflecting the low-income low-education nature of this special population. Under the assumptions of the model the statistical significance of the training variable in the pretraining periods is clear evidence of correlation between the effects and the training variable. Ashenfelter (1974) consequently estimates an effect of a training program by the difference between the coefficient of a training dummy in a posttraining period and in a pretraining period.

If a trainee-control earnings contrast in the third quarter after training was used to estimate the impact of training, training would be found to be significantly associated with an 11 percent fall in earnings. As can be seen from table 2 and from estimates to be presented, this inference from the cross-section evidence is misleading.

TABLE 2

PERIOD-BY-PERIOD WAGE-RATE REGRESSIONS

| | COEFFICIENT | | | | | |
| | Quarter before Training | | | Quarter after Training | | |
VARIABLE	3	2	1	1	2	3
Constant	.026	.171	.325	.383	.217	−.001
	(.091)	(.636)	(1.22)	(1.47)	(.846)	(.005)
Age	.042	.029	.022	.030	.037	.054
	(2.08)	(1.52)	(1.15)	(1.62)	(2.00)	(3.07)
Education	.014	.018	.016	.011	.019	.020
	(1.81)	(2.58)	(2.25)	(1.53)	(2.84)	(3.14)
Age squared/100	−.059	−.037	−.027	−.050	−.056	−.081
	(1.72)	(1.12)	(.839)	(1.59)	(1.79)	(2.73)
Black	−.028	−.034	−.022	−.009	−.030	−.026
	(.798)	(.990)	(.662)	(.281)	(.925)	(.840)
Married	.113	.087	.105	.124	.073	.052
	(2.89)	(2.33)	(2.83)	(3.40)	(2.04)	(1.55)
Training	−.129	−.096	−.132	−.115	−.077	−.106
	(3.57)	(2.78)	(3.87)	(3.44)	(2.34)	(3.39)
F	10.14	7.81	8.97	7.22	5.57	8.89

NOTE.—N observations = 608; absolute t-statistics in parentheses.

Table 3 presents generalized least-squares estimates of equation (2). The error terms μ_{it} were assumed to be independent across individuals, but the intertemporal covariance was unrestricted (though the same for each individual). The variance-covariance matrix was estimated from the residuals obtained from an equation-by-equation ordinary least-squares regression of log wages (minus the individual's mean wage over time) on a constant term, training status, and age. The estimated impact of training is 0.0148, about 1.5 percent, and is not significantly different from zero. The time effects indicate an upward drift in wage rates with less growth for older people, as expected. Ignoring the effect of age on wage growth gives the coefficients reported in table 4. The training coefficient is increased to 0.0296, capturing the fact that the trainees are younger. If the wage growth is assumed to be a simple trend (i.e., the intercept is constrained to be identical across equations in [2]) then the training variable takes the value 0.116 with an associated t-statistic of 5.39, attributing a large significant wage increase to training.

The estimates in this section lead to the conclusion that wages were higher for trainees by an average of about 1.5 percent during the 3 quarters following training than they would have been in the absence of training. The estimate is not significantly different from zero. The training variable was found to be significantly correlated with the

TABLE 3

GENERALIZED LEAST-SQUARES ESTIMATES OF EQUATION (2)

| | COEFFICIENT | | | | |
| | Quarter before Training | | Quarter after Training | | |
VARIABLE	2	1	1	2	3
Intercept	−.092	−.073	.103	.126	.094
	(2.70)	(2.10)	(2.63)	(3.09)	(2.44)
Age	.0017	.0011	−.0030	−.0025	−.0005
	(1.41)	(.890)	(2.13)	(1.70)	(.356)
Training	...	...	.0148	R	R
			(1.01)		

NOTE.—Absolute *t*-statistics in parentheses; R = restricted.

individual effects, indicating that the cross-section trainee-nontrainee contrast gives misleading estimates of the training program's impact on wages. In using the panel aspects of the data to control for individual effects, the importance of modeling time effects adequately becomes apparent. A simple linear trend in (log) wages was not adequate, and a model with time dummies and time dummies interacted with age gave sensible results in terms of the implied time path of earnings by age.

III. Endogenous Training

An additional problem in measuring the returns to schooling is that schooling is likely to be endogenous to the individual and therefore schooling coefficients may be subject to simultaneity bias. Griliches

TABLE 4

GENERALIZED LEAST-SQUARES ESTIMATES OF EQUATION (2)
WITH δ_t (Effect of Age on Wage Growth) = 0

| | COEFFICIENT | | | | |
| | Quarter before Training | | Quarter after Training | | |
VARIABLE	2	1	1	2	3
Intercept	−.045	−.042	.028	.058	.078
	(4.3)	(3.96)	(1.97)	(4.86)	(6.86)
Training	...	.0296	R	R	R
		(1.06)			

NOTE.—Absolute *t*-statistics in parentheses; R = restricted.

TABLE 5

Period-by-Period Earnings Regressions: Instrumental Variable Estimates

| | COEFFICIENT | | | | | |
| | Quarter before Training | | | Quarter after Training | | |
VARIABLE	3	2	1	1	2	3
Constant	.205	.287	.523	.468	.190	.004
	(.633)	(.939)	(1.70)	(1.59)	(.659)	(.014)
Age	.039	.027	.018	.029	.038	.054
	(1.85)	(1.38)	(.919)	(1.51)	(2.01)	(3.04)
Education	.015	.019	.017	.011	.019	.020
	(1.89)	(2.64)	(2.33)	(1.58)	(2.79)	(3.12)
Age squared/100	−.058	−.036	−.026	−.050	−.056	−.081
	(1.65)	(1.08)	(.774)	(1.56)	(1.79)	(2.73)
Black	−.052	−.049	−.048	−.020	−.026	−.026
	(1.26)	(1.26)	(1.23)	(.547)	(.716)	(.759)
Married	.081	.066	.069	.108	.078	.052
	(1.66)	(1.45)	(1.49)	(2.46)	(1.81)	(1.27)
Training	−.332	−.227	−.356	−.211	−.046	−.111
	(1.95)	(1.42)	(2.20)	(1.37)	(.307)	(.781)

NOTE.—Absolute t-statistics in parentheses.

(1977) notes this potential bias and presents two-stage least-squares estimates of the rate of return from a regression including ability measures. In this volume, Willis and Rosen model the choice of whether to go to college as the result of an explicit comparison of future earnings with and without college and obtain sensible estimates of the model's parameters. Most of the work on brothers has not treated the problem of endogenous schooling.

In the case of training, the instrumental variable approach to eliminating potential simultaneity bias can be combined with the model allowing individual effects in a straightforward way. Instrumental variable estimates of the period-by-period regressions presented in table 2 are reported in table 5.[4] Again, a simple cross-section analysis for the third quarter after training leads to the conclusion that training significantly and substantially reduces wages.

The model with explicit individual effects can be estimated by noting that an instrumental variable for the deviation from mean over time-in-training status (the regressor $\bar{d}$) is simply $-\frac{1}{2}\hat{d}$ in the pre-

[4] The instrumental variables were age, schooling, race, marital status, and region, and squared and cross-product terms in these variables. The first-stage regression had an F of 5.62 (with 608 df), indicating that the training variable is not very well predicted. These instrumental variables may enter the wage function directly and may be correlated with the individual effects without introducing bias in the panel-based estimates.

training periods and ½ $\hat{d}$ in the posttraining periods where $\hat{d}$ is the instrument for training. Instrumental variable estimates of the model with individual effects are given in table 6. The resulting point estimate of the effect of training (0.073) is larger than the estimate reported in the previous section. Griliches's (1977) finding was in the same direction; instrumental variable estimates implied a larger return to schooling than ordinary estimates.

The cross-section regressions in table 5 can be criticized on the grounds that the variables used as instruments are variables which potentially influence wages directly and are therefore not legitimate instruments. The problem of finding instruments to use in wage equations is well known; some arguments can be made to include virtually any variable in a wage equation. Without instruments the training (or schooling) coefficient will not be identified in the cross section, but it will be identified in the panel. This holds in models with or without individual effects and provides an example in which a panel is more informative than a cross section even in the absence of considerations of heterogeneity.

The two alternative estimates of the effect of training, obtained with and without treating training as exogenous, present a puzzle. On one hand the instrumental variable estimates are unambiguously better asymptotically than the ordinary estimates if training is endogenous. On the other hand, the argument for correlation between training and the error term is not that strong; correlation between training and the individual effects is allowed (indeed correlation between the instrument for training and the individual effect is permitted), and it is the remaining correlation which concerns us. If this correlation is zero, then the estimates presented in the previous section are unambiguously more efficient. A reasonable approach might be to combine

TABLE 6

INSTRUMENTAL VARIABLE ESTIMATES OF EQUATION (2)

| | COEFFICIENT | | | | |
| | Quarter before Training | | Quarter after Training | | |
VARIABLE	1	2	1	2	3
Constant	−.067	−.048	.077	.101	.069
	(1.24)	(.872)	(.115)	(1.71)	(1.19)
Age	.0012	.0006	−.0025	.0020	.0000
	(.800)	(.383)	(1.49)	(1.15)	(.017)
Training	...	...	.073	R	R
			(.722)		

NOTE.—Absolute t-statistics in parentheses; R = restricted.

these two estimates with weights inversely related to their respective variances. Such an analysis is beyond the scope of this paper, but note that the variance of the instrumental variable estimate is much larger than the variance of the ordinary estimate, and consequently the implied point estimate would be near the ordinary estimate. In the classical framework a test of the hypothesis of zero correlation is available along the lines suggested by Wu (1973), Hausman (1976) and Dufour (1977). The test consists of including as regressors both the instrument for the deviation of the training variable from its mean over time and the actual value of that variable and testing the significance of the instrument. If the variable is uncorrelated with the error, then the instrument will plainly add nothing to the regression and will not be significant. If the variable is correlated with the error, then the instrument can pick up some of the effects of systematic variation of the variable in question while the variable itself picks up the effect of some of the correlation between itself and the error. Using this test, the hypothesis of zero correlation between the training variable and the error term cannot be rejected. The absolute t-statistic on the instrumental variable is 0.63 (the coefficient was -0.66) indicating little evidence of correlation between training and the error term. Consequently, by this criterion, the estimates presented in the previous section are the preferred estimates.[5]

IV. Conclusion

The coefficient of the training variable reported in Section II is 0.015, implying a 1.5 percent increase in wages associated with training. This coefficient reflects both employment and wage-rate effects of training. In a previous paper (Kiefer 1978), I considered employment and earnings separately but did not control completely for individual effects. That paper gave the effect of training as a function of weeks in training and found essentially no effect of training evaluated at the mean number of weeks trained. This is well within a reasonable confidence interval around the present estimate, so the conclusions are compatible though the techniques of analysis were quite different.

The panel-data model described in Section I incorporates time

---

[5] The fact that the instrumental variable point estimate of the training coefficient is larger than the ordinary point may say something about posttraining on-the-job training, paid for by the trainees through lower wages. The ordinary estimate of 0.015 may be the actual (percentage) wage differential between trainees and nontrainees in the posttraining period, and the higher instrumental variable estimate may correct for posttraining choices of levels of on-the-job training. However, the data available here are too limited to explore the reasons for the difference between the instrumental variable and the ordinary estimate of the training coefficient; indeed in these data the difference is not significant.

effects and individual effects. These were not assumed to be orthogonal to the regressors. It was argued that time effects should vary across individuals according to their ages, reflecting the nonlinearity of age-earnings profiles. Incorporating this into the model gave sensible results, with total time effects smaller in magnitude for older workers. An instrumental variable extension was given in Section III, where an example was given in which a parameter not identified in the cross section is identified in the panel, even in the absence of individual effects. The instrumental variable estimate of the effect of training was larger than the ordinary estimate, but not significantly so.

The analysis exploited both the before-after comparisons possible in a panel and the trainee-nontrainee comparison. The first is typically not available in studies of the effect of formal schooling, and a number of models have been developed to avoid the potential cross-section bias, due to worker heterogeneity, which arises when before and after information is not available. The results of this paper show that the bias in the cross section can be substantial.

References

Ashenfelter, Orley. "The Effect of Manpower Training on Earnings: Preliminary Results." In *Proceedings of the 27th Annual Meeting of the IRRA*. Madison, Wis.: IRRA, 1975.

———. "Estimating the Effect of Training Programs on Earnings with Longitudinal Data." *Rev. Econ. and Statis.* 60 (February 1978): 47–57.

Becker, Gary S. *Human Capital*. 2d ed. New York: Nat. Bur. Econ. Res., 1975.

Chamberlain, Gary. "Education, Income and Ability Revisited." *J. Econ.* 5 (1977): 241–57.

Chamberlain, Gary, and Griliches, Zvi. "Unobservables with a Variance Components Structure: Ability, Schooling and the Economic Success of Brothers." *Internat. Econ. Rev.* 16 (June 1975): 422–49.

Dufour, Jean-Marie. "A Test of Independence between a Stochastic Regressor and the Disturbance Term." Mimeographed. Univ. Chicago, 1977.

Griliches, Zvi. "Estimating the Returns to Schooling: Some Econometric Problems." *Econometrica* 45 (January 1977): 1–22.

———. "Sibling Models and Data in Economics: Beginnings of a Survey." *J.P.E.*, this volume.

Hausman, Jerry A. "Specification Tests in Econometrics." Mimeographed. Massachusetts Inst. Tech, 1976. Forthcoming in *Econometrica*.

Heckman, James J. "The Common Structure of Statistical Models of Truncation, Sample Selection and Limited Dependent Variables, and a Simple Estimator for Such Models." *Annals Econ. and Social Measurement* 5 (Fall 1976): 475–92.

———. "A Simple Statistical Model for Discrete Data Developed and Applied to Test the Hypothesis of True State Dependence against the Hypothesis of Spurious State Dependence." Mimeographed. Univ. Chicago, 1977.

Kiefer, Nicholas M. "Federally Subsidized Occupational Training and the Employment and Earnings of Male Trainees." *J. Econ.* 8 (1978): 111–25.

Kiefer, Nicholas M., and Neumann, George R. "An Empirical Job-Search Model with a Test of the Constant Reservation-Wage Hypothesis." *J.P.E.* 87, no. 1 (February 1979): 89–107.

Lillard, Lee, and Willis, Robert. "Dynamic Aspects of Earnings Mobility." *Econometrica* 46, no. 5 (September 1978): 985–1012.

Mincer, Jacob. *Schooling, Experience and Earnings.* New York: Nat. Bur. Econ. Res., 1974.

Mundlak, Yair. "On the Pooling of Time Series and Cross-Section Data." *Econometrica* 46 (January 1978): 69–86.

Taubman, Paul. "The Determinants of Earnings: Genetic, Family and Other Environments: A Study of White Male Twins." Mimeographed. Univ. Pennsylvania, 1975.

U.S. Department of Labor and U.S. Department of Health, Education and Welfare. *Cost Effectiveness Analysis of Four Categorical Employment and Training Programs: MDTA, JOBS, Job Corps, and NYC-OS: A Report to the General Accounting Office.* 4 vols. Edited by G. Goodfellow and E. W. Stromsdorfer. Washington: Dept. of Labor, 1979, in press.

Willis, Robert J., and Rosen, Sherwin. "Education and Self-Selection." *J.P.E.*, this volume.

Wu, D. M. "Alternative Tests of Independence between Stochastic Regressors and Disturbances: Finite Sample Results." *Econometrica* 41 (July 1973): 733–50.

15

This chapter is of interest on several counts. Methodologically, it presents regression-adjusted experimental/control comparisons, and these include the use of Heckman's Mills ratio term (Table 4, panel C). Substantively, the results suggest that an employment and training program for "difficult" youths can be a success. (This finding is particularly important in light of the relatively weak results of Supported Work for youths. See the article by Masters and Maynard in Part II.)

In light of the importance of these findings, we present updated results here. These are experimental/control group employment rate differences for two target groups during the postprogram period:[1]

Months After Termination	Target Group	
	Males	Females Without Children
0-6	.008	.027
6-12	.054	.057
12-18	.079	.099*
18-24	.114**	.045

* = statistically significant at the 10% level.
** = statistically significant at the 5% level.

There is a clear suggestion that program effects increase over time, at least for the spans examined.

NOTE

1. For these results, see Mallar (1980: Table III.2). These results may differ from those reported below due to different data availability at different times.

REFERENCE

MALLAR, C. (1980) Draft of Chapter III of Evluation of the Economic Impact of the Job Corps Program: Second Follow-Up Report. Personal communication, C. Mallar to E. Stromsdorfer.

The Short-Term Economic Impact of the Job Corps Program

Charles D. Mallar, Stuart H. Kerachsky, and
Craig V.D. Thornton

One of the primary goals of Job Corps is to help participants improve their lifetime economic prospects. In this paper we present findings on how successful Job Corps is in meeting this goal for the first few months after Corpsmembers leave the program. More specifically, we provide evidence on whether Job Corps is having the desired impacts of (1) increasing employment and earnings; (2) improving future labor-market opportunities through additional education, training, and work experience, as well as improving job mobility, health, and the opportunities for entering the military service; (3) reducing dependence on welfare programs (both cash and in-kind programs like Food Stamps and subsidized housing), and other cash transfer programs (e.g., Unemployment Insurance and Workers' Compensation); and (4) reducing antisocial behavior, such as drug and alcohol abuse and criminal activities. The estimates of these desired impacts are broken down further by duration of stay in Job Corps (according to program completion categories) and by differences in the characteristics of both Corpsmembers and centers. Furthermore, we present graphic estimates of the time path of impacts from the point at which Corpsmembers leave the program until eight months later. Sections A through D present detailed findings for each of the four areas of desired impacts listed above.

Mathematica Policy Research, Inc. The research discussed in this paper was done under a contract with the Office of Program Evaluation of the Employment and Training Administration, U.S. Department of Labor. Authors undertaking such projects under government sponsorship are encouraged to state their findings and express their judgements freely. Therefore, any points of view or opinions stated do not necessarily represent the official position of the Department of Labor. The paper benefited from the exceptional research assistance of Patricia Lapczynski and Anne Mozer.

From Charles D. Mallar, Stuart H. Kerachsky, and Craig V.D. Thornton, "The Short-Term Economic Impact of the Job Corps Program." Unpublished manuscript, 1980.

A. FINDINGS FOR LABOR MARKET ACTIVITIES

In general, we found large and statistically significant increases in employment and earnings for program completers and erratic effects for early dropouts and partial completers (sometimes negative and almost always statistically insignificant). The positive effects showed up most prominently in the data covering the week before the follow-up interview but became greatly attenuated, and even negative, when they were averaged over the entire postprogram period. The estimates by the length of time out of the program show that this is caused by the temporarily low earnings of Corpsmembers as they re-enter the labor market during the first few months after leaving Job Corps. These periods of low earnings cancel out the positive impacts observed for the time period just prior to the first follow-up interview.

1. Impacts for the Week Before the First Follow-Up Interview

The findings for the week prior to the follow-up interview (an average of seven months after the participant sample left Job Corps) are summarized in Tables 1 through 3. Estimates are presented separately for males, females without children, and females with children, respectively. Separate estimates need to be computed for these three subgroups because of significant differences in their behavior.

For all measures of work activities (i.e., labor-force participation, looking for work, employment, military service, earnings, and hours), there are positive, large, and statistically significant effects for male program completers. (as is discussed later, however, unobserved differences among Corpsmembers by completion category may cause the effects for program completers to be overstated.) For the measures of civilian work activities, males who completed the Job Corps program were more likely to be in the labor force by almost 10 percentages points, and they had an increase in employment of approximately 13 percentage points and in full-time employment (i.e., working at least thirty-five hours per week) of approximately 14 percentage points. They worked almost six hours more per week, and they earned over $23 more per week (i.e., an increase of over $1,200 in annual earnings). Furthermore, their probability of being in the military service was approximately 8 percentage points higher.

In contrast, the impacts for males who were only partial completers, while still positive, are small and statistically insignificant. The estimated impacts for early dropouts are negative, but are also small and not significantly different from zero. As shown in the last two columns of Table 1, the average effect for all enrollees is still quite large, especially if the statistically insignificant effects for noncompleters are set equal to 0, as in the final column. For all Corpsmen, the most precise estimate of overall earnings gains attributable to Job Corps (including military earnings) from our sample (i.e., without assuming zero effects for noncompleters) is $3.30 during the week before the follow-up survey. This average weekly earnings gain for all male enrollees is just over $171 at an annual rate, and is based on reweighting the observations to correct for the fact that our sample overrepresents completers. (Note that our sample of Corpsmembers contained 49 percent program

TABLE 1

ESTIMATES OF EMPLOYMENT AND RELATED EFFECTS IN WEEK PRIOR TO INTERVIEW: MALES[a]

Variable	Unweighted Sample Mean For Corpsmembers At Follow-Up	Average Job Corps Effect For Program Completers	Average Job Corps Effect For Partial Completers	Average Job Corps Effect For Early Dropouts	Average Job Corps Effect For All Enrollees	Average Job Corps Effect For Enrollees With Noncompleters Assumed To Be Zero
Civilians in labor force	0.888	0.097	0.028	0.007	0.040	0.029
In labor force or military	0.898	0.100	0.031	-0.002	0.038	0.030
Active, including military[b]	0.656	0.124	0.025	-0.004	0.043	0.037
° Employment, civilians	0.546	0.132	0.016	-0.035	0.030	0.040
° In military	0.091	0.079	0.018	-0.013	0.024	0.024
In training or work-experience program, civilians[b]	0.044	0.025	0.013	0.029	0.023	0.007
° In school, civilians[b]	0.110	-0.017	-0.012	0.009	-0.005	-0.005
Earnings per week, civilians	$62.46	23.25	1.65	-8.57	3.43	6.98
Earnings per week, including military	$69.31	26.69	2.53	-13.66	3.30	8.01
° Civilian employment	$56.70	15.74	0.03	-11.84	0.00	4.71
° Military	$12.61	10.95	2.50	-1.82	3.30	3.30
Employed full-time, civilians	0.342	0.143	0.025	-0.025	0.040	0.043
Civilians in union jobs[b]	0.095	0.046	-0.012	-0.014	0.005	0.014
Hours per week on civilian jobs	18.33	5.65	1.31	-1.25	1.59	1.70
Hours per week if employed in civilian job	33.29	3.03	3.43	-0.14	1.88	0.91
Hourly wage rate for civilian employment	$3.47	-0.13	-1.74	-0.70	-0.84	-0.04

a/ The estimates of Job Corps effects are adjusted for preenrollment differences in the variables between the Job Corps and comparison samples, except where noted.

b/ Appropriate baseline measures were not available for these variables, and the estimates are simple Job Corps minus comparison group means at postprogram.

TABLE 2

ESTIMATES OF EMPLOYMENT AND RELATED EFFECTS IN WEEK PRIOR TO INTERVIEW: FEMALES WITHOUT CHILDREN[a]

Variable	Unweighted Sample Mean For Corpsmembers At Follow-Up	Average Job Corps Effect For Program Completers	Average Job Corps Effect For Partial Completers	Average Job Corps Effect For Early Dropouts	Average Job Corps Effect For All Enrollees	Average Job Corps Effect For Enrollees With Noncompleters Assumed To Be Zero
Civilians in labor force	0.768	0.202	0.033	-0.051	0.050	0.061
In labor force or military	0.773	0.216	0.039	-0.051	0.056	0.065
Active, including military[b]	0.517	0.058	-0.071	-0.082	-0.039	0.015
° Employment, cililians	0.388	0.086	-0.029	-0.080	-0.015	0.026
° In military	0.024	0.024	0.009	-0.006	0.008	0.007
° In training or work-experience program, civilians	0.032	-0.010	-0.020	0.030	0.003	-0.003
° In school, civilians[b]	0.146	-0.067	-0.111	-0.030	-0.066	-0.020
Earnings per week, civilians	$38.30	22.52	3.51	1.12	8.26	6.76
Earnings per week, including military	$40.53	23.38	5.48	-0.34	8.52	7.01
° Civilian employment	$37.20	20.05	4.23	0.49	7.47	6.01
° Military	$3.33	3.33	1.25	-0.83	1.05	1.00
Employed full-time, civilians	0.229	0.073	0.017	0.023	0.036	0.022
Civilians in union jobs[b]	0.079	0.061	0.058	-0.027	0.025	0.018
Hours per week on civilian jobs	12.83	4.76	1.23	-0.96	1.41	1.43
Hours per week if employed in civilian job	32.57	2.87	9.08	4.01	5.19	0.86
Hourly wage rate for civilian employment	$2.96	0.45	-0.45	0.69	0.29	0.14

a/ The estimates of Job Corps effects are adjusted for preenrollment differences in the variables between the Job Corps and comparison samples, and the estimates are simple Job Corps minus comparison means, except where noted.

b/ Appropriate baseline measures were not available for these variables, comparison means at postprogram.

TABLE 3

ESTIMATES OF EMPLOYMENT AND RELATED EFFECTS IN WEEK PRIOR TO INTERVIEW: FEMALES WITH CHILDREN[a]

Variable	Unweighted Sample Mean For Corpsmembers At Follow-Up	Average Job Corps Effect For Program Completers	Average Job Corps Effect For Partial Completers	Average Job Corps Effect For Early Dropouts	Average Job Corps Effect For All Enrollees Assumed To Be Zero	Average Job Corps Effect For Enrollees With Noncompleters Assumed To Be Zero
Civilians in labor force	0.594	0.154	-0.036	-0.247	-0.063	0.046
In labor force or military	0.594	0.155	-0.035	-0.245	-0.062	0.046
Active, including military[h]	0.271	-0.008	-0.141	-0.068	-0.072	-0.002
° Employment, civilians	0.198	-0.029	-0.071	-0.190	-0.106	-0.009
° In military	0.0	0.0	0.0	0.0	0.0	0.0
° In training or work-experience program, civilians	0.052	0.004	-0.016	0.141	0.053	0.001
° In school, civilians[b]	0.052	-0.044	-0.133	0.042	-0.070	-0.013
Earnings per week, civilians	$18.48	-1.09	-6.16	-1.50	-2.78	-0.33
Earnings per week, including military	$18.48	-2.60	-6.39	-2.32	-3.63	-0.78
° Civilian employment	$18.48	-2.60	-6.39	-2.32	-3.63	-0.78
° Military	$0.00	0.0	0.0	0.0	0.0	0.0
Employed full-time, civilians	0.094	-0.033	-0.045	-0.137	-0.078	-0.010
Civilians in union jobs[b]	0.052	0.027	-0.015	0.051	0.024	0.008
Hours per week con civilian jobs	5.65	1.99	-3.49	-7.36	-3.39	0.60
Hours per week if employed in civilian job	25.22	8.72	-8.05	0.00	0.20	2.62
Hourly wage rate for civilian employment	$4.42	-3.21	2.42	0.00	-0.24	-0.96

a/ The estimates of Job Corps effects are adjusted for preenrollment difference in the variables between the Job Corps and comparison samples, except where noted.

b/ Appropriate baseline measures were not available for these variables, and the estimates are simple Job Corps minus comparison group means at postprogram.

completers, 40 percent partial completers, and 11 percent early dropouts, as compared to 30, 30, and 40 percent, respectively, for Job Corps as a whole in fiscal year 1977. (Mallar et al., 1978, explains the procedures and justification for this reweighting of observations) If the insignificant effects for noncompleters are set equal to 0, the overall earnings gain is $8.01, or over $400 per year.

The labor-market and related effects for females without children (85 percent of the Corpswomen sample; on average they had been out of the program for an average of seven months) are similar to those for males in the week prior to the first follow-up interview (see Table 2). For Corpswomen who completed the full program, the estimated labor-market impacts are similar to those for male Corpsmembers--of a similarly large magnitude and high statistical significance. The estimated impacts are slightly larger for labor-force participation and slightly smaller for most other variables. For noncompleting females without children, as compared to male noncompleters, the impacts tended to be approximately the same for partial completers and slightly larger for early dropouts. However, these patterns between females and males are not always clear, partly because the estimates for partial completers and early dropouts have large standard errors for both females and males.

The average reweighted effects for all enrollees tended to be larger for childless females than for males, particularly for earnings and hours worked. These large estimated impacts on average for female enrollees (as compared to males) are due primarily to more positive effects for early dropouts. For female enrollees without children, we observe an average gain in weekly earnings of $8.52 (approximately $443 on an annual basis) if all categories of completion are averaged in, and $7.01 (approximately $365 on an annual basis) if the insignificant effects for noncompleters are set equal to 0. This compares to $3.30 and $8.01, respectively, for males.

There were very few Corpswomen with children in the sample. Only 100 Corpswomen (accounting for less than 5 percent of the entire Corpsmember sample) had children (including stepchildren and foster children) living with them at the time of the first follow-up interview (on average, seven months after leaving Job Corps). The impacts for Corpswomen with children (presented in Table 3) appear to be very small, and the estimates are not very precise. All impacts for females with children are not only close to 0 in magnitude, but are also statistically insignificant. Because of the small number of observations for females with children and the generally small magnitude and insignificance of estimates of Job Corps impacts for them, we will not discuss their results further in the text. However, we continue to present tabulations of findings for all groups.

Two anomalous effects show up in the estimates for labor-market and related impacts in the week prior to the first follow-up interview. First, the effects on activity rates (work, military, training, or school) tend to show reductions for female Corpsmembers. These estimated reductions in overall

activity for females are basically small and statistically significant, however, and occur primarily because of reductions in high school attendance among
former Corpsmembers. These reductions in high school attendance are due at
least in part to the timing of terminations from Job Corps within our sample
(late summer and early fall) and to the GEDs Corpsmembers earned while they were
in the program (See Section, C below).

Second, the findings for wage rates among male Corpsmembers are puzzling.
Our estimates suggest that Corpsmen tended to earn slightly less per hour than
they would have earned had they not enrolled in Job Corps. In contrast, we find
that Corpswomen without children received slightly higher wages. However, the
negative wage impacts for males are statistically insignificant (i.e., they
easily could be 0 or above); hence, it is not clear how to interpret them. On
the other hand, the positive wage impacts for females are statistically significant. A zero wage rate effect, as observed for Corpsmen, could occur even
with increased employability if that employability manifests itself only through
hours of work and earnings, and not through wage rates--perhaps because of (1)
an excess supply of youth labor combined with a minimum wage law, or (2) some
youths trading off additional hours (and earnings) for slightly lower wage rates.

A concern that pervades the analysis is that the differences we observe
among completion categories may be attributable not only to separate treatment
effects, but also to differences in the underlying characteristics of youths who
select into the different completion statuses. However, we obtain similar results to those presented here even when we control (i.e., adjust) for several
potential differences among Corpsmembers (including factors such as preenrollment values of the dependent variables, age, race—ethnicity, education, training,
previous work history, and health). Completers include both youths with high
abilities and those with low labor-market opportunities (i.e., lower opportunity
costs to staying in the program), which results in opposite biases when we estimate the impacts attributable to program completion, as opposed to impacts
attributable to underlying differences among completers. (Estimates of the
latter would embody upward bias from youths with high innate abilities and downward bias from youths with low labor-market potential. See Mallar et al., 1978,
Chapter VII.) Our best estimate with the current data is that the biases are
largely offsetting after controlling for preenrollment differences, which we do
throughout this paper, so that the impacts we estimate for program completers
can be attributed in general to program completion.

The robustness of the findings is shown in Table 4. The various estimates are made with alternative sets of assumptions regarding observable and unobservable differences between the Job Corps and comparison groups and observable
differences among the three Job Corps completion categories. Estimates are presented by sex and completion category and, in the last two columns, for the overall Job Corps program using the distributions by sex and completion category in
fiscal year 1977 (the primary year that our sample covers) to reweight the
individual estimates.

TABLE 4

ESTIMATES OF EFFECT ON WEEKLY EARNINGS IN WEEK PRIOR TO INTERVIEW UNDER ALTERNATIVE ECONOMETRIC SPECIFICATIONS[a]

Econometric Specification	Males			Females			Overall Impact	
	Program Completers	Partial Completers	Early Dropouts	Program Completers	Partial Completers	Early Dropouts	Weighted Average[b] for All Enrollees	Weighted Average[c] with Zero for All Noncompleters
A. Estimates Presented in the Main Volume								
1. Pre- to Post-program Change in Difference in Sample Mean	23.25***	1.65	-8.57	22.52***	3.51	1.12	4.93*	6.61***
B. Estimates Assuming Treatment Allocations are Exogenous[d]								
1. Difference in Sample Means	21.65***	1.22	-1.05	29.92***	-1.05	-7.77	5.47*	6.38***
2. Pre- to Post-program Change in Difference in Sample Mean	21.88***	1.38	-12.17	22.06***	5.09	0.10	3.56*	6.28***
3. Controlling for Preenrollment Earnings	21.72***	1.27	-4.77	23.23***	8.13	-4.84	5.40**	6.34***
4. Controlling for Several Exogenous Variables	19.21***	6.25	2.97	21.46***	11.48**	-7.34	7.95***	5.68***
5. Controlling for Exogenous Variables and Preenrollment Earnings	19.77***	5.54	-0.66	21.04***	9.87*	-6.16	6.87***	5.76***
C. Estimates Adjusting for Endogeneity of Treatment Allocations by Correcting Error Terms for Unobserved Differences Between Job Corps & Comparison Groups[e]								
1. Difference in Sample Means	23.31***	2.88	0.67	28.14***	14.76*	-2.90	8.67*	7.05***
2. Pre- to Post-program Change in Difference in Sample Means	18.38**	-2.11	-15.78	22.58***	5.69	0.70	1.23	5.59***
3. Controlling for Preenrollment Earnings	21.66**	1.21	-4.83	26.08***	11.40	-1.56	6.16*	6.54***
4. Controlling for Several Exogenous Variables	28.67***	15.81	12.58	27.36***	17.55*	-1.13	16.18**	8.11***
5. Controlling for Exogenous Variables and Preenrollment Earnings	26.72***	12.57	6.42	24.60***	13.55	-2.44	12.72**	7.49***

Table 4 (continued)

* Statistically significant at the 90 percent level of confidence
** Statistically significant at the 95 percent level of confidence
*** Statistically significant at the 99 percent level of confidence

a/ The dependent variable in this table is the respondent's earnings for the week prior to the first follow-up interview (on average seven months after Corpsmembers left the program).

b/ The overall impact estimates presented in this column were computed with a weighting by sex and program completion category corresponding to the observed distributions for Job Corps in fiscal year 1977 (the primary year that Job Corps sample members were in the program). Thus, the estimates in this column are representative of the average impacts from the program in fiscal year 1977. The effects for women with children (approximately 4.5 percent of Corpsmembers seven months after leaving Job Corps) are assumed to be equal to zero. (The estimates were always very small in magnitude and statistically insignificant.)

c/ The estimates in this column were computed with a weighting by sex and program completion category as in the previous column (see footnote c above), except that the effects for all partial completers and early dropouts are assumed to be equal to zero.

d/ The next ten alternative sets of estimates were computed on a common set of observations that had complete data for all of the variables used in any of the estimates. The five alternative sets of estimates shown in this section are adjusted by regressions for observable differences among the program-treatment and comparison groups ranging from no adjustments (difference in sample means) to adjustments for 14 exogenous variables and for the preenrollment value of the dependent variable (controlling for exogenous variables and preenrollment earnings).

e/ The five alternative sets of estimates presented in this section control both for varying degrees of observable differences and for unobservable differences (i.e., endogeneity of Job Corps participation corrected by a Heckman adjustment of the error terms).

The first row of Table 4 repeats the estimates presented for civilian earnings in Tables 1 and 2. The next five rows show alternative estimates under various levels of control for observable differences among the groups (program completer, partial completer, early dropouts, and comparison group).[1/] The bottom five rows show alternative estimates that control both for unobservable differences between the Job Corps and comparison groups (using the Heckman, 1979, approach)[2/] and for observable differences among all four groups. These last ten rows of estimates are based on a common set of observations that had complete data for all of the exogenous and lagged dependent variables needed in the most complex regression (row C.5). Hence, the underlying samples have a slightly small number of observations than used for the estimates presented in the earlier tables which did not require complete data on all of these explanatory variables. (The econometric procedures used in row B.2 were the same for those for A.1, except that the smaller set of observations was used for B.2.)

All of these estimates show basically the same impacts: (1) a large gain in earnings for program completers (statistically significant), (2) small and insignificant effects for noncompleters, and (3) a moderate impact on earnings for the overall sample. Only the insignificant effects for noncompleters exhibit much sensitivity to the alternative specifications, which is typical of insignificant parameters. From our empirical tests thus far, the basic findings seem to be insensitive to changes in the econometric specifications regarding observable and unobservable differences between the program-treatment and comparison groups and observable differences between completion categories within the program-treatment group. If anything, the more complete specifications suggest that the gains in earnings reported in the earlier tables are on the conservative side and biased toward zero (for example, compare row A.1 to row C.5, the most complete specification).

So far we have been unable to obtain reliable estimates that control for unobserved differences among Corpsmembers by completion categories because of identification problems. Thus, there may be biases among completion categories even though the estimates for overall impacts are consistent. (We do know the "true" proportion in each category.) However, the general findings by completion category are probably representative, since the estimated effects for the

---

[1/] Fourteen variables were included in the equations that control for age, education, race/ethnicity, health, and preenrollment earnings.

[2/] See Barnow, Cain, and Goldberger (1978) and Mallar (1979) for more details on the application of the Heckman approach to program evaluations. A probit equation was estimated for the probability of being in Job Corps in order to obtain a consistent estimate of the unobservable "Mills Ratio" variable which needs to be included in the Heckman formulation. In addition to the explanatory variables outlined in the previous footnote the probit equation for the probability of being in Job Corps included three variables representing access to Job Corps recruitment, knowledge of the program, and proximity to Job Corps centers. The resulting probit equation had good predictive ability and identified the earnings equation quite well (see Mallar, 1979). The main assumption needed here is that the comparison and program sites do not differ in unobserved ways that affect earnings behavior (which is borne out by secondary data).

group with near zero treatment (early dropouts) are usually close to zero and the overall program effects are statistically significant in general.

The exogenous variables that were included in the fourth and fifth equations for Table 4 control for differences in age, preenrollment education, race-ethnicity, and preenrollment health. The estimating probit equations for Job Corps versus comparison group status (needed for the adjustments for unobservable differences) additionally included variables for proximity to a Job Corps center (living in a three-digit zip code area where a Job Corps center is located), the number of youths from home areas (three-digit zip code areas) who enrolled in Job Corps in fiscal year 1975, and the number of youths per capita from home areas who enrolled in Job Corps in fiscal year 1975. These three additional variables for the Job Corps participation equation are highly significant, enable the earnings equation to be clearly identified, and provide very good predictors of Job Corps participation for our sample. Thus, we obtain very good estimates of Job Corps participation that are uncorrelated with errors in the earnings equations.

Our empirical findings suggest that any unobservable differences between the Job Corps and comparison groups are small in magnitude overall. This may seem surprising since researchers generally think that (1) more highly motivated youths will self-select into the program and into the program completer group and (2) this higher motivation is unobserved. We can control for motivational differences at least approximately, however, and there are equally strong reasons to suspect unobservable differences in the opposite direction. Preenrollment measures of labor-market and related activities and other observable variables are useful to adjust for differences in motivation.

Because of the relatively short follow-up period, there is some potential for additional biases in these results. Once again, however, the biases will work in opposite directions so that the net bias is probably small. The estimated impacts for <u>completers</u> may be biased upwards because nearly one-half of the baseline sample of Corpsmembers were still in the program at the cut-off date for the first follow-up survey (this is true even though we obtain similar estimates of effects by completion status after controlling for all types of variables). Therefore, the first follow-up sample of completers probably over-represents youths who have high inate abilities and, hence, complete the Job Corps program quickly (as opposed to youths who move through the program more slowly and, hence, are more likely to still be in Job Corps at the cut-off date). Similarly, the first follow-up sample may underrepresent completers from the youngest age cohort because younger Corpsmembers will have entered the program a shorter time ago, on average, than older Corpsmembers. In contrast, there may be some downward bias for completers because they will have been out of Job Corps a shorter time, on average, than noncompleters and, hence, their employment and earnings may be temporarily low as a result of their recent reentry into the labor market. This downward bias for completers is likely to be especially strong when data are averaged over the entire postprogram time period, because the postprogram period for completers will contain disproportionately fewer months beyond the initial transition period than the postprogram period for noncompleters.

2. Impacts for the Initial Months after Leaving Job Corps

Estimates for the average Job Corps effects on employment and earnings over the entire first follow-up period (from the time of termination to the first follow-up interview—an average of six full months[1]) provide a decidedly different picture from the effects observed in the week prior to interview. When Corpsmembers' work histories for the entire postprogram observation period are averaged, they show much more negative impacts. As summarized in Table 5, there were small increases in labor-force participation (looking for work or employed), employment, hours worked, weeks worked, and earnings for males who completed the program. However, Corpsmen who did not complete the program generally showed decreases in each of these measures of labor-market activity. The effects for both completers and noncompleters are significant at approximately the 95 percent level of statistical confidence, except for those associated with earnings. Taken together, the effects for Corpsmen who completed the program and those who did not yield an estimated impact on employment and earnings for the average enrollee that is negative and statistically insignificant for the first few months after leaving Job Corps, while the effect on labor-force participation is positive and significant.

The employment and earnings impacts for childless females are more positive but less significant statistically. The impacts for Corpswomen who completed the program are positive, on average, but are small and, except for labor-force participation and earnings, insignificantly different from 0 for the first six months after leaving Job Corps. However, for females, the effects for early dropouts are similar to those for completers, although they are less significant in terms of statistical confidence. The estimated impacts for partial completers are negative, but are also insignificantly different from zero. Overall, for Corpswomen we find positive but small and statistically insignificant impacts for the first few months after they left the program.

At first glance, the findings for the first six months after leaving Job Corps may seem puzzling or even contradictory when contrasted to estimates for the week before the interview.[2] As shown graphically in Figures 1 and 2, however, the findings are quite consistent. When Corpsmembers left the program, they initially experienced a period of unemployment as they reentered the regular labor market; not until after a few months did the positive impacts of

---

[1] Although the postprogram period covers an average of seven months, the beginning and end months with partial data are excluded from this analysis.

[2] A minor factor that may contribute to the observed differences is that, while jobs for the monthly data must have lasted at least two weeks to have been recorded in the interview, all current jobs were recorded. Consequently, the most recent week's data, contains transitory jobs that are missed for earlier periods.

Job Corps begin to emerge. Rather than a diminishing of the effects over time, as had been previously suggested (see Harris, 1969), we found a sizeable increase in impacts over the short-term period. Only after about six months from the point of termination did the positive impacts of Job Corps begin to predominate. The labor force participation rates were relatively high initially for Corps-members, but it appears to have taken them a few months to find jobs (and for the positive impacts on employment and earnings to be observable).

It is important to consider what causes this time pattern of first nega-tive and then positive impacts in the short-run. There seems to be two plausible and reinforcing explanations. First, as suggested by Corpsmembers (See Mallar et al., 1978), there seems to be a need for better placement and related ser-vices in the postprogram period (Corpsmembers' perceptions seem to be borne out by their short-term work histories after leaving Job Corps). Second, the main postprogram impacts on employment and earnings were for program completers who finished a training program and received GEDs (See Section B), and, because these youths had been out of the labor market for up to two years, it may have taken them a few months to "catch up" to youths in the comparison group who had been in the labor force more regularly.

3. <u>Impacts on Employment and Earnings During the Program</u>
Of course, while Corpsmembers are in the program, they forego some amount of employment and earnings in the regular labor market. The earnings foregone by the average <u>participant</u> amounted to $29.74 per week (the per-participant basis is appropriate for in-program impacts). As discussed further in the benefit-cost analysis (see Thornton, Long, and Mallar, 1979), however, Job Corps participants produced as part of their training in work projects and work-experience programs output whose social value was estimated to be approximately $29.59 per week on average.[1]

4. <u>Differences in Impacts Among Corpsmembers and Centers</u>
The analysis of impacts on employment and earnings was further extended to evaluate differences in impacts that are associated with characteristics of Corpsmembers and features of centers. The particular impact associated with each factor is adjusted via regression to net out the independent effects of all other variables. No differences in the labor-market impacts of the Job Corps program resulted from the alternative features of centers that we have been able to measure thus far in our evaluation. Neither center administration, operator, size, location nor coed status had any significant effects on the pre- to post-program changes in employment or earnings for either males or females.

In contrast, the characteristics of Corpsmembers did seem to affect the impacts of the program on their employment and earnings. Caution is necessary in interpreting these differences in Job Corps impacts among Corpsmembers,

---

[1] This value of program output estimate represents an alternative supplier's price and may be in excess of the demand value. It includes only a small amount of output consumed by Corpsmembers and the value of only a few materials and supplies provided by Job Corps. For more details, see Long (1979).

TABLE 5

ESTIMATES OF EMPLOYMENT AND RELATED EFFECTS FOR CIVILIANS AVERAGED OVER THE ENTIRE FOLLOW-UP PERIOD[a]

Variable	Unweighted Sample Mean For Corpsmembers At Follow-Up	Average Job Corps Effect For Program Completers	Average Job Corps Effect For Partial Completers	Average Job Corps Effect For Early Dropouts	Average Job Corps Effect For All Enrollees
A. MALES					
Percent of time looking for work or employed[b]	0.819	0.077	0.035	-0.012	0.029
Percent of time employed	0.487	0.053	-0.094	-0.081	-0.045
Earnings per week	$63.30	12.78	-16.10	-22.37	-9.94
Hours per week	18.86	1.52	-3.43	-3.90	-2.13
Weeks worked per six months	12.69	1.37	-2.44	-2.11	-1.17
B. FEMALES WITHOUT CHILDREN					
Percent of time looking for work or employed[b]	0.729	0.209	0.152	0.104	0.150
Percent of time employed	0.358	0.018	-0.049	0.012	-0.005
Earnings per week	$37.29	14.75	-2.31	10.04	7.75
Hours per week	12.76	0.78	-1.03	2.42	0.89
Weeks worked per six months	9.33	0.48	-1.27	0.31	-0.11
C. FEMALES WITH CHILDREN					
Percent of time looking for work or employed[b]	N.C.	N.C.	N.C.	N.C.	N.C.
Percent of time employed	0.213	0.064	-0.099	-0.224	-0.100
Earnings per week	$20.92	4.80	-9.92	-24.89	-11.49
Hours per week	7.70	3.21	-4.11	-11.43	-4.84
Weeks worked per six months	5.54	1.66	-2.58	-5.83	-2.61

[a] The estimates of Job Corps effects are adjusted for preenrollment differences in the variables between the Job Corps and comparison samples, except where noted.

[b] Appropriate baseline measures were not available for these variables, and the estimates are from regressions of "Looking for Work or Employed" on several sample characteristics.

N.C. = Not calculated

FIGURE 1

ESTIMATES OF TIME PATHS OF INCREASES IN EMPLOYMENT FOR MALES[a/]

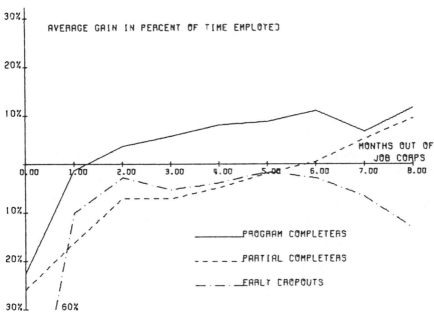

AVERAGE GAIN IN PERCENT OF TIME EMPLOYED

MONTHS OUT OF JOB CORPS

_____ PROGRAM COMPLETERS

_ _ _ _ _ PARTIAL COMPLETERS

_ . _ . _ EARLY DROPOUTS

FIGURE 2

ESTIMATES OF TIME PATHS OF INCREASES IN EMPLOYMENT

FOR FEMALES WITHOUT CHILDREN[a/]

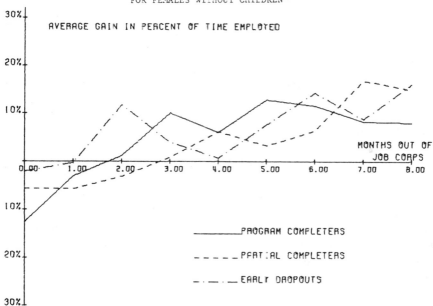

AVERAGE GAIN IN PERCENT OF TIME EMPLOYED

MONTHS OUT OF JOB CORPS

_____ PROGRAM COMPLETERS

_ _ _ _ _ PARTIAL COMPLETERS

_ . _ . _ EARLY DROPOUTS

[a/] These estimates are from error-component regressions with data pooled over months and controlling for several sample characteristics.

however, because the causality of the differences is largely unknown. For example, significantly larger than average beneficial impacts are found for Hispanics, but these are likely to be partly determined by their higher program completion rates. At the same time, better postprogram experience for a group undoubtedly causes longer participation and more completions (Corpsmembers mainly learn about the program from friends and relatives. See Kerachsky and Mallar, 1978).

Among male Corpsmembers, both race-ethnicity and age at termination influenced their labor-market experience. Hispanics and whites tended to have much larger gains in employment and earnings than did either blacks or American Indians. In addition, those who were at least 18 years of age when they left the program tended to receive greater benefits in terms of employment and earnings.

For females without children, those who already had a high school diploma received greater gains, as measured by employment and earnings. In addition, Corpswomen who were at least 18 years of age when they left Job Corps tended to have higher earnings. While there are race-ethnicity differences for females, the subgroup differences for this characteristic are not significantly different from the overall means for either employment or earnings.

5. Potential for Future Gains in Employment and Earnings

The time paths of impacts in Figures 1 and 2 show a great deal of potential for future gains in employment and earnings among Corpsmembers. Other evidence for larger future gains, in addition to improvements in current earnings and employment rates, are shown by the higher incidence of union jobs among current employment (see Tables 1 through 3), as well as by the Job Corps' impact on high school diplomas or their equivalent (see below). The potential for gains in future earnings is discussed in more detail in the following section.

B. IMPACTS ON INVESTMENTS IN HUMAN CAPITAL

For the most part, the impacts on investments in human capital are quite positive. Therefore, there appears to be great potential for future gains in earnings. The only possible negative finding is for high school education-- former Corpsmembers were less likely to be enrolled in high school during the postprogram period than they would have been in the absence of Job Corps. However, this high school effect can be attributed, in part, to both the receipt of GEDs while in Job Corps and the fixed entry dates for high school, which effectively excluded Corpsmembers who left Job Corps during the late summer and early fall. Corpsmembers were more likely to be in college and working toward advanced degrees. For other types of investments in human capital, the impacts of Job Corps are uniformly positive. On average, Corpsmembers (1) were more likely to be in a training or work-experience program, (2) had higher job mobility, (3) had improved health, and (4) were more likely to be in the military.

1. Education and Training

One effect of Job Corps is to reduce participation in high school education programs. This is shown in Table 6 for the week prior to the follow-up

TABLE 6

ESTIMATES OF EDUCATION AND TRAINING EFFECTS IN WEEK PRIOR TO INTERVIEW[a]

Variable	Unweighted Sample Mean For Corpsmembers At Follow-Up	Average Job Corps Effect For Program Completers	Average Job Corps Effect For Partial Completers	Average Job Corps Effect For Early Dropouts	Average Job Corps Effect For All Enrollees
A. MALES					
In school[b]	0.108	-0.020	-0.015	0.004	-0.009
° High school	0.036	-0.046	-0.026	0.001	-0.021
° College	0.026	0.032	-0.007	-0.007	0.006
° Vocational[c]	0.011	0.004	-0.010	0.003	0.003
° Other	0.035	-0.001	0.004	0.007	0.004
High school diploma or GED	0.195	0.149	0.025	0.010	0.056
In training program[b]	0.044	0.025	0.013	0.029	0.023
B. FEMALES WITHOUT CHILDREN					
In school[b]	0.145	-0.067	-0.116	-0.018	-0.062
° High school	0.026	-0.107	-0.102	-0.065	-0.089
° College	0.064	0.067	0.0001	0.016	0.027
° Vocational[c]	0.023	-0.002	0.003	-0.002	-0.001
° Other	0.032	-0.025	-0.018	0.034	0.001
High school diploma or GED	0.410	0.172	0.003	0.010	0.057
In training program[b]	0.032	-0.010	-0.020	0.030	0.003
C. FEMALES WITH CHILDREN[d]					
In school[b]	0.052	-0.044	-0.133	0.042	-0.070
High school diploma or GED[b]	0.250	0.034	0.043	0.081	0.056
In training program[b]	0.052	0.004	-0.016	0.141	0.053

a/ The estimates of Job Corps effects are adjusted for preenrollment differences in the variables between the Job Corps and comparison samples, except where noted.

b/ Appropriate baseline measures were not available for these variables, and the estimates are simple Job Corps minus comparison-group means at postprogram.

c/ Vocational schools are defined to include technical, business, and secretarial schools.

d/ Females with children attend school very rarely in a one-week period. Consequently, the detailed results for this group are not very meaningful and are not included here.

interview, and in Table 7 for the entire postprogram period. This effect is most pronounced for childless females, who have a reduced probability of attending high school (approximatley 8 percentage points), that is statistically significant for both the week prior to the survey and when averaged over the entire first follow-up period. This reduction, together with the sometimes negative (but small and statistically insignificant) effects on vocational schools and the "other" category of schools (primarily adult education), results in a large overall reduction in school attendance. However, Corpswomen without children have a significantly higher probability of attending college. The impacts on attending high school for male Corpsmembers are also negative and statistically significant. However, the magnitude of these negative impacts are much smaller for Corpsmen than for Corpswomen (only about one-third to one-fourth as large, depending on the time period covered).

It is unclear whether the impact on high school attendance should be considered a net benefit or a net cost to participants. To the extent that former Corpsmembers are less likely to return to high school because they obtain GEDs and other education benefits while in Job Corps, the impact on high school attendance is a net benefit. Table 6 shows large (and statistically significant) impacts from Job Corps on the probability that youths (both males and females) had a high school diploma or equivalent degree (i.e., either a regular diploma or GED). For program completers, there is a 15 percentage-point increase for males and a 17 percentage-point increase for childless females in the probability that they had a high school diploma or equivalent degree.

An alternative explanation for part of the effects on high school attendance is less positive: some Corpsmembers simply may have left the center too late to enroll for the 1977-78 academic year. Over 20 percent of the sample did not terminate from Job Corps until after September 1.

Neither of the above reasons for lower high school attendance applies to early dropouts from Job Corps. The increase in high school degrees was only about 1 percentage point for both males and females who were early dropouts (statistically insignificant), and they were all out of Job Corps in time to register for the fall semester. This may explain why the reductions in high school attendance are much smaller and statistically insignificant for early dropouts. (In fact, there is a very slight increase for male Corpsmembers in the week prior to the interview.)

A more encouraging Job Corps effect is the increase in college attendance shown by program completers among both male and childless-female Corpsmembers. Although the size of this effect is modest in absolute terms, it is more impressive both in percentage terms (approximately a 59 percent increase over the number that would have attended college) and when viewed in the context of the small proportion of sample members who had a high school diploma or GED and, thus, who were nominally eligible for college (only approximately one-fifth of the sample were eligible for college in this sense, even after including the Job Corps impact on GEDs).

TABLE 7

ESTIMATES OF EDUCATION AND TRAINING EFFECTS AVERAGED OVER THE ENTIRE FOLLOW-UP PERIOD[a]

Variable (Percent of Time)	Unweighted Sample Mean For Corpsmembers At Follow-Up	Average Job Corps Effect For Program Completers	Average Job Corps Effect For Partial Completers	Average Job Corps Effect For Early Dropouts	Average Job Corps Effect For All Enrollees
A. MALES					
In school	0.099	-0.025	-0.021	-0.090	-0.050
○ High school	0.058	-0.029	-0.024	-0.014	-0.022
○ College[b]	0.017	0.021	0.0005	-0.0005	0.006
○ Vocational[b]	0.016	0.006	0.009	0.003	0.006
○ Other	0.020	-0.002	-0.002	-0.002	-0.002
In training program	0.010	0.017	0.006	-0.005	0.005
B. FEMALES WITHOUT CHILDREN					
In school	0.114	-0.051	-0.085	-0.051	-0.061
○ High school	0.042	-0.070	-0.075	-0.049	-0.066
○ College[b]	0.050	0.050	0.003	0.018	0.023
○ Vocational[b]	0.027	0.006	-0.013	-0.015	-0.008
○ Other	0.023	-0.022	-0.018	-0.014	-0.018
In training program	0.022	0.004	-0.011	-0.001	-0.003
C. FEMALES WITH CHILDREN					
In school	0.066	-0.017	-0.095	0.011	-0.029
○ High school	0.021	-0.069	-0.040	-0.080	-0.065
○ College[b]	0.016	0.006	-0.004	-0.016	-0.006
○ Vocational[b]	0.004	-0.019	-0.027	-0.027	-0.025
○ Other	0.047	0.040	-0.022	0.097	0.044
In training program	0.021	-0.022	0.007	0.032	0.008

a/ Appropriate baseline measures were not available for any of the variables in this table, and the estimates are all simple Job Corps minus comparison group means for the postprogram period. All of these variables are measured as the percent of time participating in the program.

b/ Vocational schools are defined to include technical, business, and secretarial schools.

Male Corpsmembers were also more likely to be enrolled in training and work-experience programs (statistically significant) during the week prior to the interview. (Evidence on training and work-experience impacts for all groups are shown in Tables 1 through 3, as well as in Tables 6 and 7.) Overall, female Corpsmembers were more likely to be in a training or special work-experience program during the week prior to the interview, but the impact is smaller than for males. This impact for Corpswomen is very small and statistically insignificant. When averaged over the entire postprogram period, attendance in training programs increases for Corpsmen and decreased slightly for Corpswomen, but is statistically insignificant for both groups.

2. Other Human Capital Effects
The impacts of Job Corps on other investments in human capital (see Table 8) were generally positive. Corpsmembers had greater mobility, better health, and were more likely to have joined the military. Even without counting the moves that coincided with their leaving centers and the program (i.e., moving from a center to a city other than the one in which the Corpsmember had resided before entering Job Corps), Corpsmembers were much more mobile than youths in the comparison sample. The encouraging aspect of these moves is that, except for females with children, they were usually in response to job opportunities or, to a lesser extent, school or training. These effects are significantly different from zero at greater than the 99 percent level of statistical confidence. This pattern of effects was particularly evident for program completers. There was also a strong mobility effect for noncompleters, but they were proportionately less likely to report that the effect was in response to job opportunities or for school or training.

Former Corpsmembers also tended to show small improvements in health status, as shown by reductions in serious health problems. However, this effect is weak and not significantly different from 0. Finally, as noted earlier, Job Corps increases the probability that individuals will enter the military service. While this was also reported above as an employment effect, it also has human-capital implications, both because entering the military (i.e., passing the Armed Forces Qualifying Examination) indicates the attainment of a certain level of human-capital development and because participation in the military provides additional human-capital development through training and job-experience benefits. Finally, the increases in civilian employment discussed earlier should also produce some longer-run human-capital benefits through job experience.

C. DEPENDENCE ON PUBLIC TRANSFER PROGRAMS
As shown in Table 9, former Corpsmembers experienced reduced participation in most transfer programs. Overall (i.e., for all enrollees), the percent of time receiving cash welfare, Food Stamps, public housing, Unemployment Insurance, and Workers' Compensation were all reduced in the postprogram period. For males, the only statistically significant reduction was for Unemployment Insurance, and this was concentrated among program completers and partial completers

TABLE 8

ESTIMATES OF MOBILITY AND HEALTH EFFECTS AVERAGED OVER THE ENTIRE FOLLOW-UP PERIOD

Variable	Unweighted Sample Mean For Corpsmembers At Follow-Up	Average Job Corps Effect For Program Completers	Average Job Corps Effect For Partial Completers	Average Job Corps Effect For Early Dropouts	Average Job Corps Effect For All Enrollees
A. MALES					
Number of Moves per Six-Month Period[a]					
° For job opportunity	0.252	0.321	0.135	0.136	0.191
° For school or training	0.076	0.097	0.029	0.062	0.063
° All outside of city	0.355	0.391	0.214	0.206	0.264
° Outside of city, excluding move coinciding with leaving Job Corps	0.245	0.223	0.131	0.176	0.177
Serious helath problem[b]	0.027	0.001	-0.009	-0.025	-0.012
B. FEMALES WITHOUT CHILDREN					
Number of Moves per Six-Month Period[a]					
° For job opportunity	0.248	0.340	0.165	0.109	0.195
° For school or training	0.070	0.081	0.021	0.049	0.050
° All outside of city	0.514	0.469	0.314	0.225	0.325
° Outside of city, excluding move coinciding with leaving Job Corps	0.338	0.230	0.189	0.157	0.189
Serious health problem[b]	0.045	-0.006	0.007	0.008	0.004
C. FEMALES WITH CHILDREN					
Number of Moves per Six-Month Period[a]					
° For job opportunity	0.063	0.057	0.024	-0.020	0.016
° For school or training	0.042	0.036	0.014	0.084	0.049
° All outside of city	0.240	0.173	0.319	-0.026	0.137
° Outside of city, excluding move coinciding with leaving Job Corps	0.156	0.088	0.184	-0.040	0.066
Serious health problem[b]	0.062	0.013	0.015	-0.073	-0.021

[a] Appropriate baseline measures were not available for these variables, so the numbers presented in this table are from regressions of number of moves per six-month period on sample characteristics.

[b] These estimates of Job Corps effects are adjusted for preenrollment differences in serious health problems between the Job Corps and comparison samples.

353

TABLE 9

ESTIMATES OF WELFARE DEPENDENCE EFFECTS AVERAGED OVER THE ENTIRE FOLLOW-UP PERIOD[a/]

Variable (Percent of Time Receiving)	Unweighted Sample Mean For Corpsmembers In Follow-Up	Average Job Corps Effect For Program Completers	Average Job Corps Effect For Partial Completers	Average Job Corps Effect For Early Dropouts	Average Job Corps Effect For All Enrollees
A. MALES					
Cash welfare[b/]	0.014	-0.007	-0.006	0.001	-0.004
Food Stamps	0.192	-0.009	-0.022	-0.030	-0.021
Public Housing	0.124	-0.017	-0.029	-0.007	-0.017
Unemployment Insurance	0.002	-0.010	-0.010	-0.005	-0.008
Workers' Compensation	0.002	-0.002	-0.002	-0.003	-0.002
B. FEMALES WITHOUT CHILDREN					
Cash welfare[b/]	0.023	-0.086	-0.059	-0.042	-0.060
Food Stamps	0.201	-0.071	-0.013	-0.139	-0.081
Public housing	0.104	-0.055	0.025	-0.014	-0.015
Unemployment Insurance	0.002	-0.003	-0.004	-0.006	-0.005
Workers' Compensation	0.001	0.002	-0.0001	0.0001	0.001
C. FEMALES WITH CHILDREN					
Cash welfare[b/]	0.292	-0.344	-0.028	0.146	-0.053
Food Stamps	0.363	-0.070	0.0003	-0.194	-0.099
Public housing	0.125	0.056	0.035	-0.236	-0.067
Unemployment Insurance	0.000	-0.006	-0.007	-0.003	-0.005
Workers' Compensation	0.000	-0.0004	-0.0004	-0.0003	-0.0004

[a/] These estimates of Job Corps effects are all adjusted for preenrollment differences in the variances between the Job Corps and comparison samples. All of the variables are measured as the percent of time receiving the source of assistance.

[b/] Cash welfare includes all of the various forms of Aid to Families with Dependent Children (AFDC) and general assistance.

(in part caused by the loss of entitlements while participating in Job Corps). For childless females, the significant reductions were concentrated among program completers for cash welfare, Food Stamps, and public housing. Reductions in the receipt of cash welfare were also noteworthy for females with children who were completers. Naturally, there were also substantial reductions in the receipt of these types of transfer payments whild Corpsmembers were in residence at the centers. Not surprisingly (as shown in Thornton, Long, and Mallar, 1979), these in-program reductions were even larger than the postprogram reductions.

D. DRUG USE AND CRIMINAL BEHAVIOR

Corpsmembers showed reductions both in drug and alcohol abuse and in criminal behavior in the postprogram period. As summarized in Table 10, there were small impacts on the probability of entering drug- or alcohol-treatment programs. The small size of the effects is due in part to the low overall use of these treatment programs. The effect for male program completers is note-worthy both on a percentage basis and for its statistical significance.

Reductions in criminal behavior are evidenced by reductions in the number of postprogram arrests for all crimes (arrests for minor motor-vehicle violations were not counted) and in the reduced probability of being in jail or prison during the week of the survey; however, except for males, the effects tend to be statistically insignificant. The arrest data for males show very large and statistically significant reductions in criminality. There were more than eight fewer arrests for every 100 Corpsmen during the first six months after leaving Job Corps (significant at greater than the 99 percent level of statistical confidence). These arrest data almost certainly greatly under-estimate the impacts on crimes, for two reasons: (1) there are typically several crimes associated with each arrest, and (2) the data are from self-reports of arrests, and other studies have found substantial underreporting of arrests in self-reports as compared to official court records.[1]

The reductions in crime are continuations of effects observed during the program. During the program, however, the reductions in arrests were approxi-mately twice as large. These reductions contribute greatly to the social benefits associated with Job Corps participation.

E. CONCLUSIONS

The empirical analysis summarized in this paper finds that Job Corps is successful in achieving most of the desired impacts during the short-term post-program period. The desired impacts are particularly evident for Corpsmembers who complete the program, which appears to be at least in part attributable to program completion and not just to the underlying characteristics of completers. We also find that the beneficial impacts are not deteriorating as rapidly as

---

[1] Schore, Maynard, and Piliavin (1979), for example, have found that the underreporting was about 50 percent for a sample of ex-addicts and ex-offenders.

TABLE 10

ESTIMATES OF EFFECTS ON ANTISOCIAL BEHAVIOR AVERAGED OVER THE ENTIRE FOLLOW-UP PERIOD[a]

Variable	Unweighted Sample Mean For Corpsmembers In Follow-Up	Average Job Corps Effect For Program Completers	Average Job Corps Effect For Partial Completers	Average Job Corps Effect For Early Dropouts	Average Job Corps Effect For All Enrollees
A. MALES					
Participation in a drug- or alcohol-treatment program per six-month period	0.011	-0.035	-0.017	-0.006	-0.018
Number of arrests per six-month period	0.124	-0.064	-0.069	-0.114	-0.086
In jail or prison during the week of the survey[b]	0.026	-0.023	0.007	0.007	-0.002
B. FEMALES WITHOUT CHILDREN					
Participation in a drug- or alcohol-treatment program per six-month period	0.006	-0.002	-0.009	0.002	-0.003
Number of arrests per six-month period	0.025	-0.007	-0.020	0.022	0.001
In jail or prison during the week of the survey[b]	0.002	-0.003	-0.003	0.018	0.005
C. FEMALES WITH CHILDREN					
Participation in a drug- or alcohol-treatment program per six-month period	0.0	0.006	-0.020	0.009	-0.001
Number of arrests per six-month period	0.007	-0.078	0.011	-0.111	-0.065
In jail or prison during the week of the survey[b]	0.0	0.0	0.0	0.0	0.0

[a] The estimates of Job Corps effects are adjusted for preenrollment differences in the variables between the Job Corps and comparison samples.

[b] This includes commitments to "reform schools," "detention centers," and similar criminal justice facilities for youth, as well as regular jails and prisons.

had been previously suspected, and, in fact, employment and earnings impacts increase rapidly during the first three months that the Corpsmembers are out of the program after some initial problems for Corpsmembers when they reenter the labor market upon terminating from Job Corps.

The analysis was performed separately for males, childless females, and females with children. For each of these groups we estimated separate effects by length of stay in the program, as measured by completion status. For all groups of Corpsmembers, the immediate time period after leaving Job Corps represented an adjustment period during which the program impacts appear confusing or even counter to the expected impacts that are subsequently observed. Males and females who are program completers followed this brief period with positive and usually statistically significant responses in all areas--increased employment and earnings, increased investments in human capital, reduced dependence on welfare and other transfer income, reduced drug and alcohol abuse, and reduced criminal behavior. (Exceptions are noted in this paper.)

The results for noncompleters and females with children are less consistent and rarely significantly different from zero. Early dropouts from the program receive small amounts of program treatments at best, and they are likely to include the least able enrollees as well as overqualified enrollees who immediately leave Job Corps for better opportunities (see Mallar et al., 1978). Females with children have constraints or opportunities that appear to reduce responses to employment, schooling, training or other opportunities. However, so few former Corpsmembers have children living with them that is difficult to form statistically confident conclusions about them from our sample.

The overall short-term impacts for the Job Corps program in fiscal year 1977 are presented in Table 11. The primary findings in terms of magnitude and statistical significance discussed in this paper are summarized in this table. The pattern of the averages for all Corpsmembers follows that for program completers--increased employment and earnings (after the immediate postprogram period), increased military service, increased education and training (except for high school), increased mobility (extremely large effects), reductions in health problems, reductions in welfare assistance, reductions in other transfers, reductions in drug and alcohol abuse, and reductions in criminal behavior. As shown in Table 11, the impacts of Job Corps are especially large in percentage terms.

Beyond the generally positive results, the most noteworthy finding is that these results appear to persist to the end of the seven-month observation period. In fact, if there is any trend after the first few months of postprogram experience, it appears to be toward increased program benefits. This pattern bears further examination, particularly with a longer observation period.

TABLE 11

SUMMARY OF MAIN FINDINGS FOR OVERALL IMPACTS OF JOB CORPS[a]

Variable	(1) Estimated Sample Mean For All Enrollees	(2) Estimated Sample Mean For All Enrollees in the Absence Of Job Corps	(3) Estimated Differential For All Enrollees (1) - (2)	(4) Estimated Percentage Impact For All Enrollees (3)÷(2)x100
A. Civilian labor supply in week prior to interview				
° In labor force	0.816	0.778	0.C38	5%
° Employed	0.451	0.439	0.C12	3%
° Employed full time	0.270	0.236	0.C34	14%
° Hours	14.85	13.53	1.32	10%
° Earnings	$49.04	$44.66	$4.38	10%
B. In military during week prior to interview	0.052	0.033	0.019	58%
C. Education and training in week prior to interview				
° In high school[b]	0.043	0.083	-0.040	-48%
° In college[b]	0.027	0.017	0.010	59%
° Have high school diploma or GED	0.207	0.151	0.056	37%
° In training program[b]	0.049	0.030	0.019	63%
D. Number of moves in six-month period				
° For job opportunity[c]	0.208	0.024	0.184	767%
° For education or training[c]	0.071	0.012	0.059	492%
° All moves out of city[c]	0.362	0.089	0.273	307%
E. Percent of time having serious health problems	0.042	0.050	-0.008	-16%
F. Percent of time receiving public assistance				
° Cash welfare	0.035	0.056	-0.021	-38%
° Food Stamps	0.213	0.253	-0.040	-16%
° Public housing	0.103	0.149	-0.019	-13%
G. Percent of time receiving other transfers				
° Unemployment Insurance	0.003	0.010	-0.0C7	-70%
° Workers' Compensation	0.001	0.002	-0.0C1	-50%
H. Participation in drug/ alcohol treatment program per six-month period	0.015	0.028	-0.013	-46%
I. Number of arrests per six-month period	0.113	0.176	-0.063	-36%

[a] All of the estimates presented in this table are based on observations that were weighted according to the distributions of sex and program completion categories for Job Corps in fiscal year 1977 (the primary year that our Job Corps sample members were in the program). Thus, the estimates in this table are representative of (i.e., unbiased for) the average Job Corps impacts from the program in fiscal year 1977. The base for the percentage impacts shown in the fourth column is the estimated sample mean for all enrollees in the absence of Job Corps from the second column. The estimates are adjusted for preenrollment differences in the variables between the Job Corps and comparison samples, except where noted.

[b] Appropriate baseline measures were not available for these variables, and the estimated impacts presented in this table are simple Job Corps minus comparison-group means at postprogram.

[c] Appropriate baseline measures were not available for these variables, and the estimated impacts presented in this table are from regressions of number of moves per six-month period on sample characteristics.

REFERENCES

Barnow, Burt S., Glen G. Cain, and Arthur S. Goldberger. "Issues in the
  Analysis of Selection Bias." Paper presented at the 1978 Meetings of
  the Econometrics Society, Chicago, Illinois, August 1978.

Harris, Louis, and Associates. A Survey of Ex-Job Corpsmen. New York:
  Harris Associates, April 1969.

Heckman, James J. "Sample Bias as a Specification Error." Econometrica,
  47, January 1979, pp 153-161.

Long, David A. "Value of Output in Work Activities." Princeton, New Jersey:
  Staff Paper SP 79C-02, Mathematica Policy Research, 1979.

Mallar, Charles D. "Alternative Econometric Procedures for Program Evaluations:
  Illustrations from an Evaluation of Job Corps." In Papers and Proceedings of
  the American Statistical Association, Business and Economics Section, 1979.

Mallar, Charles D., Stuart H. Kerachsky, Craig V. D. Thornton, David A. Long,
  Thomas Good, and Patricia Lapczynski. "Evaluation of the Economic Impact
  of the Job Corps Program: First Follow-Up Report." Princeton, New Jersey:
  Project Report 78-14, Mathematica Policy Research, December 1978.

Schore, Jennifer, Rebecca Maynard, and Irving Piliavin. "The Accuracy of
  Self-Reported Arrest Data." In Papers and Proceedings of the American
  Statistical Association, Survey Research Methods Section, 1979.

Thornton, Craig V. D., David A. Long, and Charles D. Mallar. "A Comparative
  Evaluation of the Benefits and Costs of the Job Corps After Seven Months
  of Postprogram Follow-up." Princeton, New Jersey: Staff Paper SP 79C-01,
  Mathematica Policy Research, 1979.

16

Farkas et al. undertake two tasks. First, they raise a number of issues of evaluation strategy in the context of the Youth Entitlement Demonstration. And, second, they present models and methods for analyzing youth labor supply that are closely related to the methods presented in Part I. The empirical results with preprogram data are also of some interest.

The evaluation design, in which random samples are collected from experimental and comparison sites, enables self-selection bias for the coefficient on an experimental/control site dummy variable to be totally eliminated since the treatment can be regarded exogenous. This design also permits estimating a participation function to correct for possible selectivity in a model that compares program participants to nonparticipants in experimental and control sites. The reduced-form impact models will resemble those employed by the other articles in this section. Work is now underway on the first estimates of in-program impacts, and there are preliminary indications of a positive school enrollment effect.[1]

The theme of the chapter is that structural as well as reduced-form models must be a part of program evaluation. The model of youth summer labor supply extends the selection and tobit models employed by Barnow et al. and Heckman in Part I, and by Keeley et al. and Moffitt in Part II in several ways. Non-normal residuals are accounted for, as is the possibility that the tobit is too restrictive a specification to fit data well. (It is replaced with a probit and a truncated normal.) In addition, reservation wages are calculated within a model explicitly representing (the sum of) demand side distortions and fixed costs of working.

We review the steps by which the results presented in Tables 3, 4, and 5 are calculated. First, a wage offer equation is estimated jointly with a probit for employed at all so that selectivity bias is eliminated. Then the predicted wage offer is entered alongside exogenous variables in a truncated normal regression to predict total hours worked.

The results for the wage offer equation are presented in Table 3. The value of time at zero hours of work (W^*) is calculated from the truncated normal coefficients, with B_0, the estimated coefficient for the wage offer, used to deflate the coefficients for the exogenous variables. These are presented in Table 4. Finally, the coefficients for the disemployment index are calculated from the probit in two steps: First, the coefficient for the exogenous variable (age) is used to identify the standard error in the probit. (This is possible because, although the reduced-form specification for the probit contains all exogenous variables, the structural specification for the probit excludes age.) This deflates the coefficients to arrive at W^* + Disemployment Index. Second, we already know W^*, the coefficients for the Disemployment Index are calculated by subtraction. The result is reported in Table 5.

The results of these procedures tell a very reasonable, substantive story. For further calculations with the full sample (the results here are only for younger members of the sample), as well as further discussion of likely selectivity bias in these data, see Farkas et al. (forthcoming, b).

NOTE

1. See Farkas et al. (forthcoming b).

REFERENCES

FARKAS, G., D. A. SMITH, C. BOTTOM, E. W. STROMSDORFER, and R. J. OLSEN (forth-
coming a) The Youth Entitlement Demonstration: Program Impacts During the First 18 Months.
New York: MDRC.
FARKAS, G., E. W. STROMSDORFER, and R. J. OLSEN (forthcoming b) "Youth labor supply
during the summer: evidence for youths from low-income households," in R. Ehrenberg (ed.)
Research in Labor Economics. Greenwich, CT: JAI.

Reduced-Form and Structural Models in the Evaluation of the Youth Entitlement Demonstration

George Farkas, Randall J. Olsen, and Ernst W. Stromsdorfer

I. INTRODUCTION

With the passage of the Youth Employment and Demonstration Projects
Act (PL 95-93, August 5, 1977), the Congress provided for an experiment, the
Youth Incentive Entitlement Pilot Projects (YIEPP), which involves the explicit tying together of youth employment and school enrollment. In 17 labor
markets, eligible youths (economically disadvantaged 16-19-year olds who
have not graduated from high school) are being offered a full-time job during
the summer and a part-time job during the school year so long as they are enrolled in school and performing adequately. This is an entitlement program—
sufficient funds have been provided to serve all eligibles who apply. Nevertheless, it remains to be seen whether or not publicly provided, minimum wage
job guarantees for the youth target population will furnish meaningful work
experience and encourage those in school to stay and those out of school to
return. In addition, so little is reliably known concerning the decision-making
of low-income youths about schooling and labor force behavior that until a
good deal more basic conceptualization, measurement, and estimation is accomplished we will continue to lack the intellectual foundation to properly identify
and address the relevant policy issues.

Authors' Note: This work is funded under contract to the Manpower Demonstration Research
Corporation, New York City. The authors are solely responsible for the results reported here.
Sections of this paper were presented at the winter meetings of the Econometric Society, December
30, 1979, Atlanta, Georgia.

From George Farkas, Randall J. Olsen, and Ernst W. Stromsdorfer, "Reduced-Form and Structural Models in the Evaluation of the Youth Entitlement Demonstration." Original manuscript,
1980.

This article describes research design work undertaken preparatory to the evaluation of Entitlement program impacts. Our theme is the need for both reduced-form and structural models when evaluating complex social programs. Examples of these models, the issues and techniques involved in their estimation, and their fit to data on the preprogram behavior of Entitlement eligible youth provide the substance. The essay closes with a summary of issues to be addressed and models to be estimated on this project.

The Program and the Research Design

Youth Entitlement began in the spring of 1978, enrolling youths in 17 local labor markets. Four of these—Baltimore, Cincinnati, Denver, and eight rural counties in southern Mississippi—were chosen as study (experimental) sites, and for each a matched comparison (control) site was selected. These are Cleveland, Louisville, Phoenix, and a subset of counties in western and eastern Mississippi. During February-July, 1978, a study sample was captured in the eight sites as follows. First, household screening interviews were administered to a probability sample of about 130,000 households to determine the presence of program eligible youths. Next, enumerators returned to each of the program eligible households and secured baseline interviews with the eligible youths and their parents. This baseline survey obtained information on demographic and family background characteristics, including family income and its sources, as well as on preprogram behavior about schooling, training, and work experience. These data contain information on program eligibles for whom Entitlement is not available (those in the control sites) as well as for eligibles in experimental sites, some of whom will and some of whom will not subsequently choose to become program participants. The survey was conducted prior to, or contemporaneous with, program start-up and was in no way identified with the program. Three subsequent waves of reinterviews, at approximately one-year-intervals, will permit the measurement of program participation rates, program impacts during program operation, and postprogram impacts. In addition, school records (which will be obtained for each youth in the sample) and program MIS records for those sample members who participate in Entitlement will supplement and help to verify the information collected in the survey. (See Barclay et al., 1979, for further description of the research design.)

Despite the best efforts of the Manpower Demonstration Research Corporation (who coordinate Entitlement for the Department of Labor), program implementation varies considerably across the experimental sites (Ball et al., 1979; Diaz et al., 1980). Since the program is locally managed by CETA prime sponsors of varying experience and capacity, and since each of these must coordinate its activities with the local school system, difficulties are to be expected. Nevertheless, the resulting natural variation in the "program treatment" places a greater burden on the impact analysis to report not only "what happened," but also to estimate structural models that reveal "why it happened." Outcome measures divide according to whether they are labor market related (employment, hours employed, wage rates, earnings) or schooling related (school enrollment, attendance, performance, grade attainment, high school graduation, postsecondary school enrollment). Particularly important is the ability of the program to attract and hold potential or actual school dropouts, and the role played in this by the nature of program monitoring and verification of school enrollment and attendance and the availability of program-provided alternative schooling (Graduate Equivalency Degree qualifying) opportunities. Other issues include:

- guaranteed, minimum wage employment as a program treatment; how effective a guarantee? (That is, were sufficient jobs always available to serve all comers?) how desirable an opportunity? (That is, what are the true parameters of youth labor supply?); consequences of an upward shifting minimum wage; consequences of constraints on work hours; consequences of local labor market conditions;

- the schooling requirement and the GED opportunity; Why offer a school-constrained job guarantee? How effective is the constraint? (That is, is the schooling requirement enforced?) What are the true parameters governing youths' investments in human capital, and through what mechanisms can Entitlement be expected to increase such investments?

- what is the extent, composition, and consequences of the full range of program services provided? the role of competing programs, and prime sponsor commitment to Entitlement;

- other outcome measures, particularly fertility and marriage, youth splitoff from primary family, criminal activity; measures of psychological well-being, achievement motivation, and the allocation of time across a wide range of competing activities.

The Organization of This Article

The following section describes some reduced-form models to be used in the evaluation and reports the results of estimating them with baseline data on youth preprogram behavior. Section III describes a structural model of youth summer labor supply and the results of estimating this model (also with preprogram data). The article closes with a summary of future work.

II. REDUCED-FORM MODELS AND THEIR ESTIMATION

Variables

The data for this evaluation include a number of variables exogenous to the outcome variables of interest. Chief among these is geographic location—the 8 labor market areas are to be regarded as 4 experimental, and 4 matched control sites. For outcome variables whose values are strongly associated with self-selection into program participation—school enrollment is one example[1]— before/after comparisons of experimental and control sites are the most reliable measures of program effect. In this view the "treatment" is the existence of the program applied to the site as a whole. As a result of this exogenous shock, endogenous choices, including school enrollment and labor force participation, may be altered.[2] Such alterations are detected by before/after intersite comparisons, which aim to improve on an "after only" design by permitting adjustment for preprogram differences. (This is particularly important when analyzing variables such as school enrollment and employment, which exhibit strong over-time correlation.) It is therefore of interest to fit models which reveal how well experimental and control sites are matched in the preprogram period, a task we undertake below.

A number of other exogenous variables are covariates for the site dummy variables. They define intersite compositional differences that must be adjusted for, as well as subpopulations across which we wish to measure differential program impacts. These variables include age, race, sex, and family background characteristics (household composition, parents' education, and the like).

Statistical Models

A number of technical difficulties arise with any attempt to perform an analysis of variance or covariance for dichotomous dependent variables (such as school enrollment and employment). This is because OLS regression can no longer provide efficient and unbiased parameter estimates or reasonable, fitted values.

Fortunately, recent work by Nerlove and Press (1973, 1976) provide methods well-suited to this situation. These models are an extension of the log-linear model for contingency tables (Bishop et al., 1975; Goodman, 1972) in which the "main effects" in the log-linear model for the cross-tabulation of the endogenous variables are a function of exogenous variables, some of which may be continuous. Estimation is by maximum likelihood, and provides parameter estimates for the effect of each explanatory variable on each binary dependent variable, as well as an estimate of the bivariate interaction for the dependent variables. (This interaction term functions as a correlation coefficient for dichotomous variables. See Bishop et al., 1975.) When the independent variables are discrete, the resulting models are a special case of the general log-linear model. And in the case of only one dependent variable (as when we analyze the determinants of summer employment), the model is identical to the univariate logistic.[3]

More formally in the case of two dependent variables, if A and B are jointly dependently binary variables with states denoted by $i_1 = 0,1, i_2 = 0,1$, and k denotes a particular cell of the A×B cross-tabulation (k = 0,1; 1,1; 1,1), then the model defines p_k, the individual's propensity to assume state k, to be

$$p_k = \frac{e^{\theta_k}}{\underset{\text{All k}}{\Sigma} e^{\theta_k}}$$

where $\theta = \alpha_{i_1}^A + \alpha_{i_2}^B + \alpha_{i_1 i_2}^{AB}$ and the α's are log-linear model parameters (with the usual restrictions). Then, α^A and α^B are written as linear functions of the explanatory variables (for example, for the ith individual, $\alpha_{i_1}^A = x_{ij}\alpha_{i_1 j}^{A*}$, where x_{ij} is the vector of the ith individual's values for the explanatory variables, and α^{A*} is the vector of coefficients to be estimated) and coefficients are reported for the determinants of A and B. (That is, α^A and α^B are estimated. With additive restrictions, each is unique.) In addition, the value of α^{AB}, which in the calculations reported below is assumed to be independent of the explanatory variables, is reported.[4] This binary interaction ties the equations for the dependent variable main effects together, so that its value must be combined with α^{A*} and α^{B*} to produce fitted $\hat{p}_k$'s.

This model has a number of desirable properties. It appropriately models simultaneously determined dummy endogenous variables, is parsimonious, and is computationally tractable. Not only is the overall model logistic, but the probability distribution for one of the dependent variables, conditional on the other, is also logistic. And if the bivariate interaction is zero, the model produces identical results to those forthcoming from two univariate logistics, one for each dependent variable. The model can be used to fit data for one or more endogenous variables at one point in time (this use is illustrated below) or at several points in time (for example, the preprogram, during-program, and post-program periods). In the latter situation, we can fit a variety of over-time patterns (first-order Markov, second-order Markov, and so on) and measure the extent to which these have been altered by introducing the Entitlement program into experimental sites.

Results

Our baseline data represent 16-19-year olds who have not yet graduated from high school and are from low-income households. The older youths in the sample, however, are not fully representative of their birth cohorts, since many older youths will have graduated from high school and therefore be ineligible for the sample. To present estimates that fully represent the population in a particular age range, we have arrayed the sample by age (in months) and eliminated those youths above the age at which counts begin to decline. As a result, we have restricted attention to youths born between March, 1960 and December, 1963, so that models are estimated for youths aged 14-17 in January, 1977 (and, therefore, 15-18 by the close of the year). This sample has 5695 observations.

Table 1 reports the means and variances of the exogenous variables and the distribution of the sample across the eight sites. The sample is relatively evenly divided between males and females, and is 72% black, 15.6% white, and 12.4% Hispanic. The predominance of blacks results from their overrepresentation in innercity and southern-rural poverty areas.

Age is measured in months, with a "1" recorded for the youngest members of the sample, those born in December, 1963. The mean sample age is 28.7, or approximately 15½ years of age at the beginning of 1977. The average family earned income for 1977 was $3,129, and the average family welfare income for this year was $2,151. Mean parent education was 8.46 years of schooling (where available, this was recorded as the average of mother's and father's education, otherwise it was recorded as the education of the single parent or guardian). We find 11.4% of the sample living with neither natural (biological) parent, 58.6% living with the natural mother only, 2.7% living with the natural father only, and 27.3% living with both natural parents.

Table 2 reports a univariate logistic for the determinants of employment during the summer, and a bivariate logistic for the joint determination of employment and school enrollment during the fall. The summer equation contains several results of interest. Females exhibit a lower employment rate than males, a result we have observed across a variety of time periods. Interestingly, we

Table 1   Means and Variances of the Exogenous Variables

Variable	Mean	Variance
Sex		
Male	.480	.250
Female	.520	.250
Race		
Black	.720	.202
White	.156	.131
Hispanic	.124	.108
Age (In months, by Date of Birth; 1 = December 1963)	28.7	100.0
Family Earned Income (Minus that due to the youth)	3129	2266×10^4
Family Welfare Income (Minus that due to the youth)	2151	5574×10^3
Parent's Education (Years of Schooling)	8.46	12.4
Household Type		
Living with Neither Natural Parent	.114	.101
Living with Natural Mother only	.586	.243
Living with Natural Father only	.027	.027
Living with Both Natural Parents	.273	.198

Distribution by Site:			
Denver	.156	Phoenix	.069
Cincinnati	.186	Louisville	.094
Baltimore	.222	Cleveland	.087
Mississippi Pilot	.118	Mississippi Control	.068

TABLE 2   Reduced-Form Estimates of the Determinants of Employment During the Summer and Employment and School Enrollment During the Fall Preprogram Periods

	Summer, 1977 Employment Equation	Fall 1977 Employment Equation	Fall 1977 School Enrollment Equation
Constant	- .622 (7.4)*	-1.409 (14.3)	1.813 (18.2)
Female	- .340 (11.7)	- .305 (9.9)	- .127 (3.9)
White	.045 (1.1)	.226 (5.2)	- .419 (9.5)
Hispanic	.013 (C.2)	.036 (0.6)	- .336 (5.3)
Age (Months)	.0142 (9.6)	.0167 (10.2)	-.0268 (15.8)
Family Earned Income (000)	-.0050 (1.4)	.0069 (1.9)	.0085 (2.2)
Family Welfare Income	.0064 (0.9)	.0098 (1.3)	-.0023 (0.3)
Parents' Education	.011 (2.4)	.008 (1.7)	.026 (5.3)
Living with Neither Natural Parent	.032 (0.6)	.035 (1.5)	- .209 (3.7)
Living with Natural Mother Only	.006 (0.2)	.001 (0.0)	- .100 (2.5)
Living with Natural Father Only	- .087 (1.0)	.068 (0.7)	- .258 (2.7)
Site Dummy Variables**			
D12	.293 (3.6)	.510 (5.7)	- .104 (1.1)
D34	- .184 (2.5)	.143 (1.7)	- .144 (1.7)
D56	.308 (4.3)	.400 (4.8)	.047 (0.5)
PD1	.061 (1.0)	.193 (2.9)	.188 (2.7)
PD3	.214 (3.6)	.259 (4.2)	.080 (1.3)
PD5	- .458 (8.2)	- .257 (4.2)	- .205 (3.1)
PD7	- .511 (6.8)	- .209 (2.4)	- .088 (1.1)
Bivariate Interaction		- .156 (9.1)	

*t-statistics in parentheses.
**The site dummy variables are defined as follows. D12 indicates the first matched pair (Denver, Phoenix), D23 the second matched pair, etc. PD1 indicates the pilot (experimental) site in the first pair (in this case Denver), etc.

observe no racial employment differences during this preprogram summer. This is in sharp contradiction to the situation during the preprogram school year. This is apparently due to summer youth employment programs. Enrollment in these programs has been skewed toward blacks and other minorities. Such is not the case for females, so that male/female employment differences exist throughout the year. The existence of such programs, which may compete with Entitlement in the experimental sites and render the other sites something other than pure "controls" will create a continuing complication for the analysis of program impact.

We find that age exerts a significant positive effect on summer employment, but that neither earned income, welfare income, nor household structure are significant. Parents' education, however, does exert a small positive effect.

The site dummy variables are perhaps of greatest interest in this analysis. We find large intersite summer employment differences, with Denver, Phoenix, and Cleveland showing the highest rates, while the lowest is experienced by the Mississippi control. These and other result (Barclay et al., 1979) confirm that the Southwestern sites generally exhibit the best youth employment situation in the preprogram period, while the rural Mississippi sites exhibit the worst. In the case of Denver and Phoenix this seems to be due to a relatively strong local economy, the lack of which is at least partially compensated for in other sites by the existence of relatively large, subsidized summer employment programs.

During the fall, females continue to show lower employment rates than males, but we also now observe blacks and Hispanics with lower employment than whites. Family background characteristics exert no significant effect on employment, but we once again observe large intersite differentials. Even more than before, Denver and Phoenix are relatively high employment sites, while the Mississippi sites exhibit low employment.

The fall school enrollment equation generally supports the notion that school and work are substitutes at any particular point in time. Thus, the bivariate interaction term (correlation) between the two dependent variables is significantly negative, and although females engage in less of each activity than males, the higher school enrollment rate of blacks can plausibly be attributed to their lower employment opportunities. We also find that as youths age they leave school relatively rapidly—in fact more rapidly than they begin work.

Both family earned income and parents' education exert significant, positive effects on school enrollment, and disrupted household arrangements (living with other than both natural parents) are negatively associated with school enrollment. Intersite school enrollment differences are generally smaller than those for employment, but they are not negligible. The highest rates occur in Mississippi and Denver, whereas the lowest occur in Phoenix, Cincinnati, Louisville, and Baltimore. Further examination of the time pattern of school enrollment across sites in the preprogram period will be an important aspect of the before/after comparison in the impact analysis to come.

III. STRUCTURAL MODELS AND THEIR ESTIMATION

III.1 Introduction

Models such as those of the previous section will be sufficient to answer the question "what happened as a result of the Entitlement demonstration?" by comparing before/after differences in pilot and control sites. Answers to the more difficult questions "why did these outcomes occur?" and "what would have occurred under somewhat different circumstances?" require formulating and estimating more elaborate models. For the Entitlement demonstration these are generally models of time allocation—in particular, youth labor supply and youth investment in human capital. As one aspect of our preparatory work with preprogram data, we have fit models of youth summer labor supply to the baseline data. This model and the results it generates are described below. Other work (not reported here) focuses on the school enrollment decision and on youth labor supply during the school year.

Issues in the study of youth labor supply include (a) the nature and determinants of the wage offers available to target population youths in the absence of the program; (b) the nature and determinants of the "asking wages" of these youths; (c) the wage elasticity of youth labor supply; and (d) the extent to which the determinants of being employed differ from the determinants of hours worked by those who are employed. Such differences may be attributed to differential job search costs, fixed costs of working, and demand side "distortions" (such as the existence and differential coverage of minimum wage legislation) experienced by youths from differing demographic and economic categories. Preprogram conditions in this regard are particularly important, since the principal operational accomplishment of Entitlement is to act as an employer of last resort, guaranteeing a job to all eligible youths who apply.

The model we fit is also of some interest. The wage offer equation is estimated under a variety of specifications designed to correct for selectivity bias, including a new method that eliminates the assumption of normality for the regression residuals (Olsen, 1979). Labor supply is estimated by a generalization of the Tobit model, in which a truncated, normal regression for hours of work is combined with a probit equation for whether the individual works at all. Distortions associated with fixed costs of working, differential job search costs, and the failure of wage rates to freely adjust downward are modeled by calculating the supply side "disemployment index" necessary to account for the observed employment rates. That is, the probit equation is based on a comparison of an individual's (predicted) wage offer and an index which is the sum of two terms, the first being the individual's reservation wage (calculated from the hours equation) and the second being the "disemployment index" necessary to account for observed employment rates given the calculated offer and asking wages. With the assumption that this index acts only to ration jobs (once the individual obtains a job, his hours of work are determined solely by his reservation wage and wage offer), relevant parameters are identified and estimation proceeds by maximum likelihood (Olsen, 1977, 1978a, 1978b).

This section is organized as follows. We begin by describing our model within the context of its previous use for studying female labor supply. First the specification and estimation of the wage offer equation are summarized, and this is combined with a discussion of the hours of work and participation equations. The section closes with an account of the results of fitting this model to data for the preprogram summer.

III.2 The Wage Offer Equation[5]

For some time now, the possibility of selectivity bias arising when a wage equation is estimated solely for individuals currently at work has been prominently featured in the econometric literature (Gronau, 1974; Heckman, 1974, 1976, 1979; Lewis, 1974). This issue arises whenever employment rates are significantly below 100%, and first came to public attention in estimating wage offers for married women. Selection, however, is likely to assume even greater importance where youths are concerned.

The basic problem is estimating a regression equation when some observations are missing values for the dependent variable. If the residuals for these missing value observations are not a random sample of the entire population of residuals, ordinary least squares produce inconsistent estimators. Broadly speaking, there are three sources of information about selection. First, the mean of the least squares residuals will shift with the probability of having missing data. This is the basis of Heckman's (1976, 1979) test for selection. The second source of information is in the distribution of the residuals. If the population distribution of the residuals is normal, selection will cause the residuals corresponding to the observed wage offers to have a nonnormal distribution. The third source of information is heteroscedasticity. If the population of residuals is homoscedastic, but selection is present, the residuals in the sample without missing values will be heteroscedastic. Maximum likelihood methods pool these three sources of information. We show below how the distribution of the least squares residuals can be used to make inferences about selection. This provides an interesting contrast to methods based on shifts in the mean of the residuals. We will see that the assumption of normality when using maximum likelihood is substantive in that a lack of normality may be confused with selection. This suggests that a more cautious approach to the selection problem is called for. We develop such an approach by showing how to perform maximum likelihood estimation without requiring normality for the regression residuals. This method is then used to fit a wage offer equation for the youths in our sample.

Formal Description of the Problem

The objective is to estimate the regression equation

$$y_{2i} = X_{2i}\beta_2 + u_{2i} \qquad [1.1]$$

which is assumed to hold over some population. This population is sampled randomly yielding a set of observations Ψ; for some subset of Ψ, however, say Ψ_0, y_2

is not observed, whereas for $\Psi - \Psi_0 = \Psi_1$, y_2 is observed. The X's are assumed to be observed for both subsets. The problem is to estimate [1.1] taking into account the possibility that with respect to u_{2i}, Ψ_1 may not be a random sample of the population.

In the absence of some structure, the problem cannot be solved. We should not be under the illusion that the nature of the solution to this problem does not depend on the structure imposed on it. Here we will examine the extent to which the results reflect the assumptions made. To solve the problem, we will assume that the model determining whether y_2 is to be observed is

$$y_{1i} = 1 \ (y_{2i} \text{ observed}) \text{ if } u_{1i} \leqslant X_{1i}B_1 \tag{1.2}$$

$$y_{1i} = 0 \ (y_{2i} \text{ not observed}) \text{ otherwise.}$$

We will assume that u_{1i} and u_{2i} have some bivariate density and that

$$E(u_{1i}) \quad = \mu$$

$$E(u_{2i}) \quad = 0$$

$$Var(u_{1i}) \ = \sigma_1^2$$

$$Var(u_{2i}) \ = \sigma_2^2$$

$$E(u_{1i}u_{2i}) = \rho\sigma_2\sigma_1$$

$$E(u_{1i}u_{2j}) = E(u_{1i}u_{1j}) = E(u_{2i}u_{2j}) = 0 \text{ all } i \neq j$$

all X's are nonrandom and fixed in repeated samples.

If we assume that the conditional expectation of u_{2i} given u_{1i} is linear in the u_{1i} then from probability theory we can write

$$u_{2i} = \rho(u_{1i} - \mu)\sigma_2/\sigma_1 + \epsilon_i \tag{1.3}$$

$$Var(\epsilon_i) = \sigma_2^2(1 - \rho^2),$$

where ϵ_1 is uncorrelated with u_{1i}. Substituting [1.3] into [1.1] we obtain

$$y_{2i} = x_{2i}\beta_2 + \rho(u_{1i} - \mu)\sigma_2/\sigma_1 + \epsilon_i. \tag{1.4}$$

When this regression is estimated using the subsample for which y_2 is observed, least squares will yield the condition expectation $E(y_{2i}|X_{2i}, y_{1i} = 1)$ or $E(y_{2i}|X_{2i}, u_{1i} \leqslant X_{1i}B_1)$. The mean of this conditional expectation is

$$E(y_{2i}|X_{2i}, u_{1i} \leqslant X_{1i}B_1) = X_{2i}B_2 + \rho\sigma_2 E(u_{1i}|u_{1i} \leqslant X_{1i}B_1)/\sigma_1 - \rho\mu\sigma_2/\sigma_1,$$

$$\tag{1.5}$$

and the variance of this conditional expectation is

$$\text{Var}(y_{2i} | X_{2i}, u_{1i} \leqslant X_{1i}B_1) = \rho^2 \sigma_2^2 \, \text{Var}(u_{1i} | u_{1i} \leqslant X_{1i}B_1)/\sigma_1^2 + \sigma_2^2(1 - \rho^2).$$

[1.6]

If it is assumed that the distribution of u_{1i} is standard normal, that is, that a probit model is appropriate for estimating [1.2], then

$$E(u_{1i} | u_{1i} \leqslant X_{1i}B_1) = f(X_{1i}B_1)/F(X_{1i}B_1) = \lambda_i$$

where $f(\cdot)$ and $F(\cdot)$ are the standard normal density and cumulative distribution functions. As a result, the appropriate regression for [1.1] when using the sub-sample for which y_2 is observed is

$$y_{2i} = X_{2i}B_2 + \gamma\lambda_i + \eta_i$$

[1.7]

where $\text{Var}(\eta_i) = \sigma_2^2 \{1 + \rho^2 \lambda_i(X_{1i}B_1 - \lambda_i)\}$ and $\gamma = \rho\sigma_2$.

This approach to selection has been suggested by Heckman (1976, 1979) and Lee (1976) and is also the basis of a method used by Gronau (1974) and Lewis (1974).

This method introduces an auxiliary regressor which is a decreasing function of the probability of observing y_2. If the vector of least squares residuals from [1.1] is denoted $\hat{u}_2$, then we can express the regression coefficient of λ_i as

$$\hat{\gamma} = \hat{u}_2' \lambda / [\lambda'(I - X_2(X_2'X_2)^{-1}X_2')\lambda],$$

where $\hat{u}_2$, and λ are column vectors consisting of the u_{2i} and λ_i, and X_2 is the matrix formed by the row vectors X_{2i}. Note that the matrix $(\lambda \, X_2)$ must have full rank. Even when $X_1 = X_2$ this rank condition is usually satisfied because λ is a non-linear function of X_1. Examining the numerator of this expression we see that inferences concerning the direction of the selectivity bias (i.e., the sign of ρ) are based on the sign of the correlation between the least squares residuals for [1.1] and the auxiliary regressor. Equivalently, if the mean of the least squares residuals increases (or decreases) as the probability of observing y_2 increases, then this is taken as a sign of the presence of selectivity bias. Heckman has also shown that the residuals in [1.7] are heteroscedastic. If the u_{2i} have equal variances then the variance of the residuals in [1.7] will decline as the probability of observing y_2 increases.

One alternative to the use of λ_i to correct for selection is to estimate the model [1.1] − [1.2] by maximum likelihood. Typically it is assumed u_{1i} and u_{2i} have a bivariate normal density. This implies the marginal density of u_1 is normal and that the conditional expectation of u_2 given u_1 is linear so that [1.7] can be viewed as a limited information solution to the model.

Insight into the working of these methods is provided by considering the case where the model determining the observability of y_{2i} is

$$u_{1i} \leqslant K \text{ iff } y_{2i} \text{ observed} \tag{1.8a}$$

$$u_{1i} > K \text{ iff } y_{2i} \text{ not observed.} \tag{1.8b}$$

Here, we cannot use [1.2] to correct for selection since λ_i will be constant and will thus be perfectly collinear with the intercept of [1.1]. In this case it is impossible to determine whether the mean of the least squares residuals for [1.1] is related to the probability of observing y_2, since we observe no variation in the latter probability. Yet, even if we replace [1.2] with [1.8] the maximum likelihood estimator still exists. The reason for this is that the likelihood estimator is using information in the higher order moments of the $\hat{u}_2$. When [1.8] replaces [1.2] the marginal probability of observing y_2 is constant over all observations, so that there are no differences in the means or variances of the residuals within the subsample for which y_2 is observed. We will show that if the population distribution of u_2 is normal, the distribution of the residuals for the subsample for which y_2 is observed will not be normal. The reason the likelihood estimator exists when [1.8] holds instead of [1.2] is that a departure from normality of the least squares residuals u_2 is taken as evidence of the existence of selection. A corollary to this result is that the assumption of normality may not be innocuous when applying maximum likelihood to the selectivity bias model.

The Likelihood Estimator and the Distribution of the Residuals

The likelihood function for the model [1.1] and [1.2] when we assume bivariate normality is

$$\prod_{i=1}^{N} [F(-X_{1i}B_1)]^{1-y}{}_{1i} \cdot \left[\frac{1}{\sigma_2} f_N [[y_{2i} - X_{2i}\beta_2]/\sigma_2] \right]^{y}{}_{1i}$$

$$\left[1 - F \left[\frac{-X_{1i}B_1 - \rho(y_{2i} - X_{2i}\beta_2)/\sigma_2}{\sqrt{1-\rho^2}} \right] \right]^{y}{}_{1i}. \tag{1.9}$$

Because the log likelihood function has a unique maximum for given values of ρ, a simple search over ρ can be used to find the neighborhood of the global maximum. This procedure costs roughly five times as much as a comparable probit model. It can be shown that the regression model in [1.7] can be interpreted as a single Newton iteration of the likelihood function from the point $\rho = 0$ under the null hypothesis that $\rho = 0$. Note that when $\rho = 0$, expression [1.9] reduces to an ordinary least squares regression with no selectivity bias and a simple probit model. When $\rho = 0$, it is fully efficient to estimate these equations separately.

The joint density of y_{1i} and u_{2i} when y_{2i} is observed is a combination of continuous and discrete densities of the form

$$\int_{-\infty}^{X_{1i}B_1} h(u_{1i}, u_{2i}) \, du_{1i}, \qquad\qquad [1.10]$$

where $h(\cdot)$ is the bivariate normal density. From Bayes' theorem, the conditional density of u_{2i} given $y_{1i} = 1$ is [1.10] divided by the marginal probability that $y_{1i} = 1$. The joint density $h(u_{1i}, u_{2i})$ can be expressed as the product of two normal densities—the marginal density of u_{1i} times the conditional density of u_{2i} given u_{1i} or vice versa.[6] Using these results from probability theory we obtain the conditional density of u_{2i} given $y_{1i} = 1$

$$g(u_{2i} | y_{1i} = 1) = \frac{\displaystyle\int_{-\infty}^{X_{1i}B_1} \frac{1}{\sigma\sqrt{1-\rho^2}} \, f\left(\frac{u_{2i} - \rho\sigma u_{1i}}{\sigma\sqrt{1-\rho^2}}\right) f(u_{1i}) \, du_{1i}}{F(X_{1i}B_1)}, \qquad [1.11]$$

where again $f(\cdot)$ is the standard normal density. This density is not normal except in the case $\rho = 0$, so that when the population distribution of u_2 is normal, the distribution of the observed u_2's is not, unless $\rho = 0$, i.e., unless selectivity bias is absent. The density function in [1.11] can be interpreted as a convolution formula. If v and w are independent, random variables then the distribution of $z = v + aw$ is $\int_w h_v(z-aw) h_w(w) dw$ from probability theory. In [1.11] we have the distribution of $u_{2i} = v_i + \rho\sigma u_{1i}$ where the distribution of v_i is normal with mean zero and variance $\sigma^2(1 - \rho^2)$ and u_{1i} is a truncated normal variable formed by truncating a standard normal variable from above at $X_{1i}B_1$. This truncation of u_{1i} reflects the fact that by conditioning on $y_{1i} = 1$ we have also conditioned upon $u_{1i} < X_{1i}B_1$. The interpretation of [1.11] in terms of the independent variables v_i and u_{1i} makes it possible to derive the moments of u_{2i} in terms of the moments of v_i and u_{1i}. If we let $K = X_{1i}B_1$ for notational convenience, then

$$E(u_{2i}) = E(v_i) + \rho\sigma E(u_{1i})$$

$$= -\rho\sigma f(K)/F(K) = \rho\sigma\lambda(K)$$

$$\text{Var}(u_{2i}) = \text{Var}(v_i) + \rho^2\sigma^2 \, \text{Var}(u_{1i})$$

$$= \sigma^2(1 - \rho^2) + \rho^2\sigma^2 \left\{1 + \lambda(K) \, [K - \lambda(K)]\right\}.$$

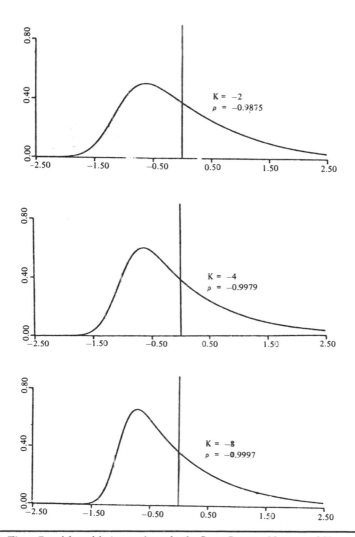

Figure 1: Three Densities with Approximately the Same Pearson Measure of Skewness

The moments of the truncated normal density have been tabulated. (See Pearson and Lee [1908] for an early discussion.) By varying K and ρ one can generate a family of nonnormal density functions. In Figures 1 and 2 this has been done with the resulting densities being standardized to have a mean of zero and variance one. In Figure 1 the densities have roughly the same Pearson measure of skewness—the mode minus the mean. Figure 2 illustrates three other members of this family of distributions. As ρ approaches zero, the densities approach the normal. Large positive values of ρ were used in the figures to heighten the visual effect. A reversal of

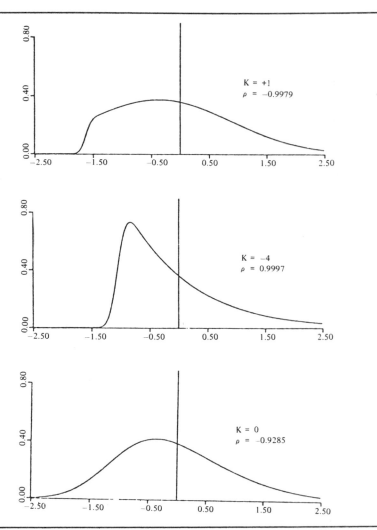

Figure 2: Representative Members of the Family of Density Functions in (1.11)

the sign of ρ produces mirror images. This two-parameter family of densities contains the normal density as a special case, and if we set $K = 0$, a subfamily of densities results that appears in the boundary production function literature. There the error term in a production function has been modeled as a sum of two components, a half normal (i.e., truncated normal with the truncation point at zero), and a normal component (see Aigner, 1975; Aigner et al., 1977; Lee and Tyler, 1978). The likelihood estimator in [1.9] uses information on the distribution of the residuals in estimating the extent and direction of selection bias. In the case where the probability of observing y_2 is a constant, this is the only information available, since the mean and variance of the residuals will be constant for the sample. In this particular case, inference crucially depends on the assumption that the population residuals are normal. If the population residuals are not normal and instead follow a normal-truncated normal convolution of the sort in [1.11] or some other skewed density function, then even if there is no selection present, a nonnormal density may be fit to the residuals leading to the inference that selection is present. The value of K will be largely determined by the fraction of the sample for which y_2 is observed with the estimated value of ρ producing the density that, together with K, best fits the residuals within the family or normal-truncated normal densities. For example, if, in a sample, half the values of y_2 are observed and the population distribution of the residuals is similar to the density at the bottom of Figure 2, then we would expect a value of $\hat{\rho}$ of about 0.9285. As a result, one may be led to infer that selection causes the sample mean to overstate the true mean when in fact $\hat{\rho} = 0.9285$ merely reflects a rightward skewness of the population density. An inference of no selection would result when the observed residuals are normally distributed. Clearly, in the case where there is no exogenous variation in the probability of observing y_2 the assumption of bivariate normality is central.

The importance of distribution of the residuals implies the importance of the specification of the dependent variable. The use of $\ln y_2$ or some other transformation may affect the distribution of the residuals. In fact, the use of the family of densities in [1.11] provides an interesting contrast to the Box-Cox (1964) method. They consider a family of transformations of the random variable with the objective of finding the transformation that produces normality. Here the objective is to consider a family of density functions with the objective of selecting the member that best matches the distribution of the residuals. This two-parameter family of densities is

$$g(\eta \mid K, \rho) = \phi f(\phi \eta + \theta) \, F\left[\frac{K - \rho(\phi \eta + \theta)}{\sqrt{1 - \rho^2}}\right] \Big/ F(K),$$

[1.12]

where

$$\theta = \rho \lambda(K)$$

$$\phi^2 = 1 + \rho^2 \lambda(K) [K - \lambda(K)].$$

This distribution has zero mean and unit variance and so is standardized. These nonnormal densities result because the selection leads to the observed residuals being disproportionately drawn from one tail of the population distribution. In the case of normal populations when the left tail is oversampled, the resulting sample distribution is skewed left since residuals from the right tail will be more sparse.

Nonnormal Maximum Likelihood

To relax the restriction that the population of the residuals is normally distributed, we will assume the conditional density of u_2 given y_2 is observed is

$$\frac{\int_{-\infty}^{X_{1i}B_1} \int_{-\infty}^{K} f_3(u_2,u_1,u_0)\, du_0\, du_1}{\int_{-\infty}^{\infty} \int_{-\infty}^{X_{1i}B} \int_{-\infty}^{K} f_3(u_2,u_1,u_0)\, du_0\, du_1\, du_2}, \qquad [1.13]$$

where the correlation matrix of $(u_2 u_1 u_0)$ is

$$\Omega \begin{pmatrix} 1 & \rho_1 & \rho_2 \\ \rho_1 & 1 & \rho_1\rho_2 \\ \rho_2 & \rho_1\rho_2 & 1 \end{pmatrix},$$

that is, the correlation between u_2 and u_1 is ρ_1, between u_2 and u_0 is ρ_2 and between u_1 and u_0 is $\rho_1\rho_2$. Once again X_{1i} is a vector of exogenous variables that explain the propensity to observe y_2. The extent and direction of selection are governed by ρ_1; ρ_2 and K are additional parameters that allow for nonnormal populations.

This correlation was used because the joint density of u_1 and u_0 given u_2 is the product of two univariate densities that simplifies computation greatly. When we set $X_{1i}B_1 = \infty$ we have the marginal density for u_2 which will be normal in the event $\rho_2 = 0$; otherwise, the marginal of u_2 will be a normal-truncated normal convolution. If $\rho_1 = 0$ there is no selection. This more general model allows the residuals to be nonnormal without this necessarily being taken as evidence of selection. Depending on the values of K and ρ_2 chosen, a great variety of distribution can be considered. If the population distribution of u_2 does not happen to be in this family of normal-truncated normal convolutions then we have committed an error of the same general type as when we impose normality on the residuals. We hope that such an error will be less serious having allowed two additional degrees of freedom to the error distribution.

III.3 Labor Supply: The Hours of Work and Participation Equations[7]

Following Gronau (1973a, 1973b, 1974), Heckman (1974), Schultz (1974), and others, we suppose that the youth will wish to work if his wage offer exceeds the value of his time at zero hours of work (his reservation wage). In this section we describe a model that generalizes Heckman's tobit equation approach by separating out the hours and participation equations. As a result, we are able to estimate the "disemployment index" associated with the differential job search costs, fixed costs of working, and labor market distortions experienced by different demographic/economic groups. The wage offer equation described above serves as an instrumental variable for these calculations. In what follows we shall assume that this has been estimated as

$$W^O = a_1 X_1 + a_2 X_2 + u_1,$$

where W^O is the natural log of the wage offer facing the individual.

Heckman's Model

More formally, we recall that Heckman adopts a model of hours and participation based upon the specification

$$H = b_0 (W^O - b_1 X_1 - b_3 X_3) + u_2, \qquad [2.1]$$

where H is hours of work. If the right hand side (RHS) of [2.1] is positive, H is determined by [2.1], but if the RHS of [2.1] is zero or negative, then H = 0. This is, of course, basically, the limited dependent variable model of Tobin (1958). It departs from the tobit model since W^O is not assumed uncorrelated with u_2, and, moreover, W^O is not observed for all individuals. It is assumed u_2 is normally distributed with mean zero and variance σ_2^2, and so when

$$W^O = b_1 X_1 + b_3 X_3,$$

The probability that the individual works is one-half. This event can be interpreted as indifference between working and not working, since this particular wage is equal to the value of the individual's time at the margin at zero hours of work. We have already referred to this wage as the reservation wage. Equation [2.1] can also be expressed as

$$W^O = H/b_0 + b_1 X_1 + b_3 X_3 - u_2/b_0. \qquad [2.2]$$

It is assumed that the individual can freely vary his hours of work and so will select H such that his wage rate equals the value of an additional hour at home. Thus imbedded in [2.2] is the reservation wage equation

$$W^* = b_1 X_1 + b_3 X_3 - u_2/b_0,$$

and the individual will work if and only if

$$W^O > W^*$$

assuming no fixed costs, minimum hours of work, or other labor market distortions. It is also assumed the wage offer does not depend on hours worked so that [1.1] is a correct specification of the wage offer equation.

The simple fact that if the individual works, H must be positive imposes some restrictions upon u_2, notably from [2.1]

$$u_2 > -b_0(W^O - b_1X_1 - b_3X_3).$$ [2.3a]

Likewise, if he does not work, it must be that

$$u_2 < -b_0(W^O - b_1X_1 - b_3X_3),$$ [2.3b]

and so the probability of working is

$$Pr[u_2 > -b_0(W^O - b_1X_1 - b_3X_3)] = 1 - F\left[\frac{-b_0(W^O - b_1X_1 - b_3X_3)}{\sigma^2}\right]$$

[2.4]

where $F(\cdot)$ is the standard normal cumulative distribution function. The density function for hours given participation is not normal, but truncated normal, because given that the individual works, hours must be positive.

A More General Model

While there are strong reasons for specifying a model for which participation and hours are generated by the same function, it is quite restrictive. Consider the following less restrictive model. The hours of work equation for working youths is

$$H = B_0(W^O - B_1X_1 - B_3X_3) - B_0v_3$$ [2.5]

Here H is restricted to be positive, and we assume that v_3 follows a truncated normal distribution.[8] Substituting the wage offer equation into [2.5] yields

$$H = B_0(a_1X_1 + a_2X_2) - B_0(B_1X_1 + B_3X_3) + B_0(u_1 - v_3)$$ [2.6]

so that the reduced form density function for hours of work given hours are positive, can be written as

$$\frac{\frac{1}{\sigma_4} f_n\{[H - B_0(a_1X_1 + a_2X_2 - B_1X_1 - B_3X_3)]/\sigma_4\}}{1 - F\left[\frac{-B_0(a_1X_1 + a_2X_2 - B_1X_1 - B_3X_3)}{\sigma_4}\right]} \quad ; H > 0,$$ [2.7]

where $\sigma_4^2 = \text{Var}(B_0 u_1 - B_0 v_3)$, and we assume that u_1 and v_3 may be correlated. Since H is assumed positive, the error term $(B_0 u_1 - B_0 v_3)$ must have zero density over the range of values that would result in negative values of H. The denominator of [2.7] is used so that the area under the remaining part of the normal density function is one.

Equation [2.6] can be estimated as follows. Attention is restricted to youths at work, and their hours of work are taken to be a function of their predicted wage offer ($\widehat{\text{Lnwage}} = a_1 X_1 + a_2 X_2$, with the a's estimated consistently by one of the methods described in section II.1 above), as well as of the variables in the sets X_1 and X_3. Estimation is by maximum likelihood, using the density function [2.7], and results in estimates of coefficients for each of the right hand side variables, as well as σ_4. The coefficient for $\widehat{\text{Lnwage}}$ is an estimate of B_0, and this coefficient can also be used to deflate the coefficients in front of the X_1 and X_3 variables, thereby solving for B_1 and B_3. (Identification is assured when the X_2 variables used as predictors of the wage offer do not appear in the (X_1, X_3) set.)

We interpret the result as using hours of work information to infer the youth's value of time. That is, among youths able to find employment and at work, observed variation in hours, $\widehat{\text{Lnwage}}$, X_1, and X_3 suggests that

$$W_i^* = B_1 X_{1i} + B_3 X_{3i} + v_3$$

is the Lnwage at which zero hours would be forthcoming. This is the value of their time at zero hours of work, the reservation wage at which they are indifferent between working and not working.

In the presence of labor market imperfections, however, this may not define the wage at which a youth's probability of being employed is ½. Rather, we may suppose that a given youth will be at work iff

$$W_i^O > W_i^* + t_i \qquad\qquad [2.8]$$

where t_i is the "disemployment index" that measures the total effect of job search costs, fixed costs of working, minimum wage legislation, and the like.[9] Since W_i^O, W_i^*, and t_i are each a function of exogenous variables, this specification permits the effects of these variables to be expressed and measured by three distinct channels of influence. In addition, we are able to explore intergroup comparisons such as the following: (a) For two groups (such as black and white youths) experiencing different wage offers but assumed to have identical values of time, does the effect of wages in increasing hours of work carry over with a similar magnitude as an effect increasing the propensity to be employed? And (b) For two groups exhibiting different values of time but assumed to experience similar wage offers (such as youths with and without their own children), does the effect of a higher value of time in decreasing hours of work carry over with a similar magnitude as an effect decreasing the propensity to be employed? Answering these and related questions begins to provide a sense for the regularities which are most important, and the unresolved issues which are most vexing, in understanding the labor supply behavior of youths from low-income households.

An alternative approach to the specification of labor supply is to introduce fixed costs of working instead of our "disemployment index," with fixed costs expressed as a function of the exogenous variables. But these methods of summarizing market distortion are equivalent, so we have chosen the representation in [2.8] since it is somewhat simpler to work with.

More formally, by permitting random components (assumed normally distributed) to the reservation wage and disemployment index,

$$W_i^* = B_1 X_1 + B_3 X_3 + v_3$$

$$t_i = B_1^t X_1 + B_3^t X_3 + v_4$$

we have

$$\text{Prob(Work)} = \text{Prob}(W_i^O > W_i^* + t_i)$$

$$= \text{Prob}(a_1 X_1 + a_2 X_2 + u_1) > (B_1 + B_1^t)X_1 + (B_3 + B_3^t)X_3 + (v_3 + v_4)$$

$$= \text{Prob}((u_1 - v_3 - v_4) > ((B_1 + B_1^t)X_1 + (B_3 + B_3^t)X_3$$

$$- (a_1 X_1 + a_2 X_2))).   [2.9]$$

If $\sigma_5^2 = \text{Var}(u_1 - v_3 - v_4)$ we can express this in probit form. With $v = u_1 - v_3 - v_4$ as a standard normal variate, we have

$$\text{Prob(Work)} = \text{Prob}\left(v > \left(\frac{(B_1 + B_1^t)X_1 + (B_3 + B_3^t)X_3}{\sigma_5} - \frac{(a_1 X_1 + a_2 X_2)}{\sigma_5}\right)\right).$$

$$[2.10]$$

In section III.2 we discussed in detail the joint estimation of the wage offer equation with a participation model in order to take selectivity bias into account. We may view [2.10] as a structural interpretation of our participation model. The existence of a variable that influences the wage offer, but not either the value of time or the disemployment index, enables us to identify σ_5 and therefore calculate $B_1 + B_1^t$ and $B_3 + B_3^t$. Once we have the wage offer equation we may use it to impute wage rates for the hours of work equation in [2.6]. Estimating [2.6] gives us B_0, B_1 and B_3 so that we are able to solve for the disemployment coefficients by subtraction. For example, we obtain $B_1 + B_1^t$ from the probit model of participation, and we then substract the value of B_1 obtained from the hours of work equation.

In principle, it is possible to identify the full covariance matrix for u_1, v_3 and v_4, but this would require more complex estimation techniques. Since these covariances are of little substantive interest, they are not reported here.

III.4 The Data for this Calculation

Accurately measuring employment and wage rates is not always easy. In our case, a questionnaire administered during late spring 1978, asked youths to fill out a history of their work beginning January 1977. On a calendar, they noted each job held during this period, the enumerator recorded the beginning date, ending date, beginning wage rate, ending wage rate, average weekly hours, as well as other information, for each of these jobs.

, For the purposes of studying summer labor supply, we have treated these data as follows. A youth was recorded as employed during the summer if he had any work period that overlapped June 1, 1977-August 30, 1977. For each such work period that either began and ended during the summer or began before the summer and ended after the summer, the average of the beginning and ending wage rates was calculated. If a work period began before the summer and ended during the summer, the ending wage rates was used. If a work period began during the summer and ended after the summer, the beginning wage rate was used. If a youth had more than one summer work spell, the average of the wage rates resulting from the above procedure was used. Hours were conceptualized as total hours worked during the summer and were calculated by multiplying the average hours per week by the number of weeks.

The full case was printed out for every individual reporting less than $1 per hour or more than $15 per hour. These were verified or adjusted on a case-by-case basis (fewer than 100 cases required this attention), and hopeless cases were omitted from the sample.

We have not used educational attainment as an explanatory variable, because the decision to drop out of school is very closely related to the decision to work during the summer. Rather than have our results confounded by a variable that is likely to be endogenous, we have chosen to omit it.

By dropping cases with poor employment data, we ended up with a sample of 5462 observations, slightly fewer than those reported in section II. The mean values for this sample are so close to those of Table 1, however, that we do not repeat them here. We find that 1949, or 35.7% of the sample were employed during the summer of 1977 at an average Lnwage of .7953. This translates to $2.22 per hour and is therefore below the posted $2.30-per-hour minimum wage in force at that time. Among those employed, mean total summer hours were 271.4.

III.5 Results: The Wage Offer Equation

We have simplified the problem of unbiased estimation by focusing on the summer months and restricting attention to the younger members of the total data set. We continue in this vein by choosing an empirical specification for the wage offer equation consisting of unambiguously exogenous variables. These are dummy variables for the different sites and race/sex groups, a continuous variable for age (in months), and dummy variables for being young (less than 16 years at the beginning of summer, 1977) and for being very young (less than 15 years at the beginning of the summer). These latter two variables permit estimation of an age-wage profile for youth without contamination by the special labor market conditions faced by youths whose age may be a particularly significant aspect of the demand for their services.

Table 3 reports the results of two calculations. The first is an OLS fit for the sample of working youths. The second applies maximum likelihood with nonnormal residuals to the full sample in order to correct for selectivity bias. In each case the dependent variable is LnWage (as a result, the coefficient estimates can be interpreted as percentage changes in the wage), and the right hand side variables have been expressed as deviations from their means (as a result, the constant term represents the mean of the dependent variable).

The OLS coefficients show Phoenix to be a particularly high wage site, white males to be the highest paid race/sex group, age to be positively associated with wages, and younger workers to be particularly poorly paid. We then re-estimated this equation by maximum likelihood to correct for possible selection with and without the assumption of normally distributed residuals. We excluded family earned income, family welfare income, living with parents, family size, male youth with child, and female youth with child from the wage equation but retained them as determinants of the probability of working. These restrictions satisfy the identification requirements for the λ method described in section III.2 (see expression [1.7]). Maximum likelihood does not formally require such restrictions since it uses information regarding the form of the distribution of the errors and their possible heteroscedasticity, but it is better to have such restrictions imposed on the model to make the solution depend less on the stochastic specification of the error term for the wage equation.

Under the assumption that the wage equation residuals are normally distributed, maximum likelihood indicates strong and statistically significant selectivity bias. To test formally for the presence of such bias we use the likelihood ratio test based on minus twice the difference between the log likelihood statistic when selection is assumed absent (expression 1.9) maximized with ρ constrained to be zero) versus the unrestricted maximum likelihood estimator. According to this test we must reject the null hypothesis that selection is absent based on a chi-squared statistic of 50 with one degree of freedom.

To test the sensitivity of this result to the assumptions concerning the distribution of the regression errors, the best strategy would be to search over the various members of the family of normal-truncated normal convolutions to find the parameters of the probability density function for the wage equation residuals which maximize the likelihood function. Given our sample sizes, this is prohibitively expensive. Instead, we estimated a least-squares wage equation

Table 3 Coefficient Estimates for the Wage Offer Equation, Estimation by Maximum Likelihood* (Dependent Variable = LnWage, Independent variables as deviations from their means)

Variable	Normal Residuals, No Selection (Coefficients Identical to OLS)		Nonnormal Residuals, Selection Permitted	
Constant	.7953	(82.8)**	.7484	(90.9)
Denver	.0332	(1.02)	.0406	(1.28)
Phoenix	.1105	(2.84)	.0979	(2.59)
Cincinnati	−.0194	(0.68)	−.0196	(0.71)
Louisville	−.0188	(0.48)	−.0235	(0.62)
Baltimore	.0000	(−−)	.0000	(−−)
Cleveland	.0353	(1.09)	.0074	(0.23)
Mississippi Pilot	.0285	(0.67)	.0203	(0.49)
Mississippi Control	−.0369	(0.93)	−.0261	(0.67)
White Male	.0000	(−−)	.0000	(−−)
Black Male	−.0047	(0.15)	−.0677	(2.19)
Hispanic Male	−.0190	(0.45)	−.0543	(1.31)
White Female	−.1732	(3.87)	−.1588	(3.66)
Black Female	−.0122	(0.37)	−.0772	(2.39)
Hispanic Female	−.0331	(0.73)	−.0899	(2.05)
Age (In Months)	.0030	(1.57)	.0021	(1.14)
Young	−.0301	(0.89)	−.0253	(0.77)
Very Young	−.0324	(0.90)	−.0422	(1.20)
Std. Error	.3808		.3719	
Log Likelihood	−4132.5		−4066.6	
K	−−−		2.0	
ρ_2	−−−		+.9285	
ρ_1	0.0000		−.0259	

*In each case, a probit participation model is estimated jointly with the wage offer equation. The probit coefficients are not shown here. However, their values from the maximum likelihood calculation with nonnormal residuals are used in the calculation of the disemployment index coefficients shown in Table 5.
**t-statistics in parentheses.

and calculated the residuals. A normal-truncated normal density was then fit to these and this error density used for the maximum likelihood selection model in [1.13]. We used K = 2.0 and ρ_2 = 0.9285, which fit the least-squares residual distribution quite well. (This density is almost a mirror image of the third panel in Figure 2.)

Interestingly, assuming normally distributed errors provides a log likelihood function of −4107.8 with strong selection, using the normal-truncated normal distribution on the wage residuals provides a log likelihood of −4066.6, with virtually no selection (ρ_1 = −.0259). Thus, by dropping the assumption of normality we have both eliminated the finding of selectivity bias and substantially improved the fit. The likelihood ratio test is not formally correct here since our estimates using K = 2, ρ_2 = 0.9285 do not represent the global maximum. Wherever the global maximum might be in the parameter space, however, we must be able to reject the normal residuals selection model with a chi-square statistic of at least 82.4 with two degrees of freedom.

In Table 3 we compare the wage equation estimated by nonnormal maximum likelihood with the least squares results. The corrected coefficients in Table 3 provide small but significant alterations to those estimated via OLS. The mean of the dependent variable declines to .7484 (equivalent to a wage offer of $2.11 per hour), suggesting that, on average, not-employed youths experienced slightly lower wage offers than employed youths with the same characteristics. (This is not a tautology.) Phoenix is still the highest wage site, but it is now joined by Denver, a result which is consistent with previous findings (Barclay et al., 1979).

White males are the highest paid race/sex group, and black and hispanic males receive wage offers approximately 6% lower. All females are paid less than all males, with white females receiving 15.9% less than white males, while black and hispanic females receive 7.7% and 9.0% less than white males. These results are perhaps the most significant change resulting from the introduction of a correction for selectivity bias. We speculate that the earnings advantage enjoyed by black and hispanic over white females may be due to the participation of the former in subsidized summer job programs paying the minimum wage. Whatever the cause, it appears that, overall, the black/white earnings differential is small, whereas the male/female differential is significant.

Age exerts a positive effect on wage rates—every month of age increases wages by 0.2%, so that aging by one year increases wages by 2.4%. Youths below 16 years of age, however, suffer a loss of 2.5% in their wage rates, and those below 15 lose an *additional* 4.2%. This result confirms the supposition that the very young face particularly low wage offers for summer work.

III.6 Results: The Labor Supply Equations
The Value of Time at Zero Hours of Work

As described in section III.3, $\hat{Ln}$wage from the coefficients of the previous section can be used with other right-hand-side variables to predict hour worked by those at work, thereby identifying the effects of these other variables as determinants of an individual's value of time at zero hours of work (reservation wage). Table 4 reports the results of this calculation. The additional right-hand-side variables are a dummy variable for Mississippi (possibly representing such rural/urban differences as price levels, the hours structure of offered employment, the availability of alternate activities to work, and tastes regarding hours of work), dummy variables for being young or very young (possibly representing taste or parental or employer constraints particularly salient to the youngest

Table 4   Coefficient Estimates for Determination of the
Value of Time at Zero Hours of Work*

Variable	Coefficient	
Constant	.2497	(43.8)**
Mississippi	−.1422	(5.08)
Young	.0181	(0.77)
Very Young	−.0234	(0.62)
Family Earned Income $\div 10^2$	−.0089	(0.43)
Family Welfare Income $\div 10^4$	.0038	(0.09)
Living with Parents	.0008	(0.02)
Male Youth with own Child	−.2140	(1.42)
Female Youth with own Child	−.0422	(0.95)
B_0 for LnWage in Hours Equation	482.7	(5.09)
Std. Error in Hours Equation	169.1	

*These are calculated from the hours equation by deflating those coefficients by B_0, the coefficient for the impact of the wage offer. See expression [2.7] and the discussion.
**t-statistics for the (untransformed) coefficients from the truncated normal regression in parentheses.

members of our sample), family earned or welfare income (possibly representing an income effect on the youth's consumption of leisure), and family size and whether the youth is a male with own child or a female with own child (possibly representing differential needs for an earned income flow or differential demands or opportunities for time spent at home as opposed to at work). By comparing the variables present in Tables 3 and 4 we see that the hours equation is heavily overidentified.

We find that hours respond positively to wage offers, with B_0 in expression [2.5] estimated to be 482.7 (t = 5.09). This value is smaller than has usually been found for married females (Heckman, 1974; Olsen, 1977, 1978b), but is significant and appears reasonable as an estimate for youths. With this coefficient used as a deflator, coefficients for the value of time can be calculated, and are shown in Table 4. The most significant of these is for the Mississippi dummy variable, which shows a 14% decrease in the value of a youth's time. That is, among otherwise identical working youths receiving the same wage offer, youths in Mississippi respond by working significantly longer hours. This result is consistent with a lower, rural price level, so that a given nominal wage offer represents a higher real wage in Mississippi. (Other explanations, such as urban/rural differences in the availability of competing activities, are not ruled out.)

Other results are that young age and family income exert little effect on the youth's value of time, while having one's own child decreases this value, by 21.4% for males and by 4.2% for females. These latter results suggest that once employment has been undertaken (and search, fixed, and other costs of employment have been paid or at least agreed to), the net effect of a youth's own child is to increase his hours of work.

Only the dummy variables for Mississippi and for young ages appear in both the wage offer and value-of-time equations. Comparing coefficients across the two equations we see that Mississippi residence exerts little effect on offered wages, but that these youths respond as though their leisure time is less valuable—Mississippi youths work significantly longer hours than those from other sites. As for youths aged less than 16 or 15 years, the former receive wage offers 2.5% lower than might be expected from an average age/wage trajectory, and the latter suffer a 6.7% decrement. Since the value of their time varies relatively little from the average, these youths work fewer hours than they would with higher wage offers.

The Disemployment Index

The disemployment index measures the extent to which a youth's probability of being employed departs from that expected on the basis of his wage offer and the value of his time at zero hours of work (calculated from the hours equation). Thus, it includes effects exerted by differential job search costs, differential fixed costs of working, and differential labor market distortions regarding the availability of job offers, as well as restrictions on the hours of work available to those who take these offers. With this much included, almost any variable could qualify as a potential determinant of such an index. We have included the following: site dummy variables (potential intersite differences in industrial structure and minimum wage coverage, as well as in the geographical access of youths to jobs), sex/race and young age dummy variables (potential differential availability of job offers due to discrimination), family income, family size, and whether living with parents (potential job search assistance; see Rees and Gray, 1979; Farkas and Stromsdorfer, 1980b), and whether or not the youth is himself a parent (fixed costs of working—child care). Age in months is excluded and identifies this relation.

Table 5 reports the result of this calculation, coefficient estimates calculated from a probit equation for the probability of employment, with the $\hat{\text{Lnwage}}$ coefficient used to identify (so as to deflate by) the standard error of the residuals. We see that among the site dummy variables the largest effects are for the two Mississippi sites, with disemployment indexes of .217 and .097. That is, the employment rates of youths in these sites behave *as if* these youths' values of time are 21.7 and 9.7% higher than is the case for Baltimore. The Mississippi youths experience close to average wage offers (Table 3), whereas their hours of work suggest that they have a lower than average value of time (Table 4). We now see (Table 5) that for whatever reason (possibly higher costs of job search and transportation to work in rural areas), Mississippi youth employment rates are significantly lower than would be expected on the basis of wage offers and hours of work in that location.

Table 5   Coefficient Estimates for Determination cf the
          Disemployment Index*

Variable	Coefficient	
Constant	.4633	(19.8)**
Denver	−.0361	(0.47)
Phoenix	.0308	(0.43)
Cincinnati	−.0449	(1.23)
Louisville	−.0140	(0.35)
Baltimore	.0000	(−−)
Cleveland	−.0560	(0.84)
Mississippi Pilot	.2166	(1.15)
Mississippi Control	.0973	(1.04)
White Male	.0000	(−−)
Black Male	−.0531	(1.53)
Hispanic Male	−.0311	(0.65)
White Female	−.0943	(1.28)
Black Female	−.0251	(0.43)
Hispanic Female	−.0392	(0.61)
Young	−.0396	(0.66)
Very Young	−.0077	(0.88)
Family Earned Income $\div 10^4$	.0122	(0.61)
Family Welfare Income $\div 10^4$	−.0244	(0.99)
Living with Parents	.0105	(0.78)
Male Youth with own Child	.2056	(1.82)
Female Youth with own Child	.1055	(1.10)
Family Size	.0003	(0.33)
Std. Error in Probit Equation	.1188	

*These are calculated by taking the coefficients from the probit equation, deflating these by the estimated standard error (calculated from the coefficient for LnWage), and subtracting the coefficients for the value of time (Table 4). See expression [2.10] and the discussion.
**t-statistic for $(B_i + B_i^t)$, that is, directly from the probit equation in parentheses.

As for the effects of the race/sex dummy variables, these show a negative value for each of the five groups compared to white males. That is, these groups exhibit higher employment rates than would be expected on the basis of their wage offers (their values of time have been assumed identical; recall their exclusion from Table 4). While at first glance somewhat surprising, this result becomes clearer by recalling the wage offer results for these groups (Table 3). In each case, the wage offer was significantly below that for white males, so that the probability of employment should be also. The coefficients for the disemployment index signify that these employment probabilities are not, in fact, as low as expected. The resulting situation is clarified by examining the expression (wage offer—disemployment index) for each of the groups:

Wage Offer–Disemployment Index

White Male	.000
Black Male	−.015
Hispanic Male	−.023
White Female	−.065
Black Female	−.052
Hispanic Female	−.051

We see that racial employment differences are slight, but that females have significantly lower employment rates than males. This is consistent with other results with these data (Barclay et al., 1979).

Finally, we find young age, family income, living with parents, and family size exerting relatively little effect on employment, but the presence of a child exerts a significant, positive effect on the disemployment index. That is, for both males and females, the presence of their own child causes a significant decrease in the propensity to be employed. This appears to be strong evidence for the existence of fixed costs of working and shows that the presence of a child is one of the strongest factors driving a wedge between individual probabilities of employment and the hours worked by employed youths. Combining the results of Tables 4 and 5, we see that employed male youths with a child work many more hours than employed youths without a child, but male youths with a child are no more likely to be employed than are other youths. Employed female youths with a child work slightly more hours than employed youths without a child, but female youths with a child are significantly less likely than other youths to be employed at all.

We have not formally tested the hypothesis that the simpler Heckman tobit labor supply model is correct, but an examination of the reduced form hours and participation models indicate rejection is assured. One indication of this is the large constant term in Table 5.

IV. IMPLICATIONS AND PLANS FOR FUTURE WORK

The results of the previous sections show how a structural model can provide a relatively rich interpretation of reduced-form findings. The impacts of such exogenous variables as race, sex, age, and family background characteristics occur via their effect on the youth's wage offer, asking wage, and disemployment index. We find that the youth's own wage exerts a powerful positive effect on total hours at work by those who are employed. Wage offers are generally far in excess of asking wages ("value of time at zero hours of work"), yet only 36% of the sample is employed, suggesting that fixed costs of working or demand side distortions are quite powerful. This situation is evidenced by the large, constant term for the disemployment index (a finding which also demonstrates the inappropriateness of the simple tobit model). The relatively large, positive coefficients associated with the effect of a youth's own child on his disemployment index suggest the existence of fixed costs associated with child care, but also important are the relative insignificance of the other variables as predictors of the disemployment index. It appears that demand deficiency *is* present (and most strongly so in the Mississippi sites), but that, at least during the summer of 1977 (when subsidized jobs programs for low-income youth were operating at relatively high levels), the available jobs were rationed in close to a random manner. Early results on program participation (Diaz et al., 1980; Farkas and Stromsdorfer, 1980a) suggests that across the four study sites, between 36 and 50% of eligibles chose to participate in Entitlement during the program's first 9 months of operation. This is further evidence for the existence of demand deficiency under current labor market conditions and for the proposition that youths do very much wish to work, even at minimum wage jobs.

Future impact analysis plans call for reduced-form examination of program participation, as well as program impacts on school enrollment and performance, employment and wage rates, and on school and work, jointly considered. Structural models of youth labor supply and educational investment will also be estimated. Where the school enrollment decision is concerned, models such as those of Willis and Rosen (1979) and Lazear (1979) can be used to value the program income guarantee within the context of the youth's present value calculation for his future income stream with and without high school dropout. Where labor supply is concerned, we can exploit the panel nature of our data as follows.

Having estimated a wage offer equation, we can impute a wage to all the control youths in both before and during program periods and calculate the change in wages. For the experimentals we can calculate the mean wage offer before the program in the same way. When the program is underway, the mean imputed wage is the program guarantee plus the expected value of the wage offer distribution (for employment outside the program) above the program guarantee times the probability of obtaining one of these relatively favorable jobs.

If the wage offer equation outside the program is

$$W = ZB + u,$$

then if the subscript b stands for before the program and d for during the program, for the controls

$$\Delta \hat{W} = (Z_d - Z_b) \, \hat{B},$$

and for the experimentals it is

$$\Delta \hat{W} = (1 - P)G + P(E(W|W > G)) - Z_b \hat{B}$$

$$= (1 - P)G + P(Z_d \hat{B} + E(u|Z_d \hat{B} + u > G)) - Z_b \hat{B}.$$

where G is the guaranteed minimum wage and $P = PR(Z_d \hat{B} + u > G)$ is the probability of finding a job above the guarantee.

The simplest labor supply model is thus

$$\Delta L = L_d - L_b = a_o + a_1 \Delta \hat{w},$$

where L is some measure of labor supply such as total hours worked. (Estimating this equation requires techniques for limited dependent variables where the limit point is endogenous, so that estimation will proceed by maximum likelihood.) By examining the fit of this equation, both within and between pilot and control sites, it will be possible to learn a good deal about the importance of wage variation in explaining the behavior of target population youth.

Of course this is only one of the analyses we shall undertake with the several waves of data ultimately available to us. In addition, each of these will involve a variety of corrections for possible self-selectivity and attrition bias. As with other evaluations of large experimental programs, we expect to develop certain of the methods as we proceed and occasionally discover an unexpected, but true, result.

NOTES

1. Those youths who would have been in school anyway are most likely to participate in the program, since for them the school requirement is no hardship. Thus, the program *could* enroll a great many youths while still having no influence on overall school enrollment rates.

2. School enrollment is simply a choice variable, since it is easily available to those who want it. Labor force participation, "being employed or looking for work," is also a matter of choice. However, being employed, an outcome variable of particular interest, depends on the availability of a job, which cannot always be taken for granted.

3. In a purely data descriptive sense, anything done with the cumulative logistic function (logit or log-linear model) can also be done with the cumulative normal (probit). However, the logistic is generally less computationally burdensome. For other models based on the probit specification see Hausman and Wise (1978), Heckman (1978a, 1978b), Smith (1979), and for continuous-time models based on the logit see Tuma et al. (this volume). Chamberlain (1978) extends and synthesizes these models.

4. Future work with this model will permit all interaction terms to depend on the exogenous variables.

5. This section draws heavily on Olsen (1979).

6. The form of the likelihood function in [1.9] resulted from factoring the joint density into the marginal u_{2i} times the conditional of u_{1i} given u_{2i} and then integrating which yields the second term in [1.9]. The first term in [1.9] is simply the marginal probability of not observing y_2.

7. This section draws heavily on Olsen (1977, 1978b).

8. With a slight relaxation of formal correctness, this equation can be estimated via OLS. Or, OLS coefficients can be corrected by a simple transformation to yield estimates for the truncated normal (Olsen, 1980).

9. If costs of search and working, minimum wage laws, and other distortions are unimportant, then $t_i \equiv 0$ and our labor supply specification reduces to a simple tobit model. Thus the Heckman specification is a nested hypothesis within our framework.

REFERENCES

AIGNER, D. J. (1975) "Alternative error specification for the estimation of production frontiers." Madison, WI. (mimeo)

AIGNER, D. J., C. A. KNOX LOVELL, and P. SCHMIDT (1977) "Formulation and Estimation of Stochastic Frontier Production Function Models." J. of Econometrics 6: 21-37.

BALL, J., W. DIAZ, J. LEIMAN, S. MANDEL, and K. McNUTT (1979) The Youth Entitlement Demonstration: An Interim Report on Program Implementation. New York: Manpower Demonstration Research Corporation.

BARCLAY, S., C. BOTTOM, G. FARKAS, E. W. STROMSDORFER, and R. J. OLSEN (1979) Schooling and Work Among Youths from Low-Income Households: A Baseline Report from the Entitlement Demonstration. New York: Manpower Demonstration Research Corporation.

BISHOP, Y.M.M., S. FIENBERG, and P. W. HOLLAND (1975) Discrete Multivariate Analysis. Cambridge, MA: MIT Press.

CHAMBERLAIN, G. (1978) "On the use of panel data." Delivered at the SSRC Conference on Life Cycle Aspects of Employment and the Labor Market.

DIAZ, W., J. BALL, N. JACOBS, L. SOLNICK, and A. WIDMAN (1980) The Youth Entitlement Demonstration: Second Interim Report on Program Implementation. New York: Manpower Demonstration Research Corporation.

FARKAS, G. and E. W. STROMSDORFER (1980a) "Social policies to reduce youth unemployment: lessons from experience and the potential of recent initiatives." U.S. Congress, Committee on Education and Labor. Washington, DC: Government Printing Office.

——— (1980b) "Comment on the paper by Rees and Gray," in Freeman and Wise (eds.) The Youth Employment Problem: Its Nature, Causes, and Consequences (NBER): Chicago: Univ. of Chicago Press.

FARKAS, G., C. BOTTOM, and E. W. STROMSDORFER (1979) "Program effects on school enrollment during program start-up: a preliminary report from the Entitlement Demonstration. Report to the Manpower Demonstration Research Corporation, October 22.

GOODMAN, L. A. (1972) "A general model for the analysis of surveys " Amer. J. of Sociology 77: 1035-1086.

GREGG, L. H. (1974) "Comments on selectivity biases in wage comparisons." J. of Pol. Economy 82: 1145-1156.

GRONAU, R. (1974) "Wage comparisons—a selectivity bias." J. of Pol. Economy 82: 1119-1143.

——— (1973a) "The effect of children on the housewife's value of time." J. of Pol. Economy 81: S168-199.

——— (1973b) "The intrafamily allocation of time: the value of the housewife's time." Amer. Econ. Rev. 63: 634-651.

HAUSMAN, J. and D. WISE (1978) "A conditional probit model for qualitative choice: discrete decisions recognizing interdependence and heterogeneous preferences." Econometrica 46: 403-426.

HECKMAN, J. (1978a) "Dummy endogenous variables in a simultaneous equation system." Econometrica 46.

——— (1978b) "Statistical models for discrete panel data developed and applied to test the hypothesis of true state dependence against the hypothesis of spurious state dependence." Annales de l'INSEE.

——— (1976) "The common structure of statistical models of truncation, sample selection, and limited dependent variables and a simple estimator for such models." Annals of Econ. and Social Measurement 5: 475-492.

——— (1974) "Shadow prices, market wages, and labor supply." Econometrica 42: 679-694.

LAZEAR, E. (1980) "Family background and optimal schooling decisions." Rev. of Economics and Statistics (February).

LEE, LUNG-FEI (1976) "Estimation of limited dependent variables models by two-stage methods." Ph.D. dissertation, University of Rochester.

————and W. A. TYLER (1978) "The stochastic frontier production function and average efficiency: an empirical analysis." J. of Econometrics 7: 385–389.

NERLOVE, M. (1976) "Multivariate log-linear probability models for the analysis of qualitative data." Discussion Paper, Center for Statistics and Probability, Northwestern University.

————and S. J. Press (1973) "Univariate and multivariate log-linear and logistic models." Santa Monica, CA: Rand.

OLSEN, R. J. (1980a) "Approximating a truncated normal regression with the method of moments." Econometrica (forthcoming).

————(1980b) "A least squares correction for selectivity bias." Econometrica (forthcoming).

————(1979) "Tests for the presence of selectivity bias and their relation to specifications of functional form and error distribution." Working Paper 812, Institution for Social and Policy Studies, Yale University.

————(1978a) "Note on the uniqueness of the maximum likelihood estimator for the tobit model." Econometrica (September).

————(1978b) "Two approaches to labor supply and selectivity bias—a reconciliation in terms of fixed costs." Working Paper 796, Institution for Social and Policy Studies, Yale University.

————(1977) "An econometric model of family labor supply." Ph.D. dissertation, University of Chicago.

PEARSON, K. and A. LEE (1968) "Generalized probable error in multiple normal correlation." Biometrika 6: 59-68.

REES, A. and W. GRAY (1978) "Family effects in youth employment." Presented at the NBER Conference on Youth Unemployment, Airlie, Virginia.

SCHULTZ, T. (1975) Estimating Labor Supply Functions for Married Women. Santa Monica, CA: Rand.

SMITH, D. A. (1979) "Labor market participation, turnover and the Gary Income Maintenance Experiment." Ph.D. dissertation, Massachusetts Institute of Technology.

TUMA, N., M. HANNAN, and L. GROENEVELD (1979) "Dynamic analysis of event histories." Amer. J. of Sociology 84 (January).

WILLIS, R. and S. ROSEN (1979) "Education and self-selection." J. of Pol. Economy 87 (October).

IV

EDUCATIONAL PROGRAMS:
DESIGNED AND NATURAL EXPERIMENTS

There is compelling evidence that schooling makes a difference in determining the cognitive skills of children. Consequently, the search for strategies to make schooling more effective is a worthwhile quest.

The primary resources that are consistently related to student achievement are teachers and other students. Other resources affect student achievement primarily through their impact on the attitudes and behaviors of teachers and students

A central problem in improving schools to develop mechanisms for incorporating into the decisionmaking process information about the priorities of the key actors, and consequently about their likely behavioral responses. The quality of public education in the future will be determined not only by the level of resources available, but also by our success in developing policy processes that take into account the behavioral responses of teachers, students, and families [Murnane, 1980: 24].

During the 1970s, a counterliterature sprung up opposing the Coleman Report's conclusion that schools do not matter. The best of these studies used microeconometric evidence to discover which resources *are* important in learning (Hanushek, 1971; Heyns, 1978; Murnane, 1975; Summers and Wolfe, 1977). Now, work in this field is taking a new turn. It is characterized by attempts to estimate behaviorally realistic models of the schooling-related choices made by teachers, students, and families. The goal (and the focus of the article by Murnane quoted above) is to formulate public policy according to a correct understanding of the parameters governing individual choice within existing institutional constraints. That is, we seek to estimate *behaviorally realistic, structural models of schooling-related choices and outcomes.*

Maynard and Murnane take a small but suggestive step in this direction. They find that the children of experimental families in the Gary Income Maintenance Experiment showed a significantly positive program impact on reading achievement. The mechanism they posit to explain this finding—experimentally induced labor supply decreases leading to greater time inputs to children—is one piece of an important (but untested) structural model of the determinants of youth cognitive development. The paper is most important as a prologue to future work with more detailed models and data.

Willis and Rosen are more ambitious. They have extended recent work on models of individual choice involving explicitly represented costs and benefits (McFadden, 1973; Domencich and McFadden, 1975; Lee, 1978) to the study of the college-attendance decision. At the heart of this model is an individual's comparison of the present-value of his future earnings stream in case he either (a) quits school after high school graduation, or (b) goes on to college. An innovation of the model is that these earnings streams differ across individuals, according to whether one's abilities are strongest in scholarship or in manual skills. Thus, the model permits the prediction that someone academically, not mechanically, smart would earn less with only a high school diploma than would the individual with the opposite distribution of abilities. Exploiting an unusual data set, the authors find empirical corroboration for their model.

Willis and Rosen's model could be expanded to explicitly incorporate non-monetary costs and benefits associated with different choices, as well as capital market imperfections that prevent individuals from making optimal schooling decisions (Lazear, 1980). Their use of an individual's discount rate (time horizon) could be given a larger role in the model and tested with a variety of dependent variables. What is important is their use of the self-selection theme running through this volume, the potentially wide applicability of models such as the one they estimate, and the key role that further work of this nature can play in advancing Murnane's (1980) program for more behaviorally realistic choice models for educational public policy analysis. (Such analyses are planned for the evaluation of the Youth Entitlement Demonstration. See the chapter by Farkas et al. in Part III.)

REFERENCES

DOMENCICH, T. and D. McFADDEN (1975) Urban Travel Demand. Amsterdam: North Holland.

HANUSHEK, E. (1971) "Teacher characteristics and gains in student achievement: estimation using micro data." Amer. Econ. Rev. 61: 280-288.

HEYNS, B. (1978) Summer Learning and the Effects of Schooling. New York: Academic.

LAZEAR, E. (1980) "Family background and optimal schooling decisions." Rev. of Economics and Statistics 62: 42-51.

LEE, L. F. (1978) "Unionism and wage rates: a simultaneous equations model with qualitative and limited dependent variables." International Econ. Rev. 19: 415-433.

McFADDEN, D. (1973) "Conditional logit analysis of qualitative choice behavior," in P. Zarembka (ed.) Frontiers of Econometrics. New York: Academic.

MURNANE, R. (1980) "Interpreting the evidence on school effectiveness," Working Paper 830. Institution for Social and Policy Studies, Yale University.

——— (1975) The Impact of School Resources on the Learning of Inner City Children. Cambridge, MA: Ballinger.

SUMMERS, A. A. and B. L. WOLFE (1977) "Do schools make a difference?" Amer. Econ. Rev. 67.

17

Maynard and Murnane observe that theirs is one of the few studies of the effect of the home environment on the educational achievement of children in which the policy variable is experimentally imposed (exogenous) rather than the result of a natural experiment (endogenous). They have exploited this opportunity to gain one very suggestive finding.

The model is reduced-form, and attention focuses on experimental/control group differences, adjusted by regression. Estimation is via OLS and tobit. The result is one regression sufficiently important to enter the literature: The Gary Experiment appears to have exerted a reasonably strong, positive effect on the reading test scores of young children.

The result whets one's appetite for further analyses of these data. Can the hypothesized causal link through parents' time and goods inputs to children be demonstrated? Does the result stand up under a variety of statistical manipulations, including regressions with different specifications? Does the effect persist through time?

The Effects of a Negative Income Tax on School Performance
Results of an Experiment

Rebecca A. Maynard and Richard J. Murnane

ABSTRACT

This paper analyzes the impact of a negative income tax experiment on the school performance of children in grades 4 through 10. The results indicate that the experimental program led to an increase in the average reading achievement of children in grades 4 through 6. This improved performance can be explained at least in part by the effect of the program on family income. No beneficial effects of the NIT program were observed for older children.

I. INTRODUCTION

Poor school performance by a large number of American children has been a major public policy concern for many years. A primary reason for this concern is that children from low-income families constitute a disproportionately large percentage of the low-achieving group. Thus, policy-makers have emphasized the need to find ways to compensate for the educational disadvantage associated with low socioeconomic status, so as to minimize the chance that children from low-income families will grow up to be as disadvantaged as their parents. In recent years, policy-makers have begun to consider whether policies aimed at improving the home environment would

The authors are, respectively, Senior Economist, Mathematica Policy Research, and Assistant Professor of Economics, Yale University.

* The authors are equally responsible for the research reported in this paper, which was performed under contract #HEW-100-76-0073 with the U.S. Department of Health, Education, and Welfare. The opinions expressed are those of the authors. We are indebted to Alicia Scott and a number of other MPR staff members who provided programming and research assistance for this project. We also thank Anthony Boardman, Kenneth Kehrer, Larry Manheim, Edward Pauly, Barbara Phillips, Douglas Wolf, and anonymous reviewers for helpful comments on an earlier draft. [Manuscript received August 1978; accepted March 1979.]

From Rebecca A. Maynard and Richard J. Murnane, "The Effects of a Negative Income Tax on School Performance: Results of an Experiment," 14(4) *Journal of Human Resources* 463-476 (Fall 1979). Copyright 1979 by the University of Wisconsin.

effectively lead to improved academic achievement. This paper explores this issue by analyzing the effects on school performance of a negative income tax (NIT) experiment that provides a guaranteed minimum income to a group of poor families and which alters incentives for labor force participation by reducing benefits levels in proportion to increases in earnings. The results of this analysis indicate that the NIT led to an increase in the average reading achievement of children in grades 4 through 6. However, no beneficial effects were observed for older children.

The next section of this paper discusses the evidence from previous research which suggests that home environmental factors affect educational performance; it also introduces a model describing mechanisms by which welfare reform may improve educational achievement, and provides a brief review of the results of the effects of income maintenance experiments on educational achievement. Section III describes the Gary Income Maintenance Experiment sample that is used in this study. Section IV discusses the empirical methodology, and Section V presents the results. Finally, the paper summarizes the findings and discusses their policy implications.

II. THE HOME ENVIRONMENT, INCOME GUARANTEE PROGRAMS, AND EDUCATIONAL ACHIEVEMENT

Evidence on the Role of the Home Environment

Researchers from many disciplines have used a variety of specifications and research designs to examine the determinants of educational achievement. The results have varied greatly; however, the one common conclusion is that the home environment exerts a powerful influence on educational achievement (Coleman et al. [5], Jencks et al. [10], Aaron [1]). Among the home environment attributes that researchers have found to be significantly correlated with school performance are the educational levels of parents, family income, socioeconomic status indices, the presence of reading materials, and durable-goods ownership.[1] Other researchers have found nutrition, health care, parental time allocation, and housing characteristics to be associated with school performance.[2]

While the results of these studies are highly suggestive, they do not provide firm evidence concerning the expected effects on educational

---

1   For example, see Averch et al. [2], Duncan [6], Flanagan [7], Birch and Gussow [4], Wray [21], and Fogelman and Goldstein [8].

2   For example, Wray [21] provides evidence that nutrition is important; Kaplan et al. [11] suggest that health care affects performance; Leibowitz [13, 14] and Lindert [15] conclude that parental time investments in their children result in improved performance; and Wilner and Walkley [20] find significant relationships between housing quality and school attendance and promotion rates.

achievement of public policy programs that directly influence the home environment (for example, by supplementing family income). The main reason is that most previous studies have used data from natural experiments in which the potential policy variables are endogenous.[3] For example, a family's income is the result of a variety of factors, such as parents' abilities, attitudes, and motivation levels. These factors may be the primary causal determinants of children's educational achievement; the correlation between family income and children's achievement may reflect simply one mechanism by which parents with high levels of motivation and skills help their children. If this is the case, then providing more income without changing parents' abilities or attitudes may not lead to greater educational achievements by children.

An important strength of this study is that it is based on data from a controlled experiment. In this experiment, families were assigned to either a treatment or control group according to a well-specified allocation model. As a result, after controlling for the effect of the assignment variables, any significant differences between experimental and control groups that are observed in the postenrollment period can be attributed solely to the experimental treatment.

Mechanisms by Which an NIT Could Influence Educational Achievement

In this section, we describe two mechanisms by which welfare reform could affect educational achievement by altering the home environment.[4] In our model, a child's achievement is influenced by three factors: (1) the quality of the home environment since birth; (2) the quality of formal schooling; and (3) a composite commodity that indicates the effects of innate ability, peer-group influence, and other factors. The critical attributes of the home environment are characterized as goods inputs and time inputs. Goods inputs include such things as nutritious food, health care, and materials that stimulate intellectual interests; time inputs include parental time reading to children, talking with them, and otherwise providing information and stimulation. It is assumed that goods inputs are positively related to family income, especially for low-income families, and that time inputs are positively related to "leisure time," which is defined as time spent not working.

The particular type of welfare reform considered in this paper is the

---

3   A few studies, such as Kaplan et al. [11], Wilner and Walkley [20], and Heber et al. [9] did involve the analysis of experimental programs which directly influenced children's home environments. However, because of both sample size and methodological limitations, the results of these studies are only suggestive of the expected effects of environmental changes.

4   A mathematical version of this model may be obtained from the authors.

negative income tax (NIT) program. The major features of this plan are (1) a guaranteed minimum annual income, which families receive if they have no other source of income, and (2) a tax rate, or benefit reduction rate, which is the amount by which the NIT payment is reduced for each dollar of income that the family earns. The main results of such a program are expected to be a reduction in parents' employment and an increase in total family income (Watts and Rees [19], Bawden et al., [3], Kehrer [12]).

Considered in this framework, the total effect of a negative income tax program on children's achievement depends on three factors:

- The extent to which an NIT program results in increased leisure and increased family income.
- The extent to which parents spend their increased leisure and income on time and goods inputs to children.
- The marginal productivity of additional time and goods inputs in raising children's achievement levels.

In this paper we do not attempt to examine these causal links that relate a negative income tax program to children's achievement. Instead, we use a reduced-form model to estimate the total effect of the NIT program on achievement. However, in the last section of the paper, this description of the causal chain provides a framework for discussing the empirical results.

Results from Other NIT Experiments

To place the results of our analysis of the Gary data in perspective, it is useful to review briefly the evidence concerning the school performance effects of the two NIT experiments that preceded the Gary experiment—the New Jersey-Pennsylvania and Rural experiments.

Educational Effects of the New Jersey-Pennsylvania NIT Experiment. As part of the evaluation of this NIT experiment, Mallar [16] investigated the short-run effects of a negative income tax program on the educational attainment of a sample of 138 young adults. The results of this study generally support the hypothesis that an NIT program will lead to improved educational achievement. It was estimated that young adults whose parents enrolled in one of the NIT plans were between 20 and 90 percent more likely than their counterparts in the control group to complete high school. Similarly (depending on the parameters of the particular NIT plan), it was estimated that participants in the NIT program had completed, on average, one-third to one-and-one-half more years of formal education than their control-group counterparts. However, this study does not provide any information concerning the more immediate performance effects, such as changes in attendance, standardized test scores, or academic grades, which may have led to the observed increase in years of education completed.

Educational Effects of the Rural Experiment. The evaluation of the Rural experiment, which was conducted in North Carolina and Iowa, did include an investigation of the effects of an NIT program on three immediate educational-achievement measures—attendance, standardized test scores, and academic grades (Maynard [17]). This study of 847 students in grades 2 through 12 revealed statistically significant experimental effects for all measures of performance for one subsample of children—elementary school students in North Carolina. However, among the other three subsamples (elementary school children in Iowa and high school students in both regions) there seemed to be no effect of the NIT program on any measure of performance.

III. THE GARY SAMPLE

The sample for this study consists of those children whose families participated in the Gary Income Maintenance Experiment and for whom information on the school performance measures is available.[5] In a number of important respects, these children are not representative of the nation's school children. All of them are black, and three-fifths of them live in female-headed households. Furthermore, their families are considerably poorer, on average, than the U.S. population. (The average annual income of the families in the Gary experiment was only $5200, compared with a national average of $9433, and 44 percent of the families had incomes below the poverty line, compared to only 10 percent of the nation's families.)

Since prior research indicates that children of different ages respond differently to environmental influences, we divided the sample into two groups: children in grades 4 through 6, and children in grades 7 through 10.[6] It is important to keep in mind that this is a sample of very low achieving children which, while not representative of the U.S. student population, does represent the group of children who are of greatest concern to educational policy-makers.

---

5 This experiment was conducted between 1971 and 1974. Thus, pre-enrollment performance data were generally from the 1969–70 school year, the one exception being that pre-enrollment reading tests for some children were administered in the fall of the 1970–71 school year. Postenrollment measures of performance were obtained for the 1973–74 school year when available, since this coincided with the end of the experiment. When we did not have data for this period, we used data for the first of the following postenrollment years for which they were available: 1972–73, 1971–72, and 1974–75.

6 We standardized the test scores to eliminate differences across grade levels in means and standard deviations. We eliminated differences across grade levels in the means of academic grades and days absent by including variables denoting grade level. There were no significant differences across grade levels in the standard deviations of these latter two performance measures.

IV. THE EMPIRICAL METHODOLOGY

The basic equation used to estimate the impact of the NIT experiment on children's school performance was specified as follows:

$$A_{i,post} = a_0 + a_1 A_{i,pre} + \Sigma_j d_j D_{ij} + \Sigma_j s_k S_{ik} + t T_i + u_i$$

where $A_{i,post}$ is a measure of the ith child's school performance during or after participation in the NIT experiment; $A_{i,pre}$ is a measure of the ith child's school performance in the year prior to enrollment in the experiment; D_{ij} is the jth variable describing the ith child or his/her family prior to enrollment in the experiment;[7] S_{ik} is the kth variable describing the schools that the ith child attended in the period between the pre- and postenrollment measures of school performance; $T_i = 1$ if the ith child's family participated in the experimental NIT program and 0 if the family was in the control group; and u_i is an error term for the ith child, which is distributed normally with a mean of zero and a constant variance.[8]

The major hypothesis examined in this analysis is that the coefficient t in this equation is positive (in the case of absences, negative) and significantly different from zero. In addition, we tested more detailed hypotheses concerning experimental effects on particular types of children by replacing the dichotomous treatment variable with a number of variables that interact treatment status with pre-experimental performance measures and background characteristics.

Ordinary least-squares was used to estimate this equation when the dependent variable was reading scores or composite grade-point averages. However, Tobit analysis was used to estimate the impact of the NIT program on the number of days absent during the school year, since this variable has a lower bound of zero.

V. RESULTS

Table 1 describes the results of the empirical work on the school performance of children in grades 4 through 6, and Table 2 describes the results for

---

7 This vector includes those variables which influenced the assignment of observations to experimental or control cells. The model does not include measures of the child's family and home environment coincident with the years of the experiment because this could have led to biased estimates of the experimental effects.

8 Our sample definition does permit multiple observations from the same household to be included in any regression. Thus, there may be some correlation in this error term among family members. We have not used an error-components model that includes a family-specific error term, however, since evaluation of the Rural experiment suggested that this error-component was generally not significant.

TABLE 1

REGRESSION ADJUSTED DIFFERENCES IN SCHOOL PERFORMANCE
MEASURES BETWEEN EXPERIMENTAL AND CONTROL GROUPS,
GRADES 4 THROUGH 6

Experimental-Control Comparison Groups	Performance Measure		
	Reading Test Scores[a]	Academic Grade Point Average	Days Absent[b]
All children	22.3**	−0.4	0.9
Grade level			
Four	53.2**	−1.8	1.3
Five	−4.5	0.2	0.1
Six	26.2*	−0.1	1.0
Years between enrollment in experiment and postenrollment performance measure			
One	−1.0	−0.6	1.1
Two	23.5	0.4	0.4
Three or four	25.0**	−0.5	0.7
Pre-enrollment income			
Less than half the poverty line	29.5*	−1.4	−0.7
Half the poverty line or higher	19.6*	0.1	1.2
Dependent variable			
Mean	0.0	81.6	12.0
Standard deviation	99.1	7.4	12.6
Number of observations	575	619	608

Note: These experimental-control differences are calculated by evaluating the estimated regression equations at the sample mean for all variables except experimental treatment variables, which are evaluated at zero for controls and one for experimentals.

a   The test score measures analyzed are standardized raw scores on the Iowa Test of Basic Skills. The mean grade equivalent scores are 4.1, 4.4, and 5.2 for the fourth, fifth, and sixth grade samples, respectively.

b   These results for this measure are based on Tobit analysis, since 11 percent of the sample had zero days absent from school during the postenrollment year.

*   Statistically significant at the .05 level on a two-tailed test.

**   Statistically significant at the .01 level on a two-tailed test.

children in grades 7 through 10. The entries in each table indicate differences between experimental and control groups for the three measures of school

TABLE 2
REGRESSION ADJUSTED DIFFERENCES IN SCHOOL PERFORMANCE MEASURES BETWEEN EXPERIMENTAL AND CONTROL GROUPS, GRADES 7 THROUGH 10

Experimental-Control Comparison Groups	Performance Measure		
	Reading Test Scores[a]	Academic Grade Point Average	Days Absent[b]
All children	−12.5	−1.6**	0.5
Grade level			
Seven	—	−1.3	−2.2
Eight	−12.5	0.2	0.9
Nine	—	−2.6*	3.3*
Ten	—	−2.5*	−0.2
Years between enrollment in experiment and postenrollment performance measure			
One	—	—	2.9
Two	−10.3	−1.8*	2.1
Three or four	−14.0	−1.6	−0.2
Pre-enrollment income			
Less than half the poverty line	−8.8	0.3	−3.0
Half the poverty line or higher	−13.7	−2.2**	1.1
Dependent variable			
Mean	0.0	78.4	10.7
Standard deviation	99.6	8.9	13.8
Number of observations	276	898	829

Note: These experimental-control differences are calculated by evaluating the estimated regression equations at the sample mean for all variables except experimental treatment variables, which are evaluated at zero for controls and one for experimentals.

a The test score measures analyzed are standardized raw scores on the Iowa Test of Basic Skills. The mean of the grade equivalent scores is 6.6.

b These results for this measure are based on Tobit analysis, since 14 percent of the sample had zero days absent during the postenrollment year.

* Statistically significant at the .05 level on a two-tailed test.

** Statistically significant at the .01 level on a two-tailed test.

performance, after controlling for the effects of demographic characteristics and pre-enrollment performance. We report experimental-control differences in school performance for the total sample and for three subsamples that are defined by the grade level of the child, the number of years since the family was enrolled in the NIT program, and family income.[9]

Findings for Fourth Through Sixth Graders

The results shown in Table 1 indicate that the experimental NIT program had positive effects on the reading test scores of the younger children considered in this study. On the scale of the standardized scores used to measure reading skills, children whose families were enrolled in the NIT program scored, on average, 22 points higher than their counterparts in the control group. This 22-point difference is the result of a significant 53-point difference between experimentals and controls in the fourth grade sample and a significant 26-point difference for the sixth grade sample. (Evaluated at the sample means, these differences correspond to a six- to nine-month difference on a grade equivalent scale among fourth graders and a two- to five-month difference among sixth graders.) There was essentially no difference between the scores of experimentals and controls in the fifth grade sample.

The results also indicate that the length of time in the program was an important determinant of test score gain. Children whose families had been in the program for only one year at the time of the performance measure scored no higher on average than their counterparts in the control group. However, children whose families had been in the program for two or more years did score substantially higher, on average, than children in the control group. The difference in scores is statistically significant only among those whose postenrollment test was administered three or four years after their families enrolled in the experiment.

Table 1 also presents estimated experimental-control group differences in test scores for two subsamples defined by family income: those with incomes less than one-half the official poverty level and those with incomes greater than or equal to the poverty level. The NIT program had a favorable effect on reading scores for both subgroups; this effect was particularly large (30 points) among those in the lower income group.

---

9   One regression equation was estimated for each set of experimental-control comparisons. We also investigated whether the experimental-control differences were sensitive to: (1) pre-enrollment performance measures; (2) the number of parents in the household; (3) the number of children in the family; (4) the number of bedrooms per person; (5) the sex of the child; and (6) the particular tax-rate/guarantee plan that applied to experimental families. In general, we did not find that experimental effects were sensitive to any of these factors.

Findings for Seventh Through Tenth Graders

Reading scores were available only for children in the eighth grade. As seen from Table 2, for this relatively small subsample, there is no evidence that the NIT program affected the reading scores of older children.

Similarly, there is no evidence to suggest that the NIT program had a positive impact on students' academic grades. This is not surprising, since academic grades contain a great deal of "noise" that could mask differences in actual achievement. However, this does not explain the significant negative relationships between participation in the NIT program and academic grades that were estimated for children in grades 9 and 10, and, consequently, for the full sample. These negative relationships were also particularly significant for children in families with pre-enrollment income greater than or equal to 50 percent of the poverty line.[10]

We considered four hypotheses to explain these unexpected results. The first is that a disproportionately large number of the children in the NIT program attended schools that gave students relatively low grades. A second hypothesis is that the negative results are an artifact of systematic sample attrition. A third hypothesis is that some older children interpreted the NIT program as an indication that "effort" was not a condition for receiving income; consequently, they reduced their efforts in school. The final hypothesis is that some children responded to the stimuli provided by the NIT program by enrolling in more difficult academic courses—for example, college preparatory courses instead of vocational courses. We were able to investigate empirically only the first two of these hypotheses; we found no evidence in support of either. Unfortunately, the data did not permit a systematic examination of the last two hypotheses.[11]

Finally, there is no evidence that the NIT program led to improved school attendance for older children. The one statistically significant result indicates that children in the ninth grade whose families participated in the program were absent, on average, three days more per year than their counterparts in the control group. Several of the hypotheses suggested to explain the academic grade-point results may also apply to this finding.

VI. SUMMARY AND CONCLUSIONS

The experimental NIT program had favorable effects on the reading

---

10 Unreported regression results indicate that the adverse effects of the NIT program on the grade-point averages of children in families with low pre-enrollment income were significant only for children in grades 9 and 10.

11 A more complete description of these hypotheses and the techniques used to test them is available from the authors.

achievement of younger children, and the effects were larger the longer the families were in the program. Children whose families had particularly low incomes before enrolling in the program experienced the greatest improvement. The NIT program had no favorable effects on the school performance of older children.

A Mechanism by Which the Experiment May Have Affected Performance

In order to understand why the Gary NIT experiment led to improved reading scores for younger children (and why the overall results are modest), it is useful to return to the causal chain described in Section II. This leads us to ask the following three questions:

· What was the effect of the experiment on parents' leisure time and on family income?
· Did the effects on leisure time of parents lead to more time inputs to children, and was there additional income which was spent on goods inputs to children?
· Did changes in goods and time inputs influence educational performance?

Below we consider the evidence relating to each of these questions.

Other findings from the evaluation of the Gary experiment suggest that the experiment had a significant effect on total family income, but only minimal effects on the employment of mothers. On average, total family income increased by almost $2000 per year (about 50 percent). For wives, there was virtually no change in hours worked, although there was a decrease of about two hours per week for female family heads. The small absolute change in hours worked for females is due to the fact that relatively few women were working prior to their enrollment in the program.[12]

We have no direct information on the ways in which parents spent their leisure time. However, since the experimentally induced changes in parental labor force participation were so small, it seem unlikely that the Gary NIT program results in substantially increased time inputs to children.[13]

The increased income resulting from the NIT program did, however, result in changes in consumption behavior that could have increased the quantity and quality of goods inputs to children. Experimental families who lived in public housing prior to enrollment were more likely than control-

---

12   The reduction in hours worked among adult males is also small (about 2.5 hours per week). In addition, there is evidence that the leisure time of males is less related to time inputs to children than is the leisure time of females (Leibowitz [13]).

13   The observed reductions in labor force time are concentrated among a few people. Children in these families may be disproportionately represented in the sample for which we observed the greatest effect. However, data are not readily available to investigate this possibility.

group families to move into private dwellings.[14] Further, in comparison to control families, experimental families purchased more clothing, medicine, and home production appliances.[15]

In large part, the modest nature of the school performance results can be explained by the facts that there were almost no experimentally induced changes in parents' leisure time, and that there were only limited experimentally induced changes in family income and the consumption of goods inputs. However, it should also be remembered that this was only a three-year experiment. It may take longer than three years for parents to fully adjust their labor supply and income allocations. Furthermore, three years may be insufficient for the educational effects of improvements in the home environment to be observed.[16]

A Comparison of the Gary Results with Those of the Rural Experiment

In many respects the results from the Gary and the Rural experiments are similar. In both experiments, the NIT program had impacts on the school performance of the youngest children, particularly those from the poorest families. Like the Gary results, the pattern of results from the Rural experiment can be explained in terms of the effects of the experiment on parental leisure time and family income. The effects of the NIT on family income and labor force participation were larger for the North Carolina sample than for the Iowa sample. The net annual income gain for North Carolina families who participated in the Rural NIT program averaged about $800, compared to about $500 for the Iowa sample (and $1700 for families in the Gary experiment).[17] Also, on average, North Carolina women in the Rural experiment reduced the time they spent working outside of the home by about four hours per week, compared to a reduction of about one hour per week for women in Iowa.[18] Changes in consumption, similar to those in the Gary experiment, were identified in the Rural experiment, especially among North Carolina families (Setzer et al., [18]).

---

14 There was no overall experimental-control differential in residential mobility rates.
15 Leibowitz [14] suggests that the availability of home production appliances is likely to result in the reallocation of time from home chores to time inputs to children.
16 The fact that this was an experiment of known, limited duration may have also distorted the participants' responses. It is not clear what the implications of such distortions would have been.
17 This comparison of income changes between the Gary and Rural experiments does not account for cost-of-living differences due to either geographic location or the timing of the experiments. An adjustment for both of these factors would tend to reduce the gap between the income changes in the two experiments.
18 The corresponding figures for Gary are two hours per week for female family heads and virtually no change for wives.

In summary, differences in family income and the employment of mothers may explain many of the differences among the experimental effects estimated for the Gary, the North Carolina, and the Iowa samples. In North Carolina, where the most consistent pattern of effects was observed, there were substantial changes in both the consumption of goods inputs and the time allocation of mothers. In Gary, where modest school performance effects were observed, there were similar changes in the consumption of goods inputs, but essentially no changes in the time allocation of mothers. Finally, in Iowa, where no effects on school performance were observed, there were almost no changes in the time allocation of mothers and only small changes in goods inputs.

Conclusion

The results of this study, together with those of the Rural experiment, suggest that an income-support program such as an NIT may lead to improved school performance among younger children. In particular, it may benefit younger children whose families have the lowest income and, consequently, receive the largest income supplements. A more thorough investigation of the relationships between specific home environment characteristics and educational achievement should provide still greater evidence as to which children would benefit most from such a change in our welfare policy.

REFERENCES

1. Henry Aaron. "Healthy, Wealthy and Wise: Backdoor Approaches to Education." Unpublished manuscript, The Brookings Institution, 1977.
2. Harvey Averch et al. "How Effective Is Schooling?" In *A Critical Review and Synthesis of Research Findings*. Santa Monica, Calif.: Rand Corporation, 1972.
3. D. Lee Bawden et al. *Rural Income Maintenance Experiment: Final Report*. Madison: Institute for Research on Poverty, University of Wisconsin, 1976.
4. H. Birch and J. Gussow. *Disadvantaged Children: Health, Nutrition, and School Failure*. New York: Harcourt, Brace and World, Inc., 1970.
5. James S. Coleman. *Equality of Educational Opportunity*. Washington: U.S. Department of Health, Education, and Welfare, Office of Education, 1966. OE-38001.
6. Greg J. Duncan. "Educational Attainment." In *Five Thousand American Families—Patterns of Economic Progress: An Analysis of the First Five Years of the Panel Study of Income Dynamics*, Vol. I, Ch. 7. Ann Arbor: Survey Research Center, University of Michigan, 1974.

7. J. Flanagan. *Studies of the American High School.* Pittsburgh: Project TALENT, University of Pittsburgh, 1962.

8. K. Fogelman and H. Goldstein. "Social Factors Associated with Changes in Educational Attainment Between 7 and 11 Years of Age." *Educational Studies* 11:2 (1976): 96–109.

9. Rick F. Heber. *Rehabilitation of Families at Risk for Mental Retardation.* Madison: University of Wisconsin, 1972.

10. Christopher Jencks et al. *Inequality.* New York: Basic Books, 1972.

11. R. Kaplan et al. "The Efficacy of a Comprehensive Health Care Project: An Empirical Analysis." *American Journal of Public Health* 62 (July 1972): 924–30.

12. Kenneth Kehrer. "The Gary Income Maintenance Experiment: Summary of Initial Findings." Indiana University, 1977.

13. Arleen Leibowitz. "Home Investments in Children." *Journal of Political Economy* 82 (March/April 1974): S111–31.

14. ————. "Parental Inputs and Children's Achievement." *Journal of Human Resources* 12 (Spring 1977): 242–51.

15. Peter Lindert. "Family Inputs and Inequality Among Children." Institute for Research on Poverty Discussion Paper 218-74. Madison: University of Wisconsin, 1974.

16. Charles Mallar. "The Educational and Labor Supply Responses of Young Adults on the Urban Graduated Work Incentive Experiment." In *The New Jersey Income Maintenance Experiment,* eds. Harold Watts and Albert Rees. New York: Academic Press, 1977.

17. Rebecca Maynard. "The Effects of the Rural Income Maintenance Experiment on the School Performance of Children." *American Economic Review* 67 (February 1977): 370–75.

18. Florence Setzer et al. *Summary Report: Rural Income Maintenance Experiment.* Washington: U.S. Department of Health, Education, and Welfare, 1976.

19. Harold W. Watts and Albert Rees, eds. *Final Report of the New Jersey Graduated Work Incentive Experiment.* Madison: Institute for Research on Poverty, University of Wisconsin, 1974.

20. D. Wilner and R. Walkley. "Effects of Housing on Health and Performance." In *The Urban Condition,* ed. Leonard Duhl, M.D. New York: Basic Books, 1963.

21. J. Wray. "Population Pressure on Families: Family Size and Child Spacing." In *Rapid Population Growth: Consequences and Policy Implications,* ed. Roger Rovelle. Baltimore: Johns Hopkins University Press, 1971.

18

The great importance of this chapter lies in its estimation of a model of choice explicitly representing the individual-specific returns from each potential outcome of the choice. This notion is central to the millions of decisions each of us makes throughout our lifetime, yet very little empirical work has been undertaken to estimate the magnitudes of the underlying parameters governing these decisions. One exception is much of the work on labor supply—an individual's wage rate represents the return to his decision to enter the labor force.[1] Another is the recent work on the choice of transit mode (Demencich and McFadden, 1975). Willis and Rosen's study is an important advance of such models into the study of the college-attendance decision.

The article is less difficult then it looks. At its heart is an expression for the present value of an individual's earnings stream according to whether he (a) goes to college, or (b) quits school after high-school graduation. These are expressions 7 and 8.[2] We see that attending college alters the level of one's earnings (expressed here as a beginning salary, $\bar{y}$, and a salary growth rate, g), and also imposes the cost of foregone earnings during the S extra years in school.

It is assumed that the individual decides whether to attend college by comparing these present values. This leads to the basic probit model of college choice (expressions 9-11).[3] It is in attempting to empirically specify and unbiasedly estimate this model that new issues arise.

Structural equations for the determinants of key model parameters—y, g, and r (the individual's discount rate)—are given in expressions 12-14. If we take no account of which exogenous variables enter each of these equations, but, rather, note than any variable entering at least one of these equations must therefore affect college choice, we arrive at a reduced form probit for this decision. This is given by expressions 15 and 16, with estimates reported in the first column of Table 2.

Structural estimates require attention to possible selection bias associated with the fact that for each individual we only observe his earnings stream from the choice actually taken. Correction for this, however, is readily available in the form of Heckman's inverse Mills ratio term method (see the chapter by Heckman in Part I) described in expressions 17-23. Assuming that individual abilities affect earnings, but net of earnings exert no other effect on college choice, identification is assured, and we are able to estimate structural earnings functions (Table 3) and also to use imputed values from these to estimate a structural probit model of choice (columns 2 and 3 of Table 2).[4]

NOTES

1. Even in this literature, other returns from working are not usually explicitly represented, nor are the full range of benefits from the competing choice outcome—staying at home.

2. The definite integrals written here are just a calculus device for adding up earnings over a sequence of years. The algebraic expression on the right-hand-side is arrived at through standard calculus theorems codified as rules for the evaluation of integrals.

3. Expression 9 is derived through the standard calculus trick of using a Taylor series expansion to linearize a function around a point.

4. For a related sequential estimation procedure, see the chapter by Farkas et al. in Part III.

REFERENCE

DOMENCICH, T. and D. McFADDEN (1975) Urban Travel Demand. Amsterdam: North Holland.

Education and Self-Selection

Robert J. Willis and Sherwin Rosen

A structural model of the demand for college attendance is derived from the theory of comparative advantage and recent statistical models of self-selection and unobserved components. Estimates from NBER-Thorndike data strongly support the theory. First, expected lifetime earnings gains influence the decision to attend college. Second, those who did not attend college would have earned less than measurably similar people who did attend, while those who attended college would have earned less as high school graduates than measurably similar people who stopped after high school. Positive selection in both groups implies no "ability bias" in these data.

I. Introduction

In this paper we specify and estimate a model of the demand for college education derived from its effect on expected lifetime earnings compared with its cost. Attention is focused on specifying the role of earnings expectations in the derived demand for schooling; these are found to be empirically important determinants of the decision to attend college. In addition to including financial incentives, the model allows for a host of selectivity or sorting effects in the data that are related to "ability bias," family effects, and tastes that have occupied

Thanks are due to Sean Becketti for excellent research assistance, to Lung Fei Lee for advice on statistical issues, and to Richard Layard and W. M. Gorman for criticism of an initial draft. This research was supported by NSF and the National Bureau of Economic Research, but this is not an official NBER publication. The order of the authors' names was selected by a random device.

other researchers. Background and motivation are presented in Section II. The structure of the model, a variant of a simultaneous-equations problem involving discrete choices, is presented in Section III. The estimates, based on data from the NBER-Thorndike sample, appear in Section IV. Some implications and conclusions are found in Section V.

II. Nature of the Problem

Estimates of rates of return to education have been controversial because they are based on ex post realizations and need not reflect structural parameters necessary for correct predictions. For example, it is well understood that college and high school graduates may have different abilities so that income forgone during college by the former is not necessarily equal to observed earnings of the latter. Our objective here is twofold. One is to estimate life earnings conditioned on actual school choices that are purged of selection bias. The other is to determine the extent to which alternative earnings prospects, as distinct from family background and financial constraints, influence the decision to attend college.

One would need to go no further than straightforward comparisons of earnings outcomes among school classes for structural rate of return estimates if educational wage differentials were everywhere equalizing on the direct, opportunity, and interest costs of schooling. For then the supplies of graduates (or "demands" for each level of education) would be nearly elastic at the equalizing wage differentials, and the distribution of human wealth would be approximately independent of the distribution of schooling.[1] However, recent evidence on the structure of life earnings based on panel data strongly rejects this as a serious possibility. Total variance of earnings among people of the same sex, race, education, and market experience is very large, and more than two-thirds of it is attributable to unobserved components or person-specific effects that probably persist over much of the life cycle.[2] The panel evidence therefore suggests that supply elasticities are substantially less than completely elastic at unique wage differentials and that there are inframarginal "ability rents." Put in another way, observed rates of return are not wholly supply deter-

---

[1] The equalizing difference model originates with Friedman and Kuznets (1945). Jacob Mincer (1974) has developed it most completely in recent years.

[2] See Lillard and Willis (1978) for additional detail and confirmation of these remarks. Related studies have reached similar conclusions, e.g.. Weiss and Lillard (1978). Of course, it is conceivable, but unlikely, that educational wage differentials are exactly equalizing for each individual, although considerable lifetime income inequality exists among individuals. This possibility is rejected in the empirical findings presented below.

mined and depend on interactions with relative demands for graduates as well.

A natural approach has been to incorporate measures of ability into the statistical analysis, either directly or as indicators of unobserved factors, in order to, in effect, impute ability rent. But merely partitioning observed earnings into schooling and ability components does not use any of the restrictions imposed on the data by a school-stopping rule, and that decision embodies all the economic content of the problem. Some of that additional structure is incorporated here.

Economic theories of education, be they of the human-capital or signaling varieties, are based on the principle of maximum capital value: schooling is pursued to the point where its marginal (private) internal rate of return equals the rate of interest. It is easy to show that this leads to a recursive econometric model in which (i) schooling is related to a person's ability and family background, and (ii) earnings are related to "prior" school decisions and ability. Earnings gains attributable to education do not appear explicitly in the schooling equation. Instead, the cost-benefit basis of the decision is embedded in cross-equation restrictions on the overall model, because the earnings equation is a constraint for the maximum problem that determines education attainment.[3] There are many estimates of recursive models in the literature, but very few have tested the economic (wealth-maximizing) hypothesis.[4]

We begin with the assumption of marked heterogeneity and diversity in the population, as in the unobserved-component approach to panel data. Costs and benefits of alternative school-completion levels are assumed to be randomly distributed among people according to their capacities to finance education, tastes, perceptions, expectations, and an array of talents that affect performance in work activities associated with differing levels of schooling. Some of these things are observed, while others are unobserved. Individuals are sorted into educational classes according to the interaction of a selection criterion (such as maximum present value) and the underlying joint distribution of tastes, talents, expectations, and parental wealth. The selection

[3] The basic model is discussed in Becker (1975). See Rosen (1977) for an elaboration of this argument and a survey of the relevant literature. Blaug (1976) also stresses the need for estimating structural demand for schooling relationships, and Griliches (1977) discusses the difficulty of doing so in conventional models. Part of Griliches's discussion is pursued in Griliches, Hall, and Hausman (1977). The model elaborated here is conceptually distinct from that work, though some of the statistical techniques are similar. A similar remark applies to the work of Kenny, Lee, Maddala, and Trost (in press).

[4] There is aggregate-time-series evidence that earnings are important determinants of professional school enrollment (see Freeman [1971] and numerous subsequent studies by the same author); but there is virtually no micro evidence even though such data have been most often studied in the human-capital and signaling frameworks.

rule partitions the underlying joint density into a corresponding realized educational distribution. The supply function of graduates at any level of schooling is "swept out" of the joint taste, talent, parental wealth distribution as increased wage differentials enlarge the subset of the partition relevant for that class.

Let Y_{ij} represent the potential lifetime earnings of person i if schooling level j is chosen, X_i a vector of observed talent or ability indicators of person i, and τ_i an unobserved talent component relevant for person i. Similarly, split family-background and taste effects into an observed vector Z_i and an unobserved component ω_i. Let V_{ij} denote the value of choosing school level j for person i. Then a general school-selection model is:

$$Y_{ij} = y_j(X_i, \tau_i), \qquad j = 1, \ldots, n; \tag{1}$$

$$V_{ij} = g(y_j, Z_i, \omega_i); \tag{2}$$

$$i \text{ belongs to } j \text{ if } V_{ij} = \max(V_{i1}, \ldots, V_{in}); \tag{3}$$

and

$$(\tau, \omega) \sim F(\tau, \omega). \tag{4}$$

Equation (1) shows how potential earnings in any given classification vary with talent and ability.[5] The earnings function differs among school classes because work activities associated with alternative levels of education make use of different combinations of talent. Equation (2) translates the earnings stream from choice j into a scaler such as present value and is conditioned on family background to reflect tastes and financial barriers to extending schooling. Equation (3) is the selection rule: the person chooses the classification that maximizes value and is observed in one and only one of the n possibilities open to him. Equation (4) closes the model with a specification of the distribution of unobservables. Since observed assignments of individuals to schooling classes are selected on (X, Z, τ, ω), earnings observed in each class may be nonrandom samples of population potential earnings, because those with larger net benefits in the class have a higher probability of being observed in it.

This formulation is suggested by the theory of comparative advantage.[6] It allows for a rather eclectic view of the role of talent in

[5] Actually, expository convenience dictates a more restrictive formulation than is necessary. The X and Z need not be orthogonal. They may have some elements in common, but identification requires that they not have all elements in common (see below).

[6] Roy (1951) gives a surprisingly modern and rigorous treatment of a selection problem based on the theory of comparative advantage. See Rosen (1978) for extensions and elaboration on this class of problems. Heckman (1976), Lee (1976), and Maddala (1977) develop the appropriate estimation theory.

determining observed outcomes, since the X's may affect earning capacity differently at different levels of schooling (see eq. [1]) and covariances among the unobservables are unrestricted. Indeed, there may be negative covariance among talent components. For example, plumbers (high school graduates) may have very limited potential as highly schooled lawyers, but by the same token lawyers may have much lower potential as plumbers than those who actually end up choosing that kind of work. This contrasts with the one-factor ability-as-IQ specifications in the literature which assume that the best lawyers would also be the best plumbers and would imply strictly hierarchical sorting in the absence of financial constraints. In effect an IQ-ability model constrains the unobserved ability components to have large positive covariances—an assumption that is probably erroneous and is not necessary for our methods. Note also that population mean "rates of return" among alternative schooling levels have no significance as guides to the social or private profitability of investments in schooling. For example, a random member of the population might achieve a negative return from an engineering degree, yet those with appropriate talents who choose engineering will obtain a return on the time and money costs of their training which is at least equal to the rate of interest.

There are difficult estimation problems associated with selectivity models. In brief, the unobservables impose distinct limits on the amount of structural information that can be inferred from realized assignments in the data. For example, it would be very desirable to know the marginal distribution of talents in (4), since it would then be possible to construct the socially efficient assignment of individuals to school classes, defined as the one that maximizes overall human wealth. Then the deadweight losses due to capital market imperfections could be computed by comparing optimal with observed assignments. However, the marginal density is not itself identified, since unobserved financial constraints and talent jointly determine observed outcomes. These issues will be made precise shortly, but, roughly speaking, we do not necessarily know if a person chose college education because he had talent for it or because he was wealthy. What can and will be done is to map out the joint effects of the unobservables embedded in the actual demand curve for college attendance, which embodies all constraints inherent in the actual market but which nevertheless is a valid structural basis for prediction. Selectivity or ability bias in unadjusted rate of return computations that do not take account of the sorting by talent inherent in observed assignments can also be computed.

A few limitations to these methods must be noted at the outset. It is crucial to the spirit of the model, based as it is on human diversity, that few covariance restrictions be placed on the distribution of unobservables. This practically mandates the assumption of joint normality, since no other nonindependent multivariate distribution offers anything close to similar computational advantages. While the general selection rule specified below is likely to emerge from a broad class of economic models of school choice, it is not known how sensitive the results are to the normality assumptions. In addition, nonindependence forces some aggregation in the number of choices considered for computational feasibility, even though the statistical theory can be worked out for any finite number.[7] This rules out of consideration other selection aspects of the problem that should be considered, such as choice of school quality.[8] All people in our sample have at least a high school education, and we have chosen a dichotomous split between choice of high school and more than high school (college attendance). Some internal diagnostic tests help check on the validity of this aggregation. Experiments with a college completion or more classification, compared with a high school graduation or some college classification, yielded results very similar to those reported below.

III. The Model

Specification of the econometric model is tailored to the data at our disposal. More details will be given below, but at this point the important feature is that earnings are observed at two points in the life cycle for each person, one point soon after entrance into the labor market and another point some 20 years later. The earnings stream is parameterized into a simple geometric growth process to motivate the decision rule. This is a reasonable approximation to actual life earnings patterns for the period spanned by the data. Two levels of schooling are considered, labeled level A (for more than high school) and level B (for high school).

If person i chooses A, the expected earnings stream is

$$y_{ai}(t) = 0, \qquad\qquad 0 < t \leq S,$$
$$y_{ai}(t) = \bar{y}_{ai} \exp[g_{ai}(t - S)], \qquad S \leq t < \infty, \tag{5}$$

[7] The problem is that the aggregates are sums of distributions that are themselves truncated and selected. Therefore the distributions underlying the aggregate assignments are not necessarily normal. We are unaware of any systematic analysis of this kind of aggregation problem.

[8] Methods such as conditional logit have been designed to handle high-dimensioned classifications (McFadden 1973) but require independence and other (homogeneity) restrictions that are not tenable for this problem. Hausman and Wise (1978) have worked out computational methods on general normal assumptions for three choices. Note also that maximum-likelihood methods are available, but are extremely expensive because multiple integrals must be evaluated. Hence we follow the literature in using consistent estimators.

where S is the incremental schooling period associated with A over B and $t - S$ is market experience. If alternative B is chosen, the expected earnings stream is

$$y_{bi}(t) = \bar{y}_{bi} \exp(g_{bi} t), \qquad 0 \leqslant t < \infty. \tag{6}$$

Thus earnings prospects of each person in the sample are characterized by four parameters: initial earnings and rates of growth in each of the two alternatives. Diversity is represented by a random distribution of the vector $(\bar{y}_a, g_a, \bar{y}_b, g_b)$ among the population.[9]

Equations (5) and (6) yield convenient expressions for present values. Assume an infinite horizon, a constant rate of discount for each person, r_i, with $r_i > g_{ai}, g_{bi}$, and ignore direct costs of school. Then the present value of earnings is

$$V_{ai} = \int_s^\infty y_{ai}(t) \exp(-r_i t)\, dt = [\bar{y}_{ai}/(r_i - g_{ai})] \exp(-r_i S) \tag{7}$$

if A is chosen and

$$V_{bi} = \int_0^\infty y_{bi}(t) \exp(-r_i t)\, dt = \bar{y}_{bi}/(r_i - g_{bi}) \tag{8}$$

if B is chosen. These are likely to be good approximations, since the consequences of ignoring finite life discount corrections and non-linearities in earnings paths toward the end of the life cycle are lightly weighted for nonnegligible values of r.

Selection Rule

Assume that person i chooses A if $V_{ai} > V_{bi}$ and chooses B if $V_{ai} \leqslant V_{bi}$. Define $I_i = \ln(V_{ai}/V_{bi})$. Substitution from (5) to (8) yields $I_i = \ln \bar{y}_{ai} - \ln \bar{y}_{bi} - r_i S - \ln(r_i - g_{ai}) + \ln(r_i - g_{bi})$. A Taylor series approximation to the nonlinear terms around their population mean values $(\bar{g}_a, \bar{g}_b, \bar{r})$ yields

$$I_i = \alpha_0 + \alpha_1 (\ln \bar{y}_{ai} - \ln \bar{y}_{bi}) + \alpha_2 g_{ai} + \alpha_3 g_{bi} + \alpha_4 r_i, \tag{9}$$

with

$$\begin{aligned}
\alpha_1 &= 1, \\
\alpha_2 &= \partial I/\partial g_a = 1/(\bar{r} - g_a) > 0, \\
\alpha_3 &= \partial I/\partial g_b = -1/(\bar{r} - \bar{g}_b) < 0, \\
\alpha_4 &= -[S + (\bar{g}_a - \bar{g}_b)/(\bar{r} - \bar{g}_a)(\bar{r} - \bar{g}_b)].
\end{aligned} \tag{10}$$

---

[9] Wise (1975), Lazear (1976), and Zabalza (1977) have used initial earnings and growth of earnings to study life earnings patterns. The distribution of potential earnings and growth is not constrained in our model, thus, e.g., allowing the possibility that $\bar{y}_a$ and g_a are negatively correlated (and similarly for $\bar{y}_b$ and g_b), as in Mincer (1974). On this see Hause (1977).

Hence the selection criteria are

$$\Pr(\text{choose A}) = \Pr(V_a > V_b) = \Pr(I > 0),$$
$$\Pr(\text{choose B}) = \Pr(V_a \leq V_b) = \Pr(I \leq 0). \tag{11}$$

Earnings and Discount Functions

Let X_i represent a set of measured characteristics that influence a person's lifetime earnings potential, and let $u_{1i}, \ldots, u_{4i}$ denote permanent person-specific unobserved components reflecting unmeasured factors influencing earnings potential.[10] Specify structural (in the sense of population) earnings equations of the form

$$\ln \bar{y}_{ai} = X_i \beta_a + u_{1i}, \tag{12}$$
$$g_{ai} = X_i \gamma_a + u_{2i}$$

if A is chosen and

$$\ln \bar{y}_{bi} = X_i \beta_b + u_{3i}, \tag{13}$$
$$g_{bi} = X_i \gamma_b + u_{4i}$$

if B is chosen. The variables on the left-hand sides of (12) and (13) are to be interpreted as the individual's expectation of initial earnings and growth rates at the time the choice is made. In order to obtain consistent estimates of $(\beta_a, \gamma_a, \beta_b, \gamma_b)$ from data on realizations it is assumed that expectations were unbiased. Hence forecast errors are assumed to be independently normally distributed, with zero means.

Let Z_i denote another vector of observed variables that influence the schooling decision through their effect on the discount rate. Then

$$r_i = Z_i \delta + u_{5i}, \tag{14}$$

where u_5 is a permanent unobserved component influencing financial barriers to school choice. The vector (u_j) is assumed to be jointly normal, with zero means and variance-covariance matrix $\Sigma = [\sigma_{ij}]$. The Σ is unrestricted.

Reduced Form

The structural model is (9), (12), (13), and (14). A reduced form of the selection rule is obtained by substituting (12)–(14) into (9):

[10] The τ's of Section II are related to $(u_1 \ldots, u_4)$ by a set of implicit prices that vary across school classifications, as in Mandelbrot (1960). See Rosen (1978) for the logic of why these differences in valuation can be sustained indefinitely and cannot be arbitraged.

$$I = \alpha_0 + X[\alpha_1 (\beta_a - \beta_b) + \alpha_2 \gamma_a + \alpha_3 \gamma_b] + \alpha_4 Z\delta + \alpha_1 (u_1 - u_3)$$
$$+ \alpha_2 u_2 + \alpha_3 u_3 + \alpha_5 u_5 \tag{15}$$
$$\equiv W\pi - \epsilon,$$

with $W = [X, Z]$ and $-\epsilon = \alpha_1 (u_1 - u_3) + \alpha_2 u_2 + \alpha_3 u_4 + \alpha_5 u_5$. Thus, an observationally equivalent statement to (9) and (11) is

$$\Pr (\text{A is observed}) = \Pr (W\pi > \epsilon) = F\left(\frac{W\pi}{\sigma_\epsilon}\right), \tag{16}$$

where $F(\cdot)$ is the standard normal c.d.f. Equation (16) is a probit function determining sample selection into categories A or B, to be estimated from observed data.[11]

Selection Bias and Earnings Functions

The decision rule selects people into observed classes according to largest expected present value. Hence the earnings actually observed in each group are not random samples of the population, but are truncated nonrandom samples instead. The resulting bias in observed means may be calculated as follows. Note that $\Pr [\text{observing } y_a (t)] = \Pr (I > 0) = \Pr (W\pi > \epsilon)$. Therefore, from (12), $E (\ln \bar{y}_a | I > 0) = X\beta_a + E(u_1 | W\pi > \epsilon)$. Define $\rho_1 = \rho (u_1/\sigma_1, \epsilon/\sigma_\epsilon) = \sigma_{1\epsilon}/\sigma_1\sigma_\epsilon$. Then $E (\ln \bar{y}_a | I > 0) = X\beta_a + \sigma_1\rho_1 E(\epsilon/\sigma_\epsilon | \epsilon/\sigma_\epsilon < W\pi/\sigma_\epsilon) = X\beta_a + \sigma_1\rho_1 [-f (W\pi/\sigma_\epsilon)/F (W\pi/\sigma_\epsilon)]$, where F is the cumulative normal density and f is its p.d.f. Define

$$\lambda_a \equiv -f(W\pi/\sigma_\epsilon)/F(W\pi/\sigma_\epsilon) \tag{17}$$

as the truncated mean (with truncation point $W\pi/\sigma_\epsilon$) of the normal density due to selection. Making use of the definition of ρ_1 and λ_a yields

$$E(\ln \bar{y}_a | I > 0) = X\beta_a + \frac{\sigma_{1\epsilon}}{\sigma_\epsilon} \lambda_a. \tag{18}$$

A parallel argument for g_a, $\bar{y}_b$, and g_b yields

$$E(g_a | I > 0) = X\gamma_a + \frac{\sigma_{2\epsilon}}{\sigma_\epsilon} \lambda_a, \tag{19}$$

$$E(\ln \bar{y}_b | I \leq 0) = X\beta_b + \frac{\sigma_{3\epsilon}}{\sigma_\epsilon} \lambda_b, \tag{20}$$

[11] For completeness, $-\epsilon$ should be redefined to take account of deviations between realizations and expectations at the time school decisions were made. Thus, let $\ln Y_{ai} = \ln \bar{y}_{ai} + v_{1i}$, where Y_{ai} is realized initial earnings, $\bar{y}_{ai}$ is expected initial earnings, and v_{1i} is normally distributed forecast error. Similarly, forecast errors v_{2i}, v_{3i}, and v_{4i} are defined for g_{ai}, $\ln \bar{y}_{bi}$, and g_{bi}. Then the complete definition of $-\epsilon$ is obtained from replacing u_{ji} with $(u_{ji} + v_{ji})$, $j = 1, \ldots, 4$, in (15). Clearly this has no operational significance for the model, given the assumption of unbiased expectations.

and

$$E(g_b \mid I \leq 0) = X\gamma_b + \frac{\sigma_{4\epsilon}}{\sigma_\epsilon} \lambda_b, \tag{21}$$

with

$$\lambda_b = E\left(\epsilon/\sigma_\epsilon \middle| \frac{\epsilon}{\sigma_\epsilon} > \frac{W\pi}{\sigma_\epsilon}\right) = f(W\pi/\sigma_\epsilon)/[1 - F(W\pi/\sigma_\epsilon)] \tag{22}$$

and

$$\sigma_{k\epsilon} = -[\alpha_1(\sigma_{1k} - \sigma_{3k}) + \alpha_2\sigma_{2k} + \alpha_3\sigma_{4k} + \alpha_5\sigma_{5k}], \, k = 1, \ldots, 4. \tag{23}$$

Note from (17) that $\lambda_a \leq 0$. Therefore the observed (conditional) means of initial earnings and rates of growth among persons in A are greater or less than their population means as $\sigma_{1\epsilon}$ and $\sigma_{2\epsilon} \lessgtr 0$, from (18) and (19). Conversely, $\lambda_b \geq 0$ (see [22]), and there is positive or negative selection bias in initial earnings and growth rates for people observed in class B according to $\sigma_{3\epsilon}$ (and $\sigma_{4\epsilon}) \gtrless 0$. Since σ_{ij} is unrestricted, $\sigma_{k\epsilon}$ is also unrestricted, and selection bias can go in either way. In particular, it is possible that the bias is positive in both groups, consistent with the comparative-advantage argument sketched above. Positive bias in A and negative bias in B would be consistent with a single-factor (hierarchical) interpretation of ability. Of course, neither finding yields a definitive "ability" interpretation because of the presence of expectational errors and financial factors (σ_{5k}) in (23): the assignments are based on talent, expectations, and wealth, not on talent alone.

Estimation

Consider the following regressions applied to observed data:

$$\begin{aligned}
\ln \bar{y}_a &= X\beta_a + \beta_a^*\lambda_a + \eta_1, \\
g_a &= X\gamma_a + \gamma_a^*\lambda_a + \eta_2, \\
\ln \bar{y}_b &= X\beta_b + \beta_b^*\lambda_b + \eta_3, \\
g_b &= X\gamma_b + \gamma_b^*\lambda_b + \eta_4.
\end{aligned} \tag{24}$$

Equations (18)–(21) suggest that β_a^* estimates $\sigma_{1\epsilon}/\sigma_\epsilon$, γ_a^* estimates $\sigma_{2\epsilon}/\sigma_\epsilon$, and so on. Including λ_a or λ_b in the regressions along with X corrects for truncation and selectivity bias, and $E(\eta_{ij}) = 0$ for $j = 1$, $\ldots$, 4. In addition, $E(\eta_{ij}^2)$ is heteroskedastic (see below), because the observations are truncated and at different points for different people. Equation (24) cannot be implemented directly because λ_a and λ_b are not known. However, it can be shown[12] that consistent estimates

---

[12] See Heckman (1976) and Lee (1976).

of (24) are obtained by replacing λ_a and λ_b with their values predicted from the reduced-form probit equation (16). These values are

$$\hat{\lambda}_{ai} = -f(W_i\widehat{\pi/\sigma_\epsilon})/F(W_i\widehat{\pi/\sigma_\epsilon}),$$

$$\hat{\lambda}_{bi} = f(W_i\widehat{\pi/\sigma_\epsilon})/[1 - F(W_i\widehat{\pi/\sigma_\epsilon})]$$

(25)

and are entered as least-squares regressors along with X_i. Estimation of (24) with λ_i replaced by $\hat{\lambda}_i$ corrects for selectivity bias in the observations. What is more interesting for the economic theory of educational choice is that these estimates provide a basis for estimating the structural selection rule or structural probit function (9) and (11). The structural probit is

$$\text{Pr (choose A)} = \text{Pr } \{[\alpha_0 + \alpha_1 (\ln \bar{y}_a - \ln \bar{y}_b) + \alpha_2 g_a \qquad (26)$$
$$+ \alpha_3 g_b + \alpha_4 Z\delta]/\sigma_\epsilon > \epsilon/\sigma_\epsilon\},$$

from (9), (11), and (14). Use the consistent estimates of structural earnings and growth described above to predict earnings gains for each person in the sample according to

$$\ln \widehat{(\bar{y}_{ai}/\bar{y}_{bi})} = X_i(\hat{\beta}_a - \hat{\beta}_b),$$

$$\hat{g}_{ai} = X_i\hat{\gamma}_a, \qquad (27)$$

$$\hat{g}_{bi} = X_i\hat{\gamma}_b,$$

where $\hat{\beta}$ and $\hat{\gamma}$ are estimated by the method above.[13] These predicted values are inserted into (26) and estimated by the usual probit method to test the economic restrictions (10).[14]

Other Tests

Alternative estimates are available to serve as an internal consistency check on the model. In particular, the model can be specified using the observed level of earnings at time $\bar{t}$ and earnings growth instead of initial earnings. From (5) and (6) it follows that

$$\ln y_a(\bar{t}) = X_i(\beta_a + \gamma_a\bar{t}) + u_1 + \bar{t}u_2,$$

$$\ln y_b(\bar{t}) = X_i(\beta_b + \gamma_b\bar{t}) + u_3 + \bar{t}u_4. \qquad (28)$$

---

[13] This method is due to Lee (1978), who used it to study unionization status. Our model differs somewhat in that there is more than one structural equation in each classification.

[14] Heckman (1976) and Lee (1977) show that OLS estimates of the standard errors of β_a, γ_a, β_b, and γ_b in (24) are biased if $\sigma_{k\epsilon}/\sigma_\epsilon \neq 0$ when estimated values of λ_b are used in place of their true values. Lee also shows that the usual estimates of standard errors for the structural probit (26) are biased when estimated values of $\ln (\bar{y}_a/\bar{y}_b)$, g_a, and g_b are used in place of their true values and derives exact asymptotic distributions for these parameters. We use Lee's (1977) results to compute consistent estimates of standard errors below.

Substitute for the level equations in (12) and (13) and this model also can be estimated as described above. However, now the structural probit is of the form

$$\Pr (A \text{ is chosen}) = \Pr (\{\theta_0 + \theta_1 [\ln y_a(t) - \ln y_b(t)] \\ + \theta_2 g_a + \theta_3 g_b\} + \theta_4 r/\sigma_\epsilon > \epsilon/\sigma_\epsilon). \quad (29)$$

Since $\ln y_a(\bar{t}) - \ln y_b(\bar{t}) = \ln \bar{y}_a - \ln \bar{y}_b + (g_a - g_b)\bar{t} - g_a S$, the following restrictions are implied:

$$\theta_1 = \alpha_1,$$

$$(\bar{t} - S)\theta_1 + \theta_2 + \alpha_2, \quad (30)$$

$$-\bar{t}\theta_1 + \theta_3 = \alpha_3.$$

Hence we have a check on the validity of the model. Of course, its main validation is the power to predict behavior and assignments on independent data.

Identification

Two natural questions regarding identification arise in this model.

1. Estimation of the selection rule or structural probit equation is possible only if the vectors X and Z have elements that are not in common. If X and Z are identical, the predicted values of $\ln \bar{y}_a - \ln \bar{y}_b$, g_a, and g_b are colinear with the other explanatory variables in (26), and its estimation is precluded. Note, however, that even if X and Z are identical, the reduced-form probit (16) is estimable, and it still may be possible to estimate initial earnings and growth-rate equations and selection bias. The reason is that, although the $\hat{\lambda}$ corrections in (24) are functions of the same variables that enter the $X\beta$ or $X\gamma$ parts of these equations, they are nonlinear functions of the measured variables. Structural earnings equations might be identified off the nonlinearity, though in any particular application there may be insufficient nonlinearity if the range of variation in $W\pi$ (see [15]) is not large enough.[15]

---

[15] Heckman (1979) raises some subtle issues regarding specification error in selection models. Elements of Z may be incorrectly specified in X and can be statistically significant in least-squares regressions because of truncation. Conversely, coefficients on selection-bias variables λ_a and λ_b can be significant because variables are incorrectly attributed to selection when they more properly belong directly in X. E.g., some might argue that family background belongs in structural earnings equations and our selectivity effects work (see below) because family background comes in the back door through its indirect effect on $\hat{\lambda}$. However, a reversal of the argument suggests that family-background variables might have significant estimated direct effects on earnings merely because they work through selection and resulting truncation. There is no statistically satisfactory way of resolving this problem. In any event, we cannot be "agnostic" about specification because both the economic and statistical theories require certain nontestable zero identifying restrictions. The problem is even more complicated

In the general discussion of Section II, X was tentatively associated with measured abilities and Z with measured financial constraints (and tastes), corresponding to the Beckerian distinction between factors that shift the marginal rate of return to investment schedule and those that shift the marginal supply of funds schedule. Evidently, if one takes a sufficiently broad view of human investment and in particular of the role of child care in the new home economics, easy distinctions between the content of X and of Z become increasingly difficult, if not impossible, to make. If X and Z are indistinguishable, the economic theory of school choice has no empirical content. In the empirical work below a very strong dichotomy with no commonalities is maintained: X is specified as a vector of ability indicators and Z as a vector of family-background variables. This hypothesis is maintained for two reasons. First, it provides a test of the theory in its strongest form. Certainly if the theory is rejected in this form there is little hope for it. Second, there have been no systematic attempts to find empirical counterparts for the things that shift marginal rate of return and marginal cost of fund schedules that cause different people to choose different amounts of schooling. The validity of the theory rests on the possibility of actually being able to find an operational set of indicators, and this distinction is the most straightforward possibility.

Given resolution of problem 1, not all parameters in the model can be estimated. Some are overidentified and some are underidentified. The selectivity-bias-corrected structural earnings equations (24) directly estimate β_a, β_b, γ_a, γ_b, and the structural probit (26) provides estimates of $(\alpha_1/\sigma_\epsilon, \alpha_2/\sigma_\epsilon, \alpha_3/\sigma_\epsilon, \alpha_4\delta/\sigma_\epsilon)$. Furthermore, from the approximations in (10), the coefficient on $\ln (\bar{y}_a/\bar{y}_b)$ in (26) estimates $1/\sigma_\epsilon$ (given that $\alpha_1 = 1$), so that it is also possible to estimate population average real rates of interest. In addition, there are 15 parameters in the unobserved-component variance-covariance matrix Σ. Following a development similar to the one leading to (18)–(21), it can be shown that the variances of residuals in (24) are

$$\text{var }(\eta_{ij}) = \sigma_{jj} + \frac{\sigma_{j\epsilon}}{\sigma_\epsilon} \left(\frac{W_i\pi}{\sigma_\epsilon} \lambda_{ai} - \lambda_{ai}^2 \right), j = 1, 2;$$

$$\text{var }(\eta_{ij}) = \sigma_{ij} + \frac{\sigma_{j\epsilon}}{\sigma_\epsilon} \left(\frac{W_i\pi}{\sigma_\epsilon} \lambda_{bi} - \lambda_{bi}^2 \right), j = 3, 4. \tag{31}$$

Similar expressions hold for covariances between η_{i1} and η_{i2} and between η_{i3} and η_{i4}. Hence it is possible to estimate the own-population variances σ_{jj} for $j = 1, \ldots, 4$, two within-group

---

in the present context because the theory is based on unobserved talent and financial constraint shifters and must have observable counterparts to be operational. Evidently choice among alternative specifications ultimately must rest on predictive performance outside the sample.

covariances, and four covariances σ_{j_ϵ} for $j = 1, \ldots, 4$. These, along with the estimate of σ_ϵ, provide only 11 statistics to estimate 15 parameters. Evidently all the covariance terms in Σ cannot be estimated without additional zero or other restrictions because we never observe the path not taken. This is the basis for the statement above that deadweight losses from assignments based jointly on wealth and talent rather than on talent alone cannot be imputed. The demand function for college attendance implicit in (26) reflects the joint density of talent, wealth, tastes, and expectations, and their separate effects cannot be disentangled.

IV. Estimation

The model has been estimated on a sample of 3,611 respondents to the NBER-Thorndike-Hagen survey of 1968–71.[16] These data refer to male World War II veterans who applied for the army air corps. They do not come from a random sample of the population, since the military screening criteria were based on certain aspects of ability and physical fitness. Therefore it is not possible to extrapolate these results to the population at large. However, the sample's advantages more than compensate for this. First, it covers more than 20 years of labor-market experience, far longer than any other panel of comparable size and most appropriate for measuring lifetime earnings effects of educational choice as the theory requires. Second, it contains extensive information on family background and talent. While several other panels are as good on family background, virtually none compare in their range of talent and ability indicators most appropriate to the theory of comparative advantage.

The sample actually used is a subset of 5,085 total respondents. Forty-two observations were dropped for not responding to the age question, another 480 persons were deleted because they were pilots, had extended military service, or did not report a job in 1969, and 952 were dropped because they did not report both initial ($\bar{y}$) and latest ($y[\bar{t}]$) earnings required for structural estimation. Definitions of variables are given in Appendix A. Individuals were put into two categories: group A represents those who entered college and group B those who stopped school after high school graduation. Not all members of group A completed college, and a substantial fraction completed more than a college education. They are labeled "college attendees" hereafter. Descriptive statistics appear in table 1. Notice that more than 75 percent of the sample chose to attend college for some period,

---

[16] These data have been extensively analyzed by other investigators, especially Taubman (1975), who also discovered them. For complete documentation see NBER (1973).

TABLE 1

Descriptive Statistics

Variable	High School (Group B) Mean	SD	More than High School (Group A) Mean	SD
Father's ED	8.671	2.966	10.26	3.623
Father's ED^2	83.99	55.53	118.4	78.09
DK ED	.0999	...	.0464	...
Manager	.3628	...	.4954	...
Clerk	.1239	...	.1450	...
Foreman	.2238	...	.1695	...
Unskilled	.1492	...	.0819	...
Farmer	.1062	...	.0720	...
DK job	.0177	...	.0124	...
Catholic	.2933	...	.2138	...
Jew	.0405	...	.0617	...
Old sibs	1.143	1.634	.9035	1.383
Young sibs	.9381	1.486	.8138	1.266
Mother works:				
Full 5	.0468	...	.0486	...
Part 5	.0392	...	.0504	...
None 5	.7168	...	.7507	...
Full 14	.0822	...	.0936	...
Part 14	.0708	...	.0851	...
None 14	.6384	...	.6713	...
H.S. shop	.2592	...	.0908	...
Read	20.57	10.17	24.06	11.63
NR read	.0291	...	.0128	...
Mech	59.24	18.27	58.88	18.96
NR mech	.0025	...	0	...
Math	18.13	11.82	28.94	17.17
NR math	.0683	...	.0188	...
Dext	50.04	9.359	50.68	9.811
NR dext	0	...	.0071	...
Exp	29.33	2.439	24.54	2.907
Exp^2	866.1	147.1	610.4	147.4
S13–15	...	...	.3106	...
S16	...	...	.3993	...
S20	...	...	.0823	...
Year 48	46.62	1.584	48.05	1.869
Year 69	69.11	.3691	69.08	.3437
ln $\bar{y}$	8.635	.4107	8.526	.3871
ln $y(t)$	9.326	.4573	9.639	.4904
g	.0309	.0251	.0535	.0283
λ_a	−1.2870	.2873	−.3193	.2256
λ_b	.4666	.3763	1.605	.5212
No. observations	791		2820	

Note.—Variables are defined in Appendix A.

reflecting the unusual ability distribution in the sample and eligibility for a liberal school subsidy (the GI Bill). However, the presence of the GI Bill is common to both college attendees and high school graduates.

There are some obvious differences between the two groups. Both mean and relative variance of earnings in both years are smaller for high school graduates, as tends to be true in other samples. In addition, high school graduates had smaller earnings growth over the period, had more siblings and were lower in birth order than college attendees, and were more likely to have taken vocational training in high school. Their fathers had less schooling and were more likely to be blue-collar workers as well. Four ability measures have been chosen for analysis, out of some 16 indicators available in the data. Math and reading scores are related to IQ type of ability (in fact, it is known that math score is highly correlated with IQ score in these data), while the other two are more associated with manual skills. The four together seem well suited to the comparative-advantage logic underlying the formulation of the model. High school graduates tend to score lower in the math and reading-comprehension tests, about the same in manual dexterity, and somewhat better on mechanical ability. In line with the previous discussion, all ability measures in table 1 are assigned to X, while the family-background measures—reflecting financial constraints, tastes, and perceptions—are assigned to Z. Experience, school-completion dummies (for group A), and year of reported earnings are used exclusively as controls in structural earnings equations.

The first columns in table 2 present estimated coefficients and asymptotic t-statistics of the reduced-form probit selection into group A—equation (16). These effects more or less parallel the summary of table 1 given above. Math score has a particularly strong positive effect and mechanical score a strong negative effect on the college attendance decision. The effect of mother's working is somewhat unexpected. Mother's home time when the respondent was 5 years old or younger has virtually no effect on college attendance, whereas the respondent was more likely to go to college if his mother worked when he was 6–14 years of age. This is more supportive of market investment through relaxation of financial constraints than of home investments in kind.[17]

Structural estimates of earnings and growth equations corrected for selection are found in table 3. These are somewhat different from the typical earnings equations found in the literature, because they in-

[17] Recall that female labor-force participation during the war increased. The normalized category for mother's work classifications is nonresponse. We do not know how many did not respond because no mother was in the home.

clude a much sparser set of regressors. For example, we know respondents' unemployment experience, weeks worked, weeks ill, marital status, and so forth but have not included them in the regressions. The logic of this lies in the model itself: at the time the college attendance decision was made, there is no reason to expect that respondents knew the outcomes of such variables. It is more in the spirit of the choice framework of the model to allow these "current" events to be captured indirectly via their correlations with included variables in order to estimate expected or anticipated values relevant to the structural probit.[18] The problem is more difficult in the case of school-completion differences among members of group A in table 3 and, in truth, raises an unresolvable aggregation problem. The anticipations argument above suggests that school-completion differences within group A may not enter the earnings equations, so that included variables pick up average completion experience in the sample. Alternatively, it can be argued that the level of schooling achieved within group A should be controlled by including school-completion dummies. This latter specification is reported in table 3 and is the one used to estimate the structural probit in table 2. Of course we do not switch on the school-completion dummies to estimate the earnings advantages of college attendance, since that would clearly stack the deck in favor of finding strong financial effects. Earnings and structural probit equations were also estimated with school dummies deleted, and the results were very similar to those reported here. However, it is clear that this issue only can be resolved by going into a more disaggregated model with multiple classifications.

With the exception of experience, most of the variables have little effect on initial earnings in either A or B (see cols. 1 and 2 of table 3).[19] Experience effects are the strongest and are known to be most important at early and late stages of career patterns, facts borne out in these data since experience has little effect on later (surveyed around 1969) earnings. The ability measure that has the largest effect on

[18] A related and thorough discussion of this issue appears in Hanoch (1967), to which the reader is referred. It has not escaped our attention that current variables such as hours of work and unemployment experience might serve as indicators of an unobserved "taste for leisure" component, but we have not experimented with that possibility.

[19] Initial earnings is recall data from the 1955 Thorndike survey and refers to a period as much as 9 years prior to that survey date. Late earnings is closer to the NBER survey date and probably has less recall error in it. The low R^2 statistics in table 3 are due to the fact that we are looking at within-group variation, whereas most results in the literature get a lot of mileage out of current variables and explanation of between-group mean variation. It is also worth noting that the standard errors in the earnings and growth equations computed from the exact asymptotic distribution reported in the table are virtually identical with those estimated by OLS.

TABLE 2

College Selection Rules: Probit Analysis

Variable	Reduced Form (16)		Structure (26)		Structure (29)	
	Coefficient	t	Coefficient	t	Coefficient	t
Constant	.0485	.20	.1512	.22	.1030	.17
Background:						
Father's ED	-.0145	-.41	-.0168	-.54	-.0152	-.49
Father's ED²	.0037	2.05	.0038	2.26	.0037	2.26
DK ED	-.4059	-3.96	-.3924	-2.79	-.4001	-2.91
Manager	.1897	2.17	.1825	2.13	.1871	2.21
Clerk	.0556	.54	.0561	.59	.0554	.59
Foreman	.0182	.19	.0210	.23	.0200	.22
Unskilled	-.0910	-.85	-.0948	-.89	-.0928	-.87
Farmer	-.2039	-2.12	-.2256	-2.27	-.2094	-2.14
DK job	-.0413	-.19	-.0629	-.29	-.0609	-.28
Catholic	-.1144	-1.91	-.0982	-1.51	-.1083	-1.66
Jew	-.0293	-.23	.0143	.12	-.0158	-.14
Old sibs	-.0162	-.93	-.0162	-.93	-.0161	-.93
Young sibs	.0122	.63	.0096	.49	.0112	.57
Mother works:						
Full 5	.1039	.66	.1168	.81	.1104	.76
Part 5	.2179	1.42	.2106	1.52	.2156	1.56

	coeff.	t	coeff.	t	coeff.	t
None 5	.0655	.63	.0677	.65	.0661	.64
Full 14	.2898	2.29	.2884	2.30	.2888	2.33
Part 14	.2709	2.20	.2768	2.02	.2693	2.03
None 14	.1980	1.91	.1990	1.92	.1966	1.92
H.S. shop	-.4411	-6.14	-.4397	-3.74	-.4379	-3.90
Ability:						
Read	.0047	1.67	...	...	...	...
NR read	-.2575	-1.41	...	...	...	...
Mech	-.0070	-4.29	...	...	...	...
NR mech	-3.0236	-1.04	...	...	...	...
Math	.0244	12.34	...	...	...	...
NR math	-.7539	-5.75	...	...	...	...
Dext	.0019	.72	...	...	...	...
NR dext	2.2797	.47	...	...	...	...
Earnings:						
ln $(\bar{y}_a/\bar{y}_b)$	...	...	5.1486	2.25	...	...
g_a	...	...	138.3850	1.83	7.6632	.11
g_b	...	...	-44.2697	-1.28	71.8981	2.34
ln $y_a(t)/y_b(t)$	...	...	...	...	5.1501	2.57
Observations	3611		3611		3611	
Limit observations	791		791		791	
Nonlimit observations	2820		2820		2820	
-2 ln (likelihood ratio)	579.5		568.8		576.6	
χ^2 degree freedom	28		23		23	

NOTE.—t is asymptotic t-statistic: DK: Don't know, dummy variable; NR: No response, dummy variable; other variables are defined in Appendix A.

TABLE 3

Structural Earnings Estimates: Equations (24) and (28), OLS

			Dependent Variable			
Regressor	$\ln \bar{y}_a$ (1)	$\ln \bar{y}_b$ (2)	g_a (3)	g_b (4)	$\ln y_a(\bar{t})$ (5)	$\ln y_b(\bar{t})$ (6)
Constant	8.7124	2.8901	.1261	.2517	10.3370	7.5328
	(16.51)	(1.37)	(3.90)	(2.11)	(5.52)	(2.08)
Read	.0009	−.0019	.0001	.0003	.0027	.0057
	(1.21)	(−1.17)	(1.11)	(3.20)	(2.80)	(3.28)
NR read	.0791	.0506	−.0034	−.0046	.0033	−.0402
	(1.24)	(.58)	(−.76)	(−.89)	(.04)	(−.42)
Mech	−.0002	−.0005	−.0001	−.0001	−.0021	−.0017
	(−.48)	(−.54)	(−2.16)	(−1.13)	(−3.59)	(−1.73)
NR mech	...	.1969	...	.0002	...	.2196
		(.69)		(.01)		(.68)
Math	.0015	−.0013	.0001	−.0000	.0030	−.0019
	(2.02)	(.74)	(1.18)	(−.20)	(3.31)	(−1.00)
NR math	−.1087	.0562	.0015	.0006	−.0877	.0712
	(−1.94)	(.83)	(.38)	(.15)	(−1.24)	(.96)
Dext	.0008	−.0019	−.0000	.0003	.0002	.0036
	(1.03)	(−1.21)	(−.78)	(2.77)	(.16)	(2.19)
NR dext	.0751	...	−.0004	...	.1466	...
	(.28)		(−.02)		(.43)	
Exp	−.0523	.4260	−.0028	−.0154	−.0129	.0776
	(−1.49)	(3.10)	(−1.11)	(−1.93)	(−.29)	(.53)
Exp²	.0015	−.0067	.0000	.0002	−.0000	−.0012
	(2.22)	(−2.95)	(.21)	(1.82)	(−.01)	(−.49)
Year 48	−.0020	−.0156	...	...	...	...
	(−.48)	(−1.72)				
Year 69	...	...	...	...	−.0067	.0039
					(−.26)	(.09)
S13–15	.1288	...	−.0062	...	.0168	...
	(5.15)		(−3.49)		(.52)	
S16	.0760	...	.0026	...	.1095	...
	(3.82)		(1.79)		(4.26)	
S20	.1318	...	.0049	...	.2560	...
	(4.10)		(2.13)		(6.15)	
λ_a	−.1069	...	.0058	...	.0206	...
	(−3.21)		(2.45)		(.49)	
λ_b	...	−.0558	...	.0118	...	.2267
		(−.66)		(2.39)		(2.48)
R^2	.0750	.0439	.1578	.0513	.0740	.0358

Note.—NR: No response, dummy variable; other variables are defined in Appendix A; t-values are shown in parentheses.

initial earnings is math score for college attendees. Ability indicators are more important for earnings growth (cols. 3 and 4) and later earnings (cols. 4 and 5). Dexterity and reading scores have positive effects on g_b and $y_b(\bar{t})$, while math and reading scores have positive effects on $\ln y_a(\bar{t})$ but exhibit much weaker effects on earnings growth. Interestingly enough, the effect on mechanical score is negative in all cases, raising obvious questions about what it is that this test supposedly measures (recall, however, the sample truncation on high-ability military personnel). Even so, it seems to have a more important negative effect for members of group A. This, along with the results for dexterity and math scores, lends support to the comparative-advantage hypothesis.

Selectivity biases are particularly interesting in that regard. The coefficients of λ_b show no selectivity bias for initial earnings of high school graduates, but positive bias for growth rates. Therefore, observed earnings patterns of high school graduates show higher rates of growth compared with the pattern that would have been observed for the average member of this sample had he chosen not to continue school. On the other hand, the coefficients of λ_a show positive selection bias for initial earnings of college attendees and negative bias for earnings growth. The latter is due to the fact that there are no selection effects for late earnings. Thus, the observed earnings pattern among members of group A is everywhere higher than the population mean pattern would have been and converges toward the population mean late earnings level. *Positive selection among both A and B also lends support to comparative advantage.*

The most novel empirical results are the structural probit estimates in table 2, which show how anticipated earnings gains affect the decision to attend college. The predicted earnings variables are statistically significant except for g_b in (26) and g_a in (29).[20] More striking, however, is the agreement of the sign patterns predicted by the theory (see eq. [10] and recall that the structural probit coefficients are normalized by σ_ϵ, from [26] and [29]). The model passes two internal consistency checks. The first is restriction (30). Working backward to normalized α estimates from directly estimated θ's in column 5 of table 2 yields[21] a predicted (α/σ_ϵ) vector of (5.15, 155.90, −52.68), which is similar to the direct estimates in column 3 of (5.15, 138.39,

---

[20] Recall (n. 14) that the t-statistics for the structural probit in table 2 are based on consistent estimates of the standard errors, as suggested by Lee (1977). The t-statistics on background variables are not very different from the biased values computed by a standard probit algorithm. However, the t-statistics on the predicted earnings and growth variables are substantially reduced when corrected for bias; e.g., the standard probit estimates of t-values for ln $(\bar{y}_a/\bar{y}_b)$, g_a, and g_b in (26) are (10.8, 8.15, −4.81), compared with the unbiased values of (2.25, 1.83, −1.28) in table 2.

[21] There are two ways of estimating $\bar{t}$ and $(\bar{t} − S)$ for these computations. First, a direct estimate of $\bar{t} − S$ is obtained as the difference between average year of 1969 job and average year of initial job for members of group A in table 1. A direct estimate of $\bar{t}$ is the average difference between 1969 job and initial job for members of group B. However, an independent estimate of S is the average years of schooling among members of group A minus 12.0. Hence another estimate of $(\bar{t} − S)$ is the direct estimate of $(\bar{t} − S)$ minus the direct estimate of S; and another estimate of $(\bar{t} − S)$ is the direct estimate of $\bar{t}$ minus the direct estimate of S. The two estimates for each parameter were averaged for purposes of these checks. They are 24.19 for $\bar{t}$ and 19.68 for $(\bar{t} − S)$.

-44.27). Working forward from actual estimates of normalized α to predicted estimates of θ gives prediction (5.15, 37.04, 80.31), compared with actual (5.15, 7.66, 71.90). These comparisons probably would not be so close if the two-parameter approximation to earnings patterns in (5) and (6) was not reasonably good. Second, equations (15) and (26) indicate that estimated coefficients on the Z variables in structural and reduced-form probits should be the same. Direct comparison of coefficients of Z in table 2 shows extremely close similarity of $\alpha_4\delta$ in all three equations. In sum, the results give direct, internally consistent evidence on the validity of the economic theory of the demand for schooling derived from its (private) investment value. The economic hypothesis cannot be rejected.

V. Conclusions

The structural probit estimates of table 2 support the economic hypothesis that expected gains in life earnings influence the decision to attend college. They also show important effects of financial constraints and tastes working through family-background indicators, a finding in common with most other studies of school choice.[22] Availability of the GI Bill might well be expected to dull the observed monetary effects, but they remain strong enough to persist for a significant fraction of the sample.

The estimates also show positive sorting or positive selection bias in observed earnings of both high school graduates and college attendees. To be clear about the implications of these results it is necessary to distinguish between the effects of measured abilities and unmeasured components on earnings prospects in A or B. The selection results refer to unmeasured components of variance. If we examine a subpopulation of persons with given measured abilities (i.e., with the same values of X in [12] and [13]), the empirical results on selectivity imply that those persons who stopped schooling after high school had better prospects as high school graduates than the average member of that subpopulation and that those who continued on to college also had better prospects there than the average member of the subpopulation. That is, the average earnings at most points in the life cycle of persons with given measured characteristics who actually chose B exceeded what earnings would have been for those persons (with the same characteristics) who chose A instead. Conversely, average earn-

---

[22] See Radner and Miller (1970) and Kohn, Manski, and Mundel (1976) for logit models of college choice. These models contain more detail in personal and college attributes but do not make any attempt to assess the effects of anticipated earnings in college attendance decisions. See Abowd (1977) for another approach to the selection problem focusing on school quality.

ings for those who actually chose A were greater than what earnings would have been for measurably similar people who actually chose B had they continued their schooling instead. This is a much different picture than emerges from the usual discussions of ability bias in the literature, based on hierarchical or one-factor ability considerations. The one-factor model implies that persons who would do better than average in A would also do better than average in B. That is, positive selectivity bias in B cannot occur in the strict hierarchical model.[23]

The most attractive and simplest interpretation is the theory of comparative advantage, because hierarchical assignments are not observed. While the results are consistent with comparative advantage, they do not prove the case because life-persistent luck and random extraneous opportunities could have played just as important roles in the observed assignments as differential talents did. For all we know, those who decided to stop school after high school may have married the boss's daughter instead, or made better career connections in the military, and so forth. The important point is that their prospects in B were higher than average.

As noted above, the population average rate of discount, $\bar{r}$, is an identifiable statistic in the model. Estimates are obtained by applying restriction (10) to the estimates in table 2. Maintain the hypothesis that $\alpha_1 = 1$. Then the estimated coefficient of $\ln(\bar{y}_a/\bar{y}_b)$ in table 2 estimates $(1/\sigma_\epsilon)$, from equation (26). Since all the equations of the structural probit are normed by σ_ϵ this estimate provides a basis for estimating the population parameters in (10).

Straightforward computations using the structural probit estimates (26) in table 2 yield

$$(\bar{r} - \bar{g}_a) = .0372,$$
$$(\bar{r} - \bar{g}_b) = .1163.$$
(32)

Estimates of $\bar{g}_a$ and $\bar{g}_b$ are necessary to impute values of $\bar{r}$, and a slight ambiguity arises because the growth rates are functions of measured characteristics (see [12] and [13]). For illustrative purposes we use the overall sample mean values of characteristics (the X's) to impute $\bar{g}_a$ and $\bar{g}_b$ from the structural earnings estimates in table 3, purged of selectivity bias. The average person in the sample would have ob-

---

[23] It should be emphasized that the special nature of this sample makes it impossible to extrapolate this result to the entire population. The reason is that the selection criteria for sample eligibility were established by entrance requirements into the army and our sample is a subset of those who volunteered for the air corps. It is possible to conceive of systematic truncation and selection rules by the military that would support the comparative-advantage argument in this subset, even though roughly hierarchical talents and positive correlations among alternative income prospects might well characterize the population at large.

tained growth rates $\bar{g}_a$ = .0591 and $\bar{g}_b$ = .0262 in A and B, respectively. The population mean discount rate, $\bar{r}$, is overidentified. The first equation of (32) yields an estimate of $\bar{r}$ = .0963, while the second gives $\bar{r}$ = .1425. Two more estimates of $\bar{r}$ are implied by the structural probit that uses the late earnings difference rather than the initial earnings differences. These are $\bar{r}$ = .0981 and $\bar{r}$ = .1240. Even if the precise derivation and specification of the model in Section III strain the reader's credulity, it is nonetheless clear that the structural specification is consistent with more casual derivations, and the estimated sign patterns in the structural probit, if not the precise restrictions among coefficients, would be predicted by virtually any economic model.

The positivity of earnings selection effects in both groups also implies that selection bias in simple rate of return estimates could go in either direction. The following procedure gives a rough and ready indication in this sample. First the two-parameterization of earnings in (5) and (6) implies that the average internal rate of return, i, is estimated by $\ln(y_a/y_b) + \ln(i - g_b) - \ln(i - g_a) - iS = 0$, where i is the rate of discount that equates average present values. Using sample mean values of $\bar{y}_a, \bar{y}_b, g_a$, and g_b in table 1 and a schooling increment of 4.11 years yields a simple unadjusted rate of return of i = 9.0 percent. This is comparable to the statistic usually presented in rate of return studies that make no allowance for differential ability between high school and college graduates. Several adjustments must be made to this number, however. First, correcting for selectivity alone yields an adjusted mean rate of return of i = 9.8 percent, which is actually larger, not smaller, than the observed mean rate of return. The 9.8 percent figure is obtained by subtracting the selectivity bias corrections from the observed sample means of $\bar{y}_a, \bar{y}_b, g_a$, and g_b and in principle could be larger or smaller than the unadjusted figure due to positive selection in both A and B. It does not make any allowance for differential measured ability effects between the two groups. A more meaningful computation in the context of the model is to use measured abilities and the parameters of the corrected earnings and growth-rate functions to answer the following question: What is the expected rate of return to college of the typical person who chose A as compared to the expected rate of return of the typical person who chose B? This is a "standardized" comparison: the rates of return differ between the typical A person and the typical B person because their measured abilities differ and because the values of these abilities (the regression coefficients in table 3) differ in A or B. Assuming that persons with the average characteristics of those who chose B would have exhibited the same values of experience and initial year of earnings as those who actually chose A and vice versa, the average rate of return for persons of type A is 9.9 percent, while the average is 9.3

percent for persons of type B. Thus, those who actually chose A had measured abilities that were more valuable in A than did those who actually chose B.

Predictions

The model passes the test of empirical verification of its structural restrictions. How well does it do in predicting assignments on independent data? The sample used is not a random drawing of the U.S. population and for this reason cannot be extrapolated to the population at large. However, only a subset of the NBER-Thorndike-Hagen sample was used to estimate it, and the remaining remnant is more likely to be a suitable group for prediction purposes. The remnant refers to those who did not report initial earnings. For this reason it may not be a random sample of the relevant population either. And while there is no reason to suppose that the censoring of initial earnings was systematically related to the selection mechanism of the model, it should be noted that a somewhat smaller proportion of these individuals (66 percent of them) chose to attend college than in the sample used for structural estimation.

One indirect test of the model's predictive content has been calculated. First, the reduced-form probit was reestimated for the remnant, which does not involve extrapolations, since the sample selection between A and B and the content of $W = [X, Z]$ is known for these people. Results appear in Appendix B. While there is some conformity with table 2, there are also many differences between reduced-form estimates in the two samples. In short, family-background coefficients are not too stable.

The second experiment involves an extrapolation. Both initial earnings differences and growth rates were predicted for members of the remnant sample from the structural earnings estimates of table 3 and then used to reestimate the structural probit of this group (no t-statistics are reported for structural probit coefficients because of the large expense of doing so). The results also appear in Appendix B. The sign reversals on family-background indicators carry over to these estimates too, though the coefficients and signs of the Z variables in the structural estimates are very close to those found in the reduced-form estimates in Appendix B. However, the coefficients on the earnings differences and growth rates for the remnant sample are very close to those estimated for the original sample of table 2.

Enrollment Functions

Perhaps the simplest and most useful summary of the results is obtained from the demand function for college attendance implicit in the structural probit estimates. Recalling the definition of the index function in (9), the probability of attending college is given by Pr (A is chosen) = $F(I/\sigma_\epsilon)$, where F is the standard normal c.d.f. Let m denote the size of the relevant population, and let N represent the number choosing to attend college. Then the number enrolled in college is given by

$$N = mF(I/\sigma_\epsilon). \qquad (33)$$

This would be equivalent to a supply function of graduates were it not for the aggregation involved in group A. The supply of graduates is somewhat different since we do not know how long people outside the sample would stay in school. The normality assumptions imply that the enrollment function (33) follows the cumulative normal curve. It therefore has zero elasticity at its extremes and positive elasticities in between. The major point of interest here is responsiveness of enrollments to earnings opportunities near the sample mean. From the definitions of present value in Section III, note that dln (V_a/V_b)/dln $(\bar{y}_a/\bar{y}_b) = 1$. A 1 percent change in relative initial earnings changes relative capital values by 1 percent. To clarify a possible point of confusion on this conceptual experiment, dln $(\bar{y}_a/\bar{y}_b)$ represents a permanent—not a transitory—change in lifetime prospects, because it increases relative differences between potential earnings in A compared with B not only initially but forevermore (see [5] and [6]). Differentiating (33) yields an elasticity formula

$$\text{dln } N/\text{dln } (\bar{y}_a/\bar{y}_b) = [F'(I/\sigma_\epsilon)(\alpha_1/\sigma_\epsilon)]/F(I/\sigma_\epsilon),$$

where I/σ_ϵ is evaluated at the desired sample proportion. For example, the elasticity evaluated at a sample proportion of .5 (half in A and half in B) is 4.1. On the other hand, the initial earnings elasticity at the observed sample proportion is 1.94, still a substantial response given the presence of marked diversity in the population. By way of comparison, an increment of father's education of 1.59 years (the difference in means of father's schooling between groups in table 1) elicits a relative response of .0337.

Appendix A
Definitions of Variables for Tables

Father's ED	Father's years of school. Nonresponse assigned mean.
Father's ED²	Square of Father's ED.
DK ED	Dummy variable: 1 if respondent did not know father's education.
Manager	Dummy variable: 1 if father was a businessman, manager, or professional.
Clerk	Dummy variable: 1 if father had white-collar occupation other than those in management.
Foreman	Dummy variable: 1 if father was a foreman, supervisor, or skilled craftsman.

Unskilled	Dummy variable: 1 if father was semiskilled operative or unskilled laborer.
Farmer	Dummy variable: 1 if father was a farmer.
DK job	Dummy variable: 1 if respondent did not know father's occupation.
Catholic	Dummy variable: 1 if respondent is Catholic.
Jew	Dummy variable: 1 if respondent is Jewish.
Old sibs	Number of older siblings.
Young sibs	Number of younger siblings.
Mother works:	
Full 5	Dummy variable: 1 if mother worked full time when respondent was less than 6 years of age.
Part 5	Dummy variable: 1 if mother worked part time when respondent was less than 6 years of age.
None 5	Dummy variable: 1 if mother did not work when respondent was less than 6 years of age.
Full 14	Dummy variable: 1 if mother worked full time when respondent was 6–14 years of age.
Part 14	Dummy variable: 1 if mother worked part time when respondent was 6–14 years of age.
None 14	Dummy variable: 1 if mother did not work when respondent was 6–14 years of age.
H.S. shop	Dummy variable: 1 if respondent majored in vocational courses in high school.
Read	Raw score on college undergraduate level reading comprehension test. Continuous variable, nonrespondents assigned mean.
NR read	Dummy variable: 1 if reading score not reported.
Mech	Raw score on pictorial representation of mechanical problem test. Continuous variable, nonrespondents assigned mean.
NR mech	Dummy variable: 1 if mechanical score not reported.
Math	Raw score on mathematics test (performance in advanced arithmetic, algebra, and trigonometry). Continuous variable with nonrespondents assigned mean.
NR math	Dummy variable: 1 if math score unreported.
Dext	Score on test of finger dexterity. Continuous variable, nonrespondents assigned mean.
NR dext	Dummy variable: 1 if dexterity score not reported.
Exp	Continuous variable: Age − Schooling − 6.
Exp^2	Square of Exp.
S13–15	Dummy variable: 1 if respondent received 13–15 years of school.
S16	Dummy variable: 1 if respondent received 16 years of school.
S20	Dummy variable: 1 if respondent received 20 or more years of school.
Year 48	Year in which initial postwar earnings are reported. Continuous variable.
Year 69	Year in which earnings at time of NBER survey are reported. Continuous variable.
$\ln \bar{y}$	Log of earnings on first job after finishing school, in 1967 prices.
$\ln y(t)$	Log of earnings at time of NBER survey in 1967 prices.
g	(ln earn 69 − ln earn 48) ÷ (Year 69 − Year 48) percentage rate of growth between the two observations.
λ_a	See equation (17), based on estimates in table 2, column 1.
λ_b	See equation (22), based on estimates in table 2, column 1.

Appendix B

COLLEGE SELECTION RULES: PROBIT ANALYSIS
(Independent Subsample of Individuals with
No Report on Initial Earnings)

VARIABLE	REDUCED FORM (16) Coefficient	t	STRUCTURE (26) Coefficient	STRUCTURE (29) Coefficient
Constant	−.4424	−.936	−.1170	−.1514
Background:				
Father's ED	−.0183	.27	.0131	.0123
Father's ED^2	.0020	.61	.0023	.0023
DK ED	−.2645	−1.69	−.2548	−.2608
Manager	.2009	1.50	.1689	.1768
Clerk	.1664	.92	.1523	.1490
Foreman	−.1276	−.83	−.1359	−.1369
Unskilled	−.3118	−1.79	−.3298	.3260
Farmer	.1353	.75	.1174	−.1332
DK job	−.3515	−1.04	−.3133	−.3426
Catholic	−.0887	−.80	−.0847	−.1024
Jew	−.2169	−.95	−.1879	−.2159
Old sibs	.0335	1.02	.0343	.0336
Young sibs	.0191	.56	.0170	.0176
Mother works:				
Full 5	−.6039	−2.06	−.6080	−.6080
Part 5	−.0470	−.18	−.0409	−.0351
None 5	−.0200	−.11	−.0345	−.0248
Full 14	.1656	.67	.1747	.1764
Part 14	−.1248	−.58	−.1258	−.1310
None 14	−.0581	−.31	−.0360	.0448
H.S. shop	−.5387	−3.95	−.5436	−.5395
Ability:				
Read	.0056	1.07	. . .	. . .
NR read	.2393	.74	. . .	. . .
Mech	−.0480	−1.64	. . .	. . .
NR mech	. . .	. . .	. . .	. . .
Math	.0251	6.80	. . .	. . .
NR math	−.4775	−2.15	. . .	. . .
Dext	.0050	1.08	. . .	. . .
NR dext	. . .	. . .	. . .	. . .
Earnings:				
ln $(\bar{y}_a/\bar{y}_b)$	. . .	. . .	4.9674	. . .
g_a	. . .	. . .	122.1460	−1.8761
g_b	. . .	. . .	−34.8393	76.4555
ln $[y_a(t)/y_b(t)]$	. . .	. . .	. . .	4.8837
Observations	952		952	952
Limit observations	321		321	321
Nonlimit observations	631		631	631
−2 ln (likelihood ratio)	184.446		179.419	184.446
χ^2 degree freedom	. . .		. . .	. . .

NOTE.—t is asymptotic t-statistic; DK: Don't know, dummy variable; NR: No response, dummy variable; other variables are defined in Appendix A.

References

Abowd, John M. "An Econometric Model of the U.S. Market for Higher Education." Ph.D. dissertation, Univ. Chicago, 1977.

Becker, Gary S. *Human Capital*. 2d ed. New York: Nat. Bur. Econ. Res., 1975.

Blaug, Mark. "The Empirical Status of Human Capital Theory: A Slightly Jaundiced Survey." *J. Econ. Literature* 14 (September 1976): 827–55.

Freeman, Richard. *The Market for College Trained Manpower: A Study in the Economics of Career Choice*. Cambridge, Mass.: Harvard Univ. Press, 1971.

Friedman, Milton, and Kuznets, Simon. *Income from Independent Professional Practice*. New York: Nat. Bur. Econ. Res., 1945.

Griliches, Zvi. "Estimating the Returns to Schooling: Some Econometric Problems." *Econometrica* 45 (January 1977): 1–22.

Griliches, Zvi; Hall, B.; and Hausman, Jerry. "Missing Data and Self-Selection in Large Panels." Discussion Paper no. 573, Harvard Inst. Econ. Res., 1977.

Hanoch, Giora. "An Economic Analysis of Earnings and Schooling." *J. Human Resources* 2, no. 3 (1967): 310–29.

Hause, J. "The Fine Structure of Earnings and the On-the-Job-Training Hypothesis." Mimeographed. Univ. Minnesota, 1977.

Hausman, Jerry, and Wise, D. "A Conditional Probit Model for Qualitative Choice." *Econometrica* 46 (March 1978): 403–26.

Heckman, James J. "The Common Structure of Statistical Models of Truncation, Sample Selection and Limited Dependent Variables and a Simple Estimator for Such Models." *Ann. Econ. and Soc. Measurement* 5 (Fall 1976): 475–92.

———. "Sample Selection Bias as a Specification Error." In *Female Labor Supply: Theory and Estimation*, edited by J. P. Smith. Princeton, N.J.: Princeton Univ. Press, 1979.

Kenny, L.; Lee, L.; Maddala, G. S.; and Trost, R. "Returns to College Education: An Investigation of Self-Selection Bias in Project Talent Data." *Internat. Econ. Rev.* (in press).

Kohn, M. G.; Manski, C. F.; and Mundel, D. S. "An Empirical Investigation of Factors Which Influence College-going Behavior." *Ann. Econ. and Soc. Measurement* 5 (Fall 1976): 391–420.

Lazear, Edward. "Age, Experience and Wage Growth." *A.E.R.* 66 (September 1976): 548–58.

Lee, Lung Fei. "Estimation of Limited Dependent Variables Models by Two-Stage Methods." Ph.D. dissertation, Univ. Rochester, 1976.

———. "On the Asymptotic Distributions of Some Two-Stage Consistent Estimators: Unionism and Wage Rates Revisited." Mimeographed. Univ. Minnesota, 1977.

———. "Unionism and Wage Rates: A Simultaneous Equations Model with Qualitative and Limited Dependent Variables." *Internat. Econ. Rev.* 19 (June 1978): 415–33.

Lillard, L., and Willis, Robert. "Dynamic Aspects of Earnings Mobility." *Econometrica* 46, no. 5 (1978): 985–1012.

McFadden, D. "Conditional Logit Analysis of Qualitative Choice Behavior." In *Frontiers in Econometrics*, edited by P. Zarembka. New York: Academic Press, 1973.

Maddala, G. S. "Self-Selectivity Problems in Econometric Models." In *Applications in Statistics*, edited by P. R. Krishnaia. Amsterdam: North-Holland, 1977.

Mandelbrot, Benoit. "Paretian Distributions and Income Maximization." *Q.J.E.* 76 (February 1960): 57–85.

Mincer, Jacob. *Schooling, Experience and Earnings.* New York: Nat. Bur. Econ. Res., 1974.

National Bureau of Economic Research. "The Comprehensive NBER-TH Tape Documentation." Mimeographed. March 1973.

Radner, Roy, and Miller, L. S. "Demand and Supply in U.S. Higher Education." *A.E.R.* 60 (May 1970): 326–34.

Rosen, Sherwin. "Human Capital: Relations between Education and Earnings." In *Frontiers of Quantitative Economics,* edited by Michael D. Intriligator. Vol. *3B.* Amsterdam: North-Holland, 1977.

———. "Substitution and Division of Labor." *Economica* 45 (August 1978): 235–50.

Roy, Andrew D. "Some Thoughts on the Distribution of Earnings." *Oxford Econ. Papers,* n.s. 3 (June 1951): 135–46.

Taubman, Paul. *Sources of Inequality of Earnings.* Amsterdam: North-Holland, 1975.

Weiss, Yoram, and Lillard, Lee A. "Experience, Vintage, and Time Effects in the Growth of Earnings: American Scientists, 1960–1970." *J.P. E.* 86, no. 3 (June 1978): 427–47.

Wise, D. "Academic Achievement and Job Performance." *A.E.R.* 65 (June 1975): 350–66.

Zabalza, A. "The Determinants of Teacher Supply." Mimeographed. London School Econ., 1977.

V

HOUSING PROGRAMS: DESIGNED EXPERIMENTS

In the 1970s, major resources were devoted to the experimental study of the economics of housing supply and demand, culminating with the research undertaken in the Experimental Housing Allowance Program (EHAP). This Housing and Urban Development (HUD)-funded program included the Housing Allowance Demand Experiment (HADE), the Housing Allowance Supply Experiment, and the Administrative Agency Experiment. The first two chapters in this section report the analysis of HADE data on housing demand, while the final two chapters report the results of complementary work with data from the Seattle/ Denver and Gary Income Maintenance Experiments. As a result, our uncertainty regarding the price and income elasticities of housing demand has been considerably reduced. (For further reviews of these results see Friedman and Weinberg, forthcoming; Mayo, forthcoming; and Mulford, 1979.)

The HADE experiment involved random assignment to a control group as well as to several different experimental groups. One of these groups was a "Percentage of Rent" group who received a percentage rebate on their rent with no housing requirements to meet. Using "Percentage of Rent" and control households, Friedman and Weinberg (1980) examined two housing expenditure functions—a log linear and a linear form (derived from a Stone-Geary utility function). They estimate the price elasticity of housing demand for low-income renters to be −.22 (a 10% price drop results in a 2.2% increase in quantity demanded) and the permanent income elasticity to be .36 (a 10% increase in income results in a 3.6% increase in housing purchase). The authors emphasize, though, that it is unnecessary and possibly misleading to consider these elasticities as constant over the range of housing prices and income. Both elasticities are likely to increase (in absolute value) as income increases.

In Part V, Hausman and Wise take a different approach. It deals with the possibility that the housing allowance produces a discontinuity in the budget constraint faced by the experimental sample. They postulate a Cobb-Douglas utility function with the share of income going to rent expressed as a function of household characteristics (including income). Within this framework, Hausman and Wise study the behavior of several experimental groups in HADE: (1) households that were offered an income-based housing allowance conditional on meeting a "minimum rent" requirement; (2) households that were offered an unconstrained housing allowance payment; and (3) households that were offered "percentage of rent" housing allowances. Their estimates of housing demand elasticities, −0.16 for price elasticity and 0.6 for income elasticity, are close to those found by Friedman and Weinberg (1980).

Friedman and Weinberg's study in this volume is directly concerned with the estimation of HADE program effects. In addition to investigating the response of the minimum rent and unconstrained groups, they also examine the housing demand response of "minimum standards" households—households receiving an allowance payment only if their dwelling units meet certain standards. (See the appendix to Friedman and Weinberg in this volume.) Since rent is not strictly correlated with these standards, the approach of Hausman and Wise could not be followed since the discontinuity points in the budget constraint are not clearly defined in the dependent variable—rent.

Accordingly, Friedman and Weinberg postulate a basically model-free approach based on their earlier work on housing demand to model the normal behavior of experimental households using the control group. To obtain an accurate estimate of program effect, they correct their estimates for selection bias that occurred because the recipient households were selected on the basis of their housing consumption—a variable endogenous to the experiment. (See Morris et al., in Part I for a discussion of the problems associated with such sample selection.) They found that the housing requirements were important for response to the program. That is, a household's initial housing requirement status had an overwhelming effect on the way that household responded to the housing allowance offer. Households that already met their housing requirements at enrollment, and so were automatically eligible for allowance payments, did not use their allowance to increase their housing expenditures or consumption. But households that met their requirements only after enrollment made large increases in their expenditures as a result of the program. Nevertheless, these increases in housing expenditure and consumption still accounted for only a portion of the allowance payment. Overall, the minimum standards and minimum rent requirements induced roughly the same increases in both expenditures and services as the unconstrained payments. Variations in program effects exist as a function of the two sites—Phoenix and Pittsburgh—which are not entirely accounted for in the analysis.

From a policy standpoint, there is at least one major problem with a housing allowance program. Even though a program can be designed to lead both to an improvement in the quality and quantity of housing and a reduction in the proportion of income spent on housing, such benefits are limited to those who participate. The plan fails if the needy do not participate. And, it appears likely, according to a study by Kennedy and McMillan (1979), that the programs with housing requirements tested in the demand experiment reached less than one-fourth of the eligible households with program-defined, substandard housing.

This raises the issue of alternative means to help the poor increase the quality and quantity of their housing—namely, via an unconstrained, income maintenance program that would reach all the poor through a mechanism such as the Internal Revenue system. The studies by Ohls and Kaluzny (Part V) test for the effects of an unconstrained, negative income tax program on the demand for housing. This alternative is of particular interest inasmuch as the negative income tax experiments (NIT) positively affect behavior other than labor supply, but most of the publicity for the NIT concerned the "negative" outcomes of reduced labor supply and increased marital dissolution. An appropriate assessment of such an NIT program thus depends on a comprehensive accounting of all effects—both "negative" and "positive" (see Weisbrod and Helming, Part VI). The use of the NIT income payments for such productive ends as housing, health, daycare, and education represent program benefits. The purchase of improved housing, apart from its immediate impact on improvement of the quality of life, also may have longer-run effects associated with better health and safety and other "neighborhood effects," to list the most obvious.

In this context, the work of Ohls on the Denver/Seattle Income Maintenance Experiment and that of Kaluzny on the Gary Income Maintenance Experiment are generally consistent with the HADE results on the unconstrained payment (see Friedman and Weinberg, Part V). In Gary, the estimated elasticity of rent (the sample was split into renters and homeowners) with respect to experimental payments was about .3—a 10% increase in income subsidy resulted in a 3% increase in rental purchase of housing. Comparable figures for Seattle and Denver were .42 and .32, respectively.

Finally, it is important to note that although an NIT program will likely reach the entire population of concern, these individuals will spend much less of their income subsidy on housing than they would under a constrained housing subsidy. For instance, the participants in the EHAP increased their net rental expenditures by 19%, which is to be compared with a 5% increase for the Gary Experiment. This highlights the dilemma inherent in the choice between in-kind subsidies and subsidies in cash. In-kind subsidies are generally preferred by (are utility increasing for) tax payers, but provide less utility to the recipient than an unconstrained income subsidy of the same cost. Society must balance these competing claims in choosing between these methods of delivering goods and services to the low-income population.

REFERENCES

FRIEDMAN, J. and D. H. WEINBERG (forthcoming) "The demand for rental housing: evidence from the Housing Allowance Demand Experiment." J. of Urban Economics.

KENNEDY, S. D. and J. McMILLAN (1979) Draft Report Participation Under Alternative Housing Allowance Programs: Evidence from the Housing Allowance Demand Experiment. Cambridge, MA: Abt Assoc.

MAYO, S. K. (forthcoming) "Theory and estimation in the economics of housing demand." J. of Urban Economics.

MULFORD, J. (1979) Income Elasticity of Housing Demand. Rand Report R-2449-HUD. Santa Monica, CA: Rand.

19

This study and that of Hausman and Wise (this section) are complementary. Both examine the effect of the Housing Allowance Demand Experiment (HADE). Hausman and Wise focus on the econometric method of measuring the impact of social programs that change the budget constraint facing individuals and households. They use the HADE data to develop a general approach to measuring the class of programs that cause kinks and discontinuities in the budget constraint. In this process, they measure the overall effect of the HADE program on the consumption of housing. Friedman and Weinberg are not unaware of this general approach, but their specific intent is to measure the effect of the different housing subsidy treatments of HADE. They discuss three of the four basic treatments: housing gap, unconstrained, and control. The formula used to determine housing subsidies was similar to those in the Negative Income Tax Experiments, except that the payment schedule was determined by housing costs (needs) rather than by more general consumption needs. The housing gap allowance was constrained because it was linked to recipients' housing. A subsidy was received only if a dwelling met the program's housing standards. There were 11 different Housing Gap allowance plans, testing three payment levels, three benefit reduction rates and two types of housing requirements—minimum standards and minimum rent. The unconstrained plan had no housing requirement and resembled a general income subsidy. The effects of such a plan operate similar to those reported by Ohls and Kaluzny (this section). A variant of the experiment's minimum standards requirement (see in the Appendix to this study) is currently in force in the Section 8 housing program operated by the Department of Housing and Urban Development. Hence, this analysis is particularly relevant from a policy standpoint.

The experimental effects are measured under the assumption that housing expenditures at two years after enrollment, R, can be separated into two effects—normal housing expenditures that would have existed in the absence of the program, R_N, and an experimentally induced effect, R_x. The experimental effect was estimated, using a log-linear specification, under the assumption that the ratio of actual to normal expenditures, R/R_N, was functionally related to the experimental treatment and a random error term. Thus:

$$\ln(R/R_N) = \ln(R) - \ln(R_N) = X\beta + \epsilon$$

where,

X = a vector of experimental variables,
β = a vector of experimental effects, and
ϵ = a random error term.

β is interpreted as the median percentage change in rent associated with a change in the relevant variable, X. The control group provided estimates of normal rent.

An interesting methodological aspect of this study is that the authors directly control for potential bias arising from selection on an endogenous variable. (See Morris et al., Part I). That is, households were selected for the experiment as a result of their preprogram housing consumption. Adjustment for the resulting bias led to lower treatment effects for both sites across all treatment variations.

Another issue concerns the short-term nature of the experiment (a common theme in most of the experiments reported in this volume) and the costs and period of time needed for the experimentally induced behavior to occur. This phenomenon may explain the differences in results that occurred between the Pittsburgh and Phoenix sites. Phoenix had a much higher mobility rate both before and during the experimental period and a vacancy rate about three times higher than Pittsburgh. This effect remained the major unresolved analytic issue in the study, since the differences between cities occurred for households that met their housing requirements after enrollment, a consequence that heavily influenced the overall result. One correction for this type of problem, which has obvious cost implications for managing such an experiment, is to set up the experiment in a variety of sites, not just one or two. Thus, the Youth Entitlement Study (Farkas et al., Part III), is operating in eight sites, four experimental and four control, while the EOPP demonstration (Bishop et al., Part VIII) is scheduled to operate in more than 20 demonstration and control sites. This design may improve the chance of controlling for site specific effects.

In terms of results and policy implications, the following findings are most significant: The housing requirements themselves were an important determinant of household response to the allowance program. Thus, the initial housing requirement status had an overwhelming effect on how households responded to the subsidy. First, households that had already met their housing requirements at enrollment, and hence were automatically eligible for the subsidy, did not make any substantial increase in housing consumption. Second, households that met their requirements *after* enrollment made large, experimentally induced increases in their housing expenditures. But these above-normal expenditures consumed only a portion of the housing allowance subsidy. Third, overall, the minimum standards and minimum rent low requirements induced about the same increases in housing consumption as the unconstrained payment. Overall, across the treatments of minimum standards, minimum rent low, minimum rent high, and unconstrained household, the proportion of allowance spent on housing expenditures ranged from 6- to 23% in Pittsburgh and from 19- to 41% in Phoenix, while, for housing services, the proportion of allowance used for housing services ranged from 0- to 7% in Pittsburgh and from 15- to 26% in Phoenix. These effects are generally larger than those reported by the studies of Ohls and Kaluzny. The subsidies in Ohls and Kaluzny were general income maintenance payments and not tied to one's housing consumption behavior in any way, unlike the HADE design.

Two policy problems remain to qualify an unequivocal endorsement of this type of program. First, specific housing requirements should be imposed only if the policy makers (or, rather, taxpayers) have very strong preferences about the requirements. This is due to the fact that the requirements distort the behavior of the subsidy recipients such that they apparently try to obtain housing that satisfies just those requirements while otherwise containing a normal level of housing quality for expenditure dollar. The well being (utility) of the tax payer or policy maker may be increased by such a program. On the other hand, the well being of recipients is potentially reduced relative to the increase in well being they could have achieved with an unconstrained income subsidy. Furthermore, the constrained housing subsidies resulted in a greater purchase of housing expenditures and services, but only by a few percentage points relative to the unconstrained housing subsidy for services in Phoenix, though by a 6 to 8 percentage point difference over the 19 percent effect in Phoenix. Also, there is the added social cost of monitoring the constrained program. In addition, unlike a universal income maintenance program that might operate through the tax system, the housing allowance program benefits only those low income households who choose to participate—apparently only by about 25% of the eligibles in the two HADE sites. Thus, the correct social choice between a general cash income transfer and a subsidy in kind, whether constrained or not, is not altogether clear. As Friedman and Weinberg note, the "best" housing program may not be one program at all. Rather, it may be a combination of programs, each taking a different approach, including supply oriented programs such as subsidized public housing.

Housing Consumption in an Experimental Housing Allowance Program
Issues of Self-Selection and Housing Requirements

Joseph Friedman and Daniel H. Weinberg

I. INTRODUCTION

The method of providing housing assistance to low-income families is currently the focus of national debate. The U.S. Congress is considering increasing the emphasis in federal housing policy toward use of existing housing as against new construction (e.g., Levine, 1978). Debate continues, as well, between advocates of an unrestricted cash transfer (such as those tested in the various Negative Income Tax (NIT) experiments) and those in favor of housing-based subsidies (e.g., Khadduri, Lyall and Struyk, 1978). The disagreement among economists and others concerned with housing policy was considered so acute that the Congress has spent over $200 million to test alternate housing assistance programs.

This paper examines evidence from the Housing Allowance Demand Experiment--an experimental housing assistance program that used the existing housing stock and provided income transfer payments in both constrained and unconstrained forms. For three years, the experiment offered monthly allowance payments to approximately 1,200 low-income households selected at random in two sites: Allegheny County, Pennsylvania (Pittsburgh) and Maricopa County, Arizona (Phoenix). Several different allowance plans were tested involving different payment formulas and housing requirements. In addition, a control group of approximately 500 households was enrolled at each site. The calendar period covered by the experiment was roughly late 1973 to early 1977. The evaluation is based on the first two years of household observation.

Financial support for this research was provided by the U.S. Department of Housing and Urban Development under Contract H-2040R to Abt Associates Inc. The authors wish to thank Stephen Kennedy, whose comments and suggestions were extremely valuable in formulating the analysis. The authors remain responsible for the results reported here.

From Joseph Friedman and Daniel H. Weinberg, "Housing Consumption in an Experimental Housing Allowance Program: Issues of Self-Selection and Housing Requirements." Unpublished manuscript, 1980.

This paper discusses three of the four basic treatment groups under which households were enrolled: Housing Gap, Unconstrained, and Control.[1] The "Housing Gap" was the difference between the cost of existing housing meeting certain standards (described below) and a fraction of income to be spent on housing. The formula used to determine payments was similar to those used in the NIT experiments:

$$(1) \qquad S = C - bY$$

where

S = the allowance payment,

C = the basic payment schedule, varied by household size and site,

b = the benefit reduction (household contribution) rate, and

Y = household income.

The main difference was that the basic payment schedule was determined by housing costs rather than more general household needs. The Housing Gap allowance payment was constrained because it was linked to recipients' housing--households received allowance payments only if their dwelling units met the program's housing standards. The Unconstrained plan offered households a payment based on the same formula (equation (1)), but without a housing requirement to be met, and thus it resembled a general income support program. Finally, the group of Control households received only a $10 monthly cooperation payment for providing the same information as Experimental households.

The experiment included 11 different Housing Gap allowance plans, testing three levels for the basic payment schedule, three values for the benefit reduction rate, and two types of housing requirements--Minimum Standards and Minimum Rent. The three basic payment schedules tested were proportional to C^*, the estimated cost of existing housing meeting the "Minimum Standards" for various household sizes in each metropolitan area. The value of the benefit reduction rate, b, varied around C.25 (corresponding to typical subsidy levels in conventional housing programs).

Households under the "Minimum Standards" requirements had to occupy units that met certain physical quality standards for the dwelling unit and had a minimum number of rooms per person in order to receive payments. (These standards are listed in Appendix A.) This type of requirement is currently used in the Section 8 housing program. Such physical requirements necessitate housing inspections, which are costly to implement and are inconvenient to both tenants and landlords. As a possible less costly alternative, a "Minimum Rent" requirement was tested. Minimum Rent plans required households to spend at least a certain minimum amount for housing in order to receive allowance payments. Two minimum rent levels were tested, $0.7C^*$ and $0.9C^*$. Minimum Standards plans, though, provide the focus for the analysis.

The paper is organized as follows: in Section II we present the methodology used to estimate the experimental effect on housing consumption, as measured both by rent changes and a hedonic index of housing services. Since participation in the program was conditioned on the level of recipients' housing consumption, the methodology used was designed to correct for possible selection bias. Section III then presents the analysis of experimental impact. Finally, in Section IV we present a summary and some concluding remarks.

II. METHODOLOGY USED TO ESTIMATE HOUSEHOLD RESPONSE

This paper examines two continuous measures of housing consumption: rent and housing services. In a competitive market with perfect information, rent and housing services are proportional to each other and no distinction need be made between the two measures (see Olsen, 1969). However, even if the average relationship between rent and housing services is proportional, this relationship might not hold for every housing unit in the market. Household behavior, such as long-term tenancy or shopping efficiency, may influence the price per unit of housing services paid by a household.[2] This section provides a simplified theoretical model for understanding the mechanisms of household response to a housing allowance offer and presents the methods used to estimate experimental effects on housing consumption.

The condition nature of the offer is likely to have a profound effect on household response. Household response to such payments can be analyzed using standard consumer theory. Assume that households normally consume the quantity of housing services (H) and nonhousing goods (Z) that maximizes household utility, $U(H,Z)$, subject to the budget constraint

(2) $Y = P_H H + P_Z Z$

where

Y = household income,

P_H = the price of housing (thus $P_H H$ = rent), and

P_Z = the price of nonhousing goods.

Assume the household initially chooses to consume housing of H_0 and non-housing goods of Z_0. Receipt of an unconstrained allowance payment (S) moves the budget line outward, inducing the household to consume more housing (H_1). However, a Housing Gap allowance is received only if the household's housing consumption is greater than some minimum (H_{min}). The response to the allowance offer depends on the relationship among H_{min}, H_0, and H_1. Three cases are illustrated in Figure 1. In Figure 1(a), initial consumption exceeds H_{min} and the household automatically receives the allowance payment. These households simply treat the payment as additional income. Because the income elasticity of demand is fairly low, not much response in terms of additional housing expenditure can be expected.[3]

Figure 1(b) illustrates a second case. This household would not normally meet the housing requirement (H_{min}). If it were to receive the allowance payment, however, the income-induced increase in housing would be sufficient for the household to meet the requirement. Such households, like those in Figure 1(a), are in effect unconstrained by the requirement and are free to treat the payment as additional income.

The final case is illustrated by Figure 1(c). Households whose housing consumption would be less than H_{min} even with the additional income represented by allowance payment are constrained to allocate more of the allowance payment to housing than they normally would. Because they are required to make a nonoptimal allocation, their benefits from the program are lower than their benefits under an unconstrained allowance offer. Nevertheless, as long as their utility with the allowance payment and the nonoptimal housing is larger than their utility without the allowance, they should choose to participate in the program. That is, the household should in theory participate as long as

$$(3) \qquad U(H_{min}, Y_0 + S - P_H H_{min}) \quad U(H_0, Y_C - P_H H_0).$$

For some households, however, the payment S will will not be large enough to compensate for their nonoptimal allocation. Such households should not in theory participate in the program. It seems plausible that the households

Figure 1

ALLOCATION OF THE ALLOWANCE PAYMENT TO HOUSING

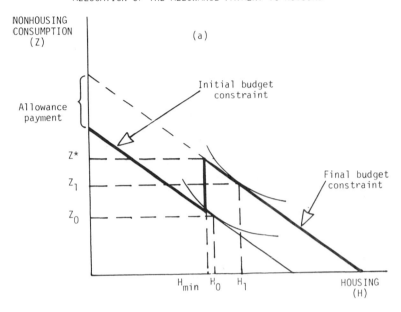

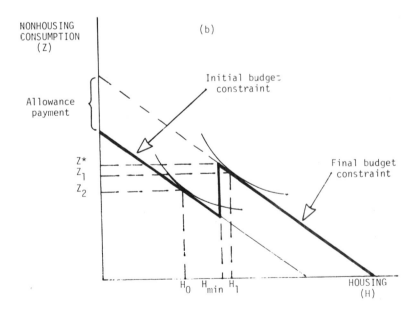

Figure 1 (continued)

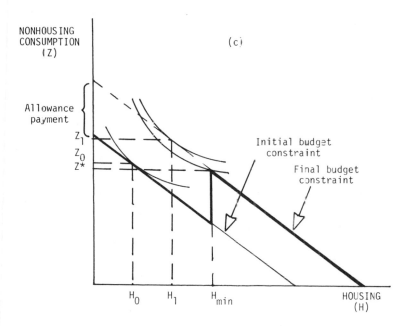

NOTE: The size of the allowance payment relative to income is exaggerated to improve clarity.

KEY: H_{min} = minimum housing requirement

H_0 = initial housing consumption

H_1 = hypothetical post-subsidy housing consumption

Z^* = consumption of nonhousing goods and services associated with consumption of H_{min}

Z_0 = initial consumption of nonhousing goods and services

Z_1 = hypothetical consumption of nonhousing goods and services associated with consumption of H_1

that do participate will have the largest increase in housing in response to the program when they fall into case (c) since such households must increase their expenditures by more than they would in response to the additional income from the allowance alone.

The average change in housing for the overall sample of Housing Gap households thus depends on the sizes of S and H_{min}, and on the proportions of participating households that fall into cases (a), (b), and (c). Two factors in particular complicate this model. First, H_{min} is not well defined for the Minimum Standards requirement. The Minimum Standards requirement merely requires certain dwelling unit features. While units that meet the Minimum Standards do on average rent for more than those which do not, it is possible for a household to meet the Minimum Standards after enrollment while reducing its housing expenditures. Second, the model posed above assumes that all households have the same tastes. For example, it is at least conceivable that the households induced to meet the requirements (case (c)) have lower income elasticities than the households that met normally, so that the response of households in case (c) could be lower than that of households in case (a).[4]

Consequently, a model-free approach is adopted. Experimental effects are measured under the assumption that the housing expenditures of housholds at two years after enrollment, R, can be separated into two parts-- the normal expenditures that would have been made in the absence of the experiment, R_N, and an additional amount that is induced by the experiment, R_X.[5] Thus,

(4) $R = R_N + R_X$

where

   R = actual expenditures two years after enrollment,

   R_N = normal expenditures two years after enrollment, and

   R_X = the experimental effect on expenditures.

Because log-linear functions proved useful in analyzing housing demand in numerous housing studies, the experimental effect was measured in terms of the ratio of actual to normal expenditures (R/R_N). Experimental effects were estimated under the assumption that this ratio was functionally related to experimental variables and a random error, specifically

(5) $\ln(R/R_N) = \ln(R) - \ln(R_N) = X_\cdot +$

where

       X = a vector of experimental variables,

       β = a vector of experimental effects, and

       ϵ = a random error term.

The vector of coefficients β may be interpreted as the median percentage change in rent associated with a change in the relevant variable, X (see, for example, Goldberger, 1968). Normal rent was estimated using Control households. The logarithm of rent at enrollment and at two years was regressed on household demographic descriptors (income, minority status, and household composition) and initial housing conditions using Seemingly Unrelated Regression (SUR). Serial correlation was then used to improve prediction. The asymptotically best linear unbiased predictor (Pindyck and Rubinfeld, 1976, pp. 170-173) of normal log rent at two years, r_N, is then

(6) $r_N = X_1 \gamma_1 - \hat{\rho} X_0 \gamma_0 + \hat{\rho} r_0$

where

      X = the vector of independent variables such as
         income,

      $\hat{\gamma}$ = the vector of estimated coefficients from the
         SUR procedure,

      $\hat{\rho}$ = the estimated serial correlation, and

      r_0 = the logarithm of initial rent.

Three statistics were used to evaluate predictive ability--the correlation between actual and predicted log rent, the percentage root mean square error, and the standard error of estimate. All three indicate good predictive power.[6]

    The overall experimental effect, r_X, is thus estimated as the mean of

(7) $\hat{r}_X = r - \hat{r}_N$

where

r = actual log rent at two years, and

$\hat{r}_N$ = estimated normal log rent at two years.

The analysis in this paper focuses on recipients of allowances, and households are recipients only if their housing requirement was met at two years after enrollment. This may introduce bias because the selection criterion is closely related to the dependent variables--rent. The estimated experimental effect, $\hat{r}_X$, is thus related to the true experimental effect, $\hat{r}_X$, as

(8) $\hat{r}_X = r_X + \delta$

where

δ = the expected value of the selection bias for recipients.

Estimation of the bias rests on the tautology that for the entire population (that is, when no subsample of households is selected), the expected value of the selection bias for the population, ε from equation (5), is zero. When the entire sample of enrolled households (for which $E(\varepsilon) = 0$) is divided into three groups, recipient households (R), households that remained in the sample but did not receive any payment because they did not meet their specified housing requirements ($\bar{R}$), and households that dropped out of the sample before the end of two years (D), the following relationship holds:

(9) $E(\varepsilon) = \dfrac{N_R}{N} E(\varepsilon | R) + \dfrac{N_{\bar{R}}}{N} E(\varepsilon | \bar{R}) + \dfrac{N_D}{N} E(\varepsilon | D) = 0,$

or

(10) $E(\varepsilon | R) = - \dfrac{N_{\bar{R}}}{N_R} E(\varepsilon | \bar{R}) - \dfrac{N_D}{N_R} E(\varepsilon | D)$

where

N = total number of enrolled households,

N_R = total number of recipient households,

$N_{\bar{R}}$ = total number of nonrecipient households,

N_D = total number of households that dropped out
of the sample, and

$E(\cdot|D)$ = the expected value of the residual for households that dropped out of the experiment.

Under the assumption that $E(\cdot|D) = 0$,[7] the bias δ ($\delta = E(\cdot|R)$) can be deter-
mined from

(11) $\qquad \delta = -\dfrac{N_R}{N_R} E(\cdot|\bar{R})$.

The method used to compute $E(\cdot|\bar{R})$ involves Control households whose units
did not meet the housing requirements at two years. These households pro-
vide a good estimate of $E(\cdot|R)$, because the experiment could not have
affected their behavior.[8]

III. THE EFFECT OF A HOUSING GAP HOUSING ALLOWANCE ON HOUSING CONSUMPTION

As discussed in Section II, the experimental effect is measured as
the percent change in housing expenditures or housing services above normal
at two years after enrollment. This section examines first the experimental
effect on expenditures and then the effect on housing services and shopping
behavior.

Section II indicated the possibility that the estimated experimental
effect for Housing Gap households may be biased. Only for Minimum Standards households was the estimated selection bias in expenditures statistically insignificant and close to zero. In contrast, and as could be
expected, the bias in the estimates for Minimum Rent households was large
and significantly different from zero. This is because a Minimum Rent
household's recipient status is directly related to the household's actual
rent outlay, while in the Minimum Standards plans, recipient status is only
indirectly related to rent. Selection on a dependent variable often leads
to bias.

Both the uncorrected and corrected estimates of the experimental effects on housing expenditures are presented in Table 1.[9] The effect for all
Minimum Standards recipient households is statistically significant only in
Phoenix, where the increase in expenditures was 14.7 percent above normal
(the effect in Pittsburgh was 3.8 percent). Separating these households
according to their enrollment unit's status with respect to the Minimum
Standards requirement indicates that while the allowance had little or no
effect on households living in units that already met the requirements at
enrollment, it did affect households whose units met the Minimum Standards
only after enrollment. For the group that met Minimum Standards after

TABLE 1

Median Percentage Increase in Housing
Expenditures Above Normal

HOUSEHOLD GROUP	PITTSBURGH MEDIAN PERCENTAGE CHANGE IN EXPENDITURES		SAMPLE SIZE	PHOENIX MEDIAN PERCENTAGE CHANGE IN EXPENDITURES		SAMPLE SIZE
	Uncorrected	Corrected		Uncorrected	Corrected	
Minimum Standards Recipients	4.3% (2.7)	3.8% (3.2)	84	16.2%** (3.9)	14.7** (4.2)	90
Did not meet requirements at enrollment	7.5* (3.9)	6.5 (4.9)	47	23.6** (5.4)	20.6** (5.8)	63
Met requirements at enrollment	1.1 (3.5)	-	37	-0.7 (3.8)	-	27
Minimum Rent Low Recipients	5.1* (2.6)	2.8 (2.5)	101	19.6** (4.5)	16.7** (4.4)	68
Did not meet requirements at enrollment	17.1** (5.3)	8.7+ (5.1)	27	51.5** (9.5)	42.0** (9.3)	26
Met requirements at enrollment	2.4 (2.9)	-	74	-1.2 (3.3)	-	42

TABLE 1 (continued)

HOUSEHOLD GROUP	PITTSBURGH				PHOENIX		
	MEDIAN PERCENTAGE CHANGE IN EXPENDITURES		SAMPLE SIZE		MEDIAN PERCENTAGE CHANGE IN EXPENDITURES		SAMPLE SIZE
	Uncorrected	Corrected			Uncorrected	Corrected	
Minimum Rent High Recipients	14.9** (3.4)	8.5* (3.6)	57		35.4** (6.0)	28.4** (6.3)	45
Did not meet requirements at enrollment	31.3** (6.1)	15.8* (6.4)	25		53.6** (9.3)	42.6** (9.7)	28
Met requirements at enrollment	4.6 (3.7)	-	32		7.4 (5.0)	-	17
Unconstrained Recipients	2.6 (3.1)	-	59		16.0** (5.6)	-	37

Note: Standard error in parentheses. No correction needed for households that met at enrollment or Unconstrained households.

**t-statistic of estimated effect significant at the 0.01 level.

*t-statistic of estimated effect significant at the 0.05 level.

+t-statistic of estimated effect significant at the 0.10 level.

enrollment, the median increase in rental expenditure was 6.5 percent above normal in Pittsburgh and 20.6 percent above normal in Phoenix, the latter statistically significant.

In Pittsburgh, the Minimum Rent Low plans had only a small effect on expenditures. In contrast, in Phoenix these plans induced rather large and significant increases in rental expenditures above normal--the median increase was almost 16 percent. Minimum Rent Low households that met the requirements only after enrollment had a median increase of 42 percent above normal while the change for similar Pittsburgh households was only 9 percent above normal (significant only at the 0.10 level).

Minimum Rent High plans had large and significant effects in both sites, with larger effects in Phoenix. Minimum Rent High plans in Pittsburgh clearly had much larger effects (8 percent overall and 16 percent for households meeting after enrollment) than the Minimum Rent Low plans. In Phoenix, the effects of the two plan types were similar for households that met the requirements only after enrollment (42 percent above normal for Phoenix Minimum Rent Low households; 43 percent for Minimum Rent High households). Overall, however, the effect of the Minimum Rent High plans was larger in Phoenix than either the Minimum Rent Low or the Minimum Standards plans.

The procedure used to estimate the impact of the housing allowance on Housing Gap households can also be used to estimate the impact of the housing allowances on Unconstrained households as well. These estimates are presented in the last line of Table 1. Only in Phoenix do Unconstrained households increase their expenditures significantly more than normal--the increase is only 2.6 percent above normal in Pittsburgh, but is 16.0 percent above normal in Phoenix. The difference in response between the sites for Unconstrained households mirrors the differences for Housing Gap households.

Since Unconstrained households receive a Housing Gap form of payment without any requirements to meet, comparison can reveal the effect of imposing the requirements above and beyond that of the allowance payment. Table 2 presents this comparison for each Housing Gap group (using the relevant requirement for determination of initial status for Unconstrained households as well). As has been pointed out earlier, Housing Gap households that already met their requirement at enrollment were essentially unconstrained in their behavior. Thus, they would be expected to show the same expenditure changes as similar Unconstrained households (controlling for payment level). In fact, while Pittsburgh Minimum Standards households that met requirements at enrollment show no significant difference in response from Unconstrained households, these households in Phoenix increase their housing expenditures significantly less. Since movers tend to increase their expenditures, this result is consistent with the hypothesis

TABLE 2

Median Percentage Increase in Housing
Expenditures for Housing Gap Households
Above that for Unconstrained Households
(Percentage Points)

HOUSEHOLD GROUP	PITTSBURGH	PHOENIX
Minimum Standards Recipients	1.1 (4.4)	-7.1 (6.1)
Did not meet requirements at enrollment	2.2 (5.8)	3.6 (7.8)
Met requirements at enrollment	6.7[a] (7.7)	-15.2+[a] (7.3)
Minimum Rent Low Recipients	0.1 (3.9)	-0.2 (3.8)
Did not meet requirements at enrollment	6.2 (7.2)	9.6 (10.9)
Met requirements at enrollment	-1.0 (4.6)	-4.6 (5.7)
Minimum Rent High Recipients	5.8+ (3.5)	10.7* (5.4)
Did not meet requirements at enrollment	10.5 (7.4)	16.8+ (10.4)
Met requirements at enrollment	6.1 (5.9)	9.1[a] (8.8)

Note: Standard error in parentheses. Housing Gap
response corrected for selection bias.

[a]Comparison based on 15 or fewer Unconstrained household observations.

*t-statistic of the comparison significant at the
0.05 level.

+t-statistic of the comparison significant at the
0.10 level.

that households in Phoenix already living in acceptable housing were reluctant to leave it. Analysis of mobility, however, showed almost exactly the
same effect of the allowance on the probability of moving in Phoenix for
Unconstrained households, Minimum Standards households that met requirements at enrollment, and Minimum Standards households that did not meet
requirements at enrollment (MacMillan, 1978, p. A-109).

Minimum Standards households that only met the requirements after enrollment increased their housing expenditures by more than Unconstrained
households in both sites. The differences are not large, however, and not
significant in either site. This is somewhat startling. Minimum Standards
households that only met requirements after enrollment increased their
housing expenditures by much more than those that already met requirements
at enrollment (about 6 percentage points in Pittsburgh and 24 percentage
points in Phoenix), and these large differences were attributed to the
different incentives of the allowance offer. It now appears, however, that
the differences could in large part reflect differences among households in
their response to the additional income.

Thus, it appears that, in comparison to a similar unconstrained income
transfer, Minimum Standards requirements neither increased housing expenditures overall nor even materially affected the allocation of increases
among households that did and did not already meet requirements at enrollment. As noted in Friedman and Weinberg (forthcoming-b), however, the
Minimum Standards requirement did induce a significant increase in the
probability that a household met those requirements whereas the Unconstrained offer did not. Thus, the lack of any differences in housing
expenditure changes may in part reflect the relatively weak link between
unit rent and meeting the Minimum Standards requirements.

The response of Minimum Rent households can also be compared to that of
Unconstrained households. Overall, Minimum Rent Low households increased
their housing expenditures by about the same percentage as Unconstrained
households in Phoenix and significantly less than Unconstrained households
in Pittsburgh. Minimum Rent High households in both sites increased their
expenditures significantly more than Unconstrained households, though the
difference is larger in Phoenix. There is no significant difference in the
response of Minimum Rent households that met their requirement at enrollment from that of comparable Unconstrained households.

Minimum Rent households that only met requirements after enrollment
would be expected to have to spend more on housing than Unconstrained
households in order to meet the requirements. While some of these households would spend enough to meet the requirements due solely to the income
effect of the payment, the requirements are large enough to induce additional expenditures. Only the difference for Minimum Rent High households

in Phoenix is significant, apparently reflecting the relatively small number of Unconstrained households (and accordingly large standard errors of estimate).

A comparison between Minimum Rent and Minimum Standards households is possible as well. Because of the direct link between additional expenditures and meeting the Minimum Rent requirements, Minimum Rent households that met requirements after enrollment are likely to have increased their rent more than the Minimum Standards households. This is in general confirmed by the data in Table 3. Minimum Rent households that met their requirements after enrollment show larger increases in expenditures than Minimum Standards households that met their requirements after enrollment. The difference is large and significant only in Phoenix and there is no significant pattern for households that met their requirements at enrollment. For all recipients, Minimum Rent High households increased expenditures more than Minimum Standards households (though significantly so only in Phoenix). Minimum Rent Low households showed the same overall increase as Minimum Standards households.

There are at least three potential reasons for the large differences in the estimated effects between the two sites: different initial housing conditions in the two sites, differences in the way the payment was used in the two sites, and differences in the size of the allowance payment itself between the sites. The first reason seems to provide at least a partial explanation for the site differences. One measure of the amount that Minimum Standards households not meeting requirements at enrollment had to pay to obtain standard units is the difference between the ratio of enrollment rent to C^* for them as compared to households actually meeting the standards. This difference was larger in Phoenix than in Pittsburgh. This implies that in order to obtain standard housing, Phoenix households needed to make larger changes in expenditures than did Pittsburgh households. Likewise, the average Phoenix Minimum Rent household that met requirements after enrollment had to make larger changes in expenditures than did the average Pittsburgh household.

Another possible explanation for the site difference in behavior is that the allowance payment was viewed differently at the two sites. Since program participants knew that the allowance payment would last for only three years, it is possible that they viewed the allowance income differently from their other income. If households in Phoenix found readjustment easier to make, then the limited duration of the experiment might have had a smaller impact on their behavior. Evidence in favor of this hypothesis is the much higher mobility rate in Phoenix, both before and during the experiment period, and the much higher vacancy rate in that site (14 versus 5 percent).[10]

TABLE 3

Median Percentage Increase in Housing Expenditures
for Minimum Rent Households Abcve that for
Minimum Standards Households

(Percentage Points)

HOUSEHOLD GROUP	PITTSBURGH		PHOENIX	
	PERCENTAGE INCREASE		PERCENTAGE INCREASE	
	Minimum Rent Low vs. Minimum Standards Households	Minimum Rent High vs. Minimum Standards Households	Minimum Rent Low vs. Minimum Standards Households	Minimum Rent High vs. Minimum Standards Households
ALL HOUSEHOLDS	-1.0% (3.9)	4.6% (4.7)	0.9% (5.4)	12.0%+ (6.9)
Did not meet requirements at enrollment	2.0 (6.7)	8.8 (7.8)	17.8* (9.6)	18.3* (9.9)
Met requirements at enrollment	1.3 (4.5)	3.6 (5.1)	-0.5 (5.1)	8.2 (6.5)

Note: Standard error in parentheses. Housing Gap response
corrected for selection bias.

*t-statistic based on estimated contrast significant at the 0.05
level.

+t-statistic based on estimated contrast significant at the 0.10
level.

A third possible explanation for site differences is that the allowance payments were typically much larger in Phoenix than in Pittsburgh.[11]   If allowance-induced rent changes were related to the size of the allowance, then the average response in Phoenix would be larger than the response in Pittsburgh.   This larger payment may have been enough to induce some households to meet requirements in Phoenix by enabling households that had to spend more on average in order to meet requirements to do so.

Shopping Behavior

Increased expenditures for housing may not always lead to changes in the amount of housing obtained. Most obviously, general inflation implies higher dollar expenditures without any change in the housing services provided by a dwelling unit. The impact on expenditures estimated above accounted for inflation by using Control households, so that this posed no problem there. Even apart from inflation, however, changes in expenditures may not reflect real changes in housing services. If allowance recipients shop for housing less carefully, then they might pay more for their units than they normally would.

This can be seen with the aid of Figure 2 for Minimum Rent households. In this figure, the vertical axis measures housing services (H) and the horizontal axis measures housing expenditures (R). The diagonal represents the average relationship between housing expenditures and housing services, that is, $R = p_H H$, or $\epsilon = 0$. Units to the left of this line would be considered good deals ($\epsilon < 0$); units to the right of the line would be considered bad deals ($\epsilon > 0$). A utility-maximizing household would normally prefer unit A over unit B, because unit A both provides more housing services and leaves more income for other purchases, that is, $U(H_A, Y - R_A) > U(H_B, Y - R_B)$. However, the allowance offer may change this relationship. Since unit B passes the Minimum Rent requirement and unit A does not, it is possible, to find an allowance payment, S, such that $U(H_A, Y - R_A) < U(H_B, Y + S - R_B)$. Of course, some units both meet the Minimum Rent requirement and are good deals ($\epsilon < 0$). However, finding these units may require additional search effort, during which the household may both spend part of its income on search costs and get no allowance payment. Thus, under these circumstances the mean value of ϵ at two years for the recipient households that met the Minimum Rent requirements only after enrollment might easily be positive ("bad deals").

For Minimum Standards households the argument is similar, although the incentive to choose overpriced units ($\epsilon > 0$) was less direct. These households were looking for units that passed the Minimum Standards, not for more expensive units. However, if in their search for units that passed the Minimum Standards, they found a unit that passed the standards but was

Figure 2

THE RELATIONSHIP BETWEEN
HOUSING EXPENDITURES AND HOUSING SERVICES

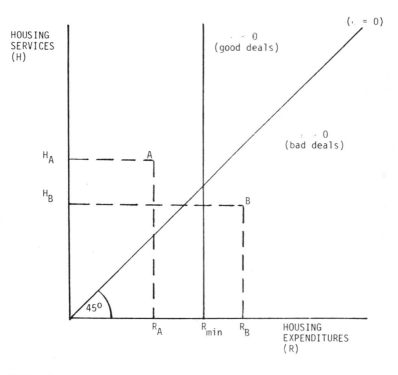

NOTE: $R = p_H H + e$

where p_H = price of housing services (p_H = 1 above) and
e = residual.

overpriced ($, > 0$), they could have chosen to occupy it even if they would normally have continued searching. To the extent that continued search for units that met Minimum Standards required additional effort, it is reasonable that, on average, this group cf households could also have positive $,$.

In order to determine the effect of the allowance payment on shopping behavior, it is necessary to measure the market value of the real housing services in a dwelling unit by using the hedonic indices developed for the Demand Experiment sites by Merrill (1977). The difference between actual rent and the rent predicted by the hedonic index is the hedonic residual, $\hat{\mu}$. This residual may represent omitted quality variables, omitted tenure variables, experimentally induced shopping efficiency or inefficiency, and luck or other random effects. These specification issues have been assessed in detail by Merrill (1977) and Kennedy and Merrill (1979) and analysis suggests that the index tends to underestimate the change in the amount of a unit's housing services in Pittsburgh but not in Phoenix.[12] Thus, the hedonic index estimates of housing services changes may be considered lower bounds of actual changes in real housing in Pittsburgh but are likely to be accurate in Phoenix.

Table 4 presents the median percentage overpayment relative to the market average at two years after enrollment. No significant overpayment relative to the market average was found for households meeting the Minimum Standards requirement in either site.[13] Nor does it appear that the Minimum Standards allowance offer induced households to overpay--there is no significant difference between the overpayment of Minimum Standards and Control households or between Minimum Standards and Unconstrained households. Table 4 also presents the median percentage overpayment for households that met the Minimum Rent requirements at two years after enrollment. The data suggest that significant overpayment occurred in both sites for both Control and Experimental households that met either Minimum Rent requirement. This is to be expected as selecting households with above average rents will to some extent select not only households with above-average housing but also households that pay more than average for the housing they obtain. There was however no significant difference between the Minimum Rent Low and the Control groups or between Minimum Rent Low and the Unconstrained households, suggesting that this allowance did not induce very substantial overpayment. Significant program effects on overpayment were found for Minimum Rent High households in Pittsburgh (the difference between all Minimum Rent High and all Control households that met the Minimum Rent High requirement at two years after enrollment is significant at the 0.05 level). Furthermore, Minimum Rent High households overpaid by significantly more than similar Unconstrained households in Pittsburgh. The fact that this did not occur in Phoenix (which had a relatively loose housing market during the experiment) suggests that the Minimum Rent High requirements themselves may

TABLE 4

Estimated Overpayment Relative to the
Market Average at Two Years After Enrollment

HOUSEHOLD GROUP	PITTSBURGH		PHOENIX	
	PERCENTAGE OVERPAYMENT	SAMPLE SIZE	PERCENTAGE OVERPAYMENT	SAMPLE SIZE
ALL HOUSEHOLDS THAT MET MINIMUM STANDARDS REQUIREMENTS AT TWO YEARS				
Control households	2.8 (1.8)	(81)	-1.7 (2.0)	(87)
Minimum Standards households	0.3 (2.3)	(83)	1.8 (3.0)	(84)
Unconstrained households	[-3.0] (4.9)	(14)	5.4 (6.2)	(17)
ALL HOUSEHOLDS THAT MET MINIMUM RENT LOW REQUIREMENTS AT TWO YEARS				
Control households	4.9** (0.6)	(214)	7.9** (1.5)	(125)
Minimum Rent Low households	6.8** (2.3)	(95)	5.5 (3.7)	(23)
Unconstrained households	2.7 (3.2)	(39)	5.5 (5.5)	(63)
ALL HOUSEHOLDS THAT MET MINIMUM RENT HIGH REQUIREMENTS AT TWO YEARS				
Control households	10.9**a (1.2)	(129)	10.4** (2.3)	(80)
Minimum Rent High households	17.7** (3.1)	(58)	14.1** (4.4)	(44)
Unconstrained households	4.4b (4.0)	(25)	[14.1]+ (7.1)	(15)

Note: Brackets indicate amounts based on 15 or fewer observations. Standard error in parentheses. Estimated overpayment of Control and Unconstrained households not significantly different from that of Minimum Standards or Minimum Rent Low households at the 0.10 level.

a Estimated overpayment significantly different from that of Minimum Rent High households at the 0.05 level.

b Estimated overpayment significantly different from that of Minimum Rent High households at the 0.01 level.

+t-statistic of residual significant at the 0.10 level.

**t-statistic of residual significant at the 0.01 level.

induce significant overpayment only in a relatively tight housing market (Pittsburgh).

IV. SUMMARY AND POLICY IMPLICATIONS

This paper has examined the effects of housing allowances on the housing consumption of low income households. Monthly payments were made to recipient households based on the difference between an expected need for expenditure on housing and a fraction (typically 25 percent) of their income. Two housing allowance plans, Minimum Standards and Minimum Rent, were examined. These are housing programs rather than income maintenance programs because the payments made to households are linked directly to housing by the imposition of housing requirements--minimum physical standards in the former plan, minimum expenditure levels in the latter. These two plans were compared to an "Unconstrained" plan in which households received payments without having to meet any housing requirements. In addition, all three plans were compared to a control group that received no allowance payments.

The housing requirements were an important determining factor for household response to the allowance program--initial housing requirement status had an overwhelming effect on the way enrolled households responded to the housing allowance offer. Households that already met their housing requirements at enrollment, and were therefore automatically eligible for allowance payments, did not use the allowance to pay for any substantial increase in their housing expenditures or consumption. Their change in housing consumption was much like what would normally have occurred in the absence of the experiment. For these households, housing allowances essentially provided a reduction in the very high preprogram proportion of income being spent on rent (rent burden).

Households that met their requirements only after enrollment made large increases in their housing expenditures, well beyond those that would have been made without the program. These above-normal increases in housing expenditures still consumed only a small portion of the allowance payment. Households that met the requirements after enrollment were able not only to meet the housing requirements and increase their housing expenditures, but also to reduce their rent burden to a reasonable level. The greatest gap is apparent for households that met their requirements after enrollment. Overall, the Minimum Standards and Minimum Rent Low requirements induced roughly the same increases in both expenditures and services as the Unconstrained payment. The Minimum Rent High requirement did induce significantly larger increases in expenditures in both sites, but much of this reflected overpayment. The increase in housing services for Minimum

Rent High households was higher than that of Minimum Standards and Unconstrained households only in Phoenix, but not significantly higher.

Table 5 shows the estimated increase in expenditures and in housing
services induced by the housing allowance in terms of average dollar increases and as a percentage of payments. Again, increases were close for
Minimum Standards, Minimum Rent Low, and Unconstrained households in both
sites. The change in expenditures for Minimum Rent High households was
larger, with a larger proportion of the allowance used for increased expenditures. Only in Phoenix, however, was this also reflected in a larger
increase in housing services. In no case were as much as half of the total
payments used for additional expenditures. It should be noted that, as a
consequence, median rent burden for all groups was substantially reduced.[14]

The major unresolved analytic issue in this paper is the difference in
response between the two experimental sites (which was larger in Phoenix
than in Pittsburgh). These differences occurred for households that met
their requirements after enrollment and consequently influenced the overall
effect heavily. Two plausible explanations were offered for the difference
and the evidence went a long way toward resolving the problem. First,
households that did not meet their requirements at enrollment in Phoenix
had to make much larger changes in their housing consumption in order to
meet requirements in their two-year units than did similar Pittsburgh
households. Second, response to the payment level and to variations in the
payment parameters was present in Phoenix, where the payment was larger,
but not in Pittsburgh. While this second finding helps to explain the
difference in response, it does raise the issue of why the payment response
differed between the sites. Finally, the distribution of preferences for
housing may well differ between the sites.

There is one major problem in giving unqualified endorsement to a
housing allowance program. Even though it appears that a program can be
designed that performs the dual purpose of leading to an improvement in
recipients' housing and to a reduction in the proportion of income that
they spend on housing, these benefits are limited to participants. To the
extent that the needy do not participate, such a plan would be a failure.

It is indeed unfortunate, therefore, that it appears to be those that
are most in need who are the least likely to participate in a housing
allowance scheme. Kennedy and MacMillan (1979) estimated that the Housing
Gap programs tested in the Demand Experiment were able to reach less than
one-fourth of the eligible households that would normally live in program-
defined substandard housing (p. S-3). Further, "because households in
housing that did not meet program requirements were unlikely to participate,
participation rates in the Housing Gap programs were significantly lower for
those in the worst housing, including the very poor, minorities, and very
large households" (p. S-5).

The "best" housing program may not be one program at all; it may be a combination of programs, each taking a different approach. Housing allowances appear to be a viable program for many of the households that Frieden and Solomon (1977) termed housing-deprived by leading to a reduction in substandardness, overcrowding, and excessive housing cost for recipients while providing freedom of choice among neighborhoods. For households choosing not to participate in a housing allowance scheme, some alternative supply-oriented program may be worthwhile. For example, a study by Mayo et al., (1979a) found that minority households participated at a higher rate than nonminority households in some of the supply-oriented housing programs (Public Housing and Section 236). While this greater participation appears to have resulted in part from the peculiar location of this housing (a tendency to be concentrated in minority areas), it appears that minority households, at least, can be served to a greater extent than nonminority households by such programs. It is worth pointing out, though, that such supply-oriented programs appear to be extremely inefficient, with costs greatly outweighing benefits (Mayo et al., 1979b).

One possible solution to the problem of the enforcement of housing standards engendering reduced participation is through a program that couples graduated standards with graduated incentives. Investigation of the participation decision of enrolled Minimum Standards households resulted in two major findings: participation increased as the subsidy level increased; and the imposition of the Minimum Standards requirement significantly reduced participation (Kennedy and MacMillan, 1979). Unfortunately, the program design did not include variation in the physical requirements themselves, so that conjectures about the impact of alternate standards must remain speculative. Nevertheless, it seems clear that less stringent physical standards are easier to meet and would result in a higher participation rate than those required in the Demand Experiment.

It is clear from the analysis of alternate housing requirements that specific housing requirements should be imposed only if the policy makers have very strong preferences about the requirements. This is because housing allowance recipients apparently try to obtain housing that satisfies just those requirements while otherwise containing a normal level of "quality" per dollar of expenditure. Once a basic level of standards is established as an irreducible minimum level of dwelling unit quality, a corresponding basic level of payment can be established which trades increased participation off against increased program cost. A second, higher level of standards could then be established that includes additional requirements by associating this higher level of requirements with a higher housing allowance payment.

TABLE 5

Proportion of Allowance Used for Increased
Housing Expenditures and Housing Services Above Normal

HOUSEHOLD GROUP	ESTIMATED AMOUNT OF INCREASE ABOVE NORMAL		MEAN PAYMENT	PROPORTION OF ALLOWANCE USED FOR:	
	Expenditures	Services		Expenditures	Services
PITTSBURGH					
Minimum Standards households	$5.6	$3.6	$65	9%	6%
Minimum Rent Low households	3.5	0.0	58	6	0
Minimum Rent High households	11.9	1.1	51	23	2
Unconstrained households	3.1	3.6	54	6	7
PHOENIX					
Minimum Standards households	22.2	13.9	81	27	17
Minimum Rent Low households	21.9	15.2	86	25	18
Minimum Rent High households	42.5	26.3	103	41	26
Unconstrained households	20.5	16.6	108	19	15

FOOTNOTES

1. The fourth basic treatment plan was "Percent of Rent." It offered households rent rebates in the form of cash payments equal to a fixed fraction of their monthly rent. The purpose of this plan was to enable estimation of the price elasticity of housing demand. It is examined in Friedman and Weinberg (forthcoming - a).

2. In this paper, housing services are measured by hedonic indices developed by Merrill (1977). The indices give a dollar value for the amount of housing services provided by a unit. The measure can be interpreted as the expected or average market rent of a unit with given location, size, and other physical characteristics.

3. In their analysis of household response to the Percent of Rent housing allowances, Friedman and Weinberg (forthcoming - a) estimated that a 10 percent increase in income would on average lead to an increase in housing expenditures of less than 4 percent. Moreover, such adjustments in housing expenditures typically occur only when households move. Other researchers have found expenditures to be slightly more responsive to income changes (see Mayo, 1978).

4. Hausman and Wise (forthcoming) have suggested a methodology that is suitable for dealing with the Minimum Rent requirement. However, their method of discontinuous budget constraints was not general enough to deal with the Minimum Standards requirement. Further, it requires strong assumptions about the functional form of household utility that we did not wish to make.

5. Expenditures are used for illustrative purposes. The methodology developed is general and was also applied to estimate the effect on the hedonic index of housing services.

6. Appendix B, available on request from the authors, presents the estimated equations. Representative statistics of fit are:

| | PITTSBURGH | | PHOENIX | |
	Rent	Housing Services	Rent	Housing Services
Correlation between actual and predicted	0.77	0.77	0.77	0.75
Percentage Root Mean Square error	0.25%	0.21%	0.35%	0.28%
Standard error of estimate	0.20	0.16	0.26	0.21
Sample size used for estimation (Control households)	289	254	256	230

7. Theoretically, there is no clear indication of the size or sign of $E(r|D)$. Voluntary dropouts consist of two groups--those whose housing consumption is so small that they have little expectation of meeting the requirements, and those whose incomes have risen so much that their allowance payment would be negligible. The former group has below-average rents ($r < 0$) while the latter has above-average rents ($r > 0$). In an attempt to evaluate the empirical importance of $E(r|D)$, the relationship of the rent of dropouts to that of all households at enrollment was determined (due to high serial correlation, this is a good measure of the expected residual at two years). This residual was very small (and insignificant):

	PITTSBURGH		PHOENIX	
HOUSEHOLD GROUP	Mean Residual	t-Statistic	Mean Residual	t-Statistic
Minimum Standards Households	-0.029	1.12	0.016	0.95
Minimum Rent Low Households	-0.012	0.37	0.017	0.78
Minimum Rent High Households	-0.021	0.74	0.006	0.30

Further, Hausman and Wise (1977b) found that their estimate of experimental effects in the New Jersey Graduated Work Incentive Experiment was unaffected by attrition when demographic covariates were included in the model.

8. Hausman and Wise (1977a) proposed a maximum likelihood procedure that deals with situations in which only the part of the sample that meets the selection criterion is observed. A variation of this technique is used by Kennedy (1978) for Demand Experiment data to test for bias due to sample attrition. The procedure developed here uses observed data on the expenditures of nonparticipants.

9. As discussed by Goldberger (1968), since log rent is used, the estimated median percentage change above normal is computed from the actual effect $\hat{\beta}$ as $\exp(\hat{\beta}) - 1$ with standard error $\exp(\hat{\beta}) \cdot [\exp(2\hat{\sigma}^2) - \exp(\hat{\sigma}^2)]^{1/2}$ where $\hat{\sigma}$ is the estimated standard error of β (for additional discussion, see Hastings and Peacock, 1975, p. 84).

10. The fact that allowance payments were only made for three years may have had less effect on housing response in Phoenix because households there would find any readjustment of their housing at the end of three years easier to make both because they moved more readily and because the market offered easy access to units. It should be noted, however, that no such site difference was found in the response of households to Percent of Rent allowances (Friedman and Weinberg, forthcoming - a), though that investigation focused on the behavior of movers alone.

11. The mean for Minimum Standards recipients was $64 in Pittsburgh and $81 in Phoenix.

12. Results of this analysis are presented in Friedman and Weinberg (forthcoming - b). The extent of the understatement of housing service change in Pittsburgh is about one-third--that is, actual changes in Pittsburgh housing services may be as much as 1.5 times the estimated change.

13. Significant overpayment relative to the market average would not necessarily imply that households obtained "bad deals." The hedonic residual $\hat{u}$ may include some omitted quality items, though this was found to be unlikely in Phoenix.

14. It is worth noting that the limited duration of the experiment may have affected the results. While the issue is unresolved, analysis of movers suggests that the long-run impact of a permanent allowance program on participant expenditures or housing services would not be substantially larger than that estimated for the two years of the experiment (see Friedman and Weinberg, forthcoming - b).

REFERENCES

Frieden, Bernard J. and Arthur P. Solomon, The Nation's Housing: 1975 to 1985, (Cambridge, Mass.: Joint Center for Urban Studies of the Massachusetts Institute of Technology and Harvard University, April 1977).

Friedman, Joseph and Daniel H. Weinberg, "The Demand for Rental Housing: Evidence from the Housing Allowance Demand Experiment' Journal of Urban Economics, forthcoming - a.

Friedman, Joseph and Daniel H. Weinberg, The Housing Choices of Low-Income Families, Cambridge, Mass., Abt Books, forthcoming - b.

Goldberger, Arthur S., "The Interpretation and Estimation of Cobb-Douglas Functions," Econometrica Vol. 35 no. 3-4, July-October 1968.

Hastings, N.A.J. and J.B. Peacock, Statistical Distributions, New York, John Wiley and Sons, 1975.

Hausman, Jerry A. and David A. Wise, "Attrition Bias in Experimental and Panel Data: The Gary Income Maintenance Experiment," unpublished manuscript, May 1977(a) (see this Volume).

Hausman, Jerry A. and David A. Wise, "Discontinuous Budget Constraints and Estimation: The Demand for Housing," Review of Economic Studies, forthcoming (see this volume).

Hausman, Jerry A. and David A. Wise, "Social Experimentation, Truncated Distributions, and Efficient Estimation," Econometrica, vol. 45, no. 4, May 1977(b), pp. 919-938.

Kennedy, Stephen D., "Sample Selection and the Analysis of Constrained Income Transfers: Some Evidence from the Housing Allowance Demand Experiment," paper presented at the meetings of the Econometric Society, June 1978.

Kennedy, Stephen D. and Jean MacMillan, Draft Report Participation Under Alternative Housing Allowance Programs: Evidence from the Housing Allowance Demand Experiment, (Cambridge, Mass.: Abt Associates Inc., October 1979).

Kennedy, Stephen D. and Sally Merrill, "The Use of Hedonic Indices to Distinguish Changes in Housing and Housing Expenditures: Evidence from the Housing Allowance Demand Experiment," paper presented at the Research Conference on the Housing Choices of Low-Income Families, Washington, D.C., March 1979.

Khadduri, Jill, Katharine Lyall, and Raymond Struyk, "Welfare Reform and Housing Assistance: A National Policy Debate," Journal of the American Institute of Planners, vol. 44, January 1978, pp. 2-12.

Levine, Martin D., Federal Housing Policy: Current Programs and Recurring Issues, Washington, D.C., Congressional Budget Office, June 1978.

MacMillan, Jean, Draft Report on Mobility in the Housing Allowance Demand Experiment, Cambridge, Mass., Abt Associates Inc., June 1978.

Mayo, Stephen K., "Theory and Estimation in the Economics of Housing Demand," paper presented at the meetings of the Econometric Society, August 1978.

Mayo, Stephen K., Shirley Mansfield, W. David Warner and Richard Zwetchkenbaum, Draft Report on Housing Allowances and Other Rental Assistance Programs--A Comparison Based on the Housing Allowance Demand Experiment, Part 1: Participation, Housing Consumption, Location, and Satisfaction (Cambridge, Mass.: Abt Associates Inc., November 1979)(a).

Mayo, Stephen K., Shirley Mansfield, W. David Warner and Richard Zwetchkenbaum, Draft Report on Housing Allowances and Other Rental Assistance Programs--A Comparison Based or the Housing Allowance Demand Experiment, Part 2: Costs and Efficiency (Cambridge, Mass.: Abt Associates Inc., August 1979)(b).

Merrill, Sally, Draft Report on Heconic Indices as a Measure of Housing Quality, Cambridge, Mass., Abt Associates Inc., December 1977.

Olsen, Edgar O., "A Competitive Theory of the Housing Market," American Economic Review, vol. 59, September 1969.

Pindyck, Robert S. and Daniel L. Rubinfeld, Econometric Models and Economic Forecasts, New York, McGraw-Hill, 1976.

APPENDIX A

COMPONENTS OF MINIMUM STANDARDS
(Program Definition)

1. COMPLETE PLUMBING
    Private toilet facilities, a shower or tub with hot and cold running water, and a washbasin with hot and cold running water will be present and in working condition.

2. COMPLETE KITCHEN FACILITIES
    A cooking stove or range, refrigerator, and kitchen sink with hot and cold running water will be present and in working condition.

3. LIVING ROOM, BATHROOM, KITCHEN PRESENCE
    A living room, bathroom, and kitchen will be present. (This represents the dwelling unit "core," which corresponds to an efficiency unit.)

4. LIGHT FIXTURES
    A ceiling or wall-type fixture will be present and working in the bathroom and kitchen.

5. ELECTRICAL
    At least one electric outlet will be present and operable in both the living room and kitchen. A working wall switch, pull-chain light switch, or additional electrical outlet will be present in the living room.[a]

6. HEATING EQUIPMENT
    Units with no heating equipment; with unvented room heaters which burn gas, oil, or kerosene; or which are heated mainly with portable electric room heaters will be unacceptable.

7. ADEQUATE EXITS
    There will be at least two exits from the dwelling unit leading to safe and open space at ground level (for multifamily building only). Effective November, 1973 (retroactive to program inception) this requirement was modified to permit override on case-by-case basis where it appears that fire safety is met despite lack of a second exit.

8. ROOM STRUCTURE
    Ceiling structure or wall structure for all rooms must not be in condition requiring replacement (such as severe buckling or leaning).

9. ROOM SURFACE
    Ceiling surface or wall surface for all rooms must not be in condition requiring replacement (such as surface material that is loose, containing large holes, or severely damaged).

10. CEILING HEIGHT
    Living room, bathroom, and kitchen ceilings must be 7 feet (or higher) in at least one-half of the room area.[a]

11. FLOOR STRUCTURE
    Floor structure for all rooms must not be in condition requiring replacement (such as large holes or missing parts).

12. FLOOR SURFACE
    Floor surface for all rooms must not be in condition requiring replacement (such as large holes or missing parts).

13. ROOF STRUCTURE
    The roof structure must be firm.

14. EXTERIOR WALLS

The exterior wall structure or exterior wall surface must not need replacement. (For structure this could include such conditions as severe leaning, buckling, or sagging, and for surface conditions such as excessive cracks or holes.)

15. LIGHT/VENTILATION

The unit will have a 10 percent ratio of window area to floor area and at least one openable window in the living room, bathroom, and kitchen or the equivalent in the case of properly vented kitchens and/or bathrooms.[a]

16. OCCUPANCY

No more than two persons per adequate bedroom.

Note: a. This housing standard is applied to bedrooms in determining the number of adequate bedrooms for the program occupancy standard (number 16).

20

Hausman and Wise proceed further down the path marked by Burtless and Hausman (1978; reprinted in Part II) in extending Heckman's (1974a, 1974b) techniques for "estimating indifference curves" to the situation where budget constraints are nonlinear or even discontinuous. The goal is to move beyond simple experimental/control comparisons to a structural model that will provide fundamental parameter estimates applicable to a variety of potential programs and individual situations. This paper examines the demand for housing, employing HADE data to estimate demand elasticities within a uniform framework that applies across the different treatment groups of the study sample, even though some of these face linear, and others nonlinear, budget constraints.

The authors first posit a utility function that has a Cobb-Douglas form. From the utility function the authors then derive a budget allocation function,

$$V(R_1, R_2) = (Y - R)^{1-\beta} R^{\beta}$$

where

R_1 = a vector of goods other than housing
R_2 = a vector of housing goods
R = expenditure on rent
$Y-R$ = expenditure on other goods
β = a taste parameter.

Tastes are incorporated in this model by allowing β to depend on family characteristics. Thus,

$$\beta = X\delta + \eta$$

where

X = a vector of family characteristics
δ = vector of parameters, and
η = an error term which incorporates unobserved household attributes.

Among the variables included in X are a measure of permanent family income (which is assumed to serve as a proxy for household tastes and is based on a household's pre-experimental income), family size, age of household head, race of household head, and a categorical variable to represent site—Phoenix or Pittsburgh. The measure of permanent income is expected to influence the tradeoff between housing and the consumption of other commodities.

An individual is assumed to spend on housing, R, the amount consistent with the relative value he attaches to that housing as indicated by the taste parameter β. In other words, he is expected to choose the value of R that maximizes the budget allocation function V specified above. This value of R is

$$R = \beta Y$$

where Y is defined as a measure of permanent income.

The idea is to let the value (of β) associated with marginal shifts in the allocation of income depend on permanent income. . . . Transitory changes in income, as might be associated with household payments, are not assumed to change β; rather β is presumed to be conditional on initial pre-experimental income which we use as a proxy for permanent income.

Finally, marginal expenditure on housing is presumed to be proportional to income, with the proportion depending on family characteristics as noted in the general function for β above. The multiplicative form is less restrictive than a linear form that implies that housing expenditure is equal to a constant that depends on family characteristics plus a fixed proportion of income.

Several other considerations must be accounted for before estimation can proceed. The unusual nature of the process whereby the data are generated requires special attention to specification of a housing expenditure functional form that does not rule out any values that are empirically observed. This is a concern because the budget constraint imposed by the experiment is discontinuous. (See the text and Friedman and Weinberg for a graphic presentation of the experimental budget constraint.) The nature of participation in the experiment is affected by this budget constraint as well as they way in which people shift between the two discontinuous portions of the budget constraint. The experimental treatment effect is nonsymmetric across individuals. Some persons are more likely to participate than others; some persons, even with a well defined preference for expenditure on housing versus other goods, may not be able to realize that preference in practice. These problems are resolved by specifying a likelihood function for estimating the parameters of tastes, β, the variance of η, the error term for β, and the variance of ϵ, a measure of the random error between observed housing expenditure and a "theoretically" preferred value. Thus,

$$R = \beta Y, \text{ above, becomes}$$
$$R = \beta Y + \epsilon.$$

One final adjustment in the model specification was made because individuals may treat the (short-term) experimental subsidy payment differently from the permanent income measure. This resulted in

$$R = \beta (Y + P-k)$$

where

P = the experimental subsidy payment, and
k = a parameter to be estimated, an approximate discount factor for moving costs.

As for the results, the parameter estimates across treatment types are very similar, especially for the permanent income variable. Likewise, the estimates are generally highly significant. These results bear out the usefulness of the model specification—similar estimates are obtained across different treatments.

As a general policy result, the elasticity of housing expenditure with respect to income, at mean family income in the sample, was about 0.6. A 10% increase in income leads to a 6% increase in housing expenditure—one of the largest measured effects in the set of four papers in this section. The elasticity of expenditure for treatment price, one minus the percent of the rent matching rate, was estimated to be –.16. A 10% change in price leads to a 1.6% change in quantity demanded. The price elasticity is a short-term measure, whereas the income elasticity reflects housing expenditures associated with more permanent levels of income.

REFERENCES

HECKMAN, J. (1974a) "Shadow prices, market wages, and labor supply." Econometrica (July): 679-694.

――― (1974b) "Effects of child care programs on women's work effort." J. of Pol. Economy (April): 491-519.

Discontinuous Budget Constraints and Estimation
The Demand for Housing

Jerry A. Hausman and David Wise

Individual choices are often characterized by economists as resulting from maximization of an implicit utility function subject to a budget constraint. Informal graphical descriptions of the outcome of this process usually presume that the budget constraint, determined by individual income and prices, is linear–that the price of a good is independent of the amount of it that is purchased, and that income is independent of the amount purchased. But governmental regulations in particular–as well as non-governmental practices–often produce non-linear, kinked, and even discontinuous budget constraints.

The relationship between hours worked and income, for example, would be linear if the wage rate didn't depend on hours worked. But, because of the progressive federal income tax structure, individuals actually face a net marginal wage rate that declines with income. The budget constraint is non-linear. Negative income tax plans often prescribe one tax rate up to a so-called "breakeven" point, and another thereafter. There is a kink at the breakeven point.[1] Social security regulations impose low tax rates on wage income up to a given level and a very high tax rate on each additional dollar of income. Most existing health insurance plans, as well as proposed national health insurance schemes, include some combination of a deductible, a coinsurance rate, and possibly a maximum health care expenditure level. The price of a dollar's worth of health care is one up to the amount of the deductible; it is the coinsurance rate between the amount of the deductible and the maximum expenditure, and is zero thereafter. Again, the implied budget constraint is non-linear; it has "kinks" in it. Some proposed housing subsidy schemes stipulate that low income families receive "housing" payments, but only after a minimum expenditure for housing. The implied budget constraint is discontinuous.

This paper proposes a rather general method of estimation when the implicit budget constraint is non-linear. But it does so by addressing a particular problem–the analysis of data generated by treatments in the recent Housing Demand Experiment, that can be thought of as creating discontinuous individual budget constraints. It rests on the assumption that the relative value that individuals attach to purchased goods can be described by a functional relationship that assigns weights to goods, or to the dollar expenditures for these goods, a "utility" function. The key parameters of this function are "taste" parameters that are assumed to depend on individual characteristics of decision makers and to be random, given measured characteristics. That is, they depend on observed as well as unobserved attributes of individuals or of their environment. In addition, we assume that persons are not always able to match expenditures to hypothetical best, or maximizing, values. Although the approach is motivated by the idea of utility

From Jerry A. Hausman and David Wise, "Discontinuous Budget Constraints and Estimation: The Demand for Housing," *Review of Economic Studies,* 67(1980): 75-96. Copyright © 1980 by The Society for Economic Analysis Limited.

maximization, the value function that we use for empirical analysis does not severely constrain our empirical estimates. We obtain separate results based on data generated under quite different budget constraint conditions, but based on the same individual model of behaviour. The estimated behavioural parameters are remarkably similar across the samples.

We begin by addressing a problem in the analysis of data generated in the Housing Allowance Demand Experiment.[2] One of the experimental treatments was a "housing gap" subsidy plan that effectively created discontinuous individual budget constraints. This plan in particular–as well as the general goals of the Experiment–are described in Section 1, together with our proposed method for analysing empirical observations generated under it. The analysis of data generated by other treatment plans is discussed in Section 2. We discuss these plans only because comparison of parameter estimates based on data generated by different treatments provides a good test of our behavioural model. Empirical results are presented in Section 3. Extension of the method to other problems is discussed in Section 4. Section 5 is a short summary. Some details of estimation are presented in an Appendix.

1. DISCONTINUOUS BUDGET CONSTRAINTS AND HOUSING SUBSIDIES

1.1. *The General Problem*

The Housing Allowance Demand Experiment was designed to provide information about the effects of particular subsidy schemes on expenditure for housing and on housing quality. In general, it is intended to provide data on the effects of different subsidy formulas on family demand for housing. The effects on the supply of housing are not addressed in this experiment. There is no attempt to estimate the effect of subsidy plans on final equilibrium values of housing expenditure.

Three basic types of subsidy serve as a basis for payments to families under the terms of the experiment. The *first* is "per cent of rent". Payments to families under this plan are proportional to rent paid. The proportions vary from 0·2 to 0·6, depending on the "particular treatment" to which a family is assigned. It is a "matching" plan and varies the effective price of housing across families. The *second* is a straight lump sum transfer payment, that depends only on family income. It is a "block grant" and has the effect of increasing the family budget, or shifting its budget constraint outward. The *third* is also a lump sum transfer plan, but payment is conditional on meeting certain housing requirements. In some cases the requirement is in terms of physical housing standards; in others it is a lower bound on the dollar amount of rent. The second and third subsidy arrangements are called "*housing gap*" plans. The payments are supposed to fill the gap between the cost of modest housing and the proportion of its income that the family might reasonably be expected to devote to housing.

A general goal of the experiment is to provide estimates, based on the data generated by the experiment, that can be used to predict the effect on housing demand of a variety of possible subsidy formulas, not only those explicitly incorporated in the experimental design. The analysis of the experimental results should also be commensurate with this goal.

The first experimental plan, as described above, provides direct evidence of the effect of price on the demand for housing. The second provides direct evidence of the income effect; that is, the effect of shifts in income without any change in the price of housing relative to other goods. One might be inclined to presume that with accurate estimates of both income and price effects one could predict the impact on demand of almost any subsidy plan. This would be true if all plans could be parameterized in terms of price and income effects only. But, of course, they cannot. The third type of plan provides a good example. In fact, the reason for incorporating such a scheme into the experiment was to estimate its experimental effect, possibly with the realization that it could not be decomposed into simple income and price effects. This highlights an important problem. We would like to be able to use the experimental data to draw inferences that can be applied to a much broader range of plans than are represented in the experimental ones. Just as we cannot, in a straightforward way, use estimates based on the first two plans to draw inferences about the effect of the third, we cannot easily use estimates based on all three to make inferences about all other possible plans.[3]

Thus, we have proposed a procedure that allows analysis of data based on all of the experimental plans–in particular, the housing gap plans with a minimum rent require-ment–in an integrated and consistent manner. It allows us to compare directly the results based on one body of data with those from the others. Because our aim is to estimate a general demand function for housing, we would like to be able to compare results based on data generated in different ways. The characteristics of the approach that allow comparison of results generated by different experimental plans also allow prediction of the effects of a wide variety of other possible plans.

The only experimental plan that the approach does not address directly is the version of the third plan that is based on minimum physical standards of housing. In addition, the procedure that is outlined below does not incorporate explicitly the movement of families from one housing unit to another. This important aspect of the problem is left for later development.[4] The procedure is directed toward the analysis of empirical results generated by the housing gap plans with a minimum rent requirement. It is further restricted to the analysis of data pertaining to the first year of experimental data–at a point in time one year after the experiment began. Although the method is motivated by the basic ideas of utility maximization, the empirical estimates are not severely constrained by the functional form of a presumed utility indicator. In particular, the elasticity of housing expenditure with respect to income is allowed to vary with income. We will see that the same basic parameters may be estimated from any of the available groups of data and compared. The exposition of this possibility also provides a demonstration of how estimates based on the existing data sets might be used individually, or jointly, to predict the effects of a wide variety of possible housing subsidy plans that are based on grants to individual families. The analysis is extended elsewhere to cover pre-experimental, as well as experimental, data.[5] The basic ideas of the approach are the same as those laid out here.

1.2. *Estimation*

The housing gap plans with a minimum rent requirement prescribe a payment to families based on family income and size. The payment is made, however, only if the family spends at least a minimum dollar amount for rent. The minimum amount depends on the experimental treatment group to which the family is assigned.[6] Let family income be denoted by Y, the subsidy payment by P, rent by R, and the minimum rent by R^*.

The family, once the experiment begins, faces a budget constraint like that depicted in Figure 1.[7] The family can spend its income for rent and other goods according to the budget constraint depicted by the solid lines in the figure. It can trade off expenditures for rent and for other purposes along the lower segment of the budget line as long as it spends less than R^* for rent. Once it spends an amount R^* or more for rent, it receives a payment P, which shifts the budget constraint outward, and tradeoffs are then made along the upper segment. Given this budget constraint, we might expect that the family would choose to spend on rent and other goods according to the relative value that it attaches to the benefits that are gained from these two kinds of expenditure. This relative value, however, should be expected to differ among families, possibly depending on family characteristics like size.

Because we observe only expenditure for housing, not its quantity or quality, we have modelled housing choice through a budget allocation function shown in equation (1.4) below. It can be derived from an explicit utility function as described in the intervening

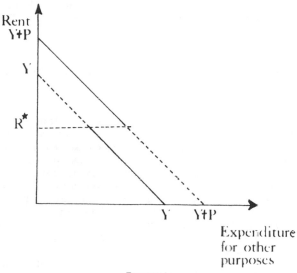

Rent

Y+P

Y

R*

Y   Y+P

Expenditure
for other
purposes

FIGURE 1

paragraphs. We shall introduce an explicit quality dimension along the lines of models proposed by Fisher and Shell (1967) and Muellbauer (1975). The specific manner in which quality enters the utility function is close to the framework used by Hausman and Wise (1978) in a discrete choice model. Assume that there exist N types of rented housing, each characterized by a price p_n, $n = 1, ..., N$. These prices reflect the underlying attributes of the housing including factors such as location, neighbourhood characteristics, and building characteristics. For any quality type n the individual purchases a quantity q_n. Person j we assume chooses the quality and quantity of housing that maximizes his utility function subject to a budget constraint. Our theory permits variation among persons in the value attached to housing versus other goods, as well as one type of housing versus another type.

Suppose we partition goods into two vectors, x_1 and x_2, with an associated utility function $U(x_1, x_2)$. Define

$$V(R_1, R_2) \equiv \max_{x_1, x_2} U(x_1, x_2), \quad \text{subject to} \quad p_1 \cdot x_1 = R_1 \quad \text{and} \quad p_2 \cdot x_2 = R_2.^8 \quad ...(1.1)$$

That is, given expenditures, R_1 and R_2, x_1 and x_2 are chosen to maximize utility. Then suppose that R_1 and R_2 are chosen to maximize V, with the result

$$\max_{R_1, R_2} V(R_1, R_2), \quad \text{subject to } R_1 + R_2 = Y. \quad ...(1.2)$$

Suppose that the utility function is Cobb–Douglas with

$$U(x_1, x_2) = \prod_{i=1}^{I_1} x_{1i}^{\alpha_i} \prod_{i=1}^{I_2} x_{2i}^{\beta_i}.$$

Then it is straightforward to demonstrate that

$$V(R_1, R_2) = R_1^{\Sigma \alpha_i} R_2^{\Sigma \beta_i} \left(\prod_{i=1}^{I_1} \left(\frac{\alpha_i}{\Sigma p_{1i} \alpha_i} \right)^{\alpha_i} \prod_{i=1}^{I_2} \left(\frac{\beta_i}{\Sigma p_2 \beta_i} \right)^{\beta_i} \right)$$

$$= A R_1^{\Sigma \alpha_i} R_2^{\Sigma \beta_i}, \quad ...(1.3)$$

where prices are included in the constant A.

Now suppose that the second vector of goods x_2 represents housing and person j chooses only one quality level of housing.[9] Define the quality adjusted quantity of housing for person j as $H^j \equiv \max_q b_n^j q_n$, where b_n^j is person j's evaluation of the quality of type n housing, q_n is the quantity purchased and $q_n = R_2/p_n$. Then substituting into equation (1.3) using the normalization $\Sigma\alpha_i + \Sigma\beta_i = 1$ and setting the constant A equal to unity we have for person j:

$$V(R_1, R_2) = \max_{x_1,q}(\textstyle\prod_{i=1}^{I_1} x_{1i}^{\alpha_i})H^\beta = \max_{x_1}(\textstyle\prod_{i=1}^{I_1} x_{1i}^{\alpha_i})\left(\max_q b_n^j \frac{R_2}{p_n}\right)^\beta$$

$$= (Y - R)^{1-\beta}R^\beta, \qquad\qquad ...(1.4)$$

where R is rent and $Y - R$ is expenditure on other goods.[10] It might be appropriate to think of V as a budget-allocation function that is derived from an underlying utility function. It is convenient for our purposes because we observe empirically only housing expenditure; we have no "quantity" measure. Expenditure for housing represents the purchase not only of housing itself, but neighbourhood characteristics, access to the central city, and other attributes associated with housing locations as well. And of course changes in expenditure under the experimental plans may reflect changes in location as well as changes in the structural quality of housing itself. (Until we discuss the per cent of rent plans, we assume that all persons face the same housing price *schedule*. They live in the same city. But prices for a given unit of housing should be expected to vary within the city depending on location.) The initial specification we have used corresponds to a Cobb–Douglas utility function. But the methodology that follows is not peculiar to this form. Analogous developments could be based on alternative specifications of V, corresponding to any well-defined utility function. As explained below, we have in fact altered this general specification so that it is not constrained to have the usual properties of Cobb–Douglas formulations.

We would like the taste parameter β to depend on family characteristics. Some of these characteristics we observe and measure, and others we do not. Thus, we suppose that β is a function of observed characteristics, X, as well as unobserved attributes represented by the random term η. We write β as

$$\beta = \delta_0 + X_1\delta_1 + X_2\delta_2 + ... + X_J\delta_J + \eta = X\delta + \eta, \qquad\qquad ...(1.5)$$

where δ is a vector of parameters. We will be particularly concerned with estimation of the elements of δ.

An individual might be presumed to choose the value of R that is most consistent with the relative value that he attaches to housing, as indicated by β. In other words, he might be expected to choose the value of R that maximizes the function V, depicted in (1.4). This value of R is given by

$$R = \beta Y. \qquad\qquad ...(1.6)$$

We see that this relationship appears to imply that rent increases proportionately with income–that the elasticity of rent with respect to income is unity. This is a strong assumption that we will not impose. We can overcome it by allowing income to enter as one of the family characteristics X in (1.2). Thus this measure of "permanent" income is expected to influence the tradeoff between housing and the consumption of other commodities. We might, for example, have

$$\beta = X\delta + Y\delta_y + \eta. \qquad\qquad ...(1.7)$$

There are any number of other possible specifications. The idea is to let the value associated with marginal shifts in the allocation of income depend on permanent income. That is, permanent income is intended to serve as a proxy for household tastes. Transitory changes in income, as might be associated with housing payments, are not assumed to change β; rather, β is presumed to be conditional on initial pre-experimental income, which we use as a proxy for permanent income.

Note that the specification $R = \beta Y$, with $\beta = X\delta$, differs from the more commonly used one, $R = \alpha + \tilde{\beta} Y$, where $\alpha = X\tilde{\delta}$. We presume that marginal expenditure on housing is proportional to income, with the proportion depending on family characteristics. The alternative specification implies that expenditure is equal to a constant that depends on family characteristics, plus a fixed proportion of income. Hypothetical examples of the two functional forms, given X, are graphed in Figure 2. Only the intercept of the linear form shifts with X. The multiplicative form is considerably less restrictive.

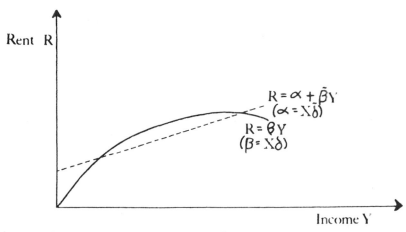

FIGURE 2

For purposes of exposition, we began the development above with the assumption of a utility function from which the function V was derived, and then introduced an expenditure function R consistent with the maximization of V. For empirical purposes, however, it is more appropriate to follow the reverse order. Observable data can be used directly to estimate the housing expenditure function R, but only indirectly to estimate the parameters of V. Thus, our first priority must be the specification of a housing expenditure function that is consistent with empirical observations. This would be sufficient by itself if it were not for the unusual nature of the process that generated our data and our desire to be able to predict expenditure under a wide range of other possible circumstances. To do this, we chose a utility function that is consistent with the empirically verifiable housing expenditure function. It is this additional function that allows us to predict, for example, what values of P would cause a particular individual to switch from the lower to the upper portion of the budget line in Figure 1. It should be thought of as a functional form, analogous to the housing expenditure functional form, but also dependent upon it.

We now want to make sure that we have a stochastic specification of housing expenditure that does not rule out any expenditure values that are observed empirically. By reproducing Figure 1 and superimposing some "indifference" curves on it, we can see that some values would seem to be improbable, given our specification as presently stated. Suppose that a person with taste parameter β^* would choose to spend an amount R^* for rent; that is, he would just meet the minimum expenditure requirement, and would thus receive the payment P. According to (1.6), $R^* = \beta(Y + P)$. There will also be a value β_*, of β, less than β^*, indicating a "weaker" taste for housing, such that an individual with taste parameter β_* would be indifferent between spending R^* for rent and receiving the payment P and spending R_* for rent and not receiving P.[11] Any person with β less than β_* would spend less than R_* on housing and would be on the lower portion of the budget line.

Any person with β greater than β^* would spend more than R^*. His expenditure would be represented by a point on the upper portion of the budget line. Persons with values of β between β_* and β^* would all spend at the "corner point", R^*. Apparently, no one would spend between R_* and R^* for housing.

To explain points between R_* and R^*, we need to realize that even if persons had a well defined preference for expenditure on housing versus other goods, they would not necessarily be able to realize that preference in practice. It may be impossible to find housing at a particular price in a particular area, for example. Or, possibly, such housing could be found only after extensive search. Thus, we suppose that observed housing expenditure differs from the "theoretically" preferred value, (1.6), by a random term ε. Equation (1.6) is replaced by

$$R = \beta Y + \varepsilon$$
$$= (X\delta + \eta) Y + \varepsilon$$
$$= (X\delta) Y + \eta Y + \varepsilon. \qquad \qquad ...(1.8)$$

Note that Y will often be replaced by $Y + P$ in expressions that follow.

Before we consider the likelihood of observing any particular value of R, we pause to note the non-symmetric effect of the experimental treatment across individuals. In particular, some persons are much more likely to "participate" in the experiment than others. Participation should be understood to mean receipt of the payment P.[12] Participating families are represented by points along the upper portion of the budget line. Persons with pre-enrolment rent R^* will almost surely participate. In general, the farther below R^* pre-enrolment rent is, or the lower β is, the less likely is participation in the experiment. The likelihood of participation, of course, should also depend on income Y and the size of the payment P.

Return now to Figure 3 and equation (1.7). Consider the likelihood $l(R)$ of observing any particular value of R, say the value R noted in Figure 2. There are many values of η

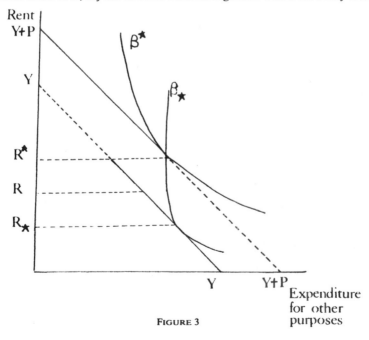

FIGURE 3

and ε, given X, Y, and P, that would lead to an observed expenditure R on housing. In particular, $l(R)$ is given by the following probability

$$l(R) = \Pr \left\{ \begin{array}{lll} & \beta < \beta_* & \text{and} \quad \varepsilon = R - \beta Y. \\ \text{or } \beta_* < \beta < \beta^* & \text{and} \quad \varepsilon = R - R^*. \\ \text{or } \beta^* < \beta & \text{and} \quad \varepsilon = R - \beta(Y + P). \end{array} \right\} \qquad \ldots(1.9)$$

That is, if β is less than β_*, the "maximizing" value of R would be less than R_*, at βY. The difference between the observed R and βY is represented by the value of the stochastic term ε. If β is between β_* and β^*, the maximizing value of housing expenditure is at R^*. The value of ε must then be the difference between the observed R and R^*. A similar argument can be made for the third term in (1.9). It may also be instructive to look at a graph of the values of ε and β, that would lead to observed rental R, given X, Y, and P. It is shown in Figure 4. Any values of β and ε represented by points on the broken solid line would lead to observed housing expenditure equal to R. This can be seen by referring back to equation (1.8). An analogous diagram could be drawn for any other observed value of R. Equation (1.9) is written precisely as shown for any value of R. Note that there are logical bounds on both β and ε. Values of β should not be outside the 0 to 1 interval, and ε should not take on values that would imply rentals of less than 0 or greater than $Y + P$. We will impose neither constraint formally, at least not initially. A constraint analogous to the theoretical bounds on ε applies to almost any stochastic specification. Ignoring it should be unimportant where few, if any, values of R are close to zero or approach $Y + P$. Imposing bounds on β should also be of no practical importance, as long as observed rents do not approach values that are close to zero as a proportion of income.

We will assume that ε is normally distributed with mean zero and variance σ_ε^2, and that β is normally distributed with mean $X\delta$ and variance σ_n^2, and is independent of ε.

$$\varepsilon \sim N(0, \sigma_\varepsilon^2),$$
$$\beta \sim N(X\delta, \sigma_n^2). \qquad \ldots(1.10)$$

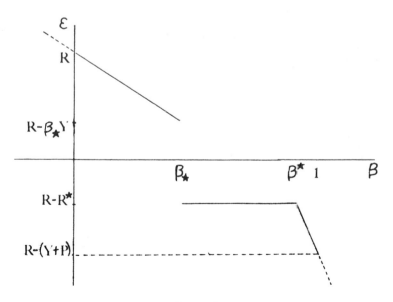

FIGURE 4

Assume that the density function relative to ε is g, and that the density of β is h. Then, referring back to (1.9), $l(R)$ is given by

$$l(R) = \int_{-\infty}^{\beta_*} g(R - \beta Y)h(\beta)d\beta + g(R - \beta^*(Y + P)) \int_{\beta_*}^{\beta^*} h(\beta)d\beta$$

$$+ \int_{\beta^*}^{\infty} g(R - \beta(Y + P))h(\beta)d\beta. \qquad \ldots(1.11)$$

This likelihood may be written simply in terms of normal density and distribution functions, as shown in equation (1.16) below. The intervening paragraphs detail the derivation of this result.

To evaluate the terms of $l(R)$, it is useful to treat each separately. In addition, it is convenient when evaluating the first and third terms to think of the random variables R and β, instead of ε and β. Consider the first term of (1.11). Note that $R = X\delta \cdot Y + \eta Y + \varepsilon$ is distributed normally with mean $X\delta \cdot Y$ and variance $\sigma_n^2 Y^2 + \sigma_\varepsilon^2$. Note also that the first term in (1.11) comes from the first term in (1.9), which in turn can be thought of as: $\beta < \beta_*$ and $R = \beta Y + \varepsilon$. Consider the joint distribution of β and R and write it as

$$f(\beta, R) = f(R) \cdot f(\beta \mid R). \qquad \ldots(1.12)$$

The conditional distribution $f(\beta \mid R)$ of β given R is distributed normally with mean $X\delta + (\sigma_n^2 Y)/(\sigma_n^2 Y^2 + \sigma_\varepsilon^2)(R - X\delta \cdot Y)$ and variance $\sigma_n^2 \sigma_\varepsilon^2/(\sigma_n^2 Y^2 + \sigma_\varepsilon^2)$.

The first term in (1.11) can then be written as

$$\int_{-\infty}^{\beta_*} f(R)f(\beta \mid R)d\beta = \frac{1}{\sqrt{\sigma_n^2 Y^2 + \sigma_\varepsilon^2}} \phi\left(\frac{R - X\delta \cdot Y}{\sqrt{\sigma_n^2 Y^2 + \sigma_\varepsilon^2}}\right) \Phi\left[\frac{\beta_* - X\delta - \dfrac{\sigma_n^2 Y}{\sigma_n^2 Y^2 + \sigma_\varepsilon^2}(R - X\delta \cdot Y)}{\dfrac{(\sigma_\varepsilon^2 \sigma_n^2)^{\frac{1}{2}}}{(\sigma_n^2 Y^2 + \sigma_\varepsilon^2)^{\frac{1}{2}}}}\right]$$

$$= \tilde{\phi}(z_1) \cdot \Phi[d_1], \qquad \ldots(1.13)$$

where ϕ is a unit normal density function, Φ is a unit normal cumulative distribution function, and the last equality defines $\tilde{\phi}$, z_1, and d_1. That is, $z_1 = (R - X\delta \cdot Y)/(\sigma_n^2 Y^2 + \sigma_\varepsilon^2)^{\frac{1}{2}}$ and d_1 equals the term in square brackets in the second equality.

The second term in (1.11) can be evaluated directly in terms of the density function of ε and β and is given by

$$g(R - \beta^*(Y + P)) \int_{\beta_*}^{\beta^*} h(\beta)d\beta = \tilde{\phi}\left(\frac{R - \beta^*(Y + P)}{(\sigma_\varepsilon)}\right)\left\{\Phi\left[\frac{\beta^* - X\delta}{(\sigma_n)^{\frac{1}{2}}}\right] - \Phi\left[\frac{\beta_* - X\delta}{(\sigma_n)^{\frac{1}{2}}}\right]\right\}$$

$$= \tilde{\phi}(z_2)\{\Phi[\bar{d}_2] - \Phi[\underline{d}_2]\}, \qquad \ldots(1.14)$$

where the last equality defines z_2, $\bar{d}_2$ and $\underline{d}_2$.

The last term in (1.11), which comes from the last term in (1.9), can be written analogously to the first as

$$\int_{\beta^*}^{\infty} f(R)f(\beta \mid R)d\beta = \frac{1}{(\sigma_n^2(Y + P)^2 + \sigma_\varepsilon^2)^{\frac{1}{2}}} \phi\left(\frac{R - X\delta(Y + P)}{(\sigma_n^2(Y + P)^2 + \sigma_\varepsilon^2)^{\frac{1}{2}}}\right)$$

$$\left\{1 - \Phi\left[\frac{\beta^* - X\delta - \dfrac{\sigma_n^2(Y + P)}{\sigma_n^2(Y + P)^2 + \sigma_\varepsilon^2}(R - X\delta(Y + P))}{\dfrac{(\sigma_\varepsilon^2 \sigma_n^2)^{\frac{1}{2}}}{(\sigma_n^2(Y + P)^2 + \sigma_\varepsilon^2)^{\frac{1}{2}}}}\right]\right\}$$

$$= \tilde{\phi}(z_3)\{1 - \Phi[d_3]\}, \qquad \ldots(1.15)$$

where the last equality defines z_3 and d_3.

Collecting the expressions in (1.13), (1.14), and (1.15), we see that the likelihood $l(R)$ can be written succinctly as

$$l(R) = \tilde{\phi}(z_1) \cdot \phi[d_1] + \tilde{\phi}(z_2)\{\Phi[\bar{d}_2] - \Phi[\underline{d}_2]\} + \tilde{\phi}(z_3)\{1 - \Phi[d_3]\}. \qquad ...(1.16)$$

Each of these terms may be easily evaluated by computer.

To evaluate the likelihood for N families, we index them by i. Thus, we need to think of R_i, Y_i, X_i, P_i, R_i^*, as well as β_i^*, β_{*i}, and R_{*i}. The z's and d's defined above will also be indexed by i. For N families, the likelihood function is given by

$$\mathscr{L} = \prod_{i=1}^{N} l(R_i),$$

and the log-likelihood function by

$$\mathscr{L} = \sum_{i=1}^{N} \ln \{l(R_i)\}$$
$$= \sum_{i=1}^{N} \ln \{\tilde{\phi}(z_{1i}) \cdot \Phi[d_{1i}] + \tilde{\phi}(z_{2i})\{\Phi[\bar{d}_{2i}] - \Phi[d_{2i}]\} + \tilde{\phi}(z_{3i})\{1 - \Phi[d_{3i}]\}\}. \qquad ...(1.17)$$

Maximization of (1.17) leads to estimates of the elements of δ in $\beta = X\delta + \eta$, as well as estimates for σ_η^2 and σ_ε^2. The maximization procedure is explained in more detail in the Appendix.

We need now to return to Figure 2 and equation (1.8) and to think a bit about what our specification implies. We need also to ask what we could predict if we had estimates for δ, σ_η^2 and σ_ε^2.

Thus far we have treated the experimental payment P as being equivalent to other income Y. The two sources of income are not distinguished, although the experimental payment does not determine the proportion β of income alloted to rent, while experimental income and other exogenous variables do. But we might expect that families do not treat them symmetrically. The payment, for example, may not be treated like other income simply because of its short term nature; it lasts at most for the two-year duration of the experiment, plus one year. We experimented with a specification of the form

$$R = \beta(Y + P - k), \qquad ...(1.18)$$

for persons in the treatment group receiving unconditioned payments ("block grants"), as an alternative to the specification $R = \beta(Y + P)$. In this formulation, k is a parameter to be estimated. It may be loosely thought of as a discount factor for moving costs. Estimates based on this specification are reported below.[13]

What could we predict if we had estimates for δ and the two variances? In the first place, we would be able to predict the expected value of β for any family for whom we had measures on the characteristics indicated by X. The predicted value would be given by

$$\hat{\beta} \mid X = X\hat{\delta}. \qquad ...(1.19)$$

For given income Y, payment level P, and minimum R^*, we would predict the likelihood of any particular value of rent by using $\hat{\delta}$, $\hat{\sigma}_\eta^2$, $\hat{\sigma}_\varepsilon^2$, and equation (1.16). Recall that X includes family income.

We would also be able to predict the probability of "participation" in a plan, such as the experimental one.[14] Analogous to our estimation procedure, we would suppose that a given family faced a budget constraint like that in Figure 2. Then the probability–given X, Y, P, and R^*–of observing housing expenditure above R^* would be given by

$$\Pr(R > R^*) = \Pr\begin{Bmatrix} \beta < \beta_* & \text{and} & \varepsilon \geq R^* - \beta Y, \\ \text{or } \beta_* < \beta < \beta^* & \text{and} & \varepsilon \geq 0, \\ \text{or } \beta^* < \beta & \text{and} & \varepsilon \geq R^* - \beta(Y + P) \end{Bmatrix}. \qquad ...(1.20)$$

The second term in (1.20), for example, derives from the supposition that for β between β_* and β^*, the maximizing value of R is at R^*. For R to be greater than or equal to R^*, ε must simply be greater than or equal to zero. Similar arguments substantiate the other terms. The probability may also be written as

$$Pr\,(R > R^*) = \int_{-\infty}^{\beta_*} \int_{R^*-\beta Y}^{\infty} g(\varepsilon)h(\beta)d\varepsilon d\beta + \int_{-\beta_*}^{\beta^*} \int_{0}^{\infty} g(\varepsilon)h(\beta)d\varepsilon d\beta$$

$$+ \int_{\beta^*}^{\infty} \int_{R^*-\beta(Y+P)}^{\infty} g(\varepsilon)h(\beta)d\varepsilon d\beta. \qquad \qquad ...(1.21)$$

To estimate the probability, the bivariate integrals would be evaluated using estimated values for $\beta(X\hat{\delta})$, σ_η^2, and σ_ε^2. The necessary computations can be made very quickly.[15]

2. THE ANALYSIS OF DATA FOR CONTROL AND PER CENT OF RENT TREATMENT GROUPS

Thus far our discussion has been largely restricted to the so-called housing gap allowance plans, those that lead to discontinuous budget constraints. Our analysis was primarily directed toward the development of a procedure for obtaining "good" parameter estimates based on data for persons faced with this constraint. The relationship whose parameters we shall estimate, however, is in no way peculiar to the experimental treatment that generated the data. The functional relationship estimated by the procedure is quite general. It simply relates the proportion of a family's income that it spends on housing to family characteristics, including income.

Since the relationship we estimated is not peculiar to, or explicitly constrained by, any particular experimental plan, estimates based on data generated by different plans should be similar. One way of testing the model is to see if this is, in fact, true. We will therefore compare estimates based on the housing gap plans with those based on the per cent of rent plans, and with estimates based on data for the control group. Assume first that we only have data for control families. They presumably face a budget constraint like that in Figure 5. A family with income Y would spend an amount on rent depending on its taste

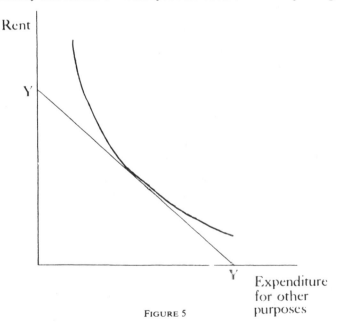

FIGURE 5

for housing, indicated by the tangency of the budget line and indifference curve in the figure, and a "maximization" error, ε. Again, we suppose that housing expenditure is given by

$$R = \beta Y + \varepsilon = X\delta \cdot Y + \eta Y + \varepsilon \qquad \qquad \ldots(2.1)$$

where

$$\beta \sim N(X\delta, \sigma_\eta^2), \qquad \varepsilon \sim N(0, \sigma_\varepsilon^2). \qquad \qquad \ldots(2.2)$$

The likelihood of any particular value of R is given simply by

$$l(R) = \frac{1}{(\sigma_\eta^2 Y^2 + \sigma_\varepsilon^2)^{\frac{1}{2}}} \phi\left[\frac{R - X\delta \cdot Y}{(\sigma_\eta^2 Y^2 + \sigma_\varepsilon^2)^{\frac{1}{2}}}\right] = \tilde{\phi}(z_1). \qquad \qquad \ldots(2.3)$$

Note that R is distributed normally with mean $X\delta \cdot Y$ and variance $\sigma_\eta^2 Y^2 + \sigma_\varepsilon^2$. Thus we can estimate the δ parameter of (2.1) by least square regression, with a correction for heteroskedasticity. A simple two-step procedure gives asymptotically efficient estimates.[16] Our results are based on this method. Or, all of the parameters could be estimated by maximum likelihood, using (1.16).

Data from the percent of rent plans can also be used after taking account of the price effect of these plans. The other plans generated no price effect. The budget constraint faced by families on these plans looks something like the solid line in Figure 6. The slope is determined by the proportion of rent that is paid under the experimental treatment, the "matching rate". We call it m. The price of a dollar's worth of housing is not 1, as for other goods, but it is $P = 1 - m$. At pre-enrolment, families on these plans face a budget constraint just like all others, something like the dashed line in Figure 6.

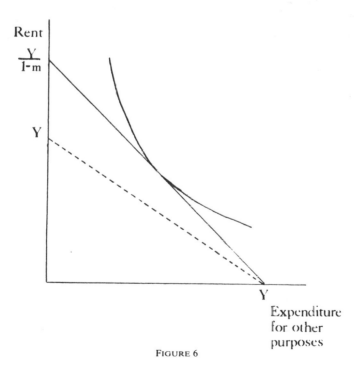

FIGURE 6

We have used a constant price elasticity form of the housing expenditure function given by,

$$R = \beta \frac{Y}{P^d},\qquad\qquad ...(2.4)$$

and estimated d along with the other parameters of the model. When P is equal to one, this formulation reduces to the housing expenditure function of equation (1.6) above. Again we suppose that the observed expenditure deviates from this presumed optimum by a random term ε. Under this formulation the elasticity with respect to price is d.[17] It equals 1 only when d is 1.[18]

There are two reasons why the price elasticity may not be one. The first is that the response of persons in the population, in general, who are faced with different prices for housing relative to other goods, may not be consistent with unit price elasticity with respect to housing expenditure. Presumably, we do not observe persons faced with "different" market housing price schedules, because they all live in the same housing "market". They do face different price schedules, though, if they are in the per cent of rent treatment group. But persons may consider these artificial price reductions to be so short-lived that they do not fully react to them during the course of the experiment. This is the second reason that a price different from unity may be observed. We, of course, cannot distinguish the two reasons. In practice, specifications implying unit price elasticity are not consistent with empirical observations.

For some purposes it is convenient to think of d as representing a "discount" factor applied to the matching rate. That is, consider the underlying long-run price elasticity to be unity, but assume that the matching rate is discounted because of its short-term nature. Families are less likely to increase their rent, which normally requires moving, because the matching rate is short-term. Even if it were not, it might take persons some time to adjust to it; that is, to move. Then d might be thought of as a short-run discount factor.[19] Thus, we might think of persons spending on housing as if they faced a budget constraint indicated by the dotted line in Figure 7, rather than the solid line as in Figure 6.

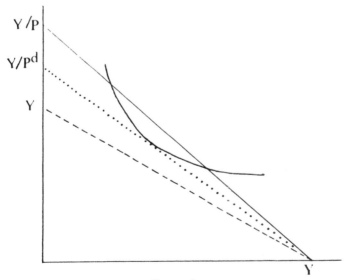

FIGURE 7

Parameter estimates for the per cent of rent treatment group were obtained using the same generalized least squares procedure that was used to obtain estimates for the control group. [In fact, the two groups were combined for purposes of estimation.]

3. EMPIRICAL RESULTS

We have obtained estimates of the parameters of equation (1.8) for housing gap families and have compared them with estimates based on controls alone–equation (2.1)–and controls plus per cent-of-rent families–equation (2.6). The experiment was conducted in two cities, Phoenix and Pittsburgh. Estimates were obtained for the two cities combined, as well as for each individually.

The proportion of rent spent on income is assumed to be a function of family income, family size, the age of the head of the household, and the race of the household head. When the two cities are combined, a dummy variable is included that takes the value 1 for persons who live in Phoenix and zero otherwise.

Results for the two cities combined are presented in Table I. Estimates based on families in Pittsburgh are presented in Table II and for Phoenix in Table III.

TABLE I

Parameter estimates (and standard errors) for Phoenix and Pittsburgh combined, by experimental treatment group

	Treatment Group			
	Housing gap families alone	Controls alone	Housing gap plus controls	Per cent of rent plus controls
Variables X determining β:				
Constant	0·4229	0·4553	0·4687	0·4583
	(0·0233)	(0·0144)	(0·0120)	(0·0109)
Family income (in hundreds)	−0·0026	−0·0025	−0·0030	−0·0027
	(0·0004)	(0·0002)	(0·0002)	(0·0001)
Family size	−0·0071	−0·0024	−0·0076	−0·0010
	(0·0030)	(0·0022)	(0·0018)	(0·0016)
Age of head > 62	−0·0066	−0·0219	−0·0277	−0·0091
	(0·0261)	(0·0138)	(0·0122)	(0·0093)
Non-white head	−0·0475	−0·0304	−0·0348	−0·0289
	(0·0155)	(0·0092)	(0·0083)	(0·0062)
Phoenix dummy	0·0260	0·0309	0·0278	0·0403
	(0·0143)	(0·0073)	(0·0072)	(0·0052)
Price variable, d	—	—	—	0·1593
				(0·0319)
Standard error of rent, σ_ε	40·55	44·16	38·43	47·18
	(01·41)		(01·07)	
Standard error of β, σ_η	0·039	0·069	0·047	0·047
	(0·009)		(0·004)	
Mean of estimated β's ($X\delta$'s)	0·2341	0·2439	0·3131	0·3183
Standard deviation of estimated β's	0·0539	0·0406	0·0598	0·0683
Sample size	555	637	1192	1384

In general, the estimates based on data for different treatment groups correspond very closely with one another. The primary parameters are measured quite precisely. In particular, the constant term and the coefficient on income, the most important parameters determining β, and the two standard errors (one for the random "maximization" term ε

TABLE II

Parameter estimates (and standard errors) for Pittsburgh, by experimental treatment group

	Treatment group			
	Housing gap families alone	Controls alone	Housing gap plus controls	Per cent of rent plus controls
Variables X determining β:				
Constant	0·4513	0·5081	0·4448	0·4376
	(0·0294)	(0·0182)	(0·0134)	(0·0126)
Family income (in hundreds)	−0·0032	−0·0033	−0·0029	−0·0027
	(0·0006)	(0·0003)	(0·0003)	(0·0002)
Family size	−0·0078	−0·0021	−0·0035	−0·0024
	(0·0050)	(0·0039)	(0·0028)	(0·0020)
Age of head >62	−0·0039	−0·0009	−0·0006	−0·0149
	(0·0235)	(0·0163)	(0·0134)	(0·0108)
Non-white head	−0·0198	−0·0239	−0·0261	−0·0165
	(0·0196)	(0·0138)	(0·0109)	(0·0077)
Pheonix dummy	—	—	—	—
Price variable, d	—	—	—	0·1434
				(0·0401)
Standard error of rent, σ_ε	35·10	41·24	33·18	40·62
	(02·03)		(1·51)	
Standard error of β, σ_η	0·036	0·080	0·0476	0·041
	(0·011)		(0·0051)	
Mean of estimated β's ($X\delta$'s)	0·3007	0·3183	0·3057	0·3240
Standard deviation of estimated β's	0·0580	0·0784	0·0570	0·0639
Sample size	313	337	650	765

and the other for the random "taste" term η) are measured with considerable precision. The coefficients on family size and age of the household head, although always negative, are measured with much less precision, and thus their estimated values vary more among the samples. The estimates are often not significantly different from zero. None of the signs or magnitudes of the variables is inconsistent with prior expectations, and all appear to be internally consistent and consistent with known average values in the sample.

Consider first the estimates in Table I for the housing gap treatment groups in both cities combined. The standard error of rent–the standard error of ε in equation (1.8) is estimated to be 40·55. The standard error of β–the standard error of η in equation (1.8), and representing the variation in "taste" for housing given any set of exogenous variables X–is estimated at 0·039. This may be compared with the mean of the estimated β's for the sample of 0·284 and their sample standard deviation of 0·054. The range in estimated β's is from 0·1245 to 0·3773, close to the range of the observed ratios of housing expenditure to income. Thus, the model does seem to capture the primary determinants of the proportion of family income that is allocated to rent.

Of the coefficients on the variables determining β, the constant term as well as the coefficients on income and the variable identifying families with non-white heads are measured with considerable precision. In particular, the coefficient on income is negative and measured quite precisely. It indicates that an increase in family income of 1000 dollars would reduce the proportion of income spent on housing by about 2·6 per cent. Families with non-white heads are estimated to spend about 4·8 per cent less on housing than families headed by whites. An increase in family size is estimated to reduce the proportion of family income going to housing. Apparently, the increase in "need" for other goods

TABLE III

Parameter estimates (and standard errors) for Phoenix, by experimental treatment group

	Treatment group			
	Housing gap families alone	Controls alone	Housing gap plus controls	Per cent of rent plus controls
Variables X determining β:				
Constant	0·3992	0·5733	0·5446	0·5254
	(0·0335)	(0·0233)	(0·0197)	(0·0186)
Family income (in hundreds)	−0·0020	−0·0032	−0·0034	−0·0028
	(0·0005)	(0·0002)	(0·0003)	(0·0002)
Family size	−0·0051	−0·0100	−0·0127	−0·0038
	(0·0033)	(0·0032)	(0·0027)	(0·0025)
Age of head > 62	−0·0182	−0·0861	−0·0753	−0·0366
	(0·0457)	(0·0216)	(0·0236)	(0·0158)
Non-white head	−0·0823	−0·0314	−0·0405	−0·0393
	(0·0244)	(0·0131)	(0·0131)	(0·0099)
Phoenix dummy	—	—	—	—
Price variable, d	—	—	—	0·1748
				(0·0504)
Standard error of rent, σ_r	47·15	45·42	44·80	53·90
	(02·34)		(01·68)	
Standard error of β, σ_n	0·028	0·0519	0·038	0·0412
	(0·012)		(0·007)	
Mean of estimated β's ($X\delta$'s)	0·2641	0·3401	0·3224	0·3534
Standard deviation of estimated β's	0·0537	0·0725	0·0660	0·0751
Sample size	242	300	542	619

outweighs the increase in the "need" for housing. Families headed by persons over 62 appear to spend about the same proportion of their income on housing as other families. The relevant coefficient is slightly negative, but measured very imprecisely.

Comparison of the estimates based on the housing gap treatment group with those based on controls and the per cent of rent groups reveals very close correspondence among them. In particular, the estimates of the constant terms and the coefficients on income are remarkably similar across the sample groups. The estimated non-white head effects are also of comparable orders of magnitude across the groups, although the estimates differ somewhat. The estimated effects of family size are all negative, but they vary substantially from group to group and are not always significantly different from zero. The age of the head of the family, if greater than 62, is estimated for each group to have a negative effect on housing expenditure, but the effect is not always significantly different from zero. Finally, families in Phoenix are estimated to spend about 3 or 4 per cent more of their income on housing than families in Pittsburgh.[20]

The elasticity of housing expenditure with respect to the price variable–or the "discount factor" applied to reductions in the price of housing–for the per cent of rent group is estimated to be −0.16. (See equation (2.4).) This may be compared to an income elasticity that according to our per cent of rent group estimates is 0·58 for a white family in Pittsburgh with a head less than 62 years old and with family income of $5000. It would be 0·75 at income equal to $3000 and 0·41 at $7000.[21] Note that the income elasticities are based primarily on "permanent" current income, while the price elasticities depend on families' response to temporary decreases in price.

The results for Pittsburgh in Table II again reveal close correspondence among the parameter estimates for the different treatment groups. The exceptions are the estimated coefficients on family size and the age of the family head. But none of them is significantly different from zero.

The estimates for Phoenix are also of the same order of magnitude for the different groups; but the coefficients on the constant term and family income are considerably smaller for the housing gap group than for the others, the control group in particular. The non-white head estimated effect is larger for the housing gap group. The mean of the estimated β's is also lower for the housing gap group, presumably because of the lower coefficient estimates.

We mentioned above the possibility that the payment under the housing gap treatment may be "discounted". That is, families may not adjust their rent because of it as much as they would if it were considered to be "permanent" income or permanent potential income. This may apply both to families who receive the payment without adjusting their rent and to those who could only receive the payment if they spent more on housing. This suggests that we may need to allow explicitly for the payment to be treated unlike income. Note that if this effect is strong but not explicitly allowed for in the estimation procedure, lower coefficients on the variables determining β would tend to compensate for it. This may be one reason for the lower estimates for the housing gap families in Phoenix.

For one treatment group we did experiment with a specification that allows families to respond to the payment as if it were less than its actual value. The specification we estimated was of the form

$$R = \beta(Y + P - k), \qquad \qquad ...(3.1)$$

TABLE IV

Parameter estimates with a discount for "moving" for controls and block grant treatment groups, by city

	Phoenix		Pittsburgh	
	Without "moving" parameter	With "moving" parameter	Without "moving" parameter	With "moving" parameter
Variables X determining β:				
Constant	0·5727	0·5786	0·3980	0·4036
	0·0216)	(0·0227)	(0·0147)	(0·0155)
Family income (in hundreds)	−0·0032	−0·0033	−0·0021	−0·0021
	(0·0002)	(0·0002)	(0·0002)	(0·0002)
Family size	−0·0020	−0·0100	0·0026	0·0025
	(0·0029)	(0·0029)	(0·0028)	(0·0028)
Age of head > 62	−0·0881	−0·0889	0·0242	0·0258
	0·0197)	(0·0198)	(0·0146)	(0·0149)
Non-white head	−0·0330	−0·0327	−0·0277	−0·0273
	(0·0119)	(0·0120)	(0·0111)	(0·0111)
Phoenix dummy	—	—	—	—
Discount for "moving"	—	19·17	—	20·12
		(06·92)		(05·57)
Standard error of rent, σ_ε	45·51	45·36	40·39	40·27
Standard error of β, σ_η	0·0382	0·0407	0·042	0·0524
Mean of estimated β's ($X\delta$'s)	0·3414	0·3292	0·3016	0·3146
Standard deviation of estimated β's	0·0742	0·0704	0·0511	0·0599
Sample size	346	346	406	406

where k is a parameter to be estimated. It is straightforward to estimate it using the control group together with the treatment group that received a flat grant independent of housing expenditure.

The variable k may be thought of as a discount factor for moving expense. If there were no moving expense or other transaction cost associated with adjusting rent, response to P would presumably be stronger.[22] In this specification, the variable associated with k takes the value 1 if the family receives a payment and is zero otherwise–i.e. for control families. This "transaction" or "moving" cost parameter is estimated to be 20·12 in Pittsburgh and 19·17 in Phoenix. (Estimates of the other parameters are shown in Table IV. The table also contains estimates based on a specification excluding the parameter k. Adding k does not alter the other estimates substantially.) These numbers pertain to monthly income. Over the three years that persons receive payments, they imply that families receiving block grants behaved on the average "as if" their incomes were $724 less in Pittsburgh and $690 less in Phoenix than they actually were.

4. SOME EXTENSIONS

Assume that the parameters of the model have been estimated for the per cent of rent treatment group. It may be informative to demonstrate how we would predict housing expenditure by persons under a plan not represented among the experimental ones. Consider, for example, a "closed-end" matching scheme like that depicted in Figure 8. The price of an additional dollar's worth of housing is $P = 1 - m$ until R^* is spent on housing. If R^* or more is spent, each additional dollar's worth of housing costs one dollar; the price is 1. The budget constraint implied by this plan is depicted by the solid line in Figure 8.

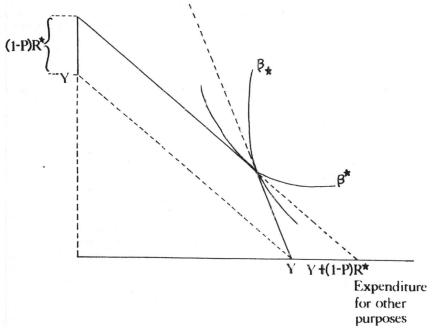

FIGURE 8

A family with taste parameter β_* for housing would spend R^* for rent if faced with an extended–by the dashed line–budget constraint like the lower part of the heavy line in Figure 8. If the family had taste parameter β^*, it would spend R^* when faced with an extended budget constraint with slope equal to that of the upper portion of the one in the figure. Families with $\beta < \beta_*$ would prefer to spend an amount less than R^* given by, $R = \beta Y / P^d$. Persons with $\beta > \beta^*$ would prefer to spend more than R^*, as if they received a flat payment equal to $(1 - P)R^*$. Their preferred expenditure would be given by $R = \beta[Y + (1 - P)R^*]$. Families with β between β_* and β^* would spend R^*.[23] We can see that $B^* = R^* / (Y + (1 - P)R^*)$.

Assuming the same stochastic specification as above, we have that

$$R = \beta \cdot \frac{Y}{P^d} + \varepsilon = X\delta \cdot \frac{Y}{P^d} + \eta \frac{Y}{P^d} + \varepsilon, \quad \text{for } \beta < \beta_*;$$

and

$$R = \beta[Y + (1 - P)R^*] + \varepsilon = X\delta \cdot [Y + (1 - P)R^*] + \eta[Y + (1 - P)R^*] + \varepsilon, \quad \text{for } \beta > \beta^*.$$

The likelihood of observing any particular value of R is now given by

$$l(R) = \Pr \left\{ \begin{array}{ll} \beta < \beta_* & \text{and} \quad \varepsilon = R - \beta \dfrac{Y}{P^d}, \\ \text{or } \beta_* < \beta < \beta^* & \text{and} \quad \varepsilon = R - R^*, \\ \text{or } \beta^* < \beta & \text{and} \quad \varepsilon = R - \beta[Y + (1 - P)R^*] \end{array} \right\}. \quad \ldots(4.1)$$

For values of β between β_* and β^*, the maximizing value of R is at R^*. This gives rise to the second term in (4.1). Similar arguments can be made for the first and third terms. Equation (4.1) can be written like similar expressions above in terms of normal density and distribution functions, which in turn could be evaluated by using estimated values for β, d, σ_m^2, and σ_ε^2. These are, of course, the estimates that we obtain from using data from the per cent of rent experimental plan.

5. SUMMARY

We have proposed a rather general method for obtaining empirical estimates based on observations of individuals who face non-linear or discontinuous budget constraints. The methodology rests on the assumption that the behavioural model to be estimated should be specified so as to be consistent with empirical observations. Then a utility function corresponding to this behavioural equation can be incorporated into the analysis and used to bridge the gap between estimation and prediction when individuals face linear budget constraints and comparable calculations when budget constraints are non-linear.

The suggested methodology has been used to estimate housing expenditure functions based on several different sets of data corresponding to different treatment groups in the Housing Demand Experiment. The different treatment groups imply different budget constraints. One of the housing gap plans in particular implies a discontinuous budget constraint. Our procedure was directed primarily to the analysis of data generated under this plan. The estimates based on the different treatment plans were surprisingly close. This similarity provides strong support for our proposed methodology. Our estimates imply an elasticity of housing expenditure with respect to income of about 0·6 at the average family income of persons in our sample. The elasticity of expenditure with respect to treatment price–one minus the per cent of rent matching rate–was estimated to be −0·16. The price elasticity reflects short term change in housing expenditure during the first year of the experiment, whereas the income elasticity reflects housing expenditures associated with more permanent levels of income.

APPENDIX ON ESTIMATION

Maximum likelihood parameter estimates were obtained using the algorithm suggested by Berndt, Hall, Hall, and Hausman (1974). It requires only the use of first derivatives of the likelihood function. For convenience, we will reproduce a few of the results from the text and then present the derivatives with respect to the parameters of the model.

The log-likelihood function is of the form

$$\mathcal{L} = \sum_i \ln \left[l(R_i) \right]. \qquad \qquad \text{...(A.1)}$$

The terms $l(R_i)$–equation (1.11) in the text–may be written as

$$
\begin{aligned}
(R_i) = &\frac{1}{\sqrt{\sigma_n^2 Y_i^2 + \sigma_\varepsilon^2}} \phi\left(\frac{R_i - X_i \delta \cdot Y_i}{\sqrt{\sigma_n^2 Y_i^2 + \sigma_\varepsilon^2}} \right) \\
&\times \Phi \left[\frac{\beta_{*i} - X_i\delta - \dfrac{\sigma_n^2 Y_i}{\sigma_n^2 Y_i^2 + \sigma_\varepsilon^2}(R_i - X_i\delta \cdot Y_i)}{\dfrac{(\sigma_\varepsilon^2 \sigma_n^2)^{\frac{1}{2}}}{(\sigma_n^2 Y_i^2 + \sigma_\varepsilon^2)^{\frac{1}{2}}}} \right] \\
&+ \frac{1}{\sigma_\varepsilon^2} \phi\left(\frac{R_i - \beta_i^*(Y_i + P_i)}{(\sigma_\varepsilon^2)} \right) \left\{ \Phi\left[\frac{\beta_i^* - X_i\delta}{(\sigma_n^2)^{\frac{1}{2}}} \right] - \Phi\left[\frac{\beta_{*i} - X_i\delta}{(\sigma_n^2)^{\frac{1}{2}}} \right] \right\} \\
&+ \frac{1}{(\sigma_n^2(Y_i + P_i)^2 + \sigma_\varepsilon^2)^{\frac{1}{2}}} \phi\left(\frac{R_i - X_i\delta(Y_i + P_i)}{(\sigma_n^2(Y_i + P_i)^2 + \sigma_\varepsilon^2)^{\frac{1}{2}}} \right) \\
&\times 1 - \Phi\left[\frac{\beta_i^* - X_i\delta - \dfrac{\sigma_n^2(Y_i + P_i)}{\sigma_n^2(Y_i + P_i)^2 + \sigma_\varepsilon^2}(R_i - X_i\delta(Y_i + P_i))}{\dfrac{(\sigma_\varepsilon^2 \sigma_n^2)^{\frac{1}{2}}}{(\sigma_n^2(Y_i + P_i)^2 + \sigma_\varepsilon^2)^{\frac{1}{2}}}} \right] \qquad \text{...(A.2)}
\end{aligned}
$$

The first, second, and third terms in (A.2) come from equations (1.13), (1.14), and (1.15) respectively, in the text. Using the same definitions as in the text, we can write (A.2) succinctly as

$$l(R) = \tilde{\phi}(Z_{1i})\Phi[d_{1i}] + \tilde{\phi}(Z_{2i})\{\Phi[\bar{d}_{2i}] - \Phi[\underline{d}_{2i}]\} + \tilde{\phi}(Z_{3i})\{1 - \Phi[d_{3i}]\}. \qquad \text{...(A.3)}$$

In fact, a comparison of (A.3) and (A.4) may be used to define the Z's and d's in (A.3). It is convenient to rewrite d_{1i} as

$$d_{1i} = \frac{\beta_{*i}(\sigma_n^2 Y_i^2 + \sigma_\varepsilon^2) - \sigma_n^2 Y_i R_i - \sigma_\varepsilon^2 X_i\delta}{(\sigma_\varepsilon^2 \sigma_n^2)^{\frac{1}{2}}(\sigma_\beta^2 Y_i^2 + \sigma_\varepsilon^2)^{\frac{1}{2}}}, \qquad \text{...(A.4)}$$

and to rewrite d_{3i} analogously. Also let $\sigma_n^2 Y_i^2 + \sigma_\varepsilon^2 = \sigma_y^2$ and $\sigma_n^2(Y_i + P_i)^2 + \sigma_\varepsilon^2 = \sigma_{\tilde{y}}^2$.

The derivatives are then given by

$$
\begin{aligned}
\frac{\partial \mathcal{L}}{\partial \delta_j} = \sum_{i=1}^N \frac{1}{l(R_i)} \Bigg\{ &\frac{\tilde{\phi}(Z_{1i})\Phi(d_{1i})X_{ij}Y_i}{\sqrt{\sigma_y^2}} + \frac{\tilde{\phi}(Z_{1i})\phi(d_1)X_{ij}\sigma_\varepsilon^2}{\sqrt{\sigma_y^2}\sqrt{\sigma_\varepsilon^2 \sigma_n^2}} \\
&+ \tilde{\phi}(Z_{2i})\left[-\frac{\phi(\bar{d}_{2i})X_{ij}}{\sqrt{\sigma_n^2}} + \frac{\phi(\underline{d}_{2i})X_{ij}}{\sqrt{\sigma_n^2}} \right] + \frac{\tilde{\phi}(Z_{3i})(1 - \Phi[d_{3i}])X_{ij}(Y_i + P_i)}{\sqrt{\sigma_{\tilde{y}}^2}} \\
&- \frac{\tilde{\phi}(Z_{3i})\phi(d_{3i})X_{ij}\sigma_\varepsilon^2}{\sqrt{\sigma_{\tilde{y}}^2}\sqrt{\sigma_\varepsilon^2 \sigma_n^2}} \Bigg\}. \qquad \text{...(A.5)}
\end{aligned}
$$

$$\frac{\partial \mathcal{L}}{\partial \sigma_\varepsilon^2} = \sum_{i=1}^N \frac{1}{l(R_i)} \left\{ \tilde{\phi}(Z_{1i}) \Phi[d_{1i}](Z_{1i}^2 - 1) \frac{1}{2\sigma_v^2} \right.$$

$$+ \tilde{\phi}(Z_{1i}) \phi(d_{1i}) \left[\frac{\beta_* - X_i \delta}{(\sigma_\varepsilon^2 \sigma_n^2)^{\frac{1}{2}} (\sigma_v^2)^{\frac{1}{2}}} - \frac{d_{1i}}{2} \left(\frac{1}{\sigma_\varepsilon^2} + \frac{1}{\sigma_v^2} \right) \right]$$

$$+ \tilde{\phi}(Z_{2i}) [\Phi[\bar{d}_{2i}] - \Phi[\underline{d}_{2i}]](Z_{2i}^2 - 1) \frac{1}{2\sigma_\varepsilon^2} + \tilde{\phi}(Z_{3i})[1 - \Phi[d_{3i}]](Z_{3i}^2 - 1) \frac{1}{2\sigma_{\tilde{y}}^2}$$

$$\left. - \tilde{\phi}(Z_{3i}) \cdot \phi(d_{3i}) \left[\frac{\beta_{*i} - X_i \delta}{(\sigma_\varepsilon^2 \sigma_n^2)^{\frac{1}{2}} (\sigma_{\tilde{y}}^2)^{\frac{1}{2}}} - \frac{d_{3i}}{2} \left(\frac{1}{\sigma_\varepsilon^2} + \frac{1}{\sigma_{\tilde{y}}^2} \right) \right] \right\} \qquad \ldots(A.6)$$

$$\frac{\partial \mathcal{L}}{\partial \sigma_n^2} = \sum_{i=1}^N \frac{1}{l(R_i)} \left\{ \tilde{\phi}(Z_{1i}) \Phi[d_{1i}](Z_{1i}^2 - 1) \frac{Y_i^2}{2\sigma_v^2} \right.$$

$$+ \tilde{\phi}(Z_{1i}) \phi(d_{1i}) \left[\frac{\beta_{*i} Y_i^2 - R_i Y_i}{\sqrt{\sigma_\varepsilon^2 \sigma_n^2} \sqrt{\sigma_v^2}} - \frac{d_{1i}}{2} \left(\frac{1}{\sigma_n^2} + \frac{Y_i^2}{\sigma_v^2} \right) \right]$$

$$+ \tilde{\phi}(Z_{2i}) \left[-\phi(\bar{d}_{2i}) \frac{\bar{d}_{2i}}{2\sigma_n^2} + \phi(\underline{d}_{2i}) \frac{d_{2i}}{2\sigma_n^2} \right] + \tilde{\phi}(Z_{3i})(1 - \Phi[d_{3i}])(Z_{3i}^2 - 1) \frac{(Y_i + P_i)^2}{2\sigma_{\tilde{y}}^2}$$

$$\left. - \tilde{\phi}(Z_{3i}) \cdot \phi(d_{3i}) \left[\frac{\beta_i^*(Y_i + P_i)^2 - R_i(Y_i + P_i)}{\sqrt{\sigma_\varepsilon^2 \sigma_n^2} \sqrt{\sigma_{\tilde{y}}^2}} - \frac{d_{3i}}{2} \left(\frac{1}{\sigma_n^2} + \frac{(Y_i + P_i)^2}{\sigma_{\tilde{y}}^2} \right) \right] \right\} \qquad \ldots(A.7)$$

Financial support for this research was provided by the US Department of Housing and Urban Development under contract H-2040R to Abt Associates Inc., and by Prime Grant SOC 76-81989 from the National Science Foundation. We wish to thank Peter Diamond, Joe Friedman, Larry Lau, Mitch Polinsky, Paul Samuelson, and a referee for their comments on an earlier draft of this paper.

NOTES

1. Subsequent to this paper an analysis of labour supply under the non-linear budget constraints imposed by the Gary Income Maintenance Experiment was done by Burtless and Hausman (1978).

2. For a detailed description of relevant parts of the Experiment, see Friedman and Kennedy (1977).

3. The paper concentrates on a methodology for estimation when faced with a situation like the housing gap plan. Our results, however, suggest that estimates based on the other plans could be used for prediction under a housing gap (or other) plan, making use of the ideas that form the basis of our methodology.

4. For a detailed specification of a procedure to handle it empirically see Wise (1977b).

5. See Wise (1977a).

6. The payment is given by $P = aC^* - bY$, where C^* is a basic payment level varying with family size and site, and a and b depend on the treatment group to which the family is assigned. The values of a are 0·8, 1 and 1·2; those of b are 0·15, 0·25 and 0·35. See Friedman and Kennedy (1977) for details.

Assignment to treatment versus control groups was random. Within the treatment groups, assignment to a particular plan depended in part on family income; but was not made on the basis of observed rent. Assignment was exogenous with respect to rent, the variable that we shall treat as endogenous.

Of those persons assigned to any housing gap plan, approximately 25 per cent of those in Pittsburgh moved during the first year of the experiment; in Phoenix, about 45 per cent moved. This provides some empirical verification that the relationships between rent and family characteristics, that we shall describe below, are not due to assignment rules.

7. The housing gap plans depicted in Figures 1 and 3 pertain to the minimum rent plans referred to in Section 1.1 as the third basic type of subsidy.

8. The V function also depends on prices, but we suppress the arguments since all persons in our sample are presumed to face the same housing price schedule.

9. Since we observe neither prices nor quantities for other commodities, it is impossible to estimate all of the α_i. But if in a given city all consumers face approximately the same prices, the conditions for the composite commodity theorem hold. Thus β which is taken to be the tradeoff between housing expenditure and other goods is the most that can be estimated.

10. This derivation assumes that p is constant for as much housing of quality n as person j purchases.

11. That is, $V(\beta_*, R^*) = (Y + P - R^*)^{1-\beta_*}(R^*)^{\beta_*} = (Y - R_*)^{1-\beta_*}(R_*)^{\beta_*} = V(\beta_*, R_*)$. A straightforward iterative technique allows the solution of this equation for β_* in terms of Y, P, and R^*–all observed variables. We need to do this to derive estimates as described below. In fact, there is a second pair of alternative values to R_* and β_* which is consistent with such a relationship. There is a value of $\beta > \beta^*$ defining an indifference curve that would be tangent to the lower segment of the budget constraint at a point above R^* and would also pass through the point where the curve represented by β^* is tangent to the upper segment.

12. Of the 581 families who were in one of the minimum rent plans one year after enrolment in the experiment, 57 per cent were participating at that time.

13. The two could also be distinguished by defining $\tilde{Y} = Y + \lambda P$, where λ may be presumed to be between 0 and 1, and may be interpreted as a "discount" factor applied to the payment P. Then we would have, $R = X\delta(Y + \lambda P) + \eta(Y + \lambda P) + \varepsilon$, when referring to values of R on the upper portion of the budget constraint. In determining housing expenditure, the family behaves as if its income were $Y + \lambda P$–or could be, if it now spends less than R^*–instead of $Y + P$. In this case, λ would be estimated along with the other parameters of the model.

A considerably more precise and rigorous treatment of this problem follows from explicit treatment of the decision to move or not and the joint estimation of the probability of moving along with the expenditure equation. Such a specification is detailed in Wise (1977b). It also yields "long-run" estimates of the effect of changes in exogenous variables.

14. "Participation" is taken to mean that a family spends more than R^* on housing and thus receives the payment P. See Note 12.

15. We will not carry out these computations based on the data used in this paper, but we will do so in later work using data based on the entire duration of the experiment.

16. Equation (2.1) is first estimated to obtain residuals e. Then σ_n^2 and σ_r^2 are estimated by a regression of e^2 on Y^2. The second step estimates (2.1) after using $\hat{\sigma}_n^2 Y^2$ and $\hat{\sigma}_e^2$ to make a correction for heteroskedasticity.

17. The elasticity of housing "quantity" with respect to price is $d - 1$.

18. Note that it is not necessary to consider a utility function in order to predict housing expenditure in this case because the implied budget constraint is linear. A direct utility function does not exist for this expenditure function, except in the special case of $P = 1$. But the indirect utility function does. As d goes to 1, this indirect function approaches the indirect function corresponding to the expenditure function in (1.6).

19. It is probably not correct to think of adjusting rent over time. It is more likely that persons adjust in one step, but only when they move. It may take some time to move, and whether a family moves or not should depend both on the degree of "disequilibrium" and on the time out of equilibrium, and on the expected duration of the disequilibrium–how long the price decrease is expected to last. Thus, the coefficient d is likely to result primarily from the proportion of persons who move versus those who don't. This is somewhat different from thinking of d as depending on expenditure effects that are basically continuous and are observed for most persons.

20. This difference may reflect different housing price schedules as well as differences in climate and other city characteristics.

21. These income elasticities correspond rather closely with those estimated by Polinsky and Ellwood (1977).

22. Transaction cost associated with moving may include such considerations as changing neighbourhoods and making new friends or finding new shopping areas, etc.

23. We can see this by noting that if β is such that $\beta Y / P^d = R^*$, then if income is given by $Y + (1 - P)R^*$, $R = \beta[Y + (1 - P)R^*]$ would be less than R^*. It would equal $R = R^*[P^d + P^c(1 - P)(R^*/Y)]$. Since $(R^*/Y) < 1$, this expression would be less than one for $P < 1$.

REFERENCES

BERNDT, E. K., HALL, B. H., HALL, R. E. and HAUSMAN, J. A. (1974), "Estimation and Inference in Nonlinear Structural Models", *Annals of Economic and Social Measurement*, 653–665.

BURTLESS, G. and HAUSMAN, J. (1978), "The Effect of Taxes on Labor Supply: Evaluating the Gary NIT Experiment", *Journal of Political Economy*.

FISHER, F. M. and SHELL, K. (1967), "Taste and Quality Change in the Pure Theory of the True Cost of Living Index", in Wolfe, J. F. (ed.) *Value, Capital and Growth: Papers in Honour of Sir John Hicks* 97–138 (Edinburgh).

FRIEDMAN, J. and KENNEDY, S. D. (1977), "Housing Expenditures and Quality, Part II; Draft Report on Housing Expenditures under a Housing Gap Housing Allowance", (Abt Associates Inc.).

HAUSMAN, J. A. and WISE, D. A. (1978), "A Conditional Probit Model for Qualitative Choice", *Econometrica*, **46**.

MUELLBAUER, J. (1975), "The Cost of Living and Taste and Quality Change", *Journal of Economic Theory*, **10**, 269–283.

POLINSKY, A. M. and ELLWOOD, D. T. (1977), "An Empirical Reconciliation of Micro and Grouped Estimates of the Demand for Housing", Harvard Institute of Economic Research, Discussion Paper Number 567.

WISE, D. A. (1977a), "Memorandum: Housing Demand, Discontinuous Budget Constraints, and Estimation" (mimeograph).

WISE, D. A. (1977b), "Memorandum: Moving and the Housing Demand Experiment" (mimeograph).

The Seattle and Denver Income Maintenance Experiments, as well as the rural, Gary, and New Jersey experiments, were designed to test the effects of a negative income tax program on labor supply. The scope of these studies expanded, however, to incorporate how the guaranteed income benefits were spent by the poor—a major policy concern in its own right. Thus, the analysis by Ohls and that following by Kaluzny complement the Experimental Housing Allowance Program (EHAP) reported on in the previous chapters in this section. They confirm certain analytical results of the EHAP studies and allow for a more informed policy choice between subsidies-in-kind and unconstrained cash payments as a means of enhancing the quality and quantity of housing for the poor.

The present study continues our theme by dealing specifically with measurement and bias problems associated with quasiexperimental designs. Thus in SIME/DIME, the allocation of households to treatment status was based on an assignment model that incorporated preexperimental income in the assignment to program treatment. A nontrivial consequence is that experimental effects cannot be measured simply by comparing mean values between experimentals and controls. (Note the discussion above by Morris et al. which argues forcefully for not selecting a sample on an endogenous variable.) Next, the sample was truncated in that only households in low-income neighborhoods with relatively poor housing were screened for sample inclusion. Households living in these areas may have a lower than average taste for housing. A major concern of these analyses is that the housing consumption responses to the net experimental income benefit is relatively low. This could be due to the selection method, although it is at least true that the results reported in this section are consistent with one another.

While Ohls and Kaluzny are concerned with identical measurement and data problems, their approach to them differs somewhat. The model used by each expresses housing consumption as a function of permanent household income, a vector of household demographic variables, and a treatment variable. Ohls calibrates permanent, after-tax income as the three-year, nonexperimental household disposable income, while Kaluzny relies on a different measure. In addition to the measures of rental and housing prices used by Kaluzny, Ohls employs an hedonic quality index independent of actual rents and housing prices and thereby provides a direct measure of housing quality. Finally, an index composed of fourteen standard housing criteria is used.

The models analyzed are demand equations that show the direct effects of the experimental payments on housing consumption. As with the analysis by Kaluzny, however, two indirect effects due to participation in the experiment may have led to biases in the experimental effect estimates. First, nonexperimental transfer income was reduced. Second, work effort was reduced and, hence, earned income. Ohls corrects for both these effects in his analysis. For instance, correction for the first effect suggests that the experimental transfer payments replaced 62% of pre-experimental transfer income. This factor was then used to adjust downward the experimental effect on housing consumption. The adjustment for reduced work effort also reduces the net experimental effect on housing consumption. In some cases, however, these two adjustments result in a net negative experimental effect on the demand for housing.

Since total income generally increased and housing is a normal good—more of it is consumed as income rises—these adjusted negative results are counterintuitive, and Ohls notes that they are unreliable. Possible causes are sampling error, or, more significantly, unknown biases in the relatively complex experimental assignment model. In any case, the net effects of the experiment on housing consumption are smaller than the gross effects.

Overall, there were statistically significant experimental effects on the consumption of rental housing. The estimated elasticity of housing demand with respect to experimental transfer payments ranged from .2 to .6—a ten% increase in transfer payments resulting in a 2% to 6% increase in housing consumption. The results were similar for the two principle measures of housing consumption—market prices and the hedonic index. And they were consistent for both Denver and Seattle. But the estimated experimental effects on home ownership were not statistically significant, even though combined analysis of the rental and home ownership samples in Denver resulted in higher estimated experimental effects than the analysis of each sample separately. This was likely due to participants switching from rental to home ownership. Finally, results based on an additional analysis of households enrolled in the experiment for five years indicate that the overall results were not sensitive to the timing of the data collection.

The Demand for Housing Under a Negative Income Tax

James C. Ohls

This paper examines the effects of income transfer payments on recipients' housing consumption. The data for the analysis were drawn from the Seattle and Denver Income Maintenance Experiments (SIME/DIME) and are of interest for at least two reasons. First, the way in which transfer payments received under various redistribution programs are spent is of considerable importance in assessing how effective alternative social welfare programs are in meeting the needs of the poor. Second, the SIME/DIME results provide evidence about the demand for housing among low income households. These data can be useful in developing efficient low income housing policies.

An important conclusion of the analysis reported below is that the income maintenance payments increased the average housing consumption of participants in the experimental program. The evidence shows that housing consumption increased within the rental sector and also that, at least in Denver, some households upgraded their housing by switching from the rental to the owner-occupant sector of the housing market.

Author's Note: The analysis was funded by the U.S. Department of Health, Education and Welfare and the U.S. Department of Housing and Urban Development under contracts with the Washington State Department of Health and Welfare and the Colorado State Department of Social Services. Thanks are due to Gary Burtless, David Horner, Richard Kaluzny, Charles Metcalf, Edgar Olsen, Cynthia Thomas, and Dan Weinberg for helpful comments, and to Asha Gangal who provided outstanding programming support. An earlier version of parts of the analysis in this paper was presented at a HUD-sponsored conference in March, 1979. (See Ohls, 1979.)

From James C. Ohls, "The Demand for Housing Under a Negative Income Tax." Unpublished manuscript, 1980.

Although the observed experimental effects are statistically significant, they are nevertheless relatively small. In particular, none of the
estimated income elasticities of demand are greater than .6, most are
below .4, and some are lower than .2. These estimates imply that a
1 percent change in income, whether from experimental payments or from some
other source, can be expected to increase housing consumption by, at most,
six-tenths of one percentage point. Consequently, if there is a specific
policy interest in increasing the housing consumption of low-income
families, income maintenance payments of the type made by the SIME/DIME
programs may not be cost effective. This paper presents a brief description
of the experimental programs, discusses the methodology used in the study,
and presents the results of the analysis.

OVERVIEW OF THE EXPERIMENTS

The Seattle and Denver experiments were undertaken in the early 1970s by
the U.S. Department of Health, Education and Welfare to test the effects of
a negative income tax [1]. Households were potentially eligible for
participation in SIME/DIME if their income fell below certain levels.
Households in low income neighborhoods were interviewed to gain information
on several criteria. To be eligible, a family had to have at least two
members which included either an adult and a dependent child or a married
couple. The head of the family (the male head, if present) had to be
between eighteen and fifty-eight years of age. One household head (again
the male, if present) had to be physically capable of employment. Blacks,
Chicanos, and single-headed families were oversampled.

Households that passed the screening tests were stratified on the basis
of race, marital status, and pre-experimental income and were assigned to
a financial treatment. Allocation to experimental or control status was
based on an assignment model designed to produce a cost effective allocation of households for analysis of labor supply responses. A consequence
of this sample assignment technique is that the effects of the experimental
treatments cannot be determined simply by comparing mean values between
experimentals and controls.

The various SIME/DIME financial treatments provided a complex set of
incentives for the experimental households. Eighty-four different
combinations of treatments were used in the combined Denver and Seattle
samples, including the households assigned to control status. The
variations included three basic support levels ($3,800; $4,800; and $5,600)
adjusted for family size and by whether the eligible family was the primary
or secondary unit in the household. These support levels were adjusted for
inflation on a quarterly basis. Families were initially assigned to the
program for three or five years of participation. A small group of control

families scheduled to be discontinued after three years and some three-year experimental families were later enrolled as twenty-year experimental families.

Varying tax rates on earnings were also used. Constant tax rates were set at levels of 50 percent and 70 percent. For some households, a tax rate that declined as earnings increased was used. Under this system, initial tax rates were set at 70 percent and 80 percent, declining at an average of 2.5 percent for every $1,000 in earnings. Other features of the payment structure included the taxation of grant income from other programs at 100 percent, and reimbursement of income-based taxes, including Social Security and income taxes.

The sample has at least one limitation for an analysis of housing consumption. All the households screened for eligibility were in low income neighborhoods with relatively poor housing. Households living in these areas may have had a lower than average taste for housing. Consequently, their reponses to the experiment may have been weaker than those of other low income families living in better neighborhoods [2]. The effects, if any, of this sample selection method cannot be fully determined. However, because the income elasticities estimated in this study are in the general range of those found in other works, there is evidence that this sample selection method may not have significantly affected the results of the analysis.

The analysis presented in this paper is based on data from periodic interviews of SIME/DIME households and on detailed housing characteristics data collected during physical inspections of participant housing units conducted toward the end of the experiment. Both the analysis and the approach to the housing characteristics data collection were designed to be as similar as possible to comparable research conducted by Abt Associates to evaluate the Demand Component of HUD's Experimental Allowance Housing Program [3].

METHODOLOGICAL APPROACH

Many factors affect family housing consumption decisions. Income is clearly an important consideration. Higher income families have greater resources with which to meet their housing needs. Similarly, the size and composition of a household is another determinant. Ethnic background may influence taste in housing and even constrain housing opportunities.

The estimation of housing demand functions provides a convenient framework within which to analyze the impact of SIME/DIME on housing consumption. The basic approach used to examine these impacts was to estimate housing demand equations of the form:

H = f(Y,D,E,b)

where   H is a measure of housing consumed

                         Y is household income

                         D is a vector of household demographic variables

                         E represents a household's position within the
                         Income Maintenance Experiments

                         b is a vector of parameters to be estimated.

After equations in this form were estimated, the relevant components of the
parameter vector, b, were then used to examine the effects of SIME/DIME on
housing consumption. Thus, the analysis in this chapter is based on the
estimation of demand equations relating housing consumption to experimental
payments, non-grant income and other variables. A number of issues were
addressed to operationalize this approach, including variable specification, equation specification, and appropriate statistical techniques.
These are discussed below [4].

MEASURING HOUSING CONSUMPTION

    Two different measures of housing consumption were used throughout the
analysis: monthly rent or estimated current market price (of owned
dwellings) and hedonic quality indices of housing services produced by
dwelling units. More limited estimation work used a third measure of
housing consumption--whether dwelling units met certain standard criteria.

    Rents and House Prices. To the extent that competition within an urban
housing market results in a uniform market-wide price per unit of housing
services, rent levels can be interpreted as measures of the amounts of
housing services provided by rented dwellings. Similarly, the estimated
current market values of owner-occupied dwelling units can be interpreted
as measures of housing services. For this analysis, rent levels were
adjusted for any differences in furnishings and utilities by subtracting
the estimated cost of furnishings from furnished dwellings and adding
estimated utility payments if utilities were not supplied by the landlord.
Ohls and Thomas (1979) describe this rent adjustment process.

    Hedonic Quality Indices. Many recent studies have demonstrated that
substantial proportions of variations in housing rents and prices can be
explained by regressing those market-determined variables on vectors of
dwelling and neighborhood characteristics [5]. The estimated equations can
be interpreted as functions which translate dwelling charactertistics into
indices of the amounts of housing services provided by dwellings. Because

these hedonic indices are independent of the actual rents and market prices of individual dwellings units, they provide a direct measure of housing quality by eliminating differences in observed housing consumption levels caused by random differences in prices per unit of housing services. Ohls and Thomas (1979) describe the hedonic indices used in this analysis.

Standard Index. One objective of housing policy has been to help families obtain housing that meets minimum quality standards. To measure success in meeting this goal, a variable based on whether individual dwelling units met each of fourteen standard criteria was used to describe "standard." These criteria are described in Ohls and Thomas (1979).

EXPERIMENTAL TREATMENT VARIABLE

Modeling of the experiment to permit statistical analysis was made complex by the many financial treatments in SIME/DIME. Experimental families were provided with a basic income support level and were then taxed at a tax rate, t, up to a point where the amount of earnings taxed away was equal to the support level. Thus, the amount of resources available to any given family was positively related to the support level and negatively related to the tax rate. The three different support levels and the different tax rates used in the experiment were described in the introduction.

In light of these variations, several ways of incorporating the experimental financial treatments into the model were considered. A single (1,0) variable for experimental versus control status would fail to capture the substantial variations in experimental treatments. At the opposite extreme, it would be difficult to interpret the estimated coefficients if dummy variables were used to represent each treatment. The latter approach would also use up degrees of freedom in the estimation work. The use of either of these dummy variable approaches to modeling the experiment would also fail to take into account different effects by income level. Experimental effects were probably greater for relatively low-income families, whose incomes were significantly supplemented by the transfer program, than for higher income families who received relatively little assistance because of the tax rates.

To avoid the potential problems associated with the use of dummy variables, experimental effects were represented in most of the analysis by a variable equal to the average annual experimental payments received by families over the three-year period prior to the collection of data on housing characteristics. The experimental variable therefore reflects differences in the level of support provided by the experimental income maintenance plans. Furthermore, because experimental payments varied inversely with non-grant income, this variable also takes into account the possibility that experimental impacts were greatest for low-income households. This variable facilitates interpretation of the results. The estimated coefficients on the payment variable can be interpreted as showing the estimated changes in consumption of housing services that resulted from a dollar-per-year increase in experimental payments [6]. While the analysis focuses on the average payments variable, it is supplemented by the use of dummy variables to represent the effects of the experiment.

INCOME VARIABLES

Income is included in the estimated demand equations for two reasons. First, income is a key determinant of housing consumption. Second, inclusion of income avoids biases in the statistical analysis that result from the structure of the SIME/DIME program. As described in the introduction, the probability of a given family being placed in either the control or experimental samples depended on income, ethnicity, and whether the family included one or two parents. Because both housing consumption and experimental status are correlated with income, the effect of income was controlled to ensure that observed correlations of assignment status with housing consumption did not result from the correlation of both of these variables with income.

Both theory and previous studies on the demand for housing suggest that the appropriate income concept to use in housing demand estimation work is permanent after-tax income rather than income in any single year [7]. Therefore, three-year average non-experimental household disposable income was used as an income variable [8].

OTHER DEMOGRAPHIC VARIABLES

As noted earlier, the assignment model used in the SIME/DIME programs resulted in a stratified sample. To avoid the possibility of inaccurate results because of correlations of ethnicity or household composition with both housing consumption and experimental status, the regression work reported below controlled for these factors by using dummy variables to indicate whether families were white, Black or Chicano and whether a family had one or two household heads.

Preliminary analysis of the data suggested that the number of people in the household was also a significant determinant of housing consumption. Therefore, a series of five dummy variables was used to indicate whether there were three, four, five, six, or seven or more individuals in the household.

EQUATION SPECIFICATION AND ANALYSIS TECHNIQUES

No "correct" functional form for housing consumption analysis is known, and previous housing analysis has used many functional forms. The statistical work reported below makes use of linear functional forms for convenience in performing the analysis and in interpreting the results. During the research planning, consideration was also given to the log-linear functional form which has also frequently been used in housing analysis. However, because the experimental payments variable in this study takes on a value of zero for the control households, the use of a simple log-linear form was inappropriate.

The ordinary least squares regression technique was used for analysis of continuous dependent variables. However, this method was not appropriate in analysis of dichotomous variables such as compliance with basic standard criteria. Probit techniques were therefore used in this work [9].

RESULTS

Tables 1 and 2 summarize the key results of the regression analyses of housing consumption [10]. The results indicate that the SIME/DIME income maintenance payments had a relatively small but statistically significant effect on rental housing consumption measured by monthly rental payment [11]. The comparable elasticities for the owner-occupant sector of the market were even smaller and were not statistically significant. One possible reason the results may have been significant for renters and not homeowners is that renters were able to adjust their housing consumption more easily during the short period of the experiment.

For the rental sector at both sites, the estimated income elasticity of expenditures with respect to experimental income maintenance payments is higher than the income elasticity with respect to non-grant income. One possible explanation for this result is that income maintenance payments were viewed as more stable than other sources of income. Another cause of the lower estimated demand elasticity for non-grant income may arise from an unavoidable equation specification problem. Data on prices per unit of housing services were not included in the demand equations because such data were not available. If there is a negative correlation between income and the prices of land and housing services, and if a price term is not included in a housing expenditures equation, the income term in the equation may pick up some of the negative price effect and, as a result, be biased downward [12].

Tables 1 and 2 also show that the estimated income elasticities based on the hedonic measures of SIME/DIME housing quality are smaller than the elasticities based on housing consumption measured by the monthly rent and sales price. This finding is comparable to results of the Experimental Housing Allowance Program Demand Experiment. Possible explanations are that variables were omitted from the hedonic equations or that not all increases in housing expenditures resulted in increased housing quality.

TABLE 1

REGRESSION RESULTS AFTER THREE YEARS, DENVER

Consumption Measure	Income Elasticity of Demand: Non-Grant Income[a]	Income Elasticity of Demand: Experimental Grants	Increased Consumption from $2,000/ Yr. in Grants	Sample Size
Renters				
Monthly Rent	.215* (5.95)[b]	.325* (4.80)	$13.00* (4.80)	824
Hedonic Monthly Rent	.160* (4.49)	.240* (3.72)	9.60* (3.72)	392
Owners				
House Value	.321* (6.94)	.179 (1.20)	784.00 (1.20)	753
Hedonic House Value	.249* (6.80)	.074 (.64)	310.00 (.64)	536

NOTE: Asterisks indicate that coefficients are significantly different from 0 at the 95 percent confidence level for a one-tailed test.

[a]Elasticities have been computed at average housing consumption, income, and grant levels for the sample. For renters in Denver, average non-grant income, average grant income, and average rent were $5,697; $1,944; and $151. The corresponding values for Denver homeowners are $10,198; $1,105; and $23,628. In Seattle, comparable values for renters are $6,132; $1,953; and $150, and the corresponding values for homeowners are $11,222; $1,007; and $20,765. Income elasticities have been computed using the sum of grant and non-grant income as the basis for measuring percentage changes. If Y_n is non-grant income, Y_g is grant income, and H is housing consumption, the elasticity shown in the first column is:

$$\frac{\delta H}{\delta Y_n} \bigg/ \frac{H}{Y_g + Y_n} .$$

That shown in the second column is: $\dfrac{\delta H}{\delta Y_g} \bigg/ \dfrac{H}{Y_g + Y_n} .$

Elasticities were computed in this way to allow direct comparability with elasticity estimates reported elsewhere in the literature where, in general, all types of income are included in the percentage bases used for elasticity estimates.

[b]Numbers in parentheses are absolute values of t statistics.

TABLE 2

REGRESSION RESULTS AFTER THREE YEARS, SEATTLE

Consumption Measure	Income Elasticity of Demand: Non-Grant Income[a]	Income Elasticity of Demand: Experimental Grants	Increased Consumption from $2,000/ Yr. in Grants	Sample Size
Renters				
Monthly Rent	.268* (6.28)	.421* (4.63)	$16.00* (4.63)	401
Hedonic Monthly Rent	.247 (1.21)	.119 (.46)	4.52 (.46)	35
Owners				
House Value	.224* (5.04)	.104 (.57)	354.00 (.57)	599
Hedonic House Value	.100* (2.00)	.088 (.42)	300.00 (.42)	120

NOTE: Asterisks indicate that coefficients are significantly different from 0 at the 95 percent confidence level for a one-tailed test.

[a]Elasticities have been computed at average housing consumption, income, and grant levels for the sample. For renters in Denver, average non-grant income, average grant income, and average rent were $5,697; $1,944; and $151. The corresponding values for Denver homeowners are $10,198; $1,105; and $23,628. In Seattle, comparable values for renters are $6,132; $1,953; and $150, and the corresponding values for homeowners are $11,222; $1,007; and $20,765. Income elasticities have been computed using the sum of grant and non-grant income as the basis for measuring percentage changes. If Y_n is non-grant income, Y_g is grant income, and H is housing consumption, the elasticity shown in the first column is:

$$\frac{\delta H}{\delta Y_n} \bigg/ \frac{H}{Y_g + Y_n}$$

That shown in the second column is:

$$\frac{\delta H}{\delta Y_g} \bigg/ \frac{H}{Y_g + Y_n}$$

Elasticities were computed in this way to allow direct comparability with elasticity estimates reported elsewhere in the literature where, in general, all types of income are included in the percentage bases used for elasticity estimates.

[b]Numbers in parentheses are absolute values of t statistics.

ANALYSIS OF NET EXPERIMENTAL EFFECTS

The regressions summarized in Tables 1 and 2 can be viewed as structural demand equations that show the direct effects of experimental payments on housing consumption. Participation in the income maintenance experiments, however, had at least two important indirect effects. First, the amount of other nonexperimental transfer income received by the households, such as Aid to Families with Dependent Children (AFDC), was reduced. Second, families reduced their work effort and hence their earned income in response to the negative work incentives created by the tax rate built into the negative income tax formula. Both of these indirect effects would be expected to lower housing consumption and decrease the potential impact of the experiment. Therefore, in addition to estimating gross effects, the net effects of the experiment were estimated by including these negative indirect effects.

Reductions in Non-Experimental Transfer Income.   For   many   of   the families in SIME/DIME, the income support payments replaced other transfer income such as AFDC payments. This section estimates the amount by which such non-grant income was decreased for a typical household, and then computes the effects of the decreased income on housing consumption.

A regression equation was estimated for the Denver sample to assess the reduction in non-grant transfer income resulting from experimental status. Three-year average annual non-grant transfer income was regressed on a (1,0) experimental status variable; a series of control variables (including ethnicity, number of household heads, and family size) and variables representing the pre-experimental income variables which were used in implementing the experimental assignment model. The estimated coefficient on the experimental status variable in this equation was -980.08, while the average annual experimental payment for households in the sample was estimated to be $1,578. Thus, it can be estimated that approximately 62 percent (980/1578) of the experimental SIME/DIME payments replaced other types of non-transfer income for participants in the experiment.

Using this factor, it was possible to adjust the estimates of gross experimental impact shown in Tables 1 and 2 to take into account the effects of the reduction in other transfer income. These adjustments, shown in Table 3, substantially reduce the magnitude of the estimated experimental effects [13]. For example, in Denver the estimated increase in the monthly rent was reduced from $13.02 to $7.79. The adjustment makes the estimated net effect negative for some owner-occupants.

Reductions in Both Transfer Income and Work Effort.   In addition to the reduction in non-experimental transfer income, the income maintenance experiments may also have encouraged families to reduce work effort and hence, their earned income. This indirect effect, like the first one, may

TABLE 3

EFFECTS OF ADJUSTING FOR REDUCED NON-EXPERIMENTAL TRANSFER INCOME,
DENVER

Consumption Measure	Increased Consumption from $2,000/Year in Grants (Gross Effect)	Increased Consumption from $2,000/Year in Grants (Net Effect)
Renters		
Monthly Rent	$13.00	$7.79
Hedonic Monthly Rent	9.60	5.63
Owners		
House Value	$784.00	-46.80
Hedonic House Value	310.00	-334.80

SEATTLE

Consumption Measure	Increased Consumption from $2,000/Year in Grants (Gross Effect)	Increased Consumption from $2,000/Year in Grants (Net Effect)
Renters		
Monthly Rent	$16.00	$9.80
Hedonic Monthly Rent	4.52	-1.31
Owners		
House Value	$354.00	-124.64
Hedonic House Value	300.00	89.20

have decreased housing consumption during the experiment. To assess these two effects together, regression equations were estimated using income and experimental variables that did not reflect changes in non-grant income and work effort in response to the experiment.

The income variables used in this work were the pre-experimental income categories used in the model that initially assigned households to experimental or control status. Three variables were used to represent the experimental treatments. One was a (1,0) dummy variable indicating experimental or control status, and the other two were the differences between household support level and $4,800, and between the marginal tax rate and .70. Thus, for experimental households with a $4,800 support level and a .70 marginal tax rate, the coefficient on the experimental variable provides an estimate of the overall effect of the experiment. For households with different support levels and marginal tax rates, differential experimental responses due to variations in these factors can be computed for given support levels and tax rates using coefficients on the other experimental variables. As in the empirical work reported earlier, ethnicity, family size, and number of household heads were also taken into account in the regressions.

Key results of this analysis are summarized in Table 4. As expected, the estimated net effects of the experiment are, in general, considerably smaller than the gross effects presented in Tables 1 and 2. The 6.40 coefficient for the experimental dummy variable in the rent equation suggests that a typical experimental family with a $4,800 support level and a .70 marginal tax rate had a net $6.40 increase in monthly rent as compared to the $13.00 gross increase in monthly rents estimated for an experimental family with $2,000 in annual payments. The estimated experimental coefficients in the rent equations of Table 4, however, are not statistically significant.

The estimated net effect on house value in Denver shown in Table 4 is negative and statistically significant. The results suggest that after controlling for other factors, the typical house value for an experimental household was more than $2,000 lower than that for a control household. The comparable effect for the hedonic index value of housing consumption by owner-occupants was also negative, although considerably smaller in absolute value and not statistically significant.

It seems unlikely that the net experimental effect on the housing consumption of owner-occupants could actually have been negative. Therefore, these results may not be reliable. They may reflect sampling error or unknown biases in the initial experimental assignment model. Indeed, results of a regression analysis of relationships between experimental status and housing consumption levels at the beginning of the experiment show evidence of a possible bias in the Denver sample. (Baseline data

TABLE 4

NET EXPERIMENTAL EFFECTS
DENVER

Consumption Measure	Regression Coefficients		
	Experimental Status	Difference in Support Levels	Difference in Marginal Tax Rates
Renters			
Monthly Rent	6.40 (1.32)[a]	.029 (0.00)	24.58 (0.89)
Hedonic Monthly Rent	7.85 (1.78)	.809 (0.23)	34.29 (1.36)
Owners			
House Value	-2,262* (2.78)	919 (1.21)	-7,769 (1.61)
Hedonic House Value	-748 (1.20)	-669 (1.15)	-1,657 (0.44)

SEATTLE

Consumption Measure	Regression Coefficients		
	Experimental Status	Difference in Support Levels	Difference in Marginal Tax Rates
Renters			
Monthly Rent	8.46 (1.37)	3.99 (0.62)	55.63 (1.36)
Hedonic Monthly Rent	-0.47 (0.03)	-9.88 (0.31)	277.89 (1.51)
Owners			
House Value	674.60 (1.00)	-837.67 (1.14)	-8,891.41 (1.83)
Hedonic House Value	547.75 (0.80)	-123.99 (0.17)	-5,911.78 (1.23)

NOTE: Asterisks indicate that coefficients are significantly different from 0 at the 95 percent confidence level for a two-tailed test.

[a]Numbers in parentheses are absolute values of t statistics.

on housing consumption are not available in Seattle, so comparable tests for bias cannot be made.)

Regressions similar to those summarized in Table 4 were run using pre-experimental rent and house values as the dependent variables. The independent variables were pre-experimental values for the same variable as those used in the regressions reported in Table 4 except that one additional variable, pre-experimental income, was added to control the effects of income. As shown in Table 5, the estimated effect of experimental status on monthly rent is small and not statistically significant. The corresponding effect for the owner-occupied sector is negative, relatively larger, and statistically significant at the 90 percent level for a two-tailed test. This result suggests that at least part of the estimated negative net experimental effect on owner-occupied housing shown in Table 4 is due to a negative relationship between experimental status and housing consumption for owner-occupants at the start of the experiment and not to the effects of the experiment itself.

Overall, the analysis of this section supports the view that the net effects of the experiment, after taking into account indirect effects through reduced work effort and reduced other transfer income, are considerably smaller than the gross effects. The net effects on rental expenditures are estimated to be somewhat less than half the gross effects. The net effects on house value are estimated to be negative in Denver, although at least some of this apparent negative effect probably is due to biases introduced through the assignment model.

STANDARD HOUSING MEASURE

The effect of experimental payments on the number of households living in "standard" housing was examined, using data on whether housing met all of a set of fourteen standard criteria. This measure is described more fully in Ohls and Thomas (1979). Probit analysis was used in this work, and the same independent variables used in the preceding regression analysis were included.

As shown in Table 6, the estimated experimental effects in Denver are statistically significant. Results suggest that $2,000 of income maintenance payments increased the probability of a household living in standard housing by approximately 6 percent. The estimated effect of experimental transfer payments in Seattle is positive but not statistically significant [14].

COMBINED ANALYSIS OF RENTERS AND OWNERS

The results reported thus far are based on analyses performed separately for the rental and the owner-occupied sectors of the housing market. The most important reason for this separation is that key measures of housing

TABLE 5

POSSIBLE BIASES IN THE ASSIGNMENT MODEL
DENVER

Consumption Measure	Regression Coefficients		
	Experimental Status	Differences in Support Levels	Difference in Marginal Tax Rates
Renters			
Monthly Renter	2.65 (1.06)	.000 (0.21)	6.17 (0.39)
Owners			
House Value	-1,086 (1.84)	.001 (1.08)	-5,462 (1.60)

TABLE 6

INCREASES IN PROBABILITY OF MEETING STANDARDS
DENVER

Consumption Measure	Increased Probability from 1% More Total Income From[a]		Increased Probability from $2,000/ Yr. in Grants	Sample Size
	Non-Grant Income	Experimental Grants		
Minimum Standards	.0026*	.0023*	.056*	940
Based on 14 Criteria	(5.22)	(1.97)	(1.97)	

SEATTLE

Consumption Measure	Increased Probability from 1% More Total Income From[a]		Increased Probability from $2,000/ Yr. in Grants	Sample Size
	Non-Grant Income	Experimental Grants		
Minimum Standards	.0016	.0061	.12	201
Based on 14 Criteria	(1.33)	(1.57)	(1.57)	

NOTE: Asterisks indicate that the coefficients are significantly different from 0 at the 95 percent confidence level for a one-tailed test.

[a]Changes in probabilities are evaluated for households with the mean sample incomes ($8,195 for Denver and $10,154 for Seattle) and with a .50 chance of living in standard housing before the changes.

[b]Numbers in parentheses are the coefficients divided by their standard errors for the associated table entries.

consumption--rents and estimated market values--were not directly comparable between sectors. This difference also precluded the direct use of
hedonic housing measures in analyzing the two sectors jointly, because the
hedonic equations were themselves estimated in terms of either rent or
estimated market value.

One disadvantage of analyzing the two sectors separately, however, was
that changes in housing consumption caused by switching from one sector to
the other were not detected. In particular, families may have improved
their housing by moving from rented apartments to better dwelling units in
the owner-occupied sector. Therefore, a method of measuring housing consumption in the two sectors on a comparable basis was developed so that
joint analyses could be performed. This method involved estimating a ratio
of house prices to rental values using the results of the hedonic regression equations. This ratio was then used to estimate the rental value of
owner-occupied units. These procedures are described in Ohls and Thomas
(1979).

The results of the joint analysis are presented in Table 7. These
results suggest that switching from rental status to owner-occupancy may
have been an important way in which Denver experimental households upgraded
their housing in response to increases in income because the estimated
experimental elasticities for Denver shown in Table 7 are all higher than
the comparable elasticities in Tables 1 and 2. Although they are larger
than those reported earlier, however, the estimated elasticities for Denver
in Table 7 are still relatively small, with .5 as an upper bound. The
combined sample of renters and owners did not generally produce higher
elasticity estimates for the Seattle data.

The Denver findings may have implications in the development of policies
to increase housing consumption among lower income households. If switching from rental status to owner-occupancy is a means of upgrading housing,
programs limited to the rental sector may fail to take advantage of an
important method of increasing housing consumption.

SENSITIVITY OF RESULTS TO ALTERNATIVE ANALYSIS SAMPLES

In addition to the work reported above, a number of supplemental lines
of analysis were undertaken in order to examine the sensitivity of the
results to alternative ways of defining the analysis samples. While space
constraints make it impossible to present complete results here, the
following paragraphs briefly summarize these findings. (Complete results
are presented in Ohls and Thomas (1979).)

Movers. Families who move have greater opportunities than families
who do not move, to adjust their housing consumption levels, so it was of
interest to determine whether the experiments had differential effects on
households who changed dwellings during the period covered by the analysis.

TABLE 7

REGRESSION RESULTS: COMBINED ANALYSIS OF RENTERS AND OWNERS
DENVER

Consumption Measure	Income Elasticity of Demand: Non-Grant Income	Income Elasticity of Demand: Experimental Grants	Increased Consumption from $2,000/ Year in Grants	Sample Size
Monthly Rent (combined measure)	.477* (15.65)	.420* (5.48)	$17.60* (5.48)	1601
Hedonic Monthly Rent (combined measure)	.291* (11.19)	.232* (3.63)	$9.72* (3.63)	1042

SEATTLE

Consumption Measure	Income Elasticity of Demand: Non-Grant Income	Income Elasticity of Demand: Experimental Grants	Increased Consumption from $2,000/ Year in Grants	Sample Size
Monthly Rent (combined measure)	.269* (8.67)	.331* (2.94)	$10.60* (2.94)	1000
Hedonic Monthly Rent (combined measure)	.116 (2.53)	.131 (.90)	$4.24 (.90)	174

NOTES: See notes to Table 1.   These elasticities are computed at the mean values of the variables for the sample used in these regressions.

Asterisks indicate that the coefficients are significantly different from 0 at the 95 percent confidence level for a one-tailed test.

Therefore, regressions similar to those in Tables 1 and 2 were performed on the sample of families who moved. The results suggest that the housing consumption of movers was somewhat more responsive to experimental payments and to differences in non-grant income than the housing consumption of the complete sample. However, the differences are relatively small, and the basic pattern of elasticities shown in Tables 1 and 2 was observed for the sample of movers as well.

Five-Year Households. The work reported above included both households that were enrolled in the experiment for three years and others that participated for five years. This is important because the housing data used in most of the preceding analysis were collected approximately three years into the experiment at about the time when disenrollment began for the three-year families. In order to examine whether the limited duration and/ or approaching end of the experiment for the three-year families significantly affected the results, parts of the analysis were repeated with a sample limited to only the five-year households.

The exclusion of three-year families raises somewhat the estimated income elasticities with respect to experimental income maintenance payments, thus suggesting that the limited duration of the experiment may to some extent have affected the results reported above. However, although these elasticities are larger than the earlier ones, their basic pattern and order of magnitude remain unchanged. This result provides additional support for the belief that the other results reported in this chapter were not seriously biased by the length of the experiment.

MAIN CONCLUSIONS

These are the principal conclusions reached in the analysis:

- There were statistically significant effects of experimental payments on housing consumption in the rental sector. The estimated elasticity of housing demand with respect to experimental payments was relatively low--in the range of .2 to .6. These results are found both when measuring housing consumption with market rent and when using a hedonic index indicator of housing quality, although the elasticities were lower with the hedonic variables. These results were similar for both Seattle and Denver.

- The positive effects of experimental payments on rental housing consumption were decreased by two other results of the experiment: reduced non-experimental transfer income, and reduced earned income resulting from changes in household labor supply. The net effects of the experiment after taking those two factors into account were less than half the estimated gross effects and were not statistically significant.

- Estimated experimental effects on housing consumption of homeowners were not statistically significant.

- The estimated effect of the experiment on the probability of meeting minimum standards was positive and statistically significant in Denver, but was not significant in Seattle.

- In Denver, combined analysis of both the rental and the owner-occupied sectors resulted in higher estimated experimental effects than analysis of either sector alone. This suggests that switching from rental housing to owner-occupancy may have been an imporant way in which households increased their housing consumption in response to the experiment.

- Analysis limited only to households that moved during the experiment resulted in somewhat higher estimated experimental effects than analysis of the entire sample. However, examination of movers alone does not alter the basic pattern or order of magnitude of the results.

- Analysis limited to households enrolled in the experiment for five years led to results similar to those obtained using combined three-year and five-year families. This finding provides additional evidence that the results were not highly sensitive to the timing of the data collection.

APPENDIX

This appendix presents complete regression results for two representative equations from those summarized in Table 1. Complete results for all regressions discussed in the paper are available in Ohls and Thomas (1979).

TABLE A-1

COMPLETE REGRESSION RESULTS FOR REPRESENTATIVE EQUATIONS
DENVER

Independent Variables	Monthly Rent			House Value		
	Coefficient	t Statistic	Mean	Coefficient	t Statistics	Mean
White	6.78	1.52	0.27	-281.53	0.38	0.34
Chicano	-10.00	2.40	0.35	-1696.08	2.15	0.29
Number of Heads	6.17	1.46	0.56	-2090.77	2.52	0.25
Three Family Members	7.15	1.45	0.26	-8.83	0.00	0.18
Four Family Members	15.06	2.85	0.24	129.08	0.11	0.30
Five Family Members	33.87	5.46	0.14	-495.89	0.40	0.21
Six Family Members	17.55	2.34	0.09	561.68	0.42	0.14
Seven or More Family Members	16.32	1.52	0.03	-1219.36	0.77	0.07
Average Experimental Grant	0.0065	4.80	1255.79	0.38	1.20	630.22
Average Non-Grant Income	0.0043	5.95	5729.72	0.67	6.94	10252.63
Constant	104.32			17716.75		
Sample Size	824			753		
Mean Value (Dependent Variable)	151.20			23528.95		
R^2	0.14			0.12		

NOTES

1   More complete descriptions of the experiments can be found in M. Kurtz and R.G. Spiegelman, The Design of the Seattle and Denver Income Maintenance Experiments. SIME/DIME Research Memorandum. Menlo Park, California: SRI International, May 1972; and Robert G. Spiegelman, "The Design of Social Experiments with Principal Reference to the Seattle/Denver Income Maintenance Experiments," paper presented at the SIME/DIME Conference, Orcas Island, Washington, May 14-17, 1978.

2   I am indebted to Philip Robins for bringing this point to my attention.

3   For a discussion of this work, see Joseph Friedman and Daniel H. Weinberg, Draft Report on Housing Consumption Under a Constrained Income Transfer: Evidence from a Housing Gap Housing Allowance. Cambridge, Mass., Abt Associates Inc., April 1979; and Joseph Friedman and Daniel H. Weinberg, Draft Report on the Demand for Rental Housing: Evidence from a Percent of Rent Housing Allowance. Cambridge, Mass., Abt Associates Inc., September 1978.

4   For additional details concerning variable specification and other aspects of the research, see Ohls and Thomas (1979).

5   For a discussion of this literature, see Sally Merrill, Housing Expenditures and Quality, Part III: Draft Report on Hedonic Indices as a Measure of Housing Quality. Cambridge, Mass.: Abt Associates Inc., December 1977.

6   In using average grant payments as the experimental variable in the analysis, household labor supply decisions are assumed to be independent of housing consumption choices. If labor supply decisions were not made independently of housing decisions, then experimental payments--which depend in part on income and therefore on labor supply--would themselves be determined simultaneously with housing decisions. It would therefore not be appropriate to treat this variable as independent in the ordinary least squares analysis of housing demand. This implicit assumption that housing consumption and labor supply decisions are independent is also made in most other housing demand studies.

7   For a discussion of this literature, see Stephen K. Mayo, Housing Expenditures and Quality, Part I: Housing Expenditures Under a Percent of Rent Housing Allowance. Cambridge, Mass.: Abt Associates Inc., January 1977.

8   This income variable is similar to the income measure used in the analysis of HUD's Experimental Housing Allowance Program Demand Experiment. An instrumental variable approach to estimating the effects of permanent income was used initially in this study. This work proved unenlightening, however, because it was not possible to identify either a single instrumental variable or a set of such variables that were highly correlated with observed income.

9   For a discussion of the probit technique and of why it is more appropriate than ordinary least squares in the present context, see Arthur Goldberger, Econometric Theory. New York: John Wiley and Sons, Inc., 1964, pp. 250-1.

10   Complete regression results for representative equations are presented in the Appendix. Complete results for all regressions reported in this paper are available in Ohls and Thomas (1979).

11   As noted earlier, the estimated treatment effects include the direct
      effect of experimental payments on housing but do not include possible
      negative effects from reduced income caused by reduced labor supply.

12   See A. Mitchell Polinsky: "The Demand for Housing: A Study in Specifi-
      cation and Grouping," Econometrica, March 1977, pp. 447-63. Polinsky
      points out that there is a negative correlation between income and the
      price of land and housing services in most cities because average income
      tends to increase with distance from the center of a city and the
      average price of housing services decreases with distance.

13   Estimates shown in the table are for a household receiving $2,000
      annually in experimental grants. The first column in the table is taken
      directly from Table 1. The second column is computed by subtracting
      from the first column $1,240 times the estimated coefficient on non-
      grant income. ($1,240 is 62 percent of the $2,000 in experimental pay-
      ments.)

      These procedures assume that households treat non-grant transfer income
      in the same way as other non-grant income when making housing con-
      sumption decisions. If non-grant transfer income actually is treated
      more like grant income, then coefficients estimated on grant income
      rather than on non-grant income should be used in adjusting for the
      effects of other reduced transfer income. If calculations are made this
      way, entries in the second column of Table 3 for Denver are $4.95,
      $3.04, $298 and $144. Comparable values for Seattle are $6.08, $1.72,
      $135 and $114.

14   All probability changes are evaluated for a household with mean income
      for the sample of $8,195 in Denver and $10,154 in Seattle and a .50
      probability of living in standard housing before the income increase.

                            REFERENCES

Ohls, James C. and Cynthia Thomas. The Effects of the Seattle and Denver
    Income Maintenance Experiments on Housing Consumption, Ownership, and
    Mobility. Princeton, N.J.: Mathematica Policy Research, Inc., December
    1979.

Ohls, James C. The Effects of the Seattle and Denver Income Maintenance
    Program on the Housing Consumption of Participating Households. Paper
    presented at HUD Conference on the Experimental Housing Allowance Program,
    March 1979. Forthcoming in U.S. Department of Housing and Urban Develop-
    ment, Occasional Papers in Housing and Community Affairs.

22

This study is of interest for two reasons. First, behavioral results are developed that are generally consistent with those found in several other negative income tax experiments (Ohls, Part V) and the Experimental Housing Allowance Program (Friedman and Weinberg and Hausman and Wise, Part V). Second, within the context of several complementary econometric specifications, the author carefully discusses the variety of problems that remain in interpreting and estimating behavior in a short-term experimental context.

Kaluzny examines the impact of several specifications of negative income payments on alternate measures of housing consumption: home purchase, increase in rental value, and the combined effect of moving and upgrading one's housing. In general, the increased demand for housing, a normal good, is seen to be a function of a person's presence or absence in the experiment, experimental income, nonexperimental income, family structure, pre-experiment poverty levels, and several other related variables. Due to the transitory nature of the experiment, it was necessary to measure permanent income to estimate program effects without bias. Although an instrumental income variable based on pre-enrollment income was used, the best specification of permanent income involves a categorical variable that measured program participation joined with a variable for the NIT experimental income and a variable for nonexperimental income. Even though this arrangement provided a better specification of permanent income and summarized the effect of the NIT tax and guarantee parameters in a single parameter, it did not resolve another problem: some of the NIT benefit replaced nonexperimental income. This could have biased the responsiveness of housing consumption to NIT benefits either upward or downward, depending on whether the income elasticity of the NIT income was smaller or larger than that of the nonexperimental income. And because of the short-run nature of the experiment—three years—the ultimate effect of the program may be understated if individuals are unwilling to commit a temporary increase in income to higher housing costs. This combines with the fact that moving one's household is costly, and individuals may not choose to incur such costs in a short-term experiment. (Even higher are the fixed costs involved in negotiating a home purchase.) Finally, there may be an upward bias in home ownership effects if the NIT benefit merely accelerated a home purchase decision taken prior to program participation.

The lesson is that experimental design can solve a major philosophical problem—the attribution of causality—and a major measurement problem—self-selection bias—but other conceptual problems can remain to bias results and perplex the careful analyst. One other problem was the necessity to make separate estimates of effects on home ownership and rental upgrading. In this case, for the rental model the result was to understate the total elasticity (the elasticity of the combined home purchase and rental upgrading) of housing expenditures because the exclusion of home owners truncated the distribution of expenditures on housing (see the Introduction). Thus, rental and home ownership behavior had to be combined. To do so, imputed rental values had to be assigned to housing consumed by home owners. But to yield more accurate measures of housing value, this analysis was confined to those who moved during the experiment. The adjustment injected selectivity bias into the analysis, which then had to be corrected.

The results of the Gary estimates of housing consumption response are similar to that from the SIME/DIME and the New Jersey experiment. Only 2.8% of gross experimental payments were devoted to increased rental housing consumption, but housing consumption out of the net increase in income due to the NIT benefit was 6.7%. The estimated elasticity of rental expenditure with respect to experimental payments was about .3—a

10% rise in experimental payments leads to a 3% rise in rental expenditure. In contrast, the conceptually comparable elasticity estimates for the Denver and Seattle Experiments are .42 and .32. In actual rental expenditures, the Gary effects are approximately one-quarter of those estimated for the Experimental Housing Allowance Program—a 19% increase in rental expenditures compared to 5% for Gary.

For home ownership, experimental households had about a 9% greater chance of becoming homeowners compared to the controls. For the pooled sample of owners and renters who moved, approximately 10.3% of the net experimental benefit was used for housing. Overall, the transitory nature of the experiment may cause these results to understate the effects of a permanent NIT program.

Evaluation of Experimental Effects on Housing Consumption
The Gary Income Maintenance Experiment

Richard L. Kaluzny

The analysis and discussion of negative income tax (NIT) programs generally emphasizes the work-leisure choice of participants. However, evidence is accumulating that such programs may influence far more than the amount of time people devote to work. Consumption patterns, especially those of durable goods and housing, also appear to be responsive to income changes generated by NIT benefits (Nicholson 1978; Ohls and Thomas 1979; Wooldridge 1978).

Analytic interest in the effects of an NIT program on housing stems from two major concerns. First, there is a general policy interest in the evaluation of both direct and indirect consequences of the NIT program. Do families receiving NIT benefits make adjustments in their consumption patterns that impact on their long-run chances of escaping from poverty? The relative importance of housing expenditures in a family budget creates an interest in the explicit analysis of housing consumption adjustments. To the extent that housing and neighborhood quality affect the health and welfare of families, this issue becomes even more important.

Second, there is a basic policy interest in housing programs. Since the 1930s, concern that the lack of decent, safe, and sanitary housing may substantially contribute to the incidence of poverty has generated a series of public policies directed toward the "housing problem." Many of these

The author is a Senior Economist at Mathematica Policy Research, Inc. Princeton, N.J. An earlier version of this paper appeared in the Journal of Human Resources XIV (No. 4) Fall 1979. David Capp, Dianna Walters, Elizabeth Beveridge and Anne Moser provided excellent research assistance over the long history of this project.

From Richard L. Kaluzny, "Evaluation of Experimental Effects on Housing Consumption: The Gary Income Maintenance Experiment." Unpublished manuscript, 1980.

programs (e.g., public housing) have focused on expanding the supply of housing for low-income households. The limited success of this approach, in conjunction with the belief that poverty is a principal cause of urban blight, has stimulated interest in policy alternatives that focus on the demand for housing services [1]. Income maintenance and housing allowance programs are two such alternatives that provide families an opportunity for using income supplements to increase housing consumption.

This paper examines the impact of NIT payments on several measures of housing consumption for households that participated in the Gary Income Maintenance Experiment, outlined below. A discussion of the expected treatment effects and of the general approach used is followed by an examination of the experimental impact on increases in home ownership, rental expenditures, and mobility. Next, the combined responses of renters and owners are presented, and in conclusion, the Gary results are contrasted with findings from the housing allowance experiment and other NIT experiments.

THE GARY EXPERIMENT

The Gary experiment was conducted between 1971 and 1974 by the U.S. Department of Health, Education and Welfare as one of four large-scale experiments designed to evaluate the effects of alternative negative income tax programs. Four different NIT plans, combining two taxe rates (40 and 60 percent) and two guarantee levels (which varied with family size) were tested. The guarantee levels of $4,300 and $3,300 per year for a family of four were approximately equal to 100 and 75 percent of the 1971 poverty level, respectively [2].

Experiment participants were drawn from the residents of low income neigborhoods in Gary, Indiana. All of the 1,799 families enrolled were Black with a high concentration (about 60 percent) of female-headed families. Families with male heads usually had low income but were not extremely poor. Families with female heads of household were generally much poorer than husband-wife families--over 80 percent of them were receiving income from the AFDC program immediately prior to enrollment.

The households were interviewed three times per year over the course of the experiment. Housing data were collected shortly after the initial enrollment period and annually in the summer interview wave thereafter. This analysis is based on 1,364 cases for which basic housing data were available for both the enrollment period (obtained retrospectively shortly after enrollment) and for the last housing interview at the end of the experiment.

NIT EFFECTS AND HOUSING CONSUMPTION

The presence of a negative income tax program can be expected to have a positive effect on the consumption of housing services. Transfer payments supplement other sources of family income and, even in light of labor disincentives, create a net positive income effect leading to increased consumption of all normal goods, including housing services [3]. Even when transfer payments are small (or even zero) because family income is near or above the breakeven level, a positive income effect may still be expected because the guarantee feature reduces the need to hold or build savings to offset potential future losses in income and may, as a result, increase spending for current consumption.

While the sign of these effects is clearly positive, the magnitude is harder to anticipate. Previous research suggests that the income elasticity of demand for housing services is under .5 and may be considerably less than .5 for low income households (Carliner, 1973; Ohls and Thomas, 1979). The effects of an NIT policy may be substantially smaller than those of a housing allowance program, both because of the unrestricted nature of the NIT payment and the reluctance among households to make adjustments in housing which extend beyond the experimental period.

The evaluation of NIT effects on housing consumption is complicated by the difficulty of making short-run housing adjustments and by the limited duration of the experimental period. Measures of changes in average consumption levels during the experiment (i.e., changes in rent expenditures or home ownership rates) can provide a useful reflection of the short-run impacts of the experimental payments. However, such a focus is potentially misleading in terms of estimating long-run effects because the aggregate impact on housing consumption depends upon the combination of NIT effects in three areas: the consumption adjustments of households that move, the number of households that move, and the extent to which non-movers (primarily owners) upgrade the housing services related to their existing unit [4].

Underestimates of long-range effects are likely in an experimental setting because a substantial proportion of the sample may choose not to move during the experimental period. Consequently, the analysis of treatment effects examines both the average treatment response during the experimental period for all experimental households and the conditional response of households that moved. It should be noted that the behavior of families that move is still a short-run response that encompasses participant perceptions about the limited duration of the experimental payments.

The basic model used in all analyses is expressed as:

$$H_t = f(Y, X_j, T_i)$$

Housing consumption, H_t, is operationally defined as homeowner status, and as private monthly rent expenditures. Homeowner status was observed for the entire three-year experimental period and for each of the annual periods. Rent expenditures, including utilities, were measured at pre-enrollment and at the end of each of the three years of the experiment.

Two alternative specifications of treatment effects and household income were examined. In the first, the household's permanent income, Y, was measured using an instrumental variable based on pre-enrollment income. The X_j vector includes measures controlling for female-headed families, initial enrollment in the AFDC program, number of children and adults, and pre-enrollment poverty levels used in the assignment of households to experimental plans. Additional control variables such as housing status at the beginning of each analysis period were included for selected analyses.

Experimental status, T_i, was entered as a set of four binary variables. This provided an estimate of the net change in housing consumption, H_t, for households in each plan compared to all households in the control group. This specification did not, however, explicitly separate the influence of experimental status from the size of the transfer payment.

In the second specification, the household's permanent income level was represented by two components, the average monthly experimental transfer payment and the average monthly income from all non-experimental sources. Both components were averaged over the entire experimental period and incorporated the labor supply effects of transfer income on non-experimental income. Treatment effects entered the model in two ways--as average monthly transfer payments and as a binary variable for experimental status to represent experimental effects that may have operated independently of the NIT benefit size. This specification provided a better measure of permanent household income than that which was available from the pre-enrollment measures. In addition, it summarized the effect of the tax and guarantee parameters in one single parameter, size of the NIT benefit, which was the variable directly observable to the household. However, the average monthly transfer payment overstated the net effect of the NIT program on family income because part of the benefit replaced non-experimental income. This may have biased the estimated responsiveness of housing consumption to experimental payments either upward or downward depending on whether the elasticity of response to the net experimental benefit was truly smaller or larger than that of non-experimental income. Comparison of these estimated elasticities with elasticities computed using net increases estimated from the first specification did not suggest a serious distortion.

INCREASES IN HOMEOWNERSHIP

The number of homeowners in the analysis sample increased substantially during the course of the experiment. At enrollment, 23 percent of the sample were owners, but by the end of the third year, 34 percent owned homes. Experimental payments to households that already own homes may have an impact on the consumption of services as existing units are upgraded or as families move to better units but payments are not expected to affect ownership status [5]. The primary policy interest was focused on whether non-owner households at enrollment were more likely to become owners during the experiment.

The probability of becoming an owner during the entire experiment or during any of the three annual periods was estimated using probit analysis [6]. Comparison of ownership rates in each of the four plans to rates for the control group (Table 1, panel A) show statistically significant increases in the first year ranging from .03 to .05 in three of the four plans. Ownership rates among households in the high guarantee 60% tax plan were also significantly higher than for the control group in the second year and over the full course of the experiment.

The results for the second specification of the treatment effects (Table 1, panel B) estimate a statistically significant mean increase of .059 in the probability of becoming an owner by the end of the experiment. Increases in ownership tended to be a positive function of the size of the experimental payment. An increase of $100 per month, for example, increased the mean probability of becoming an owner during the course of the experiment by .02.

The conditional probability of ownership for all households that moved in a given period was also examined using a specification similar to that used by Poirier (1978) on the New Jersey data (not shown). As expected, the experimental-control differences were somewhat larger than those for the full sample. The probability that experimental households that moved at some time during the experiment were homeowners was .09 higher than that for comparable controls.

The presence of a positive treatment effect is not an unambiguous indication that there was a net long-run increase in the number of households that ultimately become homeowners. One interpretation of these patterns is that the ownership increase was primarily a timing effect. The presence of guaranteed benefits for three years reduced the obstacles to ownership and the risk of making such a long-range purchase. Consequently, households that were near the threshold of becoming owners may have been induced to accelerate their decision to purchase a home. To the extent this is true, the total number of families who became owners is unlikely to be substantially larger than it would have been in the absence of the NIT

TABLE 1

EXPERIMENTAL EFFECTS ON THE PROBABILITY OF HOMEOWNERSHIP

		Enrollment to End of Experiment	First Year	Second Year	Third Year
A.	Estimated Increase in the Probability of Ownership, by Plan[a]				
	Low Guarantee 60% tax	.048 (1.64)	.028* (1.95)	-.007 (0.49)	.020 (0.89)
	40% tax	.037 (1.24)	.017 (1.09)	.005 (0.33)	.016 (0.69)
	High Guarantee 60% tax	.069** (2.06)	.046*** (3.00)	.028* (1.92)	-.019 (0.92)
	40% tax	.052 (1.55)	.033** (2.01)	.009 (0.52)	-.005 (0.23)
B.	Mean Estimated Probability of Becoming an Owner (Non-owners)[b]				
	1. experimental group	.144	.074	.022	.052
	2. control group	.085	.021	.026	.042
	difference (1-2)[c]	.059*	.053***	-.004	.010

[a]Evaluated at the point where all variables except the treatment plans have a mean value, and three of the four treatment variables are set at zero. The ratio of the maximum likelihood estimate to the standard error, which is distributed approximately as t, is shown in parentheses.

[b]Evaluated for controls at the point where all variables have a mean value except the treatment variables, which have a zero value. For experimentals, the point evaluated is at the mean value of all variables except treatment status and the mean transfer payment among experimentals, which are 1 and $212, respectively.

[c]The test statistic is based on the likelihood ratio for the constrained and unconstrained models.

*Statistically significant at the .10 level.
**Statistically significant at the .05 level.
***Statistically significant at the .01 level.

payments. The treatment effect would, however, represent a net increase in the flow of housing services consumed, measured in terms of household-years of ownership.

PRIVATE RENT EXPENDITURES

An increase in housing consumption generated by the experiment was also evident among private renters. Average rental expenses increased 30 percent from $93 per month to $121 per month during the experiment. A comparison of cross-sectional rent expenditures shows that the mean differences between the experimental and control groups, which were virtually non-existent at enrollment, became increasingly more positive and statistically significant at the end of the third year (Table 2, panel A) [7]. Expenditures at the end of the experiment by households in the treatment groups ranged from $4 to $14 per month higher than comparable households in the control groups.

The second treatment specification estimated a significant treatment-control group difference by the end of the experiment of $6.14 or 5 percent of the mean rent level. Rent expenditures were significantly related to size of the experimental payment, increasing approximately $7 per $100 in gross benefits. This implies an elasticity of rent with respect to experimental benefits which is over twice that of non-experimental income (.29 versus .12, respectively).

The cross-sectional results provide a convenient summary measure of the impact of the experiment but tend to understate the longer-run impact of the NIT payment on households that actually adjusted their consumption. Changes in rental expenditures among households in the experimental group that moved between enrollment and each cross-section were also examined using the second treatment specification (Table 2, panel B).

The mean rent difference between the control and treatment groups is positive and generally increased over time for both movers and non-movers. In the third year, the differences are statistically significant for movers with households in the treatment group paying $7.99 per month more than those in the control group.

The estimated elasticities of rent with respect to experimental payments and non-experimental income (.27 and .11, respectively) are slightly lower than for the sample as a whole but are consistent with previous results based on disaggregate data for low income households (Wooldridge, 1978; Ohls and Thomas, 1979) [8]. Housing consumption out of experimental pay-ments was low compared to other income during the first two years (perhaps reflecting lag effects), but increased markedly in the last year.

The elasticity estimates for experimental payments may be biased because the mean experimental payment measure overstated the net income increase

TABLE 2

SUMMARY OF ESTIMATED TREATMENT EFFECTS ON
MONTHLY RENTAL EXPENSES

		First Year	Second Year	Third Year
A. Estimated Treatment/Control Differences (All cases)				
Low Guarantee[a/]	60% tax	$2.20 (4.10)	$4.50 (4.12)	$7.58 (5.19)
	40% tax	2.51 (4.35)	8.79** (4.35)	7.59 (5.43)
High Guarantee[a/]	60% tax	5.38 (4.82)	6.54 (4.55)	13.95** (5.63)
	40% tax	-1.47 (5.38)	-1.48 (5.29)	3.86 (6.05)
All Plans[b/]		$2.10	$5.01	$6.14***
B. Estimated Treatment/Control Differences (Movers/Non-movers)[b/]				
Movers		$1.29	$7.06	$7.99**
Non-movers		$1.19	$2.11	$0.68
Elasticity of Rent (for movers) with Respect to:[c/]				
Experimental payments		0.15	0.13	0.27
All non-experimental income		0.16	0.14	0.11

[a/] Based on a specification including pre-enrollment income and four binary variables for type of NIT plan. Standard errors are shown in parentheses.

[b/] Differences are evaluated for the mean value of experimental payments ($212) among the experimental group.

[c/] Income elasticities have been computed using the sum of experimental payment and all other income as the basis for measuring the percentage change in income (i.e., the elasticities for experimental payment income, Y_{EP}, and all other income, Y_O, are computed as

$$\frac{dH}{dY_{EP}} \bigg/ \frac{H}{Y_{EP} + Y_O} \quad \text{and} \quad \frac{dH}{dY_O} \bigg/ \frac{H}{Y_{EP} + Y_O} \quad , \text{ respectively).}$$

**Statistically significant at the .05 level.
***Statistically significant at the .01 level.

due to the NIT program. Comparison of the mean rent increase in the third year and the mean net increase in income due to the NIT program suggests an elasticity for net experimental payments of about .32 for movers and about .26 for all experimental households [9].

PROBABILITY OF MOVING

The observed treatment effects on rental expenditures of movers and the increase in ownership, which occurs primarily as the result of a move, suggest that under an NIT program the housing consumption of movers can significantly increase over what it would be in the absence of the transfer payments. As a result, it is of interest to examine the treatment effect on the probability of moving, which may also lead to a change in aggregate consumption of housing.

The mobility models, similar to those used earlier, were estimated for the entire experimental period plus the three annual periods using probit analysis. Measures of family size and housing arrangement at the beginning of the period, and changes in family type and size during the period were included, in addition to income and treatment variables.

Almost half the total sample moved at least once during the experiment with most of the activity occurring in the first year. Households in the experimental group had higher overall mobility rates than households in the control group (.53 versus .46), but the estimated treatment effects are not statistically significant (see Table 3).

Variations by type of NIT plan show only minor differences between plans with the possible exception of the first year. However, no consistent pattern of variation is observed.

The lack of treatment effects on mobility may be the result of several factors. The expected sign of the treatment effect is ambiguous because the mobility measure does not distinguish among types of moves which may have offsetting treatment effects. Moves to upgrade a housing unit are expected to be positively related to increased experimental payments, but moves which result in declining housing consumption (e.g., following loss of income or a wage earner) are expected to be negatively related to such payments. In addition, the short duration of the experiment may have limited the amount of voluntary moves to upgrade housing which households considered making.

COMBINED ANALYSIS OF RENTERS AND OWNERS

The positive impact of experimental payments on rental expenditures and on home ownership indicates the presence of an important NIT effect on the

TABLE 3

ESTIMATED TREATMENT EFFECTS ON THE PROBABILITY
OF MOVING, BY PERIOD

		Enrollment to End of Experiment	First Year	Second Year	Third Year
A.	Estimated Differences in Probability of Moving, by Plan[a]				
Low Guarantee	60% tax	.038 (0.82)	.02 (0.57)	-.02 (0.54)	.01 (0.34)
	40% tax	.060 (1.21)	.02 (0.46)	.04 (1.13)	.03 (0.91)
High Guarantee	60% tax	.067 (1.34)	.08* (1.81)	.01 (0.28)	.02 (0.44)
	40% tax	.04 (0.77)	-.00 (0.05)	.00 (0.16)	.06 (1.49)
B.	Mean Estimated Probability of Moving[b]				
1.	experimental group	.53	.30	.16	.19
2.	control group	.46	.27	.16	.17
	difference (1-2)[c]	.07	.03	.00	.02

[a] Evaluated at the point where all variables except the treatment plans have a mean value, and three of the four treatment variables are set at zero. The ratio of the maximum likelihood estimate to the standard error, which is distributed approximately as t, is shown in parentheses.

[b] Evaluated for controls at the point where all variables have a mean value except the treatment variables, which have a zero value. For experimentals, the point evaluated is at the mean value of all variables except treatment status and the mean transfer payment among experimentals, which are 1 and $212, respectively.

[c] The test statistic is based on th likelihood ratio for the constrained and unconstrained models.

*Statistically significant at the .10 level.

consumption of housing services. From a policy perspective, the separate analysis of owners and renters is somewhat unsatisfactory because it fails to provide an estimate of the overall responsiveness of housing expenditures to the NIT benefits. This overall elasticity is an important measure which would be useful in assessing the comparative efficiency of alternative demand side policies such as housing allowance and NIT grants on housing expenditures. The elasticity of rental expenditures with respect to transfer payments may understate the overall elasticity of housing expenditures because the exclusion of owners essentially truncates the distribution of expenditures on housing services [10].

The problem in deriving an overall estimate of the elasticity of housing expenditures is to successfully assign a rental value to the benefits of ownership so that expenditures for owners and renters can be combined. Use of a hedonic price index to assign rental values to owners was precluded by limitations on the detail of the available data. An alternative-- translating the asset value of a house into a rental value requires a reasonable estimate of the house value. This poses a problem with regard to homeowners who purchased their home years ago and do not have a very good sense of its current market value.

The joint analysis of owners and renters is limited to households that moved during the experiment. This allows emphasis on the group of households observed to be the most responsive to the NIT payments while minimizing the problems of deriving reasonable estimates of the current market value of owner-occupied homes. The conventional wisdom (Muth, 1969) and empirical experience from the Seattle-Denver NIT experiments (Ohls and Thomas, 1979) suggest that the rental value is between 1/95 and 1/114 of current value. A value of 1/100 was chosen to estimate rental values for owners.

The analysis also attempted to correct for a potential source of bias arising from missing data, due primarily to attrition. The available data base did not include attrition data, so the effects of these losses could not be estimated. The data base did, however, include a number of cases that participated in the experiment but had missing or incomplete data for the last housing-related interview which precluded them from the analysis sample. The exclusion of these cases could also introduce a bias into the estimates presented above if these cases differ systematically from the remaining cases with respect to housing consumption or mobility.

The analysis in this section was conducted using a procedure developed by Heckman (1974) to adjust for the selectivity bias introduced by missing observations. The results for both the corrected and uncorrected estimates are presented in Table 4. Although the pattern of results is similar in both cases, the unadjusted results tend to be from 8 to 22 percent smaller than the corrected estimates. This suggests that the earlier results may have been similarly understated.

TABLE 4

SUMMARY OF ESTIMATED TREATMENT EFFECTS ON
HOUSING EXPENDITURES OF MOVERS
(RENTERS AND OWNERS)

		With Correction Factor	Without Correction Factor
A. Estimated Treatment/Control Differences, by Plan[a/]			
Low Guarantee	60% tax	$13.87* (6.99)	$12.44* (6.55)
	40% tax	7.01 (7.33)	5.61 (6.88)
High Guarantee	60% tax	17.58** (7.34)	16.09** (6.83)
	40% tax	-7.19 (7.85)	-8.79 (7.31)
B. Estimated Mean Treatment/Control Difference			
Mean Difference[b/]		$9.32**	$7.63**
Elasticity of Experimental Payment[c/]		.17	.14
Elasticity of Non-experimental Payment[c/]		.12	.12

[a/]Based on a specification including pre-enrollment income and four binary treatment variables. Standard errors are shown in parentheses.

[b/]Evaluated at the mean experimental payment ($212).

[c/]Evaluated as in Table 2, footnote 3. Using mean values for the sample of owners and renters who moved.

*Statistically significant at the .10 level.
**Statistically significant at the .05 level.

The level of housing expenditures for households that moved were estimated at the end of the experiment for two specifications of experimental status (see Table 4). The first specification used an estimate of pre-enrollment income and binary variables for the four NIT plans. It indicates statistically significant differences between the control group and households in the low guarantee 60% plan and high guarantee 60% plan ($13.87 and $17.58, respectively). The net experimental effect on housing expenditures does not vary consistently with the plan parameters, which suggests that the effect is not related to NIT benefit size.

The second specification used mean experimental payments and mean non-experimental income and suggests a statistically significant mean experimental-control difference of $9.32. The estimated elasticity with respect to experimental payments is somewhat larger than that for non-experimental income (.17 and .12, respectively). An alternative computation based on the mean changes in income and housing expenditures suggests an elasticity with respect to net experimental payments of about .46.

CONCLUSIONS

The changes in consumption of housing services for the households in the Gary Experiment are similar in many respects to the findings on housing consumption for households in both the New Jersey experiment and the Denver experiment. All three experiments observed statistically significant positive effects on private rental expenses.

In the Gary Experiment, average monthly rent expenses at the end of the experiment increased about 5.1 percent overall and 6.7 percent among households that moved. While only 2.8 and 3.8 percent of the gross experimental payment for all experimentals and movers, respectively, went to increased rent expenditure, spending out of the net increase in income due to the NIT benefit was substantially larger (6.7 and 8.9 percent, respectively). The estimated elasticity of rent with respect to experimental payments is about .3 for all cases as well as for movers. This estimate, while generally lower than that for the Denver and Seattle NIT experiments (.42 and .32, respectively), is still comparable.

The changes in rental expenditures induced by the Gary NIT payments, while positive and significant, are about one-quarter the magnitude of changes estimated for housing allowance benefits (HUD, 1978). Participants in the Experimental Housing Allowance Program (EHAP) increased their net rental expenditures by 19 percent compared to the 5 percent found for Gary households. The share of the benefit payment devoted to housing consumption is also smaller, as expected, for the general cash grant compared to payments specifically for use on housing. About 7 percent of the net increase in income due to the Gary Experiment payments compared to 29 percent of the EHAP benefit, were used to increase rental expenditures [11].

Experimental payments also have a small but statistically significant positive effect on a household's chances of becoming a homeowner. By the end of the experiment, households that received the average experimental payment and that moved had a 9 percent greater chance of becoming owners than did comparable controls. Similar effects were noted in the New Jersey and Denver experimentals among Black households.

Housing expenditures at the end of the experiment for a pooled sample of owners and renters who moved during the experiment were examined to provide an overall summary measure of treatment effects. The results indicate that mean housing expenditures of experimentals were $9.30 per month or 6.4 percent higher than that of controls. This suggests that about 10.3 percent of the net experimental benefit was used for housing. The estimated elasticity with respect to experimental payments is less precise than for renters but still ranges between .17 and .4.

The evidence for a positive increase in housing consumption in response to the transfer payments, while limited, is encouraging. Furthermore, the effects estimated here are likely to be lower bounds of the responses which would be observed in an ongoing NIT program. This is true for two reasons. First, more households can be expected to become movers and make long-range commitments to increased housing expenditures in an ongoing program. Second, the conditional responses of movers, which are observed to be positive in this and in several other experiments, are also likely to become stronger as more households perceive the guarantee feature of the transfer payment to be a permanent rather than a transitory element in their income flow.

NOTES

1. Muth (1969) succinctly presents the blight argument as a corollary of the positive income elasticity of housing. Low-income families demand fewer or lower-quality housing services than high-income families. This demand is met by the conversion of single-family units to multiple-family units and by reduction in quality, generated by decreased maintenance expenditures, rather than by the construction of new low-quality units.

2. See Kehrer et al. (1975) for details on the administration and design of the experiment.

3. Average gross transfer payments in the four Gary plans for households in this sample ranged from $162 to $276 per month with approximately 7.5 percent of the experimental households averaging payments of less than $50 per month. The mean payment for the entire experimental period over all plans was $212 per month; the smaller net increase of $90 per month was due to declines in hours worked (especially by husbands and female heads of households) and because part of the gross transfer payment replaced AFDC income that recipients were receiving before the experiment.

4. Data were collected at the end of the experiment on expenditures made by homeowners for repair or remodeling purposes. Analysis of these expenditures did not suggest the presence of any NIT effects during the experimental period. The subsequent discussion is presented in terms of the other two factors.

5. Transfer payments may prevent some households from involuntarily giving up a unit they own. In general, there was relatively little loss of ownership status for any reason during the experiment. Over 90 percent of all pre-enrollment owners remained owners.

6. The basic specification for all models included variables controlling for changes in household type over the period, household size at the beginning of the period and household income. This approach differs from that used in the analysis of the New Jersey Income Maintenance Experiment where Wooldridge (1978) examined cross-sectional homeownership status and Poirier (1978) examined households that moved.

7. In the models examining rent expenditures, the effects of rent subsidies or reductions in contract rent between the tenant and landlord (e.g., services in lieu of rent or below market rents for relatives of the landlord) were captured by a binary variable indicating the presence of such adjustments. Variables reflecting family size and type at the beginning of each period were also included in the specification.

8. Carliner (1973) estimates income elasticities of .5 using disaggregate cross-section data for all households. Because participants in the experiment were drawn from low income neighborhoods rather than from a general sample, it is reasonable to expect a truncation in the distribution of housing expenditures which would create a downward bias in the elasticity estimates.

9. The elasticity of net experimental payments was computed as

$$\frac{\Delta R}{R} \Bigg/ \frac{\Delta Y}{Y}$$

where R is the mean rent, ΔY is the net increase in income due to the experiment, and Y is the mean income of experimental families.

10. This is especially true if ownership reflects a relatively high taste for consumption of housing services. Households that become owners may then be willing to spend more for the benefits of ownership than they would if they had remained in the rental market.

11. The EHAP Demand Experiment also monitored the housing expenditures of a small sample of households given unconstrained cash grants. These households reacted very similarly to the Gary Experiment households, using only about 10 percent of the grant for increased housing consumption (see HUD, 1978, p. 18).

REFERENCES

Carliner, Geoffrey. "Income Elasticity of Housing Demand." Review of Economics and Statistics vol. IV (November 1973):528-32.

Heckman, James. "Shadow Prices, Market Wages, and Labor Supply." Journal of Political Economy vol 42, July 1974.

Kehrer, Kenneth C., et al. The Gary Income Maintenance Experiment Design, Administration and Data Files. Gary, Indiana. Gary Income Maintenance Experiment, July 1975.

Muth, Richard F., Cities and Housing. Chicago: University of Chicago Press, 1969.

Nicholson, Walter. "Expenditure Patterns: A Descriptive Survey," in Watts, H.W. and A. Rees (eds). The New Jersey Income Maintenance Experiment vol. III. New York: Academic Press, 1978.

Ohls, James C. and C. Thomas. "The Effects of the Seattle and Denver Income Maintenance Experiments on Housing Consumption, Ownership, and Mobility." Denver, Colorado: Mathematica Policy Research, Inc., December 1979.

Poirier, Dale. "The Determinants of Home Buying," in Watts, H.W. and A. Rees (eds), The New Jersey Income Maintenance Experiment vol. III. New York: Academic Press, 1978.

U.S. Department of Housing and Urban Development. A Summary Report of Current Findings from the Experimental Housing Allowance Program. Office of Policy Development and Research, April 1978.

Wooldridge, Judith. "Housing Consumption," in Watts, H.W. and A. Rees, (eds). The New Jersey Income Maintenance Experiment vol. III. New York: Academic Press, 1978.

VI

HEALTH AND SAFETY PROGRAMS:
DESIGNED AND NATURAL EXPERIMENTS

This set of studies on health, safety and related issues contains several important policy results and methodological lessons.

From a policy standpoint, the Weisbrod and Helming study analyzes a mental health program that strongly de-emphasizes hospitalization and favors living in the community and the provision of supporting services from skilled professionals and community agencies. A careful accounting of the costs and benefits—economic and noneconomic, both measurable and unmeasurable—in the context of an experimental design with random assignment to treatment and control, demonstrates the apparent efficacy of the treatment. These results are of considerable policy significance in view of the radical shift of our society in the past decade and a half away from institutionalized care of the mentally ill and toward treatment within the community. The experimental design and the carefully structured cost and benefit accounting suggest that this major socio-medical trend may be in the correct direction. Of course, as the authors stress, these apparent net positive results are only one input into the ultimate policy decision to move toward this method of health care. Cost/benefit analysis informs but cannot supplant the responsibility to make such a decision.

The study by Smith, on the other hand, is much less complete than that of Weisbrod and Helming. For, while it estimates the impact of safety inspections on accident rates in a variety of industrial contexts, it does not place a value on the measured reduction in the accident rate, it ignores a number of other program effects, and it fails to measure costs. The study is extremely important from a policy standpoint, however, for the Occupational Safety and Health Administration (OSHA) has been embattled since its inception both on valid and less than valid conceptual, administrative and political grounds. Smith's generally positive findings should encourage OSHA administrators to perform more complete economic and social accounting of the effects of their safety programs. We hope these results may also lead to an improvement in the data, for the OSHA program data now strain the corrective capacity of econometric models.

There is the danger that badly designed program data may result in the rejection of a program which on a priori grounds is socially justified. The question is: What is the optimum feasible program? Current data suggest we do not yet have it. The difficulty of deciding whether OSHA is justified and how to value the experimental mental health program examined by Weisbrod and Helming is highlighted by the work of Viscusi in his effort to value the economic losses in situations involving risk of death or injury. Here we face the problem that, ultimately, human life and suffering are not amenable to economic accounting. This implies that the costs and benefits of health and safety programs can never be fully meaured by conventional means. Hence, as Weisbrod and Helming note, the policy maker must always step in to make the final judgment. This problem notwithstanding, Viscusi demonstrates that workers do place an economic (as well as noneconomic) value on their health and well being.

Several methodological lessons emerge from these chapters. As with the other designed experiments in this volume, the work of Weisbrod and Helming demonstrates the advantages of random assignment—self-selection is avoided and one can ambiguously assert a causal relation between program treatment and effect. Under ideal conditions—with measures of appropriate variables—an experimental design is not necessary for unbiased measurement of program effects. (For example, see the chapter by Barnow et al. in Part I.) On the other hand, ideal measures of critical variables are rarely available. This is the case with OSHA. There is always uncertainty about whether bias has been eliminated in a natural, experimental context. The study by Smith, which represents an excellent effort to overcome problems in data, amply illustrates this fact. As noted above, the OSHA program is, a priori, potentially worthwhile. But, if it is ill-designed or ill-administered, it has potential for harm—negative, not just zero effects—as well as potential for good. Since the studies in this volume demonstrate the high cost of experimentation and that many aspects of social cost and benefit are difficult to measure no matter how extensive the experiment, it is difficult to recommend that designed experiments be employed in all cases. The effects of the OSHA program, however, are of such potential importance and have been the subject of such contention that it is reasonable to recommend an experimental design to measure the program's impact. For Smith reveals the difficulty of measuring a program's impact when, for a variety of political and economic reasons, incomplete data is collected on the program and its intended subjects and beneficiaries.

Weisbrod and Helming's discussion of the complex difficulties in accounting for social costs and benefits, as well as Smith's data difficulties, highlight the complications that arise in the proper execution of an evaluation. Officials in OHSA are partly responsible for the decision not to collect any more than the limited program data already on hand. The result of this judgment severely limited the knowledge one could gain. Weisbrod and Helming also decided not to collect certain data due to the costs to patients and their families. But the constraints on knowledge imposed by such costs were much less damaging to this study.

Ethical considerations of executing experiments in OSHA are also highlighted by the mental health study, for some of the patients assigned to the experimental group expressed a preference to be in the control group. They could always drop out, of course, but the ethical issue remains. We should point out, however, that the installation of any social program is an experiment. The fastidiousness of program managers and policy makers concerning the damage potentially caused to subjects in an experiment is partly a reflection of the point made by Viscusi—people behave differently when identified lives (known persons in an experiment) are under consideration rather than when statistical lives (an unidentified membership of a target population in a social program) are under consideration. For, to be sure, the social program as a natural experiment can also fail and cause damage to persons and society. But this point is not vigorously expressed when the same potential, negative effects of social experiments are being discussed. Experiments at least have the value of making it possible to explicitly identify and measure as many of these costs as possible. Natural experiments can only suffice if properly modeled and if proper data are collected as a result of that modeling.

Finally, we leave this introduction with a cautionary note sounded by the Viscusi study—there are no unambiguous and absolute economic measures of the loss of human life and limb.

23

One of the most fundamental problems in analyzing social programs is assessing the loss and gain to humans in situations where they may be injured or killed. This issue is important since policies to reduce the risks of death and injury are assuming an increasingly central role in the development of social policy. Apart from the relatively intractable nature of this valuation problem, this study provides insight on several issues of great importance to evaluations in the health area such as:

- the existence and nature of compensating wage differentials;
- the difficulty of assessing the value to a person or community of avoiding a very small probability of a very large loss—e.g., a nuclear reactor melt-down;
- the different values individuals and communities place on *identified* versus *statistical* lives;
- the unique characteristic of life and health that involve nontransferable commodities for which no insurance contract can provide replacement; and
- the conceptual difficulties of using any of the several economic procedures for assessing the value of a life.

These issues are discussed in the context of an attempt to measure the value that individuals (implicitly) attach to death and injury through their decisions to accept employment associated with varying degrees of risk.

Although it has conceptual difficulties, the willingness-to-pay measure is the method of valuation used in this study. For the individual, it is his or her value of life and limb that is adopted. For societal choices, the willingness to pay of other members of society must be measured to obtain the appropriate estimate of the value of life or health. Next, the study deals with measuring the value of statistical lives and not-identified lives. Finally, the conceptual basis for the analysis is the theory of compensating wage differentials. Jobs which have particular disadvantages must have offsetting advantages (such as higher wages) that make them as attractive on net as those jobs without such disadvantages. This notion was articulated by Adam Smith in *The Wealth of Nations*. Viscusi notes that, in his judgment, the underlying hypothesis of compensating wage differentials is not controversial. This may be true among economists, but the theory is not universally accepted among policy makers and program administrators. Statutes regarding occupational safety and health, environmental preservation, and consumer product safety demonstrate society's ambivalence in accepting an economic criterion as the sole basis for decision-making in this area, even when only statistical lives are under consideration.

Nevertheless, there is ample evidence that lives and health are subject to economic valuation by both individuals and society. Viscusi attempts to understand this valuation by using data from the University of Michigan's 1969-1970 Survey of Working Conditions in a multivariate model where annual earnings are regressed on job hazard indices, workers' characteristics, and job characteristics. The resulting regression coefficients on the job hazard variables measure the implicit monetary return that workers receive in compensation for risk of death or injury. These estimates are then used to estimate the monetary value that workers attach to death or injury. Where there are low probabilities of risk of death, the regression coefficient of the "death risk" variable for the earnings equation is multiplied by the number of deaths per year which correspond to a one unit change in the "death" variable. Linear and nonlinear (semilogarithmic) earnings equations were estimated; the semilogarithmic function implying a rising price differential being required as the risk of death on the job increases.

The estimated results are similar across a variety of models estimated in this general framework. The average value of a life falls in the range of $1 to $1.5 million in 1960 dollars (undiscounted). The average value of an injury, that is, the drop in earnings due to injury, range between $13,000 and $14,000. This measure includes fatal as well as nonfatal injuries. When one accounts for the death risk premium separately, the valuation of an injury falls in the $6,000 to $10,000 range.

These results differ considerably from other estimates of the valuation of life. Work by Acton based on respondents answers to questions concerning valuation of different programs to save the life of heart attack victims fall in the range of $28,000 to $43,000. These measures are faulty, however, for at least two reasons: (1) Individuals have little incentive to give thoughtful responses to such interview questions. Rather, Viscusi's data are most relevant since they express *revealed* behavior—what they say they will do in hypothetical situations. (2) Individuals find it extremely difficult to evaluate choices involving very small probabilities.

Comparing Viscusi's results with the work of Thaler and Rosen (1976) is more complex. Their estimate of the value of a life in 1969 dollars is $220,000 plus or minus $60,000—quite a large difference from Viscusi's result. The most likely reason for this difference lies in the fact that the two studies were concerned with different populations. The Michigan Survey of Working Conditions data base is a sample of the blue collar population, whereas the Thaler and Rosen sample draws on a group which is less risk averse and, hence, places a lower valuation on loss of life for any given level of risk on the job. Thus, an important scientific and policy lesson of this comparison is that different valuations of life result from samples with different tastes for risk. Risk-averse individuals self-select out of risky jobs while persons with a taste for risk self-select into those jobs. Valuations of life in any given context are subject to the worker's taste for risk and are in no sense absolute.

Finally, of the several policy and applications issues discussed, the most interesting is the set of issues arising when one substitutes the numbers of *lives* saved for the valuation concept—usually out of a distaste for attaching economic value to human beings. Briefly, the substitution of the number of lives saved by a program for the *valuation* of those lives (a) does not allow one to determine the optimal level of expenditures in life saving; (b) ignores outcomes other than lives saved; and (c) values all lives equally, regardless of length of life preserved and the quality of that life. Thus, the ideal measure continues to escape us in policy formulation.

Labor Market Valuations of Life and Limb
Empirical Evidence and Policy Implications

W. Kip Viscusi

The empirical analysis of compensating wage differentials received by 496 blue-collar workers yields the first implicit values of injuries ever obtained and the only implicit values of life that take into account compensation for other nonpecuniary characteristics. Workers behave as if they attached a dollar value of 10^4 to nonfatal injuries and 10^6 to death. This value of life estimate exceeds those found in other studies, not because these earlier estimates are wrong, but simply because there is not a unique value of life but a distribution of such values across the population. Detailed discussions indicate the pertinence of these results not only to occupational health and safety policies but also to benefit-cost analyses of other policies affecting life and limb.

Policies to reduce the risks of death and to prevent injuries or illness have become an increasingly important part of the public decision-making agenda. This interest in government intervention has been largely motivated by a growing perception that there are many important limitations to private choices. The decision-maker may have limited knowledge of the implications of his actions. This problem is especially acute for health hazards that are difficult to monitor and involve very small probabilities. If a worker is locked in by seniority rights or accumulated pension benefits, he may be reluctant to switch to a safer position after he learns of the hazards involved. The costs of altering one's past choices suggest that individuals may have limited control over a health-affecting activity.

* Financial support and able research assistance were provided by the U.S. Department of Labor and Ernest Fung, respectively. Richard Zeckhauser provided helpful comments that improved both the exposition and substance of this article.

From W. Kip Viscusi, "Labor Market Valuations of Life and Limb: Empirical Evidence and Policy Implications," 26(3) *Public Policy* 359-386 (Summer 1978). Copyright © 1978 by the Fellows of Harvard College. Reprinted by permission of John Wiley & Sons, Inc.

Finally, a person cannot fully insure himself against possible adverse outcomes. Although one can buy insurance that will provide cash or medical care in the event of death or injury, this monetary transfer may do little to restore a person to his original level of welfare. The primary difficulty is that life and health involve nontransferable commodities for which no insurance contract can provide replacements.

Many government programs have been enacted in an attempt to influence the probabilities of adverse impacts on individuals' health. Most of these have led to the promulgation of safety regulations, such as those affecting employment hazards, nuclear reactors, automobiles, and food additives. In addition to programs that alter the probabilities of adverse health outcomes, a variety of efforts is intended to improve individual well-being after illnesses or injuries have struck. Medical insurance, workmen's compensation, and welfare programs have been created to ameliorate the consequences of such unfavorable occurrences. Policies that directly influence the risks of death, injury, or illness are often justified partly on the grounds that these efforts may reduce the costs of such compensation, which are shared by society at large.

In this article, I have two principal concerns. First, I explore new bodies of data on labor market behavior in order to obtain estimates of the values that individuals implicitly attach to death and injury through their employment decisions. Second, in discussing the pertinence of these estimates to policy evaluation, I demonstrate that investigations directed at obtaining an elusive value of life number are largely misdirected. Instead, analysts should be concerned with differences in individuals' values of life and health status and the implications that the resulting distribution of values has for government policy. I do not become involved in subtle value debates as to who should be making such decisions or whether lifesaving should be used to redistribute income to the poor. These matters are thoroughly treated by Zeckhauser (1975) and Zeckhauser and Shepard (1976).

The general approach taken here follows the two basic guidelines established in 1968 by Schelling's classic essay "The Life You Save May Be Your Own." First, the principal matter of concern is, not identified lives, but statistical lives. The value society places on an identified life, such as a trapped coal miner, is likely to be substantially greater than the implicit valuations of life and health status of individuals who cannot be identified, such as the prospective beneficiaries from improved ambulance service or flood control programs. In the latter instance, the policy has a probabilistic effect on the well-being of large numbers of individuals. The lives that have been extended or improved may not be identifiable even on an *ex post* basis; the prevention of a flood, for example, provides no information on who would otherwise have died.

Second, the willingness-to-pay measure of the value of life and limb is adopted. In the case of individual choice, it is the individual's valuation that is of consequence. For public choices, the willingness to pay of other members of society must also be tallied to obtain the appropriate estimate for the value of life or health status. The willingness-to-pay measure has been adopted by all the principal economic analyses of the value of life of the past decade.

The alternative measure of the value of life that has attracted the greatest attention is the discounted value of one's earnings, which is the technique used by Rice and Cooper (1967).[1] Although this is frequently labeled the human capital approach, it has never been espoused by a prominent exponent of human capital theory. The reason for the reluctance to endorse this technique is simple. No conceptual basis exists for linking a person's future earnings to the value he would place on his life if he were faced with a lottery on life and death. Discounted income measures are not even a reasonable upper boundary for the amount he would pay to avoid certain death, for an individiaul faced with such a situation might try to earn more income, perhaps even illegitimately, in an effort to preserve his life. For use in policy decisions, the discounted income measure has unacceptable implications, particularly for the nation's elderly and housewives, as well as others with low earned incomes.

The method used to assess individuals' willingness to pay to avoid death or injury is similar to that used for obtaining dollar valuations of other components in benefit-cost analysis.[2] In particular, market prices are determined. The market context to be examined is that for potentially hazardous employment. An alternative technique used

[1] For a critique of this and other proposed measures of the value of life, see Mishan (1971), Zeckhauser (1975), and Acton (1976).

[2] As the analyses by Zeckhauser (1975) and Zeckhauser and Shepard (1976) have indicated, the use of these implicit prices is by no means straightforward or uncontroversial. I return to this matter in the third section.

by Acton (1973) and Jones-Lee (1976) is the interview method, in which individuals are asked hypothetical questions that can be used to elicit implicit valuations of life. The principal limitation of this approach is that respondents have no incentive to give thoughtful or honest answers. Moreover, if their responses are likely to influence policy decisions, they may have an incentive to misrepresent their underlying preferences. Individual labor market decisions are not subject to these limitations. It is for these reasons that analysts gather data from observed behavior to estimate supply curves, demand curves, and other objects of econometric inquiry rather than simply relying on responses to hypothetical questions.

In the first section of this article, I analyze the labor market behavior of 496 blue-collar workers in order to obtain new estimates of the implicit dollar loss associated with fatalities and to provide the first estimates of the dollar losses associated with nonfatal injuries. These estimates are discussed and compared with existing work in the second section. This section also includes the principal method-ological contribution of this article. In particular, it is not a unique value of life that should be the object of debate and econometric inquiry. Rather one should be concerned with the value of life schedules for the entire population. The application of these empiri-cal estimates to the evaluation of government policies affecting life and limb, both in the labor market and in broader contexts, is discussed in the third section. The fourth section sums up my con-clusions.

Empirical Estimates

Theoretical Foundations. Adam Smith articulated the conceptual basis of this investigation two centuries ago when he observed that "the whole of the advantages and disadvantages of the different employments of labor and stock must, in the same neighborhood, be either perfectly equal or continually tending to equality." In other words, jobs that carry with them certain disadvantages must have other offsetting advantages such as higher wages that make them as attractive overall as jobs without these disadvantages.[3]

[3] This "compensating wage differential" result holds whether or not individuals are risk-averse i.e., whether or not they will demand favorable odds to engage in a lottery. All that is required is

Although the underlying theory is not particularly controversial, it has been only recently that it has been subjected to successful empirical tests. One principal difficulty has been that the most attractive jobs in society tend to be well paid. Unless an analyst has sufficient information to be able to disentangle the role of different personal characteristics from the role of job attributes, including riskiness, the estimates of the wage premiums for risk will be seriously biased.

Description of the Sample. The data set to be used in this analysis is the University of Michigan's 1969–1970 Survey of Working Conditions (SWC). This survey provides the most detailed information available concerning the individual and his job. The analysis here uses only the data on 496 full-time blue-collar workers in the SWC sample, since the survey questions focused primarily on the types of job characteristics pertinent to this group. Using the data provided in this survey, I construct job hazard indices for each worker's job. The worker's earnings are then regressed on these job hazard indices, his personal characteristics, and the job characteristics in order to obtain the implicit monetary price workers receive for risks of death and injury. The results of this analysis are then used to estimate the dollar values that individuals attach to the loss of life or to a work injury.

The means and standard deviations of the principal variables are summarized in Table 1. The workers have a mean age of about 40, roughly 10 years of education, and 9 years of tenure, i.e., experience at their present place of employment. Just under a quarter of the sample is female, and about 12 percent is black. The percentage of workers who belong to unions, 49 percent, is about what one would expect for the blue-collar nonfarm population. In terms of occupational distribution, almost 80 percent of the workers are either operatives or craftsmen, foremen, or kindred workers. In short, the sample appears representative of the blue-collar working population.

The main independent variables of interest are of course the job hazard variables. The SWC includes a self-assessed hazard variable (DANGER) that has a value of 1 if the worker's job exposes him to dangerous or unhealthy conditions and a value of 0 otherwise. For

that individuals prefer being healthy to being dead or injured. A more formal statement of the underlying model is provided in Viscusi (forthcoming, *b*). The state-dependent utility model presented in that article is quite general. The ill health state can be interpreted as either a fatal or nonfatal job injury. Other economic analyses of compensating differentials include the work by Thaler and Rosen (1976), Oi (1973), and Smith (1976).

Table 1. SUMMARY OF SAMPLE CHARACTERISTICS[a]

Variable	Mean or fraction in sample	Standard deviation
Personal background:		
Age	39.71	13.71
Female	0.234	
Black	0.123	
Education	10.30	3.03
Tenure	9.09	10.03
Union	0.492	
Single	0.101	
Job characteristics:		
Number of employees at enterprise	562.2	915.3
EARNINGS	6,809.9	2,870.7
DANGER	0.522	
INJRATE	15.93	9.26
DEATH	5.91	8.29
NONFATAL	1,586.55	921.18
Occupation:		
Craftsmen, foremen, and kindred	0.34	
Service workers	0.17	
Private household workers	0.01	
Laborers	0.05	
Operatives and kindred	0.43	

[a] The standard deviations of the 0–1 dummy variables are omitted, since they can be computed from their fraction m in the sample, where the standard deviation is $(m-m^2)^{0.5}$.

purposes of this study, the DANGER variable is not of interest in its own right but rather is used in constructing and refining hazard indices for the worker's job. Detailed examination of worker responses and the hazards cited indicated that the self-assessed hazard variable was consistent with the worker's occupation and industry. Workers' perceptions of hazards exhibited a strong positive correlation with the industry injury rate. Moreover, the annual earnings premium for job risks was \$375 based on the self-perceived hazards variable and \$420 based on the industry injury rate—a difference well within the bounds of error.[4] All available evidence suggests that

[4] These findings are reported in Viscusi (forthcoming, *b*).

workers' subjective assessments of the risk are plausible. It is unlikely, however, that workers have perfect information about the
risks posed by their jobs. The empirical implications of imperfect
worker information are discussed in the following section.

Using information about each worker's industry, 1969 Bureau of
Labor Statistics (BLS) industry injury rate statistics were matched to
the workers in the sample.[5] The most aggregative of these measures
was INJRATE, the number of fatal or disabling on-the-job injuries
per million hours worked in a particular worker's industry. An
injury is defined as being "disabling" if it was "either caused some
permanent impairment or made the worker unable to work at a
regularly established job for at least 1 full day after the day of
injury." Injuries are divided into three categories: death, permanent
partial disability, and temporary total disability. On average, for the
industries represented by the workers in the sample, death was 0.4
percent of all injuries. Permanent partial disability accounted for 2.9
percent of all injuries, and temporary total disability for the remaining 96.7 percent. For the purposes of this analysis, the two nonfatal
injury rate classifications were pooled, for the data were not rich
enough to distinguish the compensating differentials for all three
types of hazards. The first of the disaggregative injury variables is
DEATH, which is INJRATE multiplied by the percentage of injuries
that were fatal in the worker's industry. Similarly, the variable
NONFATAL was obtained by multiplying INJRATE by the percentage of nonfatal injuries.

Assuming an average workweek of 40 hours and an average of 50
weeks worked per year, these hazard variables can be directly converted into annual probabilities of adverse outcomes.[6] On average,
the workers in the sample faced an annual probability of 0.0319 of a
fatal or nonfatal job injury, a 1.18×10^{-4} probability of death, and a
0.0317 probability of a nonfatal injury. These risks are a bit higher
than the average for all manufacturing industries but lower than the
hazard levels in many nonmanufacturing industries such as mining
and transportation. They are, of course, incremental death and

---

[5] All injury rate data are from the U.S. Department of Labor (1971).

[6] Since INJRATE is the number of fatalities and injuries per million hours, the number per
2,000 hours is INJRATE divided by 500. DEATH and NONFATAL are the percentages of
INJRATE that are fatal and nonfatal, i.e., DEATH + NONFATAL = 100 INJRATE. Hence
dividing each by 50,000 converts it to an annual probability.

injury risks, over and above the risks the workers face in the normal course of their daily life.

Three job risk variables were also constructed, using the information as to whether the worker considered his job hazardous, thereby reducing some of the measurement error associated with using an industry-wide risk index. The variables INJRATE1, DEATH, and NONFATAL1 were obtained by multiplying their former values by the 0 to 1 dummy variable DANGER. Thus, these variables are identical in value with INJRATE, DEATH, and NONFATAL except that they equal zero if the worker does not view his job as hazardous.

Empirical Results. The earnings equation was estimated in both linear and semilogarithmic form; annual earnings (EARNINGS) and its natural logarithm (LOGEARNINGS) were the two dependent variables. Ideally, one would like to use the hourly wage as the dependent variable rather than total earnings, but the SWC did not provide wage data or other information, such as weeks worked, that would make it possible to construct a wage rate. Since the analysis focuses on full-time workers and includes an overtime work variable, this shortcoming is presumably not very serious.

In addition to various combinations of job risk variables, each equation also contained 22 other independent variables. These included 11 dummy job characteristic variables reflecting the speed of work, whether the worker is a supervisor, overtime work, job security, whether the job requires that the worker make decisions, the presence of a training program, the number of other employees at the enterprise, and three dummy variables denoting the occupational group of the worker. The remaining independent variables pertained to regional economic conditions and the worker's personal characteristics, including age, race, sex, years of schooling, health status, tenure, and union membership.

It is assumed here that workers act as if the objective hazard indices correspond to their subjective assessments. Imperfect worker information generates underestimates of workers' implicit value of life for both econometric and economic reasons. First, if workers' probability assessments are randomly distributed about the true value, one encounters a conventional errors-in-variable situation in which the empirical estimates are biased downward. Second, suppose that workers' prior probability assessments correspond to the true risk of the job but that these assessments are imprecise. In normal employment situations in which workers face a sequence of lotteries in life and death and in which workers learn about the risks of the job through their on-the-job experiences, workers require less wage compensation for any mean level of risk as their initial judgment becomes less precise.[7] The empirical results consequently will understate workers' actual value of life and health.

Overall, the LOGEARNINGS equation provided a somewhat better fit. The linear form of the earnings equation implies a constant price per unit of job risk, and the semilogarithmic form implies a rising price. The death risk results are reported in Table 2. Six different specifications were estimated for both the EARNINGS and LOGEARNINGS variables. The principal differences among them are the other job risk variables that were included—the nonfatal injury rate or self-assessed dangers—and whether the hazard variables were nonzero only in instances in which the worker perceived his job as being hazardous. The most meaningful results are probably those given in lines 2 and 5 in Table 2, in which both the fatal and nonfatal components of the BLS injury rate are included in the equation. Throughout this first set of equations, the death risk coefficients tend to be somewhat lower for the job risk variables that are conditional on self-perceived hazards.

The implied value of life estimates contained in Table 2 pertain to implicit values when there are low probabilities of risk. These magnitudes were computed in straightforward fashion. As noted earlier, each unit of the death risk variable corresponds to 50,000 deaths per year. Multiplication of the death risk coefficient for the EARNINGS equation by this number yields the value that individuals place on their life for small changes in the probability of death. The valuation estimates for the LOGEARNINGS equation were obtained similarly, taking into consideration the different functional form being used.[8]

The results from one equation to the next display striking similarity; most of the death risk equations in which other job risk variables are included indicate a value of life in the range of $1 to $1.5 million in 1969 dollars. These estimates clearly exceed the amount that a representative worker in the sample could pay to avoid certain death.

---

[7] This point is formalized in Viscusi (forthcoming, a).

[8] These estimates were obtained with respect to a one unit change in the death risk evaluated at the mean income level for the sample.

Table 2. SUMMARY OF DEATH RISK REGRESSION RESULTS[a]

Death risk variable	Other job risk variables included in equation	LOGEARNINGS results		EARNINGS results	
		Death risk coefficient (std. error)	Implied value of life	Death risk coefficient (std. error)	Implied value of life
1. Industry death risk (DEATH)	. . .	0.00205 (0.00075)	1,595,000	35.39 (10.73)	1,769,500
2. Industry death risk (DEATH)	Nonfatal injury rate (NONFATAL)	0.00153 (0.00088)	1,185,000	29.20 (12.69)	1,460,000
3. Industry death risk (DEATH)	Self-assessed dangers (DANGER)	0.00183 (0.00075)	1,420,000	32.13 (10.81)	1,606,500
4. Industry death risk conditional on self-perceived hazard (DEATH1)	. . .	0.00189 (0.00072)	1,490,000	34.08 (10.38)	1,704,000
5. Industry death risk conditional on self-perceived hazard (DEATH1)	Nonfatal injury rate conditional on self-perceived hazard (NONFATAL1)	0.00076 (0.00093)	600,000	18.27 (13.33)	913,500
6. Industry death risk conditional upon self-perceived hazard (DEATH1)	Self-assessed dangers (DANGER)	0.00141 (0.00079)	1,080,000	27.93 (11.40)	1,396,500

[a] Complete regression results are not reported here, since they are similar to those reported in Viscusi (forthcoming, b); the only difference is the inclusion of death risk and nonfatal injury risk variables in this analysis. Two of the equations in the aforementioned paper correspond to those in line 1 in Table 3.

It is important, however, to note that such a magnitude is not what the valuation of life figures represent. Rather, individuals act as if their life were worth the indicated amounts when they are faced with very small incremental risks of death. An individual facing an annual additional death risk of 1.18×10^{-4} (the mean for the sample) would receive additional wage compensation of $173 based on the EARN-INGS equation coefficient in line 2. The amount that a worker would pay to eliminate the certainty of death is necessarily below the $1 to $1.5 million amount, since the worker's wealth would be reduced as he purchased reductions in the risk of death. This decline in wealth in turn would reduce the value the individual attached to his life, since one's willingness to incur such risks increases as one's wealth declines.[9] In short, there are likely to be important income effects so that the implicit value of life for small changes in the probability of death will greatly exceed the value workers would pay to avoid certain death.

In similar fashion, one can interpret the implied values of all injuries, including death. These values are reported in Table 3. Workers act as if they viewed the average industrial injury as equivalent to a $13,000 to $14,000 drop in income. This result refers to the distribution of all industrial injuries, of which 0.4 percent overall were fatalities, 2.9 percent permanent partial disability, and 96.7 percent temporary total disability. If the death risk premium is distinguished from that for nonfatal injuries, one obtains a value for nonfatal injuries in the $6,000 to $10,000 range. These results are instructive in that they indicate that, in dollar terms, a probability of death is regarded as being 100 times worse than an equal probability of a nonfatal injury.

Comparisons with Other Work

Results from Interview Studies. To date, there have been no other estimates of the implicit value of injuries. Hence these results cannot be compared with other analyses. There have been several investigations of individuals' value of life. The first of these studies was Acton's 1973 investigation in which individuals were asked their

---

[9] Supporting conceptual analysis and empirical evidence are provided in Viscui (forthcoming, b).

Table 3. SUMMARY OF INJURY RISK REGRESSION RESULTS

Injury risk variable	Death risk variable included in equation	LOGEARNINGS results		EARNINGS results	
		Injury risk coefficient (std. error)	Implied value of injury	Injury risk coefficient (std. error)	Implied value of injury
1. Unspecified job injury (INJRATE)	· · ·	0.0040 (0.0016)	13,550	26.37 (10.14)	13,185
2. Unspecified job injury conditional on self-perceived hazard (INJRATE1)	· · ·	0.0040 (0.0013)	13,550	27.72 (7.83)	13,860
3. Industry nonfatal injury rate (NONFATAL)	Industry death rate (DEATH)	0.932E-5 (0.897E-5)	5,500	0.110 (0.121)	5,500
4. Industry nonfatal injury rate, conditional on self-perceived hazard (NONFATAL1)	Industry death rate conditional on self-perceived hazard (DEATH1)	0.136E-4 (0.704E-5)	9,500	0.191 (0.101)	9,500

valuations of different programs to save the life of heart attack victims. These interviews suggested a value of life in the range of $28,000 to $43,000.

For several reasons, Acton's results are not comparable with those assessed here for the labor market. First, the lives involved are post-heart attack lives and consequently should be valued less highly. Second, the sample size was rather small (36), so that the estimates may not be very reliable.[10] Third, individuals have no incentive to give thoughtful or honest responses to questions asked in an interview.

This final observation is perhaps the most fundamental, for it highlights the inherent limitations of the interview approach. The process of thinking about choices involving small probabilities is notoriously difficult. Indeed, the principal purpose of Schelling's pathbreaking essay was to provide a methodology that would enable private decision makers to conceptualize these issues in a systematic fashion. A person confronted with information about a hypothetical lottery clearly has less of an incentive to evaluate his preferences regarding these risks than he would if he were incurring the same risks daily in his place of employment. Moreover, even if the respondent has given the issues careful consideration, he has no reason to reveal his preferences honestly. He may give the response that he believes will create a favorable impression on the interviewer, a difficulty that is more likely when the life to be saved is not that of the respondent but an anonymous member of the community. A person's altruism may be much greater when he knows he will not be required to back up his statements with out-of-pocket contributions. Finally, individuals may misrepresent their preferences if they believe their responses will affect the benefits they will receive or the taxes they must pay to support a public program to save lives; this is the familiar strategic issue. The fundamental and pervasive nature of these limitations suggests that interview results might best be used to supplement rather than supplant estimates obtained from market behavior.

---

[10] A similar interview study by Jones-Lee (1976) also has a small sample; only 30 out of 90 people polled responded. The low response rate also raises the problem that the personal characteristics and implicit valuations of life of the respondents may be quite different from those who chose not to answer the questionnaire.

Labor Market Analyses. Thaler and Rosen's 1976 analysis of implicit valuations of life in the labor market yielded estimates of $220,000 ± $66,000 in 1969 dollars. These figures are more closely comparable with those found in the first section.[11] Their study focused on 900 adult males in hazardous occupations. The death risk variable used was the Society of Actuaries' incremental death risk for a group of 37 narrowly defined occupations. This variable reflected the death risks of the occupation per se as well as the death risks that were unrelated to work but are correlated with the characteristics and life-styles and income levels of people in different occupations. As a result, the patterns of risk are surprising. Cooks face three times the death risk of firemen, elevator operators face twice the death risk of truck drivers or electricians, waiters face 67 times the death risk of linemen or servicemen, and actors face a higher death risk than fishermen, foresters, power plant operatives, and individuals in many other more physically demanding occupations. Although narrowly defined occupational risk indices may be superior to BLS industry risk data, the inclusion of death risks unrelated to work makes it unclear which variable involves less measurement error.

If, as Thaler and Rosen suggest (p. 287), the BLS injury rate involves more measurement error and if this error is random, my value of life estimates should underestimate the actual value by more than theirs. My figures, however, are already roughly five times the level of their results. Consequently, one cannot use measurement error as the explanation for this difference, because correction for this problem would make the estimates more disparate than they already are.

The principal difference in the death risk variables is that the BLS industry death risk variable pertains to a broad cross-section of industries, but the Society of Actuaries' measure pertains to only the most hazardous occupations that on average pose an annual death risk ten times larger than that faced in the SWC sample (10^{-3} versus 10^{-4}). The sample of workers in the Thaler and Rosen study includes only those workers who are least averse to job risks, but my analysis

[11] The study by Smith (1976) of death risk premiums in the labor market yielded an implicit value of life of $2.6 million. Smith, however, was not particularly confident of the reliability of the results, since all his efforts to find premiums for injuries or other variants of the components of the BLS injury rate were unsuccessful. Moreover, his analysis did not include any job characteristics other than the industry death risk. The results were therefore very likely biased upward.

Table 4. COMPARISON OF SAMPLES USED IN VALUE OF LIFE STUDIES[a]

Category	Thaler and Rosen sample mean value	SWC sample mean value
Personal characteristics:		
Age	41.8	39.7
Education	10.1	10.3
White	0.90	0.88
Union	0.45	0.49
Married	0.92	0.90
Females	0	0.23
Occupational characteristics:		
Operative and kindred	0.27	0.43
Service workers	0.45	0.17
Laborers	0.22	0.05
Annual income	7,194	6,810
Annual incremental death risk	1×10^{-3}	1×10^{-4}

[a] The annual income figures for the Thaler and Rosen sample were calculated by multiplying the average weekly salary by the average number of weeks worked in 1966. The earnings figure in 1967 dollars for the Thaler and Rosen sample was converted into 1969 dollars using the consumer price index for these two years.

focuses on the entire blue-collar population.[12] Table 4 presents detailed comparisons of the two samples. In terms of personal characteristics there is little difference except that the Thaler and Rosen study excluded women from the analysis. The occupational distribution is quite different; their sample included a much higher percentage of service workers and laborers than did the SWC sample.

The most salient difference in the two studies is that the Thaler and Rosen analysis focuses on a group who have shown themselves to be less averse to severe death risks than the rest of the population. Unlike standard consumer items, death risks do not command a single price. The risk is inextricably linked to the job; it cannot be divided to yield a constant price per unit of risk. Those individuals who are least averse to such risks are willing to accept a lower compensation per unit of risk than the rest of the working popula-

[12] Their sample was selected on the basis of the availability of death risk data, which was provided only for the most hazardous occupations.

tion. As a result, they are inclined to accept larger risks with lower wage premiums per unit of risk. Hence the Thaler and Rosen analysis yields a lower implied value of life.

The final important difference in the analysis is that the results reported in the first section are the only value of life estimates obtained from equations in which other nonpecuniary job characteristics, such as nonfatal injuries and the speed of work, were included. To the extent that job risks are positively correlated with other unattractive job attributes, the omission of these attributes leads to overestimates of the value of life.

A suggestive estimate of the extent of the bias can be obtained by examining the results in Table 2. Omission of the nonfatal injury rate from the equations boosts the implied value of life significantly. The increase ranges from 21 to 150 percent, depending on the equation in question. Omission of seven other job attribute variables alters the value of life estimates by much less—usually by about one-third and by as little as 1 percent for one equation.[13] A similar bias in other data sets could account for the fact that Smith's (1976) estimate of the BLS industry death risk premium yielded a value of life of $2.6 million, roughly double that found in this study. By similar reasoning, Thaler and Rosen's estimates may be too high, so that their value of life would actually have been less than one-fifth of the magnitude I found if additional job attribute variables had been included in their analysis.

Value of Life and Limb Schedules. Summarizing, the principal reason that my value of life estimates are several times larger than Thaler and Rosen's appears to be the difference in the level of the risk. Their analysis reflected the preferences of those least averse to risk and who consequently were in very risky jobs. One's natural inclination is to ask which estimate better reflects the value of life. Framing the issue in those familiar terms, however, is not the appropriate way to view value of life problems.

In particular, different members of the population attach different values to their life. Empirical analyses should not be directed at estimating an elusive value of life number; rather they should estimate the schedule of values for the entire population. The line *VL* in Figure 1 illustrates such a schedule. As the percentage of the popula-

---

[13] The seven variables omitted were all of the eleven job characteristic variables except the number of employees at the enterprise variable and the three occupational dummy variables.

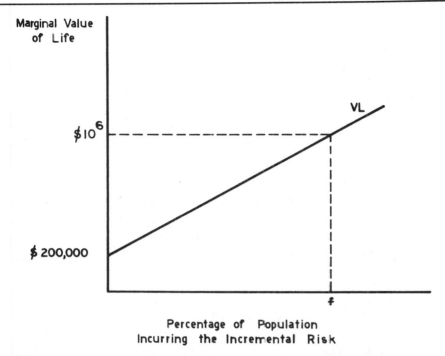

Figure 1. RELATION OF THE VALUE OF LIFE TO THE PERCENTAGE OF THE
POPULATION INCURRING THE RISK

tion incurring the incremental risk increases, so does the marginal
valuation of life. Those who price their life the cheapest are drawn
into the market first; higher wages must be paid to lure additional
workers into risky jobs. Thaler and Rosen focused on the lower tail
of the population—those who appeared to value their life at approximately $200,000. The more representative blue-collar SWC sample
yielded a value of roughly $1 million. Empirical estimates can most
accurately be viewed as weighted averages of points along the marginal valuation of life curve for the population. If the sample contains disproportionately many workers from the occupations posing
substantial risks, it generates lower average values of life and limb
than if the sample is more representative. For simplicity, the empirical results are illustrated as if they yielded single points on the curve
rather than weighted averages of points along it. Thus, for Figure 1,
Thaler and Rosen's results yield the intercept at $200,000, but my
findings correspond to a marginal value of 10^6 with percentage f of the population incurring the risk.

Table 5. HYPOTHETICAL SAMPLE OF WORKERS

	GROUP 1	GROUP 2	GROUP 3
Annual risk of death x_i	10^{-6}	10^{-5}	10^{-4}
Average total compensation y_i	$1.50	$10	$20
Implicit value of life	1.5×10^6	10^6	0.2×10^6
Number in group	10	100	10

The nature of the way the regression analysis averages workers' marginal valuations of life and limb can be illustrated with the aid of a numerical example and a bit of elementary statistics. Consider the sample of workers whose characteristics are summarized in Table 5. For simplicity, the only influences considered are the death risks posed by the job and the compensation for those risks, generating a model of the form[14]

$$y = \beta x$$

Here x is the incremental death risk incurred by the worker, y is the earnings premium for this risk, and β is the implicit value of life. The implicit value of life for each of the three groups of workers is obtained by dividing y by x for the group, yielding values ranging from 0.2×10^6 to 1.5×10^6.

Suppose that the value of life estimate to be obtained is the simple average of these marginal valuations, weighted according to the number of workers in each group. This approach would yield an average value of life equal to

$$\frac{1}{n} \sum_{i=1}^{n} \frac{y_i}{x_i} = \$9.75 \times 10^5$$

It is important to recall that regression estimates do not yield a simple linear average of this type but rather produce an estimated value of life $\hat{\beta}$ given by

$$\hat{\beta} = \frac{\sum_{i=1}^{n} y_i x_i}{\sum_{i=1}^{n} x_i^2} = \$2.73 \times 10^5$$

[14] The intercept for this simplified model is presumably zero, since workers receive no wage premium if they face no additional risk.

Thus, the implied value of life estimates obtained in regression analyses are nonlinear weighted averages of points along the value of life curve in Figure 1.

Investigations that seek a unique value of life rather than points on the value of life schedule implicitly assume that the value of life curves are flat. The stark difference, however, between the Thaler and Rosen results and those of this study combines with the investigation of likely biases in the analyses to suggest that individuals' valuations of life vary substantially.

In addition to influencing the interpretation of the empirical results, the analysis of the value of life curves is important in ascertaining the appropriate value of life to be used in government policymaking. We return to this matter in the last part of the third section.

Policy Applications[15]

Implications for Occupational Health and Safety Policy. The most immediate significance of the empirical results is their implication for labor market performance. If workers were not compensated adequately for the risks they incurred, one would conclude that the market did not function effectively, perhaps because of systematic individual misallocations. The theme of inadequate compensation runs throughout the more sociologically oriented literature on occupational safety.

As the empirical results indicate, the annual compensation for all job risks totals only about $400. Unlike stuntmen and other workers who received clearly significant hazard premiums, blue-collar workers in the more hazardous occupations do not receive additional remuneration that is sufficiently great to be visible to the casual observer. It is also important to note, however, that the risks the workers incur are not very large; the probability of a fatal injury is only about 10^{-4}. To ascertain whether workers are accepting additional risks for amounts small enough to suggest some form of market failure, one should examine, not the absolute level of com-

---

[15] For a detailed discussion of the policy issues raised by the valuation of life, see Zeckhauser (1975). In this section, I focus on the narrower issue of the implications of the empirical results for policy choice.

pensation, but the implicit values that workers associate with death or injury. The empirical results indicate that these magnitudes are quite impressive—on the order of $1 to $1.5 million for fatalities and $10,000 for injuries. Although there is no way to ascertain whether these levels of compensation are above or below those that would prevail if workers were perfectly informed, the magnitudes are at least suggestive in that they indicate substantial wage compensation for job hazards.[16] These findings do not imply that the government should not intervene. They do indicate, however, that it is doubtful that one can base the case for intervention on the absence of compensation for risks of death and injury.

The value of life and limb estimates also can be used in assigning dollar values to the impacts of occupational health and safety regulation. If safety standards reduce the death risks or injury risks faced by workers, workers' wages fall in a competitive market. Regulation of job hazards also imposes implicit costs on employers. The amounts of these costs are often difficult to compute directly, since firms have an incentive to overstate the financial burdens of prospective regulations. On a theoretical basis, however, the marginal cost of safety improvements in a competitive market equals the cost of the wage premiums for an incremental change in the level of the risk.[17] How much wages are reduced and cost increased depends on a variety of factors such as the level of risk and the extent to which it is reduced, the types of hazard, and the characteristics of the workers and the workplace, e.g., unionization. Nevertheless, application of the implicit values of life and limb to analysis of the impacts of health and safety regulation might be a useful starting point for policy evaluation.

The Need for Explicit Evaluations. More generally, the empirical results set forth here have important implications for policy analyses of projects involving risks of life and limb. To date, there has been little systematic attempt to incorporate dollar valuations of life and limb into these analyses.[18] Even federal evaluations of water resource projects, which assign somewhat arbitrary values to recreation bene-

---

[16] In addition to *ex ante* wage compensation workers also receive substantial tax-free workmen's compensation benefits—up to two-thirds of the worker's gross wages in most states—so that the injury results in particular underestimate the implicit values attached by workers.

[17] See Thaler and Rosen (1976) for elaboration of this argument.

[18] An important exception is Acton's (1973) innovative study of policies to assist heart attack victims.

fits and other project impacts, ignore the lifesaving consequences of flood control and include only reduced property damage in the tally of benefits and costs. Much of the problem derives from society's reluctance to make explicit the trade-offs between dollars and lives. People are likely to say, "If additional expenditures can save lives, we will spare no expense in doing so." Although this maxim is not entirely implausible when dealing with identified lives, it clearly does not reflect the reality of public decisions or common medical practice, or for that matter private decisions. Public decisions concerned with individual welfare implicitly assign a finite value to life and other health outcomes except in the rare instances in which additional expenditures would accomplish nothing. Ignoring the issue of valuation of life and limb may circumvent the problem of offending people's sensitivities by making the trade-offs explicit. But at the same time it may be very costly in that it sacrifices lives that could have been improved or saved by a more systematic allocation process. An important issue for society as a whole, and one that many people are unwilling to face, is whether lives will be sacrificed in an effort to maintain the illusion that we will not trade off lives for dollars.

The most systematic alternative to valuations of life and limb is the use of cost-effectiveness analysis. Instead of ascertaining which program offers the greatest net benefits to society, one estimates the costs per lives saved of different programs and allocates funds where they are most productive. Although this approach is useful in highlighting clear-cut cases of inefficiency, it has important limitations.

First, suppose that OSHA spends $2 million for each life saved through its coke oven regulations, the Medicare program spends $1 million per life saved, and nuclear safety regulation costs $0.5 million per life saved. Additional lives could be saved if funds were reallocated so that the cost per life saved would be the same across different programs. Even if such a reallocation were made, however, the policy might not be optimal, for there are no means to determine the optimal level of expenditures in the life-extending area.

The second shortcoming of cost-effectiveness analysis is that it provides no guide to action when there is a variety of project impacts of unknown value. Programs that extend lives typically have other health outcomes, such as influencing the probability of illness and the well-being of individuals who are ill. In such instances, one cannot summarize a program's effect by saying that it costs $X per life saved, since it has impacts on many objectives.

Finally, analyses of costs per life saved are not meaningful if the lives saved have different lengths and different qualities. Extending the life of an elderly individual or someone in a permanant coma differ greatly in value from reducing the incidence of fatalities among healthy individuals whose lives will be greatly extended by policy intervention. In short, the extent of life lengthening and the quality of the life that is lengthened are important matters of interest not readily subsumed into the simple cost-effectiveness calculation.

Although policy makers can choose among programs with several qualitatively described impacts, in doing so they implicitly assign dollar values, or shadow prices, to the different outcomes. Making policy decisions on this basis raises two key problems. First, there is no guarantee that the attitudes of the policy makers toward the worth of life and limb coincide with those of society as a whole. The preferences of project beneficiaries, not legislators and bureaucrats, should be of a paramount concern and should not be ignored in the decision-making process.[19] Second, if quantitative values are not assigned to different policy impacts, the most productive allocations may not even be included in the list of policy options considered by the decision maker. Typically, the processes of program design and decision are separated, because different groups of individuals are responsible for drawing up the menu of policy options and choosing among these alternatives. Including explicit values of life and limb in the early stages of policy design assists in ensuring that society's valuations are incorporated in the entire policy choice process.

Externalities and Individual Values. If dollar values are to be assigned to different impacts on life and health, the controversy centers on what these values should be. Implicit values obtained by observing market behavior are instructive in establishing the value of life to the individual. Society at large, however, also has a stake in the health of its members. The group most affected by the external effects of death or illness is the individual's family. To the extent that the

---

[19] Two important exceptions should be noted. If beneficiaries systematically misallocate resources and neglect the future, a case might be made for using implicit values of life above those revealed in the marketplace. Moreover, if there are substantial externalities, the preferences of society as a whole must also be incorporated in the analysis. This matter is discussed in the following section.

preferences of other members of the household are taken into account when making one's employment decision, the market estimates reflect such externalities. Although the outcome might not be exactly what one would observe if the external effects were evaluated, a substantial input of this type no doubt affects employment decisions.[20]

Externalities to individuals other than one's family are not reflected in market estimates. It is unlikely, however, that these amounts are significant when compared with the $1 to $1.5 million value of life estimates that were obtained. Since market behavior is not instructive, interview studies along the lines of Acton (1973) might be used to resolve this issue.

Differences in the Value of Life. The empirical estimates of the implicit values of the loss due to either death or injury pertain to the sample of the working population examined. The value that an individual implicitly attaches to different health outcomes depends on his personal characteristics and on the nature of the lottery he faces. An attempt was made to ascertain whether the job risk variables interacted with personal characteristic variables such as age, race, and health status. The only significant effect found was for the education and death risk interaction term. In the linear form of the earnings equation, the coefficient for the interaction term was positive. The interpretation of this result is unclear, since better-educated workers may be safer workers. The premium may then not reflect differences in preferences but differing efficiency in the production of workplace health and safety. Additional empirical work is required to disentangle influences such as these so that different value of life estimates for people with different characteristics can be obtained.

In the absence of empirical evidence, one can often rely on theoretical analyses to indicate directions of influence. For example, it can be shown that individual aversion to adverse health outcomes necessarily increases as one's wealth increases.[21] As a result, the values individuals place on life and limb necessarily decline as the size of the risk increases, since the reduction in wealth that occurs

---

[20] Indeed, almost all labor supply analyses of recent vintage focus on household labor supply rather than individual choice models. Many of the predictions of the household labor supply approach, particularly those pertaining to wives' labor supply, have been borne out empirically.

[21] See Viscusi (forthcoming, *b*).

with the purchase of incremental reductions in the risk also diminishes the unattractiveness of the adverse health outcome.

A related result pertains to the level of the risk faced by an individual. Suppose the individual faces a 0.5 probability of death in the coming year in situation A and a 0.2 probability in situation B. In which instance would he place a greater value on a reduction of the probability of death by 0.1? It can be shown that because assets have a higher marginal value when survival is more certain, the willingness to pay for a reduction in the death risk is greater in situation B.[22] Individuals' personal characteristics and the nature of the lotteries they face are two important classes of considerations in modifying the value of life and limb estimates to take account of the specific aspects of a policy's effect.

A further class of considerations pertains to the nature of the quality of life after a life is extended or an illness is cured. The value of extending the life of a person with a terminal form of cancer or with a spinal-cord injury that has resulted in permanent paralysis is substantially less than that for an individual who can lead a full and active life. Substantial progress in the conceptualization of quality of life issues has been made by Zeckhauser and Shepard (1976). Additional research to obtain quantitative estimates of the effect of different changes in the quality of life would enhance our understanding of the quality adjustment process. Market evidence can also be useful here. For example, if more disaggregated job hazard information were available, one could estimate the implicit monetary loss that individuals attach to a variety of health outcomes rather than simply investigate the value attached to death and the broad category of nonfatal injuries. Thus, it would be possible to assign dollar values to different qualities of life, whereas we are now forced to use estimates that assume all individuals enjoy an average quality

---

[22] For proof of this and a series of related propositions of analytic and policy interest, see Weinstein, Shepard, and Pliskin (1976). This theorem is based on a conjecture by Zeckhauser, which was first proved by Raiffa (1968) for a somewhat different analytic context. The key assumption is that the marginal utility of a given amount of wealth is greater when one is alive than when dead. Although intuitively plausible, this assumption might seem to contradict observed behavior, since many individuals purchase life insurance at actuarially unfair rates in order to transfer additional resources to their family after death. The presence of substantial death duties, however, reduces the value of one's bequest so that the level of wealth after death would be reduced below the value when alive. If, as usually assumed, the marginal utility of wealth is positive but diminishing as the level of wealth increases, the tax system in effect raises the marginal utility of wealth after death so that life insurance purchases might become attractive.

of life. Disaggregation of this type is likely to be most important when the health outcomes involved differ from the typical disabling work injury or fatality that I have investigated.

Voluntary Risks, Involuntary Risks, and Self-Selection. In analyzing the value of life and limb, one should use the information provided by the nature of the risk incurred. In particular, voluntary and involuntary risks should be treated quite differently. To date, the only distinction that has been drawn between these two types of risks is that in a market system prices reflect individuals' value of the risks to life and limb if the risks are incurred voluntarily.[23]

In the discussion below I am not concerned with obtaining value of life and health estimates in contexts in which the degree of individual volition in accepting the risk varies. Rather, I assume that the pertinent schedule of values for the population has already been obtained through prior empirical work. The key question is how these schedules are to be used in the policy evaluation process in situations in which individuals incur risks voluntarily and involuntarily. Although the degree of volition involved spans a continuum of possibilities, for simplicity I focus on the polar cases of completely voluntary and completely involuntary risk.

The nature of the risk conveys important information about the implicit value of life and limb being assigned by the affected population. Other things equal, it is those who place the lowest dollar value on the expected loss to their health who choose to incur the risk. If individuals choose to live in a flood-prone area, to drive cars while intoxicated, or to work at hazardous jobs, the government's assessment of the value of the health gains from safety regulation should be quite different from its assessment when no element of free choice is involved.

Suppose, for example, that the characteristics of the affected population are comparable with those of the SWC sample of workers that was examined and that the median value of life corresponds to that of the individual at point f in Figure 2. Consider the situation in which the risk is involuntary and affects the whole population. Then the use of the median individual's value of life gives correct estimates of the benefits of lifesaving activities if the value of life schedule is linear, as is CC; overstates the benefits if the schedule is concave, as

[23] See Mishan (1971).

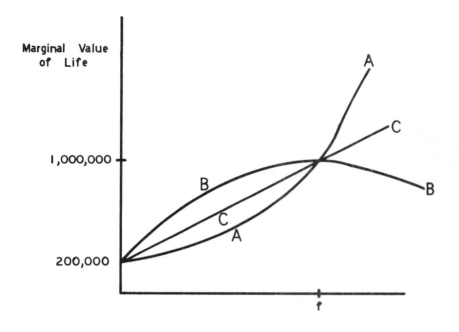

Figure 2. POSSIBLE SHAPES OF VALUE OF LIFE SCHEDULES

is *BB*; or understates the benefits for schedule *AA*. If the risk is voluntary and affects only half of the population, the use of the median individual's preferences at point *f* overstates the value of life irrespective of the shape of the value of life curve, since all other individuals who have chosen the risk value their lives at less than the amount for the median individual.

For the purposes of policy evaluation, it is the preferences of the average individual that matter in calculating consumers' surplus. The value of health-enhancing program benefits to project beneficiaries is computed by multiplying the number of lives saved or injuries prevented by the average value attached to these outcomes. In contrast, market outcomes reflect the preferences of the marginal worker. The valuation of life and limb of the worker who accepts the risky job and who is most averse to the hazards is instrumental in setting the wage rate, not the preferences of all the other inframarginal workers who would be willing to accept less than the going wage for the hazardous job.

Conclusion

Examination of implicit dollar values attached by workers to fatalities and injuries indicates that these health outcomes are evaluated at roughly 10^6 and 10^4, respectively. These estimates pertain to a particular subset of the working population and do not represent unique measures of these health outcomes. Indeed, the search for a unique value of life number is largely misguided; one should instead be concerned with obtaining measures of the distribution of individuals' assessments of different health outcomes.

Although much research remains to be done in these areas, policymakers should not be reluctant to use the estimates that are available. These dollar estimates are no less precise than most of the other dollar values assigned to project impacts in benefit-cost analyses. Moreover, the policy decision may not be very sensitive to whether the correct average value of life for the affected population is $1.1 or $1.5 million, whereas substantial welfare losses may result if the value assigned to life is only $10,000 or if the problem is ignored altogether. Although use of dollar values for life and limb may offend some individuals' moral sensitivities, the greater danger is that these trade-offs will be made without systematic analysis. Society will then be paying a substantial implicit price in lives sacrificed in an effort to preserve popular illusions.

Bibliography

Acton, Jan: "Evaluating Public Programs to Save Lives: The Case of Heart Attacks," RAND Corporation R-950-RC, 1973.

———: "Measuring the Monetary Value of Lifesaving Programs," *Law and Contemporary Problems,* vol. 40, no. 4, Autumn, 1976, pp. 46–72; also RAND Corporation, P-5675, 1976.

Jones-Lee, M. W.: *The Value of Life: An Economic Analysis,* University of Chicago Press, Chicago, 1976.

Mishan, E. J.: "Evaluation of Life and Limb: A Theoretical Approach," *Journal of Political Economy,* vol. 79, no. 4, pp. 687–705, 1971.

Oi, Walter: "An Essay on Workmen's Compensation and Industrial Safety," in *Supplemental Studies for the National Commission on State Workmen's Compensation Laws,* U.S. Government Printing Office, Washington, pp. 41–106, 1973.

Raiffa, Howard: *Decision Analysis: Introductory Lectures on Choices under Uncertainty*, Addison-Wesley, Reading, Mass., 1968.

Rice, Dorothy, and Barbara Cooper: "The Economic Value of Life," *American Journal of Public Health*, vol. 57, no. 11, pp. 1954–1966, 1967.

Schelling, Thomas: "The Life You Save May Be Your Own," in S. Chase (ed.), *Problems in Public Expenditure Analysis*, Brookings, Washington, 1968, pp. 127–162.

Smith, Adam: *The Wealth of Nations*, Modern Library, New York, 1937.

Smith, Robert: *The Occupational Safety and Health Act: Its Goals and Its Achievements*, American Enterprise Institute, Washington, 1976.

Thaler, Richard, and Sherwin Rosen: "The Value of Saving a Life: Evidence from the Labor Market," in N. Terleckyz (ed.), *Household Production and Consumption*, NBER Studies in Income and Wealth No. 40, Columbia University Press, New York, 1976, pp. 265–298.

U.S. Department of Labor, "Injury Rates by Industry, 1969," BLS Report No. 389, 1971.

University of Michigan Institute for Social Research, *Survey of Working Conditions*, SRC Study No. 45369, University of Michigan Social Science Archives, Ann Arbor, 1975.

Viscusi, W. Kip: "Job Hazards and Worker Quit Rates: An Analysis of Adaptive Worker Behavior," *International Economic Review* (forthcoming, *a*).

———: "Wealth Effects and Earnings Premiums for Job Hazards," *Review of Economics and Statistics* (forthcoming, *b*).

Weinstein, Milton, Donald Shepard, and Joseph Pliskin, "The Economic Value of Changing Mortality Probabilities: A Decision-Theoretic Approach," Discussion Paper No. 46D, Public Policy Program, Harvard, Cambridge, Mass. 1976.

Zeckhauser, Richard: "Procedures for Valuing Lives," *Public Policy*, vol. 23, no. 4, pp 419–464, 1975.

——— and Donald Shepard:"Where Now for Saving Lives?" *Law and Contemporary Problems*, vol. 40, no. 4, pp. 5–45, Autumn, 1976.

24

This study estimates the effects of safety inspections by the Occupational Safety and Health Administration (OSHA) on injury rates at the plant level. The OSHA inspections are shown to reduce injuries by about 16% in 1973 and by about 5% in 1974, though the latter estimate is not statistically significant. There was an estimated lag of about 3.5 months in effective hazard abatement.

In addition to these general beneficial effects, the following phenomena were noted:

First, it was not possible to determine whether the decline in effect from 1973 to 1974 was due to a "worst-first" strategy in inspection targeting or related to the relative inexperience of an expanded inspection staff in 1974.

Next, the largest inspection-related reduction in injury rates occurred among small and more dangerous plants.

Finally, OSHA impact on firms inspected "early" in 1973 was apparently close to the maximum potential impact suggested by several safety studies. This impact occurred with a relatively short lag.

Apart from the policy significance of these positive results—OSHA has been under consistent political attack since its origin—this study is useful in that it effectively uses a quasiexperimental design to gain maximum information from a relatively limited data base. A simple but explicit economic rationale is first developed which sets forth the conditions under which firms will reduce injury rates and the expected result of OSHA inspections on firm accident behavior.

The standard evaluation problem is faced: To measure the impact of OSHA inspections, the observed injury rate must be compared to the rate which would have existed had no inspection occurred. Because data on the determinnts of accident rates in the absence of OSHA inspections did not exist at the plant level, where information on injury rate changes and OSHA inspections is best, an autoregressive model is used to control for non-OSHA factors influencing injury rates. The yearly change in a plant's observed injury rate is assumed to be a function of the injury rate observed in an earlier year.

The assumptions of this autoregressive model are carefully developed so that potential biases in the estimation of OSHA effects can be tested for and possibly corrected. This approach proved to be critical, since a simplistic regression model that compared injury rate changes in inspected and uninspected plants suggested that OSHA inspections *increased* injury rates in 1973—a result that is not reasonably supportable by one's theoretical judgments. At worst OSHA should have *no* effect.

The above perverse result appears to have occurred since inspections are targeted to some extent on industries or plants where technological change or the pace of work suggest the existence of particularly hazardous conditions. In addition, rising hazards tend to trigger inspections and a seasonal pattern in the injury rates of inspected plants suggests the possibility of further interaction between injury rates and the inspection incident. Econometric techniques had to be developed to overcome these data difficulties. Thus, several variations of the following equation were estimated:

$$a_t = g\,(D,\ E_t/E_o,\ X_t,\ a_o;\ N) + u$$

where
a_t and a_o = the observed injury rates for the plant in the year t and the base year o; D = a vector of categorical variables indicating the industry to which the plant is attached; E_t/E_o = the ratio of plant employment in year t to plant employment in the base year o; X = a categorical variable indicating an OSHA inspection; N = a vector of categorical variables indicating the employment-size group into which the plant falls; and u = a term containing the random deviations form a_t and a_o, both of which are defined as the firm or plant injury rate consistent with profit maximization.

In addition to the main findings listed above, several additional conclusions emerge from this study. The first is that inadequate data can seriously compromise efforts to analyze a social program, and OSHA has been plagued by such problems. In addition, the use of data aggregated at the industry level to measure OSHA's impact would prove futile. Few firms are inspected out of the total eligible population, and the effects on inspected firms appear to be positive but small enough to be swamped by the aggregation process. Next, it is important to stress that it is not possible to judge the social optimality of the OSHA program and its compliance program from these results alone. Social costs of complying with the regulatory process must be measured and economic and noneconomic value must be placed on the net inspection effect. Finally, an indirect effect on accidents and, possibly, occupational disease, in uninspected firms or plants should be measured.

The Impact of OSHA Inspections on Manufacturing Injury Rates

Robert Stewart Smith

ABSTRACT

This paper estimates the effects of OSHA inspections on injury rates at the plant level. The methodology involves comparing injury rates of plants inspected "early" in a given year with those inspected "late" in the year, after controlling for prior injury rates and other factors. The results suggest that OSHA inspections in 1973 reduced injury rates by about 16 percent, but that 1974 inspections had no statistically significant impact.

The Occupational Safety and Health Act of 1970, which is enforced by the Occupational Safety and Health Administration (OSHA), is perhaps the most controversial of the recent regulatory programs. Defenders of the act contend its goal of reducing injuries and illnesses to the feasible minimum is desirable, but that achievement of the goal is thwarted by political opposition and bureaucratic inefficiency [1]. Critics of the act argue, in essence, that the act imposes costs without any significant benefits [2]. While disagreeing about the desirability of the act, both sides apparently agree that OSHA has had no measurable impact on injuries and illnesses in the workplace. Indeed, a look at Table 1 appears to confirm this view. From 1972 to 1976 there was a decline in the incidence of all injuries, a small rise in the incidence of lost-workday injuries, and a substantial increase in the number of lost workdays per 100 employees.

The author is on the faculty of the New York State School of Industrial and Labor Relations, Cornell University.

* The author wishes to thank Helen Montague of the U.S. Department of Labor for her computer assistance on this project, which was done under contract with the Department of Labor. The methodology, results, and views expressed herein are solely the author's and do not necessarily reflect those of the Department of Labor. The author wishes to thank John Burton, Aldona DiPietro, Ronald Ehrenberg, Robert Hutchens, Walter Oi, and Henry Wan for their helpful comments on an earlier draft of this paper. None is responsible for any remaining oversights. The author has also benefited from the comments of the editor and two referees. [Manuscript received July 1978; accepted October 1978.

From Robert Stewart Smith, "The Impact of OSHA Inspections on Manufacturing Injury Rates," 14 (2) *Journal of Human Resources* 145-170 (Spring 1979). Copyright 1979 by the University of Wisconsin.

TABLE 1
INJURY RATES, U.S. PRIVATE SECTOR, 1972–76

	1972	1973	1974	1975	1976
	Total Private Sector				
Incidence rate, all injuries	10.9	11.0	10.4	9.1	8.9
Lost workday injury rate	3.3	3.4	3.5	3.3	3.4
Lost workdays per 100 full-time workers	47.9	53.3	54.6	56.1	57.8
	Manufacturing				
Incidence rate, all injuries	15.6	15.3	14.6	13.0	12.6
Lost workday injury rate	4.2	4.5	4.7	4.5	4.6
Lost workdays per 100 full-time workers	62.6	68.2	72.7	75.4	76.7

Note: Injury rates are the number of injuries per 100 full-time employees per year.
Sources: U.S. Department of Labor, Bureau of Labor Statistics, *Occupational Injuries and Illnesses in the United States, 1973* (Bull. No. 1874) and *1974* (Bull. No. 1932); U.S. Department of Labor, Bureau of Labor Statistics, *Chartbook on Occupational Injuries and Illnesses in 1975* (Rep. No. 501); U.S. Department of Labor, Office of Information, "News: BLS Reports on Occupational Injuries and Illnesses for 1976," December 1, 1977.

Unfortunately, assessing the impact of OSHA cannot be accomplished satisfactorily by looking at the data in Table 1 because these data do not indicate what injury rates would have been in the absence of a federal safety and health program. It is well established, for example, that aggregate injury rates are subject to intertemporal fluctuations resulting from factors having nothing to do with OSHA.[1] Therefore, to estimate OSHA's impact one must employ a statistical model capable of distinguishing its effects from all the other factors that systematically influence injury rates.

The initial studies designed to isolate OSHA's impact on injury rates have been characterized by their use of aggregated data and their findings of statistically insignificant effects. Mendeloff [4] used time-series data for manufacturing industries and found no statistically significant post-OSHA decline in lost-workday injuries either at the national level or for California. However, he did find (for California) an OSHA-related decline in injuries where workers were caught in or between machinery—injuries which he

---

1   See, for example, Kossoris [3] and Smith [8].

argues are most likely to be affected by OSHA standards. Smith [10] used cross-sectional data on manufacturing industries and found that pre- to post-OSHA injury rate changes were statistically no different in industries that OSHA had targeted for special attention than they were elsewhere. Viscusi [15] analyzes pooled cross-sections of industries to determine the effect of the probability of inspection and the expected penalty for noncompliance on injury rates. He finds no effect.

The results of these initial evaluations are not surprising given their use of small, aggregated data sets in an environment where (as will be argued) the potential effects of OSHA are not very large and are most likely confined to the small percentage of inspected plants. Further, it is not at all clear that industries with high inspection rates are sufficiently comparable to those with low rates to enable valid comparisons. The purpose of the research reported here is to improve on these early studies by estimating the impact of OSHA inspections on manufacturing injury rates using a large sample with longitudinal, plant-specific data. The data are sufficiently rich to permit the selection of a valid comparison group and to permit estimates of the time lag between an inspection and its effects on injuries.

It should be cautioned at the outset, however, that, for two reasons, the study does not purport to estimate the total impact of OSHA in the manufacturing sector. First, because of data quality problems, OSHA's impact on occupational disease cannot be estimated. The impacts estimated here, therefore, relate only to occupational injuries. Second, the impact of OSHA on uninspected firms is not estimated in this study. The reasons for this will be discussed later.

The theory underlying the estimates and the assumptions required to specify the estimating equations are the topic of Section I. Sections II and III report on the data and the estimates of impact that were made. Concluding comments are contained in Section IV.

I. DEVELOPMENT OF THE ESTIMATING EQUATIONS

A Theory of Work Injuries

Let us begin by assuming that each plant is operated with the goal of profit maximization; then, what would determine the injury rate in plants if the cost of injuries could be avoided by the purchase of safety inputs (machine guards, protective gear, training programs, and the like)? Straightforward application of maximization principles indicates that a necessary condition for profit maximization is that safety inputs per labor hour[2] be employed to

---

2   For simplicity of exposition, it will be assumed that hours per worker are not subject to the plant's control in maximizing profits.

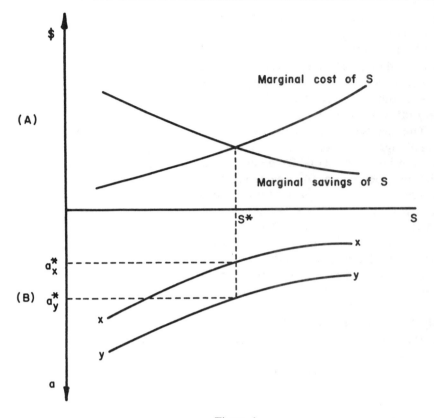

Figure 1

the point where their marginal cost is just offset by the marginal savings they create by reducing injuries (thus avoiding attendant workers' compensation premiums, compensating wage differentials, production losses, machine damage, and so on). Panel A of Figure 1 illustrates the choice of optimum safety inputs (S^*).

Once S^* is determined, the injury rate consistent with profit maximization (a^*) is given by the relationship between safety inputs per labor hour (S) and the injury rate (a). Panel B of Figure 1 illustrates the relationship between S and a, assuming diminishing marginal "productivity" of S. It is important to note that a given S^* is consistent with many different injury rates, depending on the risk inherent in the production process. For example, Panel B shows that plant y is more risky than plant x.

In sum, then, we expect that the injury rate consistent with profit maximization (a^*) will be related positively to inherent technological risk and the marginal cost of safety inputs, while being negatively related to the marginal savings of safety inputs. The intent of OSHA is to reduce a^* by requiring (1) safety inputs to be increased beyond profit-maximizing levels, or (2) the adoption of a new accident-avoidance technology. Because plants will not generally find compliance with OSHA standards profitable, and because its fines for violating standards are very low (averaging about $26 per violation and $170 per noncomplying establishment), OSHA is finding that 85 percent of the manufacturing plants it inspects for the first time are not in compliance [6, Table 6]. Thus, if OSHA standards are effective, inspected plants—those forced into compliance—should exhibit a greater fall (smaller rise) in a^* over time than uninspected plants.

An Empirically Estimable Model

The nature of accidents being inherently stochastic, observed yearly injury rates in a plant will be randomly distributed around a^*. Nevertheless, the systematic forces that determine a^*, if essentially unchanged over time, will ensure a degree of temporal stability in the observed rates. To determine the impact of OSHA inspections, the observed injury rate must be compared to an estimate of the rate which would have existed if no inspection had occurred. Ideally, data on the determinants of a^* would be used to control for non-OSHA influences on injury rates. While such data are available at the industry level of aggregation,[3] they are not available at the plant level where information on injury rate changes and OSHA inspections is best. In fact, the only data set that includes plant-specific injury rate and inspection information contains, in addition, only the number of employees in the plant, its location, and the industry the plant is in.

Given the lack of data on the determinants of a^*, the most feasible way to control for non-OSHA factors influencing injury rates is to estimate an autoregressive model using longitudinal data.[4] Listed and discussed below are the hypotheses contained in such a model—each specified up to a random error:

1. It is a maintained hypothesis that any permanent changes in inherent risk and the marginal costs and benefits of safety inputs affect the a^* in each plant within an industry to the same extent. Thus, while preexisting

---

3   See Smith [9] for an empirical test of a model containing proxies for the determinants of a^*.

4   Autoregressive models, or some variants of them, are frequently used in evaluations based on micro data to control for the myriad of plant-specific factors affecting the level of the dependent variable. An efficient way to control for unobserved, idiosyncratic influences on the dependent variable is to include the lagged dependent variable in the analysis—either as an independent variable or as part of the dependent variable. While autoregressive models may not be helpful in *explaining* the variance in the sample observations of the dependent variable, the inclusion of a lagged dependent variable is usually very effective in *controlling* for nonprogram influences on the dependent variable.

influences on a^* are summarized by the inclusion of a lagged injury rate in the estimating model, changes in these influences are assumed to be captured by industry dummy variables.

2. The a^* for each plant, regardless of industry, is hypothesized to change in some fixed proportion to percentage changes in plant employment. This allows for cyclical forces to affect a^*—forces that have been observed in studies using aggregate data (see [8]).

3. The third hypothesis is basically that OSHA inspections have an equal impact on injury rates across all plants, although this hypothesis is later altered to allow for the impact to vary with previous injury rate levels (which allows us to test the notion underlying "worst-first" inspection targeting that inspection payoffs will be larger in more risky plants).[5] It is not possible to distinguish between plants found to be in compliance and those that were cited for violations; compliance data are not included in our data set. However, the fact that in fiscal years 1973 and 1974 the percentage of manufacturing plants in compliance was only 14.7 percent, and falling, suggests that the distortions produced by this data inadequacy are probably moderate.[6]

4. In recognition of the stochastic nature of the injury rate, the yearly change in a plant's *observed* injury rate is assumed to be a function of the injury rate observed in the earlier year. This assumption allows for the phenomenon of "regression to the mean," where plants with abnormally high rates in an early year will tend to show a decline the next year, and those with abnormally low rates will tend to show an increase. This phenomenon tends to reduce the coefficient on the lagged injury rate below unity.[7]

5. The four hypotheses above are ultimately expanded to allow all influences on a^*_i to vary by plant-size category. Hazardous conditions do appear to vary by plant size, and it is therefore prudent to permit size-specific functional relationships to exist if the sample is large enough.[8]

---

5   Both variants of this hypothesis constrain the estimates to be *average* effects of inspections and do not permit such effects to vary by industry or region. There are two reasons why this approach seemed sensible at this point. First, the *average* effects are of most immediate interest in evaluating—at least initially—the *overall* impact of OSHA. Second, in the sample ultimately used for analysis, detailed industry and/or regional cells are rather thin—a fact which limits our ability to detect an impact that may be rather small. Indeed, within-region and within-industry analyses by Aldona DiPietro at the U.S. Department of Labor have produced no clear-cut results about the efficacy, or lack thereof, of OSHA inspections.

6   For the data on compliance rates, see Oi [6].

7   The presence of errors in this independent variable is of no particular consequence to the task at hand as long as the inspection variable is not correlated with the errors. In the sample ultimately utilized in this research, such correlation appears to be unlikely (as will be discussed later).

8   It is generally recognized that medium-sized plants, on the average, have higher injury rates than small or large plants. What causes this pattern is unknown, although large plants

6. Finally, it is maintained that, subject to random error, each plant achieves its a_t^* in year t, and that a_t^* changes over time owing to the influences discussed in points 1 to 5 above. The estimating equation resulting from the above briefly sketched model can therefore be represented in notational form as

(1) $a_t = a_t^* + e_t$

$a_o = a_o^* + e_o$

$a_t^* = a_o^* + f(D, E_t/E_o, X_t; N)$

thus, $a_t = g(D, E_t/E_o, X_t, a_o; N) + u$

where a_t, a_o = the observed injury rates for the plant in the year t and the base year; D = a vector of categorical variables indicating the industry to which the plant is attached; E_t/E_o = the ratio of plant employment in year t to plant employment in the base year; X = a dichotomous variable indicating an OSHA inspection; N = a vector of categorical variables indicating the employment-size group into which the plant falls; and u = a term containing the random deviations from both a_t^* and a_o^*: e_t and e_o.

The hypotheses above suggest a negative coefficient on X and positive coefficients on E_t/E_o and a_o, with the coefficient on a_o being less than unity. A priori statements about the effects of D and N cannot be made.

II. DATA AND RESEARCH METHODOLOGY

The data available for this study were compiled by the Bureau of Labor Statistics from the OSHA Form 103 employers are required to file each year. From 1973 on, these data contain month of inspection (if any) and number of injuries by month, along with the yearly injury rate, number of employees, industry, and plant location. A data set matching plant-specific information for the years 1972, 1973, and 1974 was created for purposes of this research.

In the analysis, the injury rate utilized is the lost-workday injury rate rather than the incidence of all injuries. An implicit assumption required to interpret the coefficient of X as the effect of an inspection on injuries is that the inspection does not affect the accuracy of the record-keeping system. This assumption is more likely to hold for lost-workday injuries which, because of their severity, the attention they attract, and the need to file for workers' compensation, are more apt to be recorded before inspection than are minor injuries.[9]

---

may be able to exploit scale economies and the owners of small ones may have personal relationships with employees that serve as extra incentives for safety.

9   The percentage of employers cited by OSHA inspectors for record-keeping violations is not published, but it is certainly less than 5 percent. See U.S. President [12, pp. 36, 42].

Comparisons of Inspectees and Noninspectees

The original research design called for comparing injury-rate changes in inspected and uninspected plants ($X = 1$ if inspected, 0 if not). However, using this approach yields unbiased results only if OSHA did not base its decision to inspect a plant on the contemporaneous increase in the plant's injury rate. Although there is no direct evidence on this issue (given the decentralized nature of the inspection decision), the empirical work comparing inspectees and noninspectees produced two results which called into question the assumption that inspections are made randomly with respect to injury-rate changes.

First, 1973 inspectees had significantly larger (ceteris paribus) 1972–73 increases in the injury rate than did noninspectees—a result that seemed to indicate that OSHA inspections increased injuries by well over 10 percent. While there are reasons to believe that OSHA inspections may have had no impact, it is hard to believe they made hazards worse. Further, the fact that catastrophes and employee complaints may have triggered about 16 percent of sample inspections and that inspectors are likely to become aware of industries or plants where technological change or the pace of work is posing new hazards, it is not improbable that rising hazards did tend to trigger inspections.

The second result is that the yearly injury rate increase was larger for plants inspected in the last half of 1973 than for plants inspected in the first half. This finding is inconsistent with the hypothesis that OSHA inspections made hazards worse because, if so, early inspectees ought to have the larger increases. The finding does suggest, however, that while OSHA may select its inspectees based on increases in hazards, inspections may have had some beneficial effects (those inspected early had smaller increases than those inspected later). The finding further suggests an alternate research methodology, to which we now turn.

Comparisons of "Early" and "Late" Inspectees

A potentially meaningful method of estimating the effectiveness of OSHA inspections is to compare the injury experience of plants inspected early in the year with that of plants inspected very late. The "late" group's yearly injury rate will predominantly reflect the forces at work prior to inspection; thus, this group is used as a comparison group, while the group inspected "early" is our treatment group. The fact that both groups of plants were singled out for inspection implies that they are likely to share the problem of relatively high and/or increasing hazards. Therefore, one element of non-comparability between comparison and treatment groups has been eliminated. However, the *timing* of the increase in hazards is a problem and can potentially cause some estimation biases.

First, suppose that plants in both groups experience similar increases in hazards at the same time, but that for purely random reasons some plants experiencing this increase are inspected sooner than others. If these "early" inspections are completely ineffective, both groups of plants should experience the same injury-rate changes over time, other things being equal. Hence, ineffective inspections would yield a zero coefficient on the inspection variable, while effective inspections would yield a negative coefficient. There is no problem of estimation bias caused by the timing of increased hazardousness.

Now suppose that early inspectees are those experiencing earlier increases in hazards. In cases where the increases in hazards are of a permanent nature, early inspectees will show larger increases in the yearly injury rate (ceteris paribus) unless the inspection is effective enough to offset completely the impact of increased hazards. The bias here is against finding inspection effects. A crude control for this potential difficulty can be performed, however, and the results (reported later) suggest that this bias is not a serious problem.

In cases where the increases in hazards are transitory and disappear in a relatively short period of time, early inspections might be given credit for a reduction in hazards which would have occurred anyway. Although there is a limited way (described in the next section) to control for this problem, one precaution against this bias is to attempt to ensure that any transitory increases in hazards will occur in the same year for both "early" and "late" inspectees. The method adopted involves defining "early" inspections as those occurring in March or April of the relevant year and "late" inspections as those occurring in November or December. Since OSHA is most likely to find out about transitory hazards through employee complaints and since such complaints are typically acted upon by OSHA within 8 to 11 days [11, Table 12], March-April inspections should be late enough in the year to ensure that they are not based on transitory hazards arising in the prior year.

III. RESULTS

Estimates of OSHA's inspection effects are first made for 1973 inspections, using 1972 as the base year. These effects are estimated both over the year of inspection and the following year. The within-year estimates are replicated on a set of 1974 inspectees (who were not inspected in 1973), and these estimates are augmented by data not available for 1973 inspectees to control for factors that could bias the estimates of inspection effects. The various results are then combined to calculate the implied long-run effects of inspections on injuries and the time lag involved between inspection and impact. Finally, the magnitudes of the estimated effects are considered to determine if they are consistent with what might be expected a priori.

TABLE 2
ESTIMATES OF EQUATIONS (2) AND (3),[a] 1973 INSPECTEES
DEPENDENT VARIABLE: a_{73}

Equation	Sample (Number of Observations)	Estimated Coefficient (t-statistic) on:				R^2	Joint Significance of X, Xa_{72}
		a_{72}	E_{73}/E_{72}	X	Xa_{72}		
2	All plants (2362)	.556* (33.19)	2.166* (3.29)	-.384* (-2.02)		.42	
3		.585* (25.28)	2.135* (3.24)	-.071 (-.28)	-.058** (-1.83)	.42	***
2	Small plants[b] (816)	.471* (15.45)	1.276 (.94)	-.544** (-1.32)		.34	
3		.535* (12.38)	1.148 (.85)	.204 (.37)	-.122* (-2.08)	.35	***
2	Medium-small[b] plants (799)	.509* (18.03)	3.291* (2.98)	-.354 (-1.13)		.45	
3		.501* (13.39)	3.290* (2.98)	-.448 (-1.04)	.017 (.32)	.45	
2	Medium-large[b] plants (378)	.763* (19.08)	.588 (.52)	-.329 (-.99)		.62	
3		.786 (15.83)	.617 (.54)	-.051 (-.11)	-.058 (-.79)	.62	

	Large plants[b] (369)				
2	.841* (25.69)	1.930* (1.87)	.208 (.83)		.70
3	.767* (16.18)	1.902* (1.86)	−.296 (−.87)	.138* (2.15)	.70

a The estimated coefficients on industry variables (vector D) and the constant are not reported in the table.

b Small plants are defined as those having less than 100 employees, medium-small as having between 100 and 249 employees, medium-large as having 250–500 employees, and large as having more than 500 employees.

* Indicates significance at the .05 level (one-tail test on all coefficients except the coefficients of Xa_{72}).

** Indicates significance at the .10 level.   *** Indicates the joint significance (.05 level) of the coefficients on X and Xa_{72} using the F test.

Inspections in 1973

Four versions of equation (1) were estimated on a sample of 2,362 plants inspected in March, April, November, or December 1973. Equations (2) and (3) measure the effects of an early inspection within the year, while (4) and (5) capture the differential effects of an early 1973 inspection in the following year:

(2) $a_{73} = \beta_0 + \beta_1 a_{72} + \beta_2(E_{73}/E_{72}) + \beta_3 X + \alpha D + u$

(3) $a_{73} = \beta_0 + \beta_1 a_{72} + \beta_2(E_{73}/E_{72}) + \beta_3 X + \beta_4 X a_{72} + \alpha D + u$

(4) $a_{74} = \beta_0 + \beta_1 a_{72} + \beta_2(E_{74}/E_{72}) + \beta_3 X + \alpha D + u$

(5) $a_{74} = \beta_0 + \beta_1 a_{72} + \beta_2(E_{74}/E_{72}) + \beta_3 X + \beta_4 X a_{72} + \alpha D + u$

As indicated earlier, $X = 1$ if the plant was inspected (for the first time in the year) in March or April 1973, and $X = 0$ if the plant was inspected in November or December 1973. α is a vector of coefficients on the two-digit level industry variables, and the other variables are as defined earlier. All equations were also estimated on four subsamples based on plant size.[10]

The results presented in Table 2 suggest that March-April inspectees had a 1973 injury rate that was significantly lower than it would have been without the inspection. Given that the sample mean of a_{72} was 5.4 (lost-workday injuries per 100 full-time workers), the estimated average inspection effect of $-.38$ implies a 7 percent reduction in the yearly injury rate over the first eight months after inspection. However, the coefficient on $X a_{72}$ indicates that the reductions were significantly larger in plants where the 1972 injury rate was higher. Inspection effects also clearly are not equal across plant-size categories: they are largest and statistically significant only for the smallest plants. Perhaps because they find hiring safety experts relatively expensive, the smallest plants apparently benefit the most from government inspection.

Table 3 contains estimates of equations (4) and (5). The estimated relative decline in injury rates of "early" 1973 inspectees continued through 1974, growing from .38 to .63 on the average. As before, this inspection effect tends to be greater in the more dangerous plants. The inspection-

10 If a plant was inspected more than once in 1973, all analyses were based on the first inspection (which was assumed to be an initial inspection). Because data on 1972 inspections were not available, there is a chance that some of those in our sample of 1973 inspectees were previously inspected in 1972 also—a situation that could impart conflicting biases to our results. The chances of a 1972 inspection were greater in industries earmarked for a special enforcement program (Target Industries Program), so all such industries were eliminated from the sample. The chances were also greater for large firms (where repeat inspections are more likely), thus providing further rationale for using size-related subsamples. Finally, the use of March and April 1973 inspections, rather than those in January or February, should reduce the chances of picking up 1972's follow-up inspections.

related reductions in the injury rate once again were largest in the smallest plants, although by 1974 the relative decline was statistically significant for medium-large plants also.[11]

Before discussing the results for 1974 inspections, it is useful to note briefly some other characteristics of the estimates. The coefficient on the employment ratio variable has its predicted sign, is usually significant, and is of reasonable magnitude.[12] The coefficient on the lagged dependent variable is less than unity, indicating the regression to the mean phenomenon noted earlier. Further, both the latter coefficient and R^2 rise as plant size increases—an expected result reflecting the smaller intertemporal variance in injury rates exhibited by larger plants.[13]

Inspections in 1974

Two pairs of equations were estimated on a sample of 2,492 plants inspected in March, April, November, or December 1974. The first pair were essentially replications of equations (2) and (3) above:

$$(6) \qquad a_{74} = \beta_0 + \beta_1 a_{73} + \beta_2 (E_{74}/E_{73}) + \beta_3 X + \alpha D + u$$

$$(7) \qquad a_{74} = \beta_0 + \beta_1 a_{73} + \beta_2 (E_{74}/E_{73}) + \beta_3 X + \beta_4 X a_{73} + \alpha D + u$$

The estimates of (6) and (7) are shown in Table 4. Inspections in 1974 affected injury rates in the same direction, but not to the same extent, as 1973 inspections. Injury rates of early inspectees fell relative to those of late inspectees, and these relative decreases were generally larger in smaller and more dangerous plants. The overall impact, however, was about one-third of that in 1973—an effect so small that it does not attain statistical

---

11 The results for large plants are rather puzzling, and there is no readily apparent explanation for them. However, large plants are the least satisfactory group to analyze because they are most likely to have been inspected prior to 1973, and because they are most likely (owing to their number of employees) to have been subjected to complaint-based or catastrophe-related inspections. In fact, Oi [6] presents data showing that 6–13 percent of inspections in large plants are accident-related, compared to less than 2 percent for small plants—and that the probability of an inspection's being a general schedule one is around .3 for large firms and .7 for small. Thus, it is the group of large plants which is most likely to exhibit the problems of selection bias discussed at the end of Section II.

12 The results generally are consistent with the well-known phenomenon that the injury rate of new employees is substantially higher than for older ones. For example, the coefficients in the overall regressions imply that injury rates for "new hires" are 50 percent above the sample mean—an estimate that is consistent with other evidence that the newest workers have injury rates one and one-half to two times as large as more experienced workers (Oi [7, p. 22]).

13 The greater variability of injury rates in small firms also implies heteroskedasticity in the error terms, which enlarges the estimated standard errors in the regressions run on the aggregated sample, but does not bias the coefficients. This problem is, of course, minimized in the regressions run on the size-related subsamples.

TABLE 3

ESTIMATES OF EQUATIONS (4) AND (5), [a] 1973 INSPECTEES
DEPENDENT VARIABLE: a_{74}

| Equation | Sample (Number of Observations) | Estimated Coefficient (t-statistic) on: | | | | R^2 | Joint Significance of X, Xa_{72} |
		a_{72}	E_{74}/E_{72}	X	Xa_{72}		
4	All plants (2362)	.508* (26.56)	2.185* (3.70)	-.626* (-2.88)		.35	
5		.537* (20.31)	2.177* (3.69)	-.319 (-1.09)	-.057 (-1.57)	.35	***
4	Small plants[b] (816)	.383* (11.72)	3.767* (3.20)	-1.027* (-2.34)		.30	
5		4.16* (8.97)	3.728* (3.17)	-.640 (-1.09)	-.063 (-1.00)	.30	***
4	Medium-small[b] plants (799)	.484* (14.83)	1.396 (1.38)	-.312 (-.84)		.38	
5		.512* (11.50)	1.400 (1.38)	.020 (.04)	-.059 (-.95)	.38	
4	Medium-large[b] plants (378)	.773* (16.20)	2.029* (1.98)	-.931* (-2.35)		.57	
5		.805* (13.59)	2.034* (1.98)	-.543 (-.94)	-.081 (-.93)	.57	***

4	Large plants[b] (369)	.844* (19.39)	−.015 (−.02)	.491 (1.48)		.57
5		.648* (10.43)	−.363 (−.37)	−.841* (−1.88)	.363* (4.33)	.59 ***

a,b See Table 2 footnotes.

TABLE 4
ESTIMATES OF EQUATIONS (6) AND (7),[a] 1974 INSPECTEES
DEPENDENT VARIABLE: a_{74}

Equation	Sample (Number of Observations)	Estimated Coefficient (t-statistic) on:				R^2	Joint Significance of X, Xa_{73}
		a_{73}	E_{74}/E_{73}	X	Xa_{73}		
6	All plants (2492)	.593* (36.18)	1.306* (2.14)	−.135 (−.73)		.44	
7		.604* (24.50)	1.308* (2.14)	−.033 (−.13)	−.019 (−.62)	.44	
6	Small plants[b] (889)	.417* (14.03)	.708 (.59)	−.247 (−.67)		.30	
7		.417* (9.53)	.708 (.59)	−.244 (−.50)	−.001 (−.01)	.30	
6	Medium-small[b] plants (829)	.675* (25.90)	.655 (.65)	−.069 (−.23)		.56	
7		.717* (18.26)	.615 (.61)	.336 (.82)	−.070 (−1.43)	.56	
6	Medium-large[b] plants (418)	.671* (16.12)	4.421* (3.52)	−.022 (.06)		.56	
7		.680* (11.45)	4.428* (3.52)	.060 (.11)	−.016 (−.21)	.56	

6	Large plants[b] (356)	.995* (31.87)	.572 (.68)	−.091 (−.35)		.78
7		.975* (17.84)	.541 (.64)	−.191 (−.55)	.029 (.44)	.78

a,b See Table 2 footnotes.

significance. The pattern of results for the other variables generally repeats the patterns found for 1973 inspectees.

The second pair of equations utilized data not available when analyzing 1973 inspections. In particular, two variables were added to equations (6) and (7). The first was the plant's injury rate in 1972, the addition of which gives us two lagged dependent variables as controls for the injury experience prior to inspection.

The second variable added (IR_{73}) was the ratio of injuries in the last quarter of 1973 to injuries during the entire year.[14] This variable is intended to control for either permanent or transitory increases in hazards that might trigger an early 1974 inspection, thereby reducing the chances of bias in the estimated inspection effects (discussed in the prior section). It is expected that the coefficient of IR_{73} will be positive if increasing hazards are relatively permanent in nature and negative if such hazards are essentially transitory.[15]

The modified equations can be expressed as follows:

$$(8) \qquad a_{74} = \beta_0 + \beta_1 a_{73} + \beta_2 a_{72} + \beta_3 IR_{73} + \beta_4 (E_{74}/E_{73}) + \beta_5 X$$
$$+ \alpha D + u$$

$$(9) \qquad a_{74} = \beta_0 + \beta_1 a_{73} + \beta_2 a_{72} + \beta_3 IR_{73} + \beta_4 (E_{74}/E_{73}) + \beta_5 X$$
$$+ \beta_6 X a_{73} + \alpha D + u$$

Estimates of (8) and (9) are shown in Table 5. Like the results in Table 4, the estimates in Table 5 show some evidence of inspections having reduced injuries, but the estimated effects are not statistically significant. Of almost equal interest is that the average overall inspection effect estimated in equation (8) is only slightly smaller than its counterpart in equation (6), $-.079$ vs. $-.135$, and that the coefficient on IR_{73} is insignificant at conventional levels. These results are evidence, however meager, of rather small and inconclusive biases in estimated inspection effects resulting from the omission of the IR variable in previous estimates. The fact that X and IR_{73} are essentially uncorrelated in this data set offers additional evidence that the timing of hazard increases was not particularly different for early and late inspectees—a necessary condition for the results in previous tables to be unbiased.

How credible is the estimated decline in inspection effectiveness from 1973 to 1974? Two factors suggest that the estimated decline was real rather

---

14   Monthly injury rates are not available, because employment data on the OSHA Form 103 are for the entire year only.

15   If two plants have the same injury rate in 1973, but one has experienced an unusual and transitory increase in hazards toward the end of the year, the 1974 injury rate in the latter plant will tend to be lower (reflecting its lower "permanent" injury rate).

than spurious. First, one can hypothesize that the severity of discovered hazards declined over the period. Such a decline may be expected over time in light of OSHA's attempt to inspect the most hazardous places first, and the dramatic (64 percent) rise in the proportion of "repeat initial" inspections in this period supports the view that OSHA believed it was beginning to till less fertile ground.[16] Consistent with this hypothesis is the fact that the average penalty per violation fell by 16 percent, and despite a slight rise in citations per inspection, penalties per cited plant fell by 15 percent.[17]

Second, it may well be that the ratio of discovered to actual hazards fell in 1974. The number of federal compliance officers jumped 41 percent from 1973 to 1974 (from 660 to 928), and the inexperience of these new officers may well have diluted the average productivity of OSHA's compliance staff during 1974. While any decline in inspection effectiveness owing to this cause is likely to be transitory, it still may help explain the decline found in this study.

Lags and Long-Run Inspection Effects

One means of judging the quality of the results obtained in this study is to evaluate their reasonableness in terms of the implied long-run effects on injury rates and the lags in such effectiveness. Using information from Tables 2–4, one can calculate the approximate magnitude of these variables.

Assume that the full effects of an inspection in the average firm are felt immediately after a lag of N months, that lags in effectiveness were the same in each year, that a March-April 1973 inspection was fully effective by 1974, that a November-December 1973 inspection was not effective until sometime in 1974, and that a late 1973 inspection was only one-third as effective as an early one (using the information gained from the 1974 replications). If Y = the yearly injury rate before an inspection, if Y' = the yearly injury rate after the March-April 1973 inspections are fully effective, and if $\hat{Y}$ = the yearly injury rate after November-December 1973 inspections are fully effective, then the results from the regressions can be expressed in three equations (assuming the March-April inspections took place on April 1 and the November-December ones on December 1):

---

16   A "repeat initial" inspection is not a follow-up of a prior inspection, but represents a completely new inspection of the plant. According to information received from John Katalinas, Director of OSHA's Office of Management Data and Statistical Analysis, the proportion of repeat initial inspections rose from .056 in FY 1973 to .143 in FY 1974 and .185 in FY 1975 (or from roughly .100 in calendar year 1973 to about .164 in 1974).

17   U.S. President [13, p. 23]. Penalties were $26.95 per violation and $140.58 per cited plant in 1973, and $22.51 and $119.15, respectively, in 1974.

TABLE 5

ESTIMATES OF EQUATIONS (8) AND (9),[a] 1974 INSPECTEES
DEPENDENT VARIABLE: a_{74}

Equation	Sample (Number of Observations)	Estimated Coefficient (t-statistic) on:						R^2
		a_{73}	a_{72}	IR_{73}	E_{74}/E_{73}	X	Xa_{73}	
8	All plants (2492)	.441* (23.68)	.282* (15.08)	.213* (1.47)	1.290* (2.21)	-.079 (-.45)		.48
9		.454* (17.68)	.282* (15.08)	.216* (1.49)	1.292* (2.21)	.032 (.14)	-.021 (-.70)	.48
8	Small plants[b] (889)	.316* (10.03)	.248* (7.76)	.187 (.87)	.421 (.36)	-.108 (-.30)		.34
9		.320* (7.24)	.248* (7.76)	.189 (.88)	.420 (.36)	-.067 (-.14)	-.007 (-.13)	.35
8	Medium-small[b] plants (829)	.539* (16.85)	.222* (6.95)	.275 (.97)	.782 (.80)	-.088 (-.31)		.58
9		.581* (13.56)	.223* (6.95)	.267 (.94)	.745 (.76)	.314 (.79)	-.070 (-1.47)	.58
8	Medium-large[b] plants (418)	.479* (10.61)	.333* (8.18)	.425 (.88)	4.229* (3.62)	.095 (.27)		.62
9		.479* (7.95)	.333* (8.17)	.425 (.88)	4.229* (3.61)	.098 (.20)	-.001 (-.01)	.62

596

	Large plants[b] (356)						
8	.796* (14.55)	.289* (4.40)	.374 (.94)	.870 (1.06)	−.068 (−.26)		.80
9	.766* (10.73)	.291* (4.43)	.375 (.94)	.827 (1.00)	−.213 (−.63)	.042 (.66)	.80

a,b See Table 2 footnotes. All significance tests are one-tailed except for those on the coefficients of IR_{73} and Xa_{73}.

$$(10) \quad [(3 + N)/12]Y + [(9 - N)/12]Y' - Y = [(9 - N)/12](Y' - Y)$$
$$= -.38$$

$$(11) \quad Y' - \left\{ [(N - 1)/12]Y + [(13 - N)/12)\hat{Y}] \right\} = [(N - 13)/12](\hat{Y} - Y)$$
$$+ (Y' - Y) = -.63$$

$$(12) \quad \hat{Y} - Y = (Y' - Y)/3$$

Equation (10) models the relative decline in 1973 injury rates of early 1973 inspectees, equation (11) the widening gap in 1974 between the injury rates of early and late 1973 inspectees, and equation (12) the decline in inspection effectiveness noted earlier. There are three equations and three unknowns: $(Y' - Y)$, $(\hat{Y} - Y)$, and N.

When solved, we get $Y' - Y = -.85$, $\hat{Y} - Y = -.28$, and $N = 3.6$ months. It thus appears that an early 1973 inspection, when fully effective, reduced the *yearly* injury rate by 16 percent (.85/5.4), a late inspection reduced the yearly rate by 5.3 percent, and that there was a three-and-one-half-month lag in effectiveness.[18]

The magnitude of long-run effects and short-run lags implied by our results are in the range of what is reasonable to expect, a priori, thereby lending credence to the estimates obtained. What evidence there is on the relationship between safety standards and injuries suggests that the maximum potential impact of OSHA is probably in the range of a 15 to 25 percent reduction for the average plant. However, the fact that inspections are not randomly made suggests that perhaps the maximum potential effect in our sample may be somewhat larger than average.[19]

A panel of California safety engineers concluded that roughly 26 percent of the 920 accidents they studied could have been prevented by a safety inspection [4], while a similar study in New York concluded that

---

18   To test the sensitivity of these calculations to alternative assumptions about the decline in inspection effectiveness, the equations were solved under two different specifications of equation (12):

   (12a) $Y - Y = (5/9)(Y' - Y)$, and

   (12b) $\hat{Y} - Y = 0$

   Equation (12a) reflects an assumption that the decline in effectiveness from early 1973 to early 1974 proceeded linearly over the year, while (12b) reflects an assumption that inspections late in 1973 and early in 1974 had no effect. Solving the equations using (12a) implies early 1973 inspections reduced injuries by 19 percent with a lag of four and one-half months, while the solutions using (12b) imply a 12 percent decrease with a two-month lag. Both sets of solutions closely bracket the one discussed in the text.

19   Whether this potential is reached, of course, depends on the fraction of hazardous violations actually cited by OSHA's compliance officers. There is some evidence that this fraction may not be large. See Smith [10, pp. 62–63].

although 36 percent of all injuries resulted from controllable hazards, only 22 percent were the result of a safety standard violation [5]. Investigations of permanent injuries and deaths in Wisconsin establish that 10 to 15 percent of these cases involve safety violations,[20] but another Wisconsin study concluded that roughly 25 percent of all injuries resulted from controllable hazards [16].

Given the results of the above studies for *average* plants, the difficulties in an inspector's finding all really hazardous violations, and the fact that not all inspections resulted in citations, one would probably expect OSHA's inspection effect to be something less than a 20 percent reduction in injury rates. Our point estimates, which imply a 5 to 16 percent reduction in injury rates, are thus of credible magnitudes. The estimated time lag (three and one-half months) before an inspection's effects are felt is also close to what one might expect. In May 1974, the average time period from inspection to the proposed date of abatement was 35 days for nonserious violations (which comprise 99 percent of all violations) [14, pp. 1003–1006]. With delays caused by employer foot-dragging and the appeals process, an average *effective* abatement period of three and one-half months is not at all unreasonable.[21]

---

20 Mendeloff [4, p. 15]. These investigations seek to establish injury-related violations in order to determine whether a fine (of 15 percent of workers' compensation costs) should be imposed on the employer. The probable reluctance to assign fault in cases that are not clear-cut suggests that the 10–15 percent figures may be a lower-bound estimate.

21 An assumption underlying the compliance lags in equations (10) and (11) is that injuries are not reduced until all violations in the average firm have been abated. This is a reasonable approximation to reality if violations per firm are low (the average is between three and four) or if, as seems likely, the most expensive violations to abate are both the most effective and the last to be corrected. It is instructive, however, to see how N is changed if it is assumed that compliance proceeds linearly over N months and that the decline in injuries is proportionally related to compliance. If it is assumed that compliance does not begin for one month after inspection (which both allows for appeals and avoids a computationally inconvenient nonlinearity), equations (10) and (11) are changed to

(10a) $$\frac{4}{12}Y + \frac{8-N}{12}Y' + (\frac{N}{12})\frac{(Y+Y')}{2} - Y = -.38$$

(11a) $$Y' - [(\frac{N}{12})\frac{(Y+\hat{Y})}{2} + \frac{(12-N)}{12}\hat{Y}] = -.63$$

Solving these equations using (12), (12a), and (12b) results in the same values for $(Y' - Y)$ and $(\hat{Y} - Y)$ as those obtained using (10) and (11), but the postinspection lags in complete effectiveness are lengthened to six, eight, and 2.5 months, respectively. The increased lags are the result of forcing, by assumption, the same ultimate decline in injuries to start at the very early date of one month after inspection. As such, these calculations of N are upper-bound estimates, whereas the ones reported earlier are at the lower bound. For reasons noted above, the assumptions underlying the lower-bound calculations suggest placing greater weight on these approximations of N.

IV. CONCLUSIONS

This study analyzed samples of plants inspected by OSHA in 1973 and 1974 in an attempt to estimate the impact of these inspections on injury rates. Judging from the differential changes in the injury rates of "early" and "late" inspectees, the results imply a statistically significant injury rate decrease associated with 1973 inspections and an insignificant decline associated with 1974 inspections. The point estimates of these effects imply a steady-state reduction of about 16 percent associated with inspections early in 1973, around a 5 percent reduction for 1974 inspections, and a lag of about three and one-half months in effective hazard abatement. These magnitudes, as well as those calculated under alternative assumptions, are within the bounds of what is reasonable to expect a priori. Tests for biases in the estimates owing to inspection targeting procedures (for which no controls were available in the 1973 sample) were not definitive; however, what evidence there is suggests that biases are probably small.

The estimated decline in effectiveness of OSHA inspections is particularly troubling and remains worthy of explanation. Two explanations for the decline in inspector productivity were given in the paper along with supporting evidence. There still remains, of course, the possibility that the apparent decline in effectiveness is a statistical artifact. The richness of the samples used in the study allow this possibility to be investigated further, and the evidence suggests that the results are not spurious.

Consider the possibility that the estimated effects for early 1973 inspections are "true," but that the effects of 1974 inspections are biased toward zero for unknown reasons. If so, we should let $Y' = \hat{Y}$ in equation (12), and solving equations (10) and (11) suggests a steady-state inspection effect of a 28-percent reduction in injuries operating with a lower-bound estimate of a six-month lag. These magnitudes—especially the first—are larger than a priori considerations would deem reasonable. Simply put, the pattern of injury rate changes for early 1973 inspectees, observed over the years 1973 and 1974, clearly requires a reduction in the effectiveness over that year to be consistent with a priori expectations.

Suppose, alternatively, that the within-year inspection effects for 1974 inspectees are true, but that the comparable effects for the 1973 sample are biased. If so, one would expect that the 1974 effects of 1973 inspections might be inconsistent with the 1973 effects (that is, smaller in absolute size), an expectation reflecting the suspicion that while spurious estimates might occur in one year, they are less likely to occur in two. In fact, however, the 1974 results for 1973 inspections are very consistent with those estimated for the year 1973.

In short, the results of this research lend support to a set of conclusions about OSHA's impact on the manufacturing sector, arranged below from most to least conservative:

1. It is incautious to assert, as a variety of critics have done, that OSHA inspections have no benign effects on injuries in the workplace. All estimates in this research suggest benign effects, although the evidence with respect to statistical significance of these effects is mixed. Further, the results demonstrate the relative futility of attempting to measure OSHA's impact using aggregated data. If this impact is confined to inspected firms, and inspections cover the workplaces of at most 10 percent of employees each year, the average 1973–74 impact (around a 10 percent reduction in the injury rate) suggests an overall reduction of only 1 percent in the aggregate injury rate. This overall impact surely is too small to be clearly observed in aggregated data.

2. The effectiveness of OSHA inspections declined from 1973 to 1974. It was not possible to determine whether this decline was related to the inexperience of an expanding compliance staff or to the intertemporal consequences of a "worst-first" bias in inspection targeting. The results do suggest, however, that OSHA's impact can vary over time, and the effects estimated in this paper should not be regarded as immutable or permanent.

3. The largest inspection-related reductions in injury rates have occurred among small and more dangerous plants. This finding suggests that OSHA may want to continue its policy of targeting inspections on plants with relatively high injury rates, but should consider increasing the mix of small plants among the group it inspects each year.

4. OSHA's impact on "early" 1973 inspectees was apparently close to the maximum potential impact suggested by several safety studies, and it occurred with a relatively short lag from the date of inspection. The effects on 1974 inspectees, however, were far below potential, and in fact may not have existed at all. Given that the average OSHA inspection in the manufacturing sector covered about 300 employees, the results suggest that a typical OSHA inspection saved from .8 (1974) to 2.5 (1973) lost-workday injuries per year.

To judge the social optimality of OSHA and/or its compliance program, one would have to estimate the total social costs of complying with federal safety regulations and find a way to place a dollar value on the above benefits as well as attempt to measure other possible benefits.[22] Both estimates are beyond the scope of this paper, so one cannot conclude that the benign effects reported here are socially optimal. It is hoped, however, that this study has provided a methodology and a set of results that will be of use in the task of beginning to evaluate OSHA's impact on society.

---

22 OSHA may reduce accidents due to effects on uninspected as well as inspected firms (e.g., through threat effects and/or effects on manufacturers of equipment). OSHA may also have effects on occupational diseases.

REFERENCES

1. Nicholas Ashford. "The Role of Occupational Health and Safety in Industrial Relations: Where We Are and Where We're Going." *Industrial and Labor Relations Report* (New York State School of Industrial and Labor Relations) 15 (Spring 1978): 24–28.
2. "Ford Termed Cool to 3 Key Health and Safety Agencies." *New York Times,* January 16, 1976. Pp. 1, 30.
3. Max D. Kossoris. "Industrial Injuries and the Business Cycle." *Monthly Labor Review* (March 1938): 579–94.
4. John Mendeloff. "An Evaluation of the OSHA Program's Effect on Workplace Injury Rates: Evidence from California Through 1974." Report prepared under contract to the Office of the Assistant Secretary of Labor for Policy, Evaluation, and Research, July 1976.
5. New York Department of Labor, Division of Research and Statistics. "Work Injuries Resulting from Industrial Code Rule Violations, New York State, 1966." Departmental Memorandum 243, 1966.
6. Walter Oi. "On Evaluating the Effectiveness of the OSHA Inspection Program." University of Rochester, 1975, Table 6.
7. ———. "On the Economics of Industrial Safety." University of Rochester, 1974.
8. Robert S. Smith. "Intertemporal Changes in Work Injury Rates." In *Proceedings of the 25th Anniversary Meeting, Industrial Relations Research Association.* Madison, Wis: IRRA, 1972. Pp. 167–74.
9. ———. "The Feasibility of an 'Injury Tax' Approach to Occupational Safety." *Law and Contemporary Problems* 38 (Summer-Autumn 1974): 730–44.
10. ———. *The Occupational Safety and Health Act: Its Goals and Its Achievements.* Washington: American Enterprise Institute for Public Policy Research, 1976.
11. U.S. Department of Labor, Occupational Safety and Health Administration. "Monitoring Quality and Quantity Performance of the Field Compliance Staff." Internal OSHA document, July 1974.
12. U.S. President. *The President's Report on Occupational Safety and Health.* Washington: U.S. Government Printing Office, 1973.
13. ———. *The President's Report on Occupational Safety and Health.* Washington: U.S. Government Printing Office, 1974.
14. U.S. Senate, Committee on Labor and Public Welfare, Subcommittee on Labor. *Occupational Safety and Health Act Review, 1974.* Washington: U.S. Government Printing Office, 1974.
15. W. Kip Viscusi. "The Impact of Occupational Safety and Health Regulation." Northwestern University, 1978.
16. Wisconsin Department of Industry, Labor, and Human Relations. "Inspection Effectiveness Report." September 28, 1971.

25

This intriguing study was designed to test the hypothesis that a mental health program strongly de-emphasizing hospitalization while providing professional treatment and community services within the community would be more efficacious, on net, than the prevailing treatment method of short-term hospitalization plus aftercare of the mentally ill. The experimental program—Training in Community Living—virtually eliminated hospitalization and directed patients strongly toward adjusting to community life and acquiring skills to cope with the demands of daily living.

Ideally, such a program, would be designed to have the following characteristics:

(1) Patients must learn to cope in the community environment rather than in a hospital.
(2) Patients must be motivated to *remain* in the community rather than retreat to the refuge of a hospital.
(3) Patients must have support in the community.
(4) Patients must be assisted in freeing themselves from those relationships with families and institutions that produce conflict and inhibit adjustment to the usual stresses of living.

This study is unique in several respects. First, it employs a random assignment framework in the analysis of a program to treat the mentally ill. This is rare in the analysis of social programs, much less with such a sensitive ethical subject. Second, it presents one of the more precise and complete approaches to cost-benefit analysis available, a particular rarity in the analysis of mental health programs. Finally, it succinctly deals with the appropriate scientific purpose of cost-benefit analysis.

To take the last point first, many students of social programs as well as policy makers and program managers object to the use of cost-benefit analysis as dehumanizing or artificially mechanical. But, as the authors note: "Failure to use cost-benefit analysis does not ensure more humane judgments, but only ones that are less informed." Cost-benefit analysis is fundamentally *a method of organizing knowledge.* This is its substance.

To guarantee that such as study is as informative as possible, the authors identify the full set of costs and benefits—the advantages and disadvantages—of the experimental and comparison programs without regard to the ease of measuring the variables in question. Where monetary estimates are not feasible, nonmonetary measures are devised. And, finally, some variables are listed but simply left unmeasured. Psychic costs and benefits and loss of life are a case in point. Considerable care must be taken in this exercise since one must avoid double counting of costs and benefits and mistaking a *change in the form* of costs or benefits as a *change in the total amount* of costs and benefits. The two programs compared differ also in their treatment structure, and so the *form* of the costs differ between the two treatments. This is a problem in most evaluations. In this study, for instance, the issue arose over whether to treat a person's living expenses as a cost even though he or she was living at home, self-sustaining, rather than in a hospital. The authors' chose to count such maintenance expenses as program costs to maintain a cost symmetry between the two treatments. Finally, the authors had to deal with the fact that an individual's or an institution's (e.g., a hospital) view of costs can differ in significant ways from measures of *social* cost and benefit—a full economic accounting framework.

In contrast to the difficult issues arising in the analysis of differential costs, this study faced fewer cross-program problems in the measurement of benefits. The major problem here, again a characteristic of even relatively simple programs with a uniquely defined desired outcome, is that even evaluators of simple programs may be unable to select a unique outcome measure. Usually, the outcome of a program is some combination of economic outcomes—both monetary and nonmonetary—and noneconomic outcomes. For a variety of reasons, any of these three types of outcome may not be measureable and there is no unique way to combine them into a common index. The authors recognize these factors and problems explicitly.

But what of program effects? Because some components such as loss of life and psychological stress on third parties as well as the individual are inherently difficult to measure (and in this study remained unmeasured), the balance sheet for this experiment cannot be neatly totalled. The authors suggest the following overall judgment: The experimental program *costs more* but has *greater benefits*—added benefits of $1200 per year exceed added costs of $800. Other quantitative but nonmonetary benefits and costs support the net positive monetary result.

What Benefit-Cost Analysis Can and Cannot Do
The Case of Treating the Mentally Ill

Burton A. Weisbrod and Margaret Helming

I.   INTRODUCTION

Benefit-cost analysis is an effort to bridge the gap between a conceptual model--theoretic welfare economics--and actual social policy. There are always problems of taking any theoretic construct and finding an operational proxy for it, and criticisms of benefit-cost analyses generally rest on doubts about the adequacy and completeness of the proxies:

Are all of the relevant forms of benefits and costs dealt with?

How satisfactorily are they measured?

Such criticism is warranted. The state of the art--and it is an art as well as a science--of benefit-cost analysis is such that while there is a good deal that we know about what should be measured, and about what a theoretically correct measure is, we are often unable to obtain such

AUTHOR'S NOTE: A version of this study will be published in T. Hu and F. Sandifer (eds.) Methodology of Estimating Illness (Cambridge, MA: Abt Books, forthcoming). We thank Steven La Valley, A. James Lee, Olivia Mitchell, And Steven Verrill for contributions to the design and implementation of the economic analysis.

From Burton A. Weisbrod and Margaret Helming, "What Benefit Cost-Analysis Can and Cannot Do: The Case of Treating the Mentally Ill." Unpublished manuscript, 1980.

measures within the constraints of the research budget and without
incurring unacceptably high nonpecuniary costs of some sort.

Benefit-cost analysis does have a legitimate and important role to
play nonetheless. It is not a substitute for intelligent judgment by
policymakers, but a tool to facilitate that judgment. It is the systematic collection and organization of relevant data, which, when properly
used, narrow the range of issues about which debate need occur--narrow
it but not eliminate it. Failure to use the benefit-cost analysis does
not ensure more humane judgments, but only ones that are less well informed.

Keeping perspective on the proper role of benefit-cost analysis is
particularly important in policy areas such as the provision of human
services, in which value judgments must inevitably be made. We report here
on a difficult application of this tool, a benefit-cost analysis of an
experiment in treating the mentally ill, an experiment that has potentially
major implications for public policy in determining the role of state
mental hospitals vis a vis other mechanisms for treating the mentally
ill.[1] In focusing on both the limitations of, and the attractions of
formal benefit-cost analysis, we hope to shed light on the general
questions of how to frame a useful benefit-cost analysis and what the
policymaker has when that analysis is completed.

II. THE POLICY PROBLEM: HOW TO TREAT THE MENTALLY ILL

As a case study in policy change, treatment of the mentally ill ranks
among the most dramatic examples in many decades. The change has two
major causes. One is the technological advance represented by the development of tranquilizers and the other is the change in attitudes of both
professional and lay people in favor of greater civil rights and personal
freedom for the mentally ill. As a result of both factors, there has been
a sharp reduction in the number of patients in state mental hospitals,
from 550,000 in 1955 to 340,000 as recently as 1970. And the decline
continues--to 191,000 in 1975, and to near 150,000 today. In the short
span of 20 years, a reduction of some 75 percent has occurred in the size
of the mental hospital population alone.

Treatment within the hospitals has also changed markedly. In the
short time span between 1970 and 1975 the number of patients per hospital

---

[1]The experiment was designed and directed by Leonard I. Stein, M.D.,
and Mary Ann Test, Ph.D. Readers interested in additional details
regarding the benefit-cost analysis summarized in this paper should write
to B.A. Weisbrod, Department of Economics, University of Wisconsin,
Madison, WI 53706.

staff person dropped by 40 percent, and expenditures per patient day have increased by 150 percent for the United States as a whole.[2]

Data on the aggregate social costs of mental illness, or of treating the mentally ill, are difficult if not impossible to obtain, but the magnitudes are clearly large. One recent estimate of the cost of mental illness in 1971 places the "direct care" costs at nearly $10 billion and the total costs, which include, among other things, "indirect costs" attributable to death and disability, at $25 billion.[3] Consistent information for change in these costs over time is not available. The main point, however, is that remarkable changes have occurred in the methods of treating the mentally ill, but the social costs remain high, and it is by no means clear that they are declining in real terms.

The enormous reduction in the number of hospitalized mental patients is only part of the story. Mental health professionals have become increasingly concerned with the process by which patients are hospitalized for short periods, treated, and discharged into the community, only to become sufficiently ill to be hospitalized again, and again, and again. This phenomenon has come to be called the revolving-door syndrome.

There are various hypotheses as to the causes and cures of the revolving-door syndrome. Perhaps the services and facilities available in the community are not adequate to maintain emotionally troubled people, so that turning to a hospital is the only "escape." Or perhaps mental hospitals are themselves contributors--by treating patients in ways that make patients more dependent on other people and less able to cope with the ordinary problems and frustrations of daily life in the community. But whatever the causes, concern about the mental hospitalization treatment process is growing.

III. THE EXPERIMENT

It is in this context that an unusual experiment in treating the mentally ill was launched, and that an economic benefit-cost analysis was undertaken. The experiment, which continued for about three years beginning in October 1973, was designed to test the hypothesis that a treatment program strongly de-emphasizing hospitalization while making available to patients professional treatment and supportive resources in

---

[2] Jeffrey Rubin, Economics, Mental Health and the Law (Lexington, MA: D.C. Heath and Company, 1978), pp. 130, 131.

[3] D.S. Levine and D.R. Levine, The Cost of Mental Illness-1971, National Institute of Mental Health, DHEW Publication No. (ADM) 76-265, 1975, as reported in Rubin, p. 15.

the community, would be both less costly and more efficacious than the generally prevailing system of short-term hospitalization plus aftercare. The experimental program, Training in Community Living (TCL), operated in the community, and hospitalization was virtually eliminated. Adjustment to the community was the goal; thus, the development of skills for coping with ordinary demands of daily living in the community--from preparing meals, budgeting money, using public transportation, to the satisfying use of free time--were emphasized.

To succeed, a TCL program is hypothesized to have certain character-istics: (1) patients must learn coping skills, not in a hospital but in the community; (2) patients must be motivated to remain in the community rather than to seek refuge in the sheltered environment of a hospital; (3) they must have a support system available to help solve their problems; and (4) they must be assisted in freeing themselves from those relation-ships with families or institutions that produce conflict and inhibit independent growth.

Subjects for the study consisted of persons seeking in-patient admission to Mendota Mental Health Institute, who resided in Dane County, Wisconsin (including the City of Madison and the surrounding area), who were between the ages of 18 and 62, and who had any diagnosis other than organic brain syndrome or primary alcoholism. Patients meeting these criteria were assigned randomly either to the "experimental" TCL group (hereafter referred to as E) or to the control group (C). Control subjects were admitted to the hospital in the traditional manner, and at the time of subsequent discharge--generally 2-4 weeks later--were linked with relevant community agencies in the conventional manner. Experimental subjects did not enter the hospital (except in rare instances and then only quite briefly), and even though many subjects objected, they were assigned to the TCL program for 14 months, after which they had access to the same community resources available to the control group, but received no further assistance from the professional staff of the experimental unit. Thus, not only is the TCL program unusual, but the random-assignment framework within which it has been evaluated is equally uncommon in the mental health area and, indeed, in the data underlying most benefit-cost analyses.

The process of randomized assignment of patients makes it possible to compare the costs of the two programs and their respective benefits with a minimum of concern about selection bias--that is, bias caused by patients or treatment staff in the experimental group being different from the controls in some fundamental way that affects the comparative results. No experimental design that deals with human subjects can be entirely free of such potential bias, but the random assignment process does help to minimize both it and the resulting problem of interpreting results. Further, checks can be--and in our study were--conducted to compare the participants in the two programs; it was found, for instance, that at the time of admission the E and C groups did not differ to a statistically significant degree in their sex ratios (55 percent male), marital status (46 percent never married, 27 percent divorced or separated, 27 percent married), age (average of 31), or prior time spent in a psychiatric institution (around 14 months).

There is another potential form of bias to be concerned about: sample attrition. Persons who drop out of either program may not be typical of the persons in the group; as a result, attrition may bias the calculation of costs and benefits. In our experiment, great efforts were made to minimize attrition; in the case of one patient who moved to California, a staff person flew there in order to obtain data on the patient's activities.

Data on all patients were gathered at the time of admission and at four-month intervals. The results presented here cover the 65 experimental and 65 control subjects for the 12 months following their admission.

In summary, the essential characteristics of the TCL approach are these:

1. Hospitalization is virtually eliminated.
2. Patients are aided in their neighborhoods, places of residence, and places of employment, by staff who provide support and who teach the skills necessary to maintain a satisfactory community adjustment.
3. The staff relate to patients as responsible individuals and focus on patient strengths rather than pathology.
4. The staff are assertive in their approach, in order to minimize the number of patients dropping out of treatment and to maximize their engagement in responsible, independent community living.
5. Members of the community who have contact with patients are urged to behave toward them just as they would toward "ordinary" people, and thus to become, in effect, part of the treatment staff.

IV. A BENEFIT-COST ANALYSIS

Benefit-cost analysis in the mental health area is in its infancy. The limited work that has been done has focused on the cost side of the balance, and "costs" have generally been measured by direct expenditures, thereby overlooking indirect dollar costs as well as nonpecuniary costs. Some important types of program consequences are thus often missed. In

addition, very little attention has been directed to measurement of
benefits. The economic benefit-cost analysis of the TCL experiment is
intended to investigate whether the E program is less or more costly than
the conventional C program and also whether its benefits are greater.

Ideally, the analyst should begin by identifying as fully as possible
the potential social benefits and costs--that is, the advantages and
disadvantages that might result from each program--without regard to
measurement problems. Second, the analyst should attempt to provide
monetary estimates for each form of benefit and cost for which such
estimates are appropriate. It was perfectly clear at the outset of our
economic analysis that values could not be placed on all of the consequences of treating mental patients that we had identified. "Better
health," for example, is desirable in its own right, apart from any
contribution it might make to labor productivity, earnings, reduced
hospital costs, or to any other variable for which monetary measurement
is possible. Nevertheless, even though the benefit-cost analysis is
incomplete, information on the differential monetized cost and benefit
effects of alternative treatment modes is useful, for it narrows the
range of uncertainty concerning the full benefits and costs.

It is misleading and highly undesirable, however, to neglect those
types of costs and benefits for which the analyst is unable to develop
monetary estimates; thus, when monetary estimates are not feasible,
quantitative, nonmonetary indicators should be used. For some categories
of costs and benefits, even nonmonetary measures may be unavailable; our
recommended "solution" is to list these categories nonetheless, thereby
making explicit both our belief in their relevance and our inability to
measure them. Such explicit reference is essential if these unquantified
outcomes are not to be overlooked. Because a benefit-cost analysis
implicitly or explicitly involves a comparison of alternatives, it must be
comprehensive. Otherwise one program (e.g., treatment mode) may appear
to be less costly than another, when in reality that program merely shifts
costs into forms that are not being measured. If, for example, the TCL
approach were to reduce hospital treatment costs but simultaneously to
impose increased costs on families, community agencies, or, through
offensive or criminal behavior on the general public, then an analysis
that omitted any of these latter would give an inaccurate portrayal of
the comparative costs of the two programs. The danger of mistaking a
change in the form of costs (or benefits) for a change in the total amount
of costs is an ever present source of error in any benefit-cost analysis.
Evaluations of manpower training program, for example, may count the cost
of equipment used by trainees; this would overlook the likelihood that
the alternative to a worker's participating in such a program would be

either informal training in another job, also involving equipment, or unemployment, in which case there might be cost burdens imposed on other family and community members as a result of the worker's having nothing useful and financially rewarding to do. If the capital costs were counted but the alternative costs were not, the training program could appear to be more "costly," relative to those alternatives than it really is.

In pursuit of a comprehensive accounting framework, the first step in this particular benefit-cost analysis was to list all forms of costs that were likely to be associated with either the C or E program, without regard to measurability. Table 1 lists nine major categories of costs and includes nontreatment as well as treatment costs incurred both inside and outside hospitals, whether incurred by public or private agencies. Cost categories for which no monetary estimates were made constitute a substantial part of the list. (In a later section we describe briefly the methods by which the various types of costs were measured.)

The two treatment programs incurred costs in quite different forms. Apart from direct treatment costs, all categories of monetary costs are actually lower, not higher, for the E program; indirect treatment costs are $304, or about 15 percent lower per patient per year for the E group; costs of law-enforcement and maintenance are also smaller for the average E patient, respectively $59 (10 percent) and $452 (30 percent) per patient per year; and monetized family burden costs are also lower ($48, or 40 percent).

The importance of developing a comprehensive framework is well illustrated by the detailed breakdown of costs in Table 1. Had we failed to consider the fact that mental patients may receive attention in other hospitals--some at distant locations--we would have overlooked an excess monetary cost of $1098 per patient year incurred by the C group. Badly biased estimates of relative costs would have resulted.

The E group did make greater use of some community agencies, primarily those which seek to provide employment skills. They were much heavier users of sheltered workshops, for instance. It is also notable that even though the E-group patients spent less time in hospitals and, thus, more time in the community, they got into less trouble, not more, with the law. It appears, on the basis of measured costs, not to be true, as some critics of the community-based program had predicted, that the E program shifted costs from hospitals to the law-enforcement system or to family members; both of these forms of costs were actually lower for the E-program patients.

The monetized cost of treating an average mental patient is by no means small, whichever treatment mode is considered--over $7200 per patient per year--and of that only about 40 percent is in the form of

direct treatment cost in the case of the C-group patient, or 60 percent
in the case of the experimental patient.

Whether maintenance costs should be included depends on whether they
are social costs or transfer payments, the latter reflecting shifts in
the bearer of a cost rather than changes in the total amount of cost.
After all, even if the patient were to receive no treatment at all, some
costs of housing, food, etc. would continue. The distinction between real
social costs and transfer payments is an important one. A social benefit-
cost analysis, viewed as a tool of applied welfare economics, is designed
to measure total resource costs and benefits, not simply costs incurred
by particular subgroups such as governmental agencies. The first goal of
the analysis is to identify and measure the extent to which the program
under consideration uses up societal resources (i.e., incurs costs) that
would not otherwise be used or provides benefits that would not otherwise
be realized. Flows of money per se do not necessarily reflect either

resource costs or benefits. Stipends to manpower trainees, for example,
are indeed "costs" to a program administrator but from a social
perspective they are transfers of purchasing power, not social costs.
Similarly, payments to teen-agers enrolled in Youth Corps or "Upward
Bound" education programs, food stamp program, "negative income tax"
payments, and unemployment compensation payments all involve transfer
payments, not social costs. The payments are, to be sure, costs to the
payers and benefits to the recipients, but value judgments are required
before one can judge whether the transfer (i.e., the income redistribution)
is or is not a net gain or loss from the overall societal vantage point.
It is precisely this kind of judgment that should be left to the "policymakers."

In this case it was decided that maintenance costs should be included
because (1) in the case of the E program, it is difficult to determine the
extent to which maintenance expenditures are simply transfers (and,
therefore, not social costs), and the extent to which they are, in effect,
treatment costs, since living in independent circumstances is the key to
the treatment program; and because (2) costs of in-hospital treatment
include maintenance costs, so that to count those costs when a person is
hospitalized but not otherwise would bias the analysis against the C
program. On average, E-group members received fewer transfers, as Table 1
shows, and the differences between the sources of funds for the two groups
were substantial.

Overall, we found that the E program was some 10 percent more costly
in monetary terms during the first year of the patients' treatment--$8093
compared to $7296. Measured nonmonetary costs to patients' families were
also smaller for E group members; but the number of arrests for illegal

activity (admittedly not an ideal measure of anti-social behavior) was nearly the same for both groups.

How to value patient mortality is an important issue. We have consciously chosen not to try to attach a monetary value to human lives, despite some precedent for doing so. One common basis for such valuation is lost earnings; but since many of these individuals, like retired persons and children, earn very little, if anything, in the labor force, the inadequacy of such a proxy is particularly glaring in this instance.

Two categories of deaths are reported, because they may be valued differently. Suicides are clearly symptomatic cf mental illness; deaths from other causes, such as heart attacks, may or may not be.

Some cost variables have not been measured at all. In the final analysis, any policy decision requires a judgment about the importance of such variables; this is inescapable. It is dangerous simply to neglect the unmeasured variables. Sometimes, however, judgments can be made about the probable correlation between an unmeasured variable and a measured one. For example, perhaps it can be assumed that relative family burdens of E and C groups during the first four months (for which we do have data) continued for the remainder of the year of the experiment (for which we do not have data). In general, however, the problem of making inferences about costs or benefits of unmeasured variables is one for which there is no simple solution.

We turn now to benefits. Table 2 shows that the E program brought sizably greater benefits in the form of additional labor market produc-tivity--almost $1200 more of wages per year per person; E-group patients averaged nearly twice as much in earnings as did their C-group counter-parts--$2364 per year compared with $1168. Only a small percentage of the added earnings came from employment in sheltered workshops; more than 86 percent ($1033) of the added earnings came from competitive employment, from jobs in which the patients were required to perform normal work tasks under ordinary conditions of the labor market.

Whatever the program being evaluated, but particularly in the area of human services, no single indicator of benefits is likely to capture all of the socially relevant favorable outcomes. Programs to help the educationally disadvantaged, for example, may improve their performances on tests of reading and arithmetic skills, but may also enhance self-esteem and thereby alter attitudes in important ways. By the same token, added earning power is not the only measure of benefits from treating the mentally ill. Indeed, earnings are not the only meaningful indicator even of an individual's ability to succeed in the world of work. In Table 2, labor market benefits take a variety of other forms including the number of days the patient was employed at a job, the percentage of those days that the person missed work, and whether changes in jobs did or did not represent advancement. It is noteworthy that E-group patients were employed a considerably greater number of days during the year--127 + 89, or 216 days, compared with 77 + 10, or 87 days for the average C-group patient.

Separate from labor-market performance are those benefits which represent an attempt to quantify the degree of program success in improving patients' ability to perform as consumers. Purchase of insurance was postulated to reflect thinking and planning about the future, which, according to the psychiatric specialists, was a favorable sign. Holding a savings account was also seen as an indicator of forward thinking. As the data in Table 2 show, the average E-group patient purchased more insurance, a larger percentage of E-group patients had savings accounts. (We were unable to obtain reliable information on the amounts of such savings.) Interpretation of these two results is somewhat difficult because both may result at least in part from the increased earnings and greater incidence of independent living arrangements among E-group members. Thus it is not clear whether or not these outcomes should be counted as separate benefits. In any case, both measures are favorable to the experimental program, although we do not place a monetary value on either.

Two other indicators of the comparative effectiveness of the two approaches are the patients' views of their satisfaction with life and a measure of the symptoms of mental illness that they display. E-group patients report greater satisfaction with life than did C-group patients. Other, more objective evidence, such as the E patients' greater success in holding down jobs--with all that this implies--and their lower rates of contact with law-enforcement agencies confirms this subjective measure, as does the finding that the E-group showed fewer symptoms of illness than the C-group during the course of the experimental year. Thus from both the individual patient's perspective and from the broader social perspective, our measures of the "intangible" benefits from treatment suggest that the experimental program was more beneficial.

V. METHODS AND FINDINGS

Some important, general dangers in benefit-cost analysis emerge as we describe the methods used to develop the estimates in our tables. The direct costs of hospital treatment at Mendota Mental Health Institute (MMHI) were derived in a process that accounted for (1) operating costs (including an estimate of the cost of the differing amounts of

staff time used by each group); (2) depreciation of capital in the form
of buildings and equipment; and (3) a 9 percent rate of return on the
market value of that portion of the hospital plant and land that was
used in the treatment of patients in the experiment. The resulting per
diem costs were multiplied by the average number of days of hospitalization
for the E and C groups; the results are shown in Table 1. The outpatient
cost was derived from records of amounts of time that staff spent in
outpatient treatment of C and E group patients, with staff time valued at
an average of $10 per hour.

When costs of operating facilities are involved in a benefit-cost
analysis, as is frequently the case, it is natural to turn to cost data
from the agency operating the facility. That can involve error, however,
if the cost concept used by the agency differs from the real social cost.

There were two such deviations in the accounting methods used by the
state for MMHI. One involves depreciation. The state's measures of
depreciation cost was based on the historical cost of construction--
decades earlier--rather than on the far higher current replacement cost,
which is the relevant social cost concept if treatment is to be continued
in mental hospitals. Second, no cost at all was attributed to the land on
which the mental hospital was located. (The land was potentially prime
residential property, much of it with an excellent view over Lake Mendota.)
The presumed justifications were that land does not depreciate and that
the state was not making any explicit payments to anyone for the land.
But the implicit assumption that the social cost of using the land was
zero is economically erroneous; the land has a significant opportunity cost
in the form of its potential alternative uses. Thus, in our cost accounting
we added an estimate of this opportunity cost, based on the market value
of the land. This made the C-program cost of hospitalization conceptually
equivalent to the E-program cost, because the E-program used rented
facilities, and we can assume that the rent reflected a normal market
return on the land value of the E-program center.

The program costs for the experimental center are applicable only
to the experimental group. These costs include all of the expenditures
on staff for the program, and the costs of rent, utilities, and related
expenses for maintaining the experimental staff headquarters. Also
included is the cost of some administrative services that were provided
to the E program without charge.

Indirect treatment costs and costs of contacts with the law-
enforcement system are products of data gathered from patient and family
interviews and from agencies on the extent of each patient's contacts
with each agency, and estimates, obtained in consultations with each
agency, of the average cost per patient contact. Maintenance costs are

derived primarily from the agencies involved, but where this was not possible we used patients own reports of agency contacts, together with agencies' cost data.

On the benefit side, data on competitive work experience and earnings were obtained from patients. Sheltered workshop experience and income were obtained directly from the workshops.

Some benefit and cost variables were unmeasured, not because measurement was impossible but because the costs of measurement were judged to be greater than the expected value of the information. Given a limited research budget, more or better data on one type of cost or benefit can be obtained only at the cost of less or poorer data on some other program variable. There are also nonpecuniary costs of collecting information. Thus, for example, we did not verify patients' reports of earnings from competitive employment because to do so would have required explaining the nature of our study to employers, with a resultant loss of privacy for patients. This did not seem worth the additional accuracy that might have been gained. Similarly, families were not interviewed after the patients' fourth month because the interviews themselves were a taxing process for people already under considerable stress.

Table 3 shows that neither of the two treatment programs provides labor market benefits that exceed the programs' monetized costs. The fact that either treatment approach continues to be used despite this excess of measured dollar cost over dollar benefits suggests not that treatment is wasteful, but that society has judged that some combination of compassion and nonmonetary--intangible--benefits to society, including the mentally ill, warrants incurring substantial treatment costs. (This societal commitment is not without limits, however, as the current debate over the adequacy of care provided to the "deinstitutionalized" mentally ill demonstrates.)

As between the E and C programs, there is relatively little difference between the monetized net benefits (benefits minus costs) of the two treatment modes; with both programs involving more than $7200 in cost per patient per year, the differential in net benefits of $396 per patient per year is only about 4 percent of cost, and is well within the margin of statistical and measurement error. The difference, however, does favor the E program. A reasonable valuation of benefits in the nonmonetized forms (labor market behavior, consumer decision-making, satisfaction with life and symptomatology) and of the nonmonetized costs (especially family burden costs), both of which favor the E group, also favor the experimental program. The extent of burdens placed on unrelated community members and the extent to which deaths from causes other than suicide were somehow related to the treatment modes remain unknown.

Our principal findings with respect to monetary costs and benefits
are as follows:

1. Total costs of treating mental patients are very high--more than
    $7200 per patient per year, whether a hospital-based (C-type)
    program or a community-based (E-type) program is used.

2. A very sizable proportion of costs (between 40 and 60 percent)
    are in forms other than direct hospital and medical treatment;
    again, this is true whether a hospital-based treatment program
    or a community-based program is used.

3. Although the experimental, community-based treatment program
    involves larger direct treatment costs per patient than does the
    hospital-based program, the community-based program involves
    smaller costs in every other category--indirect treatment,
    law-enforcement, maintenance, and family burdens. Considering
    all forms of costs in total, the hospital-based program is about
    10 percent cheaper per patient.

4. On the benefit side, the community-based program is associated
    with a doubling of work capacity, as gauged by the differential
    in earnings of the patients in the two programs, with a higher
    level of patient satisfaction with life, and with decreased
    medical symptomatology.

5. Considering all the forms of benefits and costs we have been able
    to derive in monetary terms, the experimental program provides
    both additional benefits and additional costs as compared to the
    conventional approach, but the added benefits, some $1200 per
    patient per year, are nearly $400 more per patient per year than
    the added costs, almost $800. Furthermore, a number of forms
    of benefits and costs that we have measured in quantitative but
    nonmonetary terms show additional advantages to the community-
    based experimental program.

VI.   CONCLUSIONS AND LESSONS

What conclusions can be drawn? Although we have made great efforts
to be comprehensive in identifying forms of costs and benefits, and to be
accurate in measuring them, we have not been able to measure satisfactorily,
let alone to value, all of the relevant benefits and costs. For instance,
we have been unable to obtain any data on the burdens that mental patients
impose on neighbors, co-workers, and others outside their families, and
we have been unable to provide monetary values for a number of forms of
costs and benefits for which we have developed quantitative measures.

Even if we had been able, however, to measure and to attach dollar values to all of the types of costs and benefits, questions would remain: How costly and how beneficial would the experimental treatment mode be if the scale of the community-based program were increased substantially; if it were introduced in larger cities or smaller towns than Madison, Wisconsin (a metropolitan area with a population of about a quarter million); if it received less cooperation from community agencies; and if it were operating under a different set of labor market conditions than existed during the recession period of the experiment?

These are the kinds of problems and questions that frequently beset the benefit-cost analyst and any prospective user of the analysis. That is, whatever the program being evaluated, and even if it is granted that the analysis is thorough and done well, how generalizable are its findings? Do they apply only to the specific project or to a larger class of that "type" of project? To a larger set of mental hospitals or only to this one? There is no easy answer to the question of generalizability, yet it cannot be ignored. If the benefit-cost analyst implies that his or her findings do apply to a wider class of projects, participants, places, and times, some justification is called for.

Any economic cost-benefit analysis, no matter how well done it may be, has its limitations, particularly when a complex human service such as health is involved. At the same time, decisions on the allocation of resources cannot be avoided; many other health programs are competing with mental health programs for the economy's limited resources, and all of these programs compete with social programs in education, housing, and welfare, not to mention the wide variety of other public and private wants. In one program area after another the claim is made that the importance of a program is so great that it is justified whatever any cost-benefit analysis may show. Benefit-cost analysis can help to structure the debate over how resources should be used. It cannot end the debate.

A cost-benefit analysis is not a mechanism for deciding mechanically on the allocation of funds and resources among programs; it is a systematic approach for weighing advantages and disadvantages—that is, for organizing knowledge. The question is not whether such analyses are desirable, for in one form or another—formal or informal—they cannot be avoided, but how to do the analyses in a useful manner. The cost-benefit analysis summarized here is unusual in its comprehensiveness (especially with respect to hard-to-measure outcomes), in its derivation from a randomized experiment, and in its origin from a cooperative effort of researchers from psychiatry, psychology, and economics. It illustrates the fact, however, that the recipe for any useful benefit-cost analysis is to mix one measure of economic science with several measures of creative art, and stir them with judgment.

Table 1

Costs Per Patient, Experimental and Congrol Groups

for the 12 Months Following Admission to the Experiment

COSTS	GROUP		
	Control	Experi- mental	E - C
Costs for Which Monetary Estimates Have Been Made			
Direct Treatment Costs			
Mendota Mental Health Institute (MMHI)			
Inpatient	$3096	$ 94	-$3002
Outpatient	42	0	- 42
Experimental Center Program	0	4704	4704
Total Direct Treatment Costs	$3138	$4798	$1660
Indirect Treatment Costs			
Social Service Agencies			
Other Hospitals (non-MMHI)			
In Madison	$ 936	$ 382	-$ 554
Out-of-Town Hospitals	808	264	- 554
Total Costs of Other Hospitals	$1744	$ 646	-$1098
Sheltered Workshops	91	870	779
Other Community Agencies			
Dane County Mental Health Center	55	50	- 5
Dane County Social Services	41	25	- 16
State Department of Vocational Rehabilitation	185	209	24
Visiting Nurse Service	0	23	23
State Employment Service	4	3	- 1
Private Medical Providers	22	12	- 10
Total Indirect Treatment Costs	$2142	$1838	-$ 304
Law-Enforcement Costs			
Overnights in Jail	$ 159	$ 152	-$ 7
Court Contacts	17	12	- 5
Probation and Parole	189	143	- 43
Police Contacts	44	43	- 1
Total Law-Enforcement Costs	$ 409	$ 350	-$ 59
Maintenance Costs			
Cash Payments			
Governmental (incl. admin.)			
Social Security (SSI, Retirement, Survivors & Disability	$ 557	$ 269	-$ 288

Table 1 continued

COSTS	GROUP		
	Control	Experi- mental	E − C
Maintenance Costs cont'd.			
Aid for Dependent Children	$ 446	$ 167	−$ 279
Unemployment Compensation,			
Welfare and Other Costs (incl.			
supervised residences)	95	98	3
Total Government Payments	$1098	$ 534	−$ 564
Private Payments to Patients	102	197	95
Experimental Center Payments to			
Patients	0	202	202
Patients Own Support	?	?	?
In-Kind Food and Lodging			
Private (from family, Salvation			
Army, etc.)	287	102	− 185
Government and Experimental Center	0	0	0
Total Maintenance Costs	$1487	$1035	−$ 452
Family Burden Costs			
Lost Earnings Due to the Patient	120	72	− 48
Total Costs for Which Monetary			
Estimates Have Been Made	$7296	$8093	$ 797

Costs for Which No Monetary Estimates Have Been Made

Other Family Burden Costs			
Percentage of Families Reporting			
Physical Illness Due to the Patient	25%	14%	− 11%
Percentage of Family Members Experi-			
encing Emotional Strain Due to the			
Patient	48%	25%	− 23%
Burdens on Other People (e.g., neighbors,			
co-workers)	?	?	?
Illegal Activity Costs			
Total Number of Arrests	1.0 times	0.8 times	− 0.2
Total Number of Arrests for Felony	0.2 times	0.2 times	0.0
Patient Mortality Costs (Percentage of			
Group Dying During the Year)			
Suicide	1.5%	1.5%	0%
Natural Causes	0%	4.6%	4.6%
Grand Total Costs	?	?	?

Table 2

Benefits Per Patient, Experimental and Control Groups

for 12 Months Following Admission to the Experiment

BENEFITS	GROUP		
	Control	Experi-mental	E – C
Benefits for Which Monetary Estimates Have Been Made			
Earnings			
From Competitive Employment	$1136	$2169	$1033
From Sheltered Workshops	32	195	163
Total Benefits for Which Monetary Estimates Have Been Made	$1168	$2364	$1196
Benefits for Which No Monetary Estimates Have Been Made			
Labor Market Behavior			
Days of Competitive Employment per Year	77 days	127 days	50 days
Days of Sheltered Employment per Year	10 days	89 days	79 days
Percentage of Work Days Attended Job	97%	93%	– 4%
Number of Beneficial Job Changes Minus Number of Detrimental Job Changes	2-2=0	3-2=1	1
Improved Consumer Decision-Making			
Insurance Expenditures	$ 33	$ 56	$ 23
Percentage of Group Having Savings Accounts	27%	34%	7%
Patient Satisfaction With Life			*
Patient Symptomatology			**
Grand Total Benefits	?	?	?

* On a 5-point scale from 1, "not at all satisfied (with friends, living situation, leisure activities)" to 5, "very much satisfied," the E group had a significantly (.05 level) higher mean score.

** A 13-symptom list, developed by the psychiatric staff but administered by trained laymen, was utilized at baseline and at 4-month intervals. At the beginning of the experiment there was no statistically significant difference between the mean number of symptoms of mental illness for the E and C groups. By the end of 12 months, however, the average E patient had significantly (.05 level) fewer symptoms.

Table 3

Summary: Valued Benefits Minus Valued Costs

	Control	Experi- mental	E - C
Valued Benefits	$1168	$2364	$1196
Valued Costs	7296	8093	706
Net (Benefits minus Costs)	-$6128	-$5732	$ 396

VII

ENERGY AND RESOURCES PROGRAMS: DESIGNED AND NATURAL EXPERIMENTS

As its title indicates, this section assesses major aspects of the problems of conserving certain natural resources: water and energy. While the analyses are specific to the resources, the analytic and policy insights, as well as the methodologies developed to measure behavioral outcomes, are generalizable to the use of other resources that are characterized by the "commons dilemma" (Berk et al., Ch. 29) such as the atmosphere, waste disposal on land and in the water, and public land and similar economic goods which can be rationed or allocated by prices—that is, any good or service, other than a pure public good of the Samuelsonian type (Samuelson, 1954). If the exclusion principle can be applied, that is, if the good or service can be priced and withheld from someone, regardless of whether it is publicly produced or regulated or privately produced, the general economic lessons expressed in this section apply. These lessons are two: First, regardless of one's ethical or political attitudes concerning the production and allocation of a good, people's behavior concerning that good can be effectively and speedily altered by manipulating its price. Elaborate governmental regulatory institutions are not the only way to deal with shortages and problems of efficiency and social equity. Second, although the economist generally takes tastes and preferences as given, it is possible to alter these even in the very short run through the use of moral suasion and information. One can affect the consumption of a good, that is, shift the demand for it, by changing tastes and preferences through various information strategies and moral appeals— "jawboning."

The study by Mead begins the articles in this section. While Mead describes in concise and painful detail the failure of a range of policies designed to efficiently and equitably produce and market hydrocarbon fuels, one should not conclude from this study that prices cannot be successfully employed as an allocative device. Indeed, if anything, Mead's study points up the fact that producers and consumers respond all too well to the changing price structure and property rights created by government regulation. It should not be surprising that policies such as the oil depletion allowance, import quotas, and oil and natural gas price controls have perverse effects and create conditions for unanticipated as well as anticipated windfall gains and losses. And, hence, such regulations become politically difficult to deal with. Given that such programs create property rights and constituencies, it is difficult for politicians to respond to Mead's prescription to return to the "free market." Indeed, it is difficult to know just what is meant when Mead talks of the "free market" since social and political conditions always affect the supply and demand of goods and services, and by defining property rights, also affect the ability to command goods and services. Nevertheless, Mead argues convincingly that different, if not less, control is advisable in the regulation of certain economic activities.

In this context, it is interesting that the studies by Berk et al., Battalio et al., and Aigner and Hausman each test the proposition that price can be used to ration and allocate goods and services. And not only that price matters, but also that the time lag between consumption and receipt of the bill helps to determine the strength of the response to price (Berk et al. and Battalio et al). These studies reflect a movement away from pricing mechanisms that do not represent the marginal cost—hence, true relative social cost—of producing the goods and services in question. With due regard to "second best" arguments (Lipsey and Lancaster, 1956-1957), it is difficult to see how marginal cost pricing can fail to be an improvement over average cost pricing, declining block rate pricing, or a fixed flat fee. And the principle justification for declining block rates—the more effective use of large scale capacity—is weakened once it is recognized that large scale capacity is in part the creation of an attitude that says capacity must be sufficient to meet any peak load demanded. Higher prices charged during peak loads (Aigner and Hausman) can result in lower peak load demands, a more uniform distribution of demand and, hence, lower capacity requirements. Excess capacity can be reduced. Different capacity and technology may be introduced as Aigner and Hausman suggest.

What is the consumer response to the price incentive structures in the three experiments in this section? For the usual economic reasons, the demand by households for water and electricity is inelastic—that is, a 1% change in price results in a less than 1% change in quality demanded. Expenditures on these two items represent a small portion of the overall household budget, and the experiments measure responses that are short run in nature. For instance, with respect to the consumption of electricity and water, households did not have sufficient time to change the quantity and quality of their water and electricity using consumer durables. They could only adjust their rate of use of the current stock. (The study by Battalio et al. excluded households that experienced large shifts in the acquisition of consumer appliances, for instance.) Finally, there is an irreducible, minimum, biological level of the consumption of resources such as water, and minimum social levels of consumption of resources such as water, and minimum social levels of consumption of energy determined by habit and custom. These change only slowly. In short, long-run price elasticities are likely to be greater in absolute value than are the short-run elasticities measured by these studies. Thus, price changes will have greater conservation effects in the long run than in the short run. As further support to the pricing policies suggested here, the study by Berk et al. shows that (as a consequence of production technology) agricultural demand for water is much more elastic than the demand of households. Hence, pricing policies that reflect marginal cost can have an even greater effect here.

Good intentions and a priori judgments should not be confused with informed public policy judgments even when we are dealing with powerful market incentives. Thus, it is important to know what the measured elasticities are in response to price changes. Price setting is an activity attendant with political as well as economic costs as noted in Berk et al. and Aigner and Hausman and, perhaps, as President Carter has discovered with his proposal to place a per gallon surcharge on gasoline. If large price changes are necessary to induce even moderate changes in behavior, other economic policies such as those tested by Berk et al. and Battalio et al. must also be considered. While these studies demonstrate that "the market works," society will reserve final judgment on any given policy until it discovers what the efficiency and equity impacts are relative to its social objectives.

REFERENCES

LIPSEY, R. G. and K. LANCASTER (1956-1957) "The general theory of second best." Rev. of Econ. Studies 24: 11-32.
SAMUELSON, P. A. (1954) "The pure theory of public expenditure." Rev. of Economics and Statistics 36: 387-389. See also several later articles by Samuelson in the same journal.

26

This study presents a concise historical summary and analysis of the major economic policies the United States has used to affect the production and consumption of energy and the distribution of income associated with the production and consumption of energy. As such, it is an effective introduction to this part of the volume. The rationale and major probable effects of the following policies are discussed:

- Subsidies, including the oil depletion allowance and expensing intangible oil drilling costs
- Prorationing rules, with well spacing regulations and depth-acreage allowable schedules
- Import quotas
- Auction of leases for outer continental shelf oil and gas fields
- Oil and natural gas price controls

Each of these policies is shown to be faulty, and the marginal effect of each is alleged to have increased the seriousness of the current oil and energy crisis.

Oil depletion allowances and expensing intangible drilling costs increased the after-tax return on investments in oil and gas exploration and production. This led to increased capital flows into exploration. Production increased. Oil prices fell. Consumption and a style of life based on inexpensive gas and oil led to the (in retrospect) excessive consumption of these nonrenewable resources. Such policies are counterproductive of a conservation goal which Mead defines as the maximization of the present value of all energy resources at any point in time.

Prorationing created idle capacity and, hence, resource waste in the form of excessive investment in oil exploration and production.

Given the excess capacity problems created in part by prorationing, import quotas were instituted to restrict the import of foreign oil. This led to increased domestic prices and accelerated depletion of domestic crude. Prorationing became inoperative in 1972, and in 1975 the Strategic Petroleum Reserve Program was instituted to reduce dependence on foreign oil.

Mead also judges that the recent (1978) movement away from cash bonus bidding has been nonoptimal. In view of his defense of the free market, however, it is hard to understand his statement that *the government has received more than a fair market value for its leases* (italics ours). Presumably, no one forced the oil companies to make "unfair" offers.

Price controls on natural gas led to excess demand and shortage of supply. These effects then had an impact on the substitute resource, oil, accelerating its use. This, too, led to increased imports and aggravated balance of payment problems. Domestically, it has apparently been the case that crude oil price controls have not had a significant effect on the final prices faced by consumers. This implies a simultaneous failure of the policy and a wholly arbitrary and unanticipated income redistribution from crude oil producers to refiners as well as among classes of refiners. In addition, the administration of controls implies real resource costs both on the part of government and industry.

Mead lists the arguments against eliminating price controls. First, world oil prices are asserted to be monopoly prices set by a cartel, the Organization of Petroleum Exporting Countries (OPEC). The argument then is that domestic oil and gas prices should not be permitted to rise to such monopoly prices. Second, it is asserted that market-clearing prices would have an unfair impact on the poor. Third, it is contended that reversion to a free market will result in windfall gains to oil and gas producers.

Mead rejects each of these arguments. He points out that market conditions plus the transfer of property rights in oil resources from the oil companies to the OPEC host countries offer a sufficient explanation of the rise in oil prices, though perhaps his case is overstated somewhat. The cartel has cracks in its facade but is still operating effectively.

He correctly points out that setting price controls on energy is a very haphazard and indirect way of helping the poor. Cash income subsidies or wage subsidies are the preferred methods to directly remove persons from poverty as is evidenced by other studies in this volume. The behavior effects of the negative income tax programs are now better understood (see Parts II, IV and V), but this policy option has been rejected for the time being as a major alternative to subsidies in-kind to the poor, such as fuel rebates to the low-income population. The actual behavior effects of wage subsidy and subsidized public service employment are less well understood (see Bishop et al., this volume). Thus, the price control arguments tend to fill this vacuum caused by ignorance or the rejection of alternative income maintenance policies.

And, finally, one notes the technical simplicity of taxing away windfall profits if sufficient political determination and cohesion exists. In fact, current tax laws will already tax away much of the profits and the oil depletion allowance has been totally removed from integrated oil companies. Excess profits taxes are not impossible to design and administer.

Mead argues for a "free market" solution to the conservation and energy shortage problem. Based on the dynamics of a democratic political system in which lobbies and pressure groups operate effectively on law makers and law makers do not bear the direct costs of their economically inefficient and market distorting actions, he feels that more intervention will not improve resource allocation. An alternative energy policy would be to let the market, that is, free market prices, allocate scarce resources. The subsequent studies in this section suggest that persons do indeed respond to price incentives as well as moral suasion.

The Performance of Government in
Energy Regulations

Walter J. Mead

An evaluation of government performance in energy regulation requires specification of a standard. Here the record of regulation will be evaluated in terms of optimum resource conservation, defined as the process of maximizing the present value of all resources at any point of time.

It is possible to distinguish two general paths by which resource conservation may be attained: free market allocation; or allocation by direct government regulations, the use of taxation, or the use of subsidies. There is wide agreement among economists that the existence of net externalities creates market failures and suboptimal resource allocation. The presence of externalities therefore has been used to rationalize government intervention in order to correct for market failures. The implicit assumption is that such regulation will in turn be economically efficient.

An influential body of opinion argues that the power of government should be used to enforce energy conservation as a means of resolving the "energy crisis." However, most of these arguments are based on naive definitions of conservation, meaning "use less" or "save energy" as if all other resources were of zero value. Concepts of this kind are found repeatedly in the Energy Policy Project report of the Ford Foundation.

The Carter "National Energy Plan" proposes a major expansion of government regulation, taxation, and subsidies. Before Congress legislates new government intervention in the energy sector, would it not be wise to evaluate the extensive record of past government intervention? In this paper five major areas of government intervention over

*Professor of economics, University of California-Santa Barbara

the past half-century will be briefly reviewed.

I. A Review of *U.S.* Energy Policy

More than a half-century ago Congress introduced percentage depletion allowance tax treatment for oil and gas production. Subsequently, provision was made for expensing of intangible drilling costs. The initial effect of these two policies was to increase the after-tax rate of return on investments in oil and gas exploration and production. These tax subsidies led to increased capital flows into exploration. Consequently, new reserves were found and production was stimulated. But increased production led to lower oil prices and established the historic *U.S.* low-price policy for energy. This in turn led consumers to treat oil and gas as cheap commodities and to consume these nonrenewable resources excessively.

Legislation in 1975 removed the benefits of percentage depletion allowances for integrated oil companies only. For the nearly 10,000 independent oil and gas producers, the depletion allowance has been retained but the tax benefits have been reduced. The benefits of expensing intangible costs have been retained in total.

These two tax policies have probably been the most important items of government interference in the petroleum industry. In the absence of these artificial stimulants the market would have delayed production. Thus they contributed directly to the energy crisis of the 1970's and in general are counterproductive of a conservation goal.

Prorationing was authorized by the federal government in the 1930's and implemented subsequently by state governments. Stephen

From Walter J. Mead, "The Performance of Government in Energy Regulations," 69(2) *American Economic Review* 352-356 (May 1979). Copyright 1979 by the American Economic Association.

McDonald has shown that MER-type prorationing rules, with their depth-acreage allowable schedules and well spacing regulations, are purely arbitrary and are economically inefficient as a solution to the common property resource externality. He has proposed an efficient solution in the form of mandatory unitization. Prorationing also included market-demand restrictions. This form of government intervention has been inoperative since 1972. For nearly four decades it created idle capacity and hence resource waste in the form of excessive investment in oil exploration and production. Thus, both MER and market-demand types of prorationing are inefficient and are counterproductive of a conservation goal.

Import quotas, introduced by President Eisenhower in 1959, were partly a consequence of market-demand prorationing. A protected domestic market is inconsistent with free trade. The effects of import quotas were to restrict the supply of imported oil. to increase domestic prices, and to artificially stimulate additional domestic production of this nonrenewable resource. Thus, $U.S.$ import quotas distorted the pattern of oil production worldwide and led to excessive production from rapidly declining $U.S.$ resources, contributing directly to the energy crisis of the 1970's. An efficient solution to the dependence problem was not introduced until 1975 when the Strategic Petroleum Reserve was authorized by Congress.

Price controls on natural gas were introduced in 1954 and those on crude oil in 1971. In both cases, controls were administered in favor of artificially low prices. In the case of natural gas, low prices led to high demand and low supply thus creating the usual shortage. Consumers who received natural gas allocations consumed it lavishly as a cheap commodity. In this respect the conservation objective has been thwarted. Part of the supply-demand gap has been filled by a close substitute, oil. This has led to increased imports and consequent dependence and balance-of-payments problems.

The effects of oil price controls are not as clear as in natural gas. Charles Phelps and Rodney Smith studied price controls and

other regulations in the oil industry and concluded that "the controls have not reduced the prices of refined products" (p. v). Another study recently completed by Robert Deacon and myself tested two hypotheses involving comparisons of domestic and foreign wholesale gasoline prices between 1971 and 1977. Both tests indicated that $U.S.$ price controls effectively lowered the price of gasoline through mid-1976. However, from that point through 1977, the evidence failed to support the hypothesis that price controls lowered gasoline prices.

If gasoline prices are not currently below levels which would be attained in the absence of price controls, then demand is unaffected by price controls. However, producers of crude oil receive artificially low prices under the price control system. Phelps and Smith pointed out that, "While the price controls on crude oil did not influence product prices, they did transfer profits within the petroleum industry" (p. vii). Wealth was transferred from crude oil producers to refiners, and from one refiner class to another. If domestic crude oil supply elasticity is greater than zero, then domestic suppliers are artificially restrained by the control system and imports are artificially stimulated, again leading to higher imports, balance of payments, and dependency problems.

Clearly, natural gas price controls have set prices below equilibrium levels. Further, evidence supports the point that oil price controls had similar effects through mid-1976. At lower prices consumers demand more. In the case of petroleum, there is an open-ended supply in the form of imports. If consumption is artificially stimulated, then conservation goals are not attained. In the case of oil and gas price controls there is further resource misallocation in the high cost of price control administration, both within the government and on the part of complying industry.

Arguments against eliminating price controls and allowing the market to allocate scarce oil and gas resources take three forms: 1) World oil prices are alleged to be monopoly prices set by an Organization of Petroleum Exporting Countries ($OPEC$) cartel. Supporters of price control argue that *U.S.* oil and gas prices should not be permitted to rise to such monopoly price levels. 2) Market-clearing prices would unfairly impact on the poor. 3) Market-determined prices would confer windfall profits on oil and gas producers.

The cartel rationale in support of price controls was recently articulated by Paul Davidson. But the evidence for the cartel thesis is mixed. On the one hand, the dominant "firm" in the alleged cartel is clearly Saudi Arabia. In the years from the strong crude oil market in 1973, to the relatively weak markets in 1975–77, Saudi Arabia expanded its market share from 24.2 to 30.4 percent of *OPEC* production. This evidence is inconsistent with either a fixed market shares or a dominant-firm price-leadership model of oligopoly behavior. On the other hand, *OPEC* output, in the aggregate, is consistent with cartel behavior. The *OPEC* share of world crude production declined from 55.5 to 52.5 percent during the increasingly weak markets from 1973 to 1977.

Some new research by Ali D. Johany has shown that crude oil price movements from approximately $3 per barrel in the early 1970's to approximately $12.50 per barrel in 1974 are rational in terms of individual oil producing countries maximizing the present value of their resources. By joining property rights theory to capital theory, Johany has carried our understanding of optimal crude oil prices beyond recent work by William Nordhaus and Robert Pindyck.

Johany pointed out that during the 1950's and 1960's there was a progressive awareness on the part of international oil companies holding oil concessions in the Middle East that their property rights were in jeopardy. Nationalization, or its euphemism, "participation," was the wave of the future. Fear of loss of property rights caused international oil companies to accelerate their foreign production. From 1950 through 1970 the compound annual growth rate in oil production from the Middle East was 10.9 percent. From 1970 through 1973, the growth rate was 15.0 percent.

Reflecting these output increases, world crude oil prices were relatively stable during the two decades from 1950 through 1970. Output increases were matched by worldwide growth in demand with only modest increases in nominal prices.

By the end of 1973, however, host countries were in complete control of output within their borders. Given firmly established property rights and lower discount rates, one would expect reduced output growth rates and sharply higher prices. The record shows that from 1973 to 1977 Middle Eastern oil output increased at a compound annual rate of only 0.7 percent. As a consequence, crude oil prices in world markets rose sharply from 1970 to date, a fact which can be explained without the aid of a cartel theory.

Johany examined the opportunity cost of capital for Saudi Arabia and concluded that for large sums of money, the *U.S.* government Treasury Bill market yielding 8 percent appeared to represent the most attractive alternative to leaving oil in the ground. Adjusting for inflation, the real opportunity cost was judged to be 1 percent. If one believes that the real price of oil fifty years hence will be approximately $21 per barrel, as determined by the cost of oil substitutes, then present values are rational. If so, the *U.S.* crude oil price controls cannot be justified in terms of a cartel theory.

Oil and natural gas price controls as methods of subsidizing the poor are haphazard tools. If additional public subsidies to the poor are warranted, then a direct approach through the negative income tax device would be a more efficient means.

Finally, decontrol would confer windfall profits on oil and gas resource owners and lease holders. But federal and state governments own most of the known and probable future productive oil and gas resources. That part of the windfall accruing to lease holders would be subject to income taxes. In 1975, the percentage depletion allowance was totally removed for all integrated oil companies. Therefore, combined federal and state income taxes would capture close to half of any windfall gains which accrue to integrated producers. For future leases issued after decontrol, the auction bidding system would totally eliminate windfalls due to decontrol.

A final element of government policy toward energy is the process used in auctioning leases. In 1978, Congress enacted a major overhaul in legislation governing outer continental shelf (*OCS*) oil and gas leasing. Under prior leasing procedures, tracts were leased after oral auction cash bonus bidding. The winning bidder obtained the right to explore for oil and gas resources. If production were undertaken, a one-sixth royalty had to be paid. However, motivated by a belief that competition under the present system is inadequate and government is not receiving "fair market value" for its resources, Congress mandated the use of bidding systems other than cash bonus bidding.

However, recent research has shown that competition for *OCS* oil and gas leases is intense and as a result the government has received more than a fair market value for its leases (R. O. Jones, the author, and P. E. Sorensen). Preliminary findings indicate that the nominal internal rate of return generated by lessees on 839 leases issued between 1954 and 1962 was 9.5 percent *before taxes*. This is a subnormal profit level and indicates that the winning bidders bid too much for their leases. Economic theory, supported by this analysis of the bonus bidding record, indicates that under the proposed bidding systems, the goals of resource conservation will be sacrificed.

II. The Political Economy of Public Policy

This short and necessarily superficial review of major past and emerging energy policies indicates that government intervention has been counterproductive with respect to resource conservation. The reasons are to be found in that ancient discipline known as political economy.

The main concerns of a politician are to get elected and to continue in office. These concerns require that politicians individually and collectively respond to dominant organized pressures brought to bear on them. Pressures from the oil industry obtained and then sustained tax subsidies and market-demand prorationing. The coal industry joined with the domestic oil industry to obtain import quotas. The political power of the oil industry has declined since the early 1970's, to be replaced by environmentalists and consumerists. These groups, together with organized labor, appear to sustain price controls. Concerns for optimum resource allocation are not primary concerns of politicians.

Second, economists advanced the externalities (market failure) concept. Informed laymen and politicians have embraced the concept. But political scientists have been slow to point out its counterpart in the political framework. If congressmen do not bear the full cost of the positions which they take and the consequent legislation which is enacted, then political market failure occurs. Where benefits of legislation are concentrated (the beneficial interests know who they are and are grateful) and costs are dispersed (those who bear the costs are not well informed and the cost per person is low) the net political externality may be significant.

Third, the legislative process is a compromising process. Economists may agree on the character and the extent of a tax subsidy or regulation necessary to correct an externality. But any agreed upon correction must pass through the political process where hearings are held and interest groups have a right to bring pressure to bear on their elected representatives. Political scientist Daniel Ogden pointed out that ". . . national policy is made through a system of power clusters," and further, . . . " administrative agencies jealously guard their subject matter 'turf.' They yield jurisdiction only after a major struggle and only in the face of overwhelming political force." Individual congressmen will approve only what is acceptable by the dominant pressure groups to which they must be responsive. What economists believe to be an appropriate correction for an externality is not what is likely to emerge from the political process.

Fourth, whatever emerges in legislation must then be administered. Another political scientists, Marver Bernstein, wrote that "the history of (regulatory) commissions indicates that they may have survived to the extent that they have served the interests of the regulated groups" (p. 73).

Finally, the presence of a net externality is not a sufficient justification for government intervention. The costs of correction, including the costs added in the legislative compromise process and actual administration accommodations referred to above, must be less than the cost of the net externality to be corrected. Failure to meet this test will lead to even greater resource misallocation.

One might assume that with the declining political power of the oil industry in the last decade, future energy policy will be legislated in the national interest. However, the only change is that the power of one interest group has been displaced by others. The structure of public policy formation as outlined above is unchanged.

President Carter has called for a "comprehensive national energy policy" and his "first principle" asserts that "we can have an effective and comprehensive energy policy only if the Federal government takes responsibility for it. . . ." (Office of the President, p. 1). The record of past energy policy does not lead one to be confident that more intervention will improve resource allocation. An alternative national energy policy would be to let the market allocate scarce resources.

REFERENCES

Marver Bernstein, *Regulating Business by Independent Commissions*, Princeton 1975.

P. Davidson, "Beware the Modern Tripoli Pirates of Natural Gas," *Los Angeles Times*, Aug. 6, 1978.

R. T. Deacon and W. J. Mead, "Price Controls and International Petroleum Product Prices," final report to the Federal Energy Administration, June 16, 1978.

A. D. Johany, "OPEC is Not a Cartel: A Property Rights Explanation of the Rise in Crude Oil Prices," unpublished doctoral dissertation, Univ. California-Santa Barbara. June 1978.

R. O. Jones, W. J. Mead, and P. E. Sorensen, "Economic Issues in Oil Shale Leasing Policy," *Oil Shale Symposium*, forthcoming.

Stephen L. McDonald, *Petroleum Conservation in the United States*, Baltimore 1971.

W. D. Nordhaus, "The Allocation of Energy Resources," *Brookings Papers*, Washington 1973, *3*, 529–70.

D. M. Ogden, Jr., "Protecting the Energy Turf: The Department of Energy Organization Act," *Natural Resources J.*, Oct. 1978, *18*.

Charles E. Phelps and Rodney T. Smith, "Petroleum Regulation: The False Dilemma of Decontrol," Rand Corp. R-1951-RC, Jan. 1977.

R. S. Pindyck, "Gains to Producers from the Cartelization of Exhaustible Resources," *Rev Econ. Statist.*, May 1978, *60*, 238–51.

Energy Policy Project of the Ford Foundation, *A Time to Choose*, Cambridge, Mass. 1974.

Office of the President, "Detailed Fact Sheet, The President's Energy Program," Washington, Apr. 20, 1977.

27

This experimental study of the household demand for energy investigates short-run responses to increases in the relative price of electricity and responses to increased information in paterns of energy use and weekly feedback on electricity use levels. It is significant from a methodological standpoint since it incorporates a two-stage experimental treatment period that involves a cross-over assignment of treatments to clarify potential ambiguities in measured experimental effects (see Morris et al., ch. 4). The study was conducted during a three-month summer period so that the results are specific to electricity consumption dominated by space cooling demands. Its results are short run in that they reflect changes in use levels for the existing capital stocks of appliances.

Though a random assignment to treatments was employed, initial cooperation in the study was voluntary. Rebates were used to reward energy conservation. This system was based on rewarding reduced consumption relative to past electricity use. Two different baseline periods were employed: a two-week period immediately prior to the assignment of subjects to the various treatment groups and electricity use during the previous summer.

The experiment had three parts. First, a two-week period during which baseline readings on electricity were taken. Subjects were not assigned to a treatment group during that time. Second, a four week experimental period in which subjects were randomly assigned to four treatment groups and a control group. And finally, a subsequent six-week period during which experimental conditions, namely a limited crossover in treatments, were changed to help clarify and expand results from the initial experimental period.

The assigned treatments were:

(1) a high price rebate group
(2) a low price rebate group
(3) a feedback group
(4) an information group
(5) a control group.

A (two-components) variance components model was used to estimate experimental effects. (See Kiefer, Part III, for a similar specification.) The dependent variable was the percentage change in kilowatt hours of electricity use relative to the pre-experimental baseline period. This variable was expressed as a function of the following categorical variables:

- whether the residence was empty during the baseline weeks
- the experimental week
- whether the residence was empty during an experimental week
- an interaction for effects between weeks and days the residence was empty during an experimental week
- the experimental treatments, including the control treatment
- two error components: a subject error component and a random error component

Additional terms were added to test for interaction effects between treatment groups and weeks. The absence of statistically significant interaction effects for these variables resulted in rejecting the hypothesis that responses to the rebate plans were sensitive to week-to-week variations in weather, or that responses to the experimental treatments varied over time.

The results for the first four-week period included several unanticipated effects. First, the low rebate group reduced electricity consumption somewhat more than the high rebate group. The information group used the most electricity—11- to 12% *more* than the high and low rebate groups, respectively. This result is difficult to interpret since we do not know what effect the data provided on household energy conservation tips had on the information group. For comparison, relative to the control group, the high and low rebate groups reduced consumption by about 2.7 and 3.6%.

Because of these unexpected results, some treatments were changed for the next six-week period. Thus, cross-over treatments were used, a unique feature of this study. The information group was placed on a modified high-price rebate plan. The control group was provided with the information on household energy conservation tips originally provided to the information group. The rebate plans for the original two rebate groups were renewed for four more weeks and then discontinued. Feedback information on energy consumption that was being supplied to these two groups was also then withdrawn. The original feedback group was left unchanged to serve as a reference group to evaluate the behavior of the other experimental groups. The variance components model was modified by including a categorical variable to reflect the changes within experimental groups and then adjusted to the data for the entire 10-week experimental period.

The result was the finding that the original information group reduced electricity consumption by about 7.6% relative to the control group. Energy conservation information given to the original control group did not result in reduced electricity consumption. This is an important finding in light of the common policy of exhorting consumers to practice conservation during periods of energy shortage. This result should be contrasted with the findings of Berk et al. (ch. 29) on water consumption where a limited test of the use of information and moral appeals suggested that such a policy option may have some effectiveness. Unfortunately, it is difficult to generalize beyond this set of results since we are dealing with behavior in just one location over a short-run summer period dominated by the use of electricity for purposes of home cooling.

Next, these experimental results replicate those of other small-scale studies of residential electrical use. For the low price rebate group, the largest estimated price elasticity of demand was −0.32—a 10% increase in price leads to a 3.2% reduction in quantity consumed. In contrast, the highest price elasticity estimate for the high price rebate group was −0.20. These elasticities lie in the bottom third of the range of short-run elasticities estimated in other studies from aggregated time series or combined time series and cross-sectional data. These estimates also suggest that price elasticities are not constant for different magnitudes of price changes.

Finally, the authors speculate on the correctness of employing as comparison groups the original three groups which did not receive rebates during the first four weeks of the experiment (the information, feedback, and control groups). Specifically, if the information component of the rebate plans resulted in increased consumption, as it appears to have done for the information group, and if its effects are strictly additive, then the information group is the relevant comparison group for the rebate groups. If the information component for the two rebate groups did not have an additive effect when combined with the rebates, the elasticities reported above are too large since the control group and the feedback group consistently used less electricity than the original information group. Discussion of these problems in the text does not resolve the issue of choice among comparison groups.

Residential Electricity Demand
An Experimental Study

Raymond C. Battalio, John H. Kagel,
Robin C. Winkler, and Richard A. Winnett

T HIS paper reports the results of a relatively inexpensive and readily replicable field experiment in the area of household demand for energy. Responses to increased information on energy use patterns in the form of written, government prepared, energy conservation pamphlets and weekly feedback on electricity use levels are investigated, along with short-run responses to increases in the relative price of electricity. The paper presents information of interest in two areas: (1) the methodology, procedures and problems encountered in designing a field experiment in household energy use; and (2) substantive findings concerning responses of households to changes in the price of electricity and information concerning electricity use.

The paper has four parts. Section I presents the design of the experiment and is primarily of interest to those readers concerned with experimental methods. Sections II and III report the empirical results of the study. The concluding section compares the results reported here with other small scale field experiments and reports estimates for price responsiveness in terms of elasticities.

I. Experimental Design

A. Monetary Rebates as Price Changes

In designing an experiment where one of the goals was to evaluate the price responsiveness of residential electricity demand, two important pragmatic considerations limited the price

Received for publication January 10, 1977. Revision accepted for publication August 24, 1978.

* Texas A&M University, Texas A&M University, University of Western Australia, and Institute for Behavioral Research, respectively.

This is a revised and shorter version of Battalio, Kagel, Winkler, and Winett (1978). At points reference is made to this research report for more details. This experiment and its analysis was partially supported by NSF Grant GS 32057 and a Texas A&M University minigrant. We thank the City Manager and Staff of the City of College Station for their cooperation, which was essential to this research project. We thank Bob Basmann, Stan Besen, Lee Brown, Gerry Dwyer, Jack Meyer, Morgan Reynolds, Tom Saving and an unusually patient referee for helpful comments on earlier drafts. All responsibility for errors rests with us.

change strategies available. First, since we were relying on voluntary cooperation, the experimental changes considered were restricted to those changes that would not result in a decline in subjects' real income. Second, since the electricity rate schedule was set by law, we could not directly bill customers in the same rate class at different rates without first obtaining special legislation permitting this action. Given these constraints, a number of alternative methods for increasing the relative price of electricity were available (Wenders and Taylor, 1976). The technique used consisted of giving rebates for reductions in electricity consumption relative to past use patterns.

A system of rebates based on past electricity use is directly interpretable in terms of the usual budget constraint with decreasing block pricing for electricity. Consider the two good case, electricity, q_1, and one composite commodity, q_2. Prior to the rebates, electricity is assumed to be purchased according to a two-part tariff with decreasing block rates as shown by the solid line in figure 1, together with an indifference curve, I^0, and its associated equilibrium, $\hat{q}_1^0$, $\hat{q}_2^0$. (We assume throughout that the equilibrium is unique and always occurs in the lowest marginal cost rate block—where $q_1 > k_2$ in figure 1.)[1]

Under the rebate schedule used this consumer is now paid γ per KWHR for each KWHR reduction in use below $\hat{q}_1^0$, the equilibrium consumption level under the pre-experimental rate structure. The dashed line in figure 1 shows the effect of the rebates on the budget line in the relevant portion of the choice space. Several special features of this change in the budget constraint are apparent. First the change corresponds to a Slutsky compensated price change since the new budget set includes the original bundle $\hat{q}_1^0$, $\hat{q}_2^0$. This satisfies the requirement that a subject's real income will not decline as a result of being in the

[1] All of the experimental subjects, except one, had pre-experimental use levels that put them in the lowest marginal cost (highest use) rate block. Under the prevailing rate structure the lowest marginal cost block began with a use level of 47 KWHR/week. The average weekly use for the subjects in the summer preceding the study was 456 KWHR/week.

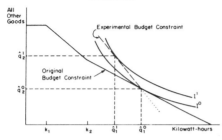

FIGURE 1.—EXPERIMENTAL CHANGE IN BUDGET
CONSTRAINT

experiment. Second, although we have not imposed penalties for use levels above $\hat{q}_1^0$ (the dotted line in figure 1), both theoretical considerations and previous empirical research indicate that the new equilibrium will have $\hat{q}_1 < \hat{q}_1^0$ and, consequently, the absence of this portion of the budget line should not cause problems in interpreting the results (Battalio, et al., 1973; Kagel, et al., 1975). Third, since the observed changes in electricity use, $\hat{q}_1^0 - \hat{q}_1$, correspond to movements along an apparent real income constant demand curve, these movements can be directly compared to conventional elasticity measures by combining our results with non-experimental measures of income elasticity. Further, given the low percentage of total income spent on electricity (on average, subjects spent a low percentage of total income on electricity during the period of the experiment), such elasticity estimates are relatively insensitive to the measure of income elasticity used following classical assumptions (Friedman, 1966, pp. 48–55).

B. Subjects

A random sample of the single family residential electricity customers (excluding trailers) in College Station, Texas, who had paid electric bills at the same residence for a minimum of one year were sent letters of invitation (followed by telephone calls to nonrespondents) to participate in the study.[2] Information collected from the more than 100 households enrolling in the study indicated that about 90% of the participants were

[2] For details of recruitment procedures along with a discussion of the potential biases introduced into the analysis as a result of using volunteer subjects, see Kagel, Battalio and Walker (in press).

married, the age range of participants was 21–76 years (median = 42) and the median net income was between $12,000 and $15,000 (range < $3,000 to > $36,000). Nearly 80% owned their residences. About 70% of the households had central air conditioning with over ⅔ of the remaining households having at least one window unit.

C. Structure and Treatments

The experiment was conducted in June, July and August, a period during which space cooling was the dominant source of electricity use. Extension of the study beyond the air conditioning season for these residences, most of which had gas heat, would have involved including measures of price responsiveness where neither space cooling nor space heating was a major source of use. Previous research, discussed below, indicates that price elasticities may vary between space cooling and other uses of electricity.

The experiment was planned to have three parts: (1) a two week period during which subjects' meters were read but they had not been assigned to an experimental condition. This period provided an updated reference point (baseline) against which to evaluate the treatment effects; (2) a four week initial experimental period during which subjects were randomly assigned to one of five treatment conditions described below; and (3) a second six week experimental period during which experimental conditions were to be changed, as needed, to follow up and clarify results obtained in the initial experimental period.

Experimental treatment conditions subjects were initially assigned to were the following.

(1) *High Price Rebate Group:* Members were eligible for weekly rebates of 30¢ for each 1% reduction in weekly kilowatt-hours of electricity use compared to their average weekly use of the past summer, up to a maximum weekly payment of $15.[3] They were also eligible for an additional $10 payment if their percentage reduction of elec-

[3] Specifying the maximum payment was designed to protect us from excessive expenses when houses were vacant for extended periods during which time air conditioning, the major component of electricity demand, would be at a minimum. All households receiving the maximum payment were vacant for 4 or more days in that week, in which case the observation was not included in the statistical analysis.

tricity use during the four week period was among the largest one-half of households in the payment group. Subjects also received information consisting of instructions on how to read their electric meter, a preprinted form on which to record each week's electricity use with their average use for the past summer printed at the top, instructions on how to compute their electric utility bill and two government prepared information booklets on sources of energy use and conservation tips for households. In addition, each subject was provided with two types of feedback about their weekly use. Each week the meter readers left a copy of their weekly meter reading and two days after each reading a form stating the week's electricity use compared to last summer's average use and the amount of payment they were entitled to for the week was mailed to them. Checks for all payments were mailed after the 4th experimental week.

(2) *Low Price Rebate Group:* Conditions were the same as for the high price rebate group with the exception that subjects were entitled to a 1.3¢ payment for each KWHR reduction in weekly electricity use compared to their average weekly use for the past summer, plus a payment of $2.00 to the one-half of the households with the largest reduction during the four week period. Given that the marginal cost of electricity at the time of the experiment was 2.6¢ per KWHR, the 1.3¢ payment increased this cost by 50% to 3.9¢ per KWHR. In contrast, the rebate schedule for the high price rebate group, calculated at the mean use level of 493 KWHR/week, amounted to a 6.1¢ payment for each KWHR reduction in electricity use, or an increase in the marginal cost of approximately 235%.

(3) *Feedback Group:* Members received all of the information and feedback given to the above two groups including mailed evaluations of use relative to the previous summer, but did not receive any rebates.

(4) *Information Group:* Members received the same government prepared booklets on household energy conservation tips and instructions on how to compute their electric bill as did the other groups, but did not receive any rebate payment or feedback.

(5) *Control Group:* Members of this group did not receive anything during these four weeks.

With the exception of the bonus payment to the two rebate groups, no mention was made of how long the experimental conditions would remain in effect. Due to the importance of space cooling requirements on electricity demand, all subjects were left post-cards to return indicating the days that the house had been empty for the week. Rebate payments were independent of whether or not the residence was empty to remove incentives for providing inaccurate information.

D. Considerations Underlying Procedures Employed

In developing a set of procedures for an experiment a number of problems are encountered that are typically ignored or left unspecified in the theory underlying the experiment (Basmann, 1975). This leaves the experimenter with several alternative methods available for implementing a given theoretical concept no one of which is, a priori, best.[4] Such problems are encountered here in using rebates as Slutsky compensated price changes, since the theory in question provides a static model of the world holding a number of factors constant which are unlikely to remain so in nature. Consequently, it is worthwhile to clarify several points regarding the procedures employed and to indicate the tests available for checking some of the more critical assumptions underlying them.

We begin with a discussion of the time frame used; one summer's air conditioning season. This means that the responses reported are short-run in the sense that they primarily involved adjustments in use levels of existing capital stocks of electricity using appliances (Taylor, 1975). The question of whether a time frame of one summer is sufficient to insure equilibrium short-run responses compared to, say, an experiment lasting several summers, or a permanent price change, although interesting, can be answered only through extended and substantially more expensive studies than the one reported here.[5] We did,

---

[4] Different procedures usually produce some differences in responses which are usually secondary in magnitude to the main experimental effects. Consequently, it is an important empirical research question to determine the robustness of any set of experimental results to the procedural alternatives available (Campbell, 1969). Further, having completed an experiment, most researchers would choose to modify a number of procedures the second time around. Unfortunately, however, hindsight ≠ foresight (Fischhoff, 1975).

[5] Of course, extending the experiment beyond one summer increases the relative frequency of changes in capital stocks

however, examine whether adjustment to the experimental conditions occurred gradually over time during the three summer months of the study. This was done by obtaining repeated (weekly) measures of electricity use under constant experimental conditions and testing whether the differences observed between groups varied systematically over time (by weeks).

The use of the repeated readings under constant experimental conditions also enables us to check whether the weekly variability in weather, and the associated changes in electricity use, had a differential effect on the various treatment groups. Such a differential effect might arise if the rebate schedule, based on the average of the previous summer's electricity use, resulted in subjects "giving up" during weeks in which the first couple of days were hotter (hence electricity use greater) than usual. The absence of interaction effects associated with weekly weather variations would indicate a constant response to the rebates, a pattern of behavior consistent with "rule of thumb" responses; e.g., electricity costs more now so change the thermostat 1° or remember to turn out lights, in conjunction with the fact that there are real economic costs to calculating expected returns from a particularly hot or cool early part of the week. In deciding on the rebate plan we were guided by the fact that an earlier, smaller scale, study using a comparable rebate plan reported no such interaction effects associated with relatively large week-to-week variations in temperature during the winter (Winett and Nietzel, 1975). We also knew that summer-to-summer variability in the weather was unlikely to be sufficiently great to result in a significant implicit increase or decrease in income as a result of unusually cool or hot weather relative to the reference period. This assumption was confirmed by an ex post examination of a random group of residences, not participating in the experiment, which showed no significant changes in average electricity use during the summer of the experiment compared to the previous summer.[6]

An additional consideration was to make our study as comparable as possible to others reported in the literature; hence, the structure of the high price rebate plan closely matched the one employed in the Winett and Nietzel study mentioned above. The cost of obtaining this comparability was that each household in the high rebate group faced a different relative price change as the rebates were based on the percentage change in use and no two households had identical base use rates. However, for no household was the increase in the relative price of electricity *less* than 110% of the marginal rate prevailing at the time of the experiment, meaning that the relative price of electricity increased at least twice as much for all subjects in the high price rebate group compared to the low price group. Given that distinctly different experimental conditions prevailed between groups, we can use dummy variables to test for differences in responses between groups. Measures of the average response differentials in arc elasticity form, divided by appropriate measures of price differentials between the rebate and the non-rebate groups (corrected for estimated income effects) provide the measures of price elasticity reported in the text.[7]

The effect of introducing the bonus was to enrich the rebate schedule and to maintain an incentive for subjects not to "give up" on energy saving practices in response to weather variability. For household j the expected value of the bonus, $E_j(B)$, was

$$E_j(B) = p_j \times \$B \qquad (1)$$

where p_j is the probability of household j winning the bonus and $\$B$ for the rebate group. A household won the bonus if it was in the top half of electricity reducers in its group with the bonus to

---

of electricity-using appliances, confounding measures of changes in utilization rates and increasing subject attrition rates due to moving, etc. A post-experiment questionnaire was used in the present study to identify and delete subjects with major changes in energy-using appliances during the experiment.

[6] Using a paired t-test, $t = 1.0$, degrees of freedom (df) = 158, probability $t \neq 0 = 0.32$. Average electricity use increased 2% between the summers. An alternative procedure which bypasses most of the problems associated with weather variation is to tie the rebates and feedback to the energy use of a control group. Studies since this one indicate ready acceptance of these procedures on the part of subjects (Winett, et al., 1978).

[7] For the high price rebate group, the price change term in the denominator of the elasticity formula was calculated at the mean level of electricity use for the group. Full evaluations of such price elasticity estimates must await the determination of the robustness of subjects' responses to the particulars of comparable rebate plans and basic research aimed at determining the differences, if any, between responses to rebate plans vs. mandated price increases of comparable magnitude (Wenders and Taylor, 1976).

be paid even if weather variability was such that no one reduced use. Since each household's change in electricity was independent of changes by others, and households only received information concerning their own use, p_j was a direct function of j's efforts to reduce use relative to the previous summer, and there was a positive expected return irrespective of weather variability.

In concluding this section we note that the decision to evaluate *changes* in electricity use relative to baseline (pre-treatment use levels) rather than to directly model actual electricity use, was based on earlier research which indicated that the residual variation when modeling individual use levels is quite large even for rather detailed models (Mayer and Robinson, 1975). All of the analyses presented below were conducted two ways; once using the previous summer's electricity use as the standard against which to measure changes in electricity use and again using the baseline period as the standard. No major differences in conclusions were reached. However, evaluation relative to the baseline period provides more updated information on household energy use, correcting for changes in household composition and energy using appliances, thereby reducing spurious between subject differences.

In the next section we report the results for the initial four week assignment of subjects to experimental conditions. Following this we describe the changes in treatment conditions instituted and the results obtained under these conditions.

II. Initial Empirical Results

In the statistical analysis dummy variables taking values of 0 or 1 were used to represent the effects of the experimental treatments, weeks and other factors affecting changes in electricity use. The dependent variable was the percentage change in KWHRs of electricity use relative to baseline (pre-experimental) use, Y. The model used was

$$Y_{ijklm} = \mu + \delta_i + \eta_j + \gamma_k + (\eta\gamma)_{jk} + \beta_l + a_{ml} + e_{ijklm} \qquad (2)$$

where we have suppressed the dummy variables, and the lower case Greek letters δ_i, η_j, . . . are unknown parameters of the dummy variables representing the following factors:

μ = constant term (average change in electricity use).

δ_i = effect of house being empty during baseline weeks, $i = 1, 2, \Sigma_i \delta_i = 0$ (one dummy variable for house empty 0 days, one dummy for house empty 1 or 2 days, all households empty greater than 2 days dropped from the analysis due to insufficient observations to estimate these effects).

η_j = experimental week, $j = 1, 2, 3, 4, \Sigma_j \eta_j = 0$ (one dummy for each week).

γ_k = effect of residence being empty during an experimental week, $k = 1, 2, 3, \Sigma_k \gamma_k = 0$ (one dummy for house empty 0 days, one dummy for house empty 1 or 2 days, one dummy for house empty 3 days, weeks in which house empty 4 or more days dropped from the analysis due to insufficient observations).

$(\eta\gamma)_{jk}$ = interaction effects between weeks and days house empty during an experimental week, $\Sigma_{j,k}(\eta\gamma) = 0$.

β_l = effects of experimental treatments, $l = 1, 2, 3, 4, 5, \Sigma_l \beta_l = 0$ (one dummy for each experimental group).

The lower case English letters represent the two error components

a_{ml} = subject error component, a random variable with zero mean, $m = 1, 2, \ldots, n_l$, where n_l is the number of subjects in treatment group l.

e_{ijklm} = the customary error term, a random variable with zero mean.

The error components, a_{ml} and e_{ijklm} were assumed to be normally distributed with the usual properties of the two component variance-components model (Maddala, 1977, p. 327).

Preliminary analysis using (2), but with additional terms to test for interaction effects between treatment groups and weeks, supported the hypothesis of no such effects $[F < 1]$. Thus, hypotheses that responses to the rebate plans would be sensitive to week-to-week variations in the weather and that responses to the experimental contingencies would vary with the simple passage of time are rejected, replicating previous results (Winett and Nietzel, 1975).

The statistic of primary interest, the results of

the F-test to determine whether the experimental treatment coefficients, β_i, were jointly equal to zero, showed we could reject this hypothesis at the 6% significance level.[8] The differences in electricity use between treatment groups, estimates of the parameters β_i in (2), are shown in table 1.

Examining the mean differences in table 1 shows a number of results we did not expect prior to the experiment. In particular, the low rebate group reduced electricity use a bit more than the high rebate group and the information group used the most electricity. Testing for statistically significant differences between treatment groups showed both rebate groups to differ from the information group at the 5% significance level.[9] Compared to the information group, the rebate groups used 11% to 12% less electricity. In addition, the difference between the control group and the information group was significant at the 10% level. No other significant differences between groups were found.

---

[8] $F = 2.29$, df $= 4,101$, probability $F \neq 1 = 0.06$ ($p = 0.06$). The error components were estimated using Henderson's method three (Henderson, 1953; Searle, 1971). The associated F-ratios and fixed effects estimates (the estimated treatment effects) are exact when the data are balanced or proportionate (Winer, 1971). Although the data are not completely proportionate (observations for the occasional residence empty for more than 4 days in a week were dropped for that week) a two-stage procedure was not employed due to the unsettled nature and associated cost of the resulting estimates (Searle, 1971). Respecifying the model (the dummy variables for δ_i) so that the data are proportionate shows the results reported to be quite robust. A more detailed account of the statistical results is in Battalio, et al., 1978.

[9] Tests were conducted using the Newman-Kuels multiple range test (Winer, 1971) which controls for the fact that multiple a posteriori paired comparisons are almost certain to result in some difference being declared significant when they are not. The advantages of the Newman-Kuels procedure are that it is easy to compute and takes into account the number of treatments in an experiment while not being quite as conservative as some of the other multiple comparison tests available (Winer, 1971, especially pp. 196–201). All multiple paired comparisons reported used this procedure.

III.   Additional Empirical Results

A.   Changes in Treatment Conditions

In designing the experiment, changes in treatment conditions were planned following the initial four week period, as needed, to follow up questions of interest. These changes and the rationale underlying them are described below.

The effect of information relative to the rebate group and the control group surprised us. We had expected, prior to the experiment, the information group (group 4) to behave like the control group. Further, the tests for interaction effects provided no basis for supposing that these differences were temporary and would change with time and/or weather variations. Consequently, the only way to replicate these results, in an effort to verify or refute them, would be to end the experiment at this point and recruit a new set of subjects, or to cross-over treatment conditions; e.g., apply the rebate treatment to the information group and see if these subjects behaved the way the between group analysis suggested. We chose to change conditions.[10]

We put the information group on a modified high price rebate plan.[11] This treatment was similar to that given to the original high price rebate group with the difference being that rebates were based on average use during the three largest use weeks of the study to date, with a 20¢ payment offered for each 1% reduction in use below this average for the first 20% reduction, and a 30¢ payment for each additional 1% reduction in use, up to a maximum weekly payment of $15. Since the modified base provided a uniformly easier target for subjects to attain than using the previ-

---

[10] In choosing which action to follow we never considered recruiting new subjects as this constituted the major time (and effort) expense in the study.

[11] This was not done right away as we waited an additional two weeks to see if this information effect would wear off. It didn't.

TABLE 1.—MEAN CHANGES IN ELECTRICITY USE BY TREATMENT GROUPS: INITIAL EXPERIMENTAL PERIOD

Experimental Group	(1) High Rebate	(2) Low Rebate	(3) Feedback	(4) Information	(5) Control
Mean Change[a]	−3.48	−4.56	+1.72	+7.25	−0.93
Number of Households	17	20	24	20	26

Note: indicates a reduction in use relative to sample average.
[a] Mean change is measured as the percentage change in KWHRs relative to the baseline period.

ous summer's average use as a base, subjects did not receive any bonus payments for being among the largest reducers in their group. These changes from the original high price rebate plan were intentionally implemented with the idea of obtaining some information regarding the sensitivity of responses to relatively modest changes in the parameters of such plans. Further, to follow up the difference between the control group and the information group, the control group (group 5) was given the government prepared booklets on household energy conservation tips and instructions on how to compute their electric bill received by the other subjects, the same treatment the information group (group 4) had received in the initial experimental period.

The rebate plans for the two original rebate groups (groups 1 and 2) were renewed for four more weeks to see if they continued to show no differences and then discontinued, along with feedback, for the last two weeks of the study. The feedback group (group 3) was left unchanged to serve as a reference group against which to evaluate the behavior over time of the other experimental groups.

B. Results of Changes in Experimental Conditions

The variance components model (2) above, with the inclusion of binary shift variables for the changes within experimental groups, was adjusted to the data for the entire experimental period. A preliminary test for treatment group by weeks interaction effects was now significant at the 1% level indicating that the differences between treatment group means were not constant during all the experimental weeks. Plotting mean values of groups, by weeks, showed that these interaction effects were a result of increased energy savings by the original high price rebate group (group 1) following the renewal of their rebate schedule and coinciding with the actual receipt of the check for the money they had earned during the initial experimental period. (Although not anticipated a priori under the procedures used here, considerable experimental evidence exists showing that response rates are frequently not independent of the timing of receipt of the rewards for responding (Rachlin, 1976)). To reflect the effect of receipt of the rebate check, an additional dummy variable was

added for both rebate groups, which eliminated the interaction effects.[12]

The effects of the changes in experimental conditions within each of the experimental groups is shown in table 2.[13] For the group ini-

TABLE 2.—MEAN CHANGES IN ELECTRICITY USE WITHIN EXPERIMENTAL GROUPS

Initial Experimental Condition	Within Group Experimental Effects	
(1) High Price Rebate Group	Receipt of Payment -8.29^a	Feedback and Rebates Withdrawn -3.24
(2) Low Price Rebate Group	Receipt of Payment $+1.44$	Feedback and Rebates Withdrawn -2.75
(3) Information Group	Modified High Price Rebate Plan -7.56^b	
(5) Control Group	Information $+0.95$	

Note: Sample sizes reported in table 1. − indicates a reduction in use compared to initial experimental conditions.
[a] Significant at the .025 level.
[b] Significant at the .01 level

tially receiving information (group 4) the rebates resulted in a statistically significant reduction in electricity use at the 1% level.[14] This result confirms the earlier findings that a price rebate plan with feedback results in decreased electricity use relative to information without any rebate. The 7.6% mean reduction in electricity use associated with eligibility for rebates is comparable in magnitude to the difference observed between the two original rebate groups (group 1 and 2) and this group (group 4) during the initial four week experimental period, indicating the robustness of the rebate plan to relatively small changes in its details.

The distribution of information to the control group (group 5) resulted in a statistically insignificant change in electricity use, although the sign of the change was consistent with the earlier findings. These results temper the original between group results. However, it seems quite clear that the energy conservation information

[12] $F = 1.18$, df $= 30.832$, $p = .32$.
[13] Analysis of the effects of changes in experimental conditions reported in table 2 weighted each household equally, regardless of the number of usable repeated measures obtained under a given experimental condition (Battalio, et al., 1978).
[14] $F = 7.48$, df $= 1,20$, $p = .01$.

distributed did not result in reductions in electricity use, suggesting that such information of and by itself is, at best, ineffective.

For the original high price rebate group (group 1), receipt of the rebate checks resulted in a significant change in use (at the 2.5% level), amounting to an 8.4% reduction compared to the initial experimental period. In contrast, receipt of the rebate check had no significant effect (at the 10% level) for the low price rebate group (group 2). Applying the variance components model (2) to subjects in groups 1–3 during the three weeks following receipt of rebate checks (during which subjects were eligible to earn additional rebates) showed group 1 using 16% less electricity than the low rebate group and 14% less than the feedback group (group 3), these differences being significant at the 1% level.[15]

Withdrawal of price rebates and feedback for group 1 resulted in a statistically significant increase in electricity use (at the 10% level) compared to the period following receipt of the first rebate check, even though subjects received a second rebate check at this time. However, withdrawal of rebates and feedback for groups 1 and 2 did not result in increased electricity use compared to the initial experimental period. We interpret this as a resistance to extinction of the energy saving behaviors developed in the initial experimental period. Although we do not know how long these behaviors persisted, similar residual effects have been reported in studies of consumer demand behavior under highly controlled laboratory type conditions (Battalio, et al., 1973; Kagel, et al., 1975) and in field experiments (Winett and Nietzel, 1975; Walker, 1979).[16]

IV. Discussion

In evaluating the results of the experiment one question which arises is the extent to which the baseline use levels correspond to "normal" use patterns. Although we have no direct evidence for this study, Hayes and Cone (1977) report no

significant differences between covert readings of electric meters obtained prior to enrollment in an energy study and overt baseline readings obtained after subjects had been enrolled in the study but prior to initiating any experimental treatments. In addition, during the experiment weekly changes in use by the control group subjects, relative to baseline use, closely matched the changes in use for a main residential feeder line in the community, relative to the same baseline period. Therefore, it appears that simply volunteering to be in the experiment did not affect electricity use either during the baseline period or afterwards.

The statistically significant, but relatively small, reductions in electricity use associated with the price rebate plans replicate results of other small scale experimental studies of residential electricity use (Winett and Nietzel, 1975; Hayes and Cone, 1977). Following procedures described earlier, measures of (arc) price elasticity were calculated for each of the rebate groups relative to the experimental groups not receiving rebates.[17] For the low price rebate group the *largest* measure of price elasticity of demand, −0.32, was obtained by comparing the difference in use between this group and the information group during the initial experimental period. In contrast, for the original high price rebate group (group 1) the *largest* price elasticity measure was −0.20, obtained by comparing the difference in use between this group following receipt of the first rebate check with the information group during the initial experimental period. If the information component of the rebate plans resulted in increased use, as it appears to have for the information only group, and its effects are strictly additive, then a comparison of the rebate groups with the information group is the relevant comparison. If, however, the information component did not have an additive effect when combined with the rebates, the elasticities obtained would be too large since the control group and the feedback group consistently used less electricity than the original information group. Even at their upper bound values of −0.32 and −0.20, respectively, these price elasticity estimates lie in the bottom third of the range of short-run elasticity

---

[15] $F = 5.71$, df $= 2,57$, $p < .01$.

[16] Theoretical models postulating irreversible demand functions (see Georgescu-Roegen, 1966, for example) receive considerable support from these results, although it must be emphasized that it is not known at present how persistent these irreversibilities are or precisely under what conditions they will or will not be found in the data.

[17] Readers can readily compute alternative price elasticities between groups following Battalio et al. (1978), note 25. For income elasticity values we used the mid-range of short-run estimates reported in Taylor (1975).

estimates reported using aggregate time series or combined time series and cross-sectional data (Taylor, 1975). Further, they suggest that price elasticities are not constant for different magnitudes of price changes, a maintained hypothesis in much of the literature in the area.

In evaluating the responses to the information condition in the present experiment it is important to note that the information was presented without any simultaneous appeals for reduced energy use and included a rate schedule that enabled subjects to readily evaluate the real costs of a number of energy using activities. Since the available evidence suggests that (at the time) most consumers didn't know the detailed costs of electricity using behaviors and/or severely overestimated these costs, the information given may well have resulted in a downward revision of the estimated costs of a number of activities, thereby promoting their use.[18] This interpretation would suggest that one explanation for why the information treatment failed to replicate (in terms of statistical significance) for the cross-over of the control group is that the controls did not read the materials as carefully as the group first receiving information; the latter getting the booklets at the beginning of the study when interest would be at a maximum, the former receiving them after being virtually ignored for six weeks. While the exact relationship between cost information and energy use require further study, all of the available data suggest that although educational materials by themselves may lead to better informed consumers and more favorable attitudes towards energy conservation, it is not likely in the short term to lead to reduced use (Wicker, 1969; Seaver and Patterson, 1976; Heberlein, 1975).[19]

The experimental group receiving weekly feedback in addition to information did not differ significantly from control conditions. Other research indicates that changes in the type or timing of feedback may have quite different results.

In a study conducted in a housing complex, where utilities were included in the fixed monthly rent, Hayes and Cone (1977) report that daily feedback (on the previous day's cost of electricity, the cost to date for the week and a projected cost for the week compared to baseline) resulted in decreases in use. In another study, Seaver and Patterson (1976) report that feedback on use alone did not reduce fuel oil consumption, but when feedback was combined with social commendation in the form of a small energy saver decal a reduction in use was observed. Even more recent studies show that when feedback is received daily or every other day marked reductions (10%–15%) in energy use occur (Seligman and Darley, 1977; Winett, et al., 1978), although these studies do not permit disentangling the effects of the information provided from the considerable amounts of prompting inherent in the procedures employed.

In concluding, we note that direct extrapolation of the results of the present study to national averages is unwarranted on a number of grounds. For example, the responses obtained were for a time period and place where space cooling demands dominated electricity use and data are available to suggest that there are important differences in price responsiveness between this and other energy using behaviors (Battalio and Kagel, 1976). Further, receiving rebate checks from an energy research project for a known, short duration is not the same as receiving changes in monthly bills directly from the utility company. The extent to which our results, or any empirical results, are reproducible under varying conditions is an empirical issue that can only be answered by further empirical research. Recognition of this is evidenced by the large and growing number of government sponsored studies currently underway in the energy field. However, based on the data available it appears that, although the short-run price elasticity for residential space cooling or heating energy is not zero, at current price levels demand is not very responsive to price increases as high as 235% or to educational materials by themselves.

[18] Using a random sample of residential customers of the public service company of New Mexico, Brown et al. (1975) report that only 5% of the subjects gave an estimate of the kilowatt-hour price of electricity and all of these overestimated the cost; most by greater than a power of ten.

[19] It is important to distinguish here between educational materials by themselves and educational materials in conjunction with major government campaigns to encourage energy conservation. The latter may be likened to advertising and have had positive effects, in terms of reduced energy use, at least for one group of consumers (Mayer, 1977).

REFERENCES

Basmann, Robert L., "Modern Logic and the Suppositious Weakness of the Empirical Foundations of Economic Science," *Schwiez Zeitschrift fur Volkswirtschuft und Statistik* (1975), 153–176.

Battalio, Raymond C., and John H. Kagel. "Household Demand Responsiveness to Peak Use Pricing: Implications Drawn from Experimental Studies of Consumer Demand Behavior of Both Humans and Animals," in *Proceedings of the Third Annual University of Missouri-Missouri Energy Council Conference on Energy* (1976), 784–792.

Battalio, Raymond C., John H. Kagel, Robin C. Winkler, Edwin B. Fisher, Robert L. Basmann, and Leonard Krasner. "A Test of Consumer Demand Theory Using Observations of Individual Consumer Purchases," *Western Economic Journal* 11 (Dec. 1973), 22–38.

Battalio, Raymond C., John H. Kagel, Robin C. Winkler, and Richard A. Winett, "Residential Electricity Demand: An Experimental Study," Technical Report No. 27, NSF Project GS 32057, Dept. of Economics, Texas A&M University, College Station, Texas (1978).

Brown, F. Lee, Lou Hoffman, and Jeffrey D. Baxter. "Towards More Accurate Measurements of Customers' Response to Electrical Price Changes," *Electrical World* 184 (Dec. 1975), 52–54.

Campbell, Donald T., "Prospective: Artifact and Control," in R. Rosenthal and R. L. Rosnow (eds.), *Artifacts in Behavioral Research* (New York: Academic Press, 1969).

Fishchhoff, Baruch, "Hindsight ≠ Foresight: The Effect of Outcome Knowledge of Judgement Under Uncertainty," *Journal of Experimental Psychology: Human Perception and Performance* 1 (1975), 288–299.

Friedman, Milton, *Price Theory*, revised ed. (Chicago: Aldine Press, 1966).

Georgescu-Roegen, N. *Analytical Economics: Issues and Problems* (Cambridge: Harvard University Press, 1966), chapter 2.

Hayes, Steven C., and John D. Cone, "Reducing Residential Electrical Energy Use Payments, Information and Feedback," *Journal of Applied Behavioral Analysis* 10 (1977), 425–435.

Heberlein, Thomas A., "Conservation Information, the Energy Crisis and Electricity Consumption in an Apartment Complex," *Energy Systems and Policy* 1 (1975), 105–117.

Henderson, C. R., "Estimation of Variance and Covariance Components," *Biometrics* 9 (June 1953), 226–252.

Kagel, John H., Raymond C. Battalio, Howard Rachlin, Leonard Green, Robert L. Basmann, and William R. Klemm, "Experimental Studies of Consumer Demand Behavior Using Laboratory Animals," *Economic Inquiry* 13 (Mar. 1975), 22–38.

Kagel, John H., Raymond C. Battalio, and James M. Walker, "Volunteer Bias in Experiments in Economics: Specification of the Problem and Some Initial Data for Small Scale Field Studies," in V. L. Smith (ed.), *Research in Experimental Economics,* Vol. 1 (Greenwich, Conn.: J. A. I. Press, in press).

Maddala, G. S., *Econometrics* (New York: McGraw-Hill, 1977).

Mayer, Lawrence S., "Estimating the Effect of Price on Energy Demand: Econometrics Versus Exploratory Data Analysis," Technical Report No. 123, Series 2, Department of Statistics, Princeton University (June 1977).

Mayer, Lawrence S., and J. A. Robinson, "A Statistical Analysis of the Monthly Consumption of Gas and Electricity in the Home," Center for Environmental Studies, Report No. 18, Princeton University (Apr. 1975).

Rachlin, Howard, *Behavior and Learning* (San Francisco: W. H. Freeman and Co., 1976).

Searle, S. R., *Linear Models* (New York: John Wiley & Sons, 1971).

Seaver, W. Burleigh, and Arthur H. Patterson, "Decreasing Fuel-Oil Consumption through Feedback and Social Commendation," *Journal of Applied Behavior Analysis* 9 (Summer 1976), 147–152.

Seligman, Clive, and John M. Darley, "Feedback as a Means of Decreasing Residential Energy Consumption," *Journal of Applied Psychology* 62 (1977), 363–368.

Taylor, Lester D., "The Demand for Electricity: A Survey," *The Bell Journal of Economics* 6 (Spring 1975), 74–110.

Walker, J. M., "Energy Demand Behavior in a Master Metered Apartment Complex: An Experimental Analysis," *Journal of Applied Psychology* (forthcoming in 1979).

Wenders, John T., and Lester D. Taylor, "Experiments in Seasonal-Time-of-Day Pricing of Electricity to Residential Users," *The Bell Journal of Economics* 7 (Autumn 1976), 531–552.

Wicker, A. W., "Attitudes Versus Actions: The Relationship of Verbal and Overt Behavioral Responses to Attitude Objectives," *Journal of Social Issues* 25 (Autumn 1969), 41–78.

Winer, B. J., *Statistical Principles in Experimental Design,* 2nd ed. (New York: McGraw-Hill, 1971).

Winett, Richard A., and Michael T. Nietzel, "Behavioral Ecology: Contingency Management and Consumer Energy Use," *American Journal of Community Psychology* 3 (June 1975), 123–133.

Winett, Richard A., Michael Neale, Kenneth Williams, James Yokely, and Hugh Kreuder, "The Effects of Individual and Group Feedback on Residential Electricity Consumption: Three Replications," mimeographed, Institute for Behavioral Research, Silver Spring, Maryland (1978).

28

This study analyzes the experiment in time-of-day electricity consumption conducted in Arizona from May to December, 1976, with particular focus on August, a peak period of use. The authors' concern is methodological. The analytic approach joins a method for analyzing a system of demand equations with the correction for sample truncation described in the Introduction to Part I of this volume. To date, none of the other analyses of these data have accounted for the truncation bias.

The experiment tests the consumer response to charging differential prices for electricity during different hours of the day, thus more nearly reflecting the marginal cost of electricity production. Time-of-day price systems could be designed that would be superior to the current constant hourly price systems or declining block rate system (where price is a function of cumulative monthly demand). Prior to installing the necessary equipment and incurring the increased costs of such a system, knowledge is needed of consumer response. The particular problem of this study is to measure the response of the particular (truncated) experimental sample and extend it to the population of electricity consumers so that the results are "representative" in the sense that they apply to the entire population of consumers who would have been eligible for the program and not just those who participated. The sample is truncated because sample households who participated in the experiment were guaranteed that they would never pay more for electricity under time-of-day prices than they would have under the prevailing rate schedule. Thus, there is an upper limit to the expenditures any given household would have to expend on purchasing electricity. In this study, however, the truncation point varies by household and over time rather than being set at a predetermined level. To assume that time-of-day price elasticities estimated from such a sample can be used to evaluate the impact of this program in a population of consumers who are not afforded the above protection may be incorrect.

The authors first present a theoretical discussion of truncation bias and its correction. (See the Introduction to this volume and to Part I). They then develop a model to analyze consumption behavior under a time-of-day pricing scheme in the form of a system of regression equations subject to various constraints and conditions including the assumption of weak separability of electricity demand from other goods (since data on the prices and consumption quantities of other goods were not available). This latter condition leads to the expression of an indirect translog utility function which is then solved for the demand functions. Imposing the assumption of homotheticity then results in a system of three monthly share equations, where there is an equation for each time-of-day pricing period in the experiment: peak, shoulder-peak, and off-peak. (The shoulder-peak period is the intervening and variable time between the pure peak and pure off-peak periods. This is assigned a price intermediate between the peak and off-peak prices.) Finally, the model allows for interaction effects among specific exogenous variables such as mean temperature, appliance capacity, and the length of the peak period. The influence of income is modeled as follows: Income is assumed to affect the level of total expenditure on electricity, which, in turn, is endogenous. The expression $\ln P_{ji}/Z_i$ is regressed on income and all other exogenous variables, where

P = the experimental prices of electricity per kilowatt hour;
Z = monthly total expenditure on electricity;
i = the households, $i = 1, 2, 3, \ldots n$; and
j = the experimental price periods, $j = 1, 2, 3$.

The resulting instrumental variable for $\ln P_{ji}/Z_i$ is then used to calculate the normalized price term for households. This instrument is included in each of the three share equations.

The authors find that all coefficients except those on the rated appliance capacity variable are estimated relatively precisely. The parameters of policy interest concern household responsiveness to price. Own-price and cross-price elasticity effects are calculated. The chi-squared test for symmetry of cross-price elasticity effects leads to rejection of the symmetry hypothesis. For the model that does not adjust for truncation, the own-price elasticity is estimated at –0.483—a 10% increase in price results in a 4.83% reduction in kilowatt hours demanded. Correction for truncation results in the own-price elasticity being –0.169—about one third as large as before, but the general pattern of complementarity holds up among the quantities of electricity consumed among the peak, shoulder-peak, and off-peak periods. This cross-complementarity among pricing periods has important implications for evaluating the effect that the introduction of time-of-day pricing will have on electrical generation capacity growth and the mix of fuels used in generating electricity.

In short, the sample truncation affects the experimental results. But the corrected results are now similar to those estimated for experimental data in Wisconsin (Caves and Christensen, 1978) where individuals were not guaranteed that their outlays under time-of-day pricing would not exceed their expenditures under the old prices.

In assessing the generality of these results, the following factors should be considered. First, the model imposes certain assumptions concerning consumer preferences. Most importantly, due mainly to the need to simplify computation, a homothetic translog demand system is employed. Second, the experiment encompasses a short duration, and an explicit model of dynamic adjustment is not estimated. To gain some idea of the nature of this problem, however, analogous results were computed for May, the first month of the experiment. The general structure of results is consistent with that of August, the period of this analysis, as well as results calculated for June. The conclusion is that the August results indicate the true effects of truncation.

Finally, participation in the experiment is voluntary and other restrictions on sample selection constrain the generality of the results. These effects can be adjusted for where they relate to truncation of the dependent variable, but they are not explicitly accounted for in the analysis.

REFERENCE

CAVES, D. W. and L. R. CHRISTENSEN (1978) "Econometric analysis of the Wisconsin residential Time-of-Use Electricity Pricing Experiment." Presented at the Electric Power Research Institute Workshop on Modeling and Analysis of Electricity Demand by Time-of-Day, San Diego, June.

Correcting for Truncation Bias
in the Analysis of Experiments
in Time-of-Day Pricing of Electricity

Dennis J. Aigner and Jerry A. Hausman

1. INTRODUCTION

Recently, an econometric literature has developed that is addressed to problems of biased estimation that arise when data are generated from samples that systematically exclude some part of the target population. An example is the data from the New Jersey negative income tax experiment, which excluded all households with incomes above certain levels dependent on family size. An investigator who uses these data to analyze labor supply response with an intention to interpret the findings for the population at large faces an obvious problem: Supply response parameters so estimated need not characterize any other part of the population than that sampled. The point is not so much that investigators make claims for their results well beyond the limited data they use, but rather that if the criterion for exclusion can itself be modeled, the parameter estimates of interest may be modified to account for this source of bias a priori, and hence *can* apply to the population.

To illustrate these ideas, we refer to the recent paper by Hausman and Wise (1977),[1] who develop consistent and efficient methods for estimating parameters in an earnings function based on the New Jersey data.

Suppose the model for the target population is

$$y_i = X_i'\beta + \epsilon_i \qquad i = 1, \ldots \qquad [1]$$

where y_i is earnings of individual (or household) i, X_i is a column vector of values of exogenous variables that affect earnings, β is the vector of regression parameters

Authors' Note: An earlier version of this paper was presented at the Workshop on Modeling and Analysis of Electricity Demand by Time-of-Day, San Diego, June 1978, sponsored by the Electric Power Research Institute. Our thanks go to Lau Christensen and Will Manning for helpful discussion and to Lester Taylor who made the data available to us. Aigner's work was supported in part by NSF Grant SOC-7909674 and in part through the DOE/California Electric Utilities Demonstration Project, administered jointly by the California Energy Commission and the California Public Utilities Commission. The views reported here are solely those of the authors and do not reflect the official positions of either of those agencies.

to be estimated, and ϵ_i is a normally distributed error with a zero mean and constant variance σ^2. Sampling is done from that portion of the population that satisfies a restriction of the form

$$y_i \leqslant z_i, \tag{2}$$

where z_i is an earnings ceiling (dependent on family size, which itself may be a variable in X_i). Thus, if $y_i = X_i'\beta + \epsilon_i \leqslant z_i$ the household is eligible to be drawn into the sample, whereas if $y_i = X_i'\beta + \epsilon_i > z_i$ it is not. Therefore, the density function of y_i, rather than being symmetric normal with mean $X_i'\beta$ and variance σ^2, is that of a truncated normal variable; in particular:

$$f(y_i) = \begin{cases} 0 \text{ if } y_i > z_i \\ \dfrac{\phi(y_i)}{\Phi[(z_i - X_i'\beta)/\sigma]} & \text{if } y_i \leqslant z_i, \end{cases} \tag{3}$$

where $\phi(y_i)$ is the normal density function with mean $X_i'\beta$ and variance σ^2, and

$$\Phi[(z_i - X_i'\beta)/\sigma] = \int_{-\infty}^{z_i} \phi(y_i) \, dy_i.$$

The relevant likelihood function is developing assuming independence in sampling over n observations and is given by

$$L = \sum_{i=1}^{n} \frac{\phi(y_i)}{\Phi[(z_i - X_i'\beta)/\sigma]}. \tag{4}$$

For computational purposes, the log-likelihood function is easier to work with, but we shall not present it here. The principles are clear enough: The relevant likelihood function is maximized with respect to σ and β given values for independent variables and the $\{z_i\}$.

That the above procedure generally will lead to different parameter estimates than least squares is illustrated by the figure below, where we assume that a single, independent variable appears in X_i, say x, and that there is a single (known) truncation point, z. If x takes on three levels, x_1, x_2, and x_3, with the associated values (replications) for y, the least squares method will consistently estimate the dotted regression line. However, the maximum likelihood procedure will estimate the solid regression line (from the origin to the point at which it intersects the z-line). Computationally, for this single-equation model the methods required to obtain the maximum likelihood estimates resemble those for the so-called Tobit model (Amemiya, 1973).

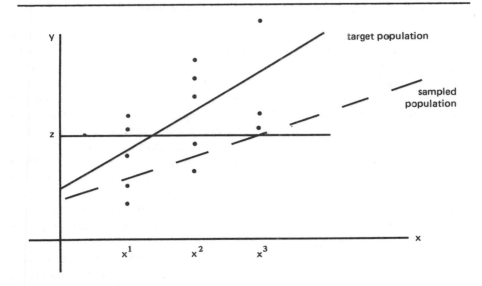

Figure 1: Attentuation of the Regression Slope from Truncation of the Dependent Variable at values $\leqslant z$.

Application of these ideas to handle the problem of sample truncation in electricity pricing experiments offers some novel features. First, rather than a predetermined level of the dependent variable determining truncation of the target population for all participants, the truncation point varies by household and over time. Second, the model to be used to analyze consumption behavior under a time-of-day (TOD) pricing scheme takes the form of a system of regression equations subject to various constraints. Depending on the particular specification used, the single-equation regression approach illustrated in equation [1] may be sufficient. But, in general, a multivariate formulation will be necessary.[2]

In the next sections we present an adaptation and application of the Hausman-Wise framework to data from an experiment in TOD pricing of electricity that took place in Arizona during 1976. These data have already received extensive analysis,[3] but none of the previous authors have accounted for the fact that in this experiment sample households were guaranteed they would never pay more for electricity under TOD prices than they would have under the prevailing rate schedule.

To assume that TOD price elasticities estimated from such a sample can be used to evaluate the impact of TOD pricing in a population of customers who are not afforded the luxury of this protection may be quite incorrect. Indeed, as the Arizona data demonstrate, major alterations in the empirical results can take place when such restrictions on the target population are explicitly considered.

2. THE ARIZONA TOD EXPERIMENT

Details of the experimental design for the Arizona TOD pricing experiment have been described elsewhere (Taylor, 1977). By way of summary, the Arizona data we use consist of monthly observations from May through October, 1976 on the consumption of 113 households in Phoenix that faced TOD prices during this period. This sample was derived from a much larger list of randomly selected households. Approximately 50% of those originally chosen were eliminated because of meter inaccessibility or an inadequate billing history. Of those left, approximately 20% refused to participate for one reason or another.[4]

The households fall naturally into three groups depending on the length of the peak and shoulder-peak periods.[5] A total of 28 different "treatments" were applied in all.[6] Comparable consumption data on each household were available for 1975, along with information on temperature, appliance capacity, and family income.[7] In this empirical work we focus on the cross-section sample for August, the month of system peak demand.

To test whether the effect of truncation is significant for these data we first construct a conventional model of electrical consumption under TOD prices. Taylor's (1977) initial attempts to fit linear and log-linear functional forms to the consumption quantities themselves were quite unsuccessful. Various reasons can be put forward to rationalize why the price effects he estimated were generally so imprecise. Among them are a weak experimental design, the fact that the fitted systems of demand equations used do not satisfy certain theoretical conditions of rational behavior, and that metering problems may have led to data inconsistencies.

For these reasons we have chosen to estimate a demand system formulated in expenditure shares, which will contain all relevant demand information. Price elasticities, for instance, can easily be calculated from a shares formulation, a popular specification of which arises naturally from the Christensen-Jorgenson-Lau (1975) translog utility function.

Given that data on the prices and consumption quantities of other goods are not available, we are forced to assume weak separability of electricity demand from other goods. This manifests itself in the *indirect translog utility function*,

$$V = \sum_{j=1}^{3} \alpha_j \ln\left(\frac{p_j}{z}\right) + \frac{1}{2} \sum_{j=1}^{3} \sum_{l=1}^{3} \beta_{jl} \ln\left(\frac{p_j}{z}\right) \ln\left(\frac{p_l}{z}\right), \tag{5}$$

written for a typical consumer,[8] where in equation [5] et seq., the following notation is used:

x_{ji} = physical quantities of electricity consumed (kwh) per month by household i in periods j = 1 (peak), j = 2 (shoulder), and j = 3 (off-peak), respectively;

y_{ji} = $p_{ji}x_{ji}$, j = 1, 2, 3, respectively, the corresponding expenditures, where $\{p_{ji}\}$ are the experimental prices per kwh;

$w_{ji} = y_{ji}/z_i$, $j = 1, 2, 3$, respectively, the shares of monthly total expenditure on electricity (z_i), where

$$\sum_{j=1}^{3} y_{ji} = z_i \quad \text{hence} \quad \sum_{j=1}^{3} w_{ji} = 1 \ .$$

Using Roy's identity to solve for the demand functions and imposing homotheticity[9] leads to the system of share equations,

$$w_1 = \alpha_1 + \sum_{l=1}^{3} \beta_{1l} \ln \left(\frac{p_l}{z} \right) + \epsilon_1 \tag{6}$$

$$w_2 = \alpha_2 + \sum_{l=1}^{3} \beta_{2l} \ln \left(\frac{p_l}{z} \right) + \epsilon_2$$

$$w_3 = \alpha_3 + \sum_{l=1}^{3} \beta_{3l} \ln \left(\frac{p_l}{z} \right) + \epsilon_3,$$

where the error terms are assumed to follow a joint normal distribution with zero means and covariance matrix $\mathbf{\Sigma}$. As previously noted because

$$\sum_{j=1}^{3} w_j = 1$$

for every observation, the system is subject to certain restrictions, namely

$$\sum_{j=1}^{3} \alpha_j = 1, \quad \sum_{j=1}^{3} \beta_{jl} = 0, \quad l = 1, 2, 3, \quad \text{and} \quad \sum_{j=1}^{3} \epsilon_j = 0.$$

Thus, the distribution specified on $\epsilon_1, \epsilon_2, \epsilon_3$ is degenerate. We proceed by discarding one equation. Its parameters are estimated by using the restrictions along with parameter estimates obtained from a consistent estimation procedure applied to the remaining two equations.

One final matter of specification remains. Both the α_j's and the β_{ji}'s may vary over individuals. Thus we allow for interaction effects in the model by defining

$$\alpha_j = \gamma_{j0} + \gamma_{j1} z_1 + \gamma_{j2} z_2 + \gamma_{j3} z_3, \tag{7a}$$

$$\beta_{jl} = \delta_{jl0} + \delta_{jl1} z_1 + \delta_{jl2} z_2 + \delta_{jl3} z_3 \tag{7b}$$

for $j, l = 1, 2, 3$

where the z_k's are exogenous variables, in particular, mean temperature, appliance capacity, and length of peak period. The α_j-functions effectively include linear influences of these exogenous variables in an otherwise standard version of the translog model. The β_{jl}-functions, however, allow for interactions between these exogenous variables and the (normalized) prices.

The influence of income is modeled in the following way. Income is taken to affect the level of total expenditures on electricity which, in turn, is allowed to be *endogenous* to the model. In the estimation, $ln(p_{ji}/z_i)$ is first regressed on income and all other exogenous variables, and the instrument for $ln(p_{ji}/z_i)$ thus created is then used in calculating the normalized price terms over households.

To test the complete specification given by [6] and [7] together, we compared it to a model where all interaction effects were assumed jointly to be zero. The former model has a total of 16 parameters per equation, whereas with $\delta_{jl1} = \delta_{jl2} = \delta_{jl3} = 0$, $l = 1, 2, 3$ for each j, 9 restrictions are imposed. The test statistic for our 2-equation estimating model is therefore χ^2_{18}. The estimated chi-squared statistic was 18.35, almost exactly its expected value under the null hypothesis that the β_{jl}'s are constants.

An additional hypothesis of interest supposes that the α_j's are constants *given* that no interaction terms appear in the model. Three additional restrictions per equation are thus imposed, implying an asymptotic χ^2_6 distribution for the likelihood ratio test statistic. The calculated value for this test is 194.62, well above rejection levels at very high confidence probabilities. Our final specification, therefore, consists of [6] with the α_j-functions of [7]. The β_{jl}'s are assumed to be constant parameters $(\beta_{jl} \equiv \delta_{jl0})$.

The results from estimating our demand system are given in Table 1. Results for the w_3-equation are derived from adding-up restrictions. Because mean temperature varies by household and rate period, the first 4 coefficients only satisfy the restriction $\hat{\alpha}_j = 1$ and not adding-up restrictions on each $\hat{\gamma}_{jk}$. We report them as if these restrictions were satisfied and contend that since temperature does not vary so much by household as by region, they are close approximations to the correct values. This suggests that the results reported are not invariant to which equation is dropped. Asymptotically, there is no such problem. The reported results still retain the consistency property.

All coefficients except those on the rated appliance capacity variables are estimated relatively precisely. The coefficients of the normalized price variables all have especially small asymptotic standard errors and large asymptotic t-statistics except for $\hat{\beta}_{32}$ (which happens to be near zero).

The main parameters of interest, of course, deal with price responsiveness. We focus on them by calculating the own-price elasticities corresponding to the $\hat{\beta}_{jl}$ estimates of Table 1.

The chi-squared test for symmetry of cross-price effects results in a test statistic of 24.4, which suggests *rejection* of the symmetry hypothesis at a significance level of 5%, and so these results are reported without the imposition of that constraint. As shown in Table 2, the own-price elasticity for the peak period is estimated at

Table 1   Estimates of Translog Share Equations for the Arizona
TOD Experiment, August 1976

Variable	Equation w_1	Equation w_2	Equation w_3 [a]
	Estimates *(asymptotic standard errors)*		
1. Constant	−1.704[b] (0.917)	−3.64 (0.639)	4.344 (1.212)
2. Rated Appliance Capacity (1000s)	−0.408[b] (1.133)	0.802[b] (0.746)	−0.394[b] (0.496)
3. Peak Period	0.0751 (0.0058)	−0.0412 (0.0039)	−0.0339 (0.0062)
4. Mean Temperature (100s)	1.853 (0.890)	4.380 (0.653)	−6.233 (1.19)
5. $\ln (P_1/Z)$	0.250 (0.0303)	−0.154 (0.0194)	−0.096 (0.0284)
6. $\ln (P_2/Z)$	−0.203 (0.0286)	0.228 (0.0182)	−0.023[b] (0.0213)
7. $\ln (P_3/Z)$	0.068 (0.0202)	−0.0535 (0.0129)	0.121 (0.0152)

a. Derived from adding-up restrictions; see text for explanation.
b. Not significantly different from zero at the 95% level.

Table 2   Corresponding Uncompensated Price Elasticities
(evaluated at the mean shares)

	Price		
	1	2	3
Period 1	−0.483	−0.423	−0.141
2	−0.419	−0.378	−0.144
3	−0.644	−0.154	−0.188

−0.483, and the pattern of numerical magnitudes resembles those estimated by Atkinson (1977) using a translog model.

The finding of gross complementarity from the cross-price elasticities indicates the importance of electricity's role as an intermediate good. Ownership of electricity using appliances that cannot be substituted across time would be expected to produce complementary relationships among the $\{x_j\}$. On the other hand, discretionary activities like operating a dishwasher can lead to substitutability across times of the day. Evidently, during the 1976 summer months in Arizona, activities that result in complementary relationships dominated. This finding also accords with that in the Connecticut project, where total usage fell during the experiment.[10] Whether complementarity across pricing periods will appear in other experiments is a question which has important implications on the effect of the introduction of TOD prices on capacity growth and the mix of generating fuels used in electricity generation.

3. CORRECTING FOR SAMPLE TRUNCATION

The available sample is constrained by the fact that participants were guaranteed that they would pay no more for electricity under TOD prices than they would have otherwise paid.[11] That is, the truncation rule is:

$$p_1 x_1 + p_2 x_2 + p_3 x_3 \leqslant p^*(x_1 + x_2 + x_3) \tag{8}$$

where p^* is the prevailing average (or flat) rate for electricity and the consumption levels are those the customer experienced while on the experiment.[12] Written in terms of the w_j's, [8] becomes

$$1 \leqslant p^* \left(\frac{w_1}{p_1} + \frac{w_2}{p_2} + \frac{w_3}{p_3} \right) \tag{9}$$

The joint density of w_1, w_2 under the self-selection hypothesis is therefore

$$f(w_1, w_2) = \begin{cases} 0 \text{ if } 1 > p^* \left(\dfrac{w_1}{p_1} + \dfrac{w_2}{p_2} + \dfrac{w_3}{p_3} \right) \\[2em] \dfrac{\phi(w_1, w_2)}{\mathrm{pr}\left[1 \leqslant \left(\dfrac{w_1}{p_1} + \dfrac{w_2}{p_2} + \dfrac{w_3}{p_3} \right) \right]} \text{ if } 1 \leqslant p^* \left(\dfrac{w_1}{p_1} + \dfrac{w_2}{p_2} + \dfrac{w_3}{p_3} \right) \end{cases} \tag{10}$$

where $\phi(w_1, w_2)$ is the bivariate normal density function with the properties ascribed by equations [6] and [7].

Correspondingly, the log-likelihood function to be maximized is as follows, assuming independent random sampling over n households:

$$\log L = \text{constant} + \sum_{i=1}^{n} \log \phi(w_{1i}, w_{2i}) \tag{11}$$

$$- \sum_{i=1}^{n} \log \phi \left\{ - \frac{1}{p_i^*} - \left(X_i' + \frac{X_i' \gamma_1}{p_{2i}} + \frac{(1 - X_i' \gamma_1 - X_i' \gamma_2)}{p_{3i}} \right) \right.$$

$$\times \left(\sigma_{11} \left(\frac{1}{p_{1i}} - \frac{1}{p_{3i}} \right)^2 + \sigma_{22} \left(\frac{1}{p_{2i}} - \frac{1}{p_{3i}} \right)^2 \right.$$

$$\left. + 2\sigma_{12} \left(\frac{1}{p_{1i}} - \frac{1}{p_{3i}} \right) \left(\frac{1}{p_{2i}} - \frac{1}{p_{3i}} \right) \right)^{-\frac{1}{2}} \Bigg\}$$

where $\phi(\cdot)$ is the standard normal distribution function,

$$X_i' = \left(1 \ z_{1i} \ z_{2i} \ z_{3i} \ ln\left(\frac{p_{1i}}{z_i}\right) \ ln\left(\frac{p_{2i}}{z_i}\right) \ ln\left(\frac{p_{3i}}{z_i}\right) \right)$$

and

$$\gamma_j' = (\gamma_{j0} \ \gamma_{j1} \ \gamma_{j2} \ \gamma_{j3} \ \beta_{j1} \ \beta_{j2} \ \beta_{j3}).$$

Because we treat z_i as endogenous and thereby create instruments for $ln(p_{1i}/z_i)$, $ln(p_{2i}/z_i)$, and $ln(p_{3i}/z_i)$, [11] should really be regarded as a pseudolikelihood function.[13]

If the truncation effect is important, the resulting parameter estimates would differ markedly from those estimated when it is ignored, as in Table 1. As Table 3 shows, some large differences do appear. Among the $\hat{\alpha}_j$'s, both the rated capacity variable and the mean temperature coefficients are quite different. But since our interest is mainly on the price effects, we concentrate our statistical testing on them. An extension of lemma (2.1) of Hausman (1978) allows us to test whether the differences are significant. Concentrating for the moment on the $\hat{\beta}_{jj}$'s (since these estimates determine the own-price elasticities), the difference in the two estimates of β_{11} is 0.152 with an asymptotic standard error of 0.0436. By using theorem 1 of Hausman (1978) under the null hypothesis of no difference, the statistic $(0.152/0.0436)^2 = 12.15$ is distributed as χ_1^2. Thus we reject the null hypothesis at all reasonable levels of significance. For β_{22} the difference in estimates is 0.035 with an asymptotic standard error of 0.0116. The test statistic (9.10) again is very significant. Finally, for β_{33} the difference in estimates is 0.026 with an asymptotic standard error 0.031 so that the test statistic (0.720) is not significant. A joint test of all 6 price terms is distributed as χ_6^2 under the null hypothesis. Yet the estimated statistic has a value of 21.8, which leads to rejection that the coefficient estimates are the same.[14]

The own-price and cross-price elasticities are also of interest and are given in Table 4. Note that the own-price elasticity for the peak period is only about one-third as large as before. Otherwise, the general pattern of gross complementarity remains, with the own-price elasticities of periods 2 and 3 increasing somewhat.[15] Thus, we may conclude that sample truncation does affect the results of an analysis

Table 3   Estimates of Translog Share Equations Corrected for Truncation
for the Arizona TOD Experiment, August 1976

Variable	Estimates (asymptotic standard errors)		
	Equation w_1	Equation w_2	Equation w_3[a]
1. Constant	1.468^b (1.203)	-1.378^b (0.748)	-0.090^b (1.352)
2. Rated Appliance Capacity (1000s)	-3.281 (1.462)	0.667^b (0.441)	2.614^b (1.576)
3. Peak Period	0.0793 (0.0094)	-0.0535 (0.0040)	-0.0258 (0.0121)
4. Mean Temperature (100s)	1.279^b (1.159)	2.068 (0.7968)	-3.347 (1.510)
5. $\ln (P_1/Z)$	0.402 (0.0531)	-0.284 (0.0224)	-0.118 (0.0567)
6. $\ln (P_2/Z)$	-0.192 (0.0461)	0.193 (0.0216)	-0.001^b (0.0424)
7. $\ln (P_3/Z)$	-0.102 (0.0362)	0.00705^b (0.0134)	0.095 (0.0342)

a. Derived from adding-up restrictions; see text for explanation.
b. Not significantly different from zero at the 95% level.

Table 4   Corresponding Corrected Uncompensated Price Elasticities
(evaluated at the mean shares)

	Price		
	1	2	3
Period 1	-0.169	-0.396	-0.684
2	-0.773	-0.474	$+0.019$
3	-0.792	-0.006	-0.362

of the Arizona data. Indeed, the pattern of results now resembles those estimated by Caves-Christensen (1978) for experimental data in Wisconsin, where no such individual protection from harm was granted.[16]

4. CONCLUSIONS AND CAVEATS

In this paper we have attempted to introduce into the conventional methodology available for estimating a system of time-of-day demand (consumption) functions the idea that the sample at hand may present a biased view of the impacts of TOD pricing in a population that is not protected from the possible adverse effects of old consumption patterns with the new rate structure. The result is a correction to the peak period, own-price elasticity toward zero and a slight increase (in absolute value) in the own-price elasticities in the other periods.

In evaluating the generality of this conclusion, we need to keep in mind several qualifications and limitations to the empirical work. First, the model structure imposes certain assumptions regarding the preferences of consumers. In particular, we have used the homothetic version of the translog demand system. Our primary reason for avoiding the more general, nonlinear (nonhomothetic) version is one of the computational necessity.

Finally, it would be of interest to compare results from an identical analysis of the remaining months of data. Given the short duration of the test data that were available to us, the results might be affected by the dynamics of adjustment to experimental rates. While an explicit model of dynamic adjustment is desirable, we have instead computed analogous results for May, the first month of the test. The estimated own-price elasticities, corresponding to the entries in Table 2, are –0.495, –0.312 and –0.227 for the peak, mid-peak and off-peak periods. Thus, again we find that the peak elasticity is largest in absolute value. Yet when truncation is accounted for, the own-price elasticities become –0.238, –0.401 and –0.363, the same phenomenon as we observed for August where the "corrected" peak period elasticity falls below those for the other two periods. While the falls is not quite so dramatic as in August, one may argue that by the later months of the experiment participants had time to adjust to the experimental rates. A similar occurrence is observed for June. Thus we conclude that the August results are not anomalous but rather are indicative of the true effects of truncation on an otherwise conventional econometric treatment of the data.

Compensation payments, participation incentives, and other forms of persuasion contribute to minimizing attrition during the course of a voluntary experiment. Attrition is an important concern, expecially if it occurs in a cell with an already low sampling rate, since the loss of observations for any reason creates difficulties at the analysis stage. Households that move for "natural" reasons may be followed and kept in the experiment if feasible.[17] Alternately, the new family may be enlisted so that installed metering equipment need not be moved. Some observations will, however, be totally unrecoverable. Attrition over the life of an experiment or the effects of voluntary participation can be dealt with explicitly in a similar fashion to the problem of truncation if the reason for (or probability of) attrition or self-selection can be modeled. An example is presented in some very recent work of Hausman and Wise (1979).

NOTES

1. Related work is by Heckman (1979).

2. It is to be noted that Hausman-Wise themselves developed results for a two-equation simultaneous equation model.

3. Cf., Atkinson (1977, 1978); Lau-Lillard (1978; Miedema, et al. (1979); Taylor (1977).

4. Thus, and inferences we make apply only to a *voluntary* program of implementation.

5. The peak period began at the same time in each case (2PM) but varied in length (3, 5, or 8 hours). The off-peak period was fixed from 10PM-9AM in all cases, the necessary adjustments taking place in the shoulder-peak period.

6. Sixteen experimental rates were associated with the 3-hour peak period and six with each of the others.

7. Unfortunately, we do not have data on appliance holdings by type, so we cannot hope to separate out how different appliances may permit altered patterns of electricity usage during the day. The temperature data is specific to rate period and household.

8. In writing [5] we have suppressed an observation subscript to converse on notation.

9. Homotheticity is imposed at the outset for two reasons. First, we believe it is a reasonable assumption given that weak separability in the utility function must be assumed due to data limitations. Secondly, it simplifies the computational work, which is formidable for the truncation problem even with the simpler linear-in-parameters model that results.

10. See Burbank (1977).

11. The population also was proscribed by such restrictions as nonseasonal dwellings only, adequate billing and payment history, and so forth. To the extent that these restrictions can be related to a truncation of the distribution of the dependent variable, they too can be handled, but we do not account for such influences here. They provide further limitations on the population to which sample results apply (see note 4).

12. During August 1976 the prevailing rate schedule was a declining block tariff subject to various surcharges and fuel cost adjustments.

The TOD prices may likewise be defined such that

$$\sum_{j=1}^{3} y_{j.} = p^* \sum_{j=1}^{3} x_{j.},$$

where the dot notation indicates summation over customers in the relevant rate class. This is a restriction that often applies to these sorts of experiments *instead* of [8], although equating current expenditure to expenditures under experimental tariffs may also involve compensation payments apart from prices.

Usually, a relatively small set of experimental price pairs is used, each of which is revenue "neutral" in this sense. Thus, prices vary over customer subgroups and not over each individual customer as the notation p_{ji} might suggest.

13. It is straightforward to prove consistency for the resulting estimators using the conventional ML theory. However, the asymptotic standard errors must be adjusted to account for the use of instruments. [See Maddala, et al. (1977).] In this application, the adjustment is small.

14. We note that the corresponding test for symmetry of cross-price effects in this case, when truncation *is* accounted for, results in *acceptance* of the null hypothesis ($\chi^2_3 = 3.34$).

15. The increase for period 3 is not statistically significant.

16. In Wisconsin, rates instead were designed to be revenue neutral (see note 12).

17. This would be the desirable way to capture the "long-run" effects of changing appliance holdings on electricity consumption as reflected in the choice of a new residence with a different mix of water heating, space heating, and air conditioning capacities, while retaining the particular behavioral characteristics of the original family.

REFERENCES

AMEMIYA, T. (1973) "Regression analysis when the dependent variable is truncated normal." Econometrica 41: 997-1016.

ATKINSON, S. E. (1978) "A comparative analysis of consumer response to time-of-use electricity pricing: Arizona and Wisconsin." Presented at the EPRI Workshop on Modeling and Analysis of Electricity Demand by Time-of-Day, San Diego, California, June.

—— (1977) "Responsiveness of time-of-day electricity pricing: first empirical results," pp. 1-197 in A. Lawrence (ed.) Forecasting and Modeling Time-of-Day and Seasonal Electricity Demands. Palo Alto, CA: Electric Power Research Institute.

BATTALIO, R. C. et al. (1979) "Residential electricity demand: an experimental study." Rev. of Economics and Statistics 61: 180-189.

BURBANK, H. D. (1977) "The Connecticut peak-load-pricing experiment," in A Lawrence (ed.) Forecasting and Modeling Time-of-Day and Seasonal Electricity Demands. Palo Alto, CA: Electric Power Research Institute.

CAVES, D. W. and L. R. CHRISTENSEN (1978) "Econometric analysis of the Wisconsin residential time-of-use electricity pricing experiment." Presented at the Workshop on Modeling and Analysis of Electricity Demand by Time-of-Day, San Diego, California, June.

HAUSMAN, J. A. (1978) "Specification tests in econometrics." Econometrica 46: 1251-1272.

—— and D. A. WISE (1979) "Attrition bias in experimental and panel data: the Gary income maintenance experiment." Econometrica 47: 455-475.

—— (1977) "Social experimentation, truncated distributions, and efficient estimation." Econometrica 45: 919-938.

HECKMAN, J. J. (1979) "Sample bias as a specification error." Econometrica 47: 153-162.

JORGENSON, D. W. and L. J. LAU (1978) "The structure of consumer preferences." Annals of Economic and Social Measurement 4: 49-102.

LAU, L. J. and L. A. LILLARD (1978) "A random response of the demand for electricity by time-of-day." Presented at the EPRI Workshop on Modeling and Analysis of Electricity Demand by Time-of-Day, San Diego, California, June.

MADDALA, G. S., T. LEE, and R. P. TROST (1977) "Instrumental variables estimation for models of self-selection." Mimeo, University of Florida.

MIEDEMA, A. K. et al. (1978) "Time-of-use electricity prices: Arizona." Report, U.S. Department of Energy, Office of Utility Systems, December.

TAYLOR, L. D. (1977) "On modeling the residential demand for electricity by time-of-day," pp. 1-221 in A. Lawrence (ed.) Forecasting and Modeling Time-of-Day and Seasonal Electricity Demands. Palo Alto, CA: Electric Power Research Institute.

29

This interdisciplinary study examines the effect of a complex set of price and non-price measures on water conservation in four California water districts over a 96-month period. Theory for the analysis of these measures is drawn from social psychology and economic theory. Autoregressive moving average and error components models measure the effect both of price changes and appeals for conservation on water consumption. Each exerts significant impacts. In contrast to the study by Battalio et al. (ch. 27), the authors demonstrate the potential importance of nonprice conservation measures. Consistent with Battalio et al., however, they also discover that conservation is enhanced if better feedback on behavior is provided by speedy billing relative to consumption.

Conceptually, this natural experiment is complicated by several problems. The first set of problems deal with the political and institutional context in which water is supplied and demanded. Namely, the price of water as it is currently produced and marketed is not simultaneously determined by supply and demand. While water can be rationed by price, it is supplied by institutions subject to regulation as with any public utility. Pricing is designed to recover costs rather than to turn a profit and finance output expansion. To some degree, consumption of water is also considered a right. These factors exacerbate the problem of the "commons dilemma"—conflict between short-run self-interest and long-run public interest when some publicly supplied or regulated good becomes relatively more scarce. Political constraints prohibit the use of price alone as a rationing and allocation device. Other methods (of doubtful a priori effectiveness) such as moral suasion and education, direct rationing, proscriptions, and moratoriums on new hook-ups, must then be relied on to accomplish what price is not permitted to accomplish.

Such measures were generally introduced in concert, though in varying combinations across the four sites, so that it is virtually impossible to unravel the independent effects of each. To help solve this second problem, the authors construct two categorical variables—one to represent the cluster of programs begun early in the study interval (the moratorium before the onset of the California drought) and the other to represent the set of programs initiated during the drought itself. The moratorium variable varies somewhat across communities, but the drought variable does not.

Finally, the authors had to adjust the nominal price structure for water to the estimates of real marginal price. The best approximation, given the complex rate structure, as well as its changes over time, was to use the real marginal price of the last unit consumed by the average user, where users were separated into domestic and agricultural consumers. Domestic users were composed of residential, commercial, and public users such as schools, though residential users dominated this category. There were, then, two dependent variables measured in units of 100 cubit feet (HCF) per account.

In addition to price and the two categorical policy variables mentioned above, consumption for the two separate sets of consumers was expressed as a function of temperature, rainfall, and a categorical variable set for site (in the error components model).

The effects of the price and nonprice policy variables are of greatest interest. For domestic users, the introduction of the package of programs associated with the moratorium was not statistically significant; but the package associated with measures introduced during the drought did exert an impact. The latter policy package reduced water consumption by 3.62 HCF—a 20% reduction from the mean level of consumption. With respect to price, each 10% per HCF increase in price reduced consumption by 3.29 HCF, again, about 20%. Price response was significant but inelastic (as predicted)—a 10% increase in price reduced consumption by 3.7%.

For agricultural users, both the moratorium and drought policy variables reduced consumption enormously—with a combined impact of 60%. Also as predicted, agricultural users responded to price incentives more than did domestic consumers. Price elasticity is -.70—a 10% increase in price reduces consumption of agricultural users by 7%.

Cross-community effects (interactions) could be ignored only at the risk of misspecifying the analytic model, so the data were pooled across communities to adjust for correlated residuals over time, correlated residuals across communities, and different residual variances across communities. After this, the drought and moratorium policy variables still retained significant but smaller effects on domestic consumption. Price elasticity dropped to -.09. Efforts to explain cross-community correlations were defeated by the nature of the data. But, the effect that did exist appeared to be the result of seasonal consumption patterns missed by the rainfall and temperature variables. This leads the authors to the judgment that the time series model for individual communities was specified correctly.

For agricultural users, the pooled results were once again relatively stronger. Price elasticity was estimated at −.57 and both nonprice policy variables reduce consumption by about 15%.

In summary, the results suggest that price is an important variable affecting demand. And perhaps of equal importance, under some circumstances, the dilemma of the commons can be alleviated by information and moral appeals.

Reducing Consumption in Periods of Acute Scarcity
The Case of Water

Richard A. Berk, Thomas F. Cooley, C. J. LaCivita, Stanley Parker, Kathy Sredl, and Marilynn Brewer

INTRODUCTION

Americans are beginning to recognize that old assumptions of unlimited natural resources are at best naive. Whether the result of real shortages, temporary market imperfections, government regulations or political maneuvering, producers and consumers alike have increasingly felt the bit of serious mismatches between supply and demand. Production bottlenecks, massive fluctuations in market price, and continuing inflation have signaled that it is possible to reach down into the horn of plenty and come up empty handed.

Responses to the perception of limits have been as diverse as explanations for why such limits exist. Some proposals have focused on supply while suggesting new technology, changes in the structure of incentives, and/or increased reliance on free market mechanisms. Especially for short-run solutions, however, even greater effort has been directed towards

This paper originally appeared in Social Science Research, March 1980, and we are indebted to a number of individuals for their support and advice. The U.S. Department of Housing and Urban Development provided funds for the research. Katharine Lyall and David Puryear of HUD were not only unusually competent project monitors, but also important sources of ideas and suggestions. Richard McCleary was enormously helpful in our early efforts to install and properly use the time-series software. During the data collection phase, Donnie Hoffman and Rebecca Cannon shouldered most of the day-to-day burdens. Finally, the research could not have been undertaken without the assistance of local water district personnel who gave freely of their time and expertise.

reducing consumption. And among the strategies readily available, conservation has become a significant option.

During 1976 and 1977, the entire West Coast of the United States experienced one of its worst droughts in recorded history, and with each passing
month, the prospect of genuine water shortages grew. Consumers were faced
with yet another natural resource that could not be squandered, and conservation seemed the only viable response. Large and small communities alike
initiated efforts to reduce their use of water. Some tried to educate consumers, while others introduced surcharges for excessive consumption. Some
communities passed local ordinances regulating when and how water might be
used, while others, apparently more concerned about the future, legislated
moratoriums on new water hook-ups. Yet, good intentions should not be confused with informed public policy, and in their hurry to reduce water use,
public officials proceeded with a melange of programs resting on unarticu-
lated principles whose effectiveness was unknown.

In this paper we will examine the impact of water conservation efforts
in four California communities selected in part because of the range of conservation programs launched.[1] The analysis will rest on eight years of
monthly data aggregated to the community level and will employ both Box-
Jenkins (1976) procedures and techniques for pooled cross-sectional and
time-series data (Kmenta, 1971: 508-517). Theory will be drawn from social
psychology and microeconomics; the former used to characterize certain
shifts in the demand curve for water, the latter used to explain changes in
consumption as a function of exogenous changes in price.

SOCIAL PSYCHOLOGICAL PERSPECTIVES ON WATER CONSERVATION

Given that programs to control water use typically rely on voluntary
measures, water conservation is often viewed within a large class of societal dilemmas created when short-run self-interest conflicts with long-run
public interest. Such problems, variously characterized as "commons dilemmas" (Dawes, 1975; Hardin, 1968), the "new Malthusianism" (Schelling, 1971),
or "social traps" (Platt, 1973) typically arise when some publicly provided
good is scarce.[2] Each individual has no incentive to reduce his/her consumption, but in the aggregate the good is rapidly depleted, and no one's
self-interest is served. With respect to water use in particular, Schelling
observes (1971):

> What we are dealing with is the frequent divergence between what
> people are individually motivated to do and what they might like
> to accomplish together. . . .We are warned of water shortages;
> leaky faucets account for a remarkable amount of waste, and we
> are urged to fit them with new washers. There just cannot be

any question but what, for most of us if not all of us, we are
far better off if we all . . . repair the leaky faucets, let the
lawns get a little browner and the cars a little dirtier, and
otherwise reduce our claims on the common pool of water. . . .
But . . .[mine] is an infinitesimal part of the demand for water
. . . and while the minute difference that I can make is multiplied by the number of people to whom it can make a difference,
the effect on me of what I do is truly negligible (pp. 68-69,
emphasis in the original).

While Schelling (1971) and Hardin (1968) provide numerous graphic illustrations of such dilemmas, more formal models have been proposed by Dawes
(1975) and Messick (1973, 1974), based on n-person extensions of the pri-
soner's dilemma decision structure. Such models provide a framework for
considering factors affecting the demand for water.

The existing theoretical models on the dilemma of the commons can be
linked to a large empirical literature of experimental studies undertaken in
laboratories (e.g., Kelly and Grzelak, 1972; Talarowski, 1977; Dawes,
McTavish and Shaklee, 1977; Marwell and Ames, 1979; Linder, 1977; Brechner,
1977; Stern, 1976; Brewer, forthcoming) and studies of conservation per se
situated in the field (e.g., Thompson and McTavish, 1976; Lipsey, 1977;
Seligman, Darley and Becker, forthcoming; Watkins, 1974; Eruvold, 1978;
Talarowski and McClintock, 1978). Taken as a whole, the available theory
and data suggest at least five social psychological factors enhancing conservation and consequently reducing the demand for water: (1) a belief that
a resource shortage exists and constitutes a problem for a group with which
an individual identifies; (2) a moral commitment to "fair" contributions to
group welfare; (3) a belief in the efficacy of personal efforts to achieve a
collective solution; (4) a belief that the personal cost of inconvenience
resulting from conservation efforts will not be great; and (5) a belief that
others in the relevant group will also conserve. We will see shortly that
in the four communities in question, "common sense" led to conservation programs that relied heavily on similar observations.

MICROECONOMIC PERSPECTIVES ON WATER CONSERVATION

It cannot be overemphasized that while attitudes no doubt affect the
demand for water, water is a market commodity; water must be purchased at a
price. When viewed solely from this perspective, there is no "commons dilemma" inherent in water shortages. In the general case of a competitive
market, if a commodity is in short supply, the price should rise to equili-
brate supply and demand at a lower quantity. Yet, the California water industry is dominated by public water purveyors or publicly regulated private
companies; price is not simultaneously determined by supply and demand.

Price is <u>exogenously</u> determined (in the short run) by water suppliers, subject to public review. Nevertheless, this means that in principle a municipality faced with a water shortage need only set the price at a sufficiently high level to produce the desired reduction in consumption.[3]

Yet, the use of price as an allocation mechanism is constrained by the fact that water is generally regarded as a basic necessity, even a right, not an economic good. As a result, most non-private water purveyors have determined their prices by using an average cost pricing scheme devised by the American Water Works Association (AWWA). The sole purpose of this scheme, called the declining-block rate structure, is to recover the historical costs incurred in operating the system. To determine prices, total annual historical costs are allocated among three different cost categories: "customer costs" associated with number of customers served (e.g., meter reading), "capacity costs" associated with the growth and maintenance of the water supply system, and "commodity costs" associated with actually delivering the water (e.g., the costs of electricity to run the pumps). In addition, the extra costs incurred by the need to meet demand during peak periods (i.e., "excess" capacity) are allocated equally to capacity and commodity costs.

Once all costs have been allocated, capacity and customer costs are added together to determine a minimum fixed monthly fee for each customer based on the customer's meter size. This fixed fee usually entitles the customer to a small amount of water that is less than his/her normal monthly consumption. The marginal (i.e., per-unit) price is then determined by using commodity costs (including 50% of the capital costs) and the expected yearly quantities of water used by wholesale, intermediate and domestic users. The result is a three-price system in which the marginal price depends on the amount of water used.

Turning to demand, aggregate demand for water is the sum of the demand curves for residential users, commercial users, and so on. However, since the determinants of demand will differ across these categories, each should be considered separately. Unfortunately, two of our four community water districts distinguish only between water used for agricultural and non-agricultural purposes. Yet, since residential water use comprises approximately 80% of the non-agricultural use, the distortions are probably not significant. Consequently, we can address demand focusing on residential and agricultural water use.

Economic theory emphasizes that for households, the position of the demand curve depends on household characteristics and income. In addition, the income elasticity of demand for water may be significant because as family income increases, households typically purchase water-using devices such as garbage disposals and, for the very wealthy, swimming pools. They also buy larger houses on larger lots.

Climate also affects the position of the demand curve. Areas with hot, dry climates will, ceteris paribus, demand more water than other areas. Climate also creates seasonal variations in demand, with greater demand in the summer months, when the temperature is higher and rainfall is lower.

The agricultural demand curve for water reflects the fact that water is a factor of production. The determinants of the agricultural demand curve include the price of the crops it is used to produce, the type of crop grown, environmental characteristics such as soil condition and climate, and technical determinants such as water quality.

Climate has much the same effect on agricultural consumers as on residential consumers. Hot, dry areas will demand more water, ceteris paribus, and more water will be demanded in the summer months than in the cooler months. Moreover, crop rotations are seasonal, and seasonal variables such as rainfall and temperature should partly capture these effects. (Soil conditions and water quality are constant in the short run for any given water supply system.)

Given this general framework, the demand curve for water by residential users should be price-inelastic for two reasons. First, there is no close substitute for water in most of its uses. A certain minimum amount of water is necessary to sustain human life and to facilitate human hygiene and health. Washing dishes and watering lawns also require water. Second, the amount of money spent on water is usually a very small percentage of the average family budget. In constrast, since water is an input to agricultural production, the price elasticity of water for agricultural purposes may be higher than for residential users. In the long run, crops that are less water-intensive can be substituted for current crops. The demand characteristics, however, depend on the elasticity of demand for the crops that can be grown as well as on the characteristics of the aggregate supply. The demand for water is thus a derived demand.

What then is the role of conservation measures within a microeconomic model? In principle, conservation measures are of two types: those that alter supply conditions and those that attempt to alter the demand curve. Measures that alter supply conditions include raising marginal prices, surcharges for water consumed in excess of an allotted amount, rationing, and moratoriums on new hook-ups to the system. Raising marginal prices will reduce quantity of water used for all consumers beyond the fixed-fee threshold as long as the price elasticity of water is less than zero. Surcharges also change the price structure, but in a different manner. The usual practice is to offer a certain amount of water at the prevailing marginal prices and then to sharply increase the marginal price for units of water in excess of the base amount. Thus, the quantity of water consumed will presumably be reduced for high-volume users. Rationing limits water use by threatening to eliminate all water deliveries if the user consumes more than the allotted amount. Moratoriums do not directly affect users who already have water hook-ups, but prevent additional hook-ups to the system. Moratoriums, however, may heighten the impact of the supply conditions for present users by emphasizing that water is in short supply.

Conservation measures that shift the demand curve itself include advertising to inform consumers of the water shortage and to promote conservation, measures to educate consumers on how to conserve water, and legislation to prohibit certain uses of water (such as car washing), under threat of punishment. All of these measures attempt to reduce consumption by shifting the demand curve, and thus its intersection with the supply curve.

Earlier we reviewed research suggesting how, through changing consumer attitudes, the demand curve for water might be affected. What is the empirical evidence for the impact of changes in supply conditions?

In brief, shifts from flat-rate to metered billing appear to discourage gross wastefulness (Hanke and Boland, 1971), but the impact of variation in price has not been especially dramatic (Hanke and Boland, 1971; Turnovsky, 1969). Part of the difficulty may stem from the low price at which water is traditionally offered, and part may result from an inability of consumers to closely monitor their consumption. In the case of the latter, water bills only report the total amount of water used in a way that does not allow consumers to disaggregate the effects of particular household activities (e.g., washing dishes versus watering lawns). Moreover, feedback is delayed since bills are typically received long after consumption has taken place. In fact, there is some evidence that at least in the case of energy consumption, conservation is enhanced if better feedback is provided (Seligman, Darley and Becker, forthcoming; McClelland, 1977).

Where does this leave us? Perhaps most important, we have embedded an analysis of water conservation campaigns in a market for water in which price is _exogenously_ determined. Social psychological perspectives and research suggest that conservation campaigns addressing appropriate consumer attitudes should shift the demand curve for water and consequently alter the quantity of water consumed. Economic theory and research suggest that consumers should respond to the conditions under which water is supplied.

DATA AND METHODS OF ANALYSIS

Our data came from four coastal California communities located about 100 miles north of Los Angeles: Goleta, Montecito, Summerland and Carpinteria. Montecito and Summerland are primarily residential areas for the well-to-do having populations around 10,000. Carpinteria, with a population of about 20,000, has a mix of primarily middle-class residential users

and agricultural users. For the latter, citrus fruit and avocados are the
major cash crops. Goleta is by far the largest community with a population
of over 70,000. In addition to being the location of the University of
California at Santa Barbara, Goleta has some light industry, a large number
of retail establishments, and a number of farms. Much as in the case of
Carpinteria, major crops include citrus and avocados.

Data Collection and Variable Construction

While we have been speaking of the community as the unit of analysis,
in fact the data are organized by water district. A water district is a
political entity much like a school district served by one or more water
purveyors. These purveyors may be public or private but in either case are
subject to extensive public regulation (like public utilities). All of the
water purveyors in our study are public, and, for all practical purposes,
each community has its own water district whose boundaries match the political boundaries of the community. Hence, one can use the terms "community"
and "water district" interchangeably (although this is often not the case in
other locales).

Within each of the communities, we would have certainly preferred to
work with data on individual consumers. However, individual-level data were
not available (in part for reasons of privacy), and we were forced to work
with aggregate figures. Thus, all of our data reflect the years 1970
through 1977 aggregated for each water district by month. We have 96 longitudinal data points for each of the four water districts. Nineteen seventy
was chosen as the first year primarily because there would be sufficient observations preceding the major policy interventions of the middle 70's. The
ending date of 1977 results from practical constraints; aggregate figures
for consumption are typically not available for about a year after primary
data are collected (e.g., from customer bills). Fortunately, the eight-year
span includes the serious drought.

Our analyses to follow employ variables suggested by the earlier theoretical discussion. To begin, water consumption should respond to seasonal
variation, and we will use mean monthly temperature and total monthly rainfall as indicators. Daily figures are routinely collected at the local air-
port, and from these aggregate measures were calculated. The same means
will be used for all four communities, but all are close enough to the air-
port so that significant variation across communities is probably not being
neglected.

Most conservation programs initiated by our sample of communities were
aimed at the kinds of attitudes discussed earlier. However, communities
varied enormously in the number, intensity and duration of conservation efforts, and capturing such complexity is no easy matter. At one extreme,
Goleta recognized as early as December 1972 that their ground water was

being overdrafted. A highly controversial moratorium on new water hook-ups
followed in an effort to restrain growing demand. In addition, a range of
measures were undertaken early in 1973 to encourage voluntary conservation:

1. news releases detailing the water shortage;

2. news releases on available water conservation practices;

3. the printing and distribution of educational brochures on
    such topics as the installation of water conservation devices;

4. monitoring and feedback to consumers about excessive water
    use (from billing records);

5. technical assistance from water district staff in finding and
    fixing leaks;

6. asking that restaurants not serve water except by request
    (washing water glasses is actually the major waste);

7. passage of an ordinance providing for emergency water rationing;

8. an elimination of the declining block price structure which had
    made the marginal cost of water less for large users.

In July of 1976 as the drought worsened, efforts escalated. Goleta
passed a local ordinance that placed a number of restrictions on how and
when water might be used. It became illegal, for example, to water land-
scapes between 11:00 a.m. and 4:00 p.m. In addition, hard-surfaced areas
(e.g., parking lots) could not be washed down, and users who exceeded established allotments were faced with extremely punitive surcharges.

At the other extreme, Carpinteria had no moratorium and limited their
later educational efforts primarily to a letter from the president of the
water district's board of directors attributing shortages to overdrafts during 1975 and 1976 and asking for voluntary conservation. In addition, information and technical assistance were made available for consumers who
requested it.

In summary, water conservation programs were initiated in two somewhat
distinct periods responding to somewhat different problems. Early efforts
were a reaction to alleged overdrafts of available supplies, and moratoriums were perhaps the most dramatic intervention. Later efforts were a reaction to the shortages produced by the severe drought.

Devising measures of these conservation efforts is complicated by a
number of problems. Perhaps the most important, in at least three of the
communities, a large number of programs were introduced in concert. Hence,
it is virtually impossible to unravel independent effects.

Faced with this difficulty and others, we settled on constructing two
dummy variables, one to represent the cluster of programs begun early in the
interval and another to represent the cluster of programs begun late. The
former we call "moratorium" to indicate the central role that hook-up moratoriums played even before the drought. The latter we call "drought" to denote programs responding to the drought itself. Moratorium varies somewhat
across communities, drought does not.

During the eight years covered by our data, all four communities experienced substantial variation in the nominal price structure for water. Early in the interval, declining block rate structures were the norm; larger users faced a smaller marginal price. In Goleta, for example, domestic users consuming less than 50 HCF (100 cubic feet) in a month paid a nominal (unadjusted for inflation) price of 22.5 cents per HCF. Domestic consumers using over 1000 HCF in a month paid only 9 cents per HCF. Late in the interval, all four communities switched to far simpler rate structures in which declining blocks were almost fully replaced by flat rates. Discussions with water district administrators suggest that much of the motivation for these changes came from a desire to put large users on the same footing as small users. (Both equity and conservation were involved.) Yet, large and/or agricultural users managed to retain a distinct price advantage even during the drought. In addition, nominal price structures responded to the revenue requirements of water districts.

Moving from a nominal price structure to estimates of the real (i.e., adjusted for inflation) marginal price was significantly complicated by the need to work with aggregate data and the fact that individual consumers were often faced with a rate structure consisting of a fixed minimum fee coupled with a declining schedule of prices. In the aggregate, our best approximation was to use the real marginal price of the last unit consumed by the average user. While this amounts to the use of an average real marginal price, it is still a substantial improvement over most past studies where the common practice has been to use an average price obtained by dividing total revenues by total consumption (see, for example, Haver and Winter, 1963; Gottlieb, 1963). The problem with using an average price of this type, of course, is that the total revenue includes the minimum monthly fee. Exceptions to this procedure can be found in the works of Sewell and Rouche (1974), Howe and Linaweaver (1967), Wong (1972) and Grima (1972).[4]

Finally, our dependent variables reflect the activities of two kinds of consumers: domestic consumers and agricultural consumers. The domestic category includes residential, commercial and public users (e.g., schools), although residential users make up the bulk of the accounts. In each water district we recorded aggregate monthly consumption in units of 100 cubic feet (HCF) and then divided by the appropriate number of water accounts (e.g., households). The result is two dependent variables measured in units of 100 cubic feet per account. This in effect standardizes for changes in the number of local accounts over time.[5]

FINDINGS AND DISCUSSION

Before turning to the multivariate results, it may prove instructive to briefly examine the means and standard deviations reported in Table 1. In particular, the findings from the multivariate models will take on more meaning if the means for domestic and agricultural consumption are kept in mind. Domestic consumers use between 18 and 41 HCF per account per month. Agricultural consumers use between 190 and 560 HCF per account per month. Clearly, agricultural consumption is larger by more than a factor of 10 and among agricultural users, the largest consumption figures are found in Goleta (where the farms are the largest). Prices also vary substantially. Mean domestic prices range from 16 cents to 23 cents per HCF. Mean agricultural prices range from 8 cents to 18 cents. Variation in mean price coupled with variation in mean consumption will take on special importance when elasticities are calculated.

Tables 2-5 show for each community the results of a multivariate time-series model (Box and Jenkins, 1976; Granger and Newbold, 1977; Box and Tiao, 1975) in which domestic consumption (Tables 2, 3) and agricultural consumption (Tables 4, 5) are regressed on the moratorium and drought dummy variables, temperature, rainfall and price. The specifications represented in the equations at the top of each table reflect our a priori theory with the exception of the impact of rainfall. Examination of the cross-correlations between rainfall and consumption indicated that a two-parameter transfer function was required. Each equation's causal parameters are reported in the first seven rows, and the omegas can be interpreted as metric regression coefficients. The last four rows include the price elasticity, the residual standard error, the estimated noise models and the chi-square (for a lag of 36 months)[6] for the noise model. For those unfamiliar with time-series analysis, the important substantive story is contained in the omegas and the price elasticity.

There is insufficient space here to consider the results reported on Tables 2-5 community by community. However, it may be instructive to briefly address the results in one community to facilitate the efforts of those readers who wish to study the tables in depth.

Consider Table 3 and the findings for domestic consumption in Summerland. Mean consumption in Summerland is a little over 18 HCF per account. Thus, Summerland's domestic users are not large volume consumers compared to those in the other four communities. If nothing else, this implies that the marginal effects of other variables may be smaller since the base from which reduction begins is somewhat lower.

Temperature and rainfall perform as one would expect and two of the three coefficients are statistically significant at the .05 level. (We are employing one-tail tests.) Each degree increase in mean temperature increases

TABLE 1

Descriptive Statistics for Variables Used in the Analysis (N = 96)

	Goleta		Montecito		Carpinteria		Summerland	
	Mean	Standard Deviation	Mean	Standard Deviation	Mean	Standard Deviation	Mean	Standard Deviation
Domestic Consumption (100 cu ft/account)	28.92	6.94	41.47	18.10	26.02	6.46	18.20	3.70
Agricultural Consumption (100 cu ft/account)	559.30	317.74	465.61	270.78	364.62	220.77	191.75	154.05
Domestic Price ($/100 cu ft)	.23	.05	.16	.03	.16	.02	.22	.03
Agricultural Price ($/100 cu ft)	.10	.02	.11	.03	.08	.04	.18	.05
Rain (inches)	1.32	2.16	1.32	2.16	1.32	2.16	1.32	2.16
Temperature (degrees)	60.36	5.32	60.36	5.32	60.36	5.32	60.36	5.32
Drought (dummy)	.27	.45	.27	.45	.27	.45	.27	.45
Moratorium (dummy)	.64	.48	.63	.49	none	none	.41	.49
Income (dollars)	12,570	789	19,475	1,222	10,427	654	12,604	791

TABLE 2

Domestic Water Use Analysis

$$DC_t = \mu + \omega_{0,1} M_t + \omega_{0,2} D_t + \omega_{0,3} T_t + (\omega_{0,4} - \omega_{1,4})R_t + \omega_{0,5} P_t + N_t$$

Parameter and Variable Name	Carpinteria		Goleta	
	Estimated Coefficient	t-value	Estimated Coefficient	t-value
μ — Mean	26.05	63.22	29.90	165.19
$\omega_{0,1}(M_t)$ — Moratorium	not applicable		-2.99	-3.55
$\omega_{0,2}(D_t)$ — Drought	-6.94	-6.31	-3.87	-3.98
$\omega_{0,3}(T_t)$ — Temperature	0.83	10.26	0.28	2.47
$\omega_{0,4}(R_t)$ — Rain	-0.21	-1.59	-0.17	-1.53
$\omega_{1,4}(R_t)$ — Rain	-0.54	-4.10	-0.42	-3.56
$\omega_{0,5}(P_t)$* — Price	-4.51	-2.21	-0.61	-0.76
Price Elasticity	-.28		-.05	
Residual Standard Error	2.54		2.36	
Noise Model for $N_t = \dfrac{\bar{\theta}(B)}{\phi(B)} a_t$**	$(1 - .24B - .15B^2 + .36B^4 - .26B^7 - .24B^{12})$ $\quad(.10)\ (.11)\ \ (.10)\ \ \ (.11)\ \ \ (.13)$		$(1 - .30B)/(1 + .25B - .43B^4 - .27B^8 + .32B^{12})$ $\quad(.14)\ \ \ \ (.08)\ \ (.13)\ \ \ (.13)\ \ \ (.12)$	
Chi-Square for N_t	40.5 (P > .05, df = 30)		37.1 (P > .05, df = 30)	

*In units of 10¢.   **Standard errors in parentheses.

TABLE 3

Domestic Water Use Analysis

$$DC_t = \mu + \omega_{0,1} M_t + \omega_{0,2} D_t + \omega_{0,3} T_t + (\omega_{0,4} - \omega_{1,4})R_t + \omega_{0,5} P_t + N_t$$

Parameter and Variable Name	Montecito		Summerland	
	Estimated Coefficient	t-value	Estimated Coefficient	t-value
μ — Mean	53.28	30.94	18.27	41.01
$\omega_{0,1}(M_t)$ — Moratorium	-17.32	-7.94	2.48	1.71
$\omega_{0,2}(D_t)$ — Drought	-6.29	-2.31	-3.62	-3.04
$\omega_{0,3}(T_t)$ — Temperature	1.88	7.85	0.35	5.87
$\omega_{0,4}(R_t)$ — Rain	-0.21	-0.46	-0.17	-1.49
$\omega_{1,4}(R_t)$ — Rain	-2.11	-4.65	-0.34	-3.15
$\omega_{0,5}(P_t)$* — Price	-5.75	-1.23	-3.29	-3.60
Price Elasticity	-0.22		-0.37	
Residual Standard Error	7.69		1.92	
Noise Model for $N_t = \frac{\theta(B)}{\phi(B)} a_t$**	$1/(1 + .16B - .28B^4)$		$(1 - .23B - .30B^2 - .35B^3)$	
	(.11) (.10)		(.10) (.11) (.11)	
Chi-Square for N_t	26.38 (P > .05, df = 33)		20.50 (P > .05, df = 32)	

*In units of 10¢. **Standard errors in parentheses.

671

TABLE 4

Agricultural Water Use Analysis

$$AC_t = \mu + \omega_{0,1} M_t + \omega_{0,2} D_t + \omega_{0,3} T_t + (\omega_{0,4} - \omega_{1,4})R_t + \omega_{0,5} P_t + N_t$$

Parameter and Variable Name	Carpinteria		Goleta	
	Estimated Coefficient	t-value	Estimated Coefficient	t-value
μ Mean	not applicable		580.63	77.76
$\omega_{0,1}(M_t)$ Moratorium	first differenced not applicable		-74.72	-4.59
$\omega_{0,2}(D_t)$ Drought	-234.03	-3.17	-6.91	-0.31
$\omega_{0,3}(T_t)$ Temperature	19.85	9.23	3.79	2.04
$\omega_{0,4}(R_t)$ Rain	-3.52	-0.71	-3.59	-1.00
$\omega_{1,4}(R_t)$ Rain	-6.11	-1.15	-6.72	-1.80
$\omega_{0,5}(P_t)*$ Price	-312.53	-8.10	-504.98	-8.22
Price Elasticity	-0.72		-0.89	
Residual Standard Error	89.30		76.43	
Noise Model for $N_t = \dfrac{\theta(B)}{\phi(B)} a_t$ **	$1/(1 - B)(1 - .65B - .32B^2)$ (.10) (.10)		$(1 - .89B)/(1 + .27B^2 - .60B^4 - .33B^6 - .38B^8)$ (.07) (.12) (.11) (.11) (.11)	
Chi-Square for N_t	24.40 (P > .05, df = 34)		29.30 (P > .05, df = 30)	

*In units of 10¢.   **Standard errors in parentheses.

TABLE 5

Agricultural Water Use Analysis

$$AC_t = \mu + \omega_{0,1} M_t + \omega_{0,2} D_t + \omega_{0,3} T_t + (\omega_{0,4} - \omega_{1,4})R_t + \omega_{0,5} P_t + N_t$$

Parameter and Variable Name	Montecito		Summerland	
	Estimated Coefficient	t-value	Estimated Coefficient	t-value
μ : Mean	631.31	26.97	204.42	20.87
$\omega_{0,1}$ (M_t) Moratorium	-221.49	-7.25	-54.20	-2.15
$\omega_{0,2}$ (D_t) Drought	-153.60	-3.65	15.70	0.50
$\omega_{0,3}$ (T_t) Temperature	26.48	6.37	11.84	4.41
$\omega_{0,4}$ (R_t) Rain	-1.52	-0.22	4.23	0.90
$\omega_{1,4}$ (R_t) Rain	-18.34	-2.57	1.82	0.34
$\omega_{0,5}$ (P_t)* Price	-296.95	-4.05	-185.41	-8.96
Price Elasticity	-0.70		-1.76	
Residual Standard Error	118.30		79.64	
Noise Model for $N_t = \frac{\theta(B)}{\phi(B)} a_t$**	$1/(1 - .25B)(1 + .26B^4)$ $\quad$ (.12) $\quad$ (.11)		1	
Chi-Square for N_t	38.77 (P > .05, df = 33)		27.13 (P > .05, df = 35)	

*In units of 10c. **Standard errors in parentheses.

water consumption by about .35 HCF. Each additional inch of rain reduces consumption by .17 HCF in the same month and .34 one month later. Clearly these effects are nontrivial compared to the mean level of consumption. For example, a 10-degree increase in mean temperature will increase water use by about 20 .

While the introduction of the package of programs associated with the moratorium has no statistically significant impact (indeed, the sign is in the wrong direction), the package of programs associated with the drought reduced water consumption by 3.62 HCF. The reduction reflects a 20% decrement from the mean level of consumption. Few would dispute that the programs associated with the drought had important effects.

Finally, price is also a powerful variable. Each 10-cent-per-HCF increase in price reduces consumption by 3.29 HCF, another 20 decrease. Actual price increases averaged closer to 5 cents, however, so that the reductions were closer to 10 . In any case, the elasticity with respect to price is -.37.

Now consider Table 5 and the results for agricultural consumption in Montecito. Mean consumption is, not surprisingly, rather large since agricultural users have greater demand per account than domestic users. From the baseline of over 600 HCF per account, it is clear that, again, temperature and rainfall have important effects (although the impact of rainfall in the same month is not statistically significant). More interesting is that both the moratorium and drought variables reduce consumption enormously. Their combined impact decreases water use by nearly 60 . The elasticity with respect to price is -.70, and each 10-cent increase in price reduces consumption by about 300 HCF. As before, however, price increases of 5 cents were closer to what actually occurred so that reductions of approximately 150 HCF were realized. Still the 150-HCF reduction translates into a 25% decrease.

To summarize the findings from Tables 2-5, while there are some interesting differences across the four communities, the results are by and large consistent with expectations. In particular, it is apparent that water consumption for both domestic and agricultural users may be altered by changes in price, conservation appeals, or both. In addition, it appears that, as anticipated, the price elasticities are somewhat larger for agricultural consumers than for domestic consumers.

With the brief discussion of individual communities behind us, we can turn to two additional questions: what are the average effects across the communities, and is there any evidence that what happens in one community affects what happens in others? The former addresses whether there are summary statements that can be made in general while the latter addresses whether we have seriously misspecified our time-series models by ignoring cross-community effects.

Both questions require that the data be combined in a pooled cross-sectional and time-series design and statistical procedures that adjust for correlated residuals over time, correlated residuals across communities, and different residual variances across communities (Kmenta, 1971: 512-514; Berk et al., 1979).

Table 6 shows the results and we will focus first on domestic consumption. As the model at the top of the table indicates, the specification is much like our earlier formulations. The major substantive difference is the introduction of dummy variables for three of the four communities to capture the variation in mean levels of consumption across water districts.

By and large, the exogenous variables perform as expected. The climatic factors have their usual effects with t-values well in excess of 1.64. The community dummy variables pick up substantial community variation in consumption per account. Conservation programs associated with the drought reduce water use by an average of over 5 HCF which amounts to about a 15 reduction relative to the overall mean across communities. The moratorium conservation programs reduce water consumption by about 2.3 HCF, while every 10-cent increase in price reduces consumption by about 1.3 HCF. The percent reduction for moratorium is about 7 (compared to the pre-moratorium mean) and the elasticity for price is -.09. These are modest, but nontrivial effects. In short, despite some variability across communities reflected in our time-series results, the predicted patterns surface when the data are pooled; the model holds "on the average."[7]

The cross-community correlations at the bottom of the table suggest that some residual shared covariation exists. In an effort to explain these correlations, we explored the possibility that conservation effects in one community affect the water consumption in others. (There is no reason to believe that changes in price in one community affect consumption in others. And the climatic factors are identical across communities.) Unfortunately, since the drought dummy variable is defined identically for all communities, it could not have such impacts. In contrast, the timing of moratoriums differ, and we introduced a variable to capture the impact of the Goleta moratorium on the other three communities. The Goleta moratorium was the earliest and most dramatic conservation effort before the drought, and we reasoned that if cross-community effects existed, they would be found for the Goleta moratorium. We were disappointed; the additional variable had virtually no impact. Consequently, we are inclined to treat the cross-community correlations as a result of seasonal patterns missed by temperature and rainfall. Perhaps more important, there is now less reason to suspect that our time-series models were in error because of a failure to include the cross-community effects of conservation programs.

The results for the pooled agricultural analysis are shown in the right-hand panel. Overall, the findings appear even stronger than for the

TABLE 6

Pooled Analysis

$$DC_{it} \text{ or } AC_{it} = \beta_0 + \beta_1 M_{it} + \beta_2 D_{it} + \beta_3 T_{it} + \beta_4 R_{it} + \beta_5 R_{i,t-1} + \beta_6 P_{it} +$$

$$\beta_7 Carp_{it} + \beta_8 Mont_{it} + \beta_9 Gol_{it} + a_{it}$$

$$E(a_{it}^2) = \sigma_{ii} \text{ (Heteroskedasticity)}$$

$$E(a_{it}a_{jt}) = \sigma_{ij} \text{ (Cross Correlation)}$$

$$a_{it} = \rho_i a_{i,t-1} + u_{it} \text{ (Temporal Correlation)}$$

Variable	Domestic Consumption		Agricultural Consumption	
	Regression Coefficient	t-value	Regression Coefficient	t-value
Intercept	-14.81	-3.08	-478.31	-3.09
Moratorium	-2.32	-2.57	-68.93	-2.72
Drought	-5.34	-5.16	-85.00	-2.63
Temperature	0.65	9.03	17.94	7.83
Rain (at t)	-0.27	-2.05	-6.89	-1.69
Rain (at t-1)	-0.60	-4.67	-12.22	-2.94
Price	-1.33	-1.82	-190.58	-8.64
Carpinteria	6.00	5.48	-40.09	-1.20
Montecito	22.81	8.80	152.41	4.47
Goleta	12.05	11.28	255.42	6.03
Price Elasticity	-0.09		-0.57	
$\hat{\rho}_{Gol}$	.17		.44	
$\hat{\rho}_{Sum}$	.70		.45	
$\hat{\rho}_{Mont}$	.54		.30	
$\hat{\rho}_{Carp}$	.21		.41	

Cross Correlations Among u_{it}

	(1)	(2)	(3)	(4)	(1)	(2)	(3)	(4)
Goleta (1)	1.00	.31	.12	.71	1.00	-.08	.28	.26
Summerland (2)		1.00	.00	.31		1.00	-.05	.18
Montecito (3)			1.00	.11			1.00	.35
Carpinteria (4)				1.00				1.00

domestic consumption data. With the exception of the dummy variable for
Carpinteria, all of the t-values are in excess of 1.64. The climatic factors behave as expected, and all of the policy-relevant variables show important effects. The moratorium conservation programs reduce consumption
by nearly 69 HCF. The drought conservation programs reduce consumption by
85 HCF. These reflect decreases of approximately 15" relative to the mean
before the conservation programs were initiated. Every 10-cent increase
in price reduces water use by over 190 HCF, and the elasticity is -.57.
Clearly, agricultural users are once again more responsive to price than
domestic users.

As in the case of domestic consumption, we introduced a variable to
capture the effects of the Goleta moratorium on the other three communities. While the cross-community correlations were not particularly large,
they were significantly different from zero. Again, however, we were disappointed. The introduction of the Goleta moratorium variable (for cross-
community effects) left the estimates of the residual standard error
unchanged and only served to inflate coefficient standard errors.[8]

CONCLUSIONS

Our findings indicate that it is indeed possible to alter consumer attitudes through water conservation programs that in many instances fall far
short of outright coercion. For water consumption at least, the dilemma of
the commons can be enormously affected by information and moral appeals. In
other words, it is possible to partially override the paradoxical and
counter-productive consequences inherent in the provision of many public
goods, and this may be accomplished without side payments or substantial restrictions on individual freedom. It is also possible to alter water consumption by manipulating its price. This gives policy makers a tool in
times of scarcity that perhaps avoids the uncertainty and vagueness of noneconomic approaches. Again, the dilemma of the commons can be altered without resorting to dictatorial measures.

On the other hand, with our data alone it is impossible to determine
whether policy makers interested in water conservation should resort to conservation programs, price increases or some combination of the two. To
begin, we have not provided estimates of the differential effectiveness of
different kinds of conservation measures. Similarly, our estimates of the
impact of price gloss over more subtle changes in pricing structure that may
well be important. With only four communities we are also unable to effectively consider how conservation programs and price alterations interact
with community characteristics: the mix of users, income levels, and the

like. Finally, the introduction of conservation programs and/or price changes has a number of implications beyond water consumption that ultimately cannot be ignored. Dramatic price increases, for example, may so reduce consumption that revenues significantly decline. We are pursuing these and other questions with a much larger sample of California communities, but at this point our overall message is quite simple: both price and conservation seem to work. One can reduce water consumption with appeals to narrow self-interest using price as the primary vehicle, or reduce water consumption with appeals to group interest using intelligent conservation programs.

FOOTNOTES

1.   Data on a much larger sample of communities across the State of California has been collected and that material is being used to extend the analyses presented here.

2.   We distinguish here between pure public goods of the Samuelsonian type and "crowdable" public goods.

3.   For a detailed application of the theory of marginal cost pricing to the water industry, see Hirshleifer, De Haven and Milliman (1960). For practical applications see Hanke (1978) and Cooley and LaCivita (1979).

4.   Sewell and Rouche use an average price weighted by the amount of consumption in each price block. This is also inapprorpate because, again, the relevant variable is the marginal price of the next unit. Howe and Linaweaver, Wong and Grima use the correct price variable, although Grima considers only communities having one marginal price.

   The aggregate data also caused serious problems in our efforts to construct a reasonable income variable to capture variation across the four communities and over time. The only income variable available was the mean family income for each community in 1970. An income series was constructed by adjusting income by the state-wide changes in disposable income over the sample period. Due to the crudeness of this variable, its performance in preliminary models in Goleta was very poor. Moreover, other empirical evidence suggests that income performs poorly in time-series regressions, but may be important when cross-sectional data are used (e.g., Headly, 1963). Consequently, income is not included in the time-series analyses for each community. In addition, for the pooled analyses, the necessity of employing dummy variables for each community (to capture different intercepts), prevented the introduction of our measure of income (due to multicollinearity). Hence, income will not figure in the results reported in this paper.

5.   This does not standardize for changes in the mix of accounts and, in particular, changes in the average size of accounts. However, while all four communities experienced some growth in the number of accounts over the eight years in question, there is no evidence that larger users were replacing smaller users (or vice versa) within either the domestic or agricultural categories. In addition, evidence of per-account temporal trends would have been revealed through our Box-Jenkins procedures and simple adjustments could have been made. None was necessary.

6.   We chose 36 months as the proper lag for the chi-square tests somewhat arbitrarily. However, we also tried several other lags and the conclusions were always the same.

7. Probably the major vulnerability of the estimation procedures we are using for the pooled data is the restriction to AR1 models in the four communities. If the AR1 models are in error, our regression coefficients are at least inefficient and the standard errors are inconsistent. In order to evaluate the appropriateness of the AR1 models, we examined the plots of the autocorrelation function and the partial autocorrelation function for the residuals of an OLS model. The plots and significance tests typically revealed modest correlations at lags of one and twelve months, but little of the more complicated patterns found for the data from single communities. Apparently, the pooling process and the (in effect) averaging of regression coefficients across communities "smooths" the patterns of serial correlation. The correlations at a lag of one are addressed in the error specification, while the correlations at a lag of twelve for each of the four communities are captured in the cross-community residual correlations.

8. Much as in the case of domestic consumption, we were concerned about the restriction of AR1 models for the serial correlations. And, as before, we examined the OLS residuals. The same patterns of correlations at lags of one and twelve months surfaced. Thus, our pooled estimates seem appropriate.

REFERENCES

Bain, J.S., R.E. Caves and J. Margolis
  1966   Northern California's Water Industry: The Comparative Efficiency of Public Enterprise in Developing a Scarce Resource. Baltimore: The Johns Hopkins Press.

Berk, R.A., D.M. Hoffman, J.E. Maki, D. Rauma and H. Wong
  1979   "An Introduction to Estimation Procedures for Pooled Cross-Sectional and Time Series Data." Evaluation Quarterly 3, 4.

Box, G.E.P., and G.M. Jenkins
  1976   Time Series Analysis: Forecasting and Control. San Francisco: Holden-Day.

Box, G.E.P., and G.C. Tiao
  1975   "Intervention Analysis with Applications in Economic and Environmental Problems." Journal of American Statistical Association 70, 1.

Brechener, K.C.
  1977   "An Experimental Analysis of Social Traps." Journal of Experimental Social Psychology 13: 552-564.

Brewer, M.B.
          "Ingroup Bias in the Minimal Intergroup Situation: A Cognitive-Motivational Analysis." Psychological Bulletin (in press).

Bruvold, W.
  1978   "Consumer Response to Urban Drought in Central California." Technical Report, University of California, Berkeley.

Cooley, T.F., and C.J. LaCivita
  1979   "Allocative Efficiency and Distributional Equity in Water Pricing and Finance: A Post-Proposition 13 Analysis." Proceedings of the Santa Barbara Tax Limitation Conference, December 1978, supplement to the National Tax Journal 32, 2: 215-227.

Dawes, R.M.
  1975   "Formal Models of Dilemmas in Social Decision Making." In M.F. Kaplan and S. Schwartz (eds.), Human Judgment and Decision Processes. New York: Academic Press.

Dawes, R.M., J. McTavish and H. Shaklee
    1977   "Behavior, Communication, and Assumptions about Other People's
        Behavior in a Commons Dilemma Situation." Journal of Person-
        ality and Social Psychology 35: 1-11.

Gottlieb, M.
    1963   "Urban Domestic Demand for Water: A Kansas Case Study." Land
        Economics 39, 2: 204-210.

Granger, C.W.J., and P. Newbold
    1977   Forecasting Economic Time Series. New York: Academic Press.

Grima, A.P.
    1972   Residential Water Demand: Alternative Choices for Management.
        Toronto: University of Toronto Press.

Hanke, S.H.
    1978   "Pricing as a Conservation Tool: An Economist's Dream Come
        True?" In D. Holts and S. Sebastian (eds.), Municipal Water
        Systems. Bloomington: Indiana University Press.

Hanke, S.H., and J.J. Boland
    1971   "Water Requirements or Water Demands?" Journal of American
        Water Works Association 63: 677-681.

Hardin, G.
    1968   "The Tragedy of the Commons." Science 162: 1243-1248.

Haver, C.B., and J.R. Winter
    1963   Future Water Supply in London: An Economic Appraisal. London,
        Ontario: Public Utilities Commission (January).

Headley, J.C.
    1963   "The Relation of Family Income and Use of Water for Residential
        and Commercial Purposes in the San Francisco-Oakland Metropoli-
        tan Area." Land Economics 39, 4: 441-449.

Hirshleifer, J., J.C. DeHaven and J.W. Milliman
    1960   Water Supply: Economics, Technology and Policy. Chicago: Uni-
        versity of Chicago Press.

Howe, C.W., and F.P. Linaweaver, Jr.
    1967   "The Impact of Price on Residential Water Demand and its Rela-
        tion to System Demand and Price Structure." Water Resources
        Research 3, 1: 13-22.

Kelley, H.H., and J. Grzelak
    1972   "Conflict Between Individual and Common Interest in an n-Person
        Relationship." Journal of Personality and Social Psychology 21:
        190-197.

Kmenta, Jan
    1971   Elements of Econometrics. New York: Macmillan.

Linder, D.E.
    1977   "Patterns of Energy Utilization and Conservation: A Social Trap
        Perspective." Symposium paper presented at the American Psycho-
        logical Association Annual Convention.

Lipsey, M.W.
    1977   "Personal Antecedents and Consequences of Ecologically Respon-
        sible Behavior." Journal Supplement Abstract Service, MS. 1521.

McClelland, L.
    1977   "Encouraging Energy Conservation as a Social Psychological Prob-
        lem." Paper presented at the American Psychological Association
        Annual Convention.

Marwell, G., and R.E. Ames
    1979   "Experiments on the Provision of Public Goods. I. Resources,
        Interest, Group Size, and the Free-Rider Problem." American
        Journal of Sociology 84: 1335-1360.

Messick, D.M.
1973   "To Join or Not to Join: An Approach to the Unionization Decision." Organizational Behavior and Human Performance 10: 145-156.

1974   "When a Little 'Group Interest' Goes a Long Way: A Note on Social Motives and Union Joining." Organizational Behavior and Human Performance 12: 331-334.

Platt, J.
1973   "Social Traps." American Psychologist 28: 641-651.

Schelling, T.
1971   "On the Ecology of Micromotives." The Public Interest 25: 59-98.

Seligman, C., J.M. Darley and L.J. Becker
   "Behavioral Approaches to Residential Energy Conservation." Energy and Buildings (in press).

Sewell, W.R.D., and L. Rouche
1974   "Peak Load Pricing and Urban Water Management: Victoria, B.C., A Case Study." Natural Resources Journal 14, 3.

Stern, P.C.
1976   "Effects of Incentives and Education on Resource Conservation Decisions in a Simulated Commons Dilemma." Journal of Personality and Social Psychology 34: 1285-1292.

Talarowski, F.S.
1977   "Effects of Moralizing and Individual Incentive in Decomposed Commons Dilemmas." Unpublished M.A. thesis, University of California, Santa Barbara.

Talarowski, F.S., and C.G. McClintock
1978   "The Conservation of Domestic Water: A Social Psychological Study." Final Report to the Water Resources Center, University of California, Davis.

Thompson, P.T., and J. McTavish
1976   "Energy Problems: Public Beliefs, Attitudes and Behaviors." Urban Environmental Studies Institute, Grand Valley State College, Allendale, Michigan.

Watkins, G.A.
1974   "Developing a 'Water Concern' Scale." The Journal of Environmental Education 5: 54-58.

Wong, S.
1972   "A Model on Municipal Water Demand: A Case Study of Northeastern Illinois." Land Economics 48, 34.

VIII

EVALUATION OF PUBLIC FINANCIAL POLICY

This section reflects a larger view of the management of the federal budget and the economy and the funding and operation of social programs. They focus on two themes: What are the causes of the increasing, and chronic inflation and unemployment? And what role can social programs and policies play in improving the current situation? As such, all of the studies concern policies that deal with some structural problem in the economy. The study by Perry attempts to explain the nature of recent inflation by developing and testing the several components of what he characterizes as a "mainline" model of the economy. In effect, this model argues that a Phillips' Curve relation holds in the economy. Prices respond fully to wages (which are the major determinant of the costs of production), but the mark-up of prices over wages is variable. Prices in the model respond not only to demand conditions but also to past changes in wages, prices, and profits as well as to expectations about future changes in these variables. Fiscal policy alone cannot be effective against inflation, because the trade-off between unemployment and inflation is small— a 1% increase in unemployment (about one million workers) buys much less than a 1% reduction in inflation. Thus, the cost of this "cure" is very high in lost employment and output. Perry also considers the argument that monetary and fiscal policies have not worked because the federal government lacked the political commitment and will to state that it intends to restrain demand until inflationary inertia is broken. While not denying that this is an issue, he doubts that a more determined stance on fiscal and monetary restraint is the entire answer. Thus, Perry argues that measures should be adopted that create disinflationary "shocks," though specific examples are not given. His overall anti-inflationary program becomes somewhat eclectic—some combination of disinflationary shocks, a tax-based incomes policy, and monetary and fiscal policies.

The studies by Ehrenberg and by Feldstein and Pellechio point to several structural factors that may contribute to the high unemployment, slow growth nature of the current economy. Feldstein and Pellechio focus on the possibility that the Social Security program may be inducing a reduction in the private savings rate and aggregate capital accumulation. And their empirical results support this view. These require corroboration, but they are sufficiently striking to warrant special efforts on the part of the federal government to determine the true nature and extent of the effect.

Ehrenberg's study complements that by Feldstein and Pellechio, pointing out that a variety of retirement policies and programs can result in increased unemployment, misallocation of resources, and undesired income distribution effects. None of the desired beneficial effects of these programs are without their attendant costs. Thus, an effort to reduce the risk in pension investment portfolios implies that high risk but high yield investments will be avoided. This can lead to lower growth and future unemployment. In short, these programs do not operate in a vacuum. Their effects are often interdependent, and can lead to large cumulative effects even when the marginal effect of each is small. Though Ehrenberg only considers retirement policies, his theme that regulation can be responsible for inflationary distortions is a common one among policy makers, academics, and journalists. The legislation usually fails to consider these interrelations. Thus, although it is likely that certain phenomena, such as that investigated by Feldstein and Pellechio, will ultimately be dealt with after sufficient debate and prodding, subtler inefficiencies benefiting clearly defined pressure groups, but with costs widely spread across the economy, may linger on much longer (see the discussion by Mead in Part VII).

Thus, with one diverse constellation of programs having structural effects on behavior that raise the nonaccelerating inflationary rate of unemployment, the response is to look to other structural programs to counteract the resulting unemployment, since the potentially inflationary and unemployment-creating programs are either too difficult to rectify in a democratic political system or are socially valued for other functions they serve.

Finally, we come to subsidized public and private sector employment programs designed to reduce structural unemployment. Here again the debate is joined. All agree that public service employment is an effective means of combating short-run employment associated with the business cycle. The question is, what long run effects can it have on structural unemployment? The debate has been lengthy and often heated. Estimates of the displacement effect (and thus, of the net job creation) due to subsidized employment have varied widely. The range of estimates is currently between 20- to 60% (the study by Gramlich in this section yields an estimate near the upper end of this range). Different methodologies have produced different results. Thus, it is to the credit of governmental officials that a major social experiment has been mounted—the Employment Opportunity Pilot Projects—to measure the effects of such a program. The work by Bishop et al. lays out a design to assess this policy option. Success in this area awaits an equal commitment to analyzing more fully the Social Security program, the Occupational Safety and Health Act, and a host of other regulatory programs whose benefits and costs are not completely understood.

30

The U.S. economy has been beset for the past decade with simultaneous high unemployment and high and increasing inflation. Both impose real costs on society and change the income distribution in undesirable ways. And any policy designed to alleviate one seems to worsen the other. This study analyzes the determinants of the current inflation and evaluates various policy measures to overcome it. It complements the studies by Gramlich and Bishop et al. that evaluate methods of reducing unemployment and increasing output through various subsidy and grant programs while attempting to minimize inflationary effects. (The study by Ehrenberg also deals with the adverse structural effects of retirement programs, some of which contribute to unemployment and inflation.)

Perry begins with an analysis of the aggregate economy, focusing on those factors that have produced the observed inertia in the inflationary rate. This "mainline" model of the economy assumes that most prices are closely related to the costs of production, with the largest costs being labor costs. Prices respond fully to wages, but the markup of prices over wages responds sluggishly to overall demand conditions, regardless of the stage of the business cycle. Wages respond to the state of demand but also to other endogenous variables such as past wages, profits, prices, and to expectations concerning each of these. These influences on wage determination affect the inertia of wage and price inflation and vary by industry, with low wage industries responding more to unemployment, while wages in high paying industries respond more to price inflation and translate a higher proportion of price increases into wage increases.

The development of an appropriate anti-inflationary policy depends on isolating the determinants of such inflation. Policy has historically focused on three variables: past rates of wage inflation, past increases in the consumer price index, and past increases in the nonfarm private deflator (the market basket of goods produced and sold by firms). We would like to estimate the separate effects of these on current inflation, but this has proven difficult to measure accurately. And while each of these factors contributes to maintaining the inertia of the inflationary process, past wage inflation appears to explain most of the current wage inflation.

What, then, influences the rate of wage change? Perry demonstrates that unemployment slows wage inflation and that the 1970s have not departed from earlier periods in this regard. But anti-inflationary effects from this source have been small and quite costly in lost output. An extra percentage point of employment, which now implies the unemployment of about one million workers, would lower the inflationary rate by 0.3 of 1% in the first year and by 0.7 of 1% if continued for 3 years. Annual lost production would amount to about $60 billion. Counteracting this, it appears that modest upward shocks in inflation from such things as rising food or import prices could offset the gains purchased by the unemployment.

The role of budget deficits and monetary growth on the inflationary process are also investigated by Perry, as are the contribution of such social welfare programs as unemployment insurance and the federal minimum wage. The latter two programs are judged to have a potentially positive but small effect on inflation, but in any case, neither program has recently changed significantly. On the other hand, considerable controversy concerns the casual role of government deficits and the money supply in the inflationary process. Empirical analysis indicates that a positive role for government deficits can be decisively rejected. Perry also argues that the growth of the money supply has no "additional, special role" in causing inflation; but deficits and changes in the money supply affect aggregate demand. This, in turn, affects the economic environment of firms, thereby influencing wages and prices. Thus, Perry is pessimistic about reliance on monetary and fiscal restraint alone to control inflation.

As a competing hypothesis, Perry considers Fellner's (1976) view that inflationary inertia results from a self-fulfilling prophecy. This expectation, in turn, is based on a judgment that the government will not take the steps and bear the costs necessary to stop inflation. Fellner proposes that a strong anti-inflationary stance, with a clear intention to restrain demand as much and as long as necessary to choke off inflation, would have the desired effect on inflation at acceptable rates of unemployment. Perry discusses this proposal and notes that much of the inflationary inertia is backward-looking rather than expectational—forward-looking. Thus, it is not clear how much an effect this strategy would have on inflation, even when linked with the small effects the resulting increased unemployment would have in restraining inflation.

In conclusion, Perry's policy proposals are designed to fit into his own interpretation of the wage-price spiral. He recommends an attempt to induce directly cost and price reductions to provide disinflationary "shocks." The disinflationary shocks would then filter through subsequent stages of the wage-price spiral. A tax-based incomes policy would break into the wage-price spiral both by influencing the decision process and also the wages and prices to which the system responds. These proposals are seen as complementary to standard fiscal and monetary policy and the strategy proposed by Fellner.

REFERENCE

FELLNER, W. J. (1976) Towards a Reconstruction of Macroeconomics: Problems of Theory and Policy. Washington, DC: American Enterprise Institute.

Slowing the Wage-Price Spiral
The Macroeconomic View

George L. Perry

OVER A DECADE has passed since the standard remedy of demand restraint was first urged to combat inflation. By the mid-1960s, many economists, including those at the Council of Economic Advisers, believed war expenditures were pushing the economy into the inflationary, excess-demand zone and recommended tax increases to help restrain aggregate demand. We cannot know how different subsequent economic performance would have been if that advice had been heeded. But it was not. Unemployment continued to decline into 1969, and the inflation rate in consumer prices rose above 5 percent. Inflation, by then, had become firmly entrenched in economic decisionmaking. When demand finally fell and unemployment rose in the recession of 1970, the inflation rate scarcely budged. Both average hourly earnings and the private nonfarm price deflator rose faster during 1970–71 than in any year of the 1960s.

Many observers concluded that a recession deeper than that of 1970 would be needed to stop inflation. In summer 1971, the Nixon administration tried a different cure, imposing wage and price controls that lasted in modified form until April 1974. These controls slowed the inflation rate for most wages and prices. But by the time the controls expired, higher prices for food and fuel, which were largely unrelated to the state of demand, and for industrial raw materials, which reflected strong world demand and speculative buying, had created double-digit rates of overall

Note: I am grateful to Jesse M. Abraham for his extensive research assistance.

Table 1. Wage and Price Inflation in the United States, Selected Periods, 1954–78

Average annual percent change

Period	Private nonfarm economy			Consumer price index
	Compensation per hour	Hourly earnings index	Price deflator	
Post-Korean War (1954–59)	4.6	4.1	2.4	1.4
Early 1960s (1960–65)	4.0	3.1	1.1	1.3
Late 1960s (1966–69)	6.4	5.6	3.7	3.8
Precontrol 1970s (1970–71)	6.7	6.8	4.7	5.1
Controls (1972–73)	6.8	6.5	3.6	4.8
Food-fuel explosion (1974–75)	9.5	8.5	10.7	10.1
1976	8.7	7.2	5.2	5.8
1977	8.8	7.3	5.4	6.5
1978:1ᵃ	9.1ᵇ	8.0ᵇ	6.3	6.6

Source: U.S. Bureau of Labor Statistics.
a. Percent change from the first quarter of 1977 to first quarter of 1978.
b. Without the large increase in the minimum wage in January 1978, the increases would have been an estimated 8.9 percent for compensation and 7.6 percent for hourly earnings.

inflation. Together with a nonaccommodating aggregate-demand policy, this price explosion also started a recession that was double the size of the average previous postwar recession and that lasted until spring 1975.

It is now three years since the trough of this deepest postwar recession. By the end of that recession, inflation had slowed sharply from its 1974 pace, but further improvement was slight once recovery began. From 1975 through 1977, all available measures of tightness in either labor markets or product markets registered ample slack. And no large upward movements have occurred in particular components of the price level since the Organization of Petroleum Exporting Countries increased oil prices in 1974. Yet despite all these disinflationary developments, the rate of inflation, by any broad measure, has continued at a historically high rate and now shows signs of creeping still further upward.

Table 1 summarizes the inflation in the economy since the Korean War as measured by four alternative indexes: compensation per hour, the hourly earnings index, and the price deflator, all of which are averages for the private nonfarm economy; and the consumer price index. Except in 1974 and 1975, when controls ended and oil prices soared, the three measures for the private nonfarm economy have moved closely together, with compensation per hour and the price deflator differing by approximately the trend rate of growth in labor productivity. The consumer price index is more volatile than the deflator. They have differed noticeably when the relative prices of food or imports changed a great deal, although the inclusion of these prices is not the only difference between the indexes. By any of these measures, inflation has been noticeably faster in the 1970s than in previous periods. It has been faster since 1975 than in the early 1970s. And it has been faster over the most recent four quarters than in previous years of the present recovery.

Inflation is unpopular. It hampers policymaking and inhibits the pursuit of high employment. This paper provides a basis for evaluating alternative approaches to slowing it.

The Mainline Model

In this section I briefly outline what I perceive to be the important characteristics of the U.S. economy that have led to the present stubborn inflation. Unlike many journalists describing the stagflation period, I do not conclude that economists fail to understand the economy. And unlike some professional writers of this period, I do not conclude that the Keynesian revolution got everything wrong. However, we have learned during the past ten years that the Keynesian analysis stops short of adequately modeling the inflation process.

Let me begin by describing the essential features of what I call the mainline model of the U.S. macroeconomy. It offers a description of macroeconomic behavior that is compatible with a broad range of more specific models that would have similar policy implications. I later discuss some alternative views of the economy and of the current stagflation that are not consistent with this mainline model and that have policy implications that I believe are basically misleading.

In the mainline model, wage and price behavior are closely linked, and there is at least some mutual causality between them. Because the effect of wages on prices is more predictable and better established, it is useful to begin analyzing the inflation problem by describing the macroeconomics of labor markets.

Wages respond to the tightness of labor markets but not enough to avoid fluctuations in employment brought about by corresponding fluctuations in demand. Thus, something like a Phillips curve exists, at least for periods that are relevant to policymakers and to the conduct of economic affairs, and for the range of unemployment actually experienced. Within this framework, average wages begin to rise at an inflationary rate while unemployment is still well above frictional levels.

Wages also respond to what has been happening to wages, prices, profit margins, or all three, or to what is expected to happen to them. All these alternatives are accommodated in the mainline model and are discussed further below. What is important is that they all predict considerable inertia in wage inflation. The response of wages to variations in demand is characteristically sluggish.

Some prices are sensitive to demand, particularly prices of industrial raw materials and goods whose costs include a large component of costs for raw materials. Agricultural prices are sensitive to world crop conditions, and prices of tradable goods respond to competition from goods produced abroad. But prices in most of the private sector are closely related to variable costs, the most important of which are labor costs. Given wages, these prices are only slightly affected by demand, and consequently their movement in response to demand variations is also sluggish.

With the possible exception of situations in which unemployment is exceptionally low or industrial operating rates are exceptionally high, variations in aggregate demand lead primarily to variations in output, employment, and unemployment. There can be sustained unemployment arising from inadequate demand. At the aggregate level, the response to variations in demand is similar whether the variation comes from fiscal policy, monetary policy, an unexplained change in velocity, or from some shift in demand from the private sector or from foreign demand for exports.

Within this general description, a number of issues that are important to the design of anti-inflation policy remain open. What is the response of inflation to alternative paths of real activity? Are wages affected by past wages, past living costs, past price margins or profitability, or all three? Is the inertia of inflation essentially backward looking or forward looking; and to the extent that expectations matter, how can they be affected? These are difficult questions that are not easily settled by empirical evidence. But that is a place to begin.

The Empirical Mainline Model

The empirical counterpart to the model of the inflation process that I have sketched has been presented before with many variations. Although the level of aggregation may differ, the essentials are an equation relating a price deflator for the private sector to wage costs, to materials costs, and possibly to some additional effects from demand and the prices of competing imports; and an equation relating wages to the tightness of the labor market and to past or expected future inflation.

I do not present any new results on the price equations. Robert Gordon has recently reviewed the aggregate evidence and reaffirmed that prices change in proportion to wage changes.[1] Other factors also have an effect, including the costs of raw materials, competing imports, and to a small extent, variations in demand. However, including them in the explanation does not diminish the importance of labor costs.

The principal unsettled issues are concerned with the causes of inertia in wage inflation. I turn first to some disaggregated evidence from the 1960s and 1970s.

DISAGGREGATED WAGE CHANGES

The first evidence of the stubbornness of inflation came when average wages and prices failed to decelerate much despite rising unemployment after 1969. The behavior of wages in particular sectors is noteworthy during this period. Some wages are set under collective bargaining agreements, frequently with three-year contracts. Many factors can enter into union wage demands in such bargaining situations, including wage levels elsewhere and living costs. There is no well-established model of what unions can successfully bargain for and, especially when contracts are negotiated infrequently and prices and other wages have changed between contracts, new settlements can bear little relation to current unemployment rates. While wages set under collective bargaining may represent an especially obvious departure from short-run market clearing in wage setting, virtually no wages are set in auction markets. Long-term attachments between firms and workers are useful to both sides and characterize a large portion of the job market. In such situations, equity, which may embrace relative wages or inflation, becomes an important consideration in wage setting. Both unionization and long-term attachments characterize some industries more than others. As a consequence, wages in different industries do not move in parallel under changing economic conditions.

High- and Low-Wage Industries. A random sample of 39 industries at the three-digit level of aggregation was divided into groups with high, medium, and low wages according to the average of their hourly earnings

1. Robert J. Gordon, "Can the Inflation of the 1970s be Explained?" *BPEA, 1: 1977*, pp. 253–77.

over the 1959–76 period. For each group, the following table shows the average wage increases during the 1960s and 1970s and the difference between the averages for the two periods.

Industry classification	Average annual percent increase in hourly earnings		Acceleration
	1959–69	1970–76	
Low wage	3.8	6.5	2.8
Medium wage	3.7	6.9	3.3
High wage	3.5	7.8	4.3

After rising slightly more slowly than wages in the low-wage group during the 1960s, wages in the high-wage group accelerated 4.3 percentage points in the 1970s, compared with an acceleration of 2.8 points for the low-wage group. The consumer price index accelerated by 4.0 points over the same interval. The acceleration of wages in the high-wage industries kept pace over the 1970–76 interval with the acceleration in the consumer price index.

The coefficient of variation of wage levels among the industries sampled declined gradually from 0.20 in 1959 to 0.18 in 1968.[2] It then rose gradually to 0.21 in 1974 and then to 0.23 in 1975 and 0.24 in 1976. Over the period from 1959 to 1976, an equation of the form developed by Wachter to explain the coefficient of variation (CV) among industry wages produced the following estimates:[3]

(1)
$$CV = 0.20 - 0.10\, u^{*-1} + 0.26\, \Delta \ln CP,$$
$$(12.0)\ (-3.2) \qquad\qquad (2.7)$$
Durbin-Watson $= 1.1$; standard error $= 0.11$,

where u^{*-1} is the inverse of the weighted unemployment rate and CP is the consumer price index. The numbers in parentheses in all equations are t statistics.

Wachter reasoned that wage dispersion was cyclical. He found that the variation was reduced by inflation, which was closely correlated with unemployment in his sample period. Equation 1 supports Wachter's cyclical conclusion that lower unemployment reduces wage dispersion; but it im-

2. Only 38 of the 39 industries were included in the coefficient of variation because wage data for industry 421–3 were available only for 1964–76.
3. Michael L. Wachter, "The Wage Process: An Analysis of the Early 1970s," *BPEA, 2:1974*, pp. 507–24.

plies that inflation independently increases it. Stagflation increases it on both counts.

Equations for annual wage increases in individual industries also reveal the relatively stronger effect of inflation and the weaker effect of unemployment in the high-wage industries. Tables 2a and 2b show simple Phillips curves for each of the 26 industries in the low-wage and high-wage groups. In each case, the change in hourly earnings adjusted for overtime was regressed on the average increase in the CPI over the two previous years and on the inverse of weighted unemployment.[4] A dummy variable equal to 1 in 1974 and 1975 was included in each equation to avoid giving undue weight to the observations for those two years. Using annual data, wages in both years were strongly affected by the combination of food and fuel inflation and the end of controls. This situation is examined more carefully below using aggregate wage equations.

Although the individual industry equations are often unsatisfactory, the average coefficient in each group fits the expected pattern. The average coefficient on unemployment is 11.5 for the low-wage industries and 6.8 for the high-wage industries; the average coefficients on the CPI are 0.6 and 0.8, respectively. Similar results are also obtained when the CPI is replaced by average hourly earnings as the lagged inflation variable. The change in the minimum wage makes no contribution as an additional explanatory variable, even in the low-wage industries. I assume this negative result reflects the poor quality of equations for individual industries. In Gramlich's careful analysis of minimum wages, a 1 percent change in the minimum adds 0.03 percent to average wages.[5] The impact on wages in low-wage industries should be many times larger than this estimate for the aggregate.

Union Wages. For the past two years, data from the employment cost index have been available for wage and salary increases in occupations both covered and not covered by collective bargaining agreements. Covered wages rose 8.1 and 7.6 percent during 1976 and 1977, respectively (fourth quarter to fourth quarter). These increases are 1.3 and 1.0 percentage points more than the rise in uncovered wages in the two years.

For years before 1976, effective union wage changes can be compared

---

4. The overtime adjustment could not be made for nonmanufacturing industries. Those equations refer to hourly earnings.

5. Edward M. Gramlich, "Impact of Minimum Wages on Other Wages, Employment, and Family Incomes," *BPEA, 2:1976*, pp. 409–51.

Table 2a. Disaggregated Wage Change Equations: Low-Wage Industries[a]

Percent

Standard industrial classification code	Independent variable			Standard error	Durbin-Watson statistic
	Unemployment	Lagged CPI	1974–75 dummy		
23	12.60 (2.4)	0.46 (2.4)	1.79 (1.2)	1.74	1.7
22	13.40 (3.9)	0.54 (4.3)	1.87 (2.0)	1.13	1.6
203	8.90 (2.8)	0.73 (6.2)	3.51 (4.0)	1.05	1.4
25	16.02 (7.0)	0.53 (6.3)	2.39 (3.8)	0.76	1.8
39	14.31 (6.7)	0.53 (6.8)	2.51 (4.3)	0.70	2.4
367	10.18 (2.7)	0.41 (3.0)	4.67 (4.5)	1.25	2.4
365	13.12 (2.9)	0.64 (3.9)	3.86 (3.1)	1.47	0.9
209	7.00 (2.5)	0.67 (6.6)	1.21 (1.6)	0.92	1.3
243	14.35 (6.8)	0.88 (11.4)	1.85 (3.2)	0.70	2.7
FIRE[b]	7.82 (3.5)	0.38 (4.6)	1.81 (2.9)	0.75	2.2
364	7.77 (2.5)	0.61 (5.5)	2.58 (3.1)	1.01	1.4
52–59	10.77 (5.6)	0.39 (5.5)	1.87 (3.5)	0.63	2.6
375–9	13.83 (2.7)	0.54 (2.8)	1.48 (1.0)	1.72	2.5
Mean	11.5	0.56	2.4	…	…

See sources and footnotes for table 2b.

with changes in the average hourly earnings index, which includes both union and nonunion workers. During most of the 1960s, effective median union wage increases lagged slightly behind the increases in average hourly earnings. Beginning in 1968, data on mean increases are available that show union increases equaling average increases outside the union sector in 1968–69 and then outpacing them in subsequent years.

Table 3 compares the percentage increase in union wages with the increases in the index of average hourly earnings for 1970–77. Union

Table 2b. Disaggregated Wage Change Equations: High-Wage Industries[a]
Percent

Standard industrial classification code	Independent variable			Standard error	Durbin-Watson statistic
	Unemployment	Lagged CPI	1974–75 dummy		
366	6.39 (2.1)	0.71 (6.3)	2.28 (2.7)	1.00	2.2
357	6.49 (1.8)	0.47 (3.5)	2.70 (2.7)	1.20	1.7
481	c	1.18 (4.2)	1.25 (0.6)	2.58	1.7
356	6.96 (3.1)	0.68 (8.2)	2.45 (3.9)	0.75	1.6
335	5.41 (1.5)	0.81 (6.0)	2.34 (2.3)	1.23	1.2
352	2.79 (0.7)	0.57 (4.0)	4.80 (4.5)	1.27	2.3
353	5.76 (2.0)	0.77 (7.4)	3.41 (4.4)	0.93	1.2
354	11.94 (6.8)	0.66 (10.3)	1.88 (3.9)	0.58	2.0
331	2.72 (0.4)	1.01 (4.1)	5.31 (2.9)	2.21	1.7
12	11.54 (1.6)	1.17 (4.4)	3.16 (1.6)	2.36	1.8
421–3	c	0.56 (1.4)	−0.86 (−0.3)	3.03	0.8
332	7.72 (2.5)	1.12 (9.7)	−0.25 (−0.3)	1.04	2.5
371	7.31 (1.5)	0.64 (3.5)	3.37 (2.4)	1.65	2.2
Mean	6.8	0.80	2.5	...	...

Sources: Data from U.S. Bureau of Labor Statistics, with wages in manufacturing industries adjusted for overtime by the author. See text for definitions of the variables.

a. All equations are estimated for the period 1959–76, with a constant term that is not reported. The dependent variable is the percent change in overtime-adjusted hourly earnings. The numbers in parentheses are t statistics. The regression for industry 421-3 is for the period 1964–76.

b. FIRE is the fire insurance and real estate industries.

c. The unemployment coefficient was negative, so the equation was reestimated without it.

wages rose much faster in 1970 and 1971 when union increases were unaffected by the recession and when unions negotiated to catch up for their small real gains during the late 1960s. During the control years, union wages moved in step with the average. And both accelerated sharply in the two subsequent years of price explosion. For the eight years

Table 3. Union and Total Private Wage Increases, 1970–77

Percent per year

Year/ Period	Effective union wage-rate change[a]	Increase in index of average hourly earnings	Difference	Real union wage-rate change[b]
1970	8.8	6.6	2.2	2.9
1971	9.2	7.0	2.2	4.9
1972	6.6	6.6	0.0	3.3
1973	7.0	6.4	0.6	0.8
1974	9.4	8.2	1.2	−1.6
1975	8.7	8.8	−0.1	−0.4
1976	8.1	7.2	0.9	2.3
1977	8.0	7.3	0.7	1.5
1970–77 average	8.2	7.3	0.9	1.7

Source: U.S. Bureau of Labor Statistics.
a. Average effective union wage-rate changes in agreements covering 1,000 or more workers.
b. Effective union wage increases less the increase in the CPI.

as a whole (1970–77), union wages have risen an average of 1 percent a year faster. But while they have outpaced average wages over this period, the 1.7 percent average annual increase in real wages in the union sector during the 1970s just maintained the average rate of real wage increase of the previous decade.

Looking Forward or Backward? The data on union wage increases during the inflationary period of the past decade can help distinguish between forward-looking and backward-looking views of the inflation process. Purely expectational models can have different implications from those that relate current wage and price developments to actual developments of the past. If the inertia in inflation arose from a purely backward-looking process, current wage setting would be influenced by wage changes that have already occurred elsewhere or by price changes that have occurred since wages currently being set were last changed. The prospect that inflation would accelerate or decelerate in the future would not enter because wage changes would be simply catching up with past events. If the process were purely forward looking, only expectations of future inflation would matter. Bygones are presumably bygones and past changes in wages or prices enter only as people form expectations from them. Unfortunately, analysis with statistical time series is unsuccessful in distinguishing between forward-looking and backward-looking processes when "expectations" are not directly observable and are modeled as

Table 4. Real and Relative Wage Gains in Major Union Contracts, 1968–75
Percentage points over three years

Contract year	Average wage gain (1)	Relative wage gain[a]		Real wage gain[a]	
		Forward looking[b] (2)	Backward looking[b] (3)	Forward looking[b] (4)	Backward looking[b] (5)
1968	19.5	0.1	3.9	4.0	9.5
1969	23.4	3.2	5.7	7.8	10.9
1970	25.9	5.7	6.5	12.4	10.4
1971	26.1	6.1	5.9	12.3	10.5
1972	24.9	3.7	4.7	4.4	11.4
1973	23.5	0.1	3.5	-2.8	9.7
1974	25.2	1.0	4.0	-0.7	4.7
1975	25.7	2.4	2.3	4.3	-0.6
Standard deviation		2.3	1.4	5.1	4.2

Sources: Union wage changes are calculated as described in notes to this table using data from U.S. Bureau of Labor Statistics on effective wage rate changes. Adjusted average hourly earnings and consumer price indexes are from BLS.

a. Relative wage gain is union wage change (defined in the next note) relative to the change in the average hourly earnings index. Real wage gain is union wage change relative to the change in the consumer price index.

b. The union wage change each year is the increase from current settlements plus average gains in the next two years from prior settlements and escalator provisions. Forward-looking gain is this change less the increase over the same time interval in average hourly earnings or the consumer price index. Backward-looking gain is this change less the increase in average hourly earnings from three years earlier or the CPI.

lagged values of past inflation. In order to distinguish between the two, it is necessary to turn to other types of evidence.

Various institutional or political arrangements whose purpose is to neutralize, at least partly, the effects of inflation on wages are based on a backward-looking approach. Adjustments in labor contracts to account for increases in the cost of living modify wages according to past changes in the CPI. Such arrangements make it possible to avoid forecasts of future inflation. The minimum wage law has typically been adjusted to take account of past changes in average wages. And the comparability rule for government wages relates them to past changes in wages of workers in the private sector in similar occupations.

Major union wage contracts are the clearest instance of wage commitments made well into the future. If the forward-looking hypothesis works anywhere, it should work in explaining these settlements. Table 4 analyzes wage gains in major union contracts for the period 1968–75. Column 1 shows the estimated average wage gain from settlements over the life of the contract, including gains from escalator provisions.[6] Columns 2 to 5 compare these settlement increases with both past and future changes in the CPI and in adjusted average hourly earnings for the private nonfarm economy. The hypothesis that settlements are forward looking is expressed in columns 2 and 4, where the percentage increases in average earnings throughout the economy and in the CPI over the three-year duration of union settlements are subtracted from the increases under the settlements. Columns 3 and 5 express the hypothesis that settlements are backward looking. There the increase in average earnings for the economy as a whole and in the CPI over the three years ending in the year of the settlement are subtracted from the increases under the settlements. Data are available for these calculations only for the years shown.

Because these major settlements are concentrated in situations that are comparatively insensitive to unemployment rates and presumably sensitive to living costs and relative wages, the hypothesis that yields the less erratic series for wage gains should be preferred. In this case, the backward-looking hypothesis is a more satisfactory one, even though the forward-looking hypothesis is given an advantage in the contest through comparing CPI gains with settlement gains that include escalator adjustments for the same years.

AGGREGATE WAGE EQUATIONS

I turn now to some aggregate wage equations to observe how well the Phillips curve and alternative specifications of lagged inflation effects predicted wages during the 1970s. Table 5 presents Phillips curve equations for the annual change in adjusted hourly earnings in the private nonfarm sector ($100 \times \Delta \ln E$), using three alternative lagged inflation variables: the dependent variable, the CPI ($100 \times \Delta \ln CP$), and the private nonfarm deflator after the effects of the rise in fuel prices in 1974–75 have been removed ($100 \times \Delta \ln DP$). Two years of lagged inflation are shown in each case, although the second year is frequently insignificant. A third-year lag invariably was insignificant and small or wrong-signed. Esti-

6. The average gain from settlements made in year t is estimated by adding the average deferred increases in years $t + 1$ and $t + 2$ to the average first-year increase in t. The deferred increases in each year are averaged over the number of workers who did not receive first-year increases in that year. This procedure is not precise and can only approximate the actual increases that occur over the life of contracts newly negotiated in any given year.

Table 5. Phillips Curve Equations for Wages in the Private Nonfarm Sector, Selected Periods, 1954–77[a]

Period and equation number	Constant	u^{*-1}	$\Delta \ln E_{-1}$	$\Delta \ln E_{-2}$	$\Delta \ln CP_{-1}$	$\Delta \ln CP_{-2}$	$\Delta \ln DP_{-1}$	$\Delta \ln DP_{-2}$	$DNIX$	Sum of lagged effects	Standard error	Durbin-Watson statistic
1954–69												
5.1	−0.37 (−0.4)	8.55 (4.5)	0.54 (2.9)	−0.05 (−0.2)	…	…	…	…	…	0.49	0.56	1.6
5.2	1.04 (1.5)	9.06 (3.8)	…	…	0.29 (1.5)	−0.05 (−0.2)	…	…	…	0.24	0.72	1.1
5.3	0.42 (0.9)	7.53 (5.0)	…	…	…	…	0.55 (3.5)	0.19 (1.2)	…	0.74	0.42	2.1
1954–71												
5.4	−1.36 (−1.4)	7.75 (3.4)	0.70 (3.3)	0.13 (0.5)	…	…	…	…	…	0.83	0.67	1.5
5.5	1.01 (1.4)	7.45 (3.0)	…	…	0.47 (2.6)	0.11 (0.5)	…	…	…	0.58	0.79	1.1
5.6	0.33 (0.7)	6.54 (4.2)	…	…	…	…	0.68 (4.4)	0.27 (1.6)	…	0.95	0.46	1.9
1954–77												
5.7	−1.88 (−2.2)	7.44 (3.5)	0.79 (4.6)	0.21 (1.1)	…	…	…	…	1.07 (2.9)	1.00	0.70	1.5
5.8	1.03 (1.3)	7.39 (2.9)	…	…	0.55 (3.8)	0.09 (0.6)	…	…	−0.02 (−0.0)	0.64	0.85	1.3
5.9	0.55 (0.6)	7.88 (3.0)	…	…	…	…	0.52 (3.7)	0.24 (1.7)	0.68 (1.3)	0.76	0.88	1.2

Sources: *Economic Report of the President, January 1978*; U.S. Bureau of Labor Statistics; and author's estimates.

a. The dependent variable is adjusted average hourly earnings ($100 \times \Delta \ln E$). The numbers in parentheses are t statistics.

b. All change variables are multiplied by 100; u^{*-1} = inverse of weighted unemployment rate; E = adjusted average hourly earnings; CP = consumer price index; DP = private nonfarm deflator with a fuel correction for 1974 and 1975 of −1.5 and −0.8 percent, respectively; $DNIX$ = dummy to account for wage and price controls with values of −1 in 1972 and 1973, +1 in 1974 and 1975.

mates are shown for periods beginning in 1954 and ending in 1969, 1971, and 1977.

The quarterly pattern of wage and price changes during 1973–74 clearly points to a discontinuity with the end of controls in the second quarter of 1974. It is difficult to model this situation. Controls were ended when the CPI was already soaring as a consequence of increases in uncontrolled prices of food and fuel and, to a lesser extent, raw materials and imports. Without these price shocks, wages might have behaved differently when controls ended. Nonetheless, in the equation estimated through 1977, I allowed for an amount of wage catch-up in 1974–75 equal to the amount wages were held down in 1972–73 by adding a dummy variable ($DNIX$) equal to -1 in 1972 and 1973 and $+1$ in 1974 and 1975. If one believes that little or no postcontrol "make-up" in wages would have occurred if it had not been for the rapid inflation caused by food and fuel prices, this procedure underestimates the response of wages to that price explosion by attributing a part of actual wage changes in 1974 and 1975 to a reversal of the wage moderation accomplished by controls.

Labor Market Effects. The labor market variable is the weighted unemployment rate, holding constant the 1966 demographic proportions of the labor force. The weighting produces a wage-bill concept of unemployed labor resources; maintaining fixed labor force proportions provides a measure that will not show a change in the tightness of the labor market if the unemployment rate of each group is constant while its relative proportions vary. This measure of weighted unemployment will not capture the possibility that some groups are on flatter or steeper portions of their "own" Phillips curves than other groups. However, it is difficult to model that possibility from available data.

A striking feature of table 5 is that the estimated short-run effect of changing labor market tightness on wages is nearly the same for any of the three periods and for any of the three measures of lagged inflation. They all indicate only a modest first-year effect on inflation from a change in unemployment. For instance, using equation 5.1, an unemployment rate 1 percentage point lower than present levels would add about 0.43 percentage point to the rate of wage inflation, while an increase of 1 percentage point of unemployment would subtract about 0.28 point. Using equation 5.7, the estimates are 0.37 point and -0.25 point, respectively. The lagged effects would continue to enlarge these impacts, but only gradually. In the third year, equation 5.1 predicts that wages would be rising 0.5 percentage point slower if unemployment were sustained at a level 1 point higher, and 0.8 point faster with unemployment sustained 1 point lower. The corresponding third-year estimates from equation 5.7 are 0.7 point slower and 1.0 point faster.

Another way to compare the estimates for different periods is to observe their characterizations of high employment. Equation 5.7, whose lagged wage effects sum to 1.0, implies that 4.0 percent weighted unemployment—corresponding today to about 5.5 percent conventional unemployment—is consistent with a steady long-run inflation rate. At this weighted unemployment rate, equations 5.1 and 5.4 predict an eventual steady rate of wage increase of 3.5 percent and 3.4 percent. Such wage increases would yield about a 1.5 percent rate of price inflation, which is about as close as the economy ever comes to price stability.

Lagged Effects. Lagged values of the unemployment measure did not enter the wage equation significantly for any period of estimation. Whatever effect there is on average wages from the state of labor markets apparently occurs promptly. However, the influence of lagged inflation is strong and the estimated size of this influence is substantially greater when the 1970s are included in the estimation period.

The straightforward interpretation of this drift in the estimated size of lagged inflation effects is that the significance of ongoing inflation has risen together with the rising rate of inflation. According to this interpretation, so long as rapid inflation was not sustained for an extended period, it was less important in setting wages. Alternatively, it may be that the importance of lagged effects are misestimated in the equations for some periods, and there exists a "true" set of lagged inflation coefficients that is unchanged.

Whether the lagged effects actually sum to 1.0 or to a little less than 1.0 is not important for understanding the current inflation predicament. There will be considerable inertia to inflation with any large value of these lagged effects. When the lagged effects sum to 1.0, the model has only one unemployment rate at which inflation is predicted to remain unchanged in the long run. For relevant time horizons, the predictions from that model are little different from the predictions of a model that has a long-run trade-off with coefficients on recent inflation summing to 0.8 or so.

The errors for the 1970s from the equations of table 5 are shown in table 6. Even the equations estimated through 1977 show persistent un-

Table 6. Prediction Errors from Wage Equations for 1970–77

Actual less predicted value in percentage points

Estimation period and equation	Errors								Sum of errors	Average error		
	1970	1971	1972	1973	1974	1975	1976	1977		1970–77	1972–75	1976–77
1954–69												
5.1	1.2	2.0	1.2	0.9	3.0	3.5	1.1	2.3	15.2	1.9	2.2	1.7
5.2	1.5	2.3	2.1	1.7	2.9	3.3	2.4	3.0	19.2	2.4	2.5	2.7
5.3	0.7	1.2	0.7	1.0	2.8	1.4	−1.6	0.6	6.8	0.9	1.5	−0.5
1954–71												
5.4	0.4	1.1	0.2	−0.1	2.1	2.3	0.1	0.9	7.0	0.9	1.1	0.5
5.5	0.4	0.8	0.9	0.9	1.7	0.7	−0.6	1.0	5.8	0.7	1.1	0.2
5.6	0.2	0.6	0.1	0.6	2.3	0.2	−3.3	−0.5	0.2	0.0	0.8	−1.9
1954–77												
5.7	−0.1	0.6	0.7	0.5	0.6	0.6	−0.7	0.2	2.4	0.3	0.6	−0.3
5.8	0.1	0.4	0.6	0.8	1.4	a	−1.1	0.7	2.9	0.4	0.7	−0.2
5.9	0.4	0.9	1.1	1.3	1.8	0.6	−2.0	0.1	4.2	0.5	1.2	−0.9

Sources: Table 5 equations.
a. Positive but less than 0.05.

derpredictions through 1975; and in the equations estimated through 1969, with their smaller lagged effects, the underpredictions are large. The catching up of union wages in 1970–71 and the price explosion of 1974–75 are two events of the period that would not be predictable from aggregate wage equations, and that may help explain the underpredictions of this period.

Lagged CPI. There is no clear preferable alternative among the measures of lagged inflation, although based on the standard errors for all three sample periods, the CPI is unsatisfactory as a single explanatory variable for inertia. The Durbin-Watson statistics for the CPI equations are also consistently low, and when the equations are reestimated with a rho correction, the sum of the lagged CPI coefficients falls to 0.2 in the 1977 regressions. Thus, the estimates give no support to the hypothesis that wages vary in order to attain some real wage level. However, the evidence in favor of *some* CPI effects on wages is considerably stronger. During the 1976–77 period when inflation slowed substantially, the CPI equations clearly outperformed the equations using the nonfarm deflator. And residuals from any of the equations show that the food-fuel price explosion did affect wage behavior in 1974–75.

Lagged Deflator. The nonfarm deflator provided the best overall fit in the equations estimated through 1969 and 1971, but also provided the worst fit when the sample period was extended to 1977.

The deflator might be expected to work in wage equations for one of two reasons: either because it represents past wage changes that affect current wages, or because changes in the price margins or profitability of firms affect wages. If it is only a proxy for the former effect, then a wage-wage model should be used directly. But occasional observations of rapid wage gains in suddenly prosperous industries—such as coal and oil after 1973 —suggest that profitability may influence wage setting.

Generalized effects of profitability are difficult to find in time-series data. Although early work on Phillips curves found an important role for profits, time-series studies that include the latest decade generally do not. A secular decline in average profitability that coincides with the acceleration of inflation may be masking a causal relation between variations around that secular decline and wage changes. Laurence Seidman, in his paper in this volume, makes such an adjustment and finds that profitability is an important explanatory variable for wages.

Attempts to use both past wages and past deflator prices in the wage equation have been unsuccessful. The effect of wage costs on prices makes them highly collinear, and one or the other dominates depending on the sample period. Competition among tradable goods makes the price of imports one source of influence on deflator prices that is independent of wage costs. When the change in the import price of manufactured goods is added to the wage-wage equations of table 5, that price is significant. However, the equation coefficients are somewhat unstable over the different sample periods. The equations could only be estimated beginning with 1960 because the import price series is not available before 1959. The equation estimated for 1960–71, the period before flexible exchange rates, is:

$$(2) \quad \Delta \ln E = -1.05 + 7.40\, u^{*-1} + 0.41\, \Delta \ln E_{-1}$$
$$ (-2.4) \quad (4.6) \qquad\quad (1.8)$$
$$+ 0.42\, \Delta \ln E_{-2} + 0.11\, \Delta \ln MP_{-1},$$
$$(1.5) \qquad\qquad (2.3)$$

Durbin-Watson = 2.6; standard error = 0.28.

where all $\Delta \ln$ terms are multiplied by 100 and MP is the price index for finished manufactured imports. For the same equation estimated through 1977, the sum of the coefficients on the lagged wage term is 0.88; and the coefficient on import prices, 0.07. These equations indicate that beyond the effects of unemployment and a lagged wage elasticity of about 0.85, a 10 percent change in the price of manufactured import goods alters the price of competing tradable goods by enough to change average wages by about 1 percent. This estimate seems high and should probably not be taken at face value. It does provide some evidence that profit margins have an independent effect on wages, although it is hardly conclusive or successfully quantified.

Lagged Wages. The most robust simple specification of the inertia process seems to be the wage-wage view modeled in equations 5.1, 5.4, and 5.7. Their errors for the two latest years are relatively small, and the two years are tracked rather well without a huge change in the error such as that produced by the deflator equations. The equations fitted through 1969 or 1971, however, greatly underpredict wage changes in subsequent years. The equation estimated through 1977 reduces these overestimates by raising the sum of the lagged wage coefficients to about 1.0.

A close look at the errors in the 1972–75 period shows some direct effect of price inflation on wages. In table 6 the errors from equations 5.1

or 5.4 declined by about 1 percentage point in 1972–73. This may be interpreted as the direct effect of controls. The errors then jump by over 2 percentage points in 1974–75. There is no wage-wage view of the inflation process that predicts this. The earlier disaggregated results show that the acceleration in 1974–75 was the same in both high-wage and low-wage industries, so the possibility can be ruled out that a distortion of relative wages in the control period led to this acceleration in the average. Even the assumption that controls suppressed a stubborn rate of wage inflation would only account for a return to 1 percent underpredictions. Something between this and no change from the 1972–73 residuals should have been expected if the actual wage experience of 1972–73 affected the wage-wage process and, therefore, wage changes in 1974–75. The actual behavior of wages indicates they responded to the actual behavior of prices.

When the lagged CPI and lagged wages are used together as explanatory variables, the coefficients on unemployment and on wage changes that lag by one year are quite uniform for the three sample periods. The estimated coefficient on the lagged CPI rises from near zero when the equation is estimated through 1969 to about 0.2 in equations estimated through 1971 or 1977. Wage changes lagged two years only become important when the estimation period is extended to 1977, raising the sum of all lagged inflation coefficients to 0.93. The equation fitted to the 1954–71 period (all logs × 100) is:

$$(3) \quad \Delta \ln E = -0.69 + 7.34u^{*-1} + 0.52 \, \Delta \ln E_{-1}$$
$$ (-0.7) \quad (3.3) \quad\quad (2.1)$$

$$+ 0.07 \, \Delta \ln E_{-2} + 0.21 \, \Delta \ln CP_{-1}.$$
$$ (0.3) \quad\quad\quad\quad (1.3)$$

Durbin-Watson $= 1.8$; standard error $= 0.66$.

The prediction errors are:

1970	1971	1972	1973	1974	1975	1976	1977	Sum
0.2	0.8	0.3	0.2	1.7	1.3	−0.4	0.9	5.0

WAGE BEHAVIOR: CONCLUSIONS

Once changes in demographics have been allowed for (by measuring tightness in the labor market with the weighted unemployment rate used here), the major change in the inflation-unemployment relation between the 1960s and 1970s is associated with the effects of lagged inflation on current wage changes. The existence of large lagged effects created inertia in inflation that transmitted past inflation to current wage changes even when current unemployment rose. In addition, the importance of these lagged effects apparently grew as inflation itself became more entrenched. Today inertia is a more important characteristic of the inflation process than it was in the 1950s and 1960s.

The disappointing experience with inflation during the 1970s can be understood as a consequence of this strong and growing inertia together with some one-time developments that added to inflation during this period. These include, in particular, the catch-up in union wages at the start of the decade and the international explosion of prices for food and fuel before the great recession.

The source of this inertia is not easily identified. Wages in high-wage industries and those set under collective bargaining are relatively insensitive to unemployment and relatively responsive to the ongoing rate of inflation. They may have been particularly important in the failure of average wages to decelerate after 1969. However, for aggregate wages to rise as fast as they have in the 1970s, the ongoing inflation rate must be an important factor in wage determination more generally, possibly as a consequence of patterning other wage changes on those in the high-wage sectors or occupations.

No single explanatory variable adequately describes the effect of past inflation on current wage changes. In general, wages responding to past wages offer a better description of the process than wages responding simply to the CPI. But to explain the developments of the mid-1970s, one needs to believe there was a substantial direct influence of prices on wages as well. This period may have been unusual, but some direct effect of past prices on wages is also estimated in equations such as 3, which are fitted to long periods that do not include the mid-1970s. In summary, to explain current wage behavior, the importance of ongoing inflation is well established, but the particular importance of ongoing price (as opposed to wage) inflation remains unsettled.

Although it is difficult to disprove the hypothesis that the inertia in aggregate wages represents expected inflation, the estimates favor the more direct hypothesis that inertia is a backward-looking phenomenon. That view is supported directly by the analysis of changes in union wages. In the aggregate equations, it is supported by the fact that inertia appears through large coefficients on recent inflation rather than through modest coefficients on inflation rates over a long past period: expectations models generally assert that expectations are adjusted gradually and therefore depend on a long past history of actual inflation. A large coefficient on recent wage changes is most naturally interpreted as a process in which wages are adjusted to keep up continuously with other wages. If these results are taken to mean that expectations are simply formed by the most recent observation of inflation, the expectations hypothesis loses any distinctive significance, for then any change in actual inflation will have a full impact on inflation in the next period, just as the backward-looking hypothesis would predict. Finally, the failure of any lagged values of unemployment to enter the wage equation argues against expected unemployment rates as an important determinant of wage changes.

Alternative Views

The mainline model that I described at the outset of this paper and the empirical evidence just presented provide a fairly general description of the macroeconomy and the inflation process. Although they leave room for alternative views about the microeconomic underpinnings of inertia and for further research on quantitative questions, they do provide a basis for discussing anti-inflation policies. The blame for inflation or the remedies for it, however, are often argued along lines that are not predicted by the mainline model or from views of the economy that are incompatible with it. Before examining what there is to learn from the mainline model about strategies for slowing inflation, I review some of these dissenting views.

BUDGET DEFICITS

If a poll were taken to sample opinions on the causes of inflation, most votes would probably go to government deficits. An economist would grant the effects of deficits on aggregate demand and would be hard pressed to find causal links between deficits and inflation over and above their effects on demand. He would also be aware that historically most deficits have come from the operation of automatic stabilizers during periods of underemployment.

Although to my knowledge no serious model predicts that actual deficits will explain inflation, equations 4 and 5 were estimated in response to the opinion polls, as follows:

(4) $\Delta \ln GP = -0.0 + 1.04 \, L\Delta \ln GP - 0.19 \, LRDG.$
         $(-0.3) \quad (5.5) \qquad\qquad (-1.4)$
Period, 1954:1 to 1973:4; Durbin-Watson = 1.7; standard error = 0.004.

(5) $\Delta \ln GP = 0.00 + 1.11 \, L\Delta \ln GP + 0.00 \, LRDG + 0.003 \, DNIX.$
         $(0.1) \quad (6.5) \qquad\qquad (0.04) \qquad\quad (1.9)$
Period, 1954:1 to 1977:2; Durbin-Watson = 1.8; standard error = 0.004.

Four-quarter percentage changes in the GNP deflator ($\Delta \ln GP$) are explained with Almon lagged values of the deflator itself ($L \Delta \ln GP$) and of the ratio of the federal deficit to the GNP ($LRDG$). The lags extend 16 quarters. The equations fitted through 1977 include the dummy variable ($DNIX$) for the control and postcontrol period of the Nixon years that sums to zero. The qualitative results are unaffected by this dummy or by a dummy for the wage-price guideposts of the 1960s. Equation 4, fitted through the end of 1973, reveals the negative effect associated with deficits, which is predicted from the fact that variations in the deficit result primarily from variations in the degree of slack in the economy. When the period is extended to 1977 in equation 5, the coincidence of the price explosion of 1974–75 and the deep recession and consequent large budget deficit raise the coefficient estimated for the deficit to zero.

The actual relationship between budget deficits and economic performance is complicated, and the equations above are not intended to summarize that relationship in any meaningful way. At a minimum, variations in the deficit would have to be decomposed into those that are induced by economic activity and those that represent changes in fiscal policy at a fixed level of utilization. Equations 4 and 5 are intended simply to dispel the view that the present inflation is caused by deficits or that cutting the deficit would help eliminate inflation without causing recession.

The lack of a causal connection between budget deficits and inflation does not deny possibly important linkages between government programs and the current inflation. One important message in Robert Crandall's paper in this volume is that government programs have contributed to inflation by pursuing goals through means that raise the price level rather than through means that show up in the budget deficit. If the costs took the form of federal expenditures or tax credits and thus appeared in the deficit, they would not affect the price level, providing that the level of aggregate demand remained the same. Paradoxically, excessive anxiety about deficits can itself be inflationary.

EXCESSIVE GROWTH OF MONEY

Besides deficits, a close contender in public opinion polls on the causes of inflation would be excessive growth of money. Unlike the deficit explanation, a positive connection between money growth and inflation is acknowledged widely by the professional community. What divides economists is the issue of whether or not a causal role can be assigned to money in addition to its role as a determinant of aggregate demand. The mainline view acknowledges the role of aggregate demand in inflation and the role of money in aggregate demand. It denies any additional, special role of money in causing inflation.

Franco Modigliani and Lucas Papademos have reported on attempts to put money into mainline inflation equations.[7] Like many other authors, they found a long mean lag for the effect of money on prices when money was used alone in a reduced-form equation. This result is entirely in accord with the view that money affects aggregate demand, thereby promptly influencing real activity and employment, and eventually the inflation rate. But they found that money was insignificant when added to equations that explain prices with the unemployment rate, import prices, and lagged inflation.

Modigliani and Papademos estimated their equations through 1971. By extending the data period, it is possible to modify these results. I explained the annual change in the GNP deflator using the current unemployment rate and three years of lagged values of the change in money and of the dependent variable. When the equation was run from 1954 to 1971, the sum of the coefficients on lagged money was only 0.13, with successive t statistics of only 0.6, 0.1, and 0.2. When the same equation was rerun for the 1954–77 period, the sum of the money coefficients rose to 0.71 with successive t statistics of 1.7, 1.2, and 0.6. Adding a dummy for the control and postcontrol period raised the sum of coefficients to 0.77. Apparently the recent interest in this type of explanation of inflation arises from the general inability of demand variables to explain the inflation of the mid-1970s and the coincidental acceleration of money growth. All the

7. Franco Modigliani and Lucas Papademos, "Targets for Monetary Policy in the Coming Year," *BPEA, 1:1975,* pp. 141–63.

independent explanatory power of money comes from this one episode. To believe that money has this independent role in causing inflation, one has to believe that the relatively rapid money growth of 1972–73 caused the subsequent explosion of prices in 1974–75, creating inflation directly rather than through demand variables for perhaps the first time in history. This interpretation not only strains the imagination, but is inconsistent with the historical evidence of long lags in reduced-form equations explaining prices with money.

SOCIAL WELFARE PROGRAMS

Government programs of income maintenance would also be high on a list of popular explanations of inflation. Unemployment compensation and the minimum wage are the two programs that are most clearly related to wage behavior. Both have been studied carefully by economists and have at least potentially significant effects on labor markets.

Table 7 shows the percentage of after-tax earnings that was replaced by unemployment benefits and the minimum wage as a percentage of average earnings during recent periods. Both measures rose gradually during the postwar period until the last half of the 1960s. Between 1966–70 and the present, the net replacement ratio under unemployment compensation increased slightly, while the relative minimum wage declined sharply.

As was noted earlier, Gramlich estimated that average wages rise by about 0.03 percent for each 1 percent change in the minimum.[8] A substantial rise in the minimum, such as the 15 percent increase of January 1978, will have a noticeable effect on aggregate wages. However, during the period that inflation was worsening, the relative minimum wage was falling. And as the disaggregated results showed, wages in low-wage industries (where increases in the minimum wage have their principal effect) were falling behind other wages. The coverage of the minimum wage was substantially expanded in the mid-1960s, adding to its impact on average wages at that time. But that episode is too remote to have any relevance to the inflation of the 1970s. Finally, by reducing the employment prospects of young workers, the minimum wage may add to their unemployment and thus have a modest effect in shifting the Phillips

8. Gramlich, "Impact of Minimum Wages."

Table 7. Unemployment Benefits and Minimum Wage Relative to Average Earnings, Selected Periods, 1951-77

Percent

Description	1951–55	1956–60	1961–65	1966–70	1971–75	1976–77
Unemployment compensation replacement ratio (net)[a]	39.4	42.9	44.4	46.0	47.3	47.1
Relative minimum wage[b]	45.4	47.6	48.3	51.1	47.2	44.3

Sources: Average weekly unemployment compensation benefits, *Economic Report of the President, January 1978*, table B-33, and updates from U.S. Department of Labor, Employment and Training Administration; spendable earnings (worker with 3 dependents), U.S. Bureau of Economic Analysis, *Business Statistics, 1975* (Government Printing Office, 1976) and *Survey of Current Business*, various issues; straight-time earnings in manufacturing, U.S. Bureau of Labor Statistics, *Employment and Earnings, United States, 1909–75*, Bulletin 1312-10 (GPO, 1975), and *Employment and Earnings*, various issues.
a. Unemployment compensation benefits as a percentage of spendable weekly earnings.
b. Minimum wage as a percentage of straight-time hourly earnings in manufacturing.

curve. Any such effect—and I would expect it to be quite small—is captured in using the weighted unemployment rate in the wage equation.

Unemployment compensation has a potential effect on wage inflation by reducing the willingness of recipients to accept available job offers. Together with other programs of income maintenance, it provides a disincentive to work compared with a situation in which no support is provided or one in which support does not depend on unemployment. However, such programs are not new to the recent years of rapid inflation. And as table 7 shows, the benefits have not become much more generous during the period when inflation has worsened.[9]

In the majority of cases, workers receiving unemployment compensation benefits have been laid off from jobs to which they expect to return. Wages in those jobs are inflexible because of the formal and informal relations binding employers and employees, not because workers who have been laid off are holding back their services waiting for better wages. While unemployment compensation may have some effect on the response of wages to unemployment, it is doubtful that the effect is large.

9. In a series of articles providing many constructive suggestions for reforming the unemployment compensation system, Martin Feldstein has pointed out that replacement ratios for certain workers can rise above the averages shown in table 7. See Martin Feldstein, "Unemployment Compensation: Adverse Incentives and Distributional Anomalies," *National Tax Journal*, vol. 27 (June 1974), pp. 231–44. However, I doubt that such calculations could alter the verdict that there has been little change in the last decade in the relative benefits of the program.

The outcome might be different if most of unemployment among those who receive benefits were well described by simple search models and if wage offers were varied by firms in response to short-run variations in labor market tightness. But this is not the case.

MISPERCEPTION, PERFECT MARKETS, AND RATIONAL EXPECTATIONS

The most serious conceptual challenge to the mainline model I have outlined comes from a view that attributes all of inflation and unemployment to misperceptions on the part of workers and firms: workers are led into more or less employment than they would normally want by their incorrect reading of wage or price trends. In a related set of models, "rational" expectations and extreme price and wage flexibility are assumed to characterize the macroeconomy. Workers are assumed to make market-clearing wage and price changes continuously, based on the best information available and constrained only by existing contracts. Except for information lags and delays until existing contracts expire, wages and prices are always adjusted to provide equilibrium levels of output and employment. Both these models have an important common feature: in contrast to the mainline model, they have variations in inflation causing variations in unemployment rather than the reverse. Without inflation surprises, unemployment would always be at a "natural rate."

The search models fail to explain the widespread phenomenon of layoffs or the cyclical pattern of quits. To the extent they predict that wages must accelerate if unemployment is to be maintained below its natural rate—their central implication—they predict wages must decelerate if unemployment is to stay above the natural rate for any sustained period. Alternatively, they may assume that misperceptions about available wage offers take a long time to be corrected. On the basis of this argument, the persistence of unemployment and inflation since the mid-1970s is understood as a continued overoptimism about available wage offers. Because most periods of unemployment have a duration measured in days or at most several weeks, it seems unrealistic to assume years of misperception to explain unemployment.

Models that combine wage and price flexibility with assumptions embodied in rational expectations about behavior have similar problems explaining persistence. Any deviation of unemployment from the natural rate can persist only until people become aware of the situation or re-negotiate existing contracts. Except for three-year wage agreements ne-gotiated with some large unions—agreements that cover only a small fraction of the work force—it is difficult to imagine price or wage arrange-ments in any important area of the economy that are bound by long-term contracts. Thus, when unemployment has deviated from past levels for any sustained period, the new unemployment level must be interpreted as a new natural rate. By contrast, the mainstream model that I have de-scribed recognizes sustained periods of underemployment and leaves open the possibility of changing unemployment through demand manage-ment.

Slowing Inflation: Aggregate Demand and Expectations

The inflation of the 1970s does not change the conclusion that slowing the economy and raising unemployment can slow and eventually elimi-nate inflation. The evidence is, however, that inflation would slow only gradually in response to holding back aggregate demand, and that the cost in lost employment and output per point of disinflation would be large. The equations of table 5 generally predict inflation will be less than one point slower in the third year of a policy that holds the unemployment rate one point higher. And the additional unemployment implies a loss of $50 billion to $60 billion a year in output in today's economy.

A different specification might alter the numerical estimates, but it could not reverse the verdict that the anti-inflation gains from restraining aggregate demand are disappointingly small. Arthur Okun recently sum-marized the estimates from six different econometric models and came to a similarly pessimistic conclusion.[10] Whatever view is held on the ur-gency of slowing inflation today, it is unrealistic to believe that the public or its representatives would permit the extended period of high unemploy-ment required to slow inflation in this manner.

Stabilization strategy since 1975 may be interpreted as an attempt to find an output path that would gradually reduce unemployment and at the same time slow inflation. The evidence of the past few years provides little hope for such a possibility. After the hourly earnings index slowed in the early quarters of recovery, it began to accelerate gradually in 1977.

10. Arthur M. Okun, "Efficient Disinflationary Policies," *American Economic Review,* vol. 68 (May 1978), pp. 348–52.

Equations based on the level of tightness in the labor market predicted a continuing deceleration given the slack labor markets of 1976–77. But the predicted unwinding of inflation in response to unemployment is so gradual that it is easily offset by other inflationary developments. Food and import prices rose faster in 1977 than in 1976, although the effect on wages of their speedup in 1977 should have been slight. Unemployment declined noticeably during 1977, and this could help explain the wage speedup if the change in unemployment as well as its level has an effect on wage inflation that is not captured in estimates using annual data.[11] But whatever the explanation is for recent wage changes, such developments further dramatize the difficulty of slowing the present inflation with demand management alone.

Slowing Inflation: Expectations

William Fellner has articulated the principal challenge to the pessimistic verdict on using aggregate demand to slow inflation.[12] He views the inertia of inflation as a consequence of generalized expectations of inflation. According to Fellner, in recent years contracts governing wages and prices have been formulated with the expectation that inflation will continue into the future.[13] So long as these expectations are maintained, they become a self-fulfilling prophecy. To stop inflation, policy must change these expectations. In Fellner's view, the only way to change them is through a convincing demonstration that monetary and fiscal policies will not accommodate the expected inflation rate.

An example will serve to illustrate this point. Assume that 4 percent

11. An effect from such changes appears in equations estimated with quarterly data. The insignificance of lagged unemployment when added to the wage equations reported in table 5 argues against any important effects from a change in unemployment over a period as long as a year. I regard the correct specification as an open question in light of the differing results with quarterly and annual data.

12. William J. Fellner, *Towards a Reconstruction of Macroeconomics: Problems of Theory and Policy* (American Enterprise Institute, 1976).

13. Martin Neil Baily, in "Stabilization Policy and Private Economic Behavior," *BPEA, 1:1978,* pp. 11–50, has recently explored the idea that the generalized expectation of prosperity has influenced the behavior of firms in a stabilizing way. Believing that the government will avoid the deep slumps of the past, firms themselves respond with hiring, stocking, and investment decisions that are more stabilizing than in the past. I interpret Fellner's views on inflationary expectations as analogous to this model of changing real behavior.

real growth is the desired path for output and that 6 percent is the expected inflation rate. A 10 percent growth rate of aggregate demand would be accommodating. If aggregate-demand growth were held to 8 percent, the econometric evidence predicts that real growth the first year would slow by nearly 2 percent while inflation would slow only slightly. After two years, real output would be more than 3 percent below the 4 percent growth path, and prices would be about 1 percent below that path. Fellner reasons that, by making the decision to slow aggregate demand convincing, expectations would change and the division between real growth and inflation would improve. The coefficients of the model that yield pessimistic projections today would be changed by the clear determination of the authorities to adopt a nonaccommodating policy.

How plausible is this remedy for inflation? The 1973–75 recession apparently did not change the coefficients. It could be argued, however, that this period did not demonstrate nonaccommodation convincingly because policies promptly turned to aiding recovery once unemployment increased. Let me bring together the scattered evidence presented earlier for questioning Fellner's optimism.

First, the evidence is that the inertia process is expectational but to only a limited extent. That does not mean that people do not have expectations about inflation, but simply that current wage and price decisions, as opposed to decisions in other spheres such as lending or investing, are not governed by those expectations. Even in the area of long-term labor contracts, in which expectations could be important, the analysis presented above shows that wage developments are better explained as backward looking and that escalators are used to avoid predicting the future. For most questions regarding inflation it is not crucial to know whether the inertia process is forward looking or backward looking. It does matter here.

Second, even if the econometric coefficients from Phillips curves are interpreted as expectational rather than backward looking, how much will an announced policy of demand restraint affect those expectations? If a nonaccommodating aggregate-demand policy is totally convincing, it will lead people to expect that unemployment will rise. But why should this affect their expectations about inflation by more than the short-run Phillips curve predicts? If inflation responds weakly to actual unemployment, why should expected inflation respond so strongly to expected unemployment?

This leaves room for a small gain in Fellner's scheme. If there are some wage contracts made with a view to the unemployment rate anticipated in the future, expecting more unemployment should modify such contracts by the amount predicted by the Phillips curve. If a restrictive nominal GNP path is to be pursued, there is thus some gain from announcing it ahead of time. My only question is whether there is reason to expect more than the improvement predicted by the Phillips curve as applied to the expected *future* course of unemployment. And if even that effect is confined to a small subset of contracts that are actually forward looking, the total benefits would be limited. On the price side, there are depletable resources whose price depends on expectations of prospective demand, but these are not important in the overall price level.

If wage and price setting were sufficiently concentrated in this economy, the possibilities for affecting inflation through Fellner's route would be greatly enhanced. A roomful of private decisionmakers who recognized that their inflationary behavior would directly affect their level of output and employment would be expected to respond favorably to a government policy of nonaccommodation. That is not what occurs in the U.S. economy.

Linking an incomes policy to an announced nonaccommodating policy on aggregate demand would help achieve Fellner's result. As discussed below, an effective incomes policy would produce a more favorable prospective split between real growth and inflation for any given path of nominal demand growth. Thus, expectations of inflation would change by more than the Phillips curve predicts. And to the extent that expectations do affect current wage decisions—which is still an open question—they would complement an incomes policy. Although it is an incomes policy that changes the immediate trade-off, the nonaccommodating demand policy is a necessary complement. Without it, the reduced inflation promised by the improved trade-off could be dissipated by a movement along the new trade-off curve.

Slowing Inflation: Tax-Based Incomes Policies

Although there are several variations of tax-based incomes policies (TIPs), their differences are primarily important in determining their acceptability, the ease of their implementation, and their effectiveness in altering individual wage and price decisions. These matters are discussed in other papers in this volume. At the macroeconomic level, the main impact of alternative TIPs affecting wages will be similar. And TIPs that act on prices primarily ensure that price restraint parallels wage restraint, which is what the macroeconomic model predicts without such policies.

It is simplest to integrate TIP effects into the macroeconomic model by assuming that the same path of real output is pursued with and without the program. Starting from the present state of the economy, a TIP that causes individual wages to rise more slowly than they otherwise would can be represented simply as a reduction in the constant term of the wage equation. Whether TIP will alter the slope of the short-run Phillips curve or whether it will reduce permanently the unemployment rate that represents full employment are separate issues that are briefly considered below. With a downward shift in the constant term of the wage equation, nominal aggregate demand must be reduced by an amount that is proportional to the shift in order to maintain the desired output path. This necessitates an appropriate combined adjustment in fiscal and monetary policies. This relatively simple procedure is all that is needed to integrate TIP and aggregate demand policies in the first year; a similar adjustment is required in subsequent years if the shift caused by TIP each year could be specified. But the macroeconomic analysis does raise some questions about the size of that shift in subsequent years and the difficulty of attaining it.

LAGGED EFFECTS

In most views of the inflation process, the slower average wage increases resulting from TIP in the first year will reduce wage pressures in the second year. If prices slow correspondingly, as would be expected, this favorable lagged effect would be predicted by any of the aggregate equations discussed earlier. Because the estimated lags are short, a major fraction of the first year's improvement in inflation will be perpetuated into the second year. In actual experience, however, some of the complications introduced by TIPs might lead to lagged effects that are different from these estimates.

Any TIP program may alter slightly the distribution of wages. The possibilities are numerous and the likely outcomes differ according to whether a penalty or reward TIP is employed. The main possibility for obtaining lagged effects that are noticeably smaller than the macromodel predicts probably arises in the case of a reward TIP that is employed for only one year. On the one hand, without a reward in the second year, workers whose wages had been restrained would tend to increase their wage demands to catch up with those that had not. On the other hand, firms that had not participated would be at a competitive cost disadvantage relative to firms that had, and that would put downward pressure on their wage offers. If these two influences cancel each other, the lagged effects from the economic equations should hold.

If the lagged wage effects in the macroeconomic model represent generalized expectations, the TIP program can be viewed in two ways. First, expectations that are based on actual experience should be favorably influenced by the initial slowdown in average wages and prices under TIP. This influence can be expected to grow if TIP effects are present over successive years. Second, expectations should be influenced by the existence of TIP as a specific and acceptable anti-inflation program. It should enhance the effects on inflationary expectations that Fellner looks for through policies of nonaccommodating aggregate demand. I have argued that these policies may be weak because their primary effect would be to change expectations of unemployment. Together with TIP, a greater part of any change in nominal demand expectations would be changes in expectations of the price level.

CHANGING THE STRUCTURE

TIPs are sometimes espoused as a means of shifting the Phillips curve in a favorable direction. This is one interpretation of shifting the constant term in the aggregate-wage equation. There is little basis, however, for judging whether such a favorable shift would be maintained in a period of substantially tighter labor markets. Because excess demand in the labor market now appears to develop gradually, TIP might make the Phillips curve more nearly L-shaped. In moderately tight markets, wages might be restrained, producing an improved trade-off; but in extremely tight labor markets, TIP might be relatively ineffective and the short-term trade-off might be the same as before.

TIPs do not have to reduce the unemployment rate that represents full employment in order to be useful. They would be a valuable tool if they were simply a shortcut to price stability and slowed the present wage-price spiral without a period of sustained high unemployment. If they were also an indirect remedy for structural problems in the labor market that produce inflation while involuntary unemployment still exists, that would be a bonus.

Measures to Cut Costs and Prices

What effect can we expect on the ongoing inflation rate from one-time increases or reductions in prices or costs? We can rely on cost changes to be reflected in prices. Beyond that, the empirical evidence is unfailingly ambiguous. The price shocks of the mid-1970s affected wages, but not proportionately. Consumer prices appear to have some persistent effect on wages, but it is modest once the effects of lagged wages themselves are allowed for. On the basis of the evidence, it appears that only a minor fraction of any shock to prices would filter through into average wage changes and thus have some multiplied effect. That still makes measures to cut prices and costs worth pursuing and their opposites worth avoiding. Even if only one-quarter of any price change influences wages, 1 percent removed from the CPI reduces wage inflation by about as much as 1 percentage point more unemployment for one year.

Measures to cut prices and costs can be effectively included as part of a larger anti-inflation strategy. In any such strategy, success will be self-perpetuating. Failure in the aggregate will almost surely cause the pieces to come apart. If the government can point to direct price-cutting measures of its own, it would stand a better chance of obtaining support from the private sector, either for voluntary restraint or for TIP. And if the government could accomplish that, it could change the inertia equations in a favorable way.

Comments
and Discussion

Martin Neil Baily: George Perry presents and discusses in an interesting and provocative way several hypotheses relevant to anti-inflationary policy. Perry describes convincingly the tremendous inertia in wage behavior during inflation and also brings out some new and informative aspects of the Phillips curve. I have a few doubts to raise, however, about his conclusions.

First, Perry shows the relatively greater inflexibility of wages in the high-wage and union sectors. The low-wage and nonunion sectors appear to be more responsive to short-run economic conditions. This result is plausible and can be rationalized, for example, on the grounds that wage contracts are more important in the high-wage and union sectors. The disaggregated wage equations that Perry estimates, however, contain no variables that will hold the wage distribution together. In *BPEA, 2:1977,* James Tobin and I developed some results suggesting the importance of the relative sectoral wage level as a determinant of the rate of change of a sector's wage. Perry does not have to accept our formulation, but one would expect some variable to be included that prevents relative wages from diverging indefinitely. In the past few years union wages have increased relative to nonunion wages. This fact is interesting in itself and relevant for wage policy. But if union wages continue to grow faster than nonunion wages, there will surely be increasing stress in the wage structure that will eventually affect the rates of change of wages in both sectors.

Second, Perry argues that the true wage equation is characterized by a "catch-up" augmented Phillips curve, rather than by an expectations-augmented Phillips curve. The arguments for this view seemed to me unconvincing. To demonstrate this would require an analysis of how expectations are formed and how the catch-up is computed, realizing that these two are different in principle and that they have in fact behaved differently enough over some historical period that the data can test the two alternatives. To be more specific, given all the shocks that have hit the economy recently and the tremendous inertia evident in wage behavior, it may have been true that the best estimate of one year's wage increase was the previous year's wage increase. If even half-true, this would make the two hypotheses difficult to distinguish.

Third, I was puzzled by two aspects of Perry's procedure and so I reran his aggregate equation. I was surprised that his wage-wage equation did not allow for serial correlation of the errors, but I discovered that this was because the correction made only a minor difference. Perry himself notes that the price feedbacks do seem to decline in importance with a serial correlation correction. However, I came to a different conclusion than Perry did regarding the stability of the equation. His predictions are made using *actual* values of the feedback variables rather than the predicted values from previous periods. This is a great help in keeping the equation on track through the 1970s. My version of Perry's equation 5.4 (the unemployment rate for adult males used in place of the weighted aggregate rate) underpredicted the rate of wage inflation in every year from 1971 through 1977 and gave a cumulative underprediction of over 16 percent by 1977.

In fairness to Perry, I should point out that he does say that the wage-wage spiral alone cannot explain the behavior of the 1970s. This is a crucial point for both theory and policy, however, and requires more emphasis. It is difficult to avoid the conclusion that the rapid price inflation and slow growth of real wages in the 1970s caused an upward pressure on wage settlements, particularly in the union and high-wage sectors, as Perry's earlier results suggested. The only other alternative is to argue that Perry has sharply underestimated the true nonaccelerating-inflation rate of unemployment (NAIRU) or natural rate. Wage acceleration has occurred, in this alternative view, because the actual unemployment rate for 1971–77, which averaged 6.5 percent, was below the NAIRU.

As a final check on the stability of the Phillips curve, I ran an F-test to see if the coefficients of the wage-wage or wage-price equations had shifted significantly. The null hypothesis was that the coefficients had remained constant across the 1956–69 and 1970–77 periods. These dates were selected because the lack of responsiveness of wages to the 1970–71 downturn was seen by many observers as an important break in wage behavior. The null hypothesis was rejected at the 5 percent level for my calculations of Perry's wage-wage and wage-price equations.

In short, therefore, I am less confident than Perry that we really do have a stable structural relation in current Phillips curve specifications. However, there are two lessons that Perry wants us to learn from the 1960s and 1970s. If the economy is wound up too much, wages and prices begin to accelerate. If unemployment is raised to slow things down again, it is a painful process. I have no quarrel with either of these lessons.

The regressions on inflation against the deficit and on inflation against money growth are fun. I hope the myth about the deficit is diminished by these findings. The improved performance of money growth as an explanation of the 1972–77 inflation does not give greater support to the monetarist than to the structuralist view of inflation. The Federal Reserve Board is not immune from political forces, nor should it be. It cannot tolerate prolonged, excessive unemployment. If structural factors push out the inflation/unemployment trade-off—resulting in inflationary price pressure even at high unemployment—the Federal Reserve Board is forced to accommodate at least some of this pressure. Consequently, high inflation and high money growth will tend to go together, even with a structuralist perspective.

Perry presents a brief discussion of the misperception theories. I think these theories can accommodate layoffs better than Perry indicates, but I share his general skepticism that expectational errors can plausibly explain the persistence of unemployment movements. And this also leads me to agree with his mistrust of the use of policy announcements to reduce inflationary pressure directly.

In conclusion, I commend Perry for his interesting and stimulating paper. If it did not convince me on all points, this merely reflects the difficulty of the issues being tackled.

William Poole: The basic message of George Perry's paper is that the Phillips curve is alive and well and that the evidence continues to support the proposition that higher unemployment buys a distressingly small rate of deceleration in inflation. I do not have any major quarrels with Perry on the matters analyzed in his paper.

For the purposes at hand it is not necessary to say much about the theory behind the Phillips curve. Perry is clearly writing within what may be called the original Phillips curve tradition, as distinguished from the more recent view of the curve developed by Milton Friedman, Edmund Phelps, and Robert Lucas. Under the traditional view, wage and price behavior—supported by contractual, collective bargaining, and other institutional considerations—reflects a substantial degree of inertia, whereas according to the view held by Friedman, Phelps, and Lucas, inertia is not inherent in behavior but reflects correctly perceived inertia in inflation caused by the monetary policies of the government. The importance of distinguishing between these two views is that according to the traditional view, demand management can reduce inflation only slowly and painfully, while under the alternative view, expectations could in principle be altered relatively quickly and, therefore, at little unemployment cost.

Perry attempts to provide evidence on this issue by examining what he calls forward-looking and backward-looking Phillips curve specifications. I find his evidence supporting the backward-looking specifications unconvincing. Consider, for example, the implications of the forward-looking theory for the apparently backward-looking wage-wage specification. Suppose wages are set on the basis of a price forecast for the next several years. Clearly, in trying to explain the wage behavior of the current year, last year's wages could be a more accurate measure of current expectations of future inflation than any proxy constructed from past or future price changes. I believe that it is simply not possible to obtain convincing evidence on this issue from the approach Perry follows.

From other evidence there can be no question that forward-looking behavior is important. The increasing use of cost-of-living clauses reflects a structural modification to contracts in anticipation of continuing inflation. In nonunion situations many companies have apparently replaced annual salary reviews with semiannual reviews so that wages can be linked more closely to changes in price level. And evidence from episodes of hyperinflation in other countries makes it clear that institutional practices seemingly anchored in bedrock are adjusted amazingly rapidly when inflation reaches triple-digit and higher rates.

If Perry underestimates the importance of forward-looking behavior, as I think he does, the near-term policy significance of this issue is nevertheless limited. Even the most ardent believer in the importance of expectations has a difficult time finding policy proposals that promise to generate a quick and lasting change in inflationary expectations. Suppose, for example, that the Federal Reserve announced that money growth would be reduced to a 4 percent annual rate immediately and then held at that rate indefinitely. It would be unlikely that this announcement would change inflationary expectations. The Federal Reserve has not always achieved its announced money growth targets; moreover, there is a possibility that the President, the Congress, or both would force a change in Federal Reserve policy if a recession occurred. From this viewpoint, the problem is not an economic policy problem at all, but rather one of constructing a political consensus for a noninflationary monetary policy.

It is unlikely that long-run inflationary expectations can be reduced without an actual decline in inflation *and* clear evidence of a commitment to less inflationary policies. For the evidence to be clear, it may well be necessary for the government consciously and deliberately to avoid following expansionary policies in the next recession.

If Perry's estimates are taken at face value, a monetary policy that kept the unemployment rate 1 percentage point above the natural rate would be consistent with a decline in the inflation rate by 0.3 percentage point each year. That policy would then call for a deceleration of money growth sufficient to slow nominal GNP growth by 0.3 percentage point a year. With this policy it would take at least twenty years of unemployment at 1 percentage point above the natural rate to reduce the inflation rate to zero. (Indeed, with Perry's two-year lag structure, it would take nearly thirty years.) It is difficult for me to believe that prediction of the results of such a monetary policy; surely in time the policy would change expectations and lead to adaptations consistent with full employment on the average. Nevertheless, Perry's estimates may well be reasonable for the time required for changed policies to become credible and to affect expectations. This period could easily be three to five years.

A number of policy proposals, including tax-based incomes policies, should be viewed in the light of their prospects for reducing the unemployment costs of the more basic anti-inflationary policy of slowing money growth. Perry mentions, but insufficiently emphasizes, the importance of reducing nominal income growth. Without monetary deceleration, other policies to reduce inflation are absolutely guaranteed to fail; with monetary deceleration, these other policies may reduce the employment costs of slowing inflation.

Perry does not discuss this possibility in detail, but I think that the importance of nonmonetary policies for the inflation issue is primarily political and expectational. The economics of these policies should be judged on efficiency and public finance considerations.

General Discussion

William Fellner amplified his views on anti-inflationary policy. He agreed with Perry that reasonably optimistic views about the output and employment consequences of his demand policy implied changes in specific regression coefficients in response to a consistent and credible policy line. He suggested that the coefficient that would change could be identified, for example, in a model of the type developed in Phillip Cagan's current work. For a slack of given size, this is the coefficient by which it is necessary to multiply the difference between the expected long-run inflation rate and the currently observed rate to obtain the current downward revision of the expected long-run rate. This revision causes current price deceleration, which either is added to the deceleration resulting from any increase in the slack or is deducted from the price acceleration resulting from any decrease. Fellner suggested that, under a credible policy of gradually reducing the rate of increase of money GNP until inflation is eliminated, the numerical value of the coefficient determining the adjustment of price-trend expectations would increase significantly. This, he argued, is because the erratic policies of the past must have made the public hesitant to lower its long-run inflation expectations during the brief periods of nondiminishing slack. Fellner also said that the alternative to the course he is advocating would be an uncomfortably controlled system, rather than the kind of economy envisaged by the advocates of incomes policy.

Michael Wachter agreed with Fellner on the importance of the changing responsiveness of inflation to government policy actions and pronouncements. Wachter said that the government had actually reduced the effectiveness of its anti-inflation policy and increased confusion during the most recent recession by frequently stating that policy was much less contractionary than it actually was.

James Tobin noted that if a TIP scheme were successful, the nominal money stock should grow less rapidly than if such a scheme were not in effect. He cautioned against accompanying a TIP scheme with aggregate demand policies that are contractionary in real terms.

Robert Gordon said that it was clear from the evidence of the 1960s and early 1970s that wages do not adjust fully to accelerations in the consumer price index; but he considered current knowledge about the effects of other wage determinants uncertain. In particular, he stated that it would be difficult to distinguish between the influence of product prices and the influence of other wages because of the high collinearity in these variables. Franco Modigliani reported that the coefficient on wages had been inappropriately negative in wage regressions with both past wages and past prices as independent variables. Perry responded that this result came from using hourly compensation as a wage variable; such compensation is currently poorly measured and is influenced by many nonmarket events such as payroll tax changes. Edward Gramlich argued that wages tend to be considerably more inflexible than prices in the U.S. economy. Thus, the use of longer lags might lend support to a price-wage hypothesis. Wachter voiced the opinion that the lagged money supply would perform as well as lagged prices or wages in explaining wage inflation. But Modigliani agreed with Perry that money supply or fiscal policy have no effect above that already captured by the excess demand variable.

Other participants at the conference discussed whether expected or past prices were more important in determining wages. Frederic Mishkin suggested that the presence in wage equations of only short lags on price inflation did not provide evidence supporting backward- rather than forward-looking wage behavior. If the inflation rate followed a random walk, for example, the most recent inflation rate would be the best predictor of future inflation rates. Therefore, even if wage behavior was forward looking, the most recent inflation rate would contain all the relevant information about expected inflation. Mishkin emphasized, however, that the relationship between past and expected price inflation need not be a stable one and might depend on the exact nature of the inflationary process. Thomas Juster said that short-run inflationary expectations were more volatile than long-run expectations and that long-run rather than short-run expectations were relevant for wage determination. This suggested the need to use longer lags.

Gardner Ackley and James Duesenberry questioned the usefulness of searching for a single determinant of wages. Duesenberry noted that there were good microeconomic reasons for product prices, consumer prices, and other wages to enter the process in both a retrospective and a prospective form. Greater disaggregation would be required to distinguish their relative importance. This uncertainty suggested that policies should not be adopted that depend too heavily on any single explanation. Ackley reasoned that each of these variables might be important to different sectors at various times. As inflation increased, institutional innovations, such as cost-of-living allowances, might well lead to changes in the relative importance of different variables.

The discussion turned to the behavior of relative wages. John Shoven suggested that the larger recent increases in wages in the high-wage industries might be explained either by the greater use of cost-of-living allowances in the high-wage unionized sector, or by the fact that as skilled wages moved into higher marginal tax brackets a larger before-tax dispersion was required to maintain the same after-tax differentials. Duesenberry mentioned Perry's evidence that wages in the high-wage sector were more sensitive to inflation and less sensitive to unemployment than those in the low-wage sectors. If the Phillips curve in the high-wage sector were flatter than that in the low-wage sector, it was likely they would intersect; if they did not, it would not lead to the cumulative divergence in wages that concerned Martin Baily in his discussion.

Modigliani and Robert Hall said that Perry had treated the rational expectations school too casually. Hall stated that Perry should have discussed the new view of this school—that recent changes in the inflation rate have been caused by changes in the natural rate because of supply shifts. Despite this omission, he agreed with Perry's Keynesian conclusion that changes in aggregate demand influence output far more than prices. Perry replied that he had not tried to present a comprehensive discussion of the rational expectations view but simply discussed where it differed from the mainline model. The principal difference is that the mainline model recognizes the possibility of extended periods of cyclical unemployment, while the rational expectations model treats such occurrences as changes in the natural rate.

31

This study argues that while structural policies such as public sector employment may be necessary to move the economy toward full employment with a nonaccelerating inflationary rate, many other public policies and social programs such as those related to retirement may have adverse effects on the level and distribution of employment and unemployment. (Though each of the programs considered also have salutary effects.) Given the current situation of simultaneous high unemployment and high inflation— stagflation—achieving lower unemployment rates without accelerating inflation may require altering social programs dealing with retirement. Ehrenberg considers five such retirement programs or policies in this study: the Social Security System (OASDHI), the Employee Retirement and Income Security Act (ERISA), the Age Discrimination in Employment Act, the Supreme Court decision in the Manhart case that prohibits sexual differentials in employee pension contributions, and early retirement provisions. The point of this study is not to criticize the intent of these policies and programs but to point out some of their unanticipated and undesirable effects on the economy and the labor market, with the objective of correcting the defects. With the Social Security system these effects are related to the payroll tax rate, the maximum taxable earnings level, the retirement earnings test, benefit rules for married women, and the unfunded, pay-as-you-go nature of the system. The tax rate itself increases the cost of labor relative to capital, and, unless it can be fully shifted to labor, will affect a firm's employment decisions. The wage tax can also affect the employment and labor force participation of workers. The maximum taxable earnings ceiling (which is now effectively being eliminated) changes the relative price of low-wage, low-skill labor vis-à-vis high-skill, high-wage labor, providing incentives for firms to shift toward the use of more skilled labor. The retirement earnings test, with its 50% marginal tax rate above the $4000 earnings exemption level, will likely discourage labor force participation and employment of the aged. (This is, however, an intended effect of the program.) Due to the benefit rules, married women face a situation wherein a lifetime of work entitles them to only small additional benefits relative to their entitlement based on their spouses' earnings. This effectively lowers their expected lifetime earnings associated with any job. Finally, the unfunded, pay-as-you-go benefit system may substantially reduce savings and thus reduce capital investment and growth, leading to reduced employment.

In an effort to increase the probability that private sector workers would receive their promised pension benefits, the ERISA includes fiduciary conditions that increase the cost of pension programs to employers. Unless these costs are fully shifted to workers, labor costs will increase and result in employers whose pre-ERISA provisions did not meet ERISA standards, reducing the level or rate of growth of employment. Finally, while private savings will increase and make possible more investment and economic growth, the conservative portfolio requirements will prevent investments in enterprises that have a high risk and thus attendant high rates of return. This will slow the rate of productivity growth and negatively affect employment.

The provisions for an older mandatory retirement age have a variety of behavioral implications, including a redistribution of jobs away from new hires (mainly younger persons), and toward the aged, along with possible changes in the stock of workers in firms—thus further affecting new hires—and, finally, possible discrimination against middle-aged workers.

The Manhart case resulted in the judgment that it was illegal sexual discrimination for employers to require females to contribute a larger portion of their salaries to pension funds than men. Since women usually live longer than men, equal contributions imply an actuarially lower benefit to women if a firm has a defined benefit plan. To maintain equal benefits for women under these conditions, the firm would have to pay the difference in premiums. Female labor will cost relatively more unless this cost can be shifted back to female workers, creating an incentive for employers to discriminate against women in their hiring.

Finally, early retirement provisions can help to hold down unemployment if, over the business cycle, workers take advantage of these provisions to leave the labor force. This can redistribute employment losses across age groups and toward older workers, and, given experience rating of the unemployment insurance payroll tax, reduce the cost of the unemployment insurance program to firms.

In summary, each of these examples (with the exception of that for early retirement) incorporate incentives that can result in unintended adverse effects on the level and distribution of employment and unemployment. While the marginal effects of each of these adverse effects may be small, their additive effect can be large. Correcting the inefficiencies of these programs can improve the economy's ability to reduce unemployment without incurring inflationary side effects. In fact, some corrections would directly act to reduce inflation. Examples include improvements in the allocation of labor by skill, age, or sex, or altering Social Security to increase aggregate saving.

Retirement Policies, Employment, and Unemployment

Ronald G. Ehrenberg

There is a growing consensus among economists that reliance on aggregate demand policies alone will not be sufficient to move the economy to full employment with a nonaccelerating inflation rate, and that policies which alter the structure of labor markets will be required. While obvious structural policies such as public sector employment programs and training programs are the focus of current debate, many other public policies affect labor markets in subtle ways which may well adversely affect the level and distribution of employment and unemployment. To help improve the inflation-unemployment tradeoff, policymakers should seek to marginally modify these policies, preserving their benefits while reducing their adverse labor market effects.

To illustrate these points, this paper discusses the influence of public and private retirement policies on the level and distribution of employment and unemployment. I focus on the Social Security system (*OASDHI*), the Employee Retirement Income Security Act (*ERISA*), the amendment to the Age Discrimination in Employment Act that raised the permissible mandatory retirement age to 70, the Supreme Court decision in the Manhart case prohibiting sex differentials in employee pension contributions, and early retirement provisions negotiated in private collective bargaining agreements. Certainly, it would be difficult to criticize the *intent* of these policies. However, each of the *public* policies adversely affects the level or distribution of employment and unemployment. I conclude by noting several reforms of the method of financing the Social Security system which would reduce the system's adverse labor market effects.

*Professor of economics and labor economics, Cornell University. Support for my research was provided by NSF Grant No. SOC 77-15800.

I. The Social Security System

The Social Security system influences labor markets in a variety of ways. First, the *retirement earnings test* for receipt of benefits and the 50 percent *marginal tax rate* on earnings above the $4,000 *earnings exemption* discourage labor force participation and employment of the aged (see Michael Boskin). These parameters, by reducing the net return to work effort after age 65, also induce a life cycle reallocation of work effort from the retirement years to earlier years (see James Smith). Empirical evidence suggests that the work week of prime age males may have *increased* by over two hours above the level it otherwise would have been because of this effect (see Richard Burkhauser and John Turner).

Second, if employers cannot shift 100 percent of the share of the payroll tax paid by them onto employees in the form of lower wages (or smaller wage increases), then firms' employment decisions will be affected. Although evidence on the extent of shifting is mixed, two recent studies concluded that less than 50 percent of employers' share of the tax is shifted onto labor (see Daniel Hamermesh, 1977a; the author, Robert Hutchens, and Robert Smith), which should induce employers to hire fewer employees than they would in the tax's absence.

Furthermore, the existence of a maximum taxable earnings level causes payroll tax rate increases to increase the cost of low-wage employees relative to the costs of high-wage employees. If relative wages do not fully adjust, increases in the tax rate should lead firms to substitute high-wage for low-wage workers. In contrast, increases in the taxable earnings level reduce the incentives for such substitution (see John Pencavel). Between 1960 and 1978, the *OASDHI* tax rate more than doubled, while the maximum taxable earnings level rose from $4,800 to $17,700. The latter change has likely dominated the former, causing a reduction in employers' incentives to substitute high-wage for low-wage employees and a shift in the distribution of employment (unemployment) towards (away from) low-skilled individuals.

The share of the payroll tax either nominally paid by employees or implicitly paid by them in the form of lower wages has a differential impact on different classes of individuals. For individuals outside the labor force it has a pure substitution effect, discouraging labor force participation. For employed individuals earning more than the taxable earnings level, it has a pure income effect, stimulating increased work effort. For employed individuals earning less than the taxable wage base, both effects are present, and the net impact is ambiguous.

The large increases in both the tax rate and maximum taxable earnings levels during the past decade may have reduced the work effort of individuals who earned more than the maximum taxable level prior to the increase, but less after. Although the impact of these changes on the unemployment rate is ambiguous, their net effect was probably to reduce the growth rate of employment. This effect may have been partially offset by the accompanying liberalization of promised future benefits. Since eligibility for *OASI* benefits depends upon career work effort, promised higher future benefit levels may stimulate greater work effort on the part of nonaged workers. However, this *entitlement effect* is likely to be greatest for low-wage workers as the benefit-earnings ratio declines as earnings rise. Moreover, since married females have the option of receiving either their own benefits or 50 percent of their husband's benefits (100 percent after he dies), their lifetime work effort entitles them to only small net additional *OASI* benefits and the entitlement effect is likely to be unimportant for them.

Finally, recent evidence suggests that the Social Security system may substantially reduce private savings (see Martin Feldstein, 1974a,b 1976; Alicia Munnell, 1974; and for contrasting evidence, Robert Barro). This net reduction is *not* offset by an increase in public savings because of the pay-as-you-go nature of the system. As a result, total savings and capital accumulation in the economy are reduced, leading to reduced growth in productivity and output, and ultimately to reduced rates of growth of employment and/or real wages. Recent increases in Social Security taxes and promised future benefits levels have likely exacerbated this effect.

In sum, the parameters of the system interact to produce numerous effects on labor markets. The reduction in labor force participation and employment of the aged is a planned effect and should not be judged a negative feature. In contrast, the *OASDHI* payroll tax on employers *and* employees and the unfunded nature of the retirement trust fund probably serve to reduce both the labor force participation rates and employment levels of the nonaged. The parameters of the system also differentially influence the distribution of employment and unemployment across sex classes and earnings classes of employees. Recent changes in the system's parameters probably have marginally slowed the growth rate of employment and reduced employers' incentives to substitute high- for low-skilled labor.

II. Employee Retirement Income Security Act of 1974 *(ERISA)*

The *ERISA* was designed to increase the probability that private sector employees receive promised retirement benefits. It includes provisions requiring liberalized vesting rules, more stringent funding requirements, and increased fiduciary responsibility. These provisions increase employers' costs of providing pensions and should lead employers to shift at least part of the increased costs to employees in the form of lower wages, smaller wage increases, or pension plan terminations. Although it is too early to assess *ERISA*'s impact on wages, recent studies show that a tradeoff exists between wages and retirement system characteristics in both the private and public sectors (see the author; Alan Gustman and Martin Segal; Randall Weiss and Bradley Schiller). If employers cannot fully shift

ERISA's costs, unit labor costs will increase, resulting in a reduction in the level (or rate of growth) of private employment. This reduction would be concentrated in those firms with pension plans whose pre-*ERISA* provisions did not meet the *ERISA* standards. Adoption of *ERISA*-type controls over public employees' retirement systems would have a similar negative impact on employment in the public sector.

The *ERISA*-type controls also affect the level of pension plan funding and composition of pension funds' portfolios. By requiring pension plans to be fully funded, they increase the stock of curent pension fund assets which, if not offset by a decline in individuals' saving, will increase the level of capital accumulation and ultimately the level of employment. On the other hand, by restricting the type of investments which pension funds may make, the controls prevent pension fund assets from being invested in projects with the highest expected rate of return (but also highest risk) and hence reduce the rate of productivity growth. Without empirical evidence, one can not ascertain which of these effects dominates.

III. Mandatory Retirement

The amendment to the Age Discrimination in Employment Act passed by Congress earlier this year, subject to a few exceptions, raises from 65 to 70 the age at which employers may compel their employees to retire. This will influence the level and distribution of employment in a number of ways. Mandatory retirement provisions tend to be found in large establishments which are unionized and in which employees usually have long actual or expected job tenure (see Edward Lazear). The typical life cycle relationship between an individual's earnings and productivity in firms, where an implicit long-term contract exists between the firm and its employees, is one in which earnings first exceed productivity, then productivity exceeds earnings, and finally earnings again exceed productivity. These stages correspond to a period of formal or informal training, a period of peak productivity, and a final period

in which productivity is declining, but informal rules or union contracts prevent wages from being cut. The age at which this latter period starts, if at all, varies widely across individuals and depends upon factors such as the employee's health and the demands of his or her specific job. The establishment of a mandatory retirement age at an age such that, *on average*, the present value of employees' earnings just equals the present value of their productivity allows a firm to maximize its expected presented value of its profits. Such rules also allow increases in the present value of employees' earnings over their life cycles (see Lazear).

If the legislation induces some individuals to postpone their retirement, then on average the present value of wages will exceed the present value of marginal productivities over employees' careers. Employers may respond by negotiating flatter or everywhere lower real wage profiles. The overall *level* of employment would be unchanged, however new hires would be reduced, because the average employee would have a longer work-life. Hence, some jobs would be redistributed from new hires, primarily youths, to the aged. Further if employers face any difficulty in making wage adjustments, then they will tend to reduce their *stock* of employees, causing still *larger* reductions in new hires.

The change may also discourage employers from hiring middle-aged employees. Prior to the legislation, a firm would be willing to hire a middle-aged worker provided that his expected present value of marginal productivities less wages was nonnegative. If expected wages at the old retirement age exceeded expected marginal productivities, the legislative-induced increase in the expected retirement age reduces the firm's incentive to hire middle-aged workers and the maximum age at which it will hire new employees. Indeed, this provides employers an added incentive to prefer young rather than middle-aged new hires, and partially offsets the legislation's negative impact on youth employment (see Barry Chiswick and Carmel Chiswick). However, to the extent that the legislation reduces the number of retirees per year, employers may be forced to increase layoffs to achieve desired lower employment levels in periods of declining aggregate demand, causing a further redistribution of employment away from those with the least seniority and increasing the measured unemployment rate.

The magnitudes of all of these effects depend upon the number of retirements postponed in response to the legislation; one recent study concluded some 200,000 aged employees would be added to the work force in the first year (see U.S. Department of Labor). However, growth in real incomes, private pensions, and Social Security benefits have reduced males' average age at retirement and as long as the Social Security retirement earnings test rules are maintained, workers aged 65 face a substantial incentive to retire. Thus, although the legislated change may marginally alter the distribution of employment and unemployment across age groups, its overall effect on the level of employment is likely to be small. It may, however, also substantially slow the progress of nonwhites into professional positions (see George Johnson and Juli Malveaux).

IV. The Manhart Case

On April 25, 1978, the U.S. Supreme Court declared that employers who require females to contribute a greater proportion of their salaries than males to contributory pension plans are committing illegal sex discrimination (see City of Los Angeles vs. Manhart). However, because female life expectancies are longer than males', to maintain the actuarial soundness of a defined benefit pension plan females must either (a) receive lower annual retirement benefits than otherwise identical males, or (b) receive equal annual retirement benefits, with larger annual contributions being made for females. The Supreme Court decision prohibits (b) unless the larger contribution is nominally paid by employers. This increases the relative costs of female employees, providing employers with an incentive to substitute males for females.

One proposal to eliminate this incentive is to use a "unisex" mortality table, calculated by weighting the relevant male and female mortality tables by the proportion of employees of each sex employed by a firm. Equal net contribution rates for *all* employees of a given age necessary to fully fund equal retirement benefits per year for retirees of each sex could then be determined. However, employers should realize that by reducing the proportion of females in their work force, they would reduce their required average net contributions (see Burt Barnow and the author). The likely magnitude of this substitution depends upon the true pension cost differential between males and female employees, and the extent to which males and females are substitutes in production. The former is likely to be quite small in plans which provide survivors benefits for spouses of beneficiaries, while precise estimates of the latter have yet to be obtained (see Hamermesh and James Grant).

V. Early Retirement

Early retirement provisions contained in many privately negotiated contracts typically allow early retirement at reduced benefit levels. While early retirement provisions are of value to employees, they also have the effect of redistributing employment losses across age groups of employees during periods of low or declining demand which may well *reduce* employers' costs.

Union contracts typically require that layoffs be inversely related to seniority; however utilizing such a policy to reduce employment may not be optimal from an employer's prospective. Due to the experience-rated nature of the unemployment insurance (UI) payroll tax, after some point layoffs raise the employer's payroll tax. Moreover, if the firm's most senior workers are in the stage of their life cycles in which wages exceed marginal productivities, the firm would best be served by reducing their employment rather than younger workers. Furthermore, if these senior workers voluntarily leave their jobs, an employer's UI tax rate would not increase as voluntary separations are not eligible for UI benefits in most states. Early retirement provisions thus allow employers to redistribute employment losses in periods of low or declining demand from younger to older workers and to reduce their *UI* payroll tax contributions (see James Medoff). Since retirees tend to be out of the labor force, these policies probably do reduce the measured unemployment rate.

VI. Conclusion

All of the retirement policies discussed in this paper, except for privately negotiated early retirement provisions, were shown to have adverse effects on the level and distribution of employment and unemployment. These examples support the contention that more explicit attention should be given to the employment effects of social programs prior to their adoption *and* that consideration should be given to restructuring existing programs to reduce their adverse labor market effects. While each of the effects is probably quite small, their sum may be sizable.

Three examples of possible changes in the financing of the Social Security system illustrate the types of restructuring one might consider. First, the use of general revenue financing from personal and corporate income tax revenues, for all or some fraction of future system revenue needs, would reduce employer's incentives to substitute capital for labor. Second, increasing system revenues by more than is necessary to fund benefits in the short-run to build up a larger Social Security trust fund, and using this fund to buy outstanding government debt, would increase the social rate of savings and capital accumulation which ultimately would result in increased rates of growth of employment (see Feldstein, 1977). Third, raising the maximum taxable earnings level, rather than the payroll tax rate, to meet future system revenue needs would reduce employers' incentives to substitute high-wage for low-wage workers. To the extent that the overall rate of wage inflation is influenced more by the level of excess demand for labor in high-wage labor markets than that in low-wage labor markets, this change will also reduce the unemployment rate associated with each level of inflation (see Martin Baily and James Tobin, George Johnson and Arthur Blakemore).

REFERENCES

M. N. Baily and J. Tobin, "Macroeconomic Effects of Selective Public Employment and Wage Subsidies," *Brookings Papers*, Washington 1977, *2*, 511–44.

B. S. Barnow and R. G. Ehrenberg, "The Costs of Defined Benefit Pension Plans and Firm Adjustments," *Quart. J. Econ.*, forthcoming.

R. Barro, "Social Security and Private Saving: Evidence from the U.S. Time-Series," mimeo, Univ. Rochester 1977.

M. Boskin, "Social Security and Retirement Decision," *Econ. Inquiry*, Jan. 1977, *15*, 1–25.

R. V. Burkhauser, and J. A. Turner, "A Time-Series Analysis on Social Security and its Effect on the Market Work of Men at Younger Ages," *J. Polit. Econ.*, Aug. 1978, *86*, 701–15.

B. R. Chiswick and C. U. Chiswick, "On Benefits of Mandatory Retirement," *New York Times*, Nov. 12, 1977.

R. G. Ehrenberg, "Retirement System Characteristics and Compensating Differentials in the Public Sector," paper presented to the Econometric Society Meetings, Chicago 1978.

———, **R. Hutchens, and R. S. Smith,** "The Distribution of Unemployment Insurance Benefits and Costs," U.S. Department of Labor. Final Report, Contract J-9-M-6-0098, Mar. 1978.

M. Feldstein, (1974a) "Social Security, Induced Retirement and Aggregate Capital Accumulation," *J. Polit. Econ.*, Sept./Oct. 1974, *82*, 905–26.

———, (1974b) "Social Security and Private Savings: International Evidence in an Extended Life Model," in his *The Economics of Public Services*, New York 1974.

———, "Toward A Reform of Social Security," *Publ. Interest*, Summer 1975, *40*, 75–95.

———, "Social Security and Saving: The Extended Life Cycle Theory," *Amer. Econ. Rev. Proc.*, May 1976, *66*, 77–86.

————, "Facing the Social Security Crisis," *Publ. Interest*, Spring 1977, *47*, 88–100.

A. **Gustman and M. Segal**, "Interstate Variations in Teachers' Pensions," *Ind. Relat.*, Oct. 1977, *16*, 335–44.

D. **Hamermesh**, (1977a) "New Estimates of the Incidence of the Payroll Tax," mimeo., Michigan State Univ. Aug. 1977.

————, "Effect of the UI System on Labor Force Behavior," tech. anal. paper no. 54, U.S. Department of Labor, Sept. 1977.

———— **and J. Grant**, "Econometric Studies of Labor—Labor Substitution and Their Implications for Policy," paper presented at the Allied Social Sciences Meetings, Chicago, Aug. 1978.

G. **Johnson and A. Blakemore**, "Estimating the Potential for Reducing the Unemployment Rate Consistent with Non-Accelerating Inflation: Methodological Issues," mimeo., U.S. Council Econ. Advisors, Mar. 1978.

———— **and J. Malveaux**, "Mandatory Retirement and Affirmative Action," mimeo., U.S. Council Econ. Advisors, Aug. 1977.

E. **Lazear**, "Why is There Mandatory Retirement?," mimeo., Univ. Chicago, Nov. 1977.

J. **Medoff**, "Layoffs and Alternatives under Trade Unions in U.S. Manufacturing," *Amer. Econ. Rev.*, forthcoming.

Alicia **Munnell**, *The Effect of Social Security on Personal Savings*, Cambridge, Mass., 1974.

————, *The Future of Social Security*, Washington 1976.

J. **Pencavel**, "Some Labor Market Implications of the Payroll Tax for Unemployment and Old Age Insurance," mimeo., Stanford Univ. 1974.

J. **Smith**, "On the Labor-Supply Effects of Age-Related Income Maintenance Programs," *J. Hum. Resources*, Winter 1975, *10*, 25–43.

R. **Weiss and B. Schiller**, "The Value of Defined Benefit Pension Plans: A Test of the Equalizing Differences Hypothesis," mimeo., Univ. Maryland 1976.

City of Los Angeles vs. Manhart, No. 76-1810, U.S. 55 L. Ed. 2d., 1978.

U.S. **Department of Labor**, "Questions and Issues Relating to the Proposed Amendments to the Age Discrimination in Employment Act of 1967," mimeo., 1977.

32

This study is the most recent in a series of studies in which Feldstein argues that the Social Security program has been a major force in depressing the private savings rate and aggregate capital accumulation. In view of the concern over the last decade with increasing inflation, rising unemployment, and an alleged decrease in the rate of productivity growth, this is a charge that deserves serious analysis and policy consideration. If the charge is empirically correct, then this is a major cost of the Social Security program that must be weighed against its benefits. The issue cannot be ignored and deserves a major research initiative on the part of the federal government to determine its significance.

The authors note that if individuals behaved rationally and if the Social Security program were actuarially fair, individuals would treat Social Security payroll taxes and savings for a private annuity as perfect substitutes. They would then save less for private pension support in their old age. But because the Social Security program does not accumulate a trust fund but is a pay-as-you-go program, the payroll taxes are converted directly to consumption. Thus, aggregate saving, and, hence, capital accumulation, is less than it would be in the absence of the program.

In contrast to this argument, the authors point out that in a more general model (one permitting more complex behavior), the effect of the Social Security program on the private savings rate is indeterminate. After rejecting irrationality and myopia as explanations of the effect of Social Security in reducing individual savings, the authors point out that the essential feature of an extended life cycle model is the joint nature of retirement and savings decisions. Exogenous variables affecting the retirement decision thus affect the decision to save. For instance, it is possible that if Social Security induces earlier retirement, it may also increase saving in the period before retirement. This "reduced retirement effect" counteracts the "wealth replacement effect" discussed in the less general model above. Hence, whether Social Security reduces savings is an empirical issue. It can not be judged a priori.

Therefore, the authors specify an econometric model using individual household data to estimate the effect of Social Security on the accumulation of wealth over one's normal working cycle. They find that differences in future Social Security benefits result in differences in ordinary saving.

Feldstein and Pellechio's model implies that each individual's desired accumulation of total wealth—private wealth plus social security wealth—will be proportional to one's final year's net labor income. This implies that consumption during retirement is proportional to the level of consumption during the preretirement years. They improve the generality of the model by taking into account the fact that the retirement decision at any age will be influenced by the value of Social Security at that age. They also relax the proportionality assumption to account for the possibility that the ratio of total retirement consumption to consumption during retirement years is a function of the individual's net labor income, α_2. (Higher earnings may induce a redistribution of lifetime income in favor of older age.) Next, they allow for differences in induced changes in gifts from children to parents, α_4, and differences in the perception of Social Security and ordinary assets (due, perhaps, to the real annuity character of Social Security benefits or its noncontractual character, λ). These considerations yield a complex parameter to be estimated, μ, where $\mu = (1 - \alpha_2 - \alpha_4)\lambda$. Unfortunately, the model does not allow the identification of these effects separately. Thus, only the net effect of Social Security on private saving can be estimated. But the coefficient estimate of μ can be interpreted as follows:

If persons are completely irrational and myopic, $\mu = 0$;

If behavior conforms to the pure traditional life cycle model, $\mu = 1$; and,

If there are completely offsetting changes in gifts from children to parents ($\alpha_4 = 1$), then $\mu \leqslant 0$. Thus, the estimated value of μ can provide some basis for choosing among the competing theories of savings behavior.

Finally, this study examines the equilibrium stock of wealth rather than the annual savings flow as the dependent variable. This variable is expressed as a function of an exogenous variable, expected Social Security wealth. Hence, this model avoids problems of bias inherent in previous models (which focussed on the annual savings flow and attempted to explain this endogenous variable with an [endogenous] lagged wealth variable).

The results suggest that each dollar of Social Security wealth reduces fungible net worth by less than one dollar. The estimated coefficient, μ, is generally significantly different from zero but is not significantly different from one. Differences among households in Social Security wealth appear to have an effect on private wealth accumulation. There are several significant qualifications, however, to these results. First, the sample is small and refers to a two-year period—1962 and 1963—when the Social Security program was substantially different. Responses cannot easily be extrapolated to the present. The two-year earnings history introduces bias of undetermined direction in estimating the effects both of the Social Security wealth and labor income variable. Finally, there is no information on either private pensions or life insurance. The effects of income on asset accumulation will therefore likely be understated and the effects of Social Security wealth will be overstated.

In summary, these results are qualified, but they point toward important policy issues and require the development of proper data to clear up the remaining uncertainty.

Social Security and
Household Wealth Accumulation
New Microeconometric Evidence

Martin Feldstein and Anthony Pellechio

T HE social security program will pay benefits of more than $100 billion in 1978.[1] Public transfers on this scale are large enough to have profound effects on the behavior of the U.S. economy. The most important effect, although not the only one, is likely to be the impact of social security on private saving and aggregate capital accumulation. The present paper contributes to the analysis of this issue by providing new evidence on the extent to which the accumulation of wealth by individual households responds to differences in social security benefits.

I. Social Security and Saving: The Theoretical Indeterminacy

The traditional life cycle model implies that an actuarially fair social security program unambiguously reduces private saving. Within a more general framework, however, the effect of social security on saving is theoretically indeterminate. Only econometric evidence can determine the extent to which social security decreases saving. Before turning to our new evidence, it is worth examining the sources of the theoretical indeterminacy.

Consider first the effect of social security in the traditional life cycle model in which the time pattern of work and labor income is exogenously fixed. In this situation, social security can alter the time pattern of consumption only if it changes the household's lifetime budget constraint. Since

an actuarially fair social security program leaves the budget constraint unchanged, there is also no change in each year's consumption. The social security tax that is paid each year therefore reduces private saving by an equal amount. For an actuarially fair social security program, this is equivalent to reducing the personal wealth accumulated before retirement by the actuarial present value of future benefits.[2]

It has been common in discussions of social security policy to reject this picture of rational life cycle saving.[3] Individuals are instead viewed as myopic nonplanners who save in a haphazard way or not at all; as a result of such myopia, the introduction of social security would have no offsetting effect on private saving.[4] We agree that there are some individuals for whom this picture of irrational saving behavior is an appropriate description but we do not believe that such behavior is universal or even typical. Irrational saving behavior among part of the population would reduce the effect of social security on private saving but would not eliminate it.[5] The econometric evidence presented below gives no support to the view that such irrationality is very widespread.

The extended life cycle model presented in Feldstein (1974, 1977) showed a quite different reason why individual life cycle saving might not be decreased and might actually be increased by the introduction or increase of social security benefits. The essential feature of the extended life cycle model is that retirement and saving decisions are made jointly. Any exogenous vari-

Received for publication December 23, 1977. Revision accepted for publication July 27, 1978.

* Harvard University and the National Bureau of Economic Research.

This research is part of the NBER program of Studies in Social Insurance. We are grateful to the NBER and the National Science Foundation for support of this research and to Robert Barro and participants in the Harvard social insurance seminar for helpful comments. This paper has not been reviewed by the NBER Board of Directors.

[1] The social security program is technically three separate programs of old age and survivors insurance, disability insurance, and health insurance for the aged (Medicare). General retirement, survivors and disability benefits alone will exceed $100 billion.

[2] The result is shown graphically for the two-period life cycle model in Feldstein (1974) and derived explicitly in Feldstein (1977).

[3] See, for example, Myers (1965), Pechman et al. (1968), Schulz (1974), and Diamond (1977).

[4] Some have even suggested that the provision of social security may actually cause some individuals to save more because it serves as a reminder of the need to provide for old age. See Katona (1965) and Pechman et al. (1968).

[5] The irrational saving behavior of a small fraction of the population might justify a compulsory saving program even if it had a small aggregate effect on saving. This is a quite separate question that will not be examined in this paper.

From Martin Feldstein and Anthony Pellechio, "Social Security and Household Wealth Accumulation: New Microeconometric Evidence," 61(3) *Review of Economics and Statistics* 361-368 (August 1979). Copyright 1979 by North-Holland Publishing Company.

able can thus influence saving indirectly by altering retirement. Social security is likely to induce earlier retirement and the resulting increase in the expected period of retirement will, as such, increase total saving during preretirement years. The net effect of social security on saving in this extended life cycle model is ambiguous. Whether and to what extent social security reduces saving depends on the relative strength of the traditional "wealth replacement effect" and the countervailing "induced retirement effect."[6]

Even if we disregard the effect of social security on retirement, there are at least four reasons why rational savers might not regard social security wealth and private fungible wealth as perfect substitutes.[7] First, social security provides an annuity rather than a fixed sum at retirement and, even before price indexing was formally incorporated, adjusted benefits for rising prices. Because of this "real annuity" character of social security, individuals might reasonably regard a dollar of social security wealth as a substitute for more than a dollar's worth of fungible assets. Second, social security benefits are not a contractual obligation of the government but are determined by legislation.[8] Pessimists might therefore underestimate the value of social security wealth while optimists overestimate it. Third, social security is not an actuarially fair program, but alters lifetime budget constraints; such changes in real lifetime resources will alter consumption and saving.[9] Fourth, the introduction of social security (or a change in an existing program) may cause offsetting changes in private intergenerational transfers, thereby reducing the depressing effect of social security on private saving.[10]

In this paper, we analyze a cross section of households and find that differences in future social security benefits cause differences in ordinary saving It should go without saying that no single econometric study can ever be conclusive. The current research should be seen as an addition to a growing body of new evidence on the effect of social security on the accumulation of wealth.[11]

II. The Econometric Specification

The present study uses individual household observations to estimate the effect of social security on the amount of wealth that individuals accumulate by the end of the normal working life. The specification of our econometric equation focuses on the stock of accumulated wealth rather than the annual flow of saving. The current section discusses our specification and the interpretation of the parameters in more detail.

It is useful to begin with the relation between labor income and accumulated individual wealth that is predicted by the traditional life cycle model in the absence of any social security. In its most general form, the traditional life cycle model implies only that each individual accumulates wealth during his working years to finance consumption during retirement; further restrictions are needed to specify an econometric equation. Under the assumption that all individuals have the same tastes with respect to consumption at different ages, that each individual's net-of-tax labor income has its own level but grows at the same exponential rate, and that intended bequests are either nonexistent or proportional to the present value of the individual's labor income, the traditional life cycle model implies that in any age cohort the value of each individual's

---

[6] See Feldstein (1977) for a formal derivation of this.

[7] We define "social security wealth" as the present actuarial value of future social security benefits. The adjective "fungible" is used to distinguish household wealth as traditionally defined from the total household wealth. The calculation of social security wealth is discussed in section III below and in Feldstein (1974).

[8] Until 1972 the law made no provision for future increases in the schedule of social security benefits. Increases occurred frequently, but required explicit acts of Congress.

[9] This important aspect is developed in Kotlikoff et al. (1977).

[10] This idea is developed by Barro (1974) and Miller and Upton (1974). Our econometric evidence deals only partially with this issue. In particular, our evidence does not preclude the possibility that the existence of social security tax liabilities on future generations could cause every household to raise its savings while the existence of benefits for the current generation of workers causes differential reduction in

savings. The direct evidence on the value of bequests by low and middle income families is, however, contrary to the prediction of the Barro-Miller-Upton theory. For a more detailed discussion of the reasons for believing that the effects of offsetting intergenerational transfers is quantitatively small, see Feldstein (1978). For those who remain agnostic about the magnitude of offsetting bequests, our evidence can be interpreted as quantifying the extent to which other reasons cause a departure from the complete replacement predicted by the traditional life cycle model.

[11] The studies to date include analyses of time series evidence (Feldstein, 1974; Munnell, 1974; Barro, 1978; Darby, 1979), household survey data (Feldstein, 1976a; Kotlikoff et al., 1977; Munnell, 1976), and cross-country data on national savings rates (Aaron, 1967; Feldstein, 1977). A brief survey of the available estimates is presented in Feldstein (1976b).

accumulated wealth is related by a unique function to his current net labor income. It has also been traditional to assume that this functional relation is one of proportionality. Consumption during retirement is then proportional to the level of consumption during the earlier working years. This implies further that the value of accumulated wealth on the verge of retirement is proportional to that final year's earnings.

Social security provides each individual with an annuity when he retires. In the traditional life cycle model, the present value of that annuity should substitute for an equal amount of private wealth at the time of retirement. The model therefore implies that each individual's desired accumulation of "total wealth" including "social security wealth" will be proportional to his final year's net labor income:

$$\frac{A_i + SSW_i}{YL_i} = \alpha_1 \qquad (1)$$

where A_i is the value of individual i's ordinary "fungible" wealth on the verge of retirement, SSW_i is the social security wealth (the present actuarial value of the benefits to be provided by social security), and YL_i is the net-of-tax labor income in the final preretirement year.

The extended life cycle model begins with the basic fact that the age of retirement is an endogenous variable. The value of social security wealth at some age at which retirement might be contemplated (say, age 60) will influence the individual's retirement decision.[12] This implies that the total wealth desired at age 60 will itself be a function of SSW relative to YL:

$$\frac{A_i + SSW_i}{YL_i} = \alpha_1 + \alpha_2 \frac{SSW_i}{YL_i}. \qquad (2)$$

Since a higher value of SSW/YL induces earlier retirement and therefore a larger desired stock of total wealth, the extended life cycle model implies $\alpha_2 > 0$.

The proportionality assumption can be relaxed to allow the possibility that the ratio of total retirement consumption to consumption during working years is a function of the individual's net labor income. This can be approximated linearly by replacing (2) by

$$\frac{A_i + SSW_i}{YL_i} = \alpha_1 + \alpha_2 \frac{SSW_i}{YL_i} + \alpha_3 YL_i \qquad (3)$$

where $\alpha_3 > 0$ if higher earnings induce a redistribution of lifetime income in favor of older age.[13] Multiplying both sides of (3) by YL_i yields the basic specification that will be used in our econometric analysis:

$$A_i + SSW_i = \alpha_1 YL_i + \alpha_2 SSW_i + \alpha_3 YL_i^2. \qquad (4)$$

This specification can be modified easily to allow for the possibility that social security induces changes in gifts from children to their retired parents.

If children reduce their gifts to their parents in proportion to the parents' receipt of social security benefits, the value of the social security wealth is reduced; total wealth should be written $A_i + (1 - \alpha_4)SSW_i$ rather than $A_i + SSW_i$.[14] Even if the induced changes in gifts from children to parents are ignored, we may wish to allow for a difference between SSW and ordinary assets because of such things as the real annuity character of social security or its non-contractual character. This suggests replacing SSW_i in (4) by some multiple of SSW_i, say λSSW_i, where λ may be either less than or greater than 1 but is not expected to differ from 1 by very much.

Combining all of these effects yields the specification[15]

$$A_i + (1 - \alpha_4)\lambda SSW_i = \alpha_1 YL_i + \alpha_2 \lambda SSW_i + \alpha_3 YL_i^2 \qquad (5)$$

or, collecting terms,

$$A_i = \alpha_1 YL_i - \mu SSW_i + \alpha_3 YL_i^2 \qquad (6)$$

where

$$\mu = (1 - \alpha_2 - \alpha_4)\lambda. \qquad (7)$$

Thus, the traditional life cycle model implies $\mu = 1$, while the effects of induced retirement (α_2)

and offsetting child-parent gifts (α_4) reduce this value. The other factors included in λ could either lower or raise μ. Thus, $\mu > 1$ cannot be precluded if, for example, there is little effect through induced early retirement or changes in intergenerational transfers but there is substantial optimism about the size of benefits or a great premium placed on the real annuity character of social security.

It is, of course, unfortunate that the estimation of an equation like (6) cannot identify the relative importance of each of the parameters in (7). An estimate of μ is sufficient to answer the policy-related question about the net effect of social security on private saving but knowledge of the individual parameters in (7) is required to evaluate the competing theories of behavior that were discussed in the preceding section. Although such individual parameter estimates cannot be obtained, the value of μ can be used to assess some of the extreme versions of these theories. For example, the pure traditional life cycle model implies $\mu = 1$ while complete myopia and irrationality implies $\mu = 0$. Similarly, completely offsetting changes in gifts from children to parents $(\alpha_4 = 1)$ imply $\mu \leq 0$. The estimated value of μ can therefore in principle help to reduce the range of admissible theories about saving behavior.

The use of a two-year average value of YL to represent a lifetime history of net earnings and of bequests and gifts received rests on the formal assumption that net earnings grow exponentially and that all other receipts are proportional to labor income. Because we are limited by the available data to only a two-year average for YL_i, we add a random error and a constant term to equation (6) to indicate that (6) cannot be expected to hold precisely:

$$A_i = \alpha_0 + \alpha_1 YL_i - \mu SSW_i + \alpha_3 YL_i{}^2 + u_i. \quad (8)$$

This is the final estimation equation used in our econometric analysis. It should be emphasized that our sample will be limited to households with men between the ages of 55 and 64 so that A_i represents fungible wealth on the verge of the normal retirement age. The sample will also be restricted in other ways that will be described in the next section.

In concluding this section, it is worthwhile to note that equation (8) avoids a very substantial bias that has been a source of serious trouble in previous tests of the traditional life cycle model based on household data.[16] The standard form of such tests has been to estimate a saving equation with a lagged wealth variable among the regressors and observe whether its coefficient is negative.[17] Since the most important source of unexplained variation among households (the u_i's of equation (8)) reflects permanent differences in taste and in risk aversion, the disturbance in a saving equation will be positively correlated with the lagged wealth variable. This is likely to cause a substantial bias that can account for the apparently poor performance of the life cycle hypothesis in previous cross-section tests. Because the current study focuses on the equilibrium stock of wealth rather than the annual savings flow and uses an exogenous variable (SSW) instead of a lagged endogenous variable, this potential source of substantial bias is avoided.

III. Data and Definitions

The data used in the present research were collected in the Federal Reserve Board's *Survey of Financial Characteristics of Consumers* (Projector and Weiss, 1966) in which detailed balance sheets and income statements were obtained from all participants. The survey was conducted in 1963 and refers to income in 1962 and wealth at the end of 1962. A follow-up survey obtained data on income in 1963. The present study uses the subsample of households in which there was an employed man aged 55 to 64 who was covered by social security. Households with very low incomes (less than half of the median) and very high incomes (more than 2.5 times the maximum covered by social security) were eliminated as were those reporting substantial bequests.[18]

The dependent variable (A) that we have used corresponds as closely as is possible with the available data to household net worth as is possible with the available data. Labor income (YL) is defined to include all income other than income from property. It is the average of the sum of wage and salary income, income from

[16] See Projector and Weiss (1966), Modigliani and Ando (1957), and, more generally, the survey of studies reported in Mayer (1972).

[17] Alternatively a consumption function is estimated and a positive coefficient is expected on the lagged wealth variable.

[18] For more details of the sample, see section III of Feldstein and Pellechio (1977).

sole proprietorships, and farm income in 1962 and 1963. The amount paid in income taxes for the two years is estimated and subtracted from total income from these sources to give disposable labor income.

The value of social security wealth was evaluated for each observation in this sample. By definition, an individual's social security wealth is the value of the benefits for which he will be eligible at age 65 less the taxes he will pay until then, discounted to the present with appropriate adjustment for actuarial survival probabilities. A married couple's social security wealth is defined in an analogous way. The survey data on the separate earnings of the husband and wife and on their ages can be used to estimate the couple's social security wealth. The procedure has been described in detail elsewhere (Feldstein, 1976a).[19]

Before turning to the econometric estimation of the wealth accumulation equation, it is important to recall some of the limitations of the current data. First, we have no information on either private pensions or life insurance. Our measure of household assets therefore understates true net worth and this understatement is likely to be an increasing function of income and perhaps of social security wealth as well. To the extent that households substitute private pensions and life insurance for other forms of asset accumulation, the regression estimates will understate the effects of income on asset accumulation and overstate the effect of social security. These biases are likely to be relatively small because pension coverage was relatively poor for this age cohort of men (born in the decade from 1898 to 1907). Second, the labor income variable bases an estimate of lifetime earnings on information for only two years. Although this would be appropriate if each individual's earnings grew exponentially, there is in fact substantial variation in earnings from year to year. To the extent that this introduces random measurement error in the estimate of both YL and SSW, their coefficients will be

biased; since the measurement errors are correlated with each other and the two values of YL and SSW are also correlated with each other, the direction of the bias cannot be determined without further information. Finally, it should be remembered that the data refer to 1963 when the social security program was much smaller and newer than it is today; the response of individuals at that time cannot be extrapolated to the present without considering the changes that have occurred during the past 15 years.

IV. The Parameter Estimates

The basic parameter estimates presented in this section imply that social security substantially reduces the accumulation of household wealth as traditionally defined. More specifically, the point estimates generally indicate that each dollar of social security wealth reduces fungible net worth by somewhat less than one dollar. The standard errors are too large to reject the implication of the traditional life cycle model that there is dollar-for-dollar replacement, but the estimates are also consistent with a rather wide range of other replacement rates. In general, however, the estimates are incompatible with the hypothesis that differences among households in social security wealth have no net effect on private wealth accumulation.

Before looking at the parameter estimates, it is useful to examine some characteristics of the sample and of the population that it represents. Our final sample contains 126 married couples plus 12 additional households with a man who was not married at the time of the survey. The sampling probabilities imply that these observations represent 4.5 million couples and a total of 4.9 million households. The mean net worth of these 4.9 million households (as of the end of 1962) was $20,801 and the corresponding standard deviation was $32,054. Their average labor income was $5,555 with a standard deviation of $2,806; median family income (including nonlabor income) for the entire U.S. population was then $6,100. Traditional net worth thus averaged about four times income. The average value of social security wealth was $24,017, about as large as all other household wealth; the standard deviation was $7,709. Finally, the men in the group had an average age of 59 years and 89% were

---

[19] A full description of the current method is described in Feldstein and Pellechio (1977); see especially the appendix. There are a number of technical improvements over the method used in Feldstein (1976a) but these do not alter the general logic of the calculation presented there. The definition used here corresponds to the net social security variable ($NSSW1$) in Feldstein (1974) but the disaggregated data permit the use of more detailed information.

married. The means and standard deviations of the income, wealth, and age variables are essentially unchanged if attention is limited to couples only.

The estimates presented below can be classified in two ways. First, separate estimates are presented for married couples and for all households. The results for the sample with only married couples are more reliable because the group of single men probably includes men who recently became widowers but who had accumulated wealth to support a couple in retirement. Combining couples and single men also raises the difficult problem of comparing the life cycle saving patterns of individuals and couples. Nevertheless, estimates for all households are presented in order not to restrict the sample unnecessarily; the combined estimates are not substantially different from the estimates for couples only.

Second, each equation is estimated with the unweighted sample of observations and with the sample weighted by the inverse of the sampling probabilities. Weighting in this way gives more weight to the middle income families around and

below the maximum social security earnings and less to the higher income families. If the equation parameters are not fixed numbers but vary among individuals in a way that is related to income, the coefficients derived in the weighted regressions are more appropriate as measures of the relevant average behavior of the population. Moreover, since the sampling probabilities were an increasing fraction of income, the method of weighting is likely to produce estimates that are statistically more efficient by reducing the problem of heteroscedasticity that arises because the variance in the error of the household assets equation is an increasing function of income.

Equation 1 of table 1 implies that each extra dollar of social security wealth reduces the accumulation of ordinary fungible net worth by 93¢. The standard error of the coefficient (0.42) and the caveats about the variables themselves that were noted in section III should caution against giving too much weight to this or any other specific point estimate in table 1. Instead, these estimates must be seen collectively and as a part of the accumulating body of evidence based on quite different types of data.

TABLE 1.—EFFECTS OF SOCIAL SECURITY WEALTH ON HOUSEHOLD ASSET ACCUMULATION

Equation	Weight[a]	Married[b]	SSW	YL	$(YL)^2 \times 10^{-3}$	AYL	MYL	Constant	$\bar{R}^2$
1	U	Mar	−0.93 (0.42)	3.49 (0.70)				25,100 (10,600)	.158
2	W	Mar	−1.26 (0.34)	2.93 (0.79)				35,270 (8,840)	.132
3	U	Mar	−0.72 (0.44)	−1.16 (3.03)	0.29 (0.18)			34,920 (12,200)	.168
4	W	Mar	−0.69 (0.34)	−9.56 (2.74)	0.86 (0.18)			57,140 (9,380)	.261
5	U	Mar	−0.96 (0.46)	2.06 (7.05)		0.025 (0.123)		25,870 (11,300)	.151
6	W	Mar	−1.12 (0.36)	12.01 (7.89)		−0.160 (0.138)		33,350 (8,990)	.134
7	U	Mar	−0.72 (0.49)	−0.99 (7.28)	0.29 (0.19)	−0.003 (0.123)		34,840 (12,600)	.161
8	W	Mar	−0.58 (0.36)	−1.66 (7.84)	0.85 (0.18)	−0.137 (0.128)		55,310 (9,530)	.261
9	U	All	−0.86 (0.79)	7.84 (5.40)	0.05 (0.33)		−5.26 (2.90)	26,880 (20,200)	.151
10	W	All	−0.51 (0.45)	−4.83 (3.51)	0.73 (0.24)		−2.54 (2.11)	44,770 (11,200)	.131
11	U	All	−1.67 (0.65)	5.45 (5.28)	−0.10 (0.32)			38,470 (19,300)	.081
12	W	All	−0.82 (0.37)	−5.86 (3.41)	0.64 (0.23)			48,480 (10,700)	.128

Note: The dependent variable in all equations is household net worth (excluding social security wealth). Standard errors are shown in parentheses.
[a] U indicates unweighted regression; W indicates regression weighted by inverse sampling probabilities.
[b] Equations 1 through 8 are restricted to the sample of married couples.

Equation 2 repeats the same specification as equation 1 but with the observations weighted by the inverses of the sampling probabilities. The coefficient of SSW becomes somewhat larger than 1 but again the standard error cautions against focusing on the specific point estimate. The homotheticity assumption is dropped and a quadratic income term is added in equations 3 and 4. The estimated coefficients of the social security wealth variables are now reduced to about 0.70; by the usual formal criteria, the coefficients are significantly different from zero but not significantly different from one.

Although the sample is restricted to men aged 55 to 64, it is possible that variations in age within this range affect the accumulation of wealth. Our failure to take this into account could in principle be a source of bias in the remaining coefficients. Age can affect the accumulation of wealth in a rather complex way. The life cycle theory implies that, because older men generally have worked longer and are closer to retirement, net worth shall increase with an individual's age. However, the relation between wealth and age for a cross section of individuals should not be the same as it is over time for a single individual or birth cohort. Even within the group of men aged 55 to 64, such events as the Depression and World War II came at very different ages and therefore could be expected to have different effects on life cycle saving. For example, the older men were in their early thirties when the Depression began while the younger men were just in their early twenties; the resulting reduction in lifetime saving can therefore be expected to be greater in the older age group. Equations 5 through 8 make a crude adjustment for the effect of age by making the equilibrium ratio of wealth to income (α_1 of equation (1)) a linear function of age. This is equivalent to adding a variable to the equation that is the product of the individual's age and labor income; $AYL = AGE \times YL$. The estimates in equations 5 through 8 show no statistically significant effect of age and no substantial effect on the coefficient of SSW of including the age-income variable.

Equations 9 through 12 drop the restriction of the sample to married couples and reestimate the basic specification with the quadratic income term. In the first two of these equations, a separate adjustment is made by adding a variable (MYL) that is equal to YL for a married couple

but otherwise equal to zero; this is equivalent to allowing a different equilibrium wealth-income ratio in equation (1) (i.e., a different value of α_1). Equations 9 and 10 have the surprising implication that couples accumulate less wealth than single individuals, but the standard errors are large relative to the coefficients.[20] The estimated effects of SSW are generally similar to the coefficients for married couples only.

In the notation of equations (7) and (8) the coefficient of the social security wealth variable is $\mu = (1 - \alpha_2 - \alpha_4)\lambda$, where (1) an induced retirement effect of social security on saving implies $\alpha_2 > 0$, (2) induced changes in child-to-parent transfers that tend to offset the effect of social security imply $\alpha_4 > 0$, and (3) such differences between social security wealth and ordinary wealth as fungibility and inflation protection imply $\lambda \neq 1$. The estimates of μ approximately equal to 1 and significantly different from 0 indicate that it is very unlikely that social security induces changes in either child-to-parent transfers or retirement plans that substantially negate the direct effect of social security on savings. The specific combination of α's and λ corresponding to the estimated value of μ obviously cannot be identified on the basis of the available evidence.

V. Conclusion

In conclusion, we wish only to reiterate that the parameter estimates presented in this paper should not be seen in isolation but as part of a larger body of evidence on life cycle savings behavior in general and on the effects of social security on saving in particular. We are as conscious as anyone of the limitations of the current data and of the problems of interpreting our results. We believe, however, that the current estimates do support the validity of the life cycle approach and of the specific conclusion that social security significantly depresses private wealth accumulation. Significant improvements in microeconometric analysis of this question must await the development of data combining accurate records of lifetime earnings, social security wealth, and private net worth.

[20] The difference between couples and single individuals may also reflect the role of life insurance.

REFERENCES

Aaron, Henry J., "Social Security: International Comparison," in Otto Eckstein (ed.), *Studies in the Economics of Income Maintenance* (Washington, D.C.: The Brookings Institution, 1967), 13–48.

Barro, Robert, "Are Government Bonds Net Wealth?" *Journal of Political Economy* 82 (Nov./Dec. 1974), 1095–1117.

———, "Social Security and Private Saving—Evidence from the U.S. Time Series," in *Studies in Social Security and Retirement Policy,* American Enterprise Institute, 1978.

Darby, Michael, "The Effects of Social Security on Income and the Capital Stock," mimeographed, American Enterprise Institute, 1979.

Diamond, Peter, "A Framework for Social Security Analysis," *Journal of Public Economics* 8 (Dec. 1977), 275–298.

Feldstein, Martin, "Social Security, Induced Retirement, and Aggregate Capital Accumulation," *Journal of Political Economy* 82 (Sept./Oct. 1974), 905–926.

———, "Social Security and the Distribution of Wealth," *Journal of the American Statistical Association* 71 (Dec. 1976a), 800–807.

———, "Social Security and Saving: The Extended Life Cycle Theory," *American Economic Review* 66 (May 1976b), 77–86.

———, "Social Security and Private Savings: International Evidence in an Extended Life Cycle Model," in Martin Feldstein and Robert Inman (eds.), *The Economics of Public Services,* an International Economic Association Conference Volume (New York: Halsted Press, 1977).

———, "Social Security and Private Savings: Reply to Barro," in *Studies in Social Security and Retirement Policy,* American Enterprise Institute, 1978.

Feldstein, Martin, and Anthony Pellechio, "Social Security and Household Wealth Accumulation: New Mi-croeconometric Evidence," National Bureau of Economic Research Discussion Paper No. 206, 1977.

Katona, George, *Private Pensions and Individual Saving.* Survey Research Center, Institute for Social Research, The University of Michigan, 1965.

Kotlikoff, Larry, Anthony Pellechio, and Christophe Chamley, "Social Security and Private Wealth Accumulation," mimeographed, Harvard University, 1977.

Mayer, Thomas, *Permanent Income, Wealth, and Consumption: A Critique of the Permanent Income Theory, the Life-Cycle Hypothesis, and Related Theories* (Berkeley: University of California Press, 1972).

Miller, M. H., and C. W. Upton, *Macroeconomics: A Neoclassical Introduction* (Homewood, Illinois: Irwin Publishing Company, 1974).

Modigliani, Franco, and Albert Ando, "Tests of the Life-Cycle Hypothesis of Savings," *Bulletin of the Oxford University Institute of Statistics* 19 (May 1957), 99–124.

Munnell, Alicia H., *The Effect of Social Security on Personal Savings* (Cambridge: Ballinger Publishing Company, 1974).

———, "Private Pensions and Saving: New Evidence," *Journal of Political Economy* 84 (Oct. 1976), 1013–1032.

Myers, Robert J., *Social Insurance and Allied Government Programs* (Homewood, Illinois: Richard D. Irwin, 1965).

Pechman, Joseph A., Henry J. Aaron, and Michael K. Taussig, *Social Security: Perspectives for Reform* (Washington, D.C.: The Brookings Institution, 1968).

Projector, Dorothy S., and Gertrude S. Weiss, *Survey of Financial Characteristics of Consumers* (Washington, D.C.: Board of Governors of the Federal Reserve System, 1966).

Schulz, James, et al. *Providing Adequate Retirement Income: Pension Reform in the United States and Abroad* (Hanover, New Hampshire: Published for Brandeis University Press by the University Press of New England, 1974).

33

While the study by Perry (Ch. 30) deals with macroeconomic policies to control inflation, this study deals with three different countercyclical stimulus programs designed to reduce unemployment and achieve a variety of related social objectives. These programs are countercyclical revenue sharing (CRS), public service employment (PSE), and local public works (LPW). Since these programs, especially PSE and LPW, are designed to have immediate effects on the employment of specific types of labor, this study serves as an analytic bridge between the conventional employment and training programs to alleviate unemployment with a minimum of inflationary increases and the broader economic stabilization programs that deal with inflation and unemployment. The net stimulative effects of these three revenue sharing programs are described, and their effects on the income distribution and other economic phenomena are also discussed briefly.

The analysis is based on a quarterly time series model of the behavior of state and local governments in the national income accounts. Consumer utility maximization theory shows how an aggregation of state and local governments would respond in their expenditure behavior to the following variable set: community disposable income, relative prices, demographic changes, interest rates, stocks of assets, and federal grants of various types. The behavioral responses affect four major dependent variables: current expenditures, capital expenditures, taxes, and the budget surplus. All variables are expressed in terms of first differences. The estimates are subject to three separate accounting or economic constraints: (1) an adding-up constraint, whereby any variable that directly enters the state and local budget must be exactly allocated to all other users of fund—the four dependent variables noted above. Any variable that does not directly enter the budget must have effects that are offset elsewhere in the budget. (2) a stock adjustment constraint deriving utility from the physical or financial assets stock and not from the budgetary flow. (3) a grant distinction treating grants differently according to the restrictions on their use—the way they affect relative prices faced by state and local governments or change their real income level.

As for results, none of the three programs fare well as stimulative countercyclical programs, but they do have other policy effects that contribute to their social value. Public service employment does have a positive impact on aggregate spending, but it is relatively weak and short-lived. With fiscal substitution, there is no impact of PSE on total expenditures after four quarters. But since the PSE funds are used to increase governmental surpluses, this effect then ultimately encourages spending and tax reduction much the same as general countercyclical revenue sharing. The timing and magnitude of the displacement effect is similar to that found in the study of Johnson and Tomola (1977). Gramlich's results, however, were not as sensitive to different assumptions in the lag structure as were the re-estimates of Johnson and Tomola performed by Borus and Hamermesh (Ch. 34). Gramlich also estimated that there would only be 60% displacement of employment compared to the much higher estimate of Johnson and Tomola. This displacement effect may be further overstated because about 26% of the CETA PSE funds pass through state and local governments to community based organizations. Accounting procedures did not adjust for this phenomenon in the estimates of state and local budget expenditures. Finally, although displacement remains high, even given the qualifications noted above, PSE is also aimed at improving the competitive position of the low-wage worker. With 100% displacement and strict enforcement of PSE wage ceilings, low-wage employment is stimulated and higher-wage employment is reduced. Other theoretical effects, such as an hypothesis that subsidized employment retards the incentive of low wage workers to invest in education and training, are not so salutary (Johnson, 1978; Baily and Tobin, 1978).

Countercyclical revenue sharing has weak short-run effects on expenditures and tax reduction. A large share of the grant pads surpluses; then as financial stocks accumulate, governments gradually raise spending and cut taxes. But the tax reduction is not necessarily different in its effects from a more direct federal tax cut. On the other hand, CRS has other potentially useful effects—programs are maintained that otherwise would have been killed by the downturn, and tax rate increases are prevented or retarded. Therefore, CRS can serve as a form of economic disaster insurance for state and local governments.

Thus, PSE and CRS show mixed social benefits and costs and the judgment on their overall policy value is not obviously negative. In contrast, the performance of the LPW program, due to the peculiar way it was set up and administered, is perverse, and, in fact, procyclical. The lesson here is that it matters a great deal how laws are designed and administered relative to the institutions and behavior they are intended to affect. With LPW, free (no matching requirement) funds were given to state and local governments for projects that could be started in 90 days. Applications totaling $24 billion were received for $2 billion worth of funds, and unfunded governments were told to wait for following year funds of $4 billion rather than begin building their projects when the initial subsidy did not materialize. Thus, LPW had a negative short-run effect on construction. At a minimum, the administrative structure of the program needs redesign to eliminate these defects.

REFERENCES

BAILY, M. N. and J. TOBIN (1978) "Inflation-unemployment consequences of job creation policies," in J. Palmer (ed.) Creating Jobs: Public Employment Programs and Wage Subsidies. Washington, DC: Brookings.

JOHNSON, G. (1978) "Structural unemployment consequences of unemployment policies," in J. Palmer (ed.) Creating Jobs: Public Employment Programs and Wage Subsidies. Washington, DC: Brookings.

——— and J. TOMOLA (1977) "The fiscal substitution effect of alternative approaches to public service employment policy." J. of Human Resources (Winter).

Stimulating the Macro Economy Through State and Local Governments

Edward M. Gramlich

The economic stimulus program of early 1977 featured a strong dose of what might be termed indirect countercyclical policy. Rather than altering federal expenditures and taxes directly, the stimulus program consisted mainly of three different grant programs for state and local governments: a) countercyclical revenue sharing (CRS); b) public service employment (PSE); c) local public works (LPW). In the parlance of the public finance literature, the first of these grants was an unconditional block grant, the second was a close-ended categorical grant with no local matching for the purpose of stimulating local government employment, and the third was a close-ended categorical grant with no local matching for the purpose of stimulating local government construction.

Stimulating, or attempting to stimulate, aggregate spending through state and local governments in this way is fiscal federalism with a vengeance. The federal government is not abdicating its stabilization responsibilities and leaving it up to states and localities to do the job,[1] but it is placing its own stabilization policy at the mercy of the behavior of state and local governments. There are no restrictions at all on the use of the CRS grants—they can be spent, used for tax reduction, or used to rebuild financial net worth (asset stocks less outstanding debt), with only the first two uses having any stimulative effect at all. There are restrictions on what can be done with the other two grants, but the well-known displacement phenomenon implies that with these grants it also may be possible for states and localities to frustrate the restrictions and use the grants as they would any other source

of revenue sharing. What happens to all three grants then is an empirical issue, and the timing and magnitude of any stabilization impact depends on how the numbers come out.

In this paper I briefly describe a model for estimating this stabilization impact and show what it suggests for the three grants. Only the PSE grant will be seen to have any positive short-run impact on aggregate spending at all, and that impact will prove to be both diluted and short-lived, indicating that the general idea of stimulating the economy through state and local governments is probably not a very good one. Plain old permanent federal income tax cuts retain their superiority as a fiscal stabilization device. But even though as *stimulation devices* the three grant programs leave much to be desired, as *policies* they may still be valuable, and the paper also suggests how one might do a more complete evaluation of each of the grant programs.

I. The Empirical Model

On three previous occasions I have tried to estimate a quarterly time-series model of the behavior of state and local governments in the national income accounts (NIA). Here I repeat and update the procedure, but I do not describe it. The underlying conception of each effort was to use consumer utility-maximization theory to show how an aggregation of state and local governments would respond to changes in community disposable income, relative prices, demographic changes, interest rates, stocks of assets, and federal grants of various types by altering current and capital expenditures, taxes, and the budget surplus. The estimates have been made subject to three separate accounting or economic constraints:

a) *The Adding Up Constraint:* Any variable that directly enters the state and

*University of Michigan. I would like to thank Michael Wolkoff for doing most of the computer work, and Laurie Bassi, Robert Cline, Alan Fechter, Daniel Hamermesh, David Levin, and John Palmer for their comments on an earlier draft.

[1]An abdication likely to result in no stabilization action being taken, see Wallace Oates, Appendix to ch. 1.

From Edward M. Gramlich, "Stimulating the Macro Economy Through State and Local Governments," 69(2) *American Economic Review* 180-185 (May 1979). Copyright 1979 by the American Economic Society.

local budget (such as federal grants) must be exactly allocated to all other uses of funds; while any variable that does not directly enter the budget must have effects that are offset elsewhere in the budget.

b) *Stock Adjustment:* For both physical capital and financial asset stocks, utility is derived from the stock itself, not the budgetary flow. In the long run the model behaves as a stock adjustment model in this regard, with both net investment and net financial saving being only temporarily altered in response to some change in an exogenous variable.

c) *Grant Distinction:* Since an important use for the model is to distinguish the effects of different types of grants, grants are treated differently according to their restrictions. Open-ended price reduction grants are viewed as altering relative prices, unconditional block grants are viewed as shifting out the budget constraint line, and close-ended categorical grants are viewed as moving

TABLE 1—CONSTRAINED ESTIMATES OF THE MODEL

Independent Variables	Dependent Variables				
	E_1	E_2	E_3	$-T$	$F_{-1} + S$
$F_{-1} + X$		.0327 (3.5)		.0580 (4.8)	.9093 (46.3)
$.67Y + .33Y_{-1}$	.0269 (4.2)	.0150 (2.0)	.0287 (2.7)	$-.0922$ (-10.0)	.0216 (−)
$.25 \sum_{j=0}^{3} PSE_{-j}$	-1.0690 (-3.9)				1.0690 (3.9)
$(1/m_1)G_1$	$-.9356$ (-25.7)				.9356 (25.7)
$(1/m_2)G_2$		$-.9453$ (-22.3)			.9453 (22.3)
K_{-1}	.0261 (8.1)	.0306 (7.1)	$-.0202$ (-3.0)		$-.0365$ (−)
W	-150.6 (-5.1)				150.6 (5.1)
LPW				-20.92 (-3.7)	20.92 (3.7)
FEM	-3.964 (-1.6)	8.228 (2.4)			-4.264 (−)
UR	.9692 (2.2)	1.600 (2.8)			-2.5692 (−)
$\bar{R}^2$ (diff)	.92	.88	.05	.28	.95

Notes: The *NIA* government accounts, eliminating all social insurance trust fund items, are the basic data set.

Definitions: Taxes T equal all taxes plus surplus of government enterprises; Discretionary spending for wages E_1 equals total wage bill payments less *PSE* grants less mandated wage expenditures on other categorical grants $(1/m_1)G_1$, where m_1 is the federal share; Discretionary spending for other current purchases and transfers E_2 equals total spending for these purposes less grant mandated expenditures $(1/m_2)G_2$; Discretionary spending for construction E_3 equals total spending less grant mandated expenditures $(1/m_3)G_3$; Exogenous budgetary inflows X equals general revenue sharing *GRS* plus countercyclical revenue sharing *CRS* less interest and debt service payments D less mandated expenditures on all federal categorical grants $\Sigma_{i=1}^{3}((1/m_i) - 1)G_i$; Financial surplus, or budget surplus S, equals $X + T - \Sigma_{i=1}^{3} E_i$; Financial stocks F equal $S + F_{-1}$; Capital stocks K equal $E_3 + (1/m_3)G_3 + (1 - \delta)K_{-1}$, where $\delta = .005$ is the quarterly depreciation rate; Local public works *LPW* equal a dummy variable building up from 1976II to 1976IV and then remaining at 1.0 through 1977IV; Income Y equals *GNP* less federal taxes; Wage rates W equal an index of the average compensation rate for state and local employees (1972 = 1.0); Demographic terms are the proportion of families headed by females *FEM* and the constant demographic weight unemployment rate *UR*; Total state and local expenditures *EXP* equals $\Sigma_{i=1}^{3} (E_i + (1/m_i)G_i) + PSE$; *PSE* grants are measured from *PSE* employment, the most reliable figure. To put the variable in real dollars, employment is multiplied by the constant 1972 annual wage of public employment workers ($8,200).

All variables are estimated as first differences of the variable in real per capita terms (except W, which is the first difference of the relative wage and the demographic terms which are simple first differences). *t*-ratios below coefficients, (−) if not calculated.

TABLE 2—SHORT- AND LONG-RUN RESPONSE OF *EXP*, *T*, AND *S* TO CHANGES IN *CRS* AND *PSE*[a]

Time Passed	Deviations from Initial Values When the Federal Government:							
	Raises *CRS* by 1.0				Raises *PSE* by 1.0			
	EXP	*T*	*S*	*F* − 1	*EXP*	*T*	*S*	*F* − 1
1	.033	−.058	.909	–	.738	–	.267	–
2	.063	−.111	.826	.909	.480	−.015	.505	.267
3	.090	−.159	.751	1.735	.229	−.045	.726	.772
4	.115	−.202	.683	2.486	−.014	−.086	.928	1.498
5	.138	−.242	.620	3.169	.016	−.141	.843	2.426
6	.158	−.278	.564	3.789	.044	−.190	.766	3.269
7	.177	−.310	.513	4.353	.069	−.234	.697	4.035
8	.194	−.340	.466	4.866	.092	−.274	.634	4.732
9	.209	−.367	.424	5.332	.112	−.311	.577	5.366
∞	.362	−.638	–	10.025	.320	−.680	–	11.720

[a]All variables are defined in notes to Table 1.

governments to the kink point in the constraint line.

The results of estimating this model quarterly from 1954 through 1977 are given in Tables 1 and 2. Table 1 presents coefficient estimates and fit statistics for a constrained estimate of the model. Blanks in the table indicate cases where the variable was not statistically significant with the proper sign, and was therefore constrained to equal zero in the final refitting. Table 2 then gives the dynamic implications of changes in *CRS* and *PSE*. As a general matter, both the coefficient estimates and the dynamic patterns in the updated version of the model are quite similar to what they were in earlier incarnations.[2]

II. The Programs

The first program examined with this model is *CRS*. The estimates of Tables 1 and 2 imply that in the short run only $.03 of a dollar's revenue sharing grant will end up as expenditures and $.06 as tax reduction, but that in the long run $.36 will go into expenditures and $.64 into tax reduction. The reason for this behavior is that in the short run a large share of the grant pads surpluses, but as financial stocks cumulate there is progressively less reason for governments to save and

[2]The most thorough description was in my 1973 paper with Harvey Galper, and the most recent in my 1978 paper.

they gradually raise spending and cut taxes until the impact on the surplus is nil.

These results as they stand imply that not much of a macro-stimulation case can be made for *CRS*: the money is spent only very slowly, and much of it is simply tax reduction which wouldn't be expected to have effects much different from the more prompt direct federal tax cuts. But such an assertion has two possible drawbacks: one econometric and one philosophical. The econometric one is that the coefficients are derived from those on *X*, budgetary inflows of all sorts. There is nothing wrong with making such an inference in theory, for *CRS* is precisely an unconstrained budgetary inflow just like every other positive or negative component of *X*. There is also little else one could do in practice, at least in a time-series context, for *CRS* grants have existed only in the last year of the estimation period (for what it's worth, the nonconstruction residuals were very small then). But it may still be risky to make such an inference. Under the present law, *CRS* exists only in high unemployment years (the overall rate must exceed 6 percent), and is paid only to governments of areas experiencing high unemployment (in excess of 4.5 percent). Hence there is a greater likelihood that *CRS* funds will be used for maintaining programs that would otherwise have to be killed in a cyclical downturn, or for preventing tax rate increases, than there is for the other components of *X*. If such is the case, the macro-stimulation benefits of *CRS* will be greater than those noted in Table 2.

There is a more basic point: *CRS* is a cyclical program, and as such only one of its possible benefits is as an automatic aggregate demand stabilizer. The other conceivable benefit is as a form of economic disaster insurance for state and local governments. More and more these governments rely on cyclically sensitive income and sales taxes, and indeed even property taxes could be somewhat cyclically sensitive with up-to-date reassessments. On the expenditure side, the growth of unions, wage contracts, and tenure arrangements implies that wage expenditures are becoming more difficult to alter in the short run, and the growth of public assistance transfers indicates these expenditures may be also. Hence it could be argued that state and local governments are now quite vulnerable to the business cycle and need a form of disaster insurance to prevent costly interruptions of services in a downturn. Whether this argument is at all convincing depends on whether various state and local governments do save for cyclical exigencies, whether this saving will be reduced by a federal cushion, and whether the politics of *CRS* enables cyclical funds to go where they are most needed. Each of these is a complex question that cannot be dealt with here, but what can be said is that looking at macro stimulation is only half of the story. If the macro-stimulation benefits of *CRS* are nil, it is somewhat harder to justify the program, but by no means impossible.

The next program is *PSE*. According to the estimates of Tables 1 and 2, the so-called displacement effect is very strong, leading to no impact of *PSE* on total expenditures after four quarters.[3] But if grant displacement is strong, state and local governments must necessarily experience a rise in their surplus, and this addition to financial stocks then encourages spending and tax reduction as with revenue sharing. Hence after hitting this nadir after four quarters, the fiscal impact of *PSE* then begins rising—following a path

approximately like delayed-reaction revenue sharing.

Again the problems in believing these results too religiously can be grouped into the statistical and the philosophical. On the statistical side, *PSE* has not been lumped with any other programs the way *CRS* was, but it has changed in character over time. In particular, the program was more tightly constrained to try to insure employment increases by the Carter Administration in early 1977 (for what it's worth, the wage bill residuals are not positive in the last two quarters of 1977). Of perhaps more importance is the fact that an estimated 26 percent of the Comprehensive Employment Training Act (*CETA*) money simply passes through local governments on the way to private nonprofit agencies known as community based organizations. Due to a soon-to-be-remedied accounting mistake, the *NIA* includes this money in the *PSE* grants but not anywhere in budget expenditures, implying that the displacement effect will inevitably be overstated.[4]

A related problem refers to the choice of the dependent variable. The equation in Table 1 uses the real wage bill from the *NIA*, a direct component of real *GNP*. But it would also be possible to use the employment of state and local governments from establishment employment data. Were this to be done, the coefficient of *PSE* would rise from -1.07 in the wage bill variant to $-.60$ in the employment variant, indicating only 60 percent displacement.[5] This suggests either

---

[3]Essentially, the timing and magnitude found by George Johnson and James Tomola. The lag structure used here is obviously arbitrary, but unlike Michael Borus and Daniel Hamermesh, I found that various simple lag polynomials gave about the same steady-state results.

[4]The 26 percent number comes from a recent Urban Institute telephone survey conducted by Laurie Bassi and Alan Fechter. The *NIA* "mistake" was candidly admitted by Bureau of Economic Analysis (*BEA*) personnel, and was corrected in the revisions of 1978. Those numbers were released too late for me to use in this paper.

[5]The equation can only be estimated over the 1967–77 period because the establishment data only go back that far. It is

$$SL\ Emp - PSE\ Emp = -.596\ PSE\ Emp$$
$$(-1.0)$$
$$+ .0016\ (.67Y + .33Y_{-1}) + .0033\ K_{-1} - 7.46\ W$$
$$(0.08) \qquad\qquad (3.5) \qquad (-0.7)$$
$$- .126\ FEM + 0.1\ UR,\ \bar{R}^2 = .07$$
$$(-0.1) \qquad (0.5)$$

G_1 is omitted from both sides of the equation because

that there may be some full-time/part-time shift (in which case the *NIA* wage bill estimate is the better one) or that *PSE* may lower the average wage paid state and local employees to a degree unaccounted for by *NIA* deflation. If the latter is the case, the best displacement estimate is that from the employment numbers, and the lower wage may also be considered a benefit of the program. If the unmeasured output of public sector workers remains constant, the lower *PSE* wages in effect generate a transfer away from public sector workers and could perhaps even make *PSE* a weapon in the government's fight against wage inflation. Before that is loudly praised, however, more effort should be expended on data collection to make sure the *NIA* can properly measure this reduction in average public sector wage rates.[6]

Finally let us turn to the basic point. The *PSE* is in part a stabilization program and in part a program aimed at improving the competitive lot of disadvantaged low-wage workers. Suppose there is 100 percent displacement. If the *PSE* wage ceilings are enforced, the program presumably is stimulating relatively low-wage *PSE* employment and reducing higher-wage regular employment. This transfer of employment demands and workers' producer surplus goes from high-wage regular employees to low-wage or underemployed *PSE* employees, and again could be very desirable from a social standpoint. As with *CRS*, macro stimulation is not everything, and the degree to which high displacement is used as evidence against *PSE* may be quite excessive.

The final grant program is *LPW*. This grant was sufficiently unique that I did not even try to incorporate the variable into the regular model, but simply used a dummy

there are no data on employees hired under categorical grant programs, and the dependent and first independent variable are in per capita difference form. The fit statistics are all substantially worse than with the wage bill equation, and the coefficients much less reliable, but they do indicate less displacement.

[6]These comments are not meant to be critical of *BEA*. Already it does try to deflate *PSE* and non-*PSE* employment separately, and its only difficulty in doing that is that there are not good data on average wages for *PSE* and regular employment.

variable. The reader may be surprised to find a negative coefficient: how can a grant to stimulate local construction actually reduce it? The answer, given in more detail and (some say) more melodramatically in my 1978 paper, can be found in a careful examination of the details of the bill. This bill gave free (no-match) money to state and local governments for construction projects that could be started within 90 days, with the intragovernment allocation of funds to be decided administratively. The Economic Development Agency was flooded with applications totalling $24 billion for the initial $2 billion of funds, and the unfunded governments were not told to go back and now build their projects but encouraged to wait until next year (1977) when another $4 billion would be forthcoming. In such circumstances it became quite rational for governments to hold up projects that would have otherwise been started to see if federal funds were to be forthcoming, and quite possible for *LPW* to have a negative short-run effect on construction. The actual estimated reduction of Table 1 of $6 billion in nominal terms (multiplying 20.92 by the price level and population) is indeed moderate both in relation to the queue of unfunded projects and the otherwise mysterious drop in state and local real construction in 1976-77.

As macro stabilizers, then, none of the grant programs come out very well. The *CRS* seems to have effects that are very small in the short run, *PSE* to have effects that are very transitory, and *LPW* to have effects that are perverse. One lesson is that an economic stimulus program should not rely only on state and local grants; some other means must be found to stabilize the national economy. But a second lesson that would appear to follow does not. It is not obvious that *CRS* and *PSE* should be scrapped even though as macro stimulants they are ineffective. In both cases a full evaluation should delve into more subtle considerations of the sort mentioned, but not dealt with, here. Conceivably one could even make a similar case for *LPW*, but there the macro-stimulation impact is so perverse and the other benefits so dubious that the evaluation reasoning would have to be very subtle indeed.

REFERENCES

M. E. Borus and D. S. Hamermesh, "Study of the Net Employment Effects of Public Service Employment—Econometric Analysis," mimeo., National Commission on Manpower Policy, 1978.

E. M. Gramlich, "State and Local Budgets the Day After It Rained: Why is the Surplus So High?," *Brookings Papers*, Washington 1978, *1*, 191–214.

_____ and H. Galper, "State and Local Fiscal Behavior and Federal Grant Policy," *Brookings Papers*, Washington 1973, *1*, 15–58.

G. E. Johnson, and J. D. Tomola, "The Fiscal Substitution Effect of Alternative Approaches to Public Service Employment Policy," *J. Hum. Resources*, Winter 1977, *12*, 3–26.

W. E. Oates, *Fiscal Federalism*, New York 1972.

34

The rediscovery of fiscal substitution and economic displacement of conventional government employment as a result of subsidized public sector employment programs caused considerable initial dismay among the proponents of these programs and sparked both a counter debate in policy discussions and a countermethodology. The results of this confrontation and debate have been salutary in the best sense of the word both for the improvement of social science and public policy. This study by Borus and Hamermesh is one of the first steps to the improvement of methods to estimate the fiscal and employment affects of subsidized public sector employment (PSE) after a shock to this type of social program (and related grant-in-aid programs) was administered by the studies of Johnson (1979), Johnson and Tomola (1977), Gramlich (1979, reprinted in Part VIII), Gramlich and Galper (1973), and others.

The message of this short study is brief but pointed—model specification is critical to the estimation of program effects. In this case, the work of Johnson and Tomola being critiqued was based on aggregate time series data of employment, subsidized employment, employee compensation, and other variables which change over time for reasons independent of the effect being measured—the impact of subsidized public service employment on total conventional (unsubsidized) public sector employment.

After restating the model and results of Johnson and Tomola, the authors point out two major and one additional problem in the specification:

(1) The Almon lag structure was constrained so that the coefficients of the variable lagged six quarters is zero. This implied that there was no net job creation in state and local governments receiving public service employees after six quarters had elapsed after the funding of a PSE slot. Substituting alternate unconstrained lag structures resulted in radically different results —some of which were erratic and conflicted with economic theory.

(2) A second constraint imposed on the model was that any reduction in non-PSE government employment when PSE slots increased had to equal the increase in unsubsidized government employment when PSE slots decreased. Removal of this constraint and providing an alternate dummy variable specification to indicate those quarters when PSE slots were declining changed the results radically, indicating that there was little fiscal substitution when PSE slots were expanding and large and unbelievable additions to conventional government employment when PSE slots were declining.

(3) Finally, the effects of income on the demand for public services and, hence, demand for government employment was allowed to be nonproportional. The inclusion of a quadratic specification of the lagged income per capita variable in the original model estimated by Johnson and Tomola resulted in a regular displacement pattern, but net jobs created by the sixth quarter were 24 per 100 PSE slots instead of –2.

In summary, this study sharply demonstrates the critical importance of model specification and the problems of using an Almon lag procedure in particular. Minor model changes produced major changes in estimates of program effect. The high degree of collinearity among the variables used in this aggregate time series data set and the very low fraction of unexplained variance guarantee these results.

A debate has ensured the significance of this issue for multibillion-dollar welfare reform, and PSE program proposals led directly to the development of the Employment Opportunity Pilot Projects by the Department of Labor in an attempt to gain more precise and reliable estimates of fiscal substitution and displacement as well as other important labor market effects of subsidized employment. The framework to estimate these effects on the demand side of the labor market is set forth in Bishop et al. (Ch. 35).

REFERENCES

JOHNSON, G. E. (1979) "The labor market displacement effect in the analysis of the net impact of manpower training programs," In F. Block (ed.), Evaluating Manpower Training Programs. Greenwich, CT: Johnson Associates.

——— and J. D. TOMOLA (1977) "The fiscal substitution effect of alternative approaches to public service employment policy." J. of Human Resources (Winter).

GRAMLICH, E. M. and H. GALPER (1973) "State and local fiscal behavior and federal grant policy." Brookings Papers on Economic Activity, 1.

Estimating Fiscal Substitution by Public Service Employment Programs

Michael E. Borus and Daniel S. Hamermesh

A recent paper by Johnson and Tomola [5] presented estimates of the extent of fiscal substitution induced by public service employment programs (PSE) in effect in the United States since 1971. It also contained a discussion of the theory of fiscal substitution of public service employment programs—the conditions under which these programs are more or less likely to produce net increases in state and local government employment. The theoretical work is a thoughtful and important presentation of an ex ante evaluation of the impact of an idealized PSE program. Recent anecdotal evidence appears to support the assertions made in the paper.[1] The empirical work, using aggregate time-series data, suffers from a serious and all-too-common econometric problem—questionable model specification.[2] This econometric difficulty has considerable importance for human resource policy since the estimates in this study, its predecessors (Johnson and Tomola [3, 4]), and others (National Planning Association [6] and Wiseman [7]) have been seized upon by government decision-makers and their critics.[3]

---

*   This comment arose out of a larger project dealing with fiscal substitution in PSE programs which was funded by the National Commission for Manpower Policy. None of the ideas expressed here necessarily represents the views of the Commission members or staff. We are deeply indebted to George Johnson who graciously provided the data used in the original paper. [Manuscript received January 1978; accepted May 1978.]

1   Jerry Wurf of AFSCME stated that, "Some cities depend on CETA to pay for twenty percent of their municipal work force." Washington Post, August 30, 1977, p. A-6. The same article noted that, "These cities have become critically dependent on CETA money for regular public services."

2   Data and other problems also exist; see Borus and Hamermesh [2].

3   In a letter to the New York Times, February 16, 1976, Charles Killingsworth challenged the use made of estimates of fiscal substitution by members of the Ford Administration. Paul MacAvoy, New York Times, March 10, 1976, responded and implied, quite incorrectly, that fiscal substitution destroys the efficacy of PSE as an employment-creation measure. George Johnson and others, New York Times, March 26, 1976, corrected this view and tried to delineate the proper role of estimates of fiscal substitution in considering PSE as a policy alternative.

From Michael E. Borus and Daniel S. Hamermesh, "Estimating Fiscal Substitution by Public Service Employment Programs," 13(4) Journal of Human Resources 561-565 (Fall 1978). Copyright 1978 by the University of Wisconsin.

TABLE 1

ALTERNATIVE ESTIMATES OF STATE AND LOCAL GOVERNMENT
NET JOB CREATION PER 100 PSE SLOTS OVER TIME

	Johnson and Tomola	Model I	Model II		Model III
Quarter After PSE Slot Is Funded	Model [5, p. 14] Assuming PSE Is Tax-Financed		When PSE Slots Decrease	When PSE Slots Increase	
(1)	(2)	(3)	(4)	(5)	(6)
1	102	142	75	−5	98
2	87	81	69	−89	86
3	64	−47	75	−155	69
4	37	109	88	−203	50
5	13	−60	103	−234	34
6	−2	−142	113	−249	24
R^2	.9982	.9992	.9992		.9985

The estimates of net job creation of PSE were produced by Johnson and Tomola [5] using quarterly data covering 1966−75. Their equation related non-PSE state and local government employment, N, to a vector of seasonal dummies, S_1, S_2, S_3; a time trend, t; the real employee compensation of state and local government employees, $w(t)$; and Almon lag terms for real personal income adjusted for taxes and grants per capita, Y; school-age children per capita, K; and PSE slots per capita, P. The Almon lags were estimated with a quadratic polynomial, with the constraint that the coefficients of the variable lagged six quarters be zero (see Almon [1]).

The estimated equation ((16) in their paper) is:

(1)
$$N(t) = -.037 + 7.19\Sigma_0^5\delta_i^1 Y(t - i) - 3.57\ w(t)$$
$$+ .184\Sigma_0^5\delta_i^2 K(t - i) - 1.02\Sigma_0^5\delta_i^3 P(t - i) + .00034t$$
$$- .00010S_1 - .000008S_2 - .00123S_3$$

where the δ_is are the coefficients of the lag distributions. Column 2 of Table 1 reproduces the Johnson-Tomola estimates of net job creation calculated under the assumption that the PSE slots are financed by a tax increase. They are of a profound importance for policy because they imply that there is no net job creation in state and local government by the time that six quarters have elapsed after the funding of a PSE slot.

The problem with the Johnson and Tomola estimates of the job-creation effects of PSE is that the effects are sensitive to minor changes in the specification of the model. Their sensitivity illustrates the difficulties inherent in using time-series data in which most of the variables are growing together over time for reasons quite independent of the behavior the researcher is trying to isolate.

ALTERNATIVE SPECIFICATIONS

One specification problem may arise from the particular way in which Johnson and Tomola used the Almon lag procedure. While they allow the job-creation effect to decline at different rates from one quarter to the next, it is specified that the declining relationship of PSE to employment must work itself out over six quarters and must decrease less rapidly in the later quarters. A less restrictive method of estimating effects of PSE over time could produce different findings.

As a first step, an equation that did not constrain the end-points of the Almon lag structure was estimated, with results very similar to those of Johnson and Tomola. Next, an even freer model—Model I—was estimated with no constraints whatsoever on the parameters of the lagged terms in income, children, and PSE slots. An ordinary least-squares regression was estimated including the current and five lagged values of each of these three variables.

The time path of net job creation implied by the estimates of Model I is presented in column 3 of Table 1. Although the equation did not explain employment significantly better than that of Johnson and Tomola, the results were extraordinary.[4] The estimates bounce erratically in the fourth quarter in a fashion inconsistent with economic theory. Further, the estimate after six quarters implies a reduction of 242 state and local government non-PSE jobs when 100 PSE slots are funded. Model I suggests that the constraints on the lag relationship implicit in the particular procedure used by Johnson and Tomola hide a very unstable basic relationship.

The Johnson and Tomola model also constrained any reduction in non-PSE state and local government employment when PSE slots increased to equal the increase in such employment when funding for PSE slots was withdrawn. We removed this constraint by defining a variable equaling the number of PSE slots for the period from the fourth quarter of 1972 through the second quarter of 1974, and the third quarter of 1975, when the number of regular PSE slots was declining, and zero otherwise. This variable was added to the Johnson and Tomola equation to produce estimates of the coefficients of a six-quarter lag using the same Almon procedure as in the Johnson and Tomola model.

---

4   The F-statistic on the null hypothesis that the Almon constraints belong on the coefficients of the terms in income, children, and PSE slots is $F(12,16) = 1.65$. The critical value at the 90 percent level with these degrees of freedom is 1.99.

The F-test on the null hypothesis that this set of Almon variables does not belong (that fiscal substitution is symmetric) is $F(2,26) = 16.72$. Since the critical value at the 99 percent level with these degrees of freedom is 5.53, we can conclude that the null hypothesis is soundly rejected. The results of this Model II are shown in Table 1, columns 4 and 5. They suggest that when the number of PSE slots is expanding, there is very little fiscal substitution. Even more startling, when PSE slots are reduced, the state and local governments add a considerably greater number of regular employees than the number of slots they lose. This (appropriate) respecification, however, changes the estimates of net job creation so greatly as to make them highly implausible. It is impossible to believe that the loss of 100 PSE slots increases regular government employment by 349 after six quarters.

A third problem is that it is unlikely that the public's demand for government services, and thus for public employees, will vary in strict proportion to increases in income. Indeed, the notion of a "taxpayers' revolt" beginning in the late 1960s suggests that this relationship is invalid. To test this hypothesis, Model III was estimated as equation (1) with a quadratic term in income per capita included, using the same Almon procedure.

The F-test on the null hypothesis that the Almon variables in Y^2 do not belong is $F(2,26) = 3.35$; the critical value at the 95 percent significance level is 3.37, and at the 90 percent level, it is 2.52, suggesting some improvement in explanatory power. The effects of 100 new PSE slots on state and local government employment are shown in column 6 of Table 1. They imply that the net impact is more substantial than that found by Johnson and Tomola—roughly 24 jobs per 100 PSE slots funded.[5]

DISCUSSION

Our minor changes in the Johnson-Tomola model demonstrate points relevant both for methodology and for policy. First, the use of the Almon lag procedure is often highly questionable. At the very least, any future study using the technique should be required to report results based on equations that do not constrain the end-point coefficients and, perhaps, even allow the lags to be free form. With the rapid expansion of use of this technique by labor economists, this admonition becomes especially important.

Second, although Johnson and Tomola [5] point out that the standard errors of their estimates of net job creation are relatively large, the situation

---

5   The coefficients of Y and Y^2 indicate that as income rose, the marginal effect on state and local employment decreased. Since income per capita increased over the 1966–75 period studied, this tends to confirm the "taxpayers' revolt" hypothesis.

is far worse than they perceived. Even minor modifications in the specification produce major changes in the point estimates of net job creation (fiscal substitution). The high degree of collinearity among the variables used in the estimates and the extraordinary low fraction of unexplained variance guarantee these results. Perhaps all one can conclude from the time-series evidence is that fiscal substitution increases with time after the funding of a new PSE slot. Point estimates based on aggregate time-series data simply do not provide a reliable guide to policy and, as Johnson and Tomola note [5, p. 23], should be used with caution if they are to be used at all.

MICHAEL E. BORUS
Ohio State University
DANIEL S. HAMERMESH
Michigan State University

REFERENCES

1. Shirley Almon. "The Distributed Lag Between Capital Appropriations and Expenditures." *Econometrica* 33, No. 1 (1965): 178–96.
2. Michael E. Borus and Daniel S. Hamermesh. "Study of the Net Employment Effects of Public Service Employment—Econometric Analyses." In *Job Creation Through Public Service Employment*. Vol. III, Report No. 6. Washington: National Commission for Manpower Policy, March 1978. Pp. 89–149.
3. George Johnson and James Tomola. "An Impact Evaluation of the Public Employment Program." Technical Analysis Paper 17, Office of the Assistant Secretary for Policy, Evaluation, and Research, U.S. Department of Labor, April 1974, processed.
4. ———. "The Efficacy of Public Employment Programs." Institute of Public Policy Studies, Discussion Paper 74, revised version, June 1975, processed.
5. ———. "The Fiscal Substitution Effect of Alternative Approaches to Public Service Employment Policy." *Journal of Human Resources* 12 (Winter 1977): 3–26.
6. National Planning Association. *An Evaluation of the Economic Impact Project of the Public Employment Program*. Final Report MEL 74-06 to the Manpower Administration, U.S. Department of Labor, May 22, 1974, four volumes, processed.
7. Michael Wiseman. "Public Employment as Fiscal Policy." *Brookings Papers on Economic Activity* (1: 1976):67–106.

35

The Employment Opportunity Pilot Projects (EOPP) are a major policy initiative of the U.S. Department of Labor to evaluate the effectiveness of a subsidized job search, employment and training program for low-income and welfare-prone families. In the debate over the appropriate policies for a major revision of the welfare system, this program offers an alternative to the various negative income tax programs. Complementary to its potential to reform welfare, such a program also offers a potential solution to the high levels of structural and cyclical unemployment which have plagued us during the 1970s. The major characteristic of this program, apart from the job search assistance, is the guarantee of a subsidized job in the public or private sector for all eligible persons who want one. Training and education are also provided, but the policy focus is on the subsidized employment and job search components.

The EOPP is the culmination of over six years of analysis and policy debate, important aspects of which were originally promoted within the Department of Labor by George Johnson (1973). The government has divided the research on this program into two broad areas—"supply-side" effects and "demand-side" effects.[1] This study examines demand-side effects, and it is that focus—incorporating effects on those who do not participate in the program—that differentiates it from all previous studies of subsidized employment and training programs.

This labor market study is an interdependent set of five substudies which address the following phenomena:

- the behavior of individuals and families in the labor market;
- the behavior of private sector firms;
- the behavior of public and private nonprofit agencies;
- the macroeconomic effects of EOPP; and
- the generalization of EOPP pilot site effects to the economy as a whole.

A concern with the extent and nature of employment displacement, including the estimation of net job creation for the target population, is one of the primary motives for the present study. Displacement is of two kinds—direct and indirect. Direct displacement occurs when a firm or agency allocates jobs to subsidized workers that would have been occupied by unsubsidized workers on the payroll. Indirect displacement occurs, in one case, when unsubsidized workers are drawn from the regular labor market into subsidized jobs, causing a reduction in labor supply to the conventional (unsubsidized) sector. This results in a new demand/supply equilibrium in the conventional sector at higher wage rates and lower employment. Some direct displacement is a likely result of the program, since subsidized workers are less expensive than other factors of production (unsubsidized workers, in particular), and employers will likely substitute the cheaper labor for these more expensive factors. The nature and extent of indirect displacement is less clear since the mandatory job search provisions may increase supply to the conventional sector and thus bid wages down. Attempts will be made to measure both types of displacement in this study, although wage rate effects in the conventional sector will be difficult to detect due to the relatively small size of the program—no more than a few thousand subsidized job slots will be injected into any given labor market.

The research objectives of the study will be accomplished with separate substudies for individuals, public sector agencies, and private sector firms. These substudies share a basic, common design: a before/after comparison of experimental and control observations within a two-equation model. The first equation explains whether and to what extent an employer or individual participates in a program. The second estimates the impact of this participation on behavior. Within a simultaneous framework, this procedure reduces or eliminates potential self-selection bias due to individual, firm, or agency self-selection into the program. Thus, the participation equations are critical for creating instrumental variables to predict participation—key explanatory variables in the structural models of the impact of EOPP on labor market variables. A variety of models will be estimated, the simplest of which compare pilot and control site averages. In contrast, the most sophisticated model employs observed behavioral differences between nonparticipants in pilot and control sites to measure direct and indirect program effects on displacement. The development and estimation of these models follow the general procedures set forth in Heckman and in Barnow et al. (Part I).

In addition, to resolve the controversy surrounding the early econometric and noneconometric methods used to measure displacement (see Borus and Hamermesh, Ch. 34 and Nathan et al., 1978) the public and private nonprofit sector study will include a field-work component modeled on the methods developed by Nathan et al. The information gained by this approach, however, will be integrated with the econometric models, using a Bayesian approach (Welch et al., 1979).

Finally, the results from the several substudies will be generalized to the economy as a whole via existing as well as planned computer simulation models. The use and modification of existing microsimulation models rests on a variety of assumptions that can be tested or revised using data from the household, employer, and applicant surveys of the study. Two major components can be improved by these data and the resulting econometric respecification—the model of participation in various aspects of the program and the model of the impact of the program on participants and nonparticipants. More reliable simulations should help resolve the concerns of Congressional and administration policy makers over the magnitudes and determinants of program participation and costs.

NOTE

1. The "supply side" effects are being analyzed jointly by Mathematica Policy Research, Princeton, New Jersey and the Urban Institute, Washington, D.C.

REFERENCES

JOHNSON, G. E. (1973) "Differences in the total employment effects of government purchases from the private sector and direct government hiring of the unemployed," Technical Assistance Paper 3. U.S. Department of Labor, Office of the Assistant Secretary for Policy, Evaluation and Research, Office of Evaluation. Washington, DC: Government Printing Office.

NATHAN, R. et al. (1978) Monitoring the Public Service Employment Program. Report prepared for the National Commission for Employment Policy. Washington, DC: Government Printing Office.

WELCH, F. et al. (1979) Research Proposal for the Labor Market Effects of the Youth Entitlement Demonstration. Submitted by Unicorn Research Corporation to the Manpower Demonstration Research Corporation, November.

A Research Design to Study the
Labor Market Effects of the
Employment Opportunity Pilot Projects

John Bishop
George Farkas
Michael C. Keeley
C. Eric Munson
Philip K. Robins

INTRODUCTION

The Employment Opportunity Pilot Projects (EOPP) are a series of major, public employment demonstrations being conducted by the Department of Labor. The demonstrations (sometimes referred to as the welfare reform demonstrations) are intended to expand the employment opportunities of a significant proportion of the low-income population without adversely affecting other segments of the economy. The program consists of two major components: a job-search assistance component to facilitate placement of participants in jobs not funded under the program and a work-training component to guarantee jobs or training opportunities for all eligible persons who want them. Each of these components are expected to affect outcomes or processes in the labor market. The key objective of the labor market analysis is to determine whether these components of the EOPP lead to an achievement of its policy objectives. The approach, most broadly defined, is to measure the overall effects of EOPP on the labor market by measuring changes in the behavior of persons, private firms, and public sector employers (state and local governments, and private nonprofit agencies). In part of the analyses, the emphasis of the research

Authors' Note: This article is based on "Design of the Study of Labor Market Impacts of Employment Opportunity Pilot Projects," prepared under Contract Number 20-55-79-30 for the Division of Experimental Operations Research, Employment and Training Administration, U.S. Department of Labor, Washington, D.C. It is based on work undertaken by many people, and included group meetings to which many individuals contributed. The Project Director was Irwin Garfinkel, whose contribution to this research was major. Other contributors not listed above include Katherine Dickinson, John Geweke, Bryce Hool, Thomas MacDonald, Stanley Masters, Donald Nichols, Aage Sorenson and Ernst W. Stromsdorfer. First drafts of the sections were written as follows: Section 1 by Keeley, Munson, and Robins, Section 2 by Keeley, Section 3 by Farkas, Section 4 by Bishop, and Section 5 by Robins. The sections were edited by Farkas and Stromsdorfer.

From John Bishop, George Farkas, Michael C. Keeley, C. Eric Munson, and Philip K. Robins, "A Research Design to Study the Labor Market Effects of the Employment Opportunity Pilot Projects." Unpublished manuscript 1980.

is on effects of EOPP on persons and firms who do not participate in EOPP. The major policy objectives of EOPP include:

- increasing the total employment opportunities of persons eligible for EOPP without reducing the employment opportunities of other persons and without adversely affecting the employers of low-wage labor;

- reducing unemployment, particularly among low-income persons, and insuring that this reduction represents a reduction in the nonaccelerating inflation rate of unemployment;

- reducing the number of welfare recipients;

- promoting a prompt transition of EOPP participants from subsidized to unsubsidized jobs without displacing persons who already hold such unsubsidized jobs; and

- improving the overall distribution of income by increasing the incomes of poor families.

Achieving these objectives (and the costs of doing so) depend critically on the effects of EOPP on the labor market. Our goal is to investigate the labor market effects of EOPP to assess whether these policy objectives have been met and to estimate the costs, budgetary and otherwise, of meeting the objectives.

Why We Expect Labor Market Impacts

We begin the discussion by presenting a simplified analysis of the expected labor market impacts of EOPP. We assume that the low wage labor market is characterized by workers and firms that are homogeneous, that eligible persons compose a fairly large portion of the total supply of labor, and that there is no involuntary unemployment. In the Design report, other more complicated scenarios in which there is unemployment are analyzed.

In analyzing the labor market effects of an open-ended public employment program such as the one being tested in EOPP, it is useful to distinguish persons who are categorically eligible for the program from persons who are categorically ineligible. In David Greenberg's (1978) original formulation of the problem, this distinction was not relevant, because all persons were assumed to be categorically eligible. For the EOPP, however, categorical eligibility is important because it excludes certain people (at least in the short run) from participation in the program. The main criterion used to determine eligibility in the EOPP is that an individual be the principal earner in a family with children. This group consists primarily of fathers and single, female heads of families. Ineligibles include (for the most part) mothers, single individuals, teenagers, and the elderly. In the following example, we assume that firms consider eligibles and ineligibles to be perfect substitutes in production. This is tantamount to saying that the characteristics that determine substitutability are similar among families and that the firms are unaware of the individual's family circumstances.

Figure 1 describes the labor market effects of public employment in this simplified low-wage labor market. Two supply curves are drawn; one for the

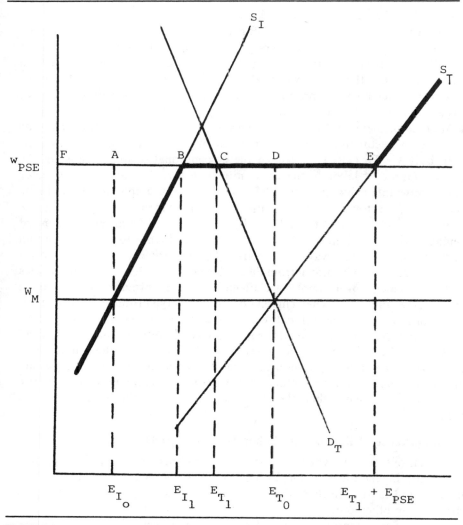

FIGURE 1: Labor Market Impacts of Public Employment

BE =	amount of Public Employment in the absence of labor market impacts (perfectly elastic demand)	
CE =	amount of Public Employment in the presence of labor market impacts (downward sloping demand)	
BC =	number of eligibles remaining in conventional sector after program	
E_{I_0} =	number of ineligibles in conventional sector before program	
E_{I_1} =	number of ineligibles in conventional sector after program	
E_{T_0} =	total employment in the conventional sector after program	
E_{T_1} =	total employment in the conventional sector after program	
$E_{T_1} + E_{PSE}$ =	total employment in the conventional and PSE sectors after program	

total population (eligibles and ineligibles), given by S_T, and one for ineligibles, given by S_I. The demand curve for labor is given by D_T.

Prior to implementation of the PSE program, E_{T_0} workers are employed at a wage rate W_m. Of these E_{T_0} workers, E_{I_0} are ineligible for public employment while $E_{T_0} - E_{I_0}$ are eligible. It is assumed that a PSE program is implemented with a wage rate above the market wage. (If the PSE wage is below the market wage, none will participate in the program and there will be no labor market impacts.) It is also assumed that there is an infinite supply of PSE jobs at this wage.

After implementing the PSE program, E_{PSE} workers (=CE) leave the conventional sector to take public employment jobs. Some eligibles, however, given by $E_{T_1} - E_{I_1}$ (=BC), remain in the conventional sector. Because of the reduced supply of labor in the conventional sector, the conventional sector market wage rate is bid up to the PSE wage rate. Total employment falls in the conventional sector from E_{T_0} to E_{T_1}, and employment of eligibles in the conventional sector falls from $E_{T_0} - E_{I_0}$ to $E_{T_1} - E_{I_1}$. Total employment of ineligibles rises to E_{I_1}, however. The supply curve of labor to the conventional sector, for a given PSE wage rate, is given by the darkened line in Figure 1.

The conclusion to be drawn from the analysis in Figure 1 is that the wage rates (and employment) of ineligibles are affected by a PSE program (i.e., there are labor market impacts). When eligibles compose a large proportion of the total supply of labor, the conventional sector wage rate rises to the PSE wage rate. (When eligibles comprise a small proportion of the total supply of labor, all eligibles will leave the conventional sector for PSE jobs, and the conventional sector wage rate rises to a level below the PSE wage rate.) Some eligibles are retained in the conventional sector and these workers receive the same wage rate as ineligibles. In essence, then, the PSE wage rate becomes the new market wage rate.

The Importance of Research on Labor Market Impacts

Evaluations of employment and training programs have focused on participants, ignoring the effects of nonparticipating eligibles and ineligibles. In the best of these studies, the effects of the program were measured as the difference in earnings (or other outcome variables) between randomly selected groups of participants and controls. None of the programs were designed to enable evaluators to detect labor market effects. Most were so small relative to the potential target population that no measurable effects on the labor market could be expected. The net social worth, however, or the social benefit-cost ratio of these programs, as well as their ultimate distributional effects, depend critically on their effects on the labor market.

Unlike previous demonstrations, pilot projects, or experiments, EOPP is designed to facilitate the measurement of its labor market effects. The scale of EOPP is large—approximately 30,000 job slots in 15 sites were first selected across the nation. In many of the sites, the program will saturate the labor market. Sufficient jobs are to be created to serve all eligibles who wish to work.

Four examples illustrate that the benefits, costs, and distributional effects of EOPP depend on the magnitude of labor market effects. First, EOPP may create pressure for conventional sector employers to raise wage offers if workers prefer EOPP jobs to lower-paying, conventional sector jobs. To the extent that conventional sector employers raise wages, their employees are indirect beneficiaries of EOPP, even though they never participate in the program. Second, EOPP may create an incentive for local public officials to substitute EOPP workers for existing workers whose salaries are paid by local funds. If conventional public sector employees are displaced by EOPP workers, they bear an important cost of the program that exceeds their share of the tax burden required to finance EOPP. Third, EOPP may lead to more effective enforcement of work requirements in welfare programs, since it will guarantee jobs to persons who otherwise might be unable to find work. This should reduce welfare payments and increase employment of actual and potential welfare recipients in both subsidized and unsubsidized jobs. Finally, unless EOPP reduces the nonaccelerating inflation rate of unemployment, it will not reduce overall unemployment in the long run. If the net impact of EOPP is to shift unemployment from those eligible for the program to those who are ineligible, then the ineligibles bear a disproportionate share of the costs of EOPP.

If EOPP guarantees jobs to a significant proportion of the low-income population, individuals and conventional sector firms are likely to perceive EOPP as an increase in the pilot community's total demand for labor. Individuals who could not find work will be offered jobs, and conventional sector employers may have more difficulty finding low-wage workers because some eligible workers may be drawn out of the conventional sector into EOPP jobs, and because some new entrants to the labor force may take EOPP jobs. This decreased supply of labor may drive up wages in low-skilled jobs and could also affect wages in higher-skilled occupations.

It is also intended to provide training for a significant proportion of eligible primary earners. During the training period, the impact on the availability of workers to the conventional sector is the same as an expansion of public service employment. It may be viewed as an increase in the overall demand for labor causing a decrease in the supply of labor available to conventional sector firms. In the long run, however, these workers return to the conventional sector with improved skills, and this produces a cumulative increase in the supply of trained workers to the conventional sector.

The effects of EOPP on labor supply and demand and, hence, its impacts on the labor market, also depend on displacement in both the public and private sectors. Displacement in the public sector occurs if total public sector employment rises by less than the number of EOPP jobs. Displacement may also occur in the private sector for several reasons. First, private sector employment might fall in response to increased public sector output. This could occur if EOPP workers are employed to produce final goods and services formerly supplied by nonsubsidized firms, or if EOPP workers are employed to produce intermediate goods that were formerly purchased from nonsubsidized employers. Second, to the extent that EOPP uses on-the-job training (OJT) in the conventional sector, OJT workers in conventional sector firms may directly displace non-EOPP workers. Third, the intensive, job-search provisions of EOPP may place EOPP eligibles in jobs that would have been filled by ineligibles. Fourth, the training component of EOPP in the long run may have a displacement effect by placing trained EOPP participants in jobs that would have been held by other trained persons.

EOPP may also have indirect, labor supply effects through the welfare system and direct labor supply effects through the job search component of the program. If the availability of an essentially unlimited number of EOPP jobs leads local welfare agencies to enforce welfare work requirements more effectively, then the employment of some welfare recipients and potential recipients should increase. In addition, the 8-week job-search assistance component of the program may improve the efficiency with which workers are matched to unsubsidized jobs, which would further increase the supply of labor to the conventional sector.

Finally, as noted above, the overall impact of EOPP must be analyzed in terms of whether it successfully reduces the nonaccelerating inflation rate of unemployment. A primary goal of EOPP is to reduce the unemployment rate for primary earners of low-income, eligible families. EOPP may succeed in reducing this unemployment rate, but it is important to determine whether other individuals will suffer increased unemployment because of displacement effects. A national guaranteed jobs program modeled after EOPP might simply shift the burden of unemployment. A study of program eligibles alone would yield different conclusions under these circumstances than would a study of both program eligibles and ineligibles.

This labor market impact analysis is designed to measure EOPP's effects on labor supply and demand, displacement rates, other transfer programs, and the inflation-unemployment tradeoff. A critical task of the labor market analysis is to measure the magnitude of the effects of EOPP on these variables. Aggregate effects on employment or unemployment are of concern, but the distributional effects on eligibles versus ineligibles and on low-wage versus high-wage workers are equally important. Since different components of EOPP (e.g., job provision versus job search) have different effects, it is of policy interest to obtain separate estimates for the effects of each component. Similarly, some kinds of job creation in the public sector and subsidization of certain kinds of jobs in the private sector may have fewer adverse effects on ineligible workers than others. Identifying and quantifying such relations will help in the design of a national program.

Overview of the Research Design

The EOPP are first being implemented in 15 sites. For each pilot site, a matched control site has also been selected. Surveys of both individuals and employers (firms and agencies) will be conducted in both pilot and control sites with the pilot site interviews including program nonparticipants and participants.

The survey design calls for reinterviews of the same respondents over time (panel data), and the collection of outcome variables for the preprogram, during program, and postprogram periods. The survey is not identified with the program and is based on stratified, random sampling that permits generalization of the results to the entire population of individuals and employers.

Under a different research contract, Mathematica Policy Research and the Urban Institute have designed a study of program implementation and program effects on participants (Metcalf et al., 1979). The present study, to be conducted jointly by SRI International, Abt Associates, and the Institute for Research on Poverty is designed to complement this, examining the program effects on nonparticipating individuals and the behavior of employing agencies and firms. This labor market study is an interdependent set of five major substudies addressing the following phenomena: the behavior of individuals and families in the labor market, the behavior of private sector firms, the behavior of public and private nonprofit agencies, the macroeconomic effects of the EOPP, the generalization of EOPP pilot site effects to the economy at large.

The design presented here summarizes these substudies with varying levels of completeness. The interested reader is referred to the full research proposal for a more elaborate description of the proposed research.

A concern with displacement—the substitution of subsidized for unsubsidized workers, with the consequent increased unemployment of the latter—is the motivation for the present study. Such an outcome can occur either (a) as a result of direct displacement, in which a firm or agency employing subsidized workers allocates work to them that would have been done by workers on regular payroll, and consequently reduces that payroll; or (b) as a result of indirect displacement, in which, to take one potential mechanism, unsubsidized workers are drawn out of the regular labor market into subsidized positions, causing a leftward shift in the supply curve of labor to the conventional sector and leading to the establishment of a new supply/demand equilibrium at higher wages but lower employment in this sector (Johnson, 1978, 1979). At least some direct displacement seems inevitable—when the cost of a factor of production is decreased (subsidized workers extract no monetary costs from their employers) employers can be expected to substitute this factor for a more expensive one (unsubsidized workers). As the fiscal distress of our city governments increases, the attraction of such actions becomes overwhelming. The existence of indirect displacement is less clear—the job search provisions of the EOPP may actually cause the price of labor in the conventional sector to be bid down rather than up, leading to increased employment. It is our intention to measure both total displacement and also the separate contributions of each type. These estimates should help to resolve issues raised by large disparities in previous results (Bassi, 1979; Borus and Hamermesh, 1979 [reprinted in this volume]; Johnson and Tomola, 1977; Nathan et al., 1978). In addition, we hope to provide a more detailed analysis of the mechanisms underlying overall displacement.

These goals will be accomplished within distinct substudies using a common design. This design involves before/after comparisons of pilot and control observations within a two equation model—one equation explaining whether or not an employer or individual participates in the program and a second equation to estimate the impact of this participation (or nonparticipation) on behavior. When these equations are estimated in a simultaneous framework it is possible to reduce or eliminate the bias potentially associated with self-selection into the program. Thus, similar econometric specifications are applied to substudies of individuals, public sector agencies, and private sector firms.

For individuals as well as for employers, participation may be conceptualized as (1) whether a given unit participates; and (2) given that it participates, the magnitude of its participation. For individuals, quantity may be measured by length of participation. For public and private nonprofit agencies and for private employers, quantity may be measured by the average number of workers it employs over some unit of time. The determinants of these are important since they contribute to our understanding of how program operations affect the labor market. For example, suppose we discover that displacement is very low in certain types of agencies and that a program variable X has strong effects on the participation of these agencies in EOPP. This information would be important to policymakers if the variable X could be influenced by the design of the program, since the displacement rate could then be manipulated.

In addition, participation studies are a necessary first step to create predicted participation variables (i.e., instrumental variables) that are key explanatory variables in structural models of the impact of EOPP on labor market variables. For example, in the studies of individual and family behavior, a predicted participation variable enables us to isolate the impact of the program on nonparticipants. In the employer studies, it makes possible the direct estimation of the rate of net job creation per EOPP job provided. And in these studies a predicted participation variable enables the separation of the direct behavioral responses of participating employers from the indirect labor market effects experienced by all employers of low-wage labor in the experimental sites.

The program impact equation (the second in our two-equation system) is based on a before/after comparison of experimental and control observations with the participation equation used to correct for possible self-selection into the experimental group. A variety of models will be estimated, the simplest of which compares pilot and control site averages, while the most complicated attempts to use observed behavioral differences between nonparticipants in pilot and control sites to separate direct from indirect displacement effects.

In addition to these econometric strategies, the public sector substudy includes a fieldwork component integrated with the econometric component. Interest in this methodology results from the fact that, until recently, studies of the impact of federal grants and expenditures on the local public sector have either been econometric (Bassi, 1978, 1979; Gramlich, 1973, 1978, 1979; Johnson, 1979; Johnson and Tomola, 1977; National Planning Association, 1974; Wiseman, 1976) or based on field interviews and observation (Nathan et al., 1975, 1977a, 1978a, 1978b); but not both. Now an attempt has been made (Adams and Crippen, 1979) to provide econometric estimates complementary to the fieldwork reports on revenue sharing produced by the Brookings group led by Richard Nathan. It is our intention to proceed further in this direction by planning for integrated fieldwork and econometric estimation early in the design of the project, thus permitting the results of the two methods to be reconciled.

Finally, the Generalization to the National Population substudy uses both existing and planned computer simulation models to fully exploit the data and results from the impact analysis. It is hoped that as a result of these efforts, new and behaviorally more realistic simulation models of labor market processes will be developed.

STUDIES OF INDIVIDUAL AND FAMILY BEHAVIOR

The models discussed in this section measure the labor market effects of EOPP using individual-level data. A primary consideration is to enable the prediction of program participation and labor market effects under alternate national employment opportunity programs. The advantage of microdata is that they may be used to study how labor market effects vary with the characteristics of individuals. Although the individual is the unit of analysis for these studies, other data such as matching employer data, aggregate predicted displacement rates, aggregate labor market data for each of the sites, fiscal data, EOPP administrative data from the pilot sites, and aggregate welfare, Unemployment Insurance, and Comprehensive Employment and Training Act data on a site basis will also be used to analyze how individuals' response to EOPP varies with their environment.

If the EOPP offers jobs to all eligible persons who want them, then wage rates for similar jobs and workers in the conventional sector (whether public or private) may rise to the EOPP wage.[1] Both program participation and the magnitude and type of labor market effects depend on six factors: the subsidized job wage rate, the length of the job search period, the nonpecuniary characteristics of the job or training provided, labor supply and demand in the conventional sector, the rate and reasons for unemployment, and the relative proportions of eligibles and ineligibles in the labor market.

In addition, labor market impacts on families and individuals are likely to depend on participation and the type of participants and on displacement and the type of displacement. Finally, both participation and labor market effects will depend to a great extent on the way in which the programs are operated. For example, if the prime sponsor's demand for EOPP labor is not perfectly elastic and is less than the quantity supplied at the subsidized wage, then subsidized jobs would have to be rationed and conventional sector market wages would not rise to the subsidized wage. Similarly, if prime sponsors substitute some subsidized workers for other, higher wage workers, labor market effects for the displaced workers might be opposite to those discussed previously for low-wage workers.

The specific outcome variables in the labor market are: wage rates, earnings and hours of work, the probability and duration of employment, the probability and duration of unemployment, the types of persons who are employed or unemployed, and migration from the site.

In addition, we intend to study the determinants of participation in EOPP, CETA, welfare and other transfer programs and also determine how participation varies with the magnitude of conventional sector labor market impacts. The analysis will (1) relate labor market effects and participation to program variables such as the length of the queue; (2) disaggregate impacts by the characteristics of the worker (eligibility status, for example), employer, or agency; (3) determine the relation between the magnitude of the impacts and economic and other conditions in the site and; (4) determine the relation of labor market effects to displacement and participation.

There are three principal reasons for wishing to determine how labor market impacts vary with individual characteristics. First, we want to determine whether in fact the programs are having beneficial effects on the target population without adversely affecting other groups. Only by looking at the entire target population, whether participants or nonparticipants, can the total effects of the program be judged. Second, because the average labor market effects, which are diffused throughout the population, may be very small, it is important to isolate the subgroups that are most likely to experience labor market effects. Third, when generalizing the results, it is important to account for differences in the characteristics of individuals in the pilot sites and in the nation.

In addition to determining how the impacts vary among different types of people and how impacts vary with differences in treatment, we also intend to determine: how impacts vary with site characteristics, how impacts vary with the magnitude of the participation rate, how impacts vary with the types of jobs created and with the magnitude of the displacement rate, and how impacts vary among eligible and noneligible nonparticipants.

The Participation Model

To measure the labor market effects of EOPP on nonparticipants, the behavior and circumstances on nonparticipants in the pilot sites are compared with similar persons in the matched control sites. Such comparisons cannot be made directly because eligible nonparticipants in the pilot sites are a self-selected sample. Therefore, it is first necessary to develop a participation model to use a two-stage, instrumental variable technique.[2] Although it is possible to model different types of participation (participation in job search only, participation in a subsidized job, participation in training), for simplicity the model below considers only one type of participation. The extension to multiple participation outcomes is straightforward. The probability of participation for a sample of eligible persons in treatment sites *only* may be modeled as:

$$P = F(X_s B_s + X_1 B_1 + X_p B_p + X_z B_Z)$$ [1]

where

P   is the probability of participation in the PSE program during some well defined time period,

X_s is a vector of site characteristics,

X_1 is a vector of individual characteristics,

X_p is a vector of program characteristics,

X_z is a vector of interactions between site, individual, and program characteristics,

B_s, B_1, B_p, and B_z are corresponding coefficient vectors to be estimated, and

F   is a cumulative probability distribution function, usually either normal or logistic.

The coefficient vectors, B_s, B_1, B_p, and B_z may be estimated by a maximum likelihood procedure.[3]

This model determines how the probability of participation in subsidized jobs varies with site characteristics, individual characteristics, program characteristics, and selected interactions of the above variables. Below, we discuss each of these factors in turn.

Variations with Site Characteristics

Site characteristics are expected to influence program participation via their effect on prevailing labor market conditions. Key factors include: proportion of the labor market being served by the pilot program, urbanization, the unemployment rate, industry composition, geographical location, and geographical mobility either into or out of the area. One of the most important variables in the participation equation is the proportion of the labor market being served by the program, since the coefficient of this variable will enable us to directly determine the sensitivity of participation to conventional sector labor market effects.

Variations with Individual Characteristics

Individual characteristics are expected to affect the supply of workers to PSE jobs, because the market labor supply function depends on the characteristics of individuals. In addition, the use of individual characteristics facilitates disaggregation of the aggregate labor market effects to workers of different types. Examples of individual characteristics likely to affect participation include: wage rate and wage rate history, employment status (current and past), occupation, receipt of welfare and type of welfare, family size and number of children, age, education, experience, marital status, geographical mobility, and race. Particularly important are wage rate and employment status since higher wage persons should be less likely to participate and unemployed persons should be more likely to participate.

Variation with Program Characteristics

Program characteristics may also affect participation. Possible program variants include: wage rate offered, length of queue or other rationing devices for subsidized jobs, length of job search period, types of jobs created, and the displacement rate. Particularly important is the wage rate offered (since it directly affects total program costs), the participation rate, and the welfare of both participants and nonparticipants. One way to model wage effects, especially if there is little variation in offered wage rates across sites, is to include each individual's *change* in wage rate as a right-hand side variable.[4] The coefficient of this variable can then be used to predict, for each individual, the probability of participation under a variety of offered wage rates.

Interactive Terms

Finally, selected interactions of site, program, and individual variables may also be included in the participation model. For example, are low-wage persons more likely to participate in sites with high unemployment rates? Also, participation rates in the program may vary over time as the conventional sector adjusts to a new equilibrium. Therefore, the effects of the variables on participation should be determined at various points in time.

The Labor Market Impact Model

A model of the determination of a labor market variable (such as earnings) is presented below. In the preprogram period, denoted as period o, the determinants of the dependent variable, Y, may be written as:

$$Y_o = X_o B_o + \Sigma_i S_i a_i + u + e_o \tag{2}$$

where

Y_o = the preprogram value of dependent variable

X_o = the preprogram vector of individual and site characteristics

S_i = a dummy variable for site i defined over all sites

u = the permanent component of the error term

e_o = a random error term, drawn independently each time period

a_i, B_o = regression coefficients.[5]

During the program period Y may be written as

$$Y_t = X_o B_t + Ek + \Sigma_i S_i a_i + \Sigma_j M_{s_i} f_j + g(TR) \delta_1 + u + e_t, \tag{3}$$

where

M_{s_i} = a dummy variable for each group of matched sites

E = an eligibility dummy variable defined for all individuals in the pilot and control sites

$g(TR)$ = a function of the program treatment (discussed below)

δ_1 = a vector of coefficients of the treatment variables

e_t = a random error term

By taking a first difference of equations 3 and 2 we have

$$Y_t - Y_o = X_o(B_t - B_o) + Ek + \Sigma_j M_{s_j}f_j + g(TR) \delta_1 + e_t - e_o. \quad [4]$$

We wish to estimate the function g(TR), since it gives us the effect of EOPP on the change in the dependent variable holding constant the other right-hand-side variables. If, however, there are systematic differences between treatment and control sites, then Y_o should be included as an additional right-hand-side variable. Including Y_o as an additional right-hand-side variable would also control for effects that might depend on the initial level of Y (proportional effects, for example) or adjustment phenomena which might also depend on the level of Y_o. If the change in Y does not depend on the level of Y_o, then including Y_o as a right-hand-side variable does not lead to any bias in the treatment coefficients.

The model of labor market effects specified in [4] has several important features:

- It allows for differences in the initial level of Y across sites.
- It allows for different rates of change over time in Y among different groups of matched sites, although not within a group of matched sites.
- It allows for imperfect matching within each matched group to the extent that this can be controlled for by the X variables and the preexperimental value of Y.

Estimating Direct and Indirect Effects of EOPP

Equation 4 can be used to measure several different treatment effects depending on the specification of g(TR). We are interested in both the direct effects of the program on the labor market and the indirect effects of the program that occur because of changes in the supply and demand for labor in the conventional sector. In conceptualizing the effects of EOPP on individuals and families, we distinguish three groups that may be affected by the program: participating eligibles, nonparticipating eligibles, and ineligibles.[6] EOPP may be expected to affect all three subgroups because of direct program effects on participants and because of indirect effects on nonparticipants through conventional sector labor markets.

The simplest impact model is

$$Y_t - Y_o = \Omega_1 Z_1 + \alpha_1 T + e \quad [5]$$

where T is a treatment dummy that is equal to 1 for pilot sites and 0 for control sites, and Z is a vector of all other right-hand-side variables such as those discussed in [4]. With this model, α_1 is an estimate of the average impact of the program on all three groups, which is an average of program effects on participants and indirect conventional sector labor market effects on nonparticipating eligibles and ineligibles. Although this model is the simplest, it is also the most constrained since the coefficient of the treatment variable, α_1, does not allow distinction between direct effects on participants and direct and indirect effects on nonparticipants.[7] For some dependent variables, such as unemployment or employment, this model would measure the overall effect of the program that is of key policy interest. However, for other variables such as wage rates or earnings, it would confound indirect conventional sector labor market effects with direct program effects.

A slightly more sophisticated model distinguishes the effects of the program on eligibles from those on ineligibles. Such a model is:

$$Y_t - Y_o = \Omega_2 Z + \alpha_2 TE + \beta_2 T(1 - E) + e \qquad [6]$$

where E is an eligibility dummy (defined exogenously). The coefficient α_2 gives the effect of the program on eligibles and the coefficient β_2 gives the effect of the program on ineligibles. Such a model is more general than the model proposed in [5] because it breaks down the overall treatment effect into effects on eligibles and ineligibles. The effects on ineligibles potentially include both direct and indirect labor market displacement. The effects on eligibles are due to both direct program effects on participants and direct and indirect labor market effects on nonparticipants. Thus, the coefficient α_2 is an average of both program and labor market effects (direct as well as indirect), and the coefficient β_2 is an average of both direct and indirect labor market effects.

A more general model than [6] separates participants and nonparticipants. Here we assume that labor market effects for eligible nonparticipants are the same as those for ineligibles. It can be written as:

$$\begin{aligned} Y_t - Y_o &= \Omega_3 Z + \alpha_3 TE\hat{P} + \beta_3((1 - \hat{P}) TE + (1 - E) T) + e \\ &= \Omega_3 Z + \alpha_3 TE\hat{P} + \beta_3(T(1 - \hat{P}E)) + e, \end{aligned} \qquad [7]$$

where $\hat{P}$ is the predicted probability of participation. This model yields more efficient estimates of labor market impacts (β_3) than [6] since more sample observations are being used to estimate β_3 in [7] than in [6]. This is because all eligibles who are nonparticipants are also being used to estimate β_3 in [7]. Even if the instrument for participation, $\hat{P}$ is not predicted well, such an equation will still give us better estimates of displacement than an effect estimated for ineligibles alone. This is because for all ineligibles, E = 0, and the treatment variable simply is a dummy variable for being in the pilot site.

A final model enables us to distinguish labor market impacts on eligibles from labor market effects on ineligibles. Equation 8 yields such estimates:

$$Y_t - Y_o = \Omega_4 Z + \alpha_4 TE\hat{P} + \beta_4 (1 - \hat{P}) TE + \Upsilon_4(1-E) T + e. \qquad [8]$$

This model is the most general since it allows the labor market effect on eligibles, β_4, to differ from the labor market effect on ineligibles, Υ_4. There may be policy interest in separately estimating these effects.

Our research strategy is to estimate all four impact models starting with the most constrained, [5], and proceeding to the most general, [8]. However, in addition to measuring the "average" treatment effects of the program, whether they be measured by the specification in [5] or the specification in [8], we also will be estimating potentially stimulative effects of participation rates, site displacement rates, and the program expenditure on the local economy (income effect). Since these variables are endogenous, instrumental variables would be used. We can determine how labor market effects vary with these variables by interacting each of them with the treatment specification.

An interactive model that addresses these questions can be written as:

$$Y_t - Y_o = \Omega_5 Z + \alpha_5 g(TR) + \beta_5 g(TR) * I_v + e \qquad [9]$$

where I_v is the interactive variable (e.g., predicted displacement rate) and all other variables are defined previously. The vector of coefficients, α_5, gives the effect of treatment when the interactive variable equals zero and the sum, $\alpha_5 + \beta_5$, gives the effect when the interactive variable is unity. Thus, with this specification, it is possible to predict the treatment effect for any given level of the interactive variable. In addition, if matched employer data are available, data concerning individual's employers (such as vacancy rates, outcontracting, receipt of subsidized employment grants) can be included as explanatory variables, and both direct and indirect displacement could be estimated from individual-level data.

Problems of Bias

This framework provides unbiased estimates of the actual labor market effects caused by the pilot programs. As specified, however, the model does not control for differences between the EOPP and a national program. There are four interrelated problems of this type of bias that should be considered:

(1) income effects caused by an infusion of additional money into the sites which presumably would not be present in a national program because other expenditures would be reduced or taxes increased to pay for EOPP

(2) increased migration of labor into the pilot sites and reduced migration out of the pilot sites in response to increased employment opportunities in the pilot sites; this also would not occur in a national program where all areas would have a guaranteed jobs program of similar structure

(3) increased outcontracting as firms in pilot sites facing localized labor shortages attempt to substitute materials purchased outside the pilot site for labor purchased within it

(4) the size of the pilot site relative to the labor market in which it is embedded; if a pilot site covers only a small portion of a large labor market, the program is not a saturation experiment and no indirect labor market effects are expected.

To ascertain correctly what the impacts of a national, guaranteed job program would be, it is important to control for these potential biases in the analysis. Below we discuss how to control for each of these types of bias.

EOPP can be conceived of as initially increasing total net wages paid by the government. In addition, the increased federal funds flowing into the site may induce the local government to lower taxes or increase government spending. To the extent that these three changes in spending result in increased factor payments *in the site*, there will be income effects of the program. The magnitude of these income effects, which we call the second round change in demand for value added in the site, ΔVA_D, is given by:

$$\Delta VA_D = kMPC_L\,[(1-t_e)\,e\Delta G_e - g\Delta T] + f\Delta G_o \qquad\qquad [10]$$

where

MPC_L = marginal propensity to spend in local firms

ΔG_e = change in government spending for labor

ΔG_o = change in government spending for goods and services

ΔT = change in taxes or transfers

t_e = the proportion of ΔG_e taxed away by state and federal government

e = the proportion of ΔG_e going to local labor

f = the proportion of ΔG_o going to local factors of production

g = the proportion of ΔT represented by taxes on local residents

k = the proportion of sales by local firms spent on local factors of production

Only a very small proportion of the dollars spent by EOPP in the community will turn up as increases in demand for value added by local private firms. At each step there are leakages: Local governments may reduce other types of spending when they receive EOPP funds (increase cash balances); substitution may result in nonlocal workers being hired ($e < 1$); the state and federal government then take their share ($t_e > 0$); part of the increase in disposable income will be saved ($MPC < 1$); and then only a small portion of spending by a community's residents increase demand for local factors of production (both k and f are likely to be less than .25). The overall effect is that only 10% or 15% of EOPP spending in a community on subsidized employment and classroom training is likely to result in greater demand for the workers employed by the community's private-for-profit firms. Since budgeted expenditures for EOPP do not in any site exceed 2% of the community's income, the EOPP induced demand shift for employment in nonsubsidized firms will certainly average less than 3/10's of a percent. In retailing, construction, and service industries the proportionate demand shift might be as large as 6/10's of a percent. While an effect of this size is large enough to bias reduced form estimates of EOPP's impact that do not control for sales, it is not large enough to give us any confidence that statistical tests for its existence (by entering the net increase in local spending produced by EOPP) would have any power. Such tests will be made nevertheless but other approaches that place more structure on the problem will be tried. Estimates of the size of EOPP induced shifts in local demand can be calculated by assuming that they are equivalent to the effects of changes in income earned in exogenous sectors like agriculture, mining, manufacturing and state and federal government. Using data on income changes in these exogenous sectors and the fiscal effects of other government programs, we will construct instrumental predictors of demand shifts and enter it into our own models.

STUDIES OF PUBLIC AND PRIVATE
NONPROFIT EMPLOYER BEHAVIOR

The studies of public, private nonprofit, and private-for-profit employers described in this and the following section are a major innovation in research design. They involve surveys of several thousand employers in pilot and control sites, a strategy that provides greater statistical precision for measuring labor market effects than is available for similar expenditures on a household survey. (This is because the employer survey gathers information on more workers per dollar of survey expenditure.) These studies also permit an increased focus on the extent and mechanisms of direct and indirect displacement. In particular, variation in prime sponsor job creation strategies can be econometrically tied to labor market outcomes for nonparticipants. In all three sectors, these include potentially both direct and indirect displacement effects, but the likely relative magnitudes of these differ across sectors. This is because the majority of subsidized slots are created in the public and private nonprofit sectors, while a smaller share of total subsidized employment is allocated to OJT positions in the private-for-profit sector. Since the total public sector is relatively small, is receiving a relatively large share of subsidized positions, and is somewhat insulated from the play of market forces, we expect direct effects to be dominant here, and these are emphasized in the public sector study. By contrast, the private sector study puts greater emphasis on indirect displacement.

Introduction

As previously noted, a major concern in all subsidized employment programs is the possibility of displacing nonsubsidized workers. Thus, with a major program concern on net EOPP job creation, it is less than ideal if total public sector employment rises by less than the number of EOPP jobs. Here we are concerned both with direct displacement—a decrease in the unsubsidized employment offered by an employer as a direct result of his receipt of (subsidized) EOPP workers[9]—and indirect displacement—a decrease in the unsubsidized employment offered by employers (either receiving or not receiving EOPP workers) as a result of program-induced changes in labor market conditions.[10]

The worst case occurs when displacement is complete, and the displaced workers resemble the target population; then the program involves no net job creation for the target population.[11] The ideal program is one in which displacement is close to zero. Unfortunately, it appears to be difficult to achieve zero displacement while employing large numbers of subsidized workers and ensuring that they engage in productive work (Haveman and Christainsen, 1978; Kemper and Moss, 1978; Kesselman, 1978). Between these extremes is a positive displacement in which some of the displaced workers are not members of the target population. Under these conditions, the program *may* be considered effective. This would more likely be the case if the subsidized workers were employed at lower wage rates than the displaced workers and if these latter workers are able to easily find new employment without having to take a cut in pay.[12]

The microsurvey data can be used to measure the total extent of worker displacement and the characteristics of those displaced. These data will provide measures of the employment rates of program nonparticipants in both pilot and control sites, and will thus yield estimates of EOPP disemployment effects. They will also provide estimates of the reemployment rates of unemployed program nonparticipants. But they provide no basis for distinguishing the magnitudes of direct and indirect displacement nor of comprehending the determinants and mechanisms underlying these magnitudes. This is because the microdata set contains no link between the way a subsidized job is created and the extent and composition of displacement resulting from that job creation.

By contrast, the study we propose will trace the flow of program funds and participants to individual employing organizations, and combine this information with data on the total unsubsidized work force and wage bill of these organizations. As a result, we will be able to answer each of the following questions:

(1) How are EOPP participants and funds distributed among projects, slots, and OJT? What is the magnitude and composition of direct displacement associated with each?[13]

(2) Which public and private, nonprofit employers are chosen for job creation? What is the magnitude and composition of direct displacement associated with different categories of these?

(3) Are the "expenditure type" effects of (1) independent of the "employer type" effects of (2)? For example, are there some public agencies in which subsidized "slots" always lead to high rates of substitution, whereas in other agencies this is not the case?

(4) What is the disposition of funds displaced from wage bill expenditures by EOPP monies? In other words, what are the consequences of fiscal substitution?

(5) What are the magnitude and determinants of the tradeoffs between the value of output of subsidized workers and the extent of direct displacement resulting from their employment?[14]

(6) How do direct and indirect displacement compare in magnitude?

(7) How does public sector displacement compare in magnitude and composition with private sector displacement?

(8) How are answers to the above questions affected by the level and composition of CETA job creation efforts in a locality?

(9) How does the existence of EOPP affect job creation efforts for regular CETA workers? Are they crowded out as additional job creation becomes difficult? Do CETA displacement rates rise as opportunities to provide "new" goods and services are exhausted?

(10) What conclusions can be drawn regarding the most effective strategies for increasing employment opportunities for the target population? What are the costs associated with alternate strategies? What job creation opportunities have been underutilized? Which, if any, strategies should be discouraged?

In addition, the public sector study will provide the data necessary to isolate (and thereby subtract) the income effect associated with the increase in federal spending in the pilot sites. That is, in a national program, EOPP expenditures might be counterbalanced by either a tax increase or a cut in other governmental programs. For the pilot projects, however, program expenditures will be concentrated in a few sites, while any counterbalancing fiscal actions are spread over the entire economy. If no statistical adjustment is made for this effect, the stimulus provided to the pilot site economies by the injection of EOPP funds renders their conventional sectors, and therefore the behavior and experiences of their program nonparticipants, incomparable with those of the control sites (Masters and Dickinson, 1979).

Data and Variables

The success of job creation under the EOPP will depend on the strategies pursued by the CETA prime sponsor and the behavior of the organizations employing EOPP workers. Accordingly, the public sector impacts study has three main foci: the CETA prime sponsor, public sector agencies and the state and local governments to which they belong, and private, nonprofit agencies. In each of the pilot and (matched) control sites, data will be collected for each of these three types of organizations.

From the CETA prime sponsors (EOPP prime sponsors) we will collect the following information regarding all EOPP and CETA job creation (PSE and OJT): type of employer; work description (in particular, project vs. slot); number of workers placed; occupational title, wage rate, hours worked, total wage bill for the subcontract; amount and purpose of nonwage bill expenditures on the subcontract. These will enable us to characterize intersite variation in prime sponsor job creation strategies and to identify the employers (public as well as private) receiving subsidized workers. The number of CETA or EOPP workers employed in a particular agency or firm, and the size of the resulting subsidized wage bill, are important right-hand-side variables in the impact equations described below.

Data will be collected for public sector employers as follows. CETA Prime Sponsor job creation lists will be used to identify and oversample government private nonprofit agencies who have employed subsidized workers. This sample will then be supplemented with a sample of agencies who have not participated in subsidized job creation. The final sample will be administered several waves of mail/telephone surveys collecting time series data on subsidized and unsubsidized employment counts by type of workers and wage rate, the accompanying wage bills by type of worker, other expenditures by type (including supplies and materials, capital expenditures, contracting for goods and services), and receipts by type. A variety of other questions will elicit information regarding employer perceptions of the supply and demand for the goods and services they produce, financial and bureaucratic opportunities and constraints affecting their operations, and the relative value and true costs (including paperwork and supervision) of subsidized and unsubsidized workers.

In addition to these telephone/mail survey data, two other sorts of data will be collected. The first of these are field interviews with a subset of the full agency sample. We will have an opportunity to gain added institutional information on the role of the subsidized workers in the production process and the associated mechanisms of displacement. Data collection will be followed by econometric estimation, with particular attention in the early stages to outliers and other departures from fit. Following this, fieldworkers will be sent to the sites with protocols developed from those used in the Nathan study. They will interview administrators from a sample of governments and nonprofits, asking both tightly structured and relatively open-ended questions. Extra effort will be expended on outliers—those exhibiting both higher and lower displacement rates than would normally be expected—in the hope that new insights can be generated regarding the necessary conditions for successful net job creation. In addition, by comparing the results of these interviews with the results achieved econometrically, we may understand why previous analyses based on these distinct methodologies have generated dissimilar results. Over a several-year study period we plan to alternate econometric work with fieldwork, iterating to a reliable and easily comprehensible description of the mechanisms of EOPP impact on net job creation in the public and private, nonprofit sectors.

The second data set will contain balance sheet information collected for local governments as a whole. These will focus on expenditures and receipts (including local tax rates and receipts), receipts from revenue sharing and other inter-governmental grants, indebtedness and debt retirement, and surplus accumulation. With these data we will seek to predict not only unsubsidized employment, but also other expenditures, receipts by type (including tax revenues), and surplus accumulation. This is done econometrically within an accounting framework in which quantities add to balance sheet totals and surplus accumulation at time t is distributed across categories at time t + 1. As a result, if EOPP grants substitute for local government expenditures on unsubsidized employment, it will be possible to trace the disposition of the "freed" funds, and thereby infer the second order employment effects of "fiscal substitution."

Thus, the econometric impact studies using public sector data will be of two sorts. The first, and the one to receive the greatest attention, will focus on how the EOPP affects the following, specific outcome variables:

- unsubsidized employment counts; total employment by occupational titles and by wage rate classes
- unsubsidized wage bills; total wage bills by occupational titles and wage rate classes

The second will also focus on these variables, but will, in addition, examine effects on the following variables within a simultaneous equation framework: nonwage expenditure by type, including capital outlays, supplies and materials, and contracting for goods and services; property tax rates and revenue; nonproperty tax revenue; indebtedness and debt retirement; and fund balances and net financial assets.

Program impacts will be ascertained by seeing how before/after changes in these outcomes vary either with a pilot/control dummy variable, or with a predicted value for the number of EOPP workers or the size of the EOPP grant. Separate variables will be created for projects, slots, and OJT. Other right-hand-side variables in these equations, functioning either to distinguish the magnitude of program impacts (e.g., interactively with the treatment variable), or as control variables to decrease the error variance and thereby increase the precision of the impact estimates (e.g., additively with the treatment variable), are the following:

- dummy variables to distinguish categories of public goods
- variables to proxy the production technology of the organization (for example, the high skill labor/low skill labor ratio in previous periods)
- variables to proxy the potential demand for the public good produced, the "service need" which measures the extent to which expanded output could be consumed
- variables to proxy the input prices faced by the organization, for example wage rates for various classes of labor
- variables to characterize the magnitudes and sources of receipts and the financial health of the organization or its government, including such measures as assessed valuation available to the property tax
- dummy variables to distinguish governmental agencies from private, nonprofits and to group agencies belonging to the same government
- predicted values of CETA employee counts and wage bills received by organizations
- site level variables such as per capita income, population density, unemployment rate, and demographic composition of the population
- political decision-making variables such as whether or not governed by town meeting

These will be used both to predict the receipt of EOPP workers and also in impact equations for the effect of these workers on unsubsidized employment in the host agencies. It is within this framework that we plan to assess the prime sponsors with respect to the success of their strategies for net job creation.

Models

The economic logic of direct displacement is clear—as inputs to production subsidized workers are cheaper than unsubsidized workers, so employers should substitute away from the latter. Of course, correct measures of relative factor prices require adjustments for the relative productivity of subsidized and unsubsidized workers, as well as for costs such as those associated with participation in federal manpower programs. Our employer survey will attempt to elicit employers' estimates of these.

The models to be estimated with these data resemble those described in the previous section. That is, a participation function and impact equation are jointly estimated to correct for possible bias arising from nonrandom selection of agencies into the program. As with the study with microdata, the participation function is also of interest in its own right. Here we are concerned with the consequences of diversity in goods and services, hiring practices, and production techniques within the public sector. For these reasons, as well as because their source of funds and bureaucratic structures vary widely, agencies will vary in their desire and ability to create new goods and services for EOPP workers to produce. Estimates of the determinants of the demand for EOPP subsidized workers can be of great use in comprehending the constraints and opportunities faced by public job creation programs.

The simplest impact model that can be estimated is

$$Y_t - Y_o = \Omega Z + \alpha \, T + e \tag{11}$$

where T is a treatment dummy that is equal to 1 for pilot site and 0 for control site, Z is a vector of all other right-hand-size variables such as those discussed above. With this model, α is an estimate of the average program impact due to direct and indirect displacement for program participants in the pilot sites and indirect displacement for program nonparticipants in the pilot sites. Other versions of this model use total EOPP monies distributed to a site (deflated by a measure of site size, for example, number of unsubsidized employees in the local public sector) as the exogenous treatment variable in place of the dummy variable, or interact either of these treatment variables with the Z variables.

A more sophisticated model separates direct and indirect displacement by using a predicted value of the EOPP grant for pilot site agencies:

$$Y_t - Y_o = \Omega Z + \alpha \, T + \beta \, \widehat{EOPP} \cdot T + e \tag{12}$$

With this model, indirect displacement is assumed to be the same for all pilot site agencies, whether participating in the program or not, and is measured by α, whereas direct displacement is measured by β. Here too, treatment variables can be interacted with Z variables.

More complex versions of this approach explicitly recognize the possibility that the presence of EOPP in a site may alter the distribution of CETA grants and (possibly) the magnitude of direct displacement for participating and non-participating agencies. One approach to these issues is to compute a new variable, PSE = EOPP + CETA, the sum of the subsidized employment received by any particular agency, and to estimate its determinants (with a tobit specification) with the total EOPP funds to any particular site included as an (exogenous) right-hand-side variable. With $\widehat{PSE}$ representing the predicted probability that an agency receives at least some subsidized workers (e.g., that PSE is greater than zero), a more complex version of equation (12) becomes:

$$Y_t - Y_o = \Omega Z + \alpha_1 \, \hat{P}T + \alpha_2(1-\hat{P})T + \beta \, \hat{P}SE \cdot T + e \tag{13}$$

This can be further expanded to break out EOPP and CETA separately:

$$Y_t - Y_o = \Omega Z + \alpha_1 \, \hat{P}T + \alpha_2(1-\hat{P})T + \beta_1 \, \widehat{EOPP} \cdot T + \beta_2 \, \widehat{CETA} \cdot T + e \tag{14}$$

Furthermore, these models will also be estimated with interactive terms between the Z's and the treatment variables, so that the agency characteristics associated with varying displacement rates can be ascertained.

Fiscal Substitution

As an extension of the estimation just described, we shall estimate a model of the sort developed by Gramlich (1973, 1978, 1979) and, in a related context, by Bassi (1978, 1979). The goal is to account for the disposition of funds displaced by EOPP and CETA monies, and to do so in such a way as to clarify the budgetary behavior of public sector employers. Thus, the unit of observation shifts to those with ultimate budgetary authority. That is, data are aggregated for the agencies of each local government so that these governments, together with the private nonprofits, are the units of observation.

This analysis proceeds within a simultaneous-equations framework, with several dependent variables added to those for discretionary expenditures on labor. As a result, we estimate a complete budgetary system, one that adds up in an accounting sense. Thus, the dependent variables are discretionary expenditures in each of several (exhaustive) categories, (−) tax revenues, and a balancing variable (surplus accumulation). This latter variable is equal to the previous stock of financial assets plus exogenous budgetary resources (such as general revenue sharing), plus tax revenues, minus the categories of discretionary spending. As a result, the sum of the dependent variables is equal to the previous stock of financial assets plus exogenous budgetary resources. This sum, treated as a single variable, is included as an independent variable in the regressions, guaranteeing that it will be completely allocated among expenditures, tax reductions, or surplus accumulation. (That is, the sum of its regression coefficients across all equations will equal 1.0.) Other independent variables include predicted values of CETA and EOPP grants, and the coefficients on these and the other independent variables are constrained to sum to 0.0 across the equations. As a result, these coefficients describe how, for a given level of exogenous budgetary resources, resources are distributed among their discretionary uses. Thus, the coefficient for the impact of the EOPP expenditures on the discretionary wage bill provides a direct measure of substitution, and the coefficients for the impact of EOPP on the other dependent variables reveal the disposition of the displaced funds. In addition, since the model advances the variables through time, allocating net financial assets at time t among competing uses at time t + 1, the time path of displaced funds initially appearing in the financial surplus can be traced to the ultimate disposition of funds. This is important, for it is in this reduced form that the consequences of EOPP public sector effects for ultimate levels of labor and commodity demand are most easily described.

The estimates of program impact on budget surpluses and tax reductions provided by this calculation are further checks for the substitution estimates gained by direct regressions of wage bills and employment counts. In a framework in which accounting identities ensure that everything adds up, behavior is more easily and fully clarified.

STUDIES OF PRIVATE EMPLOYER BEHAVIOR

As noted, EOPP labor market effects can be either direct or indirect. Private employers that contract to provide jobs for EOPP clients experience the direct effects. All low-wage employers experience the indirect effects. The indirect effects are produced by pervasive changes in the tightness of the low-wage labor market due to increased federal spending in the local economy, the exit of some workers from the private sector to take PSE jobs or to obtain training, and changes in job-seeking behavior induced by work tests or EOPP's job search component. Employers experience indirect effects as changes in the availability, quality, or cost of unskilled workers.

This section is divided into two parts. In the first part we elaborate our conceptual framework for studying the direct effects of the EOPP-OJT program in the profit-making sector. The second part develops the framework to analyze EOPP's indirect labor market effects.

Direct Impacts of the EOPP-OJT Program

The purpose of EOPP-OJT programs is to induce employers to increase the amount and intensity of the on-the-job training they provide to target population individuals. Since training must always be provided to newly hired workers, an analysis of how the receipt of an EOPP-OJT contract changes a firm's level of employment is a natural way to measure the effectiveness of the program. If, controlling for the self-selection bias, OJT contractors expand their employment more than other employers, the program is a success, and the ratio of the wages paid to the extra employees to the cost of the program is a measure of its degree of success.

Unfortunately, things are more complicated. The finding that an OJT contract has induced a firm to expand employment is neither a necessary nor a sufficient condition for concluding that it has increased employment of the target group. Increased employment in one firm may cause a decrease in employment in another firm. And even with 100% displacement, total employment of the target group may well increase. Moreover, an evaluation of the OJT program requires measures of the intensity of the training provided as well as the number of people trained. Thus, while knowing the effect of an OJT contract on a firm's employment level may be useful information, much more must be known if the success of a training subsidy strategy is to be evaluated.

The primary impact of OJT training is on the individual's specific human capital—skills and knowledge that increase the individual's productivity in that firm but not in other firms. Becker's (1964) theory of OJT training predicts that the costs and the benefits of providing this type of training are shared by the individual and his firm. The worker makes his contribution to training costs by accepting a job at a lower wage than he could get elsewhere. We can measure the amount of OJT training that is paid for by the employee by noting how much and how quickly wages rise with tenure at the firm.

The employer's contribution to training costs consists of the productivity lost by other workers who orient and train the new worker and the difference between the wage paid the worker and his actual value at a low level of productivity during the training period. The employer is compensated for incurring these costs by an increase in the worker's productivity that raises his marginal product above the wage in the post training period.

The Indirect Labor Market Effects of EOPP

If, as we expect, the components of EOPP that tighten labor markets for unskilled labor outweigh those aspects of the program that increase the availability of such labor, firms will experience a rise in quit rates and a decline in the number and quality of applicants for new jobs. How will they respond to this reduction in labor supply? There are four types of response open to the firm, listed in ascending order of the adjustment costs they impose on the firm. These are:

- increase the hours worked by current employees (i.e., by persuading part-time workers to become full time)

- hire more unskilled workers

- replace the unskilled workers with other resources (skilled workers, capital and purchased materials)

- contract output

Our research task is to determine whether EOPP reduces total, unskilled, low-wage employment, and, if that occurs, to discover how firms are induced to contract their employment. Some firms find that they have no difficulty replacing workers that quit, for even in a tight labor market there is a long queue of qualified workers willing to work for them. EOPP will not change the employment level of these firms. Other firms, however, will find that because of EOPP they are no longer able to attract workers equal in quality to the ones that are leaving. Lower-wage firms will be the first to experience such difficulties. To maintain their employment such firms must either: raise wage rates to attract extra workers; or expand their recruiting, screening, and interviewing efforts until sufficiently qualified workers are found; or lower their hiring standards.

The first alternative—raising wage rates—is quite costly, because all workers wages must be raised. In most firms, wage adjustments must be general, because wage rates are attached to jobs rather than persons, and both custom and union contracts make it difficult to only alter the wage of particular jobs. Short-run shocks to the firm's product demand and labor supply do not induce frequent upward and downward revisions of the wage rate because in the short run the benefits of raising wages are small while the potential costs of lowering them are large. The supply curve of constant quality labor faced by the firm is much less elastic in the short run than in the long run. An increase in a firm's relative wage does not immediately lead a large group of workers in other firms to leave their current jobs. Its major effect is to raise the rate at which qualified workers apply for a job. Another reason wage rates do not immediately adjust is that while wage increases are easy to implement, sharp decreases in the rate at which wage rates increase (or actually decreasing them) can impose extremely high costs on the firm. These costs take the form of long strikes, sabotage, slow downs, high quit rates and low morale. As a result most firms change their internal wage structure or general wage level (relative to other local employers) only when the changed conditions that call for such a revision are perceived to be permanent. Since EOPP is temporary and its effects hard to distinguish from normal cyclical fluctuations, we expect that any impact of EOPP on wage scales will be small and slow to appear.

The other two alternatives—intensifying recruitment and lowering hiring standards—are attractive because substantial increases in employment can be realized without large increases in average costs. Most firms have a backlog of potential new hires—workers on layoff, people who have applied for work in the past, and friends and relatives of current employees. On the down side, contractions in employment brought about by voluntary attrition, cutbacks in hours, or layoffs of the least senior workers are not perceived as unfair, and therefore warranting retaliation by workers remaining with the firm. Thus, while there *are* adjustment costs to frequently expanding or contracting a firm's work force, these are minimal when compared to those associated with attempts to manipulate pay scales.

Our mail/telephone survey will permit examination of these issues through measurement of each of the following variables on a firm-by-firm basis: level of employment and total hours worked, wage rate, the amount of training provided by employers of unskilled and semi-skilled workers, the quality of recently hired low-wage workers, prices, sales, and output of firms that employ low-wage workers, the failure rate of firms that employ low-wage workers, rates of job turnover, rates at which firms are contacted by job seekers, number and duration of job vacancies, measures of the intensity of the firms' efforts to find or select new employees.

Models

The EOPP program will affect private-for-profit employers in three distinct ways. The first arises directly from subsidizing a firm's new hiring through EOPP-OJT contracts. This impact, however, is limited to the small number of firms that participate in the program.

The second arises from the changes in the supply of labor induced by EOPP. Withdrawal of workers from the private labor market to take EOPP-provided jobs or training opportunities will tend to produce a leftward shift in the supply of low-wage labor to the private sector. The job search component of EOPP and possible tightening of work requirements by the welfare system may shift the supply of labor to the right. Consequently, the direction of the "supply" effect cannot be predicted a priori. It is, however, an effect that firms will experience roughly in proportion to their use of low-wage labor.

The third effect is a rightward shift in demand curves produced by second and later rounds of spending effects of the EOPP injection of federal dollars into the local economy. This "demand" effect will only be experienced by firms that provide services or products to local consumers or local governments, and is lessened by public sector displacement manifested as decreased contracting by local governments.

To isolate the direct effects of OJT subsidies on a firm's behavior, the behavior and circumstances of OJT contractors must be compared with similar firms in the pilot or matched control sites. Such comparison cannot be made directly, because firms that participate in the EOPP-OJT program are a self-selected sample. For example, firms planning to expand total employment may be more likely to ask for an OJT placement. This would produce a positive association between firm growth and OJT placements even if EOPP-OJT subsidies were to have no effect on employment. A two-stage, instrumental variable technique will be used for estimation. As described in the two preceding sections, this approach requires that we estimate a participation model and then substitute the predicted participation rate in our impact equations. In the resulting two-equation system, the participation equation specifies the probability of a firm negotiating an OJT contract as varying with program characteristics, firm characteristics, and selected interactions between the two.

The program characteristics used to predict firm participation will include the budgeted number of slots relative to the size of the target area employment, the nature of outreach efforts, the requirements placed on firms that participate, and the size of the subsidy offered. The likelihood that a firm will negotiate an OJT contract may depend on its plan for employment growth, the rate at which new jobs open up due to labor turnover, its wage level, and the skill requirements of entry. Other determinants are the firm's connection to information networks regarding public employment and its vulnerability to audits and Equal Employment Opportunity compliance reviews.

For the impact equation, the estimated models are designed to capture change over time. As noted previously, before/after differences between pilot and control sites and across firms of different characteristics will be used to estimate program effects. If neither the increased availability of OJT subsidies nor changes in labor supply induced by EOPP affect the sales of pilot site firms, program impacts can be estimated while controlling for changes in the firm's sales. The model developed below makes this assumption. A succeeding section outlines the models that must be estimated if this assumption is dropped or estimates of the employment response to the demand effect are desired.

A relatively simple model of program impact on the i-th employer is:

$$\Delta Y_i = X_i \beta_x + \Delta S_i B_s + \Sigma m_j f_j + \alpha \hat{P}_i + b \Delta O \hat{J} T_i + c T_i + e_i \qquad [15]$$

where

ΔY_i = change in unsubsidized employment or its associated wage bill

X_i is a vector of pre-program characteristics of the i-th firm

ΔS_i is a vector of changes of pre-program characteristics that are assumed exogenous

m_j = a dummy for each group of matched sites

$\dot{P}_i$ = the instrumental variable prediction of the probability the firm will become an EOPP-OJT contractor (P = 0 in control sites.)

$O\hat{J}T_i$ = the prediction of the change in CETA, non-EOPP OJT workers in the firm

T_i = a measure of the scale of EOPP in the site and the firm's exposure to its supply side effects (T = 0 control sites.)

e_i = a random error term

α = the estimator of the net effect of an EOPP-OJT contract on Y

b = the estimator of the net effect of changes in CETA, non-EOPP OJT contracts on Y

c = the estimator of the net effect of the pervasive supply side impacts of EOPP.

This specification has several important features:

- It allows for differences in the initial level of Y across sites and across firms.
- It allows for different rates of change over time in Y among different groups of matched sites (although not within a group of sites).
- It allows for imperfect matching within each matched group to the extent that this can be controlled for by X variables (preprogram characteristics of the firm) and the ΔS variables (exogenous changes in the characteristics of the firm).
- It produces separate estimates of the two structural effects of EOPP—the pervasive supply effects and the two components of the direct OJT effect (the direct impact of EOPP-OJT and the impact of EOPP induced changes in non-EOPP-OJT).
- It controls for the nonstructural demand effect of EOPP.

It will be possible to obtain stable estimates of the coefficients for $\dot{P}$, $\Delta O\hat{J}T$ and T only if they each contain a significant amount of variance independent both of each other and of the X's and ΔS's in the impact equation. The problem that may arise is not the technical one of identification, since the nonlinearity of the relation between $\dot{P}$, $\Delta O\hat{J}T$ and the X's insures identification. The problem is the practical one of the dangers of high multi-collinearity between the various instrumental variables. Multi-collinearity will be reduced if we can include in the models predicting OJT contractor status a group of variables that do not appear in the impact equation or do not appear interacted with location in a pilot site.

The collinearity between T and predicted OJT contractor status will depend on the way T varies across sites and across firms within a site. Where large numbers of EOPP clients are recruited and assigned to subsidized jobs and training slots, and within public sector substitution is small, T will be large. If the job search requirement is effectively enforced, the number of workers assigned to subsidized jobs and training slots is small, or substitution nearly complete, T will be small. High wage industries would also have a small T.

Variation in EOPP's impact with firm characteristics. EOPP can have very different effects on different firms. Identifying how the program's impact varies with the firm's characteristics is important both because it is of interest in its own right and because it will facilitate generalization of the pilot site results. Examples of firm characteristics that we plan to interact with either the instrumental variable for OJT contractor status ($\dot{P}$ and $\Delta O\dot{J}T$) or the supply effect proxy (T) are: proportion of the firm's work force paid less than the EOPP wage, unionization, size, industry, turnover rates, quality of newly hired labor, and whether the firm's output is constrained by the availability of labor or by sales.

Variation with program characteristics. The EOPP program is made up of two distinct elements: A job search component that comprises an 8-week, intensive job search and a subsidized employment and training component that finds a job or training slot for every eligible worker who after 8 weeks still has not found a conventional sector job. The two components have distinct effects on the labor market. The job search component, together with the possibility of toughened enforcement of work tests by welfare agencies, increases the supply of labor available to private firms. The provision of training reduces the private sector's supply of unskilled labor but increases the availability of trained labor after a lag. With only 10 observations on sites saturated by the EOPP program, separating these contrasting effects will be difficult. However, intersite variation in the relative emphasis placed on these components may allow estimation. (Of course, an orthogonal design would have been preferable.) Additional understanding of the effect of the different components may be obtained by studying the timing and mechanism of program impacts.

EOPP demand effects. If EOPP has major effects on the availability or quality of labor, firms may be forced to limit output and sales by letting order backlogs grow or increasing prices. We will test for these effects by estimating models that use an instrumental variable prediction of each firm's sales growth in place of its actual level. The variables that will be used to predict a firm's sales growth are pre-EOPP growth plans, rates of growth of national industry totals, and local growth of personal income in exogenous sectors. Since demand effects of the EOPP program are contributing to sales growth, we must also account for these.

GENERALIZATION OF EOPP TO
THE NATIONAL POPULATION

One of the principal reasons for conducting the Employment Opportunity Pilot Projects is to provide data that can be used to protect the demand for a nationwide public employment program. But, data from the pilot projects will not be available for some time (perhaps one or two years after initiation of the projects) and policy makers need information quickly to design a national program. In view of this important need, the strategy for the generalization in EOPP is to devote considerable resources during the early phases of the project to modifying existing simulation models of public employment, both to improve their structural relationships and to tie them more directly to current welfare reform efforts. During later phases of the project, when data become available for analysis, significant resources will be devoted to using the pilot project data explicitly for generalization. Such a generalization based on pilot project data may require a whole new simulation methodology or may be possible with further modification of the existing models.

This section addresses some of the issues relevant to the generalization. First, the current simulation models and possible methodological improvements in them are discussed. We then describe how labor market impacts can be integrated into the existing models. After describing this modification of the existing simulation models, we address the issue of how pilot project data can be used in the generalization. The main advantage of using pilot project data is that they provide direct information about the impacts of an open-ended, public employment program. The pilot project data will be used in the generalization in two ways: (1) to evaluate the performance capabilities of the existing models and identify weaknesses in their structure; (2) to construct behavioral relations that can be incorporated into the simulation framework by using empirical estimates of program effects.

Current Simulation Models

Estimates of the nationwide demand for PSE slots are being made using microsimulation models developed by Greenberg et al. (hereafter referred to as the KGB model)[15] and by Maxfield (hereafter referred to as the MATH model).[16] The KGB and MATH models use cross-sectional survey data (such as the Current Population Survey or the Survey of Income and Education) and behavioral response equations to estimate the number of full-time, equivalent PSE slots that would be demanded under a given environment and a given set of program rules. Predictions of the number of persons filling these slots as well as the length of time a slot is held are also available.

The KGB Model

The KGB model identifies three strategies of participation in public service employment: pure participation, mixed participation, and nonparticipation. Pure participation means that individuals devote all of their labor market time to public service employment. Mixed participation means that individuals devote part of their labor market time to public service employment and part to conventional employment. Nonparticipation means that individuals devote none of their labor market time to public service employment. In determining participation, the KGB model assumes that an individual chooses the strategy that yields the highest future stream of money income.

An important assumption of the KGB model is that individuals can choose the number of PSE hours they wish to work. Since not all want to work full-time, more than one person can occupy a given PSE slot. For a PSE program like the Program for Better Jobs and Income (President Carter's first proposal for welfare reform), the KGB model estimates that over the period of one year, about two individuals occupy a given PSE slot. Since the model is based on annual figures and does not distinguish full-time work from full-year work, this is equivalent to saying that the average length of stay in a PSE slot is about six months.

Another important assumption of the KGB model is that job search is unaffected by the program. This implies that a person holding a PSE job is just as likely to find a conventional sector job as a person who is unemployed.

A third important assumption of the KGB model is that the number of slots demanded is equal to the number of slots created—it assumes that there is a perfectly elastic supply of PSE jobs.

Finally, it assumes that nonparticipating employers respond to the PSE program by raising the wage rates of eligible workers, inducing a portion of them to remain in the conventional sector. As we describe later, there are several problems associated with the way the KGB model computes the number of eligible workers retained in the conventional sector.

The MATH Model

The MATH model differs from the KGB model in several important respects. First, the participation decision is based on future streams of full income rather than future streams of money income. Hence, the value of leisure is directly incorporated into the participation decision in the MATH model.[17]

Second, the MATH model allows for restrictions on the number of hours per week a person is allowed to work at a PSE job. But this may not be a methodological improvement over the KGB model. While PSE program regulations usually specify hours restrictions, it is not clear that they would ever be binding in practice, because individuals are free to choose the number of weeks worked in public employment per year. Only if the utility of work week leisure differs from the utility of nonwork week leisure would the hours constraint be binding.

Third, the MATH model allows for a decline in the reservation wage of an eligible person during a spell of unemployment. The KGB model assumes that the participation decision is independent of the duration of unemployment.

Fourth, the MATH model allows job search to be affected by the PSE program. Specifically, the MATH model assumes that persons holding a PSE job are just as likely to find conventional sector employment as persons working in the conventional sector who change jobs without an intervening spell of unemployment.

Finally, unlike the KGB model, the MATH model does not allow employers to respond to the PSE program. In effect, the MATH model assumes that employers have a perfectly elastic demand for labor, an assumption that is unlikely to be valid under a real program.

Because of these differences, the KGB and MATH models produce somewhat different estimates of participation and length of stay in a PSE program. Compared to the KGB model, the MATH model produces much larger estimates of both the number of PSE participants and the length of stay in a PSE job.[18] Most of the additional participants in the MATH Model come from the conventional sector or the labor force. Out of the 3.5 million participants in the MATH model, .9 million come from the conventional sector, .6 million from unemployment, and 2.0 million from the labor force. Hence, the smallest group participating in the program according to the MATH model is the group the program is intended to help the most, the unemployed.

Shortcomings of Existing Models

Despite their complexity, both of the existing microsimulation models have shortcomings that may limit their ability to predict the effects of a nationwide, public employment program. A first shortcoming is that they do not properly account for labor market effects of public employment programs. The MATH model completely ignores labor market effects while the KGB model makes an incorrect adjustment for eligibles and ignores the effects of the program on ineligibles. As indicated earlier, both the wage rate and amount of employment supplied by ineligibles is likely to increase under a PSE program. Since the existing models improperly account for these effects, they produce biased estimates of both participation in public employment and the effects of the program on the behavior of participants and nonparticipants.

They also assume that prime sponsors are able to provide jobs instantaneously to all who desire them. Such an assumption rests on the notion that prime sponsors create the jobs before the need actually arises. Whether prime sponsors and the agencies that ultimately employ PSE workers are willing and able to keep a backlog of open job slots is one of the most critical research issues for the EOPP demonstrations. If prime sponsors cannot employ eligibles immediately, then queues may develop and the simulation models will overpredict actual participation in a national program. During the early stages of the demonstrations, the sensitivity of the models' estimates to various assumptions about the short-run elasticity of supply of PSE jobs will be tested.

A third shortcoming of the existing models is that they do not account for possible displacement effects. Displacement can occur because participating firms or agencies substitute a less expensive factor (subsidized labor) for a more expensive factor (unsubsidized labor) or because nonparticipating firms reduce their employment levels in response to changes in market variables, such as the wage rate. We refer to the first type of displacement as *direct* displacement and the second type as *indirect* displacement. Both the KGB and MATH models currently overestimate the amount of indirect displacement that would occur as a result of a PSE program and ignore the possibility of any direct displacement.

A fourth shortcoming of the existing models is that they do not consider the possibility of human capital effects of PSE programs. One important component of EOPP programs is the availability of funds for training (either classroom or on-the-job). Another is the experience gained on a PSE job. If the training programs are effective or if the jobs are productive, the wage rates of participating individuals will rise. The microsimulation models should have the flexibility of allowing for such effects to occur.

A fifth shortcoming is that they assume that all eligibles are aware of the program. To the extent that outreach efforts are imperfect, the number of participants predicted by the models will be an overestimate. Efforts will be made to incorporate informational aspects about the program into the simulation models.

Neither do they allow for factors other than the wage rate to affect participation in the program. Fringe benefits, working conditions, job security, or social stigma are important factors that may affect participation rates. Attempts should be made to develop methods of determining the size of wage differentials required for participation in PSE jobs, and these methods should be incorporated into the simulation models.

Finally, the models ignore possible macroeconomic consequences of public employment programs. An implicit assumption in both models is that public employment programs shift the long-run Phillips curve to the left without exerting inflationary pressures on the economy. To the extent that this type of fiscal policy puts pressures on labor markets, however, long-run gains of a PSE program may be possible only by allowing concurrent increases in the rate of inflation (Baily and Tobin, 1977).

Modifying Existing Models to Account for Labor Market Impacts

There are several alternatives to overcoming these limitations just described; some involve modifications of behavior relations in existing models, others involve the use of pilot project data directly to respecify certain elements of the models that are particularly sensitive to the underlying assumptions. Below we discuss how the models can be modified to account for labor market impacts. Other modifications are described in the design report. Following this, we turn to more extensive respecifications that the pilot project data will make possible.

Figure 1 describes graphically how labor market effects can be incorporated into the KGB and MATH models. First, we assume that the demand for labor is perfectly elastic. Under this condition, all eligibles with wages less than the PSE wage rate will leave the private sector to take PSE jobs, and ineligibles will be unaffected by the program. This is the case assumed in the MATH model. Total PSE employment is equal to BE, which can be calculated as follows:

$$BE = AD - AB + DE \qquad [16]$$
$$= AD + a_E \Delta w,$$

where

AD = the supply of eligibles at the preprogram wage rate, W_M,

    = $E_{T_0} - E_{I_0}$,

a_E = the slope, dS_E/dW, of the labor supply curve of eligibles,[19] and

Δw = the increase in the wage rate resulting from the PSE program ($W_{PSE} - W_M$).

Total employment in the conventional sector remains constant at FA, since the market wage rate does not change. Hence, total employment of eligibles and ineligibles increases by $a_E\Delta w$, the induced increase in the supply of eligibles to the PSE sector.

When employer responses are considered, PSE employment and the supply of eligibles and ineligibles to the conventional sector will change. Assuming that employer responses can be represented by the demand curve D_T, the PSE population is reduced to CE (BC eligibles remain in the conventional sector) and the supply of ineligibles to the conventional sector increases from FA to FB. The market wage rate in the conventional sector rises from W_M to W_{PSE}.

The size of the PSE population CE, can be calculated as follows:

$$E_{PSE} = CE = BD + DE - BC$$
$$= CD + DE \qquad\qquad [17]$$
$$= (a_T - a_D)\, \Delta w$$

where

CD = induced decrease in the quantity of labor demanded caused by higher conventional sector wage,

DE = induced increase in the supply of labor (eligibles and ineligibles) caused by higher conventional sector wage,

a_T = the slope of the market supply curve, and

a_D = the slope of the market demand curve ($a_D < 0$).

The number of eligibles remaining in the conventional sector, BC, can be calculated as:

$$E_{T_i} - E_{I_i} = BC = BE - CE = AD - (a_I - a_D)\, \Delta w, \qquad [18]$$

where

a_I = the slope of the supply curve of ineligibles.

The number of ineligibles in the conventional sector can be calculated as:

$$E_{I_i} = FB = FA + AB = FA + a_I\Delta w, \qquad [19]$$

where

FA = the number of ineligibles before the PSE program, and

AB = the induced increase in the number of ineligibles resulting from the PSE program.

Conventional sector employment falls by CD, which can be calculated as:

$$E_{T_0} - E_{T_1} = CD = a_D \triangle w, \tag{20}$$

while the total supply of eligibles and ineligibles rises by DE,

$$DE = a_T \triangle w. \tag{21}$$

The KGB model allows for employers to raise wages of eligibles in order to induce them to remain in the conventional sector. This is done by assuming a value for the elasticity of demand for low wage labor (the value used is −2) and then predicting the number of potentially participating eligibles that would remain in the conventional sector. The formula used in the KGB model to calculate the number of eligibles retained in the conventional sector is given by (see Betson, Greenberg and Kasten [1979]):

$$N^* = (1 - \dot{w}E(d))N, \tag{22}$$

where

$\quad N^* \quad$ = the number of eligible workers the conventional sector employer wishes to retain;

$\quad \dot{w} \quad$ = the percentage wage increase of eligibles,

$\quad E(d) \quad$ = the absolute value of the elasticity of demand for labor, and

$\quad N \quad$ = the number of eligibles employed in the conventional sector prior to the PSE program.

In the terminology used here, N^* is equal to BC, N is equal to AD, E(d) is equal to $-a_D W_M / AD$, and $\dot{w} = \triangle w / W_M$. Thus, we can rewrite [23] in the notation used here to obtain:

$$\begin{aligned} BC \quad &= (1 + \triangle w / W_M \, a_D \, W_M / A_D) \, AD \\ &= AD + a_D \, \triangle w \end{aligned}$$

Comparing [23] with [18] derived earlier, we see that [23] is an overestimate of the number of eligibles retained in the conventional sector by the amount $a_I \triangle w$. That is, by ignoring the effects of the PSE program on ineligibles, the KGB model currently overestimates the number of eligibles that will remain in the private sector and underestimates the size of the PSE population (assuming, of course, that the elasticity of demand for labor used in the KGB model is correct).

The MATH model does not allow for employers to raise the wages of eligibles to retain them in the conventional sector. Hence, the MATH model, in contrast to the KGB model, tends to overestimate the size of the PSE population.

By incorporating the effects of the PSE program on ineligibles, it is a relatively straightforward task to modify both the KGB and MATH models to incorporate labor market effects.

Using Pilot Project Data in the Generalization Effort

Modification of the existing microsimulation models rests on a variety of untested assumptions. Many of these assumptions can be tested using data from the household surveys, the employer surveys, and the applicant surveys collected as part of the EOPP projects. Econometric analysis of these data will also enable respecification of many of the weaker behavioral components of the models.

There are two major components of the existing microsimulation models that can be improved on the basis of results obtained from analysis of the pilot project data. The first component relates to participation (and length of stay) in various aspects of the program and the second to the impact of the program on participants and nonparticipants.

Participation. The major factor determining participation in public employment in the KGB and MATH models is the difference between the program wage and the individual's wage rate in conventional employment. Apart from adjustments due to labor market effects, hours restrictions, and expected unemployment, both models assume that an individual participates in public employment if the program wage exceeds the conventional sector wage. For a variety of reasons, however, this assumption is not likely to be valid in practice.

As indicated earlier, factors that may cause participation to vary include:

- program characteristics other than the wage rate
- characteristics of individuals and their environment
- the displacement rates of EOPP and other PSE programs
- the characteristics of other welfare and transfer programs and the degree to which they enforce work requirements
- the level of government spending associated with the program
- the proportion of the labor market covered by the program
- the success of outreach efforts in informing all eligibles of the program

In principle, it is possible to control for these factors by estimating a participation equation using data collected in the various pilot project surveys. Earlier, we described how such an equation can be estimated. The participation equation, once estimated, can replace the participation algorithm being used in the KGB and MATH models.

Impacts on participants and nonparticipants. In addition to predicting the number of PSE slots, the KGB and MATH models also predict the effects of a PSE program on wage rates, hours of work, unemployment, labor force participation, and transfer program costs (such as AFDC, Food Stamps, and Unemployment Compensation) for certain groups in the population.

In the MATH model, these impacts are estimated only for program participants. In the KGB model, these impacts are estimated only for program participants and eligible nonparticipants. As discussed earlier, however, ineligibles are also likely to be affected by an open-ended, public employment program. The magnitude of the effects of public employment on ineligibles cannot be predicted a priori because the effects vary with such a wide variety of characteristics including the elasticity of the demand for labor, the unemployment rate, the characteristics of the labor force that determine eligibility, and the degree of substitutability of high-wage labor for low-wage labor and of ineligibles for eligibles.

In previous sections, we have described in detail how pilot project data can be used to estimate the effects of public employment demonstrations on a variety of outcome variables. We have also described how to control for potential biases that could arise because of differences between EOPP and a national program. In the most sophisticated version of the models presented, effects are identified for each of three major groups: participants, eligible nonparticipants, and ineligibles. These estimates, if measured precisely, can be used in the simulation models to predict the effects of alternative public employment programs—assuming, of course, that the differences between EOPP and a national program are adequately controlled in the impact equations. This eliminates the need for precise estimates of displacement and elasticities of labor supply and demand, which are required by the simulation models, and captures the effects of a wide variety of other factors that are likely to affect the size of the impacts on the various outcome measures. These equations can also be used to predict the effects of public employment programs other than the ones being tested in EOPP.

NOTES

1. If the EOPP wage rate is sufficiently high that all eligibles participate in the program, conventional sector wage rates will rise to a level lower than the program wage.

2. See Barnow et al. (this volume) and Heckman (this volume).

3. For simplicity we have written the participation function as a probability function. Participation might also be modeled using tobit where length of participation is the dependent variable (defined to be zero for nonparticipants). Participation might also be modeled as a probit and a truncated normal (Farkas et al., this volume) or as a two-state model of the type developed by Tuma et al. (this volume).

4. For a similar approach to SIME/DIME data see Keeley et al. (this volume).

5. For simplicity, we have derived the impact model as a linear regression model. However, for some dependent variables such as the probability of employment, a probit or logit model would be used. For modeling the impact of the program on rates of flows between various states such as unemployment and employment, a multistate RATE model originally developed by Tuma et al. (this volume) would be used.

6. In general, eligibility for participation in the EOPP depends on being the primary earner in a family with children and meeting an income/unemployment criterion. However, for purposes of econometric specification we wish to avoid defining as ineligible those families who could become eligible simply by changing their behavior to decrease family income. Thus, we shall consider only those families currently without children as being ineligible. Presumably, persons could also decide whether to be in families with children, but such decisions would be more difficult to implement in the short run than a decision to simply allow family income to fall.

7. Nonparticipants may suffer direct displacement if they would have been employed in a participating agency or firm in the absence of the program as well as indirect labor market effects through local economy wide supply/demand adjustments. Participants are presumably insulated from the latter. For further clarification of the distinction between "direct" and "indirect" effects see the discussions of the employer level substudies below.

8. Much of the spending in a site results in increased payments to factors outside of the site.

9. This applies to private sector employers receiving subsidized workers under an OJT agreement as well as to public sector employers receiving EOPP workers under PSE or OJT agreements.

10. For example, a leftward shift in the supply curve of labor to the conventional sector.

11. Two issues must be clarified: (1) In principle, EOPP will not allow program eligibles to displace other program eligibles. If an eligible is displaced EOPP must create another job, unless the individual does not choose to participate. From this perspective, displacement of members of the target population has implications primarily for the *number* of jobs which must be created. But if the displaced workers experience difficulty finding other employment, but are not eligible for EOPP (possibly because they are not the primary earner in a family with children), counter-productive program effects have been produced. (2) We ignore the potential stimulative effect of a jobs program which acted solely as a tax cut.

12. Assuming that they are, as seems likely, less efficient in production than the displaced workers.

13. A project is PSE involving a fixed duration set of tasks, often aimed toward producing a good or service which would "otherwise not be available." A slot is an "ongoing job" involving tasks which are a regular part of an agency's production.

14. This question can be addressed by combining our data with the data regarding value of output to be collected by Mathematica Policy Research.

15. The KGB model is described in Betson et al. (forthcoming). Details of the public service employment component of the model are presented in Greenberg (1978).

16. The jobs component of the MATH model is described in Maxfield (1978).

17. Efforts are currently underway to modify the KGB model to consider the value of leisure in the participation decision by assuming a functional form for the utility map. In the MATH model, reservation wages are estimated directly and are used to assign a money value to leisure.

18. In simulating the Program for Better Jobs and Income, President Carter's first proposal for welfare reform, the MATH model predicted 3.5 million participants with an average length of stay in the program of 34 weeks. The corresponding figures for the KGB model are 2.8 million and 24 weeks.

19. It is assumed that the slope of the market labor supply curve is equal to the sum of the slopes of the labor supply curves of eligibles and ineligibles (i.e., $a_T = a_I + a_E$). In both the KGB and MATH models, the labor supply slopes used are from the Seattle and Denver Income Maintenance Experiments (see Keeley et al., this volume).

REFERENCES

ADAMS, C. F. and D. L. CRIPPEN (1979) "The fiscal impact of general revenue sharing on local governments." Washington, DC: Department of Treasury, Office of Revenue Sharing.

AMEMIYA, T. (1974) "Regression analysis when the dependent variable is truncated normal." *Econometrica* 41: 997-1016.

AZRIN, N. (1978) Job finding club as a method for obtaining employment for welfare eligible clients. (unpublished)

BAILY, M. N. and J. TOBIN (1977) "Macroeconomic effects of selective public employment and wage subsidies." *Brookings Papers on Economic Activity*, 2, 511-541.

BARNOW, B. S., G. CAIN, and A. GOLDBERGER (1978) Issues in the Analysis of Selection Bias. Department of Economics, University of Wisconsin, Madison, WI. (unpublished)

BASSI, L. (1979) The Substitution Effect of Public Service Employment: Most Recent Evidence Report, Washington, DC: The Urban Institute.

BASSI, L. and A. FECHTER, (1978) "The implications for fiscal substitution and occupational displacement under an expanded CETA Title VI." A Final Report Submitted to the Department of Labor Under Contract No. J-9-M-7-0154, October. Washington, DC: The Urban Institute.

BETSON, D. , D. GREENBERG, and R. KASTEN (1979) "A simulation study of interactions between transfer policy and employment programs." Unpublished, Department of Health, Education and Welfare. May.

——— (forthcoming) "A microsimulation model for analyzing alternative welfare reform proposals: an application to the Program for Better Jobs and Income," in R. Haveman and K. Hollenbeck (eds.) Microeconomic Simulation. New York: Academic.

BISHOP, J. (1979) "An outline of potential uses of an employers survey for the EOPP research design." University of Wisconsin, Madison, WI: Institute for Research on Poverty.

BORUS, M. E. and D. S. HAMERMESH (1978) Study of the net employment effects of public service employment—econometric analysis. Report, National Commission for Employment Policy, Washington, D.C.

FARKAS, G. and E. W. STROMSDORFER (1979) Measuring the impact of the EOPP on the public, and private non-profit sectors, August 13. Abt Associates Inc., Cambridge, MA. (unpublished)

GRAMLICH, E. M. (1979) "Stimulating the macro economy through state and local governments." American Economic Review 69: 180-185.

——— (1978) "State and local budgets the day after it rained: why is the surplus so high?" *Brookings Papers on Economic Activity*, 1. 191-214.

——— and H. GALPER (1973) "State and local fiscal behavior and federal grant policy." *Brookings Papers on Economic Activity*, 1: 15-58.

GREENBERG, D. (1978) "Participation in public employment programs," in J. L. Palmer (ed.) Creating jobs: Public Employment Programs and Wage Subsidies. Washington, DC: Brookings.

HECKMAN, J. J. (1979) "Sample selection bias as specification error." Econometrica 47: 153-161.

JOHNSON, G. (1979) "The labor market displacement effect in the analysis of the net impact of manpower training program," in F. Bloch (ed.) Evaluating Manpower Training Programs. Greenwich, CN: Johnson Associates.

JOHNSON, G. E. and J. D. TOMOLA (1977) "The fiscal substitution effect of alternative approaches to public service employment policy." J. of Human Resources 12: 3-26.

KEELEY, M. (1979) "Measuring participation and the labor market effects of EOPP: Models and data." CA: SRI-International. Menlo Park. (unpublished)

KEMPER, P. and P. MOSS (1978) "Economic efficiency of public employment programs." in J. L. Palmer (ed.) Creating Jobs: Public employment programs and wage subsidies. Washington, DC: Brookings.

KESSELMAN, J. (1978) "Work relief program in the Great Depression," in J. L. Palmer (ed.) Creating jobs: Public employment programs and wage subsidies. Washington, DC: Brookings.

MADDALA, G. S. (1976) "Self-selectivity problems in econometric models." University of Florida, Department of Economics. (unpublished)

MADDALA, G. S. and L. LEE (1976) "Recursive models with qualitative endogenous variables." Annals of Econ. and Social Measurement 5: 525-545.

MASTERS, S. and K. DICKINSON (1979) "Effects of the EOPP program on employment: Separating income from structural factors." University of Wisconsin, Madison, WI: Institute for Research on Poverty. (unpublished)

MAXFIELD, M. Jr. (1978) "The effects of a guaranteed public service employment program on the labor force participation rate and the unemployment rate." Princeton, NJ. Mathematica Policy Research. (unpublished)

METCALF, C. E. et al. (1979) "A Research Design for the Employment Opportunity Pilot Projects." Report for the Employment and Training Administration, U.S. Department of Labor (August).

NATHAN, R. et al. (1978a) Preliminary report: Monitoring the public service employment program. February. Washington, DC: Brookings.

——— (1978b) "Monitoring the public service employment program." Report for the National Commission for Employment Policy, Washington, DC, March.

——— (1977a) Revenue sharing: The second round. Washington, DC: Brookings.

——— (1975) Monitoring revenue sharing. Washington, DC: Brookings.

National Planning Association (1974) An evaluation of the economic impact project of the public employment program. Report for the Manpower Administration, U.S. Department of Labor, Final Report, May.

ROBINS, P. (1979) Labor market impacts of EOPP and generalization to the national population. Menlo Park, CA: SRI-International. (unpublished)

——— and WEST, R. (1978) "Participation in the Seattle and Denver income maintenance experiments and its effect on labor supply." Research Memorandum 53, Menlo Park, CA: SRI-International.

TOBIN, J. (1958) "Estimations of relationships for limited dependent variables". Econometrica 26: 24-36.

TUMA, N. B., M. T. HANNAN, and L. P. GROENEVELD (1979) "Dynamic analysis of event histories." American Journal of Sociology 84: 820-854.

WISEMAN, M. (1976) "Public employment as fiscal policy." *Brookings Papers on Economic Activity*, 1.